Biographical Dictionary of World War II

Other books by Mark M. Boatner

Landmarks of the American Revolution

Encyclopedia of the American Revolution

The Civil War Dictionary

Military Customs and Traditions

Army Lore

Biographical Dictionary of World War II

By Mark M. Boatner III

Presidio

Published by Presidio Press
505 B San Marin Drive, Suite 300
Novato, CA 94945-1340

Library of Congress Cataloging-in-Publication Data

Boatner, Mark Mayo, 1921-
    Biographical dictionary of World War II / Mark M. Boatner.
        p.   cm.
    Includes bibliographical references.
    ISBN 0-89141-548-3
    1. World War, 1939-1945—Biography—Dictionaries. I. Title.
D736B63   1966
940.53'092—dc20   96-13437
[B]   CIP

Printed in the United States of America

Acknowledgments

Throughout the text I have used shortened titles and other abbreviations to cite sources—published works and individuals who helped by mail or phone. All are fully identified in the main bibliography, but again I'd like to acknowledge my debt and gratitude.

Foreseeing that Soviet entries would be the greatest challenge, and getting valuable leads from Col John F. Sloan, a Soviet specialist and encyclopedist, I was particularly fortunate in enlisting the help of two top authorities. Ironically, they turned out to be my West Point classmate Col William F. Scott and his wife Harriet Fast Scott. In addition to checking all the numerous Soviet sketches and pertinent Glossary entries the Scotts gave me their computer data bases from which I could track the careers of Red Army commanders and well over 100 major military formations from "directions" and "fronts" to the field armies that were often annihilated and reconstituted several times. I cite my capitalist comrades as "Scotts" except when the colonel's lady—who modestly favored this unliberated form—was clearly the primary authority; in such cases I cite "HFS." Due primarily to their expert and generous support the Russian portions of this book are particularly strong, if not unique in the English language.

The French posed exceptional problems because of lingering factionalism, but my long-time friend Bertrand de Seze opened doors in Paris. The most impressive of these were in the Chateau de Vincennes' splendid Pavillon de la Reine, where Col Paul Gaujac, chief of the Service Historique de l'ArmÇe, responded with far more help than I could have hoped for.

The British were a piece of cake because of their monumental Dictionary of National Biography (*DNB*), but Lionel Leventhal, publisher of Greenhill Books in London, put on the icing by carefully reading the proofs. He focused, naturally, on the British entries and checked my facts with a variety of reference books including *Obituaries From The Times* (London) and *Who Was Who*. Happily acceding to his judgment as a leading publisher of military history, I reinstated 10 people I had reluctantly culled.

The war in the Pacific being largely a US Navy show (peace MacArthur!), I needed naval expertise to balance my latent bias as a career Army officer. When Lt Gen John H. Cushman, a friend since being boys at Ft Benning, cadets at West Point, and students at the Command and General Staff College, wrote to say he had retired to live at Annapolis, I signaled back an SOS. This brought Capt Roy C Smith, USNR (Ret), aboard. An officer with editorial experience, a Navy junior of impressive genealogy who is well read in naval history, he had access to the USNA library, the US Naval Institute, and local scholars like E.

B. Potter. Capt Smith not only vetted my draft sketches but also wrote entries for naval leaders I otherwise would have omitted.

John S. D. Eisenhower and George S. Patton the younger, both old friends, provided valuable and candid material about their sires. Maestro Christoph von Dohnányi of the Cleveland Orchestra and his brother, Dr Klaus von of Hamburg, responded promptly with a fact check on the sketch of their heroic father.

It is purely fortuitous that military men provided the most assistance, but card-carrying historians also came through with moral and material support. In at the creation, so to speak, was Louis B. Morton of Dartmouth, former chief of the Pacific Section, OCMH. Another mentor, a leading authority on the anti-Hitler conspiracies and once a fellow editor-reviewer with the History Book Club, was the late Harold C. Deutsch. By mail and over the phone he shared his expertise on enigmatic figures like Wilhelm CANARIS and Elias "Cicero" BAZNA, threw new light into dark corners, and bolstered my conviction that historians have slighted outstanding field commanders like Hermann BALCK.

Donald S. Detweiler, secretary of the World War Two Studies Association, recommended specialists. D. Clayton "Jim" James, distinguished biographer of Douglas MacArthur, proved to be by far the most helpful.

Ferruccio Montevecchi, a student of my 88th Inf Div's operations in Northern Italy and a native of the region, willingly provided information on several troublesome details including Mussolini's birthplace and final resting place. (In return I put him on the trail of the battalion surgeon who delivered the twins of a teen-age partisan refugee just behind our front lines in the mountains overlooking Bologna in the fall of 1944.)

My daughter Stirling and her husband, Akira Nagura, saved me many hours of time consuming to-ing and fro-ing, and she brightened the close of each day by having a splendid supper waiting when I descended from my ivory tower on the hill. Penultimate son Spencer, a student at LSU in Baton Rouge and surrogate plantation manager, also provided valuable logistical support while making 35-mile excursions to keep the water pump, computer, and tractor running. In these home care duties, and on checking Baton Rouge libraries for me, Spencer has been joined recently by Julia Latham. Ultimate son Carter helped materially in contacts with the Library of Congress and various embassies in Washington. Donald Singer of the budget-strapped National Archives went beyond the call of duty in providing vital biographical data from their captured German records. Charles R. Shrader, a historian and research expert of Carlisle, Pa, helped fill in blank spaces.

Having begun this book a decade before personal computers arrived, I needed a lot of technical support, particularly after learning about what specialists call "dirty" rural electricity. John Nouss, a consultant who took intelligent interest in this book, eventually solved the main problems by getting an uninterrupted power system (UPS). John Nouss fortunately enjoyed occasional drives to the country.

My eldest son, Bruce, and his wife Julie, both computer experts in Silicon Valley, helped with special problems, as did Number Two son, Andrew, and his computer-savvy wife, Carolyn. Mary K. Rountree also listened to my problems in what Audubon called the "Feliciana wilderness," relieved my happy solitude, and found me regional library resources. Oliver Swan, my first agent with Paul R. Reynolds Inc. in New York City and long a good friend, worked with me on this and earlier books until his light failed. William Reiss, who took over in what became John Hawkins & Associates, has gone beyond the demands of duty.

I am grateful to Col Robert V. Kane, publisher of Presidio Press, for not sharing the view of many others in his trade that publication of *The Biographical Dictionary of World War II* was "prohibitive at today's costs."

For what is good about this book I thank all those people. Intelligent readers, whom I have tried to keep foremost in mind, will know that the rest goes without saying.

Introduction

This is a reference book for general readers, for students, teachers, writers, editors, librarians, and especially, for researchers. Browsers and casual users are welcome, of course, but the work is primarily for people who already have some intellectual investment in the history of 1939-45 and who need a concise, reliable handbook—a *vade mecum*.

Scan a few pages for an idea of what value *The Biographical Dictionary of World War II* will have for you personally. Then the following explanations will be helpful. To speed things along I'll jump the gun by using some of the cross-referencing techniques you'll find explained fully below.

How Entries Were Selected

In your hands you have about 1,000 biographical sketches of the 3,000 people whose names you are most likely to encounter in reading about the second world war. To select them I used what is called the "semantic count" or "pragmatic approach." The historian Louis B. Morton (see Acknowledgments) did not entirely approve when I began writing this book in 1970 (!), but Thomas B. Parrish, editor of *The Simon and Schuster Encyclopedia of World War II* (1978), reassures me that he found the semantic count "the only way to go."

I made very few exceptions to this purely pragmatic approach, but one was in the case of Soviet field commanders, who, after all, played the major role in Hitler's War. I included every General of the Army (equivalent to US fourstar rank) and field marshal (MSU). I also included most German commanders at the field army level, many of whom are badly neglected in other reference works. *

For the semantic count to be valid the critical first step was, of course, to compile a sound statistical "sample." For this I culled the indexes of standard works and a few specialized histories. It was important to keep in mind that wars are not exclusively military and that many other countries were heavily engaged in this one before the United States was drawn in.

Having identified about 3,000 people in all fields, and by counting the number of times they appear in the semantic count I picked about 1,000 names. The statistical exercise furthermore furnished guidance on what highlights to include in biographical sketches, just as it tells lexicographers what word definitions are in current usage.

---

*Readers with further interest in my approach to the present work should find it satisfied by "How *The Civil War Dictionary* Came into Being" (Kent State Univ Press, Vol XXXIV, No 3 [Sep 88]). Written at the editor's request, the monograph is reproduced in the Vintage Books edition of *The Civil War Dictionary.*

A book of convenient heft being limited for various reasons including print size, paper, and solid binding to about 500,000 words, I decided to make the book "comprehensive" (the most people) rather than "selective" (as in an anthology). This meant that some entries would be very short but there would be adequate space for major participants, and others would be budgeted on a sliding scale of from 250 to 1,000 words. Nobody important (as indicated by semantic count) needed to be left out, and a few marginal people could be slipped in because of topical interest (e.g., Klaus BARBIE, H. Norman SCHWARTZKOPF, and Kurt WALDHEIM.) I confess to having slipped in a few unsung heroes, and to heeding the advice of a few experts named in my acknowledgments (q.v.).

Naturally there has to be a general correlation between a subject's importance and the length at which he or she is covered. But it does not make sense to insist, like the mythical Greek innkeeper Procrustes, on stretching or truncating a "guest" to fit a prescribed bed. Thus you will find inordinately long sketches of Kiril A. MERETSKOV and Otto SKORZENY, and inordinately shorter ones of much more significant men like Enrico FERMI and "Bomber" HARRIS.

Cross References and Source Citations

Three simple "typographic techniques" need explaining. First, SMALL CAPITAL LETTERS indicate cross references to other biographical sketches. Second, **boldface** indicates a glossary entry. Third, source citations are in parentheses.

Consider this statement: "HITLER and STALIN negotiated the **Nazi-Soviet Pact** of 23 Aug 39 (Langer, Ency, 1037.)" In drawing your attention in this case to HITLER and STALIN the meaning is: "see those entries for why these leaders temporarily reconciled ancient animosities." (You may know or may not care; if so ignore the cross-reference.) The boldface says: "Further detail on the Nazi-Soviet Pact, also called the Soviet-German Nonaggression Pact or the Molotov-Ribbentrop Pact, is under that glossary entry." The example ends with a parenthetical source citation that uses a short title identified in the bibliography.

Most readers will need to check a glossary entry only once, if at all. Examples are **Barbarossa,** the **Katyn Massacre,** the **Manhattan Project,** or the **Stavka.**

About the Glossary

The glossary performs the conventional function of identifying abbreviations (like **ABDACOM**) and specialized terms (like **turning movement**). It is a mini-encyclopedia that saves space by covering events, issues, definitions, and matters that otherwise would have to be repeated in several places elsewhere. Glossary articles also are valuable in explaining commonly misused terms like the **Black**

Dragon Society and "Congressional **Medal of Honor**," not to mention "Rommel's **Afrika Korps.**"

Some very long glossary entries might have been split off as appendixes. But this conventional technique would send you scurrying to an index.

Summing up, please make two assumptions. First, that all major actors in WWII have a separate entry, and if one is cross-referenced it is for reasons explained above. Second, a cross-reference may be given to less important people merely for what editors call a "brief ID," thus saving space.

You can quickly learn to scan, to skip details, cross references, and source citations, but bear in mind that what you consider trash may be someone else's treasure.

Comparative Military Ranks

By giving German and Soviet ranks and grades in the original language (**Generalleutnant**) or style (General Lieutenant), I avoid the need for complex tables of comparative ranks. There is a separate glossary entry on each rank. Because the rank of general did not exist, strictly speaking, in the USSR, I avoid reference to "Red Army general" and, like Russian sources, use the term "Soviet military leader."

Dates

As for dates (and source citations), I repeat freely because a reference book is not necessarily read like a narrative: it frequently is skimmed, sometimes backwards, for a specific fact. Also, a careful writer does not call somebody a lieutenant general, for example, or Sir Somebody at a time in his career before the rank or knighthood was conferred. (*DNB* has the neat solution of putting "Sir" in parentheses in such a case.)

Russian dates are **New Style** unless indicated otherwise. Because of the International Date Line there is a day's difference between East and West Longitude dates. Unless otherwise noted you can assume that local dates (and times) are given.

Names of Places and People

Webster's Geographical Dictionary, which has valuable historical data, is my authority for English spellings except in a few cases where I have used the name more common in history books.

In French geographical locations I usually give a parenthetical note of the department (of which there are 96). Thus "Siradan (Hautes Pyrenées, or High Pyrenees)."

I use the form of Russian names favored by my Soviet experts, Col and Mrs Harriet F. Scott, except to delete the penultimate letter, the vowel, in words like Budennyy and Maiskiy.

Unit Identifications and Ship Designations

By long tradition the numerical designations of field armies and corps should not be given in Arabic but as, for example, "the XLVIII Panzer Corps of the Fourth Panzer Army." I have, however, rendered this as "the 48th Pz Corps, 4th Pz Army." The need to violate convention becomes obvious when one considers that the US had 11 field armies, but the Germans had more than 20 and the Soviets about 70; the US formed 31 corps, but the Germans had at least 76.

I have used US Navy designations for warships—like **BB** *Missouri* and **CV** *Lexington*—for non-US ships also. Similarly I have favored the naval idiom of "BB *Missouri*," for example, rather than "the BB *Missouri*."

Class standings for Annapolis and West Point graduates are given in parentheses. For example, in the case of Chester NIMITZ, USNA 1905 (71/144), this means he graduated No. 71 out of 144 in the Class 1905. Wartime USMA and USNA classes were graduated early, and many writers are trapped by the USNA custom of retaining the original class-year designation: the USNA Classes of 1918-20 graduated a year early, the "leap year" adjustment being made in the Class of 1921 by graduating the "upper section" a year early and the rest on schedule, 2 June 21. West Point also had accelerated wartime graduations but changed class designations, as in "Jan 43" (six months early) and "June 43" (a year early). "Passed midshipmen" is a term used because a USNA graduate is not automatically commissioned, as are USMA grads. "Ex-cadet 1933," for example, means the cadet would have been in the class of 1933 but, for some reason, did not graduate. Annapolis, which on medical or other grounds (like yearly quotas) denies graduation to a great many who pass the course, uses the term "non-graduate." "Appointed at large" is used for USMA cadets not admitted under the congressional quota of a state representative or senator. A note for careful writers: it is wrong to refer to the United States Military Academy at West Point or to the United States Naval Academy at Annapolis as the West Point Military Academy or the Annapolis Naval Academy.

Conclusion

From *DNB* I have adopted the citations "personal information" and "personal knowledge," using them only when unavoidable.

Readers should understand my heavy reliance on what real historians dismiss as "secondary sources." I have not interviewed eyewitnesses but rather have relied on published works of those who have. Secondary sources have the advantage of providing the evaluation by historians of "primary sources," which can be very tricky. But I have had many sketches reviewed by specialists (see Acknowledgments).

Much new scholarship has appeared since this book was begun, and it will continue to appear. I have tried to update sketches throughout the years but would hope to get corrections, comments and fresh material from widows, orphans, professional critics, and others to make this book even more valuable. Mail will reach me at Penrith, 10200 Col Boatner Rd, Jackson, LA 70748.

A

ABD-EL-KRIM. "The Wolf of the Rif." 1881-1963. An educated, intelligent, and vigorous man whose insurrection in 1922-26 shaped the careers of many French officers on the eve of WWII, he began by annihilating a Spanish army of 20,000 on 21 July 22 at Anual. After proclaiming the Republic of the Rif, forming a well trained army that drove the Spanish into coastal enclaves, on 13 Apr 25 he turned on the French. The army of the Rif drove south to the outskirts of Fez before being stopped by the legendary Gen Louis Lyautey. Overwhelming Franco-Spanish forces under PETAIN and FRANCO scored successes, but a discouraged Pétain had begun armistice parlays at Oudjda when Col André CORAP captured Abd-el-Krim on 26 May 26 by a coup de main (Pertinax, 327n).

The Wolf of the Rif was exiled on Réunion until 1947, when he jumped ship while en route to asylum in France. Settling in Cairo, proclaimed a national hero by Sultan Mohammed V of Morocco in 1958, the Berber chief died 6 Feb 63 in Cairo. (Dupuy et al, eds, *Harper Ency of Mil Biog.)*

ABDUL ILLAH ibn Ali. Regent of Iraq. 1913-58. In 1939 the pro-British Emir Abdul Illah became regent for his nephew, the child-king Faisal II. On 1 Apr 41 a coup by Rashid Ali Beg Gailani and the Grand Mufti of Jersualem, Amin el-HUSSEINI, forced the regent to flee to Transjordan with Faisal. But the British crushed the insurrection in a few months and reinstalled Abdul Illah. When Faisal II assumed royal prerogatives on 2 May 53 Abdul Illah became crown prince. He was shot dead in the palace by revolutionaries on 14 July 58.

ABE, Hiroaki. Japanese admiral. 1890-1949. Rear Adm Hiroaki Abe (pronounced ah-bay), easily confused with the many other flag officers named Abe (*see* Morison, V, 258n), he led the task force that gave Wake Island its first bombardment, 21-23 Dec 41. In June 42 he commanded the cruiser and battleship screen at Midway, after which he led the powerful Vanguard Group in the Battle of the Eastern Solomons (23-25 Aug 42). But Abe's force, built as usual around battleships *Hiei* and *Kirishima,* was not engaged except to support Kondo's futile night search after the battle for FLETCHER's TF 61.

Abe again commanded the Vanguard Group in the Battle of the Santa Cruz Islands, 26-27 Oct 42, a carrier action in which he had no significant part. After his promotion to vice admiral, Abe led the Striking Force of KONDO's Advanced Force through **The Slot** for another attempt to destroy Henderson Field by gunfire. The Japanese advance was detected and CALLAGHAN rushed to set up a screen. In "one of the most confused engagements in modern history" (Morison, V, 225-87), Abe disposed of a US light cruiser and two destroyers but was forced to turn back with heavy losses. "Henderson Field and its precious planes were safe for the night at least," writes Morison, "but nobody on the American side knew it" (V, 251). The other side knew it, however, and Yamamoto immediately (13 Nov 42) radioed orders from Truk to relieve Abe of command (d'Albas, 215). Abe's task force was dissolved and, on 21 Dec 42, he was sent to the Naval General Staff in Tokyo as a face-saving measure. Although only 53 years old, he was retired the following March. (Morison, V, 258n.)

ABE, Koso. Japanese admiral. 1892-1946. He was born 24 Mar/92 and became a career naval officer. Commanding the Transport Unit of the Port Moresby Invasion Group, Rear Adm Koso Abe carried HORII's South Seas Detachment and most of the "Kure" 3d Special Naval Landing Force. The invasion was frustrated by the Battle of the Coral Sea, 7-11 May 42.

The admiral subsequently had charge of bases in the Marshall Islands. After CARLSON's raid on Makin Island, 16-18 Aug 42, nine Marine prisoners were sent to Kwajalein for transshipment to Tokyo. Abe, after waiting six months in vain for further instructions, had the men executed. Based on testimony of a native witness, Vice Adm Abe was convicted of a war crime and hanged at Guam in 1946.

ABE, Nobuyuki. Japanese statesman. 1875-1953. A retired general, he headed a stopgap government formed on 28 Aug 39 in the crisis following HIRANUMA's acceptance of the **Nazi Pact**. Abe was expected to appease the Soviets and avoid further flirtation with the Axis, so he promptly announced that Japan would stay out of Europe's wars. Finally losing support from the army, which had helped install him, Abe was succeeded by YONAI on 14 Jan 40. He was appointed ambassador to China in Apr 40 and later was prominent in KONOYE's Imperial Rule Assistance Association. Abe served as governor general of Korea from July 44 until surrendering on 9 Sep 45.

ABEL, Rudolph Ivanovich, Soviet spy. *See* William FISHER.

ABETZ, Otto. German diplomat. 1903-58. Born 26 May 03 in Schwetzingen, the Third Reich's future ambassador in France became fascinated with French literature while teaching art at a girls' school in Karlsruhe. Abetz began spending more and more time in France, where he mastered the language and became prominent in Franco-German associations. The personable Francophile, tall, blue-eyed, and reddish-haired, acquired wealth and developed close ties with influential elements of Parisian society and politics. Soon after Hitler's rise to power in early 1933, Abetz was appointed to represent the Nazi Foreign Affairs Bureau in Paris, and in 1935 he joined the foreign service. The French expelled Abetz on 1 July 39 for subversive activities.

After the Germans entered Paris on 14 June 40, Abetz took up his post in the capital as Reich ambassador to the occupation authorities, but after 6 Aug 40 his title was ambassador of the Third Reich in France. (Larousse, 1068.) Operating in Paris, where he signed documents as the "Ambassador of Germany in Paris," Abetz visited Vichy only twice. The last occasion was the funeral of HUNTZINGER on 16 Nov 41. But Abetz was de facto "ambassador to France," the diplomatic link between Berlin and Vichy on all vital matters.

Although an ardent Nazi who used virulent French anti-Semitism in curtailing opposition to the German occupation, he was officially censored by Ribbentrop for objecting to Nazi excesses. Abetz left Paris in Aug 44 as Allied forces approached and was not arrested until 25 Oct 45, in Baden. Convicted of war crimes by a French military court and given 20 years at hard labor, he was freed in Apr 54. He published a memoir of his experience in France, *Das Offende Problem* (Cologne, 1951), and then a book about his imprisonment. Abetz died in a flaming crash on the Cologne-Ruhr autobahn on 5 May 58 when something mysteriously went wrong with his car's steering. "His death may have been a revenge killing for his role in sending French Jews to the gas chambers," writes Robert Wistrich.

ABRAMS, Creighton Williams, Jr. US officer. 1914-74. Born 16 Sep 14 in Maine, he graduated from West Point in 1936 (185/276) and became one of the outstanding young tank commanders in the European theater. Leading an armored battalion and a combat team in the 4th Armd Div he won two Distinguished Service Crosses, two Legions of Merit, two Silver Stars, and a Bronze Star Medal (for valor) without ever being wounded. He went on to succeed Gen William Westmoreland as commander of US forces in Vietnam (1968-72) and became army CofS in 1972. He died 4 Sep 74 at Walter Reed Army Medical Center.

ABRIAL, Jean Charles. French admiral. 1879-1962. Figuring in the Dunkirk evacuation as the "Admiral of the North" or simply "Admiral North," he was a southerner, born in Realmont (Tarn). On 23 May 40, Weygand (who had just taken over from Gamelin as Allied supreme commander), named Abrial commander in chief of French naval forces in the north. Five days later, when Allied troops began falling back on Dunkirk, the last available French port, the admiral was ordered to organize a beachhead. Abrial's deputy commander was Lt Gen M. Falgade, whose 16th Corps (composed of two French divisions) was on the perimeter's western flank.

Abrial and the French high command believed the beachhead could be held (and Falgade had some success), so no evacuation plans were made. But the British had decided on 20 May that withdrawal from the continent was essential. Vice Adm B. H. Ramsay, Flag Officer Dover, began organizing Opn Dynamo. Abrial did not know about this until the evacuation began on 26 May, Weygand having failed to inform him. The admiral then hastened to organize French maritime forces into an evacuation fleet, using the Pas-de-Calais flotilla and requisitioning all privately owned boats in the region. Abrial's first convoy was formed on 28 May, and his evacuation began the next day.

By 1 June the losses to British and French shipping and to the RAF were prohibitive (Spears, II, 5). "Abrial is very anxious to prolong the period of embarkation," said Churchill in a message that day to Reynaud, "but he is perhaps not in a very good position to judge since he is directing operations from the depths of a casemate" (ibid., 9). SPEARS broke the tension of a grim meeting with Reynaud by referring to "l'Amiral Abri," the last word meaning shelter (ibid.). The French government, increasingly embittered by what it saw as abandonment by an ally, subsequently demanded (and got) equal space aboard British ships. Of the 338,000 troops moved to England by 4 June, 123,000 were French—most but by no means all moved by the British. In a radio speech on 6 June, Reynaud referred to "Admiral Abrial, the defender of Dunkirk," as a hero. Admiral North and General Falgade reached Dover on 4 June with the last wave.

As senior officer at Cherbourg, Abrial surrendered the port to Rommel on 19 June 40 (*RP,* 83). The admiral, saved from the POW cage by the armistice, was governor general of Algeria from 20 July 40 until replaced by Weygand on 16 July 41. Succeeding AUPHAN, Abrial was Vichy's secretary of the navy from 18 Nov 42 to 26 Mar 43. Arrested after the liberation on charges of collaboration, he was sentenced on 14 Aug 46 to "national indignity" and 10 years of forced labor. The sentence was commuted to five years in prison, but on 2 Dec 47 he was granted a provisional release. (Larousse.)

ACHESON, Dean Gooderham. US statesman. 1893-1971. After serving as an assistant secretary of state under Cordell HULL, with an important role coordinating aid to the UK and the USSR, Acheson was Truman's secretary of state 1949-53. His candid, amusingly supercilious, highly literate memoir, *Present at the Creation: My Years in the State Department* (1969), has valuable material about the years 1941-53.

ADACHI, Hatazo. Japanese general. 1890-1947. Through staff and command assignments in the Kwantung Army from Mar 33, Adachi— an infantryman—rose to head the 37th Div in Aug 40 with the rank of lieutenant general. He

became chief of staff of the North China Area Army in Nov 41 and exactly a year later succeeded HORII in New Guinea. Lt Gen Adachi's three divisions were designated the 18th Army on 16 Nov 42. Forced back from Buna-Gona to the Aitape-Wewak area and isolated there with some 35,000 troops, he held off a first-rate Australian division for 10 months before surrendering with 31,000 survivors on 13 Sep 45. (Keogh, 401, 408.) Two years later, shortly after being sentenced in Rabaul to life imprisonment, he committed suicide there.

ADENAUER, Konrad. German statesman. 1876-1967. The first chancellor of the Federal Republic of Germany (1949-63) was born in Cologne and educated at the universities of Freiburg, Munich, and Bonn before practicing law in Cologne. Dr Adenauer entered municipal politics and rose to be lord mayor of Cologne in 1917. That same year he became a Center Party member of the provincial Diet and Prussian State Council. He was council chairman from 1920 until 1933, when he was dismissed by Goering from all offices. Adenauer was arrested in 1934 for political opposition. (Briggs, ed, "Adenauer.") He was among 5,000 politicians rounded up on 22 Aug 44 (after the STAUFFENBERG Attentat) and thrown into concentration camps (Hoffmann, *Resistance,* 516).

Reinstated by Allied occupation authorities as lord mayor of Cologne in 1945, he became a founder of the Christian Democratic Union and its chairman the next year. Dr Adenauer was elected chancellor of the new Federal Republic in 1949. A successful and popular statesman at a difficult time for Germany, known affectionately as *"der Alte"* (the Old Man), he was reelected in 1953, 1957, and 1961.

AGUINALDO, Emilio. Filipino elder statesman. 1869-1964. Having declared himself dictator after Spain ceded the Philippines to the US in 1898, Aguinaldo led a long and bloody insurrection put down by Douglas MacArthur's father, Arthur. The elderly rebel subsequently was on cordial terms with Douglas MacArthur. (James, *MacArthur,* I, 564.) As one of the prominent Filipinos left behind in Manila with instructions from Pres Manual QUEZON to cooperate with the Japanese for the sake of the people, Aguinaldo was prevailed on by HOMMA to broadcast a surrender appeal to MacArthur in early 1942. This "disturbed me greatly," the general remembered after the war. (MAC-ARTHUR, *Memoirs,* 134-35.)

AINSWORTH, Walden Lee. US admiral. 1886-1960. "Pug" Ainsworth was born on 10 Nov 86 in Minneapolis and graduated from Annapolis in 1910 (73/131). Tall, beefy, and genial but a strict disciplinarian, he was a gunnery and ordnance specialist.

Capt Ainsworth commanded DD Sqdn 2 in the Atlantic from 1940, then was skipper of BB *Mississippi* at the end of 1941. Promoted in July 42 to rear admiral, he became Commander, Destroyers, Pacific Fleet. After Carleton H. WRIGHT's cruiser-destroyer force (TF 67) was badly battered off Tassafaronga on 30 Nov 42, "Bull" Halsey picked Ainsworth to take it over. (Morison, V, 326.) His first action, a night bombardment of the new enemy airstrip at Munda, New Georgia, was "long regarded as a model" (ibid.).

After supporting amphibious operations with naval gunfire, Ainsworth starred in the two battles of Kula Gulf, night actions against the **Tokyo Express**. Rear Adm Ainsworth went on to lead support forces in the Marianas, at Peleliu, and at Leyte. He retired as a vice admiral on 1 Dec 48 and died 7 Aug 60 at Bethesda Naval Hospital.

AITKEN, W. M. *See* BEAVERBROOK, Lord.

ALANBROOKE. *See* BROOKE, Alan.

ALEXANDER, Harold Rupert Leofric George. British general. 1891-1969. Known from childhood as Alex, he was born 10 Dec 91 at one of two family houses in London. Alex was the third son of the 4th Earl of Caledon, who served briefly in the Life Guards and was a famous yachtsman. Caledon died when Alex was six. Alex's mother, born Lady Elizabeth Graham-Toler, daughter of the 3d Earl of Norbury, was an eccentric and imperious woman who remained aloof from her brood. But the four boys were perfectly happy on their huge ancestral estate, Caledon Castle, in County Tyrone, Ulster. Although keen on country sports, particularly running, Alex taught himself to carve wood and to paint. He decided early that he wanted to be a professional artist and, one day, president of the Royal Academy. (Principal sources for this sketch are David Hunt

in *DNB* and *Alex,* the excellent biography by Nigel Nicolson.)

Like his brothers, Alex was packed off to a preparatory school near Margate in Kent. After four years there he attended Harrow, his father's school, 1904-08, rising steadily in his studies and excelling as an athlete and in the school's Rifle Corps. He also won a prize for drawing. Alex reached the highest cadet rank at Sandhurst and had top marks in military subjects. A graduation standing of 85th among 172 assured him a commission in his regiment of choice, the Irish Guards (1911).

The pleasant-looking aristocrat, a trim five feet ten and sporting the neat moustache he would keep for life, intended to spend only a few years in uniform and retire to make his living as an artist. But war changed his plans. Alexander was on the western front from 1914 until 1918, with only short breaks to recover from two wounds or to attend military courses. He won the MC (1915), was appointed to the DSO (1916), and rose in the last two years of the war from acting commander of his battalion to acting brigadier commanding the 4th Guards Bde. Still eager for action, he volunteered to serve with one of several military missions established to save Poland and the Baltic states from the Germans or from the Bolsheviks. In 1919 he led the Baltic *Landwehr* (a brigade of ethnic Germans) in a campaign that drove the Reds from Latvia. Good at languages, he learned German and Russian.

No longer yearning for artistic life, Alexander rejoined his regiment in England in 1920 as second in command. He moved up in 1922 to the top position and took the Irish Guards to Turkey as part of the army of occupation. Ordered to Gibraltar in 1923, he returned with the regiment to England in 1924. By then a full colonel, he was reduced to major while attending the Staff College at Camberley (1926-27), then returned to his regiment (1928-30) before attending the recently established Imperial Defense College. Alexander's only two staff assignments followed, first at the War Office and then in the Northern Command. When Alexander got the coveted assignment of heading the Nowshera Bde on India's NW Frontier in 1934, he cooperated with AUCHINLECK's Peshawar Bde in several successful campaigns to repel invading tribesmen and pacify large regions. The two officers were considered at the time to be leading contenders for the highest posts in case of war *(DNB)*.

Alex was promoted to major general (T) in 1937 at the age of 45, at the time the British Army's youngest general. In 1938 he took command of the 1st Div. As one of two divisions in John Dill's 1st Corps of the BEF in France, he moved forward on 10 May 40 from SE of Lille into Belgium toward the Dyle River line. This was in accordance with the unfortunate Allied plan to meet the German assault. When the British began their desperate delaying action to avoid encirclement, Alexander was assigned briefly to Alan Brooke's 2d Corps, 18-23 May 40 (Bryant, *Tide,* 82, 90). He then returned to the 1st Corps and Montgomery succeeded BROOKE on 30 May as head of the 2d Corps. Lord GORT had orders from London to embark this corps and sacrifice the other as a covering force. But Montgomery convinced Gort that Alexander, if given charge of the 1st Corps, could save all the British troops (Montgomery, *Memoirs,* 59-60). So Alexander stepped up on 30 May to command the 1st Corps, his orders being to conduct a rear guard defense and to evacuate all the troops he could. Fortunately, German ground forces did not mount a coordinated attack against the beachhead, leaving this solely to the Luftwaffe. Thanks largely to bad weather and superhuman efforts by RAF fighters, Alexander had remarkable success during his hectic three days as rear guard commander.

The miracle of Dunkirk ended on 4 June 40, and Alexander was confirmed as 1st Corps commander in England. He then prepared coastal defenses from Scarborough to The Wash, and in Nov 40 succeeded Auchinleck as head of Southern Command. Promotion to lieutenant general followed in December. The threat of invasion ended, Alex concentrated on troop training, for which he had a remarkable talent.

After Japan entered the war (7 Dec 41) and the situation in southeast Asia became critical, Alexander reached Burma on 5 Mar 42 to succeed HUTTON. He immediately counterattacked to regroup scattered units for the defense of Rangoon but quickly accepted that he had to abandon the city. Retreating northward with his command group, the Rangoon garrison, the 17th Indian Div, and women who had disobeyed earlier orders to leave the city, he hit an enemy roadblock. But for reasons still unknown, the Japanese abandoned their trap and raced for Rangoon, which was undefended. "As Hutton later commented, 'Alex never had a greater stroke of luck in his life'" (Allen, *Burma,* 57). On 26 Apr 42 Alexander decided to abandon Burma and start the arduous retreat into India along with STILWELL's command group and Chinese troops. Recalled to England with no blot on his record for again failing to save a lost cause, Alexander was named to lead the 1st British Army in the invasion of North Africa (Opn Torch). But he served only briefly, doubling as EISENHOWER's deputy, before being sent to head the newly created Near East Command. Replaced in London by Noel ANDERSON, Alexander reached Cairo on 9 Aug 42, a day after MONTGOMERY took over the 8th Army. Alex was younger than Monty and junior in service, but BROOKE proved to be right in believing the two men would have an ideal command relationship. Alex was perhaps the only superior with the temperament to get the best out of the eccentric and idiosyncratic Monty, and Churchill had a high regard for Alexander, thus insulating the new army commander from the prime minister's meddling. After Montgomery's decisive defeat of Rommel at El Alamein (4 Nov 42) and his too-leisurely pursuit to Tripoli, Alexander took over the new 18th AG in Algeria on 19 Feb 43 and also became Eisenhower's deputy. The 18th AG included Noel Anderson's 1st Army and, after the link-up on 7 Apr it had Montgomery's 8th Army—hence the number "18." After the North African campaign ended in Tunisia on 13 May 43, Alexander led the 15th AG in the brief Sicilian campaign (10 July-17 Aug 43) and in the long, grinding Italian campaign (3 Sep 43-2 May 45). Alexander's force was composed of the 8th British and the 7th US Armies in Sicily, and the 8th British and the 5th US Armies in Italy. His promotion to field marshal dated from the capture of Rome on 4 June 44, and on 16 Dec he succeeded Henry "Jumbo" Wilson as Supreme Allied Commander, Mediterranean (SACMED). His headquarters was responsibile not only for Italy but also for Greece, the Balkans, and for liaison with advancing Red Army forces.

The British wanted Alexander in that secondary assignment primarily because the Americans liked him and thus, they hoped, would give him utmost support for the Mediterranean strategy advocated by BROOKE and Churchill but opposed by American planners. Alexander was supposed to divert maximum German strength while Churchill continued to nurse the hope that the US would go along with his idea of making the western allies' main strategic effort through the Italian Alps, Yugoslavia, and into central Europe. As commander of a large, multinational force operating independently, Alexander proved himself to be a great captain, if perhaps not in the first rank (Forrest Pogue). The main criticism of his leadership was that he was not sufficiently ruthless in sacking subordinates.

Karl WOLFF's secret surrender ended German resistance in Italy by 25 Apr 45, and Alexander rushed troops to Trieste before TITO could take Venezia Giulia from Italy. By rights, Alexander should have succeeded Alan Brooke as CIGS after the war. But he became governor general of Canada at the invitation of Mackenzie King and on the urging of Churchill. The last to hold the office, with an extended tenure from 1946 to 1952, he was exceptionally popular. After that pleasant assignment, at the start of which he became a viscount (1946) and the 1st Earl of Tunis (1952), he accepted Churchill's offer to be minister of defense. Unhappy in political life and having no great aptitude for it, Alexander resigned in the autumn of 1954 at his own request. Five years later he and Lady Alexander settled near Windsor (30 miles W of London). He died on 16 June 69, at a nearby hospital before an emergency operation could be performed for what was later diagnosed as a perforated aorta. His headstone in the churchyard of Ridge, near the family's Hertfordshire home, has the word *ALEX* above his full name, titles, and dates of birth and death.

His official dispatches were published in the *London Gazette* (5 & 12 Feb 48; 12 June 50) and were well received. The *Sunday Times* finally prevailed on him to take on a ghostwriter and publish what became titled *The Alexander Memoirs, 1940-45* (New York: McGraw Hill, 1962), edited by John North. The latter, more ghost than editor, produced a mass-appeal biography, widely condemned as journalistic, poorly organized, and misleading. Fortunately for the field marshal's place in history, there are two excellent works: Nigel Nicolson's *Alex: The Life of Field Marshal Alexander of Tunis* (New York: Atheneum, 1973) and Gen W. G. F. Jackson's *Alexander of Tunis as Military Commander* (London: Batsford, 1971).

ALLEN, Terry de la Mesa. US general. 1888-1969. "Terrible Terry" was born at Ft Douglas, Utah, on 1 Apr 88, son of a career artillery officer. His mother, from Brooklyn, was daughter of a Spanish colonel who served in the American Civil War. Allen flunked out of West Point in 1911, his final year, after being "found deficient" in his father's field, ordnance, and gunnery! After taking a year to complete college at Catholic University in Wash, DC, he was commissioned in the cavalry. Tough, profane, unorthodox, an outstanding polo player, and once a professional boxer *(CB 43)*, Allen commanded the 2d Cav and 4th Inf Divs before becoming a major general on 19 June 42. On 2 Aug 42 he took over the 1st Inf Div, "Big Red One," the regular army's premier division since 1918. Allen led it in heavy action around Oran, 8-10 Nov 42, and on into Tunisia. The division fought well after landing in Sicily on 10 July 43. But the indiscipline for which Allen and the division had been notorious in both campaigns got so bad that Eisenhower finally relieved Terrible Terry and his equally colorful assistant, Theodore ROOSEVELT, Jr. Marshall interceded to salvage both for further combat assignments (Pogue, *Marshall,* II, 40), and Allen took over the 104th "Timberwolf" Inf Div on 2 Oct 43. It reached France on 7 Sep 44, served in northern Europe, and—leading Maj Gen Clarence Huebner's 5th Corps—made contact with the Red Army on the Elbe at Pretzsch (*AA,* 571), near Torgau, on 26 Apr 45. His military reputation restored, Allen retired 31 Aug 46. He died in El Paso, Tex, on 12 Sep 69.

AMANN, Max. German publisher. 1891-1957. Hitler's first sergeant during WWI, Amann was born in Munich on 24 Nov 91. Uncouth and domineering but shrewd and intelligent, Amann was the Nazi party's business manager from 1921. In this capacity he later directed the official Nazi publishing house, Eher Verlag. The Reichsleiter earned HITLER a fortune in royalties from large sales of *Mein Kampf.* The jovial, bullet-headed little Bavarian, who lost his left arm while hunting with Franz von Epp in 1931, was stripped of property and pension rights by denazification courts in late 1948 and sentenced to 10 years in a labor camp. He died a pauper in Munich on 31 Mar 57.

AMBROSIO, Vittorio. Italian general. 1879-1958. Born in Turin, he became a cavalry officer and rose to command a squadron in the subjugation of Libya (1912-13). After holding important staff positions, he led the 3d Cav Div (1915-18). By 1940 Ambrosio was army CofS. In Apr 41 he led the 2d Italian Army into Yugoslavia when the Germans invaded the Balkans. Ambrosio resumed his former post in 1942 and succeeded CAVALLERO in Feb 43 as chief of the Commando Supremo. Although unsuccessful in his efforts to reduce German domination, Ambrosio was closely involved with King Victor Emmanuel III and others in deposing MUSSOLINI on 25 July 43. At a meeting with Ribbentrop and Keitel on 6 Aug 43 the Italian CGS requested return of Italian divisions from France and the Balkans. Hitler responded by reinforcing German troops in Italy, and KESSELRING reacted promptly to the Italian surrender by occupying Rome. Ambrosio fled with the king to Brindisi, but after the BADOGLIO government lost authority he resigned on 18 Nov 43 and took the insignificant post of army inspector general.

ANAMI, Korechika. Japanese general. 1887-1945. Born in Oita prefecture in Feb 87, Anami failed the entrance exam to the military academy twice before succeeding. He graduated in 1906 with Princes Asaka and HIGASHIKUNI, uncles of the future emperor, and was commissioned an infantryman. A sleek, burly officer, easy going and convivial but "the most perfect exemplar of the samurai ideal," he "was the most dedicated and loyal" member of the young officers who served HIROHITO from the early 1920s in what became the **Emperor's Cabal**. (Bergamini, 85.) Anami was ADC to the emperor (1926-32), commanded the 2d Imperial Guards Regt (1933-34), headed the Tokyo Military Preparatory School (1934-36), and then joined the War Ministry. There he was chief of the Military Administration Bureau before taking over the Personnel Bureau. Having been a major general since Mar 35, he was promoted exactly three years later and given command of the 109th Inf Div in China. Lt Gen Anami then was vice minister of war from Oct 39. In Apr 41 he took command of the 11th Army in central China. From July 42 he headed the 2d Area Army in north Manchuria. He was promoted in May 43 to full general. (*Kogun*, 221.) As the Japanese reorganized to cope with MacArthur's offensive, Anami's headquarters was ordered to Davao on 23 Oct 43. With five divisions of the 2d and 19th Armies, Anami was charged with organizing a counteroffensive in conjunction with the navy. But the Japanese were unable to reinforce their garrisons in New Guinea and the Solomons. (See KOGA and TOYODA, successors to YAMAMOTO.) In Mar 44, after Rabaul had been isolated, another reorganization assigned ADACHI's 18th Army in New Guinea and the 4th Air Army to the 2d Area Army (ibid., 102). Having moved his headquarters to Manado at the NE tip of Celebes Island (ibid., 78), Anami could do little more than exhort his isolated troops to fight on against hopeless odds, imposing maximum delays and hoping for a miracle. In Dec 44, after the loss of Leyte caused a command crisis in Tokyo, the emperor recalled Anami at the instigation of the imperial uncles (Bergamini, 85). The general, who by then advocated surrender under honorable terms (ibid.), was IG of Army Aviation until Apr 45, then was war minister in the SUZUKI cabinet. Informed early on 15 Aug 45 that the rebellion to stop the broadcast of HIROHITO's surrender announcement had failed, Anami took his own life by **seppuku**. Refusing to accept a coup de grace after opening his abdomen, he lived for almost an hour until a medical corpsman administered a fatal injection at 7:30 AM (ibid., 109-11).

ANDERS, Wladyslaw. Polish general. 1892-1970. The former tsarist cavalryman was seriously wounded and captured while commanding a brigade in southern Poland at the start of WWII. Refusing to join the Red Army, he spent more than a year in the harsh conditions of Moscow's Lubyanka prison. He had not fully recovered when released to raise an army of Polish POWs in Russia. His appointment was announced by SIKORSKI on 14 Aug 41. Interviewing him at the time, C. L. Sulzberger described the "stern-looking," immaculately groomed cavalryman as "about six feet tall . . . thin, well set-up, rather handsome [and], very emotional. . . ." (*Candles*, 168).

Anders soon found that many Polish POWs could not be accounted for. His worst suspicions were realized 18 months later when the Nazis revealed the **Katyn Forest massacre**. Polish forces in the USSR meanwhile grew rapidly, but the Soviets were reluctant to furnish arms and equipment. Stalin then agreed to Churchill's proposal that formation of Anders's army be completed under British auspices in the Near East.

Anders's 2d Polish Corps, consisting of three divisions, joined the British 8th Army in Italy near the end of 1943. The highly motivated, elite unit distinguished itself in two costly actions at Monte Cassino, and again in the final drive up the Adriatic coast. By V-E day, Anders had about 125,000 troops in what many senior Allied military authorities believed was the finest surviving military organization of its size. Churchill wanted it used in the British zone of occupied Germany. But the Soviets, seeing the Free Poles as a political threat, insisted that the elite corps be disbanded. Operating from a small office in London, bitter toward the British and Americans (ibid., 480), Anders was head of the many Polish exiles in England. He published *An Army in Exile* (London and New York: Macmillan, 1949), *Katyn* (Paris, 1949), and *Hitler's Defeat in Russia* (Chicago, 1953).

ANDERSON, Frederick Lewis. US bomber commander. 1905-69. Born in New York on 4 Oct 05, he was commissioned in the cavalry from West Point in 1928 (103/261). He was a pioneer in strategic air warfare, developing training methods that became standard. As CG 8th Bomber Command from 15 July 43 he experienced disappointing results and high losses initially in heavy bomber attacks on U-boat bases in France, Messerschmitt plants in Regensburg, and the controversial Schweinfurt raid on ball-bearing plants. But he helped develop innovations like shuttle-bombing, twilight raids, and bombing through cloud cover. He was promoted to major general on 4 Nov 43 at the age of 39. In Jan 44 Anderson became deputy commander of Spaatz's Strategic Air Forces in Europe and its chief of operations. Retiring for disability in 1947 as a major general, he became a partner in an investment banking firm in Palo Alto, Calif. Anderson died 2 Mar 69 in Houston, Tex.

ANDERSON, John. British administrator and statesman. 1882-1958. The only surviving son of a fancy stationer *(DNB)* and publisher, he was born in Edinburgh on 8 July 82 and graduated from the university there. After studying mathematics at the University of Leipzig, Anderson entered the Colonial Office in 1905. He was posted to Ireland as joint undersecretary, with Sir Hamar Greenwood as chief secretary. Sir John (KCB in 1919) had a major role in coping with the **Black and Tans.** For 10 years starting in 1922 he was permanent undersecretary at the Home Office. Highlights of the service that put him "among the giants" in Whitehall *(DNB)* were helping formulate air raid precautions and being chairman of the committee that got England through the general strike of 1926. In 1932 he was appointed governor of Bengal at a time when particularly dangerous disorders were starting. The proconsul showed administrative ability as well as courage in ending terrorism and coping with grave socioeconomic problems. The normal five-year term of office was extended six months so Anderson could complete critical reforms.

Returning to London, Anderson was elected in early 1938 to the House of Commons as an independent nationalist for the Scottish Universities. He continued to be reelected until the seats were abolished in 1950. During the **Munich crisis** in the fall of 1938, the dour Scot was chairman of the committee addressing the problems of emergency evacuation of civilians. In Nov 38 he accepted a call from Chamberlain to be lord privy seal with particular responsibility for man power, civil defense, and antiaircraft services.

Anderson invited the engineer Sir William Paterson to design what evolved into a small, cheap, easily erected corrugated steel shelter—"the Anderson"—that saved thousands of lives. Sir John survived bombardment from those favoring deep shelters of reinforced concrete and joined the War Cabinet in Oct 40 as lord president of the Council. In this post he had great responsibilities for organizing civilian and economic resources—to include science *(DNB)*. With experience at home and abroad in dealing with dissenters, the lean, flinty "Iron Man" took such stern measures as suppressing the *Daily Worker* for "impeding the war effort" and interning "good" aliens along with the bad. Excelling as an administrator and with a tremendous capacity for work, Anderson not only took the heat of public criticism from Churchill but also allowed the prime minister more time for meddling in military matters. Succeeded in the Council by Clement ATTLEE after the sudden death of Kingsley WOOD on 21 Oct 43, Anderson became chancellor of the exchequer but kept up his atomic energy duties until leaving the government with Churchill in 1945. His many and varied subsequent activities included being a fellow of the Royal Society (1945), a member of the BBC General Advisory Council (from 1945), chairman of the Port of London Authority (from 1946), and successor to Lord John Maynard Keynes as chairman of the Covent Garden Opera Trust (1946). He was raised to the peerage as Viscount Waverley of Westdean in 1952. Recognized in Britain as "the greatest administrator of his time, perhaps of any time in the country's history" *(DNB)*, John Anderson died 4 Jan 58 in London.

ANDERSON, Kenneth Arthur Noel. British general. 1891-1959. Born in India on Christmas Day, the only son of a distinguished railroad authority, Anderson was fluent from childhood in French, learned Italian, and traveled in Tibet and the Middle East, often on foot. He was schooled at Charterhouse and Sandhurst, from which he was commissioned (1911) in the Seaforth Highlanders. A vigorous six footer, blunt, abrasive, and difficult to know, he served in India and rose rapidly to captain in 1915. The next year he was badly wounded on the Somme, winning the MC. In 1917 he took part with the Seaforths in Allenby's campaigns in Palestine and Syria.

Between the wars he commanded the 2d Seaforths on the NW frontier of India, where he was mentioned in dispatches, and saw more service in Palestine. Promoted to colonel in 1934, he took command of the llth Inf Bde and led it as part of Montgomery's 3d Inf Div of the BEF. Toward the end of the withdrawal to Dunkirk he commanded the division. Promoted to major general, he was in England for the next two years, rising to command the 3d Div, then the 7th Corps, 2d Corps, and finally the Eastern Command. In the autumn of 1942 he became the senior British officer in Eisenhower's predominantly American headquarters in London, which was planning the North African landings (Opn Torch). The big, brash Scot was unpopular with inexperienced but ambitious US officers, especially Mark CLARK, but he soon was highly regarded by Ike himself (Buchanan, 155).

Anderson headed the Eastern TF in Opn Torch, directing the most important landings, those around Algiers. For political reasons (the French being expected to welcome American liberators but still being anti-British) the landings on 8 Nov 42 were commanded by Charles RYDER, an American general. The big Scot went

ashore on D+1 to take over from Ryder, and on 11 November he assumed command of the newly constituted 1st British Army. He was promoted concurrently to lieutenant general (T). With only four British brigades at his disposal, Anderson sent task forces forward in hopes of winning "the race for Tunis," 500 miles away. His leading elements were stopped 12 miles short of Tunis on 28 Nov 42 by Germans and Italians under Walter NEHRING. The newly formed 5th Pz Army, led by ARNIM, launched a highly successful counteroffensive on 18 Jan 43 as ROMMEL approached from Libya to link up.

A week later, on 25 Jan 43, Eisenhower prevailed on the French to give Anderson **operational control** over BARRE's battered French 19th Corps. Forward elements of FRIEDENDALL's 2d US Corps were also attached to Anderson's army. But "Anderson was no Montgomery, and could not impose his personality or a master plan on his subordinates before the two Panzer Armies joined hands" (Jackson, *North Africa,* 335). Rommel and ARNIM scored a series of victories, particularly around Kasserine Pass, 14-22 Feb 43, and they might have destroyed the British 1st Army with a panzer drive to Bone if Rommel had been given his head.

ALEXANDER's 18th AG was created about this time to coordinate efforts of the British 1st and 8th Armies (hence the designation 18). Alexander promptly concluded that Anderson was out of his depth as a field commander and asked Montgomery to release Oliver LEESE to take over the 1st Army (Nicolson, *Alex,* 177). Montgomery said he could not spare Leese. Anderson retained his post and received reinforcements from Montgomery when the two British armies linked up. Directed to make the main effort in the final phase of the Tunisian campaign, Anderson attacked on 4 May 43; his troops entered Tunis three days later. The US 2d Corps, now led by Omar BRADLEY and under Anderson's operational control, took Bizerte the same day. Enemy resistance in North Africa ended on 13 May 43, with 250,000 Italian and German forces as prisoners of war.

Though competent, courageous, and energetic, Anderson was through. Montgomery had written Alexander on 21 Mar 43 that Anderson apparently was not fit to command anything larger than a division (Nicolson, *Alex,* 177). Nor had he shown Churchill and other superiors the drive and leadership expected. Returned to

England, Anderson took over the British 2d Army Hq in June 43, began planning for the Normandy invasion, and was knighted (KCB) the following August. But the final career setback came in Jan 44, when Sir Kenneth was replaced by Miles Dempsey and given the Eastern Command. Anderson then headed the East Africa Command, Jan 45-Oct 46, and was governor and CinC Gibraltar, 1947-52, where he was promoted to full general in 1949. He retired in 1952 to live on the Riviera and he died at Gibraltar on 29 Apr 59.

ANDREWS, Adolphus. US admiral. 1879-1948. "Dolly" was born in Galveston, Tex, on 7 Oct 79. Graduated from Annapolis in 1901 (18/67), he had been on the active list for 41 years when Pearl Harbor was attacked. His presidential connections started with Theodore Roosevelt in 1904 when Dolly became junior naval aide. He commanded the presidential yacht *Mayflower* for Harding (1921-23) and was senior naval aide to Coolidge (1923-29). Meanwhile, in WWI he was XO of BB *Mississippi,* then commander of the old BB *Massachusetts.* Andrews then was assistant CofS to the navy's commander in chief. He was the US representative at the 1927 Geneva Conference. In 1936 Andrews was acting secretary of the navy for several months. In 1938 he was chief of the Bureau of Navigation briefly before being promoted to vice admiral, then he became Commander Scouting Force. On 10 Mar 41 he took over as Commandant 3d Naval District, with headquarters in New York. "President Roosevelt probably saved him from being the scapegoat for the burning of the *Normandie,*" Morison comments. When "Sea Frontiers" were created on 1 July 41, Andrews headed the North Naval Coastal Frontier, which on 6 Feb 42 became the Eastern Sea Frontier. This was a scratch force deployed from Newfoundland to northern Florida. In the spring of 1942 he created the "Bucket Brigade," a series of anchorages protected by antisubmarine nets. Next he developed the highly successful interlocking convoy system. "Monthly sinkings in the Eastern Sea Frontier [in 1942] dropped off from 23 in April . . . to 3 in July, and then to zero for the rest of 1942." (Morison, I, 257.)

On 11 Nov 43 the elderly admiral became chairman of the Navy Manpower Survey Board, and in 1945 he was on the three-member naval court of inquiry into the Pearl Harbor disaster. Dolly Andrews died 19 June 48 in Texas at the Houston naval hospital.

ANDREWS, Frank Maxwell. USAAF general. 1884-1943. A pioneer of strategic airpower and first commander (1935) of what became the US Army Air Forces, he was born in Nashville, Tenn. Andrews graduated from West Point in 1906 (42/78) as a cavalryman and entered the Air Service in 1917. He saw no action in France, but became a record-setting long-distance pilot. He was CO, Kelly Field, Tex (1923-27). Promoted directly from colonel to major general, Andrews organized and headed a force created to complement the Air Corps, the General Headquarters (GHQ) Air Force at Langley Field, Va (1935-39). He made so many enemies in the army as a champion of airpower that he was reduced to his permanent rank of brigadier general and shelved. When George C. Marshall became the army's acting CofS he made Andrews G3, the first flying officer to hold such a high position in the US Army. With his temporary rank restored, Maj Gen Andrews returned to duty in Washington (4 Aug 39-22 Nov 40). He then took over the new Panama AF, and on 19 Sep 41 was made a lieutenant general to head the new Caribbean Defense Command. After 14 anxious months, during which his earlier warnings about the danger of a European air force presence in the land of FDR's "good neighbors" was finally understood, Andrews briefly commanded US Army Forces in the Middle East, 4 Nov 42-31 Jan 43. He then succeeded Eisenhower on 4 Feb 43 in London as head of the European Theater of Operations, US Army (ETOUSA). Andrews died 3 May 43 in an aircraft accident in Iceland.

ANGELIS, Maximilian dc. German general. Born 2 Oct 89 in Budapest, he was commissioned in 1910 as a field artillery officer and had an outstanding combat record with the Austrian army in 1914-18. (Angolia, II, 272-73.) As a full colonel he was an instructor in the Vienna War Academy in 1938 when the Anschluss occurred. De Angelis was accepted into the Wehrmacht and promoted to Generalmajor on 1 Apr 38. He was chief of artillery in the 15th Mtzd Corps before starting an infantry career as commander of the 76th Inf "Berlin-Brandenburg" Div. Promoted to Generalleutnant, he led the division in Poland, France, and southern Russia, winning the RK, awarded 20 Feb 42 for action during the winter in the southern Ukraine. Promoted to head the 44th Corps (1 Mar 42), Gen of Arty de Angelis was awarded the Oakleaves (323/890) on 12 Nov 43 for his performance during six months of sustained action (to June 43) around the Kuban bridgehead (ibid.). After briefly heading the reconstituted 6th Army, he took over the 2d Pz Army on 18 July 44, and for the rest of the war was heavily engaged in Yugoslavia and his homelands, Hungary and southern Austria. The 2d Pz Army was disbanded in May 45, and the craggy Austro-Hungarian, wearing the Romanian Military Order among his many decorations, was imprisoned by the Soviets with other Wehrmacht senior officers. He was freed in 1955 to live at home in retirement after more than half a century of military service.

ANTONESCU, Ion. Romanian general and dictator. 1882-1946. Born into an aristocratic Transylvanian family, he attended French military schools and rose to head the Romanian army in 1937. But the general clashed with King CAROL II, was dismissed on 29 Nov 38 for involvement in politics, and jailed two days later after an abortive coup. He was soon released, thanks to pressure from the Iron Guard, and named minister of defense.

As the government of CAROL II collapsed, the king was forced to appoint Antonescu premier with dictatorial powers on 5 Sep 40. Highly regarded by Hitler as "ruthless but incorruptible," Antonescu got the nickname "Red Dog" from the Western press because of the original color of his thinning hair, *not* his thinning political ideology. The strongman was anti-Soviet and uneasy with the support he had to accept from the Iron Guard until he could purge his government of these Fascists. Romania joined the Axis on 23 Nov 40 and became virtually a German puppet. Antonescu assumed the rank of field marshal and actively cooperated with the Germans on field operations from the start of Barbarossa on 22 June 41. He was nominal head of the Romanian field army of 14 divisions that attacked into southern Bessarabia. In Nov 42, as disaster approached at Stalingrad, where a large body of Romanian troops supported the Germans, Hitler briefly considered raising a new AG Don under Marshal Antonescu. It would consist of the 3d and 4th Romanian Armies and the 6th German Army. Hitler moved his headquarters to Vinnitsa

and personally took command of AG A (sacking LIST), and a German-Romanian commission was already working in Rostov "to agree [on] the function of the new headquarters" (Seaton, *R-G War,* 312). Nothing came of this, but Antonescu was involved with Hitler in strategic planning.

Three days after Soviet troops attacked into Romania on 20 Aug 44, Antonescu was arrested in the coup that put MICHAEL in power. The Romanian strongman was executed on 1 June 46 for war crimes that included persecution of Jews and Gypsies.

ANTONOV, Aleksei Innokentyevich. Soviet general officer. 1896-1962. As deputy CGS in Moscow from Dec 42 he was among four officers who had the most military influence on Stalin. Antonov was born 15 Sep 95 in Grodno, son of an artillery officer. He was commissioned in 1916, saw action in WWI, and joined the Red Army in 1919. Because he was not of peasant origin, was an ex-Tzarist officer, and perhaps also because he was believed to be Jewish, Antonov was not allowed to join the CP until 1928. That year he was admitted to the Frunze MA, graduating from there in 1931 and from the Military Academy of the GS in 1937. Meanwhile Antonov had held high staff positions in the Kharkov MD (1933-36) and was a lecturer at the Frunze MA, 1938-40. (Bialer, 628.)

In June 41 he was promoted to general major, one of the "new men" filling the vacuum created by the **Great Purges**. After being an assistant to VATUTIN and deputy CofS in the Kiev Special MD for two months, Antonov was CofS of the Southern Front (Aug 41-July 42). Promoted in Dec 41, Gen Lt Antonov was CofS North Caucasus Front (July-Aug 42), of the Black Sea Group of Forces, and of the Transcaucasus Front (Nov-Dec 42).

Ordered to Moscow, he was first deputy CGS and chief of operations under VASILEVSKY from Dec 42 until relieved by SHTEMENKO on 25 May 43. He was promoted to General of the Army (No. 8) on 27 Aug 43. During the frequent absences of Vasilevsky, who spent 22 of the 34 war months at the front, Antonov bore full responsibility as CGS. On 17 Feb 45 he replaced Vasilevsky as CGS, serving also as a Stavka member.

Antonov, SHAPOSHNIKOV, VASILEVSKY, and ZHUKOV were the officers whose judgment Stalin most respected (Volkogonov, Bk 2, Pt 1, 324).

Antonov frequently signed orders in his own name. But he never became a marshal (**MSU**), remaining a general of the army for almost 19 years, until retirement, and was passed over by some 20 officers once junior to him. Part of this may be explained by his social background and early service as a tzarist officer, but Volkogonov believes that Beria carried out a whispering campaign that caused Stalin to withhold promotion although the dictator probably knew the charges were bogus (Volkogonov, 343).

In 1946 Antonov was demoted to his former post as Vasilevsky's deputy. Two years later he was further reduced to 1st Deputy Commander of the Transcaucasus MD but stepped up to be commander in 1950. After the deaths of Stalin and Beria, Antonov once again was first deputy CGS (Apr 54). The next year, when the Warsaw Pact was formed, he served as its CofS as an additional duty. Antonov died in office on 18 June 62 at the age of 66 and was buried in the Kremlin Wall.

AOSTA, Amadeus of Savoy. Italian general. 1898-1942. Grandson of King Amadeus of Spain, son of Field Marshal Emmanuel Philibert of Savoy, the tall (6 foot 4) 2d Duke d'Aosta was educated in England (including Eton), and was married to a French princess. Aosta became governor general of Italian East Africa and Viceroy of Ethiopia in 1937. Two years later he became military commander in these territories. In 1940 he was ordered to take British Somaliland (sealing the Red Sea) and invade the Anglo-Egyptian Sudan while GRAZIANI attacked from Tripoli into Egypt. The viceroy entered British Somaliland with about 25,000 troops on 4 Aug 40, and by the 17th had driven out the small garrison led by GODWIN-AUSTIN. But the Italian Northern Army from Eritrea under Gen Frusci moved only a few miles into the Sudan to Kassala and Gallabat. Both places were evacuated on 17 Jan 41, and William PLATT conquered Eritrea in a hard campaign before turning south to cooperate with the expedition from Kenya under Alan CUNNINGHAM. Aosta surrendered on 16 May 41. Italian resistance in Abyssinia ended on 27 Nov 41, and Aosta died a few months later as a POW in Nairobi, Kenya. "A chivalrous and cultivated man," he lacked the ruthlessness and military skill for his position (WC, III, 92).

APANASENKO, Iosif Rodionovich. Soviet military leader. 1890-1943. Probably Ukrainian, born 15 Apr 90 in the village of Mitrofanovskoye, Stavropol region, he was the son of a farm laborer. He had completed the third grade and was working as a shepherd when conscripted in 1911. During WWI he became a junior officer and in 1918 entered the Red Army and CP. Apanasenko formed a partisan unit near Stavropol, rose to head the 1st Cav Div, and later he commanded the 6th Cav Div. These units were the basis of BUDENNY's 1st Cav Corps. After graduating from the Frunze MA in 1932, Apanasenko took over the 4th Cav Corps in the N Caucasus MD, then was deputy commander of the Belorussian MD, 1935-38. He headed the Central Asian MD until taking over the Far Eastern Front on 14 Jan 41. Promoted on 22 Feb 41, General of the Army, Apanasenko became VATUTIN's deputy commander in the Voronezh Front on 3 June 43. Apanasenko died 5 Aug 43, during the Kharkov offensive, 40 minutes after being wounded in an air raid in which ROTMISTROV was also hit. The 53-year-old Apanasenko, young for a senior Red Army general, was buried at Belgorod.

AQUINO, Iva d'. See TOKYO ROSE.

ARAKI, Sadao. Japanese general. 1877-1966. The epitome of Japanese militarism, an intelligence specialist on the USSR, and the most eloquent spokesman for the **Strike North** faction, Baron Araki (1935) and principal members of his Imperial Way clique lost out to the Control Group in the struggle among **Japanese political factions**. (See also HIROHITO.) Araki was retired from active duty in 1936 for his political activity but he "kept various caches of secret state documents from the 1930s as guarantees for his continued health and freedom from persecution" (Bergamini, 1084). He also became minister of education, a post giving scope to his ultranationalistic convictions. Sentenced to life imprisonment in 1948 for war crimes, he was released due to bad health in June 55. He died 2 Nov 66 while on a tour of western Japan.

ARCISZEWSKI, Tomasz. Polish politician. 1877-1955. A Socialist revolutionary but strong anti-Communist, he was hunted in 1939 by both the Nazis and Soviets as a resistance leader. Arciszewski was evacuated by the RAF and reached England in July 44 with important information about German V weapons. He later headed the Polish Socialist Party in London and was prime minister of the government in exile (Nov 44-July 45).

ARGENLIEU, Georges Thierry d'. French priest and admiral. 1889-1964. After graduating from the naval academy in 1908 and seeing action in the Mediterranean during WWI he entered the Order of Discalced Carmelites in 1920. Frère Georges had risen to head the order in France in 1939, the year he was mobilized and assigned to the naval staff at Cherbourg. After becoming a POW in May 40, he escaped and joined de Gaulle in London as an assistant to Adm MUSELIER. Wounded in the abortive expedition to Dakar, he remained in Equatorial Africa as head of Free French naval forces. In Jan 41 he was named high commissioner for French Territories in the Pacific and Far East. Promoted to rear admiral, he was involved in organizing bases. In 1943 he took part in the Casablanca Conference, then commanded French naval forces in Britain, succeeding AUBOYNEAU. During the last year of the war he was CinC French Naval Forces in the North. After V-E day he was promoted to full admiral and made IG of naval forces, and he represented France at the San Francisco Conference. Argenlieu was governor general and high commissioner in Indochina until 1947, when he retired from military service to resume his religious life.

ARNIM, Hans Juergen Theodor (Dieter) von. German general. 1889-1962. After leading the 17th Pz Div and 39th Pz Corps for 18 months in Russia, Arnim commanded the 5th Pz Army in Tunisia and succeeded Rommel as head of AG Africa.

Known to friends as Dieter, the scion of an illustrious military family was born 4 Apr 89 at Ernsdorf, Silesia. After 18 months as a Fahnenjunker in the 4th Prussian Foot Guards Regt he was commissioned on 1 Oct 09. Serving on both fronts during 1914-18 and promoted to captain on 27 Jan 17, Arnim was selected for the postwar Reichswehr and earmarked as "a comer." He spent a year with the Defense Ministry, 1924-25, enhancing his reputation as a hard-working, capable, quick-thinking, genial officer. (Samuel W. Mitcham Jr, "Arnim" in Barnett, ed, *Hitler's Generals*, 335-36, cited hereafter as Mitcham.)

Oberstleutnant von Arnim (1932) took command of the elite 68th Inf Regt of the 23d Inf

Div in Berlin on 15 Oct 35 and, jumping a grade, was promoted to Generalmajor on 1 Jan 38. He was in line to succeed the outgoing division commander but was sent off instead to head Army Service Depot 4 at Schweidnitz in Silesia. Apparently he was too purely apolitical at a time when his commanding general, von WITZLEBEN, wanted recruits for an anti-Nazi conspiracy. (Mitcham, 337.) Arnim remained exiled in Silesia until 1 May 39, when he was classified as an "Extra Officer, OKH Berlin" (ibid., 358). He remained without meaningful assignment until 12 Sep 39, when he was named to head the new 52d Inf Div. But the Polish campaign was almost over, and only detachments from the division were later committed in France. Despite this lack of combat service he was promoted to Generaleutnant on 1 Dec 39 and given command of the 27th Inf Div on 5 Oct 40. This unit became the 17th Pz Div on 1 Nov 40 (B&O, 108) and was assigned to GUDERIAN's 2d Pz Gp for the invasion of Russia.

Arnim took his initial objective, Slonim, on 24 June 41 (D+2) and was seriously wounded three days later at Stolpce (Guderian, 224). He returned to duty on 17 Sep, took part in the Kiev encirclement, and seized Bryansk and its Desna River bridges. This brilliant coup de main contributed materially to the collapse of Soviet resistance in the Vyazma-Bryansk pocket by 17 Oct 41. (Guderian, 233.)

A few weeks later Arnim was promoted to Gen of Pz Troops with rank from 1 Oct 41, and on 11 Nov he left his division to command the 39th Pz Corps in AG North. (Arnim was *acting* commander of the 39th Mtzd Corps until 1 Feb 42, then officially assumed command. The unit became a panzer corps on 9 July 42. [B&O, 41-42.]) Winter had struck in full force and it took Arnim four days to reach his new headquarters near Tikhvin. The Soviet counteroffensive began two days later, and by 23 Dec the Germans had been driven back almost 100 miles from the tip of the Tikhvin salient to the Volkhov River. After holding defensive positions through the winter, the 39th Pz Corps Hq was moved out of the line, and directed to save the German hedgehog at Kholm (Cholm). In a five-day operation employing panzer and infantry units, Arnim linked up with survivors of the 5,000-man garrison on 5 May 42. Arnim was notified on 30 Nov 42 that he would command the new 5th Pz Army in Tunisia with the rank of Generaloberst. Both actions were effective 3 Dec 42, and after two meetings with Hitler, Arnim took over from NEHRING on 9 Dec as head of Axis forces in Tunisia. On Christmas Day Arnim secured his shallow beachhead by retaking Longstop Hill, a mere 25 miles from Tunis. Winter rains stopped operations, and Eisenhower had lost his race for Tunis. But "Arnim could never bring himself to co-operate with his more famous rival. This failure would materially contribute to the Axis defeat in North Africa, and would leave a permanent stain on his military reputation." (Mitcham, 344.)

After Rommel's departure on 9 Mar 43 Arnim became head of AG Africa. He withdrew to his final position the night of 1-2 May, using up almost all of his dwindling ammunition supplies. He was captured on 12 May with the Afrika Korps headquarters but refused to surrender his army group on grounds that he had lost contact with subordinate units. The last of these surrendered the next day.

Generaloberst von Arnim has been called "dour uncooperative and unsmiling . . . a difficult, secretive type of man" (Jackson, 324, 333). But British historian Paul Carrel concludes that Arnim "fulfilled his task with a consideration, courage and humanity which neither his own soldiers nor the enemy have forgotten" (Carell, as quoted in Mitcham, 353). The second highest-ranking German POW of the Western Allies when captured (after Rudolf HESS), he was held in an English country house until freed in 1947. Making a new home in West Germany, his properties in East Germany having been confiscated by the communists, Arnim was granted a pension in 1949. He died in Bad Wildungen on 1 Sep 62.

ARNOLD, Archibald Victor. US Army general. 1889-1973. "Arch" Arnold was artillery commander of the 7th Inf Div on Attu, Kiska, Kwajalein, then commanding general after 24 May 44 (when he was promoted to major general) for the landings on Leyte and Okinawa. On 9 Sep 45 he became military governor of Korea, joining the US-USSR Commission in Jan 46. From late 1946 until his retirement in 1948 he was with Army Ground Forces headquarters.

ARNOLD, Henry Harley. USAAF commander. 1886-1950. The senior US airman, builder of the world's most powerful air force, was born 25 June 86 at Gladwyne, Pa, son of a prosperous

country doctor. Like Eisenhower, eight years his junior, the future general distinguished himself primarily as a prankster at West Point, whence he graduated in 1907 (66/111). Nicknamed "Hap" because of his bright disposition, the five-feet-eleven-inch tall second lieutenant grew into a jovial, 200-pound general.

Serving on Governor's Island, which became New York City's first airport, Arnold saw Wilbur Wright and Glenn Curtiss with their early airplanes. After taking lessons from the Wright brothers, Arnold and Thomas D. Milling became the US Army's first pilots in 1911. They established the Signal Corps's first aviation school at College Park, Md, where Arnold set an altitude record of 6,540 feet, and was involved in prescribing standards for army pilot certification. But after little more than 18 months, Arnold was transferred to desk duty in Washington, missing much of the early development of army aviation, to include flying in France. Arnold was deeply involved in Billy MITCHELL's crusade for airpower. In 1934 he led 10 new Martin bombers on an 18,000-mile flight to Alaska.

At the start of 1936, Arnold was assistant chief of the Air Corps, taking over as chief when Maj Gen Oscar Westover was killed in a crash on 29 Sep 38. Revolutionary concepts of airpower by Italian military theorist Giulio Douhet (1869-1930) "came very close to conforming to the theory we had worked out," Arnold wrote in his memoir, but Americans had "a different attitude . . . toward bomber defense and a very different view of precision bombing. . . ." (Arnold, 104, 113.) The first Boeing B-17 Flying Fortress, delivered 1 Mar 37, reflected the differences. Arnold urged aircraft manufacturers to plan for unprecedented expansion. Design of the B-29 Superfortress, the B-25 Mitchell, and the B-24 Liberator was begun. Arnold also advocated strategic airborne operations (Buchanan, 407). In 1938 the US ranked seventh in military aircraft production. The Munich Crisis impressed Roosevelt with the Luftwaffe's major role in Hitler's humiliation of the Western powers. On 28 Sep 38, "Two days before the [Munich] pact was actually signed," wrote Arnold, "the President came straight out for air power. Airplanes—now—and lots of them. . . ." (Arnold, 128-29). But Arnold convinced FDR that, "A lot of airplanes by themselves . . . were not air power." There was need for a tremendous training program, research and development, and a steady flow of replacement planes and men. The US also had to supply the hard-pressed Allies, who were horrified by Arnold's idea that they were expected to hold out for a couple of years until US airpower was ready to finish the war alone.

He became a general of the army on 21 Dec 44, ranking after Marshall, MacArthur, and Eisenhower. Even before the war ended, Arnold was preparing the final moves to establish an independent US Air Force. Without warning, however, he "passed out of the picture with a heart attack," to use his words. Succeeded by SPAATZ, Arnold left Washington on 1 Mar 46 after 42 years of military service. He died on 15 Jan 50 in Sonoma, Calif.

ARNOLD, William Howard. US general. 1901-76. Born in Dyersburg, Tenn, he graduated from the USMA in 1924 (63/405), and became an infantryman. Brig Gen Arnold led troops on Guadalcanal, New Georgia, Bougainville, and the Bismarck Archipelago before being 14th Corps CofS. Promoted on 12 Nov 44, Maj Gen Arnold led the Americal Div from then until the division's inactivation on 12 Dec 45. Meanwhile, on Cebu he took the surrender of more than 10,000 Japanese when the war ended.

ARNSTEIN, Daniel. US entrepreneur. 1890-1960. A rough-hewn six-footer from Chicago's South Side, he rose from driver of a horse-drawn delivery wagon and part-time pro football player to head the NY Terminal System. In June 41 he became US Commissioner to the **Burma Road**, where inefficiency and corruption had slowed traffic to a trickle. He quadrupled the volume of shipments within four months (*CB 42*) but declined Chiang Kai-shek's offer to remain in Chungking and make a fortune running the road as a private concession (ibid.).

ARTEMYEV, Pavel Artemyevich. Soviet general officer. 1897-1979. Artemyev rose from political officer during the civil war to chief of the Operational Directorate of Troops of the NKVD in 1941. Promoted to general lieutenant in June 41 and to general colonel the next year, Artemyev headed the Moscow MD 1941-47. He then took the higher courses at the Military Academy of the GS, returned to his former post

in 1949, and was banished in June 53, after BERIA's fall, to the Ural MD as deputy commander. He rose to first deputy commander before disappearing from public view in 1960.

ASTAKHOV, Fyodor Alekseyevich. Soviet airman. 1892-1966. During the Civil War he headed aviation of the 5th Army before being appointed chief of the Siberian AF. From 1940 he was deputy CofS of the Main Directorate (or Administration) of the AF. Promoted in June 41, Gen Lt (Aviation) Astakhov took command of the SW Front AF. He was chief of the Main Directorate of the Civil Air Fleet, 1942-47, and simultaneously served as deputy commander of the Red Army AF, May 42-Aug 43, and deputy commander of Long-Range Aviation to Dec 44. He retired in 1950. Astakhov died on 12 Oct 66 after a long illness and was buried in Moscow's **ND Cemetery**.

ASTIER DE LA VIGERIE, Emmanuel R. d'. French resistance leader. 1900-69. Younger brother of François and Henri (following), the darkly handsome, Mephistophelean Baron d'Astier, whom one detractor called "an anarchist in dancing shoes," was born in Paris. He graduated in 1918 from the naval academy, left the navy in 1924, turned to journalism in 1933, and rejoined the navy when France went to war. He was head of naval intelligence at Lorient. Demobilized in the summer of 1940, he soon joined a small group of saboteurs in the south of France. In Dec 40 this expanded to form the cadre of *la Dernière Colonne* (the Last Column), a leftist group that skirted the law by using crafty propaganda against collaborators and the Vichy regime. (Larousse.) In Jan 41 the resistance leader went underground and founded *Libération,* a leftist group in the unoccupied zone. In July 41 the conspirators began putting out a clandestine weekly of the same name. The *gauchist* journalist's resistance movement was the first of real significance in France and one of the three major groups that Jean MOULIN later attempted to unite. Called to Algiers in 1943, d'Astier became commissioner of the interior in de Gaulle's **CNL**, then was minister of the interior. In this post until Oct 44, Emmanuel d'Astier was a prime mover in getting Allied aid for the Maquis. After the liberation he directed *Libération* as a daily, and it had Communist Party support until 1964. Meanwhile, in 1945 the journalist became a *progressiste* deputy from the Department of Ille-et-Vilaine. In 1958 he was awarded the Lenin Peace Prize. D'Astier published many books, including *De la chute à la libération de Paris*. He died in Paris on 12 June 69.

ASTIER DE LA VIGERIE, François Pierre Raoul d'. French general. 1886-1956. Eldest by far of three brothers who figured prominently in the Free French government, François d'Astier graduated from St Cyr in 1910. During WWI he commanded several air squadrons and became an ace. In October 1939 Gen d'Astier was given command of the critical Northern Zone of Air Operations. He used his planes effectively despite frustrating political restrictions and the failure of army commanders to request the air support he had available. Ordered to Morocco with most of his surviving force, and soon put on the inactive list, Gen d'Astier promptly went over to the resistance. In 1942 he joined de Gaulle in London, and on 20 Dec he went to Algiers with vague instructions "to assume all useful liaisons with the French leaders there" (de Gaulle, *Unity,* 71). Intramural bickering among the French had continued after the Allied landings some six weeks earlier. Greeted with hostility and suspicion, the emissary finally told DARLAN candidly that the admiral was the fly in the ointment and should remove himself. Adm Darlan reacted by asking Eisenhower to remove d'Astier! The Americans agreed, and the general was back in London the same day (24 Dec 42), when it was learned that DARLAN had been assassinated! Brother Henri d'ASTIER (below) was implicated. François d'Astier was inspector of the Free French air forces 1942-44, and attained the rank of lieutenant general. In 1945 he was named ambassador to Rio de Janiero but held the post only a year.

ASTIER DE LA VIGERIE, Henri d'. French officer. 1897-1952. Brother of Emmanuel and François, Henri d'Astier was a veteran military intelligence officer, former **cagoulard**, and dedicated monarchist. After the French collapse in June 40 he fell out with Charles Maurras, who was perhaps the most rabid theorist in the French royalist movement. D'Astier formed a small resistance group in Pamiers, in the Ariège Department of SW France, headed one of the **Chantiers de la jeunesse** in Algeria, and was one of the first to join the resistance formed in Aug 40 by André Achiary in North Africa. As "Uncle Charlie" he worked with Robert MURPHY in planning the Allied landings in North Africa (Opn Torch), attending the clandestine **Cherchell** Conference. D'Astier had a leading role in the uprising during the night of 7-8 Nov 42 that helped the Allies take Algiers with little French opposition. He subsequently occupied an important post on the High Commission (de Gaulle, *Unity,* 73). Disenchanted with Giraud and strongly hostile to Darlan, he supported the Comte de Paris, pretender to the French throne, who had come to Algiers from Morocco in hopes of conciliating French political factions. D'Astier approved of DARLAN's assassination—if he did not instigate it (Larousse). Jailed on orders from Giraud, he was held until Oct 43. (According to the authoritative Larousse encyclopedia of WWII, he was released after de Gaulle's arrival in Algiers on 30 May 43. This source also says he was freed in time to form and command a body of irregulars that fought in Tunisia. The problem is that fighting in Tunisia ended 13 May 43!)

ASTOR, Nancy Witcher. Socialite and politician. 1879-1964. The first woman to sit in the British House of Commons, she was born on 19 May 79 in Danville, Va. Her father, Chiswell Dabney Langhorne, later made a fortune in railroad development and bought an estate at Mirador, near Charlottesville. The exceptionally beautiful, brilliant, petite southern belle was 18 when she married Robert Gould Shaw. They had a son before being divorced in 1903. The next year Nancy went to England for the social and hunting seasons. In 1906 she married Waldorf Astor and made an exciting place of Cliveden, one of two stately homes of the British Astors. When her husband succeeded to the peerage as the 2d Viscount Astor in 1919, Lady Astor took his seat that year in the House of Commons. (She was the second woman *elected* to Parliament; the first was Sinn Fein Countess Markievicz in 1918, but the countess was not seated because she refused to take the oath [*DNB*].)

In the mid-1930s her "Cliveden set" of government and newspaper men was notorious for advocating appeasement of Hitler. "The idea of a conspiratorial set meeting there [at Cliveden] to promote appeasement and a sell-out to Nazi Germany was a journalistic invention," writes John Grigg in *DNB*.

Lady Astor served in parliament until 1945, by which time her performance had deteriorated and reelection prospects were dim *(DNB)*. Widowed in 1952, the dowager viscountess died 2 May 64 at her daughter's house in Lincolnshire. She is buried at Cliveden, which had recently figured innocently in the **Profumo affair**.

ATCHERLEY, Richard Llewellyn Roger. British airman. 1904-70. "Batchy" and his equally unorthodox twin brother David became legends in the RAF. After serving as a test pilot for the Royal Aircraft Establishment from 1934, Dick Atcherley pioneered night fighter operations at the start of WWII, then distinguished himself as the innovative commander of the BEF's air element in Norway. Promoted to group captain, awarded the AFC, and appointed to the DSO, he headed a night fighter training airfield in Scotland and invented a system of lighting that became standard. In 1942 the airman became a sector commander in the south of England, winning the bar to his AFC. He was downed in the Channel and wounded while flying a Spitfire. In 1943 he went to North Africa as a group commander in the Desert AF, then was on the staff of the Allied Expeditionary AF. After returning to England, Atcherley created the Central Fighter Establishment and commanded it for the rest of the war.

The brilliant, irreverent, and unorthodox airman was given to clowning—much to the dismay of his superiors. Nevertheless, he headed the RAF Cadet College, 1946-48, before becoming CinC of the new Pakistani AF, 1949-52, and being promoted to air vice marshal in 1951. Brother David's jet was reported missing over the Mediterranean in 1952, a loss that devastated his twin. Atcherly served in the US as commander of the RAF staff, British Joint Service Mission, before becoming CinC Flying Training Command, 1955-58. An air marshal from 1956, he died 18 Apr 70 in the hospital at Aldershot.

ATTLEE, Clement Richard. British statesman. 1883-1967. Son of a solicitor, he was born in London on 3 Jan 83, educated at Oxford, and called to the bar in 1906. Part-time work on the London docks led Attlee to become a socialist, and he joined the Fabian Society in 1907 and the Labour Party a year later. In WWI he became a major, serving at Gallipoli, in Mesopotamia, and in France, and suffering several bad wounds. He

was first elected to Parliament from Limehouse (London) in 1922 and remained an MP. From 1935 Attlee led Britain's Labor Party and the Opposition. When it became apparent on 9 May 40 that CHAMBERLAIN had lost Labor's support and that CHURCHILL would take over as PM, Attlee and Churchill agreed on the distribution of posts in a coalition government *(DNB)*. Attlee was in the War Cabinet as lord privy seal until Feb 42, when he was officially designated deputy PM. At this time he also became secretary for the Dominions, and from Sep 43 was lord president of the Council (succeeding Sir John Anderson).

Never wavering in his loyalty to the PM, even in the dark days of 1941-42 *(DNB)*, Attlee succeeded Churchill in 1945. Ten years later, when it became apparent that the Conservatives would elect a prime minister, Attlee announced his retirement on 7 Dec 55 and was elevated that day to the peerage as 1st Earl Attlee. A devoted family man with few political cronies, he achieved high office despite all expectations and then revealed unsuspected ability *(DNB)*. Attlee died 8 Oct 67 in Westminster Hospital.

AUBOYNEAU, Philippe Marie Joseph Raymond. French admiral. 1899-1961. Born in Constantinople (Larousse), he graduated from the Ecole Navale on 15 Mar 18 and was assigned to a destroyer. After completing the Ecole de Guerre he commanded DD *L'Orage* 1937-39 and was ordered to the Far East when war broke out. Promoted to *capitaine de frégate* in December he was liaison officer with British naval forces based at Colombo, Ceylon. In May 40, when France was invaded, Capt Auboyneau was assigned the same post in the Mediterranean under Andrew "ABC" Cunningham. Auboyneau rallied to de Gaulle three months later and took command of the 1st DD Div of the Fighting French (FF). In Mar 42 he relieved Adm MUSELIER in London as CinC FF naval forces, and naval commissioner in the **CNL**. Soon after the Allies landed in North Africa (8 Nov 42) he went to Algiers as DCGS of FF naval forces with the rank of major general (Larousse). He was replaced in London by Thierry d'ARGENLIEU. Auboyneau led the 3d Cruiser Div during the 1944 invasion of southern France. He was promoted to vice admiral in September 1945 and for two years commanded French naval forces in the Far East. Promoted to full admiral on 14 Dec 57, he held important command positions until retiring in 1960. Auboyneau died 22 Feb 61 in Paris. (Larousse.)

AUCHINLECK, Claude John Eyre. British general. 1884-1981. One of the most underestimated soldiers of the war, "the Auk" was born on 21 June 84 in Ulster of a Scots-Irish military family. Educated at Wellington College and Sandhurst, he was commissioned in 1904 into the 62d Punjab Regt. *(Concise DNB.)* Lifelong association with the regiment began with action in Egypt, Aden, and Mesopotamia. He became a brevet lieutenant colonel and in 1917 was appointed to the DSO. The Auk commanded the elite Peshawar Bde in operations on India's NW frontier, 1933-35, operating with ALEXANDER's Nowshera Bde in two successful campaigns to repel invading tribesmen and pacify large regions. Promoted to major general, he was deputy CGS, India, in 1936 and took over the Meerut District in 1938. Tall, athletic, notoriously monosyllabic, but with a highly original military mind, Auchinleck was viewed as the Indian army's most outstanding officer and was poised for fame. Soon after Britain declared war he flew to England to head 4th Corps Hq and was about to join the BEF in France when ordered to Narvik as GOC Northern Norway. He arrived on 7 May 40 to command 25,000 British, French, Polish, and Norwegian troops. The Allies took Narvik on 28 May, but Lord CORK ordered the troops withdrawn on 8 June because a German relief column was approaching from the south.

The Norwegian fiasco gave Auchinleck an appreciation of how much work was needed to bring the British up to par with the Germans, particularly in the matter of tactical air support. The Auk returned to England and took over the 5th Corps in Southern Command before moving up to head it. His duties included preparing defenses in the region most vulnerable to the expected German invasion. As an outspoken and progressive thinker in the Indian army Auchinleck had made enemies. Montgomery wrote of his brief association with the Auk in Southern Command in 1940, "I cannot recall that we ever agreed on anything" *(Memoirs, 65).* Auchinleck was promoted to full general in November 1940, knighted (GCIE), and ordered back to India as CinC. But on 5 July 41 Sir Claude changed posts with Wavell to become commander in the Middle East with headquarters in Cairo.

Although Greece was lost and Suez threatened, Churchill demanded that offensive action against Rommel be undertaken within a month or two. Auchinleck insisted on having time to prepare. After several postponements, he launched Opn Crusader on 18 Nov 41. This started off badly, and it soon was apparent that Alan CUNNINGHAM had to be replaced as head of 8th Army. Instead of leaving Cairo to take command of the army personally, Auchinleck gave the post to the untested Neil RITCHIE on 23 Nov 41. The unlikely choice seemed a good one, and by 2 Jan 42 Rommel had retreated 400 miles to El Agheila. But the "Desert Fox" struck back on 21 Jan 42 and reconquered Cyrenaica. Churchill pressured Auchinleck to counterattack immediately, but the Auk again insisted on having time for proper preparation.

Correlli Barnett points out that Auchinleck proposed in vain that true combined-arms formations be made from separate infantry, armor, and artillery forces. "As a military reformer and innovator Auchinleck has not received his due, for except for Slim he stands preeminent in this regard among British generals of the Second World War," (Carver, ed., *The War Lords,* 267).

On 26 May 42 Rommel began advancing to envelop the Gazala line and on 21 June he took Tobruk, the greatest British disaster since the loss of Singapore. Auchinleck personally assumed command of the 8th Army on 25 June and pulled it back toward Egypt. Rommel renewed his offensive the next day and drove the British to the 40-mile line between El Alamein and the Qattara Depression.

Though badly overextended, Rommel made another lunge on 1 July 42 but was stopped two days later. Auchinleck slowly gained the initiative and stopped Rommel's advance by counterattacking on 21 and 26 July in the first battle of El Alamein. By pressing on for two more days, Auchinleck might have destroyed Rommel's Panzer Army Africa. But British armor and infantry still were unable to coordinate their action, so Auchinleck broke contact 27 July and withdrew. The decision probably was correct, but Churchill had become so personally involved in eliminating Rommel that he flew to Cairo with Alan BROOKE, arriving on 3 Aug 42 to start a sweeping reorganization. Auchinleck learned by letter on 8 Aug that he would be replaced by ALEXANDER as commander of the Middle East and by Montgomery as commander of 8th Army.

AUPHAN, G. A. J.

19

Ironically, the new generals adopted about the same strategy as Auchinleck's and took more time than he had wanted. Declining the Persia-Iraq Command, the Auk returned to India and was unassigned for almost a year. On 20 June 43 he again replaced WAVELL, this time as CinC India (for the second time). Auchinleck was responsible for the "forgotten front" in Burma until MOUNTBATTEN's SEAC was created four months later. The Auk was made a field marshal on 1 June 45 and in that year was advanced in the knighthood to GCB. After MOUNTBATTEN became "the last Raj," Auchinleck was given the dismal task of splitting his beloved Indian army, unit by unit, along ethnic lines into the new armies of India and Pakistan. The former CinC India became supreme commander of the remaining forces, which promptly undertook massacres that Auchinleck was denied political authority to control. The field marshal had been accused of being partial to the Pakistanis, and Mountbatten asked him to resign (Concise DNB). The Auk complied on 15 Aug 47, shortly after India became independent, and refused a peerage (ibid.). Meanwhile his marriage had been a war casualty, the trouble starting in the summer of 1941 when he refused to take his wife to Cairo because his subordinates were not allowed to have their families in Egypt. (Auchinleck's ex-wife married Air Chief Marshal Sir Richard PEIRSE in 1946.) The field marshal held honorific posts in London until retiring in 1968 to Marrakech. Still vigorous in his 90s, "devoid of rancour, even though his career was partially blighted by injustice and calumny" (Barnett in Carver, ed., The War Lords, 260). Auchinleck died in Marrakech in 1981.

AUDET, Richard J. Canadian ace. 1922-45. As an RCAF flight lieutenant in action for the first time on 29 Dec 44, Audet downed five German planes in about two minutes. In two months he scored 10.5 victories before being hit by antiaircraft fire on 3 Mar 45 while attacking a train in Germany. Audet died in the crash of his Spitfire.

AUNG SAN, U. Burmese nationalist. 1915-47. Soon after fleeing to Japan in 1941 to avoid arrest by the British, Aung San came home to command the Burmese Independence Army. In Mar 45 he started negotiations that led to his guerrillas joining the British camp, whereas Dr BA MAW, a fellow nationalist, fled to Japan. Aung San was among seven killed 19 July 47 by political assassins.

AUPHAN, (Gabriel Adrien Joseph) Paul. French naval officer and Vichy official. 1894-1982. He was born 4 Nov 94 at Alès (Gard). As a senior staff officer and naval technician Auphan was highly regarded by Darlan and was party to high-level diplomatic negotiations in the 1930s. When France declared war on 3 Sep 39, Capitaine de Vaisseau Auphan was made under CofS of French Maritime Forces. The day before negotiations for the Franco-German armistice began, Auphan and Darlan personally gave the British their word that Hitler would never have the French fleet. In the new Vichy government Auphan served as minister of the merchant marine, under chief of maritime forces (official "Fiche Biographique"), and was Darlan's right-hand man.

In Sep 41 he became the French Navy CGS and director of the office of the secretary of state for the navy. On 18 Apr 42 Auphan took over as secretary of the navy, retaining his naval CGS title. Defenders say he took this post under LAVAL only to assure that the French fleet would never fall into German hands. (Larousse.)

Before and after the Allied invasion of North Africa, Auphan and Weygand urged Pétain to side openly with the Allies (Churchill, IV, 624, 627). After the 8 Nov 42 landings they urged Pétain to approve the cease-fire ordered by Darlan, who was in Algiers (de Gaulle, II, 52). Laval prevailed in having Pétain condemn Darlan's action (ibid.), but Auphan persuaded Pétain to approve what became known as the "Auphan telegram." Revoking previous messages on the subject, this telegram officially sanctioned and legitimized the cease-fire accord signed by Mark Clark and DARLAN at Algiers the morning of 10 Nov 42. Auphan used his secret naval code to send the telegram at 3:15 PM the same day. (Larousse.)

Auphan was prepared to arrest Laval that evening but never got Pétain's authority. On 11 Nov, after being the only minister to advocate a cease-fire throughout North Africa, Auphan sent Adm LABORDE instructions to destroy French warships in Toulon if the Germans threatened to attack the port. Finally, on 13 Nov, he sent Darlan the secret message from Pétain approving NOGUES's turning over command of all of French Africa to Darlan. Rather than approve the granting of full powers to Laval, Auphan resigned on 18 Nov 42. He went on indefinite leave *(Permission de 3 mois et Congé d'armistice).*

One of Pétain's last official acts was to empower Auphan on 11 Aug 44 to negotiate with de Gaulle on "legitimate transmission of authority" in France. De Gaulle did not deign to reply. On 9 Sep 44 the de Gaulle government revoked Auphan's pension, and on 14 Aug 46 the High Court of Justice sentenced him to forced labor "in perpetuity" and to "national indignity" for life. The charges against him included ordering destruction of the fleet at Toulon (herein). The admiral was freed from prison by an act of 25 Jan 55, and by a decision of 13 Nov 56 he was, in effect, "rehabilitated." Auphan published *les Grimaces de l'Histoire* (1951), *les Convulsions de l'Histore* (1955), and *la Marine dans l'histoire de France* (1955). With Jacques Mordal he published *The French Navy in World War II* (Annapolis, Md: US Naval Institute, 1959).

AURAND, Henry Spiese. US general. 1894-1980. The logistician was born 21 Apr 94 in Pennsylvania. He graduated from West Point in 1915 (20/165) and transferred from the coast artillery to the ordnance department. As a major general (8 Sep 42) he headed the 6th Service Cmd until becoming deputy chief ordnance officer in the ETO. In 1945 he briefly commanded the Normandy Base Section before taking over the Services of Supply in the China Theater on 25 May 45. After the war he rose through a succession of staff and command assignments to become a lieutenant general on 22 Jan 48. Director of the Pentagon's logistics division until 1949, he then commanded the US Army, Pacific, until his retirement on 31 Aug 52 as a three-star general. He died 18 June 80 at Laguna Beach, Calif. (Cullum.)

AURIOL, Vincent. French statesman. 1884-1966. The son of a village baker in Revel (just east of Grenoble), he was a university student when he joined the Socialist Party in 1905. He became a lawyer and in 1909 founded and began editing the daily newspaper *Midi Socialiste.* Auriol entered the Chamber of Deputies in 1914 as a member for Muret (near Toulouse). He was closely allied with Léon Blum, and in the latter's first Popular Front government (1936-37) was minister of finance. Auriol was among the 80

legislators at Vichy who had the courage on 10 July 40 to vote against the constitutional bill that gave Pétain dictatorial powers, and he was among the opponents of the regime arrested on one pretext or another. Released in 1941, he helped form a clandestine socialist party as well as the "Liberate and Federate" resistance movement at Toulouse. In Oct 43 he joined de Gaulle's provisional government after being extracted from the south of France by **Lysander.** First in Algiers, then in liberated Paris, Auriol presided over the socialist bloc of legislators. Closely allied with de Gaulle in forming a new French system of government, Auriol was the first president of the Fourth Republic. He held that post from 16 Jan 47 through 15 Jan 54.

AUSTEN, Godwin. *See* GODWIN-AUSTEN.

AXIS SALLY. *See* Mildred GILLARS.

AXMANN, Artur. Nazi Youth leader. 1913-. Born 18 Feb 13 in Hagen, he founded the first Hitler Youth group in his native Westphalia. Axmann was a clean-cut, well-educated young man whose sincere belief in Nazism was infectuous. In 1933 he became chief of the Social Office of the Reich Youth Leadership and was von SCHIRACH's principal assistant. Both men served briefly on the western front, Axmann until May 40. Three months later, after von Schirach became Gauleiter of Vienna, Axmann was full-time Reich Youth Leader (Reichsjugendfuehrer). In 1941 he lost an arm while serving on the eastern front. As the Red Army closed in on Berlin he commanded about 1,000 boys whose main task was to hold the Wannsee bridges until WENCK's relief column arrived. The Youth Leader reached the Fuehrerbunker just in time to hear Hitler shoot himself, to view the corpses of Hitler and Ava Braun, and to bid the GOEBBELS family farewell. The next day, 1 May 45, Axmann was among those who fled from the bunker with Martin BORMANN. He was organizing an underground when finally arrested in Dec 45. In May 49 a Nuremberg denazification court sentenced him to 39 months in prison. A Berlin denazification court had its shot some 10 years later. The Reichsjungendfuehrer, found guilty only of indoctrinating youth with Nazism, was fined 35,000 marks—about half the value of his property in Berlin. He became a businessman in the Canary Islands.

B

BA MAW. Burmese revolutionary. 1893-1977. Educated in Europe as a lawyer and becoming a violently anti-British nationalist, the cultivated Dr Ba Maw was Burma's first premier (1937-39). The British arrested him on 6 Aug 40 for infringing on the Defense of Burma Act (Allen, *Burma*, 18). Imprisoned until Jan 42, he escaped with help from the Japanese invaders, who in 1943 made Ba Maw head of a new civil administration. Although fellow nationalist AUNG SAN changed sides as Allied forces began liberating Burma, Ba Maw fled to Japan in 1945. The puppet was allowed to return in 1946. He published *Breakthrough in Burma. Memoirs of a Revolutionary, 1939-1946* (New Haven, Conn: Yale, 1968).

BACH-ZELEWSKI, Erich von dem. German general. 1899-1972. A notoriously brutal SS officer, the burly Bach-Zelewski was from an aristocratic Prussian military family. Born 1 Mar 99 in Lauenburg, Pomerania, he joined the army in 1914. After the war he served in a **Freikorps** before being commissioned in the **Reichswehr**. But in 1924 he was forced out for reasons that are not certain. He testified at Nuremberg that it was because two of his sisters married Jews, and that when reinstated in 1934 he joined the Nazi Party and SS only to protect his career. (Davidson, *Trial*, 565n.) According to other sources he was guilty of "Nazi intrigues" as an army officer and was the "S.S. organizer on the Austrian frontier" in 1931 (Brett-Smith, 159). This information squares with postwar murder charges brought against him for killings committed in 1933 (below).

Soon after being reinstated in 1934 he advanced his own career during the **Blood Purge** by seeing that Anton Freiherr von Hoberg und Buchwald's name was on the hit list. The latter's only offense was holding a post von dem Bach wanted. After commanding SS and Gestapo units in East Prussia and Pomerania he was promoted to SS general in 1939, and in the Polish campaign participated personally in massacring Jews in Riga, Minsk (his headquarters), and Mogilev. Hitler had a special affection for the energetic thug the Fuehrer said was "so clever he can do anything, get round anything."

Von dem Bach was made Higher SS and police chief in Russia with AG Center and Himmler's special representative in charge of antipartisan operations. He also was a general of the Waffen-SS and frequently commanded Waffen-SS troops. In July 43 Himmler put his hatchetman in charge of all antipartisan operations on the eastern front, then later that year sent him to Poland. There the Obergruppenfuehrer was responsible for crushing the Warsaw uprising that began on 1 Aug 44 under Bor-KOMOROWSKI. The greatest excesses of this horrible affair were committed by Kaminski's White Russian brigade of ex-POWs and Oskar Dirlewanger's brigade of German convicts on probation. (The unit was formed by Gottlob BERGER.) At the insistence of Guderian, who was supported by Himmler's SS liaison officer, FEGELEIN, Hitler ordered withdrawal of these brigades (Guderian, 356). "Von dem Bach took the precaution of having Kaminski shot and thus disposed of a possibly dangerous witness" (ibid).

The uprising ended on 2 Oct 44 after 63 days of house-to-house fighting and around-the-clock bombardment by air and siege artillery. One of the war's most famous photographs shows a bareheaded and downcast Bor-Komorowski shaking hands with a smiling von dem Bach at the surrender. (Brett-Smith, photo 17; Keegan, *Who Was Who*, 30; Mason, *Who's Who*, 30.) The Germans used the uprising as a pretext for destroying the Polish capital; Bach was ordered on 11 Oct 44 to "raze Warsaw to the ground while the war is still going on and in so far as this is not contrary to military plans for the construction of strongpoints" first removing "all raw materials, all textiles, and all furniture . . ." (as quoted in Guderian, 359).

Bach reached Budapest on 13 Oct 44 to support SKORZENY, whom Hitler had given the mission of stopping the Hungarian regent, Adm HORTHY, from making a separate peace with the Russians. To his disgust, von dem Bach was not allowed to use the monstrous 25-inch siege mortar he had gotten from Sevastopol to help in the demolition of Warsaw.

As a prosecution witness at Nuremberg the unrepentant Prussian insisted that he had only followed orders (Brett-Smith, 160). Bach, who surprisingly faced no charges at Nuremberg, escaped extradition to Russia by claiming to have protected Soviet Jews from extermination by SS **Einsatzgruppen**. But a Munich denazification court sentenced him in 1951 to 10 years of "special labor." The sentence was suspended and von dem Bach ended up merely confined to his home in Franconia (Wistrich). In 1961, however, he was arrested for involvement in the Blood Purge (herein) and ordered to serve four and a half years in prison. Indicted again in 1962, he received a life sentence for murdering six Communists in 1933. Von dem Bach died 8 Mar 72 in a prison hospital at Munich-Harlaching.

BADER, Douglas Robert Steuart. British airman. 1910-82. Born in London, the legendary "legless airman" and his elder brother were reared in straitened circumstances after their father died in 1918 of war wounds. Bader won a scholarship to St Edward's School in Oxford and excelled as a student and athlete before winning a competitive exam to the RAF College at Cranwell. Continuing to be superior in classwork and sports—captain of the rugger team and a champion boxer—Bader was commissioned in 1930. He quickly became famous as an RAF fighter pilot and athlete, but after only 18 months of flying experience he barely survived a crash that required amputation of both legs. Discharged from the RAF in 1933, he mastered artificial legs, went to work in London for the Asiatic (later Shell) Petroleum Co, and demonstrated that he could fly a plane. Still, despite his persistent efforts, Bader was not reinstated as an RAF pilot until 1939, when Britain went to war and PORTAL bent some regulations. (Sims, *Aces,* 72ff.)

Flight Lt Bader promptly removed all doubts about his fitness. He shot down an Me 109 fighter and an He 111 bomber in two missions over Dunkirk on 31 May 40. The next month he was promoted and transferred from 222 (Spitfire) Sqdn to command of 242 (Hurricane) Sqdn, which had suffered 50 percent casualties in its first few weeks of combat and was demoralized by bad leadership. The pilots, most of them Canadian, assumed that with a physically handicapped leader they would be relegated to a minor role. "It was one of the worst guesses of the war" (Sims, 78). Bader had been selected for the assignment by the air group commander, LEIGH-MALLORY, who knew him well. The new broom immediately swept out two flight commanders, imposed high standards, and raised such a fuss about inefficient logistical support that he was put on the carpet before Dowding. But two supply officers were promptly replaced by ones who produced what Bader demanded. The revitalized squadron had its baptism of fire on 30 Aug 40, in the third week of the Battle of Britain. In a one-hour sortie from Duxford the squadron claimed destruction of 12 German aircraft over the Channel, Bader himself downing two Me 110s. (Ibid., 78-90.)

Eventually leading the 12th (Duxford) Gp of up to five squadrons, Bader was outspoken to the point of insubordination. He complained that the warning system was too slow; he objected to prescribed tactics and procedures, sometimes ignoring ground control to preempt Luftwaffe pilots who almost invariably attacked out of the sun; and he championed the **big wing.** When the RAF finally took the offensive in 1941, Wing Comdr Bader (then with 12 kills) led the Tangmere wing of three Spitfire squadrons.

When caught unawares on 9 Aug 41 by an Me 109 of Adolf GALLAND's JG 26 near Le Touquet, France, Bader had 23 victories and ranked fifth among RAF aces. After barely managing to break a leather strap that trapped his right leg in the cockpit, Bader parachuted to safety but made a hard landing that badly damaged his other artificial leg. Galland sent a car to pick up his famous adversary from the hospital for a VIP tour of his base near Bethune. With a dim view of being considered a fellow "knight of the air," the class-conscious RAF hero was concerned primarily about having been done in by one of the Luftwaffe's NCO pilots! Galland, who personally had downed two Spitfires that day and had no idea who got Bader, placated his dour guest by presenting an officer who pretended to have done the deed. After a few days in the hospital Bader escaped with help from a French nurse. Lowering himself at night into the courtyard on a rope of sheets, Bader hobbled on his damaged legs to a peasant's house. But he was betrayed by another French nurse and recaptured a day before the underground could spirit him away. (Sims, 93. See Toliver and Constable,

Galland, 149–153, for a more recent and probably more reliable account, that differs in several details). The Luftwaffe meanwhile radioed the RAF that their guest needed a new set of legs and offered safe passage for a delivery plane. The British rejected the truce offer but nevertheless dropped the spare parts during a raid.

An incorrigible escape artist, Bader ended up at **Colditz**. Freed in Apr 45, he led the first postwar Battle of Britain Flypast (over London). 15 Sep 45, was promoted to group captain, but retired from the RAF in 1946. He rejoined the Shell Company that same year and was managing director of Shell Aircraft Ltd 1958-69. Bader's story is told in Paul Brickhill's *Reach for the Sky* (New York: Norton, 1954), a movie of the same title, and in an autobiography, *Fight for the Sky* (1973). Knighted in 1976 he wore the DSO with bar and two DFCs.

BADOGLIO, Pietro. Italian general and statesman. 1871-1956. Of Piedmontese peasant origin, he was a junior officer in Ethiopia (1896-97) and Tripolitania (1911-12). During WWI he rose from captain to general and became CofS to the CinC. After the war he was a senator and army CofS (1919-21). Always anti-Fascist, Badoglio was exiled as ambassador to Brazil (1924-25) but was later made a Marshal of Italy and head of the Italian armed forces.

As the Marchese del Sabotino he was governor of Libya (1928-33). Two years later he led the conquest of Ethiopia, becoming the Duke of Addis Ababa and viceroy of the new colony. From Nov 39 (two months after Hitler attacked Poland) he again headed the armed forces and opposed Italy's entry into the war on grounds that the country was not ready. He resigned 6 Dec 40 after the humiliating Italian failure in Greece.

Although apparently not active in ousting Mussolini on 25 July 43, the elderly marshal was immediately named by the king as head of government and commander of the Italian army. On 3 Sep 43 he secretly concluded an armistice with the Allies. When Gen Maxwell TAYLOR visited Rome secretly to coordinate a proposed landing of the US 82d Abn Div around the capital in conjunction with the 9 Sep 43 assault at Salerno, Badoglio had the operation called off because Kesselring had rushed in German troops. Badoglio, the royal family, and the government were besieged in the ministry of war

building during the night of 8-9 Sep 43. The next day they escaped from Pescara to Brindisi in two corvettes and set up a government under Allied auspices. Badoglio and Eisenhower signed the surrender instrument on 29 Sep 43 aboard HMS *Nelson* off Malta. On 13 Oct 43, the day after SKORZENY's dramatic rescue of Mussolini, Italy declared war on Germany. Badoglio organized a coalition government, already having established cobelligerent status with the Allies. He achieved Soviet recognition in Mar 44, which won support from Togliatti's Italian Communist Party. After the Allies occupied Rome (4 June 44) Badoglio and King Victor Emmanuel III stepped down to permit formation of a new government.

BAECK, Leo. German Jewish scholar. 1873-1956. "The central figure of German Jewry during the Nazi period, a great rabbinical scholar, teacher and community leader" (Wistrich), Leo Baeck was born 23 May 73 in Lissa, Prussia, the son of a rabbi. After completing his studies at the Berlin Institute in 1873 he was a rabbi in Oppeln until 1907, then in Duesseldorf, and in 1912 he began 30-years' service in Berlin's most prominent congregation. From publication of Das Wesendes Judentums (1905), translated as The Essence of Judaism (New York: Schocken Books, 1948), Baeck was lauded as a rabbinical scholar of the first magnitude. From the autumn of 1933, just after Hitler seized power, Rabbi Baeck was president of the central representative body of German Jews (Reichsvertretung der Juden in Deutschland), and in 1939 he became its chairman. Although quickly concluding that "the thousand-year-old history of German Jewry has come to an end" (quoted by Wistrich), he refused to seek sanctuary abroad.

The rabbi was frequently summoned for questioning by the Gestapo and arrested several times, and in 1943 he was sent to Theresienstadt. There he headed the camp's council of elders and continued to teach. He was liberated 8 May 45, a day before his scheduled execution (Briggs, ed).

Going to London, he was active as president of the Council of Jews from Germany and chairman of the World Union for Progressive Judaism. He was professor in the history of religion at Hebrew Union College in Cincinnati, and in 1954 he founded the Leo Baeck Institute for research on the history of Jews in Germany, with offices in New York and London, and was the first presiding officer. He died 2 Nov 56 in London.

BAER (Bär), Heinrich. German ace. 1913-57. Born 25 Mar 13 in Sommerfeld, son of a farmer, he joined the Luftwaffe in 1937 and became a pilot NCO. Early service in Poland, France, and the USSR was with the MOELDERS Sqdn (JG 51). In the spring of 1942, Baer took command of JG 77 in Sicily, then of JG 1 and 3. (Angolia, I, 118-120; Sims, *Aces,* passim.) In Jan 45 GALLAND organized JV 44 to refit the Me 262 jet as a fighter, and Baer took charge of the unit's flying school near Augsburg. He succeeded GALLAND as squadron commander on 26 Apr 45 and ended his military service with the rank of Oberstleutnant. "Pritzl" Baer flew more than 1,000 missions, was shot down 18 times, and had 220 victories. His score of 124 against western pilots was surpassed only by MARSEILLE (158 kills). The 16 jet victories he had with the Me 262 during the last few months of the war is still the world record.

Baer was killed 28 Apr 57 near Brunswick while demonstrating a light plane.

BAGRAMYAN, Ivan Khristoforovich. Soviet military leader. 1897-1982. An Armenian born 2 Dec 97 in Elizavetpol (now Kirovabad), Azerbaijan, he was the son of a railroad worker and became a railroad technician. Bagramyan entered the army in 1915, rose to the rank of junior lieutenant, joined the Red Army in 1920, and took the name "Dashnak" to serve as an officer in the Armenian nationalist movement (1921-30). Bagramyan did not become a party member until June 41, the year he was promoted to colonel. Having attended the Higher Cavalry School, the Frunze MA, and headed the operations section of a field army and the Kiev Special MD, Bagramyan was Budenny's operations officer in the SW Front during the early phases of Barbarossa. He escaped capture in the Kiev encirclement, was promoted to general major, and remained operations officer when Timoshenko succeeded Budenny as front commander. For planning the attack that began on 6 Dec 41 and retook Yelets, Bagramyan was promoted to general lieutenant and made Timoshenko's CofS in the SW Direction.

In July 42 he assumed command of the 16th Army, which became the 11th Guards Army in Apr 43. By June Bagramyan was a general colonel, serving initially under Sokolovsky (West Front) then under Konev. In the latter's Opn Kutuzov, Bagramyan led a large force that penetrated the northern shoulder of the Orel salient. Acclaimed for his strategic concepts in this campaign, Bagramyan succeeded Yeremenko in November as commander of the 1st Baltic Front. On 1 Dec 43 he began making the main effort of the winter offensive against AG Center. But in five successive thrusts around Vitebsk, concentrated on the German 4th Army, he had little success and incurred heavy losses.

He attacked with three field armies and a tank corps on 22 June 44, spearheading a drive toward Riga. This reached the Baltic a few miles west of the city on 31 July 44. Bagramyan took Memel on 27 Jan 45 to separate 20 divisions of Schoerner's AG North from Reinhardt's shattered AG Center and encircle Koenigsberg, cutting off "Group Samland." But the Germans reinforced Koenigsberg, and Hans Gollnick's Group Samland retained cohesion under heavy assault.

Bagramyan had been promoted to general of the army (no. 18) in Oct 44, but now he was in disfavor for failing to take his objectives in East Prussia as quickly as expected. So in Feb 45 Bagramyan's 1st Baltic Front was downgraded to the "Zemland Forces Group." His staff, plans, and troops were absorbed by Vasilevsky's 3d Belorussian Front with Bagramyan as deputy front commander. Vasilevsky took Koenigsberg on 10 Apr 45, and Group Samland surrendered nine days later.

Vasilevsky was ordered to the Far East about this time, and Bagramyan headed the 3d Belorussian Front until it was disbanded in Aug 45. After that he commanded the Baltic MD until 1954, held high army and party posts, and in 1955 was promoted to Marshal of the Soviet Union (no. 24). Twice a Hero of the Soviet Union (1944, 1977), he retired after being Deputy MoD and Chief of the Rear Services (1958-68). Bagramyan died 21 Sep 82 and is buried in the Kremlin Wall.

BAKER, George. American cartoonist. 1915–75. Staff Sgt Baker created "Sad Sack," a lumpy little GI loser featured in *Yank* magazine. The cartoonist was a tall, slim, athletic bachelor who in 1937 started working for Walt Disney Studios. Drafted in June 41, he did animation for training films. When *Yank* started publication a year later, his comic strip became the magazine's first permanent feature, ultimately reaching an estimated 10 million readers a month. *(CB 44.)*

BAKER, Josephine. Entertainer. 1906-75. A lissome, talented African-American singer and performer who had little future in racist America of the 1920s, she went to France and quickly became a music hall celebrity. After the Allied landings in North Africa on 8 Nov 42 she came out of retirement in Morocco to join the French in Algeria as an ambulance driver and troop entertainer. When her adopted country was liberated, Mlle Baker took over a chateau in the Perigord region of southern France and impoverished herself by keeping a home for children.

BALBO, Italo. Italian airman. 1896-1940. One of four top leaders in MUSSOLINI's 1922 March on Rome, he had been one of the most brutal *squadristi* in Ferrara. He was a general of Fascist militia and held several cabinet posts before becoming minister of aviation in 1929. Popular, flamboyant, and capable, Balbo made Italy one of the world's greatest air powers, personally leading several notable and highly publicized transatlantic flights. In 1933 he became Italy's first air marshal. Perceived as a political threat, he was exiled by the Duce to be governor general and CinC of the armed forces in Libya. Serious animosity developed as the spade-bearded, mustachioed hero became more openly critical of Italy's alliance with Germany. Only 18 days after Italy declared war, Balbo was returning to Libya from Rome in a plane with nine others when shot down near Tobruk on 28 June 40. A British air attack was in progress, and the Italians announced that he had died in action. But the British reported he was downed by Italian AA fire. Mussolini, who was suspected of ordering the "accident," later commented that Balbo was "the only one capable of killing me." The airman succeeded by GRAZIANI.

BALCK, Hermann. German general. 1893-1982. According to a military authority who served for a year as Balck's CofS, "if Manstein was Germany's greatest strategist during the Second World War, I think Balck has strong claims to be regarded as our finest field commander" (Mellenthin, *Panzer Battles,* 246). Yet Balck remains virtually unmentioned in standard works on Hitler's war.

He was born 7 Dec 93 at Danzig-Langfuhr into an old military family, son of a general who held the Pour le Mérite and whose book on tactics was used as a text by the US Army. The son entered Hanover Military College in Feb 14 and by 1918 commanded a company on the western front. Although a horse cavalryman, he became a lifelong friend of Guderian's and an early advocate of mechanization. Balck left OKH in late Oct 39 to command a motorized infantry regiment, then—under Guderian—led the 1st Rifle Regt, 1st Pz Div, through the Ardennes into France. The 47-year-old lieutenant colonel was awarded the RK for seizing and holding a critical bridge just north of Sedan on 13-14 May 40 (Guderian, 128; Angolia, I, 90). He went on to distinguish himself in daring operations, at one point facing de LATTRE's tough 14th Div around Rethel and remnants of the French 3d Armd Div around Juniville. Balck personally captured a set of French regimental colors. (Horn, *1940,* 561.)

Balck was promoted to full colonel shortly after leaving the Vienna area on 5 Mar 42 to fight in Greece. His 3d Pz Regt led the 2d Pz Div in turning the Metaxis Line and taking Salonika on 9 Apr 42. Through mountainous terrain notoriously unsuited for armor he led a battle group that outflanked New Zealanders trying to hold the last Allied defensive line near Mount Olympus.

Back to OKH staff duty in July 41, he served in the department responsible for panzer troops. Favorably impressing Hitler, Oberst Balck was given command of the famous 11th Pz Div in Russia on 16 May 42 and promoted 1 Aug 42 (B&O, 94 & n). Generalmajor Balck destroyed more than 500 Soviet tanks in his first two months of action. On 20 Dec 42 he received the Oakleaves for saving the 1st and 4th Pz Armies from encirclement in the Caucasus, and was promoted 1 Jan 43 to Generalleutnant (B&O, 94n). The general left his division on 4 Mar 43 and was awarded the Swords that day for having surprised and annihilated M. M. POPOV's 5th Shock Army (Angolia, I, 92).

Succeeded by von CHOLTITZ, Balck became Gen of Pz Trps on 1 Nov 43 (ibid.). Briefly replacing SCHOERNER (12-14 Nov 43) as commander of the 40th Pz Corps, Balck succeeded EBERBACH as head of the 48th Pz Corps on 15 Nov 43 (B&O, 54). On 5 Aug 44 he moved up to head the hard-pressed 4th Pz Army. With what Guderian calls "inexhaustible energy and skill," Balck immediately counterattacked. By 9 Aug he had reduced the size of the dangerous Baranov bridgehead on the upper Vistula, eliminated another minor one, and had won back some ground at Pulavy. This vigorous action prevented a major German disaster (Guderian, 261) and the front in Poland was temporarily stabilized. Balck's achievement brought him the Diamonds, awarded 31 Aug 44.

Moved to the western front, he succeeded BLASKOWITZ in Alsace as head of AG G, reaching Molsheim on the evening of 20 Sep 44, according to his CofS, F. W. von MELLENTHIN. Within three months Balck's "Cinderella among army groups" (Mellenthin, *Panzer Battles,* 314) had been driven back in Lorraine by PATTON. But his main enemy was HIMMLER, who intrigued to have Balck removed (Guderian, 394). Blaskowitz resumed his former post on 24 Dec 44, and Guderian, by then army CofS, saved Balck for further service by sending him to Hungary (ibid.).

Heading the 6th Army and again without proper military resources, Balck, still in Hitler's disfavor, Balck failed in a desperate attempt to relieve the German garrison in **Budapest.** The so-called Army Group Balck soon included Herbert Otto Gille's 4th SS Pz Corps, which had two divisions. Supported by the 96th Inf Div, the elite panzer corps failed in its heroic efforts to relieve Budapest 2 Jan-7 Feb 45. (Seaton, *R-G War,* 500-1.) Balck subsequently retreated north with AG South into Austria, surrendered 8 May 45, and was released in 1947.

US Army historians "discovered" Balck many years later and were delighted to find him living quietly in Stuttgart. He was brought to America for what turned out to be three long interviews on his experiences as a commander of large combined-arms forces. Three extensive interviews were ordered transcribed by historian Harold C. Deutsch, who made them available to student officers at the US Army War College (personal information). Still not properly recog-

nized as a field commander of large forces, Balck died in 1982.

BANDERA, Stepan. Ukrainian nationalist. 1909-59. As leader of the young faction of the Ukrainian nationalist movement and a rival of Yevhen Konovalets, he ordered the 1934 assassination of Polish minister of defense Bronislaw Pieracki (Sudoplatov, 15-16). Bandera and two others were serving life sentences in Lvov when freed by the Soviets in 1939. Breaking with the former leadership, Bandera set up a new Organization of Ukrainian Nationalists (OUN) with its capital at Lvov. There he proclaimed an independent government of Ukrainia on 30 June 41. He subsequently was confined in Sachsenhausen until Sep 44 for refusal to collaborate with the Germans, after which he headed Ukrainian resistance until the OUN was wiped out in 1950. Bandera died on the stairs of his remote Munich apartment on 15 Oct 59, apparently of a heart attack. It was revealed later that he had been killed by a KGB agent with a novel weapon that silently blew hydrogen cyanide into the victim's face (Gehlen, 240 ff).

BARBEY, Daniel Edward. US admiral. 1889-1969. The head of MacArthur's amphibious force in the SWPA was born 23 Dec 89 in Portland, Ore, and graduated from the USNA in 1912 (113/156). In 1940 he became CofS to the Commander, Training Force, Atlantic Fleet, pioneering design and development of landing operations and amphibious craft. Capt Barbey took part in all training exercises in the Atlantic, which included both US Army and USMC forces. In Nov 41 he set up an amphibious warfare section in the Navy Dept. On 10 Jan 43, a few weeks after being promoted, Rear Adm Barbey established the 7th Amphib Force Hq in Brisbane, Australia. "He demonstrated an extraordinary organizing capability," writes Hanson Baldwin in his introduction to the admiral's memoir. "Through energy, force of personality, professional competence, and common sense, he was able to fashion a smoothly functioning amphibious force from the most heterogeneous collection of craft and men in history. And he got along with MacArthur—not by any means the easiest of his tasks. . ." (Barbey, vii). The admiral directed amphibious operations from Buna to the Philippines and Borneo. Promoted again in late 1944, Vice Adm Barbey took the surrender in Seoul on 9 Sep 45 of Japanese forces under Gen Nobuyki ABE and later directed the complicated surrender negotiations in North China. "Uncle Dan" succeeded Kinkaid as 7th Fleet commander on 19 Nov 45. After heading the 4th Fleet he retired in 1951. Barbey died 11 Apr 69 in the Bremerton, Wash, US Naval Hospital. His memoir, *MacArthur's Amphibious Navy: Seventh Amphibious Force Operations, 1943-45* (Annapolis, Md: US Naval Institute) was published that same year.

BARBIE, Nikolaus (Klaus). Nazi war criminal. 1913-91. The "Butcher of Lyons," a Rhinelander of French ancestry, was born to Catholic parents on 25 Oct 13 in Bad Godesberg (near Bonn). He joined the SS in 1935, was assigned to the elite SD, and was commissioned 20 Apr 40. The chunky second lieutenant (SS Untersturmfuehrer) was with an SD detachment for Rundstedt's offensive in the west that began on 10 May 40. Moved to Amsterdam for service with the Central Bureau for Jewish Emigration and commended as a "disciplined, hardworking, friendly and honest officer . . . an honor to the SS," he was promoted in Nov 40 to Obersturmfuehrer and awarded the Iron Cross 2d Class on 20 Apr 41. Sent to Russia, the friendly Nazi served with an antipartisan force and learned the cruder methods of controlling the populace.

In the spring of 1942 he was called to Berlin for a special assignment. The Germans had an elaborate plan to kidnap Alexander FOOTE, who worked with ROESSLER's "Lucy ring" in Switzerland. Foote smelled a rat and did not step into the trap set for him in June 42 near the French border town of Gex. (Foote, 145-46.)

Barbie was transferred that month from Gex to Dijon, where he was reassigned from SS intelligence (Amt VI) to the Gestapo (Amt IV). On 11 Nov 42 the Germans reoccupied Lyons (having been there briefly in June 40). Barbie set up shop in the Hotel Terminus, operating from there until June 43, when he moved to offices and specially built torture chambers in the Ecole de Santé Militaire. He continued to use Montluc prison. Under the local SD commander, SS Lt Barbie had a domain of 15,000 square miles that included the Jura Mountains and French Alps. He had some 25 officers in sections specializing in the resistance and communists, sabotage, the

Jews, false ID cards, counterintelligence, and intelligence archives. The Germans had invaluable assistance from the Lyons police chief, René Cussonac.

Not yet 28 years old, the enterprising young Butcher of Lyons quickly destroyed all but one of five SOE networks that had operated in and around the city since the summer of 1941. On 7 June 43 he finally caught René "Didot" Hardy, who had given the Germans fits with a highly successful sabotage ring made up of his fellow railroad workers (below). It appears that Hardy traded his own skin for that of Jean MOULIN, whom Barbie arrested 21 June 43 to score his greatest coup.

As Allied troops approached to liberate Lyons on 3 Sep 44, Barbie destroyed Gestapo records and liquidated hundreds of Frenchmen, including more than 20 of his own close collaborators. An "SS leader who knows what he wants, and is enthusiastic," as a superior reported (Bower, *Barbie*, 106), he was promoted to captain (SS Hauptsturmfuehrer) effective 9 Nov 44. Before leaving Lyons to retreat north, Barbie suffered a foot wound that required hospitalization. But he soon volunteered to fight on, joining a scratch force in the north around Baranow-Bruckenkopf before ending up with an SS detachment in Duesseldorf that maintained order in slave labor camps. He then hid out until the spring of 1947, when recruited by the US counterintelligence corps (CIC) in Bavaria.

The Butcher of Lyons' crimes remained virtually unknown until René Hardy was brought to justice in 1947. Hardy had gone to Algiers after Moulin's arrest and joined the Free French. After the liberation he was director of the repatriation department in FRENAY's ministry of prisoners. Hardy's first trial, 20-24 Jan 47, ended in acquittal. A few weeks later, however, a former conductor on the Lyons-to-Paris night train came forward with a duplicate of the reservation slip Hardy had used on 7 June 43, and the new witness testified he had seen the Germans arrest Hardy. But it has never been proved that Hardy betrayed Moulin.

CIC officers protected Barbie from extradition to France because he knew too much about American counterintelligence methods. As Klaus Altmann, Barbie was evacuated from Europe with his wife and two children. He reached Bolivia in June 51, was granted citizenship, and concealed his identity until 1972. Nazi hunters Beate and Serge Klarsfeld led the effort to track down Barbie-Altmann and have him extradited. He reached Lyons on 5 Feb 83. Having been convicted in absentia for the murder of Jean MOULIN, Barbie was an acute embarrassment to the French because a public trial would remind them of something they had been trying to forget: widespread collaboration during 1940-45. Further, the death penalty had been abolished in France, and Barbie could not be retried for the same crimes. The wily and unrepentant Gestapo chief was charged with eight counts of "crimes against humanity" that included the execution of men, women, and children as hostages, torture, and mass deportations. He was sentenced in 1987 to life imprisonment and died of leukemia 25 Sep 91 in the prison hospital at Lyons. (*See* Tom Bower, *Klaus Barbie, Butcher of Lyons* [London: Michael Joseph, 1984].)

BARRE, Georges. French general. 1886-1970. Born 26 Nov 86, he began a distinguished combat career in 1912 as an officer of colonial troops in Morocco. Barré was promoted to brigadier general in Dec 39 and commanded the 7th North African Inf Div on the French frontier when the German invasion started on 10 May 40. Sustaining losses of over 30 percent, dropping back to north of Paris after being continuously in action, the colonial division was singled out for a glowing citation *à l'ordre de l'Armée*. After the armistice of June 40 Barré headed the French delegation to the Italian demilitarization commission on the Libyan frontier (Mareth line). On 2 Jan 42 the 55-year-old veteran became the senior military commander in Tunisia (like Morocco a French protectorate), and on 20 Jan 42 he was promoted to général de division. Barré adopted a neutral position when the Allies landed in North Africa on 8 Nov 42. The Americans had promised to land 5,000 troops in Tunisia but changed their plans without notifying the French. After NEHRING reached Tunisia to command reinforcements being sent from Sicily to hold an Axis beachhead, the "neutral" French general withdrew westward into the hills while parleying with the Germans. He intended to stall while waiting to see whether Allied troops would arrive in time to support him. (Jackson, *North Africa,* 316.) At 4 AM on 19 Nov 42

Nehring gave Barré an ultimatum to evacuate his strongpoint at Medjez-el-Bab within three hours (i.e., around dawn). But Barré stood fast, holding the critical communications center all day under heavy air attack and assaults by the 5th Parachute Regt as Allied troops raced forward. The French withdrew after dark under cover of the 1st British Parachute Bn and a US artillery battalion. After remaining on the ground to support an unsuccessful British advance on Tunis, Barré's division moved south to join L. M. Koeltz's French 19th Corps for the rest of the Tunisian campaign. He published *Tunisie 1942-43.*

BARUCH, Bernard Mannes. US elder statesman. 1870-1965. Born 19 Aug 70, "Bernie" Baruch was the son of a doctor who fled Poland in 1853 and settled in Camden, SC. Dr Simon B. Baruch married Belle Wolfe, descendant of a Sephardic Jew who had come to America from Portugal in colonial times. *(CB 41.)* Moving with his family to NYC in early life, but maintaining roots in South Carolina, Baruch was a Phi Beta Kappa and an athlete at the City College of New York. Over six feet tall, with aquiline features, blue-gray eyes, and a perpetual smile, he proved to have a genius for finance.

A long public service career began during the Wilson administration, but Baruch apparently lacked confidence in his own ability to hold high office and preferred the role of adviser. A close friend of ROOSEVELT's and biggest single financial contributor to the latter's first presidential campaign, the tycoon was expected to be in line for a cabinet post. But FDR "paid the old Wilsonian every compliment except following his advice." By 1940 FDR decided to make Baruch successor to Donald NELSON in a beefed-up WPB. The appointment was about to be made when Baruch fell ill for a week, and the president unaccountably decided to leave Nelson in charge. (Burns, *Roosevelt,* 52.)

Swallowing his pride, Baruch remained a major adviser to the president and to the men under whom war mobilization was reorganized, James F. BYRNES and Fred M. VINSON. So many high posts were held by Baruch's close associates that he ended up with greater influence than if he had held a top position himself. Detractors find that the tall, white-haired, amiable, egotistical, park-bench elder statesman owed his fame more to shrewd publicity than achievement. His autobiography is *Baruch: The Public Years* (New York: Holt, Rhinehart & Winston, 1960).

BASTICO, Ettore. Italian general. 1876-1972. He fought the Turks in 1911-12 before serving in the First World War, in Ethiopia, and in Spain. A close friend of Mussolini's, the hard-nosed little general suddenly succeeded the easygoing GARIBOLDI on 12 July 41 in Libya as governor and CinC. Determined to assert his authority, he immediately clashed with ROMMEL over the strategy for retaking Tobruk. This led to open hostility, German officers finding the Italian "difficult, autocratic and violent" (Irving, *Fox,* 112), and Rommel nicknaming him "Bombastico." Rommel won out by getting Mussolini's authority to deal directly with the Commando Supremo in Rome, which cut Bastico out of the chain of command. But when Hitler made Rommel a field marshal in 1942 for taking Tobruk, Mussolini made Bastico a Marshal of Italy. Returning to Italy in 1943 and retiring from the army in 1947, Bastico wrote the three-volume *Evolution of the Art of War.* (S&S.)

BATOV, Pavel Ivanovich. Soviet military leader. 1897-1985. Commander of field armies throughout the war, Batov was born in the village of Filisovo, Yaroslavl Oblast. The short, trim, ethnic Russian began military service in 1916 and joined the Red Army in 1918. During the civil war he trained volunteers and led them against White Guards at Yaroslavl. Code-named "Pablo Fritz," he was an adviser in Spain in 1936-37 and suffered a serious wound. Back in the USSR he took command of an infantry corps, leading it in Poland and Finland 1939-40 before becoming first deputy commander of the Transcaucasian MD.

Gen Lt Batov (from June 41) led the 9th Detached Rifle Corps in the Crimea. Two months later he was deputy commander of the 51st Special Army, taking over from KUZNETSOV on 22 Oct 41. Driven from the Crimea, Batov went to the Bryansk Front as head of the 3d Army in Jan–Feb 42. Until the following October he was assistant front commander, serving under CHEREVICHENKO, GOLIKOV, ROKOSSOVSKY, and REYTER. Batov then went to the Stalingrad area as commander of the 4th Tank Army, which was dubbed the "Four Tank Army" because it had so few vehicles (Erickson, *To*

Stalingrad, 447-48) and promptly redesignated the 65th Army, Don Front. Batov took part in some of the war's hardest fighting after the Soviet triumph at Stalingrad. He was in the battle of Kursk, the Dnieper crossing (becoming a HSU), and the drive through Belorussia into East Pomerania and across the Oder estuary (second HSU award).

Promoted in June 44, Gen Col Batov spent four years in the Northern Group of Forces and later was first deputy CinC of Soviet forces in Germany. Promoted again in 1955, Gen of the Army Batov took over the Carpathian MD that year. He later headed the Baltic MD (1958-59) and the Southern Group of Forces (1961-62). He was Warsaw Pact CofS (1962-65), chairman of the Soviet Veterans Committee (1970-81), and served in the **Inspectorate** until his death in 1985.

BAUDOUIN, Paul. French financier and politician. 1895-1964. Virtually unknown to the public until 1940, Baudouin figured prominently and nefariously—if briefly—in the fall of France and in the Vichy government. Born in Paris, educated at the Ecole Polytechnique (1914 and 1919-20), he was **chef de cabinet** to six finance ministers. Baudouin was an inspector of finances (1921-26) and headed the Bank of Indochina (1927-40). A protégé of Hélène de PORTES, Baudouin was Reynaud's chef de cabinet after Reynaud became premier and dismissed the faithful Gaston PALEWSKI. On 21 May Reynaud named Baudouin secretary to the War Cabinet with the official status of under-secretary of state. This made Baudouin privy to all War Cabinet business, all the better to keep his *patronne* informed. When the latter henpecked Reynaud into forming a new cabinet with more men of her political stripe (Langer, *Vichy,* 20-21), Baudouin became undersecretary for foreign affairs on 6 June. (Reynaud took the foreign minister portfolio after ousting Daladier.) From 13 June, the violently Anglophobic Baudouin was among those who advocated an armistice, and he became foreign minister in the Pétain cabinet when Reynaud resigned. Holding the post in the Laval cabinet, Baudouin opposed the premier on several important issues, particularly any effort to reestablish diplomatic relations with the British. Baudouin became minister-secretary of state (ministre secrétaire d'Etat à la présidence du Conseil) on 28 Oct 40.

After helping oust LAVAL on 13 Dec 41, he collaborated with FLANDIN, who moved up to be Pétain's deputy. When Flandin was succeeded by Darlan on 2 Jan 41, Baudouin retired from politics and returned to his post in the Bank of Indochina.

Arrested in Sep 44, he was convicted of collaboration and sentenced to five years of forced labor. He was conditionally released on 8 Jan 48. Returning to his financial affairs, Baudouin published *Neuf Mois au gouvernement* (1948), showing he was as slippery in print as in life.

BAYERLEIN, Fritz. German general. 1899-1970. "A stocky, tough little terrier of a man, full of energy and enthusiasm" (Young, *Rommel,* 92), Bayerlein was GUDERIAN's operations officer in France and Russia before seeing 19 months of almost incessant fighting in North Africa as CofS in the Afrika Korps and Panzer Army Africa. He subsequently commanded a panzer division and army corps. Bayerlein is often cited as an authority on senior German generals and their operations.

Born in Wuerzburg on 14 Jan 99, the Bavarian began his military career as a 16-year-old private in the British sector of the western front. Entering the Reichswehr in 1921 and soon selected for the **GGS**, he was attracted to the armored forces. Major Bayerlein (1 June 38) was with a panzer division in Poland then became Guderian's operations officer. After the French campaign Oberstleutnant (1 Sep 40) Bayerlein was with GUDERIAN in Russia through the Kiev encirclement. Ordered to North Africa, in Oct 41 he became CRUEWELL's CofS in the Afrika Korps and was awarded the RK on 26 Dec 41 for action at Al Agheila. He was promoted to full colonel on 1 Apr 42.

When Rommel's Italian CofS was wounded on 29 May 42, NEHRING took over the Afrika Korps from CRUEWELL (captured), and Bayerlein became Rommel's acting CofS (Young, *Rommel,* 123). Oberst Bayerlein became acting commander of the Afrika Korps on 30 Aug 42 when NEHRING was wounded at the start of the battle of Alam Halfa. Early the next day Rommel was about to call off the attack when Bayerlein convinced him to modify the planned turning movement toward Tobruk and attack British armor around Alam Halfa. But because of British bombing and shelling through the night of 1-2 Sep 42, "the worst the Afrika Korps had ever experienced . . . ,

by dawn everyone, including Rommel, had had enough" (Jackson, *North Africa,* 274). MONTGOMERY had won his first round.

Von THOMA took over the Afrika Korps but was captured at El Alamein on 4 Nov 42. Bayerlein commanded the decimated force during the next few hectic weeks of retreat until Gustav Fehn arrived on 23 Nov 42 as Thoma's permanent successor. The Bavarian returned to his staff position, remaining as commander of German units after MESSE succeeded ROMMEL. After being seriously wounded he was flown out of Tunisia shortly before the surrender on 13 May 43.

After recuperating, Oberst Bayerlein was German CofS of the new 1st Italian Army in Sicily, winning his Oakleaves and promotion to Generalmajor on 6 July 43.

After the Allies took Sicily and began moving up the boot of Italy, Bayerlein went to the Ukraine as CG 3d Pz Div 21 Oct 43-4 Jan 44 (B&O, 74). When the Panzer Lehr Div was formed of "school troops" from various training centers, Bayerlein took command of this elite unit on 10 Jan 44, four days before his 45th birthday. Promoted to Generalleutnant on 1 May 44, when his Panzer Lehr moved temporarily from France to Budapest, Bayerlein turned the division over to STRACHWITZ on D+2 of the Normandy campaign and moved up to head the 7th Army's 53d Corps Hq. In early Dec 44 he returned to command the Panzer Lehr, which was being refitted near Paderborn after being severely mauled around Caen and St Lô.

In the Ardennes counteroffensive that started on 16 Dec 44 the Panzer Lehr had a major role as spearhead of the 47th Pz Corps in Manteuffel's 5th Pz Army. Bayerlein bypassed Bastogne to the south and got within 10 miles of the Meuse. Generalleutnant Bayerlein left his shattered division on 19 Jan 45 (B&O, 130) and again headed the 53d Corps until taken prisoner in the Ruhr on 15 Apr 45. His postwar interrogations and writings have been invaluable to historians.

BAZNA, Elyesa. Spy. 1904-71. The legendary "Cicero" was born near Belgrade, at Pristina, when the region was in the Turkish empire. Although Bazna is commonly referred to as being Albanian, he and his family were oriented toward the Turks. Bazna claimed that his father was a Moslem holy man (mullah) and that his grandfather and uncles were among Mustafa Kemal's "Young Turks." (Brown, *Bodyguard*, 393.) Three of Bazna's cousins, his schoolmates at the Faith Military Academy, became prominent in the Turkish government and one was mayor of Ankara 1960-62. But the future spy was thrown out of the school and in 1919 began a life of petty crime in Allied-occupied Constantinople. Caught stealing British army property he spent time in a penal camp at Marseilles, after which he worked in the Berliet factory there and learned locksmithing. In 1925 he returned to Turkey and failed in a number of positions before becoming a *kavass* (manservant) in diplomatic households. After working for a Yugoslav ambassador, a British counselor, an American military attaché, and a German minister, he was hired by British ambassador KNATCHBULL-HUGESSEN in Ankara.

Bazna became a privileged and trusted favorite. Finding that his employer brought secret documents home to study, the *kavass* managed to have a duplicate key made to the box in which the papers were kept. On or about 20 Oct 43 he removed some documents, took them to his quarters, and used a Leica to make photographs. (He claims to have made his own rig, but Leica has an attachment for shooting time-exposure pictures with the use of a normal light bulb.)

It was the time of the **Teheran Conference** and Bazna found documents that had to do not only with the coming Allied invasion of Normandy but also with the threatened invasion of the Balkans.

Late on 26 Oct 43 the dark, insolent, shifty-eyed spy looked up a German embassy official for whom he had worked and offered to furnish photographs of documents. Initially known as "Pierre," he was turned over to the embassy's RSHA VI (intelligence) officer, Ludwig C. Moyzisch, and Opn Cicero was under way. In almost six months the spy produced 400 copies of highly classified diplomatic documents, many of them dealing with planning for major military operations. German authorities in Berlin, including Hitler, had several reasons to believe that although Bazna's documents were authentic they were planted as part of a British intrigue. The reason generally given for the Germans' failure to capitalize on what has been called their greatest coup was that jealousies and rivalries prevailed among the competing intelligence organizations of RIBBENTROP,

HIMMLER, and CANARIS. But on or about 20 Apr 44, shortly before the British allegedly found a security leak in Ankara and plugged it, Bazna quit his valet job and walked away a free man. With the equivalent of $1.2 million collected for his services the spy was prospering as developer of a Turkish luxury hotel when it was found that most of his British banknotes had been counterfeited by Opn **Bernhard.** Bazna barely escaped being jailed for fraud. He spent the rest of his life in poverty, unable to get compensation from the postwar West German government for "his valuable, though unused, information" (Strong, *Intelligence*, 145). Eking out a living as a used car dealer and singing teacher (having had some operatic training), Cicero died in Istanbul in 1971.

The English translation by Eric Mosbacher of Bazna's war memoir is *I Was Cicero* (New York: Harper, 1962). Mosbacher's own account is *Operation Cicero* (London: Wingate, 1950). Anthony Cave Brown has considerably revised the story of Cicero, presenting evidence that he was under British control as part of the **Bodyguard** deception (391-405). This would explain why Cicero was not prosecuted as a spy and why Ambassador Knatchbull-Hugessen survived professionally.

BEAVERBROOK, William Maxwell Aitken, Lord. British newspaper baron. 1879-1964. Born William Maxwell Aitken on 25 May 79 in Maple, Ontario, he was the son of a Presbyterian minister who emigrated from England. "Max" was reared in genteel poverty, his happy boyhood spent in Newcastle, New Brunswick. At the age of 16 he failed the college entrance examination and left home to make his fortune. He did this by working up through ever-more-profitable positions to hold a seat on the Montreal stock exchange and establish the Canada Cement Company. En route he married the beautiful 19-year-old Gladys Henderson in 1906. Beaverbrook's genius was in attracting backers and negotiating business combinations and alliances. In 1910 he sold out for a reputed $5 million and sought greener pastures in England.

Aided by Andrew Bonar Law (1858-1923), also from New Brunswick, Max promptly won a seat as a conservative in Parliament and bounced into the limelight. Knighthood came in 1911, followed by a baronetcy in Jan 16. Beaverbrook began building a newspaper empire that ultimately comprised the London *Daily Express* (then the world's largest selling daily newspaper), the London *Sunday Express,* and the *Evening Standard.* Although never having more than a small following as a conservative in Parliament, as a press baron Beaverbrook had a bully pulpit for powerful behind-the-scenes manipulations. To entertain political and business associates, he had a large country place in Surrey called Cherkley Court, and a tiny Tudor house with a tennis court, The Vineyard, at Fulham (a borough of London).

At the start of war in 1914 he was Canadian representative at BEF Hq. An early critic of Allied military leadership, he had a major role in the rise of Lloyd George to war minister and then to prime minister. Beaverbrook was not rewarded with the post he hoped for (president of the Board of Trade); ironically he was talked into vacating his seat in the House of Commons for the man who got the job, Sir Albert Stanley. Beaverbrook's consolation was elevation to the peerage in Dec 16. Over the king's objection, Lord Beaverbrook was made Chancellor of the Duchy of Lancaster. He was minister of information Feb-Nov 18.

After Bonar Law's death in 1923 Beaverbrook lost his political clout. A long, losing feud with Stanley Baldwin in the 1930s brought on asthma attacks that continued to be a problem. During Hitler's rise to power, the press lord advocated appeasement, assuring the public as late as the summer of 1939 that "there will be no war this year."

Beaverbrook became minister of aircraft production on 14 May 40 after his friend Churchill took over as prime minister. Famous for being blithe in the face of disaster, Max promptly showed a genius for sizing up problems and directing sweeping reorganizations to solve them. He gave priority to fighter production, shouting down opposition from RAF professionals. In six months Beaverbrook doubled factory output (WC, III, 688 ff). "Nothing that he did in his long life was as important as the part Beaverbrook played in winning the Battle of Britain," writes John Elliot in *DNB.* In the fall of 1940 he joined the first lord of the Admiralty, A. V. Alexander, in an unsuccessful effort to transfer Coastal Command from the RAF to the Admiralty. The move was defeated by PORTAL.

After rising to the initial crisis, Beaverbrook tired of his burden. In May 41 he became "simple minister of state" *(DNB),* but the next month he took over from Sir Andrew Duncan as minister of supply. Again a whirlwind, and with a genius for going to the heart of a problem, he fought for increased production of landing craft. He visited Washington in Aug 41, accompanied Averell HARRIMAN to Moscow, and returned to Washington with Churchill after the Pearl Harbor attack brought America into the war. In Feb 42 he became minister of production (again succeeding Duncan) but did not last the month; the supercharged little 146-pound "Beaver" had a nervous breakdown that forced his resignation on 26 Feb 42 (WC, IV, 75-76, 84-85). But within a few weeks he recovered sufficiently to start working on special assignments and to continue lend-lease activities. In Sep 43 he accepted the post of lord privy seal, holding the assignment until the war ended in 1945. Beaverbrook also had a leading part in Churchill's failed reelection campaign against Attlee in 1945. The Beaver was active almost to the end, remarrying in 1963. (His first wife died in 1927.) Two weeks after giving a gripping speech at a testimonial dinner, he died of cancer on 9 June 64 at Cherkley.

Beaverbrook wrote several books including one about his Canadian past, *The Rainbow Comes and Goes* (1958), the highly personal *Men and Power 1917-1918* (1956), and *The Decline and Fall of Lloyd George* (1963), *The Divine Propagandist* (1962) and *The Abdication of King Edward VIII* (published posthumously in 1966). The puckish little peer retained his Canadian twang and a Biblical vocabulary left over from his childhood as a minister's son. "Quite frankly a vulgarian" (*CB 40*), he was popular with the working classes but anathema to conservatives. American author John Gunther called him "one of the most provocative, original and lively public men in England" (ibid.).

BECK, Jozef. Polish statesman. 1894-1944. He was born 4 Oct 94, served in Pulduski's Polish Legion and was military attaché in Paris 1922-23. Trapped into revealing that he was selling documents about the French army to the Czechs, Beck was expelled. (Pertinax, 386n.)

Col Beck became foreign minister in Nov 32. Given to intrigue, hating the French, and spurning association with the Soviets, he did not wake up to the Nazi threat until too late. Even after Germany took Memel from Lithuania in Mar 39, Beck accepted the British offer of unconditional assistance only on condition that the French and Soviets be excluded from a treaty between his country and Britain. Probably having done more than Hitler to destroy Poland, Beck fled and lived obscurely in Romania until he died of tuberculosis on 6 June 44. His posthumous *Dernier rapport* (1951) has documents that "suggest a reappraisal of this controversial and elusive figure," writes Henry L. Roberts in *The Diplomats, 1919-1939* (Princeton: 1953).

BECK, Ludwig. German general. 1880-1944. A Rhinelander born in Biebrich on 29 June 80, Ludwig Beck became a soldier of remarkable intellect and urbanity. Tall and extremely slender, he had the look of a philosopher and was a fervent admirer of French literature and food. Despite these nonmilitary qualities, he rose to the top of his profession, succeeding Wilhelm Adam as head of the **Truppenamt** (and adjutant general of the Reichswehr Ministry) on 1 Oct 33. When the Wehrmacht was created on 21 May 35, Beck was promoted to Generaloberst and chief of the revived German general staff. The Rhinelander was no Nazi, but he viewed National Socialism as a political experiment of benefit to the army, and one that could be eradicated if it became a threat. (W-B, *Nemesis,* 298.) For more than three years Beck effectively directed the army's tremendous expansion. But continuing conflict with Hitler led him to resign on 18 Aug 38; he was succeeded on 1 Sep 38 by HALDER. Beck was supposed to head AG 3 if Germany mobilized, but he was permanently retired on 18 Oct 38 in Hitler's expulsion of "uncooperative" generals after the **Munich crisis**. Living quietly near Hanover, Beck remained "the secret mentor of the older generals" and the recognized head of anti-Hitler resistance. He was designated to serve as interim head of state if a putsch succeeded. Although "a man of high honour, matchless integrity and great moral courage" (W-B, *Nemesis,* 298-99), the venerable general, like most others of his caste, was a political innocent and never an effective conspirator. An operation for cancer in the fall of 1943 left him a shell of his former self. Beck's failure to act effectively on 20 July 44 is

covered in more detail under STAUFFENBERG. Among those arrested in the Bendlerstrasse, he was offered the privilege of shooting himself. After two failed attempts that merely rendered him unconscious, a sergeant administered the coup de grace: a pistol shot in the neck. The time of death apparently was shortly after midnight on 20-21 July 44.

BELL, George Kennedy Allen. British bishop. 1883-1958. The controversial Bishop of Chichester (from 1929) was born 4 Feb 83 on Hayling Island near Portsmouth. Ordained in 1907 after winning distinction as a scholar, Dr Bell began a lifelong association with the ecumenical movement in 1919. He also was prominent in the Life and Work movement.

Appointed dean of Canterbury in 1924 at the early age of 41, he directed vast changes, particularly in bringing dramatic productions to the cathedral. The most remarkable was John Mansfield's *The Coming of Christ* in 1928, the first dramatic production in an English church since the Middle Ages. Dr Bell remained a patron of the arts after becoming bishop of Chichester in 1929, inspiring T. S. Eliot to write *Murder in the Cathedral* for the Canterbury festival of 1935. *(DNB.)*

The bishop firmly supported the Confessional Church organized by Martin NIEMULLER to oppose Hitler's efforts to dominate German religion. From early in the war he loudly protested Bomber Command's indiscriminate killing of "good Germans" along with the bad. This courageous and outspoken criticism might explain why Dr Bell did not become archbishop of Canterbury in 1944 *(DNB)*.

Bell had been sought out earlier by leaders of the anti-Nazi resistance in Germany who hoped for British support. Pastor Dietrich BONHOEFFER, an associate of Niemuller's in opposing the Nazis, visited England in early 1939 and gave Bell a report on anti-Nazi efforts to that date. But the British had been fooled before and still refused to believe that any significant effort existed. In May 42, Bonhoeffer contrived to meet the English bishop secretly in Stockholm. The German pastor then gave Dr Bell rosters of prominent conspirators who would form a cabinet in a post-Hitler government. Foreign Secretary Anthony EDEN was not moved by the impressive evidence, the Gestapo was when the lists and details of the Stockholm meeting fell into their hands after the 20 July 44 attempt on Hitler's life—with fatal results for many conspirators who might otherwise have been spared.

Dr Bell was active after the war in having the German church reaccepted abroad. In 1948 he organized the first World Council of Churches. Residing in Canterbury but still Bishop of Chichester, Dr Bell died on 3 Oct 58. *(DNB.)*

BELOV, Pavel Alekseyevich. Red Army officer. 1897-1962. Belov was born at Shuya into the white-collar class (Scarecrow). He began his military career in 1916 as a private of hussars, joined the CP and Red Army three years later, and led a cavalry squadron during the civil war. From 1940 Belov headed the 2d Cav Corps, which was redesignated the 1st Guards Cav Corps. With substantial reinforcements that included the 415th Rifle and 112th Tank Divs, he had a major role in stopping HOEPPNER's 4th Pz Army short of Moscow on 5-6 Dec 41. Promoted at an unusually young age, Gen Lt Belov took over the 61st Army from M. M. POPOV in June 42. BOCK had just begun a massive counteroffensive, and the 61st Army was hard pressed in the unsuccessful actions around Kursk and Voronezh. Promoted again in July 44, after leading his army through the Ukraine and into Poland, Gen Col Belov took part in the final assault on Berlin.

After the war he headed the Southern Ural MD for 10 years, then was chairman of the Voluntary Association for Support of the army, AF, and navy. Belov retired in 1960 and died 3 Dec 63 in Moscow. He is buried in Moscow's **Novodevichy Monastery Cemetery.**

BENES, Eduard. Czech statesman. 1884-1948. A cofounder of Czechoslovakia in 1918 with Thomas G. Masaryk (1850-1937), the diminutive Benes was born 28 May 84 in Kozlany, Bohemia. Son of a farmer, he rose through his own efforts to be an internationally respected intellectual. On 18 Dec 35 he succeeded Masaryk as president and began negotiating a vast array of defensive alliances while making Czechoslovakia a nation of considerable industrial and military power. "He was ready to play against Hitler for high stakes," writes A. J. P. Taylor, "but not to fight a war" *(Origins,* 154). Sold out by the Munich Agreement of 30 Sep 38, Benes resigned five days later. Almost cer-

tainly marked for liquidation, he had significant NKVD assistance in leaving the country for England (Sudoplatov, 63, 223). Benes taught briefly at the Univ of Chicago, then established a national committee in France; on 21 July 40 he created a provisional government in London. Long a Russophile, Benes had sent Stalin information in 1936 (via the Czech ambassdor in Berlin) that allegedly triggered a devastating purge of the Soviet high command including Marshal TUKHACHEVSKY. But this long-accepted view has recently been called a "fairy tale" by an ex-NKVD official, Pavel Sudoplatov. "Benes enthusiastically supported the purge of Tukhachevsky but in no way played a role in his removal and arrest." (Sudoplatov, 92.)

After the Teheran Conference ended on 1 Dec 43, Benes realized he had to make an accommodation with the Soviets. On 12 Dec 43 he signed a treaty of friendship and alliance, returning in Mar 45 to Moscow, where he agreed that his coalition government would accept several Soviet-trained Czechs. These men accompanied Soviet liberation forces into Prague on 8 May 45. To avoid civil war, Benes allowed Klement GOTTWALD to work his communist takeover in early 1948. He resigned on 6 June 48 and died 3 Sep 48. It was suspected that the cofounder of Czechoslovakia was murdered, or that he committed suicide.

BENNETT, Donald Clifford Tyndall. RAF officer. 1910- . A civilian pilot in 1940 the Australian-born Bennett flew Polish Gen SIKORSKI from France to England. As an RAF officer he then directed the ferrying of US planes from Canada to the UK. He then joined the Air Navigation School at Eastborne in 1941 and conceived pathfinder techniques for directing bombers to their targets, a big problem for Bomber Command. But the RAF did not follow up immediately, and Bennett commanded 77 and 10 Sqdns of Bomber Command until shot down over Norway in Apr 42 and interned briefly in Sweden. In July 42, 18 months late, Bennett was promoted to air vice marshal heading the new Pathfinder Force. Putting his concepts into action with great effect, he later helped create the Light Night Striking Force of Mosquito bombers.

BENNETT, Henry Gordon. Australian general. 1887-1962. Born on 15 Apr 87 in Melbourne, he became a reserve officer. In WWI he rose from lieutenant colonel of artillery to command the 3d Inf Bde. The rangy, red-haired general had an outstanding combat record in France and at Gallipoli, acquiring the nickname "Cocky" and winning the DSO.

Between the wars he was a highly successful accountant, director of important corporations, and a member of government boards. He rose from colonel in the militia reserve in 1921 to become the youngest major general on the active list in 1939. Cocky Bennett was loudly critical of the regular army and especially of British officers (Keegan, *Who Was Who,* "Bennett"). After heading a training depot until the summer of 1940 he took over the 8th Div, the third to be formed in Australia during WWII (Keogh, 62). One of his brigade groups went to Malaya in early Feb 41; Bennett himself reached Singapore on 15 Aug 41 with the rest of the division minus one brigade group (Keogh, 68). When YAM-ASHITA began his Malayan campaign a year later, Bennett's 8th Div consisted of the 22d and 27th Bdes under H. B. Taylor and D. S. Maxwell. Bennett took command of "Westforce" in NW Johore as the Japanese moved down the western side of the peninsula. Using Maxwell's brigade plus the 8th, 22d, and 45th Indian Bdes, Bennett had some success against crack troops of the Japanese 5th and Imperial Guards Divs during the period 15-18 Jan 42 before being ordered to withdraw. (Collier, *FE,* 182-85.)

On Singapore Island Cocky Bennett com-manded the Western Area, where the Japanese main effort began on 8 Feb 42. Five days later he was among those advising PERCIVAL to sur-render (ibid., 198). With other Australian offi-cers, Bennett escaped to Johore in a sampan, and on 26 Feb 42 he reached Batavia in an ocean-going junk *(CB 42).* Cleared of misconduct and promoted to lieutenant general in Apr 42, Bennett headed the 3d Corps, which absorbed Australia's Western Command. But the general never got another field command and after con-tinued criticism for leaving Singapore he returned to private life in 1944. A postwar court of inquiry ruled that Bennett should have sur-rendered with his troops.

BERGER, Gottlob. German general. 1896-1976. Berger was a Swabian, born 16 July 96 at Gerstetten, son of a sawmill owner. He com-manded an assault group in the first world war and was severely wounded. Berger became a physical education instructor and coach, and was a champion runner, swimmer, and boxer. He also joined the **Black Reichswehr**, establishing arms depots and getting interested in military affairs. As an early member of the Brownshirts (SA), Berger showed a Machiavellian aptitude for ris-ing in the Nazi hierarchy.

Appointed SS Obergruppenfuehrer on 1 July 40, he spent the next five years as one of Himmler's principal lieutenants, heading the SS administrative office (Hauptamt) and serving as CofS for the **Waffen-SS**, where he showed genius as a recruiter. One particular triumph at a time of man power shortage was to form a unit of convicted poachers (Stein, *Waffen SS,* 266). Under his longtime friend and protégé Oskar Dirlewanger, a twice-condemned pedophile, the poachers became the NCO cadre of the infa-mous Dirlewanger brigade (below). Berger also was an adviser to Alfred Rosenberg and a major link between him and Himmler after July 42, when these men had overlapping authority in the USSR. For some months Berger directed all operations in the occupied Eastern Territories. He was elected to the Reichstag in Aug 43 from the district of Duesseldorf East. Seeing visions of postwar European unity, Berger was president of the German-Croat Society and the German-Flemish Study Group.

The portly Swabian helped establish the puppet state of Slovakia, and during the month of Sep 44 he was SS chief in Prague with responsibility for extreme pacification efforts that had become necessary. Murderously effec-tive, he brought in the SS Sonderkommando Dirlewanger, which meanwhile had been used by BACH-ZELEWESKI in Warsaw.

As the end approached and some Nazi leaders worried about war crimes charges, SCHEL-LENBERG brought Berger into a plan to save Jews and foreign internees from last-moment exter-mination and to block KALTENBRUNNER from doing this (Schellenberg, 380, 396). The deadly Berger has been characterized as "a simple, ele-mentary character, full of honest good nature, indefinite *[sic]* garrulity, and unsophisticated emotion" (Trevor-Roper, *Hitler,* 124). So the SS chieftain was all the more befuddled by his instructions on what to do with leaders of a sep-aratist threat in Bavaria and Austria and with foreign internees who might be valuable as hostages, the so-called Prominente. In a final discussion of the problems, the fuehrer shouted "Shoot them all! Shoot them all!" Berger did not understand whether, as chief of the POW administration, he should shoot all the separatists, all the internees, or all of the above. "Berger's accounts of his activities in these [last] days are all characterized by indistinct and sometimes inconsistent loquacity" (ibid.). It appears that he ended up taking considerable personal risk in saving the hostages (the **Niederdorf Group**) at the last moment. Several eyewitness accounts put him on the scene as the adventure reached its happy climax, but Berger is not mentioned in the memoirs of Fey von HASSELL, who was there. Berger was sentenced 2 Apr 49 at Nuremberg to 25 years at hard labor for killing Jews. After serving six and a half years of a commuted 10-year sentence, he was freed at the end of 1951. He died 5 Jan 75 at Gerstetten.

BERGERET, Jean Marie Joseph. French general. 1895-1956. Bergeret was born in Gray (Haute Saone). Nineteen years old when war was declared in 1914, he volunteered for the army and was selected for the special course at St Cyr. After graduation he went immediately into combat and won rapid promotion. In 1928 he entered the Armée de l'Air and had been chief of operations on the air staff for several months when promoted to brigadier general just before the war.

After the Franco-German armistice of June 40, Bergeret went to Turin, Italy, as head of a commission that negotiated armistice terms. He then was air minister in Vichy from 6 Sep 40 until resigning after Laval returned to the government on 18 Apr 42. Bergeret then became Inspector of Air Defenses. Shortly before the Allies landed in North Africa, he rallied to Giraud and on 13 Nov 42 became DARLAN's personal assistant and confidential adviser in Algiers. The airman was responsible for headquarters security when Darlan was assassinated at the door to his office on 24 Dec 42 (Murphy, *Diplomat,* 143). Under GIRAUD, who saw fit to make other security arrangements, Bergeret was deputy high commissioner of North Africa until he resigned 16 Mar 43 and was replaced by COUVE DE MURVILLE.

The man whom MACMILLAN described as charming and honest but a "wrong-headed" reactionary (*Diaries,* 44) was among those marked for revenge by the Gaullist faction of the CNL. Arrested 23 Oct 43 in a purge that included BOISSON, FLANDIN, and PEYROUTON, Bergeret was imprisoned until Sep 45. All charges against him were dropped on 25 Nov 48.

BERGONZOLI, Annibale. Italian general. 1884-1973. Known as "Electric Whiskers" (*Barba Elettrica*) because of his flaming red beard, Lt Gen Bergonzoli was highly regarded at the outset of the war in North Africa as a tough, austere field commander. On direct orders from Mussolini he made the British fight for Bardia, 3-4 Jan 41, but then abandoned four division commanders and 45,000 troops to flee on foot. Reaching Tobruk safely, he was trapped there and taken prisoner on 7 Feb 41 (the Battle of Beda Fomm).

BERIA, Lavrentiy Pavlovich. Soviet official. 1899-1953. As head of the NKVD Beria (pronounced be'ree ah) was one of the most able and most powerful men in the USSR. He was born 17 Mar 99 in the western Georgia village of Merkheuli near the Black Sea. The people there are Mingrelians, strongly nationalistic and anti-Soviet; the Mingrelian Affair was one of Stalin's final machinations (Sudoplatov, 103, 320-59).

After schooling in nearby Sukhumi, where Beria also taught younger pupils, he attended a technical engineering construction school in Baku (1915 19) and started an illegal Marxist circle. It is believed he entered the CP in 1917. The Turks occupied Baku in 1919, and the next year Beria reenrolled in his former school there when it became a polytechnic institute. But in Apr 21 he left on orders from the Transcaucasus Regional Committee to become assistant chief of the Georgian **Cheka** in Tiflis. During the next 10 years he rose from assistant chief of the Georgian **GPU** to head of the Transcaucasus GPU. After the 1924 revolt Stalin put Beria in charge of suppressing nationalist deviationists in Georgia, Armenia, and Azerbaijan. Of some five million people Beria is alleged to have arrested in 1937-38, up to 900,000 died. (Scotts, citing Volkogonov.)

Having become one of Stalin's favorites and a member of the Central Committee since 1934, Beria was made NKVD chief on 8 Dec 38. Rising steadily in power, he was a GKO member (30 June 41—4 Sep 45) and a Marshal of the Soviet Union from 9 July 45. Beria continued to head the secret police and also took charge of the Soviet atomic energy program. Despite his lack of scientific qualifications and a Neanderthalian suspicion that the program was a hoax (Scotts), he controlled slave labor needed to work the deadly uranium mines. Although exceptionally bright, the tall, heavyset, and myopic Beria—he wore pince-nez glasses—cultivated the look of an ordinary man, the better to move unnoticed around Moscow on visits to his secret agents and informers (Sudoplatov, 40). He also has been accused of using these forays to indulge unsavory biological urges. Beria had only recently become deputy premier and minister of internal affairs when Stalin died on 5 Mar 53. A marked man because of his power, he was arrested on 26 June along with his principal lieutenants and many small fry (Sudoplatov, 369). KONEV took the initiative in having Beria tried, presiding over the secret trial. Beria was shot on 23 Dec 53. *See* Pavel Sudoplatov, a close associate whose controversial memoirs did not appear until 1994, for favorable new light on this still-mysterious character.

BERNADOTTE of Wisborg, Folke. Swedish official. 1895-1948. Born 2 Jan 95, his father a brother of King Gustav V, Count Folke has been described as "a man of elegance and simplicity, of sophistication and naivete" (Toland, *Last 100 Days,* 164). His activity was limited by hemophilia, but the count had a military education and in 1918 was commissioned a lieutenant in the Swedish Royal Horse Guards. Meanwhile he worked with the Red Cross in arranging POW exchanges. The count rose in the reserves from captain (1930) to major (1941). He married an American, Estelle Romaine Manville of Pleasantville, NY, in 1928. Friends say she taught the noble Swede to laugh at himself. (Briggs, ed, *20th Cent Bio.*)

As vice president of the Swedish Red Cross, Count Folke traveled widely during the war and saved thousands of POWs and concentration camp inmates. He arranged POW exchanges and the transfer of Danish and Norwegian political prisoners to a camp supervised by the Swedish YMCA. Count Folke became president of the Swedish Scouting Association in 1943 and used his military expertise to integrate Boy Scouts into the defenses of his neutral country. (Ibid.)

During the last months of the war he was approached by KALTENBRUNNER and SCHELLENBERG on HIMMLER's behalf to feel out the Western allies on making some deal to mollify their unconditional surrender policy. The initial German proposal was to accomplish this by sparing Jews still in concentration camps. Working unofficially with Himmler and his rival Ribbentrop, Bernadotte visited Germany in mid-Feb 45 and talked to both Nazi chiefs. Knowing that Hitler had to be informed, Schellenberg leaked word of the negotiations. Himmler asked FEGELEIN to get Hitler's reaction, and he reported back on 17 Feb 45 that the fuehrer had said, "One cannot accomplish anything with this sort of nonsense in total war." (Toland, *Last 100 Days,* 163.) But as the Third Reich faced surrender, Himmler had SCHELLENBERG follow up on 24 Apr 45 with a direct appeal to Bernadotte. Seeing Himmler for the last time at Flensburg on 27 Apr, Bernadotte relayed the message to Churchill, who phoned Truman on a secure line to the Pentagon. The startled president's immediate reaction was, "What has he got to surrender?" or words to that effect. "I don't know," replied the PM. After gathering his thoughts, Truman said no such separate surrender could be considered. Although sounding disappointed, the PM promptly agreed but said he had felt obliged to relay the offer immediately. (Personal knowledge.) In his book *The Fall of the Curtain* (1945) Bernadotte describes this episode and gives a fascinating insight into the character and motives of those involved (Tunney).

In 1946 Bernadotte became president of the Swedish Red Cross, and on 20 May 48 he was appointed UN peace mediator in Palestine. With Col André Pierre Serot, a great intelligence officer of the French army (Farago, *War of Wits,* 139) at his side, the count was assassinated in Jerusalem on 17 Sep 48 by Jewish Stern Gang terrorists.

BERNHARD, Prince of the Netherlands. 1911-. A German, born 29 June 11, he was christened Bernhard Leopold Frederick Everhard Julius Coert Karel Godfried Pieter of Lippe-Bisterfeld. On 7 Jan 37 Bernhard married Princess Juliana, who became queen of the Netherlands on 6 Sep 48. The couple fled to London in 1940. As a rear admiral and lieutenant general the prince became commander of the Dutch resistance, liaison officer with the British armed forces, and chief of the Netherlands Mission to the War Office. Bernhard married

Princess Juliana, who would become queen of the Netherlands on 6 Sep 48. Meanwhile the couple fled in 1940 to London where, as a rear admiral and lieutenant general, the prince became commander of the Dutch resistance, Ln O with the British armed forces, chief of the Netherlands Mission to the War Office, and earned his wings in the RAF.

BERZARIN, Nikolai Erastovich. Soviet military leader. 1904-45. Entering the Red Army in 1918 and serving in the civil war, he led the 32d Inf Div against the Japanese at **Lake Khasan** in 1938. Gen Maj Berzarin commanded the 27th Army (May-Dec 41), then led the 34th Army to Oct 42. Promoted to general lieutenant, he headed the 39th Army from Sep 43 to May 44 and then took over the 5th Shock Army. The latter was the first to enter Berlin, and Gen Col Berzarin (May 45) was the city's first Soviet commandant. He was killed in a motorcycle or car accident. (Scarecrow.)

BESSON, Antoine. French general. 1876-1969. Born 14 Sep 76 near Lyons at St Symphorien (Rhône), Besson graduated from St Cyr in 1898 and joined the 4th Regt of Zouaves. He held command and staff positions on the western front from 1914, eventually leading the 4th Zouaves in action and winning four citations.

A full general and member of the Supreme War Council from 8 July 37, he commanded AG 3 in May 40. Located on the extreme right flank in the Colmar-Mulhouse sector, AG 3 initially had only the 8th Army. But as new positions were organized on the Somme, Besson was assigned three armies deployed from the Channel to Reims. On order he began withdrawing to the Seine on 8 June 40. Within a week—seeing that nothing but continued slaughter for his men lay ahead—he insisted that the government call for an armistice. Besson spent the rest of the war as a POW. A British general characterized the 63-year-old, much-decorated general as "a pleasant, round little man with a nice chuckle, a good officer" (Spears, II, 28).

BEST, (Karl Rudolf) Werner. Nazi official. 1903–89. With a law doctorate from Heidelberg (1927) he was chief of police in Hesse (1933) before Himmler made him head of the SD in Bavaria (1934). Dr Best, a cool, ambitious, com-

petent, amoral lawyer and devout Nazi, then was SD chief in Berlin for a very brief time, continuing to rise in Himmler's esteem. On 1 Jan 35 he took on a number of posts that gave him a major role in building the Gestapo and **SD**; he was Superior Government Councillor, the Gestapo's chief legal adviser, chief of the Bureau of the Secret State Police, and was involved in some matters of foreign intelligence. SCHELLENBERG was Best's subordinate from Aug 34. (Brissaud, 76, 85.) When the RSHA was created, Best was chief of Amt 1 from 27 Sep 39 to 12 June 40. He was charged not only with all RSHA personnel and training matters but also with counterespionage (ibid., 292). Best spent the next two years as chief of the Civil Administration in France.

In Nov 42 the Gestapo lawyer began the assignment for which he is most remembered, Reich commissioner (plenipotentiary) for Denmark. As Himmler became increasingly concerned about HEYDRICH's freewheeling independence, Best became more influential with Himmler. (Ibid., 178.) But the plenipotentiary also developed misgivings about the "final solution," which explains his rounding up fewer than 500 of more than 7,000 Jews in Denmark (Wistrich).

Sentenced to death by a Danish court, he was released in 1951. A German denazification court fined him for activities as a senior SS officer, and in Mar 69 he faced new charges of mass murder. Sentenced three years later, he was released after six months (Aug 72) for medical reasons.

BETHOUART, Marie Antoine Emile. French general. 1889-1982. One of the most prominent French generals of the war, seeing action from Norway to the Danube, Béthouart was from Dôle, in the Jura Mountains. He graduated from St Cyr in 1912 and began his career with Alpine troops. He was wounded three times in 1914-18. As MA in Belgrade, he was with King Alexander when the latter was assassinated in Marseilles on 9 Oct 34.

A general from 15 Apr 40, he led the Franco-Polish expeditionary force sent to serve under Lord CORK in Norway. His two foreign legion battalions and a Norwegian battalion retook Narvik on 28 May from a battalion of Eduard DIETL's troops.

After the Franco-German armistice, Béthouart headed the Casablanca division in southern

Morocco. Robert MURPHY reported that the general was pro-Allied and would collaborate with American forces invading Morocco. But American planners did not account for the fact that Béthouart lacked authority to order and enforce a cease-fire: he was subordinate to NOGUES (the resident-general) and JUIN (commander of land forces in North Africa). The Americans scheduled a last-minute rendezvous to coordinate details—including times and places of the landings. Béthouart had his troops occupy all critical points and ordered them to welcome the Americans as allies, then he decided to alert NOGUES that the amphibious assault would take place the night of 7-8 Nov 40. When the Americans failed to keep the planned rendezvous, Noguès—who had informed the Americans earlier that he would oppose them—believed he had been tricked. (Larousse.) The governor-general consequently had Béthouart and Col Pierre Mangin arrested for treason. After the landings on 8 Nov 42, Patton—whom Noguès had bamboozled with lavish entertainment and hunting parties—woke up just in time (on the 17th) to countermand the governor-general's order to have the two French officers executed.

Béthouart headed the mission to the US in Dec 42 to arrange for large-scale military aid. Back in Algiers he became chief of the National Defense general staff and was charged with reorganizing the army of Africa. He then joined the general staff of Army B, which became de LATTRE's 1st French Army. In due course, Béthouart took command of the army's 1st Corps and led it from southern France through the Vosges into Alsace and across the Rhine, ending the war with a sweep on the southern (right) bank of the upper Danube. Some of his heaviest action involved reducing the Colmar pocket (*see* de LATTRE).

Béthouart headed French occupation forces in Austria, and in 1949 he was promoted to full general. In 1955, after retiring, he entered politics and became a senator. The general published *Cinq Années d'espérance, Mémoires de guerre 1939-1945* (1968) and *Des hécatombes glorieuses au désastre (1914-1940)* (1972).

BEVAN, Aneurin. British politician. 1897-1960. A champion of labor, he came from the Welsh coalfields, where he was born at Tredegar, Monmouthshire, on 15 Nov 97. Big, colorful, and passionate, "Nye" Bevan had only a minor role in events of 1939-45. Churchill called him "a squalid nuisance," a characterization generally shared by the public, the press (whom Bevan called "the most prostituted in the world"), and by Labour Party associates. He was elected to Parliament in 1929 as a labor member for Ebbw Vale (Monmouthshire) and retained the seat for life. Ejected from his party in early 1939 for supporting the popular front campaign of Sir Stafford Cripps, but soon readmitted, he came close to banishment again in 1944 after feuding with Ernest BEVIN for his treatment of the coal industry. Later in 1944 he was elected for the first time to the national council, but only after promising in writing to abide by standing orders. Perennially in opposition, Nye Bevan remained prominent in national politics. As a speaker in the House of Commons he probably was second only to Churchill. *In Place of Fear* (1952) is his only book. After some months of ill health, Bevan died 6 July 69 at his home in Chesham, Buckinghamshire. (Helen M. Palmer in *DNB*.)

BEVERIDGE, William Henry. British economist. 1879-1963. The social reformer was born 5 Mar 79 in Rangpur, Bengal, eldest son of a judge in the Indian civil service. He was a precocious child but sickly and poor at games. At Charterhouse and Balliol College, Oxford, he was a brilliant student but could not find a lasting intellectual interest. Finally, after studying law in the chambers of a London commercial barrister, winning a fellowship at University College, Oxford, and becoming a bachelor of civil law (1903), he turned to the social sciences. To some the term is an oxymoron, but Beveridge proceeded on the assumption that social problems are as amenable to academic disciplines as, for example, natural phenomena. Beveridge wrote for the *Morning Post,* entered the board of trade in 1908, and became an authority on unemployment insurance. Joining the permanent civil service in 1909, he worked his way up to organize a national system of labor exchanges and to head an office that evolved into the ministry of labor. In 1914-18 he was involved in mobilizing and controlling man power. Early in 1919 he was knighted (KCB) and made permanent secretary to the ministry of food, but in June of that year he left the civil service to become director of the London School of

Economics. After making this a leading center of the social sciences, Sir William left to be Master of University College, Oxford, 1937-45.

At the start of war in 1939 Beveridge expected to be recalled by the government to take charge of controlling man power, civilian and military. After waiting a year, he finally was asked by Ernest BEVIN to study this field, but the two immediately clashed over which of them would control the wartime man power program. "Beveridge was hived off into the chairmanship of an obscure interdepartmental inquiry into the coordination of social services—an inquiry that was not expected to report until after the war. . . ." (Jose Harris in *DNB*.)

Starting work in June 41, Beveridge realized immediately that he had the long-hoped-for chance to revolutionize postwar British society (ibid.). The "Beveridge Report," worked out in collaboration with economists like Keynes and representatives of the Trades Union Congress, appeared in Dec 42 as the report on *Social Insurance and Allied Services.* A second report was published privately in 1944 as *Full Employment in a Free Society.* This "cradle to the grave" scheme was coolly received by the government, but the public bought nearly 70,000 copies within a few days. "Early in 1943 the only major parliamentary revolt of the war forced the Government to commit itself to the Beveridge proposals—with the result that Beveridge's plan eventually became the blueprint for the welfare state legislation of 1944 and 1948." (Ibid.)

To promote his plan Beveridge resigned his mastership of University College in 1944 and entered the House of Commons as a liberal for Berwick-upon-Tweed. Meanwhile, on 15 Dec 42 he had married his recently widowed second cousin Janet. "Jessy" was an "overbearing and temperamental Scotswoman" *(DNB)* who had been his secretary and aide since WWI. They established a home in Tuggal Hall, a Northumbrian country house. Beveridge hoped to have charge of postwar reconstruction, but he was defeated in the national elections of 1945. That year he was created the 1st Baron Beveridge of Tuggal and in due course was leader of the liberals in the House of Lords.

A major activity in his old age was writing his memoir, *Power and Influence* (1953). Lord and Lady Beveridge retired in 1954 to Oxford. She published *Beveridge and his Plan* that year

and died in 1959. He died 16 Mar 63 at home. Jose Harris, contributor of the *DNB* sketch cited above, wrote *William Beveridge: A Biography* (1977).

BEVIN, Ernest. British politician. 1881-1951. In the wartime coalition as minister of labor and national service, 1940-45, he was also in the war cabinet. The huge, ruddy, Bevin, a professional proletarian, had a genius for maintaining worker confidence while exhorting them to sacrifice for the national good, no mean achievement.

Bevin was born 7 Mar 81 in the Somerset village of Winsford on the edge of Exmoor. He was the illegitimate sixth son of Mercy Bevin, a 40-year-old midwife who had been separated for some years from William Bevin. The son never knew who his father was. *(DNB.)* Orphaned at the age of eight, he was taken in by an impoverished half sister in Devonshire. Two years later, with enough schooling to read, write, and do simple arithmetic, he began making his own way. From farm boy through a series of menial jobs in Bristol, frequently out of work and hungry, he grew into a tough, barrel-chested man. For 10 years beginning in 1901 he was happy as the driver of a two-horse dray for a mineral water firm. During that period he formed a lifelong partnership with the daughter of a wine taster and sired a daughter.

Bevin's hard boyhood and youth gave him identity with the working class, but he had no social rancor or desire to climb out of his class: "He preferred, instead, to help it rise and to rise with it" (Francis Williams in *DNB*). In 1911 Bevin became a full-time trade union official and three years later was one of the union's three national organizers. He developed a strident, uncompromising manner in public but a calm, conciliatory manner in negotiation *(DNB)*. Although never a great orator, harsh voiced, gesturing wildly, contemptuous of syntax and proper pronunciation, Bevin was convincing. On the eve of war in 1939 he was a top labor leader. Appreciating the urgent need for total mobilization to meet the threat from Germany, Bevin had become an ally of an ancient political foe, Churchill.

When Churchill formed his coalition government on becoming PM on 10 May 40, Bevin was made minister of labor and national service. This entailed responsibility for all matters in the two fields, including authority to withdraw workers who, in the minister's opinion, were not properly employed. Authorized to conscript workers (more than a million still were unemployed), Bevin wisely waited until the working class was ready to accept compulsion. But the new minister immediately invigorated British industry and saw that British labor performed properly for the next five years, and with a remarkable lack of industrial trouble. Although the elderly trade unionist finally was elected to Parliament in 1940, he never was at home there. After the war Ernie Bevin began a third career in 1945 as foreign minister. Despite his apparent lack of qualifications, he became one of Britain's greatest. He also was the strongman of the labor government and Attlee's closest, most loyal friend. In Mar 51 Bevin became lord privy seal, but his health was failing. He died 14 Apr 51 in London.

Standard biographies are by Francis Williams, *Ernest Bevin* (1952), and Allan Bullock, *The Life and Times of Ernest Bevin* (2 vols., 1960-70).

BIDAULT, Georges. French statesman. 1899-1982. Born in Moulins (Allier) and educated at the Sorbonne (**agrégé** in history), he was a journalist with the Catholic leftist newspaper *L'Aube* before switching in 1939 to *L'Europe Nouvelle*. Bidault was taken prisoner by the Germans in 1940 but was repatriated in 1941 because of ill health. He promptly joined the resistance and helped establish the clandestine Christian-Democrat newspaper and resistance group in the unoccupied zone named *Liberté*. After this group merged with Henri FRENAY's *Vérités* to become *Combat*, Bidault was on the steering committee. Jean MOULIN later directed him to establish a centralized agency that became known as the *Bureau d'informations et de presse* (BIP), which fed news and information to all clandestine publications. After the three major resistance groups in the unoccupied zone merged to become *les Mouvements unis de résistance*, Bidault, no longer an active resistance leader, joined former associates of *Liberté* and founded a Christian party that in 1944, after the liberation, became the powerful *Mouvement républicain populaire* (MRP). Meanwhile, Bidault allied his new party with the *Conseil national de la Résistance* (CNR) after it was formed by Jean MOULIN. Bidault succeeded Moulin as CNR president in 1943 primarily because the communist faction

favored him, although he was no fellow traveler (Aron, *Libération*, 72). Bidault kept trying to smooth relations between Gaullists and resistance leaders who aspired to power in postwar France, but his efforts were largely futile. Narrowly escaping the Gestapo before figuring prominently in the Paris uprising of Aug 44, Bidault was conspicuous in de GAULLE's Paris apotheosis. He was the only resistance leader to accept a post, that of foreign minister, in the provisional government that de Gaulle formed 10 Sep 44. Three months later Bidault accompanied de Gaulle to Moscow (Larousse).

Historian Henri Michel has concluded that French Catholics apparently played a greater part in the resistance than Catholics of any other occupied country. "As a result," wrote Michel, "on liberation, the small democrat-popular group in parliament turned into the great political party, the MRP. . . ." (*Shadow War,* 162.)

Although young for such high office, Bidault remained foreign minister in the cabinet formed in 1946 by Felix Gouin. He himself was premier in 1946, 1949-50, and 1958. Bidault was a strong internationalist, supporting the UN and working for cooperation with Russia. He was too pro-Communist for American taste, and France was the only western European country in which the Communists (under THOREZ) posed a real threat of a parliamentary takeover. But when Czechoslovakia fell into the Soviet bloc in 1948, Bidault became a staunch believer in Western defensive policies including NATO. (S&S.) In the bitter resistance to de Gaulle's Algerian policy, Bidault supported the Secret Army Organization, and in 1962 he became president of the National Resistance Council. Charged with treason in 1963, he took refuge in Brazil. The warrant for his arrest was suspended in 1968, and he returned to France. Bidault's books include *D'Une Résistance à l'autre* (1965) and *Le Point* (1968).

BIDDLE, Anthony Joseph Drexel, Jr. US diplomat. 1896-1961. Born into an illustrious and wealthy Philadelphia family of bankers and socialites, the tall, lean, suave Tony Biddle was ambassador to Oslo, 1935-37, then to Warsaw. He fled to Paris in 1939, becoming deputy to Ambassador Bullitt and the latter's designated successor in Vichy. But FDR changed his mind, and the post went to Adm LEAHY. After being ambassador to various refugee governments in

London until the invasion of Europe in 1944, Biddle was commissioned in the US Army as a lieutenant colonel. After the war he was in Paris as a brigadier general with EISENHOWER's SHAPE, then was special assistant to army CofS RIDGWAY (1953-55). Biddle was ambassador to Madrid in 1961, the year he died.

BIERUT, Boleslaw. Head of Lublin Poles. 1892-1956. A Comintern veteran, he reached Warsaw in Jan 43 to lead the clandestine Polish Worker's Party (PPR). A year later he formed the National Council of the Homeland. To challenge authority of the "London Poles," whom the west backed, the Soviets set up the Polish Committee of National Liberation in Lublin on 22 July 44 with Bierut as chairman. He became provisional president in June 45 and defeated MIKOLAJCZYK for the presidency on 5 Feb 47.

BILLOTTE, Gaston Henri Gustave. French general. 1875-1940. He was born in Sommeval (Aube), a village near Troyes, and graduated from St Cyr in 1896. Commissioned in the naval infantry, he served in Indochina and in 1930 became commander of all troops there. He was military governor of Paris in 1937. De Gaulle credits him with persuading top military authorities to order creation of the first two divisions equipped with medium tanks. (De Gaulle, *The Call*, 30.) When French and British field forces went on a war footing in Sep 39, Billotte took command of the 1st French AG. This was deployed in the frontier from the English Channel to the Maginot Line's left flank near Montmédy. As prescribed by the unfortunate **Dyle Plan,** Billotte wheeled his armies into Belgium when the Germans attacked on 10 May 40. At a conference at Casteau on 12 May attended by King Leopold III, Daladier, Lord Gort (BEF), and senior French commanders, Billotte's responsibility was extended to include coordination of Allied field armies in Holland and Belgium. The Dutch surrendered 14 May, and two days later Billotte ordered all Allied forces to withdraw from the Dyle Line to the Escaut River. The general was fatally injured in a car accident the night of 21-22 May 40 after leaving a conference with WEYGAND in Ypres. Not knowing Weygand's strategy, the Allies were left in even greater disarray than before. Command of the 1st AG passed to BLANCHARD. Billotte died after two days in a coma.

BILLOTTE, Pierre Gaston. 1906-92. Son of the general sketched above, Pierre was born in Paris, graduated from St Cyr in 1928 and was a captain when France declared war in 1939. After serving as a staff officer at GHQ he commanded a tank unit only four days before being wounded and captured on 12 May 40. He escaped in Jan 41 from a POW camp in Pomerania, reached Russia, and was interned for six months until the Soviets entered the war. Capt Billotte and a large group of former POWs left Russia with a convoy returning from Archangel. He served first as de Gaulle's CofS, then was secretary to the Free French "national defense committee" from 13 Apr 42. As one of de Gaulle's inner circle, he served in London and Algiers, and accompanied the general on his return to France after D day. Rising to the rank of colonel, Billotte took command of a brigade in Le clerc's Free French armored division and was given the honor of spearheading the French drive into Paris. The "Billotte group" overcame German rear guards to enter the capital on 25 Aug 44, and the colonel personally took the surrender of CHOLTITZ. Two months later he assumed command of the 10th Inf Div and led it for the rest of the war. In 1946 he was promoted to général de division. A founder of the Gaullist Party and MOD in 1955, he died 29 June 92 in a hospital near Paris.

BIRCH, John. US missionary. 1918-45. Robert H. W. Welch, Jr, publicized the story of John Birch and took his name for the society that became synonymous with American ultraconservatism. Birch had assisted CHENNAULT with air-ground communications and evacuating downed flyers—including DOOLITTLE and his crew after the Apr 42 Tokyo raid. An OSS captain from May 45, he was shot to death by Chinese communists on 25 Aug 45.

BISHOP, William Avery. Canadian air marshal. 1894-1956. RCAF director of recruiting in WWII, Air Marshal Bishop was a legendary ace of WWI (VC). The figures are still being disputed, but he is said to have scored 72 victories in about 175 missions. He was also the author of several widely acclaimed books..

BISSELL, Clayton Lawrence. USAAF general. 1896-1972. Born in Kane, Pa, he got a law degree before becoming an ace in 1918. In addition to being a distinguished flyer, Bissell was an outstanding instructor at the Naval War College before serving on the WDGS. On 22 Feb 42 Col Bissell took charge of air base construction in India for the 10th AF, commanding the new B-29 Superfortress outfit from 18 Aug 42. Some sources say he was promoted to major general at that time, but the *Army Almanac* gives 13 Mar 43 as his date of rank (AA, 916). Although Bissell was publicly criticized for not meeting construction schedules, even of doing this to obstruct the CHENNAULT plan, it has been pointed out that he had inadequate US logistical support and was dependent on the British for engineering (R&S, passim, particularly p. 201). A compromise over the competing STILWELL and CHENNAULT plans led to Bissell's recall on 19 Aug 43.

The general became A2, Hq AAF. He was G2, WDGS (7 Feb 44-26 Jan 46) and air attaché in London until 1948. He then he served in the USAF Hq at Wiesbaden, Germany, before retiring as a major general. Testifying before Congress in 1950, he admitted helping cover up Soviet guilt in the **Katyn Forest Massacre** by misusing the top secret classification.

BITTRICH, Wilhelm. German general. 1894-1979. Bittrich was born in Wernigerode, on 26 Feb 94. In WWI he was an army officer and pilot, winning the Iron Cross 1st Class. After serving in the Freikorps, he returned to the army as a pilot, training in the USSR. In 1934 he joined the SS.

"Willi" Bittrich led the SS Pz Regt "Deutschland" in Poland, France, and Russia. He held the rank of Oberfuehrer when awarded the RK on 14 Dec 41. Continuing to rise professionally, he headed the Das Reich and Hohenstaufen Divs before being promoted to General of the Waffen-SS and leading the 2d SS Pz Corps in Normandy. His Oakleaves (563/890) were awarded on 28 Aug 44.

For wiping out the British airhead at Arnhem (in **Market-Garden**) Bittrich became one of the last recipients of the Swords (153/159), belatedly awarded on 6 May 45. Held prisoner by the French until 1954, he died 19 Apr 79 at Muensingen. (Angolia, I, 269.)

BLACKETT, Patrick Maynard Stuart. British physicist and strategist. 1897-1974. Born 18 Nov 97 in London, educated for the RN at

Osborne and Dartmouth, he saw action in the Falkland Islands and at Jutland. He was promoted to lieutenant in May 18 and sent the following January with other young officers to Cambridge to complete their education. *(DNB.)* His eyes opened by work being done at Ernest RUTHERFORD's Cavendish Laboratory, Lt Blackett left the RN to study mathematics and physics at Magdalene College, Cambridge. This led to a fellowship and a research post at the Cavendish, where the young scientist advanced RUTHERFORD's work. His main contribution was to use a cloud chamber to obtain photographic evidence of atom splitting. Continuing his research and holding increasingly important academic posts, Blackett became interested in military problems. From 1935 he served on the TIZARD air defense committee and in Aug 40 became scientific adviser to the Antiaircraft Command. Having begun to develop **operations research**, he transferred to the Admiralty in Jan 42 as chief adviser in that new field. Becoming OR director in the Admiralty, he remained until resigning in the summer of 1945. Blackett was among the first British scientists involved in his country's atom bomb development. After attacking the majority view in a book, *Military and Political Consequences of Atomic Energy* (1948) he was long excluded from government advisory circles *(ibid.)*. Blackett was awarded the Nobel Prize for Physics in 1948 for work on cosmic radiation. He was president of the Royal Society 1965-70 and created a life peer in 1969.

BLAMEY, Thomas Albert. Australian general. 1884-1951. The senior Australian general throughout the war and the only one to become a field marshal, Blamey was born 24 Jan 84 on a farm at Wagga-Wagga, New South Wales. He was a school teacher (1899-1906) before winning a commission in the Australian permanent force. A captain in 1910, the next year he won a competitive examination for the place reserved at the staff college in Quetta, India, for Australian regular army officers. At the end of the two-year course he served in the Indian army, holding regimental and staff assignments, then was posted to England for service with the British army. Blamey was promoted to major in July 14 and in December joined the 1st Australian Div in Egypt as its intelligence officer (GSO 1). After three months at Gallipoli, he went to France with the staff of the 2d Australian

Div. Most of Blamey's service was as a staff officer, but he briefly commanded a battalion and a brigade. In May 18 he was promoted to brigadier general staff (not brigadier general).

Blamey continued to hold general staff positions in the permanent force until 1925. Then he resigned to be commissioner of police in Victoria, where the force was badly in need of reform. He concurrently held a commission in the Citizen Forces and took command of the 3d Div in 1931. Blamey handled his police duties efficiently and was knighted in 1935, but "the manner in which he handled some demonstrations by the unemployed during the economic depression brought him into disfavour with powerful political elements" (*DNB* by E. G. Keogh, official historian of the Australian army). What finally undid Sir Thomas was his attempt to conceal embarrassing facts of an incident in which a senior police officer was severely wounded in 1936. The next year he was forced to resign as police commissioner and commander of the 3d Div.

His fortunes were restored by Hitler. Soon after the UK declared war on 3 Sep 39, Blamey was made commander of Australian forces raised for service in the Middle East and given the rank of lieutenant general. Sir Thomas went to the Middle East in 1940 with 1st Australian Corps. He was WAVELL's deputy commander, Middle East, in 1941, leading the 1st Australian Corps in the latter part of Wavell's first campaign in Libya and the Anzac corps in Greece. Sir Thomas thus wore two hats: deputy CinC Middle East and commander of Australian Imperial Forces in the theater.

Blamey was called home after Japan entered the war. In Mar 42 he took command of a poorly prepared Australian army and began putting it on a war footing. Establishment of MacArthur's SW Pacific Area (SWPA) Hq in Australia created political problems. When US authorities told MacArthur that as supreme allied commander he was ineligible to head a national force (the Australians) MacArthur circumvented the instructions by publishing his General Order No. 1. This directed that (effective 18 Apr 42) all Australian fighting forces were under his **operational control** but that administrative functions—to include logistics, training, and fixed coastal defenses—remained under Blamey as CinC, **AIF**. But Sir Thomas nevertheless accepted the role of Commander, Allied Land Forces, which "raised an important question of principle and had unfortunate repercussions" (Keogh, 140-41).

On orders from MacArthur, Sir Thomas personally took command of Australian operations in New Guinea on 23 Sep 42. Soon after Buna was captured in Jan 43, Blamey returned to AIF Hq in Australia. His operational role was nominal as the Allied offensive moved on and Australian forces were relegated to mopping up. Sir Thomas remained CinC, Allied Land Forces, SWPA, if only in theory after MacArthur created the **Alamo Force** primarily to avoid placing any large body of US troops under Blamey (Keogh, 473).

After the capture of Manila, Blamey moved his forward echelon there but still was virtually ignored. MacArthur dealt direct with task force commander MORSHEAD on the planned campaign to take Borneo with Australians (Keogh, 433).

After the Japanese surrender, having quietly suffered subordination to MacArthur, Blamey retired from the army and went into business. In 1950, shortly after being restored for a brief time to the active list, he became Australia's first field marshal. Sir Thomas died in Melbourne on 27 May 51.

BLANCHARD, Jean Georges Maurice. French general. 1877-1954. He was born at Orleans on 9 Dec 77 and graduated from the Ecole Polytechnique in 1899 as an artillerist. In 1914-18 he served in frontline and staff assignments, winning two citations and ending up as a major in Marshal Joffre's headquarters. He was promoted to brigadier general at the end of 1932 and three years later got another star. In 1938 the studious sexagenarian became director of all higher military instruction.

At the start of war the general commanded the 1st French Army around Cambrai. He was part of Billotte's 1st AG (below). On 10 May 40, in accordance with the agreed strategy, Blanchard joined the advance to support the Belgians on the Dyle River line. Moving between Lord GORT's BEF, on his north flank, and CORAP's 9th French Army, he advanced about 25 miles and collided with REICHENAU's 6th Army around Hannut. Blanchard withdrew into the large pocket of Allied troops cut off by the German drive down the Somme River to the English

Channel. On 25 May 40, two days after BIL-
LOTTE was fatally injured, a bewildered Blanchard moved up to head the army group. But he
was incapable of issuing orders. Alan BROOKE
later wrote, "He gave me the impression of a
man whose brain had ceased to function"
(Bryant, *Tide,* 92). Evacuated from Dunkirk on
a French destroyer at 6 PM on 1 June 40,
Blanchard was put on the reserve list on 28 Aug
40. He faded into obscurity, but not before being
awarded the Grand Cross of the Legion of
Honor as of 4 June 40 (the date the Dunkirk
evacuation was completed).

BLANDY, William Henry Purnell. US admiral. 1890-1954. "Spike" Blandy, whom Morison
characterizes as "a Celtic type, with a humorous
Irish mouth overhung by a large red nose" (XIV,
26), was born 28 June 90 in New York and graduated first in his 59-man Annapolis class of
1913. As Chief of the Bureau of Ordnance for
two years beginning in Feb 41 "he served the
Navy well . . . in developing, adapting, and manufacturing the Swedish Bofors and Swiss
Oerlikon as the indispensable 40mm and 20mm
antiaircraft weapons" (ibid.). From early 1944,
Rear Adm Blandy led task forces of amphibious
and support carrier groups in the Central Pacific.
He took part in the capture of Kwajalein, Saipan,
and Iwo Jima, then commanded the assault on
Kerama Retto that preceded the main Okinawa
landings on 1 Apr 45. Blandy directed the atomic tests at Bikini Atoll in July 46. Promoted to
full admiral, he commanded the Atlantic Fleet
from Feb 47 until retiring on 1 Feb 50. He died
12 Jan 54 at St Albans Hospital, NY.

BLASKOWITZ, Johannes. German general.
1883-1948. Born 10 July 83 in Peterswalde,
Silesia (central Czechoslovakia), Blaskowitz
began his military career at the age of 16 as a
cadet. He joined the 18th Inf Regt at Osterode,
East Prussia (Angolia, I, 261) and by 1918 had
risen to lead an infantry company. He was
awarded the Iron Cross 1st Class.

The grimly handsome Blaskowitz, a consummate soldier of the Old Guard, universally
respected for honesty and professional ability,
was one of the Reichswehr's senior generals by
1935. As a Generalleutnant he commanded
Wehrkreis II, with headquarters at Stettin.
Although no Nazi, he staunchly admired Hitler.

"Photographs show that his mustache, in 1935
still long and thick, had become in 1937 much
smaller and by 1939 was a duplicate of
Hitler's. . . ." (Curt Riess, 231). He was one of
the few senior generals to escape Hitler's 1938
purge of the army. Promoted the next year to
General of Infantry, he led troops of his district
into Austria and Czechoslovakia before particularly distinguishing himself as commander of
the 8th Army in south Poland. This brought him
the RK, awarded on 30 Sep 39, and promotion
on that date to Generaloberst.

Blaskowitz became CinC of occupied Poland
on 23 Oct 39, but Hans FRANK was named governor general three days later. This left Blaskowitz responsible only for internal security
and strategic defense, a blatant Nazi violation
of time-honored military practice. Other senior
army officers already had objected officially to
SS atrocities in Poland, but Blaskowitz submitted his own report in Nov 39. A second protest,
dated 6 Feb 40 and drafted probably by CAN-
ARIS, was a dramatically phrased document giving further evidence of criminal SS activities in
Poland and demanding that offenders be
brought to justice. According to HASSEL the
army general wanted to press charges against
SS general Sepp DIETRICH. The Nazi hierarchy
was outraged by what it viewed as political
naivete, and Himmler put Blaskowitz on his
blacklist. His unquestioned military ability
earned Blaskowitz command of the 9th Army
when it was activated on 14 May 40 for final
operations in France, and Brauchitsch nominated him to head all occupation forces in France.
But Himmler persuaded Hitler to block the
appointment (personal information from Harold
C. Deutsch). Blaskowitz instead was relegated
to the minor post of Military Governor of Northern France until transferred in Oct 40 to command the 1st Army on the SW coast of France.
This took him out of the war for four years, and
Professor Deutsch writes that Himmler intervened on at least five occasions to impede the
general's career (Deutsch, II, 188).

But when Rundstedt, as OB West, made final
dispositions in May 44 to meet the Allied invasion of France, he created AG G under Blaskowitz. Deployed in the south of France, the new
formation comprised the 1st and 19th Armies.
The general did well against overwhelming
odds, but half his force was sacrificed because

Hitler was slow to authorize withdrawals (Manteuffel in J&R, 392). After being driven into Alsace-Lorraine, Blaskowitz launched Manteuffel's 5th Pz Army in a counteroffensive that threw the Allies into disarray until stopped by Patton around Luneville on 18-20 Sep 44. Although Hitler had begun to recognize Blaskowitz's qualities, he now made him the scapegoat for OKW's mistakes.

Balck reached AG G Hq at Molsheim, Alsace, on 20 Sep 44 as the new commander (Mellinthin, *Battles,* 303) but on 24 Dec 44 was ordered back to the eastern front. Blaskowitz returned to AG G and launched a counter-offensive on New Year's Day to exploit Allied weakness in the Vosges. After considerable initial success the Germans were stopped by 21 Jan 45 around Haguenau. AG G then was depleted by detachments sent back to the Russian front.

Now fully appreciated by the fuehrer, Blaskowitz took over from Student in Holland on 28 Jan 45 as commander of AG H. By early April Montgomery's 21st AG had driven AG H back into "Fortress Holland." But on 25 Apr 45 Blaskowitz was awarded the Swords (146/159), being one of the last recipients (Angolia, I, 261). His hawk-eyed good looks by then had taken on the aspect of a ferocious frog. He was the only officer holding the rank of colonel general in 1939 who never became a field marshal.

Taken prisoner on 8 May 45 at Hilbersum, Holland, Blaskowitz testified at Nuremberg before being indicted himself as a minor war criminal. One charge was that in Holland he had ordered the summary execution of stragglers. But the general died on 5 Feb 48, a few hours before his scheduled trial in Case No. 12, "Wilhelm von Leeb, et al." According to most accounts he dove over the railing of a prison gallery and broke his neck. But "a story of very doubtful authority became current that the general was murdered by former members of the SS who had succeeded in being taken on as prison 'trusties.'" (W-B, *Nemesis,* 462n.).

BLEICHER, Hugo. German counterespionage agent. 1899-. A human ferret who destroyed many Allied intelligence operations in France, he used the aliases "Col Henri" and "Monsieur Jean." In 1939 Bleicher was a businessman in Hamburg when recruited because of his knowledge of languages to work with the field police in occupied countries.

He served in Amsterdam before being sent to Paris. Bleicher promptly destroyed **Interallié**, the first and most important British intelligence network in France. After triumphing on his first mission, in which "Valentin" (Maj Roman GARBY-CZERNIAWSKI) and "the Cat" (Mathilde CARRE) were arrested on 17 Nov 41, Bleicher was transferred into the Abwehr and sent south with German occupation forces that began moving into Vichy France on 11 Nov 42. Here he scored another coup. Masquerading as an Abwehr colonel who wanted to defect, the seductive sergeant made contact with Odette Sansom while her chief, Peter Churchill, was visiting London. Almost exactly as he had with Czerniawski and the Cat, Bleicher caught CHURCHILL and Odette SANSOM, both on 16 Apr 43. But Col Henri never knew that Churchill was "Raoul," long-sought head of the "Spindle" network operating from near Annecy.

Bleicher worked with Henri Déricourt, a double agent who in 1944 led him to the arrest of a major secret army organizer, Maj Henry Frager. The zealous Bleicher never rose above the rank of sergeant in the clique-ridden German intelligence system. He was arrested in Amsterdam and sentenced to jail by an Allied court. On orders from his captors, Bleicher wrote his war memoirs, published as *Colonel Henri's Story* (London: William Kimber, 1954).

BLIMP, Col. *See* COLONEL BLIMP.

BLOCH, Claude Charles. US admiral. 1878-1967. A Kentuckian born 13 July 78, he was in the USNA Class of 1899 (14/53). On 6 Jan 40 he took command of the 14th Naval District in Hawaii after heading the US Fleet from 1937. "Admiral Bloch, not Admiral Kimmel, was the opposite number of General Short in Oahu. . . . But Kimmel . . . was constantly going over Bloch's head or interfering with his functions" (Morison, III, 134). Bloch contributed to the tragedy by opposing installation of antitorpedo nets, as the CNO suggested after studying the Italian naval disaster at **Taranto** (ibid., 138-39). Reaching the statutory age limit of 63, he retired on 1 Aug 42 as a full admiral and was briefly recalled to active duty that year and in 1946. Bloch died 4 Oct 67 in Washington, DC.

BLOMBERG, Werner von. German field marshal. 1878-1946. A Pomeranian born in Stargard on 2 Sep 78, he grew into a very tall, impressive-looking, intelligent officer. His progressive political and military ideas made Blomberg "refreshingly different" from others of his Prussian background (Liddell Hart, *Talk*, 21, passim). He won the Pour le Mérite in WWI but otherwise had a mediocre early record. Despite this he was accepted in the Treaty Army and rose rapidly. In 1927, at the remarkably young age of 48, he was a Generalmajor heading the **Truppenamt**. But he clashed immediately with SCHLEICHER and was exiled in 1927 to East Prussia with REICHENAU as his CofS. Both officers incurred professional criticism for associating with local Nazis. This probably is why Blomberg was scheduled for retirement in 1933 after completing a tour of duty from 1932 in Geneva as head of the German delegation to the Disarmament Conference. But the official reason was that he had not recovered from a brain concussion suffered in 1931 after falling from a horse. The politics leading to his selection to be minister of defense and Armed Forces CinC are still not fully known. There is evidence that Pres Hindenburg expected him to protect the army's position in the Nazi regime. (Keegan, ed., *Who Was Who*, 39.) Promoted immediately to general of infantry and later that year to colonel general, Blomberg came under Hitler's spell and made more concessions to National Socialism than his normal inclinations would have permitted. For example, it was he who conceived of having an oath of personal loyalty to the fuehrer imposed on the army (Deutsch, I, 20-22). Soon known as the "Rubber Lion," he was the first field marshal created by Hitler (Apr 36).

But when the Nazis decided to purge the Wehrmacht of its traditionally apolitical Old Guard, Blomberg was the first victim. His ouster was plotted by Goering, who hoped to replace the field marshal. With access to police files, Goering discovered that the woman Blomberg had just married had a record with the vice police. On saying farewell to Hitler on 26 Jan 38 the Rubber Lion rendered his final service: planting the idea that HITLER personally take over as head of the Wehrmacht. The doting old field marshal spent a happy year in exile with his alluring new wife, ignoring suggestions from visiting generals that he blow his brains out. He then lived quietly in Bavaria. Hitler had a soft spot for Blomberg until the end (Irving, *HW*, xxiv)

but rejected his request for a combat command during the war primarily because few officers would serve under a commander who had violated their social code. The pathetic, bedridden old field marshal testified at Nuremberg. He pointed out that before 1938-39 German generals had no reason to oppose Hitler "since he produced results which they desired." After that it was too late for concerted action, he lamented lamely. (Brett-Smith, 185.) Hitler's first field marshal died 14 Mar 46 while still in detention.

BLUECHER. *See* BLYUKHER.

BLUM, Léon. French statesman. 1872-1950. As the first Jew and the first Socialist to be premier of Catholic, capitalistic France, Blum was a natural scapegoat for the French national humiliation in 1940. He paid by being "more assailed in peace and longer imprisoned during the war than any other noted French leader" (Flanner, *Paris Journal*, 137).

Blum was born 9 Apr 72 in the grubby working-class Rue St Denis in Paris but moved up to prosperous bourgeois neighborhoods and excellent schools as his Alsatian father's ribbon business flourished. He won prizes in Latin and Greek and remained an intellectual even after becoming a champion of the masses. At 26 he was a member of the Conseil d'Etat even though converted to socialism at the Sorbonne.

Early in the Dreyfus Affair (1894-1906) he was an unpaid clerk to the lawyer who defended Emile Zola (1840-1902) in the libel suit brought against him in 1898 for publishing "J'accuse." Assassination of Socialist chief Jean Jaurès (1859-1914), Blum's friend and political hero, pushed the young lawyer into the Socialist Party work he had always refused to do for Jaurès (Ibid., 141). Bad vision made him unfit for military service, so Blum became executive secretary to the socialist minister of public works. In 1919 he was elected socialist deputy from the Seine, beginning his parliamentary career.

At the age of 64, virtually unknown to the public, Blum suddenly became prominent as leader of the left wing Front Populaire. His Socialist Party was joined by Radical Socialists (the party of DALADIER and BONNET), by Communists, and by others to carry the 1936 elections. Blum was premier from 5 June 36 to 19 June 37, and again from 13 Mar to 10 Apr 38, when he was succeeded by Daladier. The period was marked by domestic social reforms as Germany prepared for military conquest. "Better Hitler than the Jew Blum!" cried Frenchmen in 1936. When they did get Hitler in 1940 the Front Populaire was blamed.

In Vichy, Blum vigorously opposed granting absolute powers to Pétain, being in the "group of 80" parliamentarians to cast negative votes on 10 July 40. Although abandoned by most of his political allies, Blum declined to seek safety abroad, expecting to settle quietly in Vichy France. But on 15 Sep 40 he was arrested with five of his ministers on Pétain's orders and held at various places under reasonably comfortable conditions. Blum was the star performer in the **Riom Trials** of early 1942, turning the tables on inquisitioners and being largely reponsible for the indefinite adjournment of the proceedings (Larousse). His testimony is a rich source of historical information on why France was so vulnerable in 1940. Turned over to the Germans in Mar 43, Blum was held in isolated residences near concentration camps, finally Buchenwald, but not actually in any of them. In the last of his many books, *Le dernier mois,* he describes how he and his third wife were liberated with the **Niederdorf group**. At last respected in France and abroad as a liberty-loving liberal, Blum died 30 Mar 50 in his cottage of Jouy-en-Josas near Paris.

BLUMENTRITT, Guenther. German general. 1896-1967. A Bavarian born in Munich, and one of the German Army's finest staff officers before excelling as a field commander, Blumentritt is of historic importance because of his close association with many major personalities and events. As a young infantry officer he spent much of WWI on the Russian front. Joining the Reichswehr in 1918, he had a long association with Manstein, in whose memoirs Blumentritt looms large. The officers served together on Leeb's staff during the Sudetenland crisis, in Poland as Rundstedt's chief of operations while Manstein was CofS, and in Rundstedt's AG A in France during the autumn of 1940. Blumentritt then was Kluge's CofS in the 4th Army as part of Bock's AG Center in Russia.

For the first nine months of 1942, Generalleutnant Blumentritt was in OKH as chief of operations, succeeding Paulus. He then served in France as Rundstedt's CofS in OB West, remaining when Kluge replaced Rundstedt on

3 July 44. Blumentritt was closely associated with key officers of the anti-Hitler cabal but unaware of final plans for STAUFFENBERG's assassination attempt of 20 July 44 and not immediately a suspect. Only after the arrival of MODEL as OB West and KLUGE's suicide did Blumentritt get the long-expected news that he was being replaced. Succeeded by WESTPHAL on 5 Sep 44 and leaving OB West three days later with orders to report to Hitler's Hq on the 13th, the Bavarian was received at Rastenburg by Guderian, Keitel, and other senior officers as a condemned man. But Hitler was cordial, telling Blumentritt to take a rest before reporting to Rundstedt, who was being reinstated as OB West, for a long-sought command assignment. After his first home leave in more than two years, Blumentritt briefly commanded elite formations opposing Montgomery in the Low Countries. Toward the end of Sep 44, promoted to General of SS, he directed fanatic defenses of the 12th SS Corps in the Roermond Triangle. Driven back by HORROCKS, he took over the 25th Army in Holland in Jan 45, and from Mar 45 he headed the 1st Parachute Army in NW Germany until war's end.

BLYUKHER, Vasily Kostantinovich. Red Army officer. 1889-1938. Born 1 Dec 89 in the village of Barshchinka, Yaroslavl region, near Moscow, he became a junior officer and saw action on the southwest front in WWI. Severely wounded in 1916, he joined the CP that year, the Red Army in 1918, and was a hero of the civil war. As CinC in the Far East, one of the first MSUs created on 20 Nov 35, he was identified as the Red Army's most outstanding officer in a German army report Stalin saw just as he began to believe a coup d'état was possible if not actually planned. Having liquidated Marshal TUKHACHEVSKY (on whose court Blyukher had sat), and the other two MSUs, BUDENNY and VOROSHILOV, being too ordinary to lead a revolt, the finger pointed to the commander of the Separate Red Banner Far Eastern Army. Starting by harassing his proconsul about lack of vigor in driving the Japanese from around Lake **Khasan,** and sending MEKHLIS to substantiate this charge (Volkogonov II, 328), Stalin called the perplexed marshal to Moscow without any intention of seeing him. Arrested 22 Oct 38 on trumped-up charges of spying for Japan since 1921, he was unrecognizable when last seen on 5-6 November. "His face was a bloody pulp and one eye had been knocked out." (Ibid.) Without ever breaking, he died 9 Nov 38 in the NKVD dungeons, although this has not been confirmed until recently. Due largely to the prevalent Soviet use of code names, the Japanese believed he was alive as late as 1941 under the name "General Galin" (Scotts).

BOATNER, Haydon LeMaire. US general. 1900-77. He was born 8 Oct 00 in New Orleans, son of a federal judge. On his 17th birthday he enlisted in the Marines to pay for a year at Tulane before following his elder brother to West Point. After graduating in 1924 (146/405), Boatner served with the 15th Inf in Tientsin before getting an MA degree in Chinese language and culture (1934). The short, tough infantryman also studied Russian, gave English classes to young Chinese, played polo with Roy Chapman Andrews, and went on long hunting trips with Chinese officers. Col Boatner was visiting Washington when he found planners agonizing over a shipment of large locomotives to Chiang Kai-shek. Solving their problem by pointing out that no bridge in China could handle locomotives of the size they wanted to send (personal information), he ended up being ordered to join STILWELL in Burma.

As a rear-guard commander on the retreat to India, finally forced to ditch his radio as the Japanese closed in, the colonel concluded his last transmission with, "I expect to have a star waiting when I get back" (personal information). The first general in his West Point class, his promotion was dated 1 Nov 42.

Boatner became Stilwell's CofS and deputy commander of the Chinese army in India with primary responsibility for organization and training. He showed that the Chinese soldier, if properly fed, equipped, trained, and led, was a match for the Japanese. Boatner pioneered the development of tactics and techniques for air supply of large forces in the jungle.

But as chief of staff Boatner had periodic clashes with Stilwell over staff procedures because the commanding general's son was the G2 (bypassing the CofS) and two sons-in-law were LnOs with the Chinese (Allen, *Burma,* 367n).

Despite periodic requests to be relieved (personal information) Boatner remained Stilwell's CofS and deputy. As an Old China Hand like Stilwell whom Chiang and his generals could not gull, the straight-talking soldier was as much detested as his chief by Chiang Kai-shek and other Chinese generals including SUN LI-JEN. (Tuchman, *Stilwell,* 393, 394; personal information.)

Brig Gen Boatner headed the NCAS in Burma from its creation on 1 Feb 44. When MERRILL was medically evacuated on 19 May 44 Merrill's newly-appointed XO, Col John E. McCammon, succeeded him on 19 May 44 and was promoted to brigadier general but lasted only a week until Stilwell had to put Boatner in command of the Myitkyina TF. Japanese strength at Myitkyina proved to be much greater than suspected; Stilwell's G2 greatly underestimated Japanese strength, as postwar evidence would show; but "Vinegar Joe" blamed Boatner for lacking aggressiveness. Finally succumbing to malaria, Boatner was invalided out on 26 June 44 and replaced by Brig Gen Theodore F. Wessels. (The Allies needed regular forces to take Myitkyina on 3 Aug 44.) After convalescing, Boatner continued to be Stilwell's CofS and DCG, Chinese Combat Command (Cullum).

During the Korean War he was DCG 2d Inf Div (1951-52), winning a Silver Star for action around Heartbreak Ridge. When Chinese POWs on Koje-do took the US commander hostage in 1952 and threatened to break out and seize control of the island, Mark Clark picked Boatner to restore order. Promoted for his quick and almost-bloodless success, Maj Gen Boatner subsequently headed the JAMG in Greece, 1955-57. He was provost marshal general until retiring in 1960 to live in San Antonio, Tex, where died suddenly on 29 May 77 of a heart attack.

BOCK, (Moritz Albert Friedrich) Fedor von. German general. 1880-1945. Fedor von Bock was a Prussian of the old school, tall, slender, fine featured, and vigorous. He was an outstanding commander of army groups in Poland, France, and Russia. He was retired in July 42 because of differences with Hitler.

Born 3 Dec 80 at Kustrin, Brandenburg, son of a well-known general from an old military family, he was commissioned in 1898. Von Bock won the Pour le Merité as a battalion commander in WWI and rose to major. In 1933, when Hitler came to power, he commanded Wehrkreis II, headquartered at Stettin. Not among the "uncooperative" officers purged by the Nazis from the Wehrmacht in early 1939 after the BLOMBERG and FRITSCH affairs, Bock led troops into Austria and the Sudetenland. Promoted to Generaloberst, Bock took command of AG North for the blitz of Poland and proved to be a master of fast-moving operations of large formations. Last-minute adoption of theMANSTEIN plan relegated Bock's AG B to a secondary role in France in May 40, but he still was among the 12 field marshals created during the campaign. For the invasion of Russia he was given the main effort against Moscow. In AG Center the field marshal had KLUGE's 4th Army of 16 divisions, Strauss's 9th Army of 9 divisions, GUDERIAN's 2d Pz Gp of 5 panzer divisions and 9 others, HOTH's 3d Pz Gp of 4 panzer divisions and 7 others, plus the 51st Inf Div in reserve. Using panzers in great double envelopments and infantry armies to mop up bypassed pockets of resistance, Bock had surrounded 300,000 Russians at Minsk by1 July. In the next three weeks he pushed 450 miles to Smolensk, within 225 miles of Moscow.

But Hitler then intervened (19 July 41) to halt AG Center at Smolensk and divert its two panzer groups toward Leningrad and Kiev. After HOTH and GUDERIAN returned to AG Center, and Hitler announced publicly on 3 Oct 41 that the Red Army was incapable of further resistance anywhere (Keegan, *Mask,* 264), Bock resumed his advance on Moscow. Dubbed *Der Sterber,* (the one who preaches death), by his exhausted troops, Bock repeatedly reassured OKW that only a final lunge was needed to take Moscow. But autumn rains created a sea of mud, and Soviet resistance stiffened. By 1 Dec 41 the last, desperate, German effort had failed, an unusually severe Russian winter had set in belatedly, and Bock was suffering from severe stomach cramps. Five days later he confessed to being no longer fit physically, and on 19 Dec 41 he was replaced by KLUGE.

In less than a month (18 Jan 42), however, Bock took over AG South after REICHENAU's sudden death. Ironically, the field marshal left the area of heaviest action in Russia to find it had followed him south. On his first day at AG South he faced a Soviet counteroffensive that was not contained until about four weeks later. Then the Soviets broke through north and south of Kharkov on 12 May 42. Bock countered by attacking the Izyum salient, 17 May-25 June

42. This prelude to the large-scale German summer offensive in the south inflicted 240,000 casualties and destroyed or captured about 1,250 tanks.

Bock's initial mission, as set by Fuehrer Directive No 41 of 5 Apr 42, had been for AG South to destroy Soviet forces west of the Don, thus opening the way to the Caucusus oil fields. (Keegan, *Mask,* 287.) As for Stalingrad, no plans had yet been made beyond prescribing "an attempt" to reach that major center of production (ibid.). On his own initiative, however, Bock began his offensive with large-scale operations northward to destroy a Soviet force concentrating on his flank around Voronezh. Shedding fresh light on the campaign, John Keegan points out that Bock's unexpected initial success affected OKW's plans materially (Keegan, *Mask,* 264-65). Instead of protesting Bock's initiative, Hitler instead divided his AG South into AG B, under Bock, and AG A, to the south, under LIST (ibid.). The arrangement, ordered on 7 July, was short lived: Bock learned on 13 July 42 that he was being replaced by WEICHS. Accepting a hint to request relief for ill health, the field marshal spent the rest of the war in retirement.

Bock had proved to be the quintessential military careerist who lacked moral courage when it might jeopardize his professional future. In Poland he refused to protest the massacre of Jews by SS troops in his headquarters town of Borisov. Efforts by his nephew Henning von TRESCOW to enlist Bock in the anti-Hitler conspiracies were met with near panic. (Deutsch, I, 252; Goerlitz, *GGS,* 399).

He was killed 4 May 45 with his wife and daughter by Allied planes on a road near Hamburg.

BOHLE, Ernst Wilhelm. Nazi official. 1903-60. The "German leader overseas" was born in England, had a degree from Cape Town Univ, where his father was a German professor, and joined the Nazi Party in Mar 32. Slightly more than a year later he was Gauleiter [sic] of the Auslandsorganisation (AO), the Nazi Party's overseas branch. Having entered the foreign service, Bohle concerned himself from 7 Feb 37 with all Germans overseas, not just Nazis. He was implicated in the flight of HESS, whom he helped write a letter in English to the Duke of Hamilton. The Gauleiter saved himself by saying he assumed Hess had the fuehrer's authority.

In Apr 49 Bohle was sentenced to five years in prison for war crimes (SS membership) but was granted amnesty the same year.

BOHLEN, Charles Eustis. US diplomat. 1904-74. "Chip" Bohlen was a career foreign service officer who served five years in the Moscow embassy before 1940. He returned in 1943 as first secretary. A Soviet expert fluent in Russian, he had an important role during the war. In 1944 he was an adviser at the **Dumbarton Oaks** Conference. Bohlen was ambassador to Moscow in 1953 and later to Paris.

BOHR, Niels Henrik David. Danish nuclear physicist. 1885-1962. "The father of atomic energy," Bohr was second only to Einstein as a 20th-century scientist. He was the son of a physiology professor and got his PhD in physics from the Univ of Copenhagen in 1911. The next year he went to England, first studying at Cambridge under J. J. Thompson (1856-1940) before working from 1912 to 1916 at Manchester Univ under Ernest RUTHERFORD. By 1913 the 28-year-old Bohr had won international acclaim as a theoretical physicist, introducing quantum effects into the development of atomic theory.

Returning to Denmark in 1916, Bohr created a flourishing center for the study of physics, attracting leading authorities from all over the world. He developed the "Copenhagen interpretation," a concept that no single model could explain atomic phenomena adequately (Briggs, 70). Work on quantum theory and atomic structure won him the Nobel Prize in 1922. Visiting the US in 1938 and 1939 he warned American scientists that, based on experiments in Germany, he believed the atom could be split. Recruited for the Manhattan Project, Bohr was spirited out of German-occupied Denmark by the British secret service in 1943 and sent to Los Alamos, N.Mex, where until 1945 he contributed materially to development of the atomic bomb. He continued his scientific work after the war in Copenhagen but also campaigned for controlling the use of atomic weapons. Ex-KGB Gen Lt Pavel Sudoplatov asserts in *Special Tasks* (1994) that Bohr knowingly gave vital technical assistance to a Soviet physicist, one Yakov Terletsky.

BOINEBURG-LENGSFELD, Hans Wilhelm von. German general 1889-. A Thuringian

Freiherr of refined tastes, born 9 June 89, he was a lean, grimly handsome colonel when he began forming the 23d Pz Div around Paris on 25 Sep 41 (*B&O,* 77). Immediately promoted (1 Oct), Generalmajor von Boineburg served in Russia as Georg Stumme's CofS in the 40th Pz Corps. This was in AG Center until transferred in June 42 to the Kharkov sector in Fedor von BOCK's AG South. Thanks largely to the intercession of von Bock, Boineburg escaped punishment for the serious security violation for which STUMME was made the scapegoat. Boineburg took command of the 23d Pz Div on 26 Aug 42 and was promoted to Generalleutnant on 1 Dec 42. But on 28 Dec, while in action around Stalingrad, he was crushed by a tank. Although badly mutilated, the monocled baron recovered sufficiently from countless broken bones to take command of Greater Paris in 1943. "Paris is France," the Germans knew from many wars, and Hitler intended to make the capital a fortress. But the cultured, sybaritic new German commander evaded his instructions by establishing defenses, the "Boineburg Line," well outside the 30-square-mile urban area and did not make preparations for the prescribed heavy demolition of the bridges and buildings inside the city. OKW examined his plans on 14 Mar 44, declared them "grossly deficient," but ordered few changes.

When Heinrich von STULPNAGEL received the message on 20 July 44 that Hitler had been assassinated, Boineburg arrested the 1,200 SS and Gestapo men in Greater Paris as called for under Opn **Valkyrie.** When he learned of the snafu, Boineburg had the captives released and somehow talked himself out of trouble. But on 9 Aug 44 he was replaced by CHOLTITZ. A consummate survivor, Boineburg was taken prisoner at Erfurt by US forces.

BOISSAU, Robert. French general. Easily confused with BOISSON (below), Boissau was Vichy commander at Oran when the Allies landed on 8 Nov 42.

BOISSON, Pierre. French general. 1894-1948. A schoolmaster like his father, Boisson lost a leg at Verdun and joined the colonial service in 1919. By 1936 he was governor general of equatorial Africa, operating from Brazzaville. What Pertinax calls his "wild determination to resist" the Franco-German armistice (Pertinax, 458n) disappeared when Boisson learned that the Pétain government had ordered him to Dakar as governor general of West Africa and high commissioner for "black Africa." De Gaulle characterizes the colonial officer as "a man of energy, whose ambition—greater than his discernment—had made him choose to play on the Vichy side" (*The Call*, 113-14). Boisson did not reach Dakar until 23 July 40, after the new BB *Richelieu* was damaged there by a British air and motorboat attack. The governor general's orders were "No Germans in Dakar," but he also blocked DE GAULLE's attempt to take the city and the *Richelieu* on 23 Sep 40. The Vichy proconsul was a brutal but able and honest administrator whom Roosevelt came to admire.

Darlan ordered Boisson to bring his colony into the Allied camp after the 8 Nov 42 landings, but the Vichy official took 10 days to comply. After remaining "correct but unfriendly in Dakar" (Macmillan, *Blast,* 237), and being retained at Roosevelt's insistence over de Gaulle's objections, on 24 June 43 Boisson offered to resign after de Gaulle became head of the Provisional French National Committee. Pierre Cournaire was announced as his successor on 1 July. Marked for revenge along with BERGERET, FLANDIN, and PEYROUTON by de Gaulle despite FDR's outraged objections, the defender of Dakar was arrested on 15 Dec 43 and imprisoned. He was released after two years because of ill health. When about to be called before the high court of justice he died suddenly on 20 July 48 at Châtou, near Paris.

BOLDIN, Ivan V. Red Army leader. 1892-1965. After taking part in the Soviet-Finnish War, Gen Lt Boldin was D. G. PAVLOV's deputy in the newly constituted Western Front around Minsk. From near Grodno he counterattacked infantry divisions of the German 9th Army, 24-26 June 41; lacking air and artillery support he was driven back with heavy losses. (Seaton, *R-G War,* 119-20.) Forming stragglers into effective delaying forces, he was encircled west of Vyasma by 7 Oct 41. His 15th Army held out for 51 days, contributing materially to saving Moscow. Escaping the Vyasma encirclement with V. S. POPOV and retreating SE to Tula, Boldin worked closely with Popov from 22 Nov 41 to hold that critical place.

Promoted in 1944, Gen Col Boldin led the 50th Army in Rokossovsky's 2d Belorussian Front from the Narew bridgehead to reach the Masurian Lakes region in early 1945. Later he took part in the destruction of AG Center, serving as Chernyakovsky's deputy in the 3d Ukrainian Front. His book *Stranitsy zhizni* (1961) is quoted frequently in accounts of the first, desperate phase of the war.

BONG, Richard Ira. US airman. 1920-45. Flying the twin-engined P-38 Lightning fighter, Maj Bong downed 40 Japanese planes to become the leading American ace of all wars. The modest, blond hero was born on a farm in Poplar, Wis. His success probably was due primarily to marksmanship, Bong's modest disavowal of this indicates "that he realized how far the art could be pursued, and how skilled he might get at it" (Sims, *Aces,* 9). Repeatedly volunteering for combat missions brought him the Medal of Honor. The hero died in Aug 45 while testing an F-80 jet in California.

BONHOEFFER, Dietrich. German resistance figure. 1906-45. The brother of Klaus (following) and of Christine DOHNANYI, Dietrich was born 4 Feb 06 in Breslau, son of a well-known psychiatrist and university professor. He studied theology in Germany and at Union Theological Seminary in New York. In 1931 he began lecturing in Berlin, but when Hitler took power in 1933 the churchman moved to London, where he lectured and preached until 1935. After returning to Berlin he joined the Confessional Church and, with NIEMOELLER, attracted attention by criticizing National Socialism. He also was one of the earliest anti-Hitler conspirators. The pastor maintained contact with foreign churchmen in hopes of enlisting support for the conspirators, often visiting the Vatican. In England he told Bishop BELL in early 1939 about the growing German resistance to Hitler. Bonhoeffer's seminary was closed a second time in 1940, and the pastor was issued a gag order. Learning in May 42 that Bell had gone to Stockholm, Bonhoeffer met him incognito, using false papers supplied by Hans OSTER. In an ardent effort to prove how far the resistance had progressed, the pastor revealed not only its plans but also a list of principal conspirators! He asked Bell to find out whether the Allies might grant better peace terms to a denazified Germany.

Disappointed by earlier efforts of this nature, Anthony EDEN was unreceptive.

The pastor was imprisoned on 5 Apr 43 for subversion, shortly after his brother-in-law DOHNANYI was arrested. Investigation of the 20 July 44 putsch revealed specifics of the Stockholm meeting with Bishop Bell (above) to include identification of key conspirators. Incarcerated in Buchenwald for further interrogation, the pastor was executed 9 Apr 45 with CANARIS and OSTER.

BONHOEFFER, Klaus. German resistance figure. 1901-45. An elder brother of Dietrich (herein), he has been described as follows by a close associate:

a sturdy thick-set figure, a passionate opponent of the regime. With his thick black hair, brown eyes and brown skin he seemed to me the very prototype of his Swabian forebears, whose sense of democracy and dogged self-will he had inherited. He was extremely versatile and a good musician. He had studied international law in Geneva, had then been apprenticed to an Amsterdam bank and given up his practice as an international lawyer in Berlin because after the murders of 30 June 1934 [the **Blood Purge**] he had realized there was no future for a freelance "guardian of the law." (Otto JOHN memoirs, 24.)

So from 1936 Klaus headed the Lufthansa legal department. Meanwhile he married the daughter of historian Hans Delbrueck, and his sister Christine married Hans von DOHNANYI.

Klaus became a principal agent for Hans OSTER, hence a major figure in the anti-Hitler conspiracy. One of his major contributions was to bring BECK into contact with Wilhelm Leuschner (1888-1944), a leader of the outlawed labor movement (Deutsch, II, 47n). Incriminated during the investigation of the 20 July 44 assassination attempt on HITLER, Klaus was sentenced to death on 2 Feb 45 and shot in Berlin on 23 Apr 45.

BONOMI, Ivanoe. Italian statesman. 1873-1951. Bonomi was born into a working-class family in Mantua and was a founder of the Italian Socialist Party in 1892. During the Fascist era he was forced into retirement. As momentum gathered to oust MUSSOLINI, the tall, bespectacled, goateed independent of moderately liberal outlook was made chairman of a committee to work with the monarchy. (Buchanan, 170.) He succeeded BADOGLIO as premier on 22 June 44, retaining the influential CROCE and SFORZA but adding the communist TOGLIATTI. Bonomi was located first in Salerno, moving on 19 June 44 to liberated Rome. With two provisional governments in 12 months, Bonomi devoted most of his efforts to domestic and foreign politics. But in Nov 44 he sent the first small elements of an Italian army into action against the Germans, and for the final offensive in 1945 five combat groups, totaling about 48,000 troops, were engaged. Bonomi was succeeded as premier by Alcide de Gasperi in Dec 45 but remained active in politics.

BOR. *See* KOMOROWSKI, Tadeusz ("General Bor").

BORGHESE, Junio Valerio. Italian naval officer. 1906-74. "The Black Prince" led the 10th Light Flotilla early in the war. Using his submarine *Scirè* to launch three two-man piloted torpedo teams with **limpet mines,** Comdr Borghese had to abort a mission against Gibraltar on 29 Sep 40 because Force H was off to support de Gaulle's Dakar adventure. In several attempts during the period 27-30 Oct 40 he also failed. His first success was during the night of 20-21 Sep 41 in the Bay of Gibraltar: three teams sank a 2,444-ton freighter, the 8,145-ton naval tanker *Denbydale,* and severely damaged the 10,883-ton motor ship *Durham.* The Black Prince scored his greatest victory the night of 18-19 Dec 41. Three two-man piloted torpedo teams from *Scirè* entered Alexandria harbor through the boom gap opened for British ships. Using limpet mines, they crippled Britain's last two battleships in the Mediterranean, *Valiant* and *Queen Elizabeth* (both 31,000 tons), and the Norwegian tanker *Sagona* (7,554 tons). They also damaged the US DD *Jervis,* which was alongside *Sagona.* (R&H, I, 137, 166; S&S.) The 10th Light Flotilla's only losses were six frogmen captured. Several of Borghese's officers and men had swum on the 1935 Italian Olympic team, and some volunteered as POWs to work after the war with Comdr Lionel CRABB's Venice Underwater Working Party.

Borghese commanded a destroyer flotilla and land-based assault craft in the Anzio area after the Allies invaded Italy. But he accomplished little. The highly publicized Black Prince was associated with neo-Fascist organizations in postwar Italy.

BORIS III. King of Bulgaria. 1894-1943. Succeeding his father in 1918, Boris III believed Bulgaria's future lay in maintaining neutrality while tilting politically toward the Axis. This policy regained him South Dobruja from Romania in 1940. Still refusing to declare war against the Allies or supply troops to Hitler, he was killed 28 Aug 43 by a pro-Soviet assassin. Boris's son, Simeon II (born 1937), was the nominal king after the Russians occupied Bulgaria in early Sep 44. The monarchy was abolished in 1946.

BORMANN, Martin Ludwig. Nazi official. 1900-45. The man who became second in real power only to Hitler was born 17 June 00 in Halberstadt. His father, who died when the boy was barely three years old (Lang, *Bormann,* 17), had been sergeant major of a Prussian cavalry regiment. Martin's mother remarried within a few months, the new husband being an old friend and a well-heeled bank director some three years her junior. Although the family now could afford to give the boy a good education, Bormann dropped out of the **Realgymnasium** after a few years. His claim of having been an apprentice farmer in Mecklenburg has been generally accepted, but relatives said he worked in a mill that made oil cakes for cattle feed (ibid., 22).

Bormann was a gunner in the last months of 1918. He claims to have became general manager of a 2,000-acre estate in Mecklenburg near Parchim. Considering that he was a minor without farm experience, this is questionable, but the property, Gut Herzberg, was the scene of a famous political murder in 1923. The victim, Walter Kadow, was accused of betraying saboteur Albert Leo Schlageter to the French. Principal perpetrator of the murder in 1923 was the future commandant of Auschwitz, Rudolf Hoess, but Bormann spent a year in prison for his involvement.

After finding his calling in the rough-and-tumble paramilitary activities of postwar Germany, Bormann officially joined the Nazi Party in 1927. Two years later he married an ardent young Nazi, Gerda Buch. Hitler was official witness at the well-publicized "swastika wedding"

and godfather of the couple's first of 10 children. Frau Bormann's portraits in later life show she was strikingly handsome.

Without displaying any exceptional qualities the lumpy, publicity-shy Bormann rose steadily in the Nazi hierarchy. When Hitler became chancellor in 1933 he appointed Bormann Reichsleiter (national organizer) and chief of party headquarters (in Munich's Brown House). About this time he was elected to the Reichstag. But, more important, he became Rudolf HESS's second in command and CofS (Stabsleiter). After Hess's flight on 10 May 41 Bormann succeeded him as deputy fuehrer. A year later he was Hitler's secretary and de facto minister of the interior (Speer, *Memoirs,* 253).

"The Secretary" was far from the Nordic physical ideal. Swarthy, stocky, short-legged, and slightly knock-kneed, he looked to SCHELLENBERG like a prizefighter measuring an opponent for the kill. "He worked his way up the Party ladder with a series of limited alliances, which were lightly held or dissolved as soon as they had served their purpose," writes Davidson, "alliances with Hess, Rosenberg, Himmler, Keitel, and among others, Eva Braun" (*Trial,* 103). After the Stalingrad disaster at the end of 1942 Bormann consolidated his power by establishing the Committee of Three with Keitel and Hans Lammers. The secretariat screened all papers that Hitler signed, theoretically a useful bureaucratic exercise but one that in reality gave Bormann inordinate influence. (Speer, *Memoirs,* 252.)

Many of Hitler's mistakes stemmed from poor staff work by Bormann. He lacked the requisite intelligence, education, and experience for his sensitive post. Seldom leaving headquarters, he was out of touch with reality. As the Third Reich collapsed, Bormann became more murderous, approving death sentences even for trivial offenses. *(See* Davidson, *Trial,* 106-7.) Having been Hitler's most trusted lieutenant until the end and named executor of Hitler's political testament, he tried to maintain control by radio. The night of 1-2 May 45 he and six others left the Fuehrerbunker and undertook to break through the Soviet encirclement behind a force of tanks. Although several eyewitnesses said he was hit by tank fire, two testifying they saw his corpse, it was generally believed long after the war that Bormann reached sanctuary and remained at large. There is also good evidence that he bit a cyanide capsule and died very early on 2 May 45 on Berlin's Invalidenstrasse RR bridge. A skeleton found in the city on 8 Dec 72 was officially identified as his.

BOSE, Subhas Chandra. Indian nationalist. 1897-1945. A Bengali who graduated from Cambridge, Bose (rhymes with pose) was a tall, charismatic leader with a gift for fiery oratory He entered politics as a nationalist and became mayor of Calcutta. The British arrested Bose on 2 July 40 and jailed him for sedition. Six months later he made a dramatic escape, went to Germany, and formed a 3,000-man Indian Legion of ex-POWs from the North African campaign. German defeats at El Alamein and Stalingrad ended ideas of using the legion in an invasion of the subcontinent. Bose was taken via Madagascar by German and Japanese submarines to Rangoon to head the Provisional Government of Free India, which was created on 21 Oct 43. He formed the Indian National Army (INA) from some 40,000 Japanese-held POWs. The Subhas Bde, about 7,000 strong, accompanied Renya MUTAGUCHI's "March on Delhi" (Mar-July 44) but contributed little. The INA was disbanded as the Allies over-ran Burma. Bose escaped from Rangoon on 24 Apr 45 and moved his government to Saigon. He died of injuries sustained 18 Aug 45 in a plane crash at Taipei, Formosa, en route to Tokyo. (*Kogun,* 93, 135, 211n.)

BOTTOMLEY, Norman. British air marshal. 1891-1970. Originally an infantryman, he was senior air staff officer of Bomber Command (1938-40) before leading No 5 Gp (1940-41). He served as deputy chief of air staff (1943-45) before succeeding HARRIS as head of Bomber Command.

BOUHLER, Phillip. Nazi Chancellery chairman. 1899-1945. Described as "one of the shadowiest figures in the National Socialist elite" (Wistrich), he was born 2 Sep 99 in Munich, son of a retired colonel. He spent several years in the Royal Bavarian Cadet Corps and was still a teenager when seriously wounded in WWI. Bouhler was in publishing before becoming NSDAP business manager (Geschaeftsfuehrer) in 1925. In 1934 he became Hitler's chief of chancellery. Five years later the boyish and soft-spoken office manager took over programs for killing off the hopelessly ill and the insane. In response to public protest Hitler issued orders on 16 Aug 41 for Bouhler to stop the programs, but by then the Gruppenfuehrer had developed methods later used at death camps, notably carbon monoxide gas chambers. After BORMANN's party chancellery absorbed Hitler's private chancellery in 1944, Bouhler kept his official rank but had few duties. In the final days of the war he accompanied GOERING south. Bouhler and his wife took their own lives at Zell-am-See on10 May 45.

BOURKE-WHITE, Margaret. US photographer. 1904-71. First with *Fortune* magazine, then with *Life* from its beginning in 1936 until her retirement in 1969, she opened new frontiers in photojournalism. Known to close friends as Kit, and later as Maggie to others, she married Erskine Caldwell in 1939. That year she shot her way from blacked-out London to the oil fields of Romania and on to photograph British and French forces in the Near East. Her distinctive genre of industrial photography often required standing on cranes, freight cars, roofs, and rafters to get the desired perspective. "Bourke-White" is a combination of her mother's maiden name (Bourke) and paternal surname. The "library form" for indexing is "White, Margaret Bourke" (*CB 40*).

BOWHILL, Frederick William. British air chief marshal. 1880-1960. Son of an army officer, Bowhill was born 1 Sep 80 at Morar Gwalior, India. He spent 16 years in the Merchant Service before taking flight training as a lieutenant in the naval reserve in 1912. The next year he was certified as a pilot and appointed flying officer, RFC, Naval Wing. A spare, compact man with fierce eyebrows and hair that gave him the nickname "Ginger," he had many unique accomplishments in a long, colorful career. He was the first to fly an airplane from a ship and the first to make an air attack on an enemy fleet. Another distinction, one that says something special about the man's mettle: he was "the first high ranking officer to cut off a seaman's leg on board ship" (W. P. Hildred in *DNB*). Bowhill began his combat career as a flight lieutenant commanding CVE *Empress* in attacks on submarine bases. After staff duty in the Admiralty, Bowhill commanded a squadron in Mesopotamia, fought zeppelins off the English coast, and ended up as a wing commander in the Mediterranean. He was mentioned six times in dispatches and received a bar to his DSO. In 1919 he saw action as chief staff officer of an RAF detachment in Somaliland.

Promoted to air marshal in 1936 and knighted (KCB) the same year, Sir Frederick helped develop the system of air-ground control that was perfected in the Battle of Britain. He also advocated using barrage balloons to defend cities from low-level air attack and was involved in creating the Women's Auxiliary AF. The naval airman succeeded the RAF's Air Vice Marshal JOUBERT DE LA FERTE as head of Coastal Command in Aug 37. Highlights of this service were finding the *Altmark* (from which VIAN freed British POWs) and finding the *Bismarck* (*see* LUETJENS). But Coastal Command needed reinvigoration as the Battle of the Atlantic approached a climax, so Joubert de la Ferté, then an air marshal, was recalled from India to resume his former post in June 41.

Bowhill was ordered to Canada as head of the new Ferrying Command, an assignment that called for tact and diplomacy because the admiral had to take over work started by dedicated civilians. Sir Frederick not only succeeded but also became highly popular, as did Lady Bowhill. He stayed in Montreal until ordered home in 1943 to head the new Transport Command. Holding this post for the rest of the war, the veteran airman was four years past the normal age when he retired in 1945 as an air chief marshal. He served as chief aeronautical adviser to the Ministry of Civil Aviation (1946-57), and died 12 Mar 60 in London.

BOYINGTON, Gregory. USMC ace. 1912-88. "Pappy" Boyington scored six kills with the "Flying Tigers" in China before taking command of VMF-214 on 12 Sep 43 as a 31-year-old major. Known as the "Black Sheep" squadron his F4U "Corsair"–equipped outfit was based in the central Solomons and was a mixed bag of veterans and green replacements. The oldest member of this motley crew, Pappy was not only a remarkable pilot and marksman but also an outstanding leader and trainer. Scoring the last of his 28 kills in a sweep over Rabaul on 3 Jan 44, Pappy went down with his wingman, Capt G. M. Ashmun. After 20 months as a POW Boyington returned to duty and retired in 1947 as a colonel. He had been awarded the Medal of Honor and Navy Cross. Counting only his 22 kills in the Pacific (and excluding his six with the Flying Tigers), Boyington ranked third behind Maj Joseph J. Foss (26) and 1st Lt Robert M. Hanson (25) among USMC aces (Sims, *Aces*, 23n and 274).

BOYLE, William Henry Dudley. *See* CORK AND ORRERY.

BRACKEN, Brendan Rendall. British politician. 1901-58. The colorful Irishman was born 15 Feb 01 at Templemore, County Tipperary. Frustrated, his widowed mother, who had moved to Dublin, shipped him to Australia in 1916 after he ran away from the Jesuit College, Mungret, near Limerick. *(DNB.)* Bracken spent a short time on a sheep station but was fired for having more interest in books than the animals he was supposed to tend. Finally going to Sydney, he sought out the Christian Brothers, with whom he had long been associated. Young Bracken worked for the diocesan newspaper's advertising department before returning to Dublin in 1919 and finding that his mother had remarried and did not want him at home. With a small legacy Bracken went to England where, to conceal his politically incorrect background—it was the time of the **Black and Tans**—he pretended to be an orphan from Australia. The tall, fiery, red-haired Irishman soon made important connections that included Winston Churchill, who was making a bid to re-enter politics. Bracken and Churchill immediately hit it off as kindred spirits. After working in Churchill's unsuccessful election campaigns in 1923 and 1924, Bracken met Maj Crosthwaite Eyre of the Eyre & Spottiswoode publishing firm. The major was looking for new talent and Bracken was hired to help establish a periodical edited by Hilaire Belloc. By 1925 Bracken was a director of Eyre & Spottiswoode. From this fortuitous beginning Bracken became highly regarded as editor and publisher of *Financial News, The Banker,* and *The Economist.* He went on to control a highly regarded medical journal, *The Practitioner,* and a firm that printed Bibles. With the influence gained from these activities and the backing of Churchill, Bracken became a conservative MP from North Paddington in 1929.

Bracken supported his mentor faithfully in Parliament during the 1930s when Churchill was in political eclipse. When Churchill returned to the Admiralty on 3 Sep 39, Bracken went along as parliamentary private secretary. The Irishman retained the post when Churchill formed his wartime coalition government in May 40. A month later, Bracken was sworn to the Privy Council. (Douglas Woodruff in *DNB,* principal source of this sketch.)

Like HOPKINS with Roosevelt, Bracken was at his chief's elbow around the clock. Hopkins, whose second wife died in 1937, lived at the White House; Bracken, who never married, lived at No. 10 Downing Street or its annex.

Bracken soon moved from being a "horse holder" into the assignment for which he is best remembered, minister of information, on 21 July 41. Succeeding Alfred DUFF COOPER as the fourth to hold the post since the war started, and conspicuously successful, he retained the portfolio until the war's end. In Churchill's caretaker government, which lasted only a month in 1945, the faithful paladin was the first Lord of the Admiralty.

After the war Bracken resumed and expanded his highly successful business career. In 1952 he was elevated to the peerage as Viscount Bracken but never took his seat in the House of Lords. He refused to write or authorize a biography, and burned all his papers. Bracken died 8 Aug 58 of throat cancer in London.

BRADLEY, Omar Nelson. US general. 1893-1981. Born 12 Feb 93 on a small farm near Clark, Mo, he was named Omar Nelson for two prominent local men. Bradley's father was a country school teacher who married a 16-year-old pupil and died a month before the boy's 15th birthday. Omar's mother, left in genteel poverty and with a mortgage on the house, worked as a seamstress and took in boarders. The family background was remarkably like that of Dwight EISENHOWER, Bradley's close friend and West Point classmate.

Bradley graduated in 1915 (44/164), and like Eisenhower did not get overseas in WWI. His big break came in 1929 with assignment as an instructor at the Infantry School at Ft Benning, Ga, then directed by one Lt Col George C. Marshall. Bradley's name went into MARSHALL's famous "Black Book" as one marked for accelerated promotion. A decade later, as America mobilized, Marshall picked Lt Col Bradley to head the Infantry School. Arriving on 21 Feb 41, Bradley learned of his promotion on a special

list to brigadier general. For the next two years Bradley followed the career route picked by Marshall for officers of exceptional promise. After the attack on Pearl Harbor, 7 Dec 41, he was given command of the 82d Inf Div, one of three being activated, and promoted at that time to major general. Turning this unit over to RIDGWAY on 26 June 42, Bradley took on the task of shaping up the 28th Div, a Pennsylvania outfit "plagued with all the faults of most [National] Guard divisions" (Bradley, II, 108). In addition to being riddled with state-level politics and "hometownism," the division had been bled of manpower for OCS and cadres. After rising successfully to the challenge presented by the 28th Div, Bradley got a message from Marshall on 12 Feb 43 saying he would be moved up to command a corps. That same day, however, Eisenhower had picked Bradley from a list of officers Marshall had nominated for a special assignment to North Africa. (Ibid., 112.)

Ostensibly, Bradley was to be his classmate's "eyes and ears," recommending ways to improve training. But Eisenhower had to suspect that Marshall really wanted a special report on why American commanders and troops had failed so badly in what was supposed to be the Allied "race for Tunis." With two aides, Bradley reached Algiers on 24 Feb 43. "For the first time in 32 years as a soldier, I was off to war" (Bradley, I, 19). Sent to investigate FREDENDALL's responsibility for the Kasserine Pass fiasco, Bradley recommended on 7 Mar 43 that Fredendall be replaced as the 2d Corps commander. Patton arrived the next day to take over temporarily and was succeeded by Bradley on 15 Apr 43 for the Tunisian campaign, which ended on 13 May. Promoted 2 June 43, Lt Gen Bradley led the 2d Corps when it became part of PATTON's 7th Army for the conquest of Sicily. The campaign ended on 10 July 43 and Bradley was replaced as corps commander by John P. LUCAS a month later.

After only five months' experience as a corps commander, Bradley was jumped over PATTON and named to lead the 1st US Army in Montgomery's 21st AG for the cross-channel assault. Establishing headquarters at Bristol on 16 Oct 43, Bradley helped plan Opn Overlord and he formed the 12th AG Hq. The 1st Army began landing in Normandy on 6 June 44, and on 1 Aug 44 Bradley moved up to command the 12th AG for the rest of the war.

After promotion to four-star general (9/13) on 12 Mar 45, Bradley took over the Veterans Administration three months later. He succeeded Eisenhower as army CofS on 7 Feb 48 (*AA*, 53), then was the first permanent chairman of the JCS, sworn in on 16 Aug 49 and reappointed in 1951. Having been promoted on 22 Sep 50 to General of the Army, he was the last and youngest of WWII officers to hold that five-star rank (Bradley, II, 553). He retired from active duty on 13 Aug 53 and joined the Bulova Watch Co, becoming chairman of the board in 1958.

The first Mrs Bradley died on 1 Dec 65. Less than a year later, the 73-year-old general married 43-year-old Kitty Buhler. They had met in 1950, when as a screenwriter she interviewed him for a proposed movie. Bradley had published *A Soldier's Story* (1951), ghostwritten by his ADC, Chester B. Hansen. In 1971 the general started another autobiography but soon found the task too great for his limited literary talents. He suffered a head injury in 1975 that left him confined him to a wheelchair but mentally alert, and in 1979 Mrs Bradley brought Clay Blair to the rescue as a highly qualified collaborator.

Bradley died 8 Apr 81 in NYC of a brain clot suffered only minutes after he received an award. At the time Blair had the general's enthusiastic approval of the memoir up to the portion on WWII. Using Hanson's files and postwar historical works, Blair completed *A General's Life* (New York: Simon and Schuster, 1983).

BRANDENBERGER, Erich. German general. 1892-1955. Born in Augsburg on 15 July 92, he became an officer candidate on 1 July 11 and two years later was commissioned in the artillery. At the start of war in 1939 he was CofS, 23d Corps and had been a full colonel for three years. Promoted on 1 July 40, Generalmajor Brandenberger took over the 8th Pz Div on 20 Feb 41. For the invasion of Russia his division was in the 56th Panzer Corps of HOEPPNER's 4th Pz Gp in LEEB's AG North. Brandenberger spearheaded the drive through Soviet frontier defenses on 21 June 41 and the next day seized the critically important highway viaduct at Airogola (Manstein, *Lost Victories*, 176, 182). A Generalleutnant from 1 Aug 42, he commanded the 8th Panzers until 16 Jan 43, with three absences totaling about six months (*B&O*, 86). On 1 Aug 43 he was promoted to Gen of Pz Troops to head the 17th Army Corps and then

the 29th Army Corps. He was awarded the RK on 15 July 41 and the Oakleaves (324/890) on 12 Nov 43 for continued actions in Russia.

After Montgomery broke out of the Normandy beachhead and exploited northward across the lower Seine, Brandenberger replaced EBERBACH (captured) as 7th Army commander on 28 Aug 44. He took part in delaying actions to the Siegfried line and held positions in the Eifel. During the Ardennes counteroffensive he attacked on the south flank and held the shoulder of the penetration until hit by the counterattack of Patton's 3d Army. In Opn Lumberjack he was driven back on a broad front through the Eifel and across the Moselle River by Patton. Accused by Hitler of "defeatism" and relieved of command on about 5 Mar 45, Brandenberger took over the 19th Army in the Black Forest on 25 March. There he had to cope with the brilliant strategy of de LATTRE. After resolute delaying actions in the south of Germany the veteran German general surrendered forces in his sector to DEVERS at Innsbruck, Austria, on 5 May 45. Brandenberger was a bespectacled, jowly man of unheroic appearance, but he was one of the war's most outstanding field commanders. He died at Bonn in June 55.

BRANDI, Albrecht. U-boat commander. 1914-66. Inevitably nicknamed "Cherry," Brandi was born 20 June 14 and went to sea in 1935. His U-boat career spanned only a little more than two years starting in 1942. Commanding U-617 and then U-967, Brandi sank more than 115,000 tons while operating independently in the Atlantic. His victims included three cruisers and 12 destroyers. Kapitaenleutnant Brandi was awarded the RK on 21 Jan 43 and Oakleaves (224/890) on 11 Apr 43. Moving to U-967 and promoted, Korvettenkapitaen Brandi was awarded the Swords (66/159) on 9 May 44 for action in the North Sea and the Diamonds (22/27) on 24 Nov 44. The only earlier naval recipient of the Diamonds was Wolfgang LEUTH. The somber, unsmiling Cherry Brandi spent the last year of the war operating with small surface craft out of Holland. He died 6 Jan 66 in Cologne. (Angolia, I, 95-97.)

BRAUCHITSCH, Heinrich Alfred Walther von. German general. 1881-1948. A Junker born

4 Oct 81 in Berlin, von Brauchitsch entered the Corps of Pages. He grew into a tall, lean, powerful, handsome officer with solid professional qualifications. A man of considerable culture, he spoke several languages and was noted for his interest in economics and politics. (Brett-Smith, *Hitler's Elite*, 41; Curt Riess, *The Self-Betrayed*, 15.)

Brauchitsch began his military career in 1900 as a subaltern in the famous 3d Foot Guards but transferred the next year to the 3d Guards Field Artillery Regt. A major by 1918 he was in the **Truppenamt** from late 1922 and in 1925 took command of an artillery battalion. By 1928 he was a full colonel in the Truppenamt, first as director of training and then as a department head. Promoted to Generalmajor in 1930, he was Inspector of Artillery in 1932. In 1933 he was promoted to Generalleutnant and appointed chief of the Koenigsberg MD (Wehrkreis I) and commander of the 1st Div. From 5 June 33 he was CG 1st Army Corps at Koenigsberg.

Although a conservative of the Old Guard, the military aristocrat got along so well with the Nazis that the army high command, notably FRITSCH, thought—without real justification—that Brauschitsch was an enthusiastic National Socialist. But he clashed with Erich KOCH, Nazi president of East Prussia, and disputes between the army and SS became sufficiently alarming for Hitler himself to visit Koenigsberg to smooth things out. (Riess, 15.) This contretemps led conservative Catholics and old Social Democrats to keep contact with the general in hopes he might join in a coup d'état.

Again promoted, Gen of Arty Brauchitsch moved up in 1937 to head Gruppenkommando 4. An outstanding gunner, he is credited with developing the dual-purpose 88mm gun, probably the best artillery piece of WWII. (Brett-Smith, *Hitler's Generals*, 41.)

By 1938 Brauchitsch was considered to be just after FRITSCH, BECK, RUNDSTEDT, BOCK, and LEEB in qualifications for the top post when Hitler purged the army high command (Manstein, 75). When outgoing war minister BLOMBERG nominated REICHENAU to succeed him, and leaders of the army's Old Guard threatened to resign in protest, the Nazis found Brauchitsch heaven-sent. The elegant, aristocratic general needed money to settle a divorce and marry the "captivating though flighty Charlotte Rueffer" (Deutsch, I, 221), with whom he had been involved for some 12 years. She was an admirer of Hitler, who found her attractive (ibid.). Hitler and Goering accordingly worked out terms under which the army would accept Brauchitsch and they gave him 80,000 marks for his divorce. By this chicanery the Nazis had themselves another compliant general at the top when Brauchitsch succeeded FRITSCH on 4 Feb 38 as CinC of the army—Oberfehlshaber des Heeres (OKH)—and was promoted that day to Generaloberst.

Brauchitsch has been criticized for tamely accepting his appointment before his predecessor's case had been dealt with. He sat passively as Goering presided over the court of honor that unjustly dishonored FRITSCH and he did nothing to oppose HITLER's taking personal control of the Wehrmacht. The general was so intimidated by Hitler as to be close to physical pain when in the latter's presence (Deutsch, II, 34).

Although kept informed of the conspiracy by BECK and others to stop Hitler's rush to war, he refused to help. To his credit as a military professional, OKH opposed the **Dunkirk stop order** that saved Allied forces in the beachhead. After the fall of France, Brauchitsch was among 12 generals in the first large-scale creation of field marshals on 19 July 40.

While the war was going well and until Barbarossa stalled at the end of 1941, Hitler simply ignored the OKH chief or used him as an emotional punching bag. But as the fuehrer sought scapegoats, Brauschitsch's health collapsed. He acquired a bluish gray pallor, had difficulty breathing, spent much time in bed, and on 7 Dec 41 finally asked to be retired. Hitler ignored the request for 10 days, then told the broken general that in two days he would announce that he, Hitler, was personally taking command of the army. Brauchitsch left on 18 Dec 41 (*see* HALDER) and was retired the next day. Still suffering from heart disease and almost blind, he testified at Nuremberg but died 18 Oct 48 in a British military hospital at Hamburg-Barmbeck while awaiting trial.

BRAUN, Eva Anna Paula. Hitler's mistress. 1912-45. A simple, submissive young woman of limited intellect but some physical allure, Eva Braun was born 7 Feb 12 in Munich. She left a convent school in the summer of 1929, just barely acquiring a diploma and almost immediately becoming Heinrich HOFFMANN's laboratory assistant. That fall Hitler met her in the photographer's shop and was attracted. The fuehrer subsequently saw Fraulein Braun (pronounced "brown") when Hoffmann sent her to make weekly deliveries. In early 1932, when Hitler had recovered somewhat from his niece Geli Rabaul's suicide (18 Sep 31), Eva became his mistress. She reminded Hitler, even in her movements, of the niece with whom he had been infatuated but was quieter, less moody, and aspired to nothing more than being a mistress. Although the sexually strange Hitler had other women in his life, she was the only one to whom he consistently returned. (Payne, *Hitler,* 347). Eva was kept in the Munich Brown House before moving into the **Berghof** and living there in virtual seclusion. "She was the unhappiest woman in Germany," wrote chauffeur Erich Kempka. "She spent most of her life waiting for Hitler." (Hamilton, *Leaders,* 188.) Eva made at least two suicide attempts, both rather unconvincing. She came to be liked by most of those who knew her well and developed into a woman of considerable poise and charm. Her candid snapshots and home movies are of considerable historical value. Excluded from **Rastenburg**, Eva insisted on joining Hitler in the Berlin bunker on 15 Apr 45, where they were married on the 29th between 1 and 3 AM. Some 36 hours later they committed suicide, she by taking poison two minutes before HITLER shot himself. The bodies were carried upstairs to the chancellery garden, doused with gasoline, and set on fire. It has been said that Soviet troops found the charred cadavers but that Chuykov and Zhukov conspired to keep this a secret.It also is likely that incoming artillery scattered the remains. Eva's sister Gretl married Hermann FEGELEIN.

BRAUN, Wehrner (Magnus Maximillian) von. Rocket scientist. 1912-77. Von Braun's father, a Prussian baron, was minister of agriculture under President von Hindenburg and founder of the German Savings Bank. The son was born in Wirsitz, a city in the Polish corridor that became Wyrzysk, Poland. As an engineering student at Berlin's Charlottenburg Institute of Technology, von Braun (pronouced brown) became interested in spaceflight and worked with a rocket club. This attracted the attention of Walter DORNBERGER, who brought the young engineer into the army ordnance department on

1 Oct 32. Five years later von Braun, then 25, became a director of research near **Peenemuende** and developed the **V-2** rocket. HIMMLER saw the program's potential and, as part of his power play to take it over, had von Braun and two principal associates arrested on 14 Mar 44 and briefly imprisoned for being more interested in space travel than "victory weapons." As covered in more detail under DORNBERGER and **V-weapons**, the V-2 assault on London started 8 Sep 44; it lasted until the last launching sites were overrun seven months later on 27 Mar 45.

The Soviets were 100 miles from Peenemuende when Dornberger and von Braun left with their staff, records, and whatever else they could salvage. After hiding from the SS, and having his left arm broken in an automobile accident, the youthful, personable von Braun was nominated to make contact with approaching American troops and surrender the group. With more than 100 of his staff, 100 rockets, and their records, von Braun went to America, where he and 40 associates eventually were naturalized.

Their mission initially was to make the V-2 into a short-range nuclear missile, but the orders were changed abruptly when Russia shocked the world by putting Sputnik I into earth orbit on 31 Jan 58. Von Braun now directed modification of the Redstone rocket to meet President Kennedy's promise to land an American on the moon by 1970. That mission was accomplished in July 69 with a few months to spare. The rocket scientist, who had become director of the spaceflight center at Huntsville, Ala, then went to Washington to plan new space programs for NASA. When Nixon's administration slashed the space budget, von Braun resigned in 1972 to join Fairchild Industries. He died of cancer on 16 June 77, in Alexandria, Va, at the age of 65.

BREITH, Hermann. German general. 1892-1964. He was born 7 May 92 in Pirmasens. As a colonel commanding the 5th Pz Bde in France he won the RK on 3 June 40. Breith took over the 3d Pz Div from MODEL on 22 Oct 41, being promoted to Generalmajor and awarded the Oakleaves (69/890) the same day. On 30 Sep 42 he left his division, was promoted the next day to Generalleutnant, and on 3 Jan 43 took over the 3d Pz Corps. With several absences, Breith commanded this unit until the end, most of the time in south Russia. Several times his badly decimated forces had to be refitted.

Breith's promotion to Gen of Pz Troops was dated 1 Mar 43. He was awarded the Swords (48/159) on 21 Feb 44 (Angolia, I, 153). The following November his formation was renamed Pz Gp Breith and attached to the 3d Hungarian Army for three months as it was driven into the Alps. He fought the rest of the war with the 6th Army. Breith died 3 Sep 64. (Angolia, II, 153; B&O, 32.)

BRERETON, Lewis Hyde. US general. 1890-1967. Born 21 June 90, in Pittsburgh, Pa, he moved with his family to Annapolis, Md, at the age of 13. Although he found that the sea made him sick, figuratively *and* literally, Brereton entered the US Naval Academy after failing to get into West Point. When he graduated on 2 June 11 (56/193) the navy had too many ensigns and the army was short of second lieutenants, so the "passed midshipman" was among those permitted to resign from the navy and accept an army commission. The confirmed landlubber became a second lieutenant in the Coast Artillery Corps on 17 Aug 11.

Two years later he got his wings, and in Mar 18 assumed command of the 12th Aero Sqdn, one of the AEF's first air units. In a "brilliant and perilous reconnaissance mission" the young airman contributed materially to the success of the Aisne-Marne offensive (Arnold, *Global Mission,* 69).

Brereton became a leading proponent of strategic bombardment. A full colonel (T) in 1936, he was promoted three years later to brigadier general and given command of the 3d AF in Tampa, Fla. From there he went to the Philippines in Nov 41 to head the new US Far East AF, which was activated on 20 Sep 41. Maj Gen Brereton was receiving new aircraft with partially trained crews and trying to work out defensive plans with MacArthur's staff when the Japanese struck on 8 Dec 41 (local date). Although this was a few hours after the surprise attack on Pearl Harbor, most US aircraft were neatly aligned for defense against sabotage. Caught on the ground, 18 of 35 B-17s were destroyed along with 56 pursuit planes and 25 others. "Ever after, Brereton was in the center of the controversy over why the planes had not taken off to attack Formosa after the Philippines received news of the Japanese raid on Pearl Harbor, as Brereton claimed he had advocated" (Weigley, *ETO,* 65). MacArthur denied receiving such a recommendation, and this seems to

have been blocked by MacArthur's controversial CofS, SUTHERLAND. But authors of the USAF official history conclude that the central issue really is whether it would have been prudent to attack air bases on Formosa without proper reconnaissance (Craven and Cate, I, 204-5). Brereton delayed his own public explanation of the famous controversy for his memoirs (following), but this has not satisfied historians.

The last bomber left Luzon on 11 Dec 41 without any offensive attempt having been made. Brereton then headed the tactical air forces of **ABDACOM,** 17 Jan-24 Feb 42. Getting away from Java with only a few B-17s and transports, he flew to New Delhi, India. After briefly commanding the small 10th AF there, Brereton left with all available bombers on 26 June 42 for Egypt, where ROMMEL threatened the Suez Canal. In Cairo two days later the airman took over the newly created US Army Middle East AF Hq (USAMEAF). This was augmented by 24 B-17s that were being staged through Egypt for China. Brereton took command of the US Desert AF in October, and his pilots were integrated into RAF squadrons for experience. With a small staff at British advance headquarters he helped plan the 8th Army counteroffensive. American airmen were particularly hard pressed until MONTGOMERY won his victory at El Alamein on 4 Nov 42. Then USAMEAF then became the 9th AF, which Brereton commanded 12 Nov 42—2 Aug 44. He also headed its supporting US Army Forces in the Middle East (USAFIME) from 31 Jan to 10 Sep 43. (USAFIME was then disbanded.) The general took part in the latter phases of the North African campaign and the invasions of Sicily and Italy, also directing the costly Ploesti raid on 1 Aug 43.

Brereton took his 9th AF Hq to England as cadre for the US Army AF in the UK, activated on 15 Oct 43. Principal components were the 9th Bomber Cmd (Medium) under S. E. Anderson, the 9th Tac Cmd under QUESADA, and the 9th Troop Carrier Cmd under P. W. Williams. Brereton was promoted to lieutenant general on 28 Apr 44, and by D day (6 June 44) had 170,000 troops. Under LEIGH-MALLORY's operational control for the Normandy landings, Brereton carried "the heaviest burden of any single air organization" in Opn Overlord (Weigley, *ETO,* 66).

Although lacking airborne experience, he was given command of the 1st Allied Abn Army when it was activated on 8 Aug 44 to support MONTGOMERY's Opn Market-Garden. The "smallish, sad-faced" Brereton, characterized as "perpetually discontented and querulous" (Weigley, *ETO*, 65, 66), quickly clashed with his charismatic British deputy, "Boy" BROWNING. But a modus vivendi was reached in time for the two officers to plan history's largest airborne operation—Market-Garden. Brereton had correctly argued that he lacked the necessary resources—particularly airlift. Unfavorable weather, unexpectedly strong German resistance, and other bad luck made Montgomery's adventure a costly failure.

The 1st Abn Army was in strategic reserve thereafter, fighting the rest of the war in the ground role. RIDGWAY's component was committed to help salvage the Ardennes disaster in Dec 44. After V-E day Brereton commanded the 3d AF from 1 July 45 to 1 Mar 46, concurrently heading the 1st AF until 14 May 46.

Never attaining four-star rank, Lt Gen Brereton died 20 July 67 in Washington, DC. His memoirs are *The Brereton Diaries: The War in the Air in the Pacific, Middle East, and Europe, 3 October 1941-8 May 1945* (New York: Morrow, 1946).

BRETT, George Howard. US general. 1886-1963. The future chief of the Army Air Corps was born 7 Feb 86 in Cleveland, Ohio. He graduated from VMI in 1909 with a degree in engineering. The next year he became a second lieutenant in the Philippine Scouts and in 1911 received an RA commission in the cavalry. Brett was a 30-year-old second lieutenant when he got his wings as a pursuit pilot in 1916 and was promoted.

An officer of pleasant good looks, well built, and somewhat above average height, 1st Lt Brett was assigned to the office of the chief signal officer until Oct 17. Promoted to captain, he went to France and was in charge of purchasing and distributing all aviation materiel for the AEF's infant air service *(CB 42)*. After a TDY tour in Washington he returned to logistical duties in France and England, never seeing combat.

Between the wars he continued to excel as a logistician. By 1938 he was a brigadier general. On 1 Oct 40 he was appointed acting chief of the Army Air Corps, receiving a second star on or about that date. In May 41 he officially became

chief in a post that normally was a four-year assignment. The US meanwhile had been furnishing military aircraft to the British, and Brett made a four-month trip to study maintenance problems at RAF bases from England to Singapore. He also visited Moscow with Averell HARRIMAN. *(CB 42.)*

Soon after America entered the war, Brett flew to Chungking for a meeting on 22 Dec 41 with CHIANG KAI-SHEK on the use of heavy bombers in China. Brett then took command of "US Forces in Australia"; this future Allied supply base was redesignated US Army Forces in Australia (USAFIA) on 5 Jan 42. Promoted two days later, Lt Gen Brett joined ABDACOM in Java, returning to Australia on 23 Feb 42. As an additional duty he headed the new 5th AF, 23 Feb-4 Aug 42. (AA, 305, 594, 910, 915, 305; OCMH Chron, 6, 10, 12.)

Remaining head of USAFIA, on 21 Mar 42 Lt Gen Brett was named commander of the combined air forces in Australia and from 18 April served as deputy supreme commander and head of all MacArthur's air forces in the SWPA. But he lasted less than three months under MacArthur, who had long been dissatisfied with his air corps generals. Replaced by George KENNEY on 13 July, Brett remained in Australia as CG 5th AF to 4 Aug 42. When Frank ANDREWS was killed, Brett took over the Caribbean Defense Command in Nov 42 and held that post until the war ended.

BREZHNEV, Leonid I. Soviet official. 1906-82. Best known as KHRUSHCHEV's successor in 1964, Brezhnev held the military rank of general major in WWII. During the war he was, in turn, political administrator in the Southern Front, in the 18th Army, and chief political administrator in the 4th Ukrainian Front (1944). Brezhnev was made a Marshal of the Soviet Union in May 76 and the next year was chairman of the Presidium of the Supreme Soviet (or parliament). He died 10 Nov 82 of a heart attack and was succeeded by Yuri V. Andropov.

BROADHURST, Harry. British airman. 1905–. The youngest air vice marshal in British history, he suffered his most serious crash only 11 days after transferring into the RAF from the Royal Artillery *(CB 43)*. The daredevil pilot took part in the Dunkirk evacuation and the Battle of

Britain. Flying a Spitfire as an observer of the Dieppe raid, Gp Capt Broadhurst took a "few odd moments" to shoot down one German plane and badly damage three others. In Oct 42 he became senior air staff officer to the air commander in the western desert. In Europe, Air Vice Marshal Broadhurst led 83 Gp of the Allied Expeditionary AF. After the war he held high command positions in the RAF and NATO.

BROOKE, Alan Francis. British general. 1883-1963. Chief of the Imperial General Staff from the end of 1941, head of the British army, and chairman of the chiefs of staff committee, Brooke was Churchill's closest and most valuable military adviser throughout the war.

He was born in the south of France near Pau on 23 July 83. His father, Sir Victor Brooke of Colebrooke, had moved there from the ancestral home in the Protestant county of Fermanagh, Ulster. "Twenty-six Brookes of Colebrooke served in the war of 1914-18; twenty-seven in that of 1939-45," writes D. W. Fraser in *DNB*. Alan Brooke's elder brothers Victor and Ronnie are referred to by Churchill as "gallant . . . friends of my earlier military life" (WC, II, 265 & n). Reared in the large British colony around Pau, which to the horror of natives imported foxes to hunt, Brooke became an avid sportsman and outsdoorsman. (His war diaries include episodes of enthralled birdwatching during breaks in the Casablanca conference.) Brooke learned French and German before English *(DNB)*.

Commissioned from Woolwich in 1902 as an artillerist, he served in Ireland and India before going to France in 1914 as a lieutenant. Continually on the western front, Brooke distinguished himself as an original thinker and innovator of artillery tactics. He was mentioned six times in dispatches, breveted lieutenant colonel, appointed to the DSO, and became chief artillery officer of the 1st British Army. During eight years at Camberley and the Imperial Defense College, a full colonel from Jan 23, Brooke perfected a gift for brilliant oral presentations. He also got to know most of the officers he would be associated with in the war. A broad range of later assignments included command of Britain's first mobile division in 1937 and the new Territorial Anti-Aircraft Corps created in June 38. At this time he was promoted to lieu-

tenant general. In Aug 39 Brooke became head of Southern Command and designated commander of the 2d Corps on mobilization.

When Hitler's war broke out on 1 Sep 39 Brooke was 56 years old, three years from mandatory retirement age and without prospect of attaining the army's highest post, CIGS. He led the 2d Corps of Lord GORT's BEF to France on 28 Sep 39. After having a major role coordinating the retreat, Brooke was ordered home by Gort on 29 May 40 *(DNB)* and reached England the next day.

Knighted 11 June 40, Sir Alan (KCB) returned to France the next day to command the four British divisions still there. On several occasions he argued Churchill out of orders that would have been disastrous (Bryant, I, 135-37), then he got authority to start reembarking. "As a result of this timely decision," writes E. L. SPEARS, "136,000 British troops, 310 guns and 20,000 Polish troops were saved" (Spears, II, 256n).

Back in England on 19 June 40, Brooke resumed his post in Southern Command, where an invasion was expected. Exactly a month later he was ordered to succeed IRONSIDE as commander of Home Forces. After 17 strenuous months, Brooke learned that Churchill had picked him to succeed DILL as CIGS. This surprised Brooke because he had forcefully opposed the PM on several military matters, most recently the unrealistic scheme of sending an expediton to Trondheim, Norway. Brooke assumed his new post on 25 Dec 41, when DILL's departure was official. The new CIGS was notified 5 Mar 42 that he would succeed the ailing Sir Dudley POUND chairman of the chiefs of staff committee.

Despite strong objections from American planners, who favored a direct assault on the Continent at the earliest possible moment, Brooke had some success in advocating his Mediterranean strategy. This was "founded like Wellington's and MacArthur's on sea power [and it] . . . brought to bear on the Axis in Europe a steady and continuously growing pressure . . . that, more effectively than any premature bid to break Hitler's Western Wall, took pressure off Russia and led to Italy's collapse and Germany's growing debility" (Bryant, I, 17-18). Allied offensives in North Africa, Sicily, Italy, and threats of an offensive through the Balkans ultimately forced the Germans to disperse a third of their strength to the Mediterranean. The Germans also lost the advantage of interior lines they used in 1914-18 to shift large forces rapidly between the eastern and western fronts.

Churchill urged Brooke to take the Middle East Command when it was reorganized in the fall of 1942 to stop ROMMEL. "One of the most difficult days of my life," the general wrote in his diary on 6 Aug 42. "I had been offered the finest Command I could ever hope for and I had turned it down," he elaborated later. ALEXANDER was ideal for the post, Brooke believed (quite correctly), but the CIGS was influenced primarily by the feeling that "it would take at least six months for any successor, taking over from me, to become as familiar with [Churchill] . . . and his ways. During these six months anything might happen. . . . Winston never realized what this decision cost me. . . ." (Bryant, I, 360-63.)

A year later, however, the situation was different. On three separate occasions Churchill had promised Brooke command of the Allied forces being mustered for the cross-channel attack, Opn Overlord. But on 14 Aug 43, during the Quebec Conference, the Prime Minister casually informed Brooke that he had yielded to heavy pressure from Roosevelt to let an American take the job. (In return, MOUNTBATTEN was accepted by the US for the **SEAC** post.)

Dark, immaculately groomed, super efficient, and very, very British, Brooke was disliked by most Americans—and vice versa. A notable exception was MacArthur; their adulation was mutual (*Reminiscences,* 289-90; Bryant, I, 534n, 560). Stalin also came to admire the straight talking, no nonsense British officer's candor (WC, V, 385-87.)

Brooke was little known outside official circles until Sir Arthur Bryant published a monumental, two-volume biography a few years before the general's death (Garden City, NY: Doubleday, 1957 and 1959). This work supports the contention that Brooke may have been the war's greatest soldier.

A field marshal from Jan 44, he was created Baron Alanbrooke, of Brookeborough, in Sep 45 and the 1st Viscount Alanbrooke in Jan 45 *(DNB).* He got more official honors than any other British soldier since Frederick Roberts (1832-1914). After turning over his office to Montgomery and leaving active duty, Alanbrooke was director of the Midland Bank and

many other companies. He died at home in Hampshire on 17 June 63.

BROOKE, Charles Vyner. Rajah of Sarawak. 1874-1963. Last of the "Three White Rajahs," grandnephew of the first, he was forced out of Sarawak after the Japanese began their conquest on 17 Dec 41. Anthony W. D. Brooke, nephew and heir apparent, headed the provisional government and ceded the 48,500-square-mile territory to the British in 1946 as a crown colony.

BROOKE-POPHAM, Henry Robert Moore. British officer. 1878-1953. A pioneer in military aviation, and somewhat over age for active duty, Brooke-Popham's most conspicuous role in WWII was as CinC Far East, 1940-41. He was born 18 Sep 78 at Mendlesham in Suffolk, son of a country gentleman. Graduating from Sandhurst in 1898, he joined the Oxfordshire Light Infantry. In 1904 he assumed the additional surname of Popham, an ancestor he admired; friends thereafter called him "Brookham." He was certified as a pilot in 1911. The next year he joined the Air Bn of the Royal Engrs shortly before the battalion became the RFC.

In 1914 Brookham was a staff officer at BEF Hq in France with responsibility for logistical support of air squadrons. Seeing that the full potential of the infantry arm was not yet appreciated, he formed and directed an air wing in the battle of Neuve-Chapelle in 1915. For this he was appointed to the DSO. Having risen to be deputy adjutant and QMG, BEF, in Mar 16, with the brevet rank of brigadier, he saw the RFC through its earliest struggles. *(DNB.)* In Apr 18 Brooke-Popham was assigned to the new air ministry in London. Between the wars he was director of research in the Air Ministry from 1919 and was commandant of the RAF Staff College at Cranwell, 1921-26. Knighted (KCB) in 1927, and holding increasingly high posts, Sir Robert was the first RAF officer to head the Imperial Defense College (1931-33). He then served two years as CinC of Air Defense of Great Britain. In 1935 he was promoted to air chief marshal and made IG. During the Abyssinian crisis, when the Italian air force was a threat to Egypt, Brooke-Popham was sent to Cairo as GOC Middle Eastern AF. Returning to London, and retiring, he went to Kenya as Governor and CinC (1937-39).

Brooke-Popham returned to active duty after Britain declared war on 3 Sep 39 and visited Canada and South Africa to lay the foundations of the Commonwealth Air Training Scheme for aircrew *(DNB)*. He then directed a program for developing RAF tactical doctrine. In Oct 40 Air Chief Marshal Brooke-Popham became CinC Far East with headquarters at Singapore. His directive was "to consult and cooperate with the Navy in Far Eastern waters" and to maintain contact with CinC India (AUCHINLECK) and the governments of Australia and New Zealand. He also was responsible for operations in Burma. Although somewhat long in the tooth and inclined to nod off during conferences, the airman was lean, hard, and methodical. He fought vigorously for resources he considered necessary, but priority went to WAVELL in the Middle East. Crippling command problems in the Far East were exacerbated by Duff COOPER, who reached Singapore with Cabinet status and developed a dislike for Brooke-Popham. (Barker, *Singapore,* 51.)

Like PERCIVAL and other local commanders, Brooke-Popham considered it essential to make a forward deployment in Siam (now Thailand). But authority was denied on political grounds (Siam was a neutral country) until it was too late. The Japanese, with no moral compunctions, began landing in Siam on 8 Dec 41. A few days later, WAVELL established ABDACOM Hq in Java, making previous command arrangements in the Far East even more irrelevant. Duff Cooper had intrigued for months to have Brooke-Popham recalled (Barber, 66-67), but authorities in London procrastinated. On 27 Dec 41 the veteran airman was replaced by Lt Gen Henry R. Pownall. Unjustly criticized for his performance, he went back on the retired list in May 42 and thereafter held insignificant posts— president of the **NAAFI** and IG of the Air Training Corps. He retired again in 1945 and died 20 Oct 53 in Halton Hospital. The perceptive sketch in *DNB* is by Sir Peter Wykeham.

BROWN, Wilson, Jr. US admiral. 1882-1957. He was born in Philadelphia on 27 Apr 82 and graduated in the USNA Class of 1902 (44/59). In WWI he served in London on the staff of Adm William S. Sims and commanded DD *Parker*. He completed the Naval War College (NWC) in 1921 before being XO BB *Colorado;* naval aide to Presidents Coolidge and Hoover;

CO New London Submarine Base; CO BB *California*, CofS NWC, Commander, Training Sqdn, Scouting Force (the nucleus of the Atlantic Fleet); and superintendent of the USNA. After three years at Annapolis he became commander, Scouting Force, on 1 Feb 41 with the rank of vice admiral. (Morison, III, 211n.)

When the Japanese attacked Pearl Harbor on 7 Dec 41 he was aboard CA *Indianapolis* leading a task force that had just completed a simulated bombardment and landing exercise on Johnston Island, 700 miles SW of Oahu. Recalled to Pearl Harbor, the admiral moved his flag aboard CV *Lexington* as commander of TF 11, one of three formed in the abortive effort to reinforce the defenses of **Wake Island**. Vice Adm Brown then sailed south to help cover the approaches to New Zealand and Australia. As part of Anzac Force, Wilson was south of Papua with the CVs *Lexington* and *Yorktown* when the Japanese landed unopposed at Lae and Salamaua. To hit their amphibious fleet while it was still vulnerable, Wilson launched 104 planes across the 15,000-foot Owen Stanley Mountains on 10 Mar 42 for a "well planned and neatly executed" strike (Morison, III, 388). Little damage was done to Japanese ships because, although surprised, they were able to maneuver. But the raid was a morale builder, and only one pilot and plane were lost. (Ibid.)

Taking a voluntary reduction in rank to rear admiral, Wilson left "Lady Lex" on 3 Apr 42 to be naval aide on Roosevelt's personal staff. He retired 1 Dec 44 as a vice admiral but remained naval aide in the White House until after FDR's death to serve Truman, his fourth president. Brown died 2 Jan 57 at the New Haven USNH, Conn.

BROWNING, Frederick Arthur Montague. British general. 1896-1965. The foremost British airborne operations theorist and father of the Red Berets, Browning was born 20 Dec 86 in London. He went to Eton in 1910 and entered Sandhurst in 1914. Commissioned in the Grenadier Guards, he reached France on 19 Oct 15 to join its 2d Bn. Just short of his 19th birthday and looking even younger, he acquired the nickname "Boy" and kept it for life. Browning served in his battalion of the elite Grenadiers throughout the war except for leaves and courses. He became a specialist in trench raids, was appointed to the DSO for valor, and commanded a company before coming of age. *(DNB.)*

Between the wars the tall, handsome, and impeccably turned-out Guardsman spent four years as adjutant at Sandhurst (1924-28) and from 1935 commanded his Grenadier battalion, mainly on ceremonial duties. He also won three national championships in the high hurdles, running that event with the British Olympic team, and was a bobsledder, sailor, and airplane pilot. From 1939 he held a series of brigadier's postings in the UK.

In late 1940 Browning was selected to head an experimental airborne formation and was promoted when this became the 1st Abn Div. Maj Gen Browning organized the Airborne Command in Oct 41. It eventually had 17 brigades, one of which adopted the red beret and the name "Red Devils." Browning's elite airborne units were used first for raids, then for battalion-size drops in Eisenhower's "race for Tunis" in Nov 42.

Browning himself joined Eisenhower's staff in Algiers five months later to plan the airborne assault on Sicily, the first large Allied airborne operation and the first at night for any army. Inadequately trained pilots were thrown off course by high winds, scattering their drops over a wide area and many were shot down by "friendly fire" from convoys. Only about 12 British gliders—some 100 men—landed on or near their objectives. US parachutists under Col James GAVIN fared little better. But the scattered survivors "helped greatly to demoralize the defense of Sicily." (Morison, IX, 95; see also Craven and Cate, II, 447.)

Browning's force was expanded into an airborne corps for the Normandy invasion, and he was promoted to lieutenant general in Jan 44. The 1st Abn Div was held in reserve and never committed, but the 6th Abn Div under Maj Gen Richard Gale secured the left flank of the British beachhead. Browning also directed the Special Air Service (SAS) of about 2,000 British, French, and Belgians who achieved notable success in Brittany and in sabotaging rail lines leading to battle areas.

The 1st Allied Abn Army Hq was established 2 Aug 44 under USAAF Lt Gen Lewis H. BRERETON with Browning as his deputy and commander of the 1st British Abn Corps. After Brereton, who lacked airborne experience, came

up with one idea after another for airborne operations without allowing time for adequate planning, Browning finally threatened to resign. But their differences were resolved and the waspish British airborne authority had a major role in Opn **Market-Garden.** To control the three divisions of his airborne corps, Browning and his command group landed with Gavin's US 82d Abn Div near Nijmegen. At the final planning conference on 10 Sep 44 Browning had said to Montgomery "I think we might be going a bridge too far" (Ryan, *Bridge,* 9). This proved to be a sad epitaph for history's largest airborne operation.

Shortly thereafter Browning went to the **SEAC** as MOUNTBATTEN's CofS. Despite lack of staff experience the grim guardsman proved to be highly effective in dealing with the army, air, and naval forces of many nationalities that comprised SEAC. When the Japanese supreme commander, Hisaichi TERAUCHI, pleaded sickness Browning represented Mountbatten at the surrender formalities in Rangoon and Singapore (28 Aug and 12 Sep 45). Terauchi himself handed his swords to Mountbatten in Saigon on 30 Nov 45.

Browning returned to London to become military secretary to the war minister in late 1946. He resigned in Jan 48 and became comptroller and treasurer to the royal family. Highly successful as a courtier but beginning to suffer from bad health, he resigned in 1959 to live in Cornwall. Browning married novelist Daphne du Maurier in 1932, and one of their daughters married Montgomery's only son, David Bernard. Boy Browning died 14 Mar 65 of heart disease.

BROZ, Josip. *See* TITO.

BRUCE LOCKHART, Robert Hamilton. British diplomat and writer. 1887-1970. A Scot born 2 Sep 87 at Anstruther, County Fife, he showed early promise as a scholar. But, as recorded in *My Scottish Youth* (1937), he wasted five years "in the worship of athleticism" before being sent to study in Berlin and Paris. His eyes opened to the charms of foreign countries, Lockhart (as he is listed in *DNB*) developed a talent for their languages and literature. After three years as a rubber planter in Malaya, where his family had interests, he was invalided home in 1910 with acute malaria. The ruggedly handsome, outgoing Scot was first in examinations for the consular service and was sent to Mocow in Jan 12. Acting consul-general on the eve of the Bolshevik revolution, the fledgling diplomat was quietly recalled for improper involvement with a woman *(DNB)*. But he returned to Moscow in Jan 18 as head of a special British mission to establish unofficial relations with the new Soviet leadership. The envoy had a letter of introduction to Trotsky from Litvinov but was arrested in Sep 18 on charges of being a secret agent and imprisoned in the Kremlin. A month later he was exchanged for LITVINOV. Ill health kept Lockhart in England until Nov 19, when he became commercial secretary in Prague. He grew to love Czechoslovakia and developed a lasting friendship with Eduard BENES and Jan MASARYK. In 1922 the diplomat left government service for international banking. In 1928 he joined the London *Evening Standard* to begin a successful career as a journalist and author. The first of his many highly acclaimed books was *Memoirs of a British Agent* (1932).

Lockhart returned to the foreign service in Sep 39, when Britain declared war. In 1940 he became British representative to the Czech government in exile. The next year he was undersecretary of state in the foreign office, heading the political warfare executive. In 1951 he published Jan Masaryck's memoirs. Lockhart died 27 Feb 70 at Hove, East Sussex.

BRUENING, Heinrich. Chancellor of Weimar Republic. 1885-1970. The son of an industrialist, Bruening was born 26 Nov 85 in Muenster. He studied law, philology, and economics before serving as a machine-gun company commander on the western front and winning the Iron Cross. Entering the Reichstag in 1924, he became chancellor of the Weimar Republic on 29 Mar 30. Bruening was a financial expert whose programs showed promise of reviving the economy while preserving democracy. But even decent Germans disliked his austerity policies and proposals to establish a constitutional monarchy; the military elite resented his threatening to break up large Junker estates; and he was no match for the National Socialists. HINDENBURG replaced Bruening as chancellor on 30 May 32, first putting in von PAPEN and then HITLER. A bachelor and devoutly religious, Bruening retired to a Catholic institution. After the **Blood Purge** of June 34, undoubtedly a marked man, he took

refuge in the US. (WHEELER-BENNETT, a close friend who also was on the Nazi hit list, took considerable personal risk in helping Bruening escape.) After teaching public administration at Harvard, 1937-50, he retired to write his memoirs. Dr Bruening refused interviews on political or public events. He visited Germany in 1948 and 1951, died 30 Mar 70 at his home in Norwich, Vt, and is buried at Muenster.

BUCH, Walter. Head of Nazi Party tribunal. 1883-1949. The son of a famous judge, Buch was born in Bruschal, Baden, on 24 Oct 83 (Wistrich). He became a regular army officer but retired in 1918 as a major. Joining the Nazi Party in 1922, the sadistic, virulently anti-Semitic Buch became head of the Brownshirt (SA) commando in Nuremberg the next year. By 1926 Hitler wanted a way to purge the party of undesirables, but the first man in charge, former Generalleutnant Bruno Heinemann, did not understand what Hitler really wanted. The ex-general thought his new Committee for Investigation and Settlement (*Untersuchung und Schlichtungs Ausschuss* or USCHLA) was supposed to fight corruption and immorality within the party. (Fest, *Hitler,* 253.) So Hitler brought in the more subservient Maj Buch to head what became "the **Cheka** in the Brown House." Buch's assistants, or associate magistrates, were a young lawyer, Hans FRANK, and Ulrich Graf, a former butcher's apprentice and Hitler bodyguard (ibid.). A few months after assisting Hitler with the arrest of Ernst ROEHM and directing executions of major SA leaders in Munich's Stadelheim Prison during the **Blood Purge** of 1934, Buch was named Supreme Party Judge on 9 Nov 34. He presided over the secret investigation of the **Crystal Night** pogrom of 1938, ruling that the rank and file were following orders and had committed no crimes.

Four months after receiving a five-year sentence at forced labor and being classified by a denazification court, Buch committed suicide on 12 Nov 49 on Ammer Lake. According to Bavarian Police, he slashed his wrists and drowned.

BUCKNER, Simon Bolivar, Jr. US general. 1886-1945. Son of Confederate Maj Gen Buckner (1823-1914), who accepted U. S. Grant's "unconditional surrender" terms at Ft Donelson, Ky, 16 Feb 62, he had the unfortunate distinction of being the highest ranking American field commander killed in action during the war. Buckner was born 16 July 86 near Munfordville, Ky, and graduated from VMI before being appointed to West Point by Theodore Roosevelt. He was in the Class of 1908 (58/108), commissioned in the infantry, and became a pilot in 1917. A year later he left the Air Service without seeing action but as a believer in airpower. After being in the West Point tactical department 1919-23, he was a long-remembered commandant of cadets 1933-36. Col Buckner made a fetish of physical fitness and manliness and was known for barbed aphorisms. "If you're going to be man," he used to say on confiscating such toiletries as after-shave lotions from cadet wall lockers, "you've got to *smell* like a man." (Personal information.)

In June 40 Buckner was promoted to brigadier general and sent to Alaska. His force was designated the Alaska Defense Command in Feb 41 and the Alaskan Department in Nov 43. After 15 months of vigorously directing operations under extremely harsh conditions he was promoted on 4 May 43 and sent the next month to organize 10th Army Hq in Hawaii. Lt Gen Buckner commanded the main Okinawa landings 1 Apr 45 and on 18 June was mortally wounded by artillery fire while observing an attack by the 8th Marine Regt. He was posthumously promoted to four-star rank in 1954 (Cullum).

BUDENNY, Semen (Semyon) Mikhaylovich. Soviet military leader. 1883-1973. The future marshal, like VOROSHILOV, owed his career mostly to being "a sly and durable toady of Stalin's" (Clark, *Barbarossa,* 54). Tall, handsome, hard-drinking, and jovial, he was described to Rundstedt in 1941 by a captured subordinate as a man with "a very large moustache, but a very small brain." (As quoted in Liddell Hart, *Talk,* 222.)

Budenny was born a peasant at Kozyurin in the Rostov/Don region on 25 Apr 83. After becoming a cavalry private in 1903 and fighting in the Russo-Japanese War of 1904-5, he was an NCO of Maritime Dragoons 1908-14 and a sergeant in the First World War. In the civil war he formed the 1st Cav Corps and served in the defense of Tsaritsyn (renamed Stalingrad), becoming a principal member of Stalin's inner circle. With Stalin and YEGOROV he organized the 1st Red Cav Army, establish-

ing the legend that he created the Red Cavalry. But in the war against Poland in 1920 he showed "singular clumsiness in his handling of even divisional-size units" (Clark, *Barbarossa,* 154). Although lacking experience commanding large formations, he was one of the first five Marshals of the Soviet Union created in 1935. He and Voroshilov were the only ones to survive the Great Purges that began the next year.

In 1937 Budenny took command of the Moscow MD. He was nominal commander of the High Command Reserve in the early phases of Barbarossa and on 10 July 41 became one of three **Glavkoms**. With headquarters at Kiev he headed the Southwest **Direction**, which included all of Russia south of the Pripet Marshes and half of the entire Red Army. Kleist's 1st Pz Gp of Rundstedt's AG South threatened a strategic penetration between Kiev and Uman, critical communications centers, before the Soviets had sufficient armored strength at either place to threaten his flanks. But Budenny made the mistake of rushing reserves to Kiev and Uman even as Kleist wheeled south to penetrate between Berdichev and Kazatin on the night of 15-16 July. Resolutely pursuing faulty strategy and failing to see the need to withdraw rapidly from Uman, Budenny launched a poorly conceived counterattack on 20 July that failed within hours. As German infantry armies annihilated units trapped around Uman, and Kleist's panzers raced east, Budenny concentrated his other forces around Kiev. On 13 Sep 41 Stalin finally replaced his crony with another one, TIMOSHENKO. Evacuated from Kiev by air, Budenny never had another active field command. But the blundering Soviet field marshal, who had been successively deputy and first deputy commissar of defense, was on the Main Military Council and the Stavka from 24 July 41.

He directed the reconstituted Reserve Front until 10 Oct 41, when it was united with the Western Front. From 21 Apr 42 he led the North Caucasus Direction, then the North Caucasus Front from 20 May 42 until the following September. In 1943 he began ten years as CinC of Cavalry, then had honorific titles and appeared occasionally in official public ceremonies. A three-time Hero of the Soviet Union (1958, 1963, 1968), he died 26 Oct 73 and was buried in the Kremlin Wall.

BULGANIN, Nikolay Aleksandrovich. Soviet official. 1895-1975. Son of a clerk, he was born 11 June 95 in what is now Gorky. Bulganin joined the CP in 1917, served in the Cheka (1918-22) and Supreme Economic Council, and was director of the Moscow Electrical Plant (1927) before being Chairman of the Moscow City Council 1931-37. This appointment made him de facto mayor of Moscow, and he concurrently held other important political posts.

At the start of Barbarossa on 22 June 41 Bulganin became one of four supercommissars in the newly created Stavka. Joining the Red Army at this time, Gen Lt Bulganin appeared on 16 July 41 as commissar of Timoshenko's Western Front and then of his Western Direction. After the emergency meeting on 19 Oct 41 to organize the defenses of Moscow, Bulganin became the military member of Zhukov's staff.

As a supercharged party official who lacked military training but had a direct line to Moscow, Bulganin was a serious annoyance to Zhukov. Soon transferred to be commissar of the Northwestern Front, he intruded himself as a separate link in the chain of command between the front headquarters and the Stavka (Erickson, *To Stalingrad*, 321). He returned as commissar of the Western Front when Sokolovsky commanded it during the battle of Kursk in July 43. Bulganin then held the same post in M. M. Popov's 2d Baltic Front (Dec 43-Apr 44), 2d Belorussian Front, and finally in the 1st Belorussian Front (May-Nov 44). Then he became deputy commissar of defense, a member of the GKO, and Stalin's representative on the Polish Committee of Liberation ("Lublin Poles").

In 1944 he was promoted to full general and made a member of the war cabinet. The next year he became a General of the Army. In 1947, only 52 years old, he was made a Marshal of the Soviet Union and Stalin's successor as minister of the armed forces. Effective head of the Soviet armed forces, Bulganin held the post until 1949, being made a full member of the Politburo in 1948.

As one of the surviving intriguers after Stalin's death in 1953 he again headed the armed forces, now as minister of defense. The white-haired, goateed Bulganin became Khrushchev's alter ego, making well-publicized trips abroad as part of "the B & K show." Bulganin was chairman of the council of ministers, or prime minister, 1955-58, replacing MALENKOV. But Khrushchev personally took over as PM in Mar 58, when Bulganin was removed from the Politburo, reduced to general colonel, and exiled as chairman of the Stavropol economic council. Having shown a talent for being tolerable within a power elite intriguing for power, Bulganin was retired in 1960 on a comfortable pension. He died 24 Feb 75 in Moscow.

BULLITT, William Christian. US diplomat. 1891-1967. Although he had no significant role in public life after 1940, Bullitt was prominent up to that time as the first US ambassador to the USSR (1933-36) and the last US ambassador to the French 3d Republic (1936-40).

Bullitt started as a writer in Roosevelt's campaign headquarters and was FDR's obvious choice as ambassador to Moscow after the US announced recognition of the USSR on 18 Nov 33. Although "a fine ambassador" in the expert opinion of a close associate (KENNAN, *Memoirs 1925-1950*, 79), Bullitt resigned in the summer of 1936. He was frustrated by Stalin's refusal to honor quid pro quo promises and by Roosevelt's unwillingness to counter with a hard line. Bullitt presented his credentials as ambassador to Paris on 13 Oct 36. Although ideally qualified for the post at a critical time, he could do little more than send perceptive reports on Hitler's march to war. After the Germans swept over France in May-June 40, Bullitt remained briefly in Paris with a small staff during the first fortnight of the German occupation (14-30 June 40). He caught up with the PETAIN government at Clermont-Ferrand as it moved to Vichy, not presenting his credentials but sending Washington valuable daily reports from nearby La Bourboule. Having been told he would be succeeded in France by Anthony BIDDELL and appointed secretary of the navy (Langer, *Vichy*, 21-22), the ambassador left Robert MURPHY as charge d'affairs and on 11 July 40 went with a small staff via Barcelona and Madrid to Lisbon. The party flew into New York on 20 July 40.

Bullitt quickly sensed that his close relations with FDR had been undermined (O. H. Bullitt, ed, xi-xii). The secretary of the navy post went to Frank KNOX, and Bullitt was a special ambassador while hoping for an important assignment. The final break with the president resulted from a long vendetta between the ambassador and Sumner WELLES. Bullitt had tried to convince the president in a talk on 23 Apr 41, that the homosexual Welles should be removed from the State Department as a threat to national security and to the administration (ibid., 512). The president declined to act then but by early 1942 was convinced that Bullitt was spreading malicious gossip about his archenemy Welles and had leaked official reports. Bullitt vehemently denied this (ibid., 513-15) but was told by FDR that he was persona non grata (Burns, *Roosevelt,* 350). Deprived of his long personal association with the president, and finding that his recommendations as special ambassador were falling on deaf ears (O. H. Bullitt, ed, xii), Bullitt submitted his resignation on 20 Apr 42 but it was not accepted until 22 June 42.

This closed the door to further government service, even active military duty. So Bullitt turned to the French and was immediately welcomed. With the rank of commandant (major) from 6 June 44, he joined de LATTRE's staff in Algiers and remained through the final drive into Germany despite permanent damage to his left leg and hip from a car accident in Alsace. Returning to the States on 20 July 45, he had no further public service. The war injury left him barely able to walk in later life. Bullitt died 16 Feb 67 in Paris.

There are many books by and about Bullitt. Younger brother Orville edited one that provides valuable insight into the diplomat's life and career: *For the President, Personal and Secret, Correspondence Between Franklin D. Roosevelt and William C. Bullitt* (Boston: Houghton Mifflin, 1972).

BURKE, Arleigh Albert. US admiral. 1901-. Born in Colorado, graduating in the USNA Class of 1923 (71/413), he became an ordnance specialist. In Jan 43 he left the Washington Navy Yard to command destroyer formations in the Solomons. There Capt Burke developed tactics for independent night operations and was given the nickname "31-knot Burke." He was CNO from 17 Aug 55 to 1 Aug 61.

BUSCH, Ernst. German general. 1885-1945. Born 6 July 85 in Essen-Steele (Ruhr), Ernst Busch became an infantry officer in 1904. He won the Pour le Mérite in France during WWI, rising to command a battalion as a captain. (Angolia, II, 232.) Between the wars, Busch advanced steadily in the army and became personally devoted to Hitler and Nazism (Deutsch,

II, 372; J&R, 361 & 381; Wistrich). Because of this, Oberst Busch, as CO 9th (Spandau) Regt in the Berlin area, failed to act in 1938 on well-founded reports of his adjutant, Count Wolf Baudissin, that the Nazis were plotting against BLOMBERG and FRITSCH. (Deutsch, I, passim.) When BECK tried later that year to have the army high command officially oppose Hitler's march to war, Busch and REICHENAU were the only senior officers who declined to endorse the action at a secret meeting (W-B, *Nemesis,* 403).

Generalmajor Busch took command of the 23d Div on 1 Oct 35 and on 4 Feb 38 became a general of infantry commanding the 8th Corps. As part of LIST's 14th Army in the conquest of Poland (1-28 Sep 39) Busch figured prominently in operations that destroyed the Cracow Army. He then helped to crack the last hard nuts of resistance south of Lublin, particularly around Tomaszkow Lubeliski (some 40 miles SE of Lublin).

Moving up to command the 16th Army, Busch had a minor role in the campaign of 1940. His mission in France was to cover the southern flank opposite the Maginot Line during the Battle of Flanders. On 26 May 40 he was awarded the RK and promoted to Generaloberst (Angolia, II, 232), after which his army was involved in turning the Maginot Line.

Busch's 16th Army was on the south flank of LEEB's AG North in Opn Barbarossa. Reinforced by the 57th Pz Corps, Busch took Demyansk on 8 Sep 41. Steadily worsening weather, difficult terrain, and counterattacks stopped him short of the Valdai Hills. But he then sent his 1st Corps, reinforced by the 39th Pz Corps, on a maneuver south of Leningrad that overran the critical area around Tikhvin, 21 Oct-11 Nov 41. MERETSKOV rallied shattered Red Army forces in this sector and led a large-scale counteroffensive, 6 Dec 41-7 May 42. In desperate winter warfare Busch finally contained the northern shoulder of the major penetration, holding a line from Staraya Russa to Ostashkov while his 2d and 10th Corps formed the Demyansk hedgehog.

KUECHLER succeeded LEEB as head of AG North on 17 Jan 42 and soon had such disagreements over strategy with Busch that he finally asked for Busch to be replaced. But the durable 16th Army commander retained his post. About a year later he was promoted to field marshal in a special ceremony on 1 Feb 43. After a heroic defense around Demyansk, Busch was authorized to withdraw. The difficult operation ended successfully on 18 Mar 43. For this and continuing action in Russia the Nazi general was awarded his Oakleaves (274/890) on 21 Aug 43.

Shortly after the Soviets began a major offensive on his front Generalfeldmarschall Busch stepped up on 26 Oct 43 to succeed the injured KLUGE as head of AG Center. In another purge of field commanders blamed for the disasters on both fronts, Hitler began by sacking Busch on 28 June 44 and replacing him with MODEL.

In retirement until the last weeks of the war, Busch became head of AG Northwest at the end of Mar 45. His front extended about 200 miles from the North Sea around Bremen to Magdeburg after Blaskowitz's army group was cut off in the Netherlands. With Student's 1st Parachute Army and other remnants he opposed Montgomery's final drive on Bremen and Hamburg.

Loudly criticizing DOENITZ for "no longer acting in Hitler's spirit" (Speer, *Memoirs,* 493), Busch was denied authority to launch a final counteroffensive. Instead he was ordered by Doenitz to hold open a corridor through which Germans, civilian and military, could seek refuge in the British sector. On 3 May 45, when Hamburg fell, Busch sent Montgomery a delegation with authority from Keitel and Doenitz to surrender all German armed forces north of Berlin. Because most of these troops were in contact with the Soviets, Montgomery (as a field commander) had no authority to negotiate, but he did accept surrender of all German forces on his western and northern flanks. Busch was authorized to keep his headquarters intact to execute Montgomery's orders, but Montgomery had to rebuke the Nazi general for allowing his troops to pretend they had become allies against the Soviets. (Montgomery, *Memoirs,* 328. This attitude, obviously with some official direction, was prevalent among German POWs not only in Germany but also in Italy.)

"A soldier promoted above his ceiling, Busch lies buried in waste ground in an unmarked grave at Aldershot, where he died [17 July 45] as a prisoner of war" (Brett-Smith, 197).

BUSH, Vannevar. US scientist. 1890-1974. Born 11 Mar 90 in Everett, Mass, grandson of a whaling captain and son of a minister, Bush was a Tufts graduate with a PhD from MIT (1916). By 1932 he was dean of engineering at MIT, where he built the first electronic analogue computer to solve complex differential equations with great speed. The small, humorous genius headed the National Committee for Aeronautics. In 1939 he took over the Carnegie Institution in Washington, DC, one of the world's largest scientific organizations, and in June 40 became chairman of FDR's National Defense Research Committee (NDRC) to mobilize scientific man power and coordinate atomic research. After a year in this post he became director of the Office of Scientific Research and Development on 28 June 41 after persuading Roosevelt to set this up. Dr Bush showed that in addition to having "an unorthodox scientific mind of whiplash speed" *(CB 40)* he was a remarkable administrator. Decentralizing scientific work among colleges and universities, his office "mobil-ized research to a remarkable degree" (Buchanan, 126).

In addition to scientific books he published the highly acclaimed *Modern Arms and Free Men: A Discussion of the Role of Science in Preserving Democracy* (New York: Simon and Schuster, 1949).

BUTCHER, Harry C. US naval officer. 1902-85. A journalism graduate from Iowa State College in 1924, he was a CBS official when he met and befriended Maj Dwight D. Eisenhower two years later in Washington. After Eisenhower went to London in June 42 as commander of US forces in the ETO he wanted "an officer in naval uniform on his staff as a sort of symbol" (Butcher, xii). Adm KING gave him Butcher, a USNR officer thereafter known logically and universally if not officially as "the Naval Aide." Eisenhower told Butcher to keep a diary of "dates, places, and reminders of interesting events, official and personal" (ibid., xi). The first and almost only time the general looked at the diary he commented that it had too much detail, but he left his naval aide with a free hand (ibid., xii). Butcher published the diary as *My Three Years with Eisenhower: The Personal Diary of Harry C. Butcher, USNR, Naval Aide to General Eisenhower, 1942 to 1945* (New York: Simon and Schuster, 1946). In a letter to Montgomery in Feb 46 Eisenhower expressed regret at having selected a "confidential Aide without checking up to see whether he wanted to be a 'writer' after the war" (Montgomery, *Memoirs,* 313).

BYRNES, James Francis. US statesman. 1879-1972. The South Carolinian was born in old Charleston on 2 May 79. Without completing formal schooling but after working as a court reporter and studying law in his spare time, Byrnes was admitted to the bar in 1903. He then owned and edited the *Journal and Review* in Aiken, SC, was DA of the 2d Judicial District (1908), served as a Democrat in the US House of Representatives (1911-25), and was in the Senate (1931-41). After initially supporting the New Deal, the small, wiry, high-strung Sen Byrnes joined the Democratic opposition but remained personally loyal to the president and his foreign policy.

Appointed to the US Supreme Court in 1941, Byrnes resigned on 3 Oct 42 to head the new Office of Economic Stabilization (OES). His primary responsibility was to contain wartime inflation, but as troubleshooter on a broad variety of economic disputes he became known as "Assistant President on the Home Front." Passing his OES job to Judge Fred M. Vinson, Byrnes took over the new office of War Mobilization in Apr 43. He expected to be Roosevelt's running mate in 1944, but there was strong opposition from Labor, and FDR really wanted TRUMAN (Buchanan, 333).

When Secretary of State Cordell HULL left office, Byrnes was his logical successor. But Harry HOPKINS disliked Byrnes and also thought he would be too strong for a president who persisted in directing foreign affairs himself. The post consequently went to Edward R. STETTINIUS.

Using his court reporter experience, Byrnes made stenographic notes during the Yalta Conference, 7-12 Feb 45, that were invaluable to Truman when he took over as president on 12 Apr 45. Byrnes became Truman's secretary of state, and one of his first significant acts was to draft the **Byrnes Note,** broadcast to the Japanese on 11 Aug 45. It accelerated their decision to surrender.

With a lack of background in foreign affairs exacerbated by common American misconceptions in the field, Byrnes proved to be weak in coping with the Cold War already begun by the Soviets. (Kennan, *Memoirs: 1925-1950,* 287; Murphy, *Diplomat,* 300-1.) His lax administrative methods and long absences did the State Department great damage. As one wag put it, "The State Department fiddles while Byrnes roams" (Gaddis, 347). Another problem was that FDR had given Byrnes the task of following through with the Russians on postwar cooperation. "Part of the Grand Design," writes Robert D. MURPHY of the president's dream, "was to overcome Russian distrust of the Western Powers" (Murphy, 301). But Truman had not been taken into Roosevelt's confidence on this (nor on any other matter), and the president quickly scrapped his prececessor's Grand Design. It was common knowledge after the Moscow Conference that Truman was looking for a new secretary of state. (Murphy, 305.) Byrnes stayed long enough to complete the minor peace treaties with Italy, Romania, Hungary, Bulgaria, and Finland—work in which he excelled as an arbitrator and breaker of deadlocks. Submitting his resignation on 7 Jan 47 and being succeeded by George MARSHALL, Byrnes published *Speaking Frankly* (1947), which dealt primarily with his period in the State Department. After having a law practice in Washington, Byrnes was governor of South Carolina, 1951-55, and published his autobiography, *All in One Lifetime* (1958). With the almost unique record of having had a major role in all three branches of US government—legislative, judicial, and executive—the durable Jimmie Byrnes died three weeks before his 93d birthday.

C

CADOGAN, Alexander George Montagu. British diplomat. 1884-1968. Of ancient Welsh lineage, born 25 Nov 84 in London, Cadogan (ka-dug'an) was the seventh son of the 5th Earl of Cadogan. After the privileged but disciplined childhood of British landed gentry, his time divided between the stately Chelsea House at the corner of Cadogan Square in London and an 11,000 acre family estate in Suffolk. He was an all-around standout at Eton. Reading history at Balliol College, Oxford, he was too active in undergraduate life to gain more than second class honors (1906). Cadogan was first on entrance examinations for the diplomatic service in Oct 08 and went on to be the quintessential British foreign service officer *(CB 44)*. Returning to London from three and a half years in Turkey, 1909-12, the natty little Welsh aristocrat promptly married Lady Theodosia Louisa Augusta Acheson, daughter of the fourth Earl of Gosford. He next served 16 months in Vienna, leaving on 14 Aug 14, two days after Britain declared war. Cadogan served in the Foreign Office as a junior clerk until being promoted to first secretary in 1919 and sent to Paris. As secretary general to the UK delegation to the League of Nations, he had a major role in drafting the convention on disarmament and attended many conferences on collective security arrangements. (Ibid.) Cadogan rose to head the Foreign Office League of Nations section. In Jan 34 he was posted as minister to China, becoming ambassador in May 35, when the legation became an embassy. Returning to Whitehall on 1 Jan 36 as one of Anthony Eden's deputy under secretaries of state in the FO, Cadogan replaced Sir Robert VANSITTART on 1 Jan 38 as permanent undersecretary. Holding this post until 1946 Sir Alexander (KCB in 1941) won praise for his calm, thorough, and self-effacing performance, getting on well with Churchill and accompanying the PM on trips abroad. Cadogan led the British delegation to the Dumbarton Oaks conference and was his country's permanent UN representative 1946-50.

Retiring from public life, Sir Alexander was chairman of the BBC 1952-57, staunchly defending its independence during the Suez crisis of 1956 *(DNB)*. He died 9 July 68 in London. *The Diaries of Sir Alexander Cadogan, OM, 1938-1945* (Putnam's, 1972) are all the more valuable because of outstanding editing by David Dilks, who has added valuable biographical detail about the man who was so private in his public life.

CALLAGHAN, Daniel Judson. US admiral. 1890-1942. Born 26 July 90 in San Francisco, he graduated from the USNA in 1911 (39/193). After being Naval Aide to the President, 1938-41, Capt Callaghan commanded CA *San Francisco* for a year ending May 41. Then he was Adm GHORMLEY's CofS until Oct 42. The Guadalcanal campaign had been under way since 7 Aug 42 when Callaghan was promoted to rear admiral commanding TG 67.4. With flag aboard *San Francisco* and having 5 cruisers and 10 destroyers the admiral was supporting the Americal Div landings when Adm Hiroaki ABE led a powerful bombardment force toward Henderson Field. This resulted in a savage night of action off Savo Island on 12-13 Nov 42. At a range of only 1,600 yards Callaghan opened fire at 1:50 AM with guns and torpedoes from a force that now numbered 13 ships. It was Friday the 13th, and what followed was "one of the most confused engagements in modern history" (Morison, V, 225-87). Callaghan turned the Japanese back temporarily but he was KIA along with Adm Norman SCOTT and the five SULLIVAN BROTHERS.

CALVERT, Michael "Mad Mike." British officer. 1913-. A fanatically brave Royal Engineer officer, dashing, inventive, and methodical (Allen, *Burma,* 348-49), Mad Mike saw action in Norway, 1940, before training commandos in the UK, Australia, and New Zealand. From late 1941 he ran the Bush Warfare School in Burma, and in 1943 he led a Chindit column under WINGATE. A brigadier at the age of 30, Mad Mike commanded 77 Bde in the liberation of Burma (1944). Soon after "Vinegar Joe" Stilwell's NCAC Hq took operational control of LENTAIGNE's British Special Force (17 May 44) friction flared up among the allies. The notoriously anglophobic Stilwell favored his American-trained Chinese divisions and his friend Merrill's Marauders (Galahad force). While the Chinese advanced under secret orders from Chiang Kai-shek to husband their strength (Allen, *Burma,* 363), Calvert had increasingly heavy losses. After 77 Bde spearheaded a cautious Chinese force, taking the strongpoint at Moguang on 27 Jun 44, a BBC broadcast from NCAC Hq gave the Chinese the credit. Mad Mike signalled: "Chinese reported taking Mogaung. My Brigade now taking umbrage." (Ibid., 374.) Continuing to suffer heavy losses in clearing critical positions on the road to Myitkyina, a vital strategic objective in the Allied campaign, 77th Bde was evacuated to India on 24 June 44.

"The threat of a court-martial hung in the air" when the brigadier reported to Vinegar Joe before leaving. "You send some very strong signals, Calvert," said Stilwell. "You should see the ones my brigade-major won't let me send," replied Mad Mike. After laughing that he had the same trouble, Stilwell found the NCAC staff had misinformed him about Calvert's operations. (Ibid., 375-76.) Leaving India in late 1944, Calvert led SAS forces in Belgium, Holland, and Norway. (Tunney.) In addition to *Fighting Mad* (London: Jarrolds, 1964), Calvert wrote *Prisoners of Hope* (London: Cape, 1952; new ed, Leo Cooper, 1971), and *The Chindits* (New York: Ballantine, 1973).

CAMERON, Donald. British submarine officer. 1919–61. On 11 Sep 43, six British midget submarines ("X-craft") left Scotland under tow by large submarines to northern Norway for an attack on *Tirpitz,* which lay immobile in strongly defended Altenfiord. Early 22 Sep 43, with the two subs that were able to make the final approach, Lts Cameron, RN, and Godfrey Place, RNR, detonated two-ton charges beneath the gigantic battleship, effectively eliminating her as a threat to Arctic convoys bound for Russia. Both subs surfaced accidentally on the run-in, alerting the defenders. Cameron scuttled *X-6* and was captured with his crew. *X-7* was entangled in the sub nets and went out of control after the "side-charges" exploded, only Lt Place and one man surviving to be taken prisoner. Cameron died 10 Apr 61 at Gorport, Hampshire.

CAMM, Sydney. English aircraft designer. 1893-1966. Best remembered for designing the Hurricane fighter, he was born in Windsor on 5 Aug 93, son of a carpenter. Soon after leaving the Royal Free School at Windsor, Camm was apprenticed to a woodworker. He was involved in making gliders and model planes before joining the G. H. Martinsdyne aeroplane company at Brooklands and working there throughout WWI. Camm collaborated with Martinsdyne on aircraft design and in 1922 joined the Hawker Engineering Co at Kingston, the firm whose fortunes were built on the Sopwith line of aircraft. Starting as a senior draughtsman, he was chief designer two years later. From 1925 Camm worked on military aircraft models, producing designs noted for elegance, grace, and for integration of their Rolls Royce engines and armament into the air frame. Working closely with the Air Ministry from 1934, the Hawker Co was in full production of the Hurricane when war broke out in 1939. The plane was the RAF's first one-wing fighter, 100mph faster than anything previously flown, maneuverable, and rugged. It was built around the new Rolls Royce Merlin engine and had eight machine guns. (Later the plane had cannon, rockets, and bombs.) In the Battle of Britain, 400 Hurricanes and 200 Spitfires defeated 1,000 Me 109s and Me 110s. Final production was some 14,500 Hurricanes, many going to Russia. The second-generation Hurricane was the Typhoon fighter-bomber (1942), followed by the Tempest, which evolved into the Sea Fury. Camm went on to design jet aircraft, the Sea Hawk and its successor, the Hunter (1951). The latter won the world air speed record and remained operational for 20 years. Camm pioneered design of the vertical take off and landing (VTOL) fighter, turning out the revolutionary P-1127 Kestrel (1958).

The tall, thin, irascible, self-taught genius was knighted in 1953. He was on the board of Hawker Siddeley Aviation from 1935 until his death at Richmond, Surrey, 12 Mar 66. (Peter Wykeham in *DNB.*)

CAMPBELL, John Charles "Jock." British general. 1894–1942. He was born at Thurso, Caithness, 10 Jan 94. On the first day of war in 1914 he enlisted in the Honourable Artillery Co and a year later was commissioned from Woolwich and ordered to the western front. In 1916 he survived two wounds, one requiring a year's convalescence. By war's end he was a captain in the Royal Horse Arty and a recipient of the MC. Between the wars he was known as a first-class rider, huntsman, and polo player. In 1922 he married a grand-niece of Cecil Rhodes. *(DNB.)*

When GRAZIANI advanced toward Egypt in Sep 40, Jock had recently been promoted from command of a 4th Royal Horse Arty (RHA) battery to head the regiment. Alternating between command of the 4th and the 3d, Campbell was a master of delaying tactics. During the retreat Campbell was appointed to the DSO, and for action on 14 Dec 40, as Lt Gen Richard O'CONNOR began his counteroffensive, he won a bar to his DSO.

Campbell was promoted to brigadier on 3 Sep 41 and given command of the 7th Support Gp, which screened vast expanses of desert while the 8th Army regrouped. The innovative gunner created the famous "Jock columns," small, mobile task forces of field artillery, anti-tank guns, antiaircraft guns, and motorized infantry. "They could not hold ground against a determined attack and had to depend on their mobility to ride such blows. . . . But they did appeal to the privateering instinct of British officers, who enjoyed commanding them" (Jackson, *North Africa*, 130). Brigadier Campbell won the VC for action at Sidi Rezegh, 21-22 Nov 41. On 26 Feb 42, shortly after promotion to major general commanding the 7th Armd Div ("Desert Rats"), Campbell was killed near Halfaya Pass when his staff car skidded and overturned.

CANARIS, Wilhelm Franz. German admiral. 1887-1945. The enigmatic Abwehr chief was born in the Ruhr village of Aplerbeck near Dortmund on 1 Jan 87. His family, the Canarisi, were first identified in the northern Italian silk-spinners' village of Sala on Lake Como during the sixteenth century. The Canarisi spread to Corsica, Greece, and Germany (Hoehne, *Canaris*, 4), "Willie" grew up in a wealthy, cultured, happy Westphalian family of right-wing but liberal Protestants. Visiting Athens in 1902 the boy learned of Adm Constantine Kanaris (1790-1877) and became an ardent admirer of the legendary naval hero who was a founder of modern Greece. Canaris later kept a portrait of Kanaris in his living room and joked that the Greek was his grandfather (Hoehne, *Canaris*, 7).

Canaris came to believe that his country's future lay in seapower, and in 1905 he entered the Imperial German Navy. Six years later he was promoted to full lieutenant, assigned to CL *Dresden,* and eventually was its XO. The ship performed a number of delicate diplomatic missions in Latin American waters before being cut off from returning to Germany in 1914. Canaris improvised an intelligence net that enabled *Dresden* to operate for several months as a commerce raider. Sole survivor of the Battle of the Falklands, 8 Dec 14, the ship had to be scuttled in the Juan Fernandez Islands, 400 miles west of Santiago, Chile.

Canaris escaped on 4 Aug 15 from an island internment camp off Concepción to make a daring two-week horseback ride through the Andes, helped by local Germans in eluding pursuit by Chilean police. From the town of Neuquén in central Argentina, and masquerading as "Reed Rosas," putative son of a Chilean father and British mother, he proceeded by rail to Buenos Aires. On a Dutch ship bound for Rotterdam, Reed Rosas artfully deceived British passengers and RN security officers to pass the British blockade, even helping inspectors check on a Chilean whose accent aroused their suspicion (ibid., 34-35). He reached Germany on 4 Oct 15. Because of his work in Latin America, where he had begun a mastery of Spanish and lifelong devotion to Hispanic culture, Canaris was sent to improvise an intelligence service for U-boat operations in the Mediterranean. As "Kika," still using the passport of Reed Rosas, the crafty little (5 foot 3) Canaris performed feats of espionage in Italy and Spain. The true facts remain a mystery, but he became a legend. Having eluded British and Italian counterintelligence, he entered the submarine service on 24 Oct 16. A little less than a year later he was a successful U-boat skipper in the Mediterranean.

After the armistice of 1918 Canaris was prominent in Freikorps activities including the Kapp putsch and later was involved in covert efforts to rebuild the German armed forces. He worked in Japan with German designers on building submarines, then resumed his naval career and became increasingly involved with military intelligence. As XO of the training ship *Berlin,* 1922-24, Canaris got to know an outstanding officer candidate named Reinhard HEYDRICH. Promoted on 1 Oct 31, Capt Canaris took command of BB *Schlesien* on 29 Sep 32. It was supposed to be a "retirement tour," but after two years, when the first naval officer to head the Abwehr Section of the Reichswehr Ministry was forced to resign, RAEDER reluctantly named Canaris to succeed him. This was because the post might otherwise have reverted to the army—Canaris was the only naval officer who would not need a long "running-in" period.

The new military intelligence chief took over his office on the third floor of 72-76 Tirpitz Ufer on 2 Jan 35 at 8 AM before most of the staff appeared. One early arrival remembered that the white-haired naval captain with the Iron Cross 1st Class on his untidy tunic looked more like "the impresario of a worldwide music-hall agency . . . than a senior German officer" (ibid., 167-68). After four months on the job Canaris was promoted to admiral. He quickly reached a modus vivendi with Heydrich and Himmler, whose SS intelligence agencies had given his predecessor difficulties. And one of the admiral's first achievements was to convince Hitler to intervene promptly on the side of FRANCO in the Spanish Civil War.

As an ardent nationalist and rightist with an almost pathological aversion to communism, the Little Admiral sincerely approved of Nazism initially. But the FRITSCH affair of early 1938 seems to have been what first led him to join the already-established conspiracy against Hitler. SS atrocities in Poland, which he instructed Abwehr agents to document fully (HCD), opened the admiral's eyes further. During the Munich Crisis he was deeply involved in efforts to enlist British, American, and even French aid (HCD) in supporting a movement within the Wehrmacht to block Hitler's expansionist policies.

German military fortunes were at high tide when Hitler picked Canaris in the winter of 1940-41 to negotiate with Franco for Spanish collaboration in the capture of Gibraltar. The admiral called on his considerable resources in Spain and personally did much cloak and dagger work in planning the proposed coup de main, but he astounded Spanish friends in high places by predicting that Germany would lose the war! This encouraged FRANCO to take a hard line with Hitler.

Even before this, however, Canaris became inactive in anti-Hitler conspiracies because so many had failed (HCD). But he continued to gather and support other putschists, primarily Hans OSTER. From his extensive study of the

enigmatic little admiral Professor Deutsch finds two outstanding personality traits: an almost Oriental fatalism, and a delight in deceiving enemies as to his true feelings. Canaris fooled Heydrich and Himmler almost to the end and was one of the few who *ever* hoodwinked Hitler. (HCD.)

When HEYDRICH reached Prague in late 1941 he already was preparing a case for absorbing Canaris's Abwehr in the RSHA. After the acting protector finally unmasked the master spy Paul "Franta" THUEMMEL as chief of the Abwehr office in Prague he confronted the little admiral with evidence not only of inefficiency but also of outright treason. Canaris refuted the charges but placated his powerful antagonist by agreeing to let the SD absorb certain Abwehr functions. Less than a week after this meeting at Hradcany Castle HEYDRICH was mortally wounded (27 May 42), giving the Abwehr a new lease on life. Although he may not have known of Heydrich's initial victory in Prague, Himmler went on to compile a detailed record of Abwehr failures that led Hitler to order, on 12 Feb 44, that all intelligence services be unified in the SS. Canaris was demoted to head the Office for Commercial and Economic Warfare, an appointment as insignificant as it sounds.

A few weeks later Himmler innocently confided to Canaris that he knew about the latest anti-Hitler plots and that the SS was shadowing suspects including BECK and GOERDELER. Canaris promptly alerted the conspirators. On 23 July 44, three days after STAUFFENBERG's failed attempt to kill Hitler, the little admiral was placed in house arrest. But there were no charges against him, not even suspicion of treason. Canaris was quartered initially at Burg Lauenstein, a small Abwehr station in the Frankenwald. He was treated as a "prisoner of honor," even thanked by Hitler for his war efforts (Hoehne, 556). But on 22 Sep 44 the SS found Abwehr records of the conspiracy that DOHNANYI had so diligently compiled. These included carbons of a few pages of the Canaris diaries! Dohnanyi had pleaded in messages smuggled from his cell that these archives be destroyed, but Gen Beck insisted they be preserved to prove what "Good Germans" had done to fight Nazism. SS interrogators slowly pieced together a picture of the conspiracy's incredible scope, but Canaris was still treated with respect and he continued to outwit interrogators. Keitel saved his former subordinate from facing a People's Court. But on about 4 Apr 45 the complete Canaris diaries of perhaps 10,000 pages were found. (They later disappeared.) With this final evidence coming in the last days of the Third Reich, Hitler ordered liquidation of the surviving conspirators. Oster was the first to be brought before a summary court at Flossenbuerg the afternoon of 8 Apr 45. Having abandoned hope, he vehemently admitted that since 1938 he had worked to overthrow the Nazis. Canaris was brought in to hear Oster's accusation that the admiral had been involved in every action. "I did it for show," Canaris said in a final, desperate plea. When finally asked point-blank whether Oster was falsely incriminating him, Canaris quietly said "No." (Ibid., 595.) The diehard was beaten while en route to his cell, his nose broken (Brown, *Bodyguard*, 819). With a spoon he tapped out a farewell in prison Morse code to a neighbor, Lt Col H. M. Lunding, former chief of the Danish secret service. The next morning, 9 Apr 45, the 58-year-old Canaris was taken naked from his cell shortly after 6 AM and hustled to the execution chamber. With an iron collar around the neck he was hung from the ceiling. An SS officer told Dr Josef "Ochensepp" Mueller, also a prisoner, that the little admiral had taken half an hour to die (ibid.). Canaris was followed by Oster, Dietrich Bonhoeffer, and two others.

CANNON, John K. USAF general. 1895-1955. A pursuit pilot at Mitchell Field, NY, when the war started, Cannon was promoted to brigadier general and given command of the 1st AF briefly, 12-22 July 42. (*AA*, 593.) He led the 12th Air Support Cmd for the landings in Morocco on 8 Nov 42 before taking over the 12th Bomb Cmd in North Africa. Cannon then was Ira EAKER's deputy in the Allied Tac AF, helping plan and execute air support for the landings in Sicily and Italy. Promoted in June 43, Maj Gen Cannon succeeded SPAATZ on 21 Dec 43 as CG, 12th AF. When this air force relinquished strategic functions to DOOLITTLE's new 15th AF (created 1 Nov 43) the 12th AF became the US component of the Mediterranean Allied Tac AF (*AA*, 219). Cannon's force achieved air superiority of 30:1 in Italy (WC, VI, 330, 521) and also supported the invasion of Southern France. Promoted to lieutenant general on 17 Mar 45, Cannon replaced EAKER as CG Mediterranean Allied AF on 2 Apr 45. From Dec 46 Cannon headed the USAF element of CLAY's European Command.

CAPA, Robert. US war photographer. 1913-54. Born André Friedmann in Hungary, he became Robert Capa after moving to Paris. In 1936 he covered early actions of the Spanish civil war and became famous internationally as a combat photographer. Capa went on to cover opening phases of the Sino-Japanese war in 1938 and the London blitz in 1940 before accompanying American front-line troops in North Africa, Italy, France, and Germany. In 1947 he joined other famous photographers including Henri CARTIER-BRESSON to establish a cooperative freelance agency, Magnum Photos. One of his books, *Slightly Out of Focus*, was published that year. After covering the first Arab-Israeli war, Capa was with French troops in Vietnam when killed by a mine in 1954.

CAPRA, Frank. US film producer. 1897-1991. Born in Palermo, Sicily, he went to America with his family while still young. Capra studied chemical engineering at the California Institute of Technology and served in the army during WWI. After having odd jobs he started a career in the nascent film industry. In 1928 he joined Columbia Pictures and began turning out a long series of highly successful comedies. Oscar-winning classics were *It Happened One Night* (1934), *Mr Deeds Goes to Town* (1936), and *You Can't Take it With You* (1938). Other films were *Lost Horizon* (1937) and *Mr Smith Goes to Washington* (1939). After George C. Marshall saw the need to motivate US forces for war, Capra (as a Signal Corps major) produced a series of highly dramatic, simplistic, propaganda films. *Prelude to War* (1942) was followed in 1943 by *The Nazis Strike, Divide and Conquer*, and *The Battle of Britain*. In 1944 Capra made *The Battle of China* and *The Battle of Russia*. During the war he also made *Meet John Doe* (1941), *Arsenic and Old Lace* (1944), which were followed by *It's a Wonderful Life* (1946), and *State of the Union* (1948).

Having won six Oscars he was content thereafter to remake his own films and publish an autobiography, *The Name Above the Title* (1971). Capra died 3 Sep 91 at his home in La Quinta, Calif.

CARLSON, Evans Fordyce. USMC Raider leader. 1896-1947. The son of a Congregationalist minister, he joined the USMC, was commissioned from the ranks, and served two tours in China, 1927-29 and 1933-35, before commanding the Marine guard at the Little White House at Warm Springs, Ga, 1935-37. Characterized by Barbara Tuchman as "an American Candide," the intense young officer made a favorable impression on Roosevelt. When Carlson went to China for his third tour of duty the president asked him to send back personal reports to the White House. Reaching Shanghai less than a month after the Japanese invasion began on 7 July 37, Carlson wrote weekly letters to FDR. "Interpreting everything he met in terms of the ideals he was brought up with," he reported that "mutual confidence obtained between the Generalissimo and the leaders of China's Communist Party" because "'both had the welfare of China at heart'" (Tuchman, 175). This contributed significantly to FDR's unrealistic China policy.

Carlson made a trip to Yenan in the fall of 1937 that intensified his admiration for Chinese guerrilla tactics and was instrumental in having USMC "raider battalions" created in 1941. When Capt Carlson took command of the 2d Raider Bn he chose FDR's son James, a lieutenant in the USMC Reserve, as XO. The astute move assured "Carlson's Raiders" a high priority for their requisitions. Carlson adopted his slogan from the Chinese communist guerrillas, Gung Ho, "Work Together."

For a strategic diversion in the Guadalcanal campaign, Carlson left Pearl Harbor on 8 Aug 43 with 222 Marines aboard the submarines *Argonaut* and *Nautilus*. Under Comdr William H. Brockman, skipper of *Nautilus,* the task force moved 2,000 miles, undetected, to the lightly held Gilbert Islands. In two days of heavy fighting the raiders captured Makin Atoll, destroyed the radio station, burned equipment, captured important documents, and gained valuable experience. At the cost of 30 dead and missing, the Marines killed 86 die-hard Japanese. The task force departed for Pearl Harbor, convinced that all living Marines were on board. But nine were left behind. Quickly captured, they ended up being executed on orders from Koso ABE.

Although the raid was hailed as a great success, long range consequences were very unfortunate. Japanese patrols found and eliminated the New Zealand coastwatchers and three other men who had been a vital means of Allied intelligence. The Japanese immediately started reinforcing and fortifying the Gilbert Islands,

including Tarawa, 120 miles south of Makin. On 4 Nov 42, soon after his first raid, Carlson reached Guadalcanal to conduct a 30-day, 150-mile armed reconnaissance. Losing only 17 men, the Raiders killed more than 500 Japanese. Carlson returned to the States for medical treatment, leaving his battalion on Guadalcanal and never getting another command.

As a full colonel he was an observer at Tarawa, 20-23 Nov 43, where the Marines lost 984 killed and 2,072 wounded. As mentioned earlier, Tarawa was not heavily fortified until after the Makin raid.

On Saipan while attempting to rescue a wounded man he sustained injuries that led to his early retirement on 1 July 46 (when he was promoted to brigadier general) and to an early death the next year.

Lean, leathery, hawk nosed, bushybrowed, and brave, Carlson was an intense, complex man like such other "special forces" leaders as Bill DARBY, and Orde WINGATE.

CAROL II, King of Rumania. 1893-1957. The Hohenzollern "Playboy of the Balkans" was trained in a Prussian regiment, served in WWI, and renounced his rights to the throne in 1925. Carol's son Michael reigned under a regency from the old king's death in 1927 until 1930, when Carol returned with his mistress Magda "Bibi" Lupescu from self-imposed exile in Paris. In 1938 Carol established a corporatist dictatorship, quickly dismissing Ion ANTONESCU. The king had to play a cagey game with Hitler while hoping the British and French would be able to protect their investment in his country's great gas and oil fields. Carol also was under constant threat from the ultra-fascist Iron Guard. His regime meanwhile became more and more oppressive. On 21 June 40, a week before the Soviets invaded Bessarabia, the king was forced to form a new Party of the Nation to include the Iron Guard. Under pressure from Germany and Italy at the Vienna Conference, Romania agreed on 30 Aug to give back to Hungary about 16,600 square miles that included costly frontier defenses and almost 2,400,000 people. Carol was forced to abdicate in favor of his son Michael on 5 Sep 40 when ANTONESCU became premier, and the next day he narrowly escaped to Yugoslavia in his private armored train with Mme Lupescu, about 30 retainers, and property including three automobiles. Spanish authorities honored Antonescu's demand that the fugitives be put under house arrest but refused to return La Lupescu for trial. Most of their wealth already abroad, Carol and his mistress lived in Portugal until the end of 1940, then in Brazil, where they were married in 1947.

CARRE, Mathilde Belard "The Cat." French triple agent. 1910–60. After getting a law degree, Lily Belard became Mme Carré in 1933. At the start of WWII she was an army nurse briefly before Capt Roman "Valentin" Garby-Czerniawski recruited her as the cipher clerk and broadcaster for a spy ring he was setting up in Paris for the British. Lily introduced her messages to London with "The Cat reports." An alluring brunette who confessed to getting an almost sexual thrill out of danger, she gathered information from social contacts with German officers to supplement what Valentin was putting together from more serious sources.

The **Interallié** net was broken up on 17 Nov 41 when Sgt Hugo BLEICHER arrested Valentin and the Cat. She saved her skin by becoming a horizontal collaborator and double agent for Bleicher.

Lily did not inform London promptly of Valentin's arrest. Then, with full knowledge of all four Interallié radio stations to include security tags imbedded in messages to show that the operator was not under enemy control (West, *MI6,* 143), she proposed to the SIS that she continue reporting for Interallié but under a former code name, "Victoire." London not only approved but also asked Victoire to transmit SOE messages. The Germans had silenced the last SOE radio operator in France more than two months earlier, so London was elated to receive a properly authenticated message on 1 Jan 42 from an SOE agent who identified himself as Pierre de Vomecourt ("Lucas"). British operators did not suspect that this and subsequent messages were dictated by the Abwehr. But Lucas soon became suspicious of Lily because of her too-good-to-be-true skill at getting him information and materials including faked papers. When Lucas suddenly accused Lily of being a double agent, she broke into tears and confessed. Instead of killing her and warning his associates, Lucas decided he could turn her into a triple agent.

Now on a hot tin roof, the Cat persuaded the Abwehr to let Lucas take her on a trip to London

he had planned. Mme Carré promised to get inside information about British intelligence and also to find details of a meeting Lucas was setting up in Paris for all SOE agents. Despite German collusion the Cat and Lucas had two harrowing failures before being embarked on 26 Feb 42 from a remote cove in Brittany. The coquettish Cat spent several happy months in a comfortable London flat surrounded by sympathetic British intelligence officers—and hidden microphones. When the SIS got all they wanted they had her thrown clawing and scratching into a cage for the duration.

Repatriated in due course, Mathilde Carré was convicted of high treason in 1949. The death sentence was commuted to life imprisonment, and a reprieve was granted in Sep 54. Lily published *J'ai été la Chatte,* translated as *I Was the "Cat"* (London: Four Square Books, 1961).

CARTIER-BRESSON, Henri. French photographer. 1908-. Born in Paris, son of a wealthy textile manufacturer, he became world famous for uncommon ability to photograph ordinary people at revealing moments and to record historic events. His eye for the surreal and a life-long love of painting came from studying under the cubist painter and critic, André Lhote. (Briggs, ed.) The photographer also had a long association with the famous film director Jean Renoir (the painter's son). Cartier-Bresson was serving with the French army when captured in 1940. After nearly three years as a POW he escaped and joined the Paris resistance to make a photographic record of the German occupation and the liberation. After the war he was president of Magnum Photos (1956-66), a cooperative agency that he, Robert CAPA, and others set up. Many books of Cartier-Bresson's photographs have been published.

CARTON DE WIART, Adrian. British general. 1880-1963. Long before the second world war, Carton de Wiart (VC, DSO) was a legendary military hero. He was born 5 May 80 in Brussels of aristocratic Belgian parentage. His father, a lawyer, moved the family to Cairo. An indifferent scholar, Carton de Wiart ran away from Balliol College, Oxford, in 1899 and lied about his age to join Paget's Horse as it headed for action against the Boers. Receiving the first of 11 wounds he would have before the end of 1918, and returning briefly to his college, Carton de Wiart returned to South Africa and served for the rest of the war in the ranks of the Imperial Light Horse. He then got a regular commission in the 4th Dragoon Guards, which was serving in India. But the cushy life of polo and pig-sticking palled, so he returned to South Africa in 1905 to spend three years as ADC to Sir Henry Hilyard, the CinC. Carton de Wiart rejoined his regiment in England but was attached to a unit headed for action against the **Mad Mullah** in Somaliland. Badly WIA while storming a fort in July 14, winning the DSO, he was invalided back to England, where his left eye was removed.

"His heroic career in the war of 1914-18 was spent in the trenches or in hospital," writes E. T. Williams (a major editor for *DNB*). "He was severely wounded eight times and lost his left hand" (ibid.). He won the VC as a battalion commander and went on to lead three infantry brigades in succession. After the war, having been promoted to lieutenant colonel, he was second in command of the British Military Mission to Poland. He headed the mission, 1919-24. Carton de Wiart then resigned his commission to live on a huge Polish estate in the Pripet marshes lent him by the family of Prince Charles Radziwill, his last Polish ADC.

In July 39 Carton de Wiart served again as head of the British mission to Poland. He disagreed sharply over strategy with Marshal SMIGLY-RYDZ, Polish CinC, who put reliance on horse cavalry and made a poor deployment to meet the German threat. As Poland's armed forces collapsed, Carton de Wiart escaped through Romania to England. He was given command of the 61st Div, a territorial formation with headquarters at Oxford, and promoted to major general.

On short notice the old war horse, a tall man with a black eye patch and empty sleeve that made him resemble "an elegant pirate," was given command of the hastily formed Central Norwegian Expeditionary Force. He reached Namsos by flying boat on the evening of 15 Apr 40 with a small staff that included Peter Fleming, the future author and elder brother of Ian Fleming (creator of the fictional super spy James Bond). With nights only three hours long, Carton de Wiart disembarked his inexperienced and poorly equipped British troops in the snow. When French Chasseurs Alpins were put ashore the next night they revealed the Allied presence to the enemy by firing on German fighter-bombers. The elite mountain troops then found they had left an indispensable ski strap behind, and ships carrying their mules did not arrive. Because of this the chasseurs had to stay in Namsos when Carton de Wiart pushed south. His green, inadequately equipped troops, lacking transport and air cover, drove 50 miles south in four days despite heavy air attack until the lead elements were shelled by German destroyers. Deploying in 18-inch snow, the British were attacked by German ski troops. When the planned Allied naval attack on Trondheim never materialized, Carton de Wiart had to order a withdrawal. After dark on 3 May, two days before his 60th birthday, the old warrior skilfully extricated his troops from Namsos.

A year later Carton de Wiart was named to head the British military mission in Yugoslavia. But his plane went down from engine failure just after leaving Tobruk on 21 Apr 41 and he swam a mile to shore. With other senior officers he was a POW in central Italy, first at Sulmona and then in the Castello di Vincigliati at Fiesole, just outside Florence. He, NEAME, and O'CONNOR made several escape attempts, once evading recapture for eight days. After a fifth try, in which the other two got away (29 Mar 43), Carton de Wiart was sent to Lisbon with General ZANUSSI to begin negotiating the Italian surrender. After their arrival on 26 Aug 43 Zanussi freed his distinguished companion when this preliminary effort failed. (WC, V, 107-108.)

Less than a month later, Churchill named Carton de Wiart his personal representative to Chiang Kai-shek with the rank of lieutenant general. The famous warrior made a great impression in Chungking and accompanied the Generalissimo and Mme Chiang to the Cairo conference, 22-27 Nov 43. A year later the general made a personal report to the Cabinet. Asked by the new Attlee government in 1945 to stay at his post, Carton de Wiart remained in China until 1946 and was knighted (KBE) that year.

Carton de Wiart had married Countess Frederica, eldest daughter of Prince Fugger Babenhausen, in 1908, and they had two daughters. Two years after his first wife's death in 1949, Sir Adrian remarried and settled in County Cork to pursue a private war against fish and fowl and publish his memoirs, *Happy Odyssey* (London: Cape, 1950). He died 5 June 63.

CASEY, Richard Gardiner. Australian official. 18900–1976. Born 29 Aug 90 in Brisbane, the elder son of a rancher who had mining interests, Casey was educated at Melbourne and Cambridge Universities (1913). In WWI he won the MC (1917) and was appointed to the DSO (1918). Casey began public service with a long tour in London as Australia's first LnO with the Cabinet Secretariat, 1924-31, then came home to enter politics. Elected to the Federal Parliament in 1931 as member for Corio (Victoria) in the United Australia Party interest, he rose rapidly from assistant treasurer in 1933 to treasurer in 1935. A pleasant, direct, hardworking public servant, Casey lacked "the mental agility and political sense" to win out over Robert G. MENZIES for the Australian prime ministership in 1939 *(DNB)*. Menzies appointed Casey minister for supply and development, taking advantage of Casey's absence in London on business to consolidate his power base in Australia.

Resigning from parliament, Casey went to Washington in Mar 40 as his country's first minister to the United States. Exactly two years later Churchill sent him to Cairo as British minister of state resident in the Middle East and member of the War Cabinet. From early 1944 Casey was governor of Bengal, where he continued to show great drive and effectiveness as a civil administrator. Returning to Australia in Mar 46, he needed three years to get back into national politics *(DNB)*. Casey was minister for external affairs, 1951-60. On retiring he created a life peer, Baron Casey, of Berwick and the City of Westminster. Governor general of Australia, 1965-69, knighted (KG) in the latter year, Sir Richard died 17 June 76 at Melbourne of pneumonia.

"CAT, The." See Mathilde CARRE.

CATROUX, Georges (Albert Julien). French general. 1877–1969. As a general's son Catroux spent much of his youth in the Middle East. He left St Cyr in 1898 as an infantry officer, saw action in the colonies, and in 1916 was WIA and captured while commanding a company of Algerian tirailleurs. Returning to the colonies, he was promoted to *général de division*. Early in 1939, as commander of an army corps in Algiers, Catroux was among those shelved by GAMELIN for urging military reforms. But MANDEL recalled the trim, soldierly Catroux on 21 Aug 39 to be acting governor general of

Indo-China with the rank of full general, and on 20 May 40 (as the German overran Flanders) he was made governorgeneral. Catroux and LEGENTILHOMME, in Chad, were the only overseas commanders to reject the June 40 armistice.

Vichy consequently relieved Catroux of his duties in the Far East and ordered him back to France, effective 26 July 40. Late the next month, before Admiral Decoux arrived to take over, Catroux led an unsuccessful anti-Vichy revolt. He also had to deal with the Japanese demand for the right to establish bases in northern Indo-China in return for recognizing continued French sovereignty. Vichy acceded to these demands on 29 Aug 40.

Catroux joined de Gaulle in London on 17 Sep 40 and was appointed high commissioner and CinC Free French Forces in the Middle East on 28 Nov. But Vichy forces held the region until a Franco-British operation under Henry "Jumbo" WILSON overcame the stiff resistance of Gen Ferdinand Dentz in Syria. LEGENTILHOMME's 1st Free French Div entered Damascus on 21 June, and the convention of Acre, 15 July 41, ended Vichy's control of the region. Four days later Catroux became delegate general of the Free French in Syria and Lebanon.

De Gaulle and the British had conflicting ideas of the region's postwar political status. E. L. SPEARS, Churchill's personal representative to de Gaulle in the Middle East, found that de Gaulle was unwilling to honor CATROUX's promises of postwar independence to Syria and the Lebanon. Both were French mandates, and more about the problem is sketched under SPEARS.

Catroux figured prominently in the Byzantine negotiations in Algiers after the Allied landings on 8 Nov 42. Named CinC of (all) Free French Forces on 25 Nov, Catroux undertook the big task of establishing control over all French colonial formations. In 1943 the general joined the CNL as commissioner of state, and on 2 June of that year he became commissioner for Moslem affairs throughout the French colonies. (Larousse.)

The general was appointed governor general of Algeria on 4 June 44. That very day he issued an ordinance giving French citizenship to certain Moslems and setting conditions for granting it to the others. The elderly general was named minister for North Africa on 9 Sep 44 (ibid.).

Catroux gave his full support to the much junior de Gaulle but commented candidly to

Harold Macmillan on 2 June 43 that de Gaulle's quarrels with the British made him "a tragedy for France" (*War Diaries . . . 1943-1945*, 106).

Catroux was ambassador to Moscow, 1945-48, and de Gaulle's confidant while the latter was withdrawn from politics in 1953-58. In 1955 the veteran colonial administrator negotiated the return of Muhammad V as king of Morocco. Catroux was appointed governor general of Algeria on 1 Feb 56 but resigned four days later because European reactionaries raised violent objections; they disliked the general's views that certain French colonies should be granted independence. Having presided over the inquiry into the Indo-China war in 1954, in 1961 he headed the military court that condemned French generals in Algeria who revolted against DE GAULLE's orders to end hostilities.

CAVALLERO, Ugo. Italian field marshal. 1880-1943. After fighting in WWI Cavallero was a successful industrialist and secretary of war, 1925-28. Returning to active duty after business experience with the Pirelli Rubber Co and as director of the large Ansoldo ship yards, Gen Cavallero was CinC in East Africa, 1937-1940. Late in Nov 40 he replaced BADOGLIO as CGS. His greatest accomplishment was to turn the Italian general staff from a mere advisory body into a military high command, the Commando Supremo, and he used his industrial experience to invigorate war production. Cavallero was noted for his optimism, which endeared him to the Duce. But, although a first class organizer, Cavallero "proved excessively subservient to his German allies" (Kirkpatrick, *Mussolini*, 481).

When Hitler promoted Rommel to field marshal for taking Tobruk (21 June 42) and Mussolini bestowed the marshal's baton on Rommel's Italian superior, Ettore BASTICO, it was necessary to promote Cavallero also (as head of the Commando Supremo).

Marshal Cavallero was replaced by AMBROSIO after Montgomery took Tripoli (23 Jan 43). The former CGS already was convinced that MUSSOLINI, now a broken man, had to be removed. The marshal stayed in touch with military conspirators, and in Aug 43 was arrested and interrogated. In a signed statement he admitted advocating Mussolini's ouster, "at least from the military command," and that all military powers be turned over to the army.

(Quoted by Kirkpatrick, 611.) Knowing this statement would be found after the BADOGLIO government fled Rome on the night of 8-9 Sep 43, Cavallero committed suicide (ibid., 612n). His body was found early in the morning on a garden bench (NYT obit., 10 Sep 43). His official diary, *Commando Supremo, Diario 1940-43 del Capo di SMG* (Bologna: Capelli, 1948), is of great historical value.

CHABAN-DELMAS, Jacques. French resistance leader. 1915-. A Parisian, Jacques Delmas was a rugby and tennis star before becoming "a junior Treasury official with great charm, vitality and courage" (Aron, 165). He joined the resistance, adopting Chaban-Delmas as a nom de guerre, and specializing as a financial counselor. In June 44, when only 29 years old, he became de Gaulle's national military delegate in France with the rank of brigadier general. His almostimpossible task was to coordinate FFI operations with those of the liberating armies. With rare military acumen he worked to impress on freewheeling forces of the "interior" (FFI) that their actions must be subordinated to those of the "exterior." (Larousse.) In the Paris uprising of Aug 44 he and A. Parodi, de Gaulle's political delegate, blocked a dangerous expansion of the insurrection and had a major role in the cease fire. (Michel, 330; Larousse, 429.)

CHAMBERLAIN, (Arthur) Neville. British statesman. 18691940. He was the son of Joseph Chamberlain (1836-1914) and half brother of Austen Chamberlain (1863-1937), both of whom were distinguished statesmen. As a young man he spent seven years in a heroic but hopeless effort to grow sisal on land his father had bought on a small desert island, Andros, in the Bahamas. (See WC, I, 494-495.) Chamberlain then was a businessman in Birmingham, city council member, and lord mayor for a year. During WWI he spent some time as director general of labor recruiting. In 1918, at the age of 50, he entered Parliament. Chamberlain was head of the conservative party and had been chancellor of the exchequer for five years when he succeeded Stanley Baldwin as PM on 28 May 37. Churchill, who knew both men well, comments that:

> Baldwin was the wiser, more comprehending personality, but without detailed executive capacity. He was largely detached

from foreign and military affairs. He knew little of Europe, and disliked what he knew. He had a deep knowledge of British party politics, and represented in a broad way some of the strengths and many of the infirmities of our island race. Neville Chamberlain, on the other hand, was alert, businesslike, opinionated, and self-confident in a very high degree. Unlike Baldwin, he conceived himself able to comprehend the whole field of Europe, and indeed the world. Both as Chancellor of the Exchequer and as Prime Minister, he kept the tightest and most rigid control upon military expenditure. He was throughout this period the masterful opponent of all emergency measures. He had formed decided judgements about all the political figures of the day, both at home and abroad, and felt himself capable of dealing with them. His all pervading hope was to go down in history as the Great Peacemaker. . . . (WC, I, 221-22.)

Although Chamberlain's forte was home affairs, he had to concentrate on foreign affairs. The new prime minister adopted a policy of appeasement despite strenuous objections from foreign secretary Anthony EDEN. The latter would have shared the opinion of Soviet Ambassador Ivan Maisky, who commented that, "insofar as foreign affairs were concerned Chamberlain produced the impression of innocence bordering on idiocy." (Ulam, 251.) Apeasement nevertheless was solidly supported not only in Britain and France but also in the United States. One of Chamberlain's first concessions followed from his policy of rapprochement with Italy. Eden resigned in protest on 20 Feb 38, succeeded by HALIFAX. Having recognized the Italian conquest of Ethiopia, Chamberlain signed the Anglo-Italian Pact on 16 Apr 38. This gave Mussolini a free hand in Abyssinia and Spain in return for Italian goodwill in Central Europe. After three meetings with Hitler, Chamberlain signed the Munich Agreement on 30 Sep 1939. The PM returned with a joint agreement he had drafted and that Hitler had signed without demur. One sentence read: "We regard the Agreement signed last night, and the Anglo-German Naval Agreement, as symbolic of the desire of our two peoples never to go

to war with one another again." Chamberlain waved this paper triumphantly and read it aloud when he deplaned at Heston. Churchill writes, "As his car drove through cheering crowds from the airport, he said to Halifax, sitting beside him, 'All this will be over in three months'; but from the windows of Downing Street he waved his piece of paper again and used these words, 'This is the second time there has come back from Germany to Downing street peace with honour. I believe it is peace in our time.'" (WC, I, 318.)

But Chamberlain ordered a program of rapid rearmament, for which the Munich Agreement had bought time. When the Germans occupied Czechoslovakia in Mar 39 the PM pledged aid to Poland, thinking this would make Hitler consult him before attacking Poland. Chamberlain's government declared war on Germany a few hours after learning on 3 Sep 39 that Hitler had invaded Poland. Heartbroken and discredited, he remained in office until the Norway fiasco. (*See* CHURCHILL.) The end then came quickly for Chamberlain in 1940: he resigned as PM on 10 May; he resigned all remaining government posts on 3 Oct; and on 9 Nov 40 he died. See Keith Feiling, *Life of Neville Chamberlain* (1946).

CHAMBRUN, René Adelbert, Comte de. 1906–1962. A great great-grandson of Lafayette's, he was the son of Gen Jacques de Chambrun and Clara Longworth. The latter was a sister of a former speaker of the US House of Representatives and of Alice Roosevelt Longworth. In 1935 the dashing 29-year-old count married José Laval, Premier Pierre Laval's daughter. Gen John J. Pershing was best man.

PERTINAX presents considerable evidence that Gen Jacques de Chambrun and Amb Charles de Chambrun, René's father and uncle, were despicable characters who "played shabby parts during the last period of the Republic" (*Gravediggers,* 389n). The Free French issued reports during the war that René de Chambrun was serving Laval as a special envoy. But official charges of collaboration were never made: Chambrun was accepted in postwar Franco-American society, continuing his law practice in Paris and New York, and he was president of the Baccarat crystal company. A sour note was sounded as late as 1976 when de Chambrun was invited to participate in bicentennial celebrations of the American Revolutionary. A newspaper story was headlined, "Lafayette Kin Denounced" (*Washington Post,* 23 Jan 76, A1). He died 22 Apr 62 in Paris (NYT obit 24 Apr 62).

CHANDRA BOSE. See Bubhas Chandra BOSE.

CHANG CHING-HUI. See WANG CHING-WEI, Chinese turncoat.

CHATEL, Yves (Charles). French colonial administrator. 1885-1944. A Breton born in Rennes, Châtel became governor general of Algeria on 20 Nov 41, when WEYGAND was recalled. Châtel was visiting Vichy when the Allies landed in North Africa on 8 Nov 42. Rushing back to Algiers and urging resistance, he changed sides during the night of 10-11 Nov and became a member of Darlan's Imperial Council. As a civilian functionary Châtel opposed the council's domination by military officers, so when time came to replace DARLAN, he first nominated the Comte de Paris (Bourbon pretender). Next proposing PEYROUTON, he finally went along with GIRAUD's election. But Châtel was replaced on the council by PEYROUTON on 19 Jan 43 and not immediately given new duties. Finally sent to Lisbon, he was retired in Oct 43. Châtel died 13 Oct 44 while waiting to appear before the High Court of Justice, which dropped charges posthumously on 2 May 45. (Larousse.)

CHAUTEMPS, Camille. French politician. 1885-1963. A Radical Socialist leader, born in Paris, he was prominent in national politics from 1919 as a deputy. A long-time senator, 1934-43, a minister 11 times, he was premier (*président du Conseil*) four times between 1925 and 1940. (Larousse.) He was in Leon BLUM's first popular front cabinet (1936-37), headed the second one (1937-38), and was vice premier to Daladier and Reynaud (21 Mar–16 June 40). It was Chautemps who reconciled advocates and opponents of the Armistice by proposing on 15 June to find out what terms the Germans intended to demand. The council of ministers' adoption of this proposition the next day led to Reynaud's resignation and Pétain's selection as head of state. Reynaud said later that the Chautemps proposition was made to block French acceptance of an armistice: it was assumed that the German conditions would be unacceptable. *In Carnets secrets de l'armistice* (1939-40), 1963, Jean Chautemps wrote that on 20 June 40 his father intended, with President Albert Lebrun's blessing, to establish himself in Algiers as head of the French government (Larousse).

But Camille Chautemps remained vice premier until 12 July 40. The following November he went to Washington on an official mission but quickly broke with the Vichy government and dropped out of politics. On 26 Mar 47 he was convicted *in absentia* of treason, probably unfairly. The sentence of five years in prison, national disgrace, and confiscation of his property was revoked in Apr 54. Chautemps spent the rest of his life in Washington but made brief visits to France.

CHEN CHENG. Chinese general. 1897-1965. Born in Chekiang Province between 1897 (*China Hdbk,* 638) and 1900, he completed the Paoting Military Academy in 1922. Rising rapidly, he headed a division in 1927 and a field army in 1929. In 1938-44 he was governor of Hupeh Province, and from 1940 was commander in chief of the 6th War Area. (Ibid.) A leader of the progressive Whampao group (Tuchman, 394, 490) and close associate of Chiang Kai-shek's, Chen was thought to be the Generalissimo's political heir until Chiang's son was ready. (*CB 41;* Tuchman, 315.) When Stilwell worked with T. V. Soong to create "Y-Force" in Burma (below), Vinegar Joe found the dapper little Chen cooperative beyond all hopes and called him a "Man of Genius." (Tuchman, 398.) On 17 Feb 43, Chen was named commander of some 30 Chinese divisions comprising Y-Force. On 15 May 43 this army was sent from Burma to defend Hupeh Province when the Japanese launched Opn Ichigo, a major offensive to counter the CHENNAULT plan. Chen and Soong were in disfavor by the end of 1943 because the Japanese had overrun vital areas. On 27 Apr 44 Chen was replaced as Y-Force commander by Wei Li-huang. Wedemeyer recommended on 21 Nov 44 that Chen be given command of Alpha Forces defending Kunming, but Chiang favored War Minister Ho Ying-Ching (he of the Ho-Umezu Agreement.) The ousted general took over as war minister. In 1946-48 he was CGS, then premier, 1950-54 and 1957-63. Chen Chung also was vice president of Nationalist China from 1954 until his death in 1965.

CHENNAULT, Anna Chan. Wife of Claire L. CHENNAULT. c. 1923-. Exquisitely beautiful as a young woman and more alluring with the years, the diminutive Anna Chan, a Catholic, was the daughter of a diplomat. She had personal ties with Asian leaders including Mme Chiang Kai-shek and was a reporter for *The China Central News Agency* (1944-48) when she came to know the general in Kunming. They were married in 1947. After Chennault's death in 1958 "the Dragon Lady" (so called, inevitably, by the press) was active in Washington. In addition to being a power in the China Lobby, she was a language researcher at Georgetown University, broadcaster for Voice of America, lecturer, writer, fashion designer, and key executive of the Flying Tiger (air freight) Line.

CHENNAULT, Claire Lee. USAF general. 1890-1958. The airman was born 6 Sep 90 in Commerce, Tex, but reared in Louisiana, where his father was a cotton planter. Entering LSU to study agriculture, he soon decided to become a teacher. By 1914 a high school principal in Texas, Chennault joined the OTC soon after the US declared war. Commissioned in Nov 17, he soon transferred from the infantry to the Signal Corps aviation section but did not qualify as a pilot until 1919 and never went overseas. A few months after being discharged on 9 Apr 20 he was commissioned in the Army Air Corps. Chennault rose to be chief of fighter training at Maxwell Field, Ala, and author of a non-conformist book, *The Role of Defensive Pursuit* (1935). The pioneering airman also led a three-man "flying circus" that performed around the country.

In 1937 Maj Chennault was retired for bad hearing. With his wife and eight children he lived briefly in a cottage near Waterproof, La, before joining members of his flying circus in China. They had organized an aviation school for Mme Chiang Kai-shek, and Chennault became Chiang's air adviser. With help from T. V. SOONG and Thomas G. CORCORAN, and in flagrant violation of the Neutrality Act, Chennault created the **American Volunteer Group** (AVG) or "Flying Tigers." He also set up training for Chinese pilots and organized the air route from India to China over "the Hump." In Apr 42 he was recalled to duty in the US Army as a brigadier general.

The controversial "Chennault Plan," submitted 8 Oct 42, called for a big increase in air-

power to bomb the Japanese into submission. STILWELL's "Burma Plan" featured intensified ground action. Chiang backed Chennault, as did Roosevelt in due course, this being largely on the advice of CURRIE and HOPKINS (Burns, *Roosevelt,* 377). Chennault was promoted to major general on 14 Mar 43 and designated CG of the 14th AF, activated four days earlier at Kunming to execute his plan.

Ranging 5,000 miles over China, Burma, and Indo-China, the 14th AF supported Chinese ground operations. This strategic air offensive hurt the Japanese in 1943, but in Apr 44 they countered with Operation Ichi-go. Chiang's ground defenses crumbled as the enemy took seven of the airfields built at tremendous expense and effort for the Chennault plan. The counteroffensive in northern Burma had to be called off, and US advances in the Pacific were slowed by the diversion of logistical effort. Operation Ichi-go also deprived US forces in the Pacific of strategic air support Chennault was supposed to provide from his 14th AF bases in China. By Oct 44 these bases were no longer needed because new ones had been established in the Pacific. Discredited and out of favor even with Chiang, Chennault resigned in July 45 to protest proposals to disband the joint Chinese-American wing of Chiang's forces. The weatherworn US airman commanded the 14th AF until 10 Aug 45 (*AA,* 597).

Seeing that a fortune could be made distributing relief supplies in China after the war, Chennault helped organize the Chinese Nationalists' Civil Airline (CAT). Corcoran and Soong again were involved, and Chennault became CAT chairman in Formosa. The airman died of lung cancer in New Orleans in July 58, the month Congress promoted him to lieutenant general on the retired list. Robert Hotz edited *Way of a Fighter: The Memoirs of Claire Lee Chennault* (New York: Putnam's, 1949).

CHEREVICHENKO, Yakov Timofeyevich. Soviet officer. 1894-1976. He was born in the village of Novoselovka, Rostov/Don region, on 12 Oct 94. In WWI he rose to the rank of sergeant, joining the Red Army in 1918 and the CP in 1919. After graduating from the Frunze MA in 1935, and the having normal peacetime assignments, Gen Lt Cherevichenko led the 12th Army, a mechanized cavalry force, into Romania in June 40, taking northern Bukovina and

Bessarabia. The same month he assumed command of the Odessa MD, remaining for a year. Promoted in June 41, the month Barbarossa began, Gen Col Cherevichenko commanded the 9th Army, which was formed from the Odessa MD as part of TYULENEV's new Southern Front of three armies on the Romanian frontier.

On 5 Oct 41 Cherevichenko took command of the hard-pressed front with Antonov as CofS. (Gen Lt D. I. Ryabyshev had replaced Tyulenev, WIA.) Narrowly escaping annihilation in Rostov, the Southern Front took part in TIMOSHENKO's recapture of that place on 29 Nov 41. Moving north for the desperate defensive actions around Moscow, Cherevichenko assumed command of the reconstituted Bryansk Front on 18 Dec 41. Despite a severe shortage of ammunition and transport, the front became operational on 24 Dec for a drive on Orel-Bolkhov. Cherevichenko was an old Civil War cavalryman who infuriated subordinate army commanders with his "antiquated . . . approach to his assignments, all for the 'dashing attack'" (Erickson, *To Stalingrad,* 287). His drive stalled and stopped after a slow advance that accomplished little (ibid., 327), and on 7 Jan 42 he suffered heavy losses from a German counteroffensive.

On 1 Apr 42 Cherevichenko became D. T. Kozlov's deputy commander in the Crimean Front. As the Germans drove toward the Volga River and the Caspian Sea, the short-lived front was dissolved in May 42 and the North Caucasus Front formed under BUDENNY, who retained command of the Southern Front. (Scotts.) As Budenny's deputy Cherevichenko headed the Maritime Group, an operational group formed on 28 July with the Don Group. On 1 Sep 42 the Maritime Group was renamed the Black Sea Group and made part of the Transcaucasus Front. (Ibid.) Despite having some success around Tuapse by 7 Oct 42, Cherevichenko was replaced about a week later by I. Ye. PETROV.

Thereafter denied command of large combat formations, the old cavalryman headed the 5th Army until Feb 43. Then he was deputy commander of the Northwest Front until September and head of the Kharkov MD until Dec 43. Attached to the Stavka until Apr 45, he led the 7th Rifle Div in minor actions of the Belorussian Front and then headed a military district before retiring in 1950. (Scotts.)

CHERNYAKHOVSKY, Ivan Danilovich. Soviet military leader. 1906-45. A General of the Army and twice Hero of the Soviet Union (1943, 1944), he was the Red Army's youngest front commander when killed in the last months of the war.

Son of a railroad worker, Chernyakhovsky was a Ukrainian, born 29 June 06 in Uman. He joined the Red Army in 1924 and the CP when commissioned four years later. By 1940 he was a colonel commanding the 28th Tank Div in the Baltic Special MD. Opposing the German drive on Leningrad that started in June 41 Chernyakhovsky handled his forces well as part of the 18th Tank Corps and was promoted. Gen Maj Chernyakhovsky fought south of Leningrad until July 42 and was promoted to general lieutenant. He then led the 60th Army, taking part in the Kursk offensive of 1943 and was promoted in Mar 44 to general colonel. In Apr 44 he took over the Western Front just before it was renamed the 3d Belorussian Front (24 Apr).

In Opn Bagration, 22 June-29 Aug 44 he made the main effort in the north around Vitebsk. Opposed by G. H. Reinhardt's crack 3d Pz Army, he quickly encirled Vitebsk and trapped the 53d Corps. Chernyakhovsky was promoted on 26 June 44, just three days before his 38th birthday, to general of the army (No. 23 of 29 through 1945). After opn Bagration had destroyed AG Center, Chernyakhovsky took part in the Baltic Offensive Operation, 14 Sep-24 Nov 44, and in the drive into East Prussia that began 13 Jan 45. In these campaigns he liberated Minsk, Vilna, and Kaunas.

While inspecting outside Koenigsberg the general was mortally wounded at Melzak, Poland, dying on 18 Feb 45. One of the Red Army's finest young front commanders, he was buried in Vilna.

CHERWELL, Lord. See LINDEMANN, Frederick Alexander.

CHEVALLERIE, Kurt von der. German general. 1891-1945. A Berliner, he was commissioned in 1911 and assigned to the 5th Guards Grenadier Regt. In WWI he was decorated for valor and rose to be a captain commanding a company of the 4th Inf Regt. At the start of WWII he was a Generalmajor heading the 83d Inf Div. Promoted to Generalleutnant, he led the 99th Light Div in Russia and was awarded the RK on 23 Oct 41. Two months later he took over the 59th Corps as a General of Infantry. Remaining in the east, he was awarded the Oakleaves (357/890) on 19 Dec 43. Von der Chevallerie then went to France as commander of the 1st Army, deployed between the Loire and the Pyrenees. When the Allies broke out of the Normandy beachhead and raced east, Chevallerie was directed to leave elements to defend an enclave from La Rochelle to the Gironde River and shift the bulk of his 1st Army to defensive positions on the Seine between Paris and Fontainebleau. For failing to accomplish the impossible, Chevallerie was sacked late in August and replaced by KNOBELSDORFF. Still on the inactive list, he disappeared around 19 Mar 45 when the Red Army liberated Kolberg (now Kolobrzeg, Poland). He died about this time or later as a POW in the USSR. (Angolia, II, 298-99.)

CHIANG KAI-SHEK. Chinese leader. 1887-1975. Chiang was born in Chekiang Province, son of a wine merchant who was a village leader and regional manager of the government salt monopoly. The father died when Chiang Kai-shek was nine, leaving the family in abject poverty. The boy was sent to live with relatives who owned a shop. Running away from an odious apprenticeship, Chiang found a home in the provincial army and was devoted throughout life to soldiering. He proved to be an outstanding student, winning admission to the new national military academy at Paoting and being one of the few selected a year later (1907) to attend the Military State College in Tokyo. The frail, brooding, austere Chinaman, who detested the Japanese, became imbued with radical ideas of overthrowing the Manchu dynasty. With thousands of other Chinese students in Japan he joined the movement headed by Dr Sun Yat-sen. Chiang led a regiment around Shanghai during the revolution of 1911 and sided with Dr Sun's Kuomintang (Nationalist Party) in the counter-revolution that followed. Chiang returned to Japan after Gen Yuan ousted the Kuomintang from the new government.

In the decade 1915-25 Chiang was in China, disappearing and reappearing, "sometimes sharing in Sun's attempted coups, sometimes moving in the Shanghai mafia world of the Green Society" (Tuchman, 93). He barely survived financially until he met a leading Che-

kiang businessman who became Dr Sun's principal financial backer. This patron sent Chiang south with a letter of introduction to Sun Yat-sen.

Gen Yuan died on 6 June 16 and Dr Sun, with Russian help, gradually won enough popular support to establish a national government. With guidance from Mikhail Borodin this government was constituted along communist lines with power in the hands of a small elite. Chiang, who had served on the staff of a Fukien warlord who was alternately Dr Sun's friend and foe, collaborated with Russian advisers in building loyal and effective Chinese fighting forces. Chiang used these troops in a series of campaigns that eventually broke the power of feudal war lords. After a year of military and political training in Moscow, Chiang organized and headed the Whampoa Military Academy (1924). With this school to produce a loyal military elite needed to consolidate Kuomintang power, Chiang took command of the Nationalist army.

After Sun Yat-sen's death on 12 Mar 25 Chiang eventually won out over WANG CHING-WEI in the struggle for power. Although he was content to let others deal with political matters while he continued military operations, it became increasingly apparent that only the army could ensure survival of the revolution, so Chiang emerged as political as well as military leader of the Kuomintang. The Moscow sojourn had not made him pro-Soviet, rather the contrary (Tuchman, 92). Russian advisers under Borodin and BLUYKER were largely responsible for Chiang's successes in winning over the masses and defeating the warlords. But the Chinese leader objected to radical social changes the Soviets were imposing. So Chiang launched a sudden and bloody purge that eliminated the communists from the Kuomintang government. During the next few years he defeated communist armed forces, forcing their survivors to make the famous "long march" to the badlands of north Shensi in NW China. (*See* CHU TEH.)

After concluding the Ho-Umezu Agreement, 10 June 35, Chiang retired from five years of arduous but successful military and political struggles. But he returned to power when it was evident the Japanese intended to take over China. In Dec 36 he was kidnapped by Gen Chang Hsueh-liang, former Chinese military commander in Manchuria. Released unharmed, it was assumed he had made a deal for the Kuomintang and communists to collaborate against the invaders. Chiang denied this, and reasons for his safe release have never been clear, but he soon was cooperating with the Reds.

Full scale war started in July 37. A German military assistance program, in China since 1928, had trained 30 of Chiang's most loyal divisions to a proficiency heretofore unknown in a country where soldiers had been pariahs for centuries. The Japanese were surprised by the resistance they met around Shanghai in 1932, and now some Chinese units had several highly publicized little successes. The first was at Taierchwang, 6-7 Apr 37, followed by CHU TEH's victory over ITAGAKI at Pingsinkuan, 25 Sep 37. But by 1939 the Kuomintang's troops were driven to the interior. Chiang told a sympathetic world that all he needed was modern arms and money. Foreign military observers knew better: Col Joseph W. STILWELL reported that Chinese defeats were due to appallingly inept leadership and abysmal ignorance of the fundamentals of modern warfare; the German military mission reached a similar conclusion.

Aid to China had come from Europe until Hitler invaded Poland on 1 Sep 39. But the Chinese got US loans totaling $45,000,000 in 1939, these funds being authorized only for the purchase of civilian supplies. This "trickle" became a torrent as controversy mounted between the Old China Hands, notably Stilwell, and the China Lobby, led by the beguiling Mme CHIANG and T. V. SOONG.

The China theater of operations was created during the Arcadia conference (Dec 41) with Chiang Kai-shek as its head. "Though an Allied commander, the Generalissimo was responsible only to himself, which made him unique among those who afterward held similar posts" (R&S, CBI, 62). American lend-lease material started flowing to China in May 41 over the **Burma Road.** It was apparent from the start that the Chinese were demanding materiel they were incapable of using effectively and that was needed elsewhere. For example, T. V. Soong asked Roosevelt to give a third of the US Navy's dive bombers to Chennault's Flying Tigers, which were not yet in action. (Ibid., 40.)

But the American president persisted in believing he could make China a great power under Chiang and eventually gave into the latter's demands to recall Stilwell and the Old China Hands. They were replaced by gullible men like

Amb Patrick HURLEY and Gen Albert WEDE-MEYER. Although Chiang had the unique honor of being Allied Supreme Commander of the China Theater of Operations, the Generalissimo steadfastly refused to let any portion of China be placed under American command, much less purge Chinese leaders who were corrupt, incompetent, or both. Preoccupied with his postwar position, Chiang continued to divert lend-lease material from the war against Japan.

The frail, brooding Chinese leader, a devout, Puritanical Methodist, "read the Bible every day and frowned on sin with the intensity of one who has not sampled it," writes Theodore H. White. "He did not smoke; he rarely drank. . . . Chiang was incorruptible," adds White. "Chinese pointed out, however, that a man who has everything . . . could afford to be honest." (W&J, *China,* 123.) But Old China Hands saw Chiang as a man of low intellect who lacked military aptitude for modern war, an oriental despot who put personal survival and interests above the welfare of his people, and who was manipulated by a brilliant and charming wife.

In 1944 Chiang's world seemed to be crumbling. His armies were losing territory to the Japanese and the communists. There was famine, inflation, banditry, growing resentment of high taxes and brutal conscription, even the Young Generals' plot to oust the Generalissimo. The American press was becoming highly critical. And there were family problems that threatened to split the dynasty: T. V. SOONG had long been at odds with his brother in law, but rumors circulated in May 44 that Mme Chiang was so outraged by Chiang's taking a mistress she might break openly with her husband. (Esherick, ed., *Service,* 93-96, 130. Compare W&J, *China,* 123.)

Immediately after the Japanese surrender, Chinese communist forces under CHU TEH began a four-year civil war. The People's Republic of China was proclaimed under Mao Tse tung in 1949. Chiang fled with two million supporters to Taiwan (Formosa), where the Republic of China flourished. Chiang's son by his first marriage, Chiang Ching-kuo, became head of the Kuomintang after his father's death in 1975.

CHIANG KAI-SHEK, Madame. See SOONG SISTERS.

CHISTYAKOV, Ivan Mikhaylovich. Soviet general. 1900-79. A colonel when the Germans invaded in June 41, he was soon commanding a rifle corps in the Kiev district with the rank of general major. At Stalingrad he took over the 1st Guards Army Hq on 28 Sep 42, but on 15 Oct 42 this was disbanded to form the cadre of VATUTIN's Southwest Front Hq. Again promoted, Gen Lt Chistyakov headed this front's 21st Army, which made the main effort on the eastern flank of the Stalingrad counteroffensive. Chistyakov's troops broke out of three bridgeheads, then worked closely with MOSKALENKO's 1st Tank Army to complete encirclement of Romanian forces on 21 Nov 42. On 26 Jan 43 he made contact with Chuykov's 62d Army of the western wing. M. Ye. Katukov's 1st Guards Tank Army now was formed from the disbanded 1st Tank Army, and Chistyakov took part with Katukov in routing Knobelsdorff's crack 48th Pz Corps. The 21st Army was in the High Command Reserve until Mar 43, when released to help Zhukov stabilize the Voronezh Front (Seaton, *R-G War,* 350). His formation redesignated the 6th Guards Army at this time, Chistyakov was in Vatutin's Voronezh Front. In the Battle of Kursk, he and Katukov were hit on 4 July by their old enemy Knobelsdorff who achieved tactical surprise by jumping off late on an oppressively hot day, at 3 PM, ignoring the threat of rain (that would hamper tank movement). According to some accounts, Chistyakov's front-line infantry and hundreds of Katukov's dug-in tanks were quickly overrun as artillery defensive barrages were slow in coming, and the Germans advanced for more than a week before losing momentum (Seaton, *R-G War,* 361-64). But Mellenthin does not support this dramatic view of what KNOBELSDORFF achieved (*Panzer Battles,* 208-25).

Still in Vatutin's front, the 6th Guards Army helped capture Belgorod on 5 Aug 43. Chistyakov was promoted to colonel general shortly after his army jumped off on 22 June 44 with Bagramyan's 1st Baltic Front in Opn Bagration, the offensive that destroyed AG Center and liberated Belorussia and East Poland. In June 45, Chistyakov took command of the 25th Army of the 1st Far Eastern Front. He led this against the Japanese in the Manchurian campaign that started on 9 Aug 45.

CHISTYAKOV, Mikhail Nikolayevich. Soviet officer. 1896-1980. As a general major of artillery in June 41 he became chief of artillery

of the Western Front. After December of that year he was chief of the combat training directorate of the main directorate of the chief of artillery, and from June 42 he was Red Army deputy commander of artillery. Chistyakov became a marshal of artillery in 1944. The next year he was commander of artillery under the High Command of the Far East. (Scotts.)

CHOLTITZ, Dietrich von. German general. 1894-1966. Short and chubby, known to his troops as "Hard Guy" (*ganz harter*), Choltitz was a fourth-generation professional soldier from Silesia. As a lieutenant colonel leading a parachute infantry battalion, he probably was the first German to touch enemy soil when Hitler attacked the west. After fighting four days and nights in Rotterdam, he sent an ultimatum on 14 May 40 that the city would be bombed if resistance continued. After his emissaries, a priest and a grocer, failed to find the enemy commander, the bombing destroyed the heart of the city, killing more than 700 people and leaving 78,000 wounded and homeless. Choltitz later said he tried to stop the attack from running its full course but that his signal flare had not been seen. A year later, now a full colonel, he led the 16th (Oldenburg) Regt of Abn Inf, 22d Div, 11th Army, for 400 miles into the Ukraine before taking it to the Crimea. The Hard Guy penetrated Sevastopol's outer defenses in late Dec 41 and took Ft Stalin on 13 June 42 (Manstein, 225, 250). When the siege ended on 27 July the Oldenburgers had 347 survivors of 4,800 engaged. Promoted to command the 22d Div, Generalmajor Choltitz led it in south Russia, where the Germans were being driven back. As acting commander of the crack 48th Pz Corps (vice KNOBELSDORFF), he directed the defensive battle near Pereyaslav that began on 16 Oct 43. After finally stopping a succession of human wave assaults, Choltitz revealed to his staff and visitors including Mellenthin that he was having visions of a Russian tide swamping Germany. Apparently with authority from Manstein, Choltitz undertook a trip to warn Hitler of this specter, but the distraught general could not get past Halder. (Mellenthin, *Panzer Battles,* 243; Choltitz memoirs, 172-73.)

Promoted to lieutenant general, Choltitz took command of the 84th Corps of Dollmann's 7th Army in Normandy on 18 June 44, D+12. The carpet bombing near St Lô on 25 July virtually wiped out the elite Panzer Lehr Div, and by 31 July the rest of the 84th Corps had been driven south and east in disarray.

Choltitz's promotion to general of infantry and his appointment as commander of the Greater Paris area were announced on 7 Aug 44. After a personal briefing by Hitler at Rastenburg the hard guy reached Paris by train on the evening of 9 Aug to succeed von BOINEBURG. With Patton only 100 miles away, the hero of Rotterdam (herein) had little time and inadequate means for making Paris into a fortress to delay Eisenhower's advance. On 23 Aug 44 Choltitz received Hitler's orders to destroy the 68 Seine bridges and start large-scale demolition within the city. Choltitz made a convincing show of complying with his orders, but with covert support from SPEIDEL and others he undertook to save Paris and not to sacrifice its garrison in putting down the popular uprising that broke out in support of the French resistance. Many historians believe his role has been exaggerated, but Choltitz lost no time in surrendering to Col Pierre G. BILLOTTE, who led the first Allied troops into Paris on 25 Aug 44.

Choltitz's memoirs are *Soldat unter Soldaten* (Konstanz, Zurich, Wien: Europa-Verlaeg, 1951). The French translation is *Un soldat parmi des soldats* (Paris: Aubanel, 1964). He also wrote *Brennt Paris?* (Mannhein: UNA Weltbuecherei, n.d.).

CHRISTIE, J(ohn) Walter. US inventor. 1866?-1943. The innovative tank designer first created the wheel-and-track carriage for an 8-in gun during WWI. This experience led him to design the first postwar tank built in America, the 3-man, 13.5-ton Christie Medium Tank M1919. (C&S, *Tanks*, 169.) Its removable tracks could be stowed around the hull for road running, an important feature of subsequent Christie designs. (Tank tracks tear up roads.)

The turretless Christie M1928 astonished observers with its speed with or without tracks. Its revolutionary suspension featured eight large weight-bearing wheels on torsion bars connected to long, adjustable, vertical springs. After seeing a demonstration on 4 Oct 30 the US Army ordered five modified M1928s, which ran circles around its outclassed competitors (personal knowledge). The USSR bought two under license to become prototypes of their BT series. (Ibid.,

171.) The Soviet T-34, which had a Christie suspension, was probably the best tank of WWII.

But the US Army Ordnance Department meanwhile developed its "inverted Y" or "volute" system for the M4 series, the "Grants" and "Shermans," the first of which was standardized in Oct 41. The Army rejected other highly innovative, highspeed Christies, including adaptations of the M1932 that made it fast enough to fly short distances or to be dropped from low flying aircraft and hit the ground running. The tank was never tested in the latter model, but the Russians bought the basic M1932. (Ibid., 206.) The 6-ton, 2-man Christie M1936 was designed for a sustained cross-country speed of 60mph. Sold in Britain, it evolved into that country's first fast cruiser tank. A modified model, the Christie M1937, was demonstrated to the War Office and adoped by them. Further development, using the same suspension but a roomier hull and making maximum use of aluminum to reduce weight.

Christie had the satisfaction of finding a home abroad for his tanks--particularly their torsion-bar suspension. For his own country he created the first standard turret track for battleships, gun mounts, and carriages. His design for an amphibious automobile platform for the 75mm artillery piece led to development of the world's first amphibian tank.

CHU TEH. Chinese general. 1886-1976. Of peasant origin according to himself and official communist sources, he also is said to have been born into a rich family of landowners. (*CB 42*; Johannes Steele, 299.)

His name meaning "Red Virtue," Chu Teh was from the village of Ni Lung in Szechwan province. He taught athletics in the higher primary school there before attending the Yunnan Military Academy 1909-11 and joining SUNYAT-SEN's revolutionary party. Chu Teh fought in the first battles against the Manchus and within five years (by 1916) was a brigadier general, one of "four fierce generals" in the Southern provinces (Steele, 299). His extensive military experience in these early years included guerrilla warfare along the mountainous frontier of Indo-China. In 1921, having risen to brigade commander, he is said to have become a corrupt, dissipated, opium-addicted official in Yunnan province *(CB 42)*. But by 1922 he joined the Kuomintang and began undergoing a moral conversion (Steele, 299). Chu Teh became famous for egalitarian policies; his officers and men ate the same food and received about the same pay. He told Mrs Edgar Snow, author of *Inside Red China* (1939), that his success came from living closely with his men, paying attention to topographical details, planning carefully, and keeping on good terms with the people in whose country he fought. (*CB 42.*)

Meanwhile, he had broken his opium habit and was determined to get an education. With three much-younger students he took a ship to Marseilles, and in Oct 22 joined the emerging Chinese communist party in Berlin. After studying German and entering the University at Goettingen, he was expelled for communist activities. In 1926 he returned to China after traveling in Europe and Russia.

Chu Teh and MAO TSE-TUNG joined forces in 1927 to begin an enduring relationship from which Chu Teh emerged as the second most important leader in Communist China. In Oct 34 the communists, severely beaten by Chiang Kai-shek's armies, started the 13-month "long march" of 6,000 miles from Kiangsi to the badlands of north Shensi in NW China (Bergamini, 599). Under Chu Teh the 1st Front Army left with 200,000 men, about half of whom became casualties, but the army picked up 50,000 recruits and left underground cadres of 40,000 along the way. "The Long March is generally considered to have been the longest and fastest sustained march ever undertaken by an army on foot under combat conditions" (W&M, 50).

When the Japanese attacked in 1937 the Chinese communists reluctantly agreed to help fight the invaders. Chu Teh organized the 8th Route Army, ostensibly under Chiang's operational control. At a pass in the Great Wall on 25 Sep 37, Lin Piao's 115th Communist Div ambushed and wiped out a brigade of ITAGAKI's 5th Div at Pingsingkuan. It was a small but heartening and highly publicized guerrilla victory that STILWELL (then MA in China) spent a day studying on the ground (Tuchman, 168).

As Red Chinese Army commander with headquarters in Yunnan, Chu Teh supported the nationalists militarily while concentrating on ultimately winning the 22-year civil war. Within 48 hours of Japan's surrender Chu Teh ordered his field forces to seize and disarm all Japanese garrisons. Chungking responded by directing the 8th Route Army and New 4th Army to remain in place while nationalist troops advanced against

the Japanese. Chu Teh sent a signal back to Chungking protesting the gravely "mistaken order," and "The race for control of occupied China was on." (W&J, *China,* 279.)

Although never a contender for top political leadership, Chu Teh had a major role in the politico-military strategy that brought the Communist People's Republic into being in 1949. He commanded the Chinese People's Liberation Army until 1954.

CHUIKOV. See CHUYKOV.

CHURCHILL, Clementine Ogilvy Spencer-, Baroness Spencer-Churchill. Wife of Winston Churchill. 1885-1977. She was born in London on 1 Apr 85, daughter of Col Sir Henry Montague and Lady Henrietta Blanche Ogilvy. The parents separated in 1891, leaving Lady Henrietta and four children in straitened financial and social conditions. (*DNB.*) As a young woman Clementine was famous for beauty, brains, and charm. Her marriage to Winston Churchill on 12 Sep 08 was a love match that remained undimmed. She took a keen interest in her husband's career, sometimes showing a superior judgment on political issues and personalities. But while supporting her husband loyally, she privately remained an old-fashioned Liberal. During the war Mrs Churchill effectively supported various good works, and she was president of YWCA Wartime Fund, 1941-47. Her most consuming work from 1941 was as chairman (*sic*) of the Red Cross Aid to Russia Fund. She was appointed Dame Grand Cross, OBE, in the victory honors list. Eleven years younger than her husband, she survived him almost that length of time, dying suddenly and peacefully on 12 Dec 77 at her London home. The *DNB* sketch was written by her daughter, Lady Soames, Mary CHURCHILL.

CHURCHILL, Diana. British social figure. 1909-63. The wartime prime minister's eldest daughter, she was among the first British women to volunteer for service in WWII. After being an officer in the Women's Royal Naval Service (WRNS) she was a Red Cross nurse.

CHURCHILL, Mary, Lady Soames. Youngest of Winston Churchill's four daughters, born 1922, she was his aide on several overseas trips. Mary was a subaltern in an antiaircraft battery in Hyde Park when the V-1 attack started on 13 June 44. Lady Soames wrote her mother's sketch in DNB and published *Clementine Churchill* (1979).

CHURCHILL, Peter Morland. British secret agent. 1909-72. He was born 14 Jan 09 in Amsterdam, son of a consular officer who became consul-general in Milan when Peter was 10. At Cambridge he was a star athlete, a "half blue" in hockey, and he played several times on the national team (*DNB*). In late 1940 he became an intelligence officer and subsequently joined SOE French section.

Lt Churchill's first mission was in Jan 42. With money and instructions for the maquis he landed from a submarine in the south of France and set up a program for delivering other agents. Peter also had the mission of finding and reporting on a certain "Carte," who proved to be André Girard, a painter at Antibes who claimed to control a huge secret army. Promoted in May 42 for his achievements, Capt Churchill continued to develop methods of delivering SOE agents. The night of 27-28 Aug 42 he dropped near Montpellier (SW France) to establish his "Spindle" network, using the alias "Raoul." But he proved to be almost entirely ineffective (M. R. D. Foot in *DNB*). Carte had grossly exaggerated the strength of his maquis, and its few actual members faded away when the Germans moved into the south of France after the 8 Nov 42 Allied landings in North Africa. Raoul's main achievement was to help direct aerial delivery of arms and ammunition for the maquis. The materiel was dropped on the remote Plateau of Glières (near Annecy) for distribution throughout the High Savoy. Raoul also continued to help bring in agents from the sea. One was Odette SANSOM, who agreed to abandon her assigned mission in Auxerre and be a standby radio operator in the Spindle net. This was soon infiltrated by the Abwehr, so Churchill moved a small command group to St Jorioz, near Annecy, and left by light aircraft for London on the night of 23-24 Mar 43 for further instructions. During his absence Odette was approached by an amiable German who said he was an Abwehr colonel who wanted to defect. When she reported this to London, SOE smelled a rat and told Raoul to break contact with Odette. But she was waiting when he parachuted back on the night of 14-15 Apr 43. The next night they both were arrested by the friendly "colonel," who was Sgt Hugo BLEICHER.

But the crafty Bleicher was outsmarted by his prisoners. They stuck to a cover story that they were married, that Peter had come only for a conjugal visit, that he had nothing to do with Odette's secret operations, and that he was Winston Churchill's nephew. None of this was true, but the Germans never knew they had caught the long-sought Raoul! Both agents survived torture and cruel imprisonment. Peter was appointed to the DSO (1946) and Odette was awarded the George Cross. They were married in 1947 but divorced in 1955. Peter promptly remarried, lived as a writer and real estate agent near Cannes, where he died 1 May 72 of cancer. His lighthearted memoirs are *Of their Own Choice* (1952), *Duel of Wits* (1953), *The Spirit of the Cage* (1954), and *By Moonlight* (1958). This last book is a novel about the Glières Maquis (herein).

CHURCHILL, Randolph (Frederick Edward Spencer). British author, journalist, and politician. 1911-68. Sir Winston's only son, he was a popular journalist in the 1930s and a conservative MP, 1940-45. During the war he occasionally served on his father's staff, especially on trips abroad. As an intelligence officer in the Middle East he went on early commando raids in North Africa. Fluent in Italian, he attached himself to Robert Laycock's commandos for the landing at Vietri, near Salerno, on 9 Sep 43 and was "quite useful though he had no specific task" (Morris, *Salerno,* 72). In 1944 he was a major with Fitzroy MACLEAN's mission sent to support Tito in Yugoslavia. Having been unsuccessful three times before being elected to parliament in 1940, he failed three more times between 1945 and 1951. Randolph Churchill wrote several books about politics, and published the first two volumes of his father's official biography. The work was completed by Martin Gilbert.

CHURCHILL, Sarah. 1914-82. Winston Churchill's second daughter, Sarah was a member of the RAF. She traveled extensively with her father abroad, once making a trip of nearly three months that started on 12 Nov 43. She was with him at Yalta, 4-12 Feb 45. Married several times, Sarah had a drinking problem. She died at the age of 67 after an illness of several months.

CHURCHILL, Winston Leonard Spencer. 1874-1965. British war leader. Son of the brilliant but erratic Lord Randolph (1845-1905) and the beautiful, brainy heiress Jeanette "Jennie" Jerome of New York City, he was born 30 Nov 74 at Blenheim Palace, two months prematurely *(CB 42)*. The stately home was the Oxforshire seat of his grandfather, 6th Duke of Marlborough and a direct descendant of the victor of Blenheim.

Winston was a delicate and rather unhappy child with a lisp and slight stutter he never entirely overcame. He grew to be only 5 foot 6, but as a romantic from childhood he strove to develop courage and strength. After attending Harrow and graduating from Sandhurst (20/130), Churchill was commissioned in the 4th Queen's Own Hussars (1895). Most of his brief military career was spent on detached service as a newspaper correspondent, first in Cuba. Here, on his 25th birthday, he first heard shots fired in anger. Churchill wired a report of the action to the *Daily Telegraph* and thereafter supplemented his meager family allowance by journalism. He also picked up the Spanish custom of siestas and cigars. As for these, writes a wartime associate, Sir Ian Jacob, "he didn't really smoke them. He never inhaled and simply lit and re-lit until the cigar was half done [,] when he threw it away." *(DNB.)*

After a spell in London with his regiment, devoted mainly to polo, he accompanied it to Bangalore, India. When a punitive expedition against the Pathans on the NW frontier began in 1897, Churchill arranged to cover it for two newspapers. From this experience he wrote the first of several highly successful books, *The Story of the Malakand Field Force* (1898). Hot for further adventure, fame, and funds, he used his mother's influence with the prime minister to wrangled a temporary-duty assignment in the Sudan and rode with the 21st Lancers in their famous charge at Omdurman on 2 Sep 98.

The next year was momentous. Churchill starred on his regimental polo team in India, resigned his commission to run for Parliament, was narrowly defeated in the Oldham by-election, published *The River War* (to high acclaim), and sailed to cover the war in South Africa for the *Morning Post.* Churchill's capture by the Boers and his escape from Pretoria became world news. He then served in the elite South African Light Horse until this duty palled, returning to England in June 00. That year he published *London to Ladysmith, via Pretoria* and *Ian Hamilton's March.*

Now 26 years old and financially comfortable, he was elected to Parliament in 1900 as a Unionist from Olhman. But within less than three years he threw away early successes as a conservative and joined the liberal opposition in May 03. On 12 Sep 08 he married Clementine Ogilvy Spencer CHURCHILL, who became a mainstay of his life.

On 25 Oct 11 Churchill was appointed first lord of the Admiralty. In a whirlwind of activity he undertook to impose a modern staff structure and get the Royal Navy ready for the war he saw coming. Although hailed for accomplishing this, from the start of the German offensive in Aug 14 he showed an almost childish impetuosity and a thirst for personal glory. The first in a series of naval failures with which Churchill was associated in a major way was the intervention to defend Antwerp in early Oct 14. Churchill left London and personally directed Antwerp's defense during a hectic week, showing great panache but little sense of priority as first lord of the Admiralty. *(DNB.)* The climax was the disastrous Dardanelles campaign. This bloody repulse came from Churchill's conviction that the strategic strait could be opened primarily by naval gunfire. Forced out of office, an unrepentant Winston left the Admiralty on 22 May 15 to become chancellor of the Duchy of Lancaster (a sinecure) but remained on the various bodies set up to fix blame for the Dardanelles fiasco. Churchill repeatedly asked Prime Minister Asquith for a command on the western front but was repeatedly refused. When excluded from a new committee set up in the fall of 1915 to pursue the Dardanelles investigation, Churchill gave up hope of vindication.

Reverting to his old military rank, Maj Churchill went to the western front on 18 Nov 15 with hopes of commanding a brigade, but PM Asquith continued to block the appointment. After two months of temporary postings the ardent military amateur became CO, 6th Bn, Royal Scots Fusiliers. For the next six months he was a fearless and well liked troop leader. High combat losses throughout the BEF led to a reorganization in which Churchill's battalion was disbanded and he returned to England in

May 16 on the urging of Lord BEAVERBROOK to resume an active role in politics. The Lloyd George government took over from Asquith in December but it was not until 17 July 17 that the new prime minister felt he was strong enough to give the controversial champion of the Dardanelles fiasco a cabinet post as minister of munitions. One of Churchill's first innovative acts was to take the lead in having Jan SMUTS named to head a War Priorities Committee and working closely with the South African general in resolving inter-service squabbles that had impeded the war effort. Churchill went on to hold other cabinet posts until 1922, when he lost his Parliamentary seat and was in the political wilderness until the eve of WWII. It was during these years that Brendan BRACKEN became a devoted paladin.

Opposing appeasement and advocating rearmament, he was rebuilding a powerful following until the abdication crisis of 1937. Then his well-meaning efforts to minimize the blow dealt by Edward VIII to the monarchy were met with such public disapproval—and such skill by PM Stanley Baldwin—that "it was the almost universal view that my political life was at last ended" (WC, I, 219).

Hitler came to the rescue. On 3 Sep 39, when Britain declared war on Germany, Churchill returned to his old post as first lord of the Admiralty.

Despite a leading role in the Norway fiasco as chairman of the Military Coordinating Committee since 4 Apr 40, he craftily drew Prime Minister Chamberlain into fateful decisions that, when proved be wrong, led to the unfortunate CHAMBERLAIN's ouster. Churchill not only survived politically but was strong enough to become prime minister on 10 May 40, the day Germany attacked France and the Low Countries. Churchill formed a coalition government that included Labor leaders Clement Attlee and Ernest Bevin in key positions. Asking the House of Commons for a vote of confidence (13 May) he said "I have nothing to offer but blood, toil, tears and sweat" (WC, II, 25). In addition to rallying Britain in what seemed to be a lost cause, Churchill immediately started winning support from American President Roosevelt. On 15 May 40 the PM sent the first of 950 personal messages to FDR, whom he had met only once. "My relations with the President gradually became so close that the chief business between our two coun-

tries was virtually conducted by these personal interchanges," the PM was to write (WC, II, 23). The British Commonwealth stood virtually alone for 18 months, America remaining neutral with a large anti-British and anti-war constituency. Then the Japanese attack on Pearl Harbor, 7 Dec 41, did what Churchill had prayed for: it brought the United States into the war.

Singapore was about to fall in Jan 42 when Churchill called for and won a vote of confidence 464 to 1. Six months later the loss of Tobruk climaxed a string of British military disasters and brought on a powerful bid for a motion of no confidence in which HORE-BELISHA led the debate. Churchill survived by 475 votes to 25. (WC, IV, 408.)

But many remembered the old quip dating from 1915 that "Britain could not survive another Dardanelles nor another Churchill." Churchill lost sight of strategic priorities, as in the decision to help Greece in Apr 41, when it came too late to save that country and greatly weakened the British presence in North Africa. Churchill was so obsessed personally with defeating Rommel that he treated his field commanders badly, particularly Wavell and Auchinleck. He was a notorious meddler and his personal demands on subordinates were unreasonable to the point of being an abuse of authority. Taking long naps when others were working, he kept major subordinates up when they should have been sleeping.

A British authority gives this balanced summary:

> It would be wrong to fall into the customary trap of eulogizing Churchill, and to ignore the one great fault—his impulsive desire to throw everything into the fight regardless of considerations of balance and preparedness. But perhaps his greatest quality was that he himself accepted his faults, and allowed himself to be guided by his chiefs of staff. Hitler was the real megalomaniac . . . who surrounded himself with sycophants and admitted no denial of his own will. And it cost him the war. By comparison Churchill was a modest and reasonable human being. (David Mason, *Who's Who*, 73-74.)

As the war in Europe ended, the elderly and self-indulgent prime minister, never strong physically, was failing fast. The British public as well as the political opposition clamored for the end of wartime leadership. Herbert Morrison led the Labor party's bid to break up the coalition government. Clement ATTLEE was not willing to postpone this until Japan was defeated, so on 23 May 45 Churchill resigned to form a caretaker government. He returned to London on 25 July 45 from an intermission in the Potsdam Conference to await the final vote tally. By noon the next day it was evident that the Socialists were winning. "At four o'clock therefore . . . I drove to the Palace, tendered my resignation to the King, and advised His Majesty to send for Mr. Attlee" (WC, VI, 675). He refused the highest order of knighthood, KG, at this time but accepted it in Apr 53.

Churchill reverted to opposition leader and published *The Second World War* (6 vols) between 1948 and 1953. Again prime minister from Oct 51 to Apr 55, he was forced by failing health to resign, being succeeded by Anthony Eden. His *History of the English Speaking Peoples* (4 vols) was published in 1956-58. Churchill died 24 Jan 65 at his home in London. After a tremendous state funeral at St Paul's Cathedral he was buried beside his parents near Blenheim Palace.

Sir Winston's sketch in *DNB* by editor E. T. Williams gives copious bibliographical data.

CHUYKOV, Vasily, Ivanovich. Soviet military leader. 1900-82. Exceptionally young for a Red Army general officer, Chuykov is known primarily for his defense of Stalingrad, for the final assault on Berlin, and for his outstanding memoirs.

He was born 12 Feb 00 in the village of Serebryanye Prudy, Moscow region (Tula Prov) of peasant stock. At 14 he left home to work as a mechanic. Four years later he entered the Red Army and had his baptism of fire at Tsaritsyn (later named Stalingrad). Chuykov joined the CP in 1919 and took command of a regiment which he led in Siberia and the western Ukraine, 1919-20. *(CB 43.)*

The burly Russian with the hearty laugh and glittering smile—all teeth being crowned in gold—was marked for rapid advancement. He graduated from the Frunze MA in 1925 and the next year was at the Eastern Faculty of the Frunze MA. While still a student in the fall of 1926, he had the first of three assignments in China, that of diplomatic courier to Manchuria. After graduating in 1927 he returned to China and was involved two years later in the conflict over the Chinese Eastern RR. Then he was on the staff of the Special Far Eastern Army under BLYUKHER, having headed a staff department of the Special Red Banner Far Eastern Army in 1924-32 (Scotts).

Chuykov graduated in 1936 from a special course at the Military Academy of Armored Troops. In Dec 40 he became military attaché in China and chief military adviser to Chiang Kai-shek. This third tour of duty in China was interrupted when Chuykov, holding the rank of Komdiv, was recalled to lead the 4th Army into Poland on 17 Sep 39. He commanded the 9th Army in the Winter War against Finland, 1939-40. Promoted early to general lieutenant in June 40, he went back to China. (Scotts.)

When returned to the USSR in Mar 42 he consequently "was not filled with that bile of defeat which soured so many commanders," writes Erickson. "He possessed, moreover, great tactical flair and soon demonstrated that he had an almost unbreakable nerve." (*To Stalingrad,* 388.) After being V. N. Gordov's deputy in the newly formed 64th Army, Chuykov was its temporary commander when Gordov took over the new Stalingrad Front on 22 July 42, after TIMOSHENKO was sacked. Oddly, Chuykov remained only the "temporary," or "deputy" army commander until 10 Sep 42. His force, meanwhile, was still forming after a hurried move south when hit hard on 23 July 42 and again a few days later near Kamensk, on the Don River. (Ibid., 360, 364-66, 388.) Chuykov was supposed to withdraw into Stalingrad with Lopatin but could not do so because the Germans penetrated between the two Soviet armies. After the demoralized LOPATIN asked to be relieved of command, Chuikov reached the 62d Army Hq on Mamai Hill to take over remnants of the army on 12 Sep 42. He found that divisions had been reduced to fewer than 200 riflemen from a normal strength of about 9,000 (Erickson, 387-88).

Yeremenko's Stalingrad Front was formed 12 Sep 42 with the peripatetic KHRUSHCHEV assigned as commissar. To these superiors initially, and later to his subordinates, Chuykov said "We shall either hold the city or die there" (Werth, op. cit., 452). The general was as good as his words. Although faulted after the war for giving too much credit in his writings to himself and Khrushchev, and too little to Zhukov (see below), Chuykov is generally recognized as the hero of Stalingrad.

But he then proved to be a master of mobile war. Taking part in the 1943 offensives, his force redesignated the 8th Guards Army in April, Chuykov was promoted to general colonel in Oct 43. He spearheaded Zhukov's final drive into Germany and in Berlin on 1 May 45 received Hans KREBS, the German emissary who proposed an armistice. Berlin was surrendered the next day. There is evidence that his troops found the smoldering corpses of HITLER and Eva Braun, but that Chuykov conspired with Zhukov to keep the discovery a secret from the West.

Chuykov was promoted soon after V-E day to general of the army, the 24th of 29 given this rank through 1945. He was deputy CinC then CinC of Soviet occupation forces in Germany, 1946-53. With KHRUSHCHEV's ascent to power in 1953, Chuykov's career soared as ZHUKOV's plunged, and the men carried earlier animosities into post-war writings (and rewritings). After heading the Kiev MD, 1953-60, becoming a Marshal of the Soviet Union (No. 22) in 1955, he was deputy minister of defense and CinC of Soviet Ground Forces 1960-64. Marshal Chuykov was chief of civil defense from July 61 until 1972, after which he was in the general inspector's Group of the Ministry of Defense.

English editions of Chuykov's memoirs are *The Beginning of the Road* (1963), and *The End of the Third Reich* (1967). Russian-born Alexander Werth calls the first book the "best account of this complicated battle . . . [and] one of the most candid books published by any Russian general" (op. cit., 443). Other Western writers echo this high opinion.

CIANO, Galeazzo. Italian statesman. 1903-44. Constanzo Ciano, Galeazzo's father, was a naval captain and one of those most responsible for the initial successes of the fascist movement. Mussolini rewarded him with a title of nobility, promotion to admiral, and high offices that brought immense wealth. Title and fortune passed to the son, who graduated in law from the Univ of Rome in 1925 and entered the diplomatic service. As a student young Ciano was critical of fascism, but after marrying Mussolini's only daughter and eldest child Edda in 1930 he became an ardent supporter of the Duce and rose rapidly in the foreign service. From 1933 he was chief of Mussolini's press office. (As a university student Ciano had been a drama and art critic for a Rome newspaper.) In 1936 the 33-year-old fascist count began his career as minister for foreign affairs. In his introduction to the American edition of *The Ciano Diaries* (below) Sumner WELLES writes, "In his Diary Count Ciano shows himself to be precisely what he was in life—the amoral product of a wholly decadent period. . . . To him morality in international relations did not exist." Ciano had considerable knowledge of history, keen political insight, no illusions about Hitler's ultimate designs on Italy, and he could be a witty, charming companion, comments Sumner. "But he lacked moral courage and real patriotism." (Op. cit., xxix-xxxi.)

As Mussolini reshuffled his cabinet in a loosing effort to retain power, Ciano's appointment as ambassador to the Holy See was announced on 7 Feb 43. Ciano voted with the majority of the Grand Council on 25 July 43 to oust the Duce. About a month later the count disappeared from Rome, and on 23 Dec 43 he wrote the king that he was a prisoner of the Germans.

Both Nazis and Fascists were intent on finding and suppressing Ciano's official diaries, some incriminating portions of which he had shown to visitors as early as 1940. Himmler authorized a plan to free Ciano if he would surrender the diary and other papers, and final arrangements had been made when Hitler on 6 Jan 44 peremptorily ordered "Operation Count" canceled. A German secret agent, "Frau Beetz," had been assigned ostensibly as Ciano's interpreter but really to locate his papers. She became more interested in helping the Cianos than the Nazis. Edda Ciano, Mussolini's favorite child (Kirkpatrick, 619), had failed to persuade her father to have Ciano freed. When Operation Count collapsed, Ciano advised her to flee to Switzerland with his papers, which had meanwhile been taken from hiding near Rome by the Marchese Pucci and Frau Beetz. Six volumes of recorded conversations were surrendered to the Germans, but Edda kept the diaries and other papers and tried to trade these for her husband's freedom.

Ciano meanwhile had been sent first to Bavaria then to the Gestapo prison in Verona. On instructions from Mussolini he was charged with treason—his leading role in the 25 July 43 coup. The last entry in Ciano's diary is datelined

23 Dec 43, "Cell 27 of the Verona Jail." In what an SS officer witness described as a scene of "sordid confusion," Ciano and four others including Marshal DE BONO were shot to death in Verona's Scalzi prison on 11 Jan 44. (*See* Kirkpatrick, 609 ff.)

Countess Ciano reached Switzerland with the documents the day before her husband died and released them to the Chicago *Daily News* for world publication in serial form. Hasty translation and editorial sensationalism were corrected for the work edited by Hugh Gibson and with a long, analytical introduction by Sumner Welles, *The Ciano Diaries, 1939-1943: The Complete, Unabridged Diaries of Count Galeazzo Ciano, Italian Minister for Foreign Affairs, 1936-1943* (Garden City, NY: Doubleday, 1946).

Edda Ciano was expelled from Switzerland in 1945, interned at Lipari, and amnestied in 1946.

"CICERO." Code name for Elias BAZNA.

CLARK, Joseph James "Jocko." US carrier admiral. 1893–1971. "A picturesque and lovable character who looked (and dressed) more like a western desperado than a naval officer, he used rough and explosive language but knew his business thoroughly," writes Morison. He was "part Cherokee Indian and part Southern Methodist, but all fighter" (VIII, 238). Born 12 Nov 93 in Oklahoma, Clark was in the USNA class of 1918 (47/199) that graduated early in June 17. Known as Jocko from his days at the USNA, Clark became an aviator in 1925, and in 1931 commanded CV *Lexington*'s air squadron. After serving as air officer of CVs *Lexington* and *Yorktown*, 1940–42, Capt Clark fitted out CVE *Suwannee* and commanded her in the invasion of North Africa in Nov 42. Then he fitted out the new CV *Yorktown*. On 31 Aug 43 Clark's planes hit Marcus Island, destroying three quarters of the Japanese base. Five months later, 31 Jan 44, he was promoted to rear admiral. With his flag aboard CV *Hornet* for the rest of the war, Clark distinguished himself as commander of carrier task forces. Three strikes against Iwo Jima and Chichi Jima, including "Operation Jocko," 24 June 44, destroyed so many enemy planes that remnants of Adm Sadaichi Matsunaga's 27th Air Flotilla had to be withdrawn from Iwo Jima. "This undoubtedly contributed to the conquest of Saipan," concludes Morison (VIII, 312). After

the war Jocko Clark was assistant CNO for air until Nov 48. He then commanded naval air bases and the 7th Fleet before retiring as a full admiral in Dec 53. (Morison, VIII, 238n.) His candid memoirs, written with Clark J. Reynolds, are *Carrier Admiral* (New York; McKay, 1967). He died 30 Nov 71 at Sarasota, Fla.

CLARK, Mark Wayne. US general. 1896-1984. Son of an infantry colonel, he was born 1 May 96 and graduated from West Point in Apr 17 (110/139). Soon after entering combat in the summer of 1918, the tall (6 foot 2), lean, hard-driving and intensely ambitious Capt Clark was seriously wounded by shrapnel while leading his company of the 11th Inf Regt, 5th Div, in the Vosges Mountains. The rest of his WWI experience was with the G4 section of 1st Army Hq.

A few months after being promoted to major in 1933 and sent to the C&GSS, Wayne Clark (so known to friends) held important staff assignments before graduating from the AWC and becoming G3, 3d Inf Div, at Ft Lewis, Wash. During the critique of a field exercise in which a brigade commander raised eyebrows by ordering an unorthodox maneuver, Maj Clark pointed out that the decision was based on sound theoretical principles and practical battlefield experience. The innovative officer was George C. Marshall, whose biographer comments that the US Army's future CofS, would remember Clark (Pogue, *Marshall*, I, 316). A recommendation from Marshall helped Clark win assignment as an AWC instructor in 1940 (ibid.). When the school buildings were taken over for what became GHQ, Clark was promoted to lieutenant colonel, made G3 of GHQ on 16 Aug 40, and soon was Lesley J. MCNAIR's deputy. Clark jumped the grade of full colonel to become a brigadier general in Apr 41 and only a year later got his second star (17 Apr 42). He was two weeks short of his 46th birthday.

After helping McNair plan and conduct the **Louisiana maneuvers,** Clark went with EISENHOWER to organize the US buildup in the UK. Clark headed "American Ground Troops in Great Britain" and headquarters of the 2d Corps, which was to spearhead an early cross channel assault codenamed "Bolero." This was canceled in favor of "Torch," the invasion of North Africa. Eisenhower was named on 6 Aug 42 to command Torch with Clark as his deputy.

Only 17 days before the landings began, Clark made a daring trip to North Africa for the **Cherchell conference,** 22-23 Oct 42.

When Algiers surrendered on 8 Nov 42, Clark and GIRAUD were waiting at Gibraltar to go there and establish Eisenhower's headquarters. Because of bad flying weather, Clark did not reach Algiers until 5 PM. on the 9th. The news was bad. GIRAUD had proved to be completely ineffective in rallying French support. Worse, Adm DARLAN was on the scene and serious fighting continued between French and Anglo-American forces. Clark scrambled to arrange a cease-fire and establish order, and with Robert MURPHY arranged the controversial "Darlan deal." Clark was promoted on 13 Nov 42 to become the US Army's youngest three-star general, still only 46.

Lt Gen Clark took command of the new 5th Army on 12 Dec 42. With headquarters at Mostagenem (a port 44 mi ENE of Oran) he was responsible for rear area defense and making plans to meet an attack from Spanish Morocco. Fifth Army Hq also was charged with troop training. On 26 July 43 Clark was ordered to make an amphibious assault in Italy that turned out to be at Salerno, just south of Naples.

The landings on 9 Sep 43 had the left flank secured by William DARBY's US Rangers and British commandos, all under Robert LAYCOCK. Richard McCREERY's 10th Br Corps went ashore with Ernest J. DAWLEY's 6th US Corps on his right. Some 150 miles south of Salerno at this time, Montgomery's 8th Br Army advanced slowly against stubborn resistance.

Largely because of an excellent German defense and mistakes by DAWLEY, it looked for several days as if Salerno would be "another Dunkirk." By 15 Sep (D+6), however, the beachhead was safe, little thanks to Mongomery. (His troops made contact on the 16th some 40 miles SE of the beachhead with a 5th Army patrol.) The Allies drove back VIETINGHOFF's 10th Army, Americans taking the great port of Naples and Montgomery the vital airfields around Foggia. From a purely military viewpoint this should have ended the Italian campaign, but the 5th Army continued to push up the muddy and mountainous boot of Italy with the 8th Army on its right.

Clark's near disaster at Salerno was followed by failure to force the line of the Rapido River and open the way to Rome by taking Cassino.

Shortage of amphibious craft precluded the strategic envelopments that would have hastened the Allied advance, but the unopposed landing on 22 Jan 44 at Anzio, under LUCAS, bogged down.

The breakout from the Anzio beachhead started 23 May 44, 12 days after the successful assault began on the Gustav Line. But instead of following Alexander's instructions to make his main effort east through Valmontone, behind the German forces on the Gustav Line, the glory-hungry Clark sent troops north to Rome. The irony is that had Clark obeyed instructions he not only would have destroyed more of Vietinghoff's forces and speeded Allied operations in Italy, but he also would have taken Rome more easily. (Sidney T. Mathews, "General Clark's Decision to Drive on Rome," in *Command Decisions,* 284.)

With the first Axis capital liberated, the Italian campaign no longer had much point, assuming the Allies had abandoned the British plan of invading Germany through the Balkans. But Clark vigorously pushed his 5th Army north through the Apennines, taking heavy casualties as KESSELRING continued to direct masterful delaying actions.

That Clark was an officer of enormous ability, intelligence and drive was the opinion of McNair, Eisenhower, Brooke, that harsh critic of US Army officers, and Churchill, who called him "the American Eagle". . . . He had, however, two serious shortcomings. He lacked something granted to many lesser soldiers, that almost instinctive facility for discerning what was operationally sound and what was not. His "schemes of maneuver" were designed mechanically from a set of rules imbibed at the Staff College, drawn on a map and invariably faulty. . . . The other side of his (honorable) ambition was bitter jealousy of his rivals and an avid desire for publicity. He had suspicions amounting to paranoia that the British were stealing his limelight and trying to take credit for the achievements of his army. (G&B, *Italy,* 37.)

Clark took over from Alexander on 12 Dec 44 as head of the 15th AG, TRUSCOTT moving up to command the 5th Army. Promotion to full general came on 10 Mar 45, making Clark the seventh of 13 officers given this rank in WWII and, at 48, by far the youngest. Another costly campaign began in Aug, finally breaking the Gothic Line by Jan 45. The spring offensive into the Po Valley ended with unilateral surrender by Karl WOLFF that was effective in Italy on 2 May 45, a week before the final capitulation in Germany.

The 15 AG was disbanded on 5 July 45, and the next day Clark became commander of US Forces in Austria, American high commissioner, and member of the Vienna Inter-Allied Council. On 17 May 47, Geoffrey KEYES took over in Vienna from Clark, who assumed command of 6th Army in San Francisco on 19 Jan 47. His nomination by Truman to be the first US ambassador to the Vatican was withdrawn because of public protest.

Losing out to classmate J. Lawton COLLINS to succeed BRADLEY as US Army CofS on 16 Aug 49, Mark Clark directed Army Field Forces until taking over from RIDGWAY in Apr 52 as head of the Far East Command and UN Supreme Commander in Korea. He retired on 31 Oct 53 to spend the next 31 years in Charleston, SC. He was president of The Citadel, 1954-65, then remained active as president emeritus, serving on various boards, and being chairman of the American Battle Monuments Commission. Clark's memoirs are *Calculated Risk* (New York: Harper, 1950) and *From the Danube to the Yalu* (same publisher, 1954.)

Mark Wayne Clark died 17 Apr 84 at Charleston.

CLAUBERG, Karl. German doctor. 1898-1957. With high credentials as a gynecologist and obstetrician, Dr Clauberg developed techniques at the Ravensbrueck and Auschwitz camps for mass sterilization of Jewish and Gypsy women. The Soviets sentenced him to 25 years for his part in mass exterminations in the USSR. Repatriated, the unrepentant doctor was arrested in Kiel, 22 Nov 55, on charges pressed by the Central Council of Jews in Germany for his cruel and often-fatal experiments at Auschwitz. Clauberg died in a Kiel hospital while awaiting trial (Wistrich).

CLAY, Lucius Du Bignon. US general. 1897-1978. Like George Marshall, Lucius Clay was denied his proper niche in WWII because he was indispensable in Washington. Born 23 Apr 96 in Marietta, Ga, the son of a three-term US senator, he graduated in the three-year USMA Class of June 18 (27/137) and was commissioned in the Corps of Engineers. As a junior officer bored by garrison routine and incapable of suffering fools gladly, Clay was "as much a maverick in his way as George Patton was in another," writes Jean Edward Smith (following). Not until FDR brought in his New Deal in 1933 could Clay show his exceptional qualities. As spokesman on Capitol Hill for the Chief of Engineers, allying himself with Harry HOPKINS and working closely with Democratic majority leader Sam Rayburn, Clay aligned the army with FDR's relief programs.

After a year on MacArthur's staff in the Philippines, where he served with EISENHOWER, in 1939 Clay built Denison Dam on the Red River (in Sam Rayburn's congressional district). Recalled to Washington, he became head of the emergency Defense Airport Program in June 40, building or expanding some 250 airports before the United States entered the war. After going to Brazil to negotiate for air bases, Clay was heading for Burma to serve under Stilwell in Burma when EISENHOWER intervened to have the orders changed.

Starting in Mar 42, Maj Gen Clay was trapped in the Battle of Washington. As War Department Director of Materiel, Army member on the Munitions Assignment Board, and Brehon SOMERVELL's representative on the War Production Board, he was what John Kenneth Galbraith would call "one of the most skillful politicians ever to wear the uniform of the United States Army." (Quoted by Smith.)

Temporary escape came in the autumn of 1944 when Clay went to France to replace Eisenhower's controversial supply chief, John C. H. LEE. When that officer returned to grace, Eisenhower sent Clay to unclog the supply flow through Cherbourg, then to verify reports of an artillery ammunition shortage at the front, and finally to expedite ammunition production in the US. Clay made the mistake of visiting Washington on this business and was trapped as deputy to Mobilization Director Jimmie BYRNES. In the summer of 1944 Clay was a delegate to the Bretton Woods conference.

Finally given proper scope, Clay learned on 23 Mar 45 that he was to be Eisenhower's deputy for the military government of occupied Germany. He was promoted to lieutenant general on 17 Apr 45. The Office of Military Government for Germany was created on 1 Oct 45 under

Joseph T. McNARNEY with Clay as his deputy, and Clay moved up on 15 Mar 46 to succeed McNarney as military governor of Germany. (*AA*, 759.) Six months later, when unified commands of US Army, Air Force, and Navy forces were created world wide, Clay headed the European Command as CINCEUR. (*AA*, 26.) He was given his fourth star on 17 Mar 47.

Clay was highly effective as an enlightened military governor but even more so as the defender of Berlin. When the Soviets appeared ready to risk general war in late Mar 48 by announcing they would stop all vehicles, trains, and barges passing through their occupation zone into Berlin, Clay responded with greater toughness. He ordered guards to fire on any Soviet troops who attempted to enter an American train. Washington would not approve his plan to run a heavily-armed train through the blockade (personal knowledge) but Clay did not wait for permission to start the Berlin air lift. This turned out to be what Bradley called "our single greatest triumph in the Cold War" (*A General's Life*, 482).

Retiring from the army in 1949 at the age of only 51, Clay was CEO of Continental Can until 1962. He then headed Lehman Brothers, the investment firm, and was called on to perform many critical tasks in New York politics and in national politics. Clay's *Decision in Germany* was published in 1950. His *Papers . . . 1945-1949* were published in 1974 with an excellent biographical sketch by editor Jean Edward Smith that is the principal source for the above sketch. Lucius Clay died 16 Apr 78 in Chatham, Mass.

COCHRAN, Jacqueline. American flyer. c 1910-80. The famous woman flyer was born in Pensacola, Fla, on a date she never revealed. Orphaned at four and reared by a family in Columbus, Ga, she began running errands for a beauty shop when she was 11 years old, and eight years later owned her own beauty shop. (*CB 40*.) While working in NYC at a 5th Ave beauty salon the attractive Jacqueline sought to combine her interests in flying and the cosmetics business. She qualified as a pilot in 1932 and under the tutelage of Wesley Smith became the first woman to master blind flying. In 1934 she began competing in distance races, the first with Smith as her copilot. Plagued for three years by mishaps, due largely to flying planes of experimental design and construction (*CB 40*), she began a steady series of successes that culminated in victory over

nine men in the 1938 Bendix Air Derby. Four times in a row, 1937-40, she won the Harmon Trophy as the year's best woman flyer. By 1940 Miss Cochran had 17 records for speed and distance flying, national and international.

At the start of war in 1939 she organized American women to serve in Britain's Air Transport Auxiliary (ATA), which ferried planes of all types. Miss Cochran also pressed for programs to recruit women pilots for military duties in the US, but no action was taken until America entered the war. After Nancy Harkness Love became head of the Women's Auxiliary Ferrying Squadron (WAFS) in 1942, Jacqueline Cochran began operating the Women's Flying Training Detachment. In Nov 42 the organizations were merged under Jacqueline Cochran as the Women's Air Force Service Pilots (WASP). These were involved primarily in delivering planes from factories within the US to AAF units, whereas Mrs Love continued to direct ferrying operations. WASPs were civilians, although Miss Cochran and the AAF tried to have Congress authorize a military organization like Col Oveta Culp HOBBY's Women's Army Corps (WAC). When deactivated in 1944 because a surplus of male pilots was forecast, the WASP had 916 women on duty.

After the war Jacqueline Cochran headed a large cosmetics business. With an office and apartment in NYC, she and her husband had a house in Stamford, Conn, and a ranch near Indio, Calif.

COCHRAN, Philip G. US general. 1910-79. The short, wiry airman headed the US 5318 Air Unit or No 1 Air Commando, USAAF (*OCMH Chron*, 170, 178), that supported Orde WINGATE's Special Force in Burma. Cochran's friend Milt Caniff used the airman as as the model for Flip Corkan, hero in the cartoon strip "Terry and the Pirates." He died 25 Aug 79 in Genesco, NY.

COCKCROFT, John Douglas. British physicist. 1897-1967. A pioneer in nuclear physics and in radar development, he was born 27 May 97 near Manchester at Todmorden. His lifelong interest in technology began with early training under his father on mill machinery run by water and steam. (*DNB*.) In 1914 Cockcroft went to Manchester's Victoria Univ on a scholarship. The next year he volunteered for military service, served until 1918 as a field artillery signaler, and was twice mentioned in dispatches. After finishing at Victoria Univ he graduated from Cambridge in 1924 with honors in mathematics.

Although lacking formal training in physics he was taken on as a physicist by Ernest RUTHERFORD, who had a group studying nuclear physics in his Cavendish Laboratory at Cambridge. For the next 15 years Cockcroft worked as a creative scientist (*DNB*). He and E. T. S. Walton discovered that the atomic nucleus of a light element like lithium could be split without the tremendous bombarding energies believed to be needed for other elements. In 1932 the collaborators split lithium atoms into two helium nuclei (alpha particles), using a high-voltage particle accelerator that now bears their name. In 1935 Cockcroft began supervising the Mond Laboratory and became increasingly involved in mobilizing science for war. In early 1938 he convinced a discouraged TIZARD to continue the radar development program, accomplishing this by rallying some 80 physicists for a one-month study of coastal radar stations and by persuading some top scientists to get involved. These recruits went on to make important advances in radar development. (William George Penny in *DNB*.)

In 1939 Cockcroft became assistant director of research at the ministry of supply, which was responsibile for atomic research. He went to the US with TIZARD in Aug 40 to establish the exchange of scientific information that played such a large part in the war. Late that year he took over as chief superintendent of the Air Defense R&D Establishment and began concentrating on radar. In 1944 he became director of nuclear work being done by a team of Canadians, British, and French in Canada.

After the war Cockcroft directed construction of the atomic research establishment at Harwell, keeping up his duties in Canada until 1946. When Britain created the Atomic Energy Authority (AEA) Cockcroft was the first member for research while remaining director of Harwell. (*DNB*.) The physicist had a leading role in efforts to establish peaceful uses of atomic energy.

Sir John (KCB in 1953) shared the 1951 Nobel prize for physics with Walton (herein) for building the first "atom smasher" in 1932.

Nominated by Sir Winston, he became the first master of Churchill College at Cambridge in 1959. The pioneering atomic scientist received the Atoms for Peace award in 1961. He died 18 Sep 67 at Cambridge.

COLLINS, J(oseph) Lawton. US general. 1896-1987. "Lightning Joe" was the son of an Irish Catholic immigrant who made his way from Ohio through Texas to Louisiana after serving as a Union drummer boy in the Civil War. Collins was born in Algiers, La, a suburb of New Orleans. His uncle was the legendary political boss and long-time mayor of New Orleans, Martin Behrman, who got Collins an alternate appointment to West Point. The "principal" failed, and "with my usual Irish luck, which was to accompany me throughout my career," Collins became a cadet on 2 June 13. (Collins memoirs, 1-6.) In the class of Apr 17 (35/139), commissioned in the infantry, he did not get overseas but, despite this handicap, was identified early as a "comer." Collins had served two years as an instructor at the Army War College when the school closed in June 40 for the duration. Lacking seniority to command a regiment, Collins became CofS in the new 6th Corps Hq in Birmingham, Ala. After the Pearl Harbor disaster, 7 Dec 41, Collins and others of the 6th Corps staff were sent to organize the defenses of the West Coast under Gen DE WITT. But when Maj Gen H. A. Dargue was killed in a plane crash while en route to replace Gen Walter C. SHORT at Pearl Harbor, "Irish luck" led to Collins's appointment as CofS, Hawaiian Dept. With Gen Delos EMMONS, Short's successor, Collins reached Oahu on 17 Dec 41 and was promoted to brigadier general on 14 Feb 42. Three months later he took command of the 25th Inf "Tropic Lightning" Div and was give a second star. On 17 Dec 42 the division relieved Marine forces on Guadalcanal near the Tenaru River, and on 10 Jan it attacked. In some of the Pacific war's most bitter fighting the 25th Div took part in the seizure of Kokumbona, reduction of the Mt Austen pocket, and in the New Georgia campaign. "Lightning" being the telephone code name for his headquarters, the general came to be called Lightning Joe by his troops on Guadalcanal.

The elderly MacArthur considered Collins too young for the three-star rank of corps commander, but Eisenhower accepted Marshall's recommendation that Collins head the 7th Corps for the invasion of Europe. The orders were dated 19 Jan 44. With only 200 casualties, the corps secured Utah Beach on D day, 6 June 44, and linked up with airborne troops that dropped inland. Collins did not go ashore the first day, one reason being that he had to keep Adm Don P. Moon from suspending landing operations because he had lost a few naval vessels.

Lightning Joe had cut off the Cotentin Peninsula by the 18th, and on 27 June he took "Fortress Cherbourg." In "Operation Cobra," which featured "carpet bombing" near St Lô, Collins's three infantry divisions broke into stubborn but shallow German defenses on 25 July. The next day, disregarding standard tactical doctrine because he believed that enemy lines were about to collapse, Collins committed two of his three mobile divisions to start the exploitation phase. The bold, unorthodox generalship succeeded largely because the Germans did not have time to use their mobile reserves in the conventional manner. Lightning Joe's decision opened the door to the entire Brittany Peninsula.

Their entire coastal defense position shattered, the Germans launched a powerful counterattack through Mortain toward Avranches to trap Patton's 3d Army in Brittany. Collins wheeled east to help defend Mortain and take part in the failed effort to close the Falaise Gap.

In its toughest fighting of the war (Collins, 278), 7th Corps broke into Germany through the Aachen Gap, penetrated the Siegfried Line, and began the savage operation in the Huertgen Forest. When the Ardennes crisis forced the Allies on the defensive, Collins broke contact on his front and wheeled south to counterattack the northern shoulder of the German penetration (3-22 Jan 45). This cut the major German escape route from Houffalize through St Vith. Collins then resumed his offensive, drove into the Ruhr, and took Cologne on 11 Mar 45. Two weeks later he launched an offensive through Paderborn to meet another wing of the encirclement that trapped 300,000 Germans of MODEL's AG B. In the final campaign, Collins pushed south of the Harz Mountains through Nordhausen and Halle to the Elbe. On 20 April he learned he had been nominated for promotion to lieutenant general as of 15 Apr 45, and two days later he reported the end of resistance in his sector.

German opponents ranked Lightning Joe and Troy Middleton as the two best US corps commanders in Europe.

Collins became CofS Army Ground Forces in Sep 45 but on 15 Dec 45 took on the demanding task of US Army Chief of Information. It was a new post to cope with the usual postwar protest by former "civilians in uniform" against things military, like the so-called "caste system." Highly effective in this sensitive assignment, Collins doffed his public relations hat to take increasingly-important staff assignments: he became Eisenhower's deputy chief of staff on 1 Sep 47, remaining when Bradley succeeded DDE on 7 Feb 48, and before year's end moved into the new position of vice chief of staff. Promoted to full general in 1948, the Louisiana Irishman became army CofS on 16 Aug 49, winning out over his notoriously-ambitious classmate Mark W. CLARK. After four years at the top of his profession the general remained on active duty as US representative on the NATO Standing Group, this duty interrupted by a mission to Vietnam, 30 Oct 54–14 May 55. Collins was charged with trying to stabilize the anticommunist government of Ngo Dinh Diem. He failed, but was given this tribute by Secretary of State John Foster Dulles: "When we sent you out, we thought there was a 10 percent chance of saving Vietnam from Communism. You have raised that figure to at least 50 percent." (Collins, 411.)

Lightning Joe retired in 1956 and was a consultant with Pfizer & Co until Apr 69. He published *Lightning Joe: An Autobiography* (Baton Rouge, La: LSU Press, 1979), and died 12 Sep 87 in Washington, DC.

CONINGHAM, Arthur "Mary." Australianborn RAF officer. 1895-1948. Born 19 Jan 95 at Brisbane, son of an Australian cricketer who moved the family to New Zealand, Coningham was educated there at Wellington College. In 1914 he enlisted in the Canterbury Mounted Rifles and served with it in Samoa, at Gallipoli, and in Egypt. From this association with a New Zealand regiment he was nicknamed "Maori," which fell on English ears as Mary. Being tall, very handsome, urbane, and highly regarded as a fighter, Coningham did not mind the girlish sobriquet.

In Aug 16 he transferred into the Royal Flying Corps, and the following December he went to France as a second lieutenant. In seven months as a fighter pilot in No. 32 Sqdn before being wounded, he was appointed to the DSO, awarded the MC, and promoted to captain. After a year in England he returned to France and completed his war service as a major commanding No. 92 Sqdn, winning the DFC. Coningham remained in uniform and in 1919 was given a permanent commission as a flight lieutenant in the new RAF. In 1925 he led a flight from Cairo across Central Africa to Kano, Nigeria, establishing the vital air route used later for supplies from the US to the Middle East, India, and the USSR.

At the start of war in 1939, Coningham was a recently promoted air commodore commanding No 4 Gp of long-range night bombers based in Yorkshire. In July 41 he went to Egypt as air vice marshal commanding the Western Desert AF in Arthur TEDDER's Middle East AF. Inspired by the Luftwaffe's example, he pioneered development of tactical air support for Allied ground troops. One of Coningham's many innovations was to send out small bomber formations with exceptionally strong fighter support; this caused disproportionately heavy losses of enemy fighters, which enabled the Allies to use progressively fewer fighters and more bombers. Knighted (KCB) after the Battle of El Alamein (4 Nov 42), Sir Arthur continued to provide tactical air support for the 8th Army until after Montgomery occupied Tripoli on 23 Jan 43.

Mary Coningham then formed the 1st Tac AF, made up of US and UK formations, establishing headquarters on 17 Feb 43 alongside Sir Harold Alexander's 18th AG Hq in Tunisia. After the Allies won the Tunisian campaign (13 May 43), Coningham's tactical air forces made history by forcing the surrender of Pantelleria, a rugged, heavily fortified island 70 miles SW of Sicily. After directing tactical air force operations in the invasion of Sicily and southern Italy, Coningham went to England in Jan 44 to head the 2d Tac AF, which had a vital role in the Normandy landings and the drive into Germany. During the last year of the war his air force had some 1,800 front-line planes and 100,000 men from seven nations. (*DNB*.)

Appointed KBE in 1946 for his final campaign and promoted to air marshal, Sir Arthur headed the Flying Training Command until retiring at his own request in 1947. Making his home near London, Coningham died 30 Jan 48 in an air accident while flying as a passenger between the Azores and Bermuda.

COMPTON, Arthur Holly. US physicist. 1892-1962. Born 10 Sep 92 at Wooster, Ohio, a younger brother of Karl COMPTON, he was from a family of remarkably successful men and women (*CB 40*). Tall, rugged, athletic, and outgoing, he worked with Ernest RUTHERFORD in England during WWI on aircraft development. Returning to the US in 1920 and serving at the Washington Univ of St Louis, he was appointed in 1923 to the chair of physics at the Univ of Chicago. Among his many early scientific honors was the Nobel Prize in physics (1927). Dr Compton had been chairman of the physics department at the Univ of Chicago since 1940 when he became an early participant in the **Manhattan project.** His contribution included directing the metallurgical program and chain reaction studies. Compton consequently was closely involved in Enrico FERMI's first controlled and sustained release of nuclear energy on 2 Dec 42. The physicist also had a major part in producing plutonium used in the atom bombs. In 1945 he became president of Washington Univ in St Louis, Mo. Arthur Compton's war memoirs are *Atomic Quest* (1956).

COMPTON, Karl T(aylor). US physicist. 1887-1954. The elder brother of Arthur (herein), born 14 Sep 87 at Wooster, Ohio, he got his PhD in physics from Princeton (1912). After teaching for the next two years at Reed College in Portland, Ore, he served in WWI as an aeronautical engineer before being scientific advisor in the Paris embassy. Returning to Princeton as a full professor, he headed the physics department from 1929. The next year he became president of the Massachusetts Institute of Technology and held the position until 1948. The MIT radiation laboratory, which Compton established, became the leading center for radar research in America. Dr Compton was one of the government's leading scientific advisers, excellent at administering a large-scale academic effort and an outstanding team captain. "When I talk to Compton," said a colleague, "I come closest to telling the truth" (*CB 41*).

CONANT, James B(ryant). US chemist and educator. 1893-1978. Born 26 Mar 93 in south Boston (Dorchester Heights), he graduated from Harvard in 1913 and got his PhD in 1916. With an interruption for army service, 1917-19, he remained at Harvard and was its president for 20 years, 1933-53. Conant was chairman of the National Defense Research Committee, 1941-46, and had a vital role in developing the atomic bomb. (*CB 41*.) Having made his reputation as an organic chemist and research scientist, Dr Conant became famous as an educator. His highly acclaimed book *General Education in a Free Society* (1945) was followed by *Education in a Divided World* (1948).

CONTI, Leonardo. Nazi doctor. 1900-45. Effectively chief physician of Nazi Germany, Conti was born 24 Aug 00 in Lugano of a Swiss-Italian father. His German mother was an ardent Nazi. The son moved to Berlin, co-founded an anti-Semitic group in Nov 18, and joined a Freikorps that took part in the **Kapp putsch.** After getting his medical degree Dr Conti joined the Brownshirts (SA) in 1923, built up their medical services, and established a private practice of general medicine in 1927. He joined the SS in 1930 and treated Horst WESSEL that year. Conti had charge of medical arrangements for the 1936 Olympic Games in Berlin. From 20 Apr 39 he was Reich health leader and state secretary for health in the Reich and Prussian Ministry of the Interior. Conti briefly directed the euthanasia program that Philip BOUHLER took over in 1939. A Martin Bormann protégé, the doctor was elected to the Reichstag in Aug 41. He was promoted to Obergruppenfuehrer on 20 Apr 44 but ousted four months later as Reich health leader. Awaiting trial in Nuremberg Prison for war crimes the doctor hanged himself on 6 Oct 45.

COOPER, Alfred Duff. British politician. 1890-1954. The only son of Lady Agnes Duff and Sir Alfred Cooper, he was born 22 Feb 90. His surname baffles indexers, who frequently list him as Duff Cooper, Alfred (WC, I, 772), rather than the correct form used at the head of this sketch (*DNB*). From two elder sisters he acquired "a love of poetry, a gift for memorizing, and the habit of declamation" (ibid.). Winning no distinction at Eton (ibid.), Cooper spent a year abroad and went up to New

College, Oxford, in 1908, and won second class honors in history (1911). After another two years in Europe he entered the Foreign Office (FO) in Oct 13 and was well past his 27th birthday when, in July 17, he obtained a release from the FO and joined the army. A superannuated platoon leader with the Grenadier Guards' 3d Bn, he survived seven months of combat in the BEF, winning appointment to the DSO and a mention in dispatches for action on 21 Aug 18. He returned to the foreign office, and in 1919 married Lady Diana Olivia Winifred Maud Manners, daughter of the 8th Duke of Rutland and a celebrated beauty with some experience on the stage. Max Reinhardt gave her the lead, as the Madonna, in his 1923 American production of *The Miracle*. Finally solvent financially, and never a happy civil servant, Cooper resigned from the FO on 31 July 24 and promptly won election to Parliament as a Conservative. Losing his seat in the general election of 1929, he worked on a biography of Talleyrand that became a classic. But he returned to Parliament in 1931 and remained until resigning in 1945. Cooper was named secretary of state for war on Nov 35 and in May 37 he became first lord of the Admiralty when Prime Minister Chamberlain succeeded Baldwin. During the Munich crisis Cooper issued orders on 28 Sep 38 to mobilized the Royal Navy, having gotten the PM's reluctant authority. As debate opened on the Munich accord, Cooper delivered a memorable speech of resignation on 3 Oct 39. (WC, I, 310, 324.)

After giving 60 lectures in the US, Cooper became minister of information on 12 May 40 in Churchill's new cabinet. But he was soon in trouble for continuing public opinion studies on censorship regulations and for other measures to counter defeatism, which the press called governmental espionage. Also at odds with colleagues over censorship policies, the unhappy minister of information asked his friend Churchill for another post. Succeeded by Brendan BRACKEN on 21 July 41, Cooper was named Chancellor of the Duchy of Lancaster, a sinecure, but one carrying Cabinet rank.

As the Japanese threat grew in the Far East, Churchill sent Cooper on a special mission to see whether the government could do more about the situation. Leaving by air on 6 Aug 41, he and Lady Diana reached Singapore on about 10 Sep 41 via Pearl Harbor, Guam, and Manila, where they had supper with MacArthur. Cooper's vague terms of reference specifically excluded military affairs, but he made visits from Burma to Australia and New Zealand. Nine days after returning to Singapore on 30 Nov 41 he was awakened at 3 AM with news that the Japanese were landing in Malaya. Singapore was under air attack a few hours later. On 11 Dec Cooper was appointed resident cabinet minister at Singapore for Far Eastern affairs, and he was authorized to form a war council (WC, III, 611-12, 426). Immediately in conflict with BROOKE-POPHAN, the new minister found himself completely redundant when WAVELL set up ABDA Command Hq in Java on 28 Dec 41. The Coopers flew out of Singapore on 13 Jan 42 for London, where—guilty by association with disaster in the Far East—he was not given a significant appointment. In June he was made chairman of the cabinet committee on security, which gave him leisure to publish a romantic study of King David.

A strong supporter of de Gaulle, Duff Cooper reached Algiers on 3 Jan 44 as ambassador to the provisional Free French government. He moved the mission to liberated Paris on 13 Sep 44 and on 18 Nov 44 presented his credentials as British ambassador. For the next three years he did much to bring about the Anglo-French treaty of Dunkirk (4 Mar 47). Ousted at the end of 1946, he retired to his house at Vineuil (outside Paris near Chantilly).

Author of highly regarded works including *Talleyrand* (1932), *Earl Haig* (1935-36), and *David* (1943), Cooper was appointed GCMG in 1948. He next published the imaginative *Sergeant Shakespeare* (1949) and *Operation Heartbreak* (1950). As Lord Norwich of Aldwick (1952) he published *Old Men Forget: The Autobiography of Duff Cooper* (London: Rupert Hart-Davis, 1953). This had been out only a few weeks when he died 1 Jan 54 while on a voyage to the West Indies. The body of Viscount Norwich was landed at Vigo (Spain) and taken for burial at Belvoir Castle. Pronounced "beaver" and located in Leicestershire, this was Lady Diana's family home. Her memoirs, as rich in details about Viscount Norwich as of herself, are *The Rainbow Comes and Goes* (1958), *The Light of Common Day* (1958), and *Trumpets from the Steep* (1960). The books have been combined in the *Diana Cooper Autobiography* (New York: Carroll & Graff, 1985).

CORAP, André Georges. French general. 1878-1953. The portly, hard-faced old colonial warrior was famous for capturing Abd-el-Krim by a coup de main in 1926 (while serving under Giraud) as a discouraged PETAIN was about to sign an armistice agreement (Pertinax, 327n). "We later paid dearly for this feat of Corap's, since he was rewarded beyond his abilities" (ibid.). As head of the 2d Mil Region (Amiens), Corap commanded the 9th French Army when the "phony war" turned real on 10 May 40. As prescribed by the **Dyle plan** he wheeled north to positions on the Meuse between Namur and Flize, just west of Sedan. The French reached the Meuse on 11-12 May to find German troops had arrived first (Pertinax, 59). Under heavy air attack, hard hit frontally by the panzer corps of HOTH and REINHARDT at two points, the 9th Army was threatened with envelopment of their fight flank when Charles Huntzinger's 2d Army collapsed around Sedan. Corap's army was "pulverised" (Spears, I, 148). A few units maintained cohesion while retreating to reserve positions during the night of 14-15 May, but BILLOTTE phoned GEORGES at dawn on the 15th to recommend that Giraud replace Corap (Horne, *1940*, 368). "I left at 0400 on the 16th, heartbroken," wrote Corap. Trading posts with Giraud, Corap headed the 7th Army until the 19th, when Georges told him that Daladier had ordered his final dismissal. (Pertinax, 69n.) Reynaud publicly condemned Corap on 21 May for the disaster on the frontier, implying that the general might be charged with treason for leaving Meuse River bridges intact, but Huntzinger was promoted!

Georges later testified that it was "not fair to put all the blame on Corap, as some have done" (Shirer, *France*, 673n). After accompanying the government to Bordeaux in an futile effort to clear his name, Corap retired to his home at Fontainebleau. Finally exonerated during the **Riom trial** and in Paul Allard's book *Corap and the Loss of the Meuse Line* (1941), the general remained aloof from subsequent debate.

CORK AND ORRERY, William Henry Dudley Boyle, 12th Earl. British admiral. 1873-1967. "Ginger Boyle" was born 30 Nov 73 at Hale, Farnham, and commissioned in 1887. Knighted KCB in 1931 and promoted the next year to full admiral, Sir William became CinC Home Fleet in 1933. He succeeded to the title 12th Earl of Cork and Orrery the next year.

The short, ramrod-straight Lord Cork was called Ginger Boyle for his fiery red hair and disposition. His aristocratic air was enhanced by an ever-present monocle. The elderly salt was scheduled to retire from active service after heading the Home Fleet, but the unexpected death of Adm Sir William Fisher in 1937 left a vacancy which he was appointed to fill in the Portsmouth Command. In Feb 38 he was selected for admiral of the fleet, another vacancy having occurred.

Still fully fit for active duty after the normal two year tour at Porstmouth in 1939 and seeking a war assignment, he was given charge of an expedition raised to assist the Finns in fighting off the Soviet invasion that began on 30 Nov 39. But access was barred by Sweden, which hoped to remain neutral. Two days after Hitler attacked Norway on 8 Apr 40, Cork was appointed Flag Officer Narvik in command of the forces that had been raised to fight in Finland. At Harstad, a small port just north of Narvik being used as the Allied base, Ginger Boyle first met Maj Gen P. J. Mackesy, the designated joint commander of army troops, whose brigade was already there. When the two proved to have what Lord Cork called "diametrically opposed views" the admiral was given overall command on 21 April of all forces committed to retake Narvik. From 7 May he also had operational control of Allied troops in the Mosjoen-Bodo area (Ziemke, *GNT*, 325).

Gen Macksey directed the assault on Narvik which started 15 May 40 with landings of British, French, and Polish units north of the port. These troops were supported by Norwegians under Gen Carl FLEISCHER. French and Norwegian troops took Narvik on 28 May by direct assault, and Eduard DIETL's situation was desperate until a powerful German column moved north with air and naval support to drive Allied troops from the Mosjoen-Bodo area by 31 May. After destroying the dock facilities for Swedish iron ore that made Narvik so important strategically, Lord Cork extricated his forces on 8 June 40.

Now almost 70, he saw no further action. In 1941 he headed an inquiry that vindicated James SOMERVILLE's decision to discontinue an indecisive naval action off Spartivento. A commanding presence to the end of a long life, Ginger Boyle died 19 Apr 67 in London.

COT, Pierre. French politician. 1895-. From a *petite bourgeoise* family of the Savoy (French Alps), the small, dynamic Cot (an ardent mountaineer) was highly decorated in 1914-18. He went on to get a doctor of laws degree at Grenoble and a degree in political and economic sciences at the Sorbonne before becoming a professor of public law and of international public law at the Univ of Rennes (Brittany). Elected to the chamber of deputies in 1928 as a Radical Socialist, he represented his Savoyard constituents without interruption and with strong majorities until 1940. Meanwhile Cot was minister of aviation twice between 31 Jan 33 (in Daladier's first government) and 18 Jan 38. But he was "more concerned with vague dreams of international disarmament, and with solving the [aircraft] industry's problems at home by nationalization than with laying down any solid programme of rearmament" (Horne, *1940*, 82). When the vigorous Guy LA CHAMBRE replaced Cot it was too late.

Taking refuge in America with his American wife and their three children when France fell, Cot gave a graduate seminar in government at Yale from early 1941. In addition to writing an important, if self-serving, book *Triumph of Treason* (1944) and articles on French politics for *Foreign Affairs* and other scholarly journals, he worked for the French cause. Cot joined de Gaulle at Algiers in late 1943 and was elected to the Consultative Assembly. In Mar 44 DE GAULLE sent him to Moscow "on a special mission to study [political] rehabilitation" (*CB 44*).

In 1964 was it discovered that Cot had been an active Soviet spy since before the war. The British secret service (MI5) got the proof from **Venona** transcripts. But Pierre Cot was "left to die in peace" (Peter Wright, 239-41).

COWAN, Walter Henry. British officer. 1871-1956. Born 11 June 71 at Crickhowell, Breconshire, Sir Walter (1919) was a full admiral (1927) who went on to the retired list in 1931. Baronet of the Baltic and of Bilton (1921), the 68-year-old admiral was assistant secretary to the Warwickshire Hounds when Britain went to war in 1939. (*DNB*.) Eager for action, he wangled an appointment to the commandos that were being formed by his friend and former chief Roger KEYES. With the rank of commander he served in Egypt and the western desert until his commando unit was disbanded, then Cowan attached himself to the 18th King Edward VII's Own Cavalry, an Indian Army regiment. He saw action in the desert until captured 27 May 42 near Bir Hacheim while fighting an Italian tank crew single handed and armed only with a revolver. Repatriated in 1943, the salty septuagenarian rejoined the commandos for action in the Dalmatian Islands. In 1944 he was awarded a bar to the DSO he had won in 1898. Finally feeling his age (73), Sir William went back on the retired list in 1945. In a remarkable military career he was never wounded. Returning to Kineton, Warwickshire, he received a final military honor on 22 Nov 46 when appointed honorary colonel of the regiment he had served with in North Africa. The admiral died 14 Feb 56 in the hospital at Leamington. (*DNB*.)

COWARD, Noel Peirce. British theatrical figure. 1899–1973. Actor, playwright, composer, producer, and author, he figured in WWII as a morale builder and propagandist. Coward was born 16 Dec 99 at Teddington, Middlesex, into a musical family. He became a homosexual of "impeccable dignity . . . untainted by pretense," in the words of his close friend Dame Rebecca West (quoted in *DNB*).

The movie *In Which We Serve* (1942) was based closely on the life and death of MOUNT-BATTEN's destroyer *Kelly*. In addition to writing, directing, and producing the film, Coward played Mountbatten, his good friend. Another inspirational film was *This Happy Breed* (1942). During the war he also wrote the lighthearted *Blithe Spirit* (1941) and *Present Laughter* (1942).

But the gay British entertainer brought out the worst in Vinegar Joe Stilwell. It was the summer of 1944, a trying period in the Burma campaign, when Stilwell outraged Mountbatten, his senior as theater commander, by refusing to provide airlift for Coward and his company to entertain US troops at Ledo. Forced to renege but delighted that the performance fell somewhat flat, Stilwell wired his deputy commander of CBI, "If any more piano players start up this way, you know what to do with the piano." (Allen, *Burma*, 378.)

Coward became enchanted with Jamaica in 1948 and built two houses there. In one of

them, Firefly Hill, the artist died suddenly on 26 Mar 73.

Biographical works are Sheridan Morley (ed), *Noel Coward Autobiography* (1986); Cole Lesley, *The Life of Noel Coward* (1976); Charles Castle, *Noel* (1972); and Sheridan Morley, *A Talent to Amuse* (1969). The latter words are on the black memorial stone unveiled in Westminster Abbey in 1984. (*DNB*.)

CRABB, Lionel Philip. British frogman. 1910-56. Apprenticed to the Merchant Navy and serving on a run between Buenos Aires and NYC, he left the sea when about to be examined for a second mate's ticket. (Pugh, *Frogman*, 26-27.) An affable drifter, he pumped gas at a service station in Wingap, Pa, before joining a cousin in a London advertising business and selling out as soon as the business prospered. Crabb spent time in Singapore on two occasions before returning to London in 1938. Virtually destitute, he tried to join the navy, a childhood ambition, but was rejected for being too old at 28. Crabb was a merchant seaman gunner for a year before he was accepted by the Royal Navy Patrol Service. Lt Crabb went to Gibraltar in Nov 42 as a mine and bomb disposal officer. Prince BORGHESE's frogmen were attacking British ships here and elsewhere, and Crabb became involved in developing countermeasures. Although "opposed to any form of exercise" (Pugh, *Frogman*, 26), always a weak swimmer, and with poor vision in his left eye, the gnome-like seaman showed an aptitude for developing equipment and techniques for underwater warfare. Rising to the rank of commander, becoming legendary for his exploits in the Mediterranean, Crabb was awarded the George Medal in 1944. At end of the war he was appointed to the DSO for work as head of the Venice Underwater Working Party. He went on to perform antisabotage duties in Israel, remaining involved in diving, got interested in underwater photography, and took part in several marine rescue and salvage operations in England. The famous frogman was again running out of money when MI6 gave him a covert assignment (Peter Wright, 73-74). The Admiralty wanted to know whether there was something special about the hull or propellor of the Soviet heavy cruiser *Ordzhonikidze* to make her so fast. An earlier effort had been aborted, but the big ship and two destroyers lay in Portsmouth harbor after bringing Bulganin and Khrushchev for a state visit in the spring of 1956.

Overweight, overage, and ripe for a heart attack (ibid.), Crabb and a Bernard Smith checked into a Portsmouth hotel on 17 Apr 56 and registered under their own names. Two days later it was reported that Crabb had disappeared in the harbor, "presumed drowned." The Admiralty denied knowledge of any "dirty tricks," and PM Anthony Eden said in the House of Commons on 4 May that "It would not be in the public interest to disclose the circumstances in which Commander Crabb is presumed to have met his death." Two days later Moscow Radio broadcast a note in which the Soviets said a frogman had been seen floating between the Soviet destroyers at 7:30 AM on 19 Apr and said it was confirmed that British naval authorities had carried out secret underwater tests around the Soviet warships that "resulted in the death of the British frogman." (Pugh, 206.) A headless, mutilated, unidentifiable corpse in a frogman's suit later washed ashore near Portsmouth. (Brown, *"C,"* 724.) The British government implied that Crabb had been freelancing.

CRACE, John G. British admiral. 1887-1968. (Sir) John Crace (pronounced "Crayse") entered the RN in 1902, saw action in WWI, and as a rear admiral in 1942 commanded a squadron of the ANZAC Force covering sea approaches from Rabaul. First he had the vital if unromantic role of escorting US tankers during Adm Wilson BROWN's daring carrier assault of 21 Feb 42 on Rabaul and his brilliant transmontane strike of 10 Mar 42 on Japanese shipping off Lae and Salamaua. With his TF 14 (aka "Support Gp") he joined Rear Adm "Black Jack" FLETCHER's TF 17 (CVs *Yorktown* and *Lexington*) at 9:30 AM on 6 May in the Coral Sea. The heavy engagement was about to begin the next day when Fletcher, worried that Port Moresby would be undefended if he lost the carrier battle, finally gave the energetic British admiral his long-sought chance to do more than "chaperone oilers." Sent on what Morison calls "Crace's Chase," he sailed westward at 6:30 AM, 7 May. Just before 2 PM, when about 100 miles off the SE tip of New Guinea, the Support Gp came under a heavy attack that lasted an hour. An excellent seaman, Crace had ordered a diamond-shaped AA formation and his ships, which lacked air cover, quickly drove off ll land-

based, single-engined planes. Soon attacked by 12 "Sallys," twin-engine, land-based torpedo bombers, the Allied force downed five bombers without suffering a hit. Then DD *Farragut* narrowly escaped an attack by three bombers, which were positively identified later as B-17s from Townsville, Australia. (Gen George H. BRETT denied the charge and prohibited further discussion [ibid.]). Crace continued his course west until informed that Port Moresby was safe. Aside from providing a useful, if unintentional, strategic diversion, he had showed outstanding seamanship in not taking a single hit in an attack as strong as the one that had sent the inexperienced Adm Tom PHILLIPS to the bottom with *Prince of Wales* and *Repulse* off Malaya on 10 Dec 41. Crace also had demonstrated that ships of two nations could be trained to be an excellent tactical unit. (Morison, IV, 37-39; *S&S* map, p. 139.) Soon after sailing south to constitute the main strength of "MacArthur's Navy" the vigorous Crace retired from active duty to be superintendent of the RN dockyard at Chatham until 1946. The previous year he was promoted to admiral on the retired list.

CRERAR, Henry Duncan Graham. Canadian general. 1888-1965. The first Canadian to command a field army in battle, Crerar (pronounced kree-rahr) was born in Hamilton, Ontario, of Scots ancestry. Soon after graduating from the Canadian RMC in 1910 as a field artilleryman he resigned because the pay was insufficient. But in 1914 Crerar went overseas with the Canadian Expeditionary Force, saw action in Belgium and France, and as a 31-year-old lieutenant colonel remained in uniform.

After being director of military operations 1935-39 he was commandant of the RMC. Now a general he headed the Canadian planning staff in the UK. Here Robert G. L. McNAUGHTON arrived in Dec 39 to head the first Canadian contingent to reach England. This was built up to five divisions including those that distinguished themselves in Sicily and Italy under Guy G. SIMONDS.

In July 40 Crerar returned to Canada to be CGS. But a month after promotion to lieutenant general on 22 Nov 41 he voluntarily took a reduction in rank to head the 2d Cdn Inf Div overseas. The 1st Cdn Corps Hq was formed late in 1941 with Crerar as acting head, but it had no troops assigned.

After McNAUGHTON finally had 2d Cdn Corp Hq activated in Italy on 1 Feb 44 Crerar commanded it until 3 Mar 44 and returned to England. (Nicholson, *Italy*, 340-84.) Crerar's 1st Cdn Army Hq became operational in Normandy on 23 Jul 44 to comprise the 1st Br Corps and SIMONDS's 2d Cdn Corps. Taking over the Caen front, where Simonds already had been heavily engaged, Crerar launched phase two of Opn Totalize. Not "as vigorous and venturesome as the occasion demanded" (Wilmot, 410), he could not capitalize on the opportunity to trap and destroy most of KLUGE's forces by driving to Falaise and linking up with PATTON.

German resistance at Falaise ending on 18 Aug and the breakout finally achieved, Crerar led his two corps north. But while other Allied armies made spectacular gains through shattered enemy forces, Crerar's army became "the Cinderella of Eisenhower's forces" (Wilmot, 542). The Canadian general had the mission of overrunning missile launching sites and eliminating the "fortresses" of Le Havre, Boulogne, and Calais. But he attacked each port in turn, not appreciating until too late that these places (like Singapore) were highly vulnerable from the land side. (Wilmot, 542.) Although the assaults cost only 1,500 casualties, it was not until 1 Oct 44 that Crerar took the last fortress.

Toward the end of Opn Market-Garden, Montgomery belatedly gave Crerar the mission, on 27 Sep 44, of clearing the Schelde estuary. The delay allowed the Germans to organize defenses in the maze of waterways and islands between the sea and Antwerp. The 1st Cdn Army eventually needed help from the 1st Br Army and the 1st US Army. As the arduous campaign approached a climax, Crerar had to turn over command to his brilliant subordinate, SIMONDS, and go to England on 27 Sep 44 for dysentery treatment. Returning as Simonds's unconventional plan for taking Walchern Island, which Crerar had opposed initially, was proving to be a success, Crerar waited until 9 Nov to resume command. Promoted exactly a week later to full general, Crerar became the first Canadian to hold that rank in the field (Stacey, III, 426).

During the Ardennes crisis in December, the 1st Cdn Army remained relatively inactive around Antwerp. (Ironically, this was Hitler's main objective.) Starting 8 Feb 45 and his army augmented by the 30th Br Corps, Crerar attacked SE from the Nijmegen bridgehead. Through difficult terrain, in bitter winter weather, and against fanatic resistance, the 1st Cdn Army broke through the last defended section of the Siegfried Line (at Udem) on 27 Feb 45. All resistance in Montgomery's zone ended with the German surrender on 5 May. Having at one time or another had British, Belgian, Dutch, Polish, and US units in his Canadian army, which reached a maximum strength of 500,000, Crerar sailed for Canada on 30 July 45. The next year he retired from military service.

CRIPPS, (Richard) Stafford. British official. 1889–1952. Youngest son of the 1st Baron Parmoor, born 24 Apr 89 in London, Cripps was a brilliant chemist before becoming a lawyer in 1913. He was physically unfit for military service but drove an ambulance in France in 1914 and the next year was assistant superintendent in a munitions factory. In 1929 Cripps joined the Labour Party but was too far left politically to get along with the leadership. Sir Stafford (1930) helped found the Socialist League in 1932, and in 1936 he advocated forming a united front in Britain to include communists. When this political technique was revived in 1938 as a Liberal-Labor **popular front** to oppose CHAMBERLAIN's appeasement of fascism, Cripps was expelled from the party. On 20 May 40 he was appointed ambassador to Moscow. Finding the assignment unattractive and succeeded by Archibald Clark-Kerr, Cripps returned to London on 23 Jan 42. (WC, IV, 63.) He declined to head the ministry of supply but accepted the key posts of lord privy seal, leader of the house of commons, and a seat on the war cabinet. By Nov 42 Sir Stafford was so dissatisfied with the British war effort in general and Churchill's stewardship in particular that he resigned on 3 Oct 42 (WC, IV, 554-60). The next month he became minister of aircraft production, holding this post for the duration. In July 45 he was readmitted to the Labor party and appointed president of the London Board of Trade.

On a visit to India in 1942 Cripps had failed to reconcile factional differences that stood in the way of independence. He failed again in 1946, and MOUNTBATTEN cut the Gordian knot. During the crisis of 1947 Sir Stafford was minister for economic affairs for a few weeks before succeeding Hugh Dalton as chancellor of the exchequer. Long in poor health, he resigned on 20 Oct 50 and died 18 months later in Zurich of a spinal infection. (*DNB.*)

CRITTENBERGER, Willis Dale. US general. 1890-1980. Born 2 Dec 90 in Indiana, he graduated from West Point in 1913 (24/93) and joined the cavalry. An imposing officer, he was an instructor at the C&GSS, CofS 1st Armd Div, Patton's successor as CG 2d Armd Div (Feb-July 42), and CG 3d Armd Corps (Sep 42-Oct 43). After all this Stateside service he reached Italy on 26 Mar 44 with his 4th Corps Hq. Crittenberger commanded the coastal sector near Naples and did not enter action until June, when Truscott's 6th Corps withdrew to prepare for the campaign in southern France.

Crittenberger's corps took Leghorn on 19 July, closed on the Arno River west of Florence, and was in action for the rest of the Italian campaign. Getting his third star on 3 Jun 45 and leaving the soon-to-be-inactivated headquarters three months later, Crittenberger headed the Caribbean Defense Command Oct 45-June 48. After holding a series of international staff posts he commanded the 1st Army 1950-52 before retiring as a lieutenant general. He died 4 Aug 80 in Bethesda, Md. (Cullum.)

CRUEWELL, Ludwig. German general. 1892-1958. Described as "a real cavalier type, the son of a wealthy Dortmund family of printers whose fortunes rested on a church monopoly of hymnbook publishing (Irving, *Fox,* 130), Cruewell was born 20 Mar 92. He enlisted as an officer candidate assigned to the 9th Dragoons at Metz, was a cavalry lieutenant when war broke out in 1914. Promoted in 1916, Oberleutnant Cruewell was made a regimental adjutant, and in 1918 he was selected for retention in the Reichswehr. A colonel by 1939 he had various command assignments in Poland and France. He was promoted to Generalmajor on 1 Aug 40 and given command of the 11th Pz Div, which was activated on that date. In von Kleist's 1st Pz Gp he spearheaded von Wietersheim's 14th Pz Corps and his tanks began rolling into Belgrade from the south around 6:30 AM. on 13 April. Three columns entered the Yugoslav capital almost simultaneously, but Cruewell was awarded the RK on 14 May for "taking Belgrade." (Angolia, II, 45; B&O, 93; DA Pamph 20-260, 54.) The 11th Pz

then pursued and destroyed surviving elements of the Yugoslav army.

In Kleist's 1st Pz Gp of AG South for Opn Barbarossa, the fierce panzer commander was promoted to Generalleutnant and made such a reputation in the Ukraine that Rommel requested he be assigned to North Africa. Leaving the 11th Pz on 14 Aug 41 (B&O 94) for a long period of hospitalization and convalescent leave, Generalleutnant Cruewell was awarded the Oakleaves (34/89) on 1 Sep 41. He was the first divisional commander so honored. (Angolia, II, 46.)

The **Afrika Korps** (DAK) had been essentially leaderless for two months when Cruewell assumed command in Oct 41. He had little time before AUCHINLECK launched Opn Crusader on 17 Nov 41. But a "curious relationship" quickly developed between Cruewell and Rommel. "Intellectually . . . [Cruewell] was head and shoulders above Rommel," writes David Irving (*Fox*, 130). But the new DAK commander also revealed a psychological superiority that "often showed him acting with an independence bordering on disobedience, and in retrospect it is remarkable that the field marshal [Rommel] put up with it." (Ibid.) Col Fritz BAYERLEIN, Cruewell's brilliant CofS, to whom Rommel took an instant liking (ibid., 118), figured prominently in this "curious relationship."

Cruewell was promoted to Gen of Pz Troops on 1 Dec 41, about a month before Axis forces were driven back to El Agheila. Rommel's second offensive began 21 Jan 42, his force becoming Pz Army Africa on 30 Jan (B&O, 29n). Cruewell was acting commander of this army while Rommel was on sick leave 9-19 Mar 42. In the desperate attacks on the Gazala Line, Cruewell was trying to reach Rommel (trapped around Bir el Harmat) when his light plane was shot down on 29 May 42 by the 150th Bde Gp (Jackson, 214). While being shown through Shepheard's Hotel in Cairo, the stern, distinguished-looking POW quipped "It will make a grand headquarters for Rommel!" (Irving, op cit, 173-74). A brilliant career shortened by three years in British POW camps, Cruewell died in Essen at the age of 66.

CRUTCHLEY, Victor Alexander Charles. British admiral. 1893-1986. As captain of BB *Warspite* he became an expert at dealing with

U-boats on the high seas. On 15 May 40 his task force, built around *Warspite*, facing attack by land-based air off Narvik, he was unable to exploit WARBURTON-LEE'S gallant assault of 10 Ar 40. But three days later he sank the last eight of the 10 destroyers supporting Eduard DIETL's troops at Narvik. Crutchley left Warspite after Lord CORK withdrew the Allied expedition to Norway and he became commodore of the Royal Naval Barracks at Devonport.

Late in the spring of 1942 he took command of the Australian cruiser squadron that had been under Adm Sir John CRACE. In "MacArthur's navy" and based at Brisbane he was screening the Slot as US Marines landed on Guadalcanal in early Aug 42. After approving Crutchley's deployment, US Adm R. Kelly TURNER called Crutchley to a conference. Hence the screening force commander was 20 miles away when a powerful enemy column under Gunichi MIKAWA charged through The Slot at high speed, moving under the cover of darkness and foul weather. The US Navy, not trained for night operations in heavy seas, suffered a humiliating defeat in the Battle off Savo Island, 8-9 Aug 42. Adm D. J. CALLAHAN was among the many lost.

American attempts to make the British admiral a scapegoat were quickly proved to be unjustified (Morison, V, 64n), and he served the rest of the war in MacArthur's theater of operations.

CUNNINGHAM, Alan Gordon. British general. 1887-1983. A younger brother of the admiral (following), he saw action on the western front with the Royal Horse Artillery, winning the MC in 1915 and appointment to the DSO in 1918. In the latter year he was promoted to major general commanding the 5th AA Div. Late in 1940 Lt Gen Cunningham was appointed GOC East African Forces in Kenya. Small, handsome, and energetic, his jovial charm interrupted occasionally by flashes of temper, Cunningham directed a masterful campaign that called for outstanding logistical skill in arduous terrain and coordination of far flung columns. With the 11th and 12th African Divs and the 1st South African Div, he attacked north into Abyssinia on 24 Jan 41. The first phase of the campaign, in which a detachment from Aden linked up, ended 22 May 41 at Soddu after Cunningham's forces met a column of PLATT's troops from the Sudan.

Dogged Italian resistance in northern Abyssinia ended 27 Nov 41 when Platt and Cunninghan converged on Gondar. Sustaining only 500 casualties, the British bagged 50,000 POWs including the Duke of AOSTA. A conquering hero when these were few on the Allied side, Cunningham was honored with both the CB and KCB in 1941.

Sir Alan succeeded Richard O'CONNOR in Aug 42 as 8th Army commander in the western desert. "Cunningham was a magnificent-looking chap," commented Brigadier Gatehouse, a highly regarded veteran of earlier fighting in North Africa. "I thought, this is the man" (Barnett, *Desert Generals*, 84-85.) But Sir Alan was "rather like the successful owner of a village shop suddenly put in charge of a London department store" (ibid.). With only two months until AUCHINLECK launched Opn Crusader on 18 Nov 41, without experience in armored war, and facing the Desert Fox, Sir Alan was replaced as 8th Army commander by Neil RITCHIE on the eighth day of Crusader. Auchinleck withheld the news and persuaded Sir Alan to enter an Alexandria hospital under an assumed name for treatment. Commenting on this controversial action, Barnett concludes that "the Auk" concocted a white lie in hopes of sparing the feelings of a gallant but exhausted subordinate who was suffering a clear case of nervous breakdown (ibid., 120).

Sir Alan became commandant of **Camberley** in 1942, headed British troops in Northern Ireland from Oct 43 to the end of 1944, then was back in East Africa as GOC Eastern Command. On 21 Nov 45 he reached Jerusalem to succeed Lord GORT as high commissioner and CinC for Palestine and Transjordan. Leaving that trouble spot in 1948, he was elevated in the knighthood to GCMG. In retirement he was deputy county lieutenant of Hampshire and commandant of the Royal Artillery (1944-54).

CUNNINGHAM, Andrew Browne ("ABC"). British admiral. 1883-1963. One of two elder brothers of Sir Alan (above), he was born in Dublin on 7 Jan 83 into a prominent Scots family of doctors and churchmen. Although none of his forebears were seamen, Andrew took an early interest in boats. (*DNB.*) After three years in a preparatory school for the Royal Navy and 16 months aboard HMS *Britannia* (1897-98), he volunteered for service with the Naval Brigade during the Boer War. From this grass-roots experience Cunningham got an appreciation for the unique qualities of British seamen and also learned the importance of training.

ABC commanded DD *Scorpion* from 1911 until 1918, seeing much action in the Mediterranean learning the waters in which he would earn fame in WWII. Of medium height, compact, "with a rosy, weatherbeaten complexion," he was "a man of human warmth, sympathy, and generosity, although he did not suffer fools gladly, and had no use for slackers." (Peter Kemp in Carver, ed, *The War Lords,* 464.) He was said to have "flung out" 12 of his first lieutenants from *Scorpion* (ibid.). Crews marveled at his seamanship, claiming "he could cut an egg in half with a battleship" *(CB 41).*

A captain for 13 years, Cunningham was promoted in 1932 to "rear admiral (destroyers)" in the Mediterranean, the assignment he most coveted, and was commanding destroyer flotillas in the Mediterranean when Mussolini's empire builders were active in Libya and Abyssinia. Disgusted by not being permitted to fight, he nevertheless benefited from the planning and extensive maneuvers conducted in anticipation of war with Italy.

He was promoted to vice admiral in July 36 but prospects for other interesting duty were dim when he got the first in a long succession of advancements that followed the unexpected replacement of senior admirals for reasons of health. In 1937, Cunningham succeeded the ailing Sir Geoffrey Blake as commander of the Mediterranean fleet. Soon after the Munich crisis of 1938, Cunningham became deputy CNS in London. When 1st Sea Lord Sir Roger Backhouse fell ill and no successor was on hand, Cunningham had a key role in naval planning at a critical time. ABC never liked such duty, but in early June 39 luck intervened again: he succeeded Sir Dudley POUND as CinC Mediterranean Station, with the acting rank of full admiral, when Pound replaced Backhouse in London.

No fighting occurred in the Mediterranean until Italy entered the war on 10 June 40. France signed an armistice with the Germans a few days later and Cunningham was given the nasty task of winning over or neutralizing elements of the French navy accessible to him. In Alexandria he did this without bloodshed, but not at **Mers el Kebir.**

Cunningham's main concern thereafter was to protect convoys in his section of a 3,500-mile LofC through the Mediterranean to Egypt and the Middle East. For this task he had old ships, and not enough of them. Initially he had no long-range aircraft, almost no carrier aircraft, and no landbased fighter cover. Axis air attacks made the main British naval base at Malta virtually useless. Gibraltar and the western Mediterranean were similarly interdicted, and Egypt lacked major naval facilities.

The Italians eased Cunningham's task by refusing to risk their sleek new ships in a showdown, but they remained a threat. After failing to draw the Italians into action on 9 July 40 off Calabria, Cunningham made naval history at **Taranto,** 11 Nov 40. With German intervention in North Africa and Greece, Cunningham faced huge new problems. He may be faulted along with WAVELL for not coming out squarely against trying to help the Greeks when Churchill still might have been talked out of it. But Cunningham got the most out of his battered forces during the ill-advised adventure and his skippers defied almost constant air attack to reach new heights of valor. "Stick it out," Cunningham signaled toward the end, "we must never let the Army down."

Greece and Crete cost the Mediterranean fleet 2,000 lives, 2 of its 4 battleships, its only aircraft carrier, 5 cruisers, and 8 destroyers.

Personal leadership and optimism enabled Cunningham to muddle through the dark months that followed. His fleet was dangerously reduced just as its mission became more difficult—loss of destroyers being particularly serious—but Cunningham kept the LofC open through Gibraltar, Malta, and Tobruk. ABC left the Mediterranean in June 42 for duty in London with the combined chiefs of staff, replaced by Sir Henry Harwood. Cunningham's reputation with the enemy was so great that the change was not made public for three months. By that time the admiral's luck again intervened to relieve him from the staff duty he so detested: ABC became Eisenhower's naval CinC for the North African landings. As Allied land forces converged on Tunis, ABC got the additional title of Allied CinC Mediterranean. Based on Malta, he planned the amphibious phases of the campaign to take Sicily, the leap across the narrow Strait of Messina, and the Salerno landings. Cunningham took the surrender of the Italian fleet on 10 Sep 43 after it sailed into Malta.

Luck again created a vacancy for ABC as he completed 39 months of war in the Mediterranean, where for the first two years he faced "the heaviest odds in British naval history" (Bryant, *Tide,* 406). His appointment as first sea lord was announced on 4 Oct 43, when Churchill accepted the fatally ill Sir Dudley POUND's resignation. But the effective date was 21 Oct 43, when Pound died (WC, V, 164). Sir John CUNNINGHAM (no kin) took over as CinC Mediterranean.

Planning for the Normandy invasion being almost finished, the first sea lord sought a new role for the Royal Navy when their forces were no longer needed in European waters. Churchill convinced Roosevelt to overule the parochial and angloplobic Adm Ernest KING, CNO, who wanted no part of the Royal Navy in the Pacific. Politics aside, King was absolutely right, if largely for the wrong reasons: the US navy had perfected the use of far ranging, independent carrier strikes, which involved complex naval logistics; it was too late in the war to bring in a new partner.

Knighted in 1939, a baron in 1945, he became the 1st Viscount of Hyndhope on 1 Jan 46. Retiring that year, and succeeded again by Sir John Cunningham, he was twice lord high commissioner to the General Assembly of the Church of Scotland (1950 and 1955). During these years he published *A Sailor's Odyssey* (1951). The admiral died suddenly on 12 June 63 in London and was buried off Portsmouth.

CUNNINGHAM, John Henry Dacres. British admiral. 1885-1962. He was born 13 Apr 85 at Demerara, in what then was British Guiana. After initial naval training aboard *Britannia* (1900-01), he was a midshipman in *Gibraltar,* off South Africa, and went on to specialize in navigation.

In June 39 he was promoted to vice admiral and went to the Mediterranean as commander of the first cruiser squadron. This reinforced the Home Fleet when war broke out. Cunningham's squadron supported CARTON DE WIART in Norway, took King HAAKON VII and his party from Andalsnes to Tromso and on to Britain.

The admiral was co-commander, with Maj Gen N. M. S. Irwin, of DE GAULLE's hapless attempt to take Dakar, 23-25 Sep 40. Early the next year he began a gruelling tour of more than two years as fourth sea lord (supplies and transport).

Sir John (KCB in 1941) was appointed CinC Levant in June 43. The separate naval command was set up to comprise the eastern Mediterranean after the Tunisian campaign ended. Sir John was an acting admiral for two months in this post before getting the actual rank. He also was deputy to Andrew CUNNINGHAM (no kin), whom he succeeded in Oct 43 as Allied CinC Mediterranean. Sir John succeeded ABC in May 46 as first sea lord and **CNS**. The namesakes were quite different, Sir John being somewhat of an intellectual and a dour, sarcastic, hard-nosed man who seldom praised subordinates. *(DNB.)* He was promoted to fleet admiral in Jan 48 and retired the following September to spend the next 10 years as chairman of the Iraq Petroleum Co. The admiral died 13 Dec 62 in the Middlesex Hospital.

CURRIE, Lauchlin Bernard. US presidential assistant. 1902-83. Born in West Dublin, Nova Scotia, he got his BS from the London School of Economics in 1925. That year he went to Harvard, where he taught, wrote, earned his PhD (1931), and gained renown as a Keynesian economist. The short, self-assured Scot got US citizenship in 1934, when he became a senior analyst for Treasury Secretary Morgenthau. In July 39 Currie became Roosevelt's personal economic adviser and one of his six administrative assistants. Called by his many detractors an inflexible enthusiast, a consummate academician who looked at China through the eyes of a Keynesian economist, Currie undertook the first in a series of missions to China in Jan 41. At first he thought STILWELL had the right approach toward helping China, but on 24 Aug 42 he recommended that the general, Amb Clarence E. Gauss, and T. V. SOONG be recalled for having irreconcilable differences with Chiang Kai-shek. No action was taken, but the economist's wrongheaded convictions grew during the next two years until the China Lobby finally won out. Barbara Tuchman, an Old China Hand, dismisses Currie as "a man of small stature and compensating self-esteem."

CURTIN, John. Australian PM. 1885-1945. Born at Creswick, Victoria, on 8 Jan 85, he was the son of a policeman. After attending state schools he worked first as a printer's devil in a country newspaper and quickly became interested in labor politics. He was secretary of the Victorian branch of the Timber Worker's Union in Melbourne, 1911-15. Leaving to be secretary of the Anti-Conscription League and going to prison for his activities, Curtin turned to journalism in 1917 and became editor of the weekly *Westralian Worker* in Perth. In 1928 he was elected to represent Freemantle in the Australian parliament, holding the seat continuously except for a break in 1931-34, and rising to head the Australian Labor Party in 1935. Curtin was an uncharismatic man of frail physique and impaired eyesight, but he commanded respect for great sincerity and strong character *(CB 41; DNB)*. As opposition leader Curtin refused to join Sir Robert MENZIES's coalition government, which was formed after Britain declared war on 3 Sep 39. But this was in accordance with Labor Party rules, and Curtin pledged his party's support in the war against Germany. When the Arthur Fadden's government lost a vote of confidence on 3 Oct 41 Curtin became prime minister. Australia was not yet under direct threat from the Japanese, and the previous government had sent about four divisions to bolster British defenders of Egypt and the Near East.

Seeking more political independence for Australia, Curtin took actions that alarmed other members of the British Commonwealth: Australia separately declared war on Japan; Curtin accepted that Australia needed American help, and he frankly sought closer ties. But he also remained a strong supporter of the Commonwealth.

What Churchill calls "a painful episode in our relations with the Australian Government" involved Curtin's refusal to send troops to defend Burma. On 20 Feb 42, as Australian forces sailed home in convoy from the Middle East, Churchill asked Curtin for authority divert the leading division to Rangoon. Roosevelt supported Churchill in this crisis (WC, IV, 155-66) but Curtin refused. He said he feared (quite justifiably) "a repetition of the experiences of the Greek and Malayan campaigns." (Ibid., 162.)

The Australian PM doubled as defense minister during the worst part of the national crisis but then relinquished the post to concentrate on foreign affairs to include postwar planning. Late in 1943 he proposed creating a Commonwealth Command in SE Asia to counterbalance MacArthur's dominance, but he did not prevail (Tunney). After D day in Normandy reduced the need for Allied naval power in Europe, Curtin suggested that elements of the Royal Navy move into the Pacific, as did Churchill and Andrew CUNNINGHAM. Despite the strong objections of Ernest J. KING, US CNO, this came to pass.

Curtin had had difficulties in parliament for about the first two years of his tenure because his cabinet was inexperienced and the Labor party did not have a majority in the house. In June 43 he escaped a censure motion by only one vote, but he won a huge victory in the general election that followed. Despite a serious lung congestion that developed in Nov 44 after he had visited the UK, US, and Canada, Curtin remained in office until his death on 5 July 45 as the last Japanese resistance was ending.

CZERNIAWSKI, Roman. *See* **GARBY-CZERNIAWSKI.**

D

DAHLERUS, Birger. Swedish industrialist. Born in Stockholm, 6 Feb 91 and related to Goering's brother-in-law Count Eric von Rosen, Dahlerus had extensive business interests and personal contacts in Germany and Britain. Goering and Hitler used him extensively as a secret intermediary on the eve of war, and he is a much-cited eyewitness of Hitler's march to war in 1939. The Swede testified for Goering at Nuremberg (19 Mar 46), saying the Reichsmarschall sought peace in 1939. During one interview with Dahlerus at this time Hitler raged that he did not fear the British: in the event of war with them he would respond with "U-boats! U-boats! U-boats!" and "war planes! X-2" (ibid.). The English edition of Dahlerus's informative book is *The Last Attempt* (London: Hutchinson, 1947). He died 8 Mar 57 in Stockholm.

DALADIER, Edouard. French statesman. 1884-1970. The three-time premier was born 18 June 84 at Carpentras (Vaucluse) in the austere hill country of SE France. He studied under Edouard HERRIOT at the Lycée Duparc in Lyons and became a recognized authority on the classics and history. Urged by Herriot, Daladier entered politics as a radical socialist and in 1911 he was the mayor of Carpentras.

During four years on the western front he was decorated twice, cited for bravery three times, and promoted to captain. Daladier entered the Chamber of Deputies in 1919, and within less than decade wrested control of the Radical Socialist Party from Herriot, his long-time mentor. The "Bull of the Vaucluse," a short, swarthy, powerful man with a massive forehead, was minister of war 1932-34 and 1936-38, then minister of national defense 1938-40. He had a long tenure as premier, 31 Jan-24 Oct 33, then held the office two more times, briefly 30 Jan-7 Feb 34 and during the critical period 10 Apr 38-20 Mar 40. Largely responsible for France's lack of military preparedness, Daladier signed the Munich Agreement on 30 Sep 38 with shame, France being too weak to face Hitler, but he was astounded to be welcomed home as if capitulation were victory. For all his political faults, the Bull of the Vaucluse was utterly incorruptible and not interested in money or high living. But like his arch-rival Reynaud, whose Egeria was the Countess Hélène de PORTES, Daladier had the Marquise de Crussol. The ambitious marquise was a young-looking blonde of some allure who surrounded Daladier with her social and political intimates, developing a strong influence on the premier's unfortunate policies (Pertinax, 104-105). After the phony war continued to drag on and 300 deputies rose to protest the government's inaction, Pierre LAVAL led an attack that ousted the weary bull. He was succeeded by Reynaud as premier on 20 Mar 40 but remained minister of foreign affairs. When the Germans attacked France on 10 May 40 the two-month-old Reynaud government survived by a single vote and only with acceptance of DALADIER as minister of national defense. Reynaud tried to replace the ineffectual GAMELIN as head of the French Army but was blocked by Daladier and President Lebrun. On 5 June 40, a day after the Dunkirk evacuation ended, Daladier finally was ousted and replaced by de Gaulle.

Refusing to join the Pétain government, Daladier fled with other legislators to North Africa and was a principal victim of the *Massilia* **affair,** 20-26 June 40. After a month's absence he was returned to France, where on 8 Sep 40 he and Léon Blum were arrested and incarcerated with Reynaud and Gamelin in the chateau of Chazeron. After figuring in the **Riom Trial,** Daladier was imprisoned at various places in France until turned over to the Germans in 1943. Liberated with the **Niederdorf** group on 4 May 45, the three-time premier was among the few pre-war French politicians who remained prominent. He was active as a Radical Socialist until 1958. The Bull of the Vaucluse remarried at the age of 68 and lived another 18 years to die in Paris.

DALUEGE, Kurt. German police official. 1897-1946. The Third Reich's top cop and proconsul of Bohemia and Moravia was born in Kreuzburg, upper Silesia, on 15 Sep 97. After having an outstanding war record, he joined the notorious Rossbach Freikorps, and became a Nazi party member in 1922. Big, impressive-looking, and a swashbuckler, he specialized in organizing storm troopers. Nicknamed "Dummi-Dummi" (which means what it sounds like), he formed and led the first SA unit in Berlin before heading one in north Germany. Transferring to the SS, and stationed in Berlin while Himmler remained in the relative obscurity of Munich, Daluege worked closely with GOERING to purge the Prussian police of political opponents. In the complex matrix of **police and secret services of Nazi Germany** he headed the **Orpo** (Ordnungspolizei), or municipal uniformed police—almost all German police except Arthur Nebe's (Kripo).

Daluege got the SS rank of Obergruppenfuehrer in 1934. When an SS reorganization in Oct 39 created Heydrich's RSHA, Orpo was left directly under Himmler, not put in Heydrich's political security police (Sipo). Daluege was responsible for internal order and security for Nazi chiefs (Wistrich). Dummi-Dummi lacked the qualities needed to beat out Heydrich as Himmler's most powerful subordinate. But when Karl FRANK failed to show sufficient ruthless in avenging the assassination of HEYDRICH (who died on 4 June 42), Hitler and Himmler sent Daluege to Prague. Officially Frank's deputy but de facto Reichsprotektor of Bohemia and Moravia, the Nazi policeman had primary responsibility for murderous acts that followed, particularly the atrocity at Lidice and shipment of slave labor to Germany. He was convicted of war crimes by a Czech court and hanged in Prague on 24 Oct 46.

DANSEY, Claude (Edward Marjoribanks) "Col Z." British intelligence officer. 1876-1947. A veteran of the SIS and deputy chief of MI6 during the war, Dansey was born 21 Oct 76 in London. When barely 16 years he fell prey to the homosexual Robert Baldwin "Robbie" Ross, a 24-year-old Canadian remembered as Oscar Wilde's most loyal friend and literary executor. The affair was hushed up and the outraged father, now lieutenant-colonel of the 1st Life Guards, sent his son as soon as possible "to find adventure [,] and no doubt to prove his manhood, in foreign parts" (Read & Fisher, *Col Z*, 22).

This Claude did in spades. He fought with elite units in South Africa (1895-97; 1900-04) with a break for 10 arduous weeks in Borneo, and finally as chief political and intelligence officer fighting the **Mad Mullah** in British Somaliland (1904-09). Dansey somehow attracted the attention of the Irish-American financial tycoon Thomas Fortune Ryan (1851-1928). When the 23-year-old captain found he had no future in the Colonial Service after almost five years in East Africa, Ryan got the burly veteran of Britain's colonial wars a job as resident secretary of the Sleepy Hollow Country Club on the Hudson River in Westchester County, N. Y.

Dansey had become a spy (ibid. 67). The British were concerned about US support of the rebels in Ireland and Thomas Ryan was under suspicion. Ryan actually had no interest in the Irish problem, but he did have chores for the enterprising Dansey in Africa and elsewhere. The versatile secret agent was at Sleepy Hollow from 1 Dec 11 until just before England declared war against Germany on 4 Aug 14.

Joining Capt Vernon Kell's small MO5 staff, Dansey spent the war in security and counterintelligence work. Promoted in the spring of 1917, Lt Col Dansey left the army in 1919 but kept his contact with British intelligence. In 1929 he returned to SIS as station chief in Rome but, after performing well in a troublesome period, was brusquely dismissed in 1936. He was said to have mishandled large sums of SIS money, but this was a cover plan for exiling Dansey to Europe as creator of **Organization Z.**

When Stewart MENZIES took over MI6 from Sinclair on 28 Nov 39 he brought in the older and more experienced Dansey as his assistant chief. When deputy chief Lt Col Valentine "Vee Vee" Vivian was shunted aside to be chief security adviser, Dansey became vice chief of the secret service. (Ibid., 230, 235.) His alleged anti-American prejudice has been ascribed to his unsuccessful marriage in 1915 to an American, Mrs Pauline Cory Ulman. They were separated in 1929, when she refused to accompany him to Rome, and they later were divorced. On 1 Mar 45, the eve of his retirement, "Uncle Claude" married Mrs Frances Gurney Wilson Rylander, an attractive young physiotherapist who had treated some of his agents. In May 45 Sir Claude (KCMG in July 43) and his bride retired to Bathhampton Manor, an old country house near

Bath. He died 11 June 47 in the local nursing home of coronary thrombosis and myocardial degeneration.

D'AQUINO, Iva. See TOKYO ROSE.

DARBY, William Orlando. US officer. 1911-45. Born and reared in Arkansas, Darby graduated from West Point in 1933 (186/347) and joined the field artillery. As a major he activated the 1st Ranger Bn on 19 June 42 at Carrickfergus, Northern Ireland. Darby's men took their name from Major Robert Rogers's Rangers of the colonial wars, and survivors of the first course in the wilds of Scotland were presented with green berets. The charismatic Bill Darby led the 1st Ranger Bn in North Africa. In Apr 43 the initial force was split into cadres for the 3d and 4th Bns. Volunteers from units in North Africa filled the three battalions to a strength of 419 officers and men in six companies, each having two rifle platoons of about 30 men and a support section. The Rangers landed with the assault waves in Sicily, 10 July 43, the 3d Bn attached to Truscott's Joss Force, whose objective was Licata, and the other battalions landing with Dime Force to take Gela. At Salerno, 9 Sep 43, Maj Roy Murray's 4th Bn secured the beachhead at Maiori, and Darby led the 1st and 3d Bns to objectives held some five miles inland by the crack Hermann Goering Div. At Anzio, 22 Jan 44, the three battalions formed the 6615 Ranger Regt. They took the port of Anzio unopposed, but two battalions were virtually destroyed in defending the beachhead. Col Darby assumed command of the 179th RCT, 45th Inf Div, in early 1944, and then was assigned to staff duty in Washington. In mid Apr 45 the 34-year-old colonel was escorting War Department officials on a visit to Italy when he was recruited to replace the wounded assistant commander of the 10th Mtn Div. Darby was ending a pursuit up the east side of Lake Garda, two days before the cease-fire in Italy, when mortally wounded on the afternoon of 30 Apr 45 by a parting artillery shot from the Germans somewhere north of Riva. (Fisher, 511.) He died 45 minutes later. Promotion to brigadier general was posthumous.

DARLAN, Jean (Louis Xavier François). French admiral and politician. 1881-1942. Born 7 Aug 81 at Nérac (Lot et Garonne), the stocky little Gascon was the son of a former minister of justice and great-grandson of an officer killed while commanding a warship at Trafalgar. Darlan graduated from the prestigious Lycée St Louis in Paris (1899) and from the French naval academy (1902). Throughout the war of 1914-18 he commanded a battery of naval guns on various fronts.

For 10 years after being promoted to rear Admiral in 1929 Darlan had almost total control over rebuilding the French Navy into a powerful, modern force that was virtually his fiefdom. Having learned something about politics from his father, Darlan developed what an admiring Churchill called an "obsession to keep the politicians in their place as chatterboxes in the Chamber [of Deputies]" (WC, I, 500). Léon BLUM made the admiral chief of the navy's general staff in 1936, and Darlan was admiral of the fleet commanding all French maritime forces as of 1 Jan 37. This new rank was created to put Darlan on a level with Britain's first lord of the Admiralty (Larousse).

A frustrated by Gamelin's failure to plan joint operations of naval, air, and ground forces, the admiral used his ships to support the Royal Navy in the Atlantic (to include support of the Narvik expedition) and the Mediterranean (to include bombarding Genoa). Like most French naval officers Darlan was notoriously anti-British; but Churchill hoped as late as 12 June 40 that the little admiral was even more anti-German. As French leaders moved toward requesting an armistice, Darlan expressed determination on 14 June to continue resistance at sea (Larousse). But he sided with Laval in opposing the idea of a government in exile, which would be toothless without the French Navy. On 16 June 40, when the Reynaud government was ousted, Pétain named Darlan minister of the navy and of the merchant marine. In this capacity the admiral countermanded orders for French ships to join the Allies or head for neutral waters. But on 19 June he assured the British he would never deliver his fleet to the Germans, and the next day he issued secret orders, confirmed 24 June 40, to sabotage ships if the Germans tried to seize them in violation of the armistice agreement. But Article 8 stipulated that French ships would return to peacetime home ports, most of which were in German hands. The anglophobia of Darlan, his officers, and other Frenchmen was fired by what the admiral called the "odious assault" at **Mers el Kebir** on 3 July 40 and de Gaulle's failed attempt to take Dakar, 23-25 Sep 40.

Like Pétain, Darlan believed Germany would win the war. He therefore pursued pro-German policies in hopes of winning a better postwar position for France than could be expected from a victorious Great Britain (Larousse). The admiral remained minister of the navy until Feb 41, when he succeeded Pierre LAVAL as vice premier and foreign minister. The admiral also took over the ministries of the interior and defense, and by an act on 10 Feb 41 was designated as Pétain's successor. Although he subsequently dominated Vichy France, Darlan failed every test as a politician.

LAVAL returned to the Vichy government on 17 Apr 42, when Darlan surrendered all cabinet posts but remained Pétain's dauphin. Although past retirement age, the admiral was retained on active duty as commander of all French armed forces.

Visiting French Africa 21-29 Oct 42, Darlan exhorted officers to resist the expected American attack on Dakar. But the admiral let the Allies know a few days later he was prepared to cooperate with them (Smith, *OSS,* 58), and the US State Dept authorized Robert MURPHY to "initiate any arrangement with Darlan which . . . might assist the [planned] military operations" (Murphy, 128). Darlan kept contact with Murphy through his son Alain, who was a naval officer, and delegate general Raymond Fénard, the admiral who had replaced WEYGAND in Algiers. Eisenhower, meanwhile, devised a power-sharing plan (below) he hoped Darlan and Giraud could accept (Murphy, 118).

The Darlan Deal

Alain Darlan was stricken by infantile paralysis on 13 Oct 42. The admiral visited his son in Algiers, returned to Vichy on 1 Nov, but returned to Algiers five days later when informed that Alain was dying. Darlan was staying with Adm Fénard when, shortly after midnight on 7-8 Nov, he got a phone call from Gen JUIN saying that Robert MURPHY had just arrived with a most urgent message for him. Darlan and Fénard reached Juin's residence to learn that it was D day. (Murphy had not been authorized to give advance notice to any Frenchmen other than a few resistance leaders.) Darlan agreed after much pacing and fuming to report the situation to Vichy and ask for a free hand. But

when the admiral, his military secretary, Juin, and Fénard left Juin's residence to send the message through French naval channels they were stopped by maquisards who had taken the Senegalese guard into custody. (Murphy, 130.)

Dawn came but not the American troops who were supposed to have arrived at 2:30 AM. French army authorities discovered the strange situation and sent Gardes Mobiles (state police) to arrest resistance detachments including those at Juin's residence. But Juin prevailed on Darlan to order a cease fire, which became effective in and around Algiers at 6:45 PM on the 8th. Two days later, at about 11 AM, the admiral broadcast a cease fire order to all Vichy troops in North Africa. Pétain immediately disavowed Darlan's action and ordered Gen NOGUES to assume the admiral's powers. This was on the insistence of Laval and despite the urging of Gen WEYGAND and Adm AUPHAN. But the latter, Darlan's deputy in Vichy, got Pétain to authorize what became known as the "Auphan telegram," which gave the marshal's secret agreement *("accord intime")* to Darlan's actions and revoked previous messages to the contrary. The Auphan telegram was transmitted to Darlan in Algiers at 3:15 PM on the 10th, using the secret naval code (Larousse, "Auphan"). The next day, the 11th, the admiral ordered the French fleet in Toulon to break out and join the allies in Algiers.

Noguès rushed to Algiers after signing an armistice with Patton on 11 Nov 42 in Morocco, but when he finally saw the Auphan telegram, at 2 PM on the 13th, he turned his authority back to Darlan (Larousse). Darlan's citizenship was revoked, by demand of the Germans, on 27 Nov 42, the day the French fleet in Toulon was scuttled.

The "Darlan Deal" was vociferously protested by British and American anti-Vichy factions. Critics saw it only as accepting a notorious Fascist and collaborator, disregarding that it saved thousands of lives and greatly improved the Allies' chances to win the race for Tunis. Eisenhower said in a message to the CCS on 14 Nov: "The civil governors, military leaders and naval commanders will agree on only one man as having an obvious right to assume the Marshall's [Pétain's] mantle in North Africa. That man is Darlan" (*EP,* 707). As mentioned earlier, MURPHY had secret authority to make "any arrangement with Darlan which . . . might assist the military operations." The Darlan Deal was endorsed by authorities in London and Washington, confirmed on the 13th, and signed on 22 Nov 42.

Roosevelt had dispatched a letter of sympathy to Darlan about his son's illness, which Adm Leahy thinks helped in the tense situation. FDR later sent Mme Darlan and her son to Warm Springs, Ga, for an extended visit. (Leahy, 132.)

The Darlan Deal, along the lines previously visualized by Eisenhower (herein) made the admiral the political chief in all of French Africa. His title was High Commissioner and CinC of French Ground and Air Forces in Africa. GIRAUD became commander of all French military forces in the theater of war. But when factionalism between (and among) ex-Vichy men and de Gaulle's Free French adherents appeared to be insurmountable an assassin resolved the problem. Ferdinand Bonnier de la Chapelle, a young Royalist zealot being trained at an SOE/OSS camp for action in France, fatally wounded Darlan as the admiral returned to his office after lunch on 24 Dec 42, Christmas eve. The victim's last words before dying on the operating table of a nearby hospital are alleged to have been, "The British have finally done for me." (Brown, "C," 449.)

As luck would have it, MI6 chief Stewart MENZIES was in Algiers secretly on one of only two trips he made abroad during the war. Ostensibly he had come after learning that old friends of French secret service, Col Louis Rivet and Georges Ronin, had just escaped to Algiers. Menzies was lunching with them on the roof of a small house only a few hundred meters from where Darlan was shot. (Ibid., 453.) Adding to the mystery, C was so secretive about the trip that not even his personal assistant, Patrick Reilly suddenly given Christmas leave, did not know his chief had left his desk. Although SIS probably was not involved, the French high command spread the rumor that the British had ordered a series of murders so they could annex French North Africa to the British Empire (Ibid., 450). Gen GIRAUD moved with almost indecent haste to have the young assassin courtmartialled during the night of 25-26 Dec 42 and executed a few hours later without any review of the case.

"Let him rest in peace," wrote Churchill of Darlan, "and let us be thankful we never have to face the trials under which he broke" (WC, IV, 645-47). A shorter if less eloquent epitaph might be "Hitler never got the French fleet."

DARNAND, Joseph. Vichy police chief. 1897-1945. A military volunteer at the age of 18, he emerged from the first world war as a hero of guerrilla patrols with seven citations. Darnand was a cabinetmaker before owning a transport company in Nice. For involvement with the **cagoule** he was briefly imprisoned in 1938. During the phony war he led a "corps franc" and was one of the few Frenchmen to do any fighting. Darnand became a POW after the real war started but escaped from the camp at Pithiviers.

A man of action "with a rather confused ideology" (Larousse), he was named chief of the French Legion of War Veterans in the Maritime Alps Dept. In July 41 he formed the *Service d'Ordre Légionnaire* (SOL), which was officially recognized by Vichy the next year with Darnand as secretary-general. The SOL was rabidly right-wing, swearing to fight against democracy, Jews, and Gaullists. In Jan 43 the SOL was transformed, with some modifications, into the Milice. Many early recruits were citizens alarmed by mounting lawlessness. But the *Milice* evolved into a terror organization more notorious than the SS and Gestapo, particularly against maquisards and other underground groups.

Darnand recruited for the French Legion of Volunteers, visited them on the eastern front, was given the Waffen-SS rank of Sturmbannfuehrer (major), and took the personal oath of loyalty to Hitler. Unlike other paramilitary formations in France, the Milice had authority to recruit in the occupied zone. On 31 Dec 43 Darnand was named secretary-general for the maintenance of order, or head of all police in the free zone. Little more than a month later he was made secretary of the interior.

As the Allies liberated France, Darnand and 6,000 of his most-wanted Miliciens fled via Belfort to Ulm (Germany). He served on Pétain's refugee government at Sigmaringen, then—a fighter to the bitter end—he went to Italy for antipartisans operations.

In one of eight major postwar trials of Vichy leaders, Darnand was convicted of treason. A collaborator from genuine fascist conviction, not expediency, he was unrepentant and calm before a firing squad. At the last moment he shouted "Vive la France!"

DARRE, Richard Walther (Oskar). German official. 1895–1953. The Reich Farmers' Leader and minister of food was born 14 July 95 in Buenos Aires. His mother was Swedish, and his German father, who was of Huguenot ancestry, imported German goods to Argentina. Darré became a well schooled but eccentric agronomist whose radical theories were expounded in two early books, *The Peasantry as a Life Source of the Nordic Race* (1929), and *A New Nobility From Blood and Soil* (1930). The first of these brought the author to the rapt attention of Hitler, who commissioned Darré to draft a farm program. The agronomist, a tall, dark, non-Nordic-looking man who spoke with a slight foreign accent, was named National Farmers' Leader (Reichsbauernfuehrer) on 4 Apr 33 and minister for food and agriculture on 29 June 33. Within three months Darré had two revolutionary laws proclaimed. One reorganized the structure of agricultural production and marketing to assure higher farm prices. The other, the Hereditary Farm Law of 29 Sep 33, protected certain Aryan German farm owners under the ancient laws of entailment. All this ran counter to Hjalmar SCHACHT's free market economics and the Reichsbank's financial policy. Darré's programs also failed to stop the historic flight of farm labor to urban industry, to prevent the rise of peasant capitalism, even to increase the rural birth rate (Wistrich). To the delectation of the foreign press, it was rumored by 1940 that the Peasant Leader had established ranches (Hege-hoefe) in East Prussia to produce two-legged thoroughbreds *(CB 41)*. "Darré is supposed to have a 'stud book,' one of the largest card indexes in the world," that traces the ancestry of Aryan German peasants at least to 1800, "with all racial blemishes recorded" (ibid.).

Although academically respectable, a rarety among high Nazis, Darré was impractical and incompetent as an administrator. Goering dubbed him the "Minister of Malnutrition." Dismissed in May 42, having finally lost the high regard of Hitler and his intimate friend Himmler, Darré was a POW from 7 July 45 (Hamilton, *Leaders,* 216). He was sentenced to five years in prison by an American military tribunal at Nuremberg on charges of starving German Jews by withholding basic foodstuffs and confiscating property from Jewish farmers in Germany and Poland (Wistrich). Released in 1950, Darré lived in Bad Harzburg until hospi-

talized for liver trouble. He died 8 Sep 53 at a private clinic in Munich.

DAVIS, Benjamin Oliver. US general. 1877-1970. The US Army's first African-American general was born in Washington, DC, on 1 July 77. Having entered Howard Univ in 1887, Davis joined the 8th Inf Regt on 13 July 89 to serve in the Spanish-American War. Less than a year later, having been mustered out, he enlisted in the 9th Cav Regt, one of the Army's two black cavalry units, and in 1901 he was commissioned as a second lieutenant of cavalry. Davis was in the Philippines during WWI and was promoted to temporary lieutenant colonel. Because black officers were not assigned to command white troops, Davis spent much of his career on ROTC duty at Negro universities including two tours as **PMS&T** at Wilberforce Univ, Ohio, and one at Tuskegee Institute, Ala. He also was MA in Monrovia. Promoted to full colonel in 1930, he was back at Wilberforce and Tuskegee several more times before commanding the 369th "Harlem" Regt. When his son (below) graduated from West Point in 1936 the Davises were the only black line officers in the US Army *(CB 42)*. On 25 Oct 40 Davis was given the temporary rank of brigadier general *(AA,* 921). He retired in June 41 on reaching the statutory age limit but was immediately recalled to active duty as assistant IG in Washington. Gen Davis spent most of the war as a special adviser on Negro troops in the segregated US Army. In Oct 42 he went to the UK, where racial problems had arisen. One reason for this was that white American troops resented the way many Britons went out of their way to accept blacks socially. Having lived so long with discrimination and being a man of remarkable personal qualities, Gen Davis was a cool, rational, and effective adviser on race relations. The senior brigadier general of 184 on the permanent list *(AA,* 930), he retired for the last time in 1948 after 50 years of military service. He was later on the ABMC. Gen Davis died 26 Nov 70.

DAVIS, Benjamin Oliver, Jr. US army officer. 1912-. The only son of Gen Benjamin O. DAVIS, he was born 18 Dec 12 in Washington, DC, and appointed to West Point from Illinois. Although meeting no prejudice initially, Davis soon was "silenced" by the Corps of Cadets—ostracized socially and living without a roommate, in hopes he could be forced to resign. But he stood high in the Class of 1936 (35/276), only the third black in half a century to graduate from West Point.

Commissioned in the infantry, Davis joined the segregated 24th Inf Regt at Ft Benning, Ga, then served with the ROTC at Tuskegee before being his father's ADC in the 4th Cav Bde at Ft Riley, Kans. Capt Davis was not accepted for pilot training until the spring of 1941, when the first flight school for blacks was established at Tuskegee. Winning his wings in Mar 42, and promoted two months later, Lt Col Davis helped raise the 99th Pursuit Sqdn and commanded it in the Mediterranen theater. Davis took the squadron to North Africa and on to Sicily, leading it in aerial combat missions and in close support. In Oct 43 he assumed command of the 332d Ftr Gp at Selfridge Field, Mich, and two months later was leading it in Italy. His black airmen having won high praise for sustained performance in aerial combat and close support of ground operations, Col Davis returned to the US after V-E day. He wore the SS, LM, DFC, and 5 AMs (Cullum). The airman was promoted to brigadier general in 1954 and had three-star rank before retiring in Feb 70 as deputy CinC, US Strike Command. Davis says in his memoirs that he left in disappointment at not being offered more demanding assignments. He was director of public service in Cleveland until joining the Department of Transportation (DOT) in Sep 70. After less than a year as director of aviation security he advanced in the DOT hierarchy to be assistant secretary of transportation for safety and consumer affairs as air terrorism, piracy, and cargo threat approached epidemic proportions. Before leaving the post in 1975 the general dramatically improved air safety and cargo security, virtually eliminating hijacking in the continental US. Like all retired senior generals, he served on governmental commissions and corporate boards. In 1995 Davis was presented with West Point's Distinguished Graduate Award.

His memoirs are *Benjamin O. Davis, Jr., American: An Autobiography* (Washington, DC: Smithsonian, 1991).

DAWLEY, Ernest Joseph. US general. 1886-1973. Born in Wisconsin, he graduated from the USMA in 1910 (24/83) as a field artilleryman. With the AEF in France "Mike" Dawley had regimental and GS duty in 1918 and won the Silver Star. He became a brigadier general on 1 Oct 40, and a major general on 29 Sep 41. After commanding the 40th Inf Div, in Apr 42 he took over the 6th Corps Hq. Going overseas on 8 Feb 43 (*AA*, 506) and having rear area missions in North Africa, Dawley was assigned to Mark Clark's new 5th Army Hq, which was planning the Salerno landings.

The youthful Clark, 47, was unhappy from the start with Washington's selection of Dawley, 57. But Dawley had powerful friends, so Clark did not request a replacement. (Morris, *Salerno*, 19, 60.) The 36th Inf Div led Dawley's 6th Corps ashore at Salerno on 9 Sep 43 and drove some 10 miles to high ground overlooking the beaches. The 45th Div started landing in Dawley's sector on D+1, but by then the situation looked bad as KESSELRING rushed up German reinforcements.

Fundamental disagreements over strategy arose between Clark and Dawley on 12 Sep (D+3). Clark had moved the corps boundary about three miles left (NW) from the Sele River and wanted Dawley to shift forces across the river to plug a dangerous gap between his 6th Corps and the 10th British Corps. But Dawley wanted instead to use all his troops in continuing to drive inland. "By this stage he [Clark] had no confidence in his corps commander and should have relieved him on the spot," writes Morris (ibid., 234-35). The crisis was over when Harold Alexander and Eisenhower visited the beachhead on 15 and 17 Sep, but they agreed with Clark that Dawley was unfit. "You've got a broken reed on your hands," Alexander told Clark (Morris, 283). Eisenhower was more outspoken, turning on Dawley after a briefing and saying, "How did you ever get your troops into such a mess?" The accusation was unfair, but the exhausted Dawley "mumbled some reply and then appeared to be lost for words." Eisenhower later said to Clark, "Wayne, you had better take him out," and sent a message to this effect to Gen Marshall. (Morris, 300.) Having thus covered himself politically, Clark replaced Dawley on 20 Sep with Maj Gen John P. LUCAS, who at Anzio also was relieved of command.

Demoted to colonel, Dawley headed stateside training and replacement commands until retiring in 1947 as a brigadier general. The next year he was promoted to major general on the retired list. Dawley died 8 Sep 73 at Ft Ord, Calif.

DE BONO, Emilio (Giuseppe Gaspare Giovanni). Marshal of Italy. 1866-1944. A professional soldier who was chief of police and commander of the Fascist Militia, 1922-23, Gen De Bono had made the March on Rome, 28 Oct 22, as a member of the Quadumvirate. From 1923 he was a senator. But the general resigned as chief of police after the murder of MUSSOLINI's antagonist Giacomo Matteotti (1885-1924), which caused widespread rioting. De Bono was minister of colonies, 1929-35, then high commissioner for Italian colonies in East Africa and commander in chief of Italian forces there. He had some success at the start of the Abyssinian War, winning a victory at Adowa, and was appalled to learn that he would be replaced by Rodolfo GRAZIANI. As a price for leaving quietly, De Bono demanded and received promotion to marshal of Italy. The elderly fascist was among the 19 members of the Grand Council who voted on 25 July 43 to oust MUSSOLINI. Arrested after the Duce was reinstalled in Sep 43, De Bono, CIANO, and three others were executed on 11 Jan 44 at a firing range near Verona.

DECKER, Karl. German general. 1897-1945. An elegantly handsome man, to judge from wartime photos, Decker was born 30 Nov 97 in Bortnin. He served as an infantryman in WWI, was involved in development of panzer forces, and at the start of WWII commanded an antitank battalion. Lt Col Decker was awarded the RK on 13 June 41 for action in central Russia as commander of a panzer battalion (1/3/3). As a colonel he took command of the 5th Pz Div in the south of Russia on 7 Sep 43, was promoted to generalmajor on 1 Dec 43, and on 16 Oct 44 moved up to head the 39th Pz Corps in the Ukraine. After retreating westward through Kurland and East Prussia, he was promoted to general of panzer troops and his corps attached temporarily to the 5th Pz Army for the final phase of the Ardennes campaign. Driven back into Germany and making a last stand on the Elbe at Grossrundsrode with the 12th Army against the US 9th Army, the general committed suicide 21 Apr 45 near Gross-Brunssode/Braunschweig (Brunswick). He was posthumously awarded the Swords (149/159) on 26 Apr. (Angola, I, 265; B&O, 43, 79.)

DE GASPERI, Alcide. Italian statesman. 1881-1954. Editor of the daily *Il Nuovo Trentino* since 1906, and secretary of the Italian People's Party from 1919, he was imprisoned by the Fascists in 1926 when all political parties were suppressed. The Holy See had him released after 16 months and he was a refugee in the Vatican until Mussolini's fall on 25 July 43. The Trentino (who had been educated in Vienna and elected to the Austro-Hungarian parliament in 1911) organized the Christian Democratic Party and took part in the resistance movement. In June 44 De Gasperi joined the first BONOMI cabinet as a minister without portfolio. The following December he became minister of foreign affairs and retained this post in the government that succeeded the second Bonomi government in June 45. As prime minister for more than eight years starting 9 Dec 45, De Gasperi was highly effective, if often unpopular. He successfully opposed neo-fascist and communist attempts to take over; he took Italy into NATO and other European co-operative efforts; and he was responsible for the "Italian miracle" of economic recovery. Succeeded by Amintore Fanfani on 28 July 53, he died a little more than a year later of a heart attack.

DE GAULLE, Charles André Joseph Marie. French officer and statesman. 1890-1970. He was born 22 Nov 90 in Lille at his mother's home. Her ancestors were of the Catholic-industrial bourgeoisie of Dunkirk. Charles's father was an austere, erudite, and courtly lay headmaster of Jesuit schools; his ancestors had been members of the *petite noblesse* in Normandy for five centuries. The son was reared in Paris, where he acquired a solid education.

An outstanding student at St Cyr, graduating 13th in the class of 1912, he was assigned at his own request to the infantry regiment of an officer who had impressed him as lecturer at St Cyr, a Col Philippe PETAIN. This was the beginning of a long association that took strange turns.

De Gaulle was promoted to captain (T) on 10 Feb 15 and at Ft Douaumont (Verdun) on 2 Mar 16 was wounded for the third time and captured. During 32 months as a POW he made five escape attempts, for which he was confined in five different camps before being sent to Fort 9 at Ingolstadt. Here he met his future publisher

(Berger-Levrault), Maj Georges CATROUX, and a Russian named TUKHACHEVSKY.

Freed after the armistice of 11 Nov 18, he was assigned on 17 Apr 19, at his own request, to a Polish division of chasseurs being formed in France. As part of WEYGAND's French mission, and with Polish rank, Maj de Gaulle distinguished himself in action against Red Army forces under the future Marshals Budenny and Tukhachevsky, winning Poland's highest military decoration, *Virtuti Militari*. (Pierre Thibault in Larousse, cited hereafter as Thibault.)

Handsome as a younger man, a towering 6 feet 5, the melancholy de Gaulle acquired a reputation for arrogance and non-conformity that made him few friends and many critics. But after excelling at the French War College in 1924 he became a protégé of Pétain's, serving on his staff. In *Le fil de l'épée* (1932) and *Vers l'armée de métier* (1934), Lt Col de Gaulle (25 Dec 33) argued for a small, mobile, mechanized army of professionals. This appalled civilians and soldiers alike: they saw soaring costs (at the depth of the Depression) for modernization after so much time and money had been put into the Maginot Line; they continued to support the Napoleonic concept of a mass army of conscripts; and they feared a Praetorian guard that would threaten civil authority. "For this audacity, de Gaulle was struck from the 1936 promotion list, just as his earlier idol and patron, Marshal Pétain had suffered before 1914 for his unorthodox views on firepower" (Horne, *1940,* 72). De Gaulle's sudden and unauthorized publication of *La France et son Armée* (1938) caused a rift with Pétain, who accused de Gaulle of taking sole credit for work done by the marshal and his staff.

Meanwhile de Gaulle assumed command of a tank regiment on 7 June 37 and the following Christmas was promoted to full colonel. After France declared war, on 3 Sep 39, de Gaulle took over the 5th Army's tank force in Alsace. France had more and better tanks than the Germans (with superior armor although less maneuverable) but the elderly military hierarchy clung to the notion that tanks were infantry-support weapons—mobile pill boxes—and parceled them out in penny packets. De Gaulle was among the few who saw that armor had to be used in mass, and with logistical support that could keep up. In a memorandum of 26 Jan 40

de Gaulle again urged creation of a large armored force. But it was not until 11 May 40, after German armor broke through at Sedan, that de Gaulle was given command of the newly formed 4th Armd Div (4th DCR). Starting near Montcornet on 17 May 40 with about 200 tanks, the colonel attacked the southern flank of Guderian's panzer group in hopes of cutting its line of communications. It was the threat Hitler and Rundstedt feared most (Horne, *1940,* 452). De Gaulle's two-day operation, lacking air support, AA units, and badly outclassed, took about 600 prisoners but did little more than annoy the Germans. De Gaulle made another counterattack on 19 May, north of Laon, and on 27-29 May he came close to wiping out the German bridgehead across the Somme. Without air supremacy such operations were hopeless, but Thibault (cited earlier) points out that de Gaulle was the only French officer to force any enemy withdrawals during the Battle of Flanders. De Gaulle had proved he could command on a modern battlefield as well as write books about it, although the mythmakers have considerably exaggerated his accomplishments in both areas. Temporary promotion to *général de brigade* "for the duration of the war" was ordered on 26 May with the effective date (DOR) 1 June. Although not authorized, de Gaulle kept his "two star" rank. (See glossary sub-entry "French generals" under **general.**) Long impressed by de Gaulle's writings, Reynaud had wanted to make the obscure officer secretary of the war cabinet after the Germans attacked on 10 May 40. But the general declined to leave his new command assignment (above) or to serve under Daladier. On 5 June 40, however, the day after the Dunkirk evacuation ended, Reynaud ousted DALADIER and made de Gaulle minister of war. In a desperate bid to retain British support the new minister visited London on 16 June 40. The second trip, by British aircraft from Bordeaux, was to see Churchill about forming an Anglo-French union. The move would have blocked French efforts to arrange an armistice. When de Gaulle got back to Bordeaux at 9:30 PM on the 16th, he learned that Pétain was succeeding REYNAUD as premier and was forming a government that would seek an armistice. In real danger of arrest and resolved to fight on, de Gaulle left Bordeaux for London with E. L. SPEARS the next morning.

A day later "the man of June 18" broadcast his famous call for Frenchmen to fight on. France has lost a battle, he said, but she has not lost the war. Thibault points out that the emotional plea appealed primarily to "the humble: soldiers, NCOs and a few junior officers, plus some superior officers." A great problem with this first appeal from a virtually unknown and self-annointed savior was that it divided Frenchmen in their hour of humiliation: if the refugee de Gaulle was a national savior, Pétain and those who stayed behind with him were less than patriotic Frenchmen. The problem would fester.

The US decided to back Vichy France, but on 28 June 40 Churchill recognized de Gaulle as "chief of the Free French." Known initially as the Fighting French, they promptly adopted the Cross of Lorraine as their symbol. The British authorized de Gaulle to announce formation of the French National Committee (FNC) and to issue proclamations denying the independence of the Pétain government. The latter promptly outlawed de Gaulle, reducing him to the rank of colonel as of 22 June and putting him on the retired list as of the next day. On 4 July a court-martial convened by 17th Military Region (Toulouse) sentenced him in absentia to four years in prison and a token fine (100 francs, or about $20). On 2 Aug 40 a second court-martial, sitting in Clermont-Ferrand (13th Region), condemned him to death. These legal actions permitted the Vichy government to strip de Gaulle of French citizenship on 8 Dec 40. (Pierre Thibault.)

The Allies hoped this long, lean Joan of Arc could deliver the French colonies and their military forces, to include the powerful French navy. Most of Equatorial Africa had fallen easily to anti-Vichy forces, so Churchill and de Gaulle thought the same would happen at Dakar. This port city was of great strategic importance as the closest place in Africa to the Western Hemisphere, a jumping-off point for Axis aggression. But, for many reasons including the resistance put up by Pierre BOISSON, the Anglo-French attempt to take Dakar on 23 and 25 Sep 40 was a fiasco. Churchill manfully acknowledged his share of the blame, but the Allied press made de Gaulle the villain. The Fighting French chief nevertheless got a noisy welcome in the Cameroons, Chad, and at Brazzaville. Here on 27 Oct 40 he established the *Conseil de Défense de l'Empire,* making

himself head of all French territories in Africa. The Conseil became the Fighting French National Committee on 24 Sep 41 with headquarters in London at 4 Carlton Gardens. Thanks to British force of arms Gaullists won control of Syria (with some Free French help) and Madagascar. But on their own initiative—outraging Roosevelt—a Fighting French naval force under Adm MUSELIER occupied Saint Pierre and Miquelon on 24 Dec 43.

Roosevelt had it on good authority that Vichy might welcome an American liberation of North Africa but would not condone participation by the British and Fighting French. De Gaulle consequently was excluded from plans for Opn Torch. On the best advice of pro-US French generals advising Robert MURPHY in Algiers, GIRAUD was picked to rally French support for the Allies after they landed in Morocco and Algeria on 8 Nov 42. A tense situation resulted from the presence of Adm DARLAN in Algiers before the delayed arrival of GIRAUD, who proved to be a slender reed. De Gaulle officially protested the Darlan Deal as an unwarranted compromise with pro-Vichy officials in Algiers. DARLAN's assassination on 24 Dec 42, cleared the way for the Allies to install GIRAUD.

"Darlan's disappearance from the scene was of great consequence to French unity," writes de Gaulle in his memoirs. "I would have to turn it to my advantage." (*Unity,* 78.) To this end, he immediately offered to meet with Giraud, either in Algiers or Chad. Giraud was evasive, even about establishing regular liaison. Churchill and Roosevelt thought the Casablanca Conference in early 1943 would present an opportunity to resolve differences between the top French leaders. Still mad about being excluded from Torch, de Gaulle refused to attend the conference until pressed by Churchill. But the Free French chief rejected all solutions proposed by Giraud, Churchill, and FDR. De Gaulle's only concession was to pose (24 Jan 43) for the famous photograph in which he and Giraud shook hands as Churchill and FDR beamed in the background.

For some time de Gaulle had been making efforts to unify resistance leaders in France. Thanks to DEWAVRIN and Jean MOULIN this culminated in two critical actions. First, the United Movements of the Resistance, created in Mar 43, integrated the three major resistance organizations of the unoccupied zone, at least in principle, as the French are so fond of saying.

More important was creation of the *Conseil national de la Résistance* (CNR). In its first plenary session, in Paris on 27 May 43 with Jean MOULIN presiding, the CNR confirmed an agreement reached 12 days earlier. This said, among other things, "the French people will never tolerate the subordination of General de Gaulle to General Giraud and demands [sic] the immediate installation at Algiers of a provisional government under the presidency of General de Gaulle, General Giraud being made the military chief. . . ." (de Gaulle, *Unity,* 113.) The message was radioed to the world by American, British, and Fighting French stations.

Now recognized by the Allies as head of all the French opposing the Germans, de Gaulle finally could establish himself in Algiers. Making a great point of using a French plane, "le grand Charles" and his personal staff landed near Algiers on 30 May 43 for a grand reception by Giraud, CATROUX, and representatives of the US-UK missions. As CinC of the Fighting French he had authority in areas of French Africa that were vital to Allied success.

On 3 June 43 the French Committee of National Liberation (FCNL or "Algiers Committee") was established with Giraud and de Gaulle as co-presidents. Although Gen Alphonse GEORGES was sent to Algiers at the instigation of Churchill, and proved to be valuable as a conciliator, there were many obstacles to cooperation between civil and military authorities. But, whereas Giraud was completely inept politically, de Gaulle was masterful. He won support from Vichyites, radicals, French communists, and the Soviets. Over the protest of Giraud, and particularly infuriating FDR, de Gaulle ordered the arrest of ex-Vichyites, even those who had sided with Allies. Victims included BERGERET, BOISSON, FLANDIN, NOGUES, and PEYROUTON.

Seeing that he needed all the levers of power, de Gaulle used his superior political skills to get them. On 31 July 43 he succeeded in limiting Giraud's power to command of the armed forces. Giraud undertook the liberation of Corsica, 13 Sep-4 Oct 43, without forewarning the FCNL, so de Gaulle took the final step: on 9 Nov 43 the co-presidency arrangement was dissolved, leaving Giraud only his military hat.

On 21 April 44 the FCNL announced that a new national government was being formed under de Gaulle; on 26 May the FCNL acclaimed itself the Provisional Government of the French Republic. (de Gaulle, *Unity,* 250.) Churchill and FDR not only refused to recognize this action but also excluded de Gaulle from plans for liberating Europe and setting up new governments on the continent.

On 3 June de Gaulle transformed the FCNL into the Provisional Government of the French Republic, and the next day (the eve of D day) he went to London from Algiers, at the invitation of Churchill. The prime minister proposed a last-minute appeal to Roosevelt for recognition of de Gaulle's political leadership. "The French government exists," de Gaulle replied; he did not need any further authority. But he did want arrangements for cooperation between "the French administration and the military command." (de Gaulle, *Unity,* 252.) Allied authorities held de Gaulle in London until 14 June (D+8). Then he was allowed with a small entourage to visit the beachhead for one day, during which—exceeding the worst expectations of his mentors—de Gaulle installed two appointees. These were François Coulet, as Gaullist governor for Normandy, and Col P. de Chevigné, as commander of military subdivisions of liberated territory. Other governments in exile hailed de Gaulle a champion who challenged Anglo-American notions of post-war planning, and during the period 8-20 June, de Gaulle's Provisional Government was recognized by Czechoslovakia, Poland, Belgium, Luxembourg, Yugoslavia, and Norway, despite objections from the Americans and British. (*Unity,* 258.)

Reluctantly accepting an invitation from Roosevelt, the French leader reached Washington on 6 July 44, going on to NYC on the 10th and to Canada. During the visit he made wild appeals for the support of Franco-Americans. A day before returning to Algiers on the 13th, the eve of Bastille Day, de Gaulle learned that the US had recognized the FCNL as "qualified to exercise the administration of France." A few weeks later the Allies agreed that the FCNL, as Provisional Government of the French Republic, alone wielded the public powers in liberated portions of France (ibid., 275).

The Paris insurrection and liquidation of the Vichy government left a leadership vacuum in France. To fill this, de Gaulle reached France from Algiers on 20 Aug 44, landing near Saint Lô and going first to SHAEF Hq. When he learned that Eisenhower planned to bypass Paris, de Gaulle demanded that LECLERC be allowed to liberate the capital with his French 2d Armd Div. This came to pass on 25 Aug 44 with significant support from the 4th US Armd Div. De Gaulle entered Paris on the heels of the troops and reached the Gare Montparnasse at about 4 PM to learn from Leclerc that CHOLTITZ was ready to surrender the German garrison.

At the start of what a biographer calls his "Paris apotheosis" (Werth, *De Gaulle*, 169), de Gaulle kept resistance leaders waiting anxiously at the Hotel de Ville for what he was forewarned would be a challenge to his authority. The general established headquarters at the Ministry of War, planned the next day's victory parade, received reports, then moved slowly through cheering crowds to the Prefecture of Police. Here his highly laudatory speech to the Paris police was received with more cheers. With this reassurance from the crowds of his investiture, de Gaulle was ready for City Hall. At the Hotel de Ville he was greeted officially, introduced around, and speeches of mutual adulation were exchanged. As the messiah approached a window to address the clamoring crowd in the great square below, Georges BIDAULT suggested that he take this opportunity "formally to proclaim the Republic." The general responded that there was no need for this because the Republic had never ceased to exist, being preserved by his organizations in exile. "I myself am the President of the government of the Republic," quoth de Gaulle. "Why should I proclaim it now?" (*Unity*, 346.) After a speech in which he carefully avoided any mention of revolution, de Gaulle thanked the resistance leaders and told them their task was done. The French Forces of the Interior (FFI) would be integrated into the army and the militia would be dissolved. (Ibid., 357.) To various factions of the resistance he offered posts in his government, formed on 10 Sep, but only BIDAULT accepted.

De Gaulle precipitated a political crisis in early 1945 on learning that Eisenhower planned to abandon Strasbourg in coping with the counteroffensive launched by BLASKOWITZ. The outcome was that Eisenhower had to order that Strasbourg be defended "at all costs." De Gaulle's final wartime grievance was exclusion from the Yalta Conference, but France was one of the four countries to sign the final instrument of surrender with Germany and one of the four given an occupation zone in Germany.

"Of all the crosses I have had to bear," said Churchill when it was all over, "the heaviest has been the Cross of Lorraine." In response to a similar observation made earlier by Anthony Eden, de Gaulle succinctly summed up the problem: "I don't doubt it. France is a great power." (*Unity*, 114.)

The first constituent assembly elected the general unanimously on 13 Nov 45 to head the French government, the goal he had striven for since 18 June 40. But he resigned abruptly on 20 Jan 46. Although the "great power" was powerless economically, de Gaulle realized its people wanted party politics as usual; he decided to wait until France clamored for him to return as their savior. The general formed the right-wing *Rassemblement du Peuple Français* (RFP) but dissolved it in 1953 after some initial success. In retirement for the next five years he wrote the first three volumes of his four-volume war memoirs and prepared for a return to national power. The Algerian crisis of 1958 provided the opportunity. Elected president of the 5th Republic on 21 Dec 58, the general reshaped the government to give that office unprecedented, almost dictatorial, authority. He granted independence to all 13 French African colonies. But the costly Algerian war continued until 1962, bleeding France of men and money as Italy, Germany, and Japan staged incredible economic recoveries. Although the French army seemed to be on the brink of achieving a military solution in Algeria, de Gaulle ended the war. Without bloodshed he put down a revolt by long-established and wealthy Europeans *(pieds noirs)* in Algeria. Public confidence in his leadership brought French capital out of hiding, unleashing unprecedented prosperity and political stability. He developed a French atomic capability by early 1960, repeatedly blocked Britain's efforts to join the European Economic Community (which he had established), and withdrew France from NATO in 1966. De Gaulle was settling old scores with *les anglo saxons*. But the inevitable French boredom with political stability and the regal style of "le grand Charles" started growing. He survived five major assassination attempts without ever showing fear.

Student riots in 1968 marked the beginning of the end. Several crises were resolved by his calling for a referendum in which voters saw that the alternative to de Gaulle was a return to political chaos. But after negative results in a referendum on 27 Apr 69, de Gaulle resigned in a huff.

At his country home near Paris at Colombey-les-Deux-Eglises, de Gaulle completed his memoirs shortly before dying on 9 Nov 70. It was less that two weeks before his 80th birthday. In accordance with instructions written in 1952, he was buried at Colombey-les-Deux-Eglises without public ceremony.

DE GUINGAND, Francis Wilfred. British general. 1900-79. Born 28 Feb 00 at Acton in Middlesex, son of a briar-root pipe manufacturer, he graduated from Sandhurst in Dec 19 and joined the West Yorkshire (The Prince of Wales's Own) Regt. Two years later his brigade major was Capt Bernard Montgomery, and despite marked difference in temperament and life styles they struck up a long friendship. (Michael Carver in *DNB*.) Bored with regimental duty in England and needing more income to support his expensive gambling and hunting tastes, "Freddie" volunteered in 1926 for duty with the King's African Rifles in Nyasaland (now Malawi). After five happy years fighting the **Mad Mullah** he became adjutant of his regiment's 1st Bn in Egypt. Here he again had contact with Montgomery. In June 39 De Guingand became military assistant to HORE-BELISHA, secretary of state for war, and got valuable insights into high level military and political affairs. When Hore-Belisha was dismissed in Jan 41, De Guingand left at his own request and was posted as an instructor, with the grade of lieutenant colonel, to the newly formed Middle East Staff College at Haifa. At the end of 1941 he was reassigned to the joint planning staff in Cairo. After Auchinleck succeeded WAVELL as head of the Middle East Command, Col de Guingand became director of military intelligence in Feb 42. When Auchinleck took over the hard pressed 8th Army from Neil RITCHIE, the Auk made the colonel his **BGS.** On the road to El Alamein from Cairo de Guingand had a fortuitous meeting on 13 Aug 42 with Montgomery. The messiah had been given command of the battered 8th Army and was hastening forward to save it. After getting a lucid and candid appraisal of the dismal situation from de Guingand, Monty promptly named him his CofS with full staff authority for logistical as well as operational matters.

Although Montgomery de Guingand were complete opposites in temperament, they worked harmoniously in North Africa, Sicily, Italy, and northern Europe. Col de Guingand was appointed to the DSO in 1942 and knighted (KBE) in 1944. Their falling-out began in the last months of the war when Monty started claiming sole credit not only for his military triumphs but also for reconciling personal differences with Eisenhower in the winter of 1944-45 *(DNB)*. Montgomery was guilty of petty slights: excluding his chief of staff from the surrender ceremony on Lueneburg Heath, from any part in the victory celebration, and finally in abandoning his pledge to keep de Guingand as his deputy when Montgomery became CIGS in June 46. *(DNB.)*

Sir Francis was promoted to major general when he retired from the army in 1946 to become a successful businessman and pursue his interests as a sportsman, gambler, and bon viveur *(DNB)*. His first book was the highly-acclaimed *Operation Victory* (London: Hodder & Stoughton, 1947). This was followed by *African Assignment* (1953), *Generals at War* (1964), and *From Brass Hat to Bowler Hat* (1979). He died 29 June 79 in Cannes.

DE HAVILLAND, Geoffrey. British aircraft designer and manufacturer. 1882-1965. Born 27 July 82 at Wooburn, Buckinhamshire, son of a curate, he was a first cousin of actresses Olivia de Havilland and Joan Fontaine.

The future Sir Geoffrey (1944) founded the de Havilland Acft Co, Ltd. in 1920 and was its technical director until 1955. He designed one of the first half dozen successful British airplanes and engines (1908-09). Five of his eight military planes were produced in large numbers in 1914-18, the most important—the DH4—being on display in the Smithsonian Institute, Washington, DC. In 1925 he began producing the famous Moth, in which thousands learned to fly. The Tiger Moth was the primary RAF trainer. De Havilland aeroengines were produced from 1927.

Among his many notable aircraft was the **Mosquito.** In 1935 he began manufacturing the American controllable pitch propellers, which had a critical role in the Battle of Britain. After the war de Havilland pioneered commercial jet aviation with the Comet in 1949, followed by the Trident in 1962. He died 21 May 65 at Stanmore, Middlesex. *(DNB.)*

DELESTRAINT, Charles Antoine. French general. 1879-1945. A POW during most of WWI, then an early member of the French armored forces, he retired in 1939 but was almost immediately recalled to active duty. In 1940 he took command of an armored group that included Col de Gaulle's division and directed the counterattack on Abbeville, 3-4 June 40. Retiring after the armistice of 1940 to Bourg en Bresse, the general organized an association of former tank officers. When this brought criticism from Vichy the general formed a clandestine headquarters, complete with four staff sections, and reconnoitered the **Vercors** as the place for a national redoubt. On the recommendation of Henri FRENAY through Jean MOULIN, de Gaulle named his former chief to head the Secret Army. The appointment took effect about 24 Mar 43, when the general and Moulin returned to France from London.

But the old soldier, as "Vidal," was pathetically inept at unconventional warfare. Waiting outside La Muette metro station on the morning of 9 June 43 he was asked by two men whether he was meeting "Didot." Replying in the affirmative, the general was taken by his welcoming committee to Gestapo headquarters. The Germans promptly arrested the general's deputy, Gen Desmazes, and his adjutant, Col Castaldo. (Miller, *The Resistance,* 85.) The trap had been set by Klaus BARBIE, who had arrested and turned Didot (René Hardy), and the Butcher of Lyons quickly caught Moulin (21 June). De Gaulle's Secret Army, so beautifully set up by DEWAVRIN, was decapitated just as it gathered strength (de Gaulle, *Unity,* 287).

Delestraint was held at Fresnes before being deported through Struthof to Dachau. Here he was shot on 19 Apr 45, just 10 days before American troops arrived.

DEMPSEY, Miles Christopher. British general. 1896-1969. He was born 15 Dec 96 in New Brighton, Cheshire, son of a marine insurance broker. Graduating from Sandhurst in 1915, the tall, athletic, modest Dempsey joined the Royal Berkshire Regt for action on the western front and in Iraq. He was wounded, awarded the MC, and mentioned in dispatches. By 1939 Dempsey

was a lieutenant colonel, and the next year he showed tactical skill as commander of the 13th Inf Bde (Royal Berkshires) in France. For delaying actions in the retreat to Dunkirk he was appointed to the DSO. After two years in staff assignments he was promoted to major general and given the mission of forming and commanding an armored division. In Dec 42 "Lucky" (or "Bimbo") Dempsey relieved Horrocks as GOC 13th Corps, 8th Army. Concurrently promoted to lieutenant general (T), he planned the invasion of Sicily and led his corps in the assault on 10 July 43. The 13th Corps landed near Syracuse and Avola, on the 8th Army's right flank, with the 5th and 50th Inf Divs and an attached airborne brigade. Remaining in the coastal sector, he advanced to the Strait of Messina (3 Sep 43), directed an assault crossing by the 5th and 1st Cdn Divs, and moved up the boot of Italy.

In Jan 44 Dempsey assumed command of the 2d Br Army, which hit the beaches in Normandy on 6 June 44. The army met little resistance initially but quickly drew most of the German strength, including all of Rommel's panzers, to its front. Finally breaking out of the Normandy beachhead at the end of July, his 2d Army and Crerar's newly constituted 1st Cdn Army (along the coast) comprised Montgomery's 21st AG. While Crerar slowly cleared the Channel ports Dempsey raced through western Belgium, liberated Brussels, took Antwerp, and penetrated into Holland. Having been gazetted KCB in June, Sir Miles was dubbed by King George VI when he visited the front that winter *(DNB)*.

After a hard campaign in the Roermond Triangle, 15-27 Jan 45, his army began crossing the Rhine around Wesel on 23 March with massive artillery and air support plus a major airborne effort. Five days later Dempsey had opened the North German Plain for Montgomery's final offensive, and Sir Miles personally took the surrender of Hamburg on 3 May 45.

Still little known to the public, Dempsey was 48 years old when the war ended in Europe. He succeeded Sir William SLIM as 14th Army commander for the reoccupation of Singapore and Malaya, then followed Slim as CinC of Allied Land Forces in Southeast Asia. Advanced in the knighthood to KBE in 1945, and promoted to full general on leaving the Far East, he was CinC Middle East 1946-47. He retired at his own request in July 47 and held a number of high positions in business. Sir Miles published *Operations of the 2nd Army in Europe* (London: War Office, 1947).

As chairman of the Racecourse Betting Control Board, he indulged a long-standing interest in horses, which he bred and raced. Long a bachelor, Dempsey married in 1948. He died 5 June 69 at his home in Yattendon, Berkshire.

DE VALERA, Eamon. PM of Eire. 1882-1975. "Dev" was born 14 Oct 82 in NYC of a Spanish father and Irish mother. As a child he went to Ireland, where he was educated and became a mathematics tutor at Maynooth College. He joined the Irish Volunteers in 1913, was imprisoned for leading a battalion in the 1916 Easter Rising, and was saved by his American birth from being executed (Peter Teed). Released in June 17 after a year in prison, he was arrested again in May 18. While still in prison he was elected to Sinn Fein (Dec 18), and he became president of the rebel government set up the next year. Escaping from Lincoln Prison in Feb 19, Dev went to the US and raised £1 million for the IRA. After an absence of somewhat more than a year he returned to find a virtual civil war raging between the IRA and the **Black and Tans.** Shunning negotiations that led to the peace treaty of Dec 21, De Valera rejected the provision that six Ulster counties (in the north) be excluded from the Irish Free State. He again turned to violence in the Irish Civil War of 1922-23 and again was jailed. Released after less than a year, Dev renounced violence and pledged allegiance to the William Cosgrave government. Having been president of Sinn Fein since 1919, in 1926 he formed a new party, Fianna Fáil (Fenians of Ireland). In 1932 his Fenians came to power, and for the next decade De Valera controlled the government as president of the executive council. Under his constitution of 1938 Dev was PM or Taoiseach of the new Irish Free State, Eire. Intensely nationalistic in the Gaelic tradition of "Britain's misfortune is Ireland's opportunity," he undertook to remove every vestige of British influence. Insisting on strict neutrality, he even objected to Allied military activities in Northern Ireland during WWII. Churchill accused the Irish nationalist of aiding the Germans by denying the British use of ports and even feared that rumors of U-boats using Irish ports might be true (WC, I, 276-77; II, 600-07,

passim). Although De Valera said in 1935 he never would let any foreign power use Ireland as a base to attack Great Britain, he carried neutrality so far as to accept German and Japanese ambassadors. For reasons of military security the British cut off all normal civilian links with Eire by Apr 44. The tall, weak eyed, devoutly Catholic statesman remained in office until ousted by John A. Costello in 1948. He regained the prime ministry in 1951, was out of office 1954-57, then was back that year at the age of 75 and with the first overall majority since 1944. In 1959 he accepted that he had to pass the torch after nearly six decades of dominating the Irish scene. De Valera died 29 Aug 75 in Dublin at the age of 92. *(DNB.)*

DEVEREUX, James Patrick Sinnott. USMC officer. 1903-88. The story of his heroic role in the **Wake Island defense,** 8-23 Dec 41, is summarized in that glossary entry. Maj Devereux was a bantam Marine (5 feet 5) who was commissioned from the ranks in 1925. He surrendered on 23 Dec 41, spent the rest of the war as a POW, and retired from active duty in 1948 as a brigadier general. For eight years he represented Maryland in the Congress.

DEVERS, Jacob Loucks. US general. 1887-1979. The general who led the 6th US AG from southern France into Germany was born on 8 Sep 87 in York, Pa. Of Irish and Pennsylvania Dutch stock, "Jake" Devers graduated in the USMA class of 1909 (39/103) and was commissioned in the field artillery. At the Field Artillery School in 1925-28 he developed a method for getting guns on target with six rounds instead of the 30 needed under the old system. Over the heads of 474 other colonels he was promoted to brigadier general on 1 May 40, and five months later he had a second star. On an assignment one would expect an admiral to get, Maj Gen Devers located British bases in the Caribbean that the US would acquire in ROOSEVELT's "destroyers for bases deal."

On 9 Oct 40 he took command of the 9th Inf Div at Ft Bragg, NC, with the additional duty of directing a $40 million building program to accommodate an incoming National Guard outfit. On 17 July 41 Devers became chief of the Armored Force at Fort Knox, Ky, responsible for formulating doctrine, improving the design of vehicles, and readying armored forces for combat. He was promoted to lieutenant general in Sep 42, the month of his 55th birthday.

Four days after the death of Frank M. ANDREWS on 3 May 43, Devers took over the European Theater of Operations (ETOUSA) with headquarters in London. He directed the US buildup for the invasion of Europe and represented the US in COSSAC (under Frederick MORGAN). But when Eisenhower returned to London from Algiers he "sought to remove Jake Devers from the scene, sending him to the Mediterranean," writes Bradley. "Since Devers was a 'Marshall man,' Marshall was naturally miffed, but he finally agreed. . . . It was a comedown for Devers, and thereafter his relations with Ike were frosty." (Bradley, II, 217.) Devers headed NATOUSA 8 Jan-22 Oct 44. (AA, 605, although this source says elsewhere that Devers headed ETOUSA 7 May 43 to 16 Jan 44 (AA, 608). Devers had additional duties as deputy SACMED to Henry M. WILSON and deputy CinC AFHQ (in London). Joseph T. McNARNEY succeeded Devers as CG NATOUSA on 22 Oct 44 (AA, 605).

But since 1 Aug 44 Devers had been forming 6th AG Hq at Bastia, Corsica (AA, 489). As Deputy SACMED, he had general supervision over the initial landings in southern France, which were commanded by Alexander PATCH, CG 7th US Army. When the latter made contact with Patton on the south flank of Eisenhower's forces of SHAEF, Devers's 6th AG became operational at Lyons on 15 Sep 44. Four days later de LATTRE's Army B was redesignated the 1st French Army, passing from the operational control of Patch to Devers. The 6th AG eventually had more French troops (405,000) than Americans (345,000). (AA, 489.) Devers took more ground than any other Allied army group commander during the period 15 Sep-7 Nov 44 (West Point Atlas, 59). Patch advanced on the left (west) and de LATTRE cleared Belfort Gap before taking Mulhouse and pushing to the Swiss border. But remnants of Friedrich WIESE's 19th German Army remained in the Colmar Pocket. After this troublesome problem was eliminated, 9 Feb 45, smooth coordination between Patch's 7th Army and Patton's 3d Army in the Rhineland Campaign, and establishment of the Remagen bridgehead farther north, virtually destroyed German armies in the West by 21 Mar 45. Devers received the surrender of AG G in

Bavaria on 5 May 45. Eisenhower rated Devers behind Spaatz, Bradley, and possibly even Patton for promotion to four star rank (Bradley, op. cit., 390; Weigley, ETO, 670). Thanks to Marshall, however, Devers headed the list of five army generals in Europe to receive four star rank, DOR being 8 Mar 45 (AA, 915). Mark Clark and Bradley followed at two day intervals. But with Eisenhower succeeding Marshall as US Army CofS, Devers was relegated to command of Army Ground Forces. Retiring in 1949, and being Chairman of the American Battle Monuments Commission, 1959-69, the general died 15 Oct 79 at Walter Reed hospital in Washington, DC.

DEWAVRIN, André Pierre "Colonel Passy." French officer. 1912-. Born in Paris, Dewavrin graduated from the Ecole Polytechnique as an army engineer. He taught at St Cyr (1938) and fought in Norway (1940). Evacuated to England with BETHOUART's French Expeditionary Corps, Capt Dewavrin was 28 years old when he joined de Gaulle in London on 1 July 40. Promoted to major, he became one of de Gaulle's closest collaborators. (Larousse.)

Maj Dewavrin first headed both the 2d and 3d divisions of the French general staff in London but soon restricted his duties to the Deuxième Bureau, military intelligence. Adopting the code name "Passy" from the Paris metro station he quickly expanded his responsibilities to include unconventional warfare and clandestine operations. His office evolved by Aug 42 into the Bureau Central de Renseignements et d'Action (BCRA), responsible not only for intelligence but resistance as well. Described as "cool, steely-eyed and efficient . . . fearless, cultivated and intelligent" (Marshall, White Rabbit, 15, 17), Dewavrin has been accused of heading a Gestapo or KGB. One victim was Adm MUSELIER.

Dewavrin jumped into Normandy on 23 Feb 43 with his deputy, Pierre Brossolette, and YEO-THOMAS. Before returning by Lysander to London on 16 April the emissaries accomplished the seemingly impossible mission of locating the many scattered resistance groups and persuading them to accept de Gaulle's authority in a secret army that, when the time came, could support Allied liberation forces. Jean MOULIN followed through by pulling together eight major resistance movements including the communists. But the Germans had penetrated the resistance and promptly arrested Delestraint (9 June 43) and Jean Moulin (21 June 43), negating these triumphs.

A few months later, Dewavrin's organization was fused with the French army's conventional secret services to become the DGSS (*la Direction général des services spéciaux*), operating under Jacques Soustelle. During the period Nov 43-Mar 44 Lt Col Dewavrin was Soustelle's technical advisor in Algiers. As the liberation of France approached, Dewavrin became CofS to KOENIG, who headed the French Forces of the Interior (FFI). In Feb 45 Dewavrin succeeded Soustelle as head of the DGER *(Direction général des études et recherches)*, which had succeeded the DGSS in Oct 44.

Dewavrin ended his intelligence work in Jan 46 when de Gaulle quit as head of government. Having risen to full colonel, he retired several months later. (Larousse.) As Colonel Passy he published three volumes of memoirs, *Souvenirs* I, II, and III (Monaco: Solar, 1947 and 1949; Paris: Plon, 1951).

DEWEY, Thomas Edmund. US politician. 1902-71. The perennial presidential candidate was born 24 Mar 02 in Owosso, Mich. He got a law degree from Columbia Univ in 1925 and was a "racket busting" special prosecutor in New York for two years before being elected district attorney in 1937. Becoming governor of New York in 1943, he beat WILLKIE and MACARTHUR for the Republican nomination as presidential candidate against ROOSEVELT in 1944. But Dewey lost to FDR with 45.9 per cent of the popular vote and 99 of the 531 electoral votes *(CB 44)*. Four years later he was narrowly defeated for the presidency by TRUMAN.

DE WITT, John Lesesne. US general. 1880-1962. Remembered for his role in evacuating Japanese-Americans from the West Coast in 1942, De Witt was from a military family, the son of a general. While a sophomore at Princeton in 1898 he joined the army, fought in Cuba, and was given an RA commission as an infantryman (1898). He and George C. Marshall, three years junior, were classmates at Ft Leavenworth in 1906-7. Having found QM duties more to his temperament, De Witt sailed for France as QM of the 42d "Rainbow" Div. *(CB 42.)* At war's end he was 1st Army chief of

supply while Marshall was chief of operations. (Pogue, *Marshall,* III, 140.)

Army QMG 1930-34, Maj Gen de Witt was commandant at the AWC and one of two men senior to Marshall who were serious contenders for the army's top post when Marshall became CofS in the spring of 1939, and he was one of the few who still called Marshall "George" (ibid.). Promoted on 5 Dec 39 (*AA,* 915), Lt Gen De Witt took command of the 4th Army Area Hq in San Francisco in the fall of 1940, when the 4th Army was assigned to the field forces (*AA,* 496). Major subordinate units, deployed over the West Coast from San Diego to Puget Sound, were the 9th Corps (3d and 41st Divs), the 3d Corps (later comprising the 7th and 40th Divs), and the 9th Coast Arty District (ibid.). De Witt's Western Defense Command was established on 17 Mar 41, its headquarters combined with those of 4th Army (ibid., 600-11).

Two days after the Japanese attacked Pearl Harbor the elderly, mild-looking but obdurate general blasted San Francisco civic leaders for "criminal, shameful apathy" in ignoring blackout instructions *(CB 42)*. He ordered a curfew on the West Coast and commended antiaircraft units for firing on "unidentified planes." Less than a week after the Pearl Harbor attack De Witt was commanding a theater of operations with his paltry forces responsible for defending the western coastal frontier and Alaska (Pogue, op cit, 140). With many airplane plants in the close proximity of an estimated 117,000 Japanese, of whom 47,000 were American born, the zealous general called on Washington for speedy action to meet the alien threat. At first he thought that something short of mass evacuation would suffice, but he soon was predicting that citizens would take matters into their own hands. (See Pogue, op cit, 140-46, for a discussion of how the perceived threat evolved in the minds of US authorities involved.) Having proposed as early as 19 Dec 41 that all Japanese-Americans be evacuated from the West Coast, De Witt finally—after some vacillation—indicated on 29 Jan 42 that he was willing to assume responsibility for this drastic measure. On 11 Feb he was told to draft a plan, and on 19 Feb 42 the president signed an executive order (No. 9066) under which the still-somewhat-hesitant De Witt proceeded. (Lt Gen Hugh DRUM at this time was recommending that Italian and German aliens be moved from the east coast.) In an action that was properly the responsibility of civil agencies, and with his military forces spread thin, De Witt directed the movement of approximately 117,000 Japanese-Americans from a 2,000-mile stretch of the Pacific coast to "relocation centers."

On 12 Sep 43 the San Francisco headquarters were reorganized (*AA*, 601) and De Witt became commandant of the newly established Army and Navy Staff College at Ft Leavenworth, Kans (*AA*, 355). Marshall, whose role in the west coast evacuations had been "largely peripheral," "positively denied" that he had lost confidence in his colleague (Pogue, *Marshall*, III, 140, 146). After Leslie J. McNAIR was killed in Normandy on 25 July 44 De Witt took over McNair's "phantom army" in England.

When he retired in Nov 45 De Witt was junior only to Hugh A. DRUM as a three-star general given that rank in WWII.

DIELS, Rudolf. German official. 1900-57. Founder and first head of the Gestapo, Diels was born 16 Dec 00 in Berghaus (Hesse-Nassau), the son of a farmer. Bright, ambitious, and crafty, Diels joined the Prussian ministry of the interior in 1930 as an assessor in the political police. In two years he was assigned to the ministry's political bureau, which targeted threats including the Nazis and communists. When Goering became Prussian minister of the interior in 1933, Diels showed his new chief how secret police methods—particularly the use of incriminating files—could destroy political enemies. Diels set up Dept IA of the Prussian State Police, an office soon christened the Gestapo, and the young lawyer became Goering's deputy.

Himmler naturally coveted the Gestapo, and his first step was to coerce Goebbels into dismissing his trusty subordinate. One accusation fabricated by Heydrich was that Diels had intrigued with Hitler's SA enemy ROEHM. Goering dismissed Diels at the end of Sep 33, making him assistant director of the Berlin police. Diels had the good sense to know he was a marked man, so he fled on a forged passport to a refuge in the forests of Bohemia. Temporarily replaced as Gestapo chief by a boozy old party hack, Paul Hinkler, who drank himself out of office in less than a month, Diels won reinstatement by blackmailing Goering!

When the Reich minister of the interior, Wilhelm Frick, finally prevailed on Hitler to

incorporate the Prussian state into Nazi Germany, Goering surrendered control of the Gestapo to Himmler in a ceremony on 10 Apr 34. (Brissaud, 40.) Goering continued to protect Diels, personally striking his name from the SS hit list in the **Blood Purge** of June 34. (Brissaud, 46.) The protégé, whose wife had been married to Goering's brother, then held minor party posts: security chief of the Cologne government, chief of the Hanover government, and general manager of river navigation (ibid., 42n).

"Diels was undoubtedly very clever, but he was also dangerously unstable," wrote GISEVIUS from close association. "In spite of all his unscrupulous ambition, he never became a Fouché [Napoleon's treacherous minister of police] because he lacked the conscious self-discipline that his cold-blooded model had so overwhelmingly possessed." (Gisevius, 39.)

A witness at the Nuremberg trials, Diels was an official in Lower Saxony before serving as an undersecretary in the Bonn ministry of the interior until 1953. His self-serving memoir, *Lucifer ante portas, Von Severing bis Heydrich* (1950), was followed by a pamphlet attacking the Nuremberg trials and denouncing Otto JOHN in *Der Fall Otto John* (The Otto John Case), Goettingen, 1954. Diels died 18 Nov 57 after accidentally shooting himself with a hunting gun. (Wistrich.)

DIETL, Eduard. German general. 1890-1944. Recognizing the value of glamorous military figures for propaganda on the home front, Hitler picked two generals he could safely turn into popular heroes. He wanted "one in the sun and one in the snow." Rommel became the sun hero. (Liddell Hart, *Talk*, 45.)

The snow hero was a small, wiry, leather-tough Bavarian mountaineer, born 21 June 90 at Bad Aibling, son of an official (Angolia, I, 178). He survived hard combat service in WWI to join the Epp Freikorps in 1919 and the Nazi party a year later. A highly regarded company commander in the 19th Inf Regt in 1923, Dietl gave military instruction to the Brown Shirts (SA) and was active in the **Munich Beer Hall Putsch,** 8-9 Nov 23.

As commander of the 99th Alpine Regt he took part in the Anschluss (1938) and the conquest of Poland (1939). On 1 Apr 39 Dietl was promoted to generalmajor heading the 3d Mtn Div. Exactly a year later he was advanced to generalleutnant and leader of the expedition to Narvik. Surviving Lord CORK's relief efforts, Dietl was awarded the RK (9 May 40) and named commander of Mountain Corps Norway (16 June 40). Hitler personally awarded the first Oak-leaves (1/890) to the "Victor of Norway" in Berlin on 19 July 40 and promoted him (the same day) to Gen of Mtn Troops. (Angolia, II, 20.)

Dietl's next mission was to capture Mur-mansk. Undertaking a 60-mile offensive from around Petsamo, he advanced through rugged, unmapped terrain until stopped by 17 July 41, when it was apparent his forces were not up to the task. (Seaton, *R-G War*, 153; Ziemke, *GNT*, 154.) Hitler, who had never had confidence in Falkenhorst, issued a directive on 7 Nov 41 that created the Army of Lapland under Dietl to command German force in Finland, and Falken-horst returned to Oslo from Rovaniemi. (Ziemke, 135, 183.)

In a series of subsequent reorganizations Dietl assumed command of the Army of Lapland on 15 Jan 42 and of the 20th Mtn Army the follow-ing June (Ziemke, 326). Operations in Norway and Finland continued without significantly affecting the war. A few hours after attending the Berghof war conferences of 21-22 June 44, Dietl and his corps commanders were killed 23 June 44 in a plane crash near Hartberg. He was posthumously awarded the Swords (72/159) and given a state funeral.

DIETRICH, Josef "Sepp." German SS gener-al. 1892-1966. One of Hitler's best fighters and most devoted followers, Sepp Dietrich was born 28 May 92 in Hawangen, Bavaria, of peasant parentage. "He was of medium height, stocky and powerfully built, handsome in a pugilistic way . . . ," writes F. W. von MELLENTHIN. "His ideas and his conversation were often dis-jointed," reflecting a lack of education. "But he was always ready for anything and had a sense of humor, which was rather on the robust side." (*Generals*, 226).

Entering military service in 1911 and decorat-ed for valor in WWI, Dietrich was an artillery-man before being a crewman in one of the German army's only 25 tanks (ibid.). Called "Butcher Boy" from his days as a apprentice in Munich, Dietrich became an ardent Nazi and a favorite of Hitler's. He led a bodyguard that was mounted in three powerful Mercedes and armed with revolvers and hippopotamus whips (Bul-

lock, *Hitler,* 228). His Leibstandarte SS Adolf Hitler (LSSAH) was created in 1933 with only 120 officers and men as primarily a political force under Hitler's direct control. It had a major role in the **Blood Purge** of 1934. The LSSAH served under Guderian during the **Anschluss,** was raised to brigade size for action in Poland, then expanded into a motorized regiment for operations in France. After fighting in Yugo-slavia, Greece, and Russia, the unit was reorga-nized in France in June 42 as a **panzer grenadier** division. Having top priority in personnel and materiel, the LSSAH performed particularly well in the Donetz and Kharkov operations.

About the time Dietrich was awarded the Swords (26/159), 16 Mar 43, Goebbels noted in his diary that Hitler considered Dietrich "one of our top troop commanders and expects miracles from him" (Lochner, 288). The newly armored SS divisions "Das Reich" and "Totenkopf" were grouped in July 43 with the LSSAH to form Dietrich's 1st SS Pz Corps for action in south Russia.

But in Sep 43 Hitler ordered his miracle man to break off the desperate battles on the eastern front and rescue Mussolini's mistress from imprisonment by the Badoglio government. Dietrich's troops also shipped Allied POWs to Germany from Italian camps, handling the task with brutal efficiency. In early 1944 Dietrich's formation, redesignated the 1st SS Leibstandarte Pz Corps, was refitted in Belgium for deploy-ment in western France under GEYR VON SCHWEPPENBURG's operational control ini-tially. When Geyr's headquarters was knocked out by Allied planes on 10 June 44 (D+4), Dietrich took command of Pz Gp West and directed the desperate defensive actions around Caen, being promoted on 6 Aug 44 and award-ed the Diamonds (26/27). Heinrich EBERBACH came in to command Pz Gp West during the period 2 July-22 Aug, and Dietrich again was acting commander of Pz Gp West until MAN-TEUFFEL arrived on 10 Sep 44.

A new 6th SS Pz Army of four panzer divi-sions and five others was created under Dietrich in central Germany for the Ardennes counteroffensive. The man whom Rundstedt called "decent but stupid" quickly came a crop-per; he simply lacked the professional qualifi-cations to handle large formations, particular-ly when there was need to improvise in a fast moving situation.

The 6th SS Pz Army then was sent to cope with a desperate situation in Hungary. Dietrich attacked from the Hron bridgehead on 17 Feb 45 and achieved some success, but the odds were too great, especially for a general of his limited ability. After desperate efforts between Lake Balaton and the Danube, the SS panzer army was driven back to Vienna. Failing in a last ditch defense here, Dietrich withdrew to the foothills of the Alps, where he surrendered to US troops on 8 May 45.

After a year as a POW Dietrich was given a life sentence by an American court for complicity in the **Malmedy massacre**. The sentence was commuted to 25 years, nine years of which he served before being quietly released from Landsberg by a clemency board. The Germans arrested him in Aug 56 for involvement in the **Blood Purge** of 1934, and on 14 May 57 a Munich court sentenced him to 18 months in prison. Released from Landsberg he lived quietly until dying 21 Apr 66 in Ludwigsburg of a heart attack.

DIETRICH, Marlene. German-American actress. 1902-92. She was born in Berlin and trained at Max Reinhardt's drama school. *The Blue Angel* (1930) made her famous internationally as a movie actress and singer. Other successes followed, but she refused to work in Nazi Germany and from 1937 lived mainly in the United States. After Pearl Harbor, the exotic actress and singer abandoned a highly successful film career to broadcast anti-Nazi propaganda in German and entertain Allied troops. She made the German army's "Lili Marlene" her own song. In the 1950s the star began a new career as a cabaret singer and even later staged comebacks that dazzled audiences with her ageless charm. Marlene Dietrich died 6 May 92 in her Paris home.

DIETRICH, Otto. German press chief. 1897-1952. A professional journalist, Dr Dietrich was the Nazi Party press chief from 1931, and in 1937 he replaced Walter Funk as Reich Press Chief. A "formidable man . . . jealous of his prerogatives" (Davidson, *Trial,* 534), he feuded with Goebbels and Hans Fritzsche. In 1949 he was sentenced at Nuremberg to seven years' imprisonment but, with little longer to live, was released the next year.

DILL, John Greer. British field marshal. 1881-1944. Born in Belfast on 25 Dec 81, son of a bank official and grandson of a Presbyterian minister, Dill traced his ancestry to a Dutch soldier who had come over with William of Orange *(CB 41)*. He was commissioned from Sandhurst in 1901 and saw action in five of the last nine major actions of the Boer War. Tall, slim, and bright, an officer of "great charm and directness" (Parrish, *R&M,* 189), Dill became one of Britain's best army officers. In 1936 he was promoted to lieutenant general and sent to reestablish order in Palestine and Trans-Jordan. Here he showed ability not only as a field commander but also as a mediator. Promoted to full general and knighted in 1937 (KCB; GCB in 1942), he headed the 1st Corps of Lord GORT's BEF in France until recalled in Apr 40 to be Gen Sir Edmund IRONSIDE's vice CIGS.

On 26 May 40 Dill became CIGS. Ideally suited professionally but elderly for such a demanding assignment, Dill was not up to the strain of early military reverses and, particularly, of dealing with Churchill. He accompanied the PM to the Argentia Conference (9-12 Aug 41), but on 18 Nov it was announced that the king had conferred the rank of field marshal on Dill and approved his appointment as governor-designated of Bombay *(DNB)*. On this same day it was announced that on reaching the age of 60 on Christmas Day he would be succeeded by Alan BROOKE as CIGS. Brooke had begun "running in" when Churchill took Dill to Washington on 12 Dec 41 for a planning conference.

Dill found in Washington that "a new sphere was to open" for him (WC, III, 626). He remained in America as the senior British representative on the CCS, winning the highest respect and affection from American associates, particularly George Marshall. By 1944 Dill was very sick but refused to leave his post. The field marshal died 4 Nov 44, and George Marshall arranged for him to be buried in Arlington National Cemetery, the first foreigner so honored (Parrish, *R&M*, 469). H. M. "Jumbo" WILSON took over Dill's duties in Washington.

DIMITROV, Georgi. Bulgarian communist. 1882-1949. After being acquitted as the star defendant at the Reichstag Fire Trial in 1933, Dimitrov became general secretary of the comintern in 1935. He was leader of Bulgarian communists after the Soviet liberation and became prime minister on 6 Nov 46. He died 2 July 49 in Moscow.

DOENITZ, Karl. German admiral. 1891-1980. From CinC U-boats, 1939-43, he rose to head the German Navy from 31 Jan 43, and on 1 May 45 he succeeded Hitler as head of state.

Born in Berlin-Gruenau on 16 Sep 91, Karl Doenitz came from a family of professional men. In 1910 he enlisted as a sea cadet, entering the naval training school that year and serving at sea before being commissioned in 1913. After a few years aboard a cruiser in the Mediterranean, Doenitz transferred to submarines in Oct 16. In the last weeks of the war he was forced by mechanical problems to surface in the middle of a British convoy after sinking a large ship and preparing to attack another. A prisoner from 4 Oct 18 until July 19, Doenitz remained in uniform only because he was assured that Germany would soon have the submarines banned by the Versailles Treaty. But he had to wait 16 years. In 1935, Doenitz took charge of the new U-boat arm, which he was convinced was Germany's main hope for winning a war against Britain. ("The only thing that ever really frightened me during the war was the U-boat peril," Churchill would remember [WC, II, 529].) But Adm Raeder, head of the German navy, believed in capital ships, and Goering, head of the Luftwaffe, believed in the Luftwaffe. So instead of the 1,000 submarines he wanted at the start of hostilities, Doenitz had only 57, and a very high percentage of these were lost in the first stages of the war.

Although personal experience convinced Doenitz that the "lone wolf" method of submarine operation left much to be desired, this was standard procedure until late in 1940. By then, however, German air reconnaissance was critically deficient and the lone wolf, although relatively safe on the high seas, had a needle-in-the-haystack problem of finding targets. "Pack tactics" (die Rudeltaktik), long evolving in Doenitz's mind, called for fanning out 8 to 20 U-boats under radio control from a CP at Lorient, France. After spotting a prey, the U-boat would shadow it, radio back to Lorient, and a "wolf pack" would be formed in the critical area. The pack would make repeated night torpedo attacks on the surface, shadow the convoy in daylight hours at a safe range, then close up at dark to attack again.

The "happy time" for German submariners was from July to Oct 40, and when America entered the war on 7 Dec 41 they began sinking up to three ships a day along the Atlantic seaboard. But the rest of the German navy never had a happy time, and an increasingly exasperated Hitler (who hated the sea anyhow) finally sacked RAEDER; Grossadmiral Doenitz (who skipped the rank of Generaladmiral) became CinC of the German navy (Kriegsmarine) on 31 Jan 43. Submarines finally got priority in naval construction. On 6 Apr 43, the month U-boat strength hit its peak, Doenitz became one of the few awarded the Oakleaves (223/890) for leadership. (Angolia, II, 195.)

But just as Hitler belatedly realized that Doenitz was Germany's only hope for regaining the strategic initiative, the Allies were perfecting antisubmarine warfare. "We had lost the Battle of the Atlantic," Doenitz wrote after realizing that he had no answer to the very long-range airborne radar that the Allies had started using. On 24 May 43 he withdrew all U-boats to an area southwest of the Azores. (Doenitz, *Memoirs*, 325, 332, 341.)

Now his only hope was mass production of a radically improved U-boat designed in 1937 by a Prof Walter but never properly funded for development. Doenitz promptly (June 43) approved blueprints for the XXI. This was an all-electric boat of 1,600 tons with triple the underwater speed of existing boats and a ventilating apparatus ("snorkel") that enabled it to recharge batteries without surfacing. Albert SPEER provided mass production techniques, and the first of 107 Mark XXI boats was operational in Mar 45 (Irving, *HW*, 760). However, it was too late for the secret weapon to be decisive.

The German navy's major task from the summer of 1944 was to support the army on the eastern front. Some 50,000 naval personnel were transferred to the army or used in special ground formations against the Red Army. Along the Baltic coast in the last months of the war, Doenitz was preoccupied with evacuating more than two million Germans and delivering supplies. On 22 April 45, the Grand Admiral moved his headquarters to Ploen, in Holstein. Soon after this, 1 May, Doenitz was named head of state in accordance with Hitler's last will and testament. "He had never given me the slightest indication that he was even considering me as a possible successor," writes Doenitz. "I had never received any hint on the subject from anybody else, nor, I believe had any of the other leaders ever thought of such a possibility" (*Memoirs*, 441).

The "weekend Fuehrer," as the disgruntled GOERING called Doenitz, held office for 12 days. He tried to form a new government that might get less harsh surrender terms, he tried to coordinate actions of surviving field forces, and he continued to evacuate Germans from the path of the Red Army. After sending peace emissaries to Montgomery (who was chivalrous) and Eisenhower (who was not), Doenitz negotiated the **surrender of Germany.** Hostilities ceased the night of 8-9 May 45.

The Nuremberg tribunal cleared Doenitz of "conspiracy for war" but sentenced him to 10 years' imprisonment for "crimes against peace and for war crimes." More than 100 US naval officers wrote to Doenitz in his defense. "The testimony that undoubtedly saved Doenitz' life at Nuremberg came from Admiral Nimitz and from the British Admiralty," writes Davidson, both admitting they had waged the unrestricted submarine warfare for which the enemy admiral was facing death (*Trial*, 424). Albert Speer noted in his prison journals that the grand admiral still considered himself Germany's legal head of state (Speer, *Spandauer Tagebuecher*, especially p. 335). After being confined for 11 years and 4 months (10 years and 20 days being spent in Berlin's Spandau prison) Doenitz was released on 1 Oct 56. Retiring to his modest home he promptly published memoirs that historians find suspect in many areas. The English translation is *Memoirs: Ten Years and Twenty Days* (London: Weidenfeld and Nicholson, 1959). The frail, unassuming, unrepentant Grand Admiral Doenitz died 24 Dec 80, outliving all German field marshals.

DOHNANYI, Hans von. Anti-Hitler conspirator. 1902-45. Born 1 Jan 01 in Vienna, he was the son of the noted Hungarian musician Ernst von Dohnanyi (1877-1960). The name was pronounced DOUGH nanyee (CE), and Hans became nicknamed "Do," pronounced dough (Harold C. Deutsch). But grandson Christoph von Dohnanyi, music director of the Cleveland Orchestra since 1984, pronounces the family

name DOCK nanyee, and the maestro's brother, Dr Klaus von Dohnanyi, a former mayor of Hamburg, does not confirm Professor Deutsch's finding (above). Dohnanyi (without accent) is accepted by CE and other authorities in English-language reference to the subject of this sketch, but his sons adopted the original spelling, Dohnányi, and, like their father, have the particle of nobility "von."

Hans became a lawyer, practicing at the Mendelson International Law Institute in Hamburg and with the supreme court at Leipzig. In 1929 he went to Berlin as adjutant and chief adviser to Reich Ministers of Justice Joâl and his successor, Franz Guertner. Devoted to legal reform even before Hitler's rise to power in 1933, he opposed Hans FRANK's corruption of German law and also assisted Count Ruediger von der Goltz, a cousin of his wife, Christine BONHOEFFER, in defending Werner von FRITSCH against trumped-up charges in the winter of 1937-38. Having thus "gained the unfavorable notice of Nazi hierarchs" (Deutsch, I, 375), and there being a debate about his possibly having Jewish blood (which he never would have joined [ibid.]) but he was "Aryanized" by a "Fuehrer Order."

Presumably to get him out of Berlin, Hans was appointed a supreme court judge in Leipzig. He had long been associated with Hans Oster and other anti-Nazi conspirators, and after a year in Leipzig he was assigned to Oster's section of the Abwehr. This made him a key member of the German resistance, and with Teutonic thoroughness he kept copious records for what he hoped would be postwar criminal action by German courts against Third Reich officials.

On 5 Apr 43 an SS judge advocate, Dr Manfred Roeder, quietly entered the Abwehr offices just before 10 AM with a small group including Franz Xaver Sonderegger, a Gestapo official. Canaris was reassured to be confronted only with the accusation that Dohnanyi was taking bribes for smuggling Jews into Switzerland (Opn 7). The Gestapo had extracted this unfounded lead from the disgruntled Wilhelm SCHMIDHUBER, but the secret police also had well-founded suspicions that Dohnanyi had long been conspiring against the regime with Dietrich BONHOEFFER and others. Having a warrant to search Dohnanyi's office, the legally correct Roeder asked Oster to join Canaris in watching. Contents of the office safe were being displayed on desks when Dohnanyi noticed an Abwehr "playing card." This had instructions to Dr Josef MUELLER and Dietrich Bonhoeffer on a planned mission to the Vatican. "Dough" whispered to Oster that they should pretend the card was "disinformation" concocted to mislead the enemy. But Oster misunderstood, tried to pocket the card, and Sonderegger caught him in the act. Finding other incriminating evidence, Roeder arrested Dohnanyi. Later in the day Mueller, Dietrich Bonhoeffer, and his sister Christine were taken into custody. (Brown, Bodyguard, 302-3. Other accounts vary in details.)

Held in the Wehrmacht jail at 64 Lehterstrasse in Berlin, Dohnanyi used his skills as an attorney to fend off the interrogation of Roeder, who was also a good lawyer. The prisoner argued convincingly that he and Dietrich Bonhoeffer (held separately in Tegel Prison) had engaged only in legitimate Abwehr affairs including disinformation. After Canaris complained to KEITEL that Roeder was interested primarily in an SS effort to malign the army, Roeder was replaced by a certain Kutzmer. Now facing a less skilled interrogator, the prisoner had a respite.

In smuggled messages Dohnanyi pleaded that his voluminous records of the conspiracy be destroyed, but the ailing Gen Ludwig BECK insisted they be preserved for historical evidence of what Good Germans had done to fight Nazism. On 22 Sep 44 the Gestapo found Dohnanyi's archives, which led them to previously unincriminated officers including Kripo chief Arthur NEBE.

The strain of prison and brutal interrogation so affected Dohnanyi's health that he was transferred to a clinic. But on 22 Jan 44 the Gestapo had him moved to an SS medical facility, claiming the army no longer had jurisdiction. Determined to postpone trial, Dohnanyi had his wife smuggle him a dysentery culture. When this did not work he had her get a diphtheria culture, which on the second attempt produced a grave case of the disease that provided periodic relief from the ordeal of interrogation. Although clearly guilty of high treason, the prisoner (like others) was kept alive as a possible source of further information. But when the CANARIS diaries were discovered on about 4 Apr 45 (Hohne, 591-92) Hitler ordered the SS to liquidate all surviving conspirators. Still paralyzed, carried on a stretcher by SS guards, Dohnanyi was summarily tried on 6 April at Oranienburg/ Sachenhausen and sentenced to death for "high treason and treason in the field" (ibid., 592). Authorities do not agree on details, but the heroic Dohnanyi apparently was hanged at Sachenhausen on 9 Apr 45 (personal information), when Dietrich Bonhoeffer, CANARIS, and OSTER were executed at Flossenbuerg.

The late Harold C. Deutsch, an American authority on the anti-Hitler conspiracy who interviewed many surviving participants, was of great assistance on this troublesome sketch. Hans von Dohnanyi's sons, identified above, gave it a careful last minute review in 1996 and contributed valuable detail.

DOIHARA, Kenji. Japanese general. 1883-1948. Born poor in Okayama in Aug 83, he was first in his class at the Japanese MA, where he learned Chinese, Russian, and English *(CB 42)*. Bland, mild mannered, but vigorous, the stocky little Doihara became one of the **Eleven Reliables** and a master of intrigue. Starting his career in Manchuria as a general staff officer on undercover work in Eastern Siberia and North China, Doihara is believed to have contrived the **Mukden incident** and subsequent actions leading to Japanese intervention in China.

In 1937 he assumed command of the 14th Div in North China, where despite a bad defeat in Shansi he was promoted to head the 5th Army. After taking charge of the national military academy in Oct 40, the "Tiger of China" was made IG of military aviation in Apr 41. Doihara was promoted to full general in Oct 41, after TOJO took power, but his wartime service was restricted to commanding three large rear-area armies in succession. For pre-1937 activities in Manchuria he was among the major war criminals hanged on 23 Dec 48.

DOLLFUSS, Engelbert. Austrian statesman. 1892-1934. Son of a farmer's unmarried daughter, Dollfuss went on to get degrees in law and theology at the universities of Vienna and Berlin. As an officer in a machine gun unit during WWI he won eight decorations for bravery. In 1922 he earned a doctorate in economics and began a career in politics as a Christian socialist that led to his election as chancellor in 1932. To gain support from Mussolini in opposing union with Germany he promulgated a new, fascistic constitution (1934) and became unpopular for his authoritarianism. (Briggs, ed, *20 Cent Biog*.) In the unrest preceding the

Anschluss Dollfuss was attacked in his office on 25 July 34 by German SS troops in Austrian uniforms. Shot at close range, he died about six hours later. The bungled putsch was quickly put down by Kurt von SCHUSCHNIGG, who became chancellor.

DOLLMANN, Friedrich. German general. 1876-1944. Exceptionally tall and distinguished looking, he was from a family of civil servants. The elderly general assumed command of the 7th Army in Sep 39 and on 15 June 40, as French resistance collapsed, he penetrated the Maginot Line around Colmar. The 7th Army then had the cushy mission of occupying Normandy and Brittany. Rommel's arrival in early 1944 brought disagreement over defensive strategy: Dollmann believing his army should be strengthened in Normandy, where terrain was ideal for defense, but Rommel insisted that Hans von Salmuth's 15th Army, farther north in the Pas de Calais area, should have the major allocation of troops including all the panzers.

The beginning of the end came for Dollmann on 25 July 44, when 7th Army defenses were penetrated at St Lô by J. Lawton COLLINS's 7th US Corps (Opn Cobra). Operating far to the rear from a sumptuous chateau at Le Mans, Dollmann and his CofS, Generalleutnant Max Pemsel, began to crack when the situation around Caen got desperate. Dollmann could not decide how to commit Paul Hausser's 2d SS Pz Corps as it raced up. "Twice [on 26 June] Dollmann picked up the phone and ordered Hausser to . . . help Dietrich defend Caen, and twice he changed his mind" (Irving, *Fox,* 394-95). Two days later Dollmann gave Hausser panic-stricken orders to counterattack with his entire corps, not allowing time to plan the operation properly. At 10 AM on 29 June Dollmann took poison, but Pemsel delayed for two hours before reporting the general's death of "heart failure." (Ibid.) HAUSSER assumed command of the army.

DONOVAN, William Joseph "Wild Bill." US general. 1883–1959. An Irish Catholic born 1 Jan 83 in Buffalo, NY, son of a Republican ward heeler, he acquired the nickname Wild Bill as a football player at Columbia Univ. After getting his law degree from Columbia in 1907 Donovan practiced successfully in Buffalo and married into one of the city's oldest and richest

families. In 1916 he organized and led a National Guard cavalry troop to the Mexican border. With the Rockefeller Institute's food mission in Poland he met Herbert Hoover, later being his adviser, speech writer, and unofficial campaign manager. As colonel of New York's "Fighting 69th" Inf Regt in 1918 he won the Medal of Honor, DSC, DSM, and three Purple Hearts. Before returning to America he explored in China, was an observer with the Kolchak government in Siberia, and served as special counsel for the Fuel Commission in Europe. In 1922 he founded a major law firm in NYC and became active as a Republican in state and national politics. Having run unsuccessfully for lieutenant governor in 1922 and serving as assistant attorney general in Calvin Coolidge's administration, he was his party's nominee in 1932 for governor of New York.

The millionaire Wall Street lawyer was an outspoken advocate of military preparedness to protect American neutrality. He vigorously opposed Roosevelt's domestic programs but, having visited the war zones in Ethiopia and Spain, in July 40 he undertook the first of several confidential missions for the president overseas, traveling between London and the Middle East (*CB 41*).

In July 41, some six months before America's entry into the war, Roosevelt appointed Col Donovan "Coordinator of Information" (COI). This was the cover name for a private intelligence agency charged with espionage, black propaganda, and observation of resistance movements. COI was stripped of its propaganda mission and redesignated the Office of Strategic Services (*OSS*) in the summer of 1942. Assisted by Canada's William Stephenson and Britain's MI6 chief Stewart MENZIES, the vigorous Col Donovan built a chaotic organization of left wing activists and intellectuals, right wing corporate attorneys, and people from America's wealthiest families. (Smith, *OSS,* 11, 15.) Directly subordinate to the JCS, but under a heavy veil of secrecy that permitted little governmental oversight, the OSS eventually had up to 16,000 people behind enemy lines throughout the world. Wild Bill directed novel operations, many of dubious merit, and devoted much of his personal effort to building a bureaucratic empire while fighting off invasion by rival services, principally J. Edgar Hoover's FBI and Gen George V. Strong's military intelligence organization. The OSS, lacking the experience and traditions of secret services in other countries and often characterized by poor management, had many failures along with its triumphs. Donovan was a brigadier general in 1943 and a major general from 10 Nov 44.

Roosevelt's high regard for Donovan waned at about this time (Smith, *op cit*, 10), and on 20 Sep 45, only weeks after V-J day, Pres Truman ordered the OSS disbanded. It became the cadre for the CIA, created 26 Sep 47 under the National Security Act.

Wild Bill resumed private law practice in 1946. He was ambassador to Thailand, 1953-54, when US intelligence operations began mushrooming in Southeast Asia.

See *The Last Hero: Wild Bill Donovan,* by Anthony Cave Brown (New York: Times Books, 1983) and the work by R. Harris Smith cited above.

DOOLITTLE, James Harold. US general. 1896-1993. Born 14 Dec 96 in Alameda, Calif, he lived from his third to eighth year in Nome, Alaska. (His father, a carpenter, was prospecting for gold.) The boy attended the Los Angeles Manual Arts High School, where he was boxing champion. Doolittle fought professionally as a bantamweight before abandoning aspirations for a ring career. In 1916, a year after graduating from the Los Angeles Junior College, he enlisted as a flying cadet, and on 11 Mar 18 became a second lieutenant in the Army Signal Corps. *(CB 42.)* Disappointed by not seeing action in France, he was a stunt flyer before getting an RA commission on 1 July 20. Doolittle won major trophies and two peacetime DFCs (1922, 1924) before getting a PhD in aeronautical engineering from MIT in 1925. Five years later he resigned his RA commission to manage Shell Oil's aviation department, but as a reserve corps major he continued to be a military pilot.

Doolittle became president of the Institute of Aeronautical Sciences in Jan 40. He was recalled to active duty on 1 July 40 as a major in the Air Corps Reserve. On 2 Jan 42 he was promoted to lieutenant colonel and ordered to Washington.

For leading the **Doolittle Raid on Tokyo,** 18 Apr 42, he was awarded the Medal of Honor and promoted to brigadier general. Doolittle got his second star as the first commander of the 12th AF at Bolling Field, DC, on or about 23 Sep 42 *(AA,* 597). Elements of his air force took part in initial operations in North Africa, 8 Nov 42, and secured newly won bases (ibid.).

After directing bomber operations in Tunisia, he turned over command of the 12th to Carl SPAATZ on 1 Mar 43 and headed the NW Africa Strategic AF. Doolittle then had charge of the new 15th AF in Tunisia 1 Nov 43-3 Jan 44, and in coordination with the 8th AF in England made strategic strikes against Germany and her satellites *(AA,* 598). Doolittle also served as one of Lt Gen Carl Spaatz's chief deputies in Tedder's Mediterranean Allied Air Forces when it was activated on 20 Dec 43.

Doolittle went to the UK to succeeded EAKER on 6 Jan 44 as head of the 8th AF, being promoted to three-star rank on 13 Mar 44 *(AA,* 911). Again under Spaatz, who commanded the US Strategic AF in Europe, Doolittle directed American daylight precision bombing in the Allied air assault on Europe. Despite claims of precision, Doolittle's strategic bombers were rarely used for close support of ground operations. On one memorable occasion when it did, the St Lô carpet bombing for Opn Cobra on 25 July 44, "personnel errors" killed McNAIR and about 100 other Americans. Doolittle's insistence on a perpendicular bombing run may have led to the "friendly fire" disaster. (Irving, *The War Between the Generals,* 212, 223.)

To sum up the record of the 8th AF (which was commanded until 1 Dec 42 by Spaatz, then until 6 Jan 44 by Ira EAKER), it claimed destruction of 20,419 enemy aircraft on its 1,034,052 flights, 332,904 of which were by heavy bombers. *(AA,* 595-96.) At peak strength under Doolittle, the 8th AF dispatched a single mission on Christmas Eve 1944 that had more than 2,000 heavy bombers, almost 1,000 fighters, and 21,000 men.

After V-E day (8 May 45) Doolittle established 8th AF Hq on Okinawa, but it was too late for his planes to have much action. On 14 Sep 45 Doolittle was succeeded by Maj Gen Earle E. Partridge. The "Doolittle Board" heard grievances from disgruntled veterans and recommended social reforms of the US armed forces. Lt Gen Doolittle retired on 22 May 46 *(AA,* 911) and returned to Shell Oil as a director and VP in charge of aviation. The legendary airman died 27 Sep 93 at 96.

DOORMAN, Karel W. F. M. Dutch admiral. 1889-1942. The tall, dark-haired, highly-regarded rear admiral commanded the Royal Netherlands navy forces in the East Indies at the outbreak of hostilities. Effective 2 Feb 42 he headed the ABDA command combined striking force. Lacking air support, outgunned, and without time to integrate his international assembly of cruisers and destroyers, Doorman was decisively defeated in his first and only major operation, the Battle of the Java Sea, 27 Feb 42. The admiral went down with his flagship at about midnight. (Morison, III, 271, 357.)

DORNBERGER, Walter. German rocket developer. 1895-1980. The son of a pharmacist, Dornberger was headed for a career in architecture before war intervened. By the armistice of 1918 he was an artillery lieutenant. Selected for retention in the Treaty Army, he was sent for schooling in mechanical engineering and in 1930 became director of the army weapons department at Kummersdorf (near Berlin). By 1932, Capt Dornberger was working on a prototype rocket, the A-1, and that year he brought in a young amateur, Wehrner von BRAUN.

In 1936 the army set up R&D facilities at Peenemuende, where the Luftwaffe worked separately on the V-1 buzz-bomb. Hitler thought so little of Dornberger's efforts that he ordered them discontinued, but Brauchitsch and Goering covertly kept the rocket experiments going. Test firings of the A-4, begun in Mar 42, were failures until 3 Oct 42. Braun and Col Dornberger (as of about this time) still had technical problems to be solved. But after Himmler saw an A-4 launch in June 43 he recommended the weapon to Hitler. The fuehrer was wildly enthusiastic after a briefing on 7 July 43 by Braun and Dornberger that included a dramatic film of a test flight.

Allied intelligence was slow to discover that something important was happening at Peenemuende. But after an alert RAF photo interpreter, Constance Babington, noted an odd little shadow, magnification revealed a V-1 launching ramp. (Her book is *Evidence in Camera* [London: Chatto and Windus, 1958].) The RAF hit Peenemuende the night of 17-18 Aug 43 with a massive air attack. Most of the damage was to non-essential parts of the complex, and Dornberger craftily ordered the bomb rubble to be left undisturbed so the British believed they had destroyed the base. Enemy bombers consequently did not strike again for nine months, and with new manufacturing facilities in the Harz mountains the rocket program was set back only six months.

After surrendering to the Americans (see von BRAUN), Generalmajor Dornberger (as of Mar 43) was charged as a war criminal for the V-2 attacks on London and Antwerp. But he was never brought to trial. In the late 1940s he moved to America and was a missile consultant for the USAF. The rocket pioneer published *V-2* (London: Hurst and Blackett, 1954).

DORNIER, Claude. German aircraft designer and manufacturer. 1884-1969. Born 14 May 84 in Bavaria, son of a French father and German mother, he worked for the Zeppelin company from 1910 until establishing his own plant at Friedrichshafen in 1927. His 12-engine, 170-passenger, Do X flying boat made its first flight to NYC in 1931. The Do 17 (1934) "flying pencil" was used, with modifications, throughout the war. Many other Dorniers from the monoplane (Do 18), long-range flying boat (Do 26), (Do 217A) heavy bomber were in the Luftwaffe inventory. Dornier's highly uncoventional Do 335, a 474mph, 1,280-mi-range fighter-bomber was not operational by V-E day. (*CE; S&S.*)

DOUGLAS, William Sholto. British airman. 1893-1969. Descended from the Douglases of ancient Scotland, he was born 23 Dec 93 at Headington, Oxfordshire. From the age of seven he lived in London with his divorced mother and two younger brothers in straightened circumstances *(DNB)*. After entering Lincoln College, Oxford, in 1913 and winning a classical scholarship, he left the next year to enter the Royal Field Arty. At the beginning of 1915 he joined the Royal Flying Club for observer training but quickly qualified as a fighter pilot and saw bitter action that year. He soon became a squadron commander, opposing the Richthofen Sqdn and a pilot named Hermann Goering. "In circumstances where a pilot's life was measured in days he had lasted nearly four years," writes Peter Wyckham in *DNB*.

Maj Douglas, MC (1916), DFC (1917), was not interested in joining the RAF nor in returning to Oxford. Issued commercial pilot's license No 4, he became chief pilot for the Handley Page Co. But civilian life palled, and he joined the RAF in 1920 with the rank of squadron leader. Douglas was a student at the first course of the Imperial Defense College in 1920, one of the few RAF instructors there, and in 1936 was made director of staff studies in the air ministry. By 1938 he was an air vice marshal serving in the new post of assistant chief of air staff with responsibility for training and for specifying new equipment; in 1940 his title was changed to deputy CAS under Sir Cyril Newall.

The only fighter pilot among senior RAF staff officers, he was a leading critic of Chief of Fighter Command Hugh "Stuffy" DOWDING. The Battle of Britain was almost won when Sholto Douglas succeeded Dowding on 25 Nov 40, being promoted concurrently to air marshal and knighted (KCB, 1941). Douglas was praised for showing aggressiveness that DOWDING had been accused of lacking, but it is worth pondering whether the new chief would have been as successful *during* the Battle of Britain as his predecessor.

When the RAF took the offensive, however, the burly Scot was highly successful with the "**big wing**" concept. His other important innovations were to attack from very high altitude and to make low-level attacks when these could achieve surprise and minimize the effects of ground fire. Recognizing that night fighting presented many problems but great rewards, Douglas worked steadily to improve night-fighting equipment and tactics.

Promoted to air chief marshal, Douglas was sent to Cairo at the end of 1942 as TEDDER's deputy in the Middle East AF (MEAF). A command reorganization in Apr 43, only three months later, made Tedder head of Allied air forces under Eisenhower as the Tunisian campaign drew to a close, and Douglas stepped up to command the MEAF. He remained subordinate to TEDDER, whose other commands were SPAATZ's NW African AF (NAAF) and RAF Malta.

For the Normandy invasion Douglas was Chief of Coastal Command and Commander of British Expeditionary Air Forces. His major mission initially was to clear the Channel of German naval opposition, mainly U-boats, which he called "putting the cork into the bottle."

In July 45, after V-E day, Douglas took command of the British Air Forces of Occupation and in Jan 46 was elevated in the knighthood to GCB and promoted to marshal of the RAF. He had the distinction of being one of only two officers to have that rank without being chief of air staff. *(DNB.)* Very reluctantly Douglas succeeded Montgomery in June 46 as comman-

der of British forces in Europe, military governor of the British zone, and a member of the four-power Allied Control Council. Although doubting the propriety of the Nuremberg war crimes trials, he had to confirm the tribunal's sentences. This appointment ending in Nov 47, he returned to England, retired from active duty in 1948, and was awarded a peerage as 1st Baron Douglas of Kirtleside.

Despite his high assignments, the modest and publicity shy Sholto Douglas receives scant mention in the literature of 1939-45. He served after the war on the board of the British Overseas Airways Corporation before being chairman of British European Airways, 1949-64, and finally chairman of Horizon Travel Ltd. On the Labor benches of the House of Lords he was a moderate socialist, to the surprise of his former RAF associates (Peter Wykeham in *DNB*.)

Like his brilliant father, a noted authority on the history of Italian art who became an American citizen, Sholto Douglas was married three times (1919, 1933, and 1955). After four years of ill health Lord Douglas died 29 Oct 69 in a Northhampton hospital. He published *Years of Combat* (1963) and *Years of Command* (1966).

DOWDING, Hugh Caswell Tremenheere. British airman. 1882-1970. The man whose Fighter Command won the Battle of Britain in 1940 was a tall, gaunt, prickly Scot born 24 Apr 82 at Moffat, Dumfriesshire. He was the son of a local schoolmaster. After completing four lusterless years at Winchester in 1899 Dowding entered Woolwich and was commissioned in the Royal Garrison Arty (1900). He was a subaltern at Gibraltar, Ceylon, and Hong Kong before serving six years in India with mountain artillery troops including a native battery.

Back in the UK he learned to fly at a school run by Vickers and got a pilot's license on 20 Dec 13, hours before passing out of Camberley. At the staff college he was called "Stuffy," a not-too-affectionate but appropriate nickname that stuck. During a three-month RFC pilot training course he first met Hugh Trenchard, the school's assistant commandant. Promotion to captain had not come until the year before the war started in 1914.

After assignments in England and France, showing a talent for developing new technology, notably radio and photography, Dowding commanded No 16 Sqdn in 1915 before taking over the 9th "Headquarters" Wing. Having clashed earlier on a supply matter with Trenchard, who now was a brevet colonel commanding the RFC, Dowding ran afoul of his chief again in Aug 16 for insisting that one of his squadrons be rested after sustaining severe losses on the Somme. Calling Dowding a "dismal Jimmy," Trenchard replaced him with Cyril Newall. Spending the rest of the war in England, Dowding was promoted to brigadier general by 1917 but had no further field duty.

He entered the newly established RAF in 1919 with his nemesis Trenchard's grudging approval. Promoted to air vice marshal in 1929, he joined the Air Council in Sep 30 as member for R&D when Trenchard retired as CAS in 1930. Dowding was promoted to air marshal in Jan 33 and knighted KCB in June 34. Focusing on R&D, Sir Hugh did much to prepare the RAF for war. He started a design competition that led to the Spitfire and Hurricane, revolutionary single-wing, high performance metal land planes incorporating major features of the Supermarine seaplane. He also spurred development of radar, which was operational in 1935. But Dowding was slow to order development of self-sealing fuel tanks, and he has been faulted for backing "the short-range Battle bomber which, often armed only with two machine guns, was brushed out of the Royal Air Force in the Battle for France" (Andrews, 555-6).

When Sir Hugh took over Fighter Command in 1936 he also had operational control over Anti-Aircraft Command (including searchlights), Balloon Command, and the chain of early warning observer and radar stations. The RAF and the public were "bomber minded," but Dowding insisted, correctly, that the first priority was air defense, which was the mission of Fighter Command. He was among those who pressured Neville Chamberlain into appeasing Hitler during the Munich crisis because the RAF needed at least a year to reach a war footing— Britain bought almost exactly that amount of time with the **Munich agreement** of 30 Sep 38 (declaring war on 3 Sep 39) and a little more during the Phony War.

Winning air superiority over Dunkirk at the critical moment was Stuffy Dowding's first strategic triumph. He had led the struggle not to sacrifice Fighter Command in a futile gesture to save the ineptly led French and Belgian armies in Flanders. When Sir Hugh first committed

Spitfires and Hurricanes over Dunkirk he gave the Luftwaffe its first setback, and a very nasty surprise. But Dowding soon found himself fighting with formidable enemies in London who disapproved of his leadership. Given four successive warnings of imminent retirement for age, Dowding would say later that he faced his greatest challenge in the status of "an unsatisfactory domestic servant under notice" (Andrews, 57). At the root his problem was the **"big wing"** controversy. Accused of not being sufficiently aggressive, Dowding was criticized also for his sound policy of rotating entire squadrons through rest periods instead of taking individual pilots from the air group under the worst strain at any moment. (Shades of his trouble with Trenchard in 1916, mentioned herein.)

Friction over another matter grew between Dowding and his two top group commanders, PARK and LEIGH-MALLORY. While Park's No 11 Gp in southern England took the brunt of the Luftwaffe's initial assault, Leigh-Mallory's No 12 Gp had a relatively easy time in the industrial Midlands. Park wanted Leigh-Mallory to protect his air bases in southern England while squadrons were away on missions. But Leigh-Mallory took to sending his planes into Park's territory in search of independent, offensive action, making them usually unavailable when needed to protect Park's bases.

Fighter Command's worst day was 31 Aug 40 when most of Park's bases were destroyed and, for the first time, Dowding had greater losses (39 planes, 14 pilots) than the enemy. British pilots were at the breaking point; damaged plants could not produce planes to match losses; and repair work was slowed. Dowding needed a miracle, and he got it: in hopes of baiting Dowding into a battle of annihilation, Goering (with Hitler's willing approval) began the **blitz of London** 7 Sep. Showing steel nerves in this crisis, Dowding declined to commit his last fighter reserves, and with this desperately needed reprieve went on to be "the only man who ever won a major fighter battle" (Tunncy). Having been elevated to GCB in July 37, Sir Hugh was awarded the Knight Grand Cross in Sep 40. Trenchard had the decency to tell Dowding that he gravely underestimated him for 26 years. (Andrews, 55n, citing Boyle, *Trenchard.*) It was not revealed until long after the war (1974) that Dowding's success in the Battle of Britain was due largely to ULTRA intelligence, whose secrets had to be withheld even from his subordinate commanders (Winterbotham, *Ultra,* 62-63).

But the acknowledged winner of the Battle of Britain was ordered on 25 Nov 40 to relinquish command immediately! The abrupt order was from PORTAL, now chief of the air staff, who replaced Dowding with an arch-critic, Sholto DOUGLAS. (The latter promptly sacked PARK.) After special duty in the US for the ministry of aircraft production until June 41, Dowding retired at his own request in July 42. In 1943 he was honored with a baronetcy, and he took the style of his old headquarters, Bentley Priory *(DNB).* Dowding's first wife having died suddenly in 1920, leaving him a young son, Derek, Stuffy married an RAF widow in 1951.

Always contemplative and philosophical, Dowding studied spiritualism and theosophy, wrote and lectured on occult subjects, and became a vegetarian. (E. B. Haslam in *DNB.*) He published *Many Mansions* (1943), *Lynchgate* (1945), *Twelve Legions of Angels* (1946, the book having been suppressed in 1942 under wartime regulations), *God's Magic* (1946), and *The Dark Star* (1951). The controversy over his sacking in 1940 was refueled when the film *Battle of Britain* appeared in 1969. Still an erect, lean figure, he received a standing ovation from his former pilots, his so-called "chicks," at the film's premier in London. Dowding died 15 Feb 70 at his home in Kent, and his ashes are interred in Westminster Abbey. His son and only child, Wing Comdr Derek Hugh Tremenheere Dowding, succeeded him as the second baronet.

Biographies include Basil Collier, *Leader of the Few* (London: Jarrolds, 1957), and Robert Wright (Dowding's personal assistant), *The Man Who Won the Battle of Britain* (New York: Scribner's, 1970). An aptly named chapter, "Dowding vs Göring, and others," is in Allen Andrews, *The Air Marshals* (New York: Morrow, 1970), and there is a chapter on Dowding in Michael Carver, ed, *The War Lords* (Boston: Little, Brown, 1976).

DRUM, Hugh Aloysius. US general. 1879-1951. As the peacetime army's senior officer in permanent rank, Lt Gen Drum (as of 5 Aug 39) expected to have the highest field command when America went to war. Instead the fractious

old war horse was put to pasture within the first two years.

Drum was born 19 Sep 79 at Ft Brady, Mich, where his father, a Civil War veteran and regular army officer, was stationed. Young Drum left Boston College in 1898 to serve in the Philippines as a second lieutenant. After duty on the Mexican border he went to France in 1914, rose to be CofS, 1st US Army, and was promoted to brigadier general on 1 Oct 18. His staff included George C. Marshall, **G3**, and John L. DE WITT, **G4**.

For about 18 months ending in June 33, Drum was US Army deputy CofS under MacArthur. On 5 Nov 38 Maj Gen Drum took command of 1st Army Hq on Governor's Island, NY, and was awarded his third star on 5 Aug 39. In the 1939 and 1940 maneuvers in New York State Lt Gen Drum had troops carry wooden weapons and drive trucks with signs reading "cannon" and "tank." This achieved the intended effect of getting national publicity on the army's woeful lack of readiness, but Drum was accused of criticizing his superiors, principally George C. Marshall and Leslie J. McNair, for not doing their utmost to get the army proper materiel. (Pogue, *Marshall,* I, 90.)

Apparently assuming he would lead the invasion of Europe, Drum first declined the post in China that subsequently went to STILWELL, and then he pleaded for it. "The wretched Drum affair," as Stimson remembered it, dug the general's professional grave. (Pogue, *Marshall,* II, 357-60.) Remaining on Governor's Island, he retired 15 Oct 43 and headed the NY National Guard until 1948.

DUFF COOPER. See COOPER, Duff.

DULLES, Allen Welsh. US secret service officer. 1893-1969. Son of a Presbyterian minister and younger brother of John Foster DULLES, he graduated from Princeton in 1914. After teaching for eight months in a missionary school at Allahabad, India, he entered the diplomatic service in 1916. His first experience as an intelligence officer was in Switzerland in 1918. With Hugh Wilson, a senior colleague, Dulles built a network of European refugees and American expatriates who functioned unofficially for the American embassy. (Smith, *OSS,* 205.) After the armistice of 11 Nov 18, Allen Dulles joined his brother John Foster on the US delegation to the Versailles Peace Conference. Then he served on the American commissioner's staff in Berlin and came to share the concern of German industrialists, generals, and leaders of the Weimar Republic about the new Bolshevik menace. In 1927 Dulles abandoned a promising diplomatic career for better pay with his brother's international law firm of Sullivan and Cromwell in NYC (1927). This kept him in contact with leading German industrialists, and as legal adviser to the US delegation to the Geneva disarmament talks of 1927 and 1933 he had further insight into the threat of Hitler. His friend Hugh Wilson, US minister to Switzerland 1933-38 and ambassador to Nazi Germany for eight months until recalled in protest to **Crystal night,** 9-10 Nov 38, also kept Dulles current on German affairs. (Smith, 206.)

Col William "Will Bill" DONOVAN recruited Dulles and his friend Hugh Wilson for the OSS soon after America entered the war. Dulles opened the NYC office of OSS in Jan 42, but a few months later was sent at his own request to Switzerland. He crossed the Franco-Swiss border only minutes before the Germans closed it after moving into Vichy France on 11 Nov 42.

Officially, Dulles was an assistant to the US minister in Bern. But neutral Switzerland had been an international intelligence bazaar since early in the century, and the new spy merchant

"was known by everyone in Europe as a special envoy of President Roosevelt, particularly concerned with Intelligence duties" (Strong, 124). Dulles in effect hung out a shingle as an American spy merchant and "was besieged by a multitude of informants" (ibid.). Many proved to be valuable.

The OSS bureau chief became a point of contact for members of the anti-Nazi resistance inside Germany. His final achievement was to coordinate Karl WOLFF's secret surrender of German forces in Italy. Curiously, however, he had no knowledge of Rudolf "Lucy" ROESSLER's famous spy ring.

Returning to his law practice in 1945, Dulles was deputy CIA under Gen Walter Bedell SMITH then was the agency's first civilian director, 1953-61. Allen Dulles published *Germany's Underground* (1947), *The Craft of Intelligence* (1963), and *The Secret Surrender* (1966).

DULLES, John Foster. US statesman. 1888-1959. Like his younger brother Allen (previously), John Foster Dulles was a prominent corporation lawyer. He was presidential candidate Thomas E. DEWEY's foreign affairs adviser in 1944, head of the US delegation to the San Francisco Conference in 1945 that established the UN, and in 1953-1959 he was President Eisenhower's secretary of state.

E

EAKER, Ira Clarence. USAF general. 1896-1987. Born 13 Apr 96 at Llano, Tex (*AAF Guide,* 61), he attended Southeastern State Teachers College at Durant, Okla, before entering military service from that state. Commissioned 15 Aug 17 as an infantry reserve officer, he was given an RA commission on 15 Nov 17 (ibid.) and won his wings as a pursuit (fighter) pilot in Oct 18. Turning to bombardment, and working to extend the effective range of airplanes, Capt Eaker and with Maj Carl Spaatz set an endurance record of almost 151 hours in 1929. In 1936 Eaker made the first flight across the American continent navigating solely by instruments. Eaker and H. H. "Hap" Arnold collaborated on developing new concepts of strategic air war to include daylight precision bombing, and they were co-authors of three books: *This Flying Game* (1936), *Winged Victory* (1941), and *Army Flyer* (1942).

Getting his first star in Jan 42, Brig Gen Eaker was concurrently named to head what became the 8th Bomb Cmd of Lt Gen Spaatz's 8th AF, the latter being activated 28 Jan 42 (*AA,* 219). Reaching England on 20 Feb 42 and reporting two days later to the CG US Army Forces in the British Isles (USAFBI), Eaker set up the "US Army Bomber Cmd, USAFBI" (*OCMH Chron,* 25). As the first US air headquarters in Europe, it was located from 15 Apr 42 at High Wycombe, 29 mi WNW of London. Promoted again the following September Maj Gen Eaker succeeded Spaatz on 1 Dec 42 as CG 8th AF, which became the major instrument of American air power in Europe.

"There is nothing that can be destroyed by gunfire that cannot be destroyed by bombs," the airman said in an early press conference (*CB 42*). Against considerable opposition from US and UK planners, Eaker and Spaatz won approval at Casablanca, 14-23 Jan 43, of the "Eaker Plan," officially the combined bomber offensive. This called for round-the-clock air assault in which US heavy bombers (B-17s and B-24s) would attack by day while the RAF continued to strike at night. Despite excessive US losses initially and doubts about the accuracy of bomb drops, the Eaker plan proved to be effective. (The record is summarized under DOOLITTLE, who was CG 8th AF from 6 Jan 44.)

Eaker was promoted to lieutenant general on 13 Sep 43 and, while retaining command of the 8th AF, was designated CG USAAF in the UK on 16 Oct 43. This reorganization occurred when Lewis H. Brereton's 9th AF became the USAAF's tactical arm in the ETO. In preparation for the Normandy invasion, Spaatz took command of the USAAF in Europe on 22 Dec 43 and Eaker was named to succeed TEDDER as head of the Mediterranean Allied Air Forces (MAAF), turning over the 8th AF to Doolittle. But Eaker delayed his departure from England until 6 Jan 44 to help Spaatz and Doolittle get up to speed. Reaching his new command in mid-Jan 44, Eaker spent the rest of the war as CG MAAF. (*AA,* 595; *OCMH Chron,* 156.) He was among the senior US commanders given honorary British knighthood (KCB) in 1945.

Ordered to Washington as deputy commander of the Army Air Force, Eaker became the first CofS of the independent USAF after unification of the armed forces in 1947. Lt Gen Eaker retired on 31 Aug 47 to become a VP of the Hughes Tool Co, 1947-57, then was head of Douglas Acft, 1957-61. He died 6 Aug 87.

EBERBACH, Heinrich (Hans). German general. 1895-. The oft wounded, thrice captured soldier was born 24 Nov 95 in Stuttgart. He was an officer cadet assigned to Inf Regt 180, was commissioned on 25 Feb 15, and fought for seven months with his regiment in Flanders and Champagne before being critically wounded and captured by the French. Repatriated in 1917, he served in Macedonia and Palestine until being captured again. The British invalided him home with malaria.

From 1 Jan 20 to 1 Oct 35 he served with the police, attaining the rank of major before reentering the army as CO, 12th Pz Anti-tank Bn. Two years later he was promoted to lieutenant colonel and given command of the 35th Pz Regt. Leading this in Poland and France, Eberbach was awarded the RK on 4 July 40 and promoted to colonel.

A year later, now 46 years old, he took command of the 5 Pz Regt of the 3d Pz Div in Russia. In late Oct 41, as Guderian's 2d Pz Army was slowed by a fuel shortage while attempting to encircle Moscow from the southwest, Eberbach led an attempt to take Tula by a desperate coup de main. His improvised panzer brigade, fueled with pooled supplies of the 24 Pz Corps, was stopped with heavy tank losses by Gen Maj A. N. Ermakov's battered 50th Army. (Seaton, *R-G War,* 188-89.) Eberbach was awarded the Oakleaves (42/890) on 31 Dec 41.

He became acting commander (**mFb**) of the 4th Pz Div on 6 Jan 42. Promoted to Generalmajor when he left it temporarily (WIA?) on 1 Feb 42, Eberbach returned to lead the division for the period 4 Apr-26 Nov 42 (*B&O,* 76). Early in 1943 he became Inspector of the Tank Arm. Promoted on or before 1 Apr to Generalleutnant and on 1 Aug 43 to general of panzer troops, he was acting commander (**mFb**) of the 47th Pz Corps, 15-22 Oct, then acting commander of the crack 48th Pz Corps until 14 Nov 43. (*B&O,* 52, 54.) Eberbach then headed Pz Group Nikopol in unsuccessful efforts to hold the manganese and iron mines of the Dniepr Bend. (Hitler insisted, quite erroneously, that these were vital to the German war effort.)

Gen of Pz Troops Eberbach joined Rommel's AG Hq in May 44, shortly before D day in Normandy. As Rommel scrambled to contain the Allied beachhead, particularly around Caen, it is difficult to keep track of the changing German order of battle. One problem is that the new 5th Pz Army, which GEYR VON SCHWEPPENBURG formed 1 Jan 44, was also known as Pz Gp West. Eberbach's assignment apparently was to head SS panzer reserves, of which Hitler personally retained control, but he held various command positions. German records show that Eberbach took over the *5th Pz Army* from Geyr on 2 July 44 and was succeeded in this post by Sepp DIETRICH on 23 Aug 44 (*B&O,* 28). According to the official US Army campaign history, however, Eberbach replaced Geyr as commander of *Pz Gp West* (Harrison, 447) on the morning of 4 July, the day after KLUGE succeeded RUNDSTEDT as OB West.

Whatever his exact assignment, Eberbach was in the thick of the fierce SS panzer defenses south of Caen. The battle ended about 19 Aug 44 in the Falaise-Argentan pocket, where the Germans lost 50,000 captured and left 10,000 dead (*West Point Atlas,* text for Map 55). Among the wounded was the 7th Army commander, Paul HAUSSER, whom Eberbach succeeded as shattered elements of that army retreated under heavy pressure to form a bridgehead on the lower Seine. Driven from there toward the Somme, the panzer general was captured during the night of 30-31 Aug 44 in his pajamas. The 11th Br Armd Div proudly presented him to their corps commander, who remembers the prisoner as "scowling, unshaven and very ugly" (HORROCKS, 198). But official wartime photographs show the brilliant tank commander as a youthful, bright-eyed man with a pleasant round face that is only slightly marred by face wounds on the upper lip and around the tip of the nose (Angolia, II, 54). Eberbach was living in Notzingen when Angolia's work was published in 1980.

EDDY, Manton Sprague. US general. 1892-1962. Born 16 May 92, and a WWI veteran, Eddy was promoted to major general on 9 Aug 42 and given command of the 9th Inf Div. Regimental combat teams of his division landed on 8 Nov 42 in Morocco at Safi and Port Lyautey, and east of Algiers. (*AA,* 526, *West Point Atlas,* Map 82.) After French resistance ended on the 11th, Eddy had the mission of patrolling the Spanish Moroccan border until Mark Clark quit worrying about German intervention through Gibraltar. In Feb 43 the division moved to the Tunisian front, patrolling and fighting small defensive actions until the Allied offensive resumed. The "florid, hearty" Eddy, having shown "conspicuous boldness and skill" in North Africa (Weigley, *ETO,* 99), entered Bizerte on 7 May 43.

His division did not take part in the early phases of the Sicilian campaign, being held in Africa as part of the strategic reserve with the 82d Abn (-). Unloaded at Palermo on 1 Aug (D+21), the 9th Div took part in Patton's drive through Randazzo to Messina (*AA,* 526).

Redeployed to the UK in Nov 43 for further training, the 9th Div crossed Utah Beach on D+4 and made the main effort in the drive across the Cotentin Peninsula by "Lightning Joe" COLLINS's 7th Corps. Eddy entered Fortress Cherbourg on the corps' west flank and exploited to Cap de la Hague on the peninsula's NW tip.

Maj Gen Eddy then had a major part in the St Lô breakout (Opn Cobra) and in closing the Falaise Gap. On about 20 Aug 44 Eddy took command of the 12th Corps when Maj Gen Gilbert R. Cook became ill. The corps was on the open right (south) flank of Patton's 3d Army. When Eddy asked Patton how much he should worry about his wide-open flank as he moved east from Orleans, "Old Blood and Guts" said that depended entirely on how nervous Eddy was by nature! "He has been thinking a mile a day good going," Patton added. "I told him to go fifty and he turned pale.'" (Weigley, 242, citing Blumenson, *Patton Papers,* II, 522.)

Maj Gen Eddy commanded the 12th Corps under PATTON for the rest of the war. His corps drove into Czechoslovakia and was 30 miles SW of Prague when ordered to cease fire.

The youthful Eddy was promoted to lieutenant general on 20 Jan 48 (*AA,* 928) when he took over the **C&GSC** at Ft Leavenworth, Kans. He then headed the 7th US Army in Europe from 1950 until retiring 31 Mar 53 as a lieutenant general.

EDEN, (Robert) Anthony, 1st Earl of Avon. British statesman. 1897-1977. Eden was born 12 June 97 on a family estate of some 800 acres in County Durham in the north country. His eccentric and irascible father was of ancient lineage and his mother also had an impressive pedigree. After attending Eton, 1911-1915, he became an infantry lieutenant of the King's Royal Rifle Corps. In two years on the western front he became adjutant of his battalion in 1917, winning the MC that year for rescuing his sergeant under fire, rising to the rank of captain. In 1918, at the age of 20, he became the youngest brigade major in the British army. (*DNB.*)

At Oxford, 1919-22, Eden was a distinguished student of Oriental languages and graduated with first-class honors. He entered public life as a conservative politician in Parliament 1923-25. Then, having married well (following) and being independently wealthy, Eden traveled abroad extensively and wrote before becoming under secretary for foreign affairs, 1931-34, then lord privy seal. In the latter office Eden was charged with promoting the League of Nations, in which he believed ardently. In Oct 35 he became secretary of state for foreign affairs under Stanley Baldwin and retained the office under Neville CHAMBER-

LAIN. But Eden was at odds quickly with the new prime minister's appeasement policies, particularly toward Italy. When Eden expressed concern about slow British rearmament (11 Nov 37) Chamberlain told him to "go home and take an aspirin" (WC, I, 250). The final straw was the PM's determination to condone continued Italian intervention in Austria and Spain. Eden conducted his last business with Chamberlain on 18 Feb 38 and resigned two days later, succeeded by HALIFAX. The change distressed many British including Churchill (WC, I, 257-258) and delighted the Italians and Germans.

The folly of his policies having become apparent, Chamberlain made Eden secretary of state for dominion affairs shortly after declaring war on 3 Sep 39. When Churchill became PM on 10 May 40, he gave Eden the post of secretary of state for war and made him foreign secretary in Dec 40. Eden also was leader of the House of Commons from Nov 42 and was Churchill's political heir apparent.

Eden was a high-principled, hard-working, and well-organized statesman who maintained a thorough grasp of essential detail. "A man of elegance and wit, his diplomacy and flair for persuasion when arguing from the position of his country's limited power and influence were probably his most remarkable talents" (Tunney). He was closely associated with the unfortunate decision to divert British military forces from North Africa to oppose the German conquest of Greece. Quick to hail de Gaulle as the savior of France, Eden also was a vigorous supporter of Polish efforts to achieve independence. He led the British delegation to the San Francisco conference that set up the United Nations.

With Churchill's fall from power in July 45, Ernest Beavin succeeded Eden, but when Churchill returned to power in 1951, Eden again was foreign minister. In 1954 he became Lord Avon, and the next year he succeeded Churchill as prime minister. The bungled British-French-Israeli effort to take the Suez canal forced Eden to resign in Jan 57.

It was revealed by Sir Anthony Blunt that Guy Burgess, another homosexual of the **Cambridge five,** had been tasked by his Soviet controllers to improve his cover by marrying the woman who in 1952 became Eden's second wife. She was (Anne) Clarissa Churchill, Sir Winston's niece (*DNB,* "Eden"; Peter Wright, 243).

Eden's health was poor throughout the Suez crisis and never again good. Taken seriously ill while visiting Averell Harriman in Florida during the winter of 1976-77 and flown back to England by RAF plane, he died 14 Jan 77 at his home, Alvediston, in Wiltshire. *(DNB.)*

The last volume of his memoirs, chronologically, was published as *Full Circle* (1960). The others are *Facing the Dictators* (1962) and *The Reckoning* (1965). A memoir of his early years is *Another World, 1897-1917* (1976).

EDWARD VIII. See Duke of WINDSOR.

EHRENBURG, Ilya Grigoryevich. Soviet writer. 1891-1967. The best known Russian journalist of WWII, Ehrenburg was born 27 Jan 91 in Kiev, son of a Jewish brewery manager who moved the family to Moscow. Ehrenburg was expelled from the First Moscow High School for participating in the revolutionary movements of 1905-7. Later arrested but released without trial, he emigrated to Paris in 1908 and immediately began a long career as poet (his first works published in 1911), translator and journalist. After being a war correspondent on the western front, 1914-17, he returned to Russia and worked in Kiev, Rostov, and Tiflis with antibolshevik newspapers (Scarecrow). But in 1921 he changed sides, after much wavering (Briggs, ed, *20 Cent Biog*), and went to Paris as a special correspondent for *Izvestia*. Soon deported to Belgium, where he continued his assignment, he went on to Berlin and returned to Paris. His satirical novel attacking western values was published in Russian in 1921, and the English-language edition, *Julio Jurenito,* in 1958. He published a volume of satirical short stories in 1923. (Ibid.) As a correspondent he traveled extensively in Europe, the Far East, and America, then covered the Spanish Civil War before returning to Paris (1937-40).

When the Germans overran France the tall, gawky Ehrenburg returned to the USSR and during the war wrote for *Pravda* and *Krasnaya zvezda*. He was a party-liner of great courage and ambition who, although a member of the USSR Writer's Union from 1934, never joined the CP (Scarecrow). Despite occasional lapses, he had a wider European view and thus greater popularity in the Allied camp than his Russian confreres. But by Apr 45 Ehrenburg had become so strident in his anti-German hate propaganda

and criticism of the Western Allies that Soviet authorities finally ordered him to desist. (Werth, *Russia,* 965-67.)

Ehrenburg survived successive postwar purges of Jews and intellectuals because Stalin remained appreciative of the writer's contribution to the war as a propagandist (Briggs). English editions of his *Russia at War* appeared in London (1943) and New York (1944). His novels include the antiwestern *The Fall of France* (1941), its sequel *The Storm* (1948), *The Ninth Wave* (1951), and *The Thaw* (1954). The latter, published soon after Stalin's death and capitalizing on a temporary relaxation of censorship, was a free discussion of Soviet social problems at the start of the post-Stalin era. With *The Thaw* and the first volumes of his memoirs (below) the author became an important liberalizing influence in Soviet culture (Briggs). His voluminous memoirs, *Goda, Lyudi, Zhizn,* (1960-64), translated as *Years, People, Life* (1962-66), were a major publishing event in the USSR (ibid.). Khrushchev's hostile reaction led to the author's temporary eclipse in 1963 (ibid.). The volume covering 1953-64 was being written when the author died 1 Sep 67 in Moscow.

EIBL, Karl. German general. 1891-1943. Born 23 July 91 in Steg, Austria, he served in the 15th Austrian Inf Regt before joining the Wehrmacht. Soon given command of the 3d Bn, 131th Inf Regt, 44th Div, (Angolia, II, 60), he won both classes of the Iron Cross. As CO 132th Inf Regt, Lt Col Eibl was awarded the RK on 15 Aug 40 for action in France. Promoted to colonel and remaining with the 132d Regt, he was awarded the Oakleaves (50/890) on 31 Dec 41 for action in Russia. After almost another year on the eastern front, and moved up to head the 385th Inf Div, Eibl was awarded the Swords (21/159) on 19 Dec 42 and promoted to Generalleutnant. The day after becoming acting commander (**mdFb**), 24d Pz Corps, in the Don region *(B&O),* he was killed 21 Jan 43 when a disgruntled Italian soldier threw a grenade into his vehicle. (Angolia, II, 60.) Eibl was promoted posthumously to Gen of Inf.

EICHELBERGER, Robert Lawrence. US general. 1886-1961. Born 9 Mar 86 in Urbana, Ohio, he was the son of a prominent lawyer whose forebears came to Maryland from Heidelberg in 1728. Eichelberger's mother, whose family home was Port Gibson, Miss, could remember the Civil War skirmishes there. Reared on the farm established by his grandfather, Bob attended Ohio State Univ for two years before graduating from West Point in 1909 (68/103). Missing action in France, Maj Eichelberger served in the WDGS under Maj Gen W. S. Graves, who was executive assistant to the Army CofS. When Graves left Washington in July 18 to command a division, Eichelberger went along as his operations officer (G3). When Graves led the American expeditionary force to Vladivostok in Sep 18, Eichelberger was his G3 and G2. In the confused political and military situation in Siberia, where the AEF was supposed to help some 70,000 Czech soldiers who were trying to escape the Bolshevik revolution, Lt Col (T) Eichelberger won the DSC and DSM for action in the Suchan District around Novitskaya on 2 July 19. (*CB 43.*) He also got a liberal, grass roots education in international relations and a valuable insight into the superior discipline and tactical training of the Japanese soldier. (Eichelberger, *Dear Miss Em,* 10, hereafter cited as *Luvaas, ed.*)

Eichelberger's subsequent inter-war service was primarily in intelligence and the Adjutant General's Dept, culminating with a tour in the **SGS** office in Washington, 3 Jul 35-9 Nov 38. On the fast track for high wartime rank, he commanded a regiment, was promoted to brigadier general in the fall of 1940, awarded his second star the next year, and was superintendent at West Point from 18 Nov 40 to 11 Jan 42.

Shortly after the US went to war he took over the newly activated 77th Div in March. On 22 Jun 42 he became commander of the 1st Corps Hq. With CofS, Brig Gen Clovis E. Byers and other staff officers he reached Australia at the end of Aug 42 and established himself on eastern seaboard city of Rockhampton. (*Luvaas, ed,* 26.) Eichelberger was assigned the 32d and 41st Divs on 5 Sep 42 (*OCMH Chron,* 53) and given his third star on 15 Oct 42. The next month he was training the 41st Div in Australia when the Allied effort in New Guinea became desperate. The Japanese had occupied Buna on 22 July, and HORII had driven along the Kokoda Trail to threaten Port Moresby. Green American troops and officers of the 32d US Inf Div, getting their baptism of fire in some of the world's worst jungle terrain, were performing poorly.

Furious about Australians having to take over operations (Pogue, *Marshall,* II, 396), MacArthur ordered Eichelberger to New Guinea (ibid., 71) and gave him a simple order to "take Buna, or not come back alive" (*Buchanan,* 246-7).

Eichelberger flew to Dobodura on 1 Dec 42 and took charge of the American sector. This included Buna village and mission (the objective of Urbana force) and an airstrip about two miles to the SE (the objective of Warren force). As so often happens in such turnover situations but cannot be appreciated at the time, the tide of battle was turning: the beseiged Japanese were being weakened by starvation and disease as the Allied logistical situation improved and green US troops were maturing (*West Point Atlas,* 139). But the capable and aggressive Eichelberger promptly replaced the 32d Div commander, Maj Gen Edwin F. Harding, and the two task force commanders. By 1 Jan 43 the 32d Div had taken all its objectives and driven the Japanese into a small beachhead. The 7th Aus Div, to the west, was closing in on the Sanananda area. On 13 Jan Eichelberger replaced the Australian general Edmund F. HERRING as commander of the Advance New Guinea Force, which comprised all AIF and US troops on the Buna-Gona front in Papua. Japanese resistance ended 22 Jan 43, "the first victory of the war against Japan on land" (*OCMH Chron,* 87).

Eichelberger's 1st Corps was assigned to the 6th Army when it was established on 16 Feb 43 under Walter KRUEGER (ibid., 93). After the continuing campaigns in New Guinea, New Britain, the Admiralties, Biak, Numfoor, and Morotai, Eichelberger was ordered in May 44 to plan the Hollandia invasion, which started 4 Sep 44.

He then moved up to head the 8th Army for four years beginning 7 Sep 44, leading it in the reconquest of the Philippines and as commander of Allied Occupation Forces in Japan until 3 Sep 48. Not again promoted during the war, he retired as the senior of the army's 22 lieutenant generals. He was promoted in 1954 to full general and died 26 Sep 61 at Asheville, NC.

Eichelberger's memoirs are *Our Jungle Road to Tokyo,* New York: Viking Press, 1950. He later published a volume of wartime letters to his wife, *Dear Miss Em: General Eichelberger's War in the Pacific, 1942-1945,* edited by Jay

Luvaas, Westport, Conn: Greenwood, 1972. Thanks largely to the editor, an outstanding military historian, the book is a valuable source.

EICHMANN, (Karl) Adolf. Nazi war criminal. 1906-62. As an SS lieutenant colonel he headed the Jewish Office of the Gestapo and was largely responsible for carrying out the "final solution." Eichmann was born 19 Mar 06 in the Rhineland at Solingen. He was four years old when his mother died and the family moved to Linz, Austria, where his father headed the streetcar and power company. The boy was a shy, melancholy loner, docile and muddled, taunted because of his dark appearance and small stature as "the little Jew." (Snyder, *Hitler's Elite,* 220.)

Either for poor grades or lack of family funds he left the Linz Higher Institute for Electro-Technical Studies after two years. As a salesman with electrical and construction firms he blossomed into a loud, hard-drinking, swaggering extrovert, joining the Austrian Nazi Party on 1 Apr 32 and the SS Security Service (SD) in Sep 34. Finding scope in Berlin for his bureaucratic aptitudes and energy, he became the Nazi authority on Jewish affairs, even making a two-day trip to Palestine and visiting the pro-Nazi, Jew-hating Grand-Mufti of Jerusalem (Amin el Husseini).

Eichmann went to Vienna in Aug 38 (after the Anschluss) to head the SS Office for Jewish Emigration. With sole authority for issuing exit permits to Jews, he became a master at using extortion to make Jews emigrate. When the Reich Central Office for Jewish Emigration—modeled on the Vienna office—was established in early 1939 with Heydrich as the nominal chief, Eichmann was ordered back to Berlin as its director, and he transferred to the Gestapo in Dec 39. His office became part of Heydrich's **RSHA** when this was created on 17 Sep 39. The fox-faced, supercharged little Nazi bureaucrat began by forcing a thousand Jews in Stettin to waive all property rights and abandon their homes (13 Feb 40). In an RSHA reorganization of 1941 he became director of its sub-section **IV-A4b** (Brissaud, *SD,* 295).

After organizing the **Wannsee conference** of 20 Jan 42 the obscure SS officer was named the principal director of the **final solution.** This called for mass deportations—Eichmann working about a year on the **Madagascar plan** before

this was scrapped—and for creation of large scale extermination facilities in the concentration camps. Asked by Himmler in the summer of 1944 for statistics, Eichmann gave the often cited estimate that about six million Jews had been disposed of, four million of "natural causes" (in the camps), and the others by mobile extermination units. (Wistrich, 62-63.) One authority points out that these figures, not based on proper statistical methods, included Gypsies, Freemasons, homosexuals, and other "undesirables" (Bracher, 430 and n59).

"I will leap laughing to my grave," the killer said on an other occasion, "because the feeling that I have five million people on my conscience is for me a source of extraordinary satisfaction." In a variant of this boast he said to a subordinate, "I'll die happily with the certainty of having killed almost six million Jews" (Snyder, 217, 227).

But the scope of Eichmann's activities was not known until the spring of 1948, when Simon WIESENTHAL found the obscure SS officer's name recurring in the testimony of holocaust survivors and began dogging his trail. Late in 1953 Wiesenthal got a tip that Eichmann was living in Argentina, near Buenos Aires, where as Ricardo Klement he worked for the water company. The Israelis announced on 23 May 60 that Eichmann was their prisoner. Secret agents had found and kidnapped him in flagrant violation of Argentine sovereignty. Put in a glass cage for protection, the sullen mass murderer was on trial during the period 11 Apr-14 Aug 61. Convicted of crimes against the Jewish people, crimes against humanity, and war crimes, Eichmann was hanged on 31 May 62 at Ramle. Protesting to the end that he had only followed orders (the "Nuremberg defense") he died bravely and unrepentant. The corpse was cremated and the ashes scattered in the Mediterranean, outside Israel's territorial waters.

A controversial account of the man's career and trial is given by Hannah Arendt, *Eichmann in Jerusalem: A Report on the Banality of Evil* (New York: Viking, 1963).

EICKE, Theodor. German officer. 1892-1943. The notorious head of concentration camps and commander of the first SS Death's Head division was a Rhinelander born 17 Oct 92 in Solingen (as was Eichmann), son of a station master. In WWI he reached the rank of sub-paymaster and won the Iron Cross 2d Class. After the war he joined the border police, fought in a Freikorps, became involved in right-wing politics, and in 1920 joined the Thuringian police as an inspector. (Wistrich.)

A Brownshirt from late 1928, he became a member of the SS less than two years later. With the rank of SS-Standartenfuehrer he took command of the SS regiment of the Rhine-Palatinate on 15 Nov 31. The next year he fled to Italy on Himmler's instructions to avoid a two-year jail sentence for making political bomb attacks. After returning to the Rhine-Palatinate he fell out with Gauleiter Josef Burckel, who had Eicke confined as a "dangerous lunatic." But Himmler intervened to have his protégé released and soon appointed him commandant of Dachau.

Entrusted with reorganizing concentration camps, Eicke began in May 34 to set standards for which they became notorious. From the start he warned guards they would be punished for showing prisoners any sign of humanity. During the Blood Purge Eicke and a subordinate shot Ernst ROEHM to death in his cell on 1 July 34. Three days later Eicke was promoted to SS Gruppenfuehrer and appointed Inspector of Concentration Camps and SS Death's Head guard detachments (Totenkopfverbande). With headquarters at Oranienburg, he expanded the Totenkopfverbande into five numbered battalions which were enlarged into the Oberbayern, Brandenburg, and Thuringen Regts. After forming SS-Death's Head (Totenkopf) units for action in Poland, Eicke took command of the first SS Totenkopf division, a motorized unit, on 14 Nov 39. At this time he was succeeded in his concentration post by Brigadefuehrer Richard Gluecks.

Eicke's division fought without distinction in France. One company committed the first Waffen-SS atrocity in the west, the execution of about 100 POWs from the 2d Royal Norfolk Regt (4th Bde, 2d Div) on 27 May 40 at Le Paradis. Eicke had the affair hushed up, but two British soldiers survived to testify against the officer responsible, SS Capt Fritz Knochlein, who was condemned by a British court on 25 Oct 48 and hanged three months later. (Stein, 77.)

In Russia the Totenkopfdivision was hardened into an elite outfit, its commander awarded the RK on 25 Dec 41 for action with AG North. Group Eicke, built around his division, contin-

ued to fight fiercely, particularly at Fedorovka in the Demyansk pocket. The grim but often jovial "Papa" Eicke was awarded the Oakleaves (88/890) on 20 Apr 42. He died 26 Feb 43 when his plane was shot down behind enemy lines near Orella.

EINSTEIN, Albert. German-born physicist. 1879-1955. The great thinker was born 14 Mar 79 in Ulm of Jewish parents. Quickly developing an aversion to things German, he renounced his citizenship with parental approval at the age of 15, and after a period of statelessness and study in Zurich (from 1896) he became a Swiss citizen (1901). Not having shown sufficient academic qualifications for the teaching post he wanted, Einstein became an examiner in the patent office in Berne (1902-08). The mundane duties gave him leisure to ponder the unknown, and in 1905 he published four papers that revolutionized physics. Einstein's special theory of relativity was quickly accepted, and from 1908 he held a succession of academic posts before returning to Germany in 1914 as director of the Kaiser Wilhelm Institute of Physics in Berlin. Here he began work on the general theory of relativity that was his greatest achievement in physics. (Briggs, ed, *20 Cent Bio.*) In 1921 he was awarded the Nobel prize in physics. Now recognized universally as a scientific thinker, he began to antagonize right-wing Germans by well-publiciced support of Zionism, the League of Nations, and pacifism. (Wistrich, 65.) Einstein was visiting professor at the California Institute of Technology when Hitler became chancellor in early 1933, and a few months later his books were among those burned publicly (10 May 33). He did not return to Germany, where he was promptly banned as a traitor, and his property seized (1934). Einstein meanwhile joined Princeton's Institute of Advanced Studies, where he remained for the period 1933-45.

In a letter delivered to Roosevelt on 11 Oct 39 Einstein warned that the Germans were capable of developing the atomic bomb. Written at the request of Leo Szilard, Eugene Wigner, and Edward Teller, and delivered by FDR's friend and economic advisor Alexander Sachs, the letter led to the creation of the Manhattan Project. Einstein was a consultant and periodic visitor to Los Alamos but made little direct contribution as a physicist and he opposed use of the atomic bomb in war. (Grueff, *Manhattan Project,* 10, 321.) A US citizen from 1940, an unassuming and good natured genius whose name was a household word, Einstein died 18 Apr 55 at Princeton.

EISENHOWER, Dwight David "Ike." US general. 1890-1969. The top Allied commander in Europe, 1942-45, and 34th US president, 1953-61, was born in Denison, Tex, on 14 Oct 90, third son of David J. and the former Ida Elizabeth Stover. The Eisenhowers were Germans who emigrated to Switzerland during the 17th century to escape religious persecution. In 1741 they settled in Pennsylvania, moving west in 1878 with a branch of the Mennonite sect called Brethren of Christ and the (Susquehanna) River Brethren. Ida Stover had much the same background, coming from a Mennonite sect in the Shenandoah Valley of Va. Dwight was two years old when his father, who had failed as a merchant in Abilene, Kans, before taking work in Denison with the railroad, moved the family back to Abilene. Six sons grew up happily in a small house adjoining a little farm, reared in a frugal, old-fashioned, God-fearing way, and all going on to make their parents justifiably proud. Dwight worked summers to help his brother Edgar complete college and become a lawyer. The youngest brother, Milton, became president of Johns Hopkins Univ in 1956; Arthur was a banker; Roy a pharmacist; and Earl an electrical engineer and journalist. Their mother, widowed in 1941, became a Jehovah's Witness.

Like so many other outstanding American generals including Pershing, DDE chose a military career only because service academies offered a first-class college education free. Too old for Annapolis, his first choice, he entered West Point in July 11 as one of the older members of his class. Like Henry H. "Hap" ARNOLD, the easy-going, goodnatured Ike (his cadet nickname) was more distinguished as a prankster than as a future general. A promising football career as a back was cut short during the second season by a badly broken knee. His highest cadet rank was color sergeant. Graduating in 1915 (61/164) with "the class the [generals'] stars fell on," he was almost denied a commission because of the knee injury. This bothered him all his life, seriously in Sep 44 when his light plane made a forced landing on a beach in Belgium.

Early career

DDE became a temporary lieutenant colonel during WWI, not getting overseas but earning the **DSM** as commander of a heavy tank brigade at Gettysburg, Pa. Later serving under Patton at Ft Meade, Md, Ike became a close friend. The two pioneers in tank warfare undertook serious study to prepare for the **C&GSS.** Eisenhower also came into contact with the remarkable Fox Conner, USMA 1898 (17/59), who had been Pershing's operations officer in France (1917-18) and had a powerful influence on the early professional development of George C. Marshall. In 1922 Brig Gen Conner went to Panama as a brigade commander and took Maj Eisenhower as his CofS. (DDE was a permanent major from 2 July 20 and remained in grade for 16 years.)

"Under Conner's tutelage, Eisenhower perfected his administrative and tactical techniques by drafting formal orders for each day's operations in the brigade and by analyzing the tactical problems. The general also directed an intensive reading program that introduced Eisenhower to Plato and Tacitus, influential thinkers such as Nietzsche, the various military writers of the day, and Clausewitz, whose *On War* he read three times." (USMA *Register, 1990,* 12.) Fox Conner impressed on his pupil that WWII was inevitable and that it would be fought by a coalition. "Because of his dialogues with Conner, Eisenhower was well aware of the defects in the allied military command structure of the First World War, and he began pondering the question of coalition warfare as early as 1924." (Ibid.)

DDE entered the **C&GSS** that year and graduated two years later at the head the class. He spent the next two years in the Paris office of the American Battle Monuments Commission (ABMC). In close contact with ABMC Chairman John J. Pershing, the major furthered his understanding of military history and coalition warfare by working on the commission's monumental guide *American Armies and Battlefields in Europe.* A paper written after returning to the office of the assistant secretary of war, 1929-1933, first brought "this unassuming, friendly Kansan to the attention of George C. Marshall" (Janowitz, 297). Although "Eisenhower won a favorable entry in Marshall's little Black Book" (Pogue, *Marshall,* II, 237), he was not a Marshall protégé until 1940. (Personal information from son John Eisenhower, hereafter identified as JSDE.) Having also become known to Douglas MacArthur, Army CofS, DDE was on MacArthur's personal staff for almost six years, first in Washington (21 Feb 33–24 Sep 35) then in the Philippines. To qualify better as an adviser to the new Philippine AF he took flight training. Meanwhile he was promoted to lieutenant colonel on 1 July 36.

It is apparent from their writings that MacArthur and Eisenhower did not like each other. All the former says in his memoirs about their pre-war association was that in confronting the Bonus Army, "I . . . brought with me two officers who later wrote their names on world history," Majors Eisenhower and Patton. (*Reminiscences,* 95.) All DDE says in his war memoirs is that despite urgings of Pres Quezon he did not extend his four-year tour in Manila but returned home in Dec 39 "to take part in the work of intensive preparation which I was now certain would begin in the United States. . . . General MacArthur saw us off at the pier" (*Crusade,* 20). But John Eisenhower comments that "DDE had a *lot* to say about MacArthur in a later book, *At Ease* [1967]. None of it was very good." (JSDE.)

Although not yet a "Marshall man" (ibid.), Ike was on the fast track for rapid advancement. On 30 Nov 40, after a brief tour with the 15th Inf Regt at Ft Lewis, Wash, he was CofS at increasingly higher echelons. Soon after being promoted to full colonel (T) on 11 Mar 41, he became Walter KRUEGER's CofS in 3d Army Hq at San Antonio, Tex, on 24 June 41. That fall he was CofS in Krueger's triumphant Blue Army during the **Louisiana maneuvers,** whereas Patton was conspicuous on the losing side with Ben LEAR.

Promoted on 29 Sep 41, Brig Gen (T) Eisenhower was summoned on 12 Dec 41, less than a week after the Pearl Harbor disaster, to head the War Plans Div, WDGS. He was selected primarily because of recent service in the Philippines, and the very next Sunday, 14 Dec 41, Marshall suddenly asked DDE what should be done about MacArthur's situation in the Philippines. Granted a few hours for study, Eisenhower concluded that going to MacArthur's rescue was hopeless. "Our base must be Australia," he reported to Marshall. "We must take great risks and spend any amount of money." (*Crusade,* 37.) "I agree with you," Marshall replied simply (ibid.).

Working 18 hours a day and dealing with the British on grand strategy, DDE moved to the top of Marshall's list as candidate for command of US forces in the European theater (ETO). Temporary promotion to major general was dated 27 Mar 42, and Eisenhower reached London on 24 June to head the ETO, and on 7 July was awarded his third star. Soon named commander of the entire Allied force for the invasion of North Africa (Opn Torch), Lt Gen Eisenhower set up headquarters at Gibraltar on 7 Nov 42, D day minus one. On 23 Nov he reached Oran, then established headquarters in Algiers.

North Africa and Italy

A British critic, CIGS Alan BROOKE, has this comment: "It was a moment when bold and resolute action might have gathered great prizes," referring to the lost race for Tunis. "Eisenhower . . . was far too much immersed in the political aspects of the situation [the "deal" with DARLAN] . . . which he should have left to his Deputy, Clark. . . . He learnt [*sic*] a lot during the war, but tactics, strategy and command were never his strong points." (Bryant, *Tide,* 430.)

An American authority writes that in "his first combat experience, Eisenhower had been unsure of himself, hesitant, often depressed, irritable, liable to make snap judgments on insufficient information, defensive in both his mood and his tactics." (Stephen E. Ambrose, "Eisenhower's Generalship," *USMA Register, 1990,* 33, cited hereafter cited as Ambrose.) But DDE showed remarkable strength of character under strain and won the backing of British and American superiors. When things were particularly black he relayed a message to FDR: "Tell him I am the best damn lieutenant colonel in the U. S. Army." (Hanson BALDWIN, *NYT* obit, 29 Mar 69).

Eisenhower was promoted to full general (T) on 11 Feb 43, three months before his polyglot force of Americans, British, and French completed the conquest of Tunisia. He then directed the Sicilian campaign and the Salerno landing. At the last moment he wisely called off the airborne operation designed to capture Rome. In all these operations DDE was faulted for being overly cautious (Ambrose, 32-33), but he matured as a coalition commander. On 10 Dec 43 he learned he would command the long-delayed invasion of Europe as head of Supreme Hq, Allied Expeditionary Force (SHAEF).

Europe

The cross-Channel assault on 6 June 44 was DDE's greatest achievement. "From inception to completion," writes Ambrose of Opn Overlord, "it bore his personal stamp. He was the central figure in the preparation, the planning, the training, the deception, the organization, and the execution of the greatest invasion in history." (Ambrose, 33-34.) "His conviction that OVERLORD would work—amidst many doubters—and genuine concern for his men" should be stressed, commented his son after reviewing this sketch (JSDE).

Once ashore in Normandy, Eisenhower often had less trouble with the Germans than with Montgomery, who wanted to take over direction of the ground war. Yet American subordinates believed Eisenhower should have goaded Montgomery into more aggressive action in his sector, around Caen, or to have replaced him. Bradley and PATTON blamed DDE for failure to close the Falaise pocket, which would have annihilated most of the Germans in Normandy instead of merely forcing them back.

Eisenhower had opposed the "Mediterranean strategy" advocated primarily by Alan BROOKE, particularly any major offensive through the Balkans. But over strong objections from Churchill and other British leaders, the Allied Supreme Commander insisted on the need to invade southern France. Operation Dragoon, as it finally was called, took amphibious resources and combat strength that might have been used to better advantage by ALEXANDER in Italy or by MOUNTBATTEN in SE Asia. But from study of WWI logistical problems, DDE believed he needed the port of Marseilles. The secondary effort in southern France also supported Eisenhower's "broad front strategy," making better use of the overwhelming Allied superiority in manpower and materiel. It has been argued that Germany could have been defeated faster by Montgomery's making a "single thrust" into the North German Plain. We shall never know, but Monty's CofS finally concluded that this alone would not have won the war in Europe; "Eisenhower was right" (Ambrose, citing DE GUINGAND, *Operation Victory,* 330.)

Critique

The most serious charges against Ike were that he wanted to be liked. Subordinates often got the impression he agreed with all of them, no matter how they disagreed. Ambrose concedes that in constantly seeking compromise Eisenhower "did waver, sometimes badly, on some important issues—primarily the relative importance of Arnhem and Antwerp, and the meaning of the word priority." (Ambrose, 34.) But on major issues, including the broad front strategy and personally retaining direction of the ground war, Eisenhower stood firm.

"We are left with the picture of a commander of manifest integrity who warmed the heart and uplifted the spirit of everybody who worked with him," concludes a British authority on generalship. "His special skill was his skill at management. He managed the generals, the admirals and the air marshals, and the politicians, and he managed mighty armies." (Sixsmith, 221.)

Postwar

Promoted to General of the Army on 20 Dec 44, DDE remained in Europe briefly after V-E day and was US member of the Allied Commission governing Germany. He took over from Marshall as Army CofS, serving 19 Nov 45–7 Feb 48, and being followed by Bradley. Democrats and Republicans viewed the amiable war hero as an unbeatable candidate for President. But after showing considerable willingness to run, and possibly deterred by Marshall's strong objections (personal information of dubious validity), Eisenhower became president of Columbia Univ in June 48. Outbreak of the Korean War two years later gave rise to genuine concern that the USSR was making a strategic diversion to permit their overrunning western Europe. **NATO** being created to meet this threat, Truman acceded to the request of European allies that DDE establish and organize its military arm in Dec 50. Ike was Supreme Allied Commander Europe (SACEUR) with SHAPE Hq soon located just outside Paris. MONTGOMERY was deputy SACEUR, and JUIN commanded Allied ground forces.

President Eisenhower

The threat of WWIII contained, Eisenhower faced irresistible pressure to run for the presidency. He left active military duty in May 52 and resigned two months later from the army (Cullum). As the Republican candidate he defeated Adlai Stevenson with the largest popular vote to that time and was the 34th president of the US, 1953-61. He then retired to a farm bought on the Gettysburg, Pa, battlefield in 1950.

Wealthy from book royalties and good investment advice, still a hero of unprecedented popularity, Ike was active (despite several heart attacks) until shortly before his death on 28 Mar 69 at Walter Reed AMC. He was 78.

The general's war memoirs are *Crusade in Europe* (New York: Doubleday, 1948). Citations in the previous sketch are from the Permabooks Special Edition (New York: Garden City Books, 1952). *Crusade* was followed by *At Ease: Stories I Tell to Friends* (1967). A monumental work is *The Papers of Dwight David Eisenhower: The War Years,* (5-vols,) Alfred D. Chandler, Jr., ed.; Stephen E. Ambrose, assoc. ed. (Baltimore, Md: Johns Hopkins, 1970). An authoritative biography by Stephen E. Ambrose is *The Supreme Commander: The War Years of General Dwight D. Eisenhower* (New York: Doubleday, 1970).

EREMENKOV, Andrei I. *See* YEREMENKO

ERENBURG, Illya G. *See* EHRENBURG

ESEBECK, Hans-Karl, Baron von. German general born 9 Jun 1989, Generalmajor Baron von Esebeck assumed command of the 15 Pz Div near Tobruk on 13 Apr 41 after the death of Generalmajor Heinrich von Prittzwitz und Gaffron. After achieving total tactical surprise in an attack starting on 30 May, Esebeck lost about half of his effective strength before a severe sandstorm caused Rommel to call off his renewed effort to take Tobruk. (Irving, *Fox,* 94.)

Without seeing any significant further action, Esenbeck left the division on 24 July 41 and took command of the 11 Pz Div in the Ukraine on 24 Aug. Moving to the central front in late October, the bespectacled baron took over the 2 Pz Div on 17 Feb 42. On 1 Dec 42 he was promoted to Generalleutnant. While retaining command of the 11 Pz Div until 31 May 43, he temporarily replaced Hans ZORN as CG, 46 Pz Corps, 22 Nov 42 to 20 June 43. Esebeck had no further command assignment for almost a year. He then was in France as acting head of the 68 Pz Corps, 1 Dec 43 to 9 Feb 44, with headquarters just south of Paris at Rambouillet. He was succeeded by Friedrich Kirchner, meanwhile having been promoted on 1 Feb 44 to General of Panzer Troops. Implicated in the attempt on Hitler's life, Esebeck was sent to a concentration camp shortly after 20 July 44 but lived for 10 years after the war.

ESTEVA, Jean Pierre. French admiral. 1880-1951. Born on 14 Sep 80 at Reims, son of a cork manufacturer, Esteva was promoted to full admiral on 14 Sep 37, his 57th birthday.

Exactly a week before France declared war in 1939, the admiral took command of the *Forces maritimes du Sud,* based at Toulon. On 17 May 40, under threat of Italy's entering the war, he moved his forces to Bizerte. From there, in close collaboration with British forces under Adm A. B. C. Cunningham, he saw action in the eastern Mediterranean. After the Vichy government was established the admiral was named resident general of Tunisia on 23 July 40. Unlike Gen BARRE, Esteva did not oppose the German buildup that started in Tunisia on 9 Nov 42. As Allied forces approached Tunis in May 43 the Germans flew their collaborator back to France, where he was put on the inactive list. Adm Esteva was arrested after the liberation of Paris and charged with failure to resist the Germans in Tunisia. On 9 Sep 44 he was dismissed from the navy without a pension. The High Court of Justice sentenced the admiral on 15 Mar 45 to "military degradation" and life imprisonment. In failing health, Esteva was freed several weeks before his death on 11 Jan 51 at Reims.

F

FAIREY, (Charles) Richard. British aircraft designer and manufacturer. 1887-1956. He was born 5 May 87 in London, son of a mercantile clerk. Proud of being descended on both sides of the family from famous carriage builders, the boy was interested from early life in designing and building model aircraft *(DNB)*. He studied engineering and chemistry in a technical college, his father having died in 1898 and left the family almost penniless. After only two years as chief engineer to Short Brothers he founded the Fairey Aviation Co in 1915 and stimulated the design of more than 100 types of planes. The most famous were the fast bomber Fox (1925), the record-setting Long Range Monoplane (1928), the wartime Swordfish, the Gyrodyne helicopter (1948), the Gannet (1954), and the Fairey Delta (1956). The latter was the first plane to exceed the speed of sound. Fairey also was a famous yachtsman. Knighted (MBE) in 1942 and becoming director-general of the British Air Commission in Washington, he held that post until 1945. Fairey died 30 Sep 56 in London. *(DNB.)*

FALALEYEV, Fyodor Yakovelevich. Soviet marshal of aviation. 1899-1955. Born 31 May 99 in the village of Polyanskaya, Udmurt **ASSR,** he joined the Red Army in 1918, the CP in 1919, and commanded an infantry regiment during the civil war. In 1933-34 he took flight training and graduated from the AF Academy. By 1940 the airman was deputy commander of the AF strategic command. The next year he headed air forces of the Southern Front, then of the SW Sector (1941-42) before becoming Soviet AF CofS and deputy commander. Promoted in 1944 to marshal of aviation (No. 4), Falaleyev headed the AF Academy, 1946-50. He died 12 Aug 55 after a long illness.

FALKENHAUSEN, Alexander von. German general. 1878-1966. Freiherr von Falkenhausen was born 29 Oct 78 in the Blumenthal manor, in Silesia, scion of a venerable Junker family. In 1912 he was military attaché in Tokyo, and during WWI served with the Turks in Palestine, winning the Pour le Mérite. He headed the Dresden infantry school from 1927, retiring in 1930. Going to China in 1934 as the last German military adviser to Chiang Kai-shek's nationalists, Falkenhausen was recalled, with his staff, in May 38, when Germany mobilized for war. Back on active duty as a general of infantry, he was military governor of Belgium and northern France 1940-44. Although the elderly aristocrat disapproved of Nazi extremism he authorized deportations and the execution of hostages.

Falkenhausen and WITZLEBEN were the only senior commanders in high military office who were actively involved in the anti-Hitler conspiracy, both therefore being candidates for Wehrmacht CinC in the proposed new Reich cabinet. GOERDELER favored Falkenhausen until being convinced by left-wing advisers that the general's record in Belgium would make him unacceptable to Western statesmen with whom the conspirators hoped to negotiate more lenient surrender terms. (W-B, *Nemesis,* 579 and n.)

In July 44 Falkenhausen was recalled for having been involved romantically with an aristocratic Belgian lady. Arrested soon thereafter, the Freiherr may owe his life to the fact that the scandal distracted the Gestapo's attention from his association with the anti-Hitler conspiracy (Irving, *HW,* xxvii). The general was liberated with the **Niederdorf Group** on 4 May 45. "He was a great gentleman and an anti-Nazi," writes a family friend who was with the group (Fey von Hassell, 199). After reaching Naples with the group he and other German officers were arrested by the Americans and sent to a prison in Germany (ibid., 211). Turned over to the Belgians and tried for executing hostages and deporting Jews and workers, he was sentenced 9 Mar 51 to 12 years of penal servitude. But for doing what he could to protect Belgians from the SS he was granted clemency and served only three weeks. Falkenhausen died 31 July 66 at Nassau, Germany.

FALKENHORST, Nikolaus von. German general. 1885-1968. Supreme commander of German armed forces in Norway for most of the war, he was born 17 Jan 85 at Breslau into an old military family originally named Jastr-zembski. He joined the army in 1907 and by 1918 was a staff officer with German forces in Finland. The next year was in a Freikorps before entering the Reichswehr. In 1925-27 he served in the War Ministry's operations division. Promoted in 1932, Oberst Falkenhorst was military attaché in Prague, Belgrade, and Bucharest, 1933-35.

His career having prospered despite lack of command assignments, Generalleutnant Falken-horst headed the 21st Army Corps of KUECH-LER's 3d Army in East Prussia as preparations were made for the Polish campaign. The corps hit SW behind the Pomorze army, which was astride the lower Vistula, and regrouped a week later for a sweeping redeployment eastward through East Prussia to strike south into Poland. Falkenhorst destroyed major pockets of resistance around Lomza and Bialystok, for which he was promoted 1 Oct 39 to general of infantry.

Primarily because his corps staff was free to undertake planning quickly, and because he had worked with the navy in Finland (above), Falkenhorst was picked to finish planning the invasion of Norway and to command it. Hitler summoned the general on 21 Feb 40 and gave him five hours to report back with a preliminary plan. Falkenhorst's only guidance was that he would have five divisions for the ground role. "I went out and bought a Baedeker travel guide," as the general later explained how he reacted (Humble, 51 ff).

After successfully planning and executing the complex operation, being promoted to colonel general on 19 Jul 40, Falkenhorst remained in what was designated the German Northern Theater of Operations. In a succession of reorganizations, and handicapped by never having the proper unity of command, Falkenhorst headed the 21st Corps from 1 Sep 39. This was redesignated the 21st Group on 1 Mar 40, the general retaining command until 19 Dec 40 but doubling as Armed Forces Commander Norway from 25 July 40. On 19 Dec 40, the day after Hitler signed the directive for Opn Barbarossa, Falkenhorst dropped those titles to become commander of the German Army of Norway, with headquarters in Oslo.

Here Falkenhorst began planning combined German-Finnish operations to support Barbarossa, which was to cross the western borders of the USSR on 22 June 41. Forward headquarters

for the Army of Norway were established on 15 June 41 at Rovaniemi, Finland. (Rovaniemi is the major communications hub near the head of the Gulf of Bothnia, on the Arctic circle.) Falkenhorst himself remained in Oslo until 21 June to deceive the Russians, then he directed the start of DIETL's offensive in the far north against Murmansk and Kandalaksha (the railhead some 125 mi south). MANNERHEIM's two Finnish armies had begun advancing in the south to reestablish the pre-1939 frontier on the Karelian Isthmus (threatening Leningrad) and to occupy some territory between Lakes Ladoga and Onega to which Finland had a historic claim. But DIETL bogged down within a month in the Arctic wilderness. Hitler, who had never had confidence in Falkenhorst, issued a directive on 7 Nov 41 that created the Army of Lapland under Dietl to command German force in Finland, and Falkenhorst returned to Oslo. (Ziemke, 135, 183.) Mannerheim halted on the Svir River without trying to make contact with the spearhead of Leeb's strategic envelopment of Leningrad. The threat by AG North consequently was stopped and driven back.

The strategic situation in Finland then stagnated, and on 18 Dec 44 Falkenhorst was recalled to Germany because of long-standing disagreements with Joseph TERBOVEN, Nazi proconsul in Norway.

For allowing execution of British POWs under the **commando order,** a British military court condemned Falkenhorst to death in 1946. The sentence was commuted to 20 years' imprisonment. Released in 1953 for ill health, the general died 18 June 68 in Holzminden.

FECHTELER, William Morrow. US admiral. 1896-1967. Born in California, he graduated from Annapolis in 1916 (18/177). A rear admiral from Jan 44, Fechteler distinguished himself as an attack group commander in the Hollandia, Leyte, and Luzon operations. In 1946 Fechteler was promoted to vice admiral, and in 1952 he became CNO with the rank of full admiral. He died 4 July 67 at Bethesda USNA, Md.

FEDORENKO, Yakov Nikolayevich. Soviet general. 1896-1947. Fedorenko was born 22 Oct 96 in the village of Tsareborisovo, Kharkov Oblast, son of a longshoreman. After being a herdsman, a miner in the Donets basin, and a merchant seaman, he was drafted into the navy in 1915. Fedorenko joined the Oct 17 revolt in Odessa, entering the Red Guard and the CP that year. During and after the civil war he commanded armored trains. After graduating from the Kharkov Higher Artillery School and the Frunze MA, in 1934 he took over a tank regiment before moving up to command the 15th Mech Bde.

After heading mechanized, armored, and tank forces of the Kiev MD from 1937, in June 40 Fedorenko succeeded D. G. PAVLOV in Moscow as chief of the Main Armored Directorate. Six months later he took action to increase production of the new **T-34** and KV heavy tanks.

In Dec 42 Fedorenko became Commander of Armored and Mechanized Troops of the Soviet Army and Deputy Commissar of Defense. Creating the first four Soviet tank armies in 1942, he showed a better grasp of mechanized warfare than the Germans and great superiority over the Americans and British, who never formed such deep-penetration forces. (Scotts.) In 1944 Fedorenko and ROTMISTROV became the Red Army's only Marshal of Armored Troops (Scotts). Having continued to hold the same post in Moscow, Fedorenko died on 26 Mar 47.

FEDYUNINSKY, Ivan Ivanovich. Soviet military leader. 1900-77. An ethnic Russian peasant, born 30 July 00 in the village of Gilevo, Sverdlovsk region, he entered the Red Army in 1919 but did not join the Party until 1930. For service at **Khalkhin Gol** as CO, 24th Mtz Regt, he was made a Hero of the Soviet Union on 29 Aug 39. In the Special Kiev MD from Apr 41 the young colonel commanded the 15th Rifle Corps with headquarters at Kovel only 30 miles from German-occupied Poland and surrounded by a hostile populace and BANDERA partisans. (The region had only recently become part of the USSR.) Winning promotion in the early phase of Barbarossa, General Major Fedyuinsky commanded the 32d Army until summoned to Moscow on 9 Sep 41. The next day he flew with ZHUKOV to Leningrad, which was under heavy attack by LEEB. "For the time being you'll be my deputy," said Zhukov, "then we'll see" (Bialer, 430). But almost immediately, on short notice, Fedyuninsky replaced the dispirited Gen Lt F. S. Ivanov as 42d Army commander in the critical sector near the Kirov Plant.

After ZHUKOV was rushed back to Moscow on 6 Oct, Fedyuninsky headed the Leningrad front until succeeded at the end of the month by KHOZIN. Fedyuninsky replaced Khozin as CG 54th Army in MERETSKOV's new front. After being involved in the recapture of Volkhov and the counteroffensive south of Leningrad, Fedyuninsky went to the Moscow sector in Apr 42 to command the reconstituted 5th Army (which had been under L. A. GOVOROV). Promoted two months later, Gen Lt Fedyuinsky had a major role in the fighting around Moscow.

Back in the Leningrad sector as deputy commander of the Volkhov Front, Oct 42-May 43, Fedyuninsky then held the same post in the Bryansk Front until July 43. He headed the 11th Army until Dec 43 before taking over the 2d Shock Army. With this he attacked from the Orienbaum bridgehead on 14 Jan 44 as the Soviets broke the German siege of Leningrad. With the 3d Baltic Front for the drive into East Prussia, his army penetrated near Tartu on 17 Sep 44 to narrow the corridor south of Riga and threaten annihilation of the German AG North. Promoted in Oct 44 and becoming part of Rokossovsky's 2d Belorussian Front, Gen Col Fedyuninsky attacked north from the Narew bridgehead into Pomerania. The 2d Shock Army took Kolberg on 18 Mar 45, speeding the final German collapse.

One of the war's best field army commanders, Fedyuninsky was deputy commander of Soviet Occupation Forces in Germany until 1952, then commander of the Transcaucasian and Turkestan MDs. Promotion to General of the Army came in 1955. He died 17 Oct 77 and was buried in Moscow's Novodevichy cemetery. The second revised edition of Fedyuinsky's *Podnyatye po trevoge (Raised by the Alarm)*, a valuable and often humorous memoir from which Bialer has taken excerpts, was published in 1964.

FEGELEIN, Hermann Otto. SS LnO to Hitler's Hq. 1906-45. Born 30 Oct 06 at Ansbach, he is said variously to have been an almost illiterate groom who became a jockey or to have had four years of schooling at the university level. In any event he was an outstanding horseman when commissioned in the SS on 12 June 33 and given command of the first SS Reiter, a formation of horse-mounted troops. He represented Germany in the 1936 Berlin Olympics.

Fegelein led SS cavalry units in Poland and Russia, rising to the rank of SS Brigadefuehrer and winning the RK on 2 Mar 42 and the Oakleaves (157/890) on 22 Dec 42. (Angolia, I, 192.) Fegelein became Himmler's LnO to OKW in the fall of 1943 and married Eva BRAUN's sister Gretl (Margarete) on 3 June 44. A few days after being slightly injured in STAUFFENBERG's 20 July 44 bomb attempt, Fegelein took command of the 8th SS "Florian Geyer" Cav Div in Russia. Promoted to Generalmajor der Waffen-SS and awarded the Swords (83/159) for action on 30 July 44 (ibid.), he quickly returned to duty as Hitler's SS adjutant and rose to the rank of Obergruppenfuehrer.

On 27 Apr 45, as the Russians pushed toward the Fuehrerbunker, an SS search party arrested Fegelein in the Berlin apartment of "Mata O'Hara," an Irish-born British spy whose true identity has never been learned. Fegelein was in civilian clothes and apparently preparing to flee the country with the lady. She outwitted her bumbling captors and escaped through a kitchen window, whereas her cavalier was led through the fiery streets to the bunker. Hitler stripped the SS adjutant of his rank and military honors, but did not immediately suspect him of any treachery. About 9 PM on the 28th Hitler learned from a BBC report that Himmler was trying to make a surrender deal through Count BERNADOTTE. Outraged that his "loyal Himmler" was a traitor, Hitler suspected that Fegelein had been preparing to leave Germany to negotiate for his chief with the western allies. Brought from the guard house and questioned further, Fegelein admitted some knowledge of the secret negotiations but denied he had intended to desert. No longer believing his future brother-in-law, whom Eva Braun no longer defended on behalf of her pregnant sister, Hitler ordered an immediate summary court-martial. A few hours later, shortly after midnight on 28-29 Aug 45, a firing squad from Hitler's SS escort—troops of the Leibstandarte Adolf Hitler—executed Fegelein in the Chancellery courtyard (Stein, *Waffen SS,* 246).

See James P. O'Donnell's *The Bunker* (1978) for new research complementing Trevor-Roper's classic, *The Last Days of Hitler* (1947).

FELLGIEBEL, Erich Fritz. German general. 1886-1944. The Wehrmacht's chief of communications throughout the war, he was born 4 Oct 86 in Poepelwitz bei Breslau. From 1939 he was chief of the Wehrmacht and army signals branches, rising to the rank of Gen of Signal Troops. Deeply involved with the anti-Hitler cabal, Fellgiebel had a critical role in the 20 July 44 bomb plot: to phone the conspirators in Berlin immediately after Stauffenberg's bomb exploded (presumably killing Hitler) and then shut down all further communications to and from Rastenburg.

Fellgiebel and Generalmajor Helmuth Stieff, chief of the OKW organization branch, tried to put through a phone call to the Bendlerstrasse on hearing the explosion at 12:50 PM and seeing Hitler stagger with Keitel and others from the shattered briefing room. Whether Fellgiebel and Stieff lost their nerve or "failed in some technical aspect will never be known" (W-B, *Nemesis,* 643). But for this failure the putsch might have succeeded, even with Hitler alive (ibid., 658). Fellgiebel and Stieff were among the first eight convicted of treason by Judge Roland Freisler's People's Court and hanged by piano wire from from butchers' hooks (Hitler's orders) in Berlin's Ploetzensee prison on 8 Aug 44.

FERMI, Enrico. Italian-born US physicist. 1901-54. Called the greatest Italian physicist since Galileo, he was the son of a senior government official. Fermi was educated at the University of Pisa (PhD 1924) and after some time in Germany took up an appointment at the Univ of Florence. After making his first major contribution to nuclear physics there he became professor of physics at the Univ of Rome in 1927. In 1938 he was awarded the Nobel prize in physics for work in producing artificial radioactivity by using neutrons to bombard the atom. Fearing for his Jewish wife's safety in Fascist Italy, Fermi sailed with her directly from the Nobel ceremony to New York.

The expatriate worked at Columbia Univ until the outbreak of WWII, then moved to the Univ of Chicago. Having failed to interest the US Navy in developing the A-bomb, Fermi and others then prevailed on Albert EINSTEIN to write the letter to Roosevelt that got the Manhattan Project started. In Chicago on 2 Dec 42 Fermi produced the first nuclear chain reaction. Soon becoming chief consultant for nuclear physics at

Los Alamos, NM, he saw the first successful A-bomb test on 16 July 45.

Having become a US citizen in 1945, Fermi was a professor of physics and nuclear science at the Univ of Chicago from the end of the war. His wife Laura published *Atoms in the Family, My Life With Enrico Fermi,* a month before he died 28 Nov 54 of cancer.

FISHER, William (Rudolph Abel). Soviet spy. 1903-71. In 1956 the FBI called him the highest-ranking espionage agent ever caught in the United States. In the 1930s and during WWII he had worked under Pavel Sudoplatov in directing radio deception games (Sudoplatov, 107). In 1947 he set up a ring in the US and worked undetected for nine years as a retired photofinisher and amateur artist. Having used at least five aliases in the US, he then took the name Col Rudolph Ivanovich Abel when arrested in NYC. He had been betrayed by Aleksandr Korotkov, who defected to the US when recalled by Moscow center. While in the US Abel also was involved in attempting to trace Aleksandr Orlov, a **Cambridge Five** recruiter. Sentenced in 1957 to 30 years for espionage, Abel was exchanged in 1962 for U-2 pilot Gary Francis Powers.

FLANDIN, Pierre Etienne. French statesman. 1889-1958. Wealthy son of a resident general of Tunis, Flandin got a diploma in political sciences from the Sorbonne (1909), a law degree from there (1913), and became a highly successful corporate lawyer. Meanwhile he was elected as a conservative in the Chamber of Deputies in May 14 at the age of 25, then became one of France's first military flyers, and in 1920 he was undersecretary of state for aeronautics. The tremendously tall, immaculately groomed, striking-looking Flandin, who spoke English from childhood, was a minister in many cabinets before being premier from Nov 34 through May 35, then foreign minister in the first half of 1936. In this capacity Flandin became stigmatized as "the Minister who lost the Rhine" (Pertinax, 392), but Churchill points out that France's only choice was to cooperate with Hitler (WC, I, 282). Flandin served briefly at Vichy as Pétain's deputy and foreign minister before taking over from LAVAL on 13 Dec 40 and being succeeded by Darlan the following February. Flandin reached Algeria in Oct 42,

still convinced that France's only hope lay in accommodation with Germany (ibid.). He was one of the ex-Vichyites arrested by de Gaulle in 1943 (along with BERGERET, BOISSON, NOGUES, and PEYROUTON). Sentenced in July 46 to five years of "national indignity" he was quickly pardoned. Flandin published *Paix et Liberté* (1939) and *Politique française* (1947).

FLEISCHER, Carl. Norwegian general. 1883-1942. As commander of forces in the far north of his country he took over the province of North Norway when it was cut off. Withdrawing into the mountains after Eduard DIETL captured Narvik, he cooperated with Allied relief forces led by Lord CORK. Counterattacking under terrible weather conditions, the Norwegian general gave German troops their first setback of the war. Feeling betrayed by Lord Cork's withdrawal, Fleischer accompanied his government to London in June 40 and became CinC of the Norwegian Army. After continuing arguments with the British he was ordered to Canada in 1942 as military attaché and commander of Norwegian troops there but he committed suicide soon after reaching Ottawa.

FLETCHER, Frank John. US admiral. 1885-1973. "Black Jack" Fletcher was born 29 Apr 85 in Iowa. He graduated from Annapolis in 1906 (26/116), won the Medal of Honor at Vera Cruz in 1914, and saw action in WWI.

During the Pearl Harbor attack Fletcher commanded the cruiser *Minneapolis,* which survived because it was at sea. Quickly promoted, Rear Adm Fletcher was ordered to lead TF 14 to reinforce Wake Island, where DEVEREUX was directing a desperate defense, but on 22 Dec 41, about 500 from Wake, he stopped to refuel. The delay proved to be fatal because Adm W. S. Pye, as KIMMEL's temporary successor, cancelled the relief effort.

With flag aboard CV *Yorktown* Fletcher headed on 3 May 42 for Tulagi, where the Japanese had just landed opposite Guadalcanal. Having attacked Tulagi he was a day late for the rendezvous scheduled for 5 May with CV *Lexington.* When Nimitz was alerted by radio intercepts that three large Japanese forces were heading for Port Moresby, the admiral ordered US and Australian naval forces to mass for what became the battle of the Coral Sea, 6-8 May 42. Fletcher had the major role in what was a strategic victory in stopping the Japanese drive but a tactical defeat in losing *Lexington,* one of the few big US carriers in the Pacific, while sinking one enemy carrier and damaging another.

Leaving Pearl Harbor on 2 Jun 42 for the battle of Midway, Fletcher turned over tactical command to SPRUANCE when his flagship, CV *Saratoga,* was taken out of action early by three bomb hits.

Fletcher was given over-all command of the Guadalcanal campaign when CNO Ernest J. KING ordered this controversial first US offensive of the war undertaken. The inexperienced and naturally cautious Fletcher was handicapped by bad command arrangements: GHORMLEY was senior US naval commander in the South Pacific but had little authority over Fletcher, Amphibious forces in the Pacific were under TURNER, who reported direct to Ghormley; and Black Jack did not get along with Turner. Justifiably concerned about the safety of his precious carriers, *Enterprise, Saratoga,* and *Wasp,* Fletcher gave notice that he would cover the landings only until D+4, or 11 Aug 42. (Morison, V, 27.)

Late in the afternoon of D+2 Fletcher learned that large enemy naval forces were approaching, and the next morning, without Ghormley's permission, he withdrew his carriers. They were low on fuel and within range of land-based enemy aircraft, so the admiral had reason for caution. But his withdrawal left supply ships highly vulnerable to air attack and it left VANDEGRIFT's Marines with virtually no air support as they struggled to enlarge a shallow beachhead on Guadalcanal.

As commander of TF 61, built around carriers *Saratoga* (flagship), *Enterprise,* and *Wasp,* Fletcher faced Yamamoto's Combined Fleet in the battle of the Eastern Solomons, 23-25 Aug 42. This was the third of the war's great carrier engagements, and it was indecisive; but the Japanese "had shot their bolt" (wrote Nimitz) in trying to save Guadalcanal (Morison, V, 107). In the attrition tactics that followed, the Japanese continuing their efforts to support the Guadalcanal garrison, Fletcher was one of 12 wounded when a torpedo from the submarine I-26 hit *Saratoga.* Having had several operations go

wrong, Vice Adm Fletcher ended his combat career on this note.

In 1943 he took over naval forces in the north Pacific, then from 15 Apr 44, when the Alaska Sector was abolished, he also headed the new Alaska Sea Frontier. Fletcher retired on 1 June 47 as a full admiral and died in Bethesda, Md, on 25 Apr 73.

FOOTE, (Alexander) Allan. British double agent. 1905-56. A key man in the **Lucy ring,** Allan Foote was born 13 Apr 05 in a suburb of Liverpool. His father, an unsuccessful poultry farmer, had just brought the family back from Ireland and soon moved it to a poultry farm in South Yorkshire. Foote's childhood at Armthorpe, near Doncaster, was unhappy. His father never made much money, had a violent temper, and always disliked his son. Growing up during the first world war Foote developed an early interest in spies and aspired to be one. (Read and Fisher, *Lucy,* 21.)

The boy left home at the age of 14 with little education and a broad North Country accent. He spent the next 15 years in Manchester as a corn merchant. Eventually taking over from the manager, Foote kept the business alive during the worst years of the great depression. But in 1935 he found himself looking for another job. Just turned 30, he was a big man, six feet two, well-built, handsome, and quick-witted. Hoping for adventure as well as security he joined the RAF on 21 July 35. After training as an airframe fitter and reaching the rank of aircraftsman first class he was recruited by Lt Col Claude DANSEY's Z Organization. His training as a double agent for insertion into the Red Army's intelligence service (GRU) began in the Spanish civil war. The resourceful Yorkshireman became a sort of aide, factotum, and scrounger for Fred Copeman, British battalion commander in the 15th International Bde. After two years in Spain and having exceeded Dansey's expectations he was invalided home in Sep 38 after being operated on for a face wound.

Foote was sent in late 1938 to infiltrate the Soviet espionage net in Switzerland. Attaining the rank of major in the Red Army he became a mainstay of the **Lucy ring** and one Dansey's channels for feeding Ultra data to Moscow Center. In June 42 Foote craftily avoided a kidnapping attempt in which Klaus BARBIE figured.

Swiss police closed on the **Lucy ring** and arrested Foote on 20 Nov 43 while he was receiving a long message from Moscow Center. He blithely told interrogators his radio set was "a cure for insomnia" and refused to admit spying or to reveal Lucy's sources. It is one thing to catch a spy and quite another thing to convict him in court, and the host nation had embarrassing secrets to protect. Anxious to rid themselves of the problem, and getting nothing of value from Foote, the Swiss agreed to release him if only he would confess to espionage; he did not even have to mention the USSR. So Foote signed a confession that he had been an agent "for one of the United Nations." Writing himself a check on his frozen bank account for 2,000 francs ($465 at the official rate) he was released on 8 Sep 44 after 10 months in prison.

With the Franco-Swiss border now open and Paris liberated, Foote reported to Moscow Center through the recently reopened Russian embassy. With an eye to the future he said that enough of the Lucy net was intact for it to resume operations. But Rado, who had been smuggled out of Switzerland with his wife, informed Moscow (from the Paris embassy) that his ring was so badly compromised that the Soviets should wait at least two years before trying to pick up the pieces. The two illegals were summoned to Moscow for an explanation of their contradictory reports. (Lène Rado, also in bad health, was excused.) The men flew out of Paris on 6 Jan 45 via Cairo, where Rado lost his nerve and bolted. The British complied with Moscow's request to find him, and the little Hungarian spent 10 years in the **Lubyanka**. (He was rehabilitated by the Hungarian CP and showered with academic honors.)

Debriefed and given a clean bill of health, Foote had regular contact with senior GRU officers and was given training in their latest techniques. He was told to learn Russian in preparation for heading a net targeted against the US. But these and other plans did not work out, so the spy came in from the cold, expecting to have a great future with British intelligence. Crossing into the British sector in Berlin, he surrendered on 2 Aug 47 to the first RAF police patrol he saw. If Claude "Col Z" DANSEY had not died only 10 weeks earlier, the reception might have

been different. But he was met with great suspicion, a common fate of double agents. The Swiss meanwhile opened their second trial of Lucy ring on 30 Oct 47 with most members in absentia. Among the latter, Foote received a sentence of 30 months in prison, a fine of 8,000 francs, and confiscation of his radio set and the rest of the money he had in Switzerland.

Foote had high hopes for his memoirs, *Handbook for Spies* (London: Museum Press, 1949, 1953), but it did not make the money he hoped for. "They mutilated my book," he told the American historian David Dallin in 1953, saying MI5 censors cut out the best parts and, without permission, inserted fabrications (Read and Fisher, *Lucy,* 223). It was the time of British security scandals. There is no proof that Foote was involved with Burgess, Maclean, and Kim Philby (of the **Cambridge five**), but it is likely that "MI5 had something on him, something that put him forever in their power" (ibid, 224).

Foote became a clerk in the Ministry of Agricultural and Fisheries, where MI5 could keep in touch. Years of adventure had given him a duodenal ulcer, which required an operation at the end of 1945 in Moscow. The trouble exacerbated by heavy drinking, Foote underwent surgery in 1956. The operation was not a success. "This is no damn good," the big Yorkshireman said when his only available next of kin, two sisters, were called to the hospital room. A few hours later, early on 1 Aug 56, the patient calmly tore off his surgical dressings and died. He was 51.

FORRESTAL, James Vincent. US official. 1892-1949. Forrestal was born 15 Feb 92 at Beacon, NY, son of an Irish immigrant. Educated at Dartmouth and Princeton, and a naval aviator in WWI, in 1938 he became president of the banking firm that evolved into Dillon, Read & Co. Forrestal left in June 40 to become a presidential assistant, and two months later was under secretary of the navy with special responsibility for procurement and production. After the death of Frank Knox on 23 Apr 44, Forrestal was secretary of the navy, 19 May 44–17 Sep 47, then the first secretary of defense.

An intense, humorless, unsociable man with an unhappy marriage, he broke under the strain of the new office and resigned as of 28 Mar 49 (succeeded by Louis Johnson).

Close associates like presidential advisor Clark Clifford had seen alarming evidence of mental instability in Forrestal for years, but the condition was not properly diagnosed when the distraught man checked himself into Bethesda USNH soon after leaving office. Doctors thought Forrestal's condition was improving, but on 22 May 49 he committed suicide by plunging through a 16th-floor hospital window.

FOULKES, Charles. Canadian general. 1903-69. He was Crerar's CofS in the 1st Cdn Army before taking over the 2d Cdn Div. After temporarily succeeding SIMONDS as corps commander during the battle of the Scheldt Estuary until 9 Nov 44, Lt Gen Foulkes led the 1st Cdn Corps in Italy. He was Canada's CGS, 1945-51, and chairman of the Chiefs of Staff Committee, 1951-60.

FRANCO, Francisco. Spanish head of state. 1892-1975. Francisco Paulino Teódulo Hermenegildo Franco y Bahamonde was born at El Ferrol in Galicia province. He graduated with honors from the Toledo military academy in 1910 as an infantryman. Fighting the Abd-el-Krim uprising in Morocco the short, stocky, puritanical martinet was known for "incomparable bravery and for extraordinary good luck under fire" (Thomas, *Spanish Civil War,* 82). He also was a brilliant strategist and administrator. When France and Spain agreed in 1925 to combine forces against Abd-el-Krim, Franco commanded his country's troops in the successful campaign led by Marshal Pétain. Mutual admiration between the men dates from this association.

Franco had been director of the Zaragoza MA since 1927 when a **popular front** took power in Madrid on 10 May 36. Being a rightist he was virtually exiled to the Canary Islands as governor, but Franco took over the Army of Africa after it revolted. He captured Medilla on 18 July 36 to touch off the **Spanish civil war,** and after three years of bloody conflict Franco became absolute dictator on 4 Aug 39.

"El Caudillo" (the leader) concentrated thereafter on consolidating his personal rule and "keeping his blooddrained people out of another war" (WC, II, 519). Although Spain joined the anti-Comintern pact on 7 April 38 the country declared neutrality when WWII began on 3 Sep 39. Hitler had many reasons for wanting Franco in his camp, and El Caudillo obviously wanted to be on the winning side. But Franco set a high asking price and kept raising it. First he demanded full economic support to compensate for what a British blockade would cost, and Hitler was in no position to take on this burden. Franco next asked that in any postwar settlement he be given Gibraltar, French Morocco, a portion of Algeria including Oran, and parts of Africa. From Aug 40 he declined to play ball until the Germans invaded England.

Hitler went to the border town of Hendaye to meet Franco on 23 Oct 40. At this time, having conquered France, the Wehrmacht appeared to be unbeatable. All Hitler wanted was free passage of a few German troops through Spain (incognito) to link up with an airborne assault on Gibraltar. CANARIS had a major role in convincing Franco not to acquiesce, astounding his incredulous Spanish friend with the prediction that Germany could not win a long war. (Harold C. Deutsch to author, 30 Dec 88.) Be that as it may, El Caudillo would not allow Germans on Spanish soil but asked instead that Hitler supply arms for Spanish forces to take Gibraltar. Refused, Franco then he said he would remain neutral until Germany took the Suez Canal.

Franco's motives were nationalistic, but he was strongly influenced by skilful British and American diplomacy (Buchanan, 151). And for two years the British kept a force ready to take the Canary Islands if they lost Gibraltar (WC, II, 519). In Oct 43 Franco requested (and got) repatriation of the **Spanish Blue Division,** a token he had sent in Germany's war against communism, and thereafter he supported the Allies more openly. After the war the UN revoked Spain's diplomatic isolation in 1950, and five years latter admitted the country to the UN. Spain was excluded from NATO, but Franco allowed the US to establish air bases. After a quarter of a century in power, El Caudillo died in 1975.

FRANCOIS-PONCET, André. French statesman, diplomat, and writer. 1887-1978. Born at Provins, François-Poncet is best known for insightful and historically valuable memoirs (following). He was educated at the *Ecole normale supérieure* (1907-10), **agrégé** in German, and a deputy from Paris (1924-1931). Meanwhile he was under secretary of state for the beaux arts and technical instruction (1928-30) then had a government post *(à la présidence du Conseil)* for the national economy (1930-31), and from 1917 he had a number of diplomatic missions. *(Larousse.)* As ambassador to Berlin from 27 Aug 31 François-Poncet attempted to persuade Hitler to adopt a non-aggression program, particularly after being notified on 16 Mar 35 that the dictator was reestablishing military service. Protesting Hitler's reoccupation of the **Rhineland** (7 Mar 36), he urged his government to undertake rearmament *(Larousse)*. The ambassador also made the appropriate French diplomatic noises against the **Anschluss** (11 Mar 38) and served as intermediary during the **Munich crisis** of late Sep 38. Deploring French fecklessness in coping with Hitler's march to war but hoping to have some influence with Mussolini, he had himself named ambassador to Rome from 18 Oct 38 *(Larousse)*. On Italy's entry into the war on 10 June 40, he returned to France.

Named a member of the national council in Vichy on 21 May 41, but under the Nazi heel as press coordinator in Paris and Vichy (Pertinax, 546 & n), the former ambassador was deported to Germany in Aug 43. He was rescued on 4 May 45 as part of the **Niederdorf group.** The veteran diplomat and expert on Germany was a counselor to his government in Dec 48 before going to West Germany as the French high commissioner (1949-55), then as ambassador to the **FRG.** He was elected to the French Academy in 1952 for his diplomatic memoirs, *Souvenirs d'une ambassade à Berlin* (1946), *De Versailles à Potsdam* (1948), *Carnets d'un captif* (1952), and *Au palais Farnèse* (1952).

He was president of the international Red Cross (1952-65), with some overlap as president of the French Red Cross (1955-67) before retiring. His final book was *Souvenirs d'une Ambassade à Rome* (1961).

FRANK, Anne. Nazi victim. 1929-45. Born 12 June 29 at Frankfort on Main, Germany, she was the daughter of Otto Frank, a Jewish businessman who moved his family to Amsterdam in 1933 to escape persecution. On 5 July 42, when the bright and imaginative child was just 13 years old, her 16-year-old sister Margot received a call-up notice from the SS. Having

planned carefully for this contingency, the family moved four days later into a warehouse behind the father's office building. They lived undetected for almost two years in several rooms until 4 Aug 44, when everybody in the family except the father, Otto, was seized. Anne died of typhus in the Belsen-Bergen concentration camp after being there seven months. Her sensitive and poignant diary, found after the war, was published by her father in 1947 as *Het Achterhuis*. Literally "the house behind," this is what she called their hideout, although the name is rendered as "the Secret Annexe" in the English edition published in 1952 as *Anne Frank: The Diary of a Young Girl*. The remarkable work has been translated into more than 30 languages, dramatized for the stage, and made into a film (1959). The Het Achterhuis in Amsterdam is now a museum.

FRANK, Hans. German governor of Poland. 1900-46. Born in Karlsruhe on 23 May 00, he was the son of an attorney who had been disbared for corruption (Wistrich). Being just 18 when WWI cndcd, Frank had only a year of military service. But he was in the Freikorps that ousted the Communist Raeterpublic from Munich in 1919. That year he joined the **DAP,** became a Brownshirt, and had a part in the **Munich Beer Hall Putsch of 1923.** Three years later he got a law degree, started practicing in Munich, and soon was the Nazis' legal champion. He defended Hitler in 150 lawsuits (Davidson, *Trial,* 429).

The youthful Dr Frank was elected to the **Reichstag** in 1930, and three years later, when Hitler became chancellor, the lawyer became minister of justice in Bavaria. He also was made head of the NSDAP law division, Reich minister of justice, and president of the Academy of German Law. A man of mediocre juridical intellect, he tailored the cloth of German law to fit the Nazi coat and came up with such "principles" as "Law is the will of the Fuehrer."

But during the **Blood Purge** of 1934 the Nazi lawyer raised legal objections to the planned execution of some 110 SA leaders including those in Munich's Stadelheim Prison with Ernst ROEHM. Hitler finally ordered only 20 men shot. The episode lost Frank influence within the Nazi hierarchy but he remained on good terms with Hitler.

Retaining his other titles, Frank became Gov Gen of Poland on 8 Nov 39. His primary mission was to eradicate the nation's leadership while bleeding the country of labor and other resources. Himmler was responsible for the death camps but Frank gave the SS his enthusiastic assistance except when it threatened his slave labor pool. Frank finally became so alienated by Nazi excesses that he made a public appeal for a return to constitutional rule. In Aug 42 he was ousted from the Nazi hierarchy. His legal offices were taken by Otto Thierack, but Frank remained Gov Gen of Poland, living high on the hog and looting Polish museums. (Davidson, *Trial,* 433.)

On 6 May 45 he was discovered in a camp of German prisoners at Berchtesgaden and tried to commit suicide (Larousse). At Nuremberg he was genuinely shocked by full evidence of Nazi war crimes. "A thousand years shall pass and this guilt of Germany shall not have been erased," he told the court. Despite speeches supporting the "final solution," Frank was one of the less repulsive members of Hitler's coterie, retaining shreds of decency and justice (Davidson, *Trial,* 437). At Nuremberg he converted to Catholicism and wrote his memoirs, published as *Im Angesicht des Galgens* (Munich: Beck Verlag, 1953). Hans Frank was hanged on 16 Oct 46.

FRANK, Karl Hermann. Sudeten German. 1898-1946. Born 24 Jan 98 in Karlsbad, he served in the Austrian army during the last years of WWI and became a fanatical Sudeten German Freikorps leader. After failing in the bookselling business in Karlsbad he joined the Sudeten German Nazi Party and became second in command to Konrad HENLEIN. Frank entered the Czech Parliament in 1937, and on 30 Oct 38 became deputy Gauleiter of the Nazi **DAP** in the Sudetenland.

When the Germans occupied Prague on 15 Mar 39, Frank became minister of state of the Nazi Protectorate of Bohemia–Moravia. Himmler, who headed the entire German police, made Frank chief of police and top SS officer of the protectorate with the rank of SS-Gruppenfuehrer. Frank succeeded HEDRICH, who died 4 June 42, and is said to have selected Lidice for extermination as part of a "special repressive action to give the Czechs a les-

son in propriety." (Michel, *Shadow War,* 352.) From 20 Aug 43 Frank was Reich minister for Bohemia and Moravia. Convicted of war crimes by a Czech court, he was publicly hanged on 22 May 46.

FREDENDALL, Lloyd Ralston. US general. 1884-1965. Born 15 Jan 83 in Wyoming and admitted to West Point with the class of 1905, he failed to graduate but was commissioned in 1907 as a second lieutenant. A "short, tough-talking infantryman" (Pogue, *Marshall,* II, 407), he became a major general in 1940 and took command of the 4th Inf Div at Ft Benning, Ga, in October of that year. Known as a troop trainer, Fredendall headed the 2d Corps from 14 Aug 41 and the 11th Corps from its activation on 15 June 42 (*AA,* 505, 507, 522). The relatively elderly general was picked by Eisenhower with some misgivings from a list of eight whom Marshall nominated to succeed Mark CLARK as 2d Corps commander in England. Taking over on 10 Oct 42, and immediately making a favorable impression on Eisenhower (*EP,* 628), the newcomer had less than a month to complete preparations for landing his Central TF on 8 Nov around Oran. His troops were the 1st Inf Div, CCB of the 1st Armd Div, and the 1st Ranger Bn. "I bless the day you urged Fredendall upon me," Ike wrote to George Marshall a few days after the landings (Pogue, *Marshall,* II, 407) and on 19 Nov he nominated Fredendall and Patton for promotion to lieutenant general (*EP,* 685n4). Six weeks later (1 Jan 43) Fredendall's 2d Corps was reconstituted with the 1st Armd Div and the 26th RCT (of the 1st Inf Div) and ordered to take the Tunisian port of Sfax. This would block the retreat of Rommel's Pz Army Africa to join forces with von ARNIM's 5th Pz Army. But the Germans frustrated Eisenhower's "race for Tunis." Forced onto the defensive, the 2d US Corps was stretched thin on a 80-mile front to cover the Allied right flank. Eisenhower ordered a standard deployment: a screen of reconnaissance forces along the wide front, strong points covering passes in the Eastern Dorsal, and a mobile reserve to counterattack when the enemy's main effort was identified. But Fredendall posted his infantry on isolated **djebels** and scattered his mobile reserve forces in bits and pieces. Further, his well dug-in corps headquarters was 80 miles behind the front, at

Tebessa. Eisenhower discovered this fatally flawed deployment on 13 Feb 43 in the course of a belated command visit.

"At dawn the following morning," writes Bradley, "German Tiger tanks surged through the gateway at Faid Pass . . . swarmed through the Dorsal . . . [and] quickly isolated and encircled the American forces on adjoining djebels" (Bradley, I, 25). This was Arnim's right (north) wing of a classic double envelopment, the left wing of which, under ROMMEL, drove through Gafsa to meet Arnim's panzers and defeat the Americans around Kasserine Pass, 19-20 Feb 43. BRADLEY was sent to investigate the fiasco, and on his recommendation Fredendall was relieved by George PATTON on 6 Mar 43. But Fredendall's promotion to lieutenant general, which Eisenhower had recommended way back on 19 Nov 42 (above), was approved on 1 June 43. Fredendall took over the 2d Army Hq at Memphis, Tenn. This was a training command, and the general doubled as head of the Central Defense Command until Jan 44 (*AA, 600*). Awarded the DSM, Lt Gen Fredendall retired 31 Mar 46 for physical disability (Cullum) and died 4 Oct 63 in La Jolla, Calif.

FREISLER, Roland. President of Berlin People's Court. 1893-1945. The "People's judge" was born of Hessian peasant stock in Celle on 30 Oct 93. Captured on the eastern front in 1915 he was sent as a POW to Siberia, where he mastered Russian and became a Bolshevik **commissar.** He returned to Germany in 1920, studied law, and became a Nazi legal authority. Because of his communist background, Freisler was passed over when Hans FRANK was ousted from his legal offices in Aug 42. But that year he was appointed president of the Berlin People's Court (Volksgericht), a sort of summary court for cases of treason. In a blood-red robe, with huge swastika flags on the walls of the great hall of the Berlin Supreme Court and concealed cameras, the sadist conducted trials of the Valkyrie conspirators. The first session began on 7 Aug 44, less than three weeks after STAUFFENBERG's Attentat. "Freisler's conduct of the proceedings became so undignified that even the official Nazi observers and Thierack, the minister of justice, complained to Bormann about him." (Hoffmann, *Resistance,* 527.) But the trials continued, and few of the accused escaped immediate execu-

tion. On 3 Feb 45, as SCHLABRENDORFF was about to be tried, a US air raid sent the court to the cellars. A direct hit collapsed the ceiling, dropping a beam on the judge, and he died that day. (Ibid.)

FRENAY, Henri. French resistance leader. 1905-88. Born in Lyons, Henri Frenay was a St Cyrien like his father and brothers. He also graduated from the Center of Germanic Studies in Strasbourg. As a captain he was captured in the Vosges during the Battle of France but escaped from a POW column in Alsace on 27 June 40. Making his way to Marseilles, he remained until 16 Dec and was assigned to army staff duty in Vichy. Late in Feb 41 he went underground and established clandestine newspapers, *Les Petites Ailes,* and then *Vérités.* Around these papers was formed a resistance group. Within less than a year this merged with the producers of *Libertés* (including François de MENTHON) to become *Combat.* The new group spoke for the most important movement in the unoccupied zone (Michel, *Shadow War,* 105), and the former army captain and St Cyrien innovated most of the techniques used within the French resistance (Larousse). After accepting Jean MOULIN's authority and praising his performance as de Gaulle's representative in France, Frenay (code name "Charvet") criticized Moulin in his memoirs for trying to seize too much authority. He also saw in the national council of the resistance (CNR), Moulin's crowing achievement, a return to fractured French politics of the Third Republic. In sum, Charvet was willing to accept de Gaulle's military authority but unwilling to sacrifice political independence. *(Larousse.)*

All this became academic in June 43 when the Germans (notably BARBIE and BLEICHER) virtually destroyed the top military and political leadership of the resistance. Victims included Gen DELESTRAINT, and MOULIN. Frenay left for Algiers on 19 June 43 to seek better support from the FCNL. Talked into remaining, Frenay was minister of prisoners, deportees, and refugees for two years from Nov 43. He returned to France with de Gaulle, retaining his cabinet position in Paris. The English translation of Frenay's book, first published in 1973, is *The Night Will End: Memoirs of a Revolutionary* (New York: McGraw Hill, 1976).

FREYBERG, Bernard Cyril. New Zealand general. 1889–1963. Churchill called him "the salamander of the British Empire," alluding to the mythical creature that thrived in fire. When Montgomery sniffed on first seeing his troops that they did not salute much, Freyberg replied cheerily "If you wave to them they'll wave back."

Born 21 Mar 89 in Surrey, at Richmond (now in Greater London), he went to New Zealand as a child when his father joined the forestry department. Bernard Freyberg dropped out of Wellington College shortly before his 16th birthday and in due course became a dentist. Drawn to military life, he was a second lieutenant in the territorials by 1912. He was an impressive man physically, powerfully built, 6 feet 11/2 inches tall *(DNB)*, a champion swimmer, oarsman, and a good boxer. But, like George Patton, he was cursed with a high voice.

Shortly after the start of war in late Aug 14 he reached London and, with the influence of Churchill, first lord of the admiralty *(DNB)*, was given a temporary commission in the Royal Navy Volunteer Res. *(DNB* and sketch by Dan Devin in Carver, ed, *War Lords,* 582 ff. The latter source is cited hereafter as Devin.)

Lt Freyberg was assigned as commander of Co A in the Hood Bn of the newly formed Naval Div. In the first of many misguided and costly military adventures conceived by Churchill, the Naval Div was sent to assist in the Belgian defenses of Antwerp in Oct 14. Withdrawn on 6 Oct 14, Freyberg led his company in the 60-mile retreat to Ostend. This was the first of four times Freyberg would be evacuated *(DNB)* after a military fiasco for which his friend and ardent admirer Winston Churchill was primarily responsible.

Still commanding Co A, Hood Bn, Naval Div, Freyberg was a hero from the first day of the Gallipoli campaign, 25 Apr 15. Freyberg made a one-man military demonstration by swimming ashore in the dark to light flares along a beach to simulate a landing party. This won him the first of three **DSOs** he would receive in WWI. Freyberg suffered a severe abdominal wound in July but returned to duty by 19 Aug 15 and was made acting commander of the Hood Bn. The appointment was confirmed after the Dardanelles evacuation in Jan 16 (his second) and the Naval Div was reconstituted as the 63d Div of the BEF. Lt Col Freyberg distinguished himself

on the Somme in Nov 16, suffering four wounds in a 48-hour action but refusing to leave his battalion until the objective was taken and secured. Sent to England for hospitalization and a long convalescence, he was awarded the VC. In Apr 17 he took over the 173d Bde, 58th Div *(DNB)*, finally leaving his companions of almost three years in the Hood Bn. Now a brigadier general (T), he distinguished himself at Bullecourt and in the 3d battle of Ypres. Sustaining wounds that required three months' hospitalization in England, he returned to the western front and a new command, the 88th Bde, 29th Div. In the last battle of Ypres he won a bar to his DSO, and for a dash that saved a bridge at Lessines from demolition just before the armistice he was awarded a second bar *(DNB)*. Wounded on six occasions (for a total of perhaps 10 individual wounds), the great antipodean warrior had been mentioned five times in dispatches and, in addition to the DSO with two bars, he wore the VC. His eldest brothers, Oscar and Paul, had died in action at Gallipoli (1915) and in France (1917) *(DNB)*.

The nationally famous war hero remained in England to undertake a regular army career. This was interrupted in 1922 by an unsuccessful run for a seat in the House of Commons as a Liberal. Freyberg also pursued an ambition of long standing to swim the Channel. His best of three attempts failed by 500 yards in 1925 *(DNB)*. Falling victim to HORE-BELISHA's military reforms, he was retired in 1937 as a major general for medical disability. He remained in England until recalled after Britain declared war on 3 Sep 39. Given only administrative assignments, the old war horse offered his services to the New Zealand government and on 23 Nov 39 was made commander of the NZ Expeditionary Force with the warm approval of Churchill and his generals. After flying home for instructions and being given wide authority, he took the 4th NZ Bde to Egypt and, as GOC New Zealand Forces, began forming the 2d NZ Div. One brigade was in England throughout most of 1940, but by the following spring all three brigades were in Egypt and ready for action. This came in Greece, where Henry M. "Jumbo" WILSON led the controversial British intervention decided on by Churchill in one of his most misguided military moments. "The essential Freyberg was revealed in his refusal to obey Wavell's orders to leave by air, staying with his men to the end" *(DNB)*, his third evacuation by sea.

When Wavell inspected the situation in Crete, where some puny defensive preparations had been made, he decided that Freyberg should take command of the island's widely dispersed and poorly equipped forces. "Freyberg performed prodigies in the three weeks before the invasion began" on 20 May 41 *(DNB)*. But on 26 May he signalled Wavell that his surviving troops at the Suda Bay beachhead could do no more. With Adm "ABC" CUNNINGHAM, naval forces continuing their heroic efforts, the New Zealand general directed the withdrawal of about 18,000 officers and men to Alexandria. The rear guard slipped out the night of 30-31 May, but Freyberg flew out the preceding night on orders from superiors in Cairo (WC, III, 300). This decision was cited later by Churchill to Roosevelt as a precedent for evacuating MacARTHUR from the Philippines.

Back in Egypt, Freyberg reorganized his division for the war against Rommel and was heavily engaged in Opn Crusader, 18 Nov-31 Dec 41, under Gen Claude Auchinleck. But the New Zealander had fundamental disagreements over tactics with his British superiors, and with fresh memories of the Greek fiasco, Freyberg now had suffered crippling losses in relieving Tobruk. With the support of statesmen down under, who were alarmed about the sacrifice of ANZAC forces under British leadership, Freyberg withdrew his division to Syria. But he had to rush back when Rommel's second offensive drove the 8th Army back the next summer. After a march of 1,200 miles in a little more than a week, Freyberg and two of his brigades took part in the battle of Mersa Matruh, 27-28 June 42, as part of W. H. E. "Strafer" GOTT's 13th Corps, being assigned to hold high ground on an escarpment at Minqar Quaim. Transport was pooled in reserve. During the afternoon of 27 June the 21st Pz Div enveloped the New Zealanders and overran its motor pool. The corps commander thought the two brigades also had been overrun and ordered the other two divisions (1st Armd and 5th Indian) to withdraw to Futa. Freyberg had a disabling neck wound from a shell fragment but his troops were easily holding their position. Without orders on where to

go, the New Zealanders fought their way out after dark and withdrew to the El Alamein position. They had suffered 800 casualties in three days and Freyberg had to be carried on a litter. (Jackson, 240-43.)

When Freyberg returned for duty on 10 Aug 42, three days after the death of GOTT, he doubled as acting commander of the 13th Corps. Meanwhile, Montgomery took over the 8th Army on 13 Aug and two days later sent to England for Brian HORROCKS to come out as GOC 13th Corps. Freyberg's division, which meanwhile had been badly bloodied in the continued efforts to gain a tactical advantage over Rommel before resuming the offensive, was heavily engaged in Montgomery's initial victory over Rommel at Alam Halfa, 31 Aug-7 Sep 42, and in the decisive phases of the breakout at El Alamein, 23 Oct-1 Nov 42. In the pursuit of Rommel the New Zealanders became famous for wide envelopments through uncharted desert on the left flank. The first "left hook" turned Rommel out of the strong El Aghela position by taking Merduma on 16 Dec 42. Freyberg was knighted (KCB and KBE) and promoted to lieutenant general during the year.

Led by the 7th Armd Div, the 2d NZ executed another wide envelopment through the desert to take Tripoli on 23 Jan 43. The final action in Africa was to turn Rommel out of the Mareth Line. For this envelopment the 2d NZ was so strongly reinforced that it was designated the NZ Corps. Joined by the 10th Corps Hq and the 1st Armd Div, this strategic envelopment broke the Axis defenses near El Hamma (just W of Gabes) and turned Rommel out of the Mareth Line in Mar 43.

Despite a rank that entitled him to remain a corps commander, Lt Gen Freyberg insisted on staying with his division. He was not committed in Sicily nor in the early actions in Italy, the 2d NZ being taken out of the line for rest and reorganized. The 4th Bde was given tanks and reincorporated. *(DNB.)*

In late 1943 the division was assigned to the 5th Corps on the Adriatic side of the Italian front and was heavily engaged in Montgomery's action on the Sangro River. In Jan 44 Sir Bernard's New Zealand Corps was formed of his division, the 4th Indian Div and the 78th Inf Div, and moved to the sector opposite Cassino. Here the 34th and 36th US Inf Divs (of the 2d US

Corps) had been unable to penetrate at the Cassino defenses. Sir Bernard Freyberg directed another assault in which even the 4th Indian Div Gurkhas could not break through.

Freyberg then was largely responsible for the controversial decision that the way to crack KESSELRING's fortified line was to bomb Cassino abbey into rubble. (Buchanan, 184n, citing Mark Clark.) But the vandalism had just the opposite effect, creating an obstacle easier for the "Green Devils" (German parachute troops) to defend. By 23 Mar 44 the first battles of Cassino ended in a costly Allied failure.

The Germans rated the 2d NZ Div and the 2d Moroccan Div of JUIN's French Expeditionary Corps as the two best Allied formations in Italy. But the government down under, notably Frederick JONES (minister of defense) objected to the price paid for this honor, so Freyberg's division was pulled out of the Cassino cauldron and his short lived corps was "disestablished."

Reassigned to the 10th British Corps of Oliver Leese on the central portion of the front, the division met no serious opposition in the Rome Campaign, 11 May-5 June 44. But Freyberg's aggressive action in July broke Kesselring defenses on the Po River line and speeded the 8th Army's advance on Florence. As the British moved on up the Adriatic coast in Aug 44, Sir Bernard was injured in an air accident and out of action until 16 Oct. Two months later his engineers used innovative techniques to break the German defenses on the Senio River.

In the final offensive that began on 9 Apr 45, the 2d NZ crossed the Po on the 25th. Under orders from Harold ALEXANDER to frustrate Yugoslav designs on Venezia Gulia, Freyberg raced into Trieste on 2 May before Tito's partisans could "liberate" the Italian port city. For this final campaign he was awarded a third bar to his DSO.

The legendary, headstrong, outspoken but modest Freyberg had commanded his division for five years. He was governor general of New Zealand, 1946-52, raised to the peerage in 1951 as 1st Baron of Wellington and Munstead. Thereafter lieutenant governor and deputy constable of Windsor Castle, he died 4 July 63 at Windsor. A biography is Peter Singleton-Gates's *General Lord Freyberg, VC* (1963). *See* also Maj Gen Howard K. KIPPENBERGER, *Infantry Brigadier* (Oxford, 1949).

FRIEDMAN, William Frederick. US cryptologist. 1891–1969. Son of a Romanian Jew from Bucharest who became an interpreter in the Russian Postal Service, Friedman was born in Kishinev, about 100 miles north of Odessa. As antiSemitism increased, the father went to Pittsburgh in 1892, sold Singer sewing machines door to door, and was joined by his wife, son and daughter the next year.

Friedman graduated from Cornell in 1914 with a BS. The next year he began doing genetic research for the eccentric millionaire Col George Fabyan on his estate just north of Chicago. Within a few months Friedman was drawn into cryptography. In 1917 he married a fellow worker, Elizebeth [*sic*] Smith. On 1 Jan 21 they became civilian cryptographers in the army's so-called Black Chamber in Washington. Officially the Code and Cipher Solution Section, this was all that remained of Herbert Yardley's Cipher Bureau. Friedman became the War Department's chief cryptanalyst at the end of 1921 and held the post for quarter of a century through its reorganization in 1930. Friedman headed the US Army team that on 25 Sep 40 broke "Code Purple," which the Japanese used for diplomatic messages. The cryptologist subsequently worked with **Opn Magic**. Having been a reserve officer in the Signal Corps, he went on active duty as a full colonel on 23 Dec 43. Two weeks later he collapsed from overwork and was in Walter Reed for three months. Although a medical board had ruled otherwise, the Adjutant General gave him an honorable discharge "by reason of physical disqualification." Friedman worked for the rest of the war as a civilian.

In 1947 he became director of Communications Research in the new Army Security Agency. Only after retiring in 1955 did declassification make it possible for Friedman to receive appropriate public recognition. After several heart attacks he died 2 Nov 69 at his home in Washington. See the biography by Ronald Clark, *The Man Who BrokePurple* (Boston: Little, Brown, 1977).

FRITSCH, Werner von. German general. 1880-1939. The senior army officer in Germany, Werner von Fritsch was born in Benrath, near Duesseldorf, on 4 Aug 80. His father's family was ennobled in the 18th century, and his mother was a Rhinelander of distinguished Protestant lineage. As a Prussian general with the traditional disdain of his caste for national politics, Fritsch was nominated by Pres Hindenburg in Jan 34 for the senior post in the army. On 2 May 35 Fritsch became CinC of the the armed forces, the Wehrmacht (OKW). But Hitler's henchmen were determined to consolidate Nazi power and, encouraged by their success in the case of War Minister von BLOMBERG, they undertook to get Fritsch.

"Dirty tricks" specialists lucked into an old vice police dossier on a cavalry officer who had been blackmailed by an ex-convict and notorious male prostitute named Hans Schmidt. Eager to cooperate, Schmidt gave the police convincing evidence that his client in one brief encounter in a Berlin railroad station had been Werner von Fritsch. Personally confronted by Hitler with the charges and the witness Schmidt on 24 Jan 38 in the library of the Chancellery, Fritsch played into Hitler's hands by not responding with violent denial. Unable to cope with such ungentlemanly deceit, and receiving no support from fellow officers, the bewildered and politically innocent general retired on 3 Feb 38. He was succeeded as OKW chief by the Fuehrer himself. When it was discovered that Schmidt's true client was an obscure cavalry officer named Achim von Frisch (no), Hitler refused to restore Fritsch to duty in any capacity.

So called rehabilitation took the form, finally, of elaborate but highly qualified apologies and the title of honorary colonel of his old outfit, the 12th Arty Regt. Fritsch's later statements that in the event of war he would accompany his regiment into battle "as a target" have been taken to mean that he contemplated suicide. Outside Warsaw on 22 Sep 39 "he walked into the field of fire of a Polish machine gunner, as if seeking his own death," writes Wistrich. Most writers relate the same general story. But Prof Harold C. Deutsch concludes after considerable research that there is "no evidence that he deliberately exposed himself to a bullet" but, instead, was mortally wounded while "leaving the immediate combat zone to keep an appointment." (Deutsch, I, 414-15.)

FRITZSCHE, (August Franz Anton) Hans. German propagandist. 1900-53. Son of a postal worker, he was born 21 Apr 00 in Bochum, Westphalia. Young Hans Fritzsche saw some action as a private in WWI, then studied liberal arts in various universities without taking a degree. After holding several editorial positions, he found a home in the relatively new field of radio. From Sep 32 he headed the Wireless News Service *(Drahtloser Dienst)* in the Papen government, keeping the office when it became part of Goebbels's Reich Ministry for People's Enlightenment and Propaganda. Fritzsche also became head of the News Section of the Press Division, holding both posts until 1937. The next summer he was deputy chief of the Home Press Division, which told the press what to publish. In Dec 38 he succeeded Albert Ingemar Berndt as chief. Goebbels personally took over his old division in Nov 42. On temporary duty for a few months at Stalingrad, Fritzsche was in a propaganda company of the 389th Div, reporting direct to PAULUS and winning praise as a soldier. (Davidson, *Trial,* 542.) For the rest of the war Fritzsche was Plenipotentiary for the Political Organization of the Greater German Radio and chief of the Propaganda Ministry's Radio Division.

Himself a party member since 1 May 33, Fritzsche resisted pressure to dismiss non-party-members and Jews. Goebbels condoned this because his subordinate appealed to decent Germans and was circumspect politically, giving high positions to party members. The propagandists worked with great mutual respect professionally but kept their distance socially. The junior partner owed much of his success to a voice and speaking manner resembling his chief, who was second only to Hitler as a Nazi orator.

Taken prisoner by the Russians in Berlin on 2 May 45, Fritzsche was tried at Nuremberg primarily as a surrogate for Goebbels. After putting up a convincing defense, Fritzsche was acquitted on 1 Oct 46. But German courts sentenced him to nine years at hard labor, permanent loss of rights to hold public office or vote, loss of his pension, and they prohibited him from ever working at anything but common labor. Freed 29 Sep 50, he died of cancer on 27 Sep 53. The American edition of his unrepentant *Memoirs* was published in 1971.

FROLOV, Valerian Aleksandrovich. Soviet military leader. 1895-1961. Born in St Petersburg on 7 June 95, Frolov headed the 14th Army in the war against Finland, 1939-40, holding the rank of Komdiv. Under the new system of rank Gen Lt Frolov led the same army during the Arctic and Karelian Defensive Operations from 29 June to Aug 41. He then commanded the Karelian Front and was promoted on 28 Apr 43. Gen Col Frolov was succeeded by MERETSKOV in Feb 44. Frolov died on 6 Jan 61. (Scotts.)

FROMM, Erich Friedrich (Fritz). German general. 1888-1945. Remembered for his ambivalent but critical role in events following the anti-Hitler bomb attempt of 20 July 44, Fritz Fromm was born 8 Oct 88 in Berlin. He was a lieutenant when the armistice was signed in 1918. Retained in the Reichswehr, he had held increasingly high staff positions. As a colonel in the **Ministeramt** he earned SCHLEICHER's high regard. Goerlitz characterizes Fromm as "The typical professional soldier of the old *Reichswehr,* who maintained a very reserved attitude toward National Socialism but had a great respect for Hitler's almost magical influence on the masses of the German people" (*GGS,* 468). Fromm headed the General Army Office when it was created in the fall of 1933. His plans to implement Hitler's directive for a large-scale mobilization were adopted in 1934 despite strong objections from BECK, who had come to resent his subordinate. As early as 1937 Fromm was promoted to Generaloberst commanding the Replacement Army, which comprised divisions raised and trained in Germany. He also was Chief of Army Equipment.

In the fall of 1941, however, the personnel expert became anathema to Hitler for stating officially that it was time to seek peace with the Russians. Goebbels noted in his diary during Mar 43 that Hitler was disgusted with the Replacement Army commander for "not being able to improvise" more effective training and replacement functions. "The Fuehrer would be quite ready to remove Fromm from office if he had a proper successor." (Lochner, 279, 283.)

The Replacement Army, in which STAUFFENBERG was Fromm's chief of staff, was to have a key role in the difficult process of establishing a post-Nazi government to negotiate with the Allied conquerors. But on 20 July 44, when the assassination attempt on Hitler failed, Fromm lost his nerve. Worse, he proved to be a coward, turning informer. This resulted in the immediate death of BECK, STAUFFENBERG, and several brother officers in the Bendlerstrasse the evening of 20 July. The next day Himmler arrested Fromm and took over his functions. For a while the trimmer was spared the fate of other senior generals who were victims of Hitler's wrath. But he eventually was brought before the People's Court. The principal charge was failure to report what he knew about the conspiracy. On 12 Mar 45 he was shot by a firing squad rather than being hanged like WITZLEBEN and the seven others who suffered deaths of calculated cruelty on 8 Aug 44 in Ploetzensee prison. He was shot "clearly as a sign of clemency" because his crime was cowardice rather than high treason. (Hoffmann, *Resistance,* 528.)

FULLER, John Frederick Charles. British soldier, military critic, and historian. 1878-1966. A prophet without honor in his own country but, like his younger friend and apostle B. H. LIDDELL HART, much honored in Germany and the USSR, J. F. C. Fuller was born 1 Sep 78 at Chichester. His father, the Revd Arthur Fuller, rector of the parish of West Itchenor, was descended from Roundheads, and his mother, Selma Marie Philippine de la Chevallerie, from Huguenots. "Known to his friends as 'Boney' [Napoleon's nickname], he was described (about 1918) as 'a little man with a bald head, and a sharp face . . . a totally unconventional soldier [whose] attacks on the hierarchy were viewed in the spirit of a rat hunt; a spirit he responded to with much vivacity and no little wit.'" (Field Marshal Sir Richard Carver in *DNB*). Fuller attributed all this to his genes (ibid.).

With a distaste for games, showing no academic brilliance but fond of reading history, Fuller detested his public school, Malvern. He chose a military career only to please his maternal grandfather. commissioned from Sandhurst in 1898, Ensign Fuller joined the 1st Bn, Oxfordshire Lt Inf, on garrison duty in Ireland and went with it to South Africa about a year later. An attack of appendicitis ended his two months of service in the field, and Lt Fuller spent the last six months of the Boer War as an intelligence officer. He was just getting interested when ordered in 1902 to India with his battalion. Fuller relieved the boredom of garrison duty by studying the Hindu religion, philosophy, and yoga, maintaining a lifelong interest in the latter (*DNB*). Promoted to captain in 1905, he was invalided home the next year to recuperate from enteric fever.

In 1906 he began a long happy marriage to Sonia Karnatzki, whose father was Polish. To avoid returning to India, he got an assignment as adjutant of a militia unit that soon became the 10th Middlesex Bn of the new Territorial Arym. Now associated with keen amateurs instead of bored professional soldiers, Fuller began writing training literature. As this tour of duty drew to a close, and still determined to escape regimental duty in India, he began boning for the Camberley entrance exam. He succeeded on his second attempt, in 1913. Now 35 years old, he began taking a serious interest in his profession, primarily by writing. In articles for military wisdom.

Decidedly an oddball—he still did like the "games" that were practically a religion of the British upper classes—Fuller believed later that his career was saved by the outbreak of war in 1914, half way through his two-year course.

Soon promoted to major (T), he saw action as a staff officer on the western front. The turning point in his life came late in 1916, when—with no special qualifications—he joined the new Tank Corrps Hq as GSO 2 (later GSO 1, or CofS). But Lt Col Fuller quickly saw the potential of armor in war, and he planned the first successful tank assault in military history, at Cambrai on 20 Nov 16. A brigadier general in late 1918, Fuller was planning the first true tank offensive, "Plan 1919," when the war ended. The revolutionary concept of using tanks in mass, not dispersed as infantry-support weapons, was promptly filed by a British Army hierarchy that had learned nothing about the potential of armored warfare.

Fuller became chief instructor at **Camberley** in 1923. Later, as assistant to the *CIGS,* he alienated superiors by persistently pressing for mechanization. Charles DE GAULLE, Heinz GUDERIAN, and pioneers of armored forces in the Red Army recognized Fuller's genius, but not the British Army.

"The breaking point came over Fuller's selection in 1927 to take command of what was intended to be an experimental mechanized force, but which was watered down to a stan-

dard infantry brigade and garrison on Salisbury Plain with only temporary *ad hoc* control over a few mechanized units." (Ibid.) Col Fuller (1920) refused the assignment, submitted his resignation, but was persuaded to withdraw it. In 1929 he got his first troop command, an infantry brigade. Promoted in Sep 30, Maj Gen Fuller was placed on half pay, retiring at the end of 1933.

As a junior officer Fuller had codified the principles of war. His seminal *Lectures on Field Service Regulations III* (1932) led to his being called "the father of modern way," a title he disliked (S. L. A. Marshall in *S&S). Generalship, Its Diseases and Their Cure* (1933) became a candid classic, as did his *Memoirs of an Unconventional Soldier* (1936). He published the two-volume *Decisive Battles* (1939-40), *Decisive Battles of the USA* (1942), and a reedited version of his 1932 work as *Armoured Warfare* (1943). *The Second World War, 1939-1945* (1948), a pot-boiler (*DNB*), was followed by his major historical work, *The Decisive Battles of the Western World and their Influence upon History* (3 vols, 1954-56).

Fuller died 10 Feb 66 at Falmouth.

FUNK, Walther Immanuel. German official. 1890-1960. The Third Reich's minister of economics was born 18 Aug 90 at Trakehnen, East Prussia. From a family of businessmen and artisans, he studied economics, law, philosophy, literature, and music before settling into financial journalism. Funk is said to have been planted in the Nazi party by industrialists who wanted to curb the radicals. But he became one of Hitler's "nodding donkeys." When Hjalmar SCHACHT resigned in Nov 37 Funk took over as minister of economics and plenipotentiary for the War Economy. On 19 Jan 39 he succeeded Schacht as Reichsbank president.

Like most conservatives, Funk saw Hitler as the only alternative to a communist take over. But he also found it easy to embrace Nazism and accept the inept economic leadership of GOERING. Although himself comparatively humane protecting individual Jews, he drew up the laws of Nov 38 that excluded Jews from economic life. He is said to have coined the phrase *"crystal night."* From 1942 he collaborated with Himmler in making the Reichsbank a depository for looted Jewish property including gold teeth from the death camps. He never opposed a measure favored by Hitler. (Davidson, *Trial,* 247, 250, 251.)

Funk was an alcoholic and probably a homosexual. But as a hearty, cheerful, story-telling, piano-playing little fat man has was the star of Hitler's otherwise dreary entourage. One of the uglier-looking major war criminals at Nuremberg, he also was among the few repentant. He was convicted of helping exploit occupied areas and of indirect involvement in slave labor operations and sentenced to life imprisonment. Frau Luise Frank was sentenced in 1947 by a denazification court to six months at hard labor. After serving about 11 years in Spandau Prison, Funk was released on 16 May 57 for ill health. He died 31 May 60 at Dusseldorf.

G

GALLAND, Adolf. Luftwaffe general. 1911-94. Germany's leading fighter ace until the start of Barbarossa in June 41, Galland then was chief of the Luftwaffe's fighter arm for three full years, 1942-44, before creating and leading the world's first jet squadron.

A Westphalian of Huguenot descent, Galland was born on 19 Mar 11 in Westerholt, Reckling-hausen, son of a well-to-do estate manager. As a teenager he won glider contests before joining the first small group of military pilots selected for covert training. He was commissioned a Leutnant in Oct 34 on entering the Aero Club of Berlin, which Goering unveiled in Mar 35 as the Luftwaffe. Three of Galland's younger brothers also became fighter pilots, two dying in action after scoring 51 and 21 victories (Sims, *Aces,* 211). Initially Galland specialized in close air support of ground troops. Volunteering for the **Condor Legion** he led a squadron of He 51 biplanes in Spain from May 37 to July 38, logging 280 combat missions. An aggressive and deadly serious pilot, brilliant innovator of ground support tactics that would be used in the blitzkrieg, Galland had a light side: for an airplane insignia in Spain he adopted Mickey Mouse, to whom the dark, dapper, bright-eyed Galland bore a striking resemblance. His good looks had been somewhat spoiled by a near-fatal crash in Oct 35, when his face hit the instrument panel. "He is not entirely a pleasant looking man," British interrogators found after the war (Toliver and Constable, *Galland,* 38). But the "knight of the air," who was known for devotion to good cigars and fine brandy, relished the attentions of many women attracted by his fame.

Turning over his squadron to his good friend MOELDERS and returning to Germany, the airman served on the OKL staff until the summer of 1939, when he formed two ground-support units. During the 27-day blitzkrieg in Poland he won the Iron Cross 2d Class and was promoted to captain on 1 Oct 39. Leaving ground support to be a fighter pilot and transferred at the end of October to the 27th Ftr Wing (JG 27), he began transition training in Me 109s.

Galland got his first three kills on 12 May 40 (D+2) over Liége, Belgium. After 10 more victories in Flanders the ace was promoted to major and given command of Group III in JG 26. Rising to head the fighter wing, he was the highest scoring pilot in the Battle of Britain with 57 victories (Sims, *Aces,* 191). JG 26 was one of two left to oppose the RAF when the rest of the Luftwaffe moved east to invade Russia.

His wing was based at Béthune, France, when it ended the career of Douglas BADER on 9 Aug 41 in a melee near the coastal town of Le Touquet. Galland had been promoted to Oberstleutnant and was Germany's top ace (69 victories—one ahead of MOELDERS)—when awarded the Swords (1/159) on 21 June 41. After the death of Oberst Moelders on 22 Nov 41, Oberst Galland succeeded him as General of the Fighter Arm (an office, not a rank). Hitler personally awarded Galland the Diamonds (2/27) on 28 Jan 42 for 94 victories (Angolia, I, 57). When promoted 19 Nov 42 to General-major, Galland was the Wehrmacht's youngest general. The 30-year old Generalmajor Erich Baerenfaenger committed suicide in the ruins of Berlin 10 days after his promotion on 20 Apr 45. (Angolia, I, 152; II, 211).

Long a national hero and a favorite of Hitler's, Galland continued to defy orders by flying combat missions when he could find a pretext. For example, after planning the air cover that enabled *Prinz Eugen, Gneisenau,* and *Scharnhorst* to escape from Brest in Feb 42, Galland flew the mission. And he was acting commander of fighters opposing the Allied landings in Sicily that began on 10 July 43.

But Galland had realized since the summer of 1940 that RAF fighters were more than a match for the Luftwaffe. By the end of 1942, as the Allied strategic bombing program hit its stride, the General of the Fighter Arm saw that radical changes were needed in the Luftwaffe's defective doctrine of air defense. He was unable to convince Hitler and Goering, who persisted in giving priority of aircraft construction and strategy to the offense and to frustrate the efforts of Galland and MILCH to build up fighter reserves for the defense of Germany. When the Luftwaffe's bomber command was rendered even more ineffective by shortage of fuel it began retraining pilots in fighters, and the bomber command hierarchy intruded more and more into Galland's domain. Looking for a scapegoat after having disregarded Galland's recommendations, the fuehrer finally turned against his long-time favorite and even considered diverting resources into antiaircraft production from fighter production. (Speer, *Memoirs,* 408.)

Generalleutnant Galland was suspended from his post as General of the Fighters at the end of 1944, replaced officially on 15 Jan 45 by Oberst Gordon M. GOLLOB) and authorized to resume the heretofore-unsuccessful effort to convert the new ME 262 jet from a "blitz-bomber" into a fighter. It was suggested that Hitler and Goering hoped their difficult subordinate would meet the fate of Walter Nowotny (259 victories) and another predecessor who had died in the attempt.

Generalleutnant Galland reverted to squadron commander and recruited about 30 of Germany's leading aces for a special fighter unit, Jagdverband (JV) 44. Its revolutionary two-engine ME 262 jets having a great speed advantage and mounting highly effective new heavy rockets and cannon (Sims, *Aces,* 211), JV 44 flew only a few operational missions, but these chilled the blood of Allied planners. Galland proved that he had been right in advocating better defensive use of fighters, particularly the Me 262. But it was too late.

On 26 Apr 45, after downing two B-26 Marauders and bringing his score to 103, Galland was caught napping and shot up by US Mustangs. He limped back to make a forced landing at Munich-Riem during an air attack by Thunderbolts that virtually destroyed the base. Having badly injuring a knee, the general turned over command to Heinz BAER but remained with JV 44 and evacuated its few survivors to Salzburg. Here the planes were demolished before tanks of the US 7th Army arrived on 3 May 45.

After two years as a POW Galland was a technical adviser in Argentina until Jan 55. Back in Germany the legendary airman was an aerospace consultant, airline president, and business exec-

utive in several fields. His historically valuable autobiography, with a foreword by Bader, is *The First and the Last* (New York: Holt, 1954). Galland's authorized biography, published 30 years later with the benefit of official documentation, has been cited above as Toliver and Constable, *Galland. (See* bibliography.)

GAMELIN, Maurice (Gustave). French general. 1872-1958. Born 20 Sep 72 in Paris, he was from a military family that included a string of Alsacian generals on his mother's side. Gamelin was a brilliant scholar in secondary school, winning top national honors in history and philosophy, and he graduated first in his St Cyr class of 1891. The man who prided himself on being a philosopher, a "Bergsonian officer," began his military career with four years in a regiment of Algerian Tirailleurs. He subsequently had a solid grounding of duty with troops along with school and staff assignments. In 1906, as a captain, he was selected by Joffre to serve as aide *(officier d'ordonnance).* He had just commanded a chasseur battalion when called back to Joffre's staff in Mar 14. Five months later he drafted the order that launched the "Miracle of the Marne." Promotion to lieutenant colonel removed him from general staff duty, except for a five-month tour, for the rest of the war. Working his way up from command of a demi-brigade of chasseurs, he became chief of the crack 9th Div in 1916 and was promoted at this time to brigadier general. At war's end, Gamelin was considered to be the outstanding officer in his age group.

On 1 Jan 30 he became WEYGAND's deputy CGS, moving up to succeed him when Weygand was made Army Inspector General (IG) in 1931. In 1935, when Weygand was retired on reaching the statutory age limit, Gamelin was given the dual assignment of Army IG and CGS. Only Joffre had had this distinction. (Larousse.) Alphonse GEORGES had been the leading candidate for the top post but DALADIER thought he was too right-wing. As the second highest ranking officer in the Army, Georges became Gamelin's deputy. The two generals, entirely different in character and military outlook, rarely communicated. When the post was created, Gamelin became National Defense chief of staff. As such he coordinated, supposedly, the French army, air force, and navy.

Actually, there was little coordination because the three services were jealous of their independence. As for the army, Gamelin had lost the touch that made him an outstanding troop leader up until 1918. He also failed to recognize the changed nature of war that resulted from modern technology, for which he little aptitude and less interest. Although retaining the French devotion to the offensive, he allowed a defensive mindset to develop in the army and did nothing to change the passive attitude of political leaders toward the aggressions of Hitler and Mussolini.

When the France declared war on 3 Sep 39, the philosopher general and a reduced staff moved into splendid accommodations in the Chateau of Vincennes, on the eastern edge of Paris. His major subordinate in the field was Georges, the general with whom Gamelin had been barely on speaking terms for five years.

Many believed that France had the greatest army in the world. Gamelin, as inspector general, had assured his head of government, Daladier, in August that the French army was ready, and the general believed it. When the Germans attacked on 10 May 40, the Allies executed the Dyle-Escaut Plan, wheeling north to support the Belgian army and establishing a defense behind the Dyle and Escaut rivers. So the western armies played into the enemy's hands, and on 17 May 40 Weygand reached the front to replace Gamelin. The official change of command came two days later.

Gamelin withdrew to his Paris apartment. Arrested on 6 Sep 40 by Vichy authorities seeking scapegoats for the recent French humiliation, Gamelin refused to defend himself at the **Riom Trial.** Remaining confined under reasonably good conditions at various places in France, Gamelin was deported to Germany in 1943. He was liberated in 1945 with the **Niederdorf Group.** Soon thereafter he published his self-serving memoirs, *Servir: Les Armées françaises de 1940* (3 vols. Paris: Plon, 1946-47).

GANDHI, Mohandas Karamchand. Indian nationalist. 1869-1948. A political and spiritual leader called Mahatma ("great soul") who headed the Congress Party, 1920-34, he ostensibly was in retirement at the start of WWII in 1939. But in Aug 42 he proclaimed a policy of passive disobedience after rejecting Stafford CRIPPS's proposal to grant India independence after the war in return for meanwhile supporting

efforts to defeat the Japanese. The British outlawed the Congress party, arrested Gandhi on 9 Aug 42 and kept him in jail until 6 May 44. Other nationalists including Jawarharla Nehru were also jailed. When MOUNTBATTEN brought about partition in 1947, a solution demanded by the Indian minority represented by Mohammad Ali Jinnah's Moslem League, a disappointed Gandhi strove to stop Moslem and Hindu factions from continuing to massacre each other. This angered Hindu fanatics, one of whom assassinated Gandhi in Delhi on 30 Jan 48 as he led a large group in prayer.

GARAND, John Cantius. Rifle inventor. 1888-1974. As chief ordnance officer at the Springfield [Mass] Armory he designed the rifle patented in 1934 and generally known by his name. In 1940 the "Garand" was accepted as the standard US infantry weapon, replacing the bolt-action Springfield 1903. Six million Garands were produced through 1957, when the M 14 (which Garand helped develop) was adopted.

"The US Garand .30 M1 Semi-automatic Rifle," which weighed 9.5 pounds, was fed from an eight-round clip, and gas operated. Semi-automatic, it fired each time the trigger was pulled, then automatically cocked the hammer, ejected the spent cartridge, and positioned another. This meant that the rifleman did not have to take his sights off the target.

A trained soldier could fire eight rounds within 20 seconds with great accuracy up to 500 yards, quickly insert a full clip, and he had a maximum effective range of about 3,500 yards. He could load with regular ball, tracer, armor-piercing, or incendiary ammunition, and with relative ease could turn the rifle into a grenade launcher.

The M1 was not so elegant as the famous and beloved Springfield 1903, but it was much more rugged, better suited to mass production, three times faster in rate of fire, only slightly less accurate, and much easier for a recruit to learn to use. Patton called it "the greatest battle implement ever devised" (Kirk & Young, 312).

The inventor was born 1 Jan 88 in St Remi, near Montreal, Quebec. At the age of 11 he moved to Connecticut with his family, and the next year he started working in a textile mill. After being a machinist, then working in a shooting gallery, he was a tool and gauge maker and held other jobs that added to his mechanical skills. Garand also took correspondence courses.

After reading about mechanical problems with WWI American weapons, he designed a light machine gun and in 1918 joined the Bureau of Standards in Washington, where he perfected his own weapons. Garand became an American citizen in 1920, qualifying for civil service with a salary of $3,500 a year and thus forfeiting the tremendous profits he would have made as a private inventor.

He retired in 1953, understanding that for having remained in government service he would receive special compensation for his work, but the US Army successfully opposed several Congressional bills to give him a compensation of $100,000. Garand died 16 Feb 74 in Springfield.

GARBY-CZERNIAWSKI, Roman. Allied secret agent. Creator of **Interallié**, the first Allied intelligence net in occupied France, Capt Garby-Czerniawski was a romantic figure who had been an Olympic skier. As a Polish AF officer with cryptanalytical training he escaped to Paris in 1939 and working there with Polish intelligence. He went underground when France fell and organized a spy ring. But the Polish captain did not have a radio of sufficient power until the SOE sent him one. The first Interallié transmission to London was on 1 Jan 41 from an apartment near the Trocadero. His cipher clerk and broadcaster was the alluring Mathilde "the Cat" CARRE.

Interallié grew to 120 agents and four transmitters, becoming so successful that Czerniawski (code name "Valentin") received Poland's highest citation for gallantry when he visited London in Nov 41 for an SIS-Polish intelligence conference. But disaster struck while he was away. The Germans arrested and "turned" Raoul Kiffer, Interallié chief in Cherbourg. He betrayed 21 helpers and revealed Valentin's hideouts. Sgt BLEICHER ("Col Henri") caught Czerniawski asleep in his apartment at St Germain en Laye the morning of 17 Nov 41, found incriminating documents, and bagged the Cat later that day in the net's headquarters in the Rue Léandre. (Some say the Cat betrayed Czerniawski in a fit of female jealousy over another woman's.)

The Cat and Kiffer helped Bleicher arrest almost 100 Interallié agents. Abwehr operators took over the Interallié radio network without arousing suspicions in London. The Abwehr offered to give POW status to the captured agents if Czerniawski would spy for them. Valentin demanded full sovereignty for Poland as part of the deal, something the Abwehr obviously could not promise. But on 22 June 40, Valentin came to realize that Stalin was a greater enemy of Poland than Hitler, so he accepted the German proposal to "work for peace." Renamed "Armand" he was taken from Fresnes on 14 July 42 (Bastille Day) by Bleicher and Kiffer for an alleged interrogation in Paris and allowed to escape. Met by Bleicher in Lyons, Armand made his way over a British escape line to Madrid and reached London in Jan 43. En route he made contact with Abwehr and MI6 handlers. Taken in by the XX ("Double Cross") Committee as "Brutus," he became one of the war's most effective double agents.

GAVIN, James Maurice. US Army officer. 1907-90. "Jumping Jim," one of the US Army's most innovative thinkers in addition to being a heroic combat leader (2 **DSCs**, 2 **SS, PH,** 4 Combat Jump Stars), was born in NY on 22 Mar 07. At the age of 16 he ran away from the hard life of an orphan in a coal town, lied about his age to enlist fraudulently, and won an army appointment to West Point. Graduating in 1929 (185/299), he took command of the 505th Parachute Regt. in RIDGWAY's 82d Abn Div in 1942. The regiment jumped into Sicily (around Gela) and to reinforce the Salerno beachhead (the night of 14-15 Sep 44). Becoming assistant division commander in Sep 43, Gavin jumped into Normandy the night of 5-6 June 44 (D-1). Succeeding RIDGWAY the following August, he is said to have been the youngest division commander (at 37) since the Civil War. In **Market-Garden** the 82d Abn Div (accompanied by "Boy" BROWNING) landed around the Nijmegen bridges on 17 Sep 44 and took its objectives after a hard, three-day fight. Gavin was promoted to major general on 20 Oct 44, the youngest in the US Army. From strategic reserve around Reims, the division began a truck movement on 19 Dec 44 to counterattack on the north shoulder of the penetration during the Battle of the Bulge. Gavin led his division across the lower Elbe near Bleckede on 30 Apr 45, taking the surrender of 150,000 troops of the German 21st Army two days later at Ludwigslust.

The general published *Airborne Warfare* (Washington, DC: Infantry Journal Press, 1947), retaining command of his "All American" Division until 14 Mar 48. Ten years later, after directing R&D programs of "sky cavalry," satellite communications, and predicting correctly that man would soon walk on the moon, Lt Gen Gavin retired in 1958 rather than continue defending military programs in which he did not believe. His views were presented in *War and Peace in the Space Age* (New York: Harper, 1958), one of Gavin's five books. The general was ambassador to Paris, 1961-62, then chairman of the board of the Arthur D. Little Co. He died 23 Feb 90 in Baltimore, Md.

GEHLEN, Reinhard. German officer. 1902-79. The "man in the shadows," as he was known for postwar intelligence work, was born on 3 Apr 02 in Erfurt. His father, stationed there as an artillery lieutenant, was from a Silesian family with no military tradition. But his mother, born Katharina Margarete van Vaernewyck, was a Flemish aristocrat who had military officers in her family tree. (H&Z, *Gehlen,* 5.) Gehlen's father retired for ill health, moved the family to Breslau in 1908, and joined a publishing firm. Young Gehlen, shy and unsociable, was an outstanding student who acquired a passion for numbers. After completing his university education with distinction and being accepted as an officer candidate in 1920, Gehlen became a cadet in an artillery regiment on 1 Jan 21 and in due course was commissioned. In 1931 he married Herta von Seydlitz-Kurzbach, a distant relative of Frederick the Great's famous cavalry general, and the ambitious young officer soon managed to leave the stifling routine of peacetime troop duty. He completed almost two years of general staff schooling in 1935, standing second in his class. A year later he joined the general staff, and on 6 Oct 36 he was assigned to the operations section.

During the Polish campaign Maj Gehlen was senior staff officer of a reserve infantry division and he began a long association with HALDER, who was Army CofS. He served in France as OKH LnO to Busch's 16th Army before moving to Guderian's Pz Gp. Back at OKH Gehlen was Halder's adjutant 1 July-7 Oct 40, then he was chief of the Eastern Group in HEUSINGER's Operations Branch of OKH. This led to a long friendship between the two officers.

Despite lack of experience in military intelligence, Gehlen became head of Foreign Armies East on 1 Apr 42. Having won Halder's

admiration for solving problems of logistics and the disposition of reserves, Gehlen now used his love of numbers to compile precise figures on the Soviet order of battle. He rose from Oberstleutnant (Lt Col) on 1 July 41 to Generalmajor on 1 Dec 44. But Hitler became so infuriated by accurate reports of impending doom that he dismissed Gehlen on 9 Apr 45. The crafty general hid voluminous files, which he used as bargaining material after surrendering to American forces on 22 May 45 with his principal colleagues. Flown to the US with his records and four colleagues, Gehlen formed an intelligence organization under the CIA's wing and headed it for a decade. Gehlen's organization then became the FRG's Intelligence Service or *Bundesnachrichtendienst* (BND) on 1 Apr 56 and was long the West's most valuable tool in the Cold War. But the Soviets infiltrated the Gehlen organization with former-SS officers, promising them amnesty for wartime crimes. Prominent moles who worked for a decade from 1950 were Heinz Felfe, Hans Clemens, and their assistant, Erwin Tiebel. (John, xiv, 210.) The Russians also made mass arrests of Gehlen agents in East Germany. Their kidnapping of Dr Otto JOHN may have been to make it appear he had betrayed the BND agents, something Gehlen charged officially. (John, xiv, 248.) Under mounting criticism, the shadowy little spymaster retired on 30 Apr 68. Living on Starnberger Lake, he remained virtually unknown to the public until investigative reporters began revealing information about his career as BND chief. Gehlen responded with *The Service: The Memoirs of General Reinhard Gehlen* (New York: World, 1972). To the vast relief of West German and foreign secret services including the CIA, the self-serving memoirs revealed few official secrets (H&Z, *Gehlen,* xxi).

GEIGER, Roy Stanley. USMC general. 1885-1947. A Floridian, he graduated from Stetson Univ (De Land, Fla), enlisted as a US Marine in 1907, was commissioned in 1909, and became a pilot. In WWI he commanded a squadron in France and won the Navy Cross.

Brig Gen Geiger reached Guadalcanal on 3 Sep 42 to command the 1st Marine Aircraft Wing a fortnight after Henderson Field began receiving its first fighters and dive bombers. In two months of desperate action he won a second Navy Cross. The general returned to the US in May 43 as head of Marine Corps aviation. He was promoted to major general, and on 9 Nov 43 took over the 1st Marine Amphibious Corps from VANDEGRIFT on Bougainville. The Marines had landed eight days earlier, and on 15 Dec 43, when the beachhead was virtually secure, Geiger's mission was taken over by army troops.

His command redesignated 3d Amphibious Corps Hq in Apr 44, Geiger planned and directed the liberation of Guam and Peleliu before leading his corps on Okinawa. The Marine Corps general commanded the 10th US Army briefly, 18-23 June 45, after BUCKNER was mortally wounded and until Stilwell arrived. The next month Geiger took over the Fleet Marine Force, Pacific.

GEORGE II. King of the Hellenes. 1890-1947. A nephew of Kaiser Wilhelm II and great-grandson of Queen Victoria, George II was born 20 July 90 at Tatoi, the royal villa near Athens. Self-consciousness about being of small physical stature (5 foot 6), the playboy prince was less concerned about his lack of intellectual achievement. But he allegedly was proficient in 10 languages. (CB 43.)

George became king in 1922 but was a mere puppet for a military junta that on 19 Dec 23 forced him into an impoverished, 11-year exile. With British support, he returned to Greece on 24 Nov 35. Childless and just divorced, George II was the virtually powerless king of what had been the Hellenic State since 1924.

METAXIS made himself dictator on 4 Aug 36. Italian forces under MESSE invaded Greece on 28 Oct 40 but were driven back by PAPAGOS. Metaxis accepted a British offer to intervene militarily, and "Jumbo" WILSON landed a BEF in Mar 41.

When Hitler ordered a punitive expedition against Yugoslavia after an anti-Nazi uprising placed PETER II on the throne, Hitler decided to secure his Mediterranean flank by overrunning Greece as well. LIST attacked 6 Apr 41 and achieved a lightning victory. King George II fled from Athens on 22 Apr 41 and was evacuated from Crete on a British destroyer.

Making his way to London with a skeleton cabinet he proclaimed a Greek government in exile on 1 Jan 42. Representatives of hostile underground factions reached Cairo from Greece on 10 Aug 43 to undertake formation of a coalition, but dissension caused a mutiny in Greek armed forces that the British were trying to organize in Egypt. On 26 Apr 44 the king finally was able to announce formation of a cabinet. This had representatives of the communist dominated EAM, whose ELAM guerrillas under Stephanos Saraphis had gotten the upper hand over EDES forces of Napoleon ZERVAS. The rest of the story of wartime Greece is outlined in the sketch of PAPANDREOU, who eventually became premier of the government in exile. A postwar plebiscite in Sep 46 called for return of King George II, who died the next year. He was succeeded by his brother Paul.

GEORGE VI. Albert Frederick Arthur George Windsor. King of Great Britain, Northern Ireland, and the British Dominions. 1895-1952. Born in London on 14 Dec 95, "Bertie" became George VI on 11 Dec 36, the day his brother abdicated as Edward VIII (see WINDSOR). The coronation was on 12 May 37. Handsome, modest and shy, he overcame natural shortcomings to acquire an intimate knowledge of government (WC, II, 379) and to make highly effective use of his symbolic office in furthering the war effort. With support from his wife Elizabeth he boosted morale at home. In his extensive visits abroad, he became the first reigning British king to visit the US, in 1939. At a critical time George II, monarch *malgré lui* (co-editor Helen M. Plamer in *DNB*), restored the luster of an office almost fatally tarnished by his brother. John W. Wheeler-Bennett wrote the official biography, *King George VI* (1958).

GEORGES, Alphonse Joseph. French general. 1875-1951. Among the large progeny of a blacksmith, he was born on 19 Aug 75 at Montlucon, in central France. Georges stood third in his class of 1897 at St Cyr. (Larousse.) His first assignment was in Algeria with a tirailleur regiment.

In 1914 he was gravely wounded while leading a battalion. After convalescing, he was assigned to the general staff of the army, where he remained unwillingly throughout most of the war. He was Ferdinand Foch's operations chief in 1918 and Pétain's CofS in Morocco during the Riff Wars. As a division and army corps commander in Algeria, 1928-32, Georges exhibited qualities that made him famous throughout the army. In Nov 32 he went to Paris as a member of the Supreme War Council. He received a serious chest wound in the attack by an assassin in Marseilles on 9 Oct 34 that killed King Alexander of Yugoslavia and Foreign Minister Louis Barthou. Georges never regained full physical strength but he was a leading candidate to succeed WEYGAND as head of French Army; Gamelin got the post because Georges was politically unacceptable to Daladier, allegedly because of his Rightist associations.

Georges was Gamelin's deputy for the next five years, but it was an arms-length association. The men differed radically in temperament and leadership style. "Gamelin . . . never appreciated his frank and direct subordinate," but kept him as deputy because Georges was so highly regarded in the Army" (Larousse). In accordance with war plans Georges took the field in Sep 39 as CinC Northeast, commanding all French field armies and the attached BEF. But Gamelin restricted his subordinate's freedom of action by not allowing him to have a separate general staff initially and by imposing a strategy that gave Georges little initiative.

The German offensive shattered the French front, and disintegration of Georges's command was exacerbated by Allied execution of the Dyle-Escaut Plan. On 19 May 40 (D+9), when Weygand replaced Gamelin, Georges was relieved of command and his headquarters abolished but he stayed on duty to assist Weygand.

Having remained aloof from prewar military intrigue Georges was IG in the armistice army from 1 July until he reached the mandatory retirement age on 19 Aug 40. Refusing to have any significant role in the Vichy government Georges was Churchill's choice for the post in **Opn Torch** (Nov 42) that went to Giraud, who was Roosevelt's candidate (de Gaulle, *Unity*, 243). But the British got Georges to Algiers late in May 43, shortly before de Gaulle's arrival, Churchill having said to de Gaulle: "Undoubtedly, my friend General Georges would make your group complete in the capacity of a third president" (ibid., 86). But Georges became merely a minister without portfolio in the FCNL, from which body de Gaulle later ousted both him and GIRAUD.

The general lived the rest of his life quietly and declined to join in postwar polemics (Larousse).

GEROW, Leonard Townsend. US general. 1888-1972. "Gee" Gerow, born 13 July 88, headed the War Plans Div, WDGS, 16 Dec 40-

15 Feb 42 as a brigadier general (*AA*, 60). Promoted to major general and given command of the 29th Inf Div, he was taking the unit to the UK as the North African invasion was about to be launched on 8 Nov 42. Eisenhower wanted Gerow, a close friend, to command US forces being built up in the UK for the invasion of northern Europe, but George Marshall did not like the selection, so the post went to Maj Gen Russell P. Hartle (*EP*, 566-68).

Gerow succeeded Hartle on 15 July 43 as CG, 5th Corps (*AA*, 506) and directed its landings on Omaha Beach (6 June 44). First ashore was the 1st Inf Div, followed by the 29th Inf Div 2d Inf Div, and 2d Armd Div. Operating on the left of Bradley's 1st Army, the 5th Corps was **pinched out** near Vire on about 13 Aug 44. Gerow was ordered to move his headquarters more than 100 miles from around Mortain to Argentan, where he picked up three divisions that had been in Wade Haislip's 15th Corps. (Haislip moved his two other divisions to Dreux for Patton's drive eastward.)

Gerow was heavily engaged around Argentan 18-19 Aug 44 but unable to close the Falaise Gap. The Germans were putting up a desperate defense, but the main problem was that British and American higher headquarters could not figure out how to coordinate a linkup of friendly forces that were approaching head on.

Remaining in Hodges's 1st Army, Gerow spearheaded the drive across France for much of the time and supported LECLERC's entry into Paris. The 5th Corps fought in the Huertgen Forest from 2 Nov 44 and reached the Roer River a month later. During the Ardennes campaign he wheeled south to hit the north shoulder of the penetration around Malmedy and Butgenbach.

Promoted on 1 Jan 45, Lt Gen Gerow assumed command of the 19th (Reserve) Army, created 14 Dec 44. He had a full plate of rear area missions that are too numerous and varied to catalogue here. (See *AA*, 502-3.) After V-E day Gerow's headquarters established the Theater General Board to evaluate ETO operations. Replaced by Patton, Gerow headed the **C&GSC** from Nov 45 to Jan 48. (*AA*, 357.) He retired 31 July 50 as a full general.

GEYR VON SCHWEPPENBURG, Leo von. German General. 1886-1974. A handsome cavalryman, the Freiherr was MA in Brussels, the Hague, and London from 1933 to 1937. During the Rhineland crisis Col Geyr sent reports from London to warn about underestimating the British (Senger, 43) and to point out the dangers of Hitler's adventurism (Deutsch, I, 69). This brought an official rebuke from BLOMBERG (Hoehne, *Canaris*, 224), and probably accounts for Hitler's subsequent political distrust of Geyr (below). But Geyr was promoted to Generalmajor while still in London, quickly thereafter to Generalleutnant, and he commanded the 3d Pz Div 1 Oct 37-6 Oct 39. Leading this into Poland under Guderian he won a victory around Kulm for which Hitler commended him on the scene. After a prolonged illness, Geyr took command of 24th Corps in the west on 15 Feb 40 and was promoted 1 Apr 40 to General of Panzer Troops (although heading an infantry corps). Reassigned 7 Jan 42, he headed the 3d Pz Corps 1 Aprl-19 July 42, and was heavily engaged in eliminating the Kharkov salient. Succeeding STUMME, Geyr led the 40th Pz Corps 20 July-30 Sep 42, moving through Rostov into the Caucasus.

Geyr had a long association with Guderian, whose memoirs have many laudatory references to "my old and trusted comrade-in-arms." Another outstanding commander calls Geyr a born leader, modern and unorthodox, and a master of military training (SENGER, 43, 355). Assigned to form and retrain units in France to meet the expected Allied invasion, he headed the new 76th Army Corps from 21 Feb to 31 Mar 43. When GUDERIAN became **IG** of Panzer Troops on 1 Mar 43 he charged Geyr with readying 10 divisions of panzers and motorized infantry for operations in the West. (Guderian, 324.) Geyr also formed and commanded the 58th Reserve Pz Corps, 5 Aug-30 Nov 43.

As "General of Panzer Troops West" he had an anomalous position. For one thing, Hitler prohibited his being given a front-line command, apparently suspecting that the former MA to London could not be trusted politically. OB West had **operational control** over Geyr's Pz Gp West, which Rundstedt established on 19 Nov 43 *as a headquarters* to control all armored units. Geyr was supposed to advise Rundstedt on their employment, but "to co-operate with and respect the wishes of army group commanders" (Harrison, *Cross-Channel Attack,* 247). But Rundstedt's and Geyr's "ideas on the proper employment of armor were so completely at variance with Rommel's that co-operation was impossible" (ibid.). Further complicating the command structure in the west, the 5th Pz Army

was reactivated under Geyr on 1 Jan 44, renamed Pz Gp West on 24 Jan 44, but still commonly called the 5th Pz Army. Geyr is listed as its commander until 2 July 44. (B&O, 26-27.)

On 7 June, the day after the Allied landings in Normandy, Rundstedt attached Geyr's Pz Gp West to the 7th Army. Geyr was about to attack on 10 June when an air strike devastated his headquarters. Sepp DIETRICH took over, using his 1st SS Pz Corps Hq to direct fierce attacks piecemeal while Geyr reconstituted his headquarters. Geyr was about to launch four panzer corps in a coordinated attack when ROMMEL intervened on 28 June to call this off. Guderian suggests several reasons: that Rommel did not believe the operation could succeed; and that Rommel had been forewarned of the assassination attempt and wanted to keep Army forces available for use against SS units. (Guderian, 333 and n.) EBERBACH replaced Geyr on 2 July as part of a new effort by Hitler to eliminate "defeatist" generals including RUNDSTEDT.

Like most other senior officers, Geyr declined to support plots against Hitler because he did not believe that either the Army's rank and file nor the general public would have "marched" in any putsch (Deutsch, I, 244 and n). Yet "Geyr" appears in Hans OSTER's records as a nominee for the post-Nazi cabinet (Hoffmann, *Resistance,* 129). The English translation of Geyr's memoirs, which adds important material to an earlier German edition, is *The Critical Years* (London, 1952).

GHORMLEY, Robert Lee. US admiral. 1883-1958. The son of a minister, he was born 15 Oct 83 in Portland, Oregon. His family moved to Moscow, Idaho, when the boy was 10 years old. Ghormley became Phi Beta Kappa at the Univ of Idaho, was quarterback of the football team, and graduated in 1902. *(CB 42.)* He was in the USNA class of 1906 (12/116) and played on the Navy football team. As a rear admiral Ghormley went to London in Aug 40 with two other senior officers to report on whether the British could hold out, and what help the US might give without violating its neutrality.

Ghormley, now a vice admiral, reached New Zealand on 19 June 42 to command the South Pacific Area (his title being COMSOPAC). Ten days later, Admiral King proposed that he immediately undertake a counteroffensive into the lower Solomon Islands. Both MacArthur and Ghormley protested that their forces were not ready and that King had picked the wrong objective for this initial effort to secure Allied lines of communications in the south Pacific. But air reconnaissance revealed on 4 July that the Japanese were building an airfield on Guadalcanal. On the 16th Ghormley issued orders for the first US offensive of WWII. The well planned operation achieved surprise, Marines landing unopposed on 7 Aug 42. But problems developed immediately because of poor command relations among Ghormley, FLETCHER (an Annapolis classmate), and "Terrible" TURNER. The need for radio silence keep Ghormley in the dark during the critical first phase of the operation. COMSOPAC moved to Noumea, but he never visited the combat area and never saw the force he commanded (Buchanan, 233). NIMITZ ordered Ghormley replaced by "Bull" Halsey on 18 Oct 42 and sent him back to Washington. He headed the Hawaiian Sea Frontier and 14th ND, 1943-44, then US Naval Forces in Germany until 1945. Retiring 1 Aug 46 as a vice admiral, he died in the Bethesda NH, Md, on 21 June 58.

GIAP, Vo Nguyen. Vietnamese general. Born 1 Sep 10 at An Xa, Quang Binh Province, he was jailed at the age of 18 after serving four years in clandestine anti-French forces. Giap later joined the new Vietnamese Communist Party, he studied law at Hanoi Univ, married the daughter of a former teacher, and in 1939 had to take political refuge in China. Meeting Ho Chi Minh, Giap joined the fledgling Vietminh organization. An ardent nationalist, further motivated by his wife's dying in a French prison, Giap proved to be a military genius. After organizing and commanding the Vietminh army that defeated the French and Americans, he became minister of defense. The acknowledged master of revolutionary warfare in the 20th cent. Giap published *People's War, People's Army* (1961) and *Military Art of People's War* (1970).

GIBSON, Guy Penrose. British bomber pilot. 1918-44. The leader of the "dam busters," for which he won the VC, was born 12 Aug 18 in Simla, the younger son of an Indian Forest Service official. His housemaster at St Edward's School, Oxford, characterized Gibson as "strongminded without obstinancy, disarmingly frank and of great charm" (quoted in *DNB*), and as a prefect he "excerted his authority without apparent effort." Not a natural athlete, he made

good teams by sheer determination and great stamina. (R. A. Cochrane in *DNB*.)

Leaving school early to join the RAF in 1936 Gibson became a bomber pilot and won the DFC in July 40 on Bomber Command's first raid of the war (on the Kiel canal). He passed up the normal assignment to a training formation on completion of his first full operational tour and within two months he wrangled a transfer to night fighters, scoring at least four kills, and winning a bar to his DFC.

Still only 23 years old, the chunky faced, modest airman was promoted to wing commander in Apr 42 and posted back to Bomber Command. For the next 11 months he led No. 106 Sqdn, flying 172 sorties himself and being twice appointed to the DSO. After only a week's break on leaving this arduous assignment he took over No. 617 Sqdn, which was being formed to knock out two of the five hydroelectric dams on which the Ruhr depended. The "dam busters" had little time to plan and execute the particularly dicey mission of delivering the bomb recently invented by Sir Barnes WALLIS for this purpose. The spherical, rotating bomb had to be dropped from precisely 60 feet to skip into the dam face and roll down it to explode at a depth that triggered a pressure fuse. The dam busters judged the critical release point by using dual spotlights whose beams converged vertically at 60 feet. (See also **skip bombing**.)

For the strike on the night of 16-17 May 43 Gibson led 18 Lancasters, each carrying one bomb, on a long, low-level flight to the Moehne dam. Diving through a ring of mountains and heavy fire to deliver the first bomb he scored a direct hit. But it took five attempts to breach the massive concrete structure. Having hovered over the site to draw fire and having flown repeatedly over the dam to machine gun AA positions, Gibson led the three remaining Lancasters to breach the Eder dam on their last attempt. Only 10 of Gibson's 18 bombers survived the mission, a loss of almost 45 percent (Keegan, ed, *Who Was Who*, "Gibson").

Awarded the VC, the modest, straightforward hero spent a year on staff appointments and made a lecture tour in America. He returned to No. 5 Bombr Gp in June 44 but it was three months before he was allowed to fly an operational mission. His Mosquito serving as pathfinder on the night of 19-20 Sep 44 against Rheydt, not far inside the Ruhr, Wing Commander Gibson bid the Lancasters good night and headed home. He never arrived. It was learned later that, for reasons unknown, he crashed in the Netherlands and was buried at Steenbergen.

The story of the dam busters is told in Gibson's book *Enemy Coast Ahead* (1946) and in Paul Brickhill's *Dam Busters* (1951).

GILLARS, Mildred Elizabeth ("Axis Sally"). 1900-88. An aspiring actress who dropped out of Ohio Wesleyan Univ, she went to Germany in the 1920s as a music student. Mildred Gillars was teaching English in Berlin when the war started, and for the love of a foreign ministry official she agreed to broadcast Nazi propaganda. After the Allies landed in North Africa on 8 Nov 42 she operated from Tunis and was dubbed "Axis Sally." With information from German intelligence she often surprised and dismayed the Allies with lighthearted comments on facts that were supposed to be secret. She welcomed new units by name and bid "bon voyage" to convoys leaving North African ports for Italy (personal knowledge). But Axis Sally did Allied morale more good than harm because her many listeners on land, sea, and in the air enjoyed the jazz music and laughed off the heavyhanded propaganda. Convicted of treason in 1949, Axis Sally served 12 years in a US federal prison for women. After teaching German, French, and music at a Catholic convent in suburban Columbus, Ohio (Snyder, *Ency,* 115) she returned to Ohio Wesleyan—50 years after first enrolling—and completed her bachelor's degree in speech at the age of 72. She died 25 June 88 in Columbus.

GIRAUD, Henri Honoré. French general. 1879-1949. Of Alsacian descent, Giraud was born 18 Jan 79 in Paris. He graduated from St Cyr in 1900, joined the 4th Zouave Regt in North Africa, and was a 35-year-old veteran of colonial warfare when his regiment went to France at the start of WWI. Capt Giraud distinguished himself in several actions before being critically wounded and captured in the battle of Guise, 29 Aug 14. He escaped on 30 Oct 14 after failing in an earlier attempt. In various disguises—"butcher, stableboy, coal man, and magician in a traveling circus" *(CB 42)*—the very tall (6 foot 3), ramrod straight Giraud made his way through the Netherlands to England.

Rejoining his outfit in 1915, Giraud remained on the western front until the armistice of 11 Nov 18 and then served on Gen Franchet d'Esperey's staff in Constantinople. Back to Morocco in 1922, promoted to colonel in 1925, Giraud won the Grand Cross of the Legion of Honor for his critical role in the subjugation of Abd-el-Krim. (CORAP is credited with capturing the Riff chieftain.) Giraud subsequently succeeded the legendary Lyautey in Morocco. On the eve of WWII he was military governor of Metz, becoming became a member of the Superior War Council in 1938, and on 2 Sep 39, as France mobilized for war, Giraud was a full general commanding the 7th Army. Allied journalists touted him at the time as "one of the greatest tacticians and strategists in the French Army" *(CB 42)*. Still a splendid military figure at 60, he was characterized by Paul Reynaud, himself a physical fitness addict, as "the most astonishing specimen of the fighting animal I have ever come across" (ibid.). But he proved to be a rather wooden soldier with little concept of modern warfare. Although an early advocate of motorization (ibid.), Giraud believed in the Maginot Line, argued against the use of armor in mass, and clashed continually with Col de Gaulle over tank tactics. It would not become critical until later, but the general also was notoriously ignorant of politics.

On 10 May 40, in accordance with the Allied strategic plan, Giraud marched his 7th Army from the Pas de Calais area into Holland. He reached Breda on 13 May and slowed the German 18th Army's advance on Antwerp. But as the Dutch army withdrew, Giraud was ordered to switch posts with CORAP, whose 9th Army had been shattered by the German main effort through the Ardennes. Confident he could stop the German onslaught but unable to pull his forces together, he was captured at Wassigny on 19 May 40 (Larousse) while getting out of a reconnaissance car (Spears, I, 157n).

This time he was a prisoner for almost two years. Perhaps because of his reputation as an escape artist, and also because Hitler mistakenly attributed authorship of DE GAULLE's book *Vers l'armée de métier* to him, Giraud ended up in the high-walled prison of Saxony's Koenigstein castle, near Dresden. Under cover of darkness on 17 Apr 42 he was lowered in an improvised rig by fellow generals and, with further assistance from Allied secret services, reached Vichy France on the 27th. Laval urged Giraud to placate the Germans by returning to captivity (Smith, *OSS,* 47), it being known that he was a man to whom the resistance would rally as an alternative to de Gaulle. The latter told Col Robert Solborg, OSS chief in Lisbon, that Giraud was the one Frenchman to whom he would subordinate himself (ibid., 47), and the ardently anti-Gaullist Roosevelt soon viewed Giraud as his favorite Frenchman.

Although promptly approached in Lyons on 19 May by agents of the Algiers conspirators to become their leader, the general preferred to concentrate on planning an uprising in metropolitan France. But he slowly realized the grass was greener in North Africa. Giraud's principal liaison agent was Jacques Lemaigre-Dubreuil, a right-wing industrialist whose "collaboration" had won him authority to operate a huge peanut-oil empire from Algiers. As a purveyor to Rommel's army and having personal contact with Pierre Laval, Lemaigre-Dubreuil could move freely in Africa and France. Gen Charles MAST, who was working closely with Robert MURPHY became Giraud's deputy in Algiers.

Pro-American French leaders knew that the Allies would invade North Africa but were not informed of the details. The **Cherchell** conference of 22 Oct 42 only obscured the matter of Giraud's role. Having no idea that D day in North Africa was imminent (8 Nov 42), Giraud agreed to meet Eisenhower at Gibraltar and resolve the issue of command. The Anglophobic Frenchman insisted that an American submarine fetch him. Because none was available, he was tricked into believing that HMS *Seraph* was an American boat. With Capt Jerauld WRIGHT, USN, posing as skipper of the British sub, Giraud was picked up from a Mediterranean port in SW France and taken to a Catalina flying boat. His staff followed in a second sub. The weary general reached Eisenhower's advance CP at Gibraltar late on the afternoon of 7 Nov 43 and, knowing nothing of Allied plans for Torch, demanded two things: 1) Eisenhower's job, and 2) an immediate Allied invasion of southern France! After six hours of testy discussion, Giraud accepted the lesser role of commanding only French forces in North Africa and prevailing on them not to oppose the Allied invasion.

But Giraud did not reach Algiers until the morning of 9 Nov 42 (D+1). The situation was confused by Adm DARLAN's being on hand and the continuation of scattered French resistance. Almost no French officers would accept Giraud's authority, and a comic opera touch was

added by Giraud's being in civilian clothes; his uniform had been misplaced and it took a day to get a new one of the proper rank. "How to make a *coup d'état* in a bowler hat?" wrote Howard Macmillan (*Blast,* 237).

After the "DARLAN deal" Giraud was "CinC of French Ground and Air Forces in North Africa." When Darlan was assassinated on 24 Dec 42, the general was nominated by the Imperial Council and blessed by Allied authorities as the the admiral's successor. As French civil and military chief in North Africa the proudly apolitical Giraud quickly became a major embarrassment to his Allied sponsors. He showed almost indecent haste in ordering the court martial and execution of Darlan's youthful assassin, Bonnier de la Chapelle, and he later ordered the arrest of several dozen ex-Vichy men including ones who had aided the Americans in Opn Torch. Giraud said at a press conference that he was heading off a wave of murders. The British SIS was supposed to be behind the assassination ring, the alleged hit list including himself, Bergeret, and Robert Murphy. (Stuart MENZIES was in Algiers when Darlan was killed.)

Giraud attended the Casablanca Conference, 14-23 Jan 43, primarily to arrange for US military aid, but he had to face de Gaulle for the first time since 1940. De Gaulle had failed in persistent invitations since the death of Darlan to meet and negotiate some accommodation with his former military superior. But the closest the two Frenchmen came at this time was to pose woodenly for the cameras and shake hands while Churchill and Roosevelt beamed archly the background.

De Gaulle reached Algiers on 30 May 43 and soon established the French Committee of National Liberation (FCNL) with himself and Giraud as co-presidents. "Le Grand Charles" then used his superior political skills to ease his former military superior out. On 31 July 43 Giraud's power was restricted to command of the armed forces, in which capacity he promptly undertook to liberate Corsica, 13 Sep-4 Oct 43, not forewarning his political chiefs, the FCNL. As further evidence of political ineptitude, the general gave arms to Corsica's "Front National," not realizing this was communist-dominated and only a minor resistance group at that (Larousse).

Under mounting criticism the general was removed from the co-presidency on 9 Nov 43. But he remained the figurehead for an anti-

Gaullist cabal centered around Henry Hyde's secret intelligence branch of OSS in Algiers. The "senior schemer" was Lemaigre-Dubreuil (above) and the "intellectual light" was Antoine de SAINT-EXUPERY (Smith, *OSS,* 180-1). "Finally, the cabal found an agent extraordinaire in Paul Dungler, the self-proclaimed leader of the non-Gaullist resistance in . . . Alsace Lorraine" (ibid.), whom Pétain had sent on a fool's errand to Algiers in the summer of 1943 to reconcile Giraud and de Gaulle. Hyde and Giraud then gave Dungler various wild missions in France including one to make contact with Abwehr agents of the anti-Hitler conspiracy. The end to all this intra-mural scheming came in Feb 44 with Dungler in the Gestapo's hands.

Giraud meanwhile refused to comply with an FCNL decision to merge his army intelligence service with Jacques Soustelle's "special services," which reported to de Gaulle. Giraud squandered his last political capital on a vain effort to get clemency for ex-Vichy Minister of the Interior Pierre Pucheu, who was executed on 20 Mar 44. The FCNL stripped Giraud of what de Gaulle calls "his theoretical function as commander in chief and appointed him inspector general," a final act that "definitively rid his status of all ambiguity and which, furthermore, corresponded to the services he could perform usefully" (*Unity,* 189-90).

Put on the retired list as of 14 Apr 44, the embittered general was living in isolation near Mostaganem, Algeria, when, on 28 Aug 44, an Algerian soldier put a rifle bullet through his jaw (Murphy, 184). Giraud magnanimously attributed the assassination attempt not to de Gaulle directly but to "certain of his partisans." Recuperation kept Giraud in North Africa until 1 Oct 44. After following Patton's troops into Metz on 20 Nov 44 and holding an insignificant administrative office in the postwar French government, the general was elected to the 2d Constituent Assembly on 2 June 46 as a member of the Republican Party of Liberty in the Moselle Dept (which includes Metz).

Giraud published *Mes Evasions* (1946), a book about his six escape attempts, and *Un seul but, la victoire—Alger 1942-1944* (1949). Three days before his death in Dijon on 13 Mar 49 the general was decorated with the Médaille Militaire for his escape from Koenigstein.

GISEVIUS, Hans Bernd. German resistance figure. 1904–74. The bulky Prussian was born

14 July 04 in Arnsberg. In July 33 he joined Goering's Prussian ministry of the interior to begin his professional career. After being involved in the intrigue that ousted Rudolf DIELS, the first Gestapo chief, Government Councilor Gisevius himself was dismissed from the Prussian ministry of the interior in Apr 36. (Gisevius, 199.)

After a variety of assignments Gisevius was transferred to the Abwehr in the winter of 1939-40 (ibid., 456) and ended up as vice consul in Zurich. Here from 1943 he was the link between Allen DULLES and the conspirators. Returning at great personal risk to Germany on 11 July 44, he was closely involved in the plot that culminated in STAUFFENBERG's assassination attempt on 20 July 44. After witnessing events that night in the Bendlerstrasse, Gisevius went into hiding the next morning (Gisevius, 576), as did NEBE. The conspicuously large fugitive (6 foot 4) eluded the Gestapo until reentering Switzerland on 23 Jan 45 with forged papers sent by Dulles. A privileged witness for the prosecution at Nuremberg, Gisevius lived some years in the US and West Berlin before settling in Switzerland. His memoirs, a rich source of inside information about people and events of the Third Reich and the German resistance, were published in two volumes in Germany in 1946. The one-volume English version, with an introduction by Allen Dulles, is *To the Bitter End* (Boston: Houghton Mifflin, 1947).

Gisevius died 23 Feb 74 in West Germany.

GLOBOCNIK, Odilo. SS commander. 1904-45. Born 21 Apr 04 at Trieste into a Croat family of petty officials, he emigrated to Austria in 1918. From 1933 he was deputy Gauleiter for Austria until the Anschluss, then was Gauleiter of Vienna, 24 May 38-30 Jan 39. Dismissed for speculating in foreign exchange but pardoned by Himmler on 9 Nov 39, he became SS and Police Leader in the Lublin District of Poland. In this capacity the brutally efficient Croat established the death camps at Belzec, Majdanek, Sobibor, and Treblinka. In 1941 he was made head of all death camps in Poland with the rank of SS Brigadefuehrer, holding this assignment until Nov 43, when work of the extermination camps was ending. For helping himself to property of victims, Globocnik was banished to Trieste (with his SS detachment) as Police Leader for the Adriatic Coast. On the approach of British forces he fled north toward Klagenfurt, Austria, country he knew. Under circumstances that are not known, killed by partisans, by a Jewish vengeance squad, or swallowing a cyanide capsule after being arrested by a British patrol, he died 31 May 45.

GODDARD, Robert Hutchings. US rocket scientist. 1882-1945. A physics professor at Clark Univ, Worcester, Mass, Goddard pioneered rocket development. Using liquid oxygen he successfully fired the first rocket on 16 Mar 26. Others used his research to develop the WWII **bazooka, V-weapons,** and post-war space rockets.

GODFROY, René Emile. French admiral. 1885-1981. Freshly promoted Vice Adm Godfroy had been commanding the 2d Cruiser Div for two months when the Franco-German armistice was signed on 22 June 40. He sensibly submitted to Adm Andrew CUNNINGHAM's ultimatum by agreeing to have his ships demobilized in Alexandria harbor, thus avoiding a tragedy like that at **Mers-el-Kebir.**

The admiral rejoined the Allies in 1943, after they liberated North Africa, but a CNL decree removed him from office with an effective date of 10 Dec 43. A Conseil d'Etat action of 1 Apr 55 rehabilited Godfroy. He died 17 Jan 81 at Fréjus. *(Fiche biographique, Marine Nationale.)*

GODWIN-AUSTEN, Alfred R. British general. 1889-1963. Godwin-Austen was rushed from Palestine to British Somaliland in early Aug 40 to oppose the Italian invasion. Facing overwhelming combat superiority, he ordered a general withdrawal on 14 Aug 40 and evacuated the garrison to Aden.

Maj Gen Godwin-Austen then led the 12th African Div in Kenya and Abyssinia under Alan CUNNINGHAM. In the fall of 1941, with John Harding as BGS, he took command of the 8th Army's 13th Corps in the western desert. With FREYBERG's 2d NZ and MESSERVY's 4th Indian Divs, both crack units, and the 1st Army Tank Bde, he had a major role in stopping Rommel's first offensive, holding Tobruk, and driving Axis forces back to El Agheila. Meanwhile AUCHINLECK had replaced CUNNINGHAM as 8th Army commander with RITCHIE, whose leadership fell apart when ROMMEL renewed his offensive on 21 Jan 42. After protesting Ritchie's meddling, Godwin-Austen

resigned in Feb 42. RITCHIE was soon sacked, but he had cost the 8th Army "an able, strong general and a much loved man" (Barnett, 134). Succeeded by GOTT, Sir Alfred became vice-QMG at the War Office, then was principal administrative officer at Army HQ in India.

GOEBBELS, Magda. Wife of Paul GOEBBELS. 1901-45. Maria Magdalena Behrend-Friedlaender, "the most interesting woman in the Third Reich" (Reimann, *Goebbels,* 121), was born 11 Nov 01 in Berlin. In 1921 she married Guenther Quandt, a wealthy industrialist, had a son, Harald, and got an amicable divorce in 1929. Meeting Hitler after becoming Goebbels's mistress, Magda found the fuehrer electrifying, and the attraction was mutual. She married Goebbels on 19 Sep 31, apparently to give Hitler a feminine element to his entourage. (Ibid., 124.) Her husband's notorious philandering and other difficulties brought the couple to the verge of divorce on several occasions, but Hitler insisted they remain together for the sake of appearances, and the Goebbels were more congenial in their final years (Lochner, 97). Magda meanwhile had six children and two miscarriages. She confided to a friend that son Helmuth (born in 1935) was sired by Hitler (Hamilton, *Leaders,* 100). Vivacious and elegant to the end, although weakened by heart attacks and spending much time in bed, she died with her husband on 1 May 45 (below).

GOEBBELS, Paul Joseph. Nazi propaganda minister. 1897-1945. He was born 29 Oct 97 at Rheydt, a smoky little textile center in the Rhineland. The financially strapped, working-class Goebbels family was devoutly Catholic, a faith the son renounced early in life. Under five feet tall at maturity, Goebbels had a puny body, an outsize head, jug ears, loose lips, and a bad limp after having a bone operation at the age of seven. Congenital birth defects being a disqualification for high office in Nazi Germany, Goebbels said at various times that his right foot was crippled by polio, an accident, or even a wound in WWI. (Reimann, *Goebbels,* 14.) Photographs show he had an abnormal right shoe, and Goebbels wore iron braces on the left leg.

Always conscious of the handicap, "Little Joe" compensated by striving to excel. He was a good student, fond of the piano, and showed aptitude in amateur theatrics. With Catholic scholarships and school loans (which he repaid) Goebbels ended up with a PhD from Heidelberg in 1921. Intent on a literary career but adopting a Bohemian life to avoid the stigma of intellectualism, he produced a bad novel, two unsuccessful plays, and was rejected as a reporter by the famous liberal newspaper *Berliner Tageblatt* (Lochner, ed., 5).

But Goebbels, impressed by hearing Hitler speak, developed an aptitude for demagogic oratory while spreading the Nazi message among university students. Winning Hitler's admiration, the new apostle was made editor of the Nazi *Voelkische Freiheit* at Elberfeld and soon thereafter was manager of Nazi business activities in the **Gau** of Rhine-Ruhr. Yet he did not join the Nazi Party until 1926.

As an additional duty, Goebbels collaborated briefly with Gregor STRASSER to establish a newspaper that brought Hitler his first real working-class support. Goebbels picked the right moment to switch allegiance to Hitler when Gregor STRASSER began falling out with the Nazi movement. For this the crafty minion was made Gauleiter of Greater Berlin on 9 Nov 26. Taking over a disorderly horde, the "Superbandit of Berlin" displayed organizational genius. The next year he founded the weekly *Der Angriff* (The Attack), which became a daily in 1930. Using the most disreputable editorial methods to rally support for the Nazis, *Der Angriff* became the foundation of the propagandist's great personal fortune.

Goebbels had entered the Reichstag in 1928 and the next year became the Nazi party's Propaganda Leader. When Hitler created the Reich Ministry for Public Enlightenment and Propaganda on 30 June 33, the portfolio went Goering, who consolidated his authority over the press, radio, and cultural life under a succession of laws. In 1931 the limping dwarf took a giant step socially by marrying Magda GOEBBELS.

Curiously, the propaganda minister did not encroach on other ministers until confidence within the Nazi high command was shaken by the Stalingrad disaster in the winter of 1942-43. After asking Walther Funk, Robert Ley, and Albert Speer to confer with him more frequently (Speer, *Memoirs*, 254), Goebbels delivered a major speech on 18 Feb 43. Sensing that the public was prepared for greater sacrifices, the strident dwarf called for total war.

But the speech also was "obliquely addressed to the leadership which had ignored all our proposals for a radical commitment of domestic reserves," writes Speer. "Basically, it was an attempt to place Lammers and all the other dawdlers under the pressure of the mob." (Ibid, 256-57.) This speech also addressed foreign policy, which Goebbels thought was being badly handled because Ribbentrop was incompetent and the fuehrer was preoccupied with military affairs. The propaganda minister struck a major chord, in Germany and abroad, by suggesting that Western allies shared Germany's interest in blocking the Soviet threat to Europe (ibid.). Hitler was cool to all this advice, but Goebbels persevered in doing what he could unilaterally.

STAUFFENBERG's attempt to assassinate Hitler on 20 July 44 brought out unexpected leadership qualities in the little cripple who had been rejected for military service. While generals agonized in indecision, Goebbels rallied loyal troops to seize putschists at the Bendlerstrasse. Named Reich commissioner for total mobilization of resources for war five days later, he promptly let Bormann and Speer know that he was now their boss. (Speer, op. cit., 398.)

As a propagandist Goebbels was vigorous to the end. An early triumph had been making a hero out of Horst WESSEL in 1930. Although another may have suggested the title "Fuehrer" (Reimann, op. cit., 327n1), Goebbels made its use compulsory. The sorcerer also introduced the almost-mandatory salutation "Heil Hitler." He perfected the "great lie" doctrine that a continually repeated falsehood—the bigger the better—becomes believed. He used the Allies' **unconditional surrender** pronouncement to stiffen German will to fight on. The **national redoubt myth** was his final coup.

As the end approached, the fearless Goebbels accepted Hitler's invitation to move into the Fuehrerbunker with his family. The evening of 1 May 45, after having his six children poisoned, the little cripple and his sick wife started up the stairs to the Chancellery garden at about 8:30 PM. According to Trevor-Roper, an SS orderly killed them with pistol shots to the back of the head (T-R, *Hitler,* 213). According to another version the attendant fired only after Magda took poison and her husband shot himself. In accordance with Goebbels's instructions, his adjutant and driver ignited four cans of gasoline over the bodies, which the Russians identified the next day.

A standard biography by Viktor Reimann is *Goebbels* (Garden City, NY: Doubleday, 1976). Louis P. Lochner edited and translated *The Goebbels Diaries, 1942-1943* (same publisher, 1948). Another work, which has a good biographical essay, is Willi A. Boelcke (ed), *The Secret Conferences of Dr.Goebbels. The Nazi Propaganda War 1939-43* (New York: Dutton, 1970).

GOERDELER, Carl Friedrich. German resistance leader. 1884-1945. The civilian head of the anti-Hitler movement was born in Schneidemuell (now Pila, Poland) on 31 July 84. He was the son of a conservative Prussian district judge. After studying law, and beginning a career in local administration, he was second mayor of Koenigsberg before being lord mayor of Leipzig, 1930-37. While retaining this office he was price commissioner in the government of Heinrich BRUENING and remained as economic adviser when Hitler came to power. In Nov 34 Goerdeler became Reich commissioner of prices but resigned in protest the next year because his economic liberalism was rejected (Wistrich). Vigorous, opinionated, almost puritanical, somewhat ambiguous in political and social outlook, the lord mayor was highly regarded by government officials, diplomats, and business leaders in Germany and abroad. He was convinced that the Western Allies would see Germany as a bulwark against communism.

The anti-Hitler conspirators picked Goerdeler to be chancellor if a coup d'état succeeded, and his major task was to draw up a cabinet list for the new government that the Western Allies would accept as grounds for softening the announced unconditional surrender terms. Told by CANARIS as early as Mar 44 that Himmler knew of the conspiracy, Goerdeler was warned early on 18 July 44 that the Gestapo chiefs finally had decided to arrest him (Hoffmann, *Resistance,* 391). That night the Lord Mayor went to ground, eluding the Gestapo until 12 Aug 44. But he then was extraordinarily forthcoming with interrogators. Gerhard Ritter (below) is convinced this was not because of duress but because "He wanted the *Gestapo,* and through it the Nazi regime, to know precisely the nature and scope of the opposition. He was still hoping that Hitler could be persuaded to reverse his policy . . ." (ibid, 516). Goerdeler was sentenced to death on 8 Sep 44

but not executed until 2 Feb 45, probably because the Gestapo hoped to get more information from him. *See* Gerhard Ritter, *The German Resistance: Carl Goerdeler's Struggle Against Tyranny* (London: Allen and Unwin, 1958), published originally as *Carl Goerdeler und die deutsche Widerstandsbewegung* (Stuttgart: Deutsche Verlags-Anstalt, 1956).

GOERING, Hermann Wilhelm. Nazi chief. 1893-1946. The Third Reich's most colorful performer was born 12 Jan 93 at Rosenheim, Bavaria. His mother, a Bavarian of Austrian descent, had returned for the event from Haiti, where her Prussian husband was consul general. Hermann, her fourth child, was left with a family friend and reunited with his parents six years later when the father retired in Berlin. Young Hermann was regaled with stories of Prussian military glories and taken to Sunday parades at Potsdam. A long-time family friend, a wealthy Jewish convert to Christianity, loaned the financially straitened Goerings an ornately furnished castle near Nuremberg. Here the young Hermann added a taste for expensive living to his military aspirations.

After schooling in the Prussian Cadet Corps, Goering saw some action as an infantry lieutenant before being disabled by rheumatism of the knees. Defying regulations, he flew as an observer, won the Iron Cross 1st Class, and in late 1915 was accepted for flight training. In May 18 Leutnant Goering was awarded the Pour le Mérite after his 20th air victory, and on 7 July 18 he succeeded Baron Manfred von Richthofen (KIA on 21 Apr 18) as squadron leader. (*See* MILCH.) Finding post-war Germany intolerable, he took odd jobs in Scandanavia as a pilot and aircraft salesman, and in Sweden met the exotic Baroness Karen von Fock-Kantzow. Five years his senior and married for 10 years to a Swedish officer, the tall Nordic beauty was the daughter of a Swedish colonel and an English-born eccentric who went in for mystic rites. After an amiable divorce, Karen became Frau Goering in Munich on 3 Feb 22. She inspired her infatuated husband to further his education—he attended the University of Munich—and to take part in the struggle for German resurrection. The 29-year-old Hermann did both with gusto.

When the Goerings first heard Hitler speak, in Nov 22, "It was political love at first sight" (Frischauer, *Goering,* 38). The war hero was just the man Hitler had been seeking to create his Brownshirts (SA), and the socially respectable ex-lieutenant proved to be not only a good organizer but also a born politician of the rough and ready sort. As SA chief in 1923 during the **Munich Beer Hall Putsch** Capt Goering fell ignominiously but painfully with two granite splinters (from a building) in the groin. To avoid arrest he fled with his wife through Austria and Italy (meeting Mussolini) to Stockholm. The mystic Karen had become a near invalid, and Goering was a physical and mental wreck because of morphine addiction, obesity, and hypochondria. But in 1927, his health restored and an amnesty granted by Hindenburg, Goering went to Berlin. He was elected to the **Reichstag** on 20 May 28, and the ailing Karen joined him in the capital. The dark, beautiful, not-too-intellectual but politically aware Karin was one of the few women with whom the fuehrer was completely at ease. "You are the mascot of my movement," Hitler said after she played hostess at a small party arranged to win the support of Schacht, Thyssen, and others. "When you are here all goes well" (ibid., 66). But she was not up to the task; going home suddenly she died 17 Oct 31 in Stockholm with a disconsolate husband at her bedside.

Goering was elected president of the Reichstag on 30 Aug 32. After Hitler became chancellor on 30 Jan 33 he made Goering a cabinet minister without portfolio, commissioner for air, Prussian minister of the interior, and soon gave his lieutenant von Papen's post of prime minister of Prussia. Goering moved quickly and ruthlessly to use the previously insignificant position to create a power base, doing this on his own initiative but with Hitler's blessing. Immediately on replacing 22 of Germany's 32 police chiefs with trusted SA and SS officers, the new minister chose Rudolf DIELS over a hundred qualified officials to be chief of the political police. This was the ministry's most important position, and Diels used secret files to create the **Gestapo.** The central office was in Berlin, and there were Gestapo branches—bases and "directorates"—throughout Germany.

If Goering was not responsible for causing the **Reichstag Fire** of 27 Feb 33, he moved fast and decisively to use the event as a pretext for launching a wave of storm trooper violence against the communists and other opponents of the forthcoming Nazi takeover. This overburdened the jail system, so Goering and Himmler began setting up concentration camps.

Goering also had a major role in the **Blood Purge** of June 34. Pleased that this massacre removed the SA threat to the army, the dying Hindenburg approved Goering's appointment as a general of infantry. Goering also became an honorary Obergruppenfuehrer-SS and resumed his SA rank (Frischauer, 102). In March 35 Goering revealed his Luftwaffe, which became Hitler's "big stick" in foreign affairs.

Goering's marriage to Emmy Sonnemann, a well-know actress and a divorcee, was celebrated in an ostentatious state ceremony on 10 Apr 35. The second Frau Goering, whose one child, Edda (named apparently for Countess CIANO, a close family friend [Frischauer, 148]) made up in heft, health, and good sense what she lacked of her delicate predecessor's mysticism.

With the bit in his teeth, and hoping to profit by becoming Wehrmacht chief (W-B, *Nemesis,* 372n), Goering took the lead in purging the high command of BLOMBERG and FRITSCH. When HITLER announced the new command structure on 4 Feb 38 and took over as head of Germany's armed forces (OKW), the fuehrer consoled his trusty lieutenant with the rank of field marshal. A law of succession dated 1 Sep 39 made the Generalfeldmarschall Hitler's deputy and legal heir; this law was later endorsed by a decree of 29 June 41.

By now, however, *Der Eiserne* (The Iron Man) was degenerating into a Teutonic Falstaff. Fondly renamed *Der Dicke* (Fatty), eventually topping the scales at 280 pounds, he again became addicted to morphine, which he had started using after being wounded in Munich. With state funds and monumental bad taste, Der Dicke converted an old Berlin palace into his official residence. A former imperial hunting lodge on 100,000 acres, 25 miles north of Berlin, became his unofficial residence and playground. This was "Karinhall." With other top Nazis he also had an elaborate establishment at Berchtesgaden. Vast income came from his many official offices, President of the Prussian State Council, Air Minister, Reichstag President, Commissioner of the Four Year Plan, Reich Chief Hunter, and Reichsmarschall (below). He made money from his official newspaper (*Essener National Zeitung*), from stock in the aircraft industry, and from the state-owned Hermann-Goering Works (created in 1937).

Further feathering his various nests, Goering extorted gifts and loans of art masterpieces. The "big little boy" did not conceal his extravagances nor the delight they gave him.

The revolutionary new German AF, developed and commanded primarily by MILCH, was a major factor in the sudden defeat of Poland in Sep 39. On 5 Mar 40, as the Norway invasion was being planned, Der Dicke said heatedly to Hitler: "The Luftwaffe is mine. The stupid Army officers cannot be expected to employ it properly!" The fuehrer agreed that henceforth all orders to the Luftwaffe would go through OKL. France fell almost as fast as Poland, German air power again being a major factor. On 19 July 40, when Hitler appointed 12 new field marshals including MILCH, KESSELRING, and SPERRLE in the Luftwaffe, Goering got the exclusive rank of Reichsmarschall. But he and his air force revealed increasingly serious shortcomings. Having failed to stop the "miracle of Dunkirk," the Luftwaffe lost the Battle of Britain and was a disappointment in Russia. Deficient from the start in strategic offensive capability, the Luftwaffe later proved weak defensively against British and American strategic air power whose creation, ironically, it had inspired.

As the war proceeded, Goering became a pathetic figure, held in contempt by the fuehrer he continued to revere, and virtually abandoning his official duties. After the 20 July 44 attempt on Hitler's life, however, the Reichsmarshall was given plenipotentiary powers; it was 18 months too late, in his opinion (Lewin, *Hitler's Mistakes,* 149). As the Soviets began overrunning Germany, the Reichsmarshall evacuated Karinhall in Apr 45 and went to Berchtesgaden, urging Hitler to move his headquarters there. A few days later, as the Red Army closed in on the Fuehrerbunker, Goering asked his fuehrer in a message on 23 Apr 45 whether he should take over in accordance with procedures prescribed for succession (herein). Knowing that communications might be cut, he added: "If I should receive no reply by 10 PM, I shall assume that you have been deprived of your freedom of action and shall act in the best interests of our country and people." It was a sensible action that Hitler apparently came around to accepting. After first ranting that Goering was "corrupt, a failure, a drug addict," Hitler decided that his Falstaff might as well be the one to negotiate surrender. BORMANN, seeing things differently

from the depths of the Fuehrerbunker, insisted that Goering be dismissed from all offices and arrested. An SS detachment undertook to carry out this last order, but a Luftwaffe unit rescued their hefty chief.

In full regalia and with a party of about 30, he surrendered on 8 May 45 to the US 36th Inf Div near Mauterndorf. Having been greeted cordially and invited to dinner, Goering was astonished the next day to be stripped of his baton and medals and confined as a war criminal. Slimmed down, off drugs, and in high spirits at Nuremberg, Goering argued that official acts should not be judged by standards set for private individuals. The senior surviving Nazi was convicted 1 Oct 46 on all four counts of **war crimes.**

Goering swallowed potassium cyanide on 15 Oct 46 at about 9 PM, apparently having learned he was to be hanged early the next morning. Either he had concealed the capsule since entering prison (Frischauer, 280) or it was smuggled in (Davidson, *Trial,* 96). Goering was cremated at Dachau, where his ashes were dumped in a trash can (Frischauer, photograph facing page 247). Frau Goering was imprisoned under harsh conditions until Mar 46.

Biographies include those by Charles Bewley, *Hermann Goering and the Third Reich* (1962), and Willi Frischauer, *The Rise and Fall of Hermann Goering* (1951).

GOLIKOV, Filip Ivanovich. Soviet military leader. 1900-80. Young for high command in the Great Patriotic War, Golikov was born 16 July 00 in Borisovo, now Kurgan Oblast, east of the Urals. He joined the Red Army in 1918, graduated from the Frunze MA in 1933 by correspondence, and specialized in armor. (*CB 43;* Scotts.) After fighting in Poland and perhaps in Finland, he was promoted to general major on 7 May 40 and assigned two months later as deputy CGS and chief of military intelligence (GRU). Golikov reported direct to Stalin, leaving the general staff ignorant of many details to include reports from Richard SORGE in Tokyo. (Zhukov, *Memoirs,* 216, 218.)

Soon after the USSR was invaded on 22 June 41, the stocky, moon-faced, shaven-headed young Gen Lt Golikov led a six-man mission to London on 8 July 41 to get military aid and arrange for combined strategic planning. Having met in London with Harry HOPKINS, who was en route to Moscow, Golikov proceeded to Washington with another general for preliminary talks about Lend Lease.

After a successful military-diplomatic mission, Golikov took over the 10th Army in Oct 41, when the Germans were within 150 miles of Moscow. The invaders were alarmed to be attacked by a brigade equipped with British tanks, evidence that the Soviets already were getting the support that Golikov had helped to arrange. After being one of the internationally publicized heroes in the desperate defense that followed, Golikov led the 4th Assault Army in Feb-Mar 42 during the winter counteroffensive, and in Apr-July 42 he commanded the Bryansk Front in opposing the powerful summer offensive launched by Bock's AG South on 28 June 42. The drive shattered the 13th Army on Golikov's left flank, creating a widening gap between the Bryansk and Southwest Fronts. The Voronezh Front under Vatutin was created around 5 July from "the debris of Golikov's divisions and some of the meagre Stavka reserves. . ." (Clark, *Barbarossa*, 236). During the Stalingrad counteroffensive Golikov commanded the Voronezh Front in July 42 and the 1st Guards Army in Aug-Oct 42. He doubled as deputy CG of the Southeast and Stalingrad Fronts from 28 Sep 42, headed the Voronezh Front again from Oct 42 to Mar 43, and took part in the Soviet drive through Kursk and Kharkov.

Promoted on 19 Jan 43, Gen Col Golikov went to Moscow three months later as chief of the personnel directorate and deputy commissar of defense for cadres. Holding these posts until 1950—finished as a field commander— he concurrently headed the Repatriation Commission of Soviet Citizens from Oct 44. Golikov was promoted to general of the army in 1945 and to marshal in 1961. He died 29 July 80. (Scotts.)

GOLLNICK, Hans. German general. 1892-. The future general of infantry and corps commander in the east was born 22 May 92 at Gut Gursen. After serving as an officer in WWI and remaining in uniform he rose from Oberstleutnant (1 Apr 36) to full colonel (1 Oct 38). As a Generalmajor (1 June 41) he was awarded the RK on 21 Nov 42 while commanding the 36th Pz Grenadier Div in the Ukraine. Promoted to Generalleutnant on 1 Jan 43, taking command of the 46th Pz Corps on 5 Aug 43 and being awarded the Oakleaves (282/890) about three weeks later. He led this corps in the general withdrawal through Svin, Chernigov, and Lyubech toward Mozyr. Promoted on 1 Oct 43, General of Infantry Gollnick commanded the 28th Army Corps from 22 Mar 44 to the end of the war. (Angolia, II, 239; *B&O*, 48-49.)

GOLLOB, Gordon M. Luftwaffe officer. 1912-. Born 16 June 12 in Vienna and commissioned in the Austrian AF (1936), Gollob won distinction as a fighter pilot, test pilot, and commander over Poland, Norway, France, Britain, and Russia. Although not on combat duty during much of the war he had 150 fighter victories in 340 missions, being awarded the Diamonds (3/27) on 30 Aug 42 while commanding the 77th Ftr Wing in Russia. Major Gollub then served in the west until assigned in early Apr 44 to GALLAND's staff in OKL.

General of the Fighters Galland was in the last throes of a losing battle against the Bomber Arm over defensive strategy, and Oberst Gollob, an ardent Nazi who bore a striking facial resemblance to Rudolf Hess (Angolia, I, 59, photo), proved to be an unscrupulous intriguer against his chief. (*See* Toliver and Constable, *Galland*, 268-82, passim.) Not surprisingly, on 15 Jan 45 Goering named Gollob to replace GALLAND, his superior in every way.

GOLOVANOV, Aleksandr Yevgenyevich. Soviet air officer. 1904-75. Born in Nizhnyy Novgorod on 25 July 04, he took pilot training in 1932, worked in civil aviation, and eventually commanded long-range bomber formations of the Red AF. Promoted in Mar 42, Gen Maj Golovanov took command the next month of new strategic bomber command. In 1943 he became a Marshal of Aviation (the second after NOVIKOV). Although his Long Range Force (or ADD) was subordinate to the **Stavka,** Golovanov had considerable autonomy. ADD became the 18th Air Army in Jun 44, still under Golovanov, and on 19 Aug 44 he was promoted to Chief Marshal of Aviation (still second to NOVIKOV). He had a critical role in the battle for **Koenigsberg.** The number-two airman of the much-purged Red AF retired in 1953. (Scotts.)

GOLOVKO, Arseny Grigoryevich. Soviet admiral. 1906-62. As commander of the Northern Fleet throughout the war, Golovko was involved not only with the Murmansk convoys but also in driving Axis forces out of the Petsamo-Kirkenes area and northern Norway. He was promoted to vice admiral in 1942 and to full admiral in 1944. After the war until 1954 he was chief of Navy General Staff. *(S&S.)*

GORDOV, Vasily Nikolayevich. Soviet military leader. 1896-1951. Gordov was born in the village of Matveyevka, Tatar **ASSR,** on 12 Dec 96. A sergeant commissioned in the Imperial Army, he joined the Red Guards, wasan officer in the Red Army, CP member from 1918, fought in the Civil War, 1925-26, and was an instructor in the Mongolian Red Army. (Scotts.) In June 41 Gen Maj Gordov moved from being CofS, Volga MD, to CofS, 21st Army, through Sep 41. He commanded the army in August, reverted to CofS, then took over the army for the period Oct 41 to 12 June 42. On this date the Stalingrad Front was formed under TIMO-SHENKO and during the period 23 July-12 Aug 42 Gordov briefly headed the front. (Scotts.) In the confusing reorganizations outlined under YEREMENKO, Gordov had virtually no authority except as one of Yeremenko's two deputies in the new, enlarged front. On 9 Sep 42 a new Stalingrad Front was created under Yeremenko, and Gordov took command of the 33d Army the next month. A general colonel from Sep 43, he led the 3d Guards Army for the rest of the war. In May 45, after having been made a **HSU,** Gordov was arrested on charges of cowardice! After a long imprisonment he was shot on 12 Dec 51, his birthday, and was buried in Kuybyshev.

GORING, *See* GOERING

GORT, Lord, 6th Viscount (John Standish Surtees Prendergast Verker). British Field Marshal. 1886-1946. An Irishman who succeeded his father to the peerage (above) in 1902, he was educated at Harrow and gazetted to the Grenadier Guards on being commissioned in 1905. After serving in France as an operations officer (GSO 2) at GHQ, he commanded in succession the 4th and 1st Bns, Grenadier Guards, 1917-18 (VC, two DSOs, MC). In 1937, after being commandant at **Camberley,** he was jumped ahead of senior officers including DILL to be CIGS. A full general in 1937, knighted (KCB) the next year, Lord Gort turned over his post as CIGS to Dill and took the BEF to France in Sep 39. Although unimag-inative and preoccupied with minutia, not an inspiring general, Lord Gort saved the BEF after it was outflanked on the Belgian frontier and driven back toward the Channel. Violating WEYGAND's strict orders against withdrawal, showing strategic sense and initiative as Belgian and French resistance collapsed on his flanks, Gort conducted a good delaying action. Late on 31 May 40 he received orders to transfer command of the rear guard to ALEXANDER and return to England (Cyril Falls in *DNB*). The venerable British general had performed with credit in his final service as a field commander, being largely responsible for saving the BEF and many French in the **Dunkirk Evacuation,** 26 May-4 June 40.

Too old for the post of commander in chief of the British Army he was elevated in the honors hierarchy to **GCB** and appointed **IG** to the Forces for Training, 1940-41. Lord Gort then was Governor and CinC at Gibraltar, where he had an invaluable airstrip built and improved relations with Spain. Turning over command to MASON-MACFARLANE he succeeded DOBBIE as Governor General and CINC on Malta, 1942-44. Worn down by his duties, which he performed well, and being made a field marshal in 1943, Lord Gort ended his career as CINC Palestine and High Commissioner for Transjordan, 1944-45. He was created the first Viscount Gort in the UK peerage in 1945.

GOTT, William Henry Ewart. British general. 1897-1942. As CG 7th Armd Div "Strafer" Gott opposed the Italians in Libya (1941). Moving up in Feb 42 to replace Sir Alfred GODWIN-AUSTEN as commander of the 13th Corps, he held Rommel on the Bir Hacheim—Gazala line from 26 May to 13 June 42 until withdrawing to avoid a strategic envelopment of KOENIG's Free French Bde at Bir Hacheim. Gott was promoted to lieutenant general and in early August was selected to succeed Auchinleck as 8th Army commander. But he was killed on 7 Aug 42 when his plane was shot down en route to Cairo. The 8th Army was taken over by Montgomery, who had been second choice for the post.

GOTTWALD, Klement. Czech politician. 1896-1953. He deserted from the Austro-Hungarian army in WWI to join the Russians and become a communist. In the new state of Czechoslovakia he rose steadily, but after the

Munich Agreement he went to Moscow and made several broadcasts to the Czech underground. Gottwald was a signer of the order that dissolved the Comintern on 22 May 43, he had a key key role in the postwar Communist takeover of his country, and in June 45 he became premier. He ramrodded adoption of a communist constitution and succeeded Eduard BENES as president on 14 June 48. Five days after catching cold at Stalin's funeral Gottwald died of pneumonia.

GOVOROV, Leonid Aleksandrovich. Soviet general. 1897–1955. Born 22 Feb 97 (**NS**) in the village of Butyrki, Kirov Oblast, Govorov was the son of an office worker. In 1916 he was conscripted, became a junior officer, and in 1918 he was drafted into the anti-Bolshevik forces of Adm Alexander V. Kolchak (1874-1920) in Siberia. He deserted in Oct 19, joined the Red Guards two months later, entered the Red Army in 1920, but nevertheless was refused admission to the Party until 1942 because of service with Kolchak. Govorov rose rapidly in the Red Army. By 1936 he commanded an artillery corps but two years later he was transferred from the Academy of the GS without any explanation being given but the action did not impede his military advancement.

Having innovated the technique of direct fire of heavy guns on fortifications during the winter war with Finland, 1939-49, Govorov was deputy IG, Main Artillery Board, then commandant of the Dzerzhinsky Artillery Academy. In the spring of 1941, however, he was proscribed because of the service with Kolchak. After KALININ intervened to have him spared, Govorov took command of the 5th Army on 17 Oct 41, was promoted a month later to general lieutenant of artillery, and he had an important part in the counteroffensives around Moscow. In 1942 he finally was allowed to join the CP and from June of that year until July 45 he commanded the Leningrad Front. On 18 Nov 43, still only 46 years old, he became a General of the Army (No. 20), and exactly seven months later he was a Marshal of the Soviet Union (No. 12). In Feb 45 the marshal succeeded Yeremenko as commander of the 2d Baltic Front a month before it was disbanded.

After the war Govorov headed the Leningrad MD, then from 1946 to 1947 he was Chief Inspector, Soviet Army, before commanding the Anti-Aircraft Defense and being Deputy MOD

Dying in office on 19 Mar 55, he was buried in the Kremlin Wall.

GRAF, Hermann. German ace. 1912-. Graf was the first fighter pilot to score 200 air victories, finishing with 212, all but 10 against the Soviets. As a colonel commanding Ftr Wing 52 he was taken prisoner by the Americans, turned over to the Russians, and held until 1950.

GRAZIANI, Rodolfo. Italian general. 1882-1955. "Lucky" Graziani, born 11 Aug 82 at Filettino (near Rome), had the craggy look of a classical Roman centurion and was over six feet tall. In 1914 he served in Libya before going to the Italian front, where as a brigade commander he was wounded twice and promoted to major.

By 1932 he was a corps commander and considered to be Italy's best desert fighter. Graziani pacified Libya in a brutally efficient campaign before doing the same in Abyssinia. Made the Marchese di Neghelli and Marshal of Italy, Graziani became Viceroy of Ethiopia in 1936 when BADOGLIO left. But his efforts to consolidate Italian control became so outrageous as opposition spread that Graziani was replaced at the end of 1937 by the Duke of AOSTA. The marshal then was honorary governor of Italian East Africa until Nov 39, when he became head of the Italian Army and commander of the Army of the Po. When Italy declared war on 10 June 40 he ordered 32 poorly equipped divisions into France. They were stopped after failing to force the Alpine passes and advancing only five miles on the Riviera.

BALBO being killed about this time, Graziani was made governor general of Libya and commander of almost 250,000 poorly equipped, poorly led, and poorly trained troops. Finally goaded into action, Graziani attacked into Egypt on 13 Sep 40. His five divisions advanced only a few miles before stopping to build an elaborately fortified camp at Sidi Barrani. This was attacked by WAVELL on 6 Dec 40 in what was supposed to be a limited effort, but Graziani's army fled in panic, abandoning all of Cyrenaica. Losing only 2,000 of his 30,000 troops Richard O'CONNOR captured 138,000 Italians including five generals; an additional 12,000 Italians were killed or missing.

Marshal Graziani was recalled 25 Mar 41 and he resigned from the army. He became

MOD of MUSSOLINI's Salo government in Sep 43, surrendering to the Allies on 29 Apr 45 and being turned over to Italian authorities in 1946. In the spring of 1950 Graziani was sentenced to 19 years in prison but he was released after a few months. He became president of the neo-Fascist Italian Socialist Movement and died 11 Jan 55 in Rome. Graziani published his memoirs in 1947 as *Ho Difenso la Patria* (I Defended the Homeland).

GRECHKO, Andrey Antonovich. Soviet general. 1903-76. An outstanding commander of field armies in 1942-45, he was MOD from 1967 until his death.

Grechko was a Ukrainian, born 17 Oct 03 in the village of Golodayevka, at the mouth of the Don river. Little is known of his origins (HFS), but he grew to be six feet three or four inches tall, slender, and dignified. As a teenager he entered the Red Army cavalry in 1919, fought in the civil war and belatedly joined the party in 1928. After attending the Frunze MA, 1932-36, and commanding a cavalry regiment, he was CofS, 36th Cav Div.

In Sep 39 he was with forces occupying Poland. Contrary to what some have written, there is no record of his leading an infantry regiment in Finland nor of being operations officer on a corps staff. The Germans were driving into Russia when on 3 July 41, only days after he had been assigned to the GS in Moscow as one of SHAPOSHNIKOV's protégés from the GS Academy, the 37-year-old colonel was ordered to Kharkov as commander of the 34th Cav Div. Quickly proving himself and promoted, General Major Grechko moved up on 18 Jan 42 to head the 5th Cav Corps, which was in action E of Dnepropetrovsk (HFS). Continuing to stand out in desperate fighting on the southern front, he commanded the 12th Army from April to Sep 42, then the 47th Army for a month before leading the 18th Army Oct 42-Jan 43. Promoted to General Lieutenant, he headed the 56th Army until Oct 43, fighting near his birthplace. The young general then was in the 2d Ukrainian Front for two months as KONEV's deputy, KHRUSHCHEV serving on the military council and BREZHNEV being the 18th Army's political officer. Friendship with these two successors to Stalin had a favorable influence on Grechko's subsequent rise to the top of his profession.

In Dec 43 he took over the elite 1st Guards Army and was promoted about this time. General Colonel Grechko led this army until the end of the war. He took part in the liberation of Kiev and the rest of the Ukraine, the fighting in the Carpathians, and the occupation of Prague on 9 May 45. (HFS.)

He commanded the Kiev MD 1945-53, when KHRUSHCHEV was political boss of the Ukraine. After Stalin's death on 5 Mar 53 Grechko was the first since 1948 to be promoted to General of the Army (No. 33). On 26 May 53 he became CinC of Soviet Troops in Germany and in a few weeks he crushed the Berlin uprising that had started after Stalin's death. In 1955 he became a MSU (No. 24) at the age of 52. Recalled to Moscow in 1957 after ZHUKOV was ousted and MALINOVSKY was appointed MOD, Marshal Grechko was made CinC of Soviet Ground Forces. Holding the post until 1960, he was 1st Deputy MOD and CinC, Warsaw Pact Armed Forces until becoming MOD on 12 Apr 67. The next year he directed the invasion of Czechoslovakia. He then "presided over transformation of the Soviet Armed Forces, bringing superpower status to the USSR" (HFS). Twice a HSU (1958, 1973) he died in office on 26 Apr 76 at the age of 72 and is buried in the Kremlin Wall.

GREIM, Robert von. Luftwaffe general. 1892-1945. The son of a Bavarian army officer, **Ritter** von Greim was born 22 June 92 at Bayreuth. As a WWI fighter ace with 28 victories he won the Pour le Mérite. Greim studied law at the Univ of Munich for three years, organized Chiang Kai-shek's AF (1924-27), and managed commercial air training centers in Germany before reentering the Wehrmacht in 1934 as a major. In Apr 35 he became Inspector of Fighters and Dive Bombers, and in 1937 he was appointed chief of the Air Ministry's personnel section. (Angolia, I, 202.)

In 1939 Greim took command of Fliegerkorps V, leading this as a Generalleutnant in the war's opening campaigns. On 24 June 40 he was awarded the RK for action in France. After the Battle of Britain, Greim's flight corps was sent to the eastern front. From Feb 43, with the rank of Generaloberst, he headed Luftflotte 6 and was awarded the Oakleaves (216/890) on 2 Apr 43 and the Swords (92/159) on 28 Aug 44.

Luftflotte 6 Hq was in Munich when Greim got a telegram on 24 Apr 45 to report to the

Fuehrerbunker in Berlin. GOERING had just created an uproar by proposing to take over from Hitler. Delayed by heavy air attacks on Munich and points north, Greim flew into Berlin with Hanna REITSCH in the early evening of 26 Apr 45. The general's right foot was shattered by ground fire as he flew low over the Tiergarten and his little passenger landed the plane by leaning over his shoulder and taking the controls. Greim was in bed having his wound dressed when Hitler walked in to announce that the general now commanded the Luftwaffe with the rank of field marshal (the last one appointed). Greim and his co-pilot, both rabid Nazis, asked to remain in the bunker, but their fuehrer insisted that they leave as soon as a plane could be delivered to Berlin. After almost three days in the bunker the heroic pair left early on 28 Apr 45 in a training plane delivered by a sergeant-pilot. The new field marshal and his companion went by stages to DOENITZ's Hq, which was then in the Austrian Alps at scenic Zell am See. Greim was now "a total wreck, his skin yellow, hobbling on two crutches; Reitsch weeping and posturing; and both singing their tedious duet, now a ferocious denunciation of Goering, now a devout litany about the Fuehrer and the Fatherland" (T-R, *Hitler,* 173). Captured by the Americans, Greim committed suicide on 24 May 45 while in prison at Salzburg.

GREW, Joseph Clark. US diplomat. 1880-1965. Born in Boston on 27 May 80, third son of a banking family, Grew attended Groton and Harvard before entering the foreign service in 1904. The next year he married a granddaughter of Commodore Matthew C. Perry (who had opened Japan to the west in 1853), and in 1932 Grew began 10 years as ambassador to Tokyo. The suave, athletic, six-foot-tall diplomat was popular in Japan and believed that by adopting a more conciliatory attitude the US could negotiate all differences between the countries. But on 27 Jan 41 he reported rumors of a surprise attack on Pearl Harbor (Buchanan, 37-38; 43-48), and on 3 Nov 41 he warned that the Japanese might risk "national hari-kiri" to attain their objectives. After internment until the summer of 1942, Grew became special assistant to the secretary of state. He recommended that the US leave the emperor on his throne. Grew was promoted in 1944 to under secretary of state, retiring in 1945. Among his many books are *My Ten Years in Japan* (New York: Simon & Schuster, 1944) and a two-volume autobiography *Turbulent Era* (Boston: Houghton Mifflin, 1952).

GROMYKO, Andrey Andreyevich. Soviet diplomat. 1909-89. Born in Minsk, and educated as an agricultural economist, he entered the foreign service in 1939. After heading the Department of American Countries for a few months, the tall, dark, taciturn, reclusive Gromyko went to Washington as counselor of embassy under Ambassador UMANKSY. LITVINOV arrived as the new ambassador on the eve of Pearl Harbor. At various times in the summer of 1943, as he had been during UMANSKY's three-months absence, Gromyko was acting ambassador. When STALIN adopted a tougher foreign policy toward the West, Gromyko became ambassador on 24 Aug 43 (Scotts) but did not present his credentials until 4 Oct 43 *(CB 43).* Meanwhile he was named ambassador to Cuba as well. (ibid.). The Soviet ambassador, said to be the youngest ever to represent a major power in Washington (ibid.), attended major international conferences including Dumbarton Oaks, Yalta, and Potsdam.

As Molotov's successor at San Francisco, Gromyko brought proceedings to a halt on 27 May 45 by insisting that the UN Security Council, dominated by the veto, could decide even whether a dispute could be discussed (Buchanan, 502). This heralded troubles to come in the UN, where "Grim Grom" was chief permanent Soviet delegate 1946-48. The next year he returned to Moscow as first deputy foreign minister. Serving until June 52, he was ambassador to London until Apr 53. Recalled, he resumed his former post and then moved up in Feb 57 to be foreign minister. In the Politburo 1973-88 and first deputy chairman of the Council of Ministers 1983-85, Gromyko nominated his protégé Mikhail Gorbachev for the post of General Secretary in Mar 85. Four months later Gorbachev made Gromyko President of the Presidium of the Supreme Soviet of the USSR, titular head of state. Retiring at his own request in Oct 88 he was succeeded by Gorbachev. Gromyko died the next year, his newspaper obituary appearing on 4 July 89.

GROVES, Leslie Richard. US general. 1896-1970. The director of the Manhattan Project was born 17 Aug 96 in Albany, NY, four months before his father, a Presbyterian minister, became an army chaplain. Dick, as he was called before army intimates nicknamed him "Goo Goo" (personal knowledge), was "a tall, serious boy, always studying and helping his family" (Groueff, 107). He attended the Univ of Washington and MIT before graduating from West Point near the top of the wartime (early graduation) Class of 1 Nov 18 (4/227). After serving on the WDGS 1939-40 and in the construction division of the QMG (which passed to the Chief of Engineers) 1940-42 the big, paunchy colonel was pushing completion of the Pentagon Building when appointed head of the "Special Weapons Project." The Manhattan Engineer District was created on 16 Aug 42 and Brig Gen Groves became its chief a month later. Gruff, considered extremely unpleasant by many academic types, he "confidently and serenely (Groueff, 107)" directed "the greatest single project ever attempted by man; the vast construction jobs alone were the equivalent of the construction of a Panama Canal each year for three consecutive years" (AA, 868). One of his major acts was to disregard the opinions of senior scientist and brush aside FBI security objectons and to make OPPENHEIMER head of the scientific team at Los Alamos.

He was promoted to major general on 26 Feb 44 and to lieutenant general on 24 Jan 48. With only the LM and DSM (and just one of each) to show for his service, he retired quickly (29 Feb 48) and was VP of Remington Rand, Inc, until 1961. Then publishing *Now It Can Be Told* (New York: Harper, 1962), president of the USMA Assn of Grads (1961-65), he died 13 July 70 in Washington, DC.

See Stephane Groueff, *Manhattan Project: The Untold Story of the Making of the Atomic Bomb* (Boston and Toronto: Little, Brown, 1967).

GUDERIAN, Heinz Wilhelm. German general. 1888-1954. The creator and foremost leader of panzer forces was born 17 June 88 at Kulm (Chelmno). His father, whose widowed mother had had to sell the family estate in the Warthegauhad, was subsequently on duty in Alsace at Colmar (1891-1900) and at St Avold in Lorraine before Heinz and his younger brother decided to become army officers. Heinz was commissioned in the Jaegers in 1908, became a communications specialist, and on 28 Feb 18 was appointed to the **GGGS**. A short, serious infantry officer of exceptional courage and professional dedication, he gravitated from

the **Freikorps** and the Frontier Defense units into motorized formations from which the panzers evolved. Guderian saw the future of mechanized warfare as written about by Basil Liddell Hart, J. F. C. Fuller, and a few others. "Since nobody else busied himself with this material, I was soon by way of being an expert" (*Guderian,* 20).

Promoted to colonel in 1933, he became CofS of the Motorized Troops Command Staff set up in the spring of 1934, and on 15 Oct 35 he took over one of the first three panzer divisions formed, the 2d Pz Div at Wuertzburg. Guderian was a colonel for almost another 10 months, whereas the 1st Pz Div at Weimar was under Gen of Cav von WEICHS and the 3d Pz Div at Berlin was under one Generalleutnant Ernst Fessmann. Promoted on 1 Aug 36, Generalmajor Guderian remained with the division until 4 Feb 38, three days after moving up again in rank (B&O, 70-71). On that historic date, when it was announced that HITLER was succeeding the ousted War Minister BLOMBERG, newly promoted Generalleutnant Guderian moved up on short notice to head the 16th Corps Hq for the **Anschluss** (Guderian, 50). As part of the corps, and without time for proper planning, the 2d Pz Div made a bad showing. With 420 miles to cover from their home station to Vienna (ibid.), having to improvise mobile supply columns and commandeer fuel from civilian sources, as many as 70 per cent of the vehicles broke down on the way to Vienna. This confirmed the doubts of conventional military thinkers. But Hitler created a special post for Guderian as Chief of Mobile Troops, with the new rank General of Panzer Troops (20 Nov 38) and direct access to the fuehrer.

In the attack on Poland that began on 1 Sep 39, Guderian's 19th Pz Corps sliced through the Polish Corridor to win a remarkable victory near his birthplace. (Hitler came forward to congratulate GEYR on the spot.) Guderian then moved through East Prussia to execute a strategic envelopment that astounded the world.

Although he was with the majority of German generals in opposing Hitler's plans to attack the west, Guderian spearheaded the drive through France as commander of an armored corps in Kleist's Pz Gp. Overcoming objections of old-school superiors, and already known as a "difficult subordinate," Guderian crossed the Meuse near Sedan without waiting for the support of infantry armies. Moving on westward, insisting (as PATTON would do later) that speed provided all the necessary flank security, Guderian clashed with Kleist on 17 May 40 and threatened to resign. LIST came forward to reconcile the dispute, and Guderian forged on to reach the English Channel at Abbeville on 21 May 40. OKH intervened to withheld part of his forces, but he turned north with the rest. Despite heavy losses to date, and against stiffening resistance, his panzers took Boulogne on 23 May and entered Calais four days later.

Guderian then served under LIST for the final operations in France. His panzers spearheaded the advance, wheeling SE to reach the Swiss border near Pontarlier on 17 June and made a 90 degree turn NE on a broad front to make contact with Dollmann's 7th Army, which was coming west through Alsace. (Guderian, 132.) This ended French resistance.

Pz Gp Guderian was dissolved in early July, the staff going to Paris. In the mass promotions of 19 July 40 he attained what proved to be his highest rank, Generaloberst.

For the attack on Russia, 22 June 41, the panzer leader headed the 2d Pz Gp in Bock's AG Center. Cooperating with Hoth's 3d Pz Gp he made the great envelopments around Minsk and Smolensk. Having been awarded the RK on 27 Oct 39 for action in Poland, he was given the Oakleaves on 10 July 41 (Angolia, II, 38). After HITLER interrupted the drive on Moscow, Guderian wheeled south on 19 July into the Ukraine for the encirclement of Kiev.

The panzer leader returned to AG Center, where on 30 Sep 41 he resumed the advance on Moscow. His group redesignated the 2d Pz Army on 5 October, Guderian bypassed strongly defended Tula to attempt a strategic envelopment of Moscow from the SE. But the Soviets gained strength as the German offensive lost momentum and the Russian winter set in. More alarming, the remarkable **T-34** tank appeared in large numbers. Guderian made limited withdrawals to better defensive ground, then flew to see Hitler in East Prussia. A five-hour conference on 20 Dec 41 failed to sway the fuehrer from his senseless no-retrograde policy. Six days later the "difficult subordinate" was sacked after clashing with KLUGE, the new AG Center commander.

On 1 Mar 43, after the German defeats at El Alamein and Stalingrad, he was recalled and made IG of Armored Troops. Decimated and weary panzer forces needed rebuilding, and although only recently recovered from a serious heart attack, Guderian undertook the task with enthusiasm. Despite some disagreements, he and Hitler got along well. Goebbels wrote in his diary on 27 July 43: "He certainly is an ardent and unquestioning disciple of the Fuehrer" (Lochner, 415). But German reverses continued in the east, another climax coming in Operation Citadel, starting 5 July 43. Attempting to eliminate the Kursk salient, the Germans lost what has been called the greatest tank battle in history. The Soviet juggernaut rolled on toward Germany, destroying AG Center, and then the long-awaited Allied second front opened in Normandy on 6 June 44.

On 21 July 44, the day after STAUFFEN-BERG's assassination attempt, Guderian succeeded ZEITZLER as CGS. "That appointment shocked many of the members of the General Staff, who regarded Guderian as a one-sided enthusiast for his specialty and a 'bull' on the battlefield, lacking the strategic sense and balanced view required" in his new position (Liddell Hart, *Talk,* 60).

As a harsh critic of the conspirators, Guderian promptly ordered the resignation of any officer who was unwilling to give wholehearted support to National Socialism. On Hitler's orders, Guderian sat with Rundstedt and Keitel on the Army Court of Honor that expelled hundreds of officers merely on suspicion of involvement in the conspiracy. This removed the accused from court martial jurisdiction, turning them over to the People's Court headed by FREISLER.

Although he had to compromise many of his military principles, the new CGS showed moral courage in standing up to Hitler on many occasions. There were several notable donnybrooks, but Guderian lacked the temperament to be effective and the men finally were at loggerheads. The final break came on 28 Mar 45, when Hitler sent Guderian on what was supposed to be six weeks' sick leave while Hans KREBS stood in as CGS. But in six weeks Hitler and the Third Reich were dead.

Guderian resumed his post as IG of Armored Troops on 1 May 45, his staff having taken refuge in the Tyrol. The general was a POW of the Americans from 10 May 45 to 17 June 48, his 60th birthday. During the first two years of captivity he was threatened with extradition to Poland on flimsy charges of war crimes. Retiring with his devoted wife to a small house at Schwangau bei Fuessen, he died there on 17 May 54 after writing his splendid memoirs.

The English translation is *Panzer Leader* (New York: Dutton, 1954).

GUILLAUME, Augustin. French general. 1895-. Born 30 July 95 at Guillestre (Hautes-Alpes), a doctor's son, he graduated from St Cyr in 1914. He was a POW through most WWI, after which he served briefly on the Allied staff in southern Russia before joining the bureau of native affairs in Morocco. After being assistant MA in Belgrade (1922-24), he was at the Ecole de Guerre (1926-28) before serving another eight years in Morocco. In 1936 he joined the staff of the Higher War Council in Paris but returned to Morocco when France declared war on 3 Sep 39. After the Franco-German armistice of 25 June 40 Guillaume was director of political affairs in Morocco. His office at Rabat and having the blessing of NOGUES and JUIN he directed the clandestine formation of colonial troops, particularly the redoubtable mountain fighters called **goumiers.** Promoted to brigadier general in 1943 Guillaume led goumiers in GIRAUD's liberation of Corsica, in the Italian campaign through the capture of Rome on 4 June 44, and in southern France, where he had a major role capturing the stoutly defended port of Marseilles. With de LATTRE's 1st French Army Guillaume commanded the 3d (Algerian) Inf Div, which fought through Alsace, across the Rhine, and on to Stuttgart and Pforzheim.

In Aug 45 he began a two-year MA assignment in Moscow. Based on that experience, which included visits to battlefields, he became an authority on the Red Army and published two highly acclaimed books on Russia's role in the war. In Mar 48 he was assigned as CinC, French Occupation Force in Germany; in early 1951 he doubled as CinC, Allied Land Forces, Central Europe, before JUIN took command. Guillaume was resident general in Morocco 1951-54, then CGS and president of the Chiefs of Staff Committee in Paris until 1956, having reached the rank of full general.

He contributed a chapter and long biographical note to *The Red Army,* edited by LIDDELL HART (New York: Harcourt, Brace, 1956).

GUINGAND, British general.
See DE/GUINGAND.

GUISAN, Henri. Swiss general. 1874-1960. Only the fourth Swiss ever to hold the rank of general, Guisan was born at Mézières, near Lausanne. He was a captain in the national militia from 1904 and in the first world war was an observer on the western front and in the Vosges. From his promotion to *colonel divisionnaire* in 1926 Guisan devoted himself exclusively to military affairs. On 30 Aug 39, two days before Hitler invaded Poland, he was elected general and CinC of the Swiss Army. By the summer of 1940 he had a force of more than 800,000 men and women. The Swiss already had an abundance of secret installations in the Alps, but Guisan developed the national redoubt concept. To support this, extensive preparations were made in the most rugged area of SE Switzerland.

Unlike his overly cautious predecessor, Ulrich Wille, in 1914-18, Henri Guisan was not afraid to run risks in being more neutral toward Germany than toward her enemies. So, while careful to preserve deniability, the Swiss army chief went along with establishment of what evolved into the spy ring headed by Rusolf ROSSELER (aka Lucy).

He also negotiated the secret Guisan-Gamelin military convention. This provided for Franco-Swiss military coordination on their flanks. Records of this incriminating deed were found with abandoned French military archives in a train at Charité-sur-Loire (19 June 40), and Swiss security chief MASSON learned that SCHELLENBERG had the documents filed under "Switzerland." Their release to the public would be an excuse for "preventive occupation" by Germany (Schellenberg, 376). This remained a sword over Guisan's head (A&Q, 177-79).

Exceptionally vigorous for a man who was 71 years old in 1945, sleeping no more than five hours a night, Guisan was highly acclaimed by Swiss crowds in his extensive travels. Army headquarters initially were in Berne, so as to be near the Federal Palace. But, unlike Ulrich Wille (above), who had stayed there, Guisan had his headquarters, successively, at Speiz, Gumligen, Interlaken, and finally at Jegenstorf. (A&Q, 55.) He published *Rapport à l'Assemblée sur le service actif,* then retired in 1947. Guisan died in Pully, near Lausanne. (Larousse.)

H

HAAKON VII. Christian Frederick Carl Georg Waldman Axel of Slesvig-Holstein-Sonderburg-Gluecksburg. 1872-1957. Born Prince Charles of Denmark on 3 Aug 72, he was a brother of Denmark's King Christian X. After Norway became independent from Sweden in 1905 Charles was elected as King Haakon VII.

He refused German demands to name QUIS-LING prime minister after German forces under FALKENHORST invaded Norway on 8 Apr 40. As Norwegian troops under FLEISCHER and RUGE continued resistance, Haakon trekked north with his government to link up with the Anglo-French relief effort. On 29 Apr 40 his party left Andalsnes on a British cruiser and established a provisional capital at Tromso (100 mi N of Narvik). When Lord CORK's Allied expedition withdrew, Haakon, his family, and most of the government were taken to London, arriving on 10 June 40. After heading one of the most effective governments in exile, the king entered Oslo harbor on 7 June 45 to popular acclaim.

HACHA, Emil. Czech statesman. 1872-1945. A former high court judge without political experience, he succeeded BENES as president of Czechoslovakia on 30 Nov 38. As Hitler moved to take over the country, which was being split by Ruthenian and Slovakian autonomists (the latter under Joseph TISO), he summoned Dr Hacha to Berlin. In a well-staged encounter beginning at 1 AM on 15 Mar 39 the fuehrer said German troops would march at dawn and occupy Prague by 9 AM. The Czechs were given the choice of resisting and having the country "trodden underfoot," or accepting the occupation peacefully and having some autonomy. (W-B, *Munich,* 344.) Hitler signed the prepared documents and left at 2 AM, whereupon Goering and Ribbentrop "hunted the unfortunate Czechs around the table, thrusting pens into their hands and the documents in front of them," writes Wheeler-Bennett (ibid.). The elderly and ailing Dr Hacha resisted for several hours, kept going only by injections from "a physician in waiting," before resigning himself,

"with death in his soul, to give his signature" (ibid., 345). Dr Hacha continued as nominal head of what had become the Protectorate of Bohemia and Moravia. He consistently supported the German occupation and urged his countrymen not to offend their masters. Two weeks after being arrested as a collaborator he died in a Prague prison on 1 June 45.

HAILE SELASSIE. Emperor of Abyssinia. 1892-1975. Born Tafiri Makonnen in Harar with royal connections, he lived in the palace as a child and became regent in 1916. He got control of the government and was crowned king in 1930. The Italian conquest started in 1935, the diminutive emperor fled to Britain in 1936, and on 30 June of that year appeared before the League of Nations. "It is us today," he said in a futile appeal for help. "It will be you tomorrow."

In June 40 the emperor went to Khartoum in the Sudan, where PLATT was preparing a counteroffensive against the Duke of AOSTA. Collaborating with Orde WINGATE, and rallying support en route, the emperor moved through western Abyssinia to meet British columns coming from Eritrea and Kenya. The emperor reentered Addis Ababa on 4 May 41, exactly five years after the capital had surrendered. The Lion of Judah, King of Kings, was deposed on 12 Sep 74 by Marxist-oriented army officers of the foreign-educated elite he had reared. Haile Selassi died in Addis Ababa the next year, having reigned 50 years, longer than any other modern monarch.

HAISLIP, Wade Hampton. US general. 1889-1971. "Ham" Haislip was a Virginian. Born 9 July 89, he graduated from West Point in 1912 (37/95) as an infantryman. Haislip saw action in France with the AEF and rose to the rank of lieutenant colonel in 1918. He attended the French War College, an experience which was valuable in working later with LECLERC (following). Haislip was on the WDGS from 1940 (Cullum), and as a brigadier general became G1 (personnel and administration) on 19 Feb 41 (*AA,* 57). Promoted a few weeks after the attack on Pearl

Harbor (7 Dec 41), Maj Gen Haislip left Washington after exactly a year as G1. On 15 May 42 he assumed command of the newly activated 85th Div at Camp Shelby, Miss. The 85th and 88th Div were the first US divisions formed primarily of draftees, and both friend and foe were anxious to see whether America's "civilians in uniform" would measure up. They did, to the distress of veteran German commanders in Italy (1944-45).

Ham Haislip moved up to head the 15th Corps Hq when it was activated 13 Feb 43, going overseas on 14 Dec 43 to join Patton's 3d Army in England. Because of his French War College background, Haislip was assigned Jacques LECLERC's 2d French Armd Div as a component of his corps.

Maj Gen Haislip led the 15th Corps from Normandy, being heavily engaged around Falaise, and across France to Strasbourg; he then fought the Rhineland campaign and drove on across central Europe. Promoted to lieutenant general on 15 Apr 45, Haislip got his fourth star in 1949 as US Army vice CofS. The general retired in 1951 to become governor of the Soldiers Home in Washington, DC, until 1966. He died 23 Dec 71 in Washington.

HALDER, Franz. German general. 1884-1972. The German army's first true chief of staff since 1918 was a Bavarian, born 30 June 84 at Wuerzburg. His family was devoutly Protestant (Deutsch, II, 31) with a strong military tradition. An outstanding military cadet, he was commissioned in the Royal Bavarian Field Artillery in 1904. After teaching at the Bavarian Army Staff College in Munich, 1911-14, Halder served throughout WWI as staff officer at various command levels to include the army group headquarters of Crown Prince Rupprecht of Bavaria. The experience gave Halder an aversion to positional warfare—a conviction that "operations demand movement." Rising to the rank of major, he also was known as a training expert.

Despite a colorless, somewhat pedantic nature and lack of front line command experience Halder was retained in the postwar Reichswehr and advanced rapidly. He served in the **Truppenamt** 1926-31, rising to colonel.

The Bavarian then was CofS of Wehrkreis VI (in Muenster) and was promoted to Generalmajor in 1934. The next year he took over the 7th Inf Div with headquarters in Munich, one of his rare command assignments. Halder then directed the well publicized Wehrmacht maneuvers of 1937 that showed off Germany's restored military might. Promoted and returned to Berlin, Generalleutnant Halder became Ob II (training) in Oct 37 and Ob I (operations) in Feb 38.

The German army's chief of the general staff (CGS), Ludwig BECK, resigned 18 Aug 38 despite Halder's urging him to stay on and continue opposing Hitler's rush to war. But at the urging of the army CinC, BRAUCHITSCH, and with Beck's approval, Halder somewhat reluctantly accepted appointment as CGS on 1 Sep 38. He was the first Bavarian ever to hold this office, with the exception technically of Gen Wilhelm Adam, who had been chief of the **Truppenamt.** The false assumption has prevailed that Halder was also the first Catholic to be CGGGS. Prof Deutsch, cited earlier, leaves no doubt that he was a devout Protestant.

The owlish, professorial general, with assistance from the more able JODL, came to be regarded as the brains behind the army in planning, directing, and administering rapid expansion to meet Hitler's war aims. In addition to being Brauchitsch's advisor and the officer responsible for executing that officer's decisions as the German army's CINC, Halder had a full plate as CGS, being responsible for the selection, education, training and assignment of GGS officers. Halder was guardian of the unique military institution's tradition, prestige, and effective functioning under a chief of state whose attitude toward the group evolved from dislike to violent contempt. "Halder understood this struggle and carried the guild spirit forward with vigor and cunning." (Charles Burdick and Hans Adolf Jacobsen, eds, *Halder War Diary,* 2.)

Generaloberst Halder (as of 19 July 40—but not promoted further—was in basic accord with Hitler's military leadership in Poland and France, and he worked with Brauchitsch in professional harmony. But crisis loomed when Barbarossa bogged down in the early Russian winter of Dec 41 and Hitler ordered a wholesale purge of the high command. After the fuehrer sacked BRAUCHITSCH on 19 Dec 41 and personally assumed command of the German army, Halder was ready to resign. But having earlier urged Beck to stay on (above) the CGS stayed on to do what he could to minimize Hitler's baneful influence (Goerlitz, *GGS,* 406).

Nine months later, in the fall of 1942, the next command crisis centered around the fuehrer's irrational determination to relieve LIST as commander of armies being hard pressed in the Caucasus. This came to a head on 7 Sep 42, when Hitler violently chastised JODL for defending List. Hitler dismissed Halder on 24 Sep 42 and replaced him with Generalleutnant Kurt ZEITZLER. Exhausted from years of diligent service under a psychopath, he was retired as a colonel general.

On succeeding Beck in 1938 Halder had promised to support the anti-Hitler conspiracy. Although he did not keep the promise, Halder told an American historian after the war that for three years he carried a pistol to meetings at the Reich Chancellery with the idea of assassinating Hitler, but that as "a human being and a Christian" he could not do it (Deutsch, II, 197 and n).

In retirement the general lived in Berlin before moving to his home in Aschau, Bavaria. He was arrested three days after STAUFFENBERG's 20 July 44 assassination attempt, although not involved. Held in Dachau initially, he spent several months in a lightless Gestapo cell in Berlin before being sent to Flossenburg, where he passed CANARIS a message to keep his chin up (Deutsch, II, 33 and n). Having showed strong nerves throughout his ordeal (ibid.), Halder was liberated by US troops on 4 May 45 with the **Niederdorf Group.**

"Those who attempt to describe Halder seem at a loss for colorful ways to denote absence of color," writes Deutsch, who interviewed the general after the war. "Certainly Halder could be lively enough, was easily aroused to vehemence, and was anything but phlegmatic." (Op. cit., 32.) Manstein comments that "He was incorruptibly objective in his utterances, and I myself have known him [to] put a criticism to Hitler with the utmost frankness." (*Lost Victories*, 79-80.)

Halder entrusted his war diaries to a neighbor in Aschau—Frau Else Schnell—after being warned of his impending arrest (above). Frau Schnell buried them in her garden before moving them to her storehouse where US authorities found them. My main bibliography gives the complex publication data on this valuable and oft-cited work. An English language abridgement is *The Halder War Diary, 1939-42* [Novato, Calif: Presidio, 1988].) Halder also wrote *Hitler as Warlord* (London, 1950).

The last true chief of the Great German General Staff died 2 Apr 72 in Aschau, Bavaria.

HALIFAX, Edward Frederick Lindley Wood, 1st Earl of. British statesman. 1881-1959. Edward Wood was born 16 Apr 81 at Powderham Castle, home of his maternal grandfather, Lord Devon. An atrophied left arm, which had no hand, never bothered the boy: his Anglo-Catholic faith and upbringing precluded self-pity *(DNB)*; the exceptionally tall youth rode to the hounds, shot, and enjoyed the traditional life of landed gentry. Three elder brothers died before Wood was nine years old, leaving him heir to the title and great estates in Yorkshire. Educated at Eton and Christ Church, Oxford, he took a first class in modern history and won a fellowship to teach at All Souls. Elected to Parliament in 1910 as a conservative, he held the seat until succeeding his father in 1934 as Viscount (Lord) Halifax. The high offices he held before WWII were viceroy of India (1925-31), war secretary (1935), lord privy seal and leader of the House of Lords (1935-37). When Neville Chamberlain became prime minister on 28 May 37, Halifax was made lord president of the council. This provided him leisure to assist the overburdened Foreign Minister Anthony Eden.

Toward the end of 1937 Halifax was invited to visit a hunting exhibit in Berlin and spend a few days "*shooting* foxes" (*sic*) in Saxony. The invitation was addressed to him as master of the Middletown hounds. Although the extremely tall, reedy, saintly-looking Lord Halifax was reputed to share Chamberlain's conciliatory attitude toward the European dictators, and although he was fascinated to learn of the Teutonic sport of shooting foxes, he accepted (he says) only because Eden thought some (undefined) advantage might accrue. (Halifax, 185.) Nothing came of meetings with Hitler, Goering, and Goebbels, 19-21 Nov 37, and Halifax makes no mention in his memoirs of going hunting. But the theory arose that the decision to accept the invitation was "made by a Prime Minister [Chamberlain], bent on appeasement, against the wishes and advice of a robust Foreign Secretary, Anthony Eden" (Halifax, 186).

But EDEN resigned as foreign secretary on 20 Feb 38, and Chamberlain gave the post to Halifax. Because Chamberlain manfully took responsibility for the failed negotiations that ensued, Halifax survived as foreign minister and was generally believed to be in line for the premiership. When that post went to Churchill on 10 May 40, Halifax remained foreign secretary until Eden returned to that post in Dec 40.

Halifax succeeded Lord Lothian (Philip Henry Kerr) as ambassador to Washington, remaining until May 46. "Halifax had a unique gift," writes A. J. P. Taylor: "he was always at the centre of [unfortunate] events, yet managed somehow to leave the impression that he was not connected with them" (*Origins,* 137). "Even the habitual ambiguity of his speeches might be . . . a form of verbal insurance against the unexpected," writes another authority in *DNB*.

On retirement to private life, Halifax had many additional honors and enjoyed his dress-up roles as chancellor of the Order of the Garter and grand master of the Order of St Michael and St George. Lord Halifax's highly literate, enjoyable, but "gently evasive" memoirs *(DNB)*, are *Fullness of Days* (New York: Dodd, Mead, 1957).

HALSEY, William Frederick, Jr. US admiral. 1882-1959. "Bull" Halsey was born 30 Oct 82 in Elizabeth, NJ, son of a naval captain (USNA 1853). Appointed **at large,** young Halsey was in the Annapolis Class of 1904 (43/62). In WWI he commanded destroyer patrol forces in the Atlantic, winning the Navy Cross. Between the wars he was naval attaché in Germany, Norway, Denmark, and Sweden *(CB 42)*. At the age of 52 he qualified as a naval aviator (1935). After commanding CV *Saratoga* for two years, and the Pensacola Naval Air Station for a year, he took command of Carrier Division 2 in June 38 and began training air squadrons for the new CVs *Enterprise* and *Yorktown*. On 3 June 40 he was promoted to vice admiral.

When the Japanese hit Pearl Harbor on 7 Dec 41 Halsey had the good fortune of being at sea with his carriers. Under NIMITZ he then led various carrier task forces in the first strikes of the war. After a few months of sick leave in the States he returned in good health *(CB 42)* to rendezvous with CV *Hornet* on 13 Apr 42 and launch DOOLITTLE's raid on Tokyo.

A serious skin ailment requiring hospitalization in the States kept him out of action for two months until early Sep 42, during which time Raymond SPRUANCE commanded Halsey's task force in the Battle of Midway. Halsey was preparing to lead a new task force in the the South Pacific Area under GHORMLEY when he received orders on 18 October that he would replace Ghormley. Promptly promoted to admiral (26 Nov 42) and infusing a fighting spirit into

the naval operations of the Guadalcanal campaign he also commanded the 3d Fleet when it was created 15 Mar 43 from what had been the South Pacific Force. Doubling as COMSOPAC, Halsey came under MacArthur's **operational control** on 29 Mar 43. Establishing excellent rapport (Buchanan, 251 ff), the rough-and-ready, bushy-browed "Bull" Halsey, who gloried in being unconventional, was responsible for MacArthur's highly successful island-skipping strategy (ibid., 261).

Relieved as COMSOPAC on 14 June 44 Halsey moved his 3d Fleet to the Central Pacific, where Nimitz was continuing his island-to-island drive. On 13 Sep 44 Halsey recommended speeding things up by leapfrogging the Palaus, Yap, Morotai, and Mindanao and assigning the additional available resources to MacArthur's landings on Leyte. It was a little late, and Halsey's otherwise brilliant suggestion assumed incorrectly that Japanese air was no longer a problem—actually it was hidden in reserve. But historians credit him in being right about the Palaus: 1,950 Americans died in taking Peleliu, on the S tip of the islands. (Morison, XII, 13-14, 33.)

In the Leyte campaign Halsey had two missions: to support the landings that began on 22 Oct 44; and to find and destroy the main Japanese fleet. The controversial "Battle of Bull's Run" occurred when the aggressive Halsey was suckered away from his first mission. It came about like this: while KURITA and SHIMA led two striking forces against Kinkaid's 7th Fleet, which was covering the Leyte landings to the south, a carrier decoy force under OZAWA approached the Philippines from the north. With discretion as to which of his missions to give priority, Halsey churned north during the night of 24-25 October to engage Ozawa. Believing that Kurita no longer was a serious threat to Kinkaid, Halsey took along TF 34, which had been guarding San Bernadino Strait. (Hoyt, 271-75.) After receiving several desperate messages from Kinkaid (one of which never arrived), Halsey got a hornet from Pearl Harbor at 10 AM on 25 Oct 44. "Where is Task Force 34?" is what Nimitz drafted. Padded for secrecy, it came through as "Turkey trots to water. Where is Task Force 34? The world wonders." Both nonsense phrases should have been stripped off, but a tired communications man removed only the first. Halsey slammed down his cap in rage, but began to worry after getting a message three minutes later from Kinkaid: "My situation is critical. Fast battleships and support by air strike may be able [to] prevent enemy from destroying CVE's and entering Leyte."

Halsey ordered part of his fleet, including TF 34, to head back for Leyte (Hoyt, 285). Two hours later Kinkaid informed him that KURITA had retreated toward San Bernadino Strait. The crisis was over, but Halsey had been had. Perhaps "the whole world" had not wondered, but Churchill was one of many who criticized Halsey for his dangerous error. (WC, VI, 183-84.). However NIMITZ went on record to defend his aggressive subordinate.

The Bull supported MacArthur's invasion of Luzon in Jan 45, and his flagship, BB *Missouri,* was the site of the historic surrender ceremony on 2 Sep 45. Halsey turned his ships over to Spruance on 20 Sep 45 and, with a 3d Fleet reconstituted at Pearl Harbor, sailed home to a hero's welcome. He hauled down his flag on 22 Nov 45 as commander of the 3d Fleet, had special assignments in Washington, was promoted in Dec 45 to admiral of the fleet, and was relieved a year later at his own request. Retiring from active duty in April 47 to live in Pasadina, Calif, and being director of several corporations, he died 16 Aug 59.

HAMMERSTEIN-EQUORD, Kurt von. German general. 1878-1943. He was born in Hinrichshagen on 26 Sep 78. In the military politics of the pre-Hitler era Freiherr von Hammerstein was a protégé of SCHLEICHER. Because of this he was promoted in Sep 30 from head of the Truppenamt to command the Reichswehr (Chef der Heeresleitung); he took over from the elderly Wilhelm Heye and was succeeded in the **Truppenamt** by Wilhelm Adam. Brilliant and courageous but notoriously lazy and self-indulgent (W-B, *Nemesis,* 199 and n.), the square-faced, pleasant-looking Generaloberst von Hammerstein also was an outspoken anti-Nazi whom Hitler quite rightly considered dangerous politically. So the Reichswehr commander was retired 1 Feb 34 (after the BLOMBERG affair) as one of the many generals the Nazi hierarchy had tagged as "uncooperative." He was succeeded by FRITSCH, whom the Nazis craftily nominated to appease Old Guard generals

who wanted to keep out the ambitions, pro-Nazi REICHENAU.

When promptly recalled with other recently ousted generals for war service, the Freiherr immediately began conspiring against Hitler. "Had the Führer but come within his reach, there is little doubt but that *'Der rote General'*, 'The Man with Iron Nerves', would have dealt faithfully and adequately with him." (Ibid., 459.) After having a command in Silesia the general again was retired. He died 25 Apr 43 in Berlin, depriving the resistance of "one of their most valuable assets" (ibid.) The general's widow and daughter were arrested under the **kinship edicts,** held in Buchenwald, and liberated with the **Niederdorf group.**

HANFSTAENGL, Ernst Franz Sedgwick. German businessman. 1887-1975. A Harvard graduate (1909) who had an American mother, he was an acquaintance of Roosevelt's and a valuable Hitler crony during the critical years 1920-24 in Munich. The 6 foot 4 "Putzi," whose childhood nickname—kept for life—means "Little Fellow," was awarded in 1933, when Hitler came to power, with the nominal post of foreign press secretary for the Nazi Party. The jovial big fellow was a practical joker, an accomplished classical pianist and a Falstaffian character whom Hitler found good company, but to other Nazi hierarchs he was a lightweight and an offensive one. Once, at a crowded reception, he loudly called Goebbels a swine.

In what apparently was an elaborate practical joke, Putzi was given sealed orders from Hitler that he was to open only when aloft in a plane. He then found that he was to parachute into Spain to report on the performance of German troops, of whom he had been critical. The blacked-out plane flew in circles to simulate the flight over the Pyrenees, landing periodically to refuel. On one of these stops Putzi made a successful break for a train station (which was in Germany) and kept going until he reached England. Despite a jocular letter from Goering on 19 Apr 37 that "We [only] wanted to give you an opportunity of thinking over some rather overaudacious utterances you have made" (Snyder, *Ency of 3d Reich,* 137), Hanfstaengl was not willing to take Goering's word of honor that he would be safe in the Third Reich.

With his son Egon, a US Army sergeant, Putzi was later held incognito at "Bush Hill," Va, an isolated country estate on 500 acres near Washington, DC. The White House and psychological warfare specialists used "Hitler's piano player" as a sounding board for how their plans would play to Hitler and his inner circle. Hanfstaengl remained interned briefly after the war before returning home. A disagreeable egotist to at least one American historian who interviewed him often after the war (HCD), he published his memoirs as *Hitler: The Missing Years* (London: Eyre & Spottiswoode, 1957); *Unheard Witness,* (Philadelphia and New York: Lippincot, 1957); and *Zwischen Weissem und Braunem Haus* (Munich, R. Pieper, 1970).

Putzi Hanfstaengl died 6 Nov 75 in Munich.

HARDING, John H. British general. 1896-1989. "That little tiger," as Montgomery came to call his former Camberley student, has been characterized as "a shrewd and exceptionally clear-thinking strategist, who played an important role in planning the campaigns of North Africa and Italy" (Tunney). In the winter of 1940-41 Harding was the brilliant little O'CONNOR's **BGS** and one of what O'Connor fondly called his "race of dwarfs in the desert." (Like so many great men, O'Connor was very small—almost birdlike.) The BGS planned the daring initial stroke that shattered the Italians around Sidi Barrani and pushed GRAZIANI back to Benghazi. When Rommel launched his shattering counteroffensive, Harding was partly responsible for the decision to hold Tobruk, creating a "flanking position" on the Axis LofC so the Desert Fox had to end his first offensive at the Egyptian frontier on 30 May 41.

Brigadier Harding was Godwin-Austen's BGS in 13th Corps Hq for Auchinleck's offensive, 18 Nov-31 Dec 41 which relieved Tobruk and drove Rommel back to El Agheila.

In the spring of 1942 Auchinleck brought Harding to Cairo as his director of military training. When Montgomery arrived on 8 Aug 42 to command the 8th Army he asked Harding, now a major general and deputy CGS, to form an armor-heavy *corps de chasse* somewhat like Rommel's Afrika corps. Harding "hastily cobbled together" the armor-heavy 10th Corps Hq. This included the 7th Armd Div, of which Montgomery gave Harding command in the shake-up after the British victory of Alam Halfa, which ended 6 Sep 42.

Harding became Alexander's CofS, 15th AG, in Italy in Jan 44. Harding convinced his chief

to pause until his troops—the 5th US and 8th British Armies with their many national and colonial contingents—could mount a final, coordinated spring offensive. This resulted in the quick capture of Rome on 4 June 44. Mark CLARK robbed the Allies of a greater triumph, but the campaign won Alexander his field marshal's baton. Harding took command of the 13th Corps in mid-Dec 44 when ALEXANDER was reassigned as SACMED.

Field Marshal Sir John Harding headed Allied occupation forces in Venezia Giulia with headquarters in troubled Trieste. Sir John (later Lord) Harding went on to hold other high positions including **CIGS**, 1952-56. He died 20 Jan 89.

HARMON, Ernest Nason. US general. 1894-1945. Born 26 Feb 94 in Lowell, Mass, he graduated from West Point in April 1917 (76/139) and in 1924 was on the US Olympic modern pentathlon team. From July 42 to Apr 43 he commanded the vaunted 2d Armd Div (which PATTON had made famous) and was promoted to major general on 9 Aug 42. But only elements of the 2d Armd fought in North Africa, Harmon being engaged in training his division while in strategic reserve. Harmon did not lead the division in Sicily nor in the first operations in France.

A major general from 2 Feb 43 (*AA*, 910), Harmon resumed command of the division in Sep 44 as it engaged in some of its toughest fighting. Relieving Maj Gen Edward H. Brooks and part of "Lightening Joe" Collins's VII Corps of the 1st Army, he continued to drive through the West Wall. The bitter winter offensive had reached the Huertgen Forest when halted by the Christmas crisis in the Ardennes. Spearheading COLLINS's movement some 75 miles SW over icy roads, Harmon hit the 2d SS Armd Div on its N flank around Celles to halt the 5th Pz Army's drive for the Meuse. Collins shifted his corps east some 30 miles to launch Harmon's 15 mile drive SE to Houffalize. Here he linked up with the 11 Armd Div of Middleton's 8th Corps, which was moving NE. On 29 Jan 45, the day Harmon assumed command of the 22d Corps in GEROW's new 15th (Reserve) Army, *Newsweek* called Harmon "probably the most profane, wisest, and sprightliest tank leader in the army" *(CB 46)*.

Although untrained in civil affairs, Harmon established the first Allied military government in Germany. His crowning achievement was a highly mobile, well-disciplined constabulary that was expanded to handle military security throughout the entire US occupation zone.

Ernie Harmon left Germany in 1947 and ended his army career on 29 Feb 48 as deputy CG, Army Ground Forces. After being president of Norwich College, 1950-65, he lived in Sarasota, Fla. The general died 13 Nov 79 at White River Junction, Vt. (Cullum).

HARMON, Millard Fillmore. US airman. 1888-1945. The son of a West Pointer appointed from Pennsylvania to the class of 1880, Harmon was born 19 Jan 88 in San Francisco and graduated from West Point in 1912 (74/95). Harmon got his wings as a pursuit pilot and served with the Punitive expedition to Mexico before flying with the French Squadron of the AEF in France (Cullum). When the Northwest Air District was redesignated the 2d AF on 9 Apr 41, Maj Gen Harmon headed it until 19 Dec 41 (AA, 593). He became USAAF CofS in Washington on 26 Jan 42 as plans were being completed for the Guadalcanal campaign.

Harmon reached New Caledonia on 26 July 42 as to command "US Army Forces in the South Pacific Area" as COMGENSOPAC (OCMH Chron, 45). On 2 Jan 43 he activated PATCH's 14th Corps on Guadalcanal. Promoted exactly a month later, Lt Gen Harmon was ordered by Halsey on 13 July 43 to take command on New Georgia, where operations under HESTER were behind schedule (OCMH Chron, 118). Harmon activated the US 13th AF Hq under TWINING at Espiritu Santo, New Hebrides, on 13 Jan 43, himself heading the formation 6 Jan-6 Jun 44 (AA, 597).

When US Army Forces Pacific Ocean Area were superseded on 1 Aug 44 by US Army Forces in the Central Pacific Area (under R. C. RICHARDSON), AAFPOA was activated under Harmon (OCMH, Chron, 241). This made him head of all USAAF units in the Pacific.

On 26 Feb 45 the general was declared missing and presumed lost on a flight to Hawaii.

HARPE, Josef. German general. 1887-1968. Born 21 Sep 87 at Recklinghausen in the former Prussian province of Westphalia (30 miles SW of Muenster), he was a "gallant and intelligent officer" (Brett-Smith, 250) who commanded large infantry and panzer formations in Russia. On his own merits—no favorite of Hitler's and not the typical hard-faced Prussian general—he rose from Generalmajor on 1 Aug 40 to General-

oberst on 20 Apr 44. He was awarded the Swords (36/159) on 15 Sep 43 (Angolia, I, 144).

Generalmajor Harpe began forming the 12th Pz Div in Stettin on 5 Oct 40 from Generalmajor Paul Bader's 2d Motorized Div. Harpe led his division in the great encirclements of Minsk and Smolensk, in July-Aug 41, before moving to the Leningrad front in Sep 41. The 12th Pz suffered heavy losses in LEEB's great strategic envelopment of Leningrad, and on 15 Jan 42 Harpe was promoted to Generalleutnant commanding the 41st Army Corps. (B&O, 46.)

On 7 July 42 "Pz Corps Harpe" was formed to keep remnants of the Soviet 39th Army troops of the Kalinin Front (NW of Moscow) from breaking out of their encirclement SE of Bely(i) (ibid.).

A month after winning the Swords (above) Harpe succeeded MODEL on 15 Oct 43 as CG, 9th Army, in the sector SE of Minsk. He was promoted on 20 Apr 44 to Generaloberst, and on 18 May 44 he took over the crack 4th Pz Army in Model's (formerly Manstein's) AG South. This had been redesignated AG Northern Ukraine when Harpe succeeded Model on 28 June. By 15 Sep 44, a month after his AG Northern Ukraine was redesignated AG A, Harpe was defending over more than 200 miles of front between from Radom, Poland, through the Carpathians into NE Hungary; from north to south he controlled the 1st Pz Army, the 17th Army and the 4th Pz Army (West Point Atlas, Map 43). Still refusing to authorize strategic withdrawals, Hitler replaced Harpe with one of his favorites, SCHOERNER, on 16 Jan 45.

Harpe was recalled on 9 Mar 45 to succeed Manteuffel on the western front as CG, 5th Pz Army. Soon encircled in the Ruhr pocket his army was destroyed by 18 Apr 45. He died 14 Mar 68 in Nuremberg.

HARRIMAN, (William) Averell. US diplomat. 1891-1986. He was born 15 Nov 91 in NYC, the elder of two sons of the "robber baron" financier and railroad tycoon, Edward Henry Harriman. Averell attended Groton, and entered Yale at the age of 17. His father died that year, leaving his two sons an estimated $100 million, which Averell augmented through a successful career in banking, shipping and other ventures. Brought to FDR's attention by Harry HOPKINS, Harriman held a succession of appointments from Jan 34 in negotiations between big business and big government. Harriman went to London as "defense expediter" *(CB 46)* shortly before the Lend Lease act passed on 11 Mar 41. He visited Moscow to coordinate the US aide that kept Russia in the war, and made a record-setting flight of almost 25,000 miles across the South Atlantic to Asia Minor on a survey of routes that the Ferrying Command would use for delivery of Lend Lease to the Soviets. (Copilot on the trip was Major Curtis LeMAY.)

As ambassador to Moscow from 1 Oct 43 to Feb 46, when he became ambassador to London, Harriman was a realistic advisor to FDR and the State Department on postwar relations with the USSR. George F. KENNAN became Harriman's minister-counselor in Moscow.

President Truman's secretary of commerce (1947-48) and governor of New York (1956-58), Harriman performed numerous special presidential missions for J. F. Kennedy, and Lyndon Johnson. Retiring from public life in 1969, he published *America and Russia in a Changing World* (1971).

HARRIS, Arthur Travers. British air marshal. 1892-1984. The capable, irascible "Bomber" Harris, a burly, reddish-haired airman known also as "Bert" and "Ginger," headed RAF Bomber Command for most of the war. He was born 13 Apr 92 at Cheltenham (S of Birmingham), son of an Indian civil servant. Young Harris left England at the age of 17 to farm in Rhodesia. Five years later, in 1914, he joined the 1st Rhodesian Regt as a bugler and saw action in SW Africa before returning to England in 1915 and joining the RFC. Qualifying the next year as a fighter pilot, Harris flew in France with No. 45 Sqdn. He also organized London's first anti-zeppelin defenses before taking command of No. 44 Sqdn in 1918 and training it for night fighting. A major by war's end, he was given the rank of squadron leader in the newly created RAF (1919) and sent to India. Serving next in Iraq and Iran, Sqdn Ldr Harris improvised bomb racks for heavy transport aircraft of his 45th Sqdn to attack Turkish armies and insurgent tribesmen in Iran (Andrews, *Air Marshals,* 48). He led No. 58 Sqdn 1925-27 *(DNB)* and was appointed to the OBE (ibid.).

Passing through the Army Staff College, he served on the air staff in the Middle East (1930-32), then commanded No. 210 (Flying Boat) Sqdn, being promoted to group captain in 1933.

As the RAF began to focus on war, the up-and-coming airman was deputy director of plans in the Air Ministry (1934-37). With army and navy associates he produced a remarkable planning document in the fall of 1936 that forecast accurately the start of war with Germany in 1939 and became the basis for British grand strategy in WWII (Andrews, 49). Promoted to air commodore in 1937 Harris took command of No. 4 (Bomb) Gp, became **AOC** Palestine and Transjordan in 1938, attained the rank of air vice marshal in 1939 and went to the US that year with a purchasing commission. The airman then commanded No. 5 (Bomb) Gp before returning to the Air Ministry in 1940 as Portal's deputy CAS. Here, from frustration over the RAF's failures at precision bombing—the main problem being lack of proper navigational equipment—Harris came to champion area bombing—very large formations dropping with incendiaries and high explosives, making up in terror for lack of accuracy.

Bomber Command (BC) was headed by PORTAL until Sir Richard PEIRSE took over on 25 Oct 40. It continued to suffer such exorbitant losses while inflicting insignificant damages that Churchill ordered a virtual ban on strategic missions. PORTAL, who had become CAS, sacked Peirse and replaced him with Harris on 22 Feb 42. An air marshal from 1941, Harris meanwhile had headed an RAF mission to the US and Canada to coordinate air strategy.

Continuing the saturation bombing in Europe but improving techniques and slowly overcoming technical shortcomings, Harris launched the first "1,000-bomber raid." This devastated 600 acres of Cologne the night of 30-31 May 42 and cost only 40 of the 1,046 RAF bombers engaged. The raid gave Bomber Harris's doubters second thoughts about his strategy and the BC chief was promptly knighted KCB in June. Sir Arthur soon worked out a program of around-the-clock strategic bombing with Ira EAKER's US 8th AF.

Harris inflicted large-scale death and destruction in Europe, the main objective being enemy morale, a concept pioneered by the German victims. PORTAL's suggestion to try some selective bombing was labeled "panacea mongering" by "the brilliant but self-governing Bomber Commander" (Andrews, 253 and n). But BC suffered a staggering loss of 57,143 killed, of whom 41,548 have no known grave (ibid.).

Harris has been faulted also for failure to target the German fighter force, leaving this principally to the USAAF (which concentrated on daylight operations), and in 1943 the RAF lost its night bomber supremacy because Luftwaffe night fighters had achieved superiority.

Leaving BC in Sep 45, Harris became a marshal of the RAF in 1946 and retired from active duty. He promptly published his war memoirs, *Bomber Command* (London: Collins, 1947). He refused a peerage *(DNB)* but in 1953 accepted a baronetcy (ibid.). Aggrieved that his achievements had not been properly appreciated *(DNB)* he went to live in South Africa.

HART, Thomas Charles. US admiral. 1877-1971. Hart was born in the small town of Davison, Michi., on 12 June 77. Second youngest member of the 1897 class at Annapolis (13/47), "Tommy" also was one of the smallest. He was superintendent at the USNA, 1931-34.

In June 39 Hart was made a full admiral and CINC of the little US Asiatic Fleet based at Cavite in the Philippines. Four days after the Japanese began landing on 10 Dec 41, Hart pulled out the few remaining patrol bombers and their three tenders, leaving MacArthur with little naval support. On 24 December, however, Hart released the 4th Marines, stationed at Olongapo, to defend the beaches of Corregidor. In accordance with a strategy worked out earlier with the British commander BROOKE-POPHAM, Hart moved to the NEI as naval commander in the short-lived ABDA command; he was succeeded by Dutch Adm Conrad Helfrich on 14 Feb 42. Eight months beyond retirement age, the starchy, irascible little admiral gave ill health as his reason for leaving a no-win situation.

Adm Hart retired 30 June 42 but was recalled to head the Naval Board for the rest of the war. He was elected US senator from Connecticut in 1945 and died 4 July 71 at Sharon, Conn.

HARTMANN, Erich Alfred. German pilot. 1922-95. "Bubi" (Boy) Hartmann scored more air victories than any other flyer in history. The ace of aces was born 19 Apr 22 in Weissach, Wurttemberg, son a physician and a pioneer aviatrix. In the fall of 1942 Leutnant Hartmann reported to the Luftwaffe's best fighter wing, Geschwader 52, in the Caucasus. Proceeding slowly and methodically to work out tactics, he did not hit stride until the summer of 1943. In the German tradition he rose in rank slowly, becoming a captain on 1 Sep 44 and a major on V-E day. The ME 109 pilot made his 352d confirmed kill, a Yak-11 over Brno, Czechoslo-vakia, only hours before the German surrender on 8 May 45. Never wounded in 30 months of combat the super-ace flew 1,425 combat missions, more than 800 engagements, was shot down 16 times and baled out twice. He attributed his success primarily to "an advantage with which I was born," incredibly good eyesight.

The US denied Hartmann POW status, under a Yalta agreement. "The Black Devil of the Ukraine" remained defiant and unbroken during 10 years of harsh treatment in the USSR.

Not for a year after repatriation did the **experte** reluctantly join the West German AF, and he proved to be a difficult subordinate. For one thing, the prison ordeal had not left him unscathed mentally, according to at least one American pilot who knew him after his release (personal information). For another thing, Major Hartmann irritated superiors by opposing procurement of the US F-104 jet, which he correctly predicted was too hot for new German pilots to handle. A high fatality rate confirmed his judgment.

Oberstleutnant Hartmann retired in 1968 to a Stuttgart suburb. His authorized biography by Raymond F. Toliver and Trevor J. Constable is *The Blond Knight of Germany* (New York: 1970).

HARTMANN, Walter. German general. 1891-. Born at Muelheim/Ruhr on 23 July 91, he enlisted in 1910. During WWI he was a gunner and staff officer. As commander of the 24th Arty Regt in 1939-4 he fought in Poland and France. On 10 Aug 41 Oberst Hartmann was awarded the RK as CO, 104th Arty Regt, chief of the 52d Corps Arty in Russia. After recovering from a serious wound he took over the 87th Inf Div with the rank of Generalleutnant and was awarded the Oakleaves (340/890) on 30 Nov 43. Again promoted, Gen of Arty Hartmann took command of the 8th Corps, 9th Army, and was awarded the Swords (139/159) on 18 Mar 45. (Angolia, I, 252; Seaton, *R-G War,* 536.) From 19 Apr 45 he headed the 24th Pz Corps (16th and 17th Pz Divs), which was driven into Silesia and disbanded on 8 May 45 (B&O, 39).

HARWOOD, Henry Harwood. British admiral. 1888-1950. The naval hero who destroyed the *Admiral Graf Spee* was born 19 Jan 88 in London, son of Surtees Harwood Harwood, a barrister. He joined the training ship *Britannia* in 1903 and was an outstanding student, and in examinations for lieutenant he won first class certificates in all subjects. Harwood became a torpedo specialist and was appointed to the OBE for service in WWI with the Grand Fleet but saw no action. Most of his duty between the wars was ashore with naval staffs and at service schools including the Imperial Defense College. But in 1936 he was appointed commodore in command of the South American division of the America [sic] and West Indies Station (DNB). The naturally genial commodore was a Roman Catholic who got on well with South Americans (ibid.).

At the outbreak of war in 1939 Harwood was sent reinforcements and alerted to watch for the German pocket battleship Admiral Graf Spee, a powerful commerce raider. Getting into his enemy's mind, Harwood found his prey early on 13 Dec 39 in the broad estuary of the Rio de la Plata, off the coast of Uruguay. Despite the odds Harwood ordered an immediate attack by cruisers Ajax (his flagship), Achilles and Exeter, closing in from different directions, as prearranged. The German captain, Hans LANGSDORFF, was surprised and confused by the speed and vigor of the unorthodox attack, which in about 20 minutes scored more than 20 damaging hits and inflicted almost 100 casualties including 37 killed. Stunned by a head blow, Langsdorff withdrew into the neutral port of Montevideo, Uruguay. As covered in more detail under LANGSDORFF, the outclassed German captain finally scuttled his ship in the shallow estuary (17 Dec 39) and committed suicide the night of 19-20 Dec 39 after being interned in Argentina.

The internationally famous Harwood was promoted to rear admiral immediately (by radio) and knighted (KCB). A year later Sir Henry became assistant chief of the naval staff in London, so impressing Churchill that in 1942 he was made CinC Mediterranean to succeed Sir Andrew Cunningham. "For a rear admiral to receive such a post was almost unknown in modern times," comments Russell Grenfell in DNB. Promoted to full admiral (T) Harwood was concerned primarily with covering the 8th Army's flank in North Africa and providing the logistic support needed to defeat Rommel. The hero of the Rio de la Plata was so aggressive that on several occasions his naval forces occupied an abandoned Axis port before British ground troops arrived (ibid.).

But ill health forced the admiral to leave the Mediterranean in early 1943. After being Flag Officer Commanding the Orkneys and Shetlands he was invalided out of the navy in 1945 with the rank of full admiral. He died 9 June 50 at his house at Goring-on-Thames.

HASHIMOTO, Kingoro. Japanese general. 1890-1957. A regular army officer and ultra-nationalist born in Okayama City, Lt Col Hashimoto and Capt Isamu Cho founded the **Cherry Society** in 1930. As a colonel from 1933 Hashimoto commanded an artillery regiment and had an attached squadron of naval aircraft when he ordered destruction of American and British gunboats *Panay* and *Ladybird* on the Yangtse in Dec 37. After figuring prominently in the rape of **Nanking** he retained command of his regiment until Mar 39.

Then retired, the colonel became executive director of KONOYE's Imperial Rule Assistance Association in 1940. For helping instigate the Pearl Harbor attack and remaining active in politics, Hashimoto was given a life sentence for war crimes. He was paroled two years before dying in 1957.

HASSELL, Ulrich von. German diplomat. 1881-1944. Born 12 Nov 81 at Anklam, Pomerania, into a noble family, he became a career diplomat and married the daughter of Grand Admiral von Tirpitz (1849-1930), founder of the German Imperial Navy. Hassell became a diplomat of the old school, rising to be ambassador to Copenhagen (1926-30), Belgrade, and Rome (1932-38). Although mildly sympathetic to Nazism, he was known in Rome as *Il Freno* (The Brake) for opposing much of Hitler's aggressive foreign policy (Deutsch, I, 262). In HITLER's purge of 4 Feb 38 Hassell was ousted along with Foreign Minister NEURATH. Quickly concluding that prospects for a coup d'état were dim, Hassell used the cover of lecturer and economics expert to support BECK and GOERDELER. On 27 Apr 42 Hassell was warned by Ernst von Weizaecker that he was under surveillance. Although not incriminated in the 20 July 44 assassination plot, Hassell and SCHULENBURG were listed by the conspirators as candidates for the foreign minister post. Arrested on 28 July, the diplomat was tried by the **People's Court** and hanged on 8 Sep 44 at Ploetzensee Prison.

To the good fortune of historians he kept a journal, which was found in his garden and published in 1948. His alluring daughter, Fey, published an enthralling and historically valuable war memoir in 1989. Publication data are in the main bibliography.

HAUSHOFER, Albrecht. German resistance figure. 1903-45. Son of Karl HAUSHOFER, Albrecht was born 7 Jan 03 in Munich. He worked with his famous father in the field of geopolitics and was professor of political geography at the Berlin School of Politics. Albrecht had a long association with Rudolf HESS. He published acclaimed works of historical drama including *Scipio* (1934) and *Sulla* (1938) and, despite having Jewish blood, Albrecht became head of the foreign office's information section.

But he developed close associations with the **Kreisau Circle,** the **Rote Kapelle,** Carl GOERDELER, and others of the anti-Nazi resistance. He also had high connections in Britain and probably inspired HESS's flight on 10 May 41. Thereafter under surveillance, Albrecht Haushofer was arrested in Dec 44 on suspicion of involvement in the conspiracy that culminated in STAUFFENBERG's 20 July 44 attempt on Hitler's life. While in the Berlin-Moabit prison he wrote a tribute to the German resistance, "Moabiter Sonette"; accidentally preserved, it was published. Albrecht Haushofer died in the **Invalidenstrasse massacre,** 22-23 Apr 45.

HAUSHOFER, Karl. German geopolitician. 1869-1946. The founder of geopolitics was born 27 Aug 69 in Munich, where from 1921 he was a professor of geography at the university. Until then he had been a career army officer, rising in to be a general in WWI. In part because his wife was half Jewish, Karl Haushofer never fully embraced Nazism and their son Albrecht (above) became a leading resistance figure. But geopolitics provided an important ideology for the Nazis. With Hitler's knowledge the Haushofers put out peace feelers to the British in 1939. Getting no response they encouraged Rudolf HESS to undertake his mad mission on 10 May 41. The professor was arrested after his son was implicated in the 20 July 44 attempt on Hitler's life. Albrecht's execution caused the father to commit suicide on 13 Mar 46.

HAUSSER, Paul. German SS general. 1880-1972. Unquestionably the best general in the Waffen-SS, whose first training programs he established, the foxy-looking Brandenberger was born 7 Oct 80. He was an officer in the war

of 1914-18, served in the Reichswehr, and retired in early 1932 as an acting General lieutnant. (Stein, 9.)

Hausser became regional leader of the **Stahlhelm** in Berlin-Brandenburg. Soon after Hitler incorporated this into the SA, at the end of 1933, Hausser joined the SS as head of its first officer academy. Promoted to SS Brigadefuehrer in 1936 and made Inspector of the SS Verfuegungstruppen, he was charged with creating what became the **Waffen-SS.**

Despite his advanced years "Papa" Hausser was a combat leader at the divisional, corps, field army, and army group level. Two months after being awarded the RK on 8 Aug 41 as commander of the SS Das Reich Div in AG North in Russia, he lost an eye. Now distinguished by a black eye patch, he saw more action in Russia, being presented with the Oakleaves (261/890) on 28 July 43 as leader of what became the 2d SS Pz Corps. Ordered to France with his headquarters Generaloberst Hausser was leading 2d SS Pz Corps forward to reinforce Friedrich DOLLMANN's 7th Army in Normandy when Dollmann committed suicide on 29 June 44. Without consulting Rommel, Hitler ordered Hausser to take over Dollmann's post, making Papa Hausser the first SS officer to command a German field army. Hausser then directed the desperate defenses of Normandy as commander of the 7th Army and Pz Gp West until a shell fragment removed part of his face during the battle of the Falaise Gap in mid-Aug 44. Replaced by Heinrich EBERBACH, Papa Hausser was evacuated on the back of a tank and awarded the Swords (90/159) on 26 Aug 44.

At war's the SS general headed AG G, whose right flank elements opposed Patton's drive to the Rhine between Coblenz and Mannheim. He died 21 Dec 72 in Landsburg at the age of 92.

HAUTECLOCQUE, Philippe de. LECLERC's nom de guerre.

HAW HAW, Lord. Nickname for William JOYCE.

HEIDRICH, Richard "Arno." German general. 1896-1947. Born 28 July 96, he saw action as an infantryman in WWI before serving in Lithuania with a Freikorps. Heidrich then joined the Reichswehr and in 1936 was in the first German parachute infantry company. By Jan 39

Maj Heidrich was on the staff of 7th Air Div Hq (Angolia, I, 160). He fought in the west, took command of the 3d Para Inf Regt, and on 14 June 41 was awarded the RK for action in Crete. Like other German airborne forces Col Heidrich's regiment was used thereafter as "straight-leg" infantry. For action around Leningrad he was promoted to Generalmajor and given command of the elite 1st Para Div in Italy. This unit distinguished itself in defending Cassino, particularly from the rubble created by the massive bombing of 12 Mar 44 (Smith, *Cassino,* 120 ff). Allied troops dubbed them "Green Devils" for the green color of their Luftwaffe uniforms.

Heidrich was promoted to Generalleutnant and awarded the Oakleaves (382/890) and Swords (55/159) on 5 Feb and 25 Mar 44. Continuing to move up, Gen of Parachute Troops Heidrich led the crack 1st Para Corps through the rest of the Italian campaign. He surrendered 3 May 45 (Angolia, I, 160) and died 22 Dec 47 at the age of 51.

HEINKEL, Ernest. German aircraft engineer. 1888-1958. The pioneering aircraft designer and principal rival of Wilhelm MESSERSCHMITT, Heinkel was a Wurttemberger, born 24 Jan 88 in Grunback. He studied mechanical engineering at Stuttgart's Technical Academy at a time when dirigibles were seen as the most promising means of air travel, but a Zeppelin disaster in 1908 convinced Heinkel otherwise (Wistrich). In WWI he was director of a factory that produced planes for the Austro-Hungarian army and the German navy.

During WWII he made a variety of float planes (principally the He 115); one of Germany's few strategic bombers, the He 177 ("Griffin"); and the world's first turbojet fighter, the He 280. Partly because Heinkel was an outspoken critic of Luftwaffe leadership he failed to get Messerschmitt's backing. His He 111, the Luftwaffe's standard level-bomber and a versatile plane, the five-place, twin-engine He 11H-6 medium bomber becoming a platform for launching V-1s. By the end of 1944 Heinkel's factories had 55,123 workers, of whom 30,455 were foreign (Wistrich).

Arrested after the war and his holdings confiscated, Heinkel was charged in 1948 with contributing to Germany's war effort. But on evidence that he had supported the anti-Hitler resis-

tance he was released. On 18 Jan 49 a de-Nazification court classified Heinkel as a Nazi "fellow traveler." Returning to aircraft construction in the 1950s he survived only by forming close bonds with the Messerschmitt-Bolkow-Blohn company, by whom he eventually was absorbed.

Publishing his memoirs, *Sturmisches Leben* (Stormy Life), in 1953, he died 30 Jan 58.

HEINRICI, Gotthard. German general. 1886-1971. "A small, precise man with a parsonical manner" (Liddell Hart, *Talk,* 178), he was one of the war's outstanding commanders of large field forces. He was an East Prussian born 25 Dec 86 at Gumbinnen, commissioned in 1906, and he served on both fronts in 1914-18. He was a Generalmajor from 1 Jan 36, a Generalleutnant on 1 Mar 38, and was promoted to General of Infantry as the assault on France was about to start. Commanding the 12th Corps in Witzleben's 1st Army, he broke through the Maginot Line south of Saarbrucken on 14 June 40 after the defenders began withdrawing on orders (ibid., 141).

As CG, 43d Corps, Heinrici was awarded the RK on 18 Sep 41 for action in Russia. The next month his two-division corps was assigned to Guderian's 2d Pz Army. Promoted 1 Jan 42, Generaloberst Heinrici commanded the 4th Army from 20 Jan 42 for more than two years in AG Center. He developed highly successful defensive tactics that featured patrolling to discover impending Red Army attacks, withdrawing front line troops some 2,000 meters to escape enemy preparatory fires, and then counterattacking to destroy the off-balance enemy with German forces that had remained intact.

On 16 Aug 44 he succeeded Erhard Raus as 1st Pz Army commander in the Carpathians, temporarily directing operations of the 1st Hungarian Army as well. Heinrici's skill in maintaining cohesion while withdrawing into Silesia won him the Swords (136/159), awarded 3 Mar 45. Heinrici succeeded Himmler as CG, AG Vistula, on 20 March (Guderian, 422). With the decimated 3d Pz and 9th Armies he held the Oder River line for almost a month until the Soviets broke through around Kustrin on 18 April.

Heinrici had no success with Hitler in advocating abandonment of Berlin and concentration on saving Germans, civilian and military, from Soviet captivity. But the general was able to collaborate with Albert SPEER in violating Hitler's scorched earth edict (Speer, *Reich,* 468). Heinrici was relieved of command late on 28 Apr 45 after informing Keitel he would disregard Hitler's orders to hold at all cost. Taken prisoner by US forces, he was interviewed by Liddell Hart and is cited at length in *The German Generals Talk.*

Generaloberst Heinrici died 13 Dec 71.

HENLEIN, Konrad. Sudeten German leader. 1898-1945. He was born 6 May 98 in Maffersdorf, Bohemia, to a German father and a Czech mother. In 1931 he became head of the German Gymnastic Union in Czechoslovakia, and in Oct 33 established the Sudetendeutsch Heimatfront. This succeeded his country's outlawed Nazi Party but operated in a way that gave authorities no grounds for questioning its loyalty. Two years later the Heimatfront became the Sudetendeutsche Partei (SDP) with Karl Hermann FRANK as deputy. Demanding autonomy for the Sudeten German minority within the Czech state, the SDP began receiving funds covertly from the Third Reich, and by 1937 it was openly pro-Nazi and anti-Semitic. The party became an effective **fifth column** but Henlein was no tool of Hitler's until they first met secretly on 28 Mar 38 after the **Anschluss.** (Schellenberg, 34.) The Czech quisling helped persuade the British to make concessions during the **Munich crisis.** After the Germans occupied the Sudetenland Henlein was Reich governor of the region. From 1 May 39 he headed the civil administration as Gauleiter in the Protectorate of Bohemia and Moravia, rising to SS Obergruppenfuehrer in June 43. But the tall, blond, athletic, bespectacled, somewhat pedantic Henlein was inconspicuous during the war because his deputy, Karl Hermann FRANK, wielded the real authority as the protectorate's secretary of state and succeeded HEYDRICH as acting protector after his death on 4 June 42.

Only days after being interned at Pilsen by US troops Henlein committed suicide on 10 May 45 by cutting his wrists with a razor blade he had concealed in a cigarette case. The traitor's apologia, written by a close associate, Walter Brand, is *Die Sudetendeutsche Tragoedie* (1949).

HERRING, Edmund Francis. Australian general. 1892-1982. A small, quiet, tough military leader, he had the diplomatic temperament needed when US and Australians were accusing each other of performing badly in New Guinea. Herring had commanded the Australian 6th Div, 1941-42, before becoming GOC Northern Territory Forces and CG, 2d Australian Corps. On 28 Sep 42 he replaced Lt Gen Sydney Rowell as head of New Guinea Force. "In one of the ironies so common in war, Rowell had hardly departed when the situation on the Kokoda Track took a dramatic turn for the better" (Mayo, *Bloody Buna,* 61). This was because HORII was withdrawing. On 29 Nov 42 Herring established Advanced New Guinea Force Hq and started directing US-Australian efforts against the Gona-Sanananda-Buna beachhead. Poor performance of US troops led a furious MacArthur to put EICHELBERGER in command of the American component on 1 Dec 43. The gruelling campaign ended on 13 Jan 43, and Eichelberger succeeded Herring as CG, Advanced New Guinea Force. The Aussie general then led the 1st Australian Corps in the capture of Lae, the Markham Valley, and in mopping up. By Mar 44 Sir Edmund was succeeded by Leslie MORSHEAD and saw no more action.

HERRIOT, Edouard. French statesman and writer. 1872-1957. Son of a captain of Zouaves, Herriot was born 5 July 72 at Troyes. From 1905 he was mayor of Lyons and from 1919 a radical-liberal in the Chamber of Deputies, president of that body 1936-40. Herriot was premier *(président du conseil)* on several occasions in the politically turbulent period 1924-32 (Larousse).

Remaining president of the Chamber and accommodating himself with the Vichy government, Herriot supported Marshal Pétain's appointment on 16 June 40 as head of the Vichy government but abstained from the vote on 10 July 40 that accorded full powers to old marshal. But after permanent bureaus of the Chamber and Senate were dissolved on 31 Aug 42, Herriot and Jules Jeanneney, president of the Senate, publicly denounced Pétain. The stout, square-faced Herriot then defied Vichy's authority in various ways—refusing to promise not to leave the country and returning his cross of the Legion of Honor after learning that French decorations were being given to members of the **LVF**

(Larousse). But in Apr 43 he went too far by publishing a letter announcing his support of de Gaulle. Vichy authorities placed M & Mme Herriot in house arrest at Bretel (ibid.), but the Germans later moved them to the east of France. Taken from Nancy to Paris on 12 Aug 44, as US forces approached from Normandy, Herriot refused Laval's invitation to form a transition government. (Laval wanted to "save Vichy.") Again arrested by the Germans, Herriot and his wife were moved from place until finally interned at Potsdam, where they were liberated by Red Army troops on 22 Apr 45. *(CB 46.)*

The politician and man of letters, almost 73 years old when repatriated via Moscow, resumed his two careers. He was reelected mayor of Lyons in May 45, elected to the French Academy (6 Dec 46), and was president of the National Assembly from 1947 until retiring from political life in 1954. Meanwhile he declined ministerial posts so as to have time for rebuilding the Radical Socialist Party. Among his many books are the autobiographical *Episodes 1940-1944* (1950) and *Jadis* (1948-52).

HERSHEY, Lewis Blaine. US Selective Service director. 1893-1977. The big, redheaded, easy-going Hoosier was born 12 Sep 93 on a farm near Angola, Indiana. He was a rural school superintendent while earning a BA in 1914, meanwhile joining the National Guard in 1911. Hershey served in Pershing's **Punitive Expedition,** then was an artillery officer in France. Rising to captain and involved in redeploying the AEF to the States in 1918, he got an RA commission and became a highly regarded military instructor and battery commander *(CB 41)*.

In 1936 Major Hershey was appointed secretary and XO to the Joint Army and Navy Selective Service Committee in Washington. The Selective Training and Service Act was signed on 16 Sep 40 with Col Hershey (a BG the next month) as deputy director from December and director from July 41.

Meanwhile the first local selective service boards were established in Oct 40, draft registration began, and a national lottery was set up for inductions into the **AUS.** Hershey's office eventually registered 40 million men *(S&S)*, and by the end of Oct 46 had sent "Greetings" to 10,110,104 draftees *(AA, 839-40)*.

Maj Gen Hershey (from 16 Apr 42) was reappointed director on 17 July 48, after a new draft act was approved on 24 June 48. Suffering through the anti-draft protests of the 1960s and appointed Selective Service chief in 1970, Hershey retired from the Army in 1973. Four years later he returned to Angola for a trustees meeting at his alma mater. A recent and grieving widower who recently had a stroke, the general and was put up in a motel. The morning of 20 May 77 he was found to have died in his sleep.

HESS, Rudolf Richard. Nazi leader. 1894-1987. The last prisoner of Spandau was born 26 Apr 94 in Alexandria, Egypt, son of a wealthy German merchant. On 20 Aug 14 he joined the 1st Bavarian Inf Regt as a volunteer and showed a reckless bravery (twice wounded). In the last weeks of the war he was an officer pilot in the 35th Ftr Sqdn.

Hess settled in Munich and entered the university to study history, economics, and geopolitics. But the ex-lieutenant, diverted by revolutionary activities, joined Freikorps Epp and in June 20 became Nazi party member number 16. One of Hitler's earliest adherents, involved in the **Munich Beer Hall Putsch** of 8-9 Nov 23, Hess was sentenced to 18 months in jail. He worked with Hitler on the first volume of *Mein Kampf,* contributing murky thoughts, turgid prose, and proofing the typescript that Hitler pecked out. (Hutton, *Hess,* 16.)

On release the pennyless revolutionary abandoned his university studies but in 1927 got a long-sought post as assistant to geopolitician Karl HAUSHOFER. After Gregor STRASSER's disaffection in Dec 32 Hess became head of the party's new Central Political Committee. Named deputy fuehrer in Apr 33, Reichsminister without portfolio by year's end, the beetle-browed crony was a member of the Ministerial Council for the Reich and the Secret Cabinet Council. Personal devotion had won Hess these posts, but Hitler realized by 1940 that his paladin was not qualified for what lay ahead. Personal traits that had been tolerated as quirkiness in the tall, dark, and mystical old party comrade now verged on true insanity, and for 20 years Hess had not been well physically.

On 10 May 41, the eve of Opn Barbarossa, the odd bird flew the coop. With the Haushofers's encouragement and a new Me 110 loaned by

Wilhelm MESSERSCHMITT, the disturbed deputy fuehrer went west. In a remarkable feat of navigation to Scotland he bailed out within 10 miles of his target, the estate of Lord Stewart, former Duke of Hamilton. At the Berlin Olympic Games in 1936 the duke had spoken to several prominent Germans (not including Hess) about reaching some modus vivendi. Hess apparently hoped His Lordship would arrange appropriate parlays with high British officials. "Hauptmann Horn," his right foot sprained, was collected by a ploughman and turned over to local authorities. The British, surprised and embarrassed, moved Hess through easy stages to the Tower of London while deciding what to do (WC, III, 50). An equally embarrassed Hitler said "Who will believe me when I say that Hess did not fly there in my name . . . ?" (Speer, *Reich,* 174-75), which is precisely what the Soviets pretended to believe.

The British kept Hess isolated under harsh prison conditions until sending him to Nuremberg on 6 Oct 45. The gaunt, mad-eyed Hess effectively pleaded amnesia but was ruled sufficiently sane to stand trial. The only one of the accused found guilty only of the first two counts of **war crimes**—specifically of actively supporting preparations for war and of willingly participating in the aggression against Austria, Czechoslovakia, and Poland.

As the last of the major war criminals imprisoned at Spandau, Hess was found dead on 17 Aug 87 at the age of 93. Allegedly he had slipped undetected into a shed of the prison's large garden yard and hanged himself with an electrical extension cord, something a sick old man would have needed supernatural powers to accomplish alone. Based on strong suspicions that the British and Soviets were covering up dark crimes, all sorts of conspiratorial theories persist.

HESSE, Prince Philip of. *See* PHILIP, Prince of Hesse.

HESTER, John Hutchison. US general. 1886-1976. John Hester was born 11 Sep 86 in Georgia and graduated from West Point in 1908 (75/108). An infantryman, he served on the **Punitive Expedition,** then in the WDGS, 1918-19 and 1936-39. In 1940 he became a brigadier general and the next year was made "Executive for Reserve Officers of the War Department"

(*AA,* 331). In Aug 41 he took command of the 43d Inf Div and on 13 Feb 42 was promoted to major general. The division reached New Zealand on 23 Oct 42 and on 23 Feb 43 landed unopposed on the Russell Islands. Elements of the division took Vangunu and Rendova Islands against minor resistance on 30 June. But his troops bogged down on New Georgia, and on 29 July 43 Hester was relieved by John R. HODGE (*OCMH Chron,* 123). Shipped home, the general headed the Tank Destroyer Center (1943-44) and the Infantry Replacement Training Center (1944-45). He retired in 1946 and died 11 Feb 76 in Atlanta. (Cullum.)

HEUSINGER, Adolf Ernst. German general. 1897-1982. Heusinger was born 4 Aug 97 at Holzminden. He became an army cadet in 1915, fought in WWI, and joined the post war Reichswehr. Admitted to the **GGS,** he was promoted 1 Oct 40 to colonel and OKH Chief of Operations, holding the post until 30 June 44 and rising from Generalmajor in 1941 and promoted again in 1943. (Wistrich.)

Generalleutnant Heusinger was acting army CofS after ZEITZLER reported sick on 30 June 44. He was standing next to Hitler on 20 July 44 and had just concluded his portion of the briefing when STAUFFENBERG's bomb exploded, slightly wounding Heusinger. Although apparently guilty only of close professional association with the major conspirators, the general was arrested on 22 July and brought before the People's Court on 7 Aug 44. Generalmajor Helmuth Stieff, who had been closely involved with FELLGIEBEL in the 20 July attentat, testified that he had alerted Heusinger that another assassination attempt was imminent. But Heusinger was exonerated and released two months later although relieved from active duty.

The former Wehrmacht general had a major role in building the postwar Bundeswehr, and with SPEIDEL was among the first Germans to hold high NATO posts. Heusinger completed his military career as chairman of the NATO Military Committee, 1961-64.

HEWITT, H(enry) Kent. US admiral. 1887-1972. He was born 11 Feb 87 in Hackensack, NJ, and graduated 12 Sep 06 from the USNA (30/209). Hewitt spent the next 12 years at sea except for a tour at the USNA in 1913-16 to teach mathematics. In the last year of WWI, 1918, he commanded two destroyers (in turn) and won the Navy Cross for patrol and convoy duty. Hewitt returned twice to the USNA between the wars, heading the mathematics department in 1933-36 after commanding a destroyer division. As skipper of CA *Indianapolis* he took the recently elected President Roosevelt on his 1936 cruise to attend the Pan American Conference in Buenos Aires.

Promoted in 1939 to flag rank, Rear Adm Hewitt took command of Cruiser Division 8 in Oct 40, when FDR ordered "all aid to Britain short of war." From Apr 42 he headed the Amphibious Force, Atlantic Fleet. The trained USMC force having been sent to the Pacific, Hewitt had the task of indoctrinating recruits with the highly specialized skills needed for amphibious warfare. (T. V. Tujela in Stephen Howarth, ed., "Hewitt.") With Patton the admiral planned the Western TF landings in NW Africa (Opn Torch) on 8 Nov 42, directing the training and commanding the naval element. Promoted to vice admiral on 20 Nov 42 he spent the rest of the war as commander of US naval forces in the Mediterranean. Off Sicily he committed 1,000 US ships in history's largest amphibious operation to that time. The admiral subsequently was Allied naval force commander in the landings at Salerno, Anzio, and in southern France. From Feb 43 he commanded US Naval Forces, NW African Waters, which became the 8th Fleet in March of that year. His second Navy Cross was awarded in Sep 43.

Hewitt was promoted to full admiral in Apr 45, a month before V-E day, and returned to the States for duty with one of the numerous **Pearl Harbor investigations.** On 1 Aug 45, two weeks before V-J day, Hewitt became commander of US naval forces in Europe. From the fall of 1946 the admiral gave lectures at the Naval War College to senior naval officers on his amphibious experiences. In 1947 he became USN representative to the UN military staff committee.

At the age of 62, with 46 years of continuous service, Hewitt retired on 1 Mar 49 to his home in Hackensack but bought a house in Orwell, Vt. A naval historian calls the chunky but firm-featured admiral "one the most professionally competent and dauntless American flag officers" of WWII, "a tolerant and modest man who shunned public clamor" (Tujela, cited herein). To the popular press this translated into "a dignified reserve verging on pompousness" *(CB 43)*.

Kent Hewitt, as he was known among colleagues, died 15 Sep 72 in Middlebury, Vt, and was buried at the USNA.

HEYDRICH, Reinhard (Tristan Engen). Nazi official. 1904-42. The Blond Beast, SS chief HIMMLER's principal lieutenant and father of the **Final Solution,** ended his brief career as the "Butcher of Prague." He has the distinction of being the only top Nazi assassinated on orders from London.

Heydrich was born 7 Mar 04 in Halle. Rumors persisted through Reinhard Heydrich's life that he had Jewish blood, and it is safe to say that Heydrich was plagued by doubts. Himmler claimed he had to reassure Heydrich that a super-Nazi could compensate for a taint of Semitism. So much ink has been spilled over all this that some discussion is warranted here.

His mother, an actress born Elizabeth Maria Anna Amalie Krantz, daughter of a Dresden professor, was said to be the daughter of a Jewess named Sarah (Brissaud, *SD,* 26). Heydrich's father, who moved the family from Dresden to Halle, was an opera composer and distinguished musician who founded the Halle conservatory of music. The father was listed in a reference book as "Heydrich, Bruno, real name Süss." Now, *Jud Süss* is the title of Lion Feuchtwanger's best-selling novel published in 1925 and made into an anti-Semitic movie in 1940, and some unfriendly people in Halle naturally called Bruno Heydrich "the Jew Suess." The surname Suess, like many others, is gentile as well as Jewish, but Bruno got this "real name" from a stepfather, not his real father. Some writers conclude from this that the Blond Beast had no Jewish blood, but this disregards his mother's alleged ancestry.

Very tall and slim, very blond, Heydrich had a long, horse-like face, a hawk-like nose, and the deep-set, slanting eyes of a wolf. The Blond Beast was a first-class fencer, excellent horseman, skilled pilot, and a talented violinist. Out of character with this almost-idealized Nordic Aryan look was a high, nasal voice.

Too young for WWI, Heydrich had joined the Maercker Freikorps at the age of 16 as a messenger and then saw action in the Halle Freikorps. (Brissaud, *SD,* 26.) On 30 Mar 22 he became a candidate for the navy, and as a brilliant student who loved outdoor life, he excelled as a midshipman. Aboard the training cruiser *Berlin,* 1922-24, he established a close and long-enduring rapport with Capt CANARIS, the ship's XO. Promoted in 1928 to lieutenant and specializing as a radio officer, he was sent the next year to the naval headquarters at Kiel to be communications officer of the intelligence service. In Dec 30 he became engaged to Lina Mathilde von Osten, the exceptionally beautiful and rabidly Nazi 19-year-old daughter of a schoolmaster on the Baltic island of Fehmarn. (He had rescued Lina from a sailing accident.) But the highly active and oversexed blond superman meanwhile was accused of getting another girl pregnant—the daughter of an I. G. Farben director and intimate friend of Grand Admiral RAEDER. The lieutenant professed innocence, refused to marry her, and consequently was cashiered in Apr 31.

Considering himself a victim of the officer-caste system and eager for vengeance, Heydrich promptly joined the Nazi Party. He was spurred on by Lina and sponsored by a powerful Nazi friend who introduced Heydrich to Himmler on 14 June 31. The chicken farmer was so impressed by the ardent young ex-officer (not realizing he had been in signals, not naval intelligence) that he ordered Heydrich to form a badly needed SS Intelligence Service (SD).

The cashiered naval officer proved to be an excellent organizer with a genius for intrigue and a greed for power. The SS secret service chief remained on close terms with Himmler and, curiously, maintained an appearance of warm personal friendship with CANARIS despite their deadly professional animosity. Heydrich rose with dizzying speed from Sturmfuehrer (2d Lt) on 10 Aug 31 to SS general officer rank on 21 Mar 33. Less than a year later he was promoted to Obergruppenfuhrer with date of rank from 1 July 34, the final day of the **Blood Purge** in which he had a key role.

Having a powerful secret police apparatus to deal with internal "enemies of the state," the Obergruppenfuhrer also claimed (falsely) to have helped the Soviets frame TUKHACHEVSKY, setting off Stalin's **Great Purges** and crippling the Red Army's leadership on the eve of war. In 1938 the Blond Beast played a major role in the BLOMBERG and FRITSCH affairs,

in **Crystal Night,** and he masterminded the incidents at **Gleiwitz** and **Venlo.**

On Heydrich's recommendations his all-powerful Reich Security Main Office (RSHA) was established by a decree of 27 Sep 39. The RSHA incorporated the **Gestapo** and **Kripo** under a new office, **Sipo (Political Security Office).** The restructured SD was divided into SD Interior and SD Exterior. All this reorganization made Heydrich effectively HIMMLER's deputy chief of the burgeoning SS empire. At the **Wannsee Conference,** set up by his principal lieutenant, Adolf EICHMANN, Heydrich put machinery in motion for the **Final Solution.** "Reinhard" was the appropriate code name for Odilo GLOBOCNIK's extermination program in Poland and in other **concentration camps.**

The Butcher of Prague

Heydrich was rewarded by being named acting Reich Protector of Bohemia and Moravia, replacing NEURATH, but keeping his RSHA hat. The new "acting protector" was expected to make up for what Neurath's performance had lacked in National Socialist vigor, and the plan was to reassign him later, possibly to greener pastures in France.

Reaching Prague on 27 Sep 41 and hoisting the SS flag over Hradcany Castle, the Blond Beast took only five days to announce his program. "We will try to Germanize these Czech vermin," he told subordinates. A police blitz earned him a new nickname, Butcher of Prague. Czech men, women, and children were killed in large-scale executions, many staged dramatically in public. Having moved initially against political and intellectual enemies of the Third Reich, the acting protector then undertook a vigorous campaign against the underground, which had grown bold during Neurath's benign regimen. Heydrich focused on the British-sponsored Central Committee for Internal Resistance (UVOD), which was kept informed of German plans by the elusive "Franta." When it became apparent in early 1942 that the superspy was Paul THUEMMEL, head of Prague's Abwehr office, Heydrich used the revelation to drive another nail in CANARIS's coffin.

But the prospect of a more efficient German counterespionage coalition so alarmed the British secret service that MENZIES, chief of MI6, decided the SOE should have Heydrich eliminated. Authorities in London and Prague fully appreciated that this assassination would bring terrible retribution, but the Czechs decided their people would suffer less in the long run if Heydrich were killed. A leading historian of the European resistance concludes, in fact, that "the operation was decided upon . . . by the Benes government alone and not by SOE" (Michel, *Shadow War,* 223). The Czech secret service in England provided British-trained assassination agents Lt Jan Kubis and Sgt Josef Gabcik. The two-man team, codenamed Anthropoid, parachuted into the Bohemian hills on 29 Dec 41 at about 2:30 AM (Ivanov, *Target Heydrich,* 46, 106) The drop was over Nehvizdy, a village five miles south of Pilsen.

Within a week the Anthropoids, lucky from the start, were located by partisans and taken in by Czech families. Kubis and Gabcik made contact with other parachutists but did not reveal their own mission. For this reason Heydrich was not alarmed when informed of their arrival but remained preoccupied with catching THUEMMEL, and the Anthropoids soon had new orders from London to help save Franta. After the latter's final arrest on 20 Mar 42 Kubis and Gabcik returned to their original task.

While the Anthropoids struggled to recruit a team (Michel, 223) they studied Heydrich's movements and habits. The butcher of Prague seemed to mock the threat of assassination. He always used the same routes between his country estate at Panenske Brezany, Hradcany Castle and the airport; he always sat in the front seat of his powerful Mercedes sports-convertible with Oberscharfuehrer Klein, the SS driver; he almost never had a bodyguard or armed escort.

The big break came on 23 May 42, when the Czech underground gave the Anthropoids Heydrich's schedule for 27 May (Brown, "*C*", 411). Meanwhile a perfect place for an ambush had been found. It was in the Holesovice suburb were Heydrich's car would have to slow for a right turn from Kirchmayer Blvd toward Troja Bridge and the center of Prague. With time for working out details of their plan Kubis and Gabcik formed their team. Josef Valcik would be on the boulevard about 100 yards from the turn, and he would flash a pocket mirror (pretending to comb his hair) when the victim came into sight. Rena Fafek, Gabcik's girlfriend, would be driven through the turn ahead of the big Mercedes and signal (by wearing a hat or not) whether the team had to deal with two cars

or just one. Adolf Opalka was on the left-hand sidewalk across the street from the hit men; Kubis was on the corner watching Valcik; a few yards from him on the right sidewalk were Gabcik and three other parachutists, Jaroslav Svarc, Josef Bublik, and Jan Hruby. Everybody was posted by 9 AM

Heydrich left his country estate just after 10 AM, half an hour behind schedule. His senior warrant officer, Herbert Wagnitz, was driven off a few minutes later after handling some final chores. The acting protector, who loved speed, ordered Klein to step on it, and Wagnitz had no hope of catching up even if that had been the plan. Just after 10:30 the Anthropoids got their signals: Valcik flashed his mirror, and the lady partisan came through the turn bareheaded. As the unsuspecting Germans followed, a streetcar clanged up from the Troja Bridge to a transfer point on the boulevard. Klein had to slow further for a couple of indecisive pedestrians, then he slammed on the brakes to avoid hitting a man who darted into the street. It was Josef Gabcik, who whipped a Sten gun from under his rain coat, leveled it at Heydrich's chest, and calmly pulled the trigger. Nothing happened!

The startled Germans recovered fast, both standing to fire pistols and hit their dumbfounded assailant twice in the leg. As the car began moving on, Jan Kubis lobbed a grenade that exploded against the side of the car behind the front seat, tearing a great hole. Heydrich got out clutching his pistol and briefcase, staggered a few steps, and fell. Klein, unscathed, pursued Gabick, who had thrown down his gun and fled on foot. Kubis, whose face had been hit by slivers of metal, escaped on his bicycle. Valcik had run to the scene of action, being hit there by fragments and escaping with blood on his trousers. All the other partisans also got away.

Heydrich was taken a few hundred yards to the Bulkova hospital, where he was hastily examined before undergoing an emergency operation. The three-inch-deep wound in his side did not appear to be life-threatening, but it was full of debris—bits of metal and car upholstery to include cloth, leather, and horse hair near the spleen (Ivanov, 177). Put under heavy guard in the hospital and reported to be recovering well, the Obergruppenfuhrer suddenly developed blood poisoning and died 4 June 42. There is considerable evidence that the powerful little British (SOE) bomb was poisoned, but

Heydrich seems to have been done in by septicemia alone.

Meanwhile, Karl Hermann FRANK, secretary of state to the protectorate, was promoted over Konrad HENLEIN's head to be acting-protector. (NEURATH, absent on extended leave, remained protector officially. Himmler personally replaced Heydrich as RSHA chief until 13 Jan 43, when most of the office was put under KALTENBRUNNER.)

Launching a program of reprisals, Frank offered a reward of 10 million Czech crowns (£125,000; $600,000) for arrest of the guilty men. "Whoever shelters these criminals, provides then with help, or, knowing them, does not denounce them, will be shot with his whole family," the ordinance said further. (Ivanov, 206-8.) Frank proclaimed a state of siege throughout the entire protectorate but successfully opposed Hitler's order for immediate execution of 10,000 Czechs suspected of anti-German activities. "World opinion must totally lose the impression than any national uprising is concerned," Frank argued wisely; "we must say that it is merely a question of individual actions" (ibid.). Although an initial sweep of the ambush scene revealed little, the Gestapo soon had the scent. Directed in their *ratissage* by Czech traitors, the Germans sent hundreds of adult hostages from Terezin prison to die at Mauthausen, and their children under 14 were sent to other camps. Retribution included the razing of **Lidice**, Lazaly, and Bernartice and other villages.

All seven men of the assassination team made their way to the church of St Cyril and St Methodius in Prague. Their refuge revealed by a traitor, Karel Curda, the men held out against great odds for three weeks. The Germans stormed the church on 18 June 42, and the seven defenders were killed or else they committed suicide. Four Orthodox Church men were sentenced to death on 3 Sep 42 for helping the fugitives, and another 252 Czechs were condemned to death at another trial that month for aiding the parachutists. (Ivanov, 272.)

HEYDTE, Friedrich August von der. German officer. 1907-. A cousin of Klaus von STAUFFENBERG, whom he supported in the 20 July 44 attempt on Hitler's life, Freiherr von der Heydte was a professor of international law. He commanded the 1st Bn, 3d Para Regt, in its drop on Alikianou, in Crete, on 20 May 41. As a full colonel commanding the German Parachute School he was ordered on 8 Dec 44 to form a special unit for use in the Ardennes counteroffensive. With little time, inexperienced parachutists and his drop zones in difficult terrain north of Malmedy, Heydte had some success before being captured on 23 Dec 44. He published a lively and highly literate book of military memoirs, *Daedalus Revisited* (London: Hutchinson, 1958).

HIGASHIKUNI, Naruhiko. Japanese official. 1887-. Born in Kyoto, Dec 87, he had many ties by marriage with both sides of the royal family. The Emperor Meiji established the House of Higashikuni in 1906, two years before the prince graduated from the military academy as an infantry officer. He had a increasingly important command and staff assignments but served primarily in military intelligence to include seven years in Europe. Although ruggedly antiroyalist he got along well with his double nephew-in-law Hirohito (Bergamini, 119). Lt Col Higashikuni was in Paris as a member of Petain's entourage when Hirohito became regent in 1921 and on a visit to Baden-Baden he held a highly secret meeting of Japanese intelligence officers on 27 Oct 21 to create the **Emperor's cabal.**

As a major general was a general staff officer in Tokyo from Dec 29. He then commanded the 5th Inf Bde and the 4th Inf Div as a lieutenant general from Aug 34 (*Kogun*, 224). Higashikuni was military councillor and chief of the army aeronautical deptartment before taking command of the 2d Army in China in 1938. Showing good sense and individualism but little aggressiveness, he was promoted to full general in Aug 39. Then he was CinC, Home Defense Hq and he instead of TOJO might have succeeded KONOYE as premier on 16 Oct 41 if it had not been for the tradition of keeping the royal family out of open involvement in politics.

Higashikuni resigned in Dec 41 but was recalled to head the "surrender cabinet" when HIROHITO indicated willingness for the royal family to accept political leadership at a time of national humiliation. Holding office only for 50 days, 17 Aug-5 Oct 45, he resigned to protest MacArthur's announcement that occupation authorities would dictate changes in Japan's internal affairs.

Succeeded by SHIDEHARA and promptly receiving permission to become a commoner,

Higashikuni operated a variety of shops before declaring bankruptcy. In 1950 he created a new religious order, the Higashikuni-kyo, which the occupation authorities promptly banned. As late as 1964 the prince was still in the news for dubious activities.

HIGGINS, Andrew Jackson. US industrialist. 1886-1952. Born in Columbus, Nebr, on 26 Aug 86, son of a jurist, he attended Creighton Univ in Omaha (1903-6) but did not graduate. Fascinated from childhood with boats, Higgins acquired a large fleet in 1930 and subsequently organized a shipbuilding company in New Orleans. Higgins Industries was ready for the war with a great variety of products, the best known being the Higgins boat, or "landing craft, vehicle, personnel" (LCVP). Like Henry J. Kaiser he was active in many fields including innovative, low cost residential construction that featured the use of expanding concrete.

HIMMLER, Heinrich. Leading Nazi politician. 1900-45. The man who became second in power only to Hitler in Nazi Germany was born 7 Oct 00 near Munich. His father, whom the boy hated, was a strict Catholic schoolmaster who had once been tutor to the Bavarian Crown Prince. Heinrich Himmler, small, mousy and bespectacled, rose from clerk in the 11th Bavarian Regt to officer cadet in 1918. After spending time in a Freikorps he got an agricultural diploma from the Munich Technical High School, joined the Nazi party, and had a minor role in Hitler's **Munich Beer Hall Putsch** of 1923.

The STRASSER brothers hired Himmler in 1925 at Landshut and he joined the local SS. In 1928 he married a nurse who was seven years his senior, and with her modest savings he bought a farm near Munich and made a small profit in poultry while beginning a political career. Himmler succeeded Erhard Heiden as leader of Hitler's SS bodyguard on 6 Jan 29. "A rare mixture of crackpot and organizational genius" (Irving, *HW,* xxviii), Himmler was "a visionary whose intellectual flights struck even Hitler as ridiculous" (Speer, *Memoirs,* 373). Although a lapsed Catholic, Himmler used Jesuit principles of absolute obedience and strict hierarchy in building the SS. By the time Hitler took power in 1933 Himmler's SS had grown to a strength of 52,000 from a few hundred officers and men who had been sub-

ordinate to the **SA.** And in 1933 the SS chief was made head of all German political police outside Prussia, where Goering held fief. When Himmler finally pressured Hitler into making Prussia part of the Third Reich Himmler took control of the Gestapo and Kripo. The change-of-command formalities were on 10 Apr 34.

Himmler and Goering instigated the **Blood Purge of 1934,** which neutered the SA and left the SS as the principal instrument of internal rule in Germany. (Bracher, 138.) In 1936 the **Gestapo** came under the SS, whereupon Himmler started creating a state within the state. An initial step was to decree that control in the political area lay not only in the normal bureaucracy but also within the police. When Heydrich's all-powerful **RSHA** was established by a decree of 27 Sep 39, Daluege's Orpo was excluded as part of Himmler's strategy of retaining personal control of certain SS organisms. (Brissaud, *SD,* 291.)

Himmler undertook to put SS men in all key political posts of the Third Reich (Schellenberg, 297). The Waffen-SS, Himmler's private army of 40 politically reliable and first- rate combat divisions, was slowly created by Sepp DIETRICH.

Hitler gave Himmler's ambitions another boost on 20 Aug 43 when he made the Reichsfuehrer-SS minister of the interior (vice FRICK). This increased SS control over the civil service and the courts. Far from fearing an SS state-within-the-state, Hitler believed this could assure perpetuation of the Third Reich. "At the beginning of June 1944," writes Speer, "Hitler asked me to assist the SS in its efforts to build up an economic empire extending from raw materials to manufacturing" (*Memoirs,* 372).

But Himmler's physical and mental health, always poor, had deteriorated since 1939. He had acute nervous headaches, stomach cramps, a predilection for quack cures and a mysticism that included faith in astrology and the power of mental suggestion. Although no philanderer, Himmler set up housekeeping with a secretary by whom he had a son and daughter in addition to the daughter born in wedlock. Despite a thrifty nature, he always was strapped for personal funds but did not take advantage of unlimited opportunities for profiteering. "During the summer of 1942," writes one insider, "a serious conflict arose between Himmler and Bormann in which Himmler continually made small tactical errors [including accepting a personal loan] which Bormann always exploited to the full." (Schellenberg, 316.) Himmler later told Schellenberg that Bormann had made his own position impregnable (ibid.).

After the 20 July 44 attempt on Hitler's life the Reichsfuehrer-SS succeeded Erich FROMM as commander of the reserve army. Hitler directed him in mid-Aug 44 to form and train the Volkssturm, a "great levy" or "people's militia" composed mostly of elderly men and 16-year-old boys. SAUCKEL called it up in the last days of the war but nobody could issue them weapons. (Speer *Memoirs*, 450.) Hitler subsequently gave his "faithful Himmler" military tasks for which for which the SS chief was completely unqualified. Army Group Oberrhein (or AG Rhine) was created 26 Nov 44 under Himmler's independent command for the Ardennes counteroffensive.

Hitler put his ardent crony in command of the newly formed AG Vistula (Weichsel) on 25 Jan 45 as Zhukov's 1st White Russian Front closed in on Berlin from the north and within 10 days was on the Vistula within 50 miles of Berlin. But it was not until 20 March that Guderian persuaded Himmler to resign his post so HEINRICI could take it over.

Himmler went to his favorite sanitorium, Hohenlychen, 70 miles south of Berlin, but remained head of the SS and Replacement Army. Having earlier rejected GUDERIAN's suggestion to start making efforts to negotiate peace, Himmler was active from 13 Apr 45 in covertly pursuing leads developed by SCHELLENBERG. Himmler put out feelers through BERNADOTTE, who visited Hohenlychen with a group seeking release of certain concentration camp inmates.

After visiting the Fuehrerbunker for Hitler's birthday party on 20 Apr 45 the SS chief left the now-threatened sanatorium for Schwerin, near DOENITZ's headquarters. On 28 April HITLER learned of overtures his "faithful Himmler" had made to negotiate a separate peace with the west, and the furious fuehrer promptly ordered the traitor's arrest. Doenitz never got the word about this but as Hitler's designated political heir he had no intention of accepting Himmler's help.

The Reichsfuehrer-SS left Flensburg on 10 May, adopted an elaborate disguise, and was at large until stopped at a British control post near Bremen on 22 May. Although dressed as a common soldier, wearing an eye patch, and minus his moustache, Himmler aroused enough suspicion to be held for interrogation. Chaim Herzog, future president of Israel, was the British officer who first smelled a rat, I am told by Lionel Leventhal, publisher of Greenhill Books, London. Late the next evening Himmler revealed his identity but chomped down on a concealed cyanide capsule before the examining doctor could intervene. Despite desperate efforts to keep the prize prisoner alive he died within 15 minutes.

HINDENBURG, Paul Ludwig von Beneckendorff. German field marshal. 1847-1934. The Reich's last president (1925-34) was born 2 Oct 47 at Poznan (Posen). He fought in the Austro-Pussian war of 1866, commanded a field army in the Franco-Prussian war of 1870-71 and retired in 1911 but was recalled in 1914 to take command in East Prussia. He and his brilliant CofS Erich Ludendorff (1865-1937) defeated vastly superior Russian forces at Tannenberg in one of history's most dramatic victories.

In 1925 the elderly field marshal was elected president of the Weimar Republic. Five years later, when Germany was in dire straits because of Versailles treaty restrictions and the Great Depression, Hindenburg allowed Heinrich BRUENING to rule by decree as chancellor. Reelected in Apr 32 the venerable war hero appointed von PAPEN to succeed Bruening, but six months later—as the Nazis gained strength in Germany—replaced him with the slippery Gen von SCHLEICHER, who had appointed his friend Col Oskar Hindenburg to be his father's **adjutant.** During a one-hour private talk on 22 Jan 33 Hitler is believed to have used a mixture of bribes and blackmail to win the younger Hindenburg's backing (Bullock, *Hitler,* 247). President Hindenburg appointed Hitler chancellor on 30 Jan 33 and made a political testament that named Hitler to succeed him as president. The long-senile national hero died 2 Aug 34.

HIRANUMA, Kiichiro. Japanese statesman. 1867-1952. The ultranationalistic Baron Hiranuma was minister of justice from 1923 and president of the Privy Council from 1936. He succeeded KONOYE as premier on 4 Jan 39 but his cabinet fell on 28 Aug 39, Gen Nobuyuki ABE becoming the new premier. Arrested in Mar 46 and given life imprisonment in 1948 for war crimes, he died on or about 22 Aug 52.

HIROHITO. Emperor of Japan. 1901-89. Shy and physically unprepossessing but devoted to his role and capable of firmness in an emergency, Hirohito became crown prince in 1916, regent in 1921, and Japan's 124th emperor in 1926.

He was born 29 Apr 01 in Tokyo, grandson of the great Emperor Meiji and son of Crown Prince Yoshihito, who was the Emperor Taisho (1912-26). "Hiro's" younger brothers by a few years were Princes Yasuhito Chichibu and Takamatsu. A puny but spunky child, Hirohito was enrolled at the age of seven in a special class of the Peers' School or Gakushuin. The headmaster was Count Maresuke Nogi (1849-1912), a remarkable ex-general with great aesthetic aptitudes who became a surrogate father and shaped his imperial charge with the values of "faith, loyalty, bravery and fanaticism" expected of a Japanese emperor and imperial deity. (Mosley, *Hirohito,* 7.) Each morning the headmaster led students in a ceremony that started with "worshiping at a distance," bowing for 60 seconds toward the imperial palace, and that ended with "What as your dearest ambition?" The response, as Japan's occidental enemies would learn to their consternation, was: "To die for the Emperor!"

General Count Nogi concluded the duties to his imperial pupil on 12 Sep 12, the evening before Emperor Meiji's state funeral. The master first called in the 11-year-old Hirohito for a three-and-a half hour review of his progress. Saying he was "not dissatisfied" and concluding with "Work hard, for your own sake and for the sake of Japan," Nogi went home to commit ritual suicide (seppuku) after dispatching his wife—a willing accomplice—with a dagger. (Mosley, *Hirohito,* 19-20.)

Finishing at the Gakushuin in 1914 Hirohito resumed his formal education at a special department of the Takanawa Palace called the Togu-gogakumonshoin. Its president was Admiral Togo, whose annihilation of the Russian fleet in the battle of Tsushima, the decisive action of the Russo Japanese war of 1904-05, was the greatest naval victory since Trafalgar. The famous admiral was incapable of estab-

lishing the rapport Count Nogi had had with Hirohito. When Tojo reported that the crown prince was expressing polite skepticism about his divine family origins, Prince Kimmochi SAIONJI first appeared as a tutor. The wise old Genro pointed out that this fundamentalist belief was vital to the Japanese people but suggested that crown prince put aside the study of "history" temporarily for some genuine academic interest. Hirohito disclosing a strong interest in butterflies, wild flowers and fungi, more time was devoted to natural science under Dr Hirotaro Hattori. When the prince subsequently complained that their field work was hindered by a retinue of court officials, his wise tutor suggested exploring marine biology in a very small boat! So began a life-long scientific interest and a friendship with Dr Hattori that lasted until the latter's retirement in 1965 at the age of 89. (Mosley, *Hirohito,* 33-34n.)

The Emperor Taisho finally being hopelessly insane, Hirohito became crown prince on 3 Nov 16 at the age of 15 1/2. In 1921 he made a six-month grand tour of Europe, the first foreign trip ever for a Japanese crown prince. (His father did not have this title when he went abroad.) Hirohito succeeded as emperor of Japan in 1926.

Despite the old Japanese tradition that the emperor "reign but not rule" Hirohito descended from the clouds on several notable occasions. The first was when **Japanese political factions** reached the point of military insurrection on **26 Feb 36;** the emperor intervened forcefully with detailed instructions to Koki HIROTA, the new premier.

As early as 1941 the emperor expressed skepticism about the prevailing military opinion that a quick victory against the west was possible, pointing out that the militarists had been wrong in saying the same thing about victory in the war against China. The emperor nevertheless endorsed Japanese war plans officially at an imperial conference on 1 Dec 41, but in approving the surprise attack on Pearl Harbor he ordered that some prior notice be given. (*See* Cordell HULL.)

Hirohito harshly criticized military planners as Japan lost one campaign after another. The US victory at Midway in June 42 showed Tojo that Japan was in for a long war that would require utmost dedication and sacrifice from the emperor's subjects, so Hirohito was referred to thereafter in public announcements. This contributed materially to Japan's superhuman war effort.

Hirohito's criticism hastened the fall of the long-lived TOJO government on 18 July 44. After the loss of Okinawa, Hirohito made a veiled hint at an imperial conference on 22 June 45 that a negotiated peace should be considered (Buchanan, 588). The government not reacting, the emperor showed increasing initiative in facing up to the inevitability of surrender. On 9 Aug 45, when the second atomic bomb obliterated Nagasaki, and a day after the Soviets invaded Manchuria, Hirohito was directly involved for the first time in decision making. This happened during a dramatic meeting with top leaders in an air raid shelter adjoining the imperial library. After hearing final arguments, the emperor said Japan should sue for peace, and on 10 Aug 45 the Japanese sent a capitulation message through representatives in Sweden and Switzerland. The **"Byrnes note"** revived debate in Tokyo, but the surrender terms were accepted. The Japanese people were informed at 7:21 AM on 15 Aug 45 that for the first time in the nation's history they would hear the emperor's voice. A defective recording made a day earlier and further garbled in transmission was broadcast despite a last-minute effort by die-hards to prevent it. But the people got the message, and the last Japanese resistance collapsed. Disregarding another imperial tradition, Hirohito named Prince HIGASHIKUNI to head the "surrender government." He then waited for instructions from MACARTHUR, the surrender instrument being signed on 2 Sep 45. The American proconsul, Japan's first foreign conqueror, did not summon the emperor but waited for him to request the initial interview. A little more than two weeks later the visit took place with minimum publicity. After an exchange of amenities, the visibly nervous Hirohito said "I come to you, General MacArthur, to offer myself to the powers you represent as the one to bear sole responsibility for every political and military decision made and action taken by my people in the conduct of the war." The emperor's name had only recently been stricken from the war trials list, largely at the general's insistence, but Hirohito did not know this. MacArthur wrote later that he was "moved . . . to the very marrow of my bones" by "this courageous assumption of a responsibility implicit with death. . ." (*Reminiscences*, 288).

The two men met frequently thereafter, and MacArthur comments that Hirohito "played a major role in the spiritual regeneration of Japan, and his loyal co-operation and influence had much to do with the success of the occupation" (ibid.).

The American-imposed Japanese constitution of 1945 reduced the emperor to a ceremonial role, and on 1 Jan 46 Hirohito renounced the theory of imperial divinity. Another centuries-old tradition was broken when Crown Prince Akihito married a commoner. Highly respected in Japan and abroad, an old man "slouching around the Palace in frayed, baggy trousers and crooked tie, dreamily peering through glasses as thick as portholes" (Toland, *Sun*, 24) but having shown qualities of greatness, Hirohito died 7 Jan 89 after a long illness.

HIROTA, Koki. Japanese official. 1878-1948. Born 14 Feb 78 in Fukuoka, son of a stone mason, he became a diplomat. After being ambassador to Moscow, 1930-32, he was foreign minister in 1934 (vice UCHIDA), surviving the fall of the SAITO government, and becoming prime minister on 9 Mar 36. HIROHITO personally gave the new PM instructions on restoring civilian control, the **26 Feb 36** uprising having just been suppressed. Hirota succeeded initially, thanks largely to the help of War Minister TERAUCHI, who concentrated on purging the army of officers his faction found undesirable. The Hirota government signed the **Anti-comintern pact,** gaining more freedom to expand in China. But after Terauchi achieved his goals he began criticizing the Diet for obstructionism, threatening to resign in protest. Hirota resigned 23 Jan 37, allegedly to save the Diet, and was elevated to the peerage. He was foreign minister under KONOYE, 2 June 37 to 4 Jan 39.

As his country faced final defeat the diplomat was TOGO's intermediary with Soviet Ambassador Malik, but he accomplished nothing because Japan had no bargaining power left. Being a civilian who had opposed the militarists, Hirota expected to escape charges of war crimes. But occupation authorities discovered Hirota's alleged early links with the Genoysha, forerunner of the **Black Dragon Society.** Convicted on all major counts of war crimes Hirota was hanged on 23 Dec 48. See Saburo Shiroyama, *War Criminal: The Life and Death of Hirota Koki* (1977).

HITLER, Adolf. German dictator. 1889-1945. The ex-corporal who cowed Prussian generals was born 20 Apr 89 in the Austrian border village of Braunau am Inn.

The Hitler name in its many phonetic variations from Hytler in 1457 to Hitler in 1702 (Payne, 4) may well be of Czech origin (Bullock, *Hitler,* 24). But the future fuehrer of Nazi Germany may not have had any Hitler family blood, his adoptive father being illegitimate. Most homophonic Hitlers were concentrated in and around the hamlets of Spital and Walterschlag, located in a small NW corner of the Waldviertel ("wooded quarter") within a few hours' march of the Bohemian border. Waves of invaders have swarmed through the hardscrabble region, notably the Bohemian King Ottakar II in the 13th century and Jan Huss, two centuries later. There were many other foreign armies, but the Slavs left the most enduring traces.

Alois Hitler.

Hitler's father, Alois, was the illegitimate child of Maria Anna Schicklgruber, a dirt-poor, 42-year-old peasant. She gave birth in her home village of Strones in the Waldviertel of NW Austria. Generations of genealogists have never cleared up the paternity problem, and even Anna may not have known whom the father was (Payne, *Hitler,* 6).

Hans FRANK dimly remembered that Hitler asked him late in the 1930s to check a story that the Reichsfuehrer's grandsire was the 19-year-old Jewish son of a Frankenberger family in Gratz. Dr Frank found letters showing that the Frankenbergers sent Maria Schicklgruber child-support for 14 years, but Adolf Hitler steadfastly professed to believe what his father had told him: that the missing link was Johann Georg Hiedler. No proof has been found for the persistent rumor that Alois was conceived while his mother was a servant in the Rothschild household in Vienna. There is no reason to believe that Adolf Hitler had a Jewish ancestor.

Alois Schicklgruber was five years old when his mother married Johann Georg Hiedler (1792-1857), a "poor cottager" of Strones (Hitler, *Mein Kampf,* 6). Georg's brother Johann Nepomuk Hiedler (1807-88) soon took Alois into his hard-up household at Spital for reasons that can only be surmised. There has been speculation that either George or Johann Nepomuk fathered Alois.

The woods colt's birth record in the parish of Doellersheim was altered in 1876 by a compliant village priest. Three illiterate witnesses put their marks to "confirm that Georg Hitler, who was well known to them, acknowledged paternity of the child Alois, son of Anna Schicklgruber. . . ." Georg had been dead for nearly 20 years (Anna for almost 30) but the priest was led to believe Georg was alive and "living in Spital." Even more curious, Johann Nepomuk, very much alive, was not party to what has all the earmarks of a "deliberate deception." (Payne, 7.) It is often stated that Alois's uncle engineered the action, but there is better reason to believe that Alois—on the brink of professional advancement (below)—was the architect. Use of the name Georg Hitler rather than Hiedler has no special significance; it was simply an accepted variation of the family name (ibid.). After the records change became official on 6 Jan 77 Alois was known thereafter only as Alois Hitler. This saved the future German fuehrer's followers from having to shout "Heil Schicklgruber!"

Young Alois was apprenticed to a cobbler in Spital, but before turning 13 he left his uncle's home for Vienna. After four hard years in the trade he qualified as an apprentice cobbler but aspired to better things. Despite his lack of education Alois got into the Imperial Customs Service (1855) and by 1872 was posted to Braunau am Inn as an assistant customs inspector. He reached his career ceiling in 1875 as a senior assistant inspector and changed his name (above).

The stubby bachelor has been described as a "vigorous, opinionated, bullet-headed man [with] sweeping mustaches, beetling brows, and jutting jaw" set off by a fancy cocked hat and "resplendent uniform with many gilt buttons" (Payne, 10-11). Although he struck some as being pompous and officious (befitting a *Finanzwacher*), Alois was also known for a wry sense of humor and "a gift for enduring friendships" (Payne, 10). The weight of evidence does not support the picture of Alois as the drunken, tyrannical elderly husband and father (Payne, 13). Adolf Hitler naturally was much closer to his indulgent young mother.

She was Alois's third wife. The first marriage, to the 50-year-old widow Anna Glassl-Hoerner in 1873, ended with legal separation in 1880 and her death of TB in 1883. The free-wheeling

Finanzwacher meanwhile had a son, Alois, in 1882, by Franziska "Fanni" Matzelberger (1861-1884), who was six months pregnant with Angela when she became an honest woman in 1883. To jump ahead in time, Angela would marry one Leo Raubal, who fathered Geli and Friedl before dying in 1910. The widowed Angela Rabaul and her daughters joined Adolf Hitler's household in 1925, as we shall see.

Fanni had hardly left Braunau for medical treatment when her husband sent for Klara Poelzl, a quiet, attractive young woman born 12 Aug 60 in Spital and reared there. She was a granddaughter of Johann Nepomuk Hitler (herein), hence her protector's second cousin. Fanni died of TB in 1884, leaving Alois free to marry Klara. It was necessary to get a papal dispensation on grounds of "affinity," and the bride was nearly four months pregnant when the quick ceremony took place at 6 AM on 7 Jan 85. The conscientious customs officer thus lost no time in reporting to work, the bride remembered. (Payne, 12.)

A dedicated and docile hausfrau, 23 years junior to the husband she at first called "uncle," Klara had six children. Only two survived childhood, the future Reichsfuehrer and the younger Paula (1896-1960). Alois Hitler retired on a pension in the summer of 1895, and in early 1899 moved the family from Braunau to a garden house in Leonding, a village SW of Linz. Adolf entered the Linz Realshcule (17 Sep 00).

The Fuehrer's Childhood

As a substandard student who blamed "the system" Adolf had an unhappy relationship with his domineering father. After the latter's death in Jan 03 the "moonstruck" son (his mother's term) dropped out of school to spend most of his time moping around the house with delusions of becoming an artist or architect. The house in Leonding was sold in the summer of 1905 and the family moved to Linz. Here Hitler acquired his lifetime devotion to Wagnerian music. In the summer of 1906 he visited Vienna for the first time and was enchanted. In the autumn of 1907 Adolf's mother gave him her reluctant blessing to return for the entrance exam to the Academy of Fine Arts. He failed the test in 1907 and was not even allowed to take it again the next year but advised to try for the School of Architecture. With no "school leaving certificate" but four years of Realschule, he was not qualified. He

had "the artist's temperament without either talent, training, or creative energy" (Bullock, 31).

Vienna, Munich, and WWI

Crushed by this experience, Hitler spent the next five years (1908-13) as a lone drifter in Vienna, without money, friends, or a home, not seeking regular work but posing as an art student and eking out a livelihood by painting post cards and posters for store windows. No evidence supports the popular belief that he was a house painter or paper hanger—such work would have been too regular. Klara Hitler meanwhile had died, 21 Dec 07, leaving him an orphan's pension that stopped in May 11. From time to time he also had some financial help from Johanna Hiedler Poelzl, his putative aunt and Klara's mother, who died in Mar 11 and probably left him a small legacy. (Bullock, 35; Payne, 592.)

Hitler's political awakening came in Vienna. He admired the city's anti-Semitic Mayor Karl Lueger. He watched social democrats in action and learned about propaganda and the management of mass movements. "The importance of physical terror against the individual and the masses also became clear to me" (*Mein Kampf,* 58).

Wine, women, and song were no distraction for the brooding vagrant, who didn't even smoke. But there is evidence that he got syphilis during his Vienna period and also that he was impotent (Bullock, *Hitler,* 35, 392). Hitler read avidly, then and later, but (like Mussolini) primarily to reinforce his preconceptions.

To evade the draft in Austria, where he would have had to serve with Czechs, Croats, and Jews he despised (Keegan, *Mask,* 237). Hitler went to Munich in May 13. Loving the gay Bavarian capital from first sight, he continued a shiftless existence. As an Austrian he was not liable for service in the Bavarian army, which was separate from the German military establishment. But Hitler was determined to enlist, and did so on 16 Aug 14, immediately after the outbreak of war. "His selection for the 16th Bavarian Reserve must be seen as the key ingredient of Hitler's life," writes Keegan, "for the regiment was composed of exactly that class of young Germans to which Hitler had long aspired but failed to be granted admission. They were, in high proportion, high-school boys, university students and trainees for the professions who, by deliberate polity of the German military authorities, had not hitherto been drafted for military service." (Ibid.) With the regiment's 1st Co he left for France on 21 Oct 14. A good and brave soldier, Hitler enjoyed the orderly existence, comradeship, and excitement. Although not a front-line fighter, he served mostly at or near the front as a message runner for the 3d Bn Hq, 16th Bavarian Reserve, and was awarded the Iron Cross 2d Class on 14 Dec 14. The most serious of several wounds was from a British shell fragment in the left thigh on 7 Oct 16 during the fighting near Bapaume. Released after five months of hospitalization in Germany, he was promoted 17 Mar 17 to lance corporal and awarded the Iron Cross 1st Class on 4 August. The night of 13-14 Oct 18 Hitler was temporarily blinded by gas but stumbled to battalion headquarters with his last message. He spent the rest of the war in hospitals. Despite this undeniably good military record, Lance Corporal Hitler had showed little ambition. That would come.

Between the wars

Early in 1919, having returned to the Lechfeld barracks in Munich, he was an instructor in "Enlightenment Courses" designed to protect soldiers from leftist ideas (Davidson, *Trial,* 43n). Making his first speeches in beer halls, beginning to perfect a style of demagogic oratory that most Germans found irresistible, and discovering the obscure little German Workers' Party (DAP), Hitler took his discharge on 31 Mar 20. He increased his hold on the DAP, showing genius by combining the country's two strongest political ideologies to rename it the Nationalist Socialist German Workers' Party (NSDAP).

Arrested in the **Munich Beer Hall Putsch,** 8-9 Nov 23, Hitler used his trial to make his name known throughout Germany. During a pleasant detention in the fortress prison of Landsberg, 11 Nov 23-20 Dec 24, he wrote the first volume of what he proposed to publish as *Four and a Half Years of Struggle Against Lies, Stupidity, and Cowardice.* Rudolf HESS was a major collaborator, and Max AMANN picked the title *Mein Kampf (My Struggle).*

Hitler should have been finished politically, but he left prison a nationally known figure and built up the NSDAP with support from Germans in all walks of life. For that the world could blame the Versailles peace treaty and unreasonable reparations claims as Germany struggled through the Great Depression and unprecedented inflation.

The Nazis created an army of brown shirted storm troopers, the SA. The force of bully boys was formed initially by GOERING to maintain order at NSDAP rallies and disrupt meeting of opponents but ROEHM expanded the SA into a paramilitary force that could to defy Versailles treaty restrictions on the size of Germany's army while satisfying the national longing for militarism. The SA threatened to become the national army, and we shall see herein how that played out.

Meanwhile Hitler began spending time at Berchtesgaden, were in 1925 he rented a villa (Haus Wachenfeld) on the Obersalzberg. His widowed half-sister, Angela Rabaul (herein), moved in with her teenage daughters Angela (Geli) and Friedl to keep house. Eventually buying and rebuilding the villa on a grand scale as the Berghof, this is where Hitler spent "the finest hours of my life" (Bullock, 134). The attractive, if flighty, Geli was her infatuated uncle's frequent companion in public until her sudden suicide on 17 Sep 31. The relationship was platonic, according to a Berghof housekeeper, Anny Brunner-Winter, and photographer Heinrich Hoffmann, but Hitler never fully recovered from her death. Eva BRAUN became Hitler's mistress in early 1932 but was kept sequestered, virtually unknown outside the Berghof.

President Hindenburg named Hitler chancellor on 30 Jan 33 because he was the only one capable of getting a majority in the Reichstag. When Hitler refused to form a coalition government the Reichstag was dissolved pending new elections on 5 Mar 33. But before these could be held the Nazis used the **Reichstag fire** of 27 Feb 33 to outlaw the communist party, picking up the 25 per cent vote the communists would have polled. Hitler quickly got dictatorial powers for four years by railroading through the Enabling Act of 23 Mar 33, then used well-organized terrorism and propaganda to effect one of history's most dramatic and all-encompassing revolutions. On Hindenburg's death, 2 Aug 34, Hitler succeeded to the German presidency.

Early Nazi Triumphs

In foreign affairs Hitler started quickly by withdrawing from the Disarmament Conference and the League of Nations on 14 Oct 33. His non-aggression pact with Poland, long Germany's *bête noire,* was a diplomatic coup when signed 26 Jan 34. A long-time admirer of fellow-dictator Mussolini, Hitler paid him a showy official visit on 14 June 34.

Germany denounced the disarmament clauses of the Versailles Treaty on 16 Mar 35 and promptly created the high commands of the Army, Luftwaffe, and Navy (OKH, OKL, and OKM), openly beginning to rebuild the German armed forces. The **Rhineland crisis of 1936** was Hitler's first big triumph of political intuition. Meanwhile, a ham-handed putsch by Austrian Nazis on 25 July 34 resulted in the death of DOLLFUSS, but Hitler's plans for gobbling up his German-speaking neighbor were frustrated by Mussolini's announcing his support of Austria. This merely postponed the **Anschluss** until 12-13 Mar 38, and Hitler never forgot Mussolini's support on this occasion. The **Munich crisis** of 12-29 Sep 38 ended with Hitler's annexing the **Sudetenland,** which deprived Czechoslovakia of her formidable permanent frontier defenses. Having achieved all this peacefully and pledging that he had no further territorial ambitions, Hitler gobbled up the rest of Czechoslovakia. He gave nominal independence to Slovakia and established a protectorate (15 Mar 39) in what was left of Bohemia and Moravia. World opinion now turned against Hitler.

Embarrassed by Hjalmar SCHACHT's resignation on 8 Dec 37, Hitler gave GOERING charge of a new four year plan. With dizzying speed he purged the armed forces and diplomatic service of "uncooperative" opponents and ousted War Minister BLOMBERG and Army Chief FRITSCH. "From now on I take over personally the command of the whole armed forces," he announced on 4 Feb 38.

The Great Depression of 1929 had shattered the world economy and brought both Hitler and Roosevelt to power, but these leaders addressed the problem differently. The Nazi dictator bolstered the German economy by a massive military buildup, whereas the timorous western powers failed to take the hint.

Hitler's War

Another diplomatic bombshell was the **Nazi-Soviet Pact** of 23 Aug 39. The attack on Poland quickly followed on 1 Sep 39, but Hitler was surprised and badly shaken when Britain and France declared war against Germany three days latter. The bluffing over and the shooting starting, Hitler thereafter devoted himself almost exclusively to military affairs.

Heading the high command of the armed forces *(OKW),* an office he had created in early 1938 (herein), Hitler had more than a dozen wartime CPs built but used only about half of these facilities. He occasionally sought solace in Munich and the **Berghof** during the war, but spent most of the time at **Rastenburg.** In the headquarters train "Amerika" he visited the Polish front in 1939 and Yugoslavia for the Balkan invasion in Apr 41. During a critical period on the eastern front he was established in the Ukraine near Vinnitza at "Werwolf," 16 July-1 Nov 42 and 17 Feb-13 Mar 43. During the Normandy campaign Hitler visited his forward CP at Margival, near Soissons, on 17 June 44 (D+11); Rundstedt and Rommel had just left a highly unsatisfactory meeting when a rogue V-1 exploded near the fuehrer's air-raid shelter and sent him scurrying that night for Berchtesgaden! (Speidel, 99.) In Dec 44 the fuehrer spent some time at Amt 500 in the Eifel to direct the Ardennes counteroffensive. Keegan gives the code names, locations (including a map), and occupation dates of all Hitler's wartime headquarters *(Mask,* 274-77).

Like Stalin, Hitler had a mind and a memory for detail that made it almost impossible for subordinates to debate him successfully.

After the quick German victory in Poland, 1-23 Sep 39, followed a few months later by those in Denmark, Norway, the Benelux, and France, 9 Apr-25 June 40, the Wehrmacht appeared to be invincible. But at this high tide of victory the fuehrer suffered a maddening diplomatic defeat—his first—at the hands of FRANCO. Although Hitler probably never intended to invade England, preferring merely to neutralize the British and let them continue policing their vast empire, his first military defeat was in the **Battle of Britain.**

Still refusing to face the prospect of a long war but still having no grand strategy, Hitler astounded his generals by announcing Opn **Barbarossa.** This was supposed "to destroy the Soviet Union in a spring campaign in 1941" (Seaton, *R-G War,* 27). But the fuehrer first had to rescue Mussolini from fiascos in North Africa and Greece, then he had to deal with Britain's intervention in Greece and the anti-German coup in Yugoslavia. "Whether or not the Balkan diversion robbed Hitler of the time and good weather in which he might have brought his 'short war' against Russia to a successful conclusion is now disputed," warns John Keegan (*Mask,* 263). "Certainly it seems more significant to striking a judgement that Barbarossa was itself a flawed plan; like Schlieffen's it hovered uncertainly between the aim of destroying the enemy's armies and the aim of neutralizing his capital" (ibid.). The conventional wisdom is that Barbarossa might have succeeded if left to the generals, who wanted to make Moscow the main objective. The Great German General Staff knew full well that one does not defeat a nation by taking its capital. But military planners assumed that the Red Army could be drawn to sacrifice itself it the defense of Moscow, not appreciating that the Soviets were prepared to continue the war from behind the Urals.

Bock's AG Center seemed about to take Moscow when, on 19 July 41, the Bohemian Corporal diverted AG Center's two panzer groups to AG North and AG South. On 21 August, after a period of confusion, Hitler stopped what was left of Bock's drive on Moscow and directed that Guderian's 2d Pz Gp and KLUGE's 2d Army wheel south toward Kiev. Bock's army group boundary was shifted north, where HOTH's 3d Pz Gp and Adolf STRAUSS's 9th Army drove NE toward the Valdai Hills. Even the most atheistic Russians considered that Moscow had been saved by a miracle.

After this fateful strategic intermission Hitler told Bock to resume AG Center's drive on Moscow, and the fuehrer decided not to take encircled Leningrad but starve it out, saving him the burden of sustaining its population. The Wehrmacht had taken Kiev and was overrunning vast regions of the Ukraine. But by 6 Dec 41 the drive on Moscow had failed and the Russians launched a massive—if not sustainable—counteroffensive that retook much ground and inflicted heavy casualties.

Against the almost unanimous call from the generals for a strategic withdrawal Hitler ordered the Wehrmacht to form **hedgehogs** around key communications centers and hold at all cost. The Wehrmacht stopped the Russian winter counteroffensive and survived with morale and offensive capability unbroken. On the other hand, Hitler's decision—which has been called one of his greatest and best intuitive judgments—has been faulted for costing the Wehrmacht more casualties than would have been suffered from following the conventional strategy of dropping back to good defensive terrain.

Meanwhile Hitler had undertaken the first of many wartime purges, dismissing 35 generals and four field marshals including all three army group commanders and BRAUCHITSCH. Accepting the latter's resignation on 19 Dec 41, Hitler told a dumfounded HALDER: "Anybody can do that bit of operational planning. The task of a Commander in Chief is to educate the Army in a National Socialist sense. I don't know a single general in the Army who is capable of doing that in the way I want it done. That is why I have decided to assume command of the Army myself [from BRAUCHITSCH]." (Goerlitz, *GGS,* 406.)

Launching the second stage of the still-mighty Wehrmacht's efforts against the USSR, Hitler published a directive dated 23 July 42 that John Keegan calls "the most disastrous of all issued over his signature" (*Mask,* 288). Having split BOCK's AG South, Hitler ordered LIST's AG A to move south 600 miles into the Caucasus and for WEICHS's AG B to advance 200 miles and take Stalingrad.

The Third Reich reached high tide with ROMMEL's defeat at El Alamein, 4 Nov 42, and the loss of Paulus's 6th Army at Stalingrad by 2 Feb 43. Hitler's most serious mistake after 1942 had been to persist in ordering all ground gains to be held at all costs. Another cause of the Wehrmacht's ultimate annihilation is that few of Hitler's generals disobeyed his orders without being sacked: some of history's greatest victories in war have been won by generals who disobeyed orders.

Attentat!

Hitler had long taken extraordinary security precautions that frustrated several assassination attempts, mainly by never announcing his travel plans and frequently changing them at the last moment. After surviving STAUFFENBERG's bomb attempt on 20 July 44 at Rastenburg the fuehrer unleashed a ruthless campaign of vengeance. The principal conspirators and some relatively innocent men were turned over to Roland FREISLER's People's Court in Berlin; their trial and brutal executions were recorded by sound cameras. The films were so horrible that Hitler had to cancel his plans for general distribution to "*encourager les autres,*" as Voltaire has one of his characters put it in *Candide.* Thousands were sent to concentration camps, where many perished.

Another action of Hitler's, "unpublicized at the time, has remained strangely unnoticed even by historians; and it is usually linked with the persecution of the conspirators of 20 July with which it had nothing to." On 22 Aug 44 the fuehrer "ordered the arrest and detention of some 5,000 former Ministers, mayors, Members of Parliament, party leaders and political civil servants of the Weimar Republic," men he thought would be likely—like so many in 1918—to oppose fighting to the bitter end. (Sebastian Haffner, *The Meaning of Hitler* [New York: Macmillan, 1979], 152.)

The fuehrer left Rastenburg on 20 Nov 44 and was in Berlin until 10 December, when he went to direct the Ardennes counteroffensive from field headquarters in the Eifel. On 16 Jan 45, with the Red Army only 100 miles from Berlin Hitler returned to the rubble of his capital. He had one CP in the Chancellery building and another in a large air raid shelter in the Chancellery garden, the **Fuehrerbunker,** where Hitler spent most of his last month.

By now he was a physical and mental wreck, ash-grey, dragging his right foot, suspicious of everything, and kept going by Dr MORELL's injections. Since the war began turning against Germany in 1942 the fuehrer had hoped to regain the initiative with long-heralded secret weapons. One was the improved U-boat that DOENITZ was preparing to use; others were **V-weapons** and the Me 262 jet. But Hitler also consoled himself with historical examples of a lucky turn of events that saved a desperate situation. Foremost in his mind and table talk was Frederick the Great's lucky break in 1762: Prussian forces were faced with certain defeat by an overpower-

ing alliance when Peter III suddenly succeeded Russian Empress Elizabeth and, a great admirer of Frederick's, promptly negotiated a truce that was followed by a peace treaty. So when President Roosevelt suddenly died on 12 Apr 45 Hitler exhibited elation that the alliance against him would act like the alliance against Frederick. This not happening, Hitler then fell back on the theme of Goetterdaemmerung, the twilight of the gods climax to Richard Wagner's "Nibelungen Ring" having long been one of the fuehrer's few aesthetic delights.

On Sunday 22 Apr 45 Hitler finally announced he would not go the Berghof, as Goering and others urged, but would remain in the bunker. The fuehrer authorized others to leave Berlin. This prompted GOERING to send his unfortunate message from the Berghof about taking over. But the last straw for Hitler was learning late on 28 April from Allied newscasts that HIMMLER was working through BERNADOTTE to negotiate a surrender to the Western Allies. Although his rat pack faced sordid extermination rather than an exalted twilight of the gods, Hitler directed the final drama in the bunker as the Russians fought through the last few blocks of Berlin rubble.

Hitler's Last Days

In the wee hours of Sunday 29 Apr 45 Hitler married Eva BRAUN. He then finished dictating his political testament, composed his personal will and slept to noon. Later that Sunday he learned of MUSSOLINI's ignominious end in Milan. On Monday 30 Apr 45 Hitler and Eva committed suicide in their room at 3:30 PM, she with poison and he with a pistol shot through the mouth (Trevor-Roper, post., 201). Full details probably will never be known, but the bodies were taken immediately into the Chancellery garden where 180 liters of gasoline had been gathered for their cremation. With Russian shells falling occasionally, a burning rag was tossed on the gasoline-drenched bodies at about 4 PM. Two and a half hours later they were seen to be still smoldering, and around 11 PM a three-man detail found nothing to bury and concluded that the remains had been scattered by Russian artillery fire. It has been believed that no traces were ever found (ibid., 205), but it also has been alleged that CHUYKOV's troops found the corpses.

Alan Bullock's biography stands out in an overcrowded field that includes excellent works by Joachim C. Fest, Konrad Heiden, and Robert Payne. Walter C. Langer's secret wartime report has been published as *The Mind of Adolf Hitler* (1972). Many historians still consider H. R. Trevor-Roper's *The Last Days of Hitler* (1947) to be the final word on that still-controversial subject, but they now have valuable updated research in James P. O'Donnell's, *The Bunker* (1978). Full publication data on these works are in the main bibliography.

HO CHI MINH. Vietnamese statesman. 1890-1969. Born Nguyem That Thanh in Kim-lien, central Annam (N Vietnam), of peasant stock, he was educated at a Franco-Annamite colonial school. He was a school teacher 1907-11 and a seaman before living in England (1915). He then lived in Paris as a photo retoucher, a writer for socialist newspapers and he helped found the French Communist Party. Nguyem That Thanh, as he still was called, studied at Moscow's East University 1923-24 before working in Canton for a year as a translator with the Soviet consulate and becoming associated with the Chinese communist movement. In Canton he recruited Vietnam exiles during this early stage of the nationalist revolution in China. After CHIANG suddenly and brutally purged his government of communists in 1927 Nguyem That Thanh took refuge in Moscow until 1930. Returning to his homeland as an ardent nationalist he founded the Indochinese Communist Party. This being fiercely repressed by the French colonial administrators after uprisings in 1930-31, the Annamite revolutionary fled to Hong Kong, where the British arrested him for sedition but sent him home secretly to lead another coup. (Peter Teed, 198.) When this failed, Nguyem That Thanh returned to China and founded the Viet Minh or League for the Independence of Viet Nam in 1941, as Japan prepared to take on the western allies. Chiang's Nationalists jailed the Vietnamese nationalist as a communist agitator in 1942 but released him the next year, at the request of the American OSS, to organize anti-Japanese intelligence activities throughout Indochina. At this time he adopted the name Ho Chi Minh, "He Who Enlightens." Drawing US arms at Kunming (terminus of the **Burma Road**), Ho performed his intended mission initially but soon pulled most

of his guerrillas into the highlands to prepare for the postwar period.

The Viet Minh consequently were the only organized force in the field when the Japanese surrendered. They quickly took Hanoi, forced Emperor Bao Dai to abdicate on 20 Aug 45 (ending a 1,000-year monarchy) and on 2 Sep 45 the Democratic Republic of Vietnam was proclaimed with Ho as president.

In the postwar era he directed a long insurgency that drove out the French, despite considerable initial success by LECLERC and de LATTRE DE TASSIGNY. He then won a war of attrition in which desperate US leaders employed strategic bombers against snipers, defoliated ancient jungles to find guerrilla camps, and inflicted huge "body counts" of noncombatants along with Vietcong fighters. The US public watched this for years on their evening television before finally demanding a halt to the war.

Although forced by failing health to become less and less active, and long reported to be on the brink of death from cancer, "Uncle Ho" lived to see the start of negotiations that unified his country in June 76 as the Socialist Republic of Viet Nam with its capital in Hanoi. Saigon had been renamed Ho Chi Minh City in 1975, when it fell to the communists.

HO YING CHIN. Chinese general. 1889-1987. Ho was born into an ancient and wealthy family in Hsingi, Kweichow Province *(CB 42)*. In 1925 he rose from command of a brigade suppressing insurrections in Kwantung to lead a field army. From their student days at the Whampoa MA, Ho and Chiang Kaishek were close associates—Chiang never lost trust his comrade-in-arms. From 10 Mar 30 until 1944 the short, stocky, smiling Gen Ho was Chiang's devoted CofS and war minister. US advisers commented that conferences with him were a round of "double talk and tea" (Tuchman, *Stilwell*, 263). Despite his lack of professional military knowledge in any modern sense, however, Ho gradually eclipsed CHEN CHENG and on 21 Nov 44 Chiang nominated his crony to command Chinese troops in the Alpha Force established to defend the Kunming area. In May 45 Ho stopped the Japanese drive on Chichiang.

After representing Chiang in the final surrender negotiations, he was CinC, Chinese Armed Forces, China Theater; Minister of National

Defense, 1948-49; and Premier in 1949. He died 21 Oct 87 in Taipei.

HOARE, Samuel John Gurney, Viscount Templeton. British statesman. 1880-1959. A brilliant if unwordly statesman who held more high governmental offices in Britain than any other modern minister but Churchill. (Charles Mott-Radclyffe in *DNB*, primary source of most of what follows in this sketch).

Sam Hoare was born 24 Feb 80 in London the son of Sir Samuel Hoare (later first baronet) of Sidestrand Hall, Norfolk. Educated at Harrow and New College, Oxford, taking a double first in the classics and playing on the university tennis and rackets teams, Sam also excelled as an ice skater, and from boyhood in Norfolk was keen naturalist, sportsman, and first-class shot.

Hoare was assistant private secretary to Colonial Secretary Alfred Lyttleton in 1905. After failing in a run for Parliament in 1906 he served on the London County council (1907-10), and was elected in 1910 as a conservative MP. He was invalided out of active military service in WWI for rheumatic fever but learned Russian during six months of convalescence. In 1916 he joined the military mission to Russia as an intelligence officer with rank of lieutenant colonel. Having succeeded to the baronetcy in 1915, Hoare left Russia on 4 Aug 17 when the Kerensky regime began, and—knowing Italian—he went to Italy with the same rank and position.

Demobilized in 1918 he returned to politics as a conservative MPs. He was prominent among those who brought down the Lloyd George government in Oct 22. Hoare was air minister (1922-29) in Bonar Law's cabinet. He learned to fly, did much to develop the newly created RAF and promoted public acceptance of air travel: Sam Hoare and his wife made the first civil air flight from England to India, reaching New Delhi on 8 Jan 27. For this he was knighted GBE in June 27, and she was appointed dame of the British empire.

After being closely involved from 1929 in planning dominion status for India, Sir Samuel became secretary of state for India in 1931. During the next four years he dealt masterfully with the immense task of preparing a constitution for India, even finding some common ground with GANDHI. Hoare piloted the highly controversial and tremendously complex government of India bill through the House of Commons against fierce opposition from Churchill, who led the Conservative Party's right wing. Churchill went so far as to charge Hoare with breaching parliamentary privilege at a dinner for the Manchester chamber of commerce, which had a vital interest in tariff features of the bill. The House of Parliament's committee of privileges was unanimous in clearing Hoare's name. He was knighted (GCSI) in 1934, and the India bill received the royal assent in Aug 35.

Meanwhile Stanley Baldwin became PM in June 35 and was undecided on whether to make Hoare viceroy of India or foreign secretary. Still suffering from the strain of his recent accomplishment, Sir Samuel opted for the viceregency but got the post in London, and at a particularly tough time. Italy, Germany and Italy were flouting the League of Nations covenant and threatening to join forces at a time when collective security was being exposed as a hollow hope. Hoare therefore undertook to buy time, and he made a real impact on foreign affairs before being done in by what became notorious as the **Hoare-Laval proposal.** Sir Samuel (since 1934) manfully refused to withdraw his approval of the plan and had no choice but to resign. Replaced by Anthony EDEN in Oct 35 he reentered the Baldwin government in June 36 as first lord of the Admiralty. A year later he became home secretary in the Chamberlain cabinet, but in the words of Churchill he "seems to have believed that prison reform . . . would become the prevailing topic in the immediate future" (WC, I, 221). Hoare stoutly supported CHAMBERLAIN during the **Munich crisis** but, as home secretary, did take steps to prepare the home front for war.

When this came on 3 Sep 39 Hoare was appointed lord privy seal and made a member of the war cabinet. In Apr 40 he returned to the air ministry and served a month until Churchill succeeded Chamberlain as PM. Having lost out to Churchill for the top post for which he had been on track, Hoare was appointed ambassador to Spain in May 40. He performed well in this haven for secret agents, the neutral country that Hitler coveted for access to Gibraltar. One of Sir Samuel's achievements was to secure release from Spanish jails of some 30,000 Allied POWs and refugees who had escaped through the Pyrenees. *(DNB.)*

Shortly before retirement after leaving Madrid in Dec 44 Hoare was created Viscount Templeton. The title was fabricated from the villa (temple) he had built in a wood on his Norfolk estate *(DNB)*. Templeton wrote the last of his many books here, remaining active until a year before his death in London on 7 May 59. *(DNB.)*

HOBBY, Oveta Culp. US WAC commander. 1905-95. Oveta Culp was born 19 Jan 05 in Killeen, Texas. After taking an early interest in her father's law practice, in 1931 the petite, attractive brunette married Governor William Pettus Hobby of Texas, who was publisher of the Houston *Post*. Becoming involved in newspaper work and Texas politics Mrs Hobby was called on to organize the War Department's Women's Interest Section. This led to creation of the Woman's Auxiliary Army Corps (WAAC) on 15 May 41, Mrs Hobby being sworn in the next day as director with the rank of major. On 1 July 43 one A (for Auxiliary) was dropped to make the WAC a regular component of the **AUS,** and the director was promoted to colonel. WACs performed more than 200 noncombatant jobs at more than 400 US installations and in every oversea theater, and on 30 Apr 45 the WAC reached its peak strength of 100,000 including 6,000 officers *(AA, 167)*.

Col Hobby resigned on 12 July 45 for ill health but lived another 50 years to die 16 Aug 95.

HODGE, John Reed. US general. 1893-1963. Born 12 June 93 and a WWI veteran, Hodge took command of the American Div in May 43. The division had been withdrawn from Guadalcanal to the Fiji Islands, where its mission was to defend Viti Levu and to train. On 29 July 43 Hodge took command of the 43d Div on New Georgia temporarily when Maj Gen John H. HESTER was sent home for lack of success in taking Munda. The strategic air and naval base was stoutly defended by Japanese under the resolute Minoru SASAKI. Within four days Hodge had **pinched out** one of his regiments and pushed the two others to the outer runways of Munda airfield. *(OCMH Chron, 123-24.)* After this brief interlude Hester returned in early August to his troops on Viti Levu.

On 25 Dec 43 he began landing elements of the American Div piecemeal on Bougainville to relieve the 3d Marine Div on a defensive perimeter and prepare to resume the offensive. Hodge led the Americal Div. on Bougainville until he assumed command of the newly activated 24th Corps Hq in Hawaii on 9 Apr 44. He directed this for the rest of the Pacific war, in the Ryukyus, Southern Philippines, Western Pacific, Leyte and on Okinawa, getting his third star on 6 June 45.

Virtually unknown outside close professional circles, Lt Gen Hodge headed the US Army Military Government in Korea 9 Sep 45-26 July 47. Back in the States he took over the 5th Corps on 1 Nov 48 with headquarters at Ft Bragg, NC and was chief of Army Field Forces for a year before retiring 30 June 53 as a full general, having just passed his 60th birthday.

HODGES, Courtney Hicks. US general. 1887-1966. "Without the flair of Patton's Third Army and the breeziness of Simpson's Ninth," writes Omar Bradley, Hodges's 1st Army was the first into Paris, the first to enter Germany, the first to cross the Rhine, and the first to make contact with the Russians. "En route it ticketed more prisoners than any other American Army . . . [and] buried more American dead in the wake of its long advance." (Bradley, I, 226.) Hodges also commanded more tanks than Patton ever did.

Courtney Hodges was born 5 Jan 87 in Perry, Ga, some 70 miles east of Ft Benning. An avid outdoorsman not attracted to his father's newspaper business, he entered West Point in June 04 at the age of 17. After plebe year he was "found deficient" in mathematics and sent home with the advice that he was not meant to be a soldier (Bradley, I, 225-26). Unlike his classmate PATTON, who also was "found" but reentered to graduate with the next class, Hodges became an infantry private in 1906 and was commissioned three years later. He knew EISENHOWER while serving in the Philippines and was with PATTON on the **Punitive expedition** in Mexico. Going to France he rose to command a battalion in the Meuse Argonne, winning the SS and DSC.

In 1938 Lt Col Hodges was assistant commandant of The Infantry School at Ft Benning, Ga, then he was commandant 7 Oct 40-3 Mar 41 with the rank of brigadier general. Promoted to major general, Hodges was Chief of Infantry, 30 May 41-9 Mar 42 before heading the new Replacement and School Command in Birmingham, Ala. He headed 10th Corps Hq from its activation 12 May 42 in San Antonio until the following February. Again promoted, Lt Gen Hodges headed 3d Army Hq and the Southern Defense Command, the combined headquarters being at Ft Sam Houston, Texas. (*AA*, 269, 382, 507, 600.)

In the spring of 1943 Lt Gen Hodges reached England to be his friend BRADLEY's deputy and commander designate in 1st Army Hq. Army CofS George Marshall commented in a message to Eisenhower on 28 Dec 43 that "Hodges is exactly [the] same class of man as Bradley in practically every respect" (Pogue, *Marshall*, II, 647n20). The quiet Georgian took over the 1st Army Hq from BRADLEY on 1 Aug 44.

After helping destroy German forces in Normandy, Hodges led the 1st Army across France into Germany. Resistance, terrain, and weather were particularly tough in the Siegfried Line and Huertgen Forest. Concentrating on taking the Roer dams, 1st Army was spread thin in the Ardennes when the surprise German counteroffensive hit on 16 Dec 44. Hodges and Bradley both believed at first that this was merely a spoiling attack with limited objectives (Weigley, *ETO*, 465). But when this proved to be a bad miscalculation, Hodges was put under Montgomery's operational control on 20 Dec 44. The British field marshal, now directing action north of the Bulge, promptly told Eisenhower that Hodges and other American commanders might have to be relieved for exhaustion. Replying that "Hodges is the quiet reticent type and does not appear as aggressive as he really is," Eisenhower had no choice but to give Montgomery authority to relieve him if necessary. (Pogue, *Marshall*, II, 510; Weigley, 538.) Hodges indeed was shaken by being surprised in the Ardennes, but he recovered quickly and continued to win honors with his 1st Army for the rest of the war, as summarized at the start of this sketch.

Although Marshall retained his opinion that Hodges was in a class with Bradley, the Georgian's final promotion on 15 Apr 45) made him the last of 13 US full generals of WWII. The 14th was Jonathan M. WAINWRIGHT, promoted just after attending the formal Japanese surrender in Tokyo Bay. (The complete pecking order can be found under the glossary heading **Generals.**)

Shortly before V-E day (which was 8 May 45) Hodges got orders to start moving his headquarters to the Far East for the invasion of Japan, and he took an advance party to Manila. When the operation was canceled, 1st Army Hq went to Ft Sam Houston, Texas, where Hodges remained CG until 28 Mar 49. He retired in the San Antonio area and died there on 16 Jan 66.

HOEPNER, Erich. German general. 1886-1944. But for being a victim of Hitler's "house cleaning" after leading his 4th Pz Army to within sight of the Kremlin's spires on 6 Dec 41 (Guderian, 259) Hoepner would not have such an obscure place in history. He was born 14 Sep 86 at Frankfurt on the Oder. Politically minded, he took part in the **Kapp putsch** and was an early opponent of Nazism. During the Munich crisis of 1938 Generalmajor Hoepner, characterized by Walter Goerlitz as "a very talented soldier, and Guderian's chief rival for the leadership of the tank arm" (Goerlitz *GGS*, 334), was brought into the plot to "arrest Hitler at the Chancellery and turn him over to as a warmonger to the judgment of the German people." Leading his 1st Light Div through Thuringia to assembly areas on the Czech border, he had orders to bar the way to Berlin by Sepp DIETRICH's **LSSAH.** But the German people—and much of the frightened world—declined to see a threat of general war in the fuehrer's conduct, and the army lost its first and best chance for a coup d'état.

Succeeding GUDERIAN as CG, 16th Army Corps, he led this through Bohemia to enter Prague on 15 Mar 39 and was promoted 1 Apr 39 to General of Cavalry (*B&O*, 24). In Poland his 16th Corps of Reichenau's 10th Army comprised the 1st and 4th Pz Divs with the 14th and 31st Inf Divs, being designated in some accounts a panzer corps (Manstein, 54). In June 40 his 16th Corps spearheaded Reichenau's 6th Army through Belgium to Liége, then moved south to support Rundstedt's pursuit to Dunkirk. In the second phase of the campaign in France he served in Kleist's group (on GUDERIAN's right), taking Dijon while Guderian's tanks raced to the Swiss border at Pontarlier and wheeled NE to link up in Alsace with Dollmann's 7th Army.

For Opn **Barbarossa** Generaloberst Hoepner (as of 19 July 40) commanded the 4th Pz Gp in

Leeb's AG North. With three panzer divisions in Manstein's 38th and Reinhardt's 41st Pz Corps) plus six other types of division he attacked toward Leningrad through difficult and heavily defended terrain of the Baltic coast. He was fighting through prepared defenses on the Luga River, S of Leningrad, when pulled out in late Sep 41. In Hitler's wholesale reshuffle of mobile units, Hoepner was moved with his staff to AG Center. Picking up three panzer corps near Roslavl (having left his others behind) and now forming the southern wing of the Vyasma encirclement, he attacked on 2 Oct 41. After this triumph he came under the operational control of Kluge's 4th Army Hq. With the mission of encircling Moscow from the NW in terrain unsuited for armor and in bitter winter weather, he attacked 15 Nov 41 with 12 divisions (four of them panzers, one a motorized division and the rest infantry). The night of 5-6 Dec he and Reinhardt (3d Pz Gp) were only 20 miles north of Moscow (Guderian, 259)—his leading elements in sight of the Kremlin's spires—when they could do no more. On 8 Dec 41, as the Soviet counteroffensive was under way with fresh troops from Siberia, Hitler authorized Hoepner to break off the offensive but not to withdraw. On 1 Jan 42 the 4th Pz Group was redesignated the 4th Pz Army.

Putting his career on the line, Hoepner started pulling back from around Sukhinichi on 8 Jan 42 to save his troops from certain annihilation. Kluge had been pleading with Hitler for freedom of action but reported his subordinate's complaint to him about "civilian leadership," assuming the general was criticizing their commander in chief (Guderian, 273). Seeking scapegoats for the failure of Barbarossa, Hitler was conducting a large-scale purge. He had already ordered the dismissal of Hoepner, Guderian, Rundstedt, and Geyer—Leeb and Kuebler left at their own request, and Strauss reported he was physically unfit to go on. But the fuehrer ordered extraordinary action against Hoepner: cashiering without a hearing or trial, denial of the right to wear his uniform or decorations, cancellation of his pension, and denial of a house he had been allotted. "Hoeppner refused to recognize these illegal orders and the lawyers of the *OKH* and the *OKW* showed sufficient courage on this occasion to stand up to Hitler. . . ." (Ibid.) Hitler's OKH adjutant, SCHMUNDT, supported the lawyers' argument that a hearing was required

by law and that its findings probably would exonerate Hoepner. Hence the general was not cashiered—properly retired in June 42—but Hitler had the Reichstag pass a law on 26 Apr 42 that gave him power to change laws by decree. (Ibid.).

Living in retirement at Grunewald-Berlin and active in the anti-Hitler conspiracy, he was the candidate to command the Home Army should Erich FROMM cop out. Fromm did, and in the confusion following STAUFFENBERG's 20 July 44 Attentat Hoepner was one of those who could not react decisively. But he declined Fromm's option to join BECK in suicide—"I am not a swine that I should have to condemn myself." He decided to take his chances with the law. The Army **Court of Honor** ruled that he should be dismissed, which meant facing the People's Court. After a brutal interrogation and an unconvincing defense before Judge Roland Freisler he was hanged brutally with the seven other eight principals in Berlin's Ploetzensee prison on 8 Aug 44.

A biography is *Generaloberst Erich Hoepner* (1969) by W. Chales de Beaulieu, who also has covered Hoepner's drive to Leningrad in *Der Vorstoss der Panzer Gruppe 4 auf Leningrad* (1961).

HOFFMANN, Heinrich. Nazi court photographer. 1885-1957. Born 12 Sep 85 in Fuerth, he learned photography from his father, the Bavarian court photographer. He worked at his trade in London, set up shop in Munich (1909), serving as a Bavarian army photographer during WWI, and published the first of many books of his pictures in 1919. Becoming Hitler's intimate friend in Munich after the war the vulgar, jolly, bibulous Bavarian, a superb cameraman, contributed greatly to the fuehrer's earliest popularity and for some time was the only one allowed to take Hitler's picture. This brought Hoffmann a fortune, and his patron later became wealthy from royalties on the many denominations of postage stamps bearing his image.

The photographer introduced Hitler to Winifred WAGNER, Theodor MORELL and Eva BRAUN, and his daughter married Baldur von SCHIRACH. In Jan 40 he was elected to the Reichstag for the district of Duesseldorff East.

Hoffmann was sentenced by a West German court in 1947 to 10 years in prison for war profiteering, his title of professor (conferred by Hitler in 1938) was withdrawn, and all but 3,000 marks of his great fortune was confiscated. The next year his sentence was reduced to three years but in 1950 it was raised to five years. Freed in 1955, he died 16 Dec 57 in Munich at the age of 72.

HOLCOMB, Thomas. USMC commandant. 1879-1965. The genial, easy-going marine officer was born 5 Aug 79 in New Castle, Del. He attended Western HS in Washington, DC. and joined the USMC three years later (1900). A distinguished marksman, he headed the first Marine team ever to compete in the national matches and was world champion in long range shooting (CB 42). With the AEF in France he rose from a major commanding a battalion of the 6th Regt to second in command of the regiment. Holcomb also was one of the most highly decorated US officers, holding the Navy Cross, four Silver Stars and Purple Heart. After serving in the office of naval operations, he was promoted to brigadier general in 1935 and made commandant of the Marine Corps Schools at Quantico, Va. In Nov 36 he was advanced over senior officers to be US Marine Corps commandant, being reappointed in 1940.

By 7 Dec 41 the Corps had grown to a strength of about 143,000 from 16,000, and in 1945 it had more than 300,000 men and women. The Fleet Marine Force (FMF) comprised four combat divisions and four aircraft wings.

Holcomb had responsibility only for administration and training, operational control over the FMC being vested in overseas commanders. When promoted on 20 Jan 42, Lt Gen Holcomb became the highest ranking US Marine in history. Believing that a younger man (VANDEGRIFT) should take over, he retired 31 Dec 43 and was promoted to full general. In Apr 44 he began four years as Minister to South Africa.

HOMMA, Masaharu. Japanese general. 1888-1946. The conqueror of the Philippines was born into a wealthy family of landowners on Sado Island in Niigata Province. Nearly five feet ten at maturity, clean cut, artistic and highly intelligent, he was noted for lack of samurai spirit, and long association with the British Army in England, France and India (Kogun, 224) made him even more of a Japanese anomaly.

Homma was decidedly non-Japanese also in seeking romantic matrimony. His first attempt, to the daughter of an ex-geisha who married a general, was unfortunate because the wife, left in Japan during her husband's absence abroad, sought the way of her mother. After failing in a sincere effort to get his wife back on the right path Homma was involved with another geisha before finding happiness with Fujiko Takata, a divorcee whose father had spent many years in the US as a businessman. (Swinson, Four Samurai, 40-41.)

Commissioned in the infantry (1907) and a war college graduate (1915), Capt Homma served with the army general staff before going to England in Aug 18. He was an observer with the BEF in France. After being assigned in June 21 to teach at the war college he was sent some 14 months later to India as resident Japanese officer. In Jan 27 he was appointed ADC to Prince Yasuhito Chichibu, Hirohito's younger brother and crown prince until Akihito's birth in 1933. A colonel in 1930 and a lieutenant general by July 38, he commanded the 27th Div around Tiensin. In Dec 40 he became CG, Formosa Army.

Despite lack of high command experience he was ordered in Nov 41 to take the Philippines. As Supreme Commander of Japanese Army Forces in the Philippines, with his 14th Army and supporting air forces, initially about 43,000 officers and men, he was expected to complete the mission in 50 days, by 31 Jan 42. Homma deserves top marks for planning an extremely complex operation and directing its initial phases. He took Manila in 22 days, by 3 Jan 42.

But in an astounding failure of military intelligence, the Japanese did not know that MacArthur had long planned to maneuver his main forces onto Bataan. When Homma reported on 10 Feb 42 that he needed time to reorganize, CGS SUGIYAMA was so infuriated he recommended that Homma and his CofS be replaced. But only the latter was sacked, the Japanese being reluctant to admit publicly that they had suffered a setback.

Homma got reinforcements and started preparatory artillery fires on 3 Apr 42. Four days later his troops began penetrating the Bataan defenses and the peninsula was conquered by 9 April. WAINWRIGHT surrendered all forces in the Philippines on 6 May. Despite a not inconsiderable achievement, the general had taken more than three months longer than expected, using forces needed in the **NEI**. Swinson appraises "this most Europeanized of Japanese generals" as a desk general "far too soft for a *samurai*" (op ci 244-45). Homma further infuriated superiors by quashing anti-American propaganda among subjugated Filipinos and by restraining Japanese troops from the orgy they expected as reward for victory. In late-Aug 42 the general was recalled, and in Aug 43 he was transferred to the First Reserve List (Hayashi, 224). When KOISO succeeded TOJO in Dec 43 Homma was made minister of information.

US authorities in Japan arrested Homma on 15 Sep 45 as a war criminal. On 9 Dec 45, the day after being moved from a POW camp near Tokyo to Sugamo Prison, he was presented with 42 charges that included the **Bataan death march** (which he claimed to have known nothing about), bombing and shelling the open city of Manila, and various acts of his troops. Trial in Manila began 3 Jan 46; the death sentence was announced 11 February; he was shot on 3 Apr 46 at Los Baños, Luzon; and Homma's remains were disposed of secretly. But three Japanese shrines have hair and fingernails collected by his wife at one of their last meetings.

HONDA, Masaki. Japanese general. 1889-1964. From heading the 20th Army in Manchukuo Lt Gen Honda took command of the newly formed 33d Army in Burma on 30 Apr 44. MUTAGUCHI's 15th Japanese Army was pressing westward toward Imphal, India, and Honda's mission was to cover the Chinese threat to Mutaguchi's rear. The core of Honda's army was Lt Gen Shinichi Tanaka's 18th Div, facing three Chinese divisions in the Hukawng Valley of N Burma, and Lt Gen Yuzo Matsuyama's 56th Div, which faced some 10 Chinese divisions that had crossed the upper Salween in the Yunnan region.

Mutaguchi's "march on Delhi" (Opn **U**) was stopped by the British-Indian Army as the rainy season made further Japanese efforts hopeless. On 8 July Burma Area Army commander KAWABE belatedly ordered Mutaguchi to retreat, and or about 30 Aug 44 he was succeeded by Heitaro KIMURA.

Honda was ordered in Jan 45 to hold a north-south line from Lashio to Mandalay, but he deployed forces as far north as Mogaung and Myitkyina to delay Stilwell's efforts with US-Chinese troops to reopen the Burma road. When Gen SLIM feinted toward Mandalay but sent MESSERVY 60 miles farther south to take the virtually undefended Japanese supply base at Meiktila (27 Feb-3 Mar 45), Honda's 33d Army was threatened with annihilation. But Kimura—fooled into assuming he was dealing with a mere raid, charged Honda with holding Mandalay and cutting off the British spearhead at Meiktila. Honda nearly succeeded; the British had to use air resupply for three weeks; but the 17th Indian Div held at Meiktila and Stopford's 33d Corps, its task facilitated, took Mandalay during the period 9-20 Mar 45. Stopford then moved down the Irrawaddy, switching flanks with Messervy, and splitting central Burma down the middle. It was the beginning of the end for the Burma Area Army, and the British took Rangoon without opposition on 3 May. But Lt Gen Honda performed well in a long and bitter retreat against overwhelming air, ground forces and logistical resources.

Honda's earlier service had been as CofS in the Chinese Expeditionary Army from his promotion to lieutenant general in Dec 39. On 28 Oct 40 he had taken over the 8th Div, then headed the Military Education Branch Armored Dept 1941-43, before commanding the 20th Army in Manchukuo.

HOOVER, J(ohn) Edgar. US FBI Chief. 1885-1972. Born 1 Jan 95 in Washington, DC, J. Edgar Hoover lived in the family house for 43 years, until his mother's death and he never married. As a vigorous 110-pound runt known for a booming parade ground voice, "Speedy" Hover graduated from Washington's Central HS in 1913 as valedictorian and captain of the cadet company.

Becoming a messenger at the Congressional Library after his father's death, the intensely ambitious young Hoover put himself through night law school at George Washington Univ. Getting his master's degree in 1917 and being in private practice briefly, he entered the Dept of Justice that same year as an attorney. Hoover had some experience in wartime counter-espionage and began his obsession with pursuing "radicals." In 1919 he became special assistant to the US attorney general. "I was assigned to prepare a legal brief of the newly formed Communist Party [of America] and Communist Labor Party [of America]," he wrote four decades later. "This necessitated an extensive and penetrating study." Federal ghosts—who must share blame for this federal prose style—expanded the extensive and penetrating study into Hoover's much-touted *Masters of Deceit: The Story of Communism in America and How to Fight It* (New York; Henry Holt, 1958).

Meanwhile, in 1921 the short, pudgy police attorney became assistant director of the Bureau of Investigation, and a mere three years later he was appointed director. Hoover's agency, promptly redesignated the Federal Bureau of Investigation, was in disrepute, and the new director was charged with remedying this. He set up high standards of recruiting and training, established the FBI National Academy, began building a massive file of fingerprints and criminal dossiers, and formed a laboratory that broke new ground in scientific crime detection. The FBI grew quickly into a highly scientific force of honest, clean-living G-men. The agency's size and power ballooned as Congress reacted with new legislation to curb an upsurge in crime and corruption caused largely by Prohibition and the Great Depression.

The autocratic police tsar kept his bureau free from political control and did not hesitate to use his extensive secret police resources to blackmail enemies, including congressmen who might curtail his powers. Hoover saw that the FBI's triumphs were trumpeted by the national news and entertainment media.

Although he made the FBI a household name for fearless pursuit of public enemies, Hoover never targeted organized crime. He steadfastly denied that it even existed! It has been conjectured that the mafia bought immunity by threatening to reveal one or more instances of homosexual transgression in a public place by Hoover, a confirmed bachelor.

On the outbreak of Hitler's war 1939 the FBI was given primary responsibility for counterintelligence, antisabotage and associated national security matters. Hoover's G-men continued to performed conventional police duties well, scoring some sensational and highly publicized triumphs. But America's arrogant, parochial top cop proved to be an inept spy catcher. Preoccupied with gaining quick and highly publicized glory for himself and the FBI, he was incapable of learning from British veterans in

Stewart MENZIES's Secret Intelligence Service (**SIS**). Hoover's shortcomings are epitomized in his failure to pass on a report by the SIS double agent Dusko "Tricycle" POPOV that the Japanese had specific questions about Pearl Harbor's defenses.

When the Pearl Harbor disaster of 7 Dec 41 brought America into the war, and William DONOVAN's OSS was created, Hoover continued to be preoccupied with roles and missions. In the Battle of Washington he feuded with Donovan and other military intelligence chiefs. When it was all over he strongly opposed creation of the CIA to succeed the OSS.

Having directed the FBI for 48 years under eight presidents, and increasingly a target of social and political activists, Hoover died in office in 1972. He took many secrets to the grave, and revisionist biographers will be busy for generations.

HOOVER, John Howard. US admiral. 1887-1970. He was born 15 May 87 in Ohio and graduated from the USNA (73/86) on 12 Sep 06. At the start of WWII he was a rear admiral heading the Caribbean Sea Frontier. Becoming a vice admiral in 1942 Hoover then commanded all land-based air operations in the Gilbert, Marshall and Marianna Islands in the Pacific. Hoover then commanded the Forward Areas of the Pacific. He retired 1 July 48 as an admiral and died 2 Dec 70 at the Bethesda, Md, USHN.

HOPE, Victor Alexander John, 2d Marquess of Linlithgow. 1887-1952. The large, shy, stubborn Scot was born 24 Sep 87 at Hopetoun House, South Queensferry, West Lothian. *DNB* lists him as "Hope" but refers to him consistently as "Linlithgow." He was 7th Earl of Hopetoun before acquiring his father's titles in 1908 *(DNB)*. Educated at Eton, he was an active Territorial, serving in WWI and reaching the rank of colonel. He saw action with the Lothians and Border Horse and commanded a battalion of the Royal Scots. He remained a regular army officer until accepting political office as civil lord of the Admiralty 1922-24, then he was president of the Navy League 1924-31. Meanwhile he was chairman, Royal Commission on Indian Agriculture 1926-28, then was on the Joint Select Committee on Indian Constitutional Reform 1933-34.

With this background he was Viceroy of India 1935-43, the longest tenure since 1856. In a period of exceptional stress Lord Linlithgow introduced provincial autonomy (as called for in the Act of 1935), persuaded the (Indian) Congress to take office (1937), and ensured stability of the NW Frontier by directing military operations (1936-38). Despite civil unrest, opposition from Congress, withdrawal of provincial ministries, and Indian rejection in 1942 of Lord CRIPPS's constitutional proposals *(DNB)*, the viceroy mobilized the subcontinent of 400 million people to support the Allied war effort. Succeeded by WAVELL on 19 June 43, Lord Linlithgow added KG to his many other honors (KT in 1928; GCIE the next year; and GCSI in 1936). He was appointed to the privy council in 1935. Lord Linlithgow retired in Oct 43 to his Scottish estate at Southqueens Ferry. He was chairman of the Midlands Bank from 1944 until his sudden death on 5 Jan 52 while out shooting at Hopetoun. *(DNB.)*

HOPKINS, Harry Lloyd. US presidential advisor. 1890-1946. As Roosevelt's closest and most trusted adviser he looms large in the literature of the WWII. The son of a harness maker, Hopkins was born in Sioux City, Iowa. (The exact date is not given in standard references.) He graduated cum laude from Grinnell Univ in 1912 and went to work in a succession of social welfare organizations, mainly as an administrator. Because of bad eyesight he was rejected for military service. After being director of the ARC southern division in New Orleans (1917-22) and returning north, he moved through various charitable organizations to become chairman of the New York State Temporary Relief Administration in 1932. First meeting FDR in 1928, the rustic Iowan and the Hudson Valley patrician immediately established a strong personal and professional rapport. Harry Hopkins consequently was named administrator of the Federal Emergency Relief Act as President Roosevelt launched his first term in 1933. In 1935 he took over direction of the short-lived Civil Works Administration and went on to head the monumental Works Progress Administration (WPA), 1935-38. After gaining national acclaim and strong political criticism in these New Deal, depression-era activities, Hopkins became Secretary of Commerce in Dec 38. He had no

professional qualifications, and tongues wagged over what Roosevelt's true motives might be. It was speculated that FDR wanted to crack down on business, but some had just the opposite view: that the president was proffering an olive branch! Others thought "that man in the White House" was grooming his crony for the 1940 presidential nomination *(CB 41)*.

With a fast mind and a great capacity for absorbing facts, the high-strung, hard-driven administrator addressed staggering problems of labor, taxation, utilities, railroads, business, and trade with Latin America (ibid.). But Hopkins was hit hard by his second wife's death at the end of 1937 and began to suffer the bad health that would persist. He resigned in Aug 40 but—at FDR's insistence—as Special Adviser and Assistant to the President he moved into the White House. When ROOSEVELT set up **Lend Lease** he made Hopkins its first administrator. Taking over in Mar 41 Hopkins turned the gigantic program over to STETTINIUS on 28 Aug 41. The long, lanky, intense, no-nonsense Iowan undertook the first of his special presidential missions to the UK and USSR in July-Aug 41, favorably impressing Churchill and Stalin. Hopkins was a member of the War Mobilization Committee. In 1942 he made another trip to London, and in 1945—after FDR's death—he went to Moscow as Truman's representative in talks about postwar **Poland.** *(CE.)*

Having continued to drive himself, Hopkins left public life in July 45 and died 29 Jan 46. *See* Robert E. Sherwood, *Roosevelt and Hopkins* (New York: Harper, 1948).

HORE-BELISHA, (Isaac) Leslie. British statesman. 1893-1957. Scion of a prominent family of Sephardic Jews that had been in England since the Spanish Inquisition, Leslie Belisha was born 7 Sep 93 in the London suburb of Kilburn. He was left fatherless before the age of one and his devoted mother made sacrifices to give him a first-class education at Clifton College and, for brief periods, at the Sorbonne and Heidelberg. When his mother married (Sir) Adair Hore in 1912 she asked her son to couple his name with his stepfather's. Leslie Hore-Belisha distinguished himself for a year as an essayist and author of political poems at St John's College, Oxford, before enlisting for war service. Commissioned in the Army Service Corps, he served in France from early Nov 14 with an infantry brigade. Having shown great enterprise for a year in "developing local supply" *(DNB)* he was transferred to 3d Army Hq. Subsequently promoted to major the enterprising supply officer was sent to army headquarters in Salonika. He was invalided home in early 1918 with malaria. Back at St John's to continue a sparkling career, he became president of the Oxford Union and had enough success in free lance journalism to read law and be called to the bar by the Inner Temple in 1923.

Adopted by the Devonport division of Plymouth as a Liberal, Hore-Belisha held the seat from 1923 until 1945. He became minister of transport in 1934 and in Oct 35 was sworn of the Privy Council and given cabinet rank. In May 37 Hore-Belisha succeeded Duff COOPER as secretary of state for war. With Chamberlain's mandate to make "drastic changes" *(DNB)*, the impatient, intolerant Hore-Belisha did so in spades. He stimulated recruiting by raising pay and allowances, by improving life in barracks, by reducing obsolete restrictions on off-duty time, and by providing recruits with more technical training that would be useful in civilian life. (Ibid.) The minister of war revitalized the officer corps by measures including earlier retirement for over-age-in-grade generals and colonels. With Capt Basil LIDDELL HART as his military adviser at one time Hore-Belisha fought conventional wisdom to give the British army a capacity for mechanized war.

Taking "his political life in his hands" on 27 Apr 39 (WC, I, 355), Hore-Belisha forced CHAMBERLAIN to introduce conscription. The controversial minister soon came under mounting criticism after Britain went to war on 3 Sep 39. Some of his enemies were anti-Semitic, but this did not deter the man who had aspired since undergraduate days to be another Disraeli. *(DNB.)*

Hore-Belisha's political demise stemmed from criticizing Lord GORT for the BEF's slowness in setting up defenses in France. Two dominion ministers with war service, Australia's R. G. CASEY and South Africa's Deneys Reitz, had been even sharper critics after visiting the front. But Gort's explosive protest to men in high places, including the king, and support of Gort from the French high command finally convinced a reluctant PM to oust the abrasive war minister. The news dismayed "most of the press and many of the public," comments Liddell Hart *(DNB)*. Declining to head the Board of Trade or the Ministry of Information, Hore-Belisha resigned on 4 Jan 40 and was replaced by Oliver Stanley. For the rest of the war Hore-Belisha was a vociferous back-bencher and one of Churchill's severest critics. He led the unsuccessful debate for a motion of no confidence after the fall of Tobruk on 21 June 42.

The stormy petrel returned briefly to public office in May 45 as Minister of National Insurance in Churchill's Caretaker Government but lost his seat in Parliament when Attlee's labor government took power. Persuaded to join the Conservative Party, but not offered a suitable seat, Hore Belisha was no longer a political power. He accepted a peerage in 1954 and was regaining Parliamentary influence when he died suddenly on 16 Feb 57 at Reims while leading an official delegation to France.

HORII, Tomitaro. Japanese general. 1890-1942. Maj Gen Horii was sent to Guam in Aug 40 as commander of the South Seas Detachment. This was an elite unit formed around the reinforced 144th Inf Regt to include six-foot giants of extraordinary physique. A "small, stout gentleman no longer young, with gray hair and spectacles and an air of natural dignity and command" (Mayo, *Bloody Buna*, 45), Horii took Rabaul from an Australian detachment on 23 Jan 42 in a matter of hours. He then was reinforced by Yazawa Force (veterans of Malayasia) and Col Yosuke Yokoyama's crack 15th Indep Engr Regt. Yokoyama's regiment reached the Buna area on 21 July 42 to establish a beachhead and push a reconnaissance up the Kokoda Trail. Horii followed three weeks later with the main body, eventually having about 8,000 combat troops and 3,000 naval construction personnel. (Keogh, 103, 104, 184; Morison, VI, 33.)

The Japanese knew little about the Kokoda Trail, a slippery track to Port Moresby whose main branch crossed the 7,000-foot contour in the rugged and mist-shrouded Owen Stanley Range. Before the war it was used only by barefoot natives and experienced explorers, but it might be improved into a significant military road. With some opposition from the Australian

39th Bn, Horii was within 30 miles of Port Moresby by mid-Sep 42. Ahead of schedule, he dug in and waited to cooperate with an amphibious force that was to attack Port Moresby a month later.

An earlier Japanese attempt to take Port Moresby by amphibious assault had been frustrated by the Battle of the Coral Sea, 4-8 May 42. Horii and his troops had been in Rear Adm Koso ABE's Transportation Unit of the Port Moresby Invasion Group, which had to turn back.

Now the strategy was upset by the American landing on Guadalcanal, 7 Aug 42, and failure of the amphibious operation at Milne Bay, 25 Aug-6 Sep 42. So Horii went on alone with what had been an improvised operation from the start. He was getting reinforcements along the trail from Buna, but wounds, malnutrition and pneumonia took such a toll that on 24 Sep 42 a bitterly disappointed Horii was ordered to withdraw. Ironically, the Australian commander was replaced four days later by HERRING as what initially was a good Japanese delaying action turned into a disorderly rout. Horii was nearly back to his base when he decided to take a short cut across the turbulent Kumusi River from Wairopi on the night of 12-13 Nov 42. An improvised log raft broke apart, and Horii (refusing assistance) was drowned along with his CofS, Lt Col Toyanari Tanaka, and two others. (Mayo, 84; Keogh, 240.) His death was confirmed 10 days later, and he was promoted posthumously to lieutenant general (Hayashi, *Kogun*, 224). Hatazo ADACHI took over Horii's command.

HORROCKS, Brian Gwynne. British general. 1895-1985. The colorful "Jorrocks" was a corps commander under Montgomery in the Western Desert and then in northern Europe. He was born at Ranniket, India, son of an army doctor, and educated at Uppingham and Sandhurst. In 1914 he was commissioned in the Middlesex Regt. He received an abdominal wound at Ypres on 21 Oct 14, was captured, and spent the next four years as a POW. Serving as a volunteer with the mission to the White Russians in Siberia, he won the **MC** and was a Soviet POW in 1919-20.

As the British modern pentathlon champion in 1924 he took part in that year's Olympics. The athletic but unacademic Horrocks needed four attempts to enter Camberley in 1931 but later was a chief instructor there. As a tempo-

rary lieutenant commanding the 2d Bn of his regiment Horrocks went to France in 1939 with the BEF as part of Montgomery's division. Promoted during the Dunkirk evacuation to brigadier *(DNB)*, a year later he took command of the 9th Armd Div the UK. On 15 Aug 42 he got a phone call that he was going overseas and moving "one up" (Horrocks, 102-3). Montgomery had taken over the 8th Army in the Western Desert and wanted Horrocks to succeed the late "Strafer" GOTT as 13th Corps commander. With the customary temporary rank, Lt Gen Horrocks led the "infantry heavy" 13th Corps at Alam Halfa and El Alamein before succeeding Herbert LUMSDEN as commander of the "tank heavy" 10th Corps. On 30 Apr 43 Horrocks joined Noel ANDERSON's 1st British Army in Tunisia, succeeding John Crocker (WIA) as 9th Corps commander.

The campaign in North Africa was long over when Horrocks was badly wounded at Bizerte in early June 43. The bullet from a strafing German fighter traversed his torso from top to bottom! Much surgery was required and Horrocks concealed the fact that he was far from recovered when he answered Montgomery's call to command the 30th Corps in the Normandy bridgehead around Falaise. Taking over on 1 Aug 44, and being in DEMPSEY's 2d British Army, the corps broke out, and Horrocks's 11th Armd Div moved so fast in taking Amiens on 31 Aug 44 that it captured EBERBACH in his pyjamas (Horrocks, 198). The corps liberated Brussels on 3 Sep 44 and the next day entered Antwerp.

In Opn **Market-Garden** Horrocks was involved in the failed attempt to make the ground link-up in. During the Ardennes counteroffensive Horrocks's corps was the only strategic reserve available, and it took up a defensive position behind the Meuse to cover Brussels. For the Reichswald campaign (Opn **Veritable**), 8 Feb-5 Mar 45, Horrocks was attached to CRERAR's 1st Cdn Army; his corps had some 200,000 troops supported by 1,400 guns. Against fanatical young Nazis in the 1st Parachute Army, and moving through lowlands flooded waist deep, by 23 Feb 45 the 30th Corps and 2d Cdn Corps overran the first German line of defense at Cleves and Goch. British troops made contact with Simpson's US 9th Army at Geldern on 3 Mar 45. Back in Dempsey's army for the Rhine crossing, Jorrocks's 30th Corps took Bremen on 27 Apr 45 and was clearing the Cuxhaven Peninsula when the Germans capitulated.

Sir Brian was retired in 1949 to become Gentleman Usher of the Black Rod and do a series of military programs on TV. His memoirs were published first as *A Full Life* (London, 1960) then as *Escape to Action* (New York: St Martin's, 1961).

HORTHY de Nagybánya, Miklós (Nicholas) Vités. Regent of Hungary. 1868-1957. Horthy was born in Kenderes, Hungary, of a long line of Protestant landed gentry. Tall, slender, handsome, and with an impressive military bearing, he became ADC to Emperor Franz Joseph in 1909. During WWI he commanded BB *Hapsburg* and a cruiser. Capt Horthy became a national hero in 1917 for breaking through the Allied blockade in the Straits of Otranto and getting his ships to friendly waters.

In Jan 18 he took command of the Austro-Hungarian navy when it was transferred to Yugoslavia. At this time he was promoted to vice admiral. Soon after the Hungarian monarchy collapsed (16 Nov 18) and Emperor Charles I went into exile, Horthy led the new Hungarian army against Béla Kun's communist forces. The admiral entering Budapest with the Romanian invaders on 4 Aug 19. On 1 Mar 20 the Hungarian parliament appointed Horthy CinC of Hungarian forces, regent and head of what nominally was a restored monarchy.

Horthy's government undertook the "white terror" in which many communists, fellow travelers and Jews were killed or imprisoned. The regent prevented Charles I from reclaiming the throne on returning from exile (27 Mar 21), and in 1932 Horthy became a virtual dictator. (Langer, *Ency,* 1012-13.)

A fervent national desire to recover territories lost by the Trianon settlement of 1920 put Hungarian public opinion solidly behind the Germans. (Hungary had about 500,000 Germans.) As Hitler gobbled up Austria and Czechoslovakia, Horthy reclaimed lost territories in southern Slovakia and the Carpatho-Ukraine. Hungary withdrew from the League of Nations in Apr 39, joined the Anti-Comintern Pact, and in Nov 40 became a member of the Axis. Sending troops to support Hitler's invasion of Yugoslavia in Apr 41 and the invasion of Russia

two months later, Horthy was rewarded by return of Hungary's lost provinces in Czechoslovakia and Romania.

But in 1943 relations between Horthy and Hitler started deteriorating. When the admiral asked that his troops be withdrawn from the eastern front, the Germans responded promptly by occupying Hungary on 19 Mar 44. The Soviets were within 50 miles of Budapest when the regent undertook to conclude a separate peace in Oct 44. Hitler had reacted too slowly to save Romania (*see* CAROL II), but he did not repeat the mistake. As the admiral's son and political heir, Nicholas, met with Soviet agents on Sunday 15 Oct 44 to initial the surrender pact, the swashbuckling Otto SKORZENY seized young Horthy, trussed him up, and sent him by special air delivery to Germany. Meanwhile the admiral escaped to seek protection from a German general, Pfeffer-Wildenbruch, who was related to the former kaiser. Skorzeny took custody of Horthy and escorted him to Germany in style—the regent's own train—to spend the rest of the war under close surveillance in a Bavarian castle. After about seven months in German hands he was taken by US forces in May 45. The next year Horthy was released without trial from prison in Nuremberg. He spent his remaining years in Estoril, Portugal, writing *A Life for Hungary* (1953) and *Memoirs* (1956) before dying on 9 Feb 57.

HOSSBACH, Friedrich. German general. 1894-1980. "The last Prussian . . . all but immune to intimidation" even by Hitler (Deutsch, I, 149-50), Hossbach was born 21 Nov 94 at Unna, near Dortmund in Westphalia. Starting his career in 1913 and spending WWI on the eastern front, he was a regimental adjutant in 1918, remained in uniform, and in 1927 was assigned to the Reichswehr ministry as a captain. On 3 Aug 34 Major Hossbach became "Adjutant of the Wehrmacht with Hitler" but remained chief of the Central Section of the General Staff. Because BLOMBERG did not have the fuehrer's ear, Hossbach (soon promoted to colonel) was "a kind of watchdog for the General Staff" (Goerlitz, *GGS,* 322). He is remembered in history for the **Hossbach memorandum.** The colonel was dismissed on 28 Feb 30 after stoutly refusing to go along with Hitler and Goering in the plot against FRITSCH. (See Deutsch, I, 115, 154, 171-175.)

Succeeded by Rudolf SCHMUNDT, Hossbach retained his OKH post but was on Hitler's black list. He was CofS of Adolf Strauss's 2d Corps Hq at Stettin when Hitler learned of this on 5 Nov 39 and "harshly intervened to transfer him to a troop command" (Deutsch, II, 230). As colonel of the 82d Inf Regt, 31st Div, in France, Hossbach was awarded the RK on 7 Oct 40. The colonel headed the division briefly, 21 Jan-28 Feb 42, was promoted to Generalmajor on 1 Mar 42, and took command of the 82d Div exactly a month later. Hossbach returned to the 31st Div on 16 May 43, and on 2 Aug 43 (*B&O,* 57) took over the 56th Pz Corps. Hossbach was a Generalleutnant when awarded the Oakleaves on 11 Sep 43 for action in Russia (Angolia, II, 250-71). He was promoted to General of Infantry on 1 Nov 43 according to Angolia (ibid.), but other authorities show him getting this rank on 2 Aug 43 (*B&O,* 57). Replaced by Anton Grasser for the period 15 Nov-9 Dec 43, Hossbach led the 56th Pz Corps back from around Roslav to the Dnieper River. Early the next year he was forced back through the Pripet Marshes to the Kovel and Brest-Litovsk areas. Then the general led "Gruppe Hossbach," his corps reinforced by "Gruppe Gille" and several divisions, in a successful counteroffensive (*B&O,* 57).

Leaving the 56th Pz Corps on 14 June 44, Hossbach took command of the 4th Army on 19 July 44. The army was on the SE border of East Prussia as part of Reinhart's hardpressed AG Center. In late October and early Nov 44 he attacked successfully around Gumbinnen (Seaton, *R-G War,* 562), but two months later was in a highly vulnerable position forward of the Mansurian Lakes. Without authority, Hossbach started pulling back on 23 Jan 45, causing heavily fortified Loetzen to be lost without a fight. But the 4th Army attacked west to break out of the encirclement and had Romanekno's 48th Soviet Army in serious trouble when Hossbach learned by telephone on 28 Jan 45 that he was dismissed. His often-cited memoirs are *Zwischen Wehrmacht und Hitler, 19341938,* first published in 1949 and the second revision appearing in 1965.

HOTH, Hermann. German general. 1885-1971. "One of the most underestimated Germany generals and Panzer experts" (Brett-Smith, 273.) "Papa" Hoth was born 12 Apr 85 in Neuruppen,

near Berlin. He was the son of an army medical officer. In 1935-38 he commanded the 18th Div at Liegnitz, rising to the rank of Generalleutnant and being 15th in seniority on the Army List (ibid.). With accelerated promotion to General of Infantry, he assumed command of the new 15th Mtz Corps on 10 Nov 38. In Reichenau's 10th Army he led the corps from Upper Silesia into south Poland and was awarded the RK on 27 Oct 39.

With his Pz Gp Hoth comprising Joachim Lemelson's 5th and Erwin Rommel's 7th Pz Divs for the invasion of France in May 40 he drove through the Ardennes to the Channel, then into Normandy and Brittany. In the promotions of 19 July 40, Hoth was made a Generaloberst, and on 16 Nov 40 his formation was redesignated Pz Gp 3. For the invasion of Russia this comprised Rudolf Schmidt's 39th and Adolf Kuntzen's 57th Pz Corps. Teamed with Adolf STRAUSS's 9th Army on the north flank of AG Center, Hoth made the great strategic envelopments of Minsk and Vitebsk. Two days after being awarded the Oakleaves on 17 July 41, Hoth was ordered to leave the high road to Moscow and wheel north, where he again worked with Strauss. On 5 September his 57 Pz Corps and BUSCH's 16th Army were about to take Demyansk when Hoth was ordered back to AG Center for the delayed drive on Moscow. On the third day of his offensive, while heavily engaged in the encirclement of Vyasma from the north, Hoth was replaced by Georg Hans Reinhardt (on 4 Oct 41) and sent to command the 17th Army in the Ukraine.

From around historic Poltava he advanced more than 50 miles to the upper stretch of the Donetz River, but then he was driven back by the Soviet counteroffensive that started in mid-Jan 42. On 1 June 42 Hoth succeeded HOEPNER as head of the 4th Pz Army. In the great German summer offensive of 1942, Hoth's initial mission was to encircle Voronezh and then drive south to the lower Don. He covered the southern approaches to Stalingrad in the fall of 1942, but by then his force was a panzer army in name only and included seven Romanian divisions.

But the 4th Pz Army had three fresh panzer corps (57th, 48th, and 2d SS) after Manstein took over AG Don. Finally having full scope for his ability Hoth executed a remarkable counteroffensive that held open an escape route around Rostov for Kleist's AG A.

In the great battle of Kursk, 5-12 July 43, Hoth's 4th Pz Army had the largest mass of German armor ever assembled. But his gains in Opn **Citadel,** in which he attacked the southern face of the salient, had limited success because Hitler had so delayed the start of Citadel that the Soviets were ready, and morale of their infantry troops was greatly improved.

For his strategic withdrawal and defense of the Dnieper River line Hoth was awarded the Swords on 15 Sep 43 (Angolia, I, 142). His army was badly mauled in the Soviet counteroffensive that exploded out of its bridgeheads on 3 Nov 43 and quickly retook Kiev and Zhitomir. After Generaloberst Hoth urged withdrawal to better defensive positions, Hitler replaced him on 26 Nov 43 with Erhard Rauss (*B&O,* 23). Now approaching his 59th birthday and four years of high command behind him—he had commanded the formidable 4th Pz Army for almost 18 months—Hoth joined the Reserve of Officers. Bearing a striking facial resemblance to the gray, foxy Admiral CANARIS, Hoth has been characterized as "steady rather than dashing, cool, a good strategist and tactician, unflappable, and well liked by his troops and colleagues (Brett-Smith, 273).

But for "crimes against humanity" committed by his subordinates Hoth was sentenced on 27 Oct 48 at Nuremberg to 15 years in prison. Amnestied after serving six years, he retired to the mountains and wrote about military history and armored warfare (Angolia, I, 143). His memoirs, *Panzeroperationen,* were published in 1956.

HOWARD, Leslie. British actor, director, producer. 1893-1943. The archetypical Englishman in many film classics was the eldest son of Hungarian Jewish immigrants. Born in London on 3 Apr 93, named Leslie Howard Steiner *(DNB)* or Stainer (Briggs, ed.; *CB 43*), and educated locally, he became a bank clerk. At the start of war in 1914 he enlisted, was commissioned in the Northhamptonshire Yeomanry on 15 Mar 15, but resigned in May 16 *(DNB)* after suffering shell shock (Briggs, ed.). In 1917 he joined a touring company and adopted the name by which he was known thereafter. Leslie Howard became famous in England and

America as a stage actor. His first film appearance was in 1930.

At the start of war in 1939 he returned to England from America, having starred that year in *Gone With the Wind.* Like Noel COWARD, Leslie Howard was responsible for producing some of the best war films. One of these, *The First of the Few* (1942), dramatized the story of aircraft designer CAMM and the Spitfire.

Leslie Howard and 16 others were killed shortly after noon on 1 June 43 when a Ju 88 on routine patrol over the Bay of Biscayne shot down his unarmed DC-3 passenger plane. Hit in two cannon passes, BOAC flight 777a crashed in flames. Churchill, who had been on a well-publicized visit to North Africa, has written that after a German secret agent reported seeing him board the plane in Lisbon "a German war plane was instantly ordered out, and the defenseless aircraft was ruthlessly shot down. . . . The brutality of the Germans was only matched by the stupidity of their agents." (WC, IV, 830.) Nigel West does not bother to comment on this canard in *Operation Garbo* (1985), the book he wrote with Juan "Garbo" Pujol, the famous British double agent who frequently flew between Lisbon and England.

The Germans did not discipline the inexperienced pilot and crew, much less apologize, "but there were no further attacks on civilian aircraft flying between Portugal and England" (West, 97). The pilot, one Flight Lt Bellstedt from KG 40 based near Lorient, was later KIA. But his radio operator and navigator, when subsequently fished out of the sea by an RAF air-sea rescue launch, boasted of having shot the airliner down "for target practice." Both of these Luftwaffe heroes were badly beaten before being delivered ashore. Based on a single account, this may be another canard, but Nigel West sees fit to mention it. (Ibid.)

HOWARD, Trevor Wallace. British actor. 1916-88. The son of an English father and Canadian mother, Howard was educated at Clifton College and the Royal Academy of Dramatic Art. (Briggs, ed.) He made his stage debut in the Shakespeare Festival, Stratford-on-Avon, in 1936. After serving with the 1st Br Abn Div he returned to the stage in 1944 and made his film debut that year in *The Way Ahead.* Another film with WWII associations was *The Third Man* (1949), a spy classic. Howard went on to win acclaim until his death for stage, TV, and film performances.

HSUAN T'UNG (Henry P'U Yi). China's last emperor. 1906-67. At the age of six he abdicated as emperor when Sun Yat-sen's revolution ended the Ch'ing dynasty. The Japanese made him head of their puppet state in Manchuria in Mar 34. Taken prisoner by the Soviets in 1945, he was turned over to the Chinese communist government in 1956. His autobiography is *From Emperor to Citizen* (1964).

HSUEH, Yueh. Chinese general. 1896-. Born in Kwangtung, Hsueh graduated from the Paoting MA and by 1935 was commander of the 2d Route Army. From 1939 he was CinC, 9th War Area, and governor of Hunan Prov, "China's rice bowl." Lt Gen Hsueh was known then as "The Tiger of Hunan." When the Japanese began driving south from Hangkow in June 44 toward 14th AF bases in E China they took Changsha—capital of the rice bowl region—on the 18th. "The Tiger of Changsha" withdrew south 100 miles to Hengyang. He held out until 8 Aug 44 despite what he called Chiang's constant "meddling" by long-distance phone and the Generalissimo's persistent refusal to send the US arms he had been demanding (*OCMH* Chron, 409). But Hsueh Yeuh, whose loyalty Chiang had come to question, continued to do well against the Japanese offensive (Tuchman, *Stilwell*, 228-29, 472-73).

The general was personal CofS to the President, 1947-48; and Governor of Kwangtung and head of the Hainan Garrison Command, 1947-50; then minister without portfolio.

HUBE, Hans Valentin. German general. 1890-1944. Known as "The Man" *(Der Mensch)*, the one-armed panzer general was born 29 Oct 90 at Naumburg an der Saale in Saxony. After 18 months as a cadet in an infantry regiment in Magdeburg he was promoted to Leutnant in 1910. Despite loss of his left arm in WWI he stayed in the Reichswehr. A full colonel by 1939, and author of a book, *The Infantryman,* Hube had an outstanding record in Poland and was again wounded. He assumed command of the 16th Mtz Div on 14 May 40

and was promoted two weeks later to Generalmajor. His unit became the 16th Pz Div on 1 Nov 40, and about a month later it was sent to train the Romanian Army before taking part in Barbarossa.

Fighting in the Ukraine as part of AG South, der Mensch took part in the capture of Lvov and the exploitation that followed. He was awarded the RK on 1 Aug 41 and the Oakleaves on 16 Jan 42. On 15 Sep 42 he was promoted to Generalleutnant and given command of the 14th Pz Corps, taking over from Gustav von Wietersheim in Stalingrad. He was heavily engaged for the next three months and was promoted on 1 Oct 42 to General of Panzer Troops. Flown out of encircled Stalingrad to receive the Swords (22/159) from Hitler on 21 Dec 42 and to give a personal report, Hube pleaded for "the life of the Stalingrad army" (Kurt ZEITZLER in F&R, 163). But the fuehrer insisted that everything possible, including resupply by air, was being done and was not amused by Hube's suggestion that at least one Luftwaffe general be shot for the airlift's failure to date (ibid.). The general returned to Stalingrad on 9 Jan 43, turned over command of his doomed corps eight days later to Generalleutnant Helmuth Schloemer (*B&O,* 37) and was among the specialists evacuated (Craig, *Stalingrad,* 354). After directing the airlift from the outside, Hube took over a new 14th Pz Corps Hq on 5 Mar 43. But a few months later he was sent to Italy.

When the Allied invasion of Sicily began on 10 July 43 ROMMEL had Hube sent there to command German troops in Guzzoni's 6th Italian Army. With Kesselring's authority to use his initiative, Hube conducted masterful delaying actions before withdrawing German troops across the Strait of Messina during the period 11-17 Aug 43.

Summer vacation in Italy over, the Wehrmacht's only one-armed general returned to Russia. On 30 Oct 43 he succeeded MACKENSEN as head of the 1st Pz Army, which Konev was threatening to encircle in the Dnieper bend. Hube's counterattack around Krivoi Rog was successful against odds of 15:1 in men, 5:1 in tanks, and a considerable Soviet advantage in mortars and artillery (Manstein in Liddell Hart, ed, *The Red Army,* 146). In late Jan 44, hindered by alternating blizzards and thaws, the panzer army and the 8th Army failed in an attempt to save two German corps trapped in the Korsun salient.

Promoted 15 Feb 44 Generaloberst Hube came close to having his six panzer divisions and elements of 8th Army wiped out in KONEV's "mud offensive" that started on 5 Mar 44 (Erickson, 294). He saved his troops but had to abandon much materiel and could offer little resistance as Konev's front quickly pushed to within 30 miles of the Dniester.

Hube then got into an unfortunate controversy with Manstein, his immediate superior. Manstein thought Hube should stay north of the Carpathians while fighting his way due west to the rear, thus in position to regain contact with Erhard RAUS's 4th Pz Army. But The Man wanted to withdraw south across the Dniester into Romania. Hitler sided with Manstein, but— so fatigued by this exercise in professional decision-making—he decided to sack the army group commander! (Manstein, 542, 544.)

Now under MODEL, Hube tried it his way and failed—he could not get across the Dniester, so his 1st Pz Army had to undertake what Manstein had seen as the correct solution. Fighting day and night for almost a month, Hube linked up with the 4th Pz Army on 8 Apr 44. He saved most of his veteran panzer army and perhaps prevented the annihilation of German forces farther east in Romania by delaying for almost a month the advance southward of Zhukov's 1st Ukrainian Front. (S&E, *WWII*, 252; *West Point Atlas*, Map 40.).

After this achievement the hard, chubby-faced panzer army commander flew to Obersalzberg for Hitler's birthday. On 20 Apr 44 he was awarded the Diamonds (13/27) and promoted to Generaloberst. Returning to his headquarters he died the next day of injuries from a plane crash at Obersalzberg (*B&O*, 15n).

HULL, Cordell. US Secretary of State. 1871-1955. One of the last great Americans born in a log cabin, the Lincolnesque Cordell Hull came into this world on 2 Oct 71 in the mountain settlement of Star Point in Pickins County, Tenn. His father was a prosperous log-rafter and moonshiner, and his mother had Cherokee blood *(CB 40)*. A good student, "Cord" grew to six feet one. Studious and well spoken despite a high, rasping voice and unfortunate lisp, he was admitted to the bar before his 20th birthday and

was a circuit judge before winning election to Congress by a 17-vote margin. A Democrat, he was in the House 1906-21 and 1923-31, then in the Senate. Hull believed in the League of Nations and worked effectively on developing good relations with Latin America, but his main interest was taxation and the tariff.

When the quiet, elderly Senator Hull became Secretary of State on 4 Mar 33, much of the country wondered why. He and Roosevelt were opposites, and the Tennessee ex-frontiersman contrasted sharply with the patrician president's "brain trusters." But although Roosevelt was his own secretary of state, Hull was a good lieutenant and had a strong influence on foreign policy. He also was valuable because of his prestige on Capitol Hill, particularly among conservatives *(S&S)*. The secretary had a memorable confrontation on 7 Dec 41 with the unfortunate Kichsaburo NOMURA.

After serving longer than any other American secretary of state, past his 73d birthday, and having declining the VP post in Roosevelt's fourth administration, Hull tendered his resignation on 21 Nov 44. STETTINIUS took over officially on 30 November. Hull was awarded the Nobel Peace Prize in 1945 after having been nominated repeatedly by Roosevelt since 1934.

The two-volume *Memoirs of Cordell Hull* were published in 1948 (New York: Macmillan).

HUNTZINGER, Charles Léon Clément. French general. 1880-1941. The fervently anti-German Huntzinger was the son of an Alsacian father who in 1871 opted for French citizenship. He was born 25 June 80 in Lesneven, near Brest, of a Bretonne mother and grew up there. A graduate of St Cyr in 1901, the trim, elegant, alert, and vigorous Huntzinger was regarded in 1940 as one of France's most promising generals. He commanded the French 2d Army that was shattered around Sedan by Guderian's panzers, then he headed AG 4, which Rundstedt penetrated around Châlons-sur-Marne and through which Guderian again rushed. Huntzinger headed the armistice delegation that reached Compiègne late on 21 June 40. The general's only guidance from the new Pétain government in Bordeaux, apart from refusing dishonorable terms, was not to surrender the fleet nor any colonial territory. To revenge the German humiliation of 11 Nov 18—even using the same railroad car on the same siding in the great forest of Compägne—Keitel read a brief preamble, Hitler left to the tune of "Deutschland uebër alles," and the French were given written copies of German terms but not allowed any discussion. The French were permitted to return to Paris and phone to Bordeaux, where Pétain's cabinet debated through the night and most of the next day. Huntzinger signed the armistice on 22 June 40 at 8:50 PM, and the cease fire was effective at 35 minutes past midnight on 24-25 June 40.

As war minister in Vichy and a member of Pétain's inner cabinet with DARLAN and FLANDIN, Huntzinger cooperated with the secret army resistance. The Germans apparently learned of this, and it is probable that they engineered the plane crash in which Huntzinger died at Le Vigan, near Nîmes, on 12 Nov 41 (Brown, "C," 426).

HURLEY, Patrick Jay. US general. 1883-1963. Colorful, controversial, vain, and reckless, Pat Hurley was the son of Irish immigrants who moved from Texas to Choctaw Indian territory before his birth on 8 Jan 83 at what is now Lehigh, Okla. Six feet tall, physically fit and handsome, wealthy from corporate law, real estate, and oil, Hurley had been a artillery lieutenant colonel with the AEF in France. He was secretary of war under Herbert Hoover, 1929-33.

In the fall of 1941 Hurley was recalled to active military duty. After the Japanese invaded the Philippines and blockaded the islands he was sent to Australia with a million dollars in gold to buy ships and run supplies to MacArthur's forces. He was wounded three times in the process.

Col Hurley became the first US ambassador to New Zealand and on 24 July 42 was given the rank of brigadier general. He undertook a series of presidential missions including one to Russia, where the ex-cowboy and former coal miner hit it off well with Stalin. In Jan 43 Hurley resigned his post in New Zealand and became FDR's personal representative to the Near and Middle East. He then went to Chungking to lay the groundwork for the Cairo conference with Chiang. With the rank of temporary ambassador he next set up the Teheran conference and had a special mission to Afghanistan.

As the conflict worsened between the Nationalist and communist Chinese, Hurley was named special envoy to China on 18 Aug 44. Notoriously ignorant of the issues but boasting that he could troubleshoot in any gallery, he picked up Stilwell in India and reached Chungking with Donald M. NELSON on 6 Sep 44. The situation called for quick, drastic remedies and Hurley was a bull in the China shop. Charmed by the Chiangs, he was responsible for STILWELL's recall on 18 October; Ambassador GAUSS, another target, soon resigned. The Senate confirmed Hurley's appointment as ambassador to China in November after a delay of three months.

"Trouble moved with him like a cloud of flies around a steer," Dean ACHESON would recall (*Present at the Creation,* 133). One observer noted that he tired easily and had eye trouble (White, *China,* 246). Hurley resigned in Nov 45 to protest what he considered to be State Department interference in his efforts to mediate between the Chinese nationalists and communists. Hurley established residence in Santa Fe, N Mex, and in 1952 was only a few thousand votes short of winning election to the Senate.

HUSSEINI, Amin-el. Grand Mufti of Jerusalem. 1893-1974. With red hair and blue eyes that suggested he had European blood, Haj Amin was a Turkish army officer in WWI. For inciting Arabs to anti-Jewish terror in protesting British commitment to the Balfour Declaration of 2 Nov 17—which called for a national Jewish homeland in Palestine—he was jailed in 1920 by British authorities, who had a League of Nations mandate in Palestine and Transjordan. Sentenced to five years in prison, he promptly escaped. A year later High Commissioner Sir Herbert Louis Samuel gave Haj Amin a full pardon, soon appointing him to succeed his late half-brother as Mufti of Jerusalem. (A mufti, normally a professional jurist, interprets Muslim law.) "Amin appeared to be an innocuous and pliant youth, but he immediately took the title 'Grand Mufti'" and "incited his Moslem followers to massacre the Jews." (Hamilton, *Leaders,* 472.) The British arrested members of the Arab High Commission on 1 Oct 37 and banished many of them to the Seychelles, but the Grand Mufti took refuge in a mosque until 16 Oct 37 and escaped to Syria.

Soon after war broke out in Europe, he moved in Oct 39 to Iraq. Urging the recently installed pro-British regent, ABDUL ILLAH, and Prime Minister Nuri es-Said to remain neutral, he sent emissaries to offer Hitler and Mussolini pan-Arab cooperation in return for Axis support. The Grand Mufti, promised German arms, conspired in a coup d'état that installed the pro-Axis Rashid Ali Beg al-Gailani (1892-1965) as PM on 1 Apr 41. But the Axis support never came, and Maj Gen William J. SLIM led his 10th Ind Div in a lightening campaign, 2-30 May 41, that shattered the Iraqi army and forced an armistice the next day in Baghdad.

Fleeing to still-neutral Persia (Iran), the Grand Mufti went on to see Mussolini on 27 Oct 41 and Hitler on 28 November. Complicated negotiations for Axis support were exacerbated by a power struggle in Berlin with Rashid Ali Bed al-Gailani for leadership. It was not until 5 Apr 43 that the Axis formally supported the pan-Arab movement for independence in their separate states, and Hitler finally anoited the Grand Mufti of Jerusalem as his favcored Arab partner, perhaps for his Aryan complexion.

The shadowy, publicity-shy leader of a race notoriously incapable of cooperation, even against the Jews, remained in Berlin. He issued calls to nationalists of all Arab countries of the Middle East, which by 15 July 41 were controlled by the British and the Free French. The Grand Mufti helped form SS units from Muslims in occupied countries, and he vigorously opposed Jewish emigration to Palestine.

Haj Amin el Husseini left Germany in 1945 for house arrest in France but escaped to Cairo in May 46 (Tunney) and eventually set up shop in Lebanon as godfather of the Palestine Liberation Organization (PLO). Turning up occasionaly in Syria and Egypt the Grand Mufti died 4 July 74 in Beirut.

HYAKUTAKE, Haruyoshi (or Harukichi). Japanese general. 1888-1947. Commissioned in Dec 09 as a second lieutenant of infantry, the bespectacled, lean-faced, scholarly looking Hyakutake became a signals specialist. In addition to having normal assignments, he was posted to Poland in Dec 25 as resident officer. He headed the Hiroshima Military Prep School for a year in 1936-37 as a colonel, he was promoted in March of the latter year to major general, and five months later he became superintendent of the Army Signal School.

In Mar 39 he took command of the 4th Indep Mixed Bde, was promoted five months later to lieutenant general, and in Apr 40 he started a two-year tour as IG of Signal Training. He then took command of the 17th Army Hq, which was activated 18 May 42 at Rabaul. By this time the Japanese had made air bases on Bougainville (13 Mar 42) and at Tulagi, on Florida Is (3 May 42). Hyakutake was supposed to work with the navy in forging on to set up more outposts in the Solomons and New Guinea, perhaps as far as New Caledonia, Fiji, and Samoa. (One might see why this was a command needing a long-distance signals expert!)

In what was initially an army in name only, Hyakutake's major formations were Tomitaro HORII's South Seas Detachment, the Aoba Detachment, the 41st Inf Regt, and the 35th Inf Bde minus the 114th Regt (*Kogun,* 52). As "ranking Army general officer in Papua [SE New Guinea] and the Solomons" (ibid.) Hyakutake made two abortive efforts to take Port Moresby. The first was turned back by the Battle of the Coral Sea (4-8 May 42). The other, involving HORII's TF, was called off after US Marines landed on Guadalcanal (7 Aug 42).

With a low opinion of American troops and grossly underestimating their strength on Guadalcanal, Hyakutake first sent Col Kiyonayo Ichiki with about 900 men to destroy the Henderson Field perimeter. The effort came to grief on 21 Aug 42. Continuing his **piecemeal** approach, Hyakutake then sent KAWAGUCHI with some 6,000 men supported by air and naval gunfire. In a "masterpiece of mismanaged ferocity" (*West Point Atlas*, Map 135) the troops were driven off with heavy losses, most of them on Bloody Ridge, 13-14 Sep 42.

Still believing that only about 7,500 Americans were on Guadalcanal (there were 23,000) the general built up a force of 30,000 troops ashore and left Rabaul on 8 October to command them in person. His campaign calling for separate columns to move great distances through difficult, inadequately charted jungle. This ill-advised attempt at "concentration on the battlefield" was a costly fiasco.

Lt Gen Imamura reached Rabaul on 22 Nov 42 as commander of the new 8th Army Hq and promptly radioed Hyakutake that he would send him two fresh divisions within a month. But when YAMAMOTO failed to gain control of sea routes, IGHQ in Tokyo decided that Hyakutake's position was untenable. On 31 Dec 42 the emperor approved orders to evacuate Guadalcanal, and the disease-ridden Japanese survivors were evacuated secretly in the last two weeks of Jan 43.

Hyakutake then took command of the garrison on Bougainville. The 1st US Marine Div landed on 1 Nov 43 to eliminate this cancer, and on 15 November GRISWOLD's 14th Army Corps of two divisions relieved the Marines.

Hyakutake was driven back into defensive perimeters, the main one at Buin, on the south end of the island. He concentrated first on organizing vegetable gardens and was supplied from submarines and an occasional barge. (*Keogh,* 414-15.) After a valiant effort to break out on 8-24 Mar 44 and regain control of the island, he received orders from Imamura to "live and let live" (ibid.). At war's end he surrendered a formidable defensive position around Buin and returned to Japan in Feb 46. He died 10 Mar 47. Hyakutake's two elder brothers were outstanding admirals *(S&S).*

I

IACHINO, Angelo. Italian admiral. 1889-1976. Highly regarded professionally, Iachino (or Jachino) was naval attaché in London 1931-34. In 1940, with his 2d Cruiser Sqdn under the Italian Fleet Commander Campioni, Iachino performed well off Sardinia against SOMMER-VELL's Force B. A month after Andrew CUN-NINGHAM's devastating raid on Taranto, 11 Nov 40, Iachino succeeded Campioni as CinC, Italian Fleet on 10 Dec 40.

Cape Matapan
For the action of 28-29 Mar 41 against A. B. C. CUNNINGHAM off Cape Matapan, the southernmost part of mainland Greece, Iachino sallied forth on 26 Mar 41 with most of the Italian fleet. He was under German pressure to assist in stopping the British withdrawal from Greece to Crete.

The Italian 1st Div, from Taranto, had the heavy cruisers *Zara, Pola,* and *Fiume,* plus four destroyers. The new battleship *Vittorio Veneto,* with Iachino aboard, sailed from Naples with four destroyers. From Brindisi came the 8th Div: three light cruisers and two destroyers. The 3d Div, from Messina, comprised the heavy carriers *Trieste, Trento,* and *Bolzano,* with three destroyers. The divisions met south of the straits of Messina on the 29th.

Cunningham knew Iachino's movements through Ultra intercepts. He ordered H. D. Prideham-Whippell's Force B to steam from Piraeus, port of Athens. Force B comprised light carriers *Orion, Ajax, Perth,* and *Gloucester,* plus the 2d DD Div of four ships.

Cunningham himself led Force A—the carrier *Formidable,* the battleships *Barham, Warspite,* and *Valiant,* escorted by nine destroyers. Force C later was ordered from Alexandria, bringing the 14th DD Flotilla. Around noon on the 27th, British air recce located the Italian armada and reported that there was no Luftwaffe **CAP.** Surprise lost, Iachino abandoned the plan of forcing his way into the Aegean. But the next morning (28 Mar 41) his naval air patrols located Force B, and he ordered the 3d Div to attack.

Heavily outgunned, Prideham-Wippell dropped back. But after Iachino started a general withdrawal, Prideham-Wippell pursued and got between the 3d Italian Div and *Vittorio Veneto.*

Supported by six Swordfish from *Formidable,* Prideham-Wippell extricated himself and continued pursuit.

Cunningham followed with Force A, and Swordfish from **Formidable** and bombers from Crete each got a torpedo hit at dusk. CA *Pola* was made unmaneuverable and *Vittorio Veneto*'s two starboard screws were knocked out. Forced to continue his retreat at reduced speed (20 knots), and thinking he was followed only by destroyers, Iachino sent Adm Cattaneo's 1st Div back under cover of darkness with his two remaining heavy cruisers and four destroyers to save *Pola.* But the British found her about the time Cattaneo did. With a clear radar picture, and the Italians in the dark, Cunningham launched a surprise attack at close range with battleships and cruisers. *Fiume* and *Zara* plus the destroyers *Alfieri* and *Carducci* were quickly sunk. DD *Oriani* was damaged but escaped; only DD *Gioberti* was not hit. Early on the 29th the destroyers *Jervis* and *Nubian* sank *Pola* with torpedoes after RN and Greek ships took off 258 survivors. Italian losses were about 3,000, including Cattaneo. (R&H, *Chron,* 89.)

Ammiraglio D'Armata Iachino led forays until early Jan 42, one redoubtable antagonist being Sir Philip Louis VIAN. He escaped after the Italian surrender in 1943 and did not return to Italy until 1945. Among his books are *Gauda e Matapan* (Rome: Arnoldo Mondadore, 1946) and *Operazione mezzo giugnio* (Milan, 1955).

IAKOVLEV, A. S. *See* YAKOVLEV.

IBN SAUD (Abdu-l-Azis ibn Saud). Founder of Saudi Arabia. c1880-1953. Of the family that traditionally headed the ultra-orthodox Wahabi movement, he was born in Kuwait and spent his youth there as an exile. From 1902 he fought to regain his territories, finally taking Mecca in 1924 from the British-backed Hussein ibn Ali (favored by Lawrence of Arabia). The next year Ibn Saud proclaimed himself king of Hejez and Nejd, and in 1932 he founded Saudi Arabia. With fewer than five million people on 700,000 square miles of mostly desert land the king continued a large-scale program of modernization. This included persuading many fierce, nomadic Bedouins to settle peacefully on farms. To raise capital he sold oil drilling rights to the Standard Oil Co of California in 1933. Their discoveries, starting three years later, brought Saudi Arabia immense wealth.

In WWII the king, who was unenthusiastic about the Arab League, remained officially neutral to avoid turmoil with his neighbors. But during the Vichy-French inspired crisis in Lebanon in Nov 43 he supported the British by urging the Syrian government in Damascus to remain calm *(CB 43)*. He then sent messages to de Gaulle, Churchill, and Roosevelt to protest anti-Arab French actions in the region. In Feb 45, on his first trip outside Saudi Arabia, the king met separately with Churchill and Roosevelt in Egypt as they returned from Yalta.

A splendid six feet four, fit and muscular at 230 pounds, Ibn Saud was a good speaker and a shrewd debater *(CB 43)*. He also was a strict Moslem, opposed to alcohol, tobacco, gambling, and monogamy. In addition to a huge harem, he is said to have had about 150 wives (four at a time, in the Moslem manner). His progeny, stemming from some 40 sons, formed Saudia Arabia's princely cadre. The eldest son went to Egypt, but the second, Feisal, spent time in England and France. Ibn Saud was ardently anti-Zionist, ultimately becoming the principal financial backer of Arabs at war with Israel.

ICKES, Harold LeClaire. US public figure. 1874-1952. He was born 15 Mar 74 on a farm near Hollidaysburg, Pa. At the age of 16 he went to Chicago to live with an aunt after his mother died. Working as a teacher in evening public schools, Ickes got a BA from the Univ of Chicago in 1897 and, after being a reporter, graduated cum laude from its law school in 1907. He entered politics as a reformer and champion of the "little man."

Ickes came to national prominence after rallying support of Midwestern conservatives for the liberal Roosevelt's first campaign. The men first met on 22 Feb 33 to begin a lifelong friendship. Ickes was made secretary of the interior, and soon thereafter was head of the Public Works Administration (PWA). "Honest Harold" was charged with spending that reached more than five billion dollars (real money at the time!) and did this without a whiff of graft or scandal. Ickes endeared himself to FDR as "one of the few men around here [in 1938] who was not a candidate for President" *(CB 41)*.

Having long warned about an energy shortage in the east as the US prepared for war, Ickes assumed the additional duty of Petroleum Coordinator for Public Defense on 28 May 41. The following November, on the eve of Pearl Harbor, he also became Solid Fuels [coal and coke] Coordinator for National Defense (ibid.). In his zeal for conserving raw materials he went to odd lengths such as ordering all rubber mats in his Interior Department building donated to the scrap rubber drive, and picking up one he spotted in the White House (Lingeman, 247). He was "good press" for pungent, colorful statements about various proposals of other bureaucrats to help the war effort. (Lingeman, passim.) A distinguished scholar characterizes him as "a prowling defender of his bureaucratic turf, prickly and petty but insufferably rightminded on the big issues . . ." (Burns, 23).

His books are *The Autobiography of a Curmudgeon* (New York: Quadrangle Books, 1943) and *The Secret Diary of Harold L. Ickes* New York: Simon and Schuster, 1954).

IHLEFELD, Herbert. German ace. 1914-. He was born 1 June 14 in Pinnow. With seven victories in Spain, **Oberfeldwebel** Ihlefeld was commissioned in Aug 40 and given command of the 1st Gp of JG 77. On 16 Sep 40 Hitler personally awarded Oberleutnant Ihlefeld the RK for scoring 21 victories over England. After another four kills while remaining in the same unit he was a captain (Hauptmann) commanding JG 77 when given the Oakleaves (16/890) on 7 June 41 for his 40th victory. On 24 Apr 42 Hauptmann Ihlefeld was awarded the Swords (9/159) as the fifth Luftwaffe pilot to down more than 100 planes. By V-E day Oberst Ihlefeld had 130 victories. (Angolia, I, 122.)

ILYUSHIN, Sergey Vladimorovich. Soviet aeronautic designer. 1894-1977. He was born in Vologda Prov into a large peasant family and got interested in aviation as a laborer on the site for Russia's first international aviation show in St Petersburg in 1910. He pursued this interest as a security guard at St Petersburg's Kommanditsky airport. In WWI he qualified as a pilot. A 1926 graduate of the Zhukovsky Military Air Engineer Academy, Gen Col Engineer Ilyushin became an aircraft designer. The others were LAVOCHKIN, PETLYAKOV, TUPOLEV, YAKOVLEV, and the team of Mikhail I. Gurevich and Artem I. Mikoyan (Anastas MIKOYAN's brother). Their planes proved to be notably inferior in Spain, Finland, and in the opening months of the Russo-German War. But the Luftwaffe had a bad surprise when Ilyushin's odd-looking IL-2 "Stormovik" became operational in the spring 1941.

The single-seat IL-2 mounted two 20m cannon as main armament, had a top speed of 257 mph, and carried about 800 pounds of bombs or eight rockets. Heavy protective armor, spurned by other designers as an unwarranted trade-off for speed and maneuverability, gave Ilyushin's "tank busters" what was perhaps the highest survival rate on the eastern front. More than 36,000 were produced during the war, far surpassing the number of the YAKOVLEV fighter, the next highest. (Scotts.)

The IL-10 (1942) had a rear-facing machine gunner (12.7mm), a top speed of 335mph, two 23mm cannon, and a 2,000-pound payload.

An older plane (1936) became the IL-4, a medium bomber workhorse used also as a torpedo plane. With a crew of three or four, it carried about 4,400 pounds of bombs or one 18-inch torpedo. The four-engine IL-18 "Moskova," one of the first turbo-prop airliners, was widely used in the Third World in the 1960s. Another popular plane was the IL-62

IMAMURA, Hitoshi. Japanese general. 1888-1968. Born in Miyagi Prefecture, commissioned an infantryman in 1907, he became one of Japan's top generals. Imamura had a long association with the British Army from 1918, first in England, then with the BEF in France, and as resident officer in India 1926-30 (*Kogun*, 225). HOMMA, whom he stopped from committing suicide in England, was a close friend (Swinson, *Four Samurai*, 34-39).

Imamura was promoted to lieutenant general in Mar 35 and was vice CofS, Kwantung Army, 1936-37. Back in Tokyo as chief of the Army Administration Bureau from Jan 38 he was promoted to lieutenant general the following March and ordered to China eight months later to command the 5th Div. In Mar 40 he became deputy IG of military training, and 14 months later he returned to China as CG, 23d Army. (*Kogun*, 225-26.)

Commanding the 16th Army he landed on Java, 1 Mar 42, after losing several transports in the Battle of Sunda Straits (between Java and Sumatra). Rescued after clinging to driftwood for 20 minutes after his own ship was sunk, the soggy conqueror was welcomed ashore by an ADC who solemnly congratulated him for the successful landing! (Morison, III, 366 & n.)

Imamura took the surrender of all forces in the NEI on 9 Mar 42 (Collier, *FE*, 218), established a liberal occupation policy, and released Achmed Soekarno from jail. The general was appointed commander of the new 8th Area Army Hq which was created in Rabaul on 16 Nov 42 to control HYAKUTAKE's battered 17th Army on Guadalcanal and ADACHI's hard-pressed 18th Army in New Guinea. Exhorted personally by the emperor to perform a miracle (Toland, *Sun*, 418), and reaching Rabaul on 22 Nov 42, Lt Gen Imamura promptly promised Hyakutake two fresh divisions within a month (ibid.). But because YAMAMOTO could not regain control of sea routes the emperor approved orders on 31 Dec 42 to abandon Guadalcanal.

Although shocked by the decision, Imamura directed that the reinforcements from Java be diverted to reinforce Adachi at Lae. But when the Allied victory in the Bismarck Sea, 2-5 Mar 43, virtually destroyed a troop convoy headed for Lae, Imamura was convinced that further efforts of this sort would make New Guinea another Guadalcanal.

Having almost been shot down by an American fighter near Bougainville, Imamura tried unsuccessfully to stop YAMAMOTO from making the fatal flight on 18 Apr 43. A reorganization in mid-Mar 43 transferred the 18th Army on New Guinea to ANAMI's 2d Area Army. Promoted in May 43 to full general (*Kogun*, 226), Imamura was left with only Hyakutake's doomed 17th Army on Bougainville. On 7 Oct 43 he ordered that only delaying actions be conducted in the Solomons, and on 25 Mar 44 he called off Hyakutake's efforts to break out and retake control of the island whose airfields were so important.

As Australians completed mopping-up operations on New Britain, Imamura still had some 70,000 troops around Rabaul. Well provisioned, well equipped, and with ample ammunition, he held in hopes that this would be of some strategic advantage (*Keogh,* 412). Surrendering only when so ordered by the emperor, Imamura was convicted of war crimes but released from Tokyo's Sugamo Prison by 1954 and was a free man by 1956. Four years later he still was running unsuccessfully for election to the Diet.

INGERSOLL, Ralph McAllister. US journalist. 1900-85. Born 8 Dec 00 in New Haven, Conn, son of a prominent engineering consultant, Ralph Ingersoll graduated from Yale in 1921. He was an engineer until 1924, when he published *In and Under Mexico.* Largely on the basis of this, and attracted to journalism, he became managing editor of *The New Yorker* in 1925 and was associate editor of *Fortune* five years later. Ingersoll rose rapidly to be vice-president and general manager of Time, Inc, and publisher of *Time* in 1937. "Tall, bald, shambling . . . [and] something of a socialite" *(CB 40),* Ingersoll was a literary heir to Henry R. Luce (ibid). But he resigned after three years to publish a boldly innovative and short-lived NYC tabloid, *PM.*

After the US went to war he wrote *Battle is the Pay-Off,* a highly acclaimed book about green Americans facing ROMMEL's veterans in Tunisia. Lt Col Ingersoll later was a military intelligence officer and historian at Bradley's 12th AG Hq. During the **Ardennes campaign** he convinced Bradley to publish a statement rebutting MONTGOMERY's claim in a press conference that he—Monty—had staved off an American disaster (Bradley, *Story,* 486; *Life,* 383).

INGERSOLL, Royal Eason. US admiral. 1883-1976. He was born in Washington, DC, on 20 June 88, son of Rear Adm Royal Rodney Ingersoll and Cynthia Eason. The senior Ingersoll graduated from Annapolis in 1864 (2/81), and the son was in the USNA Class of 1905 (4/114). A rear admiral from 1938, he became a vice admiral on 1 Jan 42 when the post-Pearl Harbor reorganization put him in command of

the Atlantic Fleet. In Jul 42 he was promoted to admiral. Until the 10th Fleet was created in May 43 Ingersoll had the additional responsibility of anti-submarine warfare while performing the Atlantic Fleet's traditional mission of keeping lines of communications open in the Atlantic and defending the Western Hemisphere. Elements of the Atlantic Fleet supported the invasion of Morocco in Nov 42. Exactly two years later Ingersoll was succeeded by Jonas H. INGRAM and transferred to head the Western Sea Frontier. He retired 1 Aug 46 and died 20 May 76 in Bethesda, Md.

In the third generation of this naval family, Royal Rodney Ingersoll II, born 17 Dec 13 and graduating in the USNA Class of 1934 (71/463), died 4 June 42 as a lieutenant aboard CV *Hornet* in the Battle of Midway.

INGRAM, Jonas Howard. US admiral. 1886-1952. He was born 15 Oct 86 in Indiana. At Annapolis he was on the football, rowing, and track teams. Graduating in 1907 (187/209), and winning the Medal of Honor on the Vera Cruz Expedition (Apr 14), Ingram was head football coach at Annapolis, 1915-17. During WWI he was flag lieutenant to Adm Hugh Rodman. Back at Annapolis in 1926-30 Ingram was director of athletics.

Ingram commanded the Atlantic Cruiser Division in 1941 and the next year became Commander of Allied Naval Forces in the South Atlantic. In Nov 44 he succeeded Royal E. Ingersoll as CINC, Atlantic Fleet—concerned primarily with supervising troop convoys—and was promoted to full admiral at this time. He retired 1 Apr 47 and died 10 Sep 52.

INONU, Ismet. President of Turkey. 1884-1973. Born 24 Sep 84 at Izmir (then Smyrna), son of a judge, he became a professional army officer and close associate of Turkish strong man Kemal Ataturk (1881-1938). He took his westernized name from his two victories against the Greeks in early 1921 at Inönü in Anatolia. Having earlier joined Ataturk's political movement and been undersecretary of war (1918) and becoming foreign minister in 1922, the small, slight, distinguished-looking Inonu showed exceptional diplomatic skills at the Lausanne Conference of 1922-23 that gave Turkey recognition as a national state after "the sick man of

Europe" was virtually killed off by the Treaty of Sèvres in 1920. He was premier from the creation of the Turkish Republic on 29 Oct 23. After persistent policy differences with the ailing and fading Ataturk he resigned in 1937. After Ataturk died from cirrhosis in Nov 38 Inonu was president of Turkey and chairman of the Republican People's Party.

In 1939 he negotiated a treaty of mutual assistance with Britain and France that called for Turkish support if war spread to the Mediterranean, in return for which Turkey would get support if attacked. Turkey also pledged to help Romania or Greece defend themselves, a provision Inonu did not honor. Otherwise Turkey would be neutral. Much like FRANCO's Spain, Turkey was courted by both sides. But after Hitler's forces took Greece and the Balkans in 1941, and Turkey, like Spain, became isolated, the Western allies could not pay the asking price for open collaboration. As the tide turned, however, the Turks severed diplomatic relations with Germany in the summer of 1944. In Feb 45, after the Yalta Conference, Inonu had a meeting with Churchill and Roosevelt that led to Turkey's declaring war on the Axis.

Having been president from 1938 until 1950, when his party was defeated by that of Celal Bayar, Inonu was premier in 1961-65.

INOUYE, Shigeyoshi (Shigeyasu). Japanese admiral. 1889-tk. Inouye was born in Tokyo and graduated from the Naval Academy in 1909. He was naval attache in Rome, a senior staff officer in Tokyo, captain of the BB *Hiei*. Highly regarded, he was promotion to rear admiral in 1935. After being a bureau chief in the Navy Dept, Inouye took command of the 4th Fleet after it was created on 15 Nov 39, and he was made a vice admiral. Based on Truk, he had the mission of protecting the mandated islands. At the start of war the admiral directed the capture of Guam and Wake, on 10 and 23 Dec 41, Adm. Arimoto Goto conducting the tactical operations. Shortly thereafter, Inouye's area of responsibility was extended to Rabaul and the Gilberts. Inouye then was in charge of planning and executing the campaign against Port Moresby, Operation **Mo.** On 8 May 42 he ordered the operation abandoned after the covering force under Adm. Goto failed to destroy the carrier TF of Adm.

FLETCHER as planned. In hindsight the Battle of the Coral Sea was a tactical victory for the Japanese, but Inouye did not want to risk loss of his troop transports. A displeased Yamamoto ordered the 4th Fleet back to its primarily logistical duties at Truk. (The new 8th Fleet under Adm Gunichi Mikawa took over the 4th Fleet's operational duties.) Inouye was relieved of command in Oct 42 and made head of the Naval Academy *(S&S)*.

Known from 1943 as a peace advocate *(S&S)*, he was among those covertly approached early in 1944 by Adm Sokichi TAKAGAI. In Aug 44 he became Vice Minister of the Navy, and in May 45 was made a full admiral and member of the Supreme War Council (*Japanese Biog Ency,* 3d ed; *S&S*).

INVERCHAPEL. *See* KERR, Archibald John Clark Kerr.

IRONSIDE, William Edmund. British general. 1880-1959. A burly six-foot four-inch giant who once played rugby for Scotland, "Tiny" was a heroic figure of earlier wars who figured only briefly in the second world war. He was the first CIGS 3 Sep 39-27 May 40. Succeeded by DILL, he headed the Home Forces for a few weeks until replaced by Alan BROOKE on 20 July 40.

Tiny was born on 6 May 80 at Ironside, Aberdeenshire, Scotland. His father, a surgeon major in the Royal Horse Artillery Medical Service, died before the son was a year old. The widow frequently took her two children to the Continent because living there was cheaper. One consequence was that her son later qualified in seven languages as an army interpreter. *(DNB.)* After attending Tronbridge School he was commissioned from Woolwich in 1899 as a field artilleryman.

A wide variety of assignments in South Africa included escorting Jan SMUTS to the peace conference at Vereeniging in 1902 and masquerading as a Boer teamster to spy on German military operations in South West Africa. For this and other exploits, Tiny was the model for Richard Hannay in three of John Buchan's novels including *The Thirty Nine Steps*. After serving as a gunnery officer of the Royal Horse Artillery, he was promoted to captain in 1908 and posted to staff duty in the field.

Ironside returned to England to enter the staff college, **Camberley**, in 1913, and went to France in 1914 as a staff captain. In October of that year he was promoted to major and assigned the 6th British Div, then as **GSO 1** (Intelligence) with the 4th Cdn Div. In 1917 he saw action at Vimy Ridge and Passchendale. As a temporary colonel heading the Machine Gun Corps school in 1918, he was rushed into the line to block German penetration on the Somme in March. Successful on the defensive, he took part in the counteroffensive as commander of the 99th Inf Bde, 2d Div, at Albert and Bapaume. (*DNB.*) He went to north Russia in Sep 18 as chief of staff in the multi-national force organized to oppose the Bolsheviks. Only 38 years old, Ironside was soon promoted to temporary major general and named overall allied commander. His position becoming untenable as the Reds gained strength and his Russian troops defected, Ironside extricated his force from Archangel in the autumn of 1919. But he was knighted that year (KCB) and given the permanent rank of major general.

Sir William Ironside moved from the Arctic to the Near East, serving as commander of Ismid Force (1920) and North Persian Forces (1921). He then headed Camberley 1922-26. Promoted to full general in 1936 and appointed GOC Eastern Command that year, Tiny disqualified himself for CIGS by performing poorly in that year's major exercise. (Brian Bond in Keegan, ed, *Generals,* 19.) So GORT was the unfortunate choice of War Minister HORE BELISHA to succeed Sir Cyril Deverell as CIGS. Ironside remained with Eastern Command until 1938, was honored by advancement in the knighthood that year to GCB, and appointed Gov and CinC at Gibraltar 1938-39. He remained ADC to the king 1937-40. His active duty should have ended on leaving Gibraltar, but as HORE BELISHA continued to reshuffle senior generals as Britain prepared for war, Ironside was made IG of Overseas Forces. According to precedent, but certainly not intended by the war minister, the post made Ironside CinC-designate of any expedition abroad. But after Britain declared war on 3 Sep 39, GORT was moved from CIGS to head the BEF sent to France and Ironside became CIGS!

Lacking previous War Office experience, overwhelmed by the burdens of early military disasters and no longer young, Ironside was replaced on 26 May 40 by DILL. He briefly headed the Home Forces until 20 July 40, turning over his duties to Alan BROOKE. (Bryant, *Tide,* 155.) Promoted to field marshal (1940) and elevated to the peerage as 1st Baron of Archangel and of Ironside (1941), he retired from active duty but remained Colonel Commandant Royal Artillery until 1946. In 1925 he had published *Tannenberg: The First Thirty Days in East Prussia.* Making his home in Hingham, Norfolk, he published *Archangel, 1918-19* (1953). Ironside died 22 Sep 59.

IRWIN, Lord. *See* HALIFAX.

IRWIN, Noel Mackintosh Stuart. British general. 1892-1972. He commanded a brigade in the BEF in 1939-40 and led the British army element in the Dakar expedition of Sep 40 in which DE GAULLE was involved. (WC, II, 477.) Lt Gen Irwin later headed the Eastern Army of the India Command in Burma. On 20 May 43 he was replaced by George Gifford (*OCMH Chron,* 75, 111), who was succeeded by Sir William SLIM.

ISAKOV, Ivan Stepanovich. Soviet naval officer. 1894-1967. An Armenian born 22 Aug 94 in Adzhikend, Azerbaijan, son of a railroad worker, he was originally named Ovanes Stepanovich Isaakyan. Isakov was chief of the main naval staff from Nov 40 until 1943 but served as deputy front commander for naval forces in Leningrad before being transferred to the Caucasus. Severely wounded in Oct 42 he lost his left leg and was out of action for the rest of the war. But he was the Soviet Navy's CofS, 1946-47, and then held other high posts. In Mar 44 he and N. G. KUZNETSOV were the first to be appointed Admirals of the Fleet. Joining the General Inspector Group in Apr 58, he died in Moscow on 11 Oct 67. (Scotts.)

ISHIHARA, Kanji. Japanese general. 1889-1949. Born on 17 Jan 89, commissioned as an infantryman in Dec 09, Ishihara (sometimes spelled Ishiwara) distinguished himself in staff, command, and diplomatic assignments. "Brilliant, inspired, flamboyant, a fountain of ideas" (Toland, *Rising Sun,* 6), serving two tours as instructor at the War College, being a language officer in Germany, Lt Col Ishihara was assigned to the Kwantung Army in Oct 28. He worked closely and effectively with Seishiro ITAGAKI in the takeover of Manchuria, which the two officers thought should become a democratic nation and buffer against Russian expansion. Promoted in Aug 32, Col Ishihara was in Geneva two months later with the delegation to the League of Nations that walked out to protest the Lytton Commission report on Japanese aggression in Manchuria.

The colonel was a section chief in the general staff's operations bureau in Tokyo from Aug 35. After the mutiny of **26 Oct 36** he led a small but influential group that opposed the expansionists. Promoted and made chief of operations in Mar 37, he reluctantly approved the troop movements into North China that led four months later to the **Marco Polo Bridge** affair.

Increasingly unpopular for outspoken criticism of imperial policy, the exceptionally able officer was relegated to minor duties. Deputy CofS, Kwantung Army, for four months from Aug 37; then CG, Maizuru Fortified Zone, he was retired in Dec 38. Recalled to head the 16th Div he was retired in Mar 41 as a lieutenant general. In 1945 Prince HIGASHIKUNI pulled Ishihara out of obscurity and made him a special adviser to the "surrender cabinet." The man who had had so much to do with bringing on WWII now made speeches accusing the TOJO government of war guilt and exculpating the Throne. Long victim of wartime malnutrition and his health broken by his new duties, the general died in 1949 (Bergamini, 1090).

ISMAY, Hastings Lionel. British general. 1887-1965. The tall, soldierly "Pug" Ismay who had the pushed-in face of a pugilist, was born on 21 June 87, eldest son of Sir Stanley Ismay. Educated at Charterhouse School and graduating from Sandhurst at the age of 18, he served on India's northwest frontier and fought the dervishes in Somaliland during the First World War. He knew the Suez Canal region intimately from service with the 21st Cavalry Frontier Force. *(CB 43.)* From 1926 Ismay was associated at various times with the Imperial Defense Committee, a unique British institution. As a major general he became CofS to PM Churchill after Chamberlain resigned on 10 May 40. Six months later he was promoted to lieutenant general (6 Nov 42). All papers

between the PM and the service chiefs passed through Ismay, whose genius lay in minimizing friction within the British military machine and putting a brake on the PM's often impossible demands. Retiring in 1946 as a full general, he was made a peer, the 1st Baron of Wormington. (He had married Laura Kathleen Clegg of Wormington Grange, Broadway, Worcester, in 1921.)

Lord Ismay then was MOUNTBATTEN's CofS in India during the partition crisis of 1947. In 1951-52 he was Secretary of State for Commonwealth Relations in Churchill's second government, then the first Secretary General of NATO, 195257. *The Memoirs of General The Lord Ismay* were published in 1960 (New York: Viking, 1960).

ISOGAI, Rensuke. Japanese officer. 1882-1967. One of the **Eleven Reliables,** his name sometimes spelled Isogaya, he was a lieutenant general in Mar 37 and commander of the 10th Div stationed near Kobe. Ordered to China in 1937, he was teamed with ITAGAKI's elite 5th Div for an offensive along the line of the Tiensin-Shanghai RR. On 6-7 Apr 37, some two-thirds of the way, Isogai's division was ambushed and nearly surrounded at Taierchwang. ITAGAKI came to the rescue but at a frightful cost in Japanese casualties and prestige. Taking blame for this defeat, Isogai had no major combat assignment thereafter but was Governor General at Hong Kong during the war. He died in 1967.

ITAGAKI, Seishiro. Japanese general. 1885-1948. His family had been retainers of the Nambu clan that governed northern Japan under the Tokugawa shoguns. Commissioned an infantry officer in 1904, and becoming one of the **Eleven Reliables** (Bergamini, 598) he had extensive staff, command, and military attaché-duties in China from 1919. By 1928 he was a colonel in the Kwantung Army Hq, where he and Lt. Col. ISHIHARA made a perfect team," writes Toland. "What Ishihara envisioned, Itagaki could bring to pass." *(Rising Sun,* 6) After the **Mukden Incident** of 1931, Maj Gen.Itagaki had a succession of important assignments in China. These included two months of unsuccessful negotiations with CHIANG KAI-SHEK in Nanking during the spring of 1935 regarding Japanese sovereignty over north China (Bergamini, 598). In Mar 36 he became CofS, Kwantung Army, being promoted to lieutenant general a month later. (*Kogun,* 226.)

In Mar 37, four months before the **Marco Polo** Bridge incident touched off the Sino-Japanese war, Itagaki took command of the elite 5th Inf Div at Hiroshima. (*Who's Who in Japan,* 1938 ed.) Leading it immediately to North China in a team formed with ISOGAI's 10th Div., he saved the latter from annihilation at Taierchwang, 6-7 Apr 37. Itagaki was defeated again, on 25 Sep 37, this time at the hands of CHU TEH's guerrillas at Pingsinkuan, in the Great Wall. But the well-born, affable Itagaki remained in Hirohito's good graces despite the emperor's low opinion of his general's intelligence. After holding increasingly high staff assignments, the general was war minister in the HIRANUMA government, 5 Jan-30 Aug 39, and late in the year he became CofS of the army in China. In 1941 he was promoted to full general and made commander of the army in Korea. There until the last months of the war, he went to Singapore as head of the 7th Area Forces. On 12 June 45 he surrendered Singapore and all of Japan's southern armies to Mountbatten, TERAUCHI being indisposed.

Among the major war criminals hanged in Tokyo on 23 Dec 48, the round-faced, not-too-bright general was a favorite among his captors.

J

JACOB, Edward Ian Claud. British army officer. 1899-. As junior military assistant secretary to the War Cabinet 1939-46 Jacob was on the team with "Pug" ISMAY and senior assistant Leslie C. Hollis that handled Churchill's military correspondence. Promoted to major general in 1944 and a lieutenant general by war's end, he kept "perceptive and entertaining" war diaries that remain in manuscript. (Tunney.) Jacob was alive in 1991 when Charles Richardson's biography was published in London by Brasseys.

JARMAN, Sanderford. US general. 1884-1954. The gargantuan "Sandy" Jarman—six feet five, 250 pounds—was born 24 Nov 84 at the whistle stop of Boatner, La, about 20 miles WSW of Monroe. Graduating high in the USMA Class of 1908 (30/108), Jarman entered the Coast Artillery Corps. In 1918 he was CofS, Railroad Artillery Reserve, AEF, and was awarded the DSM. In 1939-42 he headed the coast artillery defenses of the Panama Canal Zone, being promoted 26 Oct 40 to major general. In early 1942, when there was genuine concern about air attack on the continental United States, Jarman was made head of the AAA Command. This eventually covered the 48 states and the Canal Zone with guns, a network of radio detection devices, and volunteer civilian spotters. After the invasion of Saipan, Jarman was Island Commander, 1944-45. On 25 June 44 he temporarily replaced Ralph C. SMITH as CG 27th Inf Div. Jarman retired as a major general in 1946 and died on 15 Oct 54 in Boston (Cullum).

JEANNENEY, Jules. French politician. 1864-1957. Born in Besançon, he became a lawyer in Paris and was mayor of Rioz (E outskirts of Besançon). In 1902 Jeanneney began a distinguished career in national politics, but the only ministerial post he accepted was as under secretary of war in the Clemenceau cabinet 16 Nov 17-20 Jan 20. President of the Senate from 1932, Jeanneney was among those who urged President Lebrun in June 40 to move the government to North Africa. Continuing as president of the Senate in Vichy, Jeanneney presided over delib-erations that abolished the Third Republic by a 229-1 vote on 10 July 40 and gave PETAIN full executive powers. But Jeanneney and HER-RIOT, his opposite number in the Chamber, sent Pétain a letter on 31 Aug 42 to protest unconsti-tutional acts of the Vichy government. This defiance ended the service of both men at Vichy.

Jeanneney accepted de Gaulle's offer to be minister of state in liberated Paris effective 10 Sep 44. The highly respected octogenarian oversaw the reestablishment of a permanent French government but declined to enter the elections of 21 Oct 45. Retiring to private life, he died 12 years later in Paris.

JESCHONNEK, Hans. German general. 1899-1943. The future Luftwaffe CofS was born 9 Apr 99 in Hohensalza. Originally an infantryman, he began flying in 1917 and became an ace. In Sep 33 he joined the staff of Air Minister Erhard MILCH, with whom he had flown in combat. Tall, lean, youthful, and hardworking, Lt Col Jeschonnek became OKL chief of operations in 1937 and in Nov 38 was promoted to full colonel. He became Luftwaffe CofS on 1 Feb 39 and the following August was a Generalmajor.

Caught up in the feuding that plagued OKL, Jeschonnek fell out with MILCH, who bypassed Goering more and more. Hitler long thought highly of Jeschonnek but eventually created his own little air staff, which also bypassed OKL (Irving, *Luftwaffe*, 235).

As the Luftwaffe continued to reveal short-comings, particularly in the Stalingrad airlift, Goering and Hitler made Jeschonnek a whip-ping boy. Slowly cracking under the strain Generaloberst Jeschonnek (from 1 Apr 42) said in early 1942: "If we have not won the war by December 1942 we have no prospect of doing so" (Bekker, 316).

The climax came on the night of 17-18 Aug 42 when 597 four-engine RAF bombers hit **Peenemuende** for the first time. The Germans were particularly nervous because Hamburg had recently had two heavy raids. The RAF made a masterly diversion with 20 Mosquitoes dropping flares to make it appear that Berlin was the target. Jeschonnek was taken in by the feint. Supported by Hitler but opposed by Goering, the Luftwaffe CofS ordered all the capital's air defenses to cut loose, subjecting 148 German fighters to the full force of the city's flak (Bekker, 314). Meanwhile the first wave of British bombers hit Peenemuende. Luftwaffe fighters from a base in Belgium arrived to start an engagement at 1:32 AM that destroyed 40 bombers and damaged 32 (ibid.).

Learning of the raid by phone at 8 AM on 18 Aug 43 in his quarters, Jeschonnek shot himself in the head. A suicide note said, "I can no longer work together with the *Reichsmarschall*. Long live the Fuehrer." (Ibid., 314.) In another note Jeschonnek asked that Goering not attend his funeral, but "Goering showed up . . . and deposited a wreath from Hitler" (Speer, I, 291). The Reichsmarschall issued a press statement that his CofS had died on the 19th (*sic*) from "hemorrhage of the stomach" (Bekker, 316). Guenther KORTEN took over as Luftwaffe CofS.

JODL, Alfred. German general. 1890-1946. As chief of the **Wehrmacht leader staff** he was Hitler's military CofS, hence the fuehrer's principal strategic adviser throughout the war. In Hitler's convoluted high command structure, Jodl also was chief of the OKW operational staff, making the capable, hard-working Bavarian the CofS to KEITEL, who in turn was OKW CofS!

Jodl was born 10 May 90 at Wuerzburg into an eminent Munich family of sincere but non-practicing Catholics. His father retired as a lieutenant colonel of artillery; his mother was of Austrian birth and peasant stock. A diligent but unimpressive scholar at the Theresiengymnasium in Munich, Alfred Jodl attended cadet school and in 1910 he joined a field artillery regiment as a sublieutenant. The next year he met the alluring and vivacious Countess Irma von Bullion, five years his senior, to whom he remained devoted from their marriage in 1913. Oberleutnant Jodl suffered a severe thigh wound on 24 Aug 14, soon after getting his baptism of fire, and continued to see action in France and Russia until the Armistice. An omnivorous reader of history and philosophy, he disapproved of the Kaiser's leadership, became antimonarchist, and felt that continuing warfare between

Germany and France eventually would destroy both countries. (Davidson, *Trial,* 346.) Jodl considered studying medicine after the war but, not having distinguished himself academically and being rated "suitable for higher command," he remained in the army (ibid.).

By 1920 he was in the **Truppenamt,** where he showed a grim devotion to duty and what FRITSCH saw as almost pathological ambition (Goerlitz, *GGS,* 297). Having risen steadily in the operations section from 1932, he became chief of the OKW's national defense section in 1935 and was promoted to Generalmajor. In Oct 38 he went to Vienna as head of the 44th Artillery Command, which concluded his career as a troop leader. Ordered back to Berlin after 10 months, when Germany was about to invade Poland, he became chief of the OKW operations branch on 23 Aug 39 with WARLIMONT as deputy. A mere 10 days later the placid, bald Bavarian met Hitler for the first time when he boarded the armored train *Amerika* en route to Poland. The men worked closely thereafter, and for a long time the general was genuinely awed by the fuehrer's intuitive military genius. Jodl saw national salvation in National Socialism, rejecting the German army's apolitical tradition and being sincerely contemptuous of officers who did not revere the fuehrer.

Although Jodl had little success in heading off major strategic disasters he did infuse some good sense into fuehrer directives. Field commanders accused Jodl of being a desk soldier, but Hitler (unlike Stalin) saw little need for top staff officers to visit the front. Jodl handled some 60,000 papers a year. As the German offensive of 1942 came to grief Hitler planned to sack the glacial staff officer along with his superiors. But only Franz HALDER got the ax (24 Sep 42).

Jodl's wife died in the spring of 1943 of pneumonia contracted in a damp air raid shelter in Koenignberg after having major spinal surgery. The following November Jodl married Luise von Benda, long a secret admirer, who had been secretary to three army chiefs of staff—Wilhelm Adam, Ludwig Beck, and Franz Halder. (Goerlitz in Barnett, ed, *Hitler's Generals,* 161.)

Hitler had Jodl promoted to Generaloberst on 30 Jan 44 over the heads of older and senior generals. But by the end of 1944 Jodl looked to Hasso von MANTEUFFEL like a tired old man (*F&R,* 245).

As Russians troops closed in on the Fuehrerbunker, on 20 Apr 45 Hitler had his last visit from Jodl and Keitel. Hitler ordered them two days later to abandon Zossen and Potsdam and move OKW Hq to south Germany. But they ended up reporting to DOENITZ in the north, delivering Hitler's last orders and figuring in the surrender proceedings (*see* KEITEL).

For his key role in drafting Hitler's plans and for approving orders that violated the rules of war, Jodl was condemned at Nuremberg as a war criminal and hanged on 16 Oct 46. In 1953 a Munich court found him not guilty of the main charges and annulled German penalties against his property.

The much-cited "Jodl Diaries" include the years 1937-45. Edited by Walter Habatsch for the period 13 Oct 38 to 30 Jan 40, they were published in *Die Welt als Geschichte* (1952 and 1953). Other portions are in the published documents of the Nuremberg trials. His widow preserved a manuscript biography and other papers. Warlimont's valuable "Interpretation and Commentary" is on microfilm in the US National Archives and other depositories.

JOHGN, Andrée de. Belgian underground leader. 1916-. After escorting three downed flyers from Belgium to the British consul in Bilbao, Spain, in Aug 41 she organized the "Comet Line," an escape route from Brussels through France into Spain. Personally making more that 36 frontier crossings, and being questioned by the Gestapo in 1941, she was arrested near the Spanish border in Jan 43. Mlle de Jongh was interrogated and imprisoned, first at Bayonne and Biarritz (where several rescue attempts were made), then in Fresnes near Paris, and finally in a German concentration camp. The Gestapo never discovered that the attractive young woman was responsible for saving at least 800 Allied officers and men. Her father and 23 agents were captured and executed, but she survived to work with lepers in Addis Ababa. Airey Neave sketches her accomplishments in *Little Cyclone* and *Saturday at M.I.9.*

JOHN, Otto. German resistance figure. c1909-. Until the Soviets kidnapped him in 1954 the controversial Dr Otto John was little known except to serious students of the anti-Nazi conspiracy. His father was of Russian, Polish, and Huguenot blood. "My mother's ancestors had been pastors in Hesse ever since the Reformation," he wrote, calling himself "a European cocktail" (John, 269). Dr John was born in Treysa (Hesse), son of a senior civil servant, and educated as a lawyer. On 1 Nov 37 he joined the Lufthansa legal department, which was headed by Klaus BONHOEFFER. Having become intimately involved with the anti-Hitler conspiracy, the burly German was in Madrid from Mar 42 with the local Lufthansa office. Under this cover he made contact with British intelligence in Madrid and Lisbon (Trevor-Roper in John, xi) and visited Berlin on business, Lufthansa's and his own. Dr John's brother Hans was severely wounded in Russia about this time and thereafter was Otto's link in Berlin with the German resistance. John's reports from Madrid went to London, Washington, and to the Free French in Algiers (ibid., 156). Making his way to Portugal and narrowly eluding Gestapo efforts to kidnap him, Dr John sent MI6 a warning on about 19 July 44 that an attempt on Hitler's life was imminent (Brown, "C," 604). MI6 arranged for John's flight to England, where he was interned as a Nazi refugee! Released in Dec 44 to serve in Sefton Delmar's "Soldatsender Calais," he helped broadcast "black" propaganda to German troops in Europe until V-E day.

After revisiting Germany in disguise as a British officer he returned to England for work on classifying German POWs politically as anti-Nazi, indifferent, or incorrigible (categories A, B, and C). In Oct 46 he took charge of POW Camp No. 11 at **Bridgend.**

Returning to Germany he helped prosecutors at Nuremberg prepare cases against senior German generals. Dr John had alienated many Germans by his service at Bridgend; now he made an enemy of Chancellor Conrad ADENAUER, intelligence chief Reinhard GEHLEN, and other high FRG officials by producing damning documentary evidence against MANSTEIN. Despite Adenauer's objections Dr John became head of the FRG's new political secret service (Bundesamt für Verfassungsschuts or BfV) on 4 Dec 50.

The "European cocktail" disappeared mysteriously in Berlin on 20 July 54 after attending ceremonies to commemorate the 10th anniversary of the anti-Hitler bomb attempt. Widely suspected of having defected or of committing suicide, he claims to have been kidnapped by the Russians for reasons that are unclear. Dr John thinks the KGB wanted a cover for their mass arrests of GEHLEN's agents. "Once a traitor, always a traitor," said Gehlen, falling in with this story (John, 248). John escaped to West Berlin on 12 Dec 55 to find himself charged with treason and with engaging in propaganda to overthrow the German government. Sentenced to four years in prison, he was released 28 July 58 after three years and eight months in solitary confinement.

His memoirs, *Zweimal kam ich heim* (1969), were translated, with an introduction by H. R. Trevor-Roper, as *Twice Through the Lines* (New York: Harper, 1972). The author argues that he was a victim of "unreconstructed" Germans like Gehlen and even FRG Chancellor Adenauer.

JOHNSON, Davenport. US air general. 1890-1963. A Texan, he was born 28 Mar 90 and graduated from West Point in 1912 (34/95). With the AEF he commanded the 2d Pursuit Gp, winning the SS and PH (for merit). A major general from 5 Aug 41, he succeeded Frank M. ANDREWS as CG, Caribbean AF, which became the 6th AF on 5 Feb 42 (*AA*, 219, 594). Johnson headed the 2d AF, a training command, during the periods 25 Feb-25 July 43 and 25 Aug-9 Sep 43 (*AA*, 593). He then took over the 11th AF in Alaska (officially on 6 Sep 43) and remained until 23 July 45 (*AA*, 596). The airman retired in 1945 as a major general and died 21 Oct 63 in Denver.

JOHNSON, Hiram (Warren). US Senator. 1866-1945. The diehard isolationist, conservative, and staunch individualist was born 2 Sep 66 in Sacramento, Calif. Twice elected governor of California, 1910 and 1914, he was a US senator from 1917 until his death. Johnson ran unsuccessfully for VP with Theodore Roosevelt in 1912; declined Harding's offer to be his candidate for VP; and in 1924 he made an unsuccessful bid for the presidency.

The crusading, reform-minded Senator Johnson was sympathetic initially to FDR's New Deal but declined a cabinet post because he wanted to remain politically free. The senator vociferously opposed FDR's third-term bid; denounced aid to Britain and Russia; and after voting with the Senate to declare war on Japan he opposed using National Guard and selective service troops outside the Western Hemisphere

(CB 41). The arch isolationist's dying effort was to cast the only dissenting committee vote against ratifying the UN Charter (Buchanan, 503-4).

JOHNSON, Herschel V. US diplomat. 1894-1966. The son of an insurance man, he was born 3 May 94 in Atlanta, Ga, but was reared in North Carolina, which became his official residence. Johnson graduated from the Univ of North Carolina in 1916 as a history major, taught French at a boys' school in Richmond, Va, and enlisted in the RA in 1917. Johnson became a captain and saw action in France. In 1919 he entered Harvard Law School but left to join the foreign service in Nov 20. After being stationed in Bern, Sofia, and Mexico City, he began a seven-year tour in London in 1934. Johnson was acting ambassador from Joseph KENNEDY's resignation in late 1940 until John WINANT arrived in Feb 41. A 47-year-old bachelor, thickset (five feet ten, 175 pounds), ruddy faced, and sandy-haired, Johnson reached Stockholm as ambassador on 4 Dec 41. It was the eve of Pearl Harbor, and his legation grew from 40 to 300 people as the "listening post" in neutral Sweden became increasingly important. The ambassador also had the problem of blocking Sweden's trade with Germany, and it was not until late 1944 that shipments of ball bearings were halted.

When HIMMLER put out feelers for a separate peace deal with the western allies in early 1945 Amb Johnson and British envoy Sir Victor Mallet received the unacceptable offer relayed through Count BERNADOTTE.

From Apr 46 the career diplomat was at the UN. After being STETTINUS's deputy for three months, Johnson was US representative on the Security Council for six months until Senator Warren R. Austin was seated in Jan 47. Johnson then reverted to the role of deputy.

JOHNSON, James Edgar. RAF ace. 1915-. Born in Loughborough, Leicestershire, "Johnny" (inevitably) Johnson was educated as a civil engineer. In 1936 the RAF rejected him as a flyer, but three years later, after serving in the mounted Leicestershire Yeomanry, Johnson was accepted as a flight sergeant in the RAF Volunteer Reserve. He was training in Spitfires when the war started, and an old rugby injury to his right shoulder required surgery that kept him out of the Battle of Britain. Not in action until Jan 41, the late-starting, easy-tempered Johnson quickly caught Douglas BADER's eye and benefited from the legendary ace's special attention. The neophyte got his first kill in June and was promoted to flight commander. Meanwhile he flew Bader's leading section until Bader was downed on 9 Aug 41.

Johnson saw his heaviest action as the relatively inexperienced leader of 610 Sqdn in the Dieppe raid, 19 Aug 42. His last victory was over Arnhem (Opn Market-Garden), 27 Sep 44, when he sustained the only hit on his plane in 515 sorties.

With 38 fighter kills, most of them in 1943-44, "Johnnie" Johnson was the top British-born ace in WWII. The only RAF pilot to score higher was the South African PATTLE (41 victories). Johnnie Johnson remained in the RAF and during the Korean War was attached to the USAF. Retiring as an air vice marshal, he wrote books on fighter tactics and strategy that include *Wing Leader* and *Full Circle* (London: Chatto & Windus, 1956 and 1964).

JOHNSON, Leon William. USAF general. 1904-. Born 13 Sep 04 in Missouri and appointed to West Point from Kansas, he graduated in 1926 (60/153). Leon Johnson began his WWII service as **A3**, 8th AF, then commanded the 44th Hv Bomb Gp. From 1942 to V-E day he led the 8th AF's 14th Combat Bomber Wing. Col Johnson was one of five awarded the Medal of Honor for the Ploesti Raid, 1 Aug 43, and he was promoted to BG on 6 Nov 43 (*AA*, 923).

Maj Gen Leon Johnson commanded the 15th AF from Apr 47 to 31 July 48 with headquarters at Colorado Springs (*AA*, 598). He then went to London as CG, 3d AF, serving there until 1952 (*AA*, 226; Cullum). Promoted to full general, Johnson ended his active duty as Air Deputy, SHAPE, 1958-61. Immediately recalled to active duty, he was director of an **NSC** committee until 1965. (Cullum.)

JOHNSON, Robert S. US ace. 1920-. Bob Johnson left Texas A&M two months after enrolling and on 11 Nov 41 became a US Army Air Corps aviation cadet. Although above average as a pilot he came close to washing out in other subjects, particularly gunnery. Assigned to

twin-engine training as a bomber pilot, he improved his marksmanship enough to qualify for transfer to single-seat fighters. Joining Col Hubert "Hub" Zemke's 56th Ftr Gp (48 P-47 Thunderbolts) as it was brought up to strength, he reached England on 13 Jan 43. In less than a year, 13 June 43-8 May 44, Johnson scored 28 victories. This made him second only to Col Francis S. Gabreski (31) among USAF pilots in Europe (Sims, *Aces*, 273). Johnson won the DSC on 6 Mar 44 for aggressive action against heavy odds over Berlin (Sims, 255-70). After the war, Johnson was a successful businessman.

JOLIOT-CURIE, Frédéric. French scientist and resistance leader. 1900-58. Joliot was born unhyphenated on 19 Mar 00 in Paris, the youngest of six children. His father, whose origins were in Lorraine, was a wholesale merchant of calico who had fought in the ranks of the Commune. His mother, whose family came from Alsace, was a highly cultivated woman of republican outlook whose father had been one of Napoleon III's chefs. Frédéric was an average student, interested primarily in football until he developed a taste for chemistry and moved to the top of his class. Despite this academic aptitude Joliot worked in a steel mill until he was 25. Seeking advice from a former teacher on what to do with his life, he became a lab assistant to Marie Curie, the Nobel laureate and distinguished physicist. The next year, 1926, Joliot married Mme Curie's eldest daughter, Irène (1897-1956), a fellow lab assistant who had gotten her doctorate from the Sorbonne in 1925. They became scientific collaborators and symbolized this by adopting the surname name Joliot-Curie, and in 1935 they were awarded the Nobel Prize for discovering artificial radioactivity.

When France went to war on 3 Sep 39 the scientist was mobilized as an artillery captain and directed to coordinate atomic research. He requested a loan of heavy water from Norway, received it just before that country was invaded, and got it and his research documents to England shortly before France fell. In a 12-hour session with the Gestapo he dissuaded the Germans from seizing France's only cyclotron and her valuable store of radium *(CB 46)*. Using his research lab for cover the scientist directed production of explosives, radio equipment, and forged identity papers for the resistance. Joliot-Curie became president of the National Front and joined the Communist Party. The Germans were not sufficiently suspicious of Frédéric until four months before the liberation of Paris to force him to go underground. Irène and their two children took refuge in Switzerland.

In Jan 46 the resistance hero became head of the new French commission on atomic energy, which he and Irène had helped found. But in 1950 he was dismissed because of his Communist Party affiliation. Still directing the work of his laboratories, and succeeding his wife as head of the Radium Institute in Paris when she died in 1956, Frédéric remained politically active until his early death two years later. Like Marie and Irène Curie, both of whom died of leukemia, he was a victim of radiation poisoning.

JONES, Albert Monmouth. US general. 1890-1967. Born 20 July 90 and becoming an RA officer, Col Jones went to the Philippines in 1940 and took command of the 31st US Inf Regt. The next year he was promoted to brigadier general and given command of the 51st Inf Div, Philippine army. On 24 Dec 41, when Maj Gen George M. Parker, Jr, became head of the Bataan Defense Force, Jones replaced him as CG, South Luzon Force (SLF).

Gen Jones directed the SLF's delaying action to Bataan, and took charge of US and Filipino forces that were still east of the Pampanga River on 31 Dec 41. The strategic Calumpit bridges were blown the next day after being used by most of the friendly troops including elements of WAINWRIGHT's North Luzon Force. Jones commanded his 51st Div on Bataan until 10 Mar 42, when he succeeded WAINWRIGHT as CG, I Corps, on Bataan (*OCMH Chron,* 28). After the surrender on 9 Apr 42 Jones come through the death march and survived 40 months as a POW. He was promoted to major general on 16 Mar 43. Having been awarded the DSC, DSM, SS (OLC), LM, BSM (OLC), and CR, Maj Gen Jones retired on 31 July 52.

JONES, Frederick. NZ statesman. 1884-1966. Born in Dunedin, NZ, on 16 Nov 84, Jones was a trade union leader and member of the Labor government when the war started. He gave up all posts except minister of defense and by 1943 had built his country's armed forces from a strength of 1,000 to a strength of 90,000

men and women at home and 80,000 overseas. By 1945 a third of all military-age men were overseas. The 2d NZ Div performed brilliantly in North Africa and in Italy under FREYBERG, one of the war's outstanding combat leaders; the 3d NZ Div served in MacArthur's conquest of the Solomons. New Zealand lost almost 40,000 officers and men during the war including POWs (Tunney). Jones died 22 May 66 at Dunedin.

JONES, Reginald Victor. British scientist. 1911-. Son of a Grenadier Guards sergeant, R. V. Jones (as he was commonly known) was born 29 Sep 11 in London. At the age of 22 he received a doctorate from Oxford, where he studied under LINDEMANN. On 1 Sep 39, when Germany invaded Poland, Dr Jones left a four-year assignment in the Admiralty research lab after working for the intelligence service on air defense. His initial wartime assignment was to study the Luftwaffe's use of science, but his mission was expanded to the entire field of scientific intelligence. He also was scientific advisor to MI6.

Among Dr Jones's greatest achievements was having centimetric radar put into JOUBERT DE LA FERTE's Coastal Command planes for spotting U-boats. He fooled the Germans into believing for six months that U-boats were being detected by infrared rays; by the time they adopted proper countermeasures the turning point in the battle of the Atlantic was reached. Almost alone and despite much skepticism he defeated the Luftwaffe's **Lorenz beam** system of air navigation. The boffin then was involved in identifying and attacking R&D installations (notably those at **Peenemuende),** in developing nuclear energy, in making preparations for D day in Normandy, and in coping with the V-1 and V-2.

On 30 Sep 46 Jones became professor of natural philosophy at the Univ of Aberdeen. His lively, much-lauded memoirs appeared in the UK as *Most Secret War* and in America as *The Wizard War: British Scientific Intelligence 1929-1945* (New York: Coward, McCann & Geoghan, Inc, 1978). As recently as 1995 he lived in Aberdeen.

JOUBERT DE LA FERTE, Philip Bennet. British general. 1887-1965. Philip Joubert de la Ferté was born 21 May 87 at Darjeeling, India.

His father was a colonel in the Indian Medical Service, and his French grandfather was a distinguished engraver who was naturalized in 1885 after coming to England 45 years earlier. (Edward Chilton in *DNB*.)

Philip was sent to England at the age of nine for schooling, and two years later he was traveling alone to spend vacations with an aunt in the south of France. The self-reliant boy and his three surviving siblings had a reputation for recklessness (ibid.). Despite an attraction to airplanes and submarines that came from avid reading, Philip was directed to the army by his father. He attended Harrow, qualified for Woolwich (RMC) on a second attempt, and was commissioned in 1907 as a field gunner.

At his own expense Joubert learned to fly in 1912 and became an RFC pilot in Mar 13. He was a fully qualified young army officer who had the additional advantage of speaking French, and it was the ideal time to launch a career in the new field of military aviation. (Ibid.). Within a week of reaching France in 1914 he and another pilot made history as the first to fly reconnaissance over enemy territory. After serving as an airman in France and Egypt, Joubert rose to command the RFC in Italy.

Between the wars he maintained his professional skills while specializing as a "school officer"; after attending **Camberley** in 1920 and being promoted to group captain in 1922 Joubert was an instructor at the newly formed RAF College at Andover. He was the first flying officer to teach at the Imperial Defense College (1926-29), then he was commandant of the RAF Staff College (1930-33). Promoted in 1934, Air Vice Marshal Joubert became AOC the Fighting Area of Great Britain, forerunner of Fighter Command. Again promoted, Air Marshal Joubert headed Coastal Command in 1936 before becoming AOC India, 1937-39. He was knighted (KCB) in 1938.

At the start of WWII Sir Philip was an adviser on air operations and assistant chief of the air staff. His specific duties were to advise on the use of radar and on RAF cooperation with the RN. Further advanced in rank, Air Chief Marshal Joubert returned to head the Coastal Command in June 41. The service in particular and **ASW** in general had been neglected, largely because the RAF under TRENCHARD was oriented toward land warfare. Joubert had difficulty getting suitable aircraft, more powerful

bombs, low-level bomb sights, better depth charges, search radar (*see* D. V. JONES), and a priority in operational research. All this occurred as the U-boat menace threatened Britain's very existence. The abrasive Joubert made enemies in the Admiralty and, for demanding that Bomber Command give priority to attacking submarine bases, in the RAF.

Despite his major contribution to winning the Battle of the Atlantic he was ousted from Coastal Command in 1943 and made IG of the RAF. Sir Philip soon went into retirement but had been out only a month when recalled in the fall of 1943 as Mountbatten's chief of information and civil affairs at the new SEAC Hq in New Delhi, India. Some 18 months later, after the liberation of Rangoon (3 May 45), Joubert returned to England for much-needed hospital treatment. He retired the following October, but after some nine months of rest and recuperation served as a civilian in the Air Ministry as director of public relations. During a year in this capacity he lectured extensively across the US on air power.

A robust, burly man just under six feet tall, the controversial Sir Philip died 21 Jan 65 at the RAF hospital at Uxbridge. He published *The Fated Sky* (1952), *The Third Service* (1955), *Rocket* (1956), *Look at Aeroplanes* (1960), and *The Forgotten Ones* (1961).

JOYCE, William ("Lord Haw Haw"). British traitor. 1906-46. Born in Brooklyn, NY, to an English mother and a naturalized Irishman, Joyce moved to England via Ireland in 1921. After graduating with first class honors in English from the Univ of London he joined Sir Oswald Mosley's British Union of Fascists in 1933. When ejected he founded the British National Socialist League.

The small, garrulous Joyce acquired a conspicuous facial scar in the process, allegedly during a political brawl. Shortly before the start of war he moved with his wife to Germany and began propaganda broadcasts that made him known to millions in Britain as "Lord Haw Haw."

Arrested by British soldiers on 28 May 45 in Flensburg and charged with treason, he argued unsuccessfully at the Old Bailey and in appeals up to the House of Lords that he was an American citizen. But the House held that because the unlordly Joyce had a British passport he owed allegiance to the Crown. In a marvel of quick justice, Joyce was hanged as a traitor on 3 Jan 46, in London.

JUIN, Alphonse Pierre. French general. 1888-1967. An old-stock *colon* ("colonist"), the future marshal of France was born 16 Dec 88 in the house of his grandfather, a lighthouse keeper at Cape Rosa, in Algeria near Bône (now Annaba). Juin's father was a gendarme in Constantine (NE Algeria); his mother was a Corsican who imbued her swarthy son with a strong character and sense of honor. (Col Adolphe Goutard in Carver, ed, *The War Lords,* "Juin," 597. Goutard wrote from a long personal association with Juin.)

After excelling at school in Constantine and Algiers, Juin was seventh out of almost 400 in the entrance examination for St Cyr in 1909. He graduated first in the class of 1912 that included de Gaulle, who had become a close friend. (Clayton, 13.) Eager for immediate action, he chose service with the 1st Regt of Algerian Tirailleurs (RTA) in the polyglot Armée d' Afrique, which was conducting large scale pacification operations in Morocco under resident general Louis Hubert Lyautey. Lt Juin was soon detached to command one of the French army's first formations of Moroccan irregulars, progenitors of the fearsome Tirailleurs Marocains or **goumiers.**

Going to France in Aug 14 as a platoon leader in the Moroccan Bde he was quickly thrown into a conventional war for which his light infantry colonial troops were not equipped nor trained. In the battle of the Marne, 6-10 Sep 14, Lt Juin remained in action with his platoon for more than 10 days despite a painful wound to his left hand on the first day. He was later awarded the cross of the Legion of Honor for "courage, eye for country and power of decision." At the start of the French counteroffensive in Champaign, Juin received a serious arm wound on 15 May 15. He needed eight months of hospital treatment, emerging with a permanently lamed right arm and authority to salute with his left hand.

Invalided home to Morocco in Dec 15 for convalescence and promoted to captain, he joined a native unit being trained for action in France. Capt Juin was Lyautey's ADC for six months before returning to the western front at his own request. He arrived during Christmas

1916 and Juin took command of a company of tirailleurs. For the next year he led his Moroccans in suicidal assaults ordered to justify the illusion of French generals that élan could overcome superior strength. Surviving the law of averages, Capt Juin was nominated in Feb 18 to take staff courses. He completed these a few weeks before the armistice of 11 Nov 18 and was posted to the French mission assigned to the AEF.

Juin graduated from the war college in 1921 and served in Tunisia and Morocco. There he learned much from close association with NOGUES in the Rif war against Abd-el-Krim in 1925. That year, when Lyautey was replaced in Morocco by Pétain and "kicked upstairs" to the Higher War Council in Paris, Juin volunteered to serve as one of three officers on Lyautey's staff. Promoted during his two years in Paris, Maj Juin then commanded a battalion in Algeria. In 1933, a year after another promotion, Lt Col Juin became a remarkable, nonconformist tactics instructor at the War College.

Returning to troop duty, Juin commanded the 3d Zouave Regt at Constantine. In 1937 he became NOGUES's CofS in Morocco and was promoted on 26 Dec 38 to brigadier general. The 51-year-old Juin chafed at being held in Algiers for three months after France declared war on 3 Sep 39. He then took command of the 15th Mtz Inf Div, a well equipped force of three regiments with modern artillery and armored reconnaissance units but no tanks. In Blanchard's 1st Army around Cambrai during the Phony War he trained with borrowed tanks to simulate German panzers, drawing on known lessons of the Polish campaign.

When German attacked on 10 May 40 the 15th Div moved into Belgium, as prescribed in the Dyle Plan. After advancing about 30 miles Juin was heavily engaged around Gembloux with the south flank of REICHENAU's 6th Army. Then he covered the retreat toward Dunkirk, stoutly defending Valenciennes (19-26 May 40) before dropping back to Lille. Most of his force was surrounded with elements of five other divisions. Ordering one column to break out, Juin defended the southern suburbs until his ammunition ran out on 29 May 40. The next day he was taken prisoner and sent with other senior officers to Koenigstein castle. While held under reasonably comfortable conditions Col Juin learned of his promotion to général de division, effective in Feb 41.

At the urging of WEYGAND, who was in Algiers as delegate general and CinC, Pétain prevailed on Hitler to authorize Juin's repatriation. In June 41 the "African specialist" was paroled to command all French troops in Morocco; NOGUES retained civil authority as high commissioner. When the Germans forced Vichy to recall WEYGAND on 18 Nov 41, Juin replaced him in Algiers as Commander, Land Forces North Africa.

The next month, when AUCHINLECK's offensive drove back Rommel's Pz Army Africa, Juin refused to make a deal with Goering for the Axis to use Tunisia's ports, railroads, and roads. The French general cited international law, but as an "African" he also wanted to save Tunisia—a French protectorate—from the war damage Syria had suffered. (Weitz, 67-68.) But Juin was furious on returning to Algiers to learn that Darlan had authorized the Axis to use the port of Gabés in SE Tunisia behind the Mareth Line!

The limited French forces in Tunisia were under de LATTRE, who was only slightly junior to his friend Juin and a rival for top rank. De Lattre wanted to deploy his few, lightly equipped colonials in the south, using the Mareth Line in a forward strategy, an offense-defence of the Libyan border; Juin favored a defense in depth using the Tunisian hills in the northwest. Responsible for defending all North Africa, Juin saw Tunisia as an outpost for stopping an enemy advance into Algeria. Juin argued also that de Lattre's strategy risked rapid destruction of his small force, opening the door to Algeria, and could not be supported logistically. Juin imposed his views, although, he used much of his subordinate's argument to get de Lattre reinforcements from Vichy. But in Jan 42 Juin maladroitly informed de Lattre he was being recalled because of German pressure to which Vichy finally had yielded. As on other notable occasions, "De Lattre exploded with fury [and] relations between the two were never quite the same again" (Weitz, 69).

When the Allied landings began on 8 Nov 42 the French had five fully trained mobile divisions ready for action, although they lacked adequate materiel. Juin had continued Weygand's program of establishing numerous secret military depots. Although Juin made no secret of being pro-Allied he declined to violate his parole by working with Robert MURPHY and French conspirators in Algeria. (Murphy, 127; compare WC, IV, 611.) This made for a tense situation on D day in North Africa when Murphy got Juin out of bed with news that US forces were landing. Furious about not having been forewarned (and known for not wanting his sleep disturbed) Juin phoned Adm DARLAN, who happened to be in Algiers. The admiral quickly joined Murphy and Juin, soon followed by his military secretary, Adm Battet, and the delegate general, Adm Fénard. Feeling released from his parole because he assumed Pétain no longer had any real autonomy, Juin took the lead in convincing DARLAN to order a cease fire.

Juin was promoted to général de corps d'armée and on 25 Nov 42 took command in Tunisia of the "French Army Detachment" (DAF). Seeing the need for unity of command, Juin proposed subordinating himself to Noel ANDERSON, who headed the 1st British Army in what was supposed to be the "race for Tunis." GIRAUD not only disapproved but also reprimanded his subordinate for the recommendation. (Weitz, 74.) Not until von ARNIM's counteroffensive in Jan 42 mangled the lightly equipped French colonials—now designated the 19th Corps—did Giraud agree to put Juin under Anderson's operational control.

Promoted 25 Dec 42, Général d'Armée Juin turned over the 19th Corps to Koeltz and began to plan formation of the French Expeditionary Corps (CEF) for future operations outside North Africa. But with authority to intervene in Tunisia, Juin returned to the field for the spring offensive and made a triumphal entry into Tunis on 13 May 43. He was acting resident general here until Gen Mast recovered from an air accident. Although still politically suspect in the Gaullist camp—having been a "Vichy general"—Juin became a member of the newly formed military commission on 22 June 43, the FCNL having endorsed his appointment as CinC of French Army forces in North Africa. But the next month, as de Gaulle eclipsed GIRAUD and consolidated his power in Algiers, Juin was replaced by Gen Leyer and "confirmed in his mission of preparing and, shortly, of commanding the expeditionary corps destined for Italy" (de Gaulle, *Unity*, 150).

Juin reached the Naples airport on 25 Nov 43 to find no senior British or American officer on hand to greet him. He was assigned to the 5th US Army of Mark W. CLARK, who was eight years his junior chronologically and light years junior in military experience. The first French colonial unit in Italy, the 2d Moroccan Mtn Div was committed on 10 Dec 43 to relieve the stalled and battered 34th US Inf Div in the rugged Apennines some 15 miles NW of Cassino. Attacking a day later, the **goumiers** astounded friend and foe by their fierce performance, and the Germans soon rated them with FREYBERG's 2d NZ Div as the best units they faced in Italy (*West Point Atlas,* 101). Joined in Italy by the 3d Algerian Inf Div of tirailleurs, Juin was assigned a sector on the 5th Army front on 3 Jan 44 and his force was officially designated the French Expeditionary Corps (CEF). The tirailleurs waded the icy Rapido River during the night of 25-26 Jan 44 and in hand-to-hand combat took Belevedere, NE of Cassino.

In the final drive on Rome, French colonials penetrated the Itri-Pico lateral of the Apennines, an almost trackless range the Germans considered impassable to troops. Pushing north through rugged hills, often supplied only by mule train and reinforced by the 1st FF Armd Div, the French captured Sienna on 3 July 44 and exploited toward Florence. (Both historic cities were taken by French and British colonials, one reason being that Americans were notoriously indifferent to sparing architectural treasures [personal knowledge].)

Juin was among those including Alexander, Clark, and "Jumbo" Wilson who strongly advocated a drive through Ljubljana Gap into Austria, instead of diverting strength from Italy for the invasion of southern France. But this would violate the strategy Stalin had insisted on at Teheran. The CEF was withdrawn to prepare for action in southern France, Juin handed over command to de LATTRE on 1 Aug 44 (Goutard, 610). Dreams of a Napoleonic campaign in central Europe dashed (ibid.), Juin took the top military position under de Gaulle, CofS of national defense, on 12 Aug 44.

He was resident general in Morocco, 1947-51, then for five years had his headquarters at Fontainebleau as CinC, Land Forces Central Europe (in NATO). Made a marshal of France in May 52, Juin retired from active duty in Oct 56. As troubles mounted in Algeria, his homeland, Juin struggled to remain loyal to his government. But, for opposing Algerian independence in a frank letter to de Gaulle in 1961, Juin was removed from the supreme defense council and forbidden to visit Algeria. Vigorous almost to the end, the last living marshal of France died 27 Jan 67 in Paris at the age of 79. His remains are in the crypt of the Invalides.

K

KAI-SHEK, Chiang. *See* CHIANG KAI-SHEK.

KAISER, Henry J(ohn). US industrialist. 1882-1967. "Fabulous Henry" was responsible for building about a third of all US merchant ships launched in 1940-45, a total of 1,460, and was a major producer of aluminum, steel, and magnesium for the war effort.

The burly, bald, supercharged tycoon was born 9 May 82 in Canajoharie, NY, and left school at the age of 11 *(CB 42)* to help support his family. While still a teenager he went to the West Coast and rose from selling street paving for a company in Spokane, Wash, to having a major involvement in some of the country's greatest engineering projects. These include the Boulder, Bonneville, and Grand Coulee Dams, and the piers of the San Francisco-Oakland Bay Bridge *(S&S)*. In 1939 he created the Permanente Cement Mill, south of San Francisco, one of the largest producers in America. Kaiser then bought a West Coast shipyard and was ready when the US entered the war to mass produce critically needed shipping faster than U-boats could sink it. Adopting simplified new "Liberty" designs and innovative shipbuilding methods, by Nov 42 he needed little more than four days to launch a 10,500-ton ship that formerly would have taken 150 days. *(CB 42.)* Kaiser, who still referred to the front end a ship as the front end (ibid.), went on to defy experts by mass producing 50 "baby flattops," 18,000-ton CVEs. His Permanente plant (above) tripled the national output of magnesium when a shortage became critical. Kaiser built California's first complete steel mill (in Fontana), entered the field of aluminum production, and in 1943 took control of the Fleetwing Aircraft company of Bristol, Pa. In July 42 the tycoon submitted a formal proposal, in collaboration with Glen Martin and Howard Hughes, to develop and manufacture 5,000 huge flying boats for trans-Atlantic movement of men and cargos. Although technically feasible, the project never got funding, largely because it would have required resources better used elsewhere.

After the war Kaiser directed other huge enterprises to include short-lived production of the little "Henry-J" automobile. More enduring is a huge and still-successful health maintenance organization (HMO).

Henry Kaiser died 24 Aug 67 in Honolulu.

KAISER WILHELM II. *See* WILHELM II.

KALININ, Mikhail Ivanovich. Soviet statesman. 1875-1946. The grand old man of the USSR, he was born on 19 Nov 75 in a village of Verkhanyaya Troitsa, Tver Province, north of Moscow. As a lathe operator, then gauge maker in artillery plants, he worked in Petersburg and, during periods of exile, in places including Tiflis and Revel. After the Oct 17 Revolution he became mayor of Petrograd. When the USSR was formed in Dec 22 he became chairman of the Central Executive Committee. From 1919 a Politburo candidate, Kalinin was a full member after 1926. The province and capital city of Tver were renamed for him in 1933.

In Jan 38 he became President of the Presidium of the Supreme Soviet, titular head of state. The "Old Man" to Old Bolsheviks, the "Little Father" to the peasants *(CB 42)*, Kalinin checked some excesses of Stalinism, particularly the cult of personality, collectivization, and the purges (*see* L. A. GOVOROV).

But on 7 Jan 88 *Pravda* published a letter of 1930 from Mikhail A. Sholokhov, author of *And Quiet Flows the Don,* blaming Kalinin for turning a blind eye on unlawful collection of all grain and livestock in the Don region, condemning peasants to death by starvation (Scotts). (Medvedev quotes a "revealing letter" of protest from Sholokhov to Stalin in the same vein [*Let History Judge,* 93].) Kalinin survived primarily because he was a useful figurehead with little real power and was no threat to Stalin. He died 3 June 46 and was buried in Red Square.

KALTENBORN, Hans Von. US radio newscaster. 1878-1965. The father of Hans von Kaltenborn was a baron and former officer of the Hessian Guards who married an American schoolteacher and settled in Milwaukee, Wisc. Hans was born there on 9 July 78, grew up in Merrill, Wisc, and eventually became a journalist. He entered Harvard in 1905 as a special student at the age of 27, was a Phi Beta Kappa, and graduated cum laude in 1909. During WWI the cultured but impecunious journalist changed his German particle of nobility, "von," into a middle name. In 1922 he became the nation's first radio news analyst, and eight years later he joined CBS. During the Spanish Civil War Kaltenborn made dramatic radio reports from the front, then Kaltenborn covered the **Munich Crisis**. From the spring of 1940 he was with NBC. Never using a script, and brooking no interruptions for commercial announcements, he became famous to millions as the "suave Voice of Doom" *(CB 40)*. In 1955 the tall, urbane radio pioneer retired officially but remained active as a public speaker and writer. His third book was *I Broadcast the* [Munich] *Crisis* (1938), and his last ones were *Fifty Fabulous Years* (1950), and *It Seems Like Yesterday* (1956). Kaltenborn died 14 June 65 in NYC.

KALTENBRUNNER, Ernst. German official. 1903-46. Nearly seven feet tall, with massive shoulders, a lantern jaw, and deep facial scars from student duels, Kaltenbrunner looked like the major war criminal he became. Unlike most Nazi hierarchs, however, he had a genius for combining police and political work that was underpinned by solid legal education.

Kaltenbrunner was born 4 Oct 03 in Austria near Braunau, Hitler's birthplace. The son and grandson of lawyers, he got a doctorate in law from Graz Univ in 1925 and set up practice in Linz. He became a rabid Nazi, joining the party in 1932 and being arrested in 1934 soon after becoming head of the Austrian SS. Apprehended again in May 35 and charged with conspiracy, he was disbarred and jailed for six months.

For his work with SEYSS-INQUART in events leading to the Anschluss, Kaltenbrunner became Austrian minister for state security on 2 Mar 38. He also was given the SS rank of Gruppenfuehrer and elected to the Reichstag. Kaltenbrunner's hopes to head the SD in Austria were thwarted by HEYDRICH's being given the post, but for the next three years the giant was successively chief of the SS in Austria and police chief for Vienna and the Upper and Lower Danube. In Apr 41 he became a lieutenant general of police.

When Heydrich was made acting Protector of Bohemia and Moravia in the spring of 1942 Kaltenbrunner became his deputy as chief of the SD and Gestapo. Having attracted Himmler's attention by establishing a highly effective intelligence network over his extensive domain (Wistrich), Kaltenbrunner succeeded HEYDRICH as head of the all-powerful **RSHA**, Hitler approving the appointment on 30 Jan 43.

The new chief was ruthlessly efficient, particularly in rounding up Jews for the death camps. He was feared and detested inside the SS, especially by SCHELLENBERG, but almost unknown to the public. "Kaltenbrunner had no heroes, neither Himmler, nor the Fuehrer, nor the Germans, nor the Austrians. He was a gangster filled with hatred and resentment and plans for improving his own condition." (Davidson, *Trial,* 320-1.) Even Himmler came to fear him (ibid., 318).

Kaltenbrunner's passion for intelligence and counterintelligence got fuller scope when CANARIS's Abwehr became a branch of the RSHA in Feb 44. Kaltenbrunner was a bloodhound in tracking down anti-Hitler conspirators after STAUFFENBERG's 20 July 44 assassination attempt.

In the twilight of the Third Reich Kaltenbrunner fled south with his staff and was picked up by an American patrol at Alt-Aussee in the Tyrol. Long a heavy-smoker, drunkard, and debauchee, he had deteriorated physically into a gaunt vestige of his former self. On trial at Nuremberg the Nazi bureaucrat lied brazenly, pleaded bad memory, blamed others, and missed some proceedings after having a cerebral hemorrhage on 18 Nov 45. Convicted of war crimes and crimes against humanity, he was hanged 16 Oct 46 with 10 other major Nazis.

KARMAN, Theodore von. US physicist. 1881-1963. The "father of the supersonic age," a pioneer in aerodynamics, was born in Hungary. After receiving his doctorate at Goettingen Univ in Germany, Karman became director of the new aeronautical institute at the Univ of Aachen in 1912. From 1930 he was director at the Guggenheim aeronautical laboratory at the California Institute of Technology, where he remained for almost 20 years, becoming an

American citizen. He refused the Nazi's invitation to return to Germany in 1939.

Dr von Karman did rocket research, built one of the first operable helicopters, and directed theoretical and design work that led to the Bell X-1. In 1942 his organization became the Jet Propulsion Laboratories at Cal Tech. In the last year of WWII he headed a group of scientists who made a major contribution to defense planning, especially to development of the independent USAF. Karman later founded what became Aerojet General, the world's largest manufacturer of rockets. In 1951 he established the NATO advisory council for aeronautical R&D, being chairman from 1952 until his death in 1963.

KAWABE, Masakazu (or Shozo). Japanese general. 1886-1965. An anxious, austere, emaciated little man (small even by Japanese standards) who looked sick most of the time (Swinson, *Four Samurai,* 118, 123), Kawabe is best remembered for briefly commanding Japanese forces in Burma in 1944.

He was born in Toyama Prefecture, completed the military academy in 1907, and was commissioned an infantryman. Graduating from the war college in 1915, he became a specialist in military training. Kawabe also served abroad as a "resident officer" in Switzerland, 1918-21, and MA in Berlin, 1929-31. He was assigned to the **IGS** in June 25. (*Kogun,* 226-27.) In Apr 36 he took command of an infantry brigade in North China. Promoted that year to major general and CofS, Kwantung Army, he was temporarily absent when the **Marco Polo Bridge** incident occurred. Apparently assuming that the adventure had approval in Tokyo, Kawabe fell in with the conspirators led by MUTAGUCHI.

Kawabe was CofS, Central China Expeditionary Army, for a year beginning in Feb 38. He then returned to Tokyo for high posts in the military training inspectorate, was promoted in Mar 39 to lieutenant general, and a year later assumed command of the 12th Div in China. Moving up the next year (1941) to head the 3d Army, he became CofS, China Expeditionary Army, in Aug 42. (Ibid.)

As a lieutenant general he took command of the Burma Area Army in Mar 43. Kawabe endorsed MUTAGUCHI's "March on Delhi," a monumental disaster for which both generals were sacked, Kawabe being succeeded on about

30 Aug 44 by Heitaro KIMURA and sent to head the Central District Army Command in Japan. Promoted to full general in Mar 45, the next month he was appointed CG, Air General Army, having charge of army air operations in the homeland, Korea and the Ryukuys. After the Japanese surrender he succeeded SUGIYAMA as CG, 1st General Army, which was charged with mainland defense. Torashiro KAWABE (to follow) was a younger brother.

KAWABE, Torashiro. Japanese general. 1890-1960. A younger brother of Gen Masakazu KAWABE, he graduated from the military academy in May 12 as a second lieutenant of artillery. Capt Kawabe graduated from the war college in November 1921. After serving with the operations section, Army GS Hq, Kawabe was "resident officer" in Riga, Latvia, Jan 26-Sep 28, to study Soviet military affairs. (US foreign affairs officers including George KENNAN were also posted to Riga for Russian area and language studies.) Back in Tokyo Major Kawabe (1927) taught tactics at the war college, served again in the Army GS Hq operations section, and was promoted to lieutenant colonel in 1931. Early the next year he became MA in Moscow, remaining until Apr 34. He was sent to the Kwantung Army as a GS officer (operations and intelligence), remaining until Mar 36 and being promoted to colonel. He returned to Tokyo just after the **26 Feb 36** mutiny had been put down. Col Kawabe was given command of the field artillery regiment of the Guard Div, holding the post until Feb 37, when he became operations chief, Army GS Hq. Kawabe then attended the Hamamatsu Army Flying School for six months and was promoted to major general in July 38. Three months later, on the eve of Hitler's war, he became MA in Berlin and in Aug 39 began doubling as MA in Budapest. In Sep 40 he assumed command of the 7th Air Bde in Manchuria, moving it to Canton in Feb 41. Six months later he returned to Tokyo for a succession of high staff assignments interrupted by duty in Manchuria, May 43-Aug 44, as CG 2d Air Army. As deputy chief of the army GS from Apr 45, he headed the delegation sent to Manila the following August to arrange the surrender there. After the war he was on the commission that advised his government on armaments. *(Kogun,* 227; *S&S.)*

KAWAGUCHI, Kiyotake. Japanese general. 1892-1961. Commissioned in Dec 41 as an infantryman and graduating from the war college in 1922, he spent most of his peacetime service as a staff officer. In Dec 1940 he assumed command of the 35th Inf Bde as a major general. After taking part in the invasion of Borneo he commanded a force of 3,500 that HYAKUTAKE sent from Rabaul to reinforce the garrison on Guadalcanal in late Aug 42. Despite suffering losses before landing, he was ordered to capture Henderson Field. This was one of HYAKUTAKE's unsuccessful piecemeal efforts. Returned to Japan and attached to the Eastern District Army Hq in Nov 42, Kawaguchi was put on the unassigned list in Mar 43 and on the reserve list a month later. Recalled to active duty in Mar 45, Kawaguchi was CG, Tsushima Fortress. (*Kogun,* 227; *S&S.*)

KEITEL, Wilhelm Bodewin Johann Gustav. German general. 1882-1946. Keitel was a Hanoverian born 22 Sep 82 in Helmscherode, Braunschweig, near Brunswick. Not a Prussian, from a family of large-scale farmers who would not allow his father to wear his army uniform at home, the son undertook a military career in 1900 only from economic necessity. He was severely wounded in WWI. With little other than staff experience from 1929, Keitel was known as a solid, dedicated officer but a plodder of "third-rate ability" (W-B, *Nemesis,* 429).

He nevertheless rose to head the exclusive **Truppenamt** and succeeded REICHENAU on 1 Oct 33 as chief of the new Wehrmachtamt. Without having ever commanded a division he was promoted to general of artillery in 1937. That year he married War Minister Blomberg's youngest daughter. When Hitler ousted BLOMBERG in early 1938 and took personal control of the Wehrmacht, the fuehrer asked Blomberg to nominate an officer to serve as his CofS. None of the candidates appealing to him, Hitler and Blomberg had the following dialogue:

Hitler. "Who is that general you have had at your side up to now?"

Blomberg. "Oh, Keitel. He would not come into consideration. He is no more than my chef de bureau [office manager]."

Hitler. "That is exactly the kind of man I am looking for."

The tall, ponderous, monocled Keitel took over as Wehrmacht CofS on 4 Feb 38 with the rank of Generaloberst. "So Hitler has got his *Lakaitel,*" said the wags (W-B, *Nemesis,* 429), making a pun on *Lakai,* which is pronounced "lackey" and means the same thing. Another early nickname was *Nickesel,* a toy donkey that nods its head. But Field Marshal Keitel (from 19 July 40) occasionally stood up to Hitler: he wrote a memo advising against the invasion of Russia, he joined JODL in protesting Hitler's removal of LIST in the fall of 1942, and more than once he offered to resign. Several times he contemplated suicide. Far from joining the anti-Hitler conspirators, however, Keitel condemned those who did. After being slightly wounded in STAUFFENBERG's 20 July 44 bomb attempt Keitel sat with GUDERIAN and Rundstedt on the Army Court of Honor that turned hundreds of innocent officers over to the People's Court. Keitel's one decent act was to delay the trial of CANARIS.

On the evening of 22 Apr 45, as the Allies were about to split Germany, Hitler ordered Keitel and Jodl to set up a headquarters in the south. But the two ended up in the north with DOENITZ on 1 May. Keitel signed the surrender document in Berlin on 9 May 45. (*See* also **Surrender of Germany.**)

At Nuremberg he was convicted of crimes against humanity and for planning and directing a war of aggression. Although pleading that he had merely obeyed orders, the lackey had gone beyond this: he was almost the only military officer who did not protest the **commissar order;** he issued the OKW decree implementing Hitler's **Nacht und Nebel** policy; and he condoned extermination of the Jews (Bracher, 418). After being sentenced to death, Keitel admitted his guilt, insisted that his attorney not appeal, and asked only to be shot as a soldier. Denied this request, Keitel went bravely to the gallows on 16 Oct 46.

His valuable papers were edited for publication by Walter Goerlitz as *Generalfeldmarschall Keitel, Verbrecher* [Criminal] *oder Offizier? Erinnerungen, Briefe, Dokumente des Chefs OKW* (Goettingen, 1962). The translation, edited by Goerlitz and David Irving, is *The Memoirs of Field Marshal Keitel* (New York, 1965).

KELLY, Colin Purdie, Jr. US officer. 1915-41. The first American hero of WW II was a Floridian, USMA 1937 (248/298). On 10 Dec 41,

Capt Kelly piloted a B-17 from Clark Field to attack the invasion fleet. Off Aparri, N Luzon, he hit a transport. When a Zero set the bomber on fire, the captain ordered his six surviving crewmen to jump, and Kelly died when the plane exploded. It was reported and long believed that Kelly had hit a battleship (*Haruna*), but it was learned later that no battleship was in the area *(OCMH Chron, 4)*. The first West Pointer KIA during the war (Cullum), Kelly was posthumously awarded the DSC, DFC, and (of course) PH.

KENNAN, George Frost. US diplomat. 1904-. The specialist in Soviet affairs was born in Milwaukee and spent part of his childhood in Europe. A year after graduating from Princeton in 1925, Kennan joined the recently established Foreign Service and promptly entered a program of Russian area and language studies. The US announced recognition of the USSR on 18 Nov 33, and Kennan accompanied Amb BULLITT to Moscow. With an interlude of less than a year in Vienna, Kennan was in Moscow until 1937. Then he was in Prague during the Sudetenland crisis of 1938 and remained through the occupation of Bohemia and Moravia six months later. Transferred to Berlin after Hitler invaded Poland on 1 Sep 39, he was there until the US delegation was interned on 14 Dec 41. Kennan was exchanged in June 42 and three months later was sent to Lisbon as counselor of legation. After having a major role in negotiating US base rights in the Azores, the foreign service officer was recalled at the end of 1943 and sent to London. Here he was special adviser to Amb John G. WINANT in the latter's capacity as US delegate to the new **European Advisory Commission.** Having gained a considerable knowledge of German affairs as well as of Soviet affairs, Kennan was a prophet without honor in his own state department. He returned to Moscow with Amb Averell HARRIMAN as his minister-counselor from 1 July 44 until Apr 46. Still unheeded, he warned against "the chimera of Soviet collaboration" *(Memoirs,* I, 256).

Under George C. MARSHALL and Dean ACHESON he headed the State Department Planning Staff until resigning the post to Paul Nitze shortly after 16 Sep 49. At the end of Aug 50 he left Washington to join the Institute for Advanced Study at Princeton (ibid.,

500), remaining a member until 1974 while being ambassador to Russia in 1952 and to Yugoslavia, 1961-1963. Kennan published award-winning works of diplomatic history and autobiography, some of which are listed in the main bibliography.

KENNEDY, Joseph Patrick. US businessman. 1888-1969. The future ambassador to London was born 6 Sep 88 in Boston's East Side. Son of an Irish Catholic political boss who had a coal business and part interest some saloons *(CB 40),* Young Joe went from the Boston Latin School to Harvard. He excelled in baseball, basketball, and football. With a BA in economics from Harvard in 1912, Kennedy set out to be a millionaire. Starting as a $125-a-month bank examiner, he borrowed to buy stock in a trust company. His father was a director, and the trust company was about to be taken over by the First Ward National Bank. Joe Kennedy then became that bank's president, at 25 the country's youngest. The next year (1914) he married the pretty, vivacious Rose Fitzgerald (1890-1995), whose flamboyant father was mayor of Boston. In what *Fortune* magazine characterized as a picaresque career (ibid.) in widely disparate fields—shipbuilding, investment banking, movie theaters and movie making, he had a fortune of about $5 million by 1930 (ibid.). The quest took a toll on his health that required hospitalization.

Reevaluating what the business tycoon called "his social views" (ibid.), Kennedy began contributing large sums to the Democratic party fund and was suspected of wanting to be Franklin Roosevelt's first secretary of the treasury. Failing this, he returned to Wall Street in 1933 and scored more coups. The repeal of prohibition was approaching, and the freebooting, almost teetotalling Boston Irishman cornered the market in Scotch whisky.

To the astonishment of those who knew his career as a Wall Street speculator, Kennedy was appointed by Roosevelt to be the first chairman of the **SEC** (1934-35). But in 431 strenuous days with the SEC Kennedy won praise as a champion of investors. ("For a good rat you want a good cat," as the French say.) Kennedy returned to corporate life, published a pro-New Deal campaign work, *I'm for Roosevelt* (1936), and for 75 days headed the newly formed and much-needed Maritime Commission.

In Dec 37 Kennedy became the first Irish-American-Catholic ambassador to London. "Jolly Joe," the "Nine-Child Envoy," was popular at first as a rough-cut, pro-British American Yankee. But lack of ambassadorial aptitude soon became embarrassing to Washington and to the anti-appeasement element that was gaining power in London. Kennedy became notorious for public statements that Britain could not survive the war against totalitarianism and for advocating that US isolationism continue. Increasingly controversial and out of step with ROOSEVELT, Kennedy announced his resignation late in Nov 40. (The **Battle of Britain** had just ended, and there was a pause in the **Blitz of London.**)

Succeeded as ambassador by WINANT and no longer a public figure of any stature, Joe Kennedy focused on establishing a dynasty. The dream became a Greek tragedy. It started with the death of his eldest son and namesake, a USAAF captain whose plane exploded in July 44 during an experimental use of radio-controlled aircraft against a **buzz-bomb** site. The second son, John F. Kennedy, commanded a **PT boat** in the Pacific, was a US senator from Massachusetts (1952-60), then president of the US until assassinated in Dallas on 22 Nov 63. Robert F. Kennedy was US attorney general (1960-64), then US senator from NY until assassinated in 1968 while campaigning for president. Edward M. Kennedy became a liberal US senator from Massachusetts from 1962 and was deterred by personal scandal and the fate of his brothers from becoming a serious presidential candidate. Several Kennedy daughters made celebrity marriages, and grandchildren kept the athletic, photogenic family in the public eye.

The patriarch, paralyzed in his later years, died 18 Nov 69 at the family enclave in Hyannis Port, Mass.

KENNEY, George Churchill. USAF general. 1889-1977. MacArthur's chief airman was born 6 Aug 89 at Yarmouth, Nova Scotia, while his parents were there on vacation *(CB 43)*. After three years at MIT he enlisted in June 17 as a flying cadet. In France the small (5 feet 6), dynamic airman commanded the 91st Aero Sqdn, logging more than 110 hours, destroying two enemy planes, and winning the DSC and SS.

Early in 1941 Kenney went from being chief of the production engineering section at Wright Field, Ohio, to head the Air Corps Experimental Depot there (ibid.). From 5 Mar 42 Maj Gen Kenney commanded the 4th AF at Riverside, Calif, but four months later he was named to replace BRETT as chief of the Allied Far East Air Forces (AAF) in MacArthur's SW Pacific Area (SWPA). On his first day of duty, 4 Aug 42, the outspoken airman faced down MacArthur's tyrannical CofS, SUTHERLAND, in a manner that neither Brereton nor Brett had done. (James, *MacArthur*, II, 198.) Two days later Kenney launched the biggest strike to date in the SWPA, successfully hitting airfields around Rabaul. His innovation of **skip bombing** revolutionized air tactics. Now a lieutenant general, Kenney undertook a drastic reorganization of the air forces that MacArthur had found so ineffective under BRERETON and Brett. Within two weeks Kenney shipped home five generals, who were followed by other officers who did not shape up.

To smooth troubled US-Australian relations and improve combat effectiveness, Kenney took command of the new US 5th AF on 3 Sep 42 while remaining head of the Allied Air Forces. The RAAF was given the mission of defending Australia, whereas the 5th AF concentrated on offensive action. Out-numbered by Japanese planes, the new commander achieved virtual parity by improving maintenance. While concurrently winning local air superiority in the Papuan campaign and providing almost the only line of communications for ground troops, Kenney continued to neutralize Japanese bases.

During the Admiralties campaign Kenney established the 13th Air TF on 11 Apr 44 pending arrival of the entire 13th AF. A little more than two months later, Kenney turned over the 5th AF to his capable deputy, WHITEHEAD, but continued the overall direction of SWPA air operations. His Far East AF (FEAF) then comprised the 5th AF as the assault air force, with the 13th AF having the support role. Kenney also directed carrier-based planes of the US 3d and 7th Fleets, landbased planes of 7th Fleet, B-29s of US 20th AF, and operations of the RAAF. The airman was promoted to four-star general on 9 Mar 45, and at war's end was sending bomber strikes from Okinawa against Kyushu.

Kenney later was the first head of the Air University, with headquarters at Maxwell AFB, Ala, directing all higher education for the USAF.

KERR, Archibald John Kerr Clark (Inverchapel). 1882-1951. British diplomat. Joining the diplomatic service in 1906, and enlisting in the Scots Guard in 1918, he succeeded the wounded KNATCHBULL-HUGESSEN as ambassador to China (1937-42). Kerr was ambassador to the USSR 1942-46, then to the US until 1948, being created 1st Baron Inverchapel of Loch Eck in 1946. He died 5 July 51. (*Who Was Who,* "Inverchapel.")

KERR, Philip Henry, 11th Marquess of Lothian. British diplomat. 1882-1940. Born 18 Apr 83 into an old landed family of Scots Catholics, he became a journalist. Kerr was a member of the Liberal Party and private secretary to Lloyd George, 1916-22 *(CB 40).* He was prominent in Lady ASTOR's Cliveden Set and long at odds with Churchill (WC, II, 399). But as ambassador to Washington from Aug 39, having succeeded a cousin as the Marquis of Lothian the previous year, Lord Lothian quickly became popular and effective in rallying desperately needed US support for Britain. "Well, boys, Britain's broke; it's your money we want," he allegedly told the press a few days after returning to Washington from a meeting with Churchill. Nobody realized that the ambassador, a Christian Scientist, was suffering from untreated uremic poisoning, a condition that can "induce a mental fog" (Parrish, *R&M,* 160). He died suddenly on 12 Dec 40, "in the full tide of success" (WC, II, 569). Lord Halifax took over Lothian's post after the 82-year-old Lloyd George declined it.

KESSELRING, Albert. German general. 1885-1960. A major commander of large-scale air and ground operations, derogated as "Smiling Albert," he was born 20 Nov 85 in Marktsheft, Bavaria. His father was a schoolmaster and town councillor in Bayreuth, where Albert completed the Classical Grammar School in 1904. That year he joined the 2d Bavarian Foot Arty Regt at Metz as an officer candidate. During the first world war he was selected for the **GGGS** and also was a trained balloon observer. The tall, genial Bavarian established an enduring friendship with Goering. He served in the exclusive **Truppenamt,** was promoted to Generalmajor in 1932, and the next year transferred to the Luftwaffe when Goering unveiled it. After secret flight training he joined Erhard MILCH's staff in 1935 and was highly effective as the Luftwaffe's chief of administration at a critical time. Although Kesselring lacked operational experience, Goering prevailed over the strong objections of Milch in having Kesselring named Luftwaffe CofS after Walther Wever's death on 3 June 36 in a plane crash. But Milch so effectively made the new CofS' position untenable that Kesselring left **OKL** in 1937. With a promotion to general of flyers and now firmly in Goering's camp of the faction-ridden OKL, Kesselring took command of Air Fleet 1. Supporting Bock's AG North in Poland, he developed a close tactical air support technique he called the "rolling attack." Supposedly to neutralize Warsaw as a communications hub, he also directed a terror bombing on the Polish capital. The "Victor of Warsaw" was awarded the RK on 30 Sep 39 (Angolia, I, 82).

Against Belgium and Holland he headed Air Fleet 2, supporting BOCK's AG B. But after rendering effective tactical air support, the Luftwaffe began revealing shortcomings for which Kesselring shares blame as a planner. Having received the nasty surprise that British fighter aircraft—Spitfires and Hurricanes—were superior to the Germans in many respects, the Luftwaffe's first failure was in not knocking out the Dunkirk beachhead (26 May-4 June). But Kesselring was made a field marshal on 19 July 40.

After taking exorbitant losses in the **Battle of Britain,** Kesselring moved his headquarters from Brussels to Posen on 22 May 41. Exactly a month later his Air Fleet 2 began supporting Bock's AG Center in Russia. The Luftwaffe continued to play a decisive part, but losses were severe.

Kesselring was appointed OB South on 28 Nov 41, before the worst troubles began in Russia. From Rome he commanded all German land and air forces in the Mediterranean. Relations with Rommel were stormy, but OB South held a tight rein without losing the respect and friendship of the difficult subordinate (Liddell Hart, ed, *Rommel Papers,* passim).

One of OB South's major missions was to interdict British shipping and gain air superiority. Kesselring recognized that neutralization of Malta deserved top priority, but he was frustrated by higher headquarters. An Italo-German airborne assault was planned in Rome by STUDENT but never attempted because Hitler lacked confidence in the Italian Navy; a campaign to bomb Malta out of the war was begun on 10 May 42 but halted 11 days later when Hitler ordered Luftwaffe resources sent to support the gigantic offensive toward Stalingrad and the Caucasus. Kesselring nevertheless was awarded the Oakleaves (78/890) on 25 Feb 42 and the Swords (15/159) on 18 July 42 (Angolia, I, 82).

Two days after the Allies landed in North Africa on 8 Nov 42 Kesselring became Mussolini's military deputy and commander of Italian forces in addition to Air Fleet 2 and Rommel's Pz Army. Directed to establish a bridgehead in Tunisia and throw the Allies back into the Atlantic, "Smiling Albert" was unable to do this. But he did block Eisenhower's "race for Tunis" and delayed the loss of North Africa for six months. Kesselring could not stop the Allied conquest of Sicily, 10 July-17 Aug 43, but a well-executed withdrawal across the Strait of Messina saved 100,000 Italian and German troops, 9,800 vehicles, and 47 tanks. (To the subsequent distress of the invaders, Hans HUBE got away with his three crack German divisions.)

Rommel established AG B Hq in Northern Italy on 15 Aug 43, Hitler having accepted Rommel's strategy of abandoning Italy south of the Po Valley and planning to make Rommel OB Southwest. Kesselring was to be transferred to Norway. In the interim, however, Smiling Albert was left to cope with the expected defection of the Italian Army and the Allied advance from Sicily. VIETINGHOFF's 10th German Army was created on 22 Aug 43 to face the tactical problem of this threat, freeing Kesselring to direct the grand strategy he already had decided on (G&B, *Italy,* 49). This called for economy of force in the far south, disposing mobile units to cover likely invasion beaches, particularly Salerno (ibid.), and putting engineers to work on formidable defenses of what became known as the Gustav Line.

OB South reacted so promptly on 9 Sep 43 that he came very close to destroying Mark CLARK's beachhead at Salerno. On 11 Sep 43 Kesselring proclaimed all of Italy a war zone, secured airfields around Rome so a planned Allied airborne assault was called off (*see* Maxwell TAYLOR), and he prepared to receive 20 additional divisions (400,000 men) in Italy. The Allies firmly in control of the Salerno beachhead by 8 Oct 43, Kesselring had Viet-

inghoff start a delaying action to avoid being trapped by Montgomery's advancing 8th Army.

Rommel was preparing to take over as OB Southwest and orders to this effect were actually being transmitted when Hitler suddenly changed his mind on 6 Nov 43 and gave Kesselring the post of supreme commander in Italy. "I reckoned that politically he was an incredible idealist," Hitler said later, "but that militarily he was an optimist, and I don't believe you can be a military commander unless you're an optimist" (Warlimont, *Inside Hitler's Hq,* 450-1).

Vietinghoff's 10th Army manned a line of defense in the mountains from coast to coast with its strongest positions being the Gustav Line through Cassino. But with substantial reinforcements from other theaters, Kesselring's AG C was created when MACKENSEN's 14th Army was formed after the Allies landed around Anzio on 22 Jan 44. Throughout the rest of the winter Kesselring skilfully shifted reserves to contain the Anzio beachhead while still holding the Gustav Line.

When the massive Allied offensive resumed on 11 May 44 the 15th AG broke through the last German position on 17 May and entered Rome on 4 June. ALEXANDER's strategy, devised by his brilliant CofS, John HARDING, forced the Germans into a delaying action across the Arno Valley and into the northern Apennines. Here the Germans organized the Gothic Line. Still high in Hitler's favor, Kesselring was awarded the Diamonds (14/27) on 19 July 44 (Angolia, I, 82).

The Allies pushed on vigorously, taking and inflicting heavy casualties. The 1st Cdn Corps broke through the east (Adriatic) flank of the Gothic Line in Oct 44, finally reaching the Po valley. Again using his reserves masterfully, Smiling Albert stopped the Allied spearhead in the mountains a mere nine miles from Bologna. Exhausted and having suffered heavy casualties, both sides dug in for the winter.

Kesselring meanwhile was seriously injured on 25 Oct 44 in an accident—his car collided with a gun coming out of a side road—and he was hospitalized for three months. Vietinghoff took over temporarily and then succeeded Kesselring permanently on 23 Mar 45, about a week before the final campaign began in Italy.

The Allies had captured the Remagen bridge on 7 March to start crossing the Rhine in strength and RUNDSTEDT was dismissed three days later as OB West. Kesselring took over with headquarters at Bayreuth and his front extending from the Dutch coast to the Alps. When SIMPSON's 9th US Army reached the Elbe some 75 miles WNW of Berlin on 6 Apr 45, a new OB Northwest was created under BUSCH. Two weeks later, as Germany was about to be split in two, HITLER named Kesselring supreme commander in the south and DOENITZ in the north. Soviet and US patrols met five days later (25 Apr 45) on the Elbe near Torgau.

The only one of the early field marshals to serve continuously without being relieved by Hitler, Smiling Albert was taken prisoner at Saalfelden (near Erfurt) on 6 May 45. (His troops surrendered piecemeal.) A British military tribunal in Venice charged him with war crimes including inhumane warfare against Italian civilians. The field marshal was cleared of responsibility for the **Ardeatine Caves** atrocity, but on 6 May 47 he was condemned to death for other crimes. The sentence was commuted quickly to life in prison. He was released in Oct 52 for ill health and became head of the Stahlhelm (veterans' organization).

Among other works, Kesselring published a highly praised autobiography, *Soldat bis zum letzen tag* (Bonn: Athenaeum, 1953). Only the first English language edition preserves the title, *A Soldier to the Last Day* (UK). The first American edition was *Kesselring: A Soldier's Record* (New York: Morrow, 1954). Reprint editions are *The Memoirs of Field Marshal Kesselring* (London: Greenhill Books, in association with Presidio Press, Novato Calif, 1989.) The field marshal died on 16 July 60 in Bad Nauheim.

KEYES, Geoffrey C. T. British officer. 1917-41. As a lieutenant colonel of the Scots Greys, the son of Adm Roger KEYES died the night of 17-18 Nov 41 in a commando raid to kill Rommel. British intelligence believed the Desert Fox still had his headquarters in a house at Beda Littoria but he was some 200 miles to the east at a forward CP near Tobruk. (Liddell Hart, *RP*, 156, 158.) Landed by Robert E. LAYCOCK, Lt Col Keyes and two others broke into the house that turned out to be occupied only by Rommel's QM staff. Killed almost instantly by a bullet near the heart and awarded the **VC** posthumously, Keyes was buried nearby with military honors by the Germans, who had lost at least five killed.

KEYES, Roger John Brownlow. British admiral. 1872-1945. "Though by no means one of the cleverest, Roger Keyes was one of the bravest and most colourful naval officers of all times," writes Bernard Fergusson (*The Watery Maze*, 31). He was born 4 Oct 72 at Tundiani, on India's NW frontier, son of a colonel who rose to be Gen Sir Charles Patton Keyes, scion of an illustrious Norman family named Guiz or Gyse. *(DNB.)*

The younger Keyes became a hero of the Boxer Rebellion (1900), of WWI, and had a prominent role in CHURCHILL's ill fated Dardanelles adventure of 1915. A master at narrow-seas-warfare and a vice admiral commanding the Dover Patrol, he planned and executed the audacious, complex, and large-scale efforts in the spring of 1918 to block German submarine bases at Ostend and Zeebrugge. Although unsuccessful, the raids were heroic and brought Keyes many honors including the KCB. Continuing an unremitting offensive in the war's final months, Keyes was appointed KCVO, created a baronet, and given a grant of £10,000. *(DNB.)*

When Britain declared war in 1939 Admiral of the Fleet Sir Roger Keyes had been on the retired list four years and was almost 67 years old. A conservative MP from North Portsmouth since 1934, he "was still young at heart and physique, and he immediately sought active service" (ibid.). Keyes supported 1st Sea Lord Churchill's vigorous efforts to mount an expedition to retake the vital Norwegian port of Trondheim, which the Germans seized on 9 Apr 40. Sir Roger, who, like Churchill, lacked judgment in advocating desperate enterprises (ibid.), strove mightily to command the effort and strongly criticized the naval staff's handling of the Norwegian campaign. In a memorable speech on 7 May 40 that did much to topple Prime Minister Chamberlain and bring in Churchill, the admiral reminded members of this record (WC, I, 658-59).

Three days later, when the Germans attacked in the west and Churchill became PM, Sir Roger went to Belgium as LnO to King Leopold III. Keyes remained until the king asked for an armistice on 27 May 40, and—back in Parliament—defended the Leopold's much-criticized conduct.

Keyes became Director of Combined Operations on 17 July 40, soon after Churchill proposed forming a special force of raiders. Succeeding Gen Sir Alan Bourne, **RM,** Commander of Raiding Operations, Keyes greatly expanded this office and had some success in gaining autonomy from the army, RN, RM, and RAF. But Churchill finally sided with those who insisted that Keyes not "direct" **combined operations** but merely form the commandos, train them, and be an advisor. At loggerheads with his superiors and furious, Sir Roger went away mad and was succeeded on 27 Oct 41 by MOUNTBATTEN. (Fergusson, *The Watery Maze,* 52, 83-84, 89.) Five weeks later the admiral's elder son, Geoffrey C. T. KEYES, was killed in a famous commando raid.

Back in Parliament Sir Roger criticized the government's conduct of the war but in Jan 43 he was raised to the peerage as Baron Keyes of Zeebrugge and of Dover. In the summer of 1944 he set off under the minister of information's auspices to lecture in the US, Canada, Australia, and NZ. In Oct 44 he was an observer of the Leyte landings.

Keyes died 26 Dec 45 at Buckingham and was buried at St James cemetery, Dover.

KHOZIN, Mikhail Semenovich. Soviet military leader. 1896-1979. Born 22 Oct 96 in the village of Skachikha, Tambov region, he was a junior officer before joining the Red Army and CP in 1918. By June 41 Gen Lt Khozin headed the **Frunze MA,** and the following October took command of the Leningrad Front. After convincing Stalin that he was better able than MERETSKOV to save VLASOV's elite 2d Shock Army, Khozin was demoted after failing to do so. Ironically, Khozin replaced MERETSKOV as head of the 33d Army in June 42, holding this post until the following October. Two months later he took over the battered 20th Army from N. I. Kiryukhin, heading this briefly before disappearing from the war in Jan 43. He died 27 Feb 79. (Scotts.)

KHRUSHCHEV, Nikita Sergeyevich. 1894-1971. Soviet statesman. 1894-1971. An ethnic Russian born 17 Apr 94 in the village of Kalinovka, Kursk Oblast, Khrushchev became a miner. During the Russian revolution he was a party worker and soldier in the 9th Rifle Regt of BUDENNY's 1st Red Cavalry Army. By

1931 the tough, ebullient, enterprising little Nikita was a party worker in Moscow, the first secretary of the Moscow Party Committee, 1935-38. Rewarded for his success in building the grandiose Moscow subway, he was appointed first secretary of the Ukrainian Central Committee. The next year, with the additional title of civilian member of the Kiev Military Council, he was with the forces occupying the Western Ukraine (which had been taken from Poland) and in 1940 he supervised sovietization of that territory.

In 1941-44 Khrushchev was a **commissar** and military council member with rank of general lieutenant from 1943. Front commanders with whom he served were, in chronological order, BUDENNY (SW Direction), TIMOSHENKO and KOSTENKO (SW Front), TIMOSHENKO, GORDOV, and YEREMENKO (Stalingrad Front) SE and Southern Front (YEREMENKO), and the 1st Ukrainian and 1st Belorussian Fronts (ZHUKOV). (Scotts.)

Having meanwhile directed the evacuation of industry and being responsible for partisan activities, Khrushchev was prime minister of the Ukraine in 1944-47. His mentor Lazar M. Kaganovich was 1st Secretary, but in 1947 Khrushchev replaced him and remained in the Ukraine until Dec 49.

Stalin then summoned Khrushchev to head the Moscow Party organization again. The brash newcomer built a power base and moved quickly after Stalin's death on 5 Mar 53 to outmaneuver the Old Stalinists. By Sep 53 he was 1st Secretary, having outwitted MALENKOV.

In 1955 Khrushchev installed BULGANIN, his alter ego, in Malenkov's place as prime minister. In Oct 57 Khrushchev dismissed ZHUKOV as defense minister, and in Mar 58 he took over from Bulganin as premier. After an 11-year tenure that featured de-Stalinization, the Hungarian revolt, Sputnik I, the Berlin Wall Crisis (for which he recalled KONEV), and the Cuban missile crisis, Khrushchev was forced in Oct 64 to resign all offices. Replaced by Brezhnev as 1st Secretary and by Kosygin as PM, Khrushchev lived under close surveillance in a house near Moscow.

In 1970 his memoirs appeared in the west but not in the USSR. Edited by Edward Crankshaw, *Khrushchev Remembers* (Boston: Little, Brown, 1970), created a sensation. The publisher included a disclaimer that the book was "made up of material emanating from various sources at various times and in various circumstances." Khrushchev denied authorship, perhaps for reasons of personal safety. Little, Brown published volume two in 1974 after Khrushchev's death, subtitling it *The Last Testament*. Volume three, with even more revealing insights, came out in 1990, subtitled *The Glasnost Tapes*.

The ebullient, impetuous man who dominated the USSR during the Cold War yet prepared the way for perestroika, died 11 Sep 71 in Moscow. Denied the highest final honors, he lies in a far corner of Moscow's **Novodevichy Monastery Cemetery**. (Scotts.)

KIDO, Koichi. Japanese official. 1889-1977. As lord keeper of the privy seal from June 40, Marquis Kido was Hirohito's permanent confidential adviser on all matters. He was a Kyoto Univ graduate who entered government service in 1930 as chief secretary to the privy seal. In various cabinets from 1937 to 1939 Kido was minister of education, of welfare, and of home affairs before becoming lord keeper of the privy seal in 1940. The diminutive marquis was direct, decisive, intellectual, orderly, and highly respected. His close friend Prince KONOYE and HIROHITO had been impressed by Prince SAIONJI, the latter's tutor, that Japan should base her foreign policy on cooperation with Britain and America. The disciples therefore deplored the course charted by the militarists.

On 9 June 45 the marquis sent the emperor a memorandum that was the first major step in steering HIROHITO toward direct involvement with seeking peace. (Toland, *The Rising Sun*, 750-51.) Kido was sentenced to life imprisonment in the Tokyo war crimes trials but paroled in 1956.

KILROY the omnipresent (US). "Kilroy was here" (with minor variations in the graffito) was seen wherever American troops went. Who was Kilroy? According to one theory he was one of the US Army's 62 real Kilroys and left a false trail while AWOL. But the widow of James J. Kilroy, an inspector at the Fore River Shipyard, Quincy, Mass, claimed that her husband chalked "Kilroy was here" after counting the holes filled by riveters who otherwise might be paid twice for the same job. (Snyder, *Guide*, 369.)

KIMMEL, Husband Edward. US admiral. 1882-1968. "Hubby" was born 14 May 82 in Henderson, Ky, son of an army major. He had many military forebears but was unable to get a West Point appointment, so he graduated from the USNA (13/62) in 1904. Becoming an ordnance specialist, a rear admiral from 1937, Kimmel spent three years as the navy's budget officer in Washington, then rose from head of a cruiser division to commander of Cruisers, Battle Force, Pacific Fleet.

Promoted 1 Feb 41 ahead of 32 others to be CINCPAC, Kimmel was thus the US Navy's senior admiral. George C. Marshall wrote the admiral's direct army opposite number, Gen Walter C. SHORT, to pass on what CNO Harold R. STARK had to say about Kimmel's personality: though brusque and "rather tough in his methods," Kimmel was said to be "a very kindly man" and "entirely responsive to plain speaking." (Quoted by Parrish, *R&M*, 201.)

But Kimmel was seriously dissatisfied with arrangements for the defense of Pearl Harbor, he informed Stark. The army was responsible for Oahu's defenses, but Rear Adm Claude C. BLOCH, commanding the 14th Naval District, was responsible for defending the naval yard itself. These problems were exacerbated by materiel shortages throughout the US armed forces. The situation had existed for 10 months when the Japanese struck Pearl Harbor on 7 Dec 41, and Chester W. Nimitz replaced Kimmel 10 days later.

The first of eight **Pearl Harbor investigations** found Kimmel and Short guilty primarily of not coordinating army-navy efforts to defend Hawaii. The admiral was retired on 1 Mar 42 for dereliction of duty, but the last Pearl Harbor investigation, four years later, found him guilty only of "errors in judgment." The admiral meanwhile had been employed immediately by Frederick R. Harris, Inc, consultants in NYC who did secret work for the Navy *(CB 42)*. Kimmel died 14 May 68 at Groton, Conn.

KIMURA, Heitaro (or Hoyotaro). Japanese general. 1888-1948. Born 28 Sep 88 and commissioned as an artilleryman in Dec 08, he graduated from the war college in 1916. Kimura was in the Siberian expedition of 1918-19 as a divisional staff officer. In early 1922 Capt Kimura became resident officer in Berlin, being promoted to major the next year, and in 1925 he was appointed to the IGS. That year he became an instructor at the war college. After commanding an artillery battalion and serving in the artillery department of the military training office, Lt Col Kimura attended the London Naval Conference with one Capt Isokoro Yamamoto. After normal career assignments, Col Kimura was in the war ministry, first as a section chief in the economic mobilization bureau then as chief of the military administration bureau. Unsoldierly looking, quiet, and almost meek, a major general from Aug 36, Kimura was TOJO's vice minister of war and close adviser from Apr 41 and was promoted to lieutenant general. Kimura was sacked in Mar 43, being a convenient scapegoat for the loss of Guadalcanal.

Around 30 Aug 44 he succeeded Masakazu KAWABE as CG, Burma Area Army. Soon in an untenable position, he withdrew his forces skilfully. For allegedly condoning atrocities and other war crimes Kimura was hanged 23 Dec 48 in Tokyo.

KING, Ernest Joseph. US CNO and Fleet CinC. 1878-1956. The brilliant, irascible chief of the US fleet and chief of naval operations (Cominch-CNO) in WWII was born 23 Nov 78 in Lorain, Ohio. His father came to America before the Civil War and had roots in Londonderry, Ireland. Ernie King's maternal grandfather had been a top sawyer in the RN dockyard at Plymouth, England.

With the USNA Class of 1901 King was commander of the brigade of midshipmen (equivalent to first captain at West Point) and fourth out of 67 academically. In 1915-19 he was on the staff of Vice Adm Henry T. Mayo (1856-1937), who commanded the Atlantic Fleet. That experience gave King valuable insight into the problems of high command within an alliance and taught him leadership principles he would use thereafter: how to decentralize authority and develop initiative among subordinates while maintaining strong control at the top. (King and Whitehill, 144-45. Hereafter cited as K&W.)

Between the Wars

Meanwhile, after five years at sea King headed the navy's postgraduate school when it reopened at Annapolis on 1 May 19. But he cut this congenial assignment short after two years because Rear Adm Henry B. Wilson, who op-

posed "book learning," was about to become superintendent at Annapolis. Chosing the only available command at sea, a refrigerator ship, King was skipper for a year before qualifying as a submariner (1922) and taking over a sub division. To improve readiness he ordered crews to move their living quarters from sub tenders to the "pig boats." Morale plummeted, and his admiral finally said, "Tell me, commander, will you rescind the order or shall I?" King said in later years that this was the only order he ever revoked. (RCS.)

Having become an aviator in 1927, King commanded CV *Lexington* in 1930-32 before attending the Naval War College. He excelled as a student but also as a socializer. Selected for flag rank, King took over the bureau of aeronautics when the post was available in Apr 33, having lobbied for the job. A year short of the normal four-year tour, Rear Adm King got sea duty to enhance his career prospects. (RCS.)

As Commander, Air Base Force, he had 1,000 seaplanes scattered from Alaska to Hawaii to Panama and to the West Coast. During the 1937 Fleet Problem (annual maneuvers) his planes were credited with sinking both of the attacking force's carriers. With temporary promotion to vice admiral commanding the Air Battle Force, King continued to advance professionally. His force grew from all three existing US carriers and their escort units to all five in 1939. When the admiral asked to be detached from the slow battleship force to join the fast cruisers and destroyers of Scouting Force the concept was rejected; it became standard practice in the war against Japan.

Despite protests from his pilots, King had them train for night carrier operations. Allowed to operate independently in the 1938 Fleet Problem the admiral used foul weather to make successful strikes on Pearl Harbor and the Mare Island Navy Yard in San Francisco Bay. In the 1939 maneuvers he was not allowed to operate separately from the battleships but for the first time was permitted to use four fleet carriers as one unit.

Despite this record he was passed over in July 39 for either the post of CNO or commander in chief of the US Fleet. Instead he was ordered to the General Board for a retirement tour of duty and reverted to two-star rank. But King so impressed Navy Secretary KNOX by increasing aircraft support capabilities and the AA armament of ships that in Jan 41 he was made Commander, Patrol Force. Again promoted, Vice Adm King directed the Neutrality Patrol, which on 1 Feb 41 was redesignated the Atlantic Fleet and King was promoted to full admiral. His force soon was expanded by the presidential order of 19 July 41, and his mission was extended to include convoy and escort duty and covert ASW operations.

The War Years

King was given the new post of Commander in Chief, US Fleet, on 20 Dec 41. The smoke having barely settled at Pearl Harbor, the normal title of CINCUS was changed to COMINCH! Despite his ambiguous command relationship with CNO "Betty" STARK as the navy's senior officer, Stark and King worked harmoniously (as did Stark and George C. Marshall).

King succeeded Stark in Mar 42 as CNO but remained COMINCH. The first of several **Pearl Harbor investigations** had held STARK partly responsible for the fiasco and he was posted to London. "Even after the war King was unable to understand why Roosevelt demoted Stark but not Marshall" (K&W, 356), and this helps explain King's discourtesy toward Marshall initially. But the notoriously arrogant, short tempered admiral was soured also by the army's earlier reluctance to recognize Marine Corps supremacy in developing doctrine for amphibious war (ibid., 321-22). Friction was caused also by Marshall's belief in "unity of command" as a principle of war, whereas the navy had officially replaced this maxim with "cooperation." Other major disagreements will be pointed out later.

Relegated to supporting the US Army in earlier wars, the US Navy finally had the chance to play a decisive role. King was not about to miss the main chance, which he saw in the Pacific, against Japan.

With considerable justification, King believed the British were preoccupied with Europe and with preserving their colonial empire. At the first JCS meeting on 13 Jan 43 he urged US delegates to insist that adequate resources be allocated to contain the Japanese advance and keep them from consolidating a position that would be impregnable. This is precisely what the Japanese hoped to do. As for how much was enough to contain the Japanese while pursuing the approved Germany-first grand strategy, there could never be agreement between King and his adversaries.

King opposed plans to land in North Africa, and objected even more vigorously to British efforts to pursue the Mediterranean strategy advocated so strongly by Churchill and CIGS Alan BROOKE. Supported by a US president whose sympathies lay with the US Navy, King succeeded in making the Pacific war a navy show, and MacArthur was relegated to a secondary role in the SWPA while NIMITZ made the main effort in the central Pacific. Debate continues over whether this was in the best US interest, particularly in view of what MacArthur achieved with fewer resources and much less loss of life, American and Japanese. MacArthur was using what LIDDELL HART termed "the indirect approach," contending that this, rather than "the direct approach," has been the secret of strategic success throughout military history.

The Guadalcanal campaign was undertaken at King's insistence despite the protests of MacArthur and GHORMLEY that their forces were not ready. It also was questioned whether the Solomons were the proper objective for the first major US counteroffensive. (K&W, 388.) Events bearing out the skeptics, the Guadalcanal campaign, 7 Aug 42-9 Feb 43, took much longer than expected and came close to failure. Press criticism was strident, and King's confidence that the Navy could go it alone was seriously shaken. (Pogue, *Marshall,* II, 394.)

The admiral was a leading advocate of bypassing the Philippines, favoring a main strategic effort into China, linking up with forces of CHIANG KAI-SHEK. He opposed invading Japan, reasoning that the submarine blockade and strategic bombing made this unnecessary (RCS), and he did not think Russian intervention was desirable (OCMH, *Command Decisions,* 394, 397). The Anglophobic and parochial US admiral also fought against Churchill's strong urging that elements of the Royal Navy be moved to the Pacific as they became unneeded in the Atlantic (Sulzberger, *Candles,* 684). But a sound professional objection was that bringing the Royal Navy into the Pacific at this late stage would create unjustifiable logistical problems (RCS).

King was given the new five-star rank of Fleet Admiral on 17 Dec 44, two days after Leahy and two days ahead of Nimitz. The Cominch-CNO had gotten on well with Secretary of the Navy KNOX, but after the latter's death on 23 Apr 44 the old salt began his disagreements with FORRESTAL, the new secretary. King's final months of active duty were plagued by conflict, and Forrestal curtailed what he thought was King's excessive power by having the post of COM-INCH abolished on 10 Oct 45. The final clash came when King nominated Nimitz to succeed him as CNO, but President Truman sided with King against Forrestal.

The admiral retired 17 Dec 45 to live in Washington. With his friend Walter Muir White-hill he wrote what has been called "the best autobiography of an American in the High Command in World War Two," *Fleet Admiral King: A Naval Record* . . . (1952). King's three official reports were reprinted as the *U. S. Navy at War, 1941-1945,* and *War Reports of . . . Marshall . . . Arnold . . . and King* (Phila-delphia and New York: Lippincott, 1947).

The admiral spent his last summers at the Portsmouth Naval Hospital in New Hampshire and his winters in Washington. He died 26 June 56 at the hospital, a day after suffering a heart attack and lapsing into a coma. After a state funeral he was buried at the Naval Academy.

KING, William Lyon Mackenzie. Canadian statesman. 1874-1950. King was born 17 Dec 74 in Kitchener, Ontario, and became well known as a scholar and author in political economy and political science. He was prime minister from 1921 to 1930 except for a short break in 1926, and from 1935 to 1948. King also held the portfolio of external affairs from 1935 to 1946. From being an isolationist he became a vigorous and effective war leader. After ill health forced him to retire from public life in 1948 he worked on his memoirs with a staff at McGill University and a grant from the Rockefeller Foundation. King died 22 July 50 near Ottawa.

KINKAID, Thomas Cassin. US admiral. 1888-1972. Six feet tall, wiry, soft-spoken, and professorial, sometimes deploring his lack of charisma, "Kink" is said to have seen more action in big battles than any other American admiral.

The son of a rear admiral, Kinkaid was born 3 Apr 88 at Hanover, NH. He was appointed to Annapolis by President Theodore Roosevelt *(CB 44)* and was barely 16 on becoming a midship-man at the USNA. He graduated in 1908 (136/201), became an expert in ordnance and gun-nery, and in 1932 was a technical adviser at the Geneva Disarmament Conference. After being promoted to captain on 1 Jan 37 he was NA in Rome and Belgrade until Mar 41. Eight months later, on the eve of war, he was promoted to rear admiral and ordered to Hawaii. Reaching Pearl Harbor on 12 Dec 41 he spent two weeks as an observer with Adm Frank FLETCHER's TF 14 on its aborted mission to support the **Wake Island defense.** Kinkaid then succeeded Rear Adm Fletcher as commander of Cruiser Div 6, which joined Wilson Brown's TF 11 for raids on the Gilbert and Marshals, Wake, and Marcus Islands. Kinkaid's cruisers continued to screen TF 11 when Rear Adm Aubrey Fitch, a naval aviator, led it to join FLETCHER near the Fiji Islands. In the Battle of the Coral Sea, 6-8 May 42, Kinkaid controlled the heavy cruisers *Minneapolis* and *New Orleans* plus four destroy-ers to protect CV *Lexington.* When the latter had to be abandoned after a massive fuel explosion, Kinkaid stayed behind to rescue survivors and administer the coup de grace. At Midway, 4-7 June 42, the admiral's cruisers were in Rear Adm Raymond Spruance's TF 16, built around CVs *Enterprise* and *Hornet.* So far Kinkaid had been little more than an observer of the carrier task force operations in which he soon had a major role.

The admiral took over TF 16, built around CV *Enterprise,* for the Guadalcanal landings, 7-8 Aug 42. With his force essentially unchanged, Kinkaid then was heavily engaged in a series of battles against the masterful Nobutake KONDO. In the Battle of the Eastern Solomons, 23-25 Aug 42, *Enterprise* survived only because of outstanding damage control and good luck. On 18 Oct 42 Kinkaid's TF 16 (*Enterprise*) was combined with TF 17 (*Hornet*) to form TF 61, under Kinkaid. He thus commanded the only surviving US fleet carriers in the Pacific. Still opposing KONDO, in the hard fought Battle of the Santa Cruz Islands, 26-27 Oct 42, Kinkaid inflicted severe damage on the heavy carriers *Zuiho* and *Shokaku* but failed to hit CV *Zuikaku* and never located CL *Junyo.* Hondo launched attacks on the two US carriers while their planes were away. The Japanese hit *Enterprise* with three bombs, immobilizing her forward eleva-tor, and so severely damaged *Hornet* that she eventually sank. Both sides had to withdraw from what was a tactical victory for Hondo. But the loss of almost 100 pilots crippled the Japanese carrier forces for more than a year. No carriers were involved in the naval battle of Guadalcanal off **Savo Island,** 12-13 Nov 42. But Kinkaid's aircraft from the badly damaged *Enterprise* operated from Henderson Field with Marine Corps and army planes. Having no enemy air opposition, they kept all but about 2,000 reinforcements from landing, sealing the fate of the Japanese on Guadalcanal.

"In leading TF 61, Kinkaid demonstrated a [rare] characteristic that was appreciated by Admirals Halsey, Nimitz and King: he did the best with what he was given" (Gerald E. Wheeler, "Kinkaid," Stephen Howarth, ed, 346).

After turning over command to Carleton Wright on 28 Nov 42 and reporting to Pearl Harbor, Kinkaid was Commander, North Pacific Force. Personal conflicts between his predecessor, Adm THEOBALD, and the army had paralyzed operations in the Aleutians for months. The picture changed quickly as Kinkaid made plans to reconquer the Aleutians. He recommended leapfrogging the estimated 5,000 Japanese on Kiska and taking Attu, the westernmost island (Wheeler, 346). Working closely and cordially with the local army commander, S. B. BUCKNER, Kinkaid planned an amphibious operation that took Attu in a hard fought campaign, 11-29 May. Kinkaid was promoted to vice admiral on 9 June, and on 19 July he approved plans for US-Canadian assault on bypassed Kiska. Allied forces landed on 20 Aug 43 to find themselves duped: the Japanese had secretly withdrawn their garrison.

After being replaced by FLETCHER on 11 Oct 43 and having home leave, Kinkaid took over the 7th Fleet on 26 Nov 43, replacing Vice Adm Arthur S. Carpender, who had become intolerable to MacArthur (Barbey, 108). As in the north Pacific, Kinkaid proved his skills in inter-service cooperation and enhanced his reputation as a tactician.

The Battle for Leyte Gulf, 24-25 Oct 44, was his finest hour. Virtually abandoned by Bull HALSEY's covering forces, threatened by Takeo KURITA's powerful surface forces, but blessed by good luck, his outgunned and outnumbered 7th Fleet put up a valiant and successful defense. Kinkaid was heavily engaged in the amphibious assaults on Mindoro and Luzon. After the Lingayen Gulf phase of this campaign, where kamikazes added a deadly new dimension, 7th Fleet Hq was at Tolosa, in Leyte Gulf. Kinkaid supported 27 assaults throughout the

Philippines and three in Borneo. His promotion to admiral (four star rank) with DOR of 3 Apr 45, his 57th birthday, made Kinkaid the most junior of the navy's high command of three fleet admirals and nine admirals. (Wheeler, 346.) In Seoul with BARBEY for the surrender of Japanese army and navy forces in Korea on 2 Sep 45, Kinkaid was among those signing for the US.

Turning over command of the 7th Fleet to Barbey on 19 Nov 45, he was Commander, Eastern Sea Frontier, and Commander, Reserve Fleet, Atlantic, from Jan 46 until retiring 30 May 50 to his home in Washington, DC. He died there on 17 Nov 72.

KIPPENBERGER, Howard Karl. New Zealand general. 1897-1957. A solicitor and Territorial officer commanding the 20th Bn when war broke out, Kippenberger was involved in the initial mobilization and was aboard the first troop transport from NZ to Egypt. A year later he led his battalion in Greece and on Crete (Apr-May 41) as part of Sir Bernard FREYBERG's crack 2d NZ Div. In the last days of this desperate campaign he briefly commanded a composite brigade. As part of the 4th NZ Bde defending Belhamed ridge SE of Tobruk against the Afrika Korps, Kippenberger was wounded and captured on 1 Dec 41. He escaped to see further action, rising to command the 5th NZ Bde in North Africa. Brigadier Kippenberger headed the 2d NZ Div during FREYBERG's frequent absences.

After the Tunisian campaign Kippenberger led the 5th Bde in Italy and rose to command the 2d NZ Div at Cassino. On 2 Mar 44 he stepped on a mine that cost him one foot immediately; the other had to be amputated later (Tunney). The brigadier had control of a repatriation program for NZ POWs before going home in 1946 to be editor-in-chief of the official NZ war history. His *Infantry Brigadier* (Oxford, 1949) is one of the war's liveliest and oft-cited memoirs. Rev 15 July 94 and 23 July 95.

KIR, Felix Adrien. French ecclesiastic. 1876-1968. Canon Kir, born 22 Jan 76, was editor of the Dijon weekly *Le Bien du Peuple* when France fell. Named to the "delegation" that succeeded the municipal council of Dijon, the ardent priest was arrested in Oct 40 for aiding the resistance, condemned to death, but freed on 7 Dec 40. He maintained an anti-Nazi line in his paper and helped more than 4,000 POWs escape. Father Kir was forced into hiding after the **Milice** tried to assassinate him in Jan 44. After the liberation he became mayor of Dijon, a post he held along with a number of national offices until his death on 25 Apr 68 at the age of 92.

Le Père Kir's favorite aperitif became internationally popular as "the Kir." It should be made from a good dry white wine (chilled, no ice), a dash of a good cassis (black currant liqueur, preferable from Dijon), and a twist of lemon peel.

KIRK, Alan Goodrich. US admiral. 1888-1963. Born 30 Oct 88 in Philadelphia, he graduated from the USNA in 1909 (45/174). In the early 1920s, Kirk was a White House aide and XO of the presidential yacht *Mayflower*. On 7 June 39 Capt Kirk reached London as naval attaché and the press characterized him as "discreet, personable, and leanly academic" *(CB 44)*. He covertly got much-needed technical information from the RN. Back to Washington at the end of 1940, he was a highly effective director of naval intelligence from the following March. A little more than six months later he took command of a destroyer division that escorted Atlantic convoys, and in Nov 41 he was promoted to rear admiral.

After the surprise attack on Pearl Harbor, 7 Dec 41, Kirk was among those criticized publicly for failures of US naval intelligence. *(See L. F. SAFFORD for more about this complex matter.)* In Mar 42 Kirk went to London as CofS to H. R. STARK, who was Commander, US Naval Forces, Europe. In Feb 43 Kirk succeeded H. K. HEWITT at Norfolk, Va, as Commander, Amphibious Forces, Atlantic Fleet.

For the assault on Sicily, Kirk commanded the Central TF, which Adm Hewitt and Patton viewed as the most important of three landings (Morison, IX, 162). Having planned the operation, he put Troy MIDDLETON's 45th Inf Div ashore around Scoglitti on 10 July 43.

After trips to England for planning conferences, on 20 Feb 44 Kirk was named commander of the Western TF for the cross-channel attack. With 1,000 allied vessels, his flag aboard CA *Augusta*, Kirk began landing BRADLEY's 1st US Army on 6 June 44. In Oct 44, a month after being promoted, Vice Admiral Kirk took command of USN Forces in France.

The jaunty, youthful, hot-tempered, chain-smoking admiral, known for unwavering optimism, retired on 1 Mar 46 as a full admiral and was ambassador to Belgium and minister to Luxembourg 1946-49. Then he was ambassador to Moscow until 1952. After entering business he was ambassador to Nationalist China from 1962 until shortly before his death on 15 Oct 63 in a NYC hospital.

KIRK, Norman Thomas. US surgeon general. 1888-1960. As an orthopedic surgeon credited with treating at least a third of all major amputees in the US armed forces in WWI, he published *Amputation: Operative Techniques* (1924), the standard text. A brigadier general from 12 Mar 43, he was promoted to major general on 1 June 43 to be Chief of the US Army Medical Service, or Surgeon General, holding the post until 31 May 47. *(AA, 94, 923.)*

KIRPONOS, Mikhail Petrovich. Soviet military leader. 1892-1941. A Ukrainian born 9 Jan 92 in the village of Vertiyevka, Chernigov Province, he was drafted in 1915. As a medical orderly he saw action on the Romanian front. Kirponos distinguished himself during the Russo-Finnish War as CG, 70th Inf Div, in the action around Vyborg. In June 40 he succeeded MERETSKOV as head of the Leningrad MD.

Around 12 Feb 41 Kirponos replaced ZHUKOV as commander of the Kiev Special MD, which in June 41 became the Southwest Front. Like the unfortunate D. G. PAVLOV, Kirponos was unable to convince Moscow that invasion was imminent. But with support from a strong-nerved CofS, Maksim A. PURKAYEV, Gen Col Kirponos had some success in slowing the German onslaught. He recommended abandoning Kiev, a course of action strongly endorsed by ZHUKOV after visiting the front on 22-26 June 41, but the Stavka did not give approval until much too late, on 17 Sep 41. Three days later Kirponos's command group and that of Potapov's shattered 5th Army—some 1,000 in all—were ambushed. Already wounded in the leg, Kirponos was hit in the head and chest by mine splinters and died almost immediately (20 Sep 41).

KLEIST, (Paul Ludwig) Erwin von. German general. 1885-1954. From a Junker family that produced about 30 generals, Erwin von Kleist was born 8 Aug 85 at Braunfels, in Hesse. He entered the army in 1900, and in 1914 was a captain in the "Death's Head" Hussars.

A general of cavalry in 1938, Kleist was retired after the BLOMBERG and FRITSCH affairs but was recalled a year later to lead the 22d Corps of LIST's 19th Army into Poland.

For operations a year later in the west, Pz Gp Kleist was formed on 5 Mar 40. It comprised Guderian's five panzer divisions and Reinhard's three motorized divisions. Kleist had no experience with armor and—like so many other German generals at this stage of the war—was skeptical about its capabilities for large-scale independent operation. But OKW picked Kleist as the man to handle a notoriously "difficult subordinate" like GUDERIAN. The panzer group spearheaded the drive through the Ardennes and across northern France until 17 May 40 (D+7), when Kleist berated GUDERIAN for disregarding orders to slow down and let the infantry catch up for flank protection. Guderian threatened to resign, but LIST resolved the dispute (Guderian, 101-10), and the race to the Channel continued.

Kleist remained nervous about his exposed south flank, particularly when de GAULLE attacked, and with Kluge and Rundstedt he shares blame for Hitler's halting the panzers short of Dunkirk. Kleist made other mistakes in his first experience with panzer troops. A fundamental one was using tanks rather than infantry in attempting to establish a bridgehead in early June 40 on the Somme River around Amiens and Peronne. (Mellenthin, *Panzer Battles,* 20.) But the old hussar quickly mastered mobile warfare, thanks largely to his brilliant CofS ZEITZLER.

Generaloberst Kleist, as of 19 July 40, was ordered south to command the 1st Pz Gp in the Balkans campaign. With his 14th Pz Corps and 11th Army Corps he moved into Bulgaria north of Sofia. On 6 Apr 41 he attacked with two widely separate columns to converge on Nis. Shattering all resistance, Kleist then moved down the Moravia River to enter Belgrade on 12 April from the south as other forces converged from the north and west.

For Opn Barbarossa, which kicked off on 22 Jun 41, Kleist's 1st Pz Group was in Rundstedt's AG South. Initially he had five panzer divisions and nine divisions of other types. Again making the main effort, he drove into the Ukraine and destroyed almost 20 Soviet divisions around Uman before wheeling north to meet GUDERIAN's panzers and close the Kiev encirclement in mid-Sep 41. Diverted north to join Bock's AG Center, he formed the southern arm of the Vyasma encirclement. His 48th Pz Corps, under Werner Kempf, was attached to Guderian's Pz Gp 2 for the battles of Orel and Bryansk (Guderian, 226) while Kleist himself went back south with the rest of his panzer group, which on 6 October was redesignated the 1st Pz Army. By 20 Nov 41 its tanks entered Rostov, "Gateway to the Caucasus." But logistical and maintenance difficulties were developing, the temperature dropped to- 20 C (about 0 F), and TIMOSHENKO retook Rostov.

After a hard winter on the defensive, Kleist had the major role in the summer counteroffensive of 1942. Attacking from the Stalino region across the Mius River toward the Donetz basin, he wheeled south to the lower Don (9-24 July 42). Penetrating defenses along the Kuban River he drove south to Maikop, then deep into the Caucasus. Kleist became commander of AG A on 22 Nov 42.

The Germans had reached high tide in the Caucasus but were overextended, and the Soviets had mounted a large-scale counteroffensive. On 28 Dec 42 Hitler finally authorized Kleist to begin withdrawing and promoted him to field marshal effective 1 Feb 43. (This is remarkable because that is the date Field Marshal PAULUS surrendered, prompting the outraged fuehrer to threaten he would create "no more field marshals!") The Soviet counteroffensive drove through the Ukraine, and by 1 Feb 43 Kleist's army group had only the 17th Army. This was in the Crimea with orders to hold at all cost.

By the spring of 1944, when he was assigned the newly constituted 6th Army, Kleist was forced to abandon the 17th Army to its fate and move his AG A Hq to Nikolayev, NE of Odessa. The Red Army had launched a new counteroffensive on 6 Mar 44 and Soviet propagandists claimed Hitler was losing support of his senior commanders. To rebut this, Hitler summoned field marshals including Kleist and Manstein to Bergtesgaden on 19 Mar 44 to sign a document manifesting their loyalty.

Then, writes Manstein, "On the morning of the 30th March, I was awakened with the startling news that Hitler's condor aircraft, which had already picked up v. Kleist from his headquarters, would shortly land at Lwow and take the pair of us to the Obersaltzberg" (*Lost Victories,* 544). Replaced by SCHOERNER, Kleist was head of the "commanders' reserve pool" when taken captive in May 45. He was extradited to Yugoslavia for trial as a war criminal and sentenced in 1948 to 15 years. But in 1949 he was handed over to the Soviets, who gave him another sentence and announced on 5 Nov 54 that the field marshal had died as a POW at Wladimorowka.

KLOPPER, Hendrik Balzazer. South African general. 1902-. After directing military training in South Africa he was promoted to major general in May 42 and given command of the 2d South African Div. Klopper was made commander of Tobruk on 12 June 42 when it was apparent that Rommel intended to invest the vitally important Mediterranean port. Tobruk's once-formidable defenses were in disrepair and Klopper had a polyglot force that his green staff never got under control. Rommel, on the other hand, was at the top of his game. After realizing that further resistance would not benefit the overall campaign and would lead to useless loss of life, Maj Gen Klopper raised the white flag as dawn broke on 21 June 42. It was the most humiliating British defeat since the Japanese took Singapore Rommel got his marshal's baton. German POW camps were swollen by 19,000 prisoners from elite formations, including elements of the Coldstream Guards, crack Indian troops, and 10,500 South Africans.

Klopper escaped in Oct 43 and eventually was Commandant-General of Union Defense Forces.

KLUGE, Guenther Hans von. German general. 1882-1944. Known aptly as "Cunning Hans," Kluge became one of Hitler's favorite field commanders. He led a field army in Poland, Belgium, France, and Russia before heading AG Center on the eastern front. Succeeding Rundstedt as OB West, and soon replaced by MODEL, he committed suicide rather than face Hitler's unfounded accusations of trying to make a deal with the enemy.

Kluge was born 30 Oct 82 in Poznan. He was commissioned in the field artillery (1901),

served with distinction in WWI, and took time to become a pilot. A Generalmajor from Sep 33 and a Generalleutnant seven months later, from Sep 34 Kluge headed Wehrkreis VI in Westphalia. He was among 16 "uncooperative" senior generals retired on Hitler's orders in early 1938 after the BLOMBERG and FRITSCH affairs. Recalled a little more than a year later and promoted to General of Artillery, Kluge took command of the 4th Army for the war on Poland. As part of Fedor von BOCK's AG North, and with **operational control** over GUDERIAN's 19th Pz Corps, he cut east across the Polish Corridor to link up with the Georg von KUECHLER's 3d Army which had attacked southward from East Prussia. This complex operation completed masterfully, and GUDERIAN passing to Kuechler's operational control for a wider strategic envelopment, Kluge pushed SE with two infantry corps to end resistance in his zone on 17 Sep 39. He was awarded the RK on 30 Sep 39.

For the assault in the west that began on 10 May 40 Kluge's 4th Army was on the right flank of Rundstedt's AG A. Kluge had operational control over Hermann HOTH's small panzer corps. This mechanized force spearheaded the German drive while infantry units followed in a sustained forced march to exploit Rommel's unsupported crossing of the Meuse near Dinant. The invaders crossed the Sambre River before CORAP's 9th French Army could man prepared defenses on the south bank.

The battle of Flanders was followed by the Battle of France, which started on 5 June 40. Kluge drove SW on a broad front from bridgeheads on the lower Somme around Abbeville. Hoth's panzers overran Normandy, taking the ports of Cherbourg and Brest on 18 and 19 June 40. Infantry corps crossed the lower Loire to take Nantes and exploit southward. Kluge was just short of Bordeaux before hostilities ended on 25 June and was in the mass creation of field marshals on 19 July 40.

For Opn *Barbarossa,* the invasion of Russia, Kluge's 4th Army was the most powerful of 11 armies in Bock's AG Center. He had 16 infantry divisions, and had operational control over Guderian's 4th Pz Gp, which comprised five panzer divisions and nine others initially. (*West Point Atlas,* Map 24.) AG Center made spectacular gains, but Kluge clashed continually with Guderian over tactics and was jealous of the panzer leader's successes. Bock tried to resolve the problem on 30 June by authorizing Guderian more freedom of action, but Kluge continued to feud violently with Guderian.

After closing the trap around Smolensk by 19 July 41 Kluge's 4th Army was reconstituted, and Guderian's panzer group was again placed under Kluge's operational control. When HITLER interrupted the drive on Moscow to send Kluge SE into the Ukraine, Cunning Hans had illusions of directing this effort. But the 4th Army got locked into a struggle along the Desna River, whereas Guderian's panzers raced to more glory in closing the Kiev pocket.

When the advance on Moscow was resumed, Kluge's 4th Army began its encirclement of Vyasma on 2 Oct 41 and then drove NE through Maloyaroslavets toward Moscow. Early on 1 December he sent his 20th Corps on a well planned final lunge along the Minsk-Moscow Hwy to seize the shortest route to the Russian capital. The Germans penetrated YEFREMOV's defenses but that general quickly launched a successful counterattack. "Von Kluge's thrust had been a deadly one, perfectly aimed, but it had finally been parried" (Erickson, *To Stalingrad,* 267).

With Barbarossa stalled short of Moscow and Leningrad, and Hitler beginning to purge the high command, Kluge replaced BOCK in mid-Dec 41 as head of AG Center and flogged his exhausted, frostbitten forces forward in a final, futile effort to take Moscow. Thereafter AG Center was heavily engaged, under conditions of incredible hardship and danger, in slowing the large-scale Soviet winter counter-offensive and holding defensive positions through 1942. Meanwhile the blow-up with GUDERIAN on Christmas eve had led Hitler to sack the panzer pioneer two days later.

Kluge had become one of Hitler's favorites. A non-smoker and virtual teetotaller with a rep-utation for fearlessness, the brilliant field com-mander jokingly, but not unreasonably, com-pared himself to Napoleon's Marshal Ney, "the bravest of the brave." Kluge's nickname Cunning or Clever Hans, merits explanation. Klug is a popular German word that has many foxy synonyms including "clever," "cunning," or even "crazy" (as in *"nicht recht klug,"* for "half crazy"). The field marshal had been known since 1938 for finding excuses to keep a safe distance from anti-Hitler conspiracies. But

after the fuehrer gave Kluge a gift of 250,000 marks ($62,500) for his 60th birthday, on 30 Oct 42, the persistent TRESCKOW convinced his chief that posterity would condone accep-tance of the gift (not unusual in German history) only if Kluge pretended to be covering himself as a conspirator. (Hoffmann, *Resistance,* 271.) Clever Hans accepted that reasoning but still refused to give more than passive support until others eliminated Hitler.

After Guderian came off the shelf to be IG of Armored Troops on 1 Mar 43 he and Kluge resumed feuding. The principal bone of con-tention this time was primarily over controver-sial planning for the Kharkov offensive, Opn **Citadel,** which Kluge favored and Guderian opposed. Disagreements led Kluge to propose a duel and ask Hitler to be his second! On Hitler's insistence Guderian prevailed on Kluge, whom the panzer general characterized as a somewhat "unstable character," to withdraw the challenge. (Guderian, 308, 312.)

The fearless field marshal was very badly injured when his car overturned on the Minsk-Smolensk road on 27 Oct 43. Two days later he was awarded the Swords (40/159), having received the Oakleaves on 18 Jan 43 (Angolia, I, 147). BUSCH took over AG Center.

Kluge was still convalescing seven months later when summoned by Hitler on 1 July 44. It was D+25 of the Normandy invasion, and Keitel interrupted the meeting after talking to Rund-stedt on the phone. "Make peace, you fools," OB West had barked when asked what OKW could do about the desperate situation in France. Hitler ordered Kluge to replace Rundstedt immediately, and the sanguine new OB West reached St Germain, near Paris, on 3 July 44. Two days later he paid his first visit to AG B Hq at La Roche Guyon and heatedly accused Rommel of making unduly pessimistic reports, even of refusal to obey orders. But Kluge quick-ly saw after visiting the front that OKW had no appreciation of how desperate the situation was.

When ROMMEL was wounded on 17 July and OKW did not name a replacement, Kluge took over AG B as an additional duty. He moved to La Roche Guyon on the 19th, the day before STAUFFENBERG's bomb exploded under Hitler's conference table at Rastenburg. About a month later Kluge was visiting the Falaise area when his radio truck was knocked out. The date was 12 Aug 44, according to Kluge's CofS

(Speidel, *Invasion,* 134), but the 15th, according to other authorities. He went "presumably to seek death" (Hoffmann, 518-19, citing Speer, *Memoirs,* 394).

With OKW not knowing for several hours where Kluge was, Hitler concluded that the field marshal had been trying to desert. MODEL reached La Roche Guyon on the afternoon of 16 August (Speidel, 137) with a letter from Hitler telling Kluge to take a rest in Germany but keep OKW informed of his exact location. US artillery and mortar fire were falling as Kluge drove off on the 18th at 5 PM, leaving Hitler a final report and professing undying personal loyalty. A phone call from Metz on the 19th informed OKW that Kluge had died near there, apparently of a heart attack. Intuition aquiver, Hitler had the SS check on the cause of death. Learning that it was suicide—cyanide— the fuehrer was "completely convinced that Kluge had been engaged in treasonous activities" (Speer, *Memoirs,* 394-95). But Kluge's body lay in state for almost two weeks in the church at Boehme (Altmark) before being buried there in the family vault.

KNATCHBULL-HUGESSEN, Hughe Montgomery. British diplomat. 1886-1971. He was born 26 Mar 86 into an ancient Kentish family. Educated at Eton with EDEN and MENZIES and at Oxford, he joined the foreign office in 1908. Tall, slender, "fastidious, ducal and clever" (Brown, *Bodyguard,* 392), "Snatch" was an outstanding linguist and trouble-shooter. Appointed ambassador to Peking in 1936 and knighted the same year (KCMG), Sir Hughe was severely wounded on 27 Aug 37 when the Japanese strafed his clearly marked official car on the road between Nanking and Shanghai. Replaced by Archibald KERR, he had a long convalescence from temporary spinal paralysis and never recovered fully.

As ambassador to Ankara from 25 Feb 39 he cultivated his Soviet opposite number, gave short shrift to von PAPEN, and had a major role in drawing Turkey to the Allied camp. The British diplomat was at the center of **Operation Cicero** involving the spy BAZNA. Commonly considered to have been a victim, the ambassador may actually have been involved with British intelligence in a disinformation scheme. Credence is lent to this little-known theory by the fact that the diplomat's career was not terminated: Knatchbull-Hugessen was ambassador to Brussels and minister to Luxembourg after the Belgium government returned on 4 Sep 44, remaining until 1947. Sir Hughe was crippled in his final years by the injuries suffered in China. *(Concise DNB.)*

His memoirs are *Diplomat in Peace and War* (London: John Murray, 1949). He also published *Kentish Family* (1960), a history of the Knatchbulls.

KNOBELSDORFF, Otto Heinrich Ernst von. German general. 1886-1966. An unimpressive-looking little man who had a long, outstanding combat record up to the field army level, Knobelsdorff was born 31 Mar 86 into a famous military family that included Manteuffels in his mother's line. As an infantryman commissioned in 1906, he saw heavy action on both fronts in 1914-18 and was twice WIA, critically during the last month.

By 1 Jan 39 he was a Generalmajor commanding the 19th Inf Div. After the campaign in France this was converted to the 19th Pz Div. Promoted to Generalleutnant on 1 Dec 40, Knobelsdorff led the division into Russia as part of AG Center. In the final desperate offensive against Moscow he was awarded the RK on 17 Sep 41 for actions around Kholm and Demyansk, then he spearheaded the drive N of Gorki across the Nara River on 16-22 Oct 41. (Angolia, I, 209-10.)

Seriously wounded in the spring of 1942, promoted to General of Panzer Troops on 1 Aug 42, Knobelsdorff commanded the 24th Pz Corps, 10 Oct-30 Nov, in AG Center. He then took over the 48th Pz Corps from EBERBACH on 1 Dec 42, and in heavy action on the Chir River, 4-22 Dec 42, knocked out more than 700 tanks (Mellenthin, *Panzer Battles,* 178). With MELLENTHIN as CofS, Knobelsdorff continued to excel as part of AG Don in MANSTEIN's masterful retrograde. Knobelsdorff made the main effort on the S side of the Kursk salient in Opn **Citadel,** attacking with Hoth's 4th Pz Army, 4-23 July 43. Despite considerable success against CHISTYAKOV's 21st Army and M. E. Katukov's 1st Tank Army, he finally was driven back with heavy losses.

By 27 Sep 43, when assigned to Otto Woehler's 8th Army, Knobelsdorff had pulled his corps from the Kremenchug bridgehead to relative safety behind the wide Dnieper River. But on that day Woehler ordered him to liquidate a new Soviet foothold near Veliki Bukrin, 50 mi S of Kiev and just W of Pereyaslav. Moving quickly with two divisions, he surprised Soviet forces moving S from their crossing site and drove them back into a bridgehead. Knobelsdorff was on home leave while CHOLTITZ, as acting corps commander 1-21 Oct 43, began having visions of a Red tide drowning Germany!

The German situation on the eastern front was not yet hopeless, but Knobelsdorff's 48th Pz Corps, now in HOTH's 4th Pz Army, was heavily engaged in beating back Soviet armor that was advancing SW from Kiev (Manstein, *Lost Victories,* 488). After being awarded the Oakleaves (322/890) on 12 Nov 43 (Angolia, I, 209), Knobelsdorff won victories at Zhitomir, Brussilov, and Radomyshl while directing counterattacks against the Kiev salient, 15 Nov-23 Dec 43. Knobelsdorff took over the 40th Pz Corps from SCHOERNER, commanding it 1 Feb-2 Sep 44. In heavy defensive actions from the Dniester into Romania he headed "Gruppe von Knobelsdorff," 26 Feb-31 May 44, being awarded the Swords (100/159) for action near Nikopol (Angolia, I, 209-10).

Leaving the 40th Pz Corps on 3 Sep 44 (*B&O,* 45), he took over the 1st Army from Kurt von der CHEVALLERIE near Paris in late-Aug 44. In BALCK's Alsace-Lorraine counteroffensive, Knobelsdorff attacked on 24 Sep 44 to reach Chateau Salins. He was beaten back by PATTON, whose 3d Army went on to penetrate the West Wall and take a Saar River bridge on 3 Dec 44 before the Germans could set off prepared demolitions. "The Fuehrer demanded a victim," writes MELLENTHIN, and "the highly capable commander of First Army was sacrificed" (op. cit., 326). Knobelsdorff was replaced by Hans Obstfelder and retired.

KNOX, William Franklin. US Secretary of the Navy. 1874-1944. Born 1 Jan 74 in Boston, "Frank" Knox spent his childhood there and in Nova Scotia before moving with his family to Grand Rapids, Mich. After getting a BA in 1889 from Alma College, the stocky, pleasant-faced, reddish-haired Knox was a "rough rider" with Theodore Roosevelt in Cuba. He became a successful newspaperman and a power in the Republican Party.

Enlisting at the age of 43 he went to France with the 78th Inf Div and rose to be a colonel of field artillery. Between the world wars he was a prominent journalist, ending up as publisher of the Chicago *Daily News.* After being the unsuccessful candidate for VP on the Republican ticket in 1936 he began to tone down his strong anti-New Deal line and supported Roosevelt's foreign policy. After the Germans attacked the west in May 40 Col Knox called for the US to rearm, and FDR nominated him to be Secretary of the Navy. (This had been long expected—Knox and STIMSON being the two big Republicans in FDR's coalition government.)

Knox relieved Charles Edison on 11 July 41 and became one of the best secretaries the navy ever had (Morison, I, 29), working harmoniously with CNO Ernest KING. Dying 23 Apr 44, Knox was replaced by FORRESTAL, his deputy.

KNUDSEN, William S. US production director. 1879-1948. Born Signius Wilhelm Poul Knudsen on 25 Mar 79 in Copenhagen, he went to America at the age of 20. In WWI he was Henry Ford's production manager and close associate. Disagreements led to Knudsen's joining General Motors in 1919, and by 1937 he was president of the company.

In 1940 the great Dane—six feet three and once a boxer—became head of the seven-member National Defense Commission. From 3 June 40 he had the additional task of mobilizing machine tools, and on 7 Jan 41 Knudson became director general for production in the new Office for (Emergency) Production Management. When FDR's executive order of 16 Jan 42 created the War Production Board under Donald M. Nelson to replace Knudson's office, the War Department recruited Knudson as its director of production with the rank of lieutenant general (28 Jan 42-1 June 45). He settled labor disputes and sped up production, principally in the aircraft industry, earning Secretary of War Stimson's tribute as "the master troubleshooter on the biggest job the world has ever seen" (*S&S*).

KOCH, Erich. Nazi official. 1896-1986. A Rhinelander born 19 June 96 at Elberfeld, he was a railroad worker when called into military service in 1915. After serving with no particular distinction he returned to the Rhineland and became a railroad clerk, trade unionist, and a member of the resistance movement against

French occupation authorities. Koch joined the Nazi Party in 1925, supported Gregor STRAS-SER's radical wing (Wistrich) and became a close friend of Alfred ROSENBERG, one of Hitler's principal lieutenants.

Koch was deputy **Gauleiter** for the Ruhr by 1927 and the next year became Gauleiter of East Prussia. He was in the Reichstag from 1930. Koch became a member of the Prussian State Council in July 33, and two months later was made Oberpraesident of East Prussia.

A "veritable cock-sparrow of a man" (Winterbotham, *The Nazi Connection,* 153)—a stocky five feet six with blue eyes, a square face, and a Hitlerian mini-moustache—he sincerely wanted to create a socialist paradise. This called for breaking up large but inefficient Junker estates. The earnest proconsul kept Himmler's SS from undermining his authority, as happened in other Gaue, but he soon faced a greater problem: the Wehrmacht was taking over his out-of-the-way province as a major military base for the war against the USSR. (*See* Winterbotham, ibid., 151-60, 168-71, for a sympathetic, eyewitness account.)

After the Germans took Bialystok in 1941, Koch headed its civil administration as an additional duty. But he again clashed with Himmler's minions, refusing to let the SS and SA have their way. Hitler solved the problem in Oct 41 by leaving Koch as titular Gauleiter of East Prussia but naming him Reich commissar for the Ukraine.

With headquarters at Rovno the porky Reichskommisar used his Gestapo and police to create a brutal administration of "Germanization" that turned the Ukrainians against Nazi forces they had welcomed as liberators. When the Red Army approached Rovno in the spring of 1944, Koch went back to his post as Gauleiter of East Prussia. Fleeing Koenigsberg before its surrender on 9 Apr 45, Koch was a fugitive in West Germany until arrested by the British in May 49. Eventually he was turned over to the Poles as a major war criminal but not tried until 19 Oct 58. Seriously ill but unrepentant and defiant, Koch received the death sentence on 9 Mar 59 but Polish law prohibiting execution of a bedridden person, Koch spent the rest of his life in prison. He died at Barczewo on 12 Nov 86 (Wistrich).

KOCH, Ilse. German war criminal. 1906-67. The strapping, red-haired Beast or Bitch of Buchenwald, also called the Red Witch, was a Dresden shop foreman's daughter. After being a librarian she was a secretary in Berlin. In 1936 she married SS Standartenfuehrer (Col) Karl Koch, senior officer at nearby **Sachsenhausen.** He became commandant of **Buchenwald** in 1939.

Frau Koch threw herself into her husband's work. A keen horsewoman, the redheaded beast rode through the camp and lashed out with a whip at any unfortunate inmate who caught her eye. Another hobby of the woman whom a postwar psychiatric examination found to be "a perverted, nymphomaniacal, hysterical, power-mad demon" (Snyder, *Ency of 3d Reich,* 198) was collecting items made from the skin of dead prisoners, particularly those who had had interesting tattoos.

Commandant Koch finally committed the ultimate military sin of embarrassing his superiors. Rumors of his excesses led to an SS investigation in 1941 that ended in a whitewash; Koch was assigned briefly to another camp but restored to his post at Buchenwald. He continued his criminal career until tried by an SS court in 1944 on charges that included murdering an SS man who was a material witness against him. Karl Koch was hanged early in 1945. His widow was tried at this time on charges of receiving stolen goods (!) but acquitted. After two years in obscurity and becoming pregnant with her son Uwe, Frau Koch was arrested in 1947 and sentenced by a US military tribunal to life imprisonment for murder. Lucius CLAY commuted the sentence to four years, leniency that brought violent objections in Germany and abroad. A US Senate committee concluded on 27 Dec 48 that "This bestial woman's guilt in specific murders is irrefutably established." In 1949 she was charged by a German court for crimes against her fellow nationals and given another life sentence on 15 Jan 51. (Ibid.) After 17 years of maniacal appeals, never admitting any guilt, the Red Witch hanged herself on 1 Sep 67 with a bed sheet in the prison of Aichach, Bavaria.

KOENIG, Marie Pierre Joseph François. French general. 1898-1970. Of Alsacian stock, he was born 10 Oct 98 at Caen, in Normandy. As a teenager he was decorated during WWI and saw action during the 1930s with the French foreign legion in Morocco. In 1940 he was a major in the legion's demi-brigade that was heavily engaged in Lord CORK AND ORRERY's operations in Norway around Narvik. Returning to France for the last-ditch stand in Normandy, he escaped to England in a fishing boat. De Gaulle promoted Koenig to colonel and he became LEGENTILHOMME's CofS in the 1st Free French Div being formed in the Sudan. That unit took part in Maitland WILSON's campaign of 7 June-12 July 41 in Syria and Lebanon that overcame Ferdinand Dentz's Vichy forces. Promoted to general and given command of the 1st FF Bde in Egypt, Koenig was assigned to RITCHIE's British 8th Army in the summer of 1942. In an epic defense of Bir Hacheim, a critical position on the 8th Army's exposed S flank, the French held off an envelopment by the Afrika Korps from 27 May until ordered on 10 June 42 to withdraw. A Seine River bridge and Paris metro station now bear the name Bir Hachiem for the action that restored French military honor after the humiliation of 1940.

GIRAUD blocked de Gaulle's efforts to give Koenig a higher command, but the Alsatian had a high staff post in the unified Free French force created in North Africa in July 43. Koenig was reassigned to London in Apr 44, and on 25 June 44 (D+20 in Normandy) he took command of the French Forces of the Interior (FFI) as a member of Eisenhower's staff. On 21 Aug 44 DE GAULLE appointed Koenig military governor of Paris, and a week later the FFI were made part of the French army (de Gaulle, *Unity*, 348, 357).

Koenig headed the French occupation zone in Germany (1945-49) before retiring from the army. He was a Gaullist deputy from Strasbourg in 1951 and—despite a notable lack of political aptitude—was minister of defense under Pierre Mendes-France and Edgar Faure. The general died 2 Sep 70 in the Paris suburb of Neuilly.

KOGA, Mineichi. Japanese admiral. 1885-1944. CinC, Combined Fleet, after YAMAMOTO, Koga was born in Saga Prefecture in Sep 85. (*Who's Who in Japan, 1938.* Other sources give 1882 as the year.)

He served as naval attaché in Paris, commander of the Yokosuka Naval Station, and from Dec 37 as vice chief of the Naval Staff Board. The admiral also took part in the capture of Hong Kong on 25 Dec 41.

Koga's appointment as YAMAMOTO's successor was announced on 21 Apr 43. An uninspiring leader but efficient in a cool, plodding way, the new CinC immediately issued Plan Z,.which was prompted by an assumption that the Combined Fleet needed a decisive victory in 1943 before the odds were overwhelming. (Morison, VI, 23.) US forces captured a copy of the plan on Hollandia after landing in April, but the strategy was being overtaken by events: KINNEY's SWPA air forces were achieving air supremacy; and MITSCHER's fast carrier TF hit Truk on 17-18 Feb 44. Koga consequently withdrew his forward elements to the Palaus but soon decided to move them farther back to the southern Philippines. The admiral's plane left Palau for Davao after dark on 31 Mar 44 and—lost in fog—went down at sea. His death was not announced until 5 May 44, when Soemu TOYODO was named to replace him.

KOISO, Kuniaki. Japanese general. 1880-1950. Born in Yamagata prefecture, Koiso joined the 30th Inf Regt as a second lieutenant in June 01. Affable, deeply religious, capable, and courageous, Koiso rose to company commander in the 30th in Mar 05 and was promoted three months later to captain. (*Kosun,* 228.) He graduated from the war college in Nov 10 and thereafter was primarily a headquarters officer. Lt Gen Koiso (1931) was vice minister of war (1932), concurrently the Kwantung Army's CofS and chief of its special service department (from Feb 32), before taking command of the 5th Div at Hiroshima in Mar 34. He was CinC, Japanese Army in Korea, from Dec 35, being promoted to full general (Nov 37). Returning to Tokyo, Koiso was "retired to the first army list" in July 38. After being minister of overseas affairs (foreign minister) in 1939-40—the cabinets of HIRANUMA and YONAI—he became governor general of Korea in May 42.

Although he had joined Yonai and others to oust TOJO on 18 July 44, Koiso became prime minister. In a muddle-headed evocation of "history" he compared the losing struggle on Leyte with the 16th century Battle of Tennozan that decided who should rule Japan (Toland, *Sun*, 603). As Japan lost more outposts including Iwo Jima, Koiso made desperate and confused efforts to save his government—failing in peace overtures to Chiang Kai-shek and proposing a drastic cabinet reorganization. Gen Koiso announced his resignation on 5 Apr 45 and on that day was succeeded by Kantaro SUZUKI. In the Tokyo war crimes trials he was convicted on 12 Nov 48, sentenced to life imprisonment, and he died 3 Nov 50.

KOJEDUB, Ivan. *See* KOZHEDUB.

KOLLER, Karl. German general. 1898-1951. A dour, capable Bavarian commissioned from the ranks, Koller rose from colonel in SPERRLE's Luftflotte 3 Hq to be its CofS. Promoted to General of Flyers, Koller was CofS, Luftflotte 2, in 1942. Then appointed OKL director of operations, he was passed over by the less-well-qualified KREIPE to succeed KORTEN as Luftwaffe CofS. Although disgusted with Goering's incompetence, Koller became the Luftwaffe's last CofS on 2 Nov 44.

KOMOROWSKI, Tadeusz. Polish general. 1895-1966. The tall, slender, courtly Col Komorowski was an internationally known equestrian who commanded the Grudziad cavalry school when it was overrun by the Germans in Sep 39. Authorized by Wladislaw SIKORSKI to head a national resistance movement, he adopted the cover name Bor (meaning forest). Although unsuited like most other regular army officers to lead irregulars, he rose from Home Army Commander in the Cracow region to head the Polish Home Army in July 43 with the rank of lieutenant general. Bor had a million dollar price on his head and was captured once, but he escaped before the Germans discovered his identity.

As the Red Army approached Warsaw in July 44 Radio Moscow exhorted the population to "become a million soldiers." The Polish capital was critically important as a communications hub, but it also had tremendous political and cultural significance. Anxious to beat the Soviet-sponsored "Lublin Poles" in establishing postwar political control of his homeland, MIKLOLAJCZYK authorized Bor to order the long planned uprising when the general thought the time was right (Michel, *Shadow War,* 327-28). Although the necessary Allied air support had not yet been arranged, Bor was so worried about being preempted by the Warsaw communists that he set 1 Aug 44 for the uprising. The

"London Poles," intending to prove they could act independently, did not notify the Allies (ibid.). With the Warsaw communists having agreed to take orders from Bor, his forces had remarkable success initially. But Stalin was alarmed by the magnitude of the insurrection, which he saw was not pro-Soviet, so he decided cold-bloodedly not only to withhold support but also to keep the western Allies from using Russian bases to provide it (ibid.).

The Germans seized the opportunity to destroy what Himmler described to Hitler as "the capital, the brains, the nerve center of this . . . nation that has barred our passage to the east for seven centuries . . ." (ibid.).

The Red Army spearhead under ROKOS-SOVSKY remained immobile on the far bank of the Vistula until 10 September, the Soviet AF did not challenge the Luftwaffe's local air supremacy, and Stalin condemned leaders of the revolt as "criminals" and "provocateurs."

After 63 days, during which BACH-ZELEWSKI used 600mm siege guns to supplement the Luftwaffe's around-the-clock bombardment, Bor surrendered on 2 Oct 44. The Home Army of 46,000, fewer than half of them armed, lost 10,000 killed. About 50,000 citizens died, 300,000 were deported, and the Germans systematically demolished surviving buildings.

Bor and his staff were given POW status. FEGELEIN has been credited with interceding on behalf of his fellow equestrian, but it is more likely that the Poles were spared because senior Nazis were beginning to worry more about being charged with war crimes.

Bor-Komorowski (as he came to call himself) joined ANDERS and other Free Poles in England after being liberated in May 45 at Innsbruck by US forces. Many blamed Bor-Komorowski for being duped by the Soviets and for bad judgment in ordering the uprising prematurely. After serving briefly in 1947 as premier of the Polish government in exile, the resistance hero lived quietly in a London suburb. He wrote about the war and worked for the Polish Welfare Association. Bor-Komorowski's books include *The Secret Army* (1952).

KONDO, Nobutake. Japanese admiral. 1886-1953. As a vice admiral commanding the

Southern Fleet, he operated in the China Sea, Indian Ocean, and Java Sea. As the Japanese began landing on 10 Dec 41 in Malaya to capture Singapore, Kondo's planes made naval history by sinking HMS *Prince of Wales* and *Repulse,* which were commanded by Sir Tom PHILLIPS.

Kondo had overall responsibility for amphibious operations in the Philippines, his 2d Fleet operating initially about 250 miles west of Luzon as the Distant Cover Force. In the Battle of Midway, 3-6 June 42, Kondo commanded the Midway Occupation Force, composed of his own 2d Fleet, Raizo TANAKA's Transport Group, and Takeo KURITA's Support Group. But YAMAMOTO's main body and Chuichi NAGUMO's 1st Carrier Striking Force were defeated decisively and Kondo had to abandon his mission and withdraw.

After VANDEGRIFT's US Marines landed on Guadalcanal, 7 Aug 42, Kondo led the first major Japanese effort to destroy the beachhead. Kondo sailed from Truk with the main element of YAMAMOTO's combined fleet and also commanded Raizo TANAKA's "reinforcement group" that escorted 800 naval landing troops and 700 army personnel. In the Battle of the Eastern Solomons, 23-25 Aug 42, against FLETCHER and KINKAID, Kondo used clever decoy tactics that nearly succeeded in sinking CV *Enterprise.* Tanaka's force, not spotted until the day after this action, was turned back with some losses, but the **Tokyo Express** subsequently landed surviving troops on Guadalcanal. Kondo's action "marked the end of aggressive action by Japanese carrier planes and heavy ships" in the Guadalcanal campaign (Morison, V, 103), but he was involved in many subsequent engagements.

In Oct 42 Kondo faced KINKAID's TF 16 and George MURRAY's TF 17 in the Battle of Santa Cruz. With a false report that the Japanese had recaptured Henderson Field, and not knowing where Kinkaid and Murray were, Kondo turned back north after his advance force was spotted around noon on 25 Oct 42. That night he continued to withdraw, followed and attacked by American ships. The Japanese CVL *Zuiho* took two hits that knocked out her flight deck, but CV *Hornet* was put out of action by bombs and torpedoes and eventually lost. CV *Enterprise,* BB *South Dakota,* and CL *San Juan*

sustained damage. Having scored a tactical victory, Kondo withdrew.

In the decisive naval battle of Guadalcanal, 12-13 Nov 42, off **Savo Island,** Kondo led a bombardment group that covered troop transports under TANAKA. The Japanese began the heavy night action in Ironbottom Sound by sinking two destroyers and depriving Willis LEE of his destroyer screen. BB *South Dakota* took 42 gun hits, lost power, but survived. The other US battleship, *Washington,* quickly knocked out BB *Kirishima,* which was scuttled early the next morning, the only battleship lost in a surface-to-surface duel during WWII (*S&S*). Kondo broke off the two-hour engagement shortly after midnight (12-13 Nov 42) and withdrew. This sealed the fate of the Japanese on Guadalcanal. After covering a masterful evacuation of Japanese survivors, Kondo was replaced by KURITA. His fighting career finished, the admiral became a member of the Supreme War Council in May 45.

KONEV, Ivan Stepanovich. Marshal of the Soviet Union. 1897-1973. Konev and Zhukov are generally considered to be the best Soviet field commanders of the war. They had a personal antipathy that began in 1939 and peaked in postwar intrigues for which Konev had a flair.

Ethnically, Konev was Russian, born in the village of Ladeino, near Kirov, on 28 Dec 97. He completed formal schooling at the age of 12, then rose from wood chopper and common laborer in a lumber yard to lumberjack. The tough, square-faced, broad-shouldered Konev was conscripted in the spring of 1916 as an artilleryman. He became a junior officer (Scotts) but by the end of Nov 17 was demobilized back in his home district.

Konev's early political affiliations are a puzzle to historians (Erickson in Carver, ed, *War Lords,* 286), but he eventually sided with the Bolsheviks, joining the CP and the Red Army in 1918. Leaving a fierce little civil war he had been fighting in the rear, Konev became a private on the eastern front and military commissar on Armored Train No. 102. He showed skill and courage in raids the train conducted in the Siberian and Transbaikal regions. Having worked his way up to command a division, Konev was a delegate to the 10th Party Congress in 1921 and carried a rifle in helping put down the Kronstadt rebellion. After several years as a commissar in the Far East, Konev took courses in 1926-27 at the Frunze MA that qualified him for regular military service.

By Sep 37 he commanded a corps in the Belorussian MD, and a year later, having headed the 57th Special Corps under BLUYKHER in Outer Mongolia, Konev took over the new 2d Independent Red Banner Far Eastern Army. ZHUKOV arrived nine months later to become the hero of **Khalkhin Gol** (1939) and anathema to Konev thereafter. Stalin would exploit this rivalry (ibid, 287).

A general lieutenant from June 40, Konev headed the Transbaikal MD until he became acting commander of the North Caucasus MD in Jan 41. The following June, as the Germans invaded Russia, Konev took command of the 19th Army as it formed around Vitebsk for a last-ditch defense of Moscow. The new army, which Konev had to commit piecemeal, included units rushed from the Far East. On 12 Sep 41, a day after being promoted, Gen Col Konev succeeded TIMOSHENKO as commander of the Western Front. Fedor von BOCK unleashed the final assault of his AG Center on 30 Sep 41 and destroyed huge Red Army forces in great encirclements around Vyazma and Bryansk. The Germans claimed more than 650,000 just in prisoners. Stalin blamed Konev for the disaster and replaced him on 10 Oct 41 with ZHUKOV, who persuaded Stalin to let Konev remain a week as deputy front commander.

Having narrowly survived professionally, Konev then took over the Kalinin Front on 17 Oct 41. The Stavka had created this new army group to cover Moscow's northern approaches, where HOTH's 3d Pz Group was attempting a strategic envelopment. The panzers came within sight of the Kremlin's towers before running out of momentum, and on 6 Dec 41 the Soviets launched a large-scale winter offensive in which Konev pushed the Germans back more than 100 miles.

Konev resumed command of the Western Front on 27 Aug 42, after ZHUKOV was recalled to Moscow for duty with the Stavka. Stopping Bock's last lunge toward Moscow, Konev was succeeded as CG, Western Front, by Sokolovsky before the great Russian winter counteroffensive began on about 2 Feb 43. Konev then replaced Timoshenko in the Northwest Front, remaining until June 43. (Scotts.)

An entirely new phase of Konev's career began on 19 July 43 when he took command of the Steppe Front. This short-lived organization was, in effect, a strategic reserve to back up the Kursk salient. But for the first time Konev had powerful armored forces and he quickly was recognized as a top field commander. He was promoted 26 Aug 43 to general of the army along with Zhukov, Vasilevsky, Rokossovsky, and Vatutin. On 20 Oct 43 Konev assumed command of the 2d Ukrainian Front. He was promoted to MSU (No. 13) in Feb 44.

About this time a staff officer described the 48-yearold marshal as follows: "He . . . can be very stern. But usually there is a gay twinkle in his eyes. . . . He is very austere in his habits; doesn't drink, and objects to others getting drunk. . . . He admires Stalin both as a leader and as a writer, and is a strong Party man. . . ." (Quoted in Werth, *Russia at War,* 786.)

Konev launched his famous "mud offensive" on 5 Mar 44 when spring thaws had made terrain of the Ukraine untrafficable by normal standards. Hitting HUBE's 1st Pz Army when its vehicles were thoroughly bogged down but **T-34**s of ROTMISTROV's 5th Guards Tank Army could navigate, Konev suddenly wheeled them north against weak resistance to take the large and vital German base at Uman on 10 Mar 44. With six panzer divisions and elements of the 8th Army stuck in the mud, Konev quickly pushed to within 30 miles of the Dniester. (Erickson, cited above, 293-94.)

The marshal then moved north to take command of the 1st Ukrainian Front on 15 May 44. He overran southern Poland and by 7 Aug 44 had a strong bridgehead on the Vistula at Baranow. Soviets in the center now paused for their logistical tail to catch up while others to the south and north began making the **main effort.** On 12 Jan 45 Konev broke out of the Baranow bridgehead in overwhelming strength, encircled the fortress city of Breslau, and by 15 Feb 45 reached the line of the Niesse River.

Stalin gave ZHUKOV the honor of taking Berlin; Konev's mission was to move south of the capital to the Elbe. Konev proposed that after the initial breakthrough he divert armored forces north against Berlin. The general staff endorsed Konev's strategy but Stalin disapproved until after ZHUKOV met unexpectedly stubborn resistance. Getting his way, Konev drove north, and on 25 Apr 45 his tanks linked up with ZHUKOV's to isolate Berlin. On the same day patrols from Konev's front made contact with those of HODGES's 1st US Army on the Elbe at Torgau, splitting Germany.

From shortly after V-E day, 7 May 45, Konev headed Soviet occupation forces in Austria. But as STALIN began removing war heroes from public view, Konev started using his prewar political experience as a commissar. In Apr 46 he superseded his archenemy ZHUKOV as head of occupation forces in Germany, and three months later replaced his rival as CinC of Soviet ground forces. Konev left this post in 1950 to serve tours as Chief Inspector of the Soviet Armed Forces, commander of the Transcarpathian MD (1952-55), then he returned for a year as CinC, Ground Forces (1955-56).

Konev was CinC of the new Warsaw Pact Forces, 1956-60. As he had been a foil for Stalin against Zhukov, Konev now performed this role for KHRUSHCHEV, who had come to power (Erickson, cited above, 297). In a speech supporting Khrushchev's removal of ZHUKOV in 1957, Konev "venomously catalogued Zhukov's military shortcomings" (ibid.). Along with MALINOVSKY, ROTMISTROV, and YEREMENKO, he then was useful to Khrushchev in rewriting the official history of WWII. But by 1960, as Khrushchev sought to cut conventional forces and rely more on missiles, Konev had the same objections that had led to ZHUKOV's demise. The marshal consequently was retired to the **Inspectorate.**

Khrushchev brought Konev back during the Berlin crisis in 1961 to head Soviet Forces in Germany until Apr 62. The two-time HSU (1944, 1945) died 21 May 73 and was buried in the Kremlin Wall.

KONOYE, Fumimaro. Japanese statesman. 1891-1945. "Very dark, very sad, very tall . . . a bundle of nerves" *(CB 40)*, Konoye was premier three times before being succeeded by TOJO on the eve of the war.

A scion of the Fujiwara clan, the prince was born in Oct 91. His mother died eight days later. His father, who had been a protégé of Prince SAIONJI's, died at the age of 42, leaving Konoye a debt-ridden orphan at the age of 13. Hounded by creditors and deserted by family friends, Konoye developed an admiration for Marxism and fascism (ibid.). But on graduating in law from Kyoto Imperial University (1917)

he reluctantly became Saionji's secretary at the Paris Peace Conference of 1917. Konoye revived the family fortunes and by 1933 was president of the House of Peers. After declining the post of PM in 1936, on the chronic excuse of ill health, he accepted on 4 June 37. As the first civilian to hold that post since the rise of the militarists, Konoye was a white hope—so to speak—for curbing the war-bent ultranationalists and forming a one-party, coalition government. The prince had been in office only three days when the **Marco Polo Bridge** incident occurred, but his cabinet survived because it was not quickly apparent that the militarists would escalate this affair into all-out war with China. Konoye approved sending reinforcements to "stabilize the situation" but protected his friend HASHIMOTO, who went on to perpetrate outrages including the **Panay incident.**

The PM persisted in trying to reconcile political, bureaucratic, military, and diplomatic factions, but in 1938 his government passed the National Mobilization Law and proclaimed the "new order in East Asia." Having lasting a mere seven months, Konoye's cabinet was followed in rapid succession by those of Generals HIRANUMA and Nobuyaki ABE, then by Admiral YONAI's on 16 Jan 40. The prince formed his second cabinet on 22 July 40. This promptly negotiated the Rome-Berlin-Tokyo Axis and formed the Imperial Rule Assistance Association to replace all other political parties in Japan. Under the executive directorship of retired Col Hashimoto (above) this helped mobilize the home front *(CE)*. In an elaborate scheme to oust Foreign Minister MATSUOKA, Konoye resigned his second cabinet on 16 July 41 with the emperor's assurance that he could form another one immediately. Soemu Toyoda replacing Matsuoka, Konoye's third cabinet operated from 18 July 41. When this failed to reach an accommodation with the US, TOJO was instructed on 16 Oct 41 to form a new government.

Unable to build his one-party association, (above), Konoye was politically inactive thereafter but remained a close adviser to the emperor. But when he might have been useful as Hirohito's personal representative in negotiations to accelerate Japan's acceptance of the **Potsdam Proclamation** before it was public knowledge, thus sparing Japan from the atomic bomb and Soviet intervention (Mosley, *Hirohito,*

308), the melancholy prince moved his household to safety at Karuizawa, in the mountains some 100 miles NE of Tokyo. After having six months "to brood on Japan's fate and his own lost opportunities" (ibid.), Konoye poisoned himself on 16 Dec 45 after learning he would be tried for war crimes.

KOO, V. K. Wellington. Chinese diplomat. 1888-. With the Mandarin name of Ku Weichun, he became Vi Kuiyuin Wellington Koo. (The Duke of Wellington was one of his father's heroes.) Born into a wealthy Shanghai family, he had a remarkable record at Columbia Univ in NYC, 1905-12, not only academically but also as a debater, editor of college publications, and runner on the track team *(CB 41)*. With a PhD, having specialized in international affairs, V. K. Koo (the name he preferred) was secretary to the president of China, Yuan Shih-kai. In 1915, three months after being appointed ambassador to Mexico, he became the youngest ever to hold that post in Washington, DC (ibid.). Subsequently minister to London, 1921-22, and China's foreign minister at various times from 1921 and PM, 1926-27, Koo was in Paris from 1932 as minister, then became ambassador in 1936. He held this position in London, 1941-46, then in Washington until 1956. During his diplomatic career Dr Koo represented China at almost all international conferences after becoming a diplomat, and from establishment of the UN was a judge in the International Court of Justice. "Cultured, polished and tremendously educated politically" (ibid.), born wealthy and marrying money, Dr Koo had his principal residence after the war at 1185 Park Ave, NYC. (*China Yrbk, 1970-71,* 579.)

KORTEN, Guenther. German air officer. 1898-1944. After being on MILCH's staff until 1936, the highly regarded Generaloberst Korten commanded Luftflotte 1 when selected to succeed JESCHONNEK as Luftwaffe CofS. Taking over on 25 Aug 43, with the able KOLLER as deputy, the new CofS was drawn into the bitter disputes over using increasingly limited resources into strengthening the now-discredited Luftwaffe. Korten was among the first to advocate giving priority to heavy bombers and GALLAND's fighter arm. Although gaining Hitler's high regard, he quickly despaired of working effectively with Goering. (Irving, *Milch,* 235.) By June 44 he had decided to resign no later than August, but was mortally wounded in STAUFFENBERG's bomb attempt on 20 July 44. A fragment of the conference table driven into his body, Korten died after two days of agony. He was succeeded by KREIPE.

KOSTENKO, Fyodor Yakovlevich. Soviet military commander. 1896-1942. He was born 22 Feb 96 in the village of Bolshaya Martynovka, Rostov Oblast, spent two years in the local school and was drafted in 1915. A civil war veteran, wounded four times as a cavalry commander, Gen Lt Kostenko headed a cavalry group in June 41 before taking over the 26th Army that month. He was captured with his army around Kiev but escaped to become TIMOSHENKO's deputy commander in the SW Front. Concurrently he led an operations group that liberated Yelets on 9 Dec 41 (Scarecrow). The general then took over the SW Front from Timoshenko on 18 Dec 41, leading it in what the Soviets call the Moscow Offensive Operation, 5 Dec 41-7 Jan 42. With TIMOSHENKO doubling at times as SW Front and SW Theater commander, Kostenko alternated as Timoshenko's deputy and as front commander. On 12 Apr 42, when he reverted to being deputy front commander, Kostenko launched the Kharkov offensive. After weeks of confused fighting the Germans cut off the Soviet salient, capturing 1,200 tanks, 2,000 guns, and 214,000 prisoners. Trapped with his command group, Kostenko was killed on 26 May 42 while trying to break out. Other casualties were 6th Army commander Gen Lt A. M. Gorodnyansky (suicide), 57th Army commander Gen Lt K. P. Podlas, and operational group commander Gen Maj L. V. Bobkin. (Seaton, *R-G War,* 261; Erickson, *To Stalingrad,* 347).

KOZHEDUB, Ivan Nikitovich. Soviet airman. 1920-. A Ukrainian who was a cadet at the start of Opn **Barbarossa** in June 41 and rose to be a guards major, Kozhedub was officially the leading Soviet fighter ace with 62 victories. German pilots say another Red AF pilot, not listed by the Soviets, had more than 80 kills. (Sims, *Aces,* 17.) Flying LA-5s and LA-7s, he had 120 air battles in about 330 combat sorties. The ace was a three-time HSU, the only others being Aleksandr Pokryshkin (another pilot) and Zhukov. Kozhedub became a Marshal of Aviation on 7 May 85.

KOZLOV, Dmitriy Timofeyevich. Soviet military leader. 1896-1967. He was born 4 Nov 96 near Gorki in the village of Razgulyayka. At the start of WWII Gen Lt Kozlov headed the Transcaucasus MD. This went through a series of name changes, being the Transcaucasus Front from August to 30 Dec 41, then the Caucasus Front until 28 Jan 42, and finally the Crimean front until 19 May 42 (Scotts). Stalin meanwhile subordinated the Sevastopol defensive zone to Kozlov's front as MANSTEIN's 11th Army closed in on the Black Sea base, then Stalin ordered the Kerch-Feodosiya landing operations, 25 Dec 41-2 Jan 42, and gave Kozlov the mission of reconquering the Crimea. Large scale Soviet amphibious operations forced the German 11th Army to fight for its life, but Manstein launched a counterattack on 15 Jan 42 that within a month took "some 170,000 prisoners, 1,133 guns and 258 tanks" (Manstein, *Lost Victories,* 238). Kozlov, his commissar (one Shamanin), and MEKHLIS were among many demoted and dismissed for the debacle.

Gen Maj Kozlov took over the reconstituted 24th Army at Stalingrad in Aug 42, and two months later he became deputy commander of the Voronezh Front under F. I. GOLIKOV. Kozlov also was Stavka representative on the Leningrad Front, then he moved to the Transbaikal Front as deputy commander in Aug 43; he was under M. P. Kovalev until Malinovsky took over in July 45 for the offensive against Japan.

Postwar assistant commander of several military districts, he retired in 1954 and died 6 Dec 67 in Minsk.

KRANCKE, Theodor. German admiral. 1893-1973. Having quickly drafted the first plans for conquest of Norway before FALKENHORST took over, Capt Krancke became "Admiral Norway." He was at Trondheim until Apr 40.

On 23 Oct 40 Krancke took the "pocket battleship" *Admiral Scheer* to sea from Gotenhaven for "the war's most successful cruise of a lone German warship" (Porten, 141). After sinking a 5,389-ton "independent" (R&H, *Chron,* 64) the raider was engaged east of Newfoundland 5 Nov 40 by HMS *Jervis Bay.* Continuing to operate alone, refueled and resupplied at sea, Krancke proceeded through the West Indies to the south Atlantic and on into the Indian Ocean. (WC, II, 597.) Here Krancke eluded a trap set by seven British cruisers and a carrier, having meanwhile forced the RN to start

providing naval escorts in the north Atlantic at a time when fleet units were needed in the Mediterranean. After five months at sea, sinking 19 ships (137,000 tons), and taking two tankers as prizes (Doenitz, *Memoirs,* 164), he returned safely to German waters on 30 Mar 41.

From Sep 42 to 1 Mar 43, Krancke was permanent naval LnO at OKW. Promoted to full admiral, he then was Naval CinC West. With H. J. Brennecke he published a book about his historic raid which was translated as *The Battleship Scheer* (London: Kimber, 1956) and *Pocket Battleship: The Story of the "Admiral Scheer"* (New York: Norton, 1958).

KRAVCHENKO, Grigory Panteleyevich. Soviet air officer. 1912-43. He was born 10 Oct 12 in the Ukrainian village of Golubivka, Dnepropetrovsk Oblast. Kravchenko got his wings in 1932 and commanded fighter units before becoming a test pilot in 1936. As a major he flew in China, 1938-39 (Scotts), then commanded an air regiment in the Transbaikal that took part in the **Khalkhin Gol** campaign. Twice a HSU and promoted in 1940, General Major of Aviation Kravchenko commanded a special air brigade on the Finnish border. He then was air commander, Baltic MD. From 1941 he was in the 3d Army, Bryansk Front, as commander of an air group, then as head of the front's air force. Along with Pavel V. RYCHAGOV he was a leading advocate of tactical air support.

A general lieutenant of aviation at the age of 28, Kravchenko was commanding an air division when KIA on 23 Feb 43 (Scarecrow).

KREBS, Hans. German general. 1898-1945. A small, plump man known for his ingratiating manner with superiors (Brett-Smith, 205), Krebs was an infantry officer in WWI. He was retained in the "treaty army," selected for service in the **Truppenamt,** and was in Moscow as deputy MA on the eve of Opn Barbarossa. Col Krebs knew Russia well, spoke the language, and had increasingly high staff positions ending as MODEL's CofS, first in Russia and then in France. Thanks largely to his old friend Gen Wilhelm Burgdorf, who headed the OKW personnel office, Krebs finally got command of a front-line unit. In mid-Feb 45 he replaced Walther Wenck as Guderian's CofS when Wenck left to be HIMMLER's CofS in AG Vistula. After Wenck was badly injured in a car accident on 17 Feb 45 Krebs took over from him on Himmler's staff but within a few weeks proved unequal to the task (Guderian, 451). Krebs consequently took over Wenck's former position as head of the OKH operations staff and Guderian's deputy CGS. Thanks largely to the odious Burgdorf's influence (ibid., 416), Krebs quickly joined Hitler's inner circle. On 28 Mar 45 he succeeded GUDERIAN to be the German army's last, least worthy and most subservient CofS.

Hours after Hitler's suicide late on 30 Apr 45 Goebbels and Bormann sent Generaloberst Krebs under a white flag through the hotly contested ruins of Berlin to parley with the Russians. With a small group Krebs met from 3:50 AM to 1:08 PM on 1 May 45 with Chuykov, who coordinated by phone with Zhukov, who was on the line to Moscow. Chuykov devotes two chapters of his memoirs to the nine-hour parley in which he made a persistent efforts to negotiate a surrender of Berlin. Krebs steadfastly insisted he had authority only to arrange an armistice under which the new DOENITZ government could deal with the Allies on peace terms. After giving the impression he was sorely tempted to surrender himself, Krebs returned to the Fuehrerbunker with a negative response for Goebbels and Bormann. The Soviets resumed their assault on the Tiergarten.

Krebs and Burgdorf almost certainly committed suicide on 1 or 2 May 45 (T-R, *Hitler,* 215), although some authorities believe Krebs was taken prisoner (Goerlitz, *GGS,* 498).

KREIPE, Werner. Luftwaffe general. 1905-. From chief of operations in Luftflotte 3 in 1940, Col Kreipe had risen to Generalleutnant by 1 Aug 44 when he succeeded KORTEN as Luftwaffe CofS. Goering passed over the more able von GREIM (whom Hitler favored) and KOLLER because he thought Kreipe would be more easy to dominate. But the new CofS became troublesome as he got a better insight into how much damage Goering and Hitler were doing to the German air effort. Within less than two months, on 21 Sep 44, Hitler ordered Kreipe banished from Rastenburg, and it was not for two months that the Luftwaffe got its fourth and last CofS, KOLLER. Kreipe later had posts within the **FRG.**

KRETSCHMER, Otto. German naval officer. 1912-. Born 1 May 12 in Heidau, he was cred-

ited with sinking between 266,000 and 314,000 tons of Allied shipping in the Atlantic before his U-99 was sent down on 17 Mar 41. As a POW in Canada for the duration he was promoted to Fregattenkapitaen, and on 25 Dec 41 he was presented the Swords (5/159) by the Bowmanville POW camp commander. After the war Kretschmer became a Flotilenadmiral in the Bundeswehr. (Angola, I, 117.)

KRUEGER, Walter. US general. 1881-1967. Born at Flatow, West Prussia, on 20 Jan 81, he came to America at the age of eight with his parents and grew up in Madison, Ind. At the age of 17 he left the Technical High School in Cleveland, Ohio, to fight in the Spanish-American war. Despite his youth Krueger rose to be a sergeant major in Cuba and decided on a military career. In June 99 he reenlisted in the RA as a private and in his spare time studied texts used at West Point.

After seeing action in the Philippine Insurrection, Krueger was commissioned in 1901. The next month the well seasoned 2d Lt Krueger met a very green 2d Lt George C. Marshall, and friendship between the two non-West Pointers was enhanced by service together a few years later as instructors at Ft Leavenworth. Krueger was G3 of the 26th Div in France until July 18. After brief tour in the US he returned to France with the 84th Div. In Oct 18 he became chief of the AEF's Tank Corps, rising to the rank of colonel (T) and winning the DSM. *(CB 43.)*

Krueger attended top service schools between wars and taught at both the Army and Navy War Colleges. He had two assignments with the War Plans Division before being brought back to Washington by MacArthur. Later, as a brigadier general Krueger headed the division, 29 May 36-30 June 38. He was succeeded by George C. Marshall. *(AA,* 60.) Krueger then commanded a brigade until promoted to major general on 1 Feb 39 and given command of the 2d Div at Ft Sam Houston, Tex. Still at "Fort Sam," he headed 8th Corps Hq from Oct 40 and on 16 May 41 took command of 3d Army Hq as a temporary lieutenant general. With Col Dwight D. EISENHOWER as its CofS, Krueger's army, won a decisive "victory" in the **Louisiana maneuvers of 1941.**

Krueger headed the Southern Defense Command until the 6th Army Hq at San Francisco was activated on 25 Jan 43, with a cadre from 3d Army Hq, for duty in Australia. (*AA*, 497-98.) The 6th Army Hq trained fresh US divisions as they arrived in Australia, whereas combat operations were carried out only by elements of his army that were designated TF Alamo (*AA*, 600) or **Alamo Force.**

Not until the Leyte campaign, 17 Oct-25 Dec 44, did Krueger himself command his army in action. MacArthur became so dissatisfied that he considered relieving Krueger (Eichelberger, 176), but the 6th Army commander retained his post, occupied Mindoro, and went on to take part in the reconquest of Luzon, 9 Jan-30 June 45 (*AA*, 498). Because of his slow advance on Manila he was again in MacArthur's disfavor (ibid., 225). But the Prussian-born general remained high on Marshall's list and was promoted to full general (8/13) on 5 Mar 45.

Krueger took his 6th Army Hq to Japan on 25 Sep 45 for occupation duties with Eichelberger's 8th Army. He remained only until 31 Dec 45, and a month later retired to live in San Antonio. For his slow and methodical ways Krueger was compared by MacArthur with the Civil War general George G. Meade (ibid., 248) and by others with Bernard L. Montgomery. But "for a certain type of frontal advance [Krueger] was equal to anyone in our military history," wrote Eichelberger (ibid., 280-81). Krueger left no memoirs.

KRUPP FAMILY. The world's most famous munitions empire began as an iron and steel manufactory in Essen in 1810. The only child of the third head of the firm was Bertha (1886-1957), for whom the gun that fired on Paris in the spring of 1918 was named "Big Bertha." Little Bertha married (1906) a diplomat who added "Krupp" to his venerable moniker in legally changing it to Gustav Krupp von Bohlen und Halbach (1870-1950). Like many others including Fritz THYSSEN, Gustav supported the unsavory Hitler in his rise to power, believing this was Germany's only hope. In 1933 Krupp began regular production of tanks, disguising this as the "Agricultural Tractor Scheme" (Goerlitz, *GGS*, 274).

Bertha and Gustav's eldest son Alfried (1907-67), took over the firm in 1942. The Krupp combine's heads and directors were tried as war criminals, mainly for using slave labor. Gustav was physically unfit to face trial. Alfried was

convicted in July 48 and sentenced to 12 years but released early in 1951. Despite war damage he rebuilt the Krupp corporation into the world's 12th largest.

KUECHLER, Georg von. German general. 1881-1968. Scion of a Junker family, Kuechler was born 30 May 81 near Hanau. He was commissioned in 1901 as an artillery second lieutenant. By 1918 Kuechler was a captain with an excellent combat record and wore the crimson trouser stripes of the **GGGS.** From late 1934 he commanded the 1st Div in East Prussia. Promoted the next year to Generalleutnant and made IG of service academies, he caught Hitler's eye in 1936 (*CB 43*). The professorial and somewhat unkempt Kuechler was promoted on 1 Apr 37 to General of Artillery commanding the 1st Army Corps in Koenigsberg. When the Nazis announced on 23 Mar 39 that the Lithuanian province of Memel was being incorporated into the Third Reich, Kuechler marched in with Himmler and Erich KOCH.

When the Germans attacked Poland, 1 Sep 39, Kuechler's 3d Army moved south from East Prussia as part von Bock's AG North. Linking up with Hans von Kluge's 4th Army and assuming operational control over GUDERIAN's 19th Pz Corps, he directed the northern arm of the great strategic envelopment east of Warsaw. Kuechler was awarded the RK at the end of the campaign (Angolia, II, 230). Although viewed as a "Nazi general," in Poland he defied Himmler's protests and ordered courts-martial of those who committed atrocities in his army area (Davidson, *Trial*, 566).

For the western offensive of 1940 Kuechler again had a critical mission on the strategic northern flank: in Bock's AG B he commanded the 18th Army of about 10 divisions including the 7th Pz. The army advanced rapidly in Holland with three columns on a broad front of more than 100 miles to link up with the highly vulnerable airborne troops after they took Moerdijk, Rotterdam, the Hague, and key bridges over the Meuse and Waal on D day, 10 May 40. The main effort was through Gennap toward Breda, where the Germans brushed aside the advance guard of Giraud's 7th French Army and the panzers raced north to link up on the afternoon of D+2 with elements of Student's 7th Abn Div at Moerdjke and Dordrecht. Dutch counterattacks on the airheads succeeded only at the Hague. After the "horror raid" on Rotterdam (*see* CHOLTITZ), the Dutch surrendered early on 15 May 40. Three days later the 18th Army occupied Antwerp and forced the line of the Scheldt to exploit westward toward Ghent. After Belgium surrendered on 28 May, Kuechler drove his tiring troops into the coastal region despite bad weather, flooded terrain, and stubborn resistance. Because of the famous "halt order" issued to panzer units south of the Dunkirk beachhead, Kuechler's 18th and other infantry armies arrived too late to stop the evacuation. This ended the night of 4-5 June 40 but the 18th Army had the mission of mopping up. "Dunkirk" Kuechler, as he was now nicknamed, then led his army through Amiens to enter Paris on 14 June and continue south until the cease fire was effective about a week later.

Included in the mass promotions of 19 July 40, Generaloberst Kuechler led his 18th Army into Russia alongside Busch's 16th Army in Leeb's AG North. Again on the north flank, he moved toward Leningrad against stubborn resistance in exceptionally difficult and heavily mined terrain of the Baltic States. In addition to using POWs for clearing mines and enforcing the **commissar** order, he had partisans and Gypsies executed. "Kuechler apparently had first gotten used to atrocities and then had come to approve of them," writes Davidson in commenting on war crimes charges against the general at Nuremberg (ibid., 566).

When LEEB asked to be relieved (after his drive on Leningrad stalled) Kuechler took over AG North on 17 Jan 42. Within two weeks the new broom asked Hitler to recall BUSCH, who had been a fellow army commander, but Hitler refused. Kuechler was promoted to Generalfeldmarschall on 30 June 42, and given the Oakleaves (273/890) on 21 Aug 43. Soon after the Soviets launched a major counteroffensive around Leningrad and threatened to cut off the 18th Army, Kuechler ordered a withdrawal on 28 Jan 44 to the line of the Luga River. The next day Hitler gave MODEL temporary command of AG North, and on 31 Jan 44 Kuechler was officially relieved and placed on the retired list.

At Nuremberg the field marshal was convicted of war crimes (above) but sentenced only to a short imprisonment at Landsberg. He died 25 May 68. (Angolia, II, 230-1.)

KUHN, Fritz. German-American Bund leader. 1896-1951. Fritz Kuhn's German-American People's League (or Bund) was a highly visible quasi-military body with a peak membership in 1939 of about 8,300 and more than 80 active cells throughout the US. The German ambassador in Washington deplored their "stupid and noisy activities" and German nationals were forbidden to join (Buchanan, I, 21-22n). The Bund did little but spread propaganda and anti-Semitism, never becoming an effective **fifth column.** Imprisonment in Nov 40 for embezzlement and forgery cut short the German-born American Nazi's brief career.

KULIK, Grigory Ivanovich. Soviet official. 1890-1950. A Ukrainian born 9 Nov 90 in the village of Dudnikovo, Poltava region, the son of a peasant, Kulik entered the Tsarist Army in 1912. He became an NCO and joined the Red Guards and the CP in 1917. The next year Kulik began his career in the Red Army and, performing well at **Tsaritsyn** as an artillery commander, was thereafter a life-long crony of Stalin's. He graduated from the Frunze MA in 1932. From May 37 to 1941 he was chief of the Red Army's main artillery directorate and simultaneously, from Jan 39, deputy commissar of defense. Although Zhukov informed Stalin candidly that Kulik was of no help to him in the victory at **Khalkhin Gol,** (Zukhov, *Memoirs,* 170), Stalin promoted his crony the next year, 1940, to marshal and made him a Hero of the Soviet Union.

Stupid, incompetent, corrupt, and unpleasant, Marshal Kulik failed conspicuously around Leningrad in Aug-Sep 41 as head of the 54th Army. He was removed from the Central Committee in Feb 42 and demoted the next month to general major (Scotts). Working his way back up, Gen Lt Kulik headed the 4th Guards Army in Apr 43. In action around Kharkov the next month his army was decimated, and in Sep 43 Kulik was once more sacked and demoted.

At war's end he was expelled from the Communist Party (Apr 45). But the durable Kulik was deputy commander of the Volga MD until arrested on 11 Jan 47. On 24 Aug 50 he was tried and shot at Kuibyshev. Posthumous rehabilitation came in Apr 56, and the next year his rank as MSU was restored.

KUNG Hsiang Hsi. Chinese official. 1881-1967. The tycoon banker and industrialist, a Christian convert who claimed direct descent from Confucius in the 75th generation (*China Hdbk 1937-1945,* 666), was born in Taiku,

Shansi province. As the husband of Ai-ling (Eling) Soong he was the brother-in-law of T. V. SOONG, of Dr SUN YAT-SEN, and of CHIANG KAI-SHEK.

H. H. Kung (the name form he favored) received his BA from Oberlin in 1906 and his MA from Yale the next year. Kung held prominent posts in China but is known primarily as governor of the Central Bank of China, 1933-45, succeeding T. V. Soong, and getting the huge foreign loans that China needed. After the communist takeover over he went to the US and died in NYC.

KURITA, Takeo. Japanese admiral. 1889-1977. He is remembered primarily for lack of aggressiveness in the battle for Leyte Gulf on 25 Oct 44, which ended Kurita's career and saved "Bull" HALSEY's.

Kurita was from a family of scholars but he decided to become a naval officer. By 1941 he was a highly regarded rear admiral whose experience had been primarily with destroyers and cruisers. After heading the Western Covering Force and the Western Attack Group, he directed a successful amphibious assault on the NW tip of Java at St Nicholas Point that started late on 28 Feb 42. (Morison, III, 334, 338, 365.)

Serving under KONDO, first as head of the Close Support Group that was supposed to provide a bombardment for troops landing on Midway, he was ordered to withdraw early 5 June 42 when the Japanese were turned back in the battle of Midway. In the Guadalcanal campaign Kurita was a vice admiral commanding the Support Group of KONDO's Advance Force, Guadalcanal Supporting Forces (Morison, V, 206). With flag aboard BB *Kongo,* his Combat Div 3 included BB *Haruna* and a destroyer escort. From just after midnight on 13-14 Oct 42 until 2:30 AM he delivered a bombardment that left Henderson Field in shambles, and he withdrew unscathed. (Morison, V, 173-75.) About a month later Combat Div 3 was augmented to support KONDO's Attack Group. Kurita was in the great naval battle of Guadalcanal, 12-14 Nov 42, but saw little action.

About a year later he succeeded KONDO as head of the 2d Fleet. Leading OZAWA's 1st Mobile Fleet toward Saipan, soon after US forces started landing on 15 June 44, Kurita's Van Force of three light carriers (CVLs) and supporting ships was about 100 miles in the lead when his search planes reported two US carrier

planes at 7:30 on the morning of the 20th. OZAWA later admitted he should have delegated tactical command to Kurita, who "would have hightailed out promptly," writes Morison (VIII, 288, 300). But Marc MITSCHER gave Ozawa a decisive and costly beating remembered as the "Great Marianas Turkey Shoot."

This left the Japanese with only one principal surface fleet, Kurita's, and Ozawa's decimated carrier force. Because merchant ships could not deliver enough fuel to the home islands for both fleets, Kurita took his to Lingga Roads, near Singapore; Ozawa went to the Sea of Japan, where much needed air crews were training. (Morison, XII, 163.)

Leyte Gulf

When MacArthur invaded Leyte on 20 Oct 44 the Japanese decided they had to stop him there or nowhere. The Sho-1 Plan called for convergence of four Japanese naval forces on the Philippines. Ozawa's big carriers, no longer good for much else, would move south from Japan as a decoy. This "Yankee bait" was supposed to lure HALSEY's 3d Fleet north, putting KINKAID's 7th Fleet in Leyte Gulf at the mercy of surface attack by three other converging columns.

Kurita left Singapore on 18 Oct 44 with two of these columns—known collectively as the 1st Striking Force. Fueling in Borneo at Brunei Bay, he proceeded on the 22d. North of Borneo, NISHIMURA broke away with his Force C and headed for Suriago Strait to approach Leyte Gulf from the south. Sailing south from Japan to follow Nishimura into Suriago Strait and take overall command in the south was SHIMA's 2d Striking Force. (*See* KINKAID for additional detail.)

Kurita plowed ahead with Force A into the Sibuyan Sea of the central Philippines. From here he would debouch through San Bernadino Strait and turn south to cooperate with Nishimura's and Shima's forces in a strategic double envelopment of Kinkaid's 7th Fleet in Leyte Gulf. Force A included the world's two largest battleships, *Yamato* and *Musashi,* plus the old BBs *Nagato, Konga,* and *Haruna,* 10 CAs, two CLs, and more than 12 DDs. The ships bristled with exceptionally heavy AA defenses.

Less than 24 hours after leaving Borneo, at 6:32 AM on 23 Oct 44, Kurita's column was spotted in the Palawan Passage and attacked by two US submarines. Making his first mistake,

Kurita had not thrown out a destroyer screen. His flagship, CA *Atago,* and CA *Maya* were sunk, and another CA was damaged. Kurita was fished out of the water to hoist a wet flag aboard *Yamato.* The next morning at about 10 o'clock he was heavily attacked in the Sibuyan Sea by carrier planes, and around 3 PM he turned back temporarily. The great *Musashi* was sinking, other ships were damaged, but Force A remained formidable. At 5:14 PM Kurita resumed course and at 11 P.M. was passing unmolested through San Bernadino Strait.

Bull Had Taken the Bait.

Japanese planes from Luzon meanwhile had unleashed "the most vigorous and successful air counterattack of the Leyte operation" (Morison, XII, 177). Frederick C. SHERMAN's TG 38.3 lost CVL *Princeton,* and damage was inflicted on a light carrier and five destroyers.

About 7 AM on 25 Oct 44 Kurita was sailing south when a lookout on *Yamato* (Kurita's flagship) reported "ships ahead." Out of radio contact with Ozawa, Kurita did not know what he had encountered. Wildly conflicting reports indicated that he faced Halsey, even that he had collided with Ozawa (Morison, XII, 248). All the Japanese commander knew for certain was that he was about to be attacked by carrier aircraft. Opening fire at long range, Kurita ordered deployment from column into a circle for maximum AA protection while he evaluated the situation. But before this maneuver could be completed, the befuddled Kurita ordered "general attack."

What opposed him was a force he could have wiped out in minutes: Clifton SPRAGUE's "Taffy 3" of six escort carriers (CVEs), three destroyers, and three destroyer escorts (DDEs). But US ships and pilots showed exceptional valor in almost two and a half hours of confused action. At 9:11 AM Kurita ordered his ships to disengage, and at 12:35, after circling to assess damages, he started withdrawing! Kurita cleared San Bernadino Strait at 9:30 PM. with only DD *Yukikaze* intact (d'Albas, 332-33). The next morning (26 October) in "the last convulsion of the battle" (ibid.), exhausted Japanese AA crews inflicted a heavy toll on 80 planes from Halsey's big carriers and on 27 Morotai-based B-17s of George Kenney's FEAF. The US carrier planes put two bombs on BB *Yamato* and sank CL *Noshiro.* The B-17s put 12 bombs so near *Yamato* that splinters mowed down the crew and seriously wounded Kurita's CofS, Rear Adm Koyanagi. (Ibid.) At 9:30 PM on the 28th the badly battered squadron returned to Brunei Bay without further major losses, but none of Kurita's capital ships is known to have seen action for another six months.

In defense of Kurita, whose apparent blunder might have been caused by memories of the "Great Marianas Turkey Shoot" (herein), Hanson Baldwin gives us additional food for thought. First, a mere two-hour delay in starting back to San Bernadino Strait could have been fatal. Second, Kurita had much to lose and little to gain by continuing on: he would have faced six battleships and overwhelming air power; Nishimura and Shima had been defeated, which Kurita knew; and most of the US amphibious ships in Leyte Gulf had been unloaded. (*Battles Lost and Won,* 309, 313.)

The unfortunate admiral survived the war and told his story in detail to US naval historians. In 1947 an American journalist described him as a "trim, hazel-eyed . . . little man with a winning smile now living in poverty in a wood-and-paper shack on Tokyo's outskirts." (Gilbert Cant, *Life,* 24 Nov 47, page 86.)

KUROCHKIN, Pavel Alekseyevich. Soviet military leader. 1900-89. Kurochkin was born 19 Nov 00 in the village of Gornevo, Smolensk region, son of a peasant. In 1917 he took part in storming the Winter Palace, joining the Red Army cavalry the next year and the CP in 1920. When the Germans invaded Russia he was a general lieutenant heading the Orlov MD. In July 41 he took command of the 20th Army, and the next month headed the 43d Army briefly before commanding the Northwest Front for 14 months. Exceptionally young for a front commander, he took part in the defensive of Leningrad with VATUTIN as his CofS. Turning over the front to Timoshenko in Oct 42, he stepped down to lead the 11th Army from Nov 42, then the 34th Army until June 43. From then he again commanded Northwest Front until it was disbanded on 20 Nov 43, being promoted 28 Aug 43 to general colonel.

In the reorganization of early 1944 when Rokossovsky's Belorussian Front became the 1st Belorussian Front, Kurochkin's command was redesignated the 2d Belorussian Front on 17 Feb 44. With his old staff he moved south to the Kovel area to form his new front from units of the high command reserve: P. A. Belov's 61st Army, N. I. Gusev's 47th Army, and V. S. Popov's 70th Army (Seaton, *R-G War,* 420). After opposing MANSTEIN's AG South until Apr 44, Kurochkin was replaced as front commander by SOKOLOVSKY and succeeded Ivan D. CHERNYAKHOVSKY as commander of the new 60th Army for the rest of the war.

An HSU in 1945, he was deputy CinC of Soviet Troops in Germany, then deputy commandant of the GS Academy (1951) before being commandant of the Frunze MA for 14 years, 1954-68. Pavel A. Kurochkin died 31 Dec 89 and was buried in the Kremlin Wall.

KURUSU, Saburo. Japanese diplomat. 1888-1954. The foreign service officer and NOMURA had the unenviable role of representing Japan in Washington when the sneak attack hit Pearl Harbor on 7 Dec 41. Kurusu was born at Yokohama in 1888. In 1910 he entered the foreign service after graduating from Tokyo Commercial College. He married an American while serving as consul in Chicago, 1913-19.

Short, dapper, and of slight build, Kurusu has been described a "silky" man whose smile was "thin but frequent" *(CB 42).* As director of the Commercial Bureau of the Foreign Office he conducted long and difficult negotiations with oil companies, whose product Japan so desperately needed. Considered pro-American, he had talks in Washington on Japanese-American commercial relations while en route in 1937 to be ambassador to Brussels. Then he was ambassador to Rome before being transferred in this capacity to Berlin in Oct 39. Kurusu signed the pact that took Japan into the **Axis,** and he signed the protocols that brought in Hungary, Romania, and Slovakia.

Returning to Tokyo as Japan moved toward war with the US, Kurusu was given ambassadorial rank and sent as a special envoy to assist NOMURA in Washington. Doomed peace negotiations were coming to a head; Kurusu had only two days' notice and was given no new instructions; and apparently knew nothing about Japan's intention to attack Pearl Harbor. Reaching Washington on 15 Nov 41, the special envoy accompanied *Nomura* on the memorable appointment with Cordell HULL on 7 Dec 41, the "day of infamy."

Repatriated in 1942 with Nomura, he retired in 1945 to be a professor at Tokyo university.

The prosecution called him as a witness at the war crimes trials.

Two of Kurusu's hyphenated daughters received western upbringing, but son Ryo was reared in Japan and became an aircraft designer. A lieutenant in 1941, Ryo Kurusu was mortally wounded in single combat with a swarm of US carrier planes on 16 Feb 45 but lived long enough to give a complete after-action report

.

KUZNETSOV, Fedor Isadorovich. Soviet military leader. 1898-1961. One of many Russians with this prevalent surname (below), Fedor Isadorovich was born 29 Sep 98 in Balbechino, a village of Mogilev region, son of a peasant. As a hard-charging junior officer in WWI he was wounded twice. He joined the Red Army in 1918, rose to command a regiment, and suffered two more wounds in the civil war.

After this distinguished combat career Kuznetsov excelled on the staff of service schools: he was commandant of the Moscow Red Banner Infantry School 1932-35 before holding the chair of tactics at the **Frunze** MA. He did not join the CP until 1938, when he became D. G. PAVLOV's deputy in the Western Special MD. In 1940 he took command of the Baltic Special MD and was promoted in Feb 41 to general colonel. At the start of Barbarossa, 22 June 41, his formation was redesignated the Northwest Front. It had two field armies, F. S. Ivanov's 8th in Latvia and V. I. Morozov's 11th in Lithuania. These were hit by LEEB's AG North, which included HOEPPNER's 4th Pz Gp.

Reacting poorly, Kuznetsov dissipated his strength with piecemeal attacks that had "little or no effect" (Erickson, *To Stalingrad,* 142). Within a fortnight his front was split and the two armies routed. Around 4 July 41 (D+12), when the Russians were struggling to slow the German steamroller, Kuznetsov succeeded V. F. Gerasimenko as CG, 21st Army.

The Central Front was created under Kuznetsov on 24 July 41, being made up of his old 21st Army (now under V. N. Gordov) and Gerasimenko's 13th Army; its mission was to plug the widening gap between the NW and Western Fronts. "Small and disorganized as it was, the Central Front formed the main Soviet barrier to the North Ukraine" (Erickson, 197).

After leg wounds hampered his movements, the general went to eastern Crimea as head of the new 51st Independent (or Special) Army, 8

Aug-22 Oct 41. But he was soon a casualty of MANSTEIN's brilliant operations. Replaced by his deputy, P. I. BATOV, Fedor Isadorovich shuttled through a baffling succession of postings during the next six weeks or so. For a few days at the end of October he resumed command of the 21st Army until it was taken over again by Gordov. F. I. Kuznetsov was I. V. TYULENEV's CofS in the 28th Army until it was reconstituted in Nov 41, then was Zhukov's deputy in the Western Front before briefly commanding the newly formed 61st Army in Nov 41. After various other assignments the often-wounded general became commandant of the GS Academy in Apr 42. He then suffered a bad concussion (Scotts) with complications that limited his performance of field duty. From Aug 43 to Feb 44 he was MERETSKOV'S deputy in the Volkhov Front, then was in the Karelian Front until sent in Feb 45 to head the Ural MD. Placed in the reserve in 1947, the peripatetic Fedor Isadorovich died 22 Mar 61 in Moscow.

KUZNETSOV, Nikolay Gerasimovich. Soviet naval officer. 1902-74. Called the father of the modern Soviet Navy, this buoyant sailor was twice a rear admiral, three times a vice admiral, and twice an admiral of the fleet! (Scotts.)

He was born in the village of Medvedki, Arkhangelsk Oblast. Joining the Red Navy in 1919, and serving in the civil war, he was not a party member until 1925. In 1937 he was an adviser in Spain. The **great purges** struck the navy particularly hard, creating vacancies in the high command and leading to N. G. Kuznetsov's being People's Commissar of the Navy and CinC of the Navy at the age of 37. He held this top post from Apr 39 to 1946. A full admiral from 1940, and admiral of the fleet in May 44, he commanded of the Soviet Pacific Fleet that supported Maksim A. PURKAYEV's operations against the Japanese. Kuznetsov became a HSU in 1945.

He built up the Soviet Navy's cruiser and submarine strength. Popular with Stalin as a disciplinarian who discarded egalitarian reforms, he was promoted in Mar 55 along with I. S. Isakov to the new rank of admiral of the fleet of the Soviet Union (HFS). But a year later Nikolay Gerasimovich Kuznetsov was demoted and retired. (Scotts.)

KUZNETSOV, Vasily Ivanovich. Soviet military leader. 1894-1964. During the war Vasily I. Kuznetsov commanded eight field armies. After surviving annihilation of his 3d Army around Grodno and of his 21th Army at Kiev (breaking out on about 20 Sep 41), Gen Lt V. I. Kuznetsov subsequently led the 58th Army briefly in November before taking over the 1st **Shock Army.** He led this until May 42, fighting in the Ukraine before moving north to have a major role in the battle of Moscow. On 12 July 42, when the Stalingrad Front was formed under Timoshenko, he commanded the new 63d Army along a 100-mile stretch of the Don with a small bridgehead at Verkhnyi Mamon. On 4 Nov 42 Kuznetsov's 63d Army Hq was the cadre of the second formation to be designated the 1st Guards Army. In VATUTIN's SW Front he had a major role in the battle of Stalingrad. After being Vatutin's deputy front commander briefly he headed the second recreation of the 1st Guards Army for a year from Dec 42. Meanwhile he was promoted to general colonel in May 43.

Reassigned in Dec 43, V. I. Kuznetsov was without another field command until heading the 3d Shock Army during the period Mar-May 45. Having served first under VATUTIN, then ROKOSSOVSKY, and finally under ZHUKOV, he took part in the liberation of Belorussia, the conquest of southern Poland and Pomerania, and the assault on Berlin.

Col Gen V. I. Kuznetsov was with Soviet occupation forces in Germany before heading the Volga MD 1952-57. He was retired in 1960 for disability.

L

LABORDE, Jean (Joseph Jules Noël). French admiral. 1878-1977. His name sometimes rendered as de la Borde, Laborde is remembered for scuttling the French fleet at Toulon on 27 Nov 42. He was born 29 Nov 78 at Chantilly. Becoming a pioneer in naval aviation, he might have reached the top of his profession if DARLAN, almost two years his junior in age, had not shown far superior political skills (*CB 43* citing Pertinax). Tall, blond, a strict disciplinarian, and a full admiral in 1938, Laborde was elevated the next year to command the French high seas fleet in the Atlantic. He conducted joint maneuvers with the Royal Navy and was highly regarded by the British. Unlike most French naval officers, who despised the British, Laborde was an admitted anglophile. (Larousse.)

In June 40 the admiral ordered his ships into British ports, but Pétain and Darlan prevailed on him to honor naval paragraphs of the Franco-German armistice signed that month. After Hitler authorized the Vichy government to create the French high seas fleet, based at Toulon, Laborde was made its commander in chief. The more-or-less disarmed remnant of the main French fleet also was at Toulon, under Adm Marquis as the port admiral. (de Gaulle, *Unity,* 54.)

Laborde and German Ambassador ABETZ met in Paris on 6 Nov 42 to plan for sending a 20,000-man expeditionary force to retake **Chad** (Larousse), little suspecting that it was D-2 for the Allied landings in North Africa, Opn **Torch.** After this Pétain extended the admiral's active duty status beyond the statutory retirement age.

When all French resistance ended in North Africa on 11 Nov 42 with the "DARLAN deal," and the Germans occupied southern France, Laborde's fleet was a great prize. But when Darlan "invited" Laborde to "direct the fleet towards West Africa" the Vichy admiral used the classic *mot de Cambronne* (Merde!) in refusing flatly (Verrier, 169), and he subsequently refused Darlan's request to take the fleet to North African ports (Larousse). The admiral also ignored de Gaulle's plea to take "the course both duty and honor commanded" (*Unity,* 55). Laborde announced publicly on 12 November,

with Adm Marquis's backing, that he would defend his base against all comers. He sacked three senior officers who refused to swear obedience (Larousse), but then took steps to weaken the port's strong land defenses. (Napoleon started his rise to fame by driving the British fleet from Toulon after taking the surrounding hills, from which field artillery can dominate the harbor.) On 18 Nov 42 Laborde authorized the withdrawal of 20 infantry battalions that had been sent a few days earlier as reinforcements. On the 26th he prescribed a system of leave–granting that crippled normal security precautions. (Larousse.)

The Germans had abandoned an attempt to take Toulon on 11 November, meeting unexpected resistance, but before dawn on 27 November they launched a surprise attack that quickly secured a foothold. At 5:29 AM Laborde ordered his demolition plan executed, this in accordance with orders Darlan had given back on 24 June 40 and that AUPHAN reiterated on 11 Nov 42. The decision cost France her most powerful surviving force, three battleships, eight cruisers, 17 destroyers, 16 PT boats, 16 submarines, and about 60 transports (*Unity,* 55). Five submarine skippers braved German minefields to leave the harbor, and three made it (ibid.). The French also blew up much of Toulon's naval infrastructure.

Many including Hitler assumed that the French admiral acted from anglophobia. But Laborde was known to be pro-British, *calling himself* an anglophile! (Larousse.) Critics argued that the French should have fought their way out, but Toulon was ringed by German mine fields and Laborde's ships were sitting ducks for the Luftwaffe, not to mention field artillery.

On 28 Mar 47 the High Court of Justice condemned Laborde to death, but Vincent AURIOL had the sentence commuted to "perpetual detention."

LA CHAMBRE, Guy. French politician. 1898-1975. Born in Paris and admitted to the bar there, he was a member of Aristide Briand's staff (1920-21) before turning to politics. La

Chambre started as an independent deputy of the left. He was mayor of Saint Servan (1932-40) and held a number of high posts at the national level before becoming a radical socialist deputy from St Malo in 1938 and succeeding Pierre COT as air minister 18 Jan 38. French air power had hit new lows (Pertinax, 133n), and La Chambre worked effectively to improve combat readiness, but French industry was so flabby that he had to purchase many planes in America.

La Chambre left his ministry on 21 Mar 40, during the Phony War, and three days later was mobilized as a captain of reserves (Larousse). Still a deputy, he followed the government to Vichy and was among those who made Pétain head of state on 10 July 40. La Chambre visited the US but returned to face charges of treason. Interned on 19 Sep 40 with other top officials of the Third Republic, the former air minister argued effectively at the **Riom Trial** on 4-5 Mar 42 that he had helped put the French-British air forces on a par with those of Germany and Italy in the spring of 1940 (Larousse).

La Chambre reentered politics after the liberation, resumed the mayoralty of St Malo on 26 Oct 47, and had a major role in rebuilding the historic city. (Larousse.)

LA GUARDIA, Fiorello (Henry). US politician. 1882-1947. The "Little Flower" (*fiorello*), "short, swart, tousled" and dynamic (CB 40), was born 11 Dec 82 in NYC. His immigrant Italian parents, the mother a Sephardic Jewess from Venice, were accomplished musicians. After being reared on various frontier posts, where his father was an army bandmaster, and returning to Europe around 1901, he joined the US Consular Service. He returned to NYC, became an attorney, US congressman, and was mayor of NYC, 1933-45. Concurrently he served from Aug 40 on the Canada-US Joint Defense Board, and in 1941 became the first director of the **Office of Civilian Defense.** Eleanor ROOSEVELT was assistant director. La Guardia resigned on 10 Feb 42 and was succeeded by James M. Landis. In Mar-Dec 46, the year before his death, La Guardia was director general of UNRRA.

LAMMERS, Hans Heinrich. German jurist. 1879-1962. The unimaginative, brutal bureaucrat was born 27 May 79 in Lublinitz, Upper Silesia. He became an expert on constitutional law, was chief of Reich chancellery from 1933, and in late 1939 became ministerial counselor for Reich defense. The jurist was Hitler's most important subordinate in matters of state until BORMANN succeeded Rudolf HESS in 1941 and thereafter dictated law to judges of the Third Reich (Davidson, *Trial,* 106). But from Jan 43 Lammers presided over cabinet meetings in Hitler's absence, and with BORMANN and KEITEL cleared orders signed by Hitler. Finally a victim of Bormann's intrigues, Lammers was arrested for involvement in GOERING's initiative on 23 Apr 45 about to take from Hitler as head of state.

The Nuremberg tribunal charged Lammers with giving legal authority to anti-Semitic acts and sentenced him to 20 years prisonment. But the Nazi jurist was freed on 16 Dec 52. He died 4 Jan 62 in Duesseldorf.

LANGSDORFF, Hans. German naval officer. 1890-1939. Aboard *Admiral Graf Spee* Langsdorff tied the Royal Navy in knots for 10 weeks while ranging from the **Denmark Strait** to South America, Madagascar, and back to the mouth of the Rio de la Plata off Uruguay. Here he finally was spotted early 13 Dec 39 by a cruiser squadron under Henry HARWOOD, who directed an audacious attack despite the great German advantage in guns and armor. With almost two dozen damaging hits, 37 dead, and 57 wounded, and himself stunned by a blow to the head, Langsdorff withdrew into the neutral port of Montevideo. Failing to get further extension of time allowed in neutral waters, the confused captain sailed at 6:15 PM on the 17th as an immense crowd watched. Convinced that Harwood had been reinforced by *Ark Royal* and CA *Renown* (actually 1,000 miles away), Langsdorff scuttled *Spee* in the shallow estuary. Having transferred his crew and 299 captured British merchant seamen to his supply ship, *Altmark,* and being interned in Argentina, Langsdorff shot himself the night of 19-20 Dec 39. (Philip VIAN liberated the *Altmark* prisoners.)

LATTRE DE TASSIGNY, Jean-Marie Gabriel de. French general. 1889-1952. De Lattre was born 2 Feb 89 at Mouilleron-en-Pareds (Vendée). He entered St Cyr in 1908, chose the cavalry, and was assigned to the 12th Deragoon Regt. From the opening engagements of 1914 Lt de Lattre saw action with his horse-mounted regiment, but in 1915 he transferred to the infantry. With the Vendée Regt (93d Inf) he survived 16 months in the Verdun sector. By war's end he was a captain, a battalion commander, four times WIA, and he had won eight citations.

Highlights of de Lattre's normal "peacetime" assignments included four years of war in the Rif, where he was CofS of the Taza region. Capt de Lattre was invalided home in 1926 with a severe wound. Toward the end of 1932 he was selected to serve on the staff of WEYGAND in the Superior War Council. Now a lieutenant colonel, he retained the post under GEORGES until 1935, when he was promoted to full colonel and given command of a regiment at Metz. In Mar 39 he attained general officer rank.

Général de Brigade de Lattre de Tassigny took command of the elite 14th Inf Div soon after France declared war on 3 Sep 39. Rushed to the Sedan area when the Germans broke through, the division ended up around Rethel and defended it for three weeks. De Lattre held his division together in the retreat southward—the Battle of France—fighting delaying actions on the Marne, on the Loire, at Nevers, and ending up in the Massif Central near Clermont-Ferrand.

De Lattre maintained command of the 14th Div in the Armistice Army but served as military commandant of the Puy-de-Dôme Dept (W of Lyons), then headed the XIII Military Region. With headquarters in the Château d'Opme he created the first officer cadre school, on which others in France and one in Algeria were modelled. As a disciple of Marshal Lyautey, de Lattre stressed moral values, social conscience, and the vital role of civil-military relationships. (Larousse.)

The general was ordered to Tunisia in Sep 41. He had serious disagreements with JUIN, an old friend and rival, who was his superior in French North Africa. Recalled in Jan 42 on suspicion of having pro-Allied sentiments he had time to begin restoring the Mareth Line, which the Italians—with designs on Tunisia— had insisted on having demilitarized. Replaced by BARRE, de Lattre was assigned to the 16th Inf Div Hq at Montpellier, in SE France near the Mediterranean. Ten months later, when the Allies landed in North Africa and the Germans started marching into the unoccupied zone on

11 Nov 42, the Armistice Army was ordered to greet the enemy with open arms. But de Lattre left Montpellier with his staff in hopes of resisting. He was arrested and held at Toulouse before being sent to Ft Montluc in Lyons. On 9 Jan 43 he was sentenced to 10 years of prison for abandoning his post and for "attempted treason." Transferred on 2 Feb 43 to the prison at Riom, de Lattre escaped on the night of 2-3 Sep 43. The jail break was planned by his wife and son Bernard and executed by Free French agents. The general was flown to London by **Lysander,** and in late Dec 43 he reported to GIRAUD in Algiers. De Lattre became largely responsible for reorganizing, rearming, and training the French. (*EP,* 1644.)

On 15 Apr 44 de Lattre was named commander of all French forces earmarked for the invasion of southern France (Opn **Anvil-Dragoon**). With headquarters in Naples, the French were organized into the 1st and 2d Corps comprising the 1st Armd Div and five infantry divisions: the 1st French, 3d Algerian, 2d Moroccan, and 9th Colonial (Senegalese) plus the Group of Tabors (**Goumiers**). The first mission, executed primarily by the Senegalese and at great cost, was to take Elba, 17-20 June 43.

For Anvil-Dragoon de Lattre served initially under the operational control of Alexander PATCH, CG 7th US Army. Gen Joseph de Monsabert sailed from Taranto with his 2d Corps (1st French Light Div and 3d Algerian Div) as the follow up force behind TRUSCOTT's 6th US Corps. BETHOUART's 1st Corps (the other French divisions listed above) were the "build up force." While the Americans drove rapidly north, the French entered Arles on 24 Aug 44 and Avignon the next day, while others had the grinding task of taking Toulon and Marseilles on the 27th and 28th. (Eisenhower insisted on having these ports quickly to sustain his drive through northern France into Germany.) Now free to join the exploitation phase of the campaign, de Lattre pursued up the right (west) bank of the Rhone. (Allied strategy is sketched under TRUSCOTT.)

Jake Devers's 6th AG became operational at Lyons on 15 Sep 44, and four days later de LATTRE's Army B was redesignated the 1st French Army. About this time he absorbed thousands of French recruits and redeployed thousands of black African troops who could not function in cold weather.

After overcoming heavy resistance in the Vosges, the French took strategic Belfort on 20 Nov 44, a day after an armored task force became the first Allied troops to reach the Rhine (Larousse). In an attempt to consolidate all French forces de Lattre had LECLERC's 2d Div transferred to his army in late November. But a strategic difference of opinion developed between the two national heroes during the campaign to reduce the **Colmar pocket,** and Leclerc rejoined Patch's 7th Army in mid-Dec 44 at his own request *(EP*, 2362n).

When the Germans counterattacked into Alsace on 16 Dec 44 de Lattre sided with de Gaulle in protesting Eisenhower's plans to abandon Strasbourg. So while Patch moved on into Germany, the 1st French Army had to send detachments to defend northern Alsace. And reduction of the Colmar pocket, 20 Jan-9 Feb 45, required heavy US reinforcements, substantially delaying the Allied advance; de Lattre could not resume the strategic offensive until 28 March. Three days later two French colonial divisions crossed the Rhine at two points SW of Heidelberg. De Lattre then wheeled south. The 1st Corps took Karlsruhe and Baden Baden and drove into the Black Forest for a brilliant maneuver through the heights above Kehl before entering Wurtemberg. The 2d Corps took Pforzheim and turned toward the army's eastern boundary to cooperate with the 6th US Corps in taking Stuttgart. Bypassing large pockets of German resistance, de Lattre drove across the upper Danube to the border of Switzerland (Lake Constance) and to Bregenz (just inside Austria).

Since 17 Aug 44 the 1st French Army had liberated a third of their country, had overrun 50,000 square kilometers of Germany, and had taken 250,000 prisoners. French casualties were 14,000 killed and 42,000 wounded. (Larousse.)

De Lattre represented France at the formal German surrender in Berlin on 9 May 45. Three months later, after deactivating his army in Germany, he became CGS in Paris. After the Western European Union was created, de Lattre was commander of its ground forces. On 6 Dec 50, when a crisis developed in Indo-China, de Lattre was sent there as high commissioner and CinC of French forces. Within a month he restored morale and inflicted a severe defeat on Vietminh regulars at Vinh Yenh, 14-17 Jan 51 and followed through to outwit the insurgents.

But from March of that year his health began to decline from what was later diagnosed as cancer in the right hip, which caused him increasing pain. His son Bernard, a lieutenant serving with a Vietnamese unit, was killed in an outpost action on 30 May 51.

The general had the situation under control, politically and militarily, when he took a month's leave in August. His illness now diagnosed as a serious cancer, he returned to find GIAP undertaking the new strategy of drawing the French north into the jungle so he could infiltrate rice-producing areas, particularly the Mekong Delta. Knowing he did not have long to live but wanting to show his successor how to carry on, de Lattre mounted an assault of waterborne, parachute, and mechanized troops under Salan and de Linaräs that took the vital communications center of Hoa Binh on 15 October. Saying farewell in the town on 19 November and handing over command to Salan he was invalided home the next day. (See Clayton, 139-64, for de Lattre's post-WWII career.)

After several major operations the general died 11 Jan 52 in Paris. His last words two days earlier in a brief period of consciousness, and having been told he would be created a Marshal of France, were "Where is Bernard?" The promotion was dated 15 Jan 52.

LAUREL, José Pacaino. Filipino politician. 1891-1959. A wealthy lawyer educated in England, France, the US, and the Philippines, Laurel became secretary of the interior in 1923 and associate justice of the supreme court in 1936. In Oct 43 the Japanese installed him as president of the Philippines. The anti-American puppet's government never won popular support, and the Japanese evacuated it to Tokyo in 1945. Laurel's trial in Manila on 143 counts of treason was never completed. Amnestied in 1948, Laurel was in the Senate 1951-57 and lost to Elpidio Quirno in a bid for the presidency.

LAVAL, Pierre. French politician. 1883-1945. A notorious collaborator who became head of the Vichy government, the swarthy, saturnine little Laval epitomized the worst morality and the best skills of French politics.

He was an Auvergnac, born 28 June 83 at Châteldon, 20km SE of Vichy. Of petit bourgeois origins, earning degrees in law and natural sciences, he quickly showed a genius for business and politics. In 1903 Laval became a Socialist Party member and in 1907 was admitted to the Paris bar. He was an effective orator and politician who quickly became known as a master of compromise, duplicity, and opportunism.

As a recently elected radical socialist member of the Chamber of Deputies in 1914 and a pacifist, he nevertheless served in the war. Defeated for reelection in 1919, he resumed law practice and achieved financial success as a newspaper publisher. Having gone through a Leninist phase and abandoned socialism, Laval returned to the Chamber of Deputies as a conservative. (It has been observed that "Laval" reads the same from the Left or the Right.)

The next year he held the first in a long series of ministerial posts in the constantly changing French governments. A senator in 1927, foreign minister at various times, he was premier in 1931-32 and 1935-36. Laval worked with Aristide Briand to establish friendly relations with Germany and in 1935 negotiated the mutual assistance pact with Russia. But his financial policies, pro-Axis leanings—particularly the collaboration with Sir Samuel HOARE to oppose application of sanctions against Italy—and defeatist outlook, sent Laval into political eclipse as Hitler's war approached.

Back in private life for four years, but still a senator and vocal critic of the government, Laval continued to build a commercial empire based on newspapers, printing, and radio. Although in Bordeaux from 14 June 40, he had no important role in bringing Pétain to power. (Pierre Thibault sketch of Laval in Larousse, hereafter cited as P.T.) On 16 June he declined to join the new government, spurning the portfolio of foreign minister. He did not figure in the political debate until 21 June, when he headed the opposition to President LEBRUN's taking refuge in North Africa. On 1 July he had a decisive role in seating the new government at Vichy, conveniently close to Châteldon (above).

As VP of the council of state Laval used persuasion, intrigue, and threat in the national assembly vote of 10 July 40 that gave Marshal Pétain full constitutional powers. Two days later, having won the elderly marshal's begrudging respect as a politician (P. T.), Laval was officially designated as Pétain legal successor and was de facto head of government. Laval believed sincerely that the future of France—

hence of himself—lay in siding with Germany, politically and idealogically (P. T.). He made contact in Paris on 16 July 40 with Otto ABETZ, who as the soon-to-be German ambassador had instructions to exploit existing political differences in France. Laval had the right man.

Pétain announced a decision on 11 Oct 40 to find ways of "collaboration in all domains." (Thus the odious word collaboration became current in France.) Laval met Hitler at Montoire on 22 Oct 40, followed two days later by the old marshal. As covered more fully under PETAIN, the Montoire meetings signified little other than a vague willingness of France and Germany to work together.

Although viewed with contempt by Hitler and ignored by Mussolini, Laval had strong support from Otto ABETZ. Meeting with the ambassador in Paris on 31 Oct 40 and 10 days later with Goering, Laval proposed military collaboration. Now truly a loose cannon and not keeping anybody else in the government informed of his initiatives, Laval was abruptly dismissed on the evening of 13 Dec 40 and arrested on suspicion of planning a coup d'état. DARLAN took over Laval's functions. Laval was only briefly under home arrest at Châteldon until Abetz had him released on 17 December and brought to Paris with a German escort. Abandoning his fiefdom in the Massif Central near Vichy, Laval chose to live under German protection in Paris. But a pistol-wielding youth named Paul Collette scored four hits on Laval during a departure ceremony on 27 Aug 41 for the first **LVF** contingent to join the Wehrmacht in Russia.

The Germans were in no hurry to reinstall Laval because they already had the collaboration of Pétain, who mustered great popular support. But Abetz, whose career depended on the closest possible collaboration, wanted Laval back in Vichy and Pétain was finding he needed a strong arm. Pétain had his first of four meetings with Laval on 18 Jan 41, and Abetz put on pressure by threating that Hitler would give France a Gauleiter. Repudiating the "men of 13 December" (above), the marshal agreed on 18 Apr 42 to recall Laval.

Now the evil Auvergnac became head of government, the old marshal a figurehead. With the ministerial portfolios of the interior, foreign affairs, and information, Laval purged the government of his enemies and reduced all but three ministers to the role of clerk. The survivors, loyal supporters, were Pierre Cathala, Aben Bonnard, and Jean Bichelonne. (P. T.) "I'll bring the French happiness whether they want it or not," said Laval. "I hope for a German victory because without it bolshevism will install itself tomorrow everywhere."

Laval agreed to send the Germans three skilled laborers for each POW repatriated. He authorized creation of a fascist militia to combat the resistance, and he increased the role of terror. The private, volunteer LVF was reorganized on 18 July 42 as the official "Légion tricolore." Jews in both French zones were rounded up by French police, 2-23 July 42, and sent to camps. From 28 Sep 42 the Gestapo was authorized to hunt resistance people in the unoccupied zone. (P. T.)

Hitler summoned Laval after occupying Vichy France on 11 Nov 42 and demanded use of facilities in Tunisia. Gen Alphonse JUIN had opposed this a year earlier, but the Germans now were allowed to send major forces to Tunisia. Wanting to be less dependent on the Third Reich for internal order, Laval created the French Milice by a law of 30 Jan 43, making himself its chief. He instituted a mandatory labor law (16 Feb 43), and offered incentives for collaboration.

Three months after the Allies consolidated their beachhead in Normandy the Germans ordered Laval on 18 Aug 44 to move his government to Belfort. Three weeks later they installed it at Sigmaringen (on the Danube in S Germany). Pétain and Laval renounced all political activity and began preparing to face French justice. On 2 May 45 Laval got permission to spend three months in Spain, where he was interned near Barcelona. Leaving there on 30 July for to Linz, Austria, he was turned over to US authorities and extradited to France. On 1 August he entered Fresnes prison and was called to testify in court against PETAIN. Himself charged with aiding the enemy and with violating state security, Laval put up a brilliant defense before the high court of justice despite insufficient time to prepare. (A French election was coming.) Quickly condemned on 9 Oct 45 to death, national indignity, and loss of all possessions, he died bravely before a firing squad at Fresnes Prison in Paris on 15 Oct 45.

"Laval was considerably less than the legend," writes an American scholar. "He was neither an invincible cajoler nor an unscrupulous turncoat." (Paxton, *Vichy,* 25.) His prison notes were edited by daughter Josée, wife of Count René de CHAMBRUN, and published as *The Diaries of Pierre Laval* (1948). "The essential study of Laval in any language," wrote Paxton in 1972, is Geoffrey Warner, *Pierre Laval and the Eclipse of France* (1968). As is apparent from my numerous source citations, I have relied heavily on Pierre Thibault's biographical essay in Larousse.

LAVOCHKIN, Semyon Alekseyevich. Soviet aircraft designer. 1900-60. Son of a teacher, Lavochkin was born 29 Sep 00 in Smolensk. From 1927 he was an aviation engineer. In 1935 he stepped up to be Russia's chief aircraft designer but went underground in 1937-38, escaping incarceration with PETLYAKOV and TUPELOV in an NKVD "design bureau." He was not a party member until 1953. With military rank, Gen Maj (Engineer-Technical Service) Lavochkin meanwhile supervised design of the LAGG-3, LA-5, LA-7, and LA-9 fighters along with other WWII aircraft. After the war he designed the first Soviet plane to reach the speed of sound, the LA-176. Lavochkin died 9 June 60 in Moscow. (Scarecrow).

LAYCOCK, Robert Edward. British commando leader. 1907-68. "Lucky" Laycock was born 18 Apr 07 in London, son of a brigadier with an outstanding military record as a Territorial officer of the Royal Artillery (DSO, KCMG). Bob Laycock's mother was the marchioness of Devonshire. *(DNB.)* Inspired by his father, young Laycock went from Eton to Sandhurst and in 1927 was commissioned in the Royal Horse Guards. Although a keen outdoorsman, the tall, pleasant young officer was an avid reader, an excellent mathematician, and he became expert in several fields of military engineering and chemical warfare. *(CB 44;* Fergusson, *The Watery Maze,* 294.)

After being with BEF Hq in France in 1939 Maj Laycock missed action in the battle of Flanders because he was selected for the first wartime course at **Camberley.** Fearing another chemical warfare staff assignment, Laycock volunteered for the first commandos being formed under Sir Roger KEYES and was accepted. Promoted to lieutenant colonel he took three new commando battalions from the UK to reach Suez in mid-Mar 40. His commandos were augmented by a local unit to become known as "Layforce."

Much went wrong as raiders discovered the limitations of their boats in rough water and the difficulties of working with supporting aircraft and mother ships including submarines and destroyers. An attack on Bardia had limited success the night of 19-20 Apr 40 after being aborted three nights earlier (Fergusson, 97).

Laycock took about 800 officers and men by destroyer from Alexandria to Crete, landing at Suda Bay the night of 26-27 Mar 41, when the British were beginning to evacuate troops from Greece to Crete . Serving under Gen Bernard FREYBERG, Laycock's lightly armed troops could do no more than help in the rear guard action. Only about 200 commandos got away in the British evacuation, which ended the night of 30-31 May. On the last ship with Laycock was his personal assistant, Capt Eveyn Waugh, who used the experience in his novel *Officers and Gentlemen* (1955). Largely because of the high losses in Crete, Layforce was disbanded four months later except for No. 11 (Scottish) Commando. Now a full colonel, Laycock was on orders to return home for a new assignment (below) when he led the Scottish Commando on a raid which struck the night of 17-18 Nov 41 on what was erroneously reported to be ROMMEL's Hq. Lt Col Geoffrey KEYES, the admiral's son, was among those KIA, and the only survivors were Laycock and a Sgt Terry. After 41 harrowing days in the desert they reached friendly forces, who soon got a hornet from higher headquarters: "Please state why Laycock was 1 hr. 20 mins. late for Christmas dinner." Lucky Laycock said later he owed survival to knowing the habits of foxes and never hunted again *(DNB)*. The commando leader had a copy of Kenneth Grahame's *The Wind in the Willows,* which he read aloud to his companion during quiet moments of their ordeal. Sgt Terry's first words on reaching safety were, "Safe at last! and now, thank God, I shan't have to hear any more of that bloody Mr Toad." (Fergusson, 105.)

"From the ashes of Layforce there arose Major David Stirling's Special Air Service Regiment, which, sometimes in association with the Long Range Desert Group, was to perform such astonishing feats in the Desert and later on the Continent," writes Fergusson in his story of Combined Operations *(The Watery Maze,* 102).

Again promoted, Brigadier Laycock became head of the Special Services Brigade. In concert with MOUNTBATTEN's Combined Operations Command, the brigadier organized and trained all "special forces" in the UK and directed commando raids on the Continent. In 1943 he led a commando assault in Sicily, winning the DSO, and at Salerno he commanded US Rangers and British Commandos in an 11-day fight on the left flank. More than half of the 738 British officers and men were casualties, including the 6th Duke of Wellington (KIA).

The 36-year-old Laycock was promoted to major general in Oct 43 and two months later succeeded his close friend MOUNTBATTEN as chief of combined operations, holding the post until 1947. He retired to the family estate at Wiseton, near Doncaster (West Riding, Yorkshire).

Knighted in 1954 (KCMG) and made governor and CinC at Malta at a time of dicey negotiations with the Independence Party. These broke down in 1958, but Laycock was hailed as "a much esteemed and effective governor" *(DNB)*. His term of office extended twice, Sir Robert retired again in 1959 and held honorific posts including colonel commandant of the Special Air Service and of the Sherwood Rangers Yeomanry (1960); high sheriff, Nottinghamshire, (1954-55); and lord-lieutenant, Nottinghamshire (1960) He died 10 Mar 68 of heart attack suffered while walking from church at Wiseton. *(DNB.)*

LEAHY, William Daniel. US admiral. 1875-1959. He was STARK's predecessor as CNO, ambassador to Vichy (1941-42), then CofS to President Roosevelt from 21 July 42 and chairman of the JCS. Leahy then was President Truman's CofS until 1949.

Born in Hampton, Iowa, on 6 May 75, Leahy graduated from the USNA in 1897 (35/47) and spent almost half of his 46 years of active duty at sea. As skipper of the secretary of the navy's dispatch boat, *Dolphin,* 1915-16, he began a close friendship with Franklin D. Roosevelt, who appointed him CNO in Jan 37. The admiral retired on 1 Aug 39 after reaching the statutory age; meanwhile he was named governor of Puerto Rico on 6 June 39.

This pleasant assignment was cut short by a telegram from FDR that sent him to Vichy as ambassador. Adm and Mrs Leahy reached Vichy on 5 Jan 41, the day Robert MURPHY left Algiers to draft what became the Murphy-Weygand Agreement. Having put this in final form the ambassador found he could do little about accomplishing his primary mission of saving the French fleet at Toulon for the Allies. Nor could he keep the Germans from tightening their grip on Vichy. When Pierre LAVAL was made the supreme authority in occupied France, 27 Apr 42, the US ambassador made his final call on Pétain. But because Mrs Leahy had died on 21 April from a postoperative embolism, the admiral did not leave Vichy until 1 May 42. He did not resign the ambassadorship.

America had gone to war, and George Marshall saw that FDR needed a senior military officer as personal adviser and point of contact with the three service chiefs. Earnest KING opposed the idea until Marshall suggested that Adm Leahy be given the job (Leahy, *I Was There,* 95-96). FDR procrastinated—not understanding why he needed any help. But the appointment was made on 6 July 42. The admiral resigned as ambassador on 18 July, assumed his new duties two days later, and FDR announced to the press on the 21st that Leahy would be "chief of staff to the commander in chief of the United States Army and Navy" (Parrish, *R&M,* 251). With his contempt for orderly bureaucracy and still not fully understanding what Marshall had in mind, the president said the admiral would perform leg work for the commander in chief (ibid.).

"The office was without precedent in American military annals," Leahy would write, and its scope had not been prescribed. Gen ISMAY held a similar position under Churchill but was not a member of the British chiefs of staff. Leahy would belong to the comparable American body, the JCS, and also to the CCS. Further, the admiral was adviser to the American *commander in chief* whereas Ismay was military adviser to the British *prime minister.* It is remarkable that Leahy, Marshall, King, and Hap Arnold were able to work together so effectively. Leahy served as chairman of the JCS, maintaining daily contact with the president. He and Harry Hopkins were the only advisers authorized to originate messages from the White House to Churchill and other British leaders *(S&S).*

Characterized as merely "a forthright naval officer, more affected by personal likes and dislikes than by partisan issues" (Murphy, *Diplomat,* 269), blunt-speaking (Buchanan), and "cranky" (Bernard Feis), the admiral did not have a decisive role on issues of military strategy *(S&S).* Rather, he was FDR's primary source of information in this field and the president's senior military adviser at international conferences.

Leahy's promotion to the five-star rank of fleet admiral was confirmed on 15 Dec 44 but backdated a month to make him the senior active-duty officer. On the death of FDR (12 Apr 45) Leahy retained his post under Truman until retiring on 25 Mar 49. He died on 20 July 59 at Bethesda Naval Hospital, Md.

Leahy's excellent memoirs are *I Was There* (New York: Whittlesey House, 1950).

LEAR, Ben. US general. 1879-. Born at Hamilton, Ontario, on 12 May 79, at the age of two he moved with his family from Canada to Colorado. During the Spanish-American War he was an NCO, 1st Colorado Inf Vols, in the Philippines. On 12 June 01 Lear was commission as a regular in the 15th Cav. He became a crack marksman and horseman, participating in the 1912 Olympic Games in Stockholm. In WWI he became a temporary colonel with the WDGS in Washington. More than six feet tall, physically fit, and a stern disciplinarian, Lear was one of the army's senior generals on the eve of WWII. He was promoted to lieutenant general on 1 Oct 40. Three weeks later he took command of 2d Army Hq when it was formed in Chicago. Responsible for training new units, he moved to Memphis, Tenn, in December. His force was defeated decisively in the **Louisiana maneuvers of 1941.**

The crusty general then had a fatal career setback. He was on a Memphis golf course when a truck convoy of the 110th QM Regt rolled by. The unit was part of the 35th Div, Missouri NG, one of several the War Department had directed Lear to bring up to an acceptable standard of discipline. At the sight of women golfers, the troops began whistling and emitting wolf calls. Seeing a golfer teeing off, they gave forth such high spirited civilian-in-uniform cries as "Fore!" and "Hey buddy, need a caddy?" *(CB 42).* Lear happened to be the "buddy." When he ordered the troops to behave, these fearless freedom fighters told him to shut up. (Pogue, *Marshall,* II, 100-1.) The general directed that the convoy drive on to Ft Robinson, North Little Rock, Ark, a distance of 150 miles, then come back to Memphis and return to Ft Robinson. Further, each soldier was to dismount and march 15 miles in the record-breaking heat *(CB 42).* The prestigious *Arkansas Gazette* broke the story (personal knowledge) and the national press blew it up. Sen Bennett Clark of Missouri later tried, unsuccessfully, to block Lear's permanent promotion to lieutenant general.

"Yoo-Hoo" Ben Lear, accused of seeking personal vengeance, maintained that his response to "loose conduct and rowdyism" was appropriate. (*CB 42;* Pogue, *Marshall,* II, 100-1.) Lear headed the Central Defense Command from July 41 to his retirement on 31 May 43 (succeeded by FREDENDALL). After Lesley J. McNAIR was killed in Normandy, Lt Gen Lear was recalled briefly as CG, AGF, from July until Dec 44 (*AA,* 603). Succeeded by STILWELL, he left on 25 Jan 45 to become Eisenhower's deputy theater commander with special duties for personnel and morale as head a new Theater Manpower Section. The shortage of front line troops had become critical and Marshall had nominated Lt Gen Lear as a "loyal, stern and drastic" officer to take action *(EP,* 2408-11; Weigley, *ETO,* 662-64). In grade since 1 Oct 40, Lear was promoted after the war to general on the retired list.

LEBER, Julius. German resistance figure. 1891-1945. He was born poor at Biesheim, Alsace, on 16 Nov 91 and became a Social democrat (Wistrich). After completing his doctorate in political science at Freiburg in 1920 he was editor of the *Volksbote* in Luebeck and from 1924 was in the Reichstag. A marked man when the Nazis came to power on 30 Jan 33, Leber was arrested the next day but released after being ill-treated. He was arrested again on 23 Mar 33 and imprisoned until 1937 as a "danger to the state" (Hoffmann, *Resistance,* 34). Dr Leber then became a major resistance figure. In various cabinet lists of the conspirators he was long the nominee for minister of the interior, and even as an alternate to GOERDLER as Reich chancellor (Hoffmann, 367).

Leber and fellow social democrat Adolf Reichwein were intermediaries with the central committee (CC) of the German CP. On 5 July 44

the two men, betrayed by a Gestapo agent (Hermann Rambow) who had penetrated the CC, were arrested. (Hoffmann, 363-64.) On 20 Oct 44 the people's court condemned Leber to death for high treason. Like many others including GOERDLER he was kept alive for many months while the Gestapo undertook to get more information. On 5 Jan 45 Leber was hanged in Ploetzensee prison. (Hoffmann, 519.)

LEBRUN, Albert François. French statesman. 1871-1950. From a farming family of Mercy-le-Haut in Lorraine, Lebrun was first in his class the Ecole Polytechnique (1890) and two years later at the Ecole Superieure des Mines. He entered politics early, held a number of ministerial posts, and headed an unsuccessful effort to extend the Maginot Line to the Channel. (Larousse.) Lebrun was elected president of France in 1932 and reelected in 1939. As an honorable but somewhat ineffectual politician, his primary role had been to choose premiers for the rapidly changing governments of the Third Republic. He left Paris with the government and continued to preside over its deliberations, first at Cangé, 12 and 13 June 40, then in Bordeaux. On the evening of the 16th he tried unsuccessfully to block Paul Reynaud's ouster. Passing the office of premier to PETAIN and remaining president, Lebrun mustered the votes to move the government to North Africa. Many ministers left to be caught up in the **Massilia** affair, and in a stormy confrontation on the 21st Laval threatened Lebrun with charging the fugitive ministers with desertion. (The president of the republic had been misled into believing that the Germans were not advancing beyond the Loire.) Lebrun kept his post as the government moved to Clermont-Ferrand on 29 June and on to Vichy three days later. But on 13 July 40 Lebrun moved to Vizille in the Italian occupation zone but without formally resigning, as FLANDIN proposed 7 July.

In 1943, after the Allies found GIRAUD incapable of rallying French support in North Africa, Churchill and Roosevelt considered replacing the general with the man who was still the legitimate president of France (de Gaulle, *Unity,* 181). Nothing came of this, but Lebrun was sounded out a few months later by emissaries acting for BADOGLIO. The Italians apparently hoped that if the Frenchman later accepted sanctuary in Rome he could somehow be used as a bargaining chip. Lebrun declined, telling the Italians they still were enemies of France. But when Hitler learned of this contact he had Lebrun arrested. Imprisoned at Lyons on 23 Aug 43, then deported and held only briefly at Itter, Austria, 3 Sep-6 Oct 43, Lebrun was sent home because of failing health and kept under surveillance. (Larousse.) He died in Paris on 6 Mar 50, the year his second volume of memoirs, *Témoignage* (1949-50), was published.

LECLERC de Hautecloque, Jacques Philippe. French general. 1902-47. Philippe François Marie Leclerc de Hautecloque was born 22 Nov 02 at his ancestral estate in Picardy near Amiens. His lineage has been traced back eight centuries (Larousse). Hautecloque was a brilliant student of the humanities before entering St Cyr in 1922 and was commissioned in the cavalry. Small, birdlike, and fragile looking, he became a rugged combat veteran in Morocco. When the battle of Flanders began on 10 May 40 he was a captain serving as an operations officer in the 4th Div, which—in accordance with the Dyle plan—advanced into Belgium. By 28 May his division was among five others (including JUIN's) whose survivors were driven back for a stand in Lille. Hautecloque got authority to make his way back to the French lines when these troops were encircled. He ended up with the armored group that Gen Buisson was forming NE of Paris around Meaux. On 15 June Capt de Hautecloque received a serious head wound during a delaying action on the Aube River, and he was evacuated to a hospital at Tonnerre, 190km SE of Paris. Again evading capture he reached Paris and on 25 June heard of de Gaulle's "call to honor" from London. (Larousse.)

Joining his wife and six children in their temporary haven near Bordeaux he left them on 3 July 40 and fled through Spain and Portugal to London. On 25 July, his head still bandaged, he reported to de Gaulle and was ordered to immediately join a delegation headed for French Equatorial Africa to rally anti-Vichy resistance. At this time he adopting the nom de guerre Jacques Philippe Leclerc to protect his family from German retribution. Having been promoted, Maj Leclerc left England on 6 Aug 40 by hydroplane with René Pleven and Hettier de Boislambert. In Lagos they were met by Col de Larminat, who came from Syria. Pleven went to Chad and Larminat to the Congo. Leclerc and Boislambert went to the Cameroons where, joined by others already on the ground, they overcame all Vichy resistance in a series of well-planned, bloodless operations. De Gaulle's emissaries quickly brought the Equatorial Africa-Cameroons block into the Free French camp (de Gaulle, *Unity,* 111-12).

On 22 Nov 40, just after these operations had ended, Col Leclerc (promoted early in the campaign) became military commandant of Chad. The French colony had a 1,200km frontier with the Italian colony of Libya. Leclerc promptly mounted a raid across the border to Mourzouk in Jan 41, and two months later he took the oasis of Koufra from its 350-man garrison. The 39-year-old Leclerc was promoted in Aug 41 to *général de brigade*.

In Nov 41 he was ordered to launch an offensive northward to liberate the **Fezzan** from the Italians and then consider linking up with the British 8th Army. (Montgomery was facing Rommel at El Alamein.)

Phase 1 involved incredible logistical problems, vast distances, arduous terrain including the 10,000-foot Tibesti mountains; desert temperatures reached 140 degrees Fahrenheit in the sun and 160 degrees inside a tank. Leclerc had 1,000 vehicles and a mixed bag of 3,250 exotic troops: the *Régiment de Tirailleurs Sénégalais du Tchad,* the Tibesti Meharistes camel corps, a recently trained French tank unit, some British officers, and the Bretagne squadron of veteran pilots in 12 obsolescent planes. *(CB 44.)*

Delayed by Montgomery's halt on the Al Agheila line, Leclerc launched his offensive on 16 Dec 42. A month later he overcame the last major Italian resistance in southern Libya—France's first major military accomplishment since the defeat of 1940. In two years Leclerc had accomplished "a series of tours de force: the formation of desert columns, the establishment of supply lines, the . . . advance of reconnaissance elements into the heart of the Italian positions" (de Gaulle, *Unity,* 68).

After moving another 1,500 miles north through the desert the "Chad column" entered Tripoli on 25 Jan 43 as the 8th Army arrived. Readily placing himself under Montgomery's command to comprise "Force L," Leclerc had a significant role on the left flank in breaking the Mareth Line and the subsequent advance on

Tunis. Force L was moved quickly to Sabratha in Tripoli, where on 14 May 43 it was redesignated the 2d French Light Infantry Div. Promoted again on 5 May 43, *Général de Division* Leclerc then was ordered to Morocco to form the 2d French Armd Div (2ème Div Blindée). He was re-equipped with US materiel and reinforced by Free French units from Syria and Dakar, and by volunteers from elsewhere.

In Wade HAISLIP's 15th Corps of Patton's 3d Army Leclerc's division reached Normandy on 1 Aug 44. The 2ème Blindée was heavily engaged around Argentan but had few casualties in the drive on Paris. Transferred to GEROW's 5th Corps of Hodge's 1st Army, Leclerc fought his way into the French capital on 25 Aug 45 (with considerable US support), and at 3:15 PM he formally accepted CHOLTITZ's surrender. A few minutes later Leclerc met DE GAULLE at the Gare Montparnasse.

Having rejoined Haislip's corps, Leclerc's division was given the honor of being the first into Strasbourg on 23 Nov 44, symbolizing his country's final liberation. As part of de LATTRE's effort to consolidate French troops Leclerc's division was assigned to the 1st French Army. But the two national heroes clashed over strategy for reducing the **Colmar pocket,** and in mid-Dec 44 Leclerc was transferred at his own request to the 7th US Army. (*EP,* 2362n.) He subsequently rejoined Frank W. Milburn's 21st Corps to have a prominent role in the US drive south through Colmar on 5 Feb 45. Leclerc's 2ème Blindée finished the war in the rush to Berchtesgaden that ended 4 May 45.

A month later he was ordered to form an expeditionary force to fight the Japanese. He left France on 18 Aug 45 as CinC of French troops in the Far East but reached Indochina in time only to sign the surrender document. As Vicomte Philippe François Marie Leclerc de Hautecloque, legally adopting his nom de guerre, Leclerc was in Saigon until recalled on 19 July 46 because his tough anti-insurgency policies met with public disapproval in France. As a full general and inspector of land troops in North Africa (Feb 47), a post becoming important because of rising nationalism, Leclerc was less than a week past his 45th birthday when killed on 28 Nov 47. His plane hit a rock while coming in to land at Colomb-Béchar after a bad weather flight from Oran (Clayton, 137). "The modern d'Artagnan" was made a marshal of France on 23 Aug 52.

LEE, John Clifford Hodges. US general. 1887-1958. Eisenhower's highly controversial but exceptionally capable logistics chief was born in Junction City, Kan, on 1 Aug 87. He graduated near the top of his West Point class in 1909 (12/103) and as an army engineer officer had a record of achievement in civil works before serving with the AEF as a divisional **G2, G3,** and CofS. Reaching the wartime rank of colonel the stern, sturdy, soldierly Lee won the **DSM** and **SS.**

He was known in the Old Army as "Jesus Christ Himself," from the triple initials J. C. H. and from his inflated ego. Lee was promoted to brigadier general on 1 Oct 40, ahead of Eisenhower. After commanding the 2d Inf Div at Ft Sam Houston, Tex, from 6 Nov 41 and promoted again in Feb 42, Maj Gen Lee reached England on 23 May 42. Two months later, not getting the field command he wanted, Lee became Eisenhower's logistics chief.

Lee's **SOS** performed brilliantly in the UK and North Africa. Without Eisenhower's prior approval, but at the urging of SOMERVELL that "one of his supply people be made a three-star general," Lee's nomination was announced in the newspapers on 3 Mar 44. (*EP,* 1759-60, 1766.) The promotion came through with retroactive rank from 21 Feb 44. About this time Lee was named Eisenhower's deputy theater commander for US forces with special responsibility for administration and supply. A directive of 14 July 44 established Lee's **COM Z, ETOUSA,** on the Continent, succeeding the SOS. (*EP,* 2005n.)

Eisenhower had praised his stern, vigorous, highly religions logistics chief as a "modern Cromwell" who had done well in an "appalling task." But the imperious Lee was a notorious "empire builder," and in early Sep 44 he caused a furor by moving forward elements of his headquarters to Paris. Lee argued that Com Z could perform better from the capital because Paris was the communications hub of France. But the logistics boss also was flouting Eisenhower's policy of keeping US troops—particularly noncombatants—out of large cities because they would burden the economy and cause public relations problems. Lee's billeting officers nevertheless demanded accommodations for 8,000 officers, 21,000 EM, threatened to take over all hotels, and wanted space in schools (Pogue, *The Supreme Command,* 322). Com Z commandos were too fast for SHAEF to stop, and the move caused much adverse publicity. Lucius D. CLAY was sent in the autumn of 1944 to replace Lee, but the latter was soon reinstated. Subsequent criticism of Lee's supply empire led to SOMERVELL's being sent in Jan 45 to investigate, but the SOS chief found that no drastic reform of COM Z was needed.

Rating subordinates on 1 Feb 45 in "value of services" Eisenhower placed Lee as No. 19 of 38 senior generals, characterizing him as "A commander rather than a supply type; extremely loyal, energetic, tireless." In a revealing comment of meaning only to US Army insiders, Eisenhower added, "Places too much value on the 'Engineer' label." (*EP,* 2467.)

Lt Gen Lee succeeded McNARNEY in Rome as to as head of **MTOUSA** in Dec 45 and quickly fell victim to journalist Robert Ruark. With leads from disgruntled GIs and assistance from the Italian Communist Party (personal knowledge), Ruark made a quick tour of Italy and published a scurrilous series of articles accusing Lee and his officers of high living while neglecting the creature comforts of enlisted men. Eisenhower, now army CofS in Washington, not only did not defend Lee but also refused his subordinate permission to publish a rebuttal. (Personal knowledge.) J. C. S. Lee retired on 31 Dec 47 as a lieutenant general. He worked quietly with the Brotherhood of Saint Andrew, lay Episcopalians based in York, Pa, were the general died on 30 Aug 58.

LEEB, Wilhelm Joseph Franz von. German general. 1872-1956. Leeb was born 5 Sep 72 at Landsberg into an old military family of Bavarian Catholics. He became an army cadet in 1895, was commissioned in the artillery, served in China (1901-02), and was a Prussian general staff officer (1909-11). As CofS to Gen Otto von Lossow in Munich, Oberstleutnant Ritter von Leeb had a minor role putting down the **Munich Beer Hall Putsch** of 1923. Some writers have confused Ritter von Leeb with one Capt (later Gen) Emil Leeb, who figured somewhat more prominently in opposing the putschists. (Gordon, *Putsch,* passim.)

In 1929 von Leeb was promoted to Generalmajor. Returning to Munich the next year he headed Wehrkreis VII until Hitler took power in 1933. Leeb and Rundstedt collaborated in blocking BLOMBERG's effort to install

the "Nazi general" REICHENAU instead of FRITSCH in the top Reichswehr post. Leeb was promoted to General of Artillery and given command of AG 2 in 1934. At this time he was one of the five most highly regarded generals of the German army, the others being BECK, BOCK, FRITSCH, and RUNDSTEDT (Manstein, *Lost Victories,* 75). In 1937-38 Leeb published *Die Abwehr* (Defense), a book to rebut champions of offensive warfare that made a great impression in Germany and abroad. Leeb argued that Germany could not defeat Russia quickly in a two-front war. (Edward Mead Earle, ed, *Makers of Modern Strategy,* 201, 360, 373.)

Long-faced, smooth-pated, and gimlet-eyed, with the ferocious looks to delight Hollywood central casting, Generalleutnant Leeb was among the "uncooperative" generals whom HITLER ordered retired in 1938. But Leeb was among those recalled in Aug 39, the month before Hitler invaded Poland. Promoted to Generaloberst, Leeb commanded AG C in the Westwall, covering the secondary front against France. Leeb made several attempts through official army channels to muster opposition against the fuehrer's continued aggression. Morally the devoutly religious general objected to the violation of **Benelux** neutrality (Deutsch, II, 81). Militarily he considered Hitler's strategy "insane" (as he wrote in his diary). On 9 Nov 39 Leeb asked Bock and Rundstedt to join him in threatening to resign rather than lead troops in the proposed offensive against the west. But these two generals, like most others, thought the suggestion mutinous (Goerlitz, *GGS,* 366). Leeb considered resigning alone, but his CofS, Georg von SODENSTERN, convinced him this would serve no useful purpose (Deutsch, II, 249). Unaware of what others were doing, then or later, in secretly opposing Hitler, Leeb virtually abandoned his own efforts (ibid., 255).

During the **"twilight war"** Leeb's AG C waged a masterful campaign of psychological and propaganda warfare. He attacked during the second month of the short campaign in France, with Witzleben's 1st Army making a penetration around Saarbruecken on 14 June 40. The next day Dollmann's 7th Army broke through near Colmar. Guderian's panzer group came under Leeb's control to race in behind the demoralized and disorganized French AG 2. Leeb got his field marshal's baton in the mass creation of 19 July 40.

In Opn **Barbarossa** he commanded AG North. It comprised BUSCH's large 16th Army of 12 divisions on the right (south), and KUECHLER's 18th Army of eight divisions on the left flank. In the center of AG North was HOEPPNER's 4th Pz Gp, which had three panzer divisions and six others. Jumping off from East Prussia on 22 June 41, Leeb's offensive moved rapidly despite difficult terrain and a heavily mined coastal region of woods and water unsuited to mechanized warfare—not "tank country." And Leeb proved to be inept at handling armor.

The 16th Army became increasingly involved in AG Center's offensive toward Moscow, but on 19 July 42 Hitler stopped the latter effort and gave Leeb HOTH's 3d Panzer Group (from AG Center) for a quick final move on Leningrad. The city's outskirts were penetrated early in September, but Hitler then had another brainstorm: instead of continuing the grinding effort to occupy Russia's second largest city and the "cradle of Bolshevism," where a large civilian population would be a burden, it would be better to isolate the city and starve it out. So AG North shifted its main effort to encircling Leningrad from the south and—it was hoped—linking up with the Finns, who had reclaimed their territory north of the city. Leeb's offensive drove a deep salient to take strategically vital Tikhvin on 8 Nov 41. Kirill A. MERETSKOV swiftly rallied Soviet forces to blunt the German assault and start building up a massive counteroffensive.

Leeb's many errors in Russia included failure to wipe out a large enemy beachhead some 30 miles west of Leningrad; the Soviet 8th Army held this "Oranienbaum sector," which was resupplied over the frozen Gulf of Finland. Barbarossa having failed, the champion of defense advocated withdrawing completely from Russia, regrouping, and then resuming a general offensive. (Goerlitz, *GGS*, 405.) Most other German generals concurred, but HITLER correctly foresaw that this could turn into a disaster like Napoleon's retreat in 1812. Hitler authorized only limited retrograde actions, and on 13 Jan 42 the field marshal asked to be relieved, allegedly for ill health. KUECHLER took command of AG North two days later. Leeb spent the rest of the war in retirement and died 29 Apr 56 at Hohenschwangau, Bavaria.

His valuable MS diaries, held by Leeb's heirs, were published in the late 1970s by the FRG.

LEESE, Oliver William Hargreaves. British general. 1894-1978. Leese led the 30th Corps in North Africa, Sicily, and Italy under Montgomery and succeeded him as 8th Army commander. Leese then headed Allied Land Forces in Burma.

He was born 26 Oct 94 in London, the eldest son of a baronet, and educated at Lundgrove and Eton. A huge six feet four, toothy, quiet, and good-natured—a P. G. Wodehouse character— he was an outstanding athlete in school (cricket and what Americans call soccer).

Leese was commissioned in the Coldstream Guards at the start of WWI. Fighting in the BEF he was wounded three times, twice mentioned in dispatches, and appointed to the DSO. Between the wars he commanded the 1st Bn of the Coldstreams, succeeded to the baronetcy in 1937, was chief instructor at the Quetta staff college in NW India (1938-40), and became a tank specialist. In the battle of Flanders (1940) he was on Lord GORT's BEF staff. Then heading the 29th Bde in the Dover area, Leese converted a guards division to armor. When Montgomery took over the 8th Army he sent for Leese to replace LUMSDEN as 30th Corps commander.

Leese led the corps across North Africa from El Alamein to the final victory. To his great professional disadvantage Leese was denied the opportunity of commanding the British 1st Army (vice Noel Anderson) because Montgomery would not release him at Alexander's request. (Ion M. Calvocoressi, *DNB*.) Spearheaded in Sicily by Guy G. SIMONDS's 1st Cdn Div, and operating on the eastern side of Montgomery's 8th Army, Leese overcame some of the toughest German resistance while Patton chased glory on the flank the Germans cared less about. The general whom Montgomery had earlier told CIGS Alan Brooke was "the best soldier out here" (ibid.) then took his staff to England. At the end of Dec 43 Leese succeeded Montgomery as 8th Army commander in Italy. (Ibid., although *West Point Atlas* Map 99 shows Leese as CG 13th Corps on 15 Jan 44 with "Monty" still heading the 8th Army.)

On 1 Oct 44, after ANDERS's Polish Corps took Cassino and the 8th Army cracked the

Gothic Line on its Adriatic flank, Leese turned over command to McCREERY. As CinC, Allied Land Forces in SE Asia (SEAC) Leese reached India on 12 Nov 44. The easygoing, humorous, informal general—who nevertheless could sometimes show an "explosive, petulant temper" *(DNB)*—had handled many nationalities successfully in the 8th Army, British, Canadian, Indian, Italian, Gurkha, Polish, and South African forces. Now, in addition to British and Indian army units, he had East and West Africans, Nigerians, and Burmese. Major ground formations were Slim's British 14th Army (advancing on Mandalay) and the British 15th Corps in the Akyab coastal area, but Leese also had operational control over SULTAN's **NCAC.** This comprised British and American forces, US-trained Chinese units, and about 12 weak Chinese divisions under WEI Li-huang. Lines of Communications Troops also were under Leese. A frontline general with a penchant for casual dress, Leese capitalized on his subordinates' strengths.

After Burma was reconquered Sir Oliver, whom King George VI had knighted (KCB) in Italy in 1943, was CinC, Eastern Command, 1945-46. He then retired to an active life of horticulture and working with numerous associations including the British Legion (1962-70), Combined Cadet Force, Old Etonians, several cricket clubs, and he was colonel of the Shropshire Yeomanry. He died childless on 22 Jan 78 at his home in Wales.

LEGENTILHOMME, Paul Louis. French colonial officer and administrator. 1884-1975. He was born at Valognes (near Cherbourg), graduated from St Cyr in 1907, and was commissioned in the Colonial Army. His first assignment was in Tonkin, until 1912, after which he fought for two years on the western front and rose to the rank of captain before being captured in 1915. After more service in the Far East Legentilhomme had a long tour in Madagascar, 1922-31. He was promoted to brigadier general in 1938, made the commander in French Somaliland, and then he headed Franco-British troops in Somaliland, 1939-40. (Larousse.) After Italy entered the war on 11 June 40 Legentilhomme led a raid into Abyssinia along the Djibouti-Addis Ababa RR, pushing Italian forces back and not stopping when the armistice was signed on 24 June in Rome.

Legentilhomme and Georges CATROUX were the only French generals to answer de Gaulle's "call to honor." The British had high hopes for using Jibouti as an additional base to support Alan CUNNINGHAM's move across the Gulf of Aden to conquer Italian East Africa. But Legentilhomme could not count on support from subordinates, so he left Djibouti secretly on the night of 1-2 Aug 40. Three months later he was in London with de Gaulle.

Promoted 1 Jan 42, *Général de Division* Legentilhomme was ordered to join the British in the Anglo-Egyptian Sudan. On 11 April he received orders to take command of various Free French forces in the Middle East that were being formed into the 1st Free French Div. In Henry Maitland WILSON's Syrian campaign of 7 June-12 July 41 the 1st FF Div revealed the normal shortcomings of a new formation. After some reverses at the hands of Vichy forces under Ferdinand Dentz, the Free French entered Damascus on 21 June and Nebek five days later. Legentilhomme retained command despite a serious wound, but it was his last combat service.

Court-martialled in absentia by Vichy authorities, he was condemned to death on 25 Sep 41. That same month the general was named CinC of Free French Africa, and on 1 Dec 42 he became high commissioner of French possessions in the Indian Ocean. Five weeks later, after William PLATT had defeated Vichy forces on Madagascar, Legentilhomme was given administrative control of the island. "This we have been keeping for his [de Gaulle's] consolation prize," Churchill said in a message to FDR on 5 Nov 42 (WC, IV, 605), alluding to de Gaulle's exclusion from planning for the North Africa invasion that began three days later.

Promoted again in Mar 43, *Général de corps d'armée* Legentilhomme was called to Algiers on 31 July 43 as de Gaulle began his showdown with Giraud. (de Gaulle, *Unity,* 149.) The colonial officer first was assistant commissioner of national defense (5 Aug 43), then the commissioner, 2 Oct—8 Nov 43 (Larousse). On the latter date, after de Gaulle had purged the FCNL of adversaries including GIRAUD and Alphonse GEORGES, Legentilhomme requested a transfer to London (de Gaulle, *Unity,* 149).

On 27 June 44 Legentilhomme became head of the 3d Military Region, which encompassed Normandy (Larousse). On 20 July 44 he succeeded Koenig as military governor of Paris. Legentilhomme was promoted to full general on 21 Jan 47, shortly before being put on the inactive list. He died at Nice at the age of more than 90 years.

LEIGH-MALLORY, Trafford Leigh. British air marshal. 1892-1944. He was born 11 July 92 at Mobberley, Cheshire, where his father and grandfathers had been rectors; his mother was a clergyman's daughter. Leigh-Mallory was commissioned in the 4th Bn, Lancaster Fusiliers, in Aug 14. This year his father changed the family name by royal assent to Leigh Leigh-Mallory from Leigh. *(CB 44.)*

After being wounded at Ypres the young officer joined the RFC in July 16. By 1918 he was mentioned in dispatches and awarded the DSO. He began a legal career but in 1919 joined the new RAF with the rank of squadron leader.

Leigh-Mallory pioneered air-ground cooperation and was a life-long advocate in a field that attracts few aeronauts. In 1930 he left a three-year assignment as head of the School of Army Cooperation to instruct at **Camberley** for a year. After a year as deputy director of staff studies in the Air Ministry and command of No. 2 Flying Training School, he was senior air staff officer in Iraq, 1936-37. Then he assumed command of No. 12 Ftr Gp, based in the Midlands at Hucknall.

Keeping this post for the Battle of Britain he had a relatively easy time while PARK's No. 11 group in southern England bore the brunt of the Luftwaffe's first attacks. Leigh-Mallory only reluctantly obeyed orders of his chief, DOWDING, to use his group in defending Park's hard-hit bases rather than hunt for easier prey in Park's territory. But L-M (as the RAF knew him) had a leading part in Britain's "finest hour." By July 40 his fighters had destroyed some 150 Luftwaffe aircraft in seven engagements. Shortly after taking over as Chief of the Air Staff, Charles PORTAL replaced DOWDING with Sholto DOUGLAS as Chief of Fighter Command (25 Nov 40) and also relieved PARK, whose No. 11 Ftr Gp Leigh-Mallory took over in Dec 40. With the Air Staff's support Leigh-Mallory and the rest of Fighter Command began changing to an offensive strategy, adopting the **"big wing"** concept that Douglas BADER and others had long advocated.

Leigh-Mallory had the additional duty of helping organize the Polish AF in the UK. During the otherwise disastrous Dieppe Raid on 19 Aug 42 he established complete air superiority. A little more than three months later (28 Nov 42), Leigh-Mallory took over Fighter Command from Sholto DOUGLAS and performed so well he was knighted in the New Year's honors list of 1943. A year later he was picked to command the Allied Expeditionary Air Forces in the Normandy invasion and promoted to air chief marshal on 31 Dec 43.

Sir Trafford headed the Allied tactical air force but fought to control at least some of the strategic bombing efforts of HARRIS and SPAATZ. The latter both objected vigorously and were supported by their RAF and USAF superiors. When Leigh-Mallory finally got some authority, thanks to Eisenhower's British deputy, TEDDER, he clashed with Harris and Spaatz over bombing priorities. The fussy, hot-headed, L-M fought even with the patient and diplomatic Tedder. Largely because of American pressure, notably from Spaatz, it was announced on 15 Oct 44 that Leigh-Mallory would be replaced in Europe by Tedder and made Mountbatten's air CinC in Burma. En route to this assignment Leigh-Mallory and his wife were killed, their plane reported missing on 14 Nov 44.

LeMAY, Curtis Emerson. US bomber commander. 1906-90. Tough, taciturn Curt LeMay was born 14 Nov 06 in Cleveland. On graduating from Ohio State Univ he promptly joined the army, becoming an artillery officer in June 28. A few months later he transferred to the recently created Army Air Corps and took flight training with the famous Kelly Field (Texas) class of 1929. On 13 Oct 29, a day after being commissioned in the Air Reserve, he was put on active duty as a pursuit (fighter) pilot, and three months later he was made a second lieutenant in the regular army. *(CB 44.)*

In Jan 37 he joined the Air Force GHQ at Langley Field, Va, and was introduced to the B-17 Flying Fortress. This began his career as a pioneer in strategic air warfare at a time when the American air force was coming of age under "Hap" ARNOLD. Maj LeMay (as of 21 Mar 41) was co-pilot of a B-24 Liberator that in Aug 41 made a record-setting flight of almost 25,000 miles across the South Atlantic to Asia Minor. The plane took W. Averell HARRIMAN on a survey of routes the Ferrying Command would use to deliver Lend Lease to the Soviets.

Profiting from the accelerated mobilization that followed Pearl Harbor Col LeMay (1 Mar 42) took over the 305th Bomb Gp (B-17s) at Muroc, Calif. Five months later he flew the group to England. As part of the 8th US AF he pioneered daylight bombing, which the RAF had abandoned as being too costly. But the B-17, as modified, had tremendous firepower on board (hence "Flying Fortress"), and the Americans had devised special defensive tactics: tight formations for mutual support and the standard three-plane formation varied so the "Forts" flew at different heights. It took iron discipline from "fly-boys" not heretofore noted for this quality, and it took confidence in a new concept of air war. Soon LeMay developed pattern bombing from lower altitudes and with another American innovation, the NORDEN bomb sight. Despite the lack of good fighter escort initially, the 305th lost only 13 planes during 25 missions flown in the year ending in mid-Nov 43. Longer-range P-47 Thunderbolt fighters made B-17 missions much more effective. In the first notable example of shuttle bombing LeMay accompanied 126 "Forts" with P-47 escort to bomb Regensburg on 17 Aug 43. From this target in southern Bavaria the Forts went on to bases in North Africa, then hit the Focke-Wulf plant in southern France (Bordeaux) on their return flight.

LeMay was promoted to brigadier general on 28 Sep 43 and got his second star on 2 Mar 44. The tough young airman, only 37 years old, did not look or act like a hero. Below middle height (about five feet eight) and not charismatic, he was notoriously taciturn—virtually incapable of small talk. But the airman was a stickler for discipline, training, and maintenance. He also was a great innovator, something that was about to be tested severely.

The gigantic B-29 Superfortress, "Hap" ARNOLD's brainchild, had become operational, if only barely. After visiting installations in the US, LeMay took over the 20th Bomb Cmd from K. B. Wolfe in July 44. The 20th had flown its first mission on 5 June, hitting Bangkok, and it struck Yawata, Japan, nine days later. But these were shakedown operations with a plane that still was, essentially, experimental.

The 20th Bomb Cmd warmed up further by hitting targets in China, Manchuria, Japan, and Sumatra. Then three 100-plane raids during the period 8-30 Sep 44 hit targets in Anshan, Manchuria's great metallurgical center 55 miles SW of Mukden. On 14 Oct came what LeMay called "the best show yet," a strike on Okayama, Formosa *(CB 44)*. But better ones followed, some hitting the southernmost of Japan's home islands.

The first B-29 loss was on the 16th mission, 11 Nov 44. It apparently was caused by hurricane weather that diverted some planes to alternate targets on the China coast from Kyushu, Japan. The first fighter opposition came 10 days later over Kyushu when two bombers were shot down and another reported missing.

LeMay operated at first from forward bases created in China under the CHENNAULT plan. When the Japanese began overrunning these fields and it became apparent that newly captured islands of the Pacific would provide better bases .LeMay was ordered in mid-Jan 45 to regroup in India. While there he honed his crews' skills with "tactical" strikes on such targets as Rangoon, Bangkok, and Singapore.

LeMay succeeded Brig Gen Haywood S. Hansell, Jr, on 20 Jan 45 as head of the 21st Bomb Cmd on Guam. The 21st had attacked Tokyo on 24 Nov 44, in daylight, the first time the Japanese capital had been hit since DOOLITTLE's raid of 18 Apr 42. Now field commander of the 20th AF *(AA,* 220) LeMay turned raids from nuisance to catastrophe. One reason was that he started making lower-level incendiary runs (from an average of 9,000 feet) on main Japanese cities. Some 100,000 tons of incendiaries on 66 cities killed about 260,000 people, injured more than 412,000, left 9,200,000 homeless, and destroyed an estimated 2,210,000 dwellings. (*West Point Atlas,* 166.) LeMay had a major role in selecting targets for the A-bombs dropped on Hiroshima, 6 Aug 45, and on Nagasaki three days later. The Japanese estimate that 240,000 died immediately or from lingering radiation effects. US estimates are as high as 78,000 dead in Hiroshima and 39,000 in Nagasaki.

After the war Maj Gen LeMay commanded the USAF in Europe. He directed the 1947 Berlin airlift, an operation of tremendous scope and complexity that the Soviets and many in the western world did not think could be possible. For many years he headed the Strategic Air

Command (SAC), a principal deterrent against the Soviet threat during the most critical phases of the Cold War. He went on to be USAF vice CofS, then chief of staff until 1961 and retired from active military duty in 1965.

Having called US defense policy "too soft," the general was picked by presidential candidate George C. Wallace as his running mate in the newly formed American Independent Party. Wallace had a 21 per cent approval rating in opinion polls (but no serious chance) when LeMay dropped a political bomb on 3 Oct 68. Said LeMay in a nationally televised press conference, "anything that we could dream up, including nuclear weapons," should be used to end the Vietnam war. The general withdrew to private life and died 1 Oct 90 at March AFB, Calif. His memoirs, written with his friend McKinley Kantor, are *Mission with LeMay* (1965).

LEMELSEN, Joachim. German general. 1888-1954. An artilleryman, Lemelsen became a Generalmajor on 1 Apr 37. After commanding the 29th Inf Div, Gen Lt Lemelsen succeeded Gen Lt Max von Hartlieb (**gennant** Walsporn) as 5th Pz Div commander on 22 May 40 in Flanders. (*B&O*, 78). Having been promoted on 1 Aug 40 to General of Artillery he left the division on 24 Nov 40 and the next day assumed command of the new 47th Mtz Corps. This was redesignated the 47th Pz Corps on 11 June 41, Lemelsen's rank having been changed on 4 June 41 to General of Panzer Troops. (*B&O*, 51-52.)

In Russia with GUDERIAN's 2d Pz Gp he had the panzer divisions of von ARNIM and NEHRING plus a motorized infantry division (Guderian, *Panzer Leader*. 145-46). Lemelsen was in the offensive to Smolensk, then in the advance through Yelna to the vicinity of Tula. Thereafter on the defensive and engaged in anti-partisan operations, Lemelsen fought more defensive actions in the Bryansk area for the first half of 1943. After this he led his corps for the retrograde actions in the Ukraine. The general was awarded the RK on 27 July 41 and the Oakleaves (294/890) on 7 Sep 43 (Angolia, II, 248).

Lemelsen turned the 47th Pz Corps over to Erhard RAUS on 4 Nov 43 after leading it for almost three years! Succeeding MACKENSEN, Lemelsen took command of the 14th Army in Italy on 5 June 44, the day after the Allies entered Rome. The dismounted panzer general, now a mountain fighter, took part in KESSELRING's delaying actions through the Apennines. He quietly went along with Karl WOLFF's arrangements for the secret surrender in Italy. About three weeks after the cease fire of 2 May 45, Lemelsen went into captivity. He died at Goettingen in 1954 (*B&O*, 52).

LEMNITZER, Lyman Louis. US general. 1899-1988. Of Bavarian ancestry, "Lem" was born 12 Nov 99 in Honesdale, Pa. The swarthy, lumbering Pennsylvania Dutchman was in the two-year USMA Class of 1920 (86/271), a catcher on the baseball team. Commissioned in the coast artillery and quickly known as a brilliant staff officer, Col Lemnitzer joined the war plans division, WDGS, in 1940. On 25 June 42 he was promoted to brigadier general and given command of the 34th AA Brig in the UK. Three months later he was G3 of Eisenhower's AFHQ. With Mark CLARK he undertook the harrowing secret mission to Algeria on 23 Oct 42. Two weeks later he was involved in another hair-raising event: the B-17 piloted by Jimmie DOOLITTLE and carrying a group of staff officers to join Eisenhower at Gibraltar for Opn Torch was jumped by Ju 88s. Proud of his Army Distinguished Marksman's Medal, Lemnitzer manned a machine gun and was credited with an "assist" in downing one of the attacking planes.

Resuming command of his AA brigade, the general took part in the North African and Sicily campaigns, interrupted by TDY in Jan 43 to help organize Mark Clark's 5th Army Hq. Succeeding Clarence R. Huebner, he then was the US G3 in AFHQ and Alexander's American deputy later. Promoton to major general was dated 30 Nov 44 (*AA*, 929). TOLBUKHIN's 3d Ukrainian Front pushed into Yugoslavia about this time, and Lemnitzer represented Alexander in talks between the Soviet marshal and TITO.

When SS General Karl WOLFF undertook his secret surrender, Lemnitzer and British Gen Terence Airey entered Switzerland in Mar 45 wearing civilian clothes and took part in preliminary arrangements directed by Allen DULLES. After the war Lemnitzer rose to four-star rank as army CofS in 1959, chairman of the JCS until 1962, and SACEUR, 1963-69. He died 12 Nov 88 at Walter Reed AGH.

LENTAIGNE, Walter David Alexander. British general. 1899-1955. Born in Burma on 15 July 99, son of a judge, he was educated in England. Six feet four, reed thin, and bespectacled, "Joe" Lentaigne was commissioned in 1917 and had most of his service on India's NW Frontier. In Feb 42 he reached Burma with his battalion of the 4th Gurkha Rifles just before Rangoon fell. Getting back to India with his original 700 men augmented to 2,500 by stragglers he was appointed to the DSO. *(CB 44.)*

When WINGATE's force was expanded in 1943 Lentaigne raised the 111th Bde on **Chindit** principles. Although he "regarded Wingate as an upstart, held his theories in contempt, and thought them unsound and unproven" (Allen, *Burma, 348*) Brigadier Lentaigne succeeded Wingate after the latter was killed on 24 Mar 44 in a plane crash. William Slim passed over "Mad Mike" CALVERT and others because he thought Lentaigne was more able to "defend Special Force against hostility in the higher echelons of command" (ibid.). This proved to be a false hope. Under Lentaigne, a major general on succeeding Wingate and a lieutenant general when the war ended, "the Chindits were villainously misused, and he was powerless to prevent it" (ibid.).

LEOPOLD III. King of the Belgians. 1901-83. Born 3 Nov 01, educated at Eton and Ghent Univ, Leopold became king after his father was killed on 17 Feb 34 in a mountain climbing accident near Namur. Queen Astrid, a Swedish beauty he had married in 1926 and who was much loved by the Belgians, died in an automobile accident in 1935.

Belgian frontier defenses crushed by assaults starting on 10 May 40, Leopold surrendered his armed forces on 28 May. Remaining with his people, but refusing to collaborate with occupation forces under FALKENHAUSEN, the king was evacuated to Germany with his second wife and children after the Allies landed in Normandy on 6 June 44. The Belgian government in exile reentered Brussels on 4 Sep 44 with British liberators. Leopold's younger brother Charles was made prince regent on 20 Sep 44. The Belgians officially exonerated Leopold for his role in the defeat of 1940, but he remained a symbol of national humiliation and the people disapproved of his remarriage in Sep 41 to a commoner. Leopold III was permanently rejected in 1951, his son by Queen Astrid becoming King Baudouin I.

LEWIS, John Llewellyn. US Labor leader. 1880-1969. Son of a Welsh immigrant coal miner, the ferocious John L. Lewis was born 12 Feb 80 near Lucas, Iowa. His formal education ended at seventh grade when he entered the coal mines. *(CB 42.)* Lewis became president of the United Mine Workers of America in 1920, then he was a power in the American Federation of Labor (AFL). In 1935 he split with the AFL to found the Congress of Industrial Organizations (CIO), which organized mass-production industries in single unions rather than by individual crafts. (Ibid.)

He supported Roosevelt initially but backed Wendell WILLKIE in 1940; when FDR won reelection Lewis resigned as head of the CIO, as he had promised. In 1942 he took his AFL out of the CIO. Lewis had joined in a pledge to refrain from action that would hamper the war effort. When CIO steel workers ("Little Steel") demanded a cost of living wage boost, the War Labor Board granted a 15 per cent raise (16 July 42) that led to the Little Steel Formula, the basis for later cost-of-living wage adjustments (Buchanan, 139). But in Apr 43 Lewis threatened a coal strike, and Roosevelt ordered Harold ICKES to take over the mines. Lewis won in the long run, breaking the Little Steel Formula and, in effect, getting his men premium pay and additional work (ibid.). But he lost in that miners were not satisfied and Congress passed tougher anti-strike legislation.

Lewis continued to influence the US economy powerfully until retiring in 1960. The beefy curmudgeon, a man of medium height but weighing 230 pounds, was a cartoonist's delight with his bushy eyebrows and ever-present cigar. He died 11 June 69 in Washington.

LEY, Robert. Nazi official. 1890-1945. Dr Ley headed the German Labor Front from 2 May 33. He was a Rhinelander born 15 Feb 90 in Niederbreidenbach to a family of poor peasants. As a military aviator he was shot down in 1917, captured by the French, and held prisoner for nearly three years.

Ley was a chemist with I. G. Farben until dismissed for habitual drunkenness. Joining the

Nazi Party in 1925 he was named Gauleiter that year for Rhineland-South. In 1931 he became Reich Inspector of the NSDAP and a year later was Reich Organization Leader of the party. He also published a party organ, *Westdeutscher Beobachter,* "a Cologne gossip paper" (Thyssen, 269) that brought Ley a fortune along with a considerable political following.

On 2 May 33 Dr Ley began forming the German Labor Front (*Deutsche Arbeitsfront,* or DAF), which on 24 Oct 34 replaced the outlawed trade unions. But the DAF was "in reality a vast propaganda organization," writes William Shirer, "and as some workers said, a gigantic fraud" (*Third Reich,* 263). Hitler's huge rearmament program and buildup of the armed forces eliminated the problem of unemployment. To keep workers' minds off their grievances Ley instituted the elaborate program of "Strength through Joy" (*Kraft durch Freude*). Ten per cent of DAF dues were used to subsidize inexpensive foreign vacations and to direct social, sports, and recreational activities. While administering his astounding conception of Nazi fun, the bibulous, emotionally unstable, uncouth Dr Ley got his own strength through joy by looting union treasuries, confiscating old-age pensions, and lowering wages while lengthening hours. For rambling speeches at mass meetings he was called the "Reich Drunk Master." Another DAF project, the "People's Car," collapsed after the Volkswagen factory was converted to war production. But Hitler gave his old crony many appointments including direction of Union of Germans Living Abroad and Chief of the Adolf Hitler Volunteer Corps of guerrilla fighters.

Awaiting trial at Nuremberg for war crimes, Ley repented his anti-Semitism in a political testament. With a rope of strips torn from a towel he then hanged himself on 25 Oct 45 from the toilet pipe in his cell.

LI Tsung-jen. Chinese general. 1890-1969. Born in Kweilin, Kwangsi Prov in 1890 (*China Hdbk,* 1947) he graduated from the Kweilin MA and by 1926 commanded the 7th Army briefly before taking over the 3d Northern Expeditionary Army. In 1927 he saved Nanking by defeating Sun Chuan-fang near Chiunkiang (Kiangsu Prov). In Feb 28 Li took over the 4th AG in Hunan and Hupeh with Pai Tsung-hsi as his deputy, but the next year Li and other Kwangsi (or southern) generals broke with Chiang Kai-shek. Li rejoined the nationalists in June 36 in Kwangtung Prov to drive back the Japanese. Many other southern war lords used the campaign to intrigue against Chiang's Nanking government, but Chiang regained control, narrowly averting civil war. As one of those who had remained in the fold (as did Pai Tsun-hsi) Li was given the mission of pacifying Kwangsi Prov. From 1937 he commanded the 5th War Area, and in Feb 45 he became director of the Hanchung Field Hq in Shensi Prov. (Ibid.)

John Gunther wrote in 1942 that the honest, genial Gen Li looked like a "hard-bitten and husky Mongoloid longshoreman" (quoted in *CB 42* from *Inside Asia*). Li and the brainy, sophisticated Pai worked as "the iron fist in the silken glove" (ibid.).

Li was VP of Nationalist China from 1941 and in 1949 he stayed behind as acting president when Chiang left for Taiwan. Later that year, however, he was hospitalized in NYC, and in 1954 he was dismissed for refusal to return to Taiwan. After 16 years of self-imposed exile Li defected in 1966 to the Chinese communists, settled in Peiking, and died there on 30 Jan 69.

LIDDELL HART, Basil Henry. British military historian and theorist. 1895-1970. The younger son of the Reverend Henry Bramley Hart (whose parsonical looks the son inherited) and the former Clara Liddell, he was born 31 Oct 95 in Paris, where his father was the Wesleyan minister (Ronald Lewin in *DNB*). Basil later inserted his mother's name to make himself B. H. Liddell Hart, although *DNB* nevertheless lists him under "Hart, Sir Basil Henry Liddell." The name is pronounced "little heart." Educated at St Paul's School and entering Corpus Christi College, Cambridge, in 1913, Liddell Hart left on the outbreak of war in Aug 14 to become an officer in the King's Own Yorkshire Light Infantry. Rising to company commander, seeing action at Ypres and the Somme, Liddell Hart was wounded twice and gassed. Starting in 1917 he developed the battle drill system and other new tactical ideas including the "expanding torrent" attack on which the **blitzkrieg** was based. He redrafted the *Infantry Training Manual* (1920) before being invalided out on half pay in 1924. Three years later he was retired as a captain.

He was military correspondent for the *Daily Telegraph* (1925-35), *The Times* of London (1935-39), military editor for the *Encyclopaedia Britannica,* and unofficial personal adviser to HORE-BELISHA (1937-38). During the war he wrote for the *Daily Mail* and other papers. From lengthy postwar interviews with top German officers (many of whom, along with Red Army officers, were unabashed admirers of his writings), he wrote *The Other Side of the Hill* (1948); of which the slightly abridged US edition is *The German Generals Talk* (New York: Morrow, 1948). Probably the leading military theoritician of modern war and an able writer, he published more than 30 books. But as a prophet without honor in his own country, Liddell Hart was not knighted until 1966.

LINDBERGH, Charles Augustus, Jr. US aviator. 1902-74. The Lone Eagle, whose solo flight across the Atlantic in 1927 inspired millions of boys (and girls) to become airmen (airwomen), was born 4 Feb 02 in Detroit. "Lindy" was the son of a rabidly isolationist Minnesotan who became a congressman in 1907 and ran unsuccessfully for state governor in 1918. Young Lindbergh was reared on a farm near Little Falls, Minn. He entered the Univ of Wisconsin in 1920 but dropped out to take flight training. In 1925 he was commissioned as a pilot in the Missouri NG. *(CB 41.)* After barnstorming and serving as a test pilot he flew with the US Mail Service.

In 1927 he won world acclaim by being the first to fly the Atlantic. "Lucky Lindy" succeeded by realizing that the secret was to fly solo in a plane whose weight was reduced to an absolute minimum. His book about the exploit, *We* (1927), laid the foundations of a personal fortune. An international hero, the tall, shy, boyish Lindbergh was sponsored by a the Guggenheim Foundation for the Promotion of Aeronautics and by government authorities on innumerable flights in the US and abroad. From 1929 the diminutive and charming Anne Spencer Morrow Lindbergh, a poet of considerable note and later an outstanding writer of prose, was his copilot.

In 1932 their infant son was kidnapped, and after a highly publicized search the body was found near his home two months later. The sub-

sequent search for the alleged kidnapper, Bruno Hoffmann, was directed by H. Norman SCHWARZKOPF. Shamelessly hounded by the press and fearing what came to be known as "copycat" criminals, the Lindberghs moved to England in 1935. From 1933 the Nazis had courted the American flyer, who was of Swedish ancestry and a strong believer in Nordic racial supremacy. After the third visit to Germany in 1938, just after the **Munich Crisis,** Lindbergh was reinforced in his earlier belief that the Luftwaffe was unstoppable. In 1939 he returned to the US and, as a colonel in the Air Corps reserve, made a four-month tour of US air bases for the War Dept. Then he began a series of increasingly strident speeches for the America First Committee. He accused US Jews of causing a war that would destroy European civilization and told audiences that social injustice in America demanded new leadership. This was taken to mean that voters should support Wendell WILLKIE's bid to defeat Roosevelt's campaign for a fourth term. After France fell, Lindbergh predicted that Britain would be crushed within weeks.

But when the US finally went to war, the famous airman made a public statement that, right or wrong in its foreign policy, America had to fight. The US air force declined Col Lindbergh's offer of service. But as a civilian consultant to the United Aircraft Corp (producers of the Vought Corsair and its Pratt and Whitney engine) he made several trips to the Pacific and Europe. In addition to teaching pilots such techniques as extending their range hundreds of miles by conserving fuel, he advised the Marines on use of the Corsair and advised George KENNEY's 5th AF on the P-38. He flew 50 combat missions in the Pacific as a civilian and downed at least one enemy plane.

A diary started in 1937 was the basis of *The Wartime Journals of Charles A. Lindbergh* (New York: Harcourt Brace Jovanovich, 1970). The book makes no excuses for the author's wrong-headed political outlook as an American Firster, shows no trace of enlightenment in later years, and continues to blame Jews for taking the US into war. An immensely complicated man, Lindbergh equated America's brutal treatment of the Japanese with Germany's atrocities. His earlier autobiographical work, *The Spirit of St Louis,* won the Pulitzer prize in

1954. Anne Lindbergh published *North to the Orient* (1935) and other works of high literary quality. The fallen hero, a victim of lung cancer, died on 26 Aug 74 in Hawaii at the age of 72 after a short illness.

LINDEMANN, Frederick Alexander, Lord Cherwell. British scientist. 1886-1957. He was born 5 Apr 86 in Baden-Baden, where his American mother was taking the cure. (Robert Blake in *DNB*.) Lindemann's father was a Catholic of French Alsacian origin who became a British citizen. The family was wealthy, and the senior Lindemann was a distinguished amateur scientist and astronomer who had a laboratory at his home near Sidmouth, Devonshire. After going to school in Scotland young Lindemann was educated at the Darmstadt Hochschule and Berlin's Physikalisch Institut, getting a PhD in physics (1910). He made important personal contributions to physics research, gaining the respect of eminent scientists including Einstein, and was elected FRS in 1920. Henry TIZARD was a fellow research student in Berlin and the two worked together in 1915-18 at the Royal Aircraft Factory at Farnborough. Although each man had defective vision in one eye they supplemented theoretical work with daring flights as test pilots, and Lindemann solved the problem of "spin." (Ibid.)

Independently wealthy, big, broad shouldered, a world class tennis player and outstanding pianist, the scientist moved easily within the upper class but knew little about how the masses lived. He was a vegetarian, a nonsmoker, and virtually a teetotaller. But a weak voice and a mumbling delivery detracted from his otherwise brilliant lectures and public speeches. (Ibid.)

In 1919 he was elected to the chair of experimental philosophy (physics) at Oxford, thanks partly to Tizard (ibid.). The post made him director of the Clarendon Laboratory, which "the Prof" (as he became known) built into one of the world's great research institutions.

Lindemann and Churchill first met in 1921. "At first sight so different, the two men quickly saw each other's qualities," writes D. V. JONES (*Wizard War,* 14). The Prof headed the statistical department on Churchill's Admiralty staff (1939-40) and followed Churchill to 10 Down-

ing St as the prime minister's scientific adviser (1940-45). The Prof consequently was the dominant scientist in the British war effort, and soon won out in a memorable feud with TIZARD. With a view to gaining clout for revitalizing air defense the Prof turned to politics. He failed in 1935-37 to enter Parliament for Oxford, but was a force in the House of Lords after becoming a peer, Baron Cherwell, of Oxford, in 1941.

Lindemann's major wartime achievements were these: use of shaped charges in bombs; development of proximity (VT) fuses; countermeasures against the **Lorenz beam;** and the H2S system of microwave radar navigation. The scientist convinced the PM and others that strategic bombing of German cities would hasten victory by breaking civilian morale. This policy proved to be highly questionable not only militarily (as TIZARD pointed out) but also on humanitarian grounds. Lindemann's uneven war record included almost a year's delay in the use of "window" to confuse German radar—like many radar experts he objected that more harm than good would come from alerting the enemy to this technique. He was slow to recognize the V-weapon threat. He has been faulted also for not giving proper priority to radar development, worried about countermeasures and needing COCKCROFT to find enough scientists to nurse the new technology to maturity.

Lord Cherwell became paymaster general in 1942 and a privy counselor in 1943. Although not a member of the war cabinet, he frequently attended its meetings. After Churchill regained power, Cherwell again was paymaster general from Oct 51 and headed the British nuclear program. His leave of absence from Oxford ran out in 1953, when Cherwell returned to head the Clarendon Lab until retiring in 1956, and that year he became the 1st Viscount Cherwell. Continuing to live at Oxford, he died in his sleep on the morning of 3 July 57.

LINDEMANN, Georg. German general. 1884-1963. Born 8 Mar 84 at Osterburg/Altmark, he was highly decorated in 1914-18. A year after being promoted to Oberst he became head of the War School at Hanover (1934). In 1936, Generalmajor Lindemann took command of the 36th Inf Div, with which he still served when awarded the RK on 4 Aug 40 for action in France. (Angolia, II, 233-34.) Promoted soon thereafter to General of Cavalry, he was given the 50th Corps (46th, 76th, and 198 Inf Divs) in LIST's 12th Army and sent to Romania. The force was detraining when the Balkan campaign began on 6 Apr 41 and saw no action. (DA Pamphlet 20-260, *Balkans*, 81.)

His corps moved to East Prussia to join KUECHLER's 18th Army of LEEB's AG North for the drive on Leningrad that began 22 June 41. On 17 Jan 42 Lindemann moved up to head the 18th Army and two months later he led the northern wing of a double envelopment that cut off some 130,000 Soviet troops in the Volkhov pocket (Seaton, *R-G War*, 243). In heavy fighting he then destroyed VLASOV's 2d Guards Army and captured its commander. Promoted for his part in this victory, Generaloberst Lindemann succeeded MODEL in early Mar 44 as CG, AG North. By now he faced the main strategic effort of the Soviets, who had shifted strength to the Leningrad sector. Unable to stop the tide, Lindemann was replaced in early July 44 by Friessner, who was quickly succeeded by SCHOERNER. (Ibid., 441.) At war's end Lindemann was CinC Denmark. He died 25 Sep 63 in Freudenstadt (Angolia, II, 234).

LINLITHGOW, 2d Marquess of. 1887-1952. *See* HOPE, Victor Alexander John.

LISCHKA, Kurt. Nazi official. 1909-. The son of a bank officer, he was born in Breslau on 16 Aug 09. After studying law and political science, he joined the Gestapo in 1935. Three years later he took over Referat IV-B (Jewish Affairs). In France from its conquest in 1940 he was prominently identified with the deportation of 80,000 Jews and other "enemies of the Third Reich." In the last major war crimes trial, ending 2 Feb 80, he was found guilty by the Cologne County Court and sentenced to 10 years imprisonment.

LIST, Siegmund Wilhelm. German general. 1880-1971. The son of a doctor, List was born 14 May 80 at Oberkirch. (This is in the Black Forest not far E of Strasbourg.)

A tall, burly, baldish, "unpleasant-looking man with the aspect of a proletarian and uncul-

tured manners" (Riess, *The Self-Betrayed*, 221), he was an expert in mountain warfare. With excellent training in the old Bavarian GS, List was highly regarded professionally as an honest, cool, and thorough—if cautious—soldier. (Brett-Smith, *Hitler's Generals*, 59, citing Riess.)

From his WWI service List retained friendships with Bulgarian and Turkish officers and was considered to be an authority on the Balkans. After being part of a Freikorps he joined the Reichswehr in 1923, became a tank specialist, and was chief of the Army Organization Dept. Promoted in 1930 to Generalmajor he looked favorably on Hitler's rise. But as head of the Dresden Infantry School, he got on the Nazi black list in 1931 for disciplining young officers involved in politics.

A Generalleutnant from 1932, List commanded the 4th Div at Dresden in 1934. He then headed the 4th Army Corps under BOCK, 1935-38, concurrently commanding Wehrkreis IV, with headquarters at Dresden. Although anti-Nazi, he was among the many senior generals who did not speak out against Hitler's dishonorable treatment of BLOMBERG and FRITSCH in early 1938 (Deutsch, I, 255-58). This is perhaps why List escaped the Nazi purge of "uncooperative" generals that year. After the Anschluss he was sent to Vienna as head of the 5th **Heeresgruppe**, which in Mar 39 he sent into Czechoslovakia.

Again promoted, Generaloberst List led the 14th Army of Rundstedt's AG South into south Poland on 1 Sep 39. Taking Cracow and encircling remnants of the Cracow and Carpathian Armies, he linked up with Guderian's panzers (of Bock's AG North) at Wlodawa, SE of Brest-Litovsk, on 17 September. Four days later other elements of List's army captured Lvov. Visiting the 14th Army's rear areas CANARIS was shocked to discover that List was condoning the mass slaughter of Jews by SS units (Deutsch, II, 182).

In the battle of Flanders that started on 10 May 40 List led his 12th Army through the Ardennes in support of Pz Gp Kleist. Making remarkable forced marches of 30 miles a day his infantry divisions reached the Meuse only a day behind the armored spearhead. On D+7, List resolved a potentially disastrous altercation between Kleist and GUDERIAN. But when this "difficult subordinate" latter came under List's operational control for the battle of France, another confrontation occurred when List berated Guderian for not pushing across the Aisne River around Rethel. The panzer leader pointed out that, having been denied authority to establish his own bridgeheads, he was letting his troops swim and sunbathe until List's other troops did the job. "It was typical of Colonel-General List's chivalrous nature that he immediately offered me his hand and proceeded calmly to discuss the future development of the attack. . . ." (Guderian, 123-24.)

List was among the 12 field marshals Hitler created on 19 July 40. Still heading 12th Army Hq for the Balkans campaign the field marshal planned and directed a complex operation against Greece and Yugoslavia. This started with List's concluding secret negotiations on 8 Feb 41 to let German troops from Romania to pass through Bulgaria. Starting 6 Apr 41 four widely dispersed columns of infantry, panzers, and mountain troops quickly accomplished their missions.

Despite this remarkable political and military achievement the field marshal remained anathema to Hitler. Goerlitz believes this was a grudge dating from the episode in 1931 mentioned above. (Davidson, *Trial,* 343.) It also was rumored, but never documented, that it was because List refused one of Hitler's large cash gifts. (Brett-Smith, *Hitler's Generals,* 61. "Cunning Hans" KLUGE accepted one on his in birthday in 1942.) So List was in the Balkans when Opn Barbarossa started, being appointed OB Southeast on 9 June 41. With headquarters at Salonika he had the problem of suppressing large-scale partisan activity in Greece and Yugoslavia and was directly responsible to Hitler for all military and political activities in Serbia, Greece, and the Greek islands including Crete.

Such was the price List paid for being a Balkan expert, but in mid-Oct 41 he was relieved by General of Pioneers Walther Kuntze. Shelved for nine months, the field marshal was named by Keitel and Halder on 7 July 42 to head the newly activated AG A in south Russia. Hitler approved only because he had no candidate (Davidson, *Trial,* 343). In Phase 3 of the summer offensive, AG A attacked eastward across the Mius River on 9 July 42. Mackensen's 1st Pz Army of AG A was to join

west of Stalingrad with Kleist's 4th Pz Army of AG B, destroying enemy in the Donets-Don area. In Phase 4, List was to drive south into the Caucasus while BOCK's AG B took Stalingrad. But on 13 July, before Phase 3 was completed, Hitler thoroughly disrupted the campaign. Now List was to break off his advance eastward and turn south to cross the Don east of Rostov. List's AG A was reinforced at the expense of Bock's AG B's by Kleist's 4th Pz Army and Richard Ruoff's 17th Army. On 23 July 42, the day Ruoff took Rostov, Hitler issued another directive: with the 17th Army and 3d Romanian Army comprising Group Ruoff, and Mackensen's weakened 1st Pz Army, List was to destroy a considerable force that had escaped from Rostov. Group Ruoff then was to seize the entire Black Sea coast to the Turkish border while, concurrently, the 1st Panzer Army overran the Caucasus! Hard enough on operational planners, all this improvisation created a nightmare for logistical personnel.

Mud and stiffening resistance by TYULENEV's Transcaucasus Front caused further problems, but Ruoff took the Black Sea port of Novorussisk on 6 Sep 43. Far to the east the 1st Pz Army occupied the Maikop-Armavir oilfields, rolled to within 150 miles of the Caspian Sea, and fought south into the Caucasus Mountains. The swastika flew over Mt Elbrus, the highest peak in Europe.

But on 30 Aug 42 Hitler brusquely summoned List to Vinnitsa from AG A Hq at Stalino and demanded why he had not done more. The fuehrer is said to have "heard List out with apparent friendliness and understanding" but to have flown into a rage as soon as the field marshal left. (Seaton, *R-G War,* 285.) Hitler ordered JODL to inspect List's sector and exploded when the emissary reported back that AG A was performing well in an almost impossible situation. This led to Hitler's refusing to have any further social contact with Halder and Jodl. The fuehrer sacked List on 9 Sep 42, ostensibly for bad health, and personally commanded AG A until Kleist took it over on 22 Nov 42.

List spent the rest of the war at his home in Garmish-Partenkirchen. Charged with war crimes committed mainly in the Balkans (above), he was sentenced in Feb 48 to life imprisonment but released on Christmas 1952 for ill health. List died 17 Aug 71 at Garmish.

LITVINOV, Maxim Maximovich. Soviet diplomat. 1876-1952. He was born Meyir Moysevevich Vallakh on 17 July 76 in the Polish ghetto of Russian-occupied Bialystok. Of many pseudonyms he came to favor Litvinov. For revolutionary activities he was arrested in 1901. En route to Siberia he escaped and fled to London, where he joined the Lenin entourage and became a close friend of Trotsky's. After the unsuccessful revolt of 1905 he edited a legal newspaper in St Petersburg before going to the Caucasus. He then was sent abroad to sell money STALIN hijacked in Tiflis. The Bolshevik had some success in Paris on this mission before being arrested and eventually expelled in 1906 to London, where for the next 10 years he held various legitimate jobs while continuing revolutionary activities. In 1916 he married Ivy Low, a radical writer whose father was a prominent lawyer and whose uncle, Sir Maurice Low, once was lord mayor of London and Washington correspondent for the London *Post*. Litvinov became fluent in English, albeit with an accent of the London slums *(CB 41)*.

In Jan 18 after receiving a wire from Trotsky the revolutionary announced his own appointment as ambassador to London. The British had long been watching him in hopes of finding cause for arrest, but they also wanted to establish unofficial relations with the Soviets. To this end BRUCE LOCKHART was sent to Russia with a letter of introduction written by Litvinov to TROTSKY, but the Russians arrested the emissary in Sep 18 as a secret agent. Titing for tat, the British arrested Litvinov and exchanged him a month later for their man.

Back in Moscow, Litvinov joined the foreign office and worked up through a series of overseas assignments to be commissar for foreign affairs 1930-39. One of his first accomplishments was to secure US recognition of the USSR in 1933. The next year the USSR was admitted to the League of Nations and Litvinov became a vocal supporter of collective security. By 1939, however, this concept had failed, and Stalin decided the USSR was strong enough to deal alone with Hitler. Although otherwise a highly effective diplomat, Litvinov was a fly in the ointment not only for his association with the failed foreign policy but also as a Jew. This was held against him in Moscow but much more so in Berlin. Apparently on an impulse while negotiating the Nazi-Soviet pact (WC, I, 366-67) Stalin had Litvinov replaced by V. M. Molotov in May 39. Litvinov was "bundled off the world stage to obscurity, a pittance, and police supervision," writes Churchill of that he calls "the end of an epoch" (ibid.). In Feb 41 the ex-diplomat was expelled from the Central Committee and marked for liquidation (*Khrushchev,* 162).

But after Hitler attacked the USSR Litvinov was made ambassador to Washington on 6 Nov 41. From Oct 42 he doubled as envoy to Cuba. On 21 Aug 43, when Stalin was preparing to reap the spoils of war, the Old Bolshevik was succeeded in Washington by Andrei A. GROMYKO, his former deputy. Hence major changes in Soviet foreign policy were marked by Litvinov's "resignation" as commissar of foreign affairs in May 39 (above) and his subsequent this recall in 21 Aug 43 as ambassador to Washington (Bialer, *Soviet Leaders,* 167). Finally the diplomat served, until retirement in Aug 46, as a deputy commissar in the department of foreign affairs he had headed for so long (*NYT* obit, 2 Jan 52).

LOCKWOOD, Charles Andrews, Jr. US admiral. 1890-1967. The WWII commander of US submarine forces in the Pacific was born 6 May 90 in Virginia and reared in Missouri. Graduating from Annapolis in 1912 (136/156), he became an "unwilling submariner" two years later but grew fond of life in the boats. (Blair, *Silent Victory,* 66; Morison, IV, 223.) He commanded Subdiv 13 from 1935 to 1937, then had the submarine desk under the CNO and was CofS to Comsubs. In Jan 41 he became GHORMLEY's CofS in London and also was naval attaché.

On 26 May 42 he relieved Capt John Wilkes as Comsubs SW, also taking over from Rear Adm W. R. Purnell as commander of all Allied naval forces based in West Australia. The new arrival, recently promoted to rear admiral, also headed TF 51, comprising surface units as well as subs in SW Australia. A short, cheerful, energetic officer, "Lockwood was almost overcome by the depression and fatigue he found all through the command" (Blair, 274). The retreat from Manila had been an exhausting ordeal for inexperienced crews, and torpedo performance had been bad (ibid.).

Lockwood conducted tests that revealed faulty torpedo design. Instead of commending him for initiative, the Bureau of Ordnance quibbled until CNO Ernest KING intervened to issue orders that eventually straightened out the technical problems. Adm Arthur S. Carpender took over as commander of TF 51 in early July 42, freeing Lockwood to concentrate on submarine matters. But Carpender and Lockwood were quickly at odds, the former fussing about what Lockwood considered to be minutiae (ibid., 283). As Lockwood shifted his fleet boats to eastern Australia in response to Japanese pressure in the Solomons and New Guinea he sent patrols into the South China Sea, Philippine waters, and the Flores Sea. (Morison, IV, 223.)

From Feb 43 Lockwood directed all submarine operations in the Pacific as Comsubpac, and late that year was promoted to vice admiral. Comsubpac claimed in a final report that his boats in the Pacific had sunk about 4,000 Japanese vessels (some 10 million tons), including a battleship, eight aircraft carriers, and 20 cruisers. US losses were 52 submarines, 375 officers, and 3,131 EM out of about 16,000 who had made war patrols. The casualty rate of almost 22 per cent was the highest for any US military service, but because of official censorship during the war it was a "silent victory." (Blair, 877.)

After the war Vice Adm Lockwood was the Navy's IG. Detesting being chief of what he called the Gestapo, and frustrated in hopes of creating a post of deputy CNO for submarines, he retired 1 Sep 47, declining further promotion and command of a fleet. (Blair, 880, 897.) He lived in Los Gatos, Calif, took part in civic affairs, hunted, and wrote. Lockwood published two autobiographical works, *Sink 'Em All* (New York: Dutton, 1951) and *Down to the Sea in Subs* (New York: Norton, 1967). With Hans C. Adamson he wrote *Hell at 50 Fathoms* (Philadephia: Chilton Books, 1962). The submariner died 6 June 67 at Monte Serena, Calif.

LOERZER, Bruno. German airman. 1892-1960. A famous ace in WWI who became Goering's lifelong friend, he headed the Air Sports League in 1933. Having provided cover for training future Luftwaffe pilots, Loerzer was an officer in that force from 1935. As a General of Flyers he commanded the 2d Air Corps in 1940. After the battle of Britain he headed the Luftwaffe personnel department.

LOERZER, Bruno. German airman. 1892-1960. A famous ace in WWI who became Goering's lifelong friend, he headed the Air Sports League in 1933. Having provided cover for training future Luftwaffe pilots, Loerzer was an officer in that force from 1935. As a General of Flyers he commanded the 2d Air Corps in 1940. After the battle of Britain he headed the Luftwaffe personnel department.

LOHSE, Heinrich. Nazi official. 1896-1964. Born 2 Sep 96 in Muehlenbarbek bei Steinburg, Lohse was gauleiter of his native Schleswig-Holstein from 1925. When Hitler took power in 1933, Lohse became president of Schles-wig-Holstein, a member of the Reichstag, and Prussian State Councillor. In Feb 34 he was given the rank of SA-Gruppenfuehrer.

From 1941 to 1944 the porky, bland-faced Nazi was in Riga as Reich Commissioner, Ostland, with authority over the Baltic States and White Russia. He mildly questioned the need for liquidating all Jews including children, women, and skilled workers but was told to support policies prescribed for the "final solution" and did little to mitigate SS excesses. In 1948 a British court sentenced him to 10 years of penal servitude but because of ill health Lohse was freed in 1951. He died 25 Feb 64 in his home town. (Wistrich.)

LOPATIN, Alexandr Ivanovich. Soviet military leader. 1897-1965. As commander of a corps in the 26th Army that was captured in the Kiev encirclement, Gen Maj Lopatin himself broke out after being given authority on 17 Sep 41 to do so. A few weeks later he took command of a new 37th Army formed SE of Voroshilovgrad from reserve units (Seaton, *R-G War,* 193) to replace VLASOV's original 37th Army that had been destroyed in Kiev. Lopatin took part in TIMOSKENKO's recapture of Rostov on 29 Nov 41, then conducted a valiant delaying action to the Don River until his army again was virtually destroyed. About 1 Aug 42 Lopatin replaced Gen Maj V. Ya. Kolpakchi as head of the 62d Army.

Conducting delaying actions through the Don country in July and August under heavy ground and air attack, his achievements not appreciated at the time (Werth, *Russia at War,* 557), Lopatin withdrew shattered and demoralized remnants of his army into the rubble of Stalingrad. The plan for Chuykov's 64th Army to join him there was frustrated by German penetrations within the city that reached the Volga.

On 7 Aug 42 the 62d Army was hit by a massive German attack that in two days isolated the remnants of its eight rifle divisions and five artillery regiments in the northern sector of Stalingrad. "He did all that was expected of him, and more," writes Zhukov. "But Lopatin chose to preserve the Sixty-second Army for a stand within the city, where the enemy forces were ultimately to be depleted and destroyed." Editor Salisbury notes that "These seemingly innocent words of praise . . . are the iceberg tip of the raging feud between Marshal Zhukov and Marshal V. I. Chuikov. . . . Chuikov in his memoirs singled out Lopatin for savage criticism [but] . . . Zhukov is saying in effect that had it not been for Lopatin there would have been no Sixty-second Army for Chuikov to command." (*Marshal Zhukov's Greatest Battles,* 129-30n.) Lopatin apparently concluded that continued efforts to defend Stalingrad were unwarranted (ibid.), and on 9 Sep 41 he let Yeremenko know that he had lost confidence in himself; and the search for a replacement ended with CHUYKOV's being told on the 12th to take over the embattled 62d Army.

Lopatin subsequently commanded the 37th Army, Oct 41 to June 42, then had a rapid succession of other field army commands: the 9th Army to July; the 62d, again, through Sep 42; the 34th until Mar 43; the 11th through July; and the 20d, Sep-Oct 43. The general was deputy CG 43d Army from Jan to July 44, when he took command of the 13th Guards Rifle Corps. After the war he commanded varous rifle corps and had staff assignments, retiring in 1954.

LORD HAW HAW. *See* William JOYCE.

LORENZ, Werner. Nazi official. 1891-1974. A wealthy man with large industrial interests, an estate near Danzig, and a reputation for living well, Lorenz became head of Volksdeutsch Mittelstelle (VOMI) in 1937. He was responsible for ethnic Germans living abroad.

Lorenz was born 2 Oct 91 in Gruenhof. He became an officer cadet and a military pilot, joined a **Freikorps** after WWI, and was an early member of the Nazi Party. In 1931 he joined the SS, rising to **Obergruppenfuehrer** in 1943. When Hitler came to power, Lorenz entered the Reichstag as a delegate from East Prussia. During the war he was involved in resettling Germans from Poland, the Baltic States, and the USSR. VOMI also exploited **fifth column** techniques, recruited Germans of foreign birth for the Waffen-SS, and undertook programs to Germanize foreign nationals in occupied territories. VOMI eventually merged with the Central Office for Race and Resettlement to form the Reich Office for the Consolidation of German Nationhood. Lorenz subsequently headed the resettlement staff with the Reich commissioner for Germanization and was in charge of the International Relations Division of the SS Central Department.

Although Lorenz was ambitious to increase personal power, he "showed great zeal and skill . . . yet never resorted to brutality" (Hamilton, *Leaders*, 305). He has been called "marginally better than some of his contemporaries when it came to the treatment of subject peoples" (Wistrich). Found guilty of war crimes and sentenced to 20 years in prison, he was amnestied in 1955 and died on 13 May 74.

LOTHIAN, Lord. *See* Philip Henry KERR.

LOVAT, Lord (Simon Fraser). British officer. 1911-. Clan Fraser's 24th chief, he served in the Scots Guards, 1934-37. Two years later Capt Fraser took command of the Lovat Scouts, a unit his father had raised in the Boer War. At Churchill's suggestion the Scouts became a commando unit in 1942. It was the last element of Robert LAYCOCK's "Layforce" retained in the Middle East order of battle.

In the Dieppe Raid, 19 Aug 42, Lovat led the wing of his 4th (Scots) Commando that destroyed a cliff-top gun battery near Le Haut. "Battery demolished 0650" was the radio report to England, and the commando was the only unit to withdraw without excessive casualties. For the Normandy landings on 6 June 44 Lovat led the 1st Special Service Bde into battle with his personal piper. Invalided out of active service for wounds, Brigadier Lovat visited the USSR with Laycock to advise the Red Army on river crossing operations. Lord Lovat was Joint Undersecretary at the Foreign Office in Churchill's caretaker government May-July 45.

LOW, David. British cartoonist. 1891-1963. The great political cartoonist, caricaturist, and satirist was born 7 Apr 91 in Dunedin, NZ. Low published his first cartoon at the age of 11. In the next six decades he produced about 13,000, publishing them every few years from 1908 in books. Low was on the Sydney *Bulletin* staff 1911-19, with the *Star* (London) until 1926, then was on Lord BEAVERBROOK's *Evening Standard*. Perhaps the cartoonist's best known work portrays an unbeaten and resolute Britain after the fall of France; it is captioned "Very well, alone" (1940). His most famous character is Colonel Blimp, a fat, pompous old British reactionary. *(CB 40.)*

From 1953 the cartoonist was with the *Manchester Guardian*. Low appears in a self caricature as a puckish man with a Shakespearean beard. He published *Autobiography* in 1956 and was knighted in 1962. (*EB* Yrbk obit.)

LUCAS, John Porter. US general. 1890-1949. Born in West Virginia on 14 Jan 90, he graduated from the USMA in 1911 (55/82), was commissioned in the cavalry and transferred to the field artillery. He served on the **Punitive Expedition** and then was in France with the 33d Inf Div, being awarded the PH.

Lucas was promoted major general (T) on 5 Aug 41 and assigned the next month as CG, 3d Inf Div, training it in the US until TRUSCOTT took over in Mar 42. A year later Lucas succeeded Harold R. Bull as Eisenhower's deputy ground commander—"eyes and ears"—in Tunisia and in Sicily.

After the near disaster at Salerno Lucas replaced DAWLEY on 20 Sep 43 as CG, 6th Corps, and began planning the Anzio landings. Churchill had proposed this amphibious assault as a "left hook" to turn Kesselring's formidable Gustav Line defenses that were anchored on Cassino (WC, V, 493). The prime minister, one for daring ventures, learned too late that Mark Clark had picked an elderly and unproven

general to command the operation and that Clark had made other decisions that—in the PM's opinion—crippled the original concept (WC, V, 486, 493.) Lucas is said to have had a premonition of failure.

On 21 Jan 44 the force sailed from Naples and achieved tactical surprise. But Lucas took too long in stabilizing his beachhead, and KESSELRING masterfully shifted reserves from the north and from quiet sectors of the Gustav Line. MACKENSEN counterattacked with his 14th Army on 15 Feb 44, making a dangerous penetration along the Albano-Anzio axis but failing to use his reserves properly for a knockout. A US counterattack on the 19th stabilized the perimeter.

"I had hoped that we were hurling a wildcat onto the shore," said Churchill, "but all we had got was a stranded whale" (WC, V, 488). Lucas was not universally blamed, particularly by the superior who mattered most, army CofS George C. Marshall. The latter informed Eisenhower by message on 1 Mar 44 that unless Lucas was needed again as eyes and ears he was to be shipped home for another high command.

Replaced by Truscott, Lucas spent the rest of the war as CG, 4th Army, at San Antonio, Tex, where his mission was to train troops and headquarters staffs.

Maj Gen Lucas was chief of the Army Advisory Group in Nanking, China, 1946-48, then deputy CG, 5th Army in Chicago. He died 24 Dec 49 at the Great Lakes USNH, Waukegan, Ill.

LUETH, Wolfgang. U-boat commander. 1913-45. Lueth destroyed more shipping, approximately 253,000 tons, than any other submarine skipper in history.

Born 15 Oct 13 in Riga, the tall, bald, scholarly looking submariner rose to Korvettenkapitaen before his 30th birthday. With U-138, U-43, and U-18 he spent more than 200 days at sea and on 9 Aug 43 was awarded the Diamonds (7/27) (Angolia, I, 69). A year later Lueth was promoted to Kapitaen sur Zee in command of the Naval School at Muerwik. Days after the German surrender, when Doenitz was using Lueth's headquarters, the captain was outside preparing to make a security check on 14 May 45 when a German guard shot him dead. For some reason Lueth had failed to answer the sentry's challenge. (Doenitz, *Memoirs,* 475.)

LUETJENS, Guenther. German admiral. 1889-1941. He is remembered primarily for a brief, fatal career as commander of the world's newest and most powerful battleship, *Bismarck.* The story is told below in some detail because it involves many famous names of the war.

In 1935 Capt Luetjens became chief of the German navy's officer personnel branch. Then he was promoted to rear admiral and appointed Officer Commanding Torpedo Boats. In the Polish campaign he was Officer Commanding Destroyers (Doenitz, 306). With a further promotion for the assault on Norway Vice Adm Luetjens led Group 1, built around BBs *Scharnhorst* and *Gneisenau.* With these he supported Eduard DIETL's expedition to Narvik, decoying Battle Cruiser *Renown* away from the scene on 9 Apr 40 for a brief duel in which *Gneisenau* was hit once. But Luetjens did not stop the Royal Navy from destroying German naval forces on which DIETL depended logistically.

Promoted after the conquest of Norway, Fleet Commander Luetjens finally got *Gneisenau* and *Scharnhorst* into the North Atlantic. Leaving Kiel on 21 Jan 41 he undertook a highly effective two-month raid; with operational control of U-boats (Doenitz, 164) he sank 21 ships totaling 115,000 tons (*H&C,* 125).

Two weeks after entering Brest on 22 Mar 41 Luetjens was ordered to transfer his flag to *Bismarck* and conduct a large scale operation RAEDER had been planning for settling scores with the Royal Navy. Various problems reduced the intended size of his force to the point that neither Hitler nor Leutjens believed it could succeed, but Raeder remained confident. The just-completed *Bismarck* (1941) was in Churchill's words "the most powerful, as she is the newest, battleship in the world" (WC, III, 319). She and CA *Prinz Eugen* (1938), whose role was that of scout, cleared the Kattegat in mid-afternoon on 20 May 41 and headed for the **Denmark Strait.** Sallying forth from here at first light on 24 May, the Germans quickly sank the venerable BC *Hood* with 95 officers and 1,321 men (*R&H,* 100). But *Bismarck* took two serious hits from BB *Prince of Wales.* With a punctured fuel tank in *Bismarck,* Luetjens broke radio

silence at 8 AM, two hours after the action ended, to say he was heading for the French coast. Rear Adm W. F. Wake-Walker continued to shadow with his two cruisers, which later in the day were diverted long enough by *Bismarck*'s heavy guns for the undamaged *Prinz Eugen* to break for the South Atlantic.

Four days earlier, on first learning of the sortie, the Royal Navy had ordered a large scale hunt. Lost in the North Atlantic for 31 hours after dropping from Wake-Walker's radar screens, *Bismarck* was picked up by a Catalina PBY when she was almost home free—690 miles from Brest and within a few hours of having land-based air cover.

But the British trap closed as the light faded on 26 May. Force H from Gibraltar—CV *Ark Royal,* BC *Renown,* and CA *Sheffield,* all under James F. SOMERVILLE—intercepted *Bismarck,* and two hits from *Ark Royal*'s **Swordfish** damaged *Bismarck*'s steering; she was forced to steam in circles while frantic repair efforts were made. *Sheffield,* which had directed the air strike, was content to wait out the night of 26-27 May as *King George V* and *Rodney* arrived to resume the action in daylight. But Capt Philip VIAN, still aboard *Cossack,* arrived during the night with his four other destroyers and made daring torpedo attacks. Shortly after midnight Luetjens signalled, "Ship unmaneuverable. We shall fight to the last shell. Long live the Fuehrer!" (WC, III, 317-18.)

At 8:47 AM on 27 May *Rodney* opened fire from 25,000 yards, followed a minute later by *King George V.* (Ibid.) The British battleships closed to 4,000 yards, after which two cruisers closed in. The last German gun was silent by 10:15 and the great ship was an inferno. A torpedo from CA *Dorsetshire* caused an internal explosion that sent *Bismarck* down at about 10:35 AM Luetjens died with some 2,100 others (*R&H,* 101).

LUETTWITZ, Heinrich, Freiherr von. German general. 1895-1970. A cavalryman, Generalleutnant von Luettwitz commanded the crack 2d Pz Div in France from 1 Feb 44. Heavily engaged in Normandy the division was virtually destroyed in the retreat eastward (*B&O,* 70). The general moved up to head the 47th Pz Corps of MANTEUFFEL's 5th Pz Army on 5 Sep 44 and was promoted to

General of Panzer Troops on 1 Nov 44 (*B&O,* 52). Comprising the reconstituted 2d Pz Div, BAYERLEIN's elite Pz Lehr Div, and the 26th Volksgrenadier Div, the 47th Corps was on Manteuffel's left (south) flank for the Ardennes counteroffensive. Luettwitz's panzers encircled Bastogne while the Volks-grenadiers attacked closer in. Luettwitz and BAYERLEIN drafted the surrender ultimatum to which Tony McAULIFFE gave his famous reply, "Nuts" (Merriam, *Bulge,* 139). On Hitler's orders the cavalryman pressed toward the Meuse with the panzers, which were virtually destroyed. In Feb 45 the general was part of Blaskowitz's AG H in the Lower Rhine region with remnants of his corps designated **Abteilung** von Luettwitz (*B&O,* 51).

LUETTWITZ, Smilo, Freiherr von. German general. 1895-1975. He was born in Strasbourg on 23 Dec 95 and joined the 8th Grenadier Regt in 1915. In June 40, Oberstleutnant Smilo, Freiherr von Luettwitz left a staff position to take over the 12th **Schuetzenregiment,** 4th Pz Div, which was on occupation duty in France. Leading it in Russia he was awarded the RK on 14 Jan 42. When the 26th Pz Div was formed in Mons, Belgium, from the 23d Potsdamer Inf Div Oberst von Leuttwitz became its acting commander on 14 July 42 and was promoted on 1 Sep 42. Generalmajor von Luettwitz took the division to France a month later for continued training and coastal defense. The 26th Pz Div was among the reinforcements rushed Italy after Allied landings started at Salerno on 9 Sep 43. Ill suited for mountain warfare, road bound and weak in infantry (Senger, 185), it nevertheless figured prominently in the Italian campaign as part of the 14th Pz Corps. SENGER, who took command of the corps on 8 Oct 43, has high praise in his memoirs for "the calm and confident commander, General Count v. Luettwitz" (ibid.). The division fought in the battles for Cassino and was among the forces KESSELRING rushed to contain the Anzio beachhead. Having been promoted to Generalleutnant on 1 Oct 43 and awarded the Oakleaves (426/890) on 16 Mar 44, Luettwitz received the Swords (76/159) on 4 July 44. (Angolia, I, 184; II, 351. *B&O,* 127.) Having been with the 26th Pz Div for almost two years Luettwitz left it to serve as acting commander of the 46th Pz Corps

in Poland, NW of Warsaw, during the period 21 July-28 Aug 44 (*B&O,* 49). On 1 September he was promoted to General of Panzer Troops and given command of the 9th Army around Warsaw. In mid-Jan 45 the Freiherr was among the generals Hitler ousted as the Red Army drove into Germany. (Seaton, *R-G War,* 536), although some authorities say he stepped down to head the 75th Army Corps (Angolia, II, 351). After the war he commanded the 3d Corps of the Bundeswehr (ibid.).

LUMSDEN, Herbert. British general. 1894-1945. Col Lumsden's 12th Lancers formed the Armored Car Regt of the BEF Hq in the retreat to Dunkirk. In England the "gay, charming, handsome, theatrical, highly-strung" cavalryman (Barnett, 278) commanded an armored brigade. In early 1942 Maj Gen Lumsden reached the Western Desert to command the 1st Br Armd Div, whose elements were being sent out piecemeal from the UK. Severely wounded almost immediately in an air attack, and replaced temporarily by MESSERVY on 6 January, Lumsden returned to duty 26 May 42 for the disastrous 8th Army defeats on the Gazala line. Lumsden was a veteran of war in the desert by the time MONTGOMERY reached Egypt on 12 Aug 42 to command the 8th Army. Monty defeated Rommel at Alam Halfa, 31 Aug-6 Sep 42, and began to purge his army of subordinates he had inherited. Not having anybody to head what was expected to be his answer to the Afrika Korps, but with high recommendations from veteran officers in the Western Desert, he picked Lumsden, whom he hardly knew (Mongtomery, *Memoirs,* 103). Lumsden's new 10th Corps was made up of the 1st and 10th Armd Divs.

Lt Gen Lumsden and his veteran subordinates disagreed sharply with Montgomery's use of armor in the battles of El Alamein to breach heavily mined areas defended by German infantry. Lumsden suffered what he considered to be exorbitant losses in "the dogfight" around Kidney Hill, 27 Oct-4 Nov 42, but broke through and led the pursuit to El Agheila. Montgomery had already decided to replace Lumsden, however, and before the strong El Agheila defenses on 13 Dec 42 he gave HORROCKS command of the 10th Corps. "I had reached the conclusion that command of a corps in a major battle was above

Lumsden's ceiling," Montgomery would write (*Memoirs,* 128). Back at the Cavalry Club in England, Lumsden was more to the point: "There just isn't room in the desert for two—like Montgomery and me." (Quoted in Strawson, *North Africa,* 159n.)

But Churchill viewed Lumsden as "one of our most distinguished and accomplished officers" (WC, V, 94) and in the fall of 1944 sent him as special British representative on MacArthur's staff. Observing preliminary bombardments in Lingayen Gulf on 6 Jan 45 he was killed aboard BB *New Mexico* with about 20 others when a kamikaze hit the port wing of the bridge. "We buried him at sea," wrote MacArthur. "He was England at its best." (*Reminiscences,* 240-41)

LUTHER, Martin. Nazi official. 1895-1945. Ribbentrop's most powerful subordinate, Luther was born 16 Dec 95 in Berlin. He served with army railroad units in WWI and was a professional furniture mover when he entered the Bureau Ribbentrop in 1936. From being a menial in charge of shipping office furniture he rose by intrigue to head the new "Germany" office, Abteilung Deutschland (Dept III). This had charge of all foreign office propaganda and was responsible for liaison with other Nazi party agencies. One of Luther's subordinates, Franz Rademacher (1906-73), drew up the **Madagascar plan** in 1940. Luther represented his chief at the **Wannsee conference** (20 Jan 42) and prodded satellite governments to use initiative in achieving the "Final Solution."

Luther conspiring with Himmler to oust Ribbentrop, drafting charges against his chief in Apr 43. But Himmler betrayed the plot by having his adjutant, Karl Wolff, send Ribbentrop an advance copy of the document. Imprisoned at **Sachsenhausen,** where he failed in a suicide attempt, Luther was released as the Red Army encircled Berlin in Apr 45. He died the next month of a heart attack while in a local hostpital. (Wistrich.)

LUTZE, Viktor. Nazi official. 1890-1943. Lutze was born in Beveregen on 28 Dec 90 and rose from the ranks of the army after enlisting in 1912. "A heavy drinker and loose talker" (Irving, *HW,* xxx), he became police president of Hanover and Oberpraesident (1933-41), member of the Prussian State Council (1933), then was CofS of the emasculated SA after the Blood Purge of 1934. Lutze died 2 May 43 in a car crash on the autobahn and was given a state funeral at which Hitler spoke.

M

MacARTHUR, Douglas. US general. 1880-1964. The third child and second son of Gen Arthur MacArthur II (following) and the formidable Mary Pinkney Hardy, he was scheduled for delivery at the ante-bellum family mansion, "Riveredge," built by her wealthy father in Norfolk, Va. But the event, on 26 Jan 80, occurred at Little Rock, where the father was serving, and a Norfolk newspaper carried the extraordinary notice that "Douglas MacArthur was born on January 26, while his parents were away." (MacArthur, *Reminiscences,* 14).

The MacArthur Heritage

Arthur MacArthur, great grandfather of Douglas, reached America in 1825 from Glasgow, Scotland, with his widowed mother. They settled in Chicopee Falls, Mass. Arthur was admitted to the New York bar in 1840, and nine years later established the family in Milwaukee, Wisc. Here he became a prominent jurist and politician.

Arthur II (1845-1912) was a legend in the Civil War as the "boy colonel" (Medal of Honor, three times WIA). He fought in the Philippines during the Spanish-American war of 1898 and in the long and bloody insurrection under Emilo Aguinaldo that followed. MacArthur was promoted to major general on 5 Feb 01, and shortly thereafter became CinC and military governor. (*Reminiscences,* 21.) But when Wm Howard Taft arrived as civil governor he quickly clashed with the veteran soldier, who went home in July 1901. Son Douglas meanwhile had entered West Point (below). In 1904-5 General Arthur MacArthur was official observer with the Japanese in the Russo-Japanese War, being joined by his son as ADC. In 1906 the senior MacArthur was promoted to lieutenant general, the top rank in the US Army and held by only one officer at a time. But Taft, now Secretary of War, denied MacArthur the Army's top post and put him on the shelf. Having reached the statutory retirement age of 64, Arthur MacArthur retired three months after President Taft took the oath of office in 1909. Three years later, the general defied doctor's orders to join veterans of his Civil War regiment for their 50th and last re-union. Asked to speak, he was recalling old days when he fell dead of a stroke. The general's wartime adjutant wrapped him in the regimental flag and, as if this were not dramatic enough, then collapsed of a fatal stroke.

In addition to remarkably strong parents, Douglas had an elder brother who was an inspiration. Arthur MacArthur III graduated from Annapolis at the age of 20 (USNA 1896 [21/38]). Considered by many to be on his way to the navy's highest position, he died suddenly of appendicitis in 1926. The brothers had been fierce competitors in childhood and were close thereafter; Arthur named a son Douglas MacArthur II. The latter had an outstanding career in the foreign service, becoming ambassador to Japan, Belgium, and Austria. (James, *MacArthur,* I, 46.)

Early Career

Although fired from childhood to follow his father's path, Douglas MacArthur found the first steps difficult. Unable to get a political appointment to West Point, he had to compete for a presidential appointment. "I never worked harder in my life," he would remember, but he beat the closest competitor by 16 points. "It was a lesson I never forgot. Preparedness is the key to success and victory." (*Reminiscences,* 18; James, I, 66.)

A classmate and competitor at "Hell on the Hudson" was Ulysees S. Grant III (1881-1968). When Mrs MacArthur learned that Mrs Grant was accompanying her son to cheer him for top honors, she packed up to follow her own. (Gen Arthur MacArthur was in the Philippines until July 01.) The ladies resided in the grubby Chaney's Hotel, just north of the parade ground. Douglas won out as first captain and graduated first in the 93-man class of 1903 with the highest grades in 25 years. Grant ranked sixth. Commissioned in the Corps of Engineers, MacArthur served briefly in the Philippines. He was promoted to first lieutenant and sent to San Francisco before being ordered to join his father in the Far East (above). In 1906 Douglas was made ADC to Pres Theodore Roosevelt. He was assigned to general staff duty in with the War Dept, 1913-17, and served in 1914 was an official observer with the Vera Cruz Expedition. After a dangerous reconnaissance made on his own initiative, Capt MacArthur was recommended by the Army chief of staff, Gen Leonard Wood, for the Medal of Honor. This was disapproved, but MacArthur was promoted to major on returning to Washington. As the junior officer on the WDGS in 1913-17 he had a major role in bringing National Guard troops into the **AEF.** Jumped to the grade of colonel in Sep 17, he transferred to the infantry and became CofS of the 42d Div. At his suggestion this division was formed of troops from many states and called the Rainbow Division.

World War I

With Gen John J. Pershing's AEF the tall, dark, strikingly handsome Col MacArthur became famous for disregarding danger as well as uniform regulations. "The Fighting Dude," "Beau Brummell of the 42nd," "d'Artagnan of the Western Front," was promoted on 26 June 18 to become (at 36) the youngest general of the AEF. He did not know that his mother had sent a long confidential letter of recommendation to "My dear General Pershing" signed "Faithfully, your friend—Mary P. MacArthur" (James, I, 304). Nor is it generally known that Pershing personally disliked the young "brilliant engineer" despite a lasting but begrudging professional admiration. (Source: Col M. M. Boatner, Jr, Corps of Engineers, Pershing's chef de cabinet, 1934-38.)

Two months after getting his star MacArthur took command of the division's 84th Bde. Following a succession of desperate defensive actions the Fighting Dude led the brigade in the AEF's three major offensives, embellishing his jaunty, "non-reg" uniform with two DSCs, a DSM, six Silver Stars, and two wound stripes. In the last week of the war he assumed command of the 42d (Rainbow) Div and was recommended for promotion to major general but the armistice intervened.

Between the Wars

In June 19 Brig Gen MacArthur became the youngest superintendent in the 117-year history of West Point. Shortened classes to meet the wartime emergency had virtually destroyed the

academy, which already was behind the times, and there was a move to close the institution. The new "Supe," himself a recent graduate, was fought every step of the way by authorities at West Point and in Washington but he prevailed in revitalizing the school, doubling its size and modernizing the curriculum. "If Sylvanus Thayer dominated West Point in the nineteenth century," writes James, "Douglas MacArthur dominated it in the twentieth." (Ibid. I, 293.) This would not be appreciated until later and MacArthur's tenure as Supe was cut short by critics including Pershing (ibid., 288-89). The announcement was made in Jan 22 that he would be replaced at the end of the academic year.

"In February 1922," writes MacArthur, "I entered into matrimony, but it was not successful, and ended in divorce [seven] years later." (*Reminiscences,* 83.) That is all the general choses to say of a painful episode in his life, but a biographical sketch demands amplification. The lady was a beautiful, jazz age socialite born to tremendous wealth in NYC. Henrietta Louise Cromwell married a rich Baltimore contractor, Walter Brooks, in 1908, had a son and daughter, and she got a divorce in 1919. Louise meanwhile had met Pershing in Paris during WWI and later was briefly his official hostess in Washington while Pershing (35 years her senior) was Army CofS. (James, I, 291, 319-24.)

Sailing for the Philippines in Sep 22 with Louise and two stepchildred (to whom he was devoted), Brig Gen MacArthur commanded the newly established Military District of Manila, then the 23d Bde, Philippine Div, and finally that division. Before Pershing left his post as Army CofS he recommended that MacArthur be promoted to major general. The son apparently never knew that Pershing again had acted on his mother's urging. (*See* her letter to Pershing in James, I, 304.)

A few months after becoming the Army's youngest two-star general (at 43), effective 17 Jan 25 (announced 23 Sep 24), MacArthur briefly headed the 4th Corps Area Hq (Atlanta) before taking over the 3d Corps Area Hq (Baltimore). As a member of Gen William ("Billy") MITCHELL's court martial (*see* also H. H. ARNOLD), "I did what I could in his behalf and I helped save him from dismissal," said MacArthur to accusations of betraying a fellow officer. "That he was wrong in the violence of his language is self-evident; that he was right in his thesis is equally true and incontrovertible." (*Reminiscences,* 85-86.)

The move to Baltimore, near Louise's "Rainbow Hill" estate, apparently was a final attempt to save the marriage. But by Aug 27 she had left for NYC and in 1929 would get a Reno divorce on grounds of "failure to provide"! (James, I, 322.) Meanwhile, a month after Louise left Rainbow Hill MacArthur's morale got a much needed boost when he was made president of the American Olympic Committee. The incumbent had died—just 10 months before the Amsterdam games of 1928——and the US effort was in disarray. The sports-minded young general worked tirelessly to resolve administrative problems, then personally exhorted American athletes to an overwhelming team victory in the unofficial final score.

In Sept 28 MacArthur was ordered back to the Philippines as commander of all US troops. In July 29 he declined the post of chief of engineers, a decision that should have alienated Washington authorities. However, on 5 Aug 30 his selection as Army CofS was announced. (*Reminiscences,* 89.) The Great Depression had struck, the army's budget was being hacked, and MacArthur was reluctant to accept the appointment. But at the strong urging of his mother he accepted.

Sworn in on 21 Nov 30 and given four-star rank, he was the youngest officer ever to hold the office. During lean year of the Depression, anti-militarism being rampant, MacArthur had considerable success in modernizing the woefully unprepared little US Army of about 135,000 officers and men. He brought mobilization plans "closer to realism than they had been before" (Weigley, *Hist of the US Army,* 407).

MacArthur's least important military action as CofS but the one most publicized was during the "Bonus Army" riots of 1932. Veterans marched on Washington to establish squatters' camps and draw world-wide attention. After most of the 17,000 protesters were appeased, a hard core of 5,000, including the "Communist bloc" (*Reminiscences,* 94), marched on the Treasury Building and the White House. Metropolitan police, roughly handled, failed to establish control. Secretary of War Patrick HURLEY then was placed in charge. Some 600 infantry

and cavalry troops from the Washington area were mustered under Gen Perry L. Miles, and President Hoover asked MacArthur to accompany him. (*Reminiscences,* 95.) In the long day of 28 July 32, without firing a shot and with no serious injuries on either side, the troops accomplished their mission. (On MacArthur's staff were Majors EISENHOWER and PATTON.) But groundless charges against MacArthur were raised by elements of the press, even in Congress, for undue use of force and grandstanding. "When I challenged such distortions, they were merely shrugged off with the expression, 'it was only politics,'" writes MacArthur. "Franklin Roosevelt once said to me, 'Douglas, I think that you are our best general, but I believe you would be our worst politician'" (*Reminiscences,* 96). When FDR assumed office in 1933 he extended MacArthur's normal tour of duty for an additional year. Now 55 years old, his first career ended, he was offered the post of high commissioner in the Philippine Commonwealth. This was being created with the inauguration of Manuel QUEZON as president. MacArthur declined because he would have had to retire from the Army. But at Quezon's request the veteran of four previous assignments in the Far East became military adviser to the Philippines. In the fall of 1935 he reached Manila with his mother and a small staff including Maj D. D. EISENHOWER. Aboard the *President Hoover* was Jean Marie Faircloth, 37, a feisty, poised, and cultured little brunette from Tennessee. She was going to visit English friends in Shanghai, and MacArthur married her in NYC 18 months after their first meeting. "It was perhaps the smartest thing I have ever done." (*Reminiscences,* 106.) Their only child, Arthur, was born in Manila on 21 Feb 38. A Chinese amah, Loh Chiu, jokingly nicknamed "Ah Cheu," soon joined the household.

World War II

When the Philippine Army was inducted into the US Army on 26 July 41, MacArthur was recalled to active duty as a lieutenant general to head the newly created US Army Forces in the Far East. (In 1935 he had reverted to his permanent rank of major general, and since 1936 had been a field marshal of the Philippines.)

Why MacArthur was caught by surprise in the Philippines remains a mystery. He had ample notice of the Pearl Harbor attack, but Japanese planes destroyed most of the air force under BRERETON on the ground. Enemy troops began landing on 10 Dec 41. On Christmas eve, MacArthur belatedly evacuated Manila and moved his headquarters to Corregidor. Shortly thereafter he was promoted to full general (again). EISENHOWER, new chief of the War Plans Div, reinforced George Marshall's conviction that the Phillipines could not be held. Instead, a new Allied base had to be created in Australia. Encouraged by Churchill, Roosevelt decided that MacArthur should be saved to fight another day. The plan initially was that he would set up a defense on Mindanao, but Prime Minister CURTIN requested that the general be evacuated to take over the new SW Pacific Area in Australia. MacArthur, his family (including Ah Cheu) and a small group left Corregidor the evening of 11 Mar 42. In the battered PT boat squadron of Navy Lt John D. Bulkeley they reached Cagayan on the 13th after a harrowing and uncomfortable trip. After more delays and narrow escapes, the party was taken (on 17 March) by two rickety B-17s to Batchelor Field, 40 miles south of Darwin. Changing planes 10 minutes before Japanese pursuers hit the field, MacArthur made a brief public statement that concluded with "I came through and I shall return." For his role in the Philippines, the general was awarded the Medal of Honor.

Appointed Supreme Commander of the SW Pacific Area (SWPA) on 18 Apr 42, he began organizing the strategic defense of Australia. SWPA Hq quickly was moved from Melbourne, to Brisbane, to Port Moresby on New Guinea. This port was being seriously threatened by a column under HORII. As the Japanese closed in, MacArthur was outraged by how poorly his American ground and air forces performed, and he had little praise for the Australians. US and Australian generals exchanged criticism, and the mood was tense. But the picture brightened. In the Battle of the Coral sea, US and Australian naval forces broke up a major enemy offensive against Port Moresby. (See Adm Frank J. FLETCHER. MacArthur's air war was taken over and turned around by George KENNEY. US forces on the Buna front were shaped up by EICHELBERGER. The capable Australian Gen Thomas BLAMEY took over direction of Allied Ground Forces. US reinforcements and increased logistical support began coming in.

By the end of 1942 MacArthur had contained the enemy advance and was on the offensive toward Tokyo.

MacArthur expected to direct the main effort against the Japanese. But Adm Ernest J. KING saw to it that the war in the Pacific was primarily a navy show directed by Chester NIMITZ. MacArthur consequently had a secondary role in a secondary theater, the agreed Anglo-American grand strategy being "Germany first." But in a brilliant display of generalship, MacArthur leap-frogged up the coast of New Guinea. During the period June 43—Mar 44 he isolated New Britain, including the principal Japanese base at Rabaul. (As head of the independent South Pacific Area, but under MacArthur's operational control, HALSEY led one wing.) The amphibious operations were remarkable for gains made with minimum loss of life. Primarily for this achievement he is considered by most military authorities as the greatest commander in WWII.

One of MacArthur's hardest fights was to scotch a proposal to bypass the Philippines, advocated most strongly by Ernest J. KING and NIMITZ (although MacArthur almost won over the latter and his CINCPAC/CINCPAO staff at Pearl Harbor). Disagreements about the Pacific war strategy were resolved by ROOSEVELT at a meeting with MacArthur and Nimitz at Pearl Harbor in June 44.

A few hours after the assault wave hit the beach on Leyte, and with snipers still at work, MacArthur provided a great "photo opportunity" by wading ashore on 20 Oct 44 with OSMENA. He had returned. The Leyte campaign was decisive because the Japanese committed their dwindling strategic resources there for a last stand. The final resistance was collapsing when MacArthur was given the new, five-star rank of General of the Army on 18 Dec 44. He now was junior (by two days) only to George Marshall, and a few days senior to EISENHOWER and "Hap" ARNOLD.

American troops began landing on Luzon in Linguyan Gulf on 9 Jan 45. After a month of heavy fighting, Japanese resistance in Manila ended on 3 March. A week later the landings began on Mindanao but it took another four months to mop up the last organized resistance in the Philippine Islands. At this time the planning for an assault on the Japanese main islands had ended when news came on 15 Aug 45 that

HIROHITO had agreed to surrender. On this date MacArthur was named Supreme Commander for the Allied Powers (SCAP), directed to receive the formal capitulation and to head the Allied occupation of Japan. The surrender ceremony was staged 2 Sep 45 aboard *Missouri* a few miles outside Tokyo Bay.

Civil Administration of Japan

Historians agree with MacArthur that the most important accomplishment of his long, illustrious career was as civil administrator of Japan. One of his first and wisest decisions was to urge that the Emperor Hirohito be left on the throne and not treated as a war criminal. MacArthur then ignored his staff's advice and waited for HIROHITO to request an audience. The emperor thereafter cooperated closely with the conqueror and helped assure that his people did likewise.

Brooking little interference from Washington as well, the imperious proconsul made sweeping and lasting reforms in Japan's political, economic, social, and cultural life. He also moved quickly and decisively to thwart Soviet efforts to muscle in. In war crimes prosecutions he was ruthless, even vindictive, incurring some just criticism in the case of YAMASHITA and others. History may prove that the constitution dictated by MacArthur was badly shortsighted in forcing the Japanese to renounce war forever as an instrument of foreign policy. This enabled the vanquished to concentrate resources on economic warfare, for which they proved to have an alarming aptitude. Japan's first big economic bounce came in the Korean War; far from being a threat while American's back was turned, as some predicted, Japan was a powerful and well remunerated US partner.

Presidential ambitions had long been associated with MacArthur. FDR called him and Huey P. Long the "two most dangerous men in America" (as his potential challengers). From the proconsul in Tokyo came professions of disinterest. An effort to draft him was started in 1943 by Senator Arthur H. Vandenberg, Robert E. Wood, newspaper publisher Frank Gannett, and others. But in the Wisconsin primary the general got only three delegates to Thomas Dewey's 17 and was persuaded to withdraw. Roosevelt was said to have been concerned earlier, but FDR's quip at the time of the Bonus Army affair (quoted above) seems to have been borne out.

The Korean War

On 25 June 50 the Soviet-supported North Koreans launched a surprise attack that quickly overran most of US supported South Korea. On 14 July, MacArthur was named Supreme Commander of the United Nations Forces in Korea retaining the former titles, SCAP and CinC Far East Command. Meanwhile he threw together combat forces from the flabby occupation troops in Japan. A precarious toe-hold was held around Pusan. Japan, far from taking advantage of US misfortune in Korea (in the Irish tradition) laid the foundation of a vigorous postwar economy.

MacArthur showed strategic audacity that is all the more remarkable considering his age and established military reputation. Against the almost universal recommendations of his advisers and higher authority, on 15 Sep 50 he sent troops ashore at Inchon. Tidal conditions and mud flats demanded such delicate timing that an amphibious operation seemed to be virtually impossible. MacArthur argued that this was all the more reason why it would succeed. He was right. Surprised, the North Koreans were forced to abandon their gains; less well known is that the North Korean army was so badly mauled that it ceased to be a major factor in the war. With authority from the **JCS,** MacArthur pursued across the 38th Parallel into Soviet-sponsored North Korea.

But then he made serious mistakes. The first was to order another amphibious envelopment, a landing at Wonsan, well above the 38th Parallel and on the east coast. This took forces that should have been used to exploit the Inchon landing. His second mistake was failure to grasp the concept of Limited War, which the US was facing for the first time in Korea and (having learned nothing) would face again in Vietnam. MacArthur's third mistake was failure to anticipate the Chinese reaction to his threat to their border, the Yalu River. Finally, he ignored evidence that Chinese forces were intervening on a massive scale. The result was a humiliating and costly defeat that forced forward elements back to the 38th Parallel and, in some places, beyond it.

In March 1951, House Minority Leader Joe Martin (R., Kansas) sent MacArthur a copy of his speech advocating use of CHIANG KAI-SHEK's Nationalist forces to invade the Chinese mainland and escalate the war. In defiance of

President Truman's orders that military leaders not publicly criticize US foreign policy, on 20 March, MacArthur wrote Martin a letter endorsing this general course of action. "As you point out," he wrote, "we must win. There is no substitute for victory." (*Reminiscences*, 385-86.) The congressman released the letter to the press, and MacArthur (like "Billy" Mitchell) was justly accused of insubordination.

MacArthur was preparing to leave Tokyo on 11 Apr 51 for a visit to the Korean front when an aide heard a radio bulletin. "President Truman has just removed General MacArthur from his Far Eastern and Korean Commands and from the direction of the occupation of Japan." (*Reminiscences*, 395.) Returning to his country for the first time in 15 years, the military hero received a tumultuous public welcome. On 19 Apr 51 he delivered a dramatic address to a joint session of Congress. Capitalizing on the fact that President Truman's popularity was at an all-time low, the general made an eloquent and theatrical apologia. He concluded by quoting from the barracks room ballad, "Old soldiers never die, they just fade away." He proceeded to do so. Ending 52 years of military service at the age of 71, with the almost-unique record of having been a general in three American wars, he became (1952) chairman of the board of Remington Rand, Inc. (later Sperry Rand). Residing with his adoring wife in the Waldorf Astoria Hotel, NYC, he outlived George MARSHALL to become, like his father, the US Army's senior officer (in 1959). He died at **WRGH** in Washington, DC, on 5 Apr 64 at the age of 84, and is buried at Norfolk, Va., in the rotunda of the MacArthur Memorial.

Although a large quantity of his records at that place now are open to researchers, the general refused to make his most closely guarded personal papers available to would-be biographers, even Douglas Southall Freeman. The sad consequence is that his own pontifical and carelessly edited *Reminiscences* (New York: McGraw-Hill, 1964) are notable primarily as evidence that few great commanders write great memoirs. The first solid biography is D. Clayton James, *The Years of MacArthur*, Vol I, 1880-1941 (1970); Vol II, 1941-45 (1975); and Vol III, 1945-64 (1985). The publisher is Houghton Mifflin. I am grateful to the author for his painstaking and gracious editing of the above sketch.

MACFARLANE, Frank Noel Mason. British general. 1889-93. Frequently identified as Noel Mason-Macfarlane, he is listed as Lt Gen Sir (Frank) Noel Mason Macfarlane in *Who Was Who, 1951-1960*, which is the source of the following sketch. Born 23 Oct 89, son of Col David Mason-MacFarlane, he was educated at Rugby and Woolwich and commissioned in the Royal Artillery. Macfarlane served in South Africa, India, France (1914-18), Belgium, Mesopotamia, and the Afghan War (1919). He then attended the Staff College at Quetta, India (1920) and the Imperial Defense College (1935). Meanwhile he had staff assignments in England, France, and India, and many tours as military attaché—in Budapest, Vienna, and Berne (1931-34), and Berlin and Copenhagen (1937-39). After being Brigadier General Royal Artillery at Aldershot 1939, he was director of military intelligence (DMI) with the BEF in France, 1939-40. Macfarlane then headed the British Mission to Moscow, 1941-42, before succeeding GORT as Governor and CinC at Gibraltar. Sir Frank (KCB 1943) became Chief Commissioner, Allied Control Commission for Italy, in 1944, serving with Robert MURPHY. Having risen to lieutenant general and appointed Colonel Commandant, Royal Artillery, in 1944, he was put on the retired list for disability in 1945. Sir Frank was an MP (Labour) for North Paddington, 1945-46, then retired to write. He died 12 Aug 53. (Ibid.)

MACLEAN, H. R. Fitzroy. British brigadier. 1911-. A famous linguist, explorer, author, and MP, he left the foreign office in 1941 to enlist in the army. He joined David STIRLING's **SAS** and took part in two commando raids on Benghazi before going to Iran in Sep 42. Here he organized the kidnapping of Gen Fazlallah Zahedi, who was conspiring to aid the Germans. (The general became premier in 1953.)

Churchill picked Maclean as "a man of daring character, with Parliamentary status and Foreign Office training . . . to go to Yugoslavia and work with Tito" (WC, V, 43). Forming a team that included the PM's son Randolph (a major with commando experience), he parachuted in to make contact with Tito's partisans. On the basis of his recommendations two months later to PM and Eden in Cairo, the last of 80 British missions with MIHAILOVIC were withdrawn in

Dec 43. All support subsequently went to Tito, whom Maclean rejoined not long before the Germans drove the partisans from their base at Drvar. "I myself was amazed, during an air raid on Drvar in February 1944, at the sight of his tall, bony frame moving about on the road as if nothing were happening," writes Djilas (*Wartime*, 348-49). With absences to cope with King PETER II's political crises, Maclean remained with TITO until the marshal became premier in Mar 45. He then resumed his career as an MP and published his war memoirs, *Eastern Approaches: Escape to Adventure*. (London: Cape, 1949; Boston: Little, Brown, 1950).

MACLEAN, Donald Duart. British traitor. 1913-83. The third son of a Liberal cabinet minister, he became one of the **Cambridge Five.** After entering the foreign service he was third secretary at the Paris embassy in 1938 and began passing classified material to the Soviets. After serving in London he went to Washington in 1944 as first secretary of the British embassy and acting head of chancery. This gave Maclean access to all classified message traffic, and as joint secretary of the Anglo-American-Canadian Combined Policy Committee in 1947 he had contact with the American Atomic Energy Commission. On trips to NYC "Homer" passed secrets to his Soviet controller, "Orphan."

US cipher experts were trying to identify Homer, whom they knew as a security leak in the British embassy in Washington, when Maclean returned to London in 1948. He was replaced in Washington by Guy Burgess, who kept his Cambridge schoolmate informed of the security search.

Posted to the Cairo embassy in 1948 as counsellor and head of chancery, Maclean was soon recalled and treated for alcoholism and homosexuality. Supposedly cured, he headed the American department of the foreign office and in November 1950 reestablished contact with Soviet intelligence. When Kim PHILBY learned in Washington of Maclean's impending arrest he sent Burgess home to warn their fellow spy. Both Burgess and Maclean defected on 25 May 51, barely escaping on the Channel ferry and making their way to Moscow. Here Maclean served in the foreign ministry before taking the British desk at the Institute of World Economic and International Relations. Having helped

shake Anglo-American relations by exposing laxity in the famous British secret service, the traitor taught graduate courses in international relations and published *British Foreign Policy since Suez* (London, 1970).

Maclean died in 1983 in Moscow.

MACMILLAN, (Maurice) Harold. British statesman. 1894-1986. Initially British Resident Minister to North Africa, he became UK Commissioner the Mediterranean and after the war was prime minister, 1957-63.

Almost six feet tall, the slim, suave diplomat was born in London on 10 Feb 94. His grandfather created the Macmillan publishing house, with whose direction Harold periodically assisted an elder brother for many years. Their "formidable" mother was American. (Macmillan, *Winds,* 30-58.) After leaving Eton, Macmillan interrupted studies at Oxford at the end of two years for service in France as a lieutenant of the Grenadier Guards. Invalided home in Sep 16 with a near-fatal wound in the pelvis, he finished Oxford with First Class Honors in 1919. The next year he married a daughter of the ninth Duke of Devonshire, Lady Dorothy, acquiring connections with one of Britain's most illustrious families.

From 1924 he was an MP with a break of two years until returning to serve from 1931 for a total of 16 years as a back-bencher. (*CB 43;* Macmillan, *Winds,* 10.) In Churchill's government, Macmillan held a minor post in the new Ministry of Supply before serving briefly in the Colonial Office. On 30 Dec 42, after **Torch,** it was announced that he would go to Algiers as British Resident Minister to North Africa (WC, IV, 645, 669). From Aug 43, with British recognition of DE GAULLE's **FCNL,** Macmillan had diplomatic status as UK commissioner. He subsequently served on the Allied Mediterranean Commission and the Italian Advisory Commission while remaining resident minister at Allied Headquarters in North Africa (*CB 43*) and being closely associated with Robert D. MURPHY.

After the war Macmillan occupied high offices in London leading to that of prime minister for almost seven years from 13 Jan 57, succeeding Anthony EDEN. His government weakened by a succession of security scandals including several involving the **Cambridge Five** and culminating in the **Profumo affair,** he retired in 1963 but remained prominent as a senior statesmen. Macmillan published historical works of exceptional merit that are listed in the bibliography of this book. Two years before his death in 1986 Macmillan accepted an earldom as first Earl of Stockton.

MAISKY, Ivan Mikhailovich. Soviet diplomat. 1884-1975. As Soviet ambassador to the UK for ten years, 1932-43, the soft-spoken, amiable, bewhiskered Maisky was dean of London's diplomatic corps. He was born 19 Jan 84 in Kirillov, Vologda Prov (N of Moscow), son of an army doctor, and named Ivan Mikhailovich Lyakhovetsky *(CB 41).* In 1908 he was expelled from the Univ of St Petersburg for revolutionary activity and arrested. Maisky then studied economics at the Univ of Munich, where he joined the social democratic movement. In 1912 he went to England and became a free-lance journalist. Shedding his Menshevik associations when the Russian revolution began, he began a diplomatic career in 1922 as press secretary for the Commissariat of Foreign Affairs. As the Soviets strove for recognition and good relations abroad, Maisky was sent for two-year assignments as counselor at the London and Tokyo embassies, and as minister to Finland. He returned to London, now as ambassador of an unpopular regime and during difficult times. Maisky was an Anglophile with a western outlook and, like LITVINOV, a staunch believer in the League of Nations and collective security. But the smiling Soviet ambassador and his gracious wife found the political and social winds of London chilling *(CB 41).* Having lived through western reaction to the **Great Purges** and **Nazi-Soviet Pact** of 23 Aug 39, the ambassador suddenly became accepted in London when Germany attacked his country on 22 June 41. (Moscow had ignored Maisky's warning.)

As London filled with governments in exile Maisky was busy negotiating agreements with them, notably the Poles, Czechs, and Free French. He was instrumental in having ANDERS's Polish army formed in the USSR. As for post-war frontiers, he wisely remained noncommittal. Like LITVINOV, Maisky was recalled in 1943. Made a deputy commissar for foreign affairs he participated in the Moscow talks of 1941, the London talks in 1942, and the Yalta and Potsdam conferences of 1945. Maisky was chairman of the Allied Commission on Repartitions in 1945 *(S&S).*

In 1946 he acquired the title academician and was involved in teaching and research until 1976. Meanwhile he was arrested 19 Feb 53 on suspicion of being a British spy (Scotts). Stalin died two weeks later, and the diplomat presumably was released then. (Scotts, citing *Mil Hist Journal,* Mar 90.) Although Maisky was an established author his *Memoirs of a Soviet Ambassador* (Moscow, 1966) are "generally unreliable" (Ulam, 251 & n.).

MALAN, Adolph Gysbert. South African ace. 1910-63. "Sailor" Malan joined the RAF in 1936. He scored the first 32 of his 35 victories by July 41, after only 14 months in action, yet was the RAF's third leading ace. The others were countryman PATTLE (41) and J. E. JOHNSON (38). A group captain from Oct 42, and spending most of the war on training assignments, Malan retired from the RAF and led campaigns against apartheid.

MALANDIN, German Kapitonovich. Soviet officer. 1894-1961. Malandin was born 15 Dec 94 in Nolinsk, Vyatka Prov, son of an office worker. In 1915 he graduated from the Military Cadet College; in WWI he was a company commander on the southwestern and Romanian fronts; and from 1918 he was in the Red Army. As an ex-Tsarist officer he was not allowed to join the CP but as a regimental commander on rear-area security duty in the civil war he crushed anti-Soviet revolts (Scarecrow). Malandin then served primarily as a staff officer. He was CofS from brigade to army level, ending in the Detached Red Banner Far Eastern Army, 1930-35. After graduation from the GS Academy in 1938, and remaining briefly as an instructor, in 1939 he was deputy CofS, Ukrainian Front, during the Galician campaign.

Politically suspect as a former officer in the old Russian army he was denied party membership until 1940. But Maladin was on the mass-promotion list of June 40, appointed general lieutenant along with Chuykov, Golikov, Konev, Vatutin, Yeremenko, and Sokolovsky. Although Malandin appeared to be in line for the fame they achieved as field commanders, he became a mere footnote.

Gen Lt Maladin was deputy CofS in the Kiev MD until his chief, ZHUKOV, became CGS on

14 Jan 41. A month later, when VATUTIN moved up from heading the operations directorate, Zhukov had Malandin transferred to Moscow as his chief operations officer. When TIMOSHENKO left Moscow to command a new Western front on 1 July 41 Malandin went along as his CofS. On 19 July Timoshenko became Glavkom of the Western **direction** and Malandin kept his post briefly, but he stepped down to be chief of the front's operations staff on 21 July 41 when SHAPOSHNIKOV arrived to be CofS.

(The 19 July 41 order making Stalin commissar of defense—vice Timoshenko—also named YEREMENKO commander of the Western Front with SOKOLOVSKY as CofS. The Scotts point out that this last part of the order apparently was never carried out. Soviet encyclopedias do not show that YEREMENKO ever commanded the Western Front.)

From Nov 41 Malandin headed the "operational art [field operations] department" at the GS Academy. From Dec 43 he was CofS to N. P. Pukhov in the 13th Army, 1st Ukrainian Front. After the war he was CofS, Central Forces Group, being promoted to general of the army (No. 31) on 12 Nov 48. Kruzhin finds he was deputy CGS at this time (RL 89/75, 5). Then Malandin was chief of the main staff, and deputy CinC of Ground Forces (Scotts). After holding other high posts he moved to the GS Academy in June 56, first as a department head then 1st deputy commandant. Malindin was commandant from June 58 until his death on 27 Oct 61.

MALENKOV, Georgi Maximilanovch. Soviet official. 1902-88. "A man of formidable intelligence, ability, toughness, and ability" (Crankshaw, ed, *Khrushchev,* 546), he became Stalin's successor.

"Yegor" Malenkov was born 5 Jan 02 in Orenburg, son of a Cossack officer in the Russian Army. Through his first wife, Valerie, who held a key post in Stalin's Orgburo, Malenkov became Stalin's personal assistant in 1927 and held the position for 25 years. A stubby five-feet-seven and later topping the scales at 250 pounds, he had a phenomenal memory. Through the Orgburo he stacked the party apparatus with Stalin supporters. Then as head of the Moscow Party Organization Dept he worked closely with NKVD chief Nikolai Yezov in getting the **Great Purges** under way. Malenkov did this by preparing dossiers on victims and nominating their successors. During the Great Patriotic War (WWII) he effectively reorganized and directed aircraft and tank production. In 1941 he was promoted to the **GKO** over KHRUSHCHEV's head. After ZHDANOV's execution in 1948 Malenkov was heir apparent to Stalin, whom he succeeded in 1953. For a short time he was both a party secretary and prime minister, but in Sep 53 he lost out to Khrushchev as first secretary and in 1955 to Bulganin as premier. Two years later Khrushchev had complete control. Branded anti-party, charged with wartime incompetence and postwar skulduggery, Malenkov was expelled in 1955 from the CC along with MOLOTOV and KAGANOVICH. Malenkov became director of a remote power station in Kazakhstan. He subsequently was seen in Moscow, where he died 14 Jan 88 at the age of 86.

MALETER, Pál. Hungarian army officer. 1911-1958. Son of a Lutheran Magyar teacher, he studied medicine before graduating in 1942 from the Budapest **MA.** He was captured by the Soviets in Jan 43, converted to communism, and he became a highly successful guerrilla leader in Hungary. After the war he graduated from the Moscow MA. As commander of the infantry division in Budapest, on 23 Oct 56 he joined the anti-Soviet uprising. The next day he became minister of defense. At a meeting the Russians called on 4 Nov 56 to negotiate their withdrawal Maléter was arrested with other nationalist leaders. On 17 June 58 the government announced he had been executed.

MALINOVSKY, Rodion Yakovlevich. Soviet military leader. 1898-1967. A Ukrainian born 23 Nov 98 in Odessa, he probably was the illegitimate son of a railroad worker and hospital cook he never knew (*Khrushchev,* 200). The boy was reared by an aunt, and in 1914 he ran away and joined the army. With three years' experience as a machine gunner he went to France in 1916 with the Russian expeditionary corps. On the western front he was wounded several times and decorated twice before being arrested by the French when his group mutinied. He was exiled to Africa, where in Jan 18 he joined a unit of the Foreign Legion headed for the Ukraine. Here he was captured while fighting on the White Russian side. Sent back to Russia via Vladivostok in 1919 as a POW (HFS) he joined the Red Army and saw action in the Far East.

After the civil war Malinovsky had formal military schooling, rising to be Timoshenko's CofS in the 3d Cavalry Corps, but, although a dedicated communist, did not enter the CP until 1926.

"Comrade Malino" was an adviser in Spain (Jan 37-May 38). Escaping the Great Purges in which so many "Spaniards" disappeared, he was a senior instructor at the **Frunze MA** until Mar 41 and was promoted. Gen Maj Malinovsky commanded the newly formed 48th Rifle Corps on the Romanian border when the Germans invaded on 22 June 40, and in the ensuing chaos showed a capacity for remaining calm no matter how hopeless the situation. In August he was moved up to command the 6th Army, was promoted in November to general lieutenant, and on 24 December succeeded Ya. T. CHERE-VICHENKO as head of the Southern Front. The young general shared blame for the Kharkov disaster in June 42 and for the loss of Rostov the next month. Among those disciplined, he was relegated to a rear-area command. During July and August, however, he headed the Don Operational Forces Group before named to command the 66th Army in August 42. In October he became Golikov's deputy CG of the Voronezh Front (Scarecrow), and the next month he took command of the crack 2d Guards Army (HFS). This army had a major role in driving back forces from Manstein's AG Don that got to within 35 miles of Stalingrad on 19 Dec 42.

Promoted to general colonel on 12 Feb 43 (HFS), Malinovsky resumed command of the Southern Front. A month later he took over the Southwest Front, and he was promoted to general of the army (No. 11) on 28 Apr 43 (HFS). His formation was redesignated the 3d Ukrainian Front in Oct 43 and became the 2d Ukrainian Front in May 44. Promotion to MSU (No. 14) was dated 10 Sep 44. After liberation of the Ukraine he led his front in the operations in Romania, Hungary, Austria, and Czechoslovakia. Malinovsky collaborated with TOLBUKHIN's redesignated 3d Ukrainian Front (on his left) in taking Vienna, and with KONEV's 1st Ukrainians (on his right) in occupying Prague.

The stocky young marshal, his staff, and two armies then moved east for the brief campaign in Manchuria. He commanded the Transbaykal Front from July 45 and the new Far East High Command from 1947 through the Korean War. Malinovsky headed the Far East MD for three years, 1953-56, after which KHRUSHCHEV made him first deputy defense minister under ZHUKOV. On the latter's ouster, Malinovsky was minister of defense from 26 Oct 57. With YEREMENKO, KONEV, and ROTMISTROV he was allied with Khrushchev in rewriting the Soviet history of WWII. Malinovsky died 31 Mar 67 of cancer while still in office.

MALYSHEV, Vyacheslav Aleksandrovich. Soviet engineer. 1902-57. Malyshev was born 16 Dec 02 at what is now Syktyvkar, Komi **ASSR,** son of a school teacher. In 1920-24 he studied in Velikie Luki to be a railroad engineer. From that city the able and ambitious Malyshev moved up with party backing through the Moscow Bauman Mechanical and Machine Building Institute (1934) to high industrial and technical offices. A specialist in diesel engines, he became commissar of heavy machine building in Feb 39 and was given the military rank of Gen Lt Engineer-Tank Service. Malyshev masterminded production of the T-34 tank. After the war he directed transport and naval construction, also being in charge of nuclear energy and weapons development. He died of leukemia on 20 Feb 57 and is buried on Red Square. (*NYT* obit.; Scarecrow; Scotts.)

MANDEL, Georges. French politician. 1885-1944. Born Jeroboam Rothschild, his father being a wealthy Parisian businessman, he turned a brilliant mind and prodigious memory to politics. Mandel became Clemenceau's protégé and was prominent in French political life from 1917 to 1920. As a deputy from the Gironde (1919-24 and 1932-40), PTT minister (1934-36), and colonial minister (10 Apr 38-18 May 40), Mandel was forceful and innovative, an opponent of the socialism, appeasement, and defeatism that crippled France.

Paul Reynaud named Mandel minister of the interior on 18 May 40. He was a hero of the dying Third Republic and Churchill's leading hope for heading a strong national government overseas (WC, II, 221). Accused of plotting political assassinations, Mandel was arrested at noon on 17 June in Bordeaux but freed by President Lebrun shortly after 2 PM; Petain's letter of apology, the terms of which

Mandel himself is said to have dictated—was delivered that evening. (Pierre Thibault in Larousse, 1170.)

Mandel was involved in the *Massilia* **affair** and charged with attempting to reestablish the French government abroad. A military tribunal in Morocco cleared the ex-minister but he was immediately interned (9 Sep 40). After being moved around in France, he was condemned in Nov 41 to further detention. Turned over to the Germans on 22 Nov 42 and held for six months in secret at **Oranienburg,** he joined Léon BLUM in a guarded house near Buchenwald. Mandel then was transferred to La Santé prison in Paris, turned over to the Milice, and murdered near the obelisk in the Forest of Fontainebleau on 7 July 44. (Larousse.)

MANNERHEIM, Carl Gustaf Emil von. Finnish statesman. 1867-1951. Baron von Mannerheim was born 4 June 67 into a Swedish-speaking family whose estate was near the port of Turku in SW Finland when that country still was part of Russia. Mannerheim became a Tsarist cavalry officer in 1889 and married the daughter of a well-to-do Russian general with close court connections. "He deeply and persistently loved the old Russia . . . [and] loathed bolshevism" (Eagles & Paananen, 30).

By 1917 Mannerheim was a lieutenant general heading an army corps. The next year he led the White Finns in driving out the Reds (with German help) and winning independence for Finland (14 Oct 18). Two months later he became regent of Finland, holding the office for seven months until the republic was established. But the aristocratic Mannerheim, who knew so little of the Finnish language in 1918 that he needed an interpreter to communicate with his White Home Guard, was purely a military leader who basically opposed democracy, parliamentary government, and scorned all political parties. (Ibid.) Not surprisingly he failed to win election as president in July 19. Now 52 years old, he retired from military service. (The Finnish army did not yet exist.)

In 1931 he was called to head the defense council. Although Finland and the USSR signed a nonaggression pact in mid-1932, construction of the "Mannerheim Line" across the Karelian Isthmus was undertaken, continuing until the Soviets struck on 30 Nov 39. At this time Field Marshal Mannerheim (since 1933) was 72 years

old but physically fit, a tall, handsome national hero who "represented unity, the flag, and everything that was strong and good in Finland." (Ibid.)

Badly underestimating Finland's will to resist, MERETSKOV suffered a bloody and humiliating repulse in Dec 39. TIMOSHENKO launched a renewed assault on 1 Feb 40 that forced Finland to surrender on 12 Mar 40. The Soviets annexed 16,200 square miles inhabited by 450,000 people. When Hitler invaded the USSR on 22 June 41, Mannerheim led an army corps that retook the Karelian Isthmus. Again allied with Germany, Finland was expected to cooperate in taking Leningrad, but Mannerheim declined to advance beyond his country's former border. On 4 June 42, his 75th birthday, Mannerheim became a marshal of Finland.

When the Soviet summer counteroffensive of 1944 started driving the German AG North back, GOVOROV directed a campaign that penetrated the Mannerheim Line and took Viipuri on 20 June 44. Surviving Finnish defenses were slowly overwhelmed, and on 4 Sep 44, exactly a month after succeeding Risto Ryti as president, Mannerheim signed a truce. Thereafter on the razor's edge of east-west relations, the durable national hero resigned on 4 Mar 46 because of declining health.

He moved to Switzerland and died in Lausanne on 27 Jan 51 at the age of 83. The posthumous *Memoirs of Marshal Mannerheim* were published in London in 1953.

MANSTEIN, Erich (Fritz) von. German general. 1887-1973. Perhaps the Wehrmacht's most brilliant strategist and field commander, Manstein was born 24 Nov 87 in Berlin. He was the 10th child of Eduard von Lewinski, an artillery officer who ultimately commanded an army corps. Retaining the right to use his original surname, Erich took the name Manstein from a childless uncle who adopted him.

Young Fritz was an Imperial court page before spending six years in the cadet corps. In 1906 he was commissioned in the 3d Footguards, his Uncle Paul von HINDENBURG's regiment.

In 1914 Manstein was adjutant of a guards regiment. He saw action in Belgium, East Prussia, and south Poland, being seriously wounded in Nov 14. Manstein then had staff assignments on both fronts and in Serbia. He was in France from the spring of 1917.

After the war he served in the Truppenamt, then was CofS in the Berlin MD. When the Truppenamt came out of the closet as the revived GGS Manstein was its chief of operations (Ia). On 1 Oct 36 he was promoted to Generalmajor and made BECK's **Oberquartiermeister I.** But as one of the "uncooperative" officers that Hitler had BRAUCHITSCH remove from Berlin after the BLOMBERG and FRITSCH affairs he was sent to Silesia as CG, 18th Div, with headquarters at Liegnitz. In the occupation of the Sudetenland, Manstein was briefly CofS in the force commanded by LEEB.

Manstein was CofS of Rundstedt's AG South in Poland and retained that post when Rundstedt took command of AG A in Oct 39 for the offensive in the west. Manstein was among those who tried, ineffectually, to block Hitler from expanding the war.

The approved OKH strategy for conquering France in 1940 was to repeat the failed Schlieffen plan of 1914, which featured a main effort through neutral Belgium. But the OKH plan did not capitalize on the German army's new capability for **blitzkrieg.** The "Manstein plan," prepared in collaboration with BLUMENTRITT and TRESCKOW and endorsed by Rundstedt, featured a main effort by panzers through the Ardennes. OKH rejected the plan in favor of their own, but this was compromised on 10 Jan 40 when an officer carrying the OKW plan made a forced landing in Belgium. A new strategy suddenly needed, Hitler approved a slightly modified form of the Manstein plan. Bur for rocking the boat Manstein was relegated to the minor role of forming the new 38th Corps in Silesia. Not taking part in executing his brilliant strategy—the drive across Flanders—he joined KLUGE's 4th Army only for the exploitation phase. The corps prepared for the aborted plan to invade England (which Manstein favored).

Gen Lt Manstein became CG, 61st Pz Corps, soon after its formation on 15 Feb 41 (B&0, 56-57). For Opn Barbarossa he was in HOEPPNER's Pz Gp of LEEB's AG North, his corps comprising the 8th Pz, 3d Mtz, and 290th Inf Divs. Attacking 22 June 41 he drove rapidly through difficult terrain of the Baltic coast, advancing more than 100 miles in the first two days and accomplishing the vital mission of seizing bridges at Dvinsk intact on 26 June. Surviving an encirclement just east of Lake Ilmen at Zoltsy in mid-July, he attacked south to inflict heavy losses. The next month his corps moved SE to Staraya Russia and drove to Demyansk and Torzhok, NW of Kalinin. (B&O, 56.)

Manstein left his corps on 12 Sep 41—after fewer than three months of fierce action—and joined Rundstedt's AG South as CG 11th Army. (The previous commander, Ritter von Schobert, had been killed with his pilot when they rolled over a mine on landing.) The 11th Army deployed on AG South's right flank, Manstein had the mission of conquering the Crimea while others drove eastward.

The Soviets stoutly defended Sevastopol (their most important Black Sea naval base) and launched a counteroffensive that took the Kerch Peninsula. Manstein repelled this threat in a brilliant riposte, but did not take Sevastopol until 2 July 42. A Generaloberst since 1 Jan 42, Manstein was made a field marshal on 1 July 42.

The great German summer offensive toward Stalingrad and the Caucasus under way, Manstein was appalled at being sent to besiege Leningrad! When MERETSKOV's Volkhov Front launched a powerful counterattack on the 18th Army south of Leningrad on 4 Sep 42, Hitler ordered Field Marshal Manstein to leave his siege operations and wipe out a deep enemy penetration. By 21 Sep 42 he destroyed the Red Army spearhead of some 10 divisions—VLASOV's elite 2d Shock Army. But Manstein lost almost as much materiel as the Soviets and had about 60,000 killed or captured. It was a victory much harder than that in the Crimea. (Manstein, 262-67; Salisbury, *The 900 Days,* 540-41.)

In late Oct 42 Hitler summoned Manstein to his forward headquarters at Vinnitsa, in the Ukraine, and alerted him to the possible mission of driving through the Caucasus to the Near East! But on 20 Nov 42, as disaster loomed at Stalingrad, Manstein was told to take over the new AG Don. Astride the Don between Kleist's AG A (in the Caucasus) and Weichs's AG B, AG Don was ordered to rescue PAULUS's 6th Army in Stalingrad. Manstein got three badly weakened panzer divisions within 35 miles of the German perimeter by 19 Dec 42; but PAULUS would not order a breakout, and Soviet counterattacks drove Manstein's panzers back. The Red Army soon launched a winter counteroffensive on a broad front. Against seven to one odds, with orders to hold all ground, AG Don kept an escape corridor open through Rostov for MACKENSEN's 1st Pz Army. AG Don was redesignated AG South on 12 Feb 43.

The Russian steamroller drove the Germans back into the Ukraine. Hitler could not long endure a Fabian general, however successful, and he personally disliked Manstein (Caidin, *Kursk*, 67, citing Guderian), who was ineffective in presenting his views to the fuehrer orally. On a rare visit to the front on 17 Feb 43 Hitler apparently intended to dismiss Manstein but changed his mind. (Lochner, ed, *Goebbels Diaries*, 265.)

Two days later Manstein undertook one of his most brilliant operations. Near Krasnograd he punched a wide hole through which the panzers exploited. He started another attack three days later, inflicting heavy losses and routing Russian units that had become careless about mutual support and fuel supply. Some 23,000 Soviets were killed, 9,000 captured, and Manstein exploited his success vigorously. AG South retook Kharkov on 14 Mar 43 and Belgorod on the 18th.

"Manstein's counteroffensive was a masterpiece of mobile warfare; it is sobering to consider what he might have accomplished if given a free hand from the beginning" (*West Point Atlas*, 36). The field marshal wanted to mass armor west of Kharkov, lure the enemy toward Odessa, and annihilate Tolbukhin and Malinovsky's South and SW Fronts with a counteroffensive that would pin them against the Sea of Azov. But Hitler had a better idea: the ex-corporal revived the idea of reducing the Kursk salient but delayed so long in awaiting new tank production that Opn Citadel was a disaster. It ruined whatever chances the Wehrmacht had left to resume the offensive in the east. Unable to make Hitler see the need for elastic maneuver rather than rigid defense of fixed positions Manstein held AG South together as the Soviets drove it back across the Dnieper and into Poland.

Hitler's final break with Manstein was looming. The field marshal epitomized the Old Guard aristocratic officer that Hitler detested, all the more because Manstein was imbued with the Prussian tradition that obedience carried with it the duty of frankly expressing his views. Liddell Hart comments that Hitler tolerated criticism from Manstein "in a way that staggered others

who were present" (foreword to *Lost Victories*, 15-16). But top Nazis faulted the field marshal, with some justification, for poor "human qualities," bad character, "excessive ambition," and "defeatism." (Lochner, op. cit., 265, 300, 473, and 503.) Another complication was that Soviet propaganda claimed Hitler was losing control of his generals. In Mar 44 Hitler summoned his senior commanders to Berchtesgaden for what was supposed to be a public show of their loyalty. Manstein returned to his headquarters on 26 Mar 44 with the belief that his heated exchanges with Hitler and arguments for a saner strategy had had some favorable reception. But Hitler was worn out by disputes over strategy. Perhaps the last straw was the one involving Hans HUBE.

"On the morning of 30th March," writes Manstein, "I was awakened with the startling news that Hitler's Condor aircraft, which had already picked up v. Kleist from his headquarters, would shortly land in Lwow to take the pair of us to the Obersalzberg." (Manstein, 544.) Hitler cordially expressed his respect for the field marshal but said Manstein needed a rest. Manstein formally transferred responsibility to MODEL on 2 Apr 44 and flew off the next day to permanent retirement.

A British military court charged Manstein with war crimes. The process did not start until Aug 49, when the FRG was being formed. Like so many other senior German commanders the field marshal claimed to have learned of genocide in his area of authority only after the war. Dr Otto JOHN did extensive research for the prosecution and found a portion the 11th Army war diary in which a line read, "A new Commander-in-Chief arrives. . . . He is an autocrat and somewhat difficult. However one can speak frankly to him." Subsequent lines were pasted over. The prosecuting council asked John to hold the page to the light and challenged the accused to read the censored passage. This had the words "The new Commander-in-Chief does not wish officers to be present at shooting of Jews. This is unworthy of a German officer." (Quoted by John, 193-94.) Unfortunately Manstein's American publishers excised this detail, so "His book makes no mention of what was really beneath the slip" (ibid.). The court found that Gypsies and Crimean Tartars also were liquidated along with Jews in Manstein's rear areas (ibid), and that he had advocated that "the

Jewish Bolshevik system be wiped out once and for all." On 24 Feb 50 the court sentenced Manstein to imprisonment for 18 years.

On medical parole from Aug 52 he was freed 6 May 53 and served for a while as a military adviser to the **FRG**. The field marshal died 12 June 73 in Irschenhausen at the age of 85.

Manstein's war memoirs appeared first in 1955 as *Verlorne Siege*. The abbreviated British and American editions, *Lost Victories* (1958), unfortunately omit "personal reminisces, often in a lighter vein" and some "detailed appendices." But the chapter on Opn Citadel substitutes new material submitted by Manstein to the US *Marine Corps Gazette* (translator's note on p. 12).

MANTEUFFEL, Hasso Eccard von. German general. 1897-1978. He was born in Potsdam on 14 Jan 97. As an early believer in mechanized warfare he quickly caught GUDERIAN's eye. After his baptism of fire in June 41 as commander of a battalion in **Schuetzen-Regiment** 7 of the 7th Pz Div the young officer moved up two months later to be colonel of Schutzen-Regiment 6. Part of Hermann HOTH's 3d Pz Gp he was awarded the RK on 27 Nov 41 for capturing a key bridge on the NW outskirts of Moscow (Angolia, I, 99). Manteuffel then moved up to head Schuetzen-Brigade 7 until July 42.

Sent to serve under von ARNIM in Tunisia he led the "Manteuffel Division" on the northern flank. In an attack on the British 46th Inf Div, 26 Feb-1 Apr 43, he was stopped after advancing almost 20 miles. Manteuffel had the good luck to be taken ill and evacuated on the last hospital ship from Tunis. (Ibid.)

On 20 Aug 43 he took command of the 7th Pz Div in the 48th Pz Corps of Hermann HOTH's 4th Pz Army. For a deep envelopment that completely surprised the Soviet 16th Army, recapturing Zhitomir and taking huge supply dumps (Mellenthin, 253-55) the "Lion of Zhitomir" was awarded the Oakleaves (332/890) on 23 Nov 43. Leaving his division on 19 Jan 44 and promoted on 1 February, Gen Lt Manteuffel headed the "Gross Deutschland" Armd Div. He was awarded the Swords (50/159) on 22 February for action in the Kiev salient around Radomyshl (Angolia, I, 100).

After being driven back into Romania the Gross Deutschland was sent to East Prussia. Attacking on 9 Aug 44 without artillery prepa-

ration the master of deception again achieved surprise and more or less stabilized the front. Promoted again, on 1 Sep 44 (*B&O,* 83), General of Panzer Troops Manteuffel took command of the 5th Pz Army in France. He was involved for the next six weeks in defensive battles around Luneville and in Lorraine until 14 Oct 44 when ordered out of the line to prepare for the Ardennes counteroffensive.

He had the greatest German successes in that operation, being awarded the Diamonds (24/27) on 18 Feb 45. Manteuffel replaced Erhard RAUSS in East Prussia as 3d Pz Army commander on 10 Mar 45. Forced out of the Stettin bridgehead on 19 March and driven back through Pomerania and Mecklenburg, he surrendered on 8 May 45 to the US 8th Inf Div with remnants of his army. A POW until Sep 47, he was active in civic affairs, industry, in the field of military history, and in politics. Manteuffel died on 28 Sep 78.

MAO TSE-TUNG. Chinese communist leader. 1893-1976. Born in the village of Shao Shan in Hunan Prov, Mao Tse-tung (or Mao Zedong and pronounced mou'dzu-dung') was the son of an ex-soldier who became a rich peasant. Mao was solidly educated in Chinese classics as well as western political and literary works. As a student he became a believer in Sun Yat-sen's revolutionary movement. After receiving a teacher's degree in 1918 and getting into student political activities, journalism, and helping found a book society, in 1920 Mao attended the Shanghai meeting that created the Chinese Communist Party (CCP). Three years later the CCP entered the Kuomintang to help eliminate the northern war lords, but in Apr 27 CHIANG KAI-SHEK purged the Kuomintang of communists. Mao had to cope with a CCP faction that favored accommodation with the Kuomintang, but in Aug 27 he began forming the Peasants and Workers Army. This soon evolved into CHU TEH's Red army with Mao as political commissar.

The communists beat off the Nationalist army in several campaigns before undertaking the Long March to Yenan (1934-35). But when full-scale war broke out with Japan in 1937 Mao decided to collaborate with Chiang against the invaders.

The Japanese eventually drove Chiang's forces inland, where he established the Nationalist capital at Chungking; Mao's capital was

Yenan in remote Shensi Prov of NE China. Here Mao perfected "revolutionary warfare," which featured innovative guerrilla tactics accompanied by political action to build solid support from the local populace. Mao also imposed strict discipline within his government, purging corrupt and unreliable elements.

But Chiang got the massive US support, much of which the Nationalists used to contain the communists. The US made repeated but ineffectual attempts during and after the war to effect a true military alliance between Chiang and Mao. One late effort was entrusted to Patrick HURLEY and the final one to George C. MARSHALL.

The Chinese civil war recommenced, with renewed vigor, immediately after the Japanese surrender. Late in 1949 Mao became head of the new People's Democratic Republic of China, his title being chairman of the central government council. By Apr 50 the communists controlled mainland China with Mao as supreme ruler and soon a controversial cult figure.

MARSEILLE, Hans Joachim. German ace. 1920-42. Of Huguenot descent, Joachim Marseille was born 13 Dec 20 in Berlin, son of a WWI flyer. (Sims, *Aces,* 132-35.) In 482 combat sorties between 10 May 40 and 27 Sep 42 the lean, darkly handsome, painfully modest fighter pilot had 158 victories. All but the first seven were in North Africa, mostly from the base at Martuba west of Tobruk. "One of the principal reasons for Marseille's success," writes Sims, "was the careful handling of his spirit and exuberance by his commanding officer in 27 Geschwader, Oberst Eduard Neumann" Another major reason was the pilot's gunnery. (Ibid.)

On 1 June 42, Marseille took command of 3 Staffel of JG 27, having the title of Staffel **Kapitaen.** The experte scored his 101st kill on 17 June, when Neumann grounded him for signs of true battle fatigue. After more than two months in Germany—where the hero was exasperatingly modest at press conferences—Marseille resumed command of 3 Staffel as the Luftwaffe's youngest captain (at 22). He was awarded the Diamonds (4/27) on 2 Sep 42 after scoring 17 victories the preceding day. This record for victories on a single day was surpassed by only one other Luftwaffe pilot, Capt Emil Lang, who downed 18 Russian planes on one day and scored 173 kills in the east before his death. (Ibid., 151, 275.)

But the Swords were never presented to Marseille personally nor to his family (Angolia, I, 62). On 30 Sep 42, three days after his final victory, the engine of his new Me 109 caught fire as he was about to recross the front near El Alamein. Waiting a few minutes to get over friendly territory and blinded by smoke, he rolled over and dropped out. But the plane's nose dipped, the pilot apparently was hit by the rudder, and the parachute never opened. (Sims, 151.)

Twenty-nine Luftwaffe pilots, almost all of them on the eastern front, led by Erich HARTMANN (352), surpassed his total score. Yet Adolf GALLAND and other authorities rated Marseille as the war's best fighter pilot.

MARSHALL, George Catlett. US Army officer and statesman. 1880-1959. From Hitler's invasion of Poland on 1 Sep 39, Marshall was the US Army's chief of staff and senior general. After these six arduous years he went on to a distinguished civilian career in high office.

Marshall's American ancestors settled in Kentucky during the American Revolution. Chief Justice John Marshall (1755-1835) was a collateral ancestor. George Marshall was born on the last day of 1880 at Uniontown in western Pennsylvania. From the age of 10, when his father fell on hard times, he knew genteel poverty. With a poor secondary schooling but a drive to excel, the tall, gangling Marshall followed an elder brother to **VMI.** It is not known why he never applied for West Point. (Pogue, *Marshall,* I, 4, 40). After making a poor initial impression he was first corporal at the end of his first year, first sergeant at the end of the second, and first captain in his final year. He graduated in 1901 with a respectable academic standing. A year later he became a second lieutenant of infantry, the commission retroactive to 2 Feb 01. This made Marshall 16 months senior to MacARTHUR, who was almost a year older but still at West Point until 1903.

A few weeks after being commissioned and ordered to the Philippines, Marshall married Elizabeth ("Lily") Carter Coles, a beautiful Lexington belle four years his senior with whom he had been smitten since his final year at VMI. The Philippine insurrection had already been put down by Douglas MacARTHUR's father, but as a "shavetail" in Co G of the 30th Inf Marshall got two years of grass-roots experience as a troop leader in a foreign environment. Then he served two more years with Co G at Ft Reno, in the Oklahoma Territory, where Lily joined him for the first time. In 1906, 2d Lt Marshall was selected for schooling at Ft **Leavenworth.** Although not heretofore an outstanding student, he began to excel. Passing the examination for promotion (effective 7 Mar 07), he went on to graduate at the top of the one-year class and to qualify for the second year of instruction, the Army Staff College. He was kept on for another two years as an instructor.

With accrued leave, he left with Lily in Aug 10 for a five-month grand tour of Europe. In England he rented a bicycle to follow army maneuvers at Aldershot. Returning to the US Marshall began getting special assignments that made his name known in the little US army. As a lieutenant in the Philippines he won high praise on maneuvers in 1913 (Pogue, I, 123-24). But he began having medical problems that would continue to dog his career. During four months of leave he spent much time on another tour with Lily, this time in Asia. Much as MacARTHUR had done, Marshall visited battlefields of the Russo-Japanese War and talked with veteran Japanese officers. Lt Marshall concluded that the US Army had much to learn about the use of bayonets, hand grenades, and night operations. But he also realized before returning to the States in May 16 that his professional prospects were dim and he seriously considered leaving the army despite a remote possibility that it might become in involved in the European war that had broken out in 1914. Promoted to captain on 14 Aug 16 he soldiered on.

1917-38.

After America entered the war (6 Apr 17) Marshall went with the first AEF contingent to France. He was quickly known as a brilliant operations officer, initially with the 1st Inf Div Hq, at GHQ under the celebrated Col Fox Connor (*see* Eisenhower), and finally as G3 of the 1st Army. Lt Col Marshall's most famous achievement was planning and supervising the complex troop movements that followed the St Mihiel offensive and preceded the Meuse Argonne drive. He was promoted to colonel and soon nominated for brigadier general. But the armistice intervened, and Marshall waited another 18 years for that star.

For five years from 1919 he was Pershing's ADC, an invaluable experience. Soon after

completing a three-year tour as **XO,** 15th Inf Regt in Tiensin, China, Lt Col Marshall was serving as a lecturer at the AWC when Lily, never strong physically, died on 15 Sep 27. Needing strenuous work to recover from this tragedy, Marshall went to the Infantry School at Ft Benning, Ga. Assistant commandant at first, he soon was virtual head of a training program that badly needed vigorous overhauling after a decade of forgetting the lessons learned in France.

Thus began "five of his most constructive years," writes Pogue (Marshall, I, 246). About 150 future generals passed through "Marshall's Benning" as students; another 50 were instructors. Marshall entered most of them in his later-famous "little black book" (Pogue, II, 95-96).

Marshall meanwhile remarried after more than two years as a childless widower. The bride was Mrs Katherine Boyce Tupper Brown, who had been a successful Shakespearian actress for several seasons before a weak heart led her to leave the stage. Mrs Brown was the recent widow of an attorney who had been killed by a mentally deranged client. Gen Pershing was best man at the wedding on 15 Oct 30.

Throughout his career Marshall sought duty with troops. In June 33 Lt Col Marshall had taken command of a battalion near Savannah, Ga, when the US Army was informed suddenly it would be responsible for carrying out Roosevelt's **CCC** program. Promoted to colonel, given command of the 8th Inf, with supervision over 34 CCC camps in Georgia, Florida, and South Carolina (Parrish, *R&M,* 59), Marshall threw himself into what he viewed as a great social experiment the army should support fully. In the fall of 1933 he was transferred to Chicago as senior instructor of the Illinois NG. Promoted to brigadier general on 1 Oct 36, shortly before his 56th birthday, Marshall then took command of the 5th Brig, 3d Inf Div, at Vancouver Barracks, Wash., with the additional duty of overseeing CCC camps in the district.

But there was a recurrence of health problems that tended to follow extended periods of exceptionally hard work. In 1912, after directing large-scale national guard maneuvers in New England, he had been found unconscious on the street: the diagnosis was "acute dilation of the heart." Eighteen months later he had an attack of "neurasthenia" after several weeks of directing the maneuvers mentioned above. Now, in

1936, he was hospitalized with a bad case of flu, then operated on for removal of a diseased portion of the thyroid gland. Rumors circulated that he would be invalided out of the service, but Marshall recovered quickly.

WWII
After only 20 months on the west coast Marshall was surprised to be made chief of the War Plans Div, WDGS, in Aug 38. Three months later, after the **Munich Crisis,** he became army CofS Malin Craig's deputy. At the White House conference on 14 Nov 38 that so delighted Hap ARNOLD Marshall flatly refused to endorse the president's decision to build 10,000 planes as a matter of first priority. But Marshall's candid, well-reasoned, and scrupulously honest military views impressed members of the administration (notably Harry HOPKINS) and the Congress (where FRD had strong opposition).

At least 35 generals were eligible to succeed Craig, although most were disqualified because they would reach the mandatory retirement age of 64 before completing the normal four-year tour. The principal contender was Hugh DRUM; and three others were senior to Marshall: DE WITT, KRUEGER, and Frank W. Rowell. In submitting his list of candidates Craig omitted Drum and De Witt, added Maj Gen Robert McC. Beck, Jr, and included four brigadier generals junior to Marshall: George Grunert, Jay L. Benedict, Clarence S. Ridley, and Adna R. Chaffee, Jr. Others including Daniel I. SULTAN, were mentioned. (Pogue, *Marshall,* I, 329-30.) Unlike Drum, Marshall refused to campaign for the top post, although well-wishers urged him to do so.

The president picked Marshall, who believed Harry HOPKINS was primarily responsible. When FDR summoned the new CofS to his study on a Sunday to give him the news, the president agreed to let the general speak his mind even when what he had to say was unpleasant. Despite entirely different personalities the men maintained a remarkably effective rapport. "I remember he called me 'George,'" the general recalled of this initial meeting. "I don't think he ever did it again [not true]. . . . I wasn't very enthusiastic over such a misrepresentation of our intimacy." (Pogue, *Marshall,* I, 323.)

The austere Virginian was promoted automatically to four-star rank on assuming his new office (1 Sep 39). Unlike all his predecessors and most of the army's senior officers, Marshall believed in air power. "He gave the army air corps virtual autonomy and supported its tremendous expansion program," writes Pogue (*Collier's Ency,* 1967 ed, "Marshall"). It has been argued that the CofS went too far in giving top personnel priority to build a corps of pilots, which caused the infantry to have many low-grade platoon leaders and company commanders; top industrial priority went to aircraft production even though there was a critical shortage of amphibious craft.

In dealing with demands of the US Navy, whose chief spokesman was Ernest J. KING, Marshall apparently accepted the political necessity of letting the navy have the major role in the Pacific. Although Arnold and King may be accused of putting parochial interests above those of the nation, nobody could make charge against the army chief. It also is generally conceded that he towered above Arnold and King as the architect of victory. The problem of giving material aid to allies while building US military strength was particularly troublesome. Marshall was fortunate in not being among the many scapegoats for the Pearl Harbor disaster, a fact resented by Ernie KING. Then came the matter of strategic planning for coalition warfare: the somber, cautious Marshall worked effectively to preserve the "Germany first" decision; and he supported the cross-channel strategy, rejecting the "Mediterranean strategy" favored by Churchill and Marshall's British counterpart, Alan BROOKE.

In the field of strategic planning, Marshall has been faulted for "innate cautiousness" that prolonged the war against Japan. (Farago, *War of Wits,* 25. Further views of this author, who was in naval intelligence, will be found in the sketch of ZACHARIAS.)

Like Alan BROOKE, Marshall suffered the disappointment of not being picked to lead his country's forces in the final defeat of Germany. He was considered indispensable in the assignment held since it all started. To sum up Marshall's achievement, he had had the major role in building the US Army from 200,000 to 8,000,000, directing them in a world-wide effort, and retaining Roosevelt's respect. When Congress created the five-star ranks of General of the Army and Fleet Admiral, Marshall was given rank as of 16 Dec 44, junior only to

LEAHY and senior to King, MacArthur, Eisenhower, and Arnold.

Postwar

After six years in office (including time as deputy before being sworn in formally), Marshall retired on 20 Nov 45 (succeeded by Eisenhower). After a special mission to China, where he could stop the civil war only temporarily, Marshall was sworn in as Truman's secretary of state on 21 Jan 47. Resignation as General of the Army (a legal requirement) was dated 28 Feb 47. Bringing in George KENNAN to head a planning staff of the sort he was used to working with in the Pentagon, he quickly undertook what became famous as the Marshall plan for European recovery (ERP). After coping effectively with staggering postwar problems around the world (see Pogue, *Marshall,* IV), the general was succeeded as secretary of state in early 1949 by Dean G. Acheson. From the following October he headed the American Red Cross. As the Korean War crisis mounted, and Louis Johnson's inadequacies became more apparent, the general accepted the post of secretary of defense in Sep 50. He planned to remain only six months but was retained for a year.

On 1 Sep 51 the general ended 50 years of public life. He retired to a house his wife had owned since 1942 in Leesburg, Va, spending winters at a cottage she had bought near the end of the war in Pinehurst, NC. Marshall was awarded the Nobel Peace Prize in 1953.

Marshall steadfastly refused to write his memoirs but in 1956 gave his papers to what became the George C. Marshall Memorial Research Library in Lexington, Va. Although now frail, he began interviews with historians of the Marshall Foundation in the fall of 1956. The first volume of Forrest C. Pogue's biography was published in 1963, the fourth in 1987. *The Papers of David Dwight Eisenhower,* for which Pogue was a consultant, has almost as much primary source material pertaining to Marshall as to Eisenhower. Publication data on both works are in my main bibliography.

After a crippling stroke in the first days of 1959, the general died 16 Oct 59 in Walter Reed and was buried in Arlington National Cemetery.

MASARYK, Jan Garrigue. Czech diplomat. 1886-1948. He was the son of Charlotte Garrigue, an American, and Thomas Masaryk (1850-1937) who in 1918 was a co-founder along with Eduard BENES of Czechoslovakia. Jan Masaryk was minister to London 1925-38. In 1940 he became foreign minister in BENES's London government in exile. Returning to Prague in 1945 with Benes, he held the same portfolio, even after the communists seized power on 25 Feb 48. Gottwald left him in office as foreign minister but, the day after adopting a communist constitution, the government announced Masaryk's apparent suicide on 10 Mar 48. Foul play was suspected, but as in the case of BENES less than three months later, was never proved *(CE).*

MASLENNIKOV, Ivan Ivanovich. Soviet military leader. 1900-54. An **NKVD-MVD** officer of no real military ability but picked by Stalin for special jobs (Erickson, *To Stalingrad,* 291), he became a general of the army, front commander, and a **HSU** (1945). In 1954 he disappeared without a trace.

Maslennikov was born 16 Sep 00, was a regular officer from 1918, and commanded a cavalry regiment in the Red Army. Transferring to border troops in 1928, he was heading border and internal troops of Belorussia in 1938. This same year, when BERIA arrived in Moscow, Maslennikov was "evidently transferred to senior work in Moscow" (Kruzhin, 11). In Mar 39 he was elected a candidate member of the central committee in the All Union **CP (B),** and an insider identifies him as "the chief of the Border Troops" at a high level meeting later that year (Sudoplatov, 98).

From 25 Feb 41 to 3 July 42 he was commissar of internal affairs with responsibility for all NKVD internal and border troops (Khruzhin, 11). Concurrently he held high-level field commands, first the 29th Army, formed in July 41 at Rybinsk, mostly of border guards and coast guards. The 29th Army fought bravely in Konev's Western Front, along with other hastily formed rear-area units, and sustained heavy losses efore abandoning Kalinin on 14 Oct 41. Konev's Kalinin Front was formed three days later, and it picked up the 29th Army.

Maslennikov took over the recently formed 39th Reserve Army around 21 Dec 41 and led it—still in the Kalinin front—from around Torzhok in the winter counteroffensive that retook Rzhev (about 120 miles WNW west of

Moscow). In June 42 his army was annihilated near Bely(i) when the Germans resumed their offensive.

Maslennikov headed the Northern Forces Group of the Transcaucasus Front, 8 Aug 42-24 Jan 43, then commanded the front for about five months. In quick succession from May 43 he was deputy commander of several fronts: Volkhov, Southwest, 3d Ukrainian, and Leningrad. Then Maslennikov led the 42d Army of the Leningrad Front from 23 Dec 43. On 18 Apr 44 he took over the 3d Baltic Front and was promoted to general of the army (No. 17) on 28 July. After taking part in the capture of Riga Maslennikov's front was disbanded in Oct 44. He was deputy CinC, Far East, June-Aug 45, and awarded the gold star of the HSU. The police general headed the Baku MD 1945-46 and the Transcaucasus MD to 1947. In June 48 he completed the higher academic courses and was made deputy minister of internal affairs. Three and a half months after BERIA's arrest on 26 June 53 (Stalin having died on 5 March) Maslennikov was interrogated on suspicion of scheming with Beria to have MVD troops arrest government leaders. "No such plan existed, and Maslennikov decided to take his own life rather than face torture or imprisonment." (Sudoplatov, 380.)

MASON-MACFARLANE, Frank Noel Mason. See MACFARLANE.

MASSON, Roger. Swiss army officer. 1894-1948. Appointed chief of the Swiss intelligence service after his country's federal council ordered mobilization on 29 Aug 39, having held the post since 1936, Col (later Brigadier) Masson had a necessarily enigmatic role in helping the Allied cause while parrying the ever-present threat of a German take-over of his small, supposedly neutral country. Playing a dangerous game in protecting Rudolf "Lucy" ROESSLER, which involved fending off Walter SCHELLENBERG's efforts by to eliminate the Lucy ring, Masson got invaluable intelligence for his country and the Allies. Switzerland also had visits from key members of the anti-Hitler resistance in Germany. But Allen DULLES had to admit after the war that he never really knew what Masson (and the Lucy ring) were doing. Masson also had to cope with strong hostile factions within Switzerland, and there were several well-publicized "Masson affairs" during and after the war. (A&Q, *Lucy,* passim.) Never betraying official secrets Masson published a series of sanitized articles in the *Tribune de Lausanne* in 1965 on the Swiss position in WWII.

MAST, Charles Emmanuel. French general. 1889-1977. A Parisian, he finished St Cyr in 1908. His early troop duty was in Algeria with the foreign legion, then in Indo-China. Starting in 1922 he had three tours of duty in Japan, the last as MA.

Col Mast commanded the 3d North Africa Div when the Germans attacked France on 10 May 40. Having been promoted, Général de Brigade Mast became a POW in June. (Larousse.) Repatriated in 1941 he became CofS to Gen Louis Marie Koeltz, who was commander of the Algiers (or XIX) military region and director of armistice services. Later that year 1941 Mast took command of the Algiers Div. Described as a "neat, stocky" little general, "very correct" (Nicholson, *Diaries,* II, 368), he already was involved in plotting an insurrection when he met and favorably impressed Robert MURPHY. In Apr 42 he helped engineer GIRAUD's escape from Germany and represented that general at the **Cherchell conference,** 22 Oct 42. Mast was promoted to général de division in Dec 42 but, vulnerable to charges of treason, held missions in Libya and Egypt before ending up in the Levant. He was named governor general of Tunisia in Aug 43 with the rank of général de corps d'armée. Four years later he was appointed director of the national defense center of higher studies with the rank of full general. He retired in 1950 on reaching the age limit.

MATSUDAIRA, Tsuneo. Japanese diplomat. 1877-1949. As imperial household minister 1936-45 Matsudaira took care of the emperor's ceremonial functions whereas KIDO handled substantive matters. Before this Matsudaira held many important diplomatic posts, including that of ambassador to Washington 1925-28 and London 1929. One of his daughters married Prince Chichibu, who was the emperor's eldest brother and heir apparent until the birth of Akihito in 1933.

MATSUI, Iwane. Japanese general. 1878-1948. A devout Buddhist, sixth son of a wealthy scholar of Chinese classics, he became a career army officer. With dreams of a unified Asia, he establish the East Asia League *(Toa Renmei)* in 1931. The sickly little General Matsui retired from the army in 1933 after learning of Japan's plans to conquer China. But after the **Marco Polo Bridge Incident** of 7 July 37 he modified his patriotic goals. Matsui advocated driving quickly up the Yangtze from Shanghai to Nanking and installing an honest, humane Japanese occupation force to win the Chinese people over from CHIANG KAI-SHEK's Nationalists. (Bergamini, 7-9.)

The emperor summoned Matsui on 15 Aug 37 and directed him to execute his plan. With two divisions (35,000 troops) Matsui reached China eight days later to reinforce the hard pressed little naval landing party in Shanghai and in a brutal four-month campaign advanced 170 miles to take Nanking (Bergamini, 4). Japanese troops ran amok in what became known as the rape of **Nanking,** which started on 13 Dec 37 (a day after the **Panay Incident** Matsui himself was appalled, as were many other Japanese, and the atrocities—witnessed by round eyed Americans, British, and French in Shanghai's international settlement—were well reported by the western press. Succeeded by Shunroku HATA, Matsui went back into retirement in the spring of 1938.

After what the insider Bergamini calls "one of the most fuzzy defense presentations in the annals of jurisprudence" (ibid., 47), the "butcher of Nanking" was convicted as a war criminal and hanged with six others in Sugamo Prison on 23 Dec 48.

MATSUOKA, Yosuke. Japanese diplomat. 1880-1946. Born into an impoverished samurai family of Choshu in SW Honshu he was 13 when he went with a cousin to Portland, Oregon. In 1900 the diminutive (five feet two) Matsuoka graduated from the Univ of Oregon with a law degree and, from, humilities suffered in menial jobs he developed an intense dislike for Americans. He became highly respected as a foreign service officer. After 18 years as a diplomat he resigned in 1920 and spent 10 years as a director of the South Manchurian RR before entering public life. In 1933 he led his delegation out of the League of Nations after it accepted the Lytton commission report that condemned Japan's occupation of Manchuria.

From 1935 until 1939 Matsuoka was president of the South Manchurian RR, then foreign minister from 22 July 40 in KONOYE's second cabinet. Long suspected of favoring the **strike-north faction,** he negotiated the **Tripartite Pact** that was signed in Berlin on 27 Sep 40.

In Jan 41 Matsuoka was authorized to make a one-month visit to Europe with instructions to get a neutrality pact with Russia, which he personally opposed. After 10 unproductive days in Moscow he was courted in Berlin by Hitler. Visiting Rome next, he retraced his steps through Berlin to Moscow. Events were moving fast, the Germans suddenly invading Yugoslavia, and there was convincing evidence that the USSR would be next. The Russian bear, who needed all possible assistance, now embraced the brilliant, mercurial, shifty little Matsuoka, who signed a nonaggression treaty with Stalin on 14 Apr 41. Matsuoka got a grand sendoff on the Trans-Siberian RR, but back in Tokyo found he now was outside the mainstream of strategic planning. Despite having accomplished his assigned mission, he was in disfavor with superiors including Hirohito, who connived with KONOYE to force a change in foreign ministers on 18 July 41. Thus Soemu Toyoda replaced Matsuoka.

"The most Westernized of Japanese leaders and the most dangerous to the West" *(CB 41)* was indicted as a major war criminal but was excused after a few days of proceedings on grounds of ill health. He died on 27 June 46.

MAULDIN, Bill. US army cartoonist. 1921-. Creator of the immortal Willie and Joe, who cheered GIs through Sicily, Italy, France, and Germany, Bill Mauldin was in the Arizona NG, which became part of the 45th Inf Div. Drawing George Patton's ire after the 45th "Thunderbirds" reached Sicily, Mauldin found a protector in Troy MIDDLETON. The easy-going, boyish-looking Mauldin continued to build troop morale, often at the expense of officers. One famous cartoon, reproduced in the official **OCMH** series, shows Willie and Joe looking from a battered jeep at a sign saying "YOU ARE ENTERING THE THIRD ARMY!" Caption: "Radio th' ol' man we'll be late on account of a thousand-mile detour." (Cole, *Lorraine,* 294.)

After a period of slow transition to civilian life, all his characters still looking like the bedraggled combat GIs Willie and Joe, Mauldin became a first-rate political cartoonist.

McAULIFFE, Anthony Clement. US general. 1898-1975. Tony McAuliffe was born 2 July 98 in Washington, DC, and appointed to the USMA from West Virginia. The peppery little Irishman graduated high in the Class of 1919 (29/284) and was commissioned in the field artillery. As a brigadier general he became Maxwell TAYLOR's artillery commander in the 101st Abn Div. Jumping into Normandy, McAuliffe coordinated the final assault on Carentan on 12 June 44 (*OCMH Chron*, 208). After taking part in Opn Market-Garden, McAuliffe was acting division commander when the Ardennes counteroffensive began on 16 Dec 44. Troy MIDDLETON delayed his departure from Bastogne a day to catch the "Screaming Eagles" as they came up to occupy an assigned blocking position much farther on. McAuliffe made the quick decision that Middleton was right in believing he should detruck in and around Bastogne, a critical road center. With approval from higher headquarters, the parachute troops were hastily organizing a defense (along with parts of the 9th and 10th Armd Divs) when hit by Heinrich von LUET-TWITZ's panzer corps. Luettwitz and Fritz BAYERLEIN sent the surrender ultimatum that evoked McAuliffe's famous reply, "To the German Commander: Nuts!" (Some will recognize the spirit of Pierre Cambronne [1770-1842], who allegedly replied "merde!" when called on to surrender remnants of the Old Guard at Waterloo [1815].)

Having been CG, 101st Abn, 5-26 Dec 44, and promoted on 3 Jan 45 (*AA*, 589, 918) Maj Gen McAuliffe commanded the 103d Inf Div until July 45. His wartime decorations included the DSC, two DSMs, and the SS. Briefly heading the 79th Inf Div until Aug 45 (*AA*, 552, 570), he was CG, Abn Center Ft Benning, Ga, 25 Sep 45-3 Jun 46. After holding high staff positions in Washington he returned to Europe as CG, 7th Army, 1953-55, then as CG, US Army in Europe, until retiring in 1956 as a four-star general. McAuliffe became VP and director of the American Cyanamid Co. A genial officer who never took fame seriously, the hero of Bastogne died 11 Aug 75 at Walter Reed Gen Hosp, Washington, DC.

McCAIN, John Sidney. US admiral. 1884-1945. Known for commanding Carrier TF 38 during the last year of the war in the Pacific, he was born 19 Aug 84 in Teoc, Miss, the nephew of Maj Gen Henry Pinkney McCain (USMA 1885), who was army adjutant general in 1914-18. John McCain was the brother of Brig Gen William A. McCain (USMA 1902). (*CB 43;* Cullum.)

The short, slightly-built "Slew" McCain graduated from Annapolis in 1906 (80/116). After 30 years in the surface navy, and rising to the rank of captain, he became a naval aviator in 1935. Capt McCain then commanded two naval air bases and CV *Ranger* before being promoted to rear admiral in Jan 41 and made Commander, Aircraft Scouting Force (which was then the Atlantic Fleet). In May 42 he became Commander, Aircraft, South Pacific. For six months he planned and directed all land-based naval air operations in the Guadalcanal campaign.

McCain went to Washington in Oct 42 to head the Naval Bureau of Aeronautics. In Aug 43 he became deputy CNO for air with the rank of vice admiral. Because he had been an aviator for only eight years there was muttering that the relatively elderly McCain owed his appointment only to seniority. But criticism ended as the air deputy showed exceptional vigor and aptitude in the assignment. In Aug 44 he was given command of a carrier group in MITSCHER's TF 58, which was the attack element of SPRUANCE's 5th Fleet. McCain took part in the Marianas campaign, the battle of the Philippine Sea, and the Leyte campaign. Now a seasoned veteran, on 30 Oct 44 he took over TF 38 from MITSCHER in HALSEY's 3d Fleet. In Jan 45 he was relieved by MITSCHER. As was the custom, McCain returned to lead the fast carrier task force, arriving on 28 May and taking it through the Okinawa campaign and on audacious raids into the China Sea and Japanese home waters.

Worn down by war's end to little more than 100 pounds, McCain requested home leave but HALSEY insisted he stay for surrender ceremonies aboard *Missouri* on 2 Sep 45. Leaving immediately thereafter for his home in Coronado, Calif, the admiral lived only until 6 Sep 45, less than a month after his 61st birthday. He was promoted posthumously to full admiral.

Adm John Sidney McCain, Jr, USNA 1931 (424/441) was CINCPAC, 1968-72. Capt John

Sidney McCain III, USNA 1958 (894/899), was shot down over North Vietnam and held for nearly seven years as a POW. He retired in 1981, was elected to the US House of Representatives from Arizona in 1984, and became a US Senator in 1986. (RCS.)

McCORMICK, Robert Rutherford. US publisher. 1880-1995. Highly controversial publisher of the Chicago *Tribune,* McCormick was born 30 July 80 in Chicago. The son of a foreign service officer who became ambassador to Austro-Hungary, Russia, and France, "Bertie" attended Eton and was Franklin D. Roovevelt's schoolmate at Groton. He graduated from Yale in 1903, was admitted to the bar in 1907, and had a brief fling in politics before becoming publisher of the Chicago *Tribune.* Six feet four inches tall, physically fit, and an avid sportsman, he fancied the title of colonel he acquired as an AEF artillery officer in France. A 1937 poll by Washington journalists rated the colonel second only to William Randolph Hearst as "least fair and reliable" *(CB 42).* But in 1941 his paper had the second largest circulation in America. On 5 Dec 41 the Chicago *Tribune* revealed highly secret US war plans, the so-called Victory Program (Wedemeyer, 15 ff). On 7 June 42, after the American victory at Midway, the *Tribune* headlined a story "Navy Had Word of Jap Plan to Strike at Sea" (Ronald Clark, *Friedman,* 189). The Federal grand jury failed to bring an indictment under the Espionage Act, and the newspaper argued that their reporter had simply made an accurate guess based on "confidential information." *(CB 42.)*

McCREERY, Richard. British general. 1898-1967. As an officer of the 12th Lancers from 1915 he won the **MC** in WWI and in 1940, with the second BEF in France, commanded a mechanized brigade. After the **Dunkirk evacuation** he was with the Home Forces before serving briefly as AUCHINLECK's adviser on the use of armor *(S&S).* In Aug 42 he became ALEX-ANDER's CofS and 13 months later led the 10th Corps at Salerno. After the drive to Cassino McCreery moved up to command the 8th Army for the rest of the war in Italy, succeeding LEESE. Sir Richard then briefly headed British occupation forces in Austria.

McINTIRE, Ross T. Roosevelt's physician. 1889-1959. From Roosevelt's first election in 1933 until the president's death on 12 Apr 45, Adm McIntire was in almost constant attendance as FDR's personal physician. The admiral therefore is of historical interest on the controversial matter of FDR's health. In his memoirs, *White House Surgeon* (1946), Vice Admiral McIntire wrote of FDR's health on the eve of his run for a fourth term in Nov 44, that "with proper care and a strict adherence to rule" the president had a good chance of living to 1948. This flies in the face of much other evidence. (*See* Parrish, *R&M,* 419-72.)

During the period 1938-46 the admiral also was surgeon general of the navy and chairman of the naval bureau of medicine and surgery. From FDR's sudden death on 12 Apr 45 the admiral held various medical offices including executive director of the International College of Surgeons, 1955-59.

McMORRIS, Charles Horatio "Soc". US admiral. 1890-1954. Born 31 Aug 90 in Alabama, McMorris was in the USNA Class of 1912 (6/156). Nicknamed "Soc" (for Socrates), he taught English and history at Annapolis and was famous during the war for being able to read and memorize a thick report while carrying on a conversation. (Garfield, 171.)

In 1939-40 Soc was operations officer, Hawaiian Dept, US Fleet. Then he was war plans officer of the Pacific Fleet until Apr 42. After going to sea as commander of CA *San Francisco* he was promoted to rear admiral. On 4 Jan 43, when KINKAID took over TF 8 in the Aleutians (replacing THEOBALD, McMorris succeeded Adm W. W. Smith as head of a cruiser-destroyer strike group under Kinkaid. With the ancient CA *Salt Lake City* ("Old Swayback Maru"), CL *Richmond,* and four destroyers, on 18 Feb 43 he gave the first naval gunfire support to the 7th Inf Div as it fought to retake Attu. Weather conditions prevented observation of results. (*OCMH Chron,* 93.) Meanwhile a US fighter strip became operational (16 February) on Amchitka as the Japanese made their last nuisance raid on the island (ibid.).

Almost 200 miles west of Attu, without air support and relying almost exclusively on radar, McMorris fought the Battle of the Komandorski

Islands on 26 Mar 43. Boshiro HOSOGAWA was sailing to reinforce and resupply the Attu garrison, having two heavy cruisers, two light cruisers, four destroyers, and two converted merchant cruisers serving as cargo ships. In the "last and longest daylight battle in the history of fleet warfare" (Garfield, 170), the superior Japanese surface force inflicted damage on DD *Nachi* and *Salt Lake City,* the latter being dead in the water by 11:03 AM after receiving a final hit from an eight inch gun. Unaware of this, however, low on fuel, and mistaking some long range shell splashes for bombs (inferring he was under air attack), Hosogaya withdrew. This left the Attu garrison without badly needed reinforcements and supplies, which subsequently came only by submarine. Attu was recaptured by 29 May 43, and the next month McMorris became CofS, Pacific Fleet. His highest wartime rank was rear admiral. Retiring 1 Sep 52 as a vice admiral, he died 11 Feb 54 at Valparaiso, Chile.

McNAIR, Lesley James. US general. 1883-1944. One of US Army's "big four," McNair was responsible for organizing and directing military training. He was born 25 May 83 in Verndale, Minn, and graduated from West Point in 1904 (11/124). As an artilleryman he served in Mexico on the Vera Cruz and Punitive Expeditions (1914 and 1918). Going to France in June 18 as a major with the 1st Div, he was closely associated with George Marshall and soon became the senior artillery staff officer in AEF Hq. A year after being promoted to brigadier general (1 Oct 18) he reverted to his permanent rank of major. McNair was assistant commandant of the Field Artillery School, 1929-33, and as a brigadier general became commandant of the **CFGSS** on 6 Apr 39. When army training was consolidated in July 40 on activation of GHQ, McNair was put in charge. Promotion to three-star rank came on 9 Jun 41 (*AA,* 910). In a major reorganization effective 9 Mar 42, GHQ was replaced by Army Ground Forces (AGF), with McNair still charged with organization and training within the US (*OCMH Chron,* 28). Short, slender, sharp-featured, and unsociable, the prematurely gray "Whitey" was hard to know. His natural reticence may have been partly due to impaired hearing. (*CB 42.*)

Leaving AGF in June 44, succeeded by Ben LEAR, he went overseas to head the 1st AG. This was a bogus force with an elaborate radio net, decoy invasion fleet, and mock-up vehicles; the mission of the 1st AG was to hold enemy forces in the Pas de Calais to oppose a landing that never came. As an observer in Normandy McNair was killed on 25 July 44 by one of many "shorts" in the carpet bombing near St Lô. De WITT took over the phantom army group. McNair was promoted posthumously to full general in 1954.

McNARNEY, Joseph Taggart. US general. 1893-1972. A dour, taciturn, ruthless, and brilliant administrator, he rose to the rank of full general on 7 Mar 45 while remaining almost unknown outside his profession.

McNarney was born 28 Aug 93 in Emporium, Pa, and graduated with the famous West Point Class of 1915 (41/164). He became a pilot in the army air corps.

Promoted to major general in Jan 42 McNarney became deputy CofS in Washington when George C. Marshall created the post in Mar 42 to give the army air corps proper status for the first time. Three months later McNarney was the army's youngest lieutenant general.

In Oct 44 he became deputy supreme Allied commander in the Mediterranean. Succeeding Jake DEVERS he was CG, NATOUSA, 22 Oct-1 Nov 44, then CG, MTOUSA, until Dec 45, being replaced by J. C. H. LEE. (*AA,* 609.) Promoted to full general on 7 Mar 45, McNarney was Eisenhower's successor as commander of US army forces in Europe from that date until 1947. He concurrently was the first head of the office of military government for Germany (OMGUS), a post turned over to his deputy, Lucius CLAY, on 15 Mar 47. He then headed the new air material command until retiring in 1952. McNarney died 1 Feb 72 in La Jolla, Calif.

McNAUGHTON, Robert George Latta. Canadian general. 1887-1966. McNaughton was born in Moosomin, Saskatchewan, on 25 Jan 87. An outstanding student and athlete, he received a BS in 1910 and MS in 1912 from McGill Univ and became a reserve officer in the artillery (*CB 42*). He served in France with the BEF, twice WIA, appointed to the DSO, and the

Canadian army commander called him the finest gunner in the British Empire *(CB 42)*. Remaining in uniform he was CGS 1929-35. McNaughton resigned to spend four years as president of the new national research bureau, where he concentrated on metal fatigue.

In Dec 39, three months after Britain declared war, Maj Gen McNaughton reached England as head of the first Canadian contingent. As Britain braced for invasion in May 40 McNaughton became the first Canadian to command an army corps that included British forces. Churchill gave him the additional duty of planning Opn **Jupiter,** an invasion of Norway to be executed by Canadians in the winter of 1942-43. In connection with Jupiter McNaughton made several trips home for consultation, touring war factories, meeting US leaders including Roosevelt. Although Churchill proposed to the American president on 22 Sep 42 that McNaughton visit Stalin to discuss the enterprise, the trip was not undertaken. (WC, IV, 436, 569, 573.)

In planning the **Dieppe raid** of 19 Aug 42 the British did not consult McNaughton until 30 April (Stacey, I, 329 & n.). The Canadian general later was falsely accused of demanding that his troops he used, but McNaughton stoutly insisted that authorities in Ottawa not issue an official denial. This would prejudice future Canadian relations with the British, being "interpreted as seeking to shift responsibility from us to them" and would give the Germans valuable information. "It was a sound and patriotic decision, but one which in the end probably did General McNaughton himself considerable harm" (Stacey, I, 395).

By the autumn of 1943 Canada's overseas force had grown to five divisions. After one of them distinguished itself in Sicily and Italy under Guy G. SIMONDS the Canadians finally got British approval to create a corps headquarters in Italy (the main problem being lack of shipping.) Partly because of his differences with military superiors in Ottawa over this problem the Canadian CinC in the UK was ready to come home. He turned over command of 1st Cdn Army to Crerar in Dec 43 and retired from the army. McNaughton was appointed minister of national defense on 2 Nov 44 (Nicholson, *Italy,* 606). Resigning in Aug 45 he was president of Canada's atomic energy control board 1946-48.

MEISSNER, Otto M. German civil servant. 1880-1953. An Alsacian born 13 Mar 80 in Bischweiler (his wife taught RIBBENTROP not far away in Metz), he was educated as a lawyer and was an infantry officer in 1915. He then joined the German military administration in the Ukraine. In 1918 he entered the foreign office and had a long tenure as chief of presidential chancery (Praesidialkanzlei), 1920-45. One of President Hindenburg's most influential advisers, he intrigued to bring Hitler to power and was rewarded by being kept in office. From 1937 the doctor of law also was minister of state and had the honorary rank of SS-Obergruppenfuehrer. He was cleared of war crimes charges at Nuremberg on 2 Apr 49, and by Jan 52 three denazification courts had cleared him. Having published his memoirs, *Staatsskretaer unter Ebert, Hindenburg und Hitler* (1950)the political trimmer—whose career resembled that of LAMMERS—died 28 Apr 53 in Munich.

MEKHLIS, Lev Zakharovich. Soviet official. 1889-1953. A police general and crony of Stalin's (Zhukov, *Memoirs,* 69n.), "an unprincipled individual whose morbid vanity overshadowed everything else" (I. T. Zamertsev quoted in Bialer, ed, 450), "I considered him a nitwit, but Stalin usually listened to him" (*Khrushchev,* 164). It may not be surprising that Mekhlis was one of Stalin's most hated underlings.

Mekhlis was born in Odessa on 25 Jan 89 **(NS),** son of a Jewish office worker. He was a private tutor and clerk before being drafted in 1911 (Scarecrow). In 1914-17 he served in artillery units, then joined the Red Army and the party in the spring of 1918. Until 1920 he commanded an infantry brigade in the Southern Front, being wounded at Kakhovka (ibid.). From 1922 he was in Stalin's secretariat, active in the campaign against Trotsky and Zinoviyev. Graduating in May 30 from the Institute of Red Professors with a doctorate in economic science, Mekhlis was chief editor of *Pravda.* As deputy commissar of defense and head of the Main Political Directorate of the Red Army from 30 Dec 37 to Sep 40 he had a leading role in the **Great Purges.** Stalin particularly valued his crony's gossip about high party members. (Scotts citing D. A. Volkogonov.) Mekhlis was Stalin's representative at **Lake Khasan** in 1938, at **Khalkhin Gol** the next year, and in the war against Finland, 1939-40. Eventually holding the military rank of general colonel (1944), he "often disorganized and disrupted operations by interference in command decisions" (Scarecrow). As commissar of State Control from Sep 40 Mekhlis was largely responsible for the fatal error of massing Soviet forces close to the western border, despite SHAPOSHNIKOV's recommendations. D. G. PAVLOV paid with his head but Mekhlis survived as deputy commissar of defense, head of the Red Army Main Political Directorate, and became the **Stavka** representative on various fronts. Mekhlis's intrigues and his reports ended the careers of many military officers. As the Germans closed in on Moscow Mekhlis was primarily responsible for the scorched earth policy of destroying villages and forests in their path. He also was involved in evacuating industry and in programs to economize on the use of power, metal, and production reserves. Another of the friendless bureaucrat's great responsibilities was to enforce **GKO** orders.

As Stavka representative on the Crimean Front in early 1942 Mekhlis shared the blame for the loss of the Kerch Peninsula. Stripped of his Moscow posts (succeeded by SHCHER-BAKOV) he also was demoted to serving in the field at the army corps level (Bialer, ed, 634). But the bad penny reappeared to serve on military councils of a long series of fronts: the Voronezh, Volkhov, Bryansk, Western, Baltic, 2d Baltic, 2d Belorussian, and 4th Ukrainian (Scarecrow).

MELLENTHIN, Friedrich Wilhelm von. German general. 1904-. An aristocrat born in Breslau he was the youngest of three brothers including Horst von MELLENTHIN. Based on his experience on all fronts as a staff officer he wrote *Panzer Battles* and *German Generals of World War II*. See main bibliography for publication data.

Soon after his mother's death in Aug 50 Generalmajor von Mellenthin emigrated to South Africa, where his wife's family had been established since 1886. Living in the Transvaal at Bryanston in he became an author and director of Lufthansa Africa.

MELLENTHIN, Horst von. German general. 1898-c1976. He was born 31 July 98 in Hanover

while his father was attached to the cavalry school there. The senior Mellenthin, killed in France on 29 June 18 as an artillery lieutenant colonel, was of a Pomeranian family tracing its roots there to 1225. His wife was a von Waldenburg from Silesia and Brandenburg, great-granddaughter of Frederick the Great's nephew Prince August of Prussia.

Horst von Mellenthin became a second lieutenant of artillery shortly before his 17th birthday. In WWI he was wounded twice and awarded the both classes of the Iron Cross. As the Nazis seized power Capt von Mellenthin was ADC to the German army's CinC, Kurt von HAMMERSTEIN-EQUORD, and his to successor, von FRITSCH. The aide arranged the first meeting between Hitler and Reichswehr commanders in early Feb 33 at Hammerstein's house.

Having a background in military intelligence Mellenthin was chief of the attaché branch 1 July 37-1 May 43. Then he rose commanding the 67th Grenadier Regt, 23d Inf Div, in northern Russia to CG, 205th Inf Div, 16th Army, on 25 Nov 43, being promoted on the latter date. Generalmajor von Mellenthin's was cited frequently in communiques for its stout delaying action against BAGRAMYAN's 1st Baltic Front. Promoted further, Generalleutnant was awarded the RK on 18 Oct 44. On 9 Jan 45 he was made acting commander of the 38th Pz Corps, which was being driven back into Latvia's Courland Peninsula. When SCHOERNER took command of AG Center in Upper Silesia he sent for Mellenthin to command his 11th Corps. The artilleryman took up this assignment on 16 Mar 45, promoted at this time to General of Artillery (B&O, 41) and awarded the Oakleaves (according to his brother [below].).

During the final weeks of the war he commanded the 7th Corps in Silesia, where his only role was to keep escape routes open to the west. Defying orders to stop withdrawing at midnight on 8-9 May 45 and surrender to the Russians, the general got most of his officers and men into American hands in Czechoslovakia.

Some POW camps already had been turned over to the Soviets in accordance with the Yalta Agreement, but Mellenthin told an American general he would shoot his way out rather than accept this fate. (US authorities had allowed German officers and 10 men to retain weapons for local security.) The Americans consequently had release papers flown in quickly and Mellenthin was set free with most of his officers and men.

In 1951 Mellenthin began five years as a deputy to Gen Reinhard GEHLEN in the latter's intelligence organization. For three and a half years beginning in 1956 the general served at the German embassy in Washington. "He died while this book was in preparation," writes his brother in the chapter from which most of the above sketch is taken (Mellenthin, *Generals,* 145).

MENGELE, Fritz. German doctor. 1911-79? One of the most notorious Nazi doctors, Mengele was a Bavarian born on 16 Mar 11 in Guenzburg. His father founded a highly successful farm-machinery factory that had a branch in Argentina. Fritz Mengele studied philosophy in Munich before getting a medical degree at the Univ of Frankfort on the Main. He joined the Nazi Party before becoming a staff member at the new institute of hereditary biology and race research. At the start of war in 1939 he entered the Waffen-SS as a medical officer. After service in France and on the eastern front he was made the deputy to Dr Hans Klein in 1943 and succeeding him as head doctor at Auschwitz when Klein went to Belsen.

Whistling gayly while performing a ghastly triage, the jaunty Mengele indicated which new prisoners would go to the gas chambers, which would do forced labor, and which would be used for spurious medical experiments. The doctor was fascinated by twins, in whom he hoped to find a way not only of accelerating population growth but also of creating a super-race.

After the war his record remained unknown while Mengele spent five years in Guenzburg with his family. Then his name began to appear in war crimes trials. (The many surviving victims had a mental block against talking about their ordeal.) The mad doctor reached Buenos Aires in 1952 via the **ODESSA** pipeline and practiced medicine while repeatedly changing identity. When Peron was ousted in 1955 the Auschwitz doctor moved to Paraguay and in due course became a citizen. As more evidence of his crimes was revealed in Germany, and the search for him began, Mengele went to ground in Brazil. Supported by his family in Germany, and presumably with help from ODESSA, Mengele fled to Cairo. From here he apparently

went to a Greek island before finally returning to Paraguay. That country's pro-German authorities denied knowledge of the Auschwitz doctor's whereabouts until 1984, when they reissued a 22-year-old order for his arrest as a fugitive. By then the dogged Beate Klarsfeld had joined the Nazi hunt that had been started by Simon Wiesethal. She had no success during a visit to South America, but a UPI news bulletin of 11 Feb 85 said Mengele was in Paraguay, living "fairly openly" under heavy guard. But there also was evidence that he had drowned, and on 6 June 85 a coffin believed to contain his remains was opened; on 1 July a team of 16 forensic experts announced that the skeleton was Mengle's "within a reasonable scientific certainty."

MENTHON, François Bernard Marie Fidèle, Comte de. French resistance leader. 1900-84. A descendant of the famous Alpine savior, St Bernard de Menthon (923-1008), the subject of this sketch was born 8 Jan 00 at Montmirey, in the Jura. He began a university career in Dijon as a political economist but turned to politics. Mobilized as a captain in 1940, he was captured by the Germans but escaped. He became editor of a clandestine newspaper, *Liberté,* which he and various law professors of Christian-Democratic outlook founded on 20 Nov 40. *Liberté* merged a year later with Henri FRENAY's *Vérités* to become *Combat.* Directed by Menthon and Frenay, the combined movement became the most important in the unoccupied zone (Michel, *Shadow War,* 105).

Much like Count Helmuth James von MOLTKE in Germany the Count de Menthon was interested primarily in combining the ideals of different resistance groups to shape a new regime for his country. (Yvert, 709.) Menthon continued to conduct university political economics courses in Lyons while co-directing *Combat.* He also served on commissions dealing with French legal reform and directed publication of *les Cahiers politiques,* a periodical. Vichy authorities harassed Menthon, first arresting him in Nov 41. DARNAND's bully boys of the SOL threw him into Lake Annecy (his home waters) on 2 May 42. With Georges BIDAULT he was a founder of the powerful *Mouvement républicain populaire* (MRP) a Catholic political party.

François de Menthon was called to Algiers and appointed commissioner of justice, 4 Sep 43-9 Sep 44. In the first government created after the liberation of Paris he was keeper of the seals, 9 Sep 44-31 May 45. Remaining in the thick of French politics, particularly in drafting the new constitution, the count served briefly as minister of national economy, 23 June-16 Sep 46, in his underground companion BIDAULT's government. When the new French constitution was adopted, 13 Oct 46, Menthon focused on efforts to create European unity. Neglecting his own political fences he lost the presidency of his party, the MRP, to Pflimlin in 1956; two years later he was beaten in parliamentary elections for the first time since 1947. He returned to an academic career, politically active only as long-time mayor of Menthon-Saint-Bernard. (The picturesque village on Lake Annecy is overlooked by the well-preserved chateau of St Bernard's birth, which the family still occupies.) Retiring in 1968, the count died 3 June 84 at Menthon-Saint-Bernard.

MENZIES, Robert Gordon. Australian PM. 1894-1978. Born 20 Dec 94 at Jeparit, a small community 250 miles NW of Melbourne, Menzies was from a line of Scottish farmers and Cornwall miners. As PM from Apr 39 to Aug 41 Sir Robert put Australia on a war footing. His government introduced compulsory military service and sent three crack divisions to the Middle East. Returning from a five-month trip through Singapore, Palestine, and Egypt to London, as Australians under British leadership suffered defeats in North Africa and Greece, Menzies found insurmountable opposition to his coalition government. Embittered by his first experience in government *(DNB)* he resigned in Aug 41 to head the new ministry for the co-ordination of defense in Arthur W. FADDEN's government. John CURTIN's Labour Party won the election of Oct 41 and was in power for eight years. (Ibid.)

Sir Robert (KT in 1963 and Order of Australia in 1976) had a long postwar tenure as PM 1949-66. It has been said that the large, bushy-eyebrowed Menzies was a noble politician with "a better mind than anybody else in and around Australia" *(DNB)*. Having so long dominated his country's politics Menzies died 15 May 78 at his home in Melbourne.

MENZIES, Stewart Graham. British SIS chief. 1890-1968. Menzies was a Scot, hence the family name is pronounced "Ming-iss." In the words of a close associate, he had "a ready smile and the assurance which had come down with the profits from the millions of gallons of whisky distilled by his ancestors" (Winterbotham, *Ultra Secret* 13). SGM was born 30 Jan 90 in London to John Graham and the beautiful Susannah West (née Wilson) Menzies, both independently rich. It is believed that Stewart was the illegitimate son of the lecherous prince who became King Edward VII in 1901; the allegation is supported by circumstantial evidence and physical resemblance— "Windsor-blue eyes; reddish hair." (Brown, *"C,"* 15-16.) In his *Who's Who* entry Menzies list only one parent, his mother.

Menzies was an outstanding athlete and sportsman at Eton and president of the influential school society Pop. Although no intellectual he won prizes for French and German. He did not go further in formal education but took a commission in the Grenadier Guards. After a year he transferred to the Life Guards, whose commander his widowed mother married in 1910. SGM had 18 months of bloody action with the 2d Life Guards Regt around Ypres in 1914-15, winning the MC and DSO. The death of four of Menzies's seven best friends, "golden boys" from Eton, has been called *"the* decisive physical and moral experience of his life" (Brown, *"C,"* 91). Turning over his post as regimental adjutant on 18 Dec 15 and promoted about this time, Bvt Maj Menzies began his military intelligence with GHQ at St Omer. "That way had been made for him is evident," writes a biographer; the major had family ties with the new CinC, Gen Sir Douglas Haig, through the Haig & Haig whisky company and Grandfather Graham Menzies of the Distillers Co Ltd (Brown, *"C,"* 91-93).

Despite lack of professional qualifications and not yet 26 years old, SGM became chief of counterespionage and security at GHQ. One of his innovation was a large card index file of known and suspected enemy agents and other people a spy hunter should know about. In 1917-18 his project led to the capture of three German spymasters, the arrest of some 128 secret agents, and surveillance of another 100 to 200. But on 22 Oct 17 he netted James Franklin Bell, one of the US Army's most distinguished and volatile generals. Bell was ostensibly on an official inspection but probably was indulging in a bit of rubbernecking during the 3d battle of Ypres—not a good time for two people with odd accents, a strange uniform, and a car of unfamiliar make to poke around behind the lines. Bell had oral authority for the trip but had not gotten written passes. British MPs did not like the look or the accent of Bell's driver, one Angelo Damoulakis, all the more so because he was licensed to drive an ambulance but not a staff car. The military police put Damoulakis under arrest while CHQ made a time consuming search of security files and concluded that the hyphenated American was a suspected enemy agent known as Anton Babel. (The name could not have had a salubrious effect on the fulminating American general.) After 50 hours the American tourists were sent on their way with apologies and the proper trip tickets, but the incident fueled the normal Anglo-American antipathy. The Bell affair also lingered as evidence that the very-British Menzies was anti-American. (Brown, *"C,"* 106-7.)

Maj Menzies married Lady Avice (Ela Muriel) Sackville on 29 Nov 18. She was a large, pretty brunette given away by her brother, the 9th Earl De la Warr. SGM proceeded to Paris for the Versailles peace conference as a member of the British delegation's security staff. Menzies's opposite number in Paris was Col Aristides Moreno, an officer of New York Puerto Rican provenience who had been SGM's opposite number in the Bell incident. Moreno was not an Anglophile in the best of circumstances, and MI6 replaced Menzies within 90 days by an older man they thought would get along better with the Americans. He was one Col Claude "Col Z" DANSEY, with whom SGM would have further contact.

Bolshevik activities in Britain now alarming, SGM became chief of the war office secret service. He had the rank of lieutenant colonel and GSO first grade in the IGS. When Lloyd George reestablished the SIS a few months later Menzies became the war office "military representative" in SIS Hq and remained responsible for military espionage.

Lt Col Menzies's mother-in-law, Countess Muriel De La Warr, was identified shortly thereafter in an official report as one of several "prominent British Subjects" conspiring with Indian seditionists. SGM's pro forma resignation was not accepted, but the experience

showed him that treason could be anywhere. He continued to head the war office military intelligence section, his career undamaged.

Sir Hugh "Quex" Sinclair took over MI6 after Capt Mansfield "C" Cunningham, the first chief, died on 14 June 23. Menzies was virtually Sinclair's deputy while still keeping the war office post. The **Arcos operation** of 1927 was his greatest achievement. But a personal crisis for Menzies developed about this time: his wife began an adulterous affair that led to divorce in 1931. (Lady Avice was novelist John le Carré's model for George Smiley's wayward wife, Lady Anne.) Divorce was still a disgrace in upper class Britain, but SGM emerged unscathed socially and professionally. He was promoted to colonel in July 32 and transferred to MI6 as C's deputy officially, not just in fact. Menzies, who was somewhat of a man with the ladies, promptly remarried (12 Dec 32); the second wife, Mrs Pamela Thetis Garton was a baby-faced, "darkly beautiful woman with an intense air" (Brown, *"C,"* 162).

On the eve of Hitler's war the colonel had primary staff responsibility for the **Ultra** material. Succeeding the ailing Sinclair on 28 Nov 39 and promoted to major general, the new chief of the secret service (CSS) took over a cozy suite on the fourth floor of 54 Broadway. A concealed door led to a passage and a semi-concealed door to his official residence at 21 Queen Anne's Gate. The CSS could come and go from meetings with colleagues or strangers without being seen on the street or getting wet. (Brown, *"C",* 225.)

But the new secret service chief had a rocky start. His world-wide intelligence organization had suffered from peacetime parsimony and needed overhauling, particularly because of the **Venlo incident** on 9 Nov 39. Menzies survived this fiasco, which wiped out the SIS apparatus in Holland and Germany, primarily because his personal blame was not known at the time. Better skilled in bureaucratic politics than in secret service work, Menzies owed his job survival initially to his control of Ultra intelligence distribution. C's deputy was the formidable and ambitious Claude "Col Z" DANSEY, the éminence grise who many thought was the real power in MI6. One of Menzies's key staff officers and virtual protégé was Kim PHILBY, for whom novelist John Le Carré would coin the designation *mole*.

But Churchill presented a greater threat to MI6 than Moscow Center. In one of his famous minutes Churchill, on 3 Aug 40, demanded two things: that he get all intercepted enemy material in its "original form," and that "Colonel Menzies should submit a report on what he had done and is proposing to do" about "improving and extending our information from France and for keeping a continual flow of agents moving to and fro." (Brown, *"C,"* 292, citing PRO, Cabinet 120/746.)

C could not comply. Either he had to resign, Churchill's private office having already proved not to be secure (ibid), or he had to meet the PM's demand in a way that would not fatally compromise British intelligence. Exactly how this was done will remain unknown until the last classified files are opened in 1995, but Menzies found a solution. Churchill directed (Sep 40) that C send him "daily all Enigma messages." This kept the PMs gossipy military assistant, Maj Desmond Morton, outside the circle of Ultra recipients. But it also established a good relationship between Churchill and Menzies for the first time. Once or twice daily an armed officer took a dispatch box of the most important decrypts to the PM, the material normally selected by Menzies personally. The box was sent to WC when he was out of the country or was radioed to him by a one-time pad held only by WC and SGM. But the SIS chief paid the price of being on call for Churchill's "midnight follies," frequently being summoned after midnight or before dawn, air raid or not, to Downing St or the central war room to talk business with Churchill or just to chat. The sessions were preceded and followed by long days at Broadway,

Among the greatest wartime accomplishments of Sir Stewart (KCMG 1943) was masterminding intricate "cover plans" and preserving the Ultra secret (by severely limiting its distribution). SGM established and maintained fruitful relations with US secret services, notably the **OSS.** His dealings with intelligence agencies of governments in exile, particularly the French, were troublesome (West, *MI6,* 147).

One of C's only two trips abroad was to Algiers in Dec 42, when DARLAN was assassinated. The French spread the rumor that Menzies had gone to see the job done right, and GIRAUD believed he was next on the SIS hit list. (SGM's other overseas trip was to Brussels during the Ardennes crisis.)

C maintained his control over Ultra despite repeated challenges and he deserves primary credit for protecting security of the program. As for turf battles, Menzies could not keep the **SOE** from taking over some MI6 functions, but he retained control over SOE's communications. (West, 246-47.)

The reputations of MI6 and its chief at war's end were at an all-time high. SGM remained CSS, director general of the Government Communications Hq (GCHQ) and brought in the wartime director of **MI,** Maj Gen John Sinclair, as his deputy and successor designate. Six years later and two and a half years past normal retirement age, Menzies announced his retirement on 30 June 52, having been advanced to KCB in 1951. That year his wife died at the age of 48, having suffered from signs of anorexia nervosa throughout much of their otherwise happy marriage. Lady Pamela left a 17-year-old daughter, Fiona, who was very close to her father.

It was assumed that Menzies resigned because of the Burgess—Maclean affair and suspicions that Philby was a Soviet spy, but his biographer concludes "these beliefs were illfounded" (Brown, *"C,"* 714). In sound health and only 62 years old, SGM thought he had better things to do after 36 years of counterespionage. His recreation from 1921, which he said was responsible for his top physical condition, was riding to the hounds with the most exclusive of all fox hunts, the Beaufort. The manhunter's London club was White's, also the most exclusive (founded 1693), and he used it as a sort of annex to Broadway. The hall porter received most of SGM's most secret official or personal mail; the only known exception to the female exclusion rule at White's was Fiona, who fetched her father's mail until reaching puberty (Brown, *"C,"* 149-50). "Although everybody at White's knew who Stewart was, and what he was doing, including the staff," writes Brown, "there was never gossip, and the higher he rose, the more difficult it became for anybody to see him." Important messengers or visitors were held by the porters until they could "see whether the colonel can see you at the moment." If so, he invariably met them in the billiard room, where SGM did not have to lower his voice.

Only a year after Menzies left Broadway it was confirmed (Apr 54) that Guy Burgess and Donald Maclean, who defected in May 51, had been "moles." SGM had backed the official finding that Philby did not tip them off in time to flee and was not himself a spy. Menzies had virtually nothing more to say about the affair, even after Philby himself defected in 1963, maintaining he had not been outwitted (Brown, *"C,"* 712).

As for SGM's appearance in spy fiction, he once said to Brown with a hint of satisfaction, "Ian Flemming tells me that I am James Bond's 'M'." (*"C,"* 10.) Asked what he thought about John le Carré's *The Spy Who Came in from the Cold,* SGM would say only, "That fellow knows something" (ibid).

But Menzies remained generally unknown (as C) until H. Montgomery Hyde published the biography of Sir William ("Intrepid") Stephenson in 1962. Philby's *My Silent War* did not appear until 1968, just after C died in a London hospital, of natural causes, on 28 May 68 in his 78th year. Brown discredits the rumor that he committed suicide in despair (Brown, *"C,"* 73). The MI6 chief's role in the cryptanalysis triumph, particularly in concealing this from the Germans, was first made public by F. W. Winterbotham in *The Ultra Secret* (New York: Harper, 1974). Anthony Cave Brown's monumental biography, *"C",* is identified in the main bibliography.

MERETSKOV, Kirill Afanasyevich. Soviet military leader. 1897-1968. The huge, brash, jovial Meretskov was born 7 June 97 in Nazaryevo, near Moscow, son of a clerk. He was a factory worker in Moscow when he joined the CP in May 17 and entered the Red Guard. The next year he became a political commissar and began a rapid rise in the Red Army, serving mostly as deputy CofS or CofS at various echelons. In 1931 he had some secret training in Germany (1931), applying himself diligently and begining to be known as something of a tactician, but he resisted learning the language. As Comrade Petrovich in Spain, "an imposing, bulky man [who] . . . looked almost comic in the beret and wide cape which he affected," he helped plan the Loyalist victory at Guadalajara (Salisbury, *Leningrad,* 111). Returning to Russia in June 37 at the height of the Great Purges he did not become one of the many military victims (Scotts) but was given the top-drawer assignment of deputy CGS to SHAPOSHNIKOV.

After serving briefly in the Volga MD, Meretskov became head of the Leningrad MD in 1938. With only three days to plan the invasion of Finland that Stalin thought would be a walkover, he attacked on 30 Nov 39 with four field armies. As SHAPSHNIKOV had warned, the Finns put up a diehard defense and within a month had repulsed the invaders. TIMOSHENKO took command of the front on 7 Jan 40, but Meretskov was merely demoted one echelon. Probably because Stalin had given him so little time to plan phase one of the war, and because he did so well in phase two of the Winter War, Meretskov emerged with his military reputation unimpaired and was one of the first three officers promoted on 4 June 40 to the new rank of General of the Army. (The others were ZHUKOV and TYULENEV.) Also made a Hero of the Soviet Union in 1940 and named to the Main Military Council on 24 July, he succeeded SHAPOSHNIKOV as CGS on 14 August. But in this top position he quickly made "a generally uncongenial impression" (Erickson, *To Stalingrad,* 24). Vasilevsky agreed with Stalin that the new CGS was "distinguished for cunning [and], circumspection," not reaching a decision until "'first finding out the opinion of the highest power in the land'" (*Stalin,* 267).

His downfall came when Stalin advanced the date for a high-level critique of recent war games and studies to revise the Field Service Regulations. Not yet fully prepared and notoriously poor at maintaining composure under pressure, Meretskov came a cropper before a large audience that included Stalin, field army commanders, military district staffs, all senior military officials in Moscow, and the Politburo. "Stalin had already decided to regroup the district commands, but first he replaced Meretskov by Zhukov," writes Erickson (op cit, 54). Both changes were effective the next day, 14 Jan 41, but not announced for almost a month, on 12 Feb 41. This has been cited as further evidence of a conspiracy to make way for Zhukov, but the explanation is simply that the latter needed the month to wrap up his affairs in Kiev (HFS).

After becoming head of the Combat Training Directorate. Meretskov was arrested on trumped-up charges of spying for the British. The action allegedly was without BERIA's knowledge, the doing of one V. S. Abakumov (Khrushchev, 103-4 & notes). It is not clear when this occurred. On 21 June 41, the eve of Barbarossa, the Politburo appears to have decided that Meretskov would command the Northern Front (Erickson, 126), but the unfortunate M. M. POPOV got that assignment.

According to some authorities Meretskov commanded the 11th Army on the East Prussian frontier in Fyodor I. KUZNETSOV's new NW Front. But Soviet records show that V. I. Morozov headed this army in June 41. Wherever he was at this time, it is known that Stalin had him released from prison in late Sep 41. (HFS, citing *Sov Voy Ent,* 8920, p. 77). "A shadow of his former self . . . hardly able to speak" (Erickson, 126), he was sent to Leningrad as Stavka representative.

Almost immediately he took over the 7th Independent Army on the Svir River facing the Finns, who were now allied with the Germans. On 8 Nov 41 the spearhead of LEEB's AG North, which had undertaken a large-scale envelopment, occupied Tikhvin. This cut Leningrad's last rail link and threatened the 7th Army's rear. When Meretskov called Moscow to report the alarming situation, Stalin picked up the phone and barked orders for Meretskov to assume command of the 4th Army remnants and whatever elements of the locally available 7th and 52d Armies he needed to wipe out the German salient. "By 11 November [within three days] the energetic and jovial Meretskov had already organized the first counter-attack and this steadily built up into an offensive" (Seaton, 137). On 9 Dec, a month after the Germans took Tikhvin, Russian troops fought their way into this city.

Meretskov's Volkhov Front was created officially on 17 December. Located between the Leningrad and Northwest Fronts, it had the three armies already available (above) plus two that were being sent in, the 26th and 59th. The new front drove the Germans back through frozen swamps and heavy woods of the Novgorod region, but a serious problem developed when the 2d **Shock Army** (the former 26th Army) was cut off. Meretskov was personally directing rescue efforts when he learned suddenly on 24 Apr 42 that his front had been deactivated. The Leningrad Front commander, KHOZIN, had convinced Stalin that he was better able to save the 2d Shock Army by using units of the disbanded Volkhov Front as an operational group (Erickson, 332).

Meretskov became deputy commander of Zhukov's Western Front and head of the 33d Army. But within a few weeks, on 8 June, the yo-yo career of this hardy survivor was up again. Stalin apologized at a full meeting of the Stavka for "a great mistake" in listening to

KHOZIN and directed Meretskov to save the 2d Shock Army, using a reconstituted Volkhov Front. But it was too late; VLASOV was taken prisoner along with remnants of his elite force.

For the next 18 months Meretskov's primary mission was to keep supply lines open to Leningrad. In phase one of the large-scale operation that broke the seige, the Novgorod counteroffensive, 1 Jan-1 Mar 44, Meretskov made a converging attack across the frozen waters and surrounding swamps of Lake Ilmen. The Volkhov Front was deactivated again on 15 Feb 44, when Meretskov and his staff took over the Karelian Front and knocked Finland out of the war in two brief but violent operations, the Vyborg-Petrozavodsk Offensive, 10 June to 9 Aug 44, and the Petsamo-Kirkenes Offensive, 7-29 Oct 44.

Promoted to **MSU** (No. 15) on 26 Oct 44, the 47-year-old Meretskov took command in Aug 45 of the new 1st Far Eastern Front, one of three under VASILEVSKY. Supported by Adm. I. S. Yumashev's Pacific Ocean Fleet in the Manchurian Offensive of 9 Aug-2 Sep 45, he helped to annihilate Japanese forces in the Far East.

Meretskov was among the many military heroes that STALIN now got out of public view. Heading in succession the Maritime, Moscow, White Sea, and Northern MD, he was assistant to the minister of defense for higher military education from 1955 (two years after Stalin's death) until retiring in 1964. He also headed the Soviet Veterans' Committee 1957-61. Dying on 30 Dec 68 in Moscow, he is buried in the Kremlin Wall.

The marshal's memoirs are *Na Sluzh-be Narodu* (Moscow, 1968). He also published *Nekolebimo Kak Rossiya* (Moscow, 1965).

MERRILL, Frank Dow. US general. 1903-55. The leader of "Merrill's Marauders" in Burma (1944) was born 4 Dec 03 in Hopkinton, Mass, and reared in Amesbury, Mass (*CB 44*). He was a regular army engineer sergeant in Panama when admitted to West Point on an army appointment. Merrill graduated in 1929 (147/ 299), was commissioned in the cavalry, and went on to get a BS from MIT in military engineering.

Prewar service included a year of special weapons study and 40 months as an assistant MA and language student in Tokyo, where he rose to captain. He was promoted to major (T) in Oct 41 and ordered the next month to

MacArthur's staff in Manila. Merrill was visiting Rangoon when the Japanese attacked Pearl Harbor on 7 Dec 41 and he remained in Burma to serve on Stilwell's staff as G3 and LnO to the British in Burma and later in India.

Formation of Merrill's 5307th Composite Unit (Provisional), to be patterned on WINGATE's Long-Range Penetration Gp ("Chindits"), was authorized at the Quebec Conference in Aug 43. Recruits were jungle-trained volunteers from the Caribbean and the US, who formed two battalions in San Francisco, and the Pacific, who joined in Perth, Australia, as the third battalion. Col Charles N. Hunter (USMA 1929), a colorful, capable infantryman and the senior volunteer, led the force to Bombay, debarking on 31 Oct, and taking them on through a British camp to a jungle training center at Deogarh. Hunter became second in command to Merrill, who was promoted in late 1943 to brigadier general *(CB 44)*. A journalist created the name Merrill's Marauders for the unit whose official codename was Galahad. (*Merrill's Marauders,* Hist Div, War Department, 1945, cited hereafter as *MM.*)

Under Stilwell in Burma the Marauders hit the veteran 18th Japanese Div's flanks and rear as the US-sponsored Chinese 22d and 38th Divs moved south. With mule trains, air supply, Kachin guides, and support from SEAGRAVE hospital units, Merrill's Marauders waged three campaigns. The first, 24 Feb-7 Mar 44, opened the way for the Chinese 38th Div to take Walawbum, giving Stilwell control of the Hakawng Valley. In the second campaign the Marauders moved south in two columns, 11 Mar-9 Apr 44, forcing the 18th Div to withdraw farther or be trapped. Midway through this operation, Col Hunter took over when Gen Merrill suffered a severe heart attack on 29 Mar and had to be evacuated from Hsamshingyang to Ledo on 31 March.

Merrill returned to duty on 17 May for the drive on Myitkyina. The Marauders having lost 700 officers and men, Stilwell reinforced them with Kachins and Chinese to a strength of 7,000. Merrill made Col John E. McCammon his XO, Hunter having taken command of H Force, which comprised the 1st Marauder Bn and 150th Chinese Regt. But Merrill lasted only two days before having another heart attack. McCammon was promoted to brigadier general and given charge of the reorganized Myitkyina TF and Hunter took command of the depleted Galahad.

But this arrangement lasted only a week until Stilwell had to replace McGammon with Gen Haydon L. BOATNER. (Allen, 367.)

Only 1,300 Marauders reached Myitkyina's defenses, and 679 of these (including Merrill) were flown out by 1 June, for hospitalization. About 200 men of the 1st Bn remained until regular forces arrived to capture Myitkyina on 3 Aug 44.

Merrill pointed out that his unit had been in action 100 days, covering 750 miles, fighting five major engagements and 32 skirmishes without a defeat. Recurring heart trouble caused Merrill's medical evacuation (under protest) on three occasions before he was flown out from near Myitkyina with malaria. The War Department having found morale within the Marauders to have almost completely broken down, the force was awarded a Distinguished Unit Citation and disbanded in Aug 44.

Promoted to major general on 5 Sep 44 the tall, lean, bespectacled Merrill headed the Allied Liaison Group for CBI until succeeded by Brig Gen Theodore F. Wessels in Dec 44. Thereafter he was deputy US commander of CBI under Daniel I. SULTAN until STILWELL took over the 10th Army on Okinawa (23 June 45). Merrill became Stilwell's CofS, then held the same post in the 6th Army until retiring in 1948. He had been awarded the LM and the BSM. Never wounded, he was awarded the **PH** *for service,* 15 Mar-1 May 42, in Stilwell's retreat from Burma *(CB 44).*

Merrill was New Hampshire commissioner of public works, 1949-55. He died 11 Dec 55, a few days past his 52d birthday, at Fernandia Beach, Fla. (Cullum.)

MESSE, Giovanni. Italian general. 1883-1968. A veteran of campaigns in Libya (1911), Ethiopia, Albania, and Greece, Messe led the Italian Expeditionary Corps in Russia, 1941-43.

Recently promoted, Generale d'Armata Messe reached Tunisia about 1 Feb 43 to command the 1st Italian Army. (*See* **Panzer Army Africa** for its antecedents.) Messe's troops were the Italian Trieste, Spezia, and Pistoia Divs, the Italian Young Fascists, and the **Afrika Korps** (under Fritz BAYERLEIN as Messe's CofS).

When ROMMEL left on 9 March, succeeded by ARNIM as AG Afrika commander, Messe repelled Montgomery's frontal attacks on the Mareth Line that began on 20 Mar 43. But a week later the NZ Corps undertook a turning movement that made the Mareth Line untenable. "Smiling Albert" Kesselring refused to authorize timely withdrawals, so Arnim could not defend the Tunisian bridgehead properly. Montgomery's slow exploitation enabled Messe to escape from the Mareth Line with few casualties, but he had insufficient time to prepare the Wadi Akarit Line (40 miles back), and he suffered heavy losses in the battle of Wadi Akarit, 5-7 Apr 43. Axis resistance in Tunisia ended on 12 May, when ARNIM was captured with the Afrika Korps Hq. Messe surrendered his army the next afternoon. Although Mussolini promoted him in absentia to Marshal of Italy, Messe was among the first to change allegiance as a POW. When the BADOGLIO government joined the Allied camp, Marshal Messe was appointed the Italian army's CofS. Criticism for serving the Germans against the Red Army led to Messe's ouster in 1945.

MESSERSCHMITT, Wilhelm. German aircraft designer and builder. 1898-1978. "Willi" was born 26 June 98 at Frankfort on the Main and was educated at the Munich Technical HS. He starting to fly at the age of 15 and became a designer for the Bavarian Acft Co. In 1923 he established the Messerschmitt Works in Augsburg and produced his first, all-metal plane three years later. (Wistrich.) Munich's Technical College gave him the honorary title Professor of Aircraft Construction in 1930.

As aircraft production stepped up in 1933 Messerschmitt's company was producing Do 11 bombers under contract (Irving, *Milch*, 34). The single-seat Me 109 fighter with its square-tipped wing was first displayed publicly at the 1936 Berlin Olympiad and tested that year in Spain; it went on to have what probably is the largest production of any combat plane in history (*S&S*, 401). But in May 40 the Luftwaffe got a shock over Dunkirk when Spitfires achieved daylight superiority over the Me 109 (Irving, *Milch*, 94).

The Me 109E remained inferior in some respects to the Spitfire, but the Me 109F outperformed the Spitfire V at altitude (*S&S*, 401). Rudolf HESS escaped to Scotland on 10 May 41 in an early model of the twin-engine Me 110. Messerschmitt's first long-range fighter, this did well until meeting the RAF and because of poor maneuverability it was withdrawn.

Hitler hailed Willi Messerschmitt as a genius. MILCH "admitted that the designer was entitled to credit for his Me 109 fighter," writes Irving. "But from the Messerschmitt drawing-offices had flowed . . . some costly white elephants. . . " (*Milch*, 152-53). The worst was the Me 210, primarily because Messerschmitt tinkered with the original blueprints of Waldemar Voight, his company's leading designer. After delays that cost some 38 million **RM** and threatened Messerschmitt with losing control of his company, the distraught Willi converted his albatross into the Me 410, a magnificent heavy fighter, interceptor, and night fighter. (*Ibid*, 155; *S&S*, 402.)

Me 262, the world's first turbojet aircraft, also had protracted birthing problems. Adolf GALLAND finally formed a squadron that made its debut in Nov 44 and scared the daylights out of Allied flyers in its relatively rare appearances.

Messerschmitt was interned after the war and convicted by a German court in 1948 of being a Nazi "fellow traveler." For the next decade he was reduced to building cabins and prefabricated houses. But when the FRG and other NATO countries needed him for the cold war he was back in business, producing jet aircraft. Messerschmitt died 15 Sep 78 in a Munich hospital at the age of 80.

MESSERVY, Frank Walter. British general. 1893-1973. A rugged, religious, and sanguine cavalryman, Messervy was born 9 Dec 93 in Trinidad. He was the eldest child of Walter John Messervy, a bank manager, and Naida de Boissiere. (*DNB* notice by R. G. Satterthwaite.) "He said repeatedly of the way to pronounce his name: 'The accent is not on the Mess, but on the Serve'" (ibid.).

Educated at Eton and Sandhurst, Messervy was commissioned in the Indian Army (1913), where he began acquiring a high handicap at polo. During the first world war he served with Hodson's Horse in France, Palestine, Syria, and Kurdistan.

Tall, spare, athletic, and fearless (ibid.), "not too calculating of odds" (SLIM, 388), he was on the 5th Indian Div staff when the division went to the Sudan in 1939. From Oct 40 he harassed Italians in East Africa with his mechanized "Gazelle Force." Assuming command of the 9th Inf Bde he took part in William PLATT's campaign that drove the Italians from Eritrea and Ethiopia. His brigade had a major role in capturing the mountain fortress of Keren on 27 Mar 41 after a costly operation lasting almost two months.

Promoted to head the veteran 4th Indian Div he was involved in the defensive operations that checked ROMMEL's first offensive. In from Lumsden AUCHINLECK's Opn Crusader he entered Benghazi on 25 Dec 41 and on 6 Jan 42 took over the 1st Armd Div temporarily while it manned forward positions facing Rommel's forces that had been driven back to El Agheila.

Rommel launched his second offensive on 21 Jan 42, virtually destroying the 1st Armd Div and routing the British 8th Army. On 26 Feb 42 Messervy succeeded Jack CAMPBELL as commander of the 7th Armd "Desert Rats" Div. The inexperienced N. M. RITCHIE was commanding the 8th Army (vice Alan CUNNINGHAM) when Rommel enveloped the Gazala line. At the start of this operation the Desert Rats caught the full force of the Afrika Korps, which was at its peak performance while Messervy and other 8th Army subordinate commanders were confused by Ritchie's orders (Strawson, 121, 141 & n.). Messervy was captured on 27 May 42 when panzers overran his headquarters. But he removed his insignia of rank, pretended to be a batman, and escaped after 18 hours. Scrambling to salvage a hopeless situation he lost all but 32 of 90 surviving tanks in a bold but foredoomed attack on 17 June. This left the 8th Army virtually defenseless against the Afrika Korps.

Sacked by Ritchie (Barnett, 164), Messervy returned to India. After various assignments including director, armoured fighting vehicles, he took over the newly formed 7th Indian Div. In due course this joined the veteran 5th Indian Div (from the Middle East) in SLIM's 15th Corps in the Arakan. The Japanese had been masters of this coastal region of Burma, but Slim's counteroffensive was moving forward when it was hit by a powerful counteroffensive. This proved to be Opn Ha-Go, a strategic diversion to support MUTAGUCHI's "march on Delhi" by quickly annihilating Slim's force.

Messervy's headquarters was attacked early 6 Feb 44 by the Tanahashi Force of Sakurai Tohutaro's 55th Div. "Clerks, orderlies, signallers, and staff officers threw off yelling rush after rush," writes Slim, "but when the Japanese mortars made the area untenable, Messervy gave the order for the whole headquarters to

fight its way through the Japanese to the Administrative Box" (Slim, 207.) This rear area installation was also was under heavy attack, but Messervy regained control of his division, brought in combat units including the 9th Bde of the 5th Div, and waged a successful two-week defense—the "Battle of the Administrative Box." For the first time British troops had repulsed a major Japanese assault, and the action was hailed later as a turning point in the campaign for Burma (Allen, *Burma,* 187-88). Messervy was then engaged in the defense of Kohima and Imphal *(DNB).*

When MOUNTBATTEN arrived as theater commander on 13 Aug 44, SLIM moved up to command the 14th Army, and in October Messervy took command of the 4th Corps. The liberation of from Scoones. Burma was on. In a bold strategy to split KIMURA's Burma Area Army Slim sent the 33d Corps south to take Mandalay on 20 Mar 45. But Messervy took a parallel route to the west. Far SW of Mandalay, he suddenly shot a column eastward across the Irrawaddy and took the major Japanese supply center at Meiktila by surprise. KIMURA counterattacked vigorously but was unable to recapture Meiktila and reestablish his LofC along the Burma Road from Rangoon. Messervy advanced on Rangoon with Indian army divisions, taking Pegu on 1 May just as the monsoon struck. This forced the enemy to abandon Rangoon and virtually ended the reconquest of Burma. Knighted on 5 July 45, Sir Frank became GOC Malaya, taking the surrender of 100,000 troops. In 1946 he headed the Northern Command in India, and the next year he became the new Pakistani government's first military commander in chief. Sir Frank (KBE in 1945, KCSI in 1947) retired in 1948 with the honorary rank of full general. He had been appointed twice to the DSO (1941 & 1944). Messervy died 2 Feb 74 at his home in Heyshott, near Midhurst. *See* Henry Maule, *Spearhead General* (1961).

METAXIS, Ioannis (John). Greek premier. 1871-1941. Born 12 Apr 71 on the island of Ithaca, Metaxis was from a line of military and political leaders. He started a distinguished army career in 1890. Entering politics in 1915 he became absolute dictator of his faction-ridden Balkan nation on 4 Aug 36. Initially pro-Axis, he rallied defenses against the Italian invasion of 1940 and invited British troops into Greece. The portly, unkempt dictator died on 29 Jan 41, less than three months before the Germans invaded Yugoslavia and forces under LIST began overrunning Greece.

MICHAEL. King of Romania. 1921-. The day after ANTONESCU seized power on 5 Sep 40 Michael came to the throne after being regent 1925-30 in the absence of his father, CAROL II. Antonescu kept Romania in the Axis camp until 23 Aug 44 when he was ousted by a coup that Michael and his advisers managed. Bucharest was liberated within a week, without the help of approaching Soviet troops. (*See* VLASOV.) The new government's unconditional surrender became official on 12 Sep 45 at a Moscow ceremony in which Stalin decorated Michael for courage and wisdom in ordering the coup. Romanian armed forces meanwhile turned on their former allies, harrying their run for the northern frontiers. Outraged by this experience in Bucharest, Hitler was ready to prevent HORTHY from staging a similar coup in Budapest. The communists progressively establishing control of Romania, Michael's abdication was announced on 30 Dec 47, and he left the country on 3 Jan 48.

MICHELIER, François Félix. French admiral. 1887-1966. Vice Adm Michelier, a friend of DARLAN's, was French naval representative on the Wiesbaden (armistice) Commission before assuming command of Vichy naval forces in North Africa. Taking instructions from NOUGUES rather than DARLAN on 8 Nov 42 he sent aircraft and more than 20 warships to engage the US armada under HEWITT. This cost the French a cruiser, six other ships, and three submarines along with 1,000 casualties. The unfinished BB *Jean Bart* in Casablanca harbor, which turned her four 14-in guns on BB *Massachusetts*, was gutted by fire and beached. The Vichy admiral also had merchantmen scuttled, including the liner *Gouverneur General Laferrièere*, which was sunk to block Oran harbor. After Noguès ordered a cease fire on 11 Nov 42, Michelier slowly became an enthusiastic supporter of the Royal Navy, thanks largely to the efforts of Adm A. B. CUNNINGHAM (Macmillan, *War Diaries*, 13 & n; WC, IV, 616, 617.)

MIDDLETON, Troy Houston. US general. 1889-1976. One of Eisenhower's best corps commanders, Middleton was born 12 Oct 89 on a plantation near Georgetown, Miss. After studying for West Point but unable to get an appointment, he enlisted in the army (1910) and rose to be the AEF's youngest colonel. Because of an irregular heart beat he resigned in 1937 to be dean of administration at the Louisiana State University, where he had been PMS&T for six years. After the LSU president was exposed in June 39 for embezzlement Middleton brought the school out of its crisis while serving as acting vice president and comptroller.

Because of physical problems which now included an arthritic knee, Middleton did not succeed in being recalled to active duty until 20 Jan 42. George Marshall discovered six months later that Col Middleton was relegated to training duty and the CofS allegedly said, "I would rather have a man with arthritis in the knee than one with arthritis in the head." J. C. H. LEE promptly had Middleton put on orders to his **SOS,** but Mark CLARK intervened to have the colonel promoted and made deputy CG 45th Inf "Thunderbird" Div. Four months later, in Oct 42, Middleton had advanced to CG and soon got his second star.

The Thunderbirds landed in Sicily on 10 July 43, overcoming light resistance before seeing heavy action in PATTON's drive to Palermo. Characteristically he called Patton's bluff when that bully general ordered him to censor the unsoldierly Bill MAULDIN. At Salerno Middleton went ashore on D+1 with two regiments for a major role: after plugging a dangerous gap along the Sele River he convinced Mark CLARK that the beachhead could be held.

Middleton was hospitalized after the breakout for trouble in what he had thought was his **good** knee. "I'll take him into battle on a litter if we have to," Eisenhower said when there was talk of invaliding the Mississippian home (Price, *Middleton,* 168-71). Middleton reached England (ambulatory) on 4 Mar 44 to head the 8th Corps Hq. On D+9, 15 June, his corps became operational north of Carentan. Moving fast to seal off the Cotentin (Cherbourg) peninsula Middleton mopped up die-hard German resistance in Brittany. B. H. RAMCKE's surrender of fortress Brest 19 Sep 44 was followed by a friendship between victor and vanquished that endured for 15 years (Price, 201).

Middleton moved to the Schnee Eifel, where battle-weary units were dispersed in lightly held defensive positions. The 8th Corps Hq was at Bastogne. When the Germans attacked in strength on 16 Dec 44 Middleton was ordered to move his command group 17 miles SW to Neufchateau. But with what Patton later called a stroke of genius, Middleton saw that it was critical to hold Bastogne. So he waited a day to meet McAULIFFE when the 101st Abn Div came through en route to Werbomont, almost 40 miles farther north. McAuliffe got authority to stop in Bastogne and organize a defense there.

After having had a major role in salvaging the situation, the 8th Corps was assigned the 4th Armd, 17th and 101st Abn, and 87th Inf Divs. Suspecting that the Germans had almost no defenders in Coblenz the corps commander ordered the 87th to make a surprise attack; it succeeded easily. Continuing to draw on his insight and knowledge of the enemy, Middleton made a successful crossing of the Rhine near the famous Lorelei: as he knew, no other invader had tried this because the terrain was so unfavorable.

Still with Patton's 3d Army Middleton drove across Germany in the last four months of the war, meeting the Red Army near the Czech border between Chemnitz and Plauen.

Despite his accomplishments during 480 days in combat during the two world wars, more than any of his contemporaries (Price, 196), Middleton did not get his third star until 5 June 45. He retired 10 Aug 45, returned to LSU as comptroller, and was president of the university, 1951-62. As president emeritus he worked closely for more than six years with Frank James Price, former head of the LSU school of journalism, to write *Troy H. Middleton: A Biography* (Baton Rouge: Louisiana State University Press, 1974).

MIHAILOVIC, Dragoliub. Yugoslav guerrilla commander. 1893?-1946. A Serb whose grandfather is said to have led the **Chetniks** and whose father was an **RA** officer, "Draja" entered the Belgrade MA at the age of 15. In 1912 he left to fight the Turks. WIA, decorated, and made a lieutenant, he returned to school in 1913 but left the next year to enlist. By 1918 he was a captain, again decorated for valor, and wounded three more times.

Mihailovic was five feet eight inches tall but so broad shouldered he looked shorter. Although studious and a nondrinker he could be a gay companion. As **IG** for fortifications soon after being promoted to colonel he made an official report that troops would fight more effectively as mobile forces than in frontier defenses. For this he was relegated to an insignificant post. Ironically the war minister who sacked him, Gen Milan Neditch, headed the Serbian government as a German puppet after the Germans invaded Yugoslavia on 6 Apr 41. The troublesome colonel found himself in the mountains as senior officer with a band of fugitives, Serbian guerrillas, and German deserters.

He began forming what King PETER II's refugee government recognized as the Free Yugoslav Army. Col Mihailovic was made a full general on 14 Dec 41 and shortly thereafter was named minister of war. Considerably before TITO began operating with his communist-dominated and largely Croatian partisans, Mihailovic was leading his Chetniks, who represented traditional monarchist and Serbian values. The rivals reached an understanding on 27 Oct 41 (Djilas, *Wartime,* 88), but two weeks later their forces had a bloody clash in Serbia. Instead of concentrating against the Germans the partisans and Chetniks became involved in a bloody civil war.

Because of German reprisals Mihailovic soon left the invaders alone and focused on plans for a postwar government dominated by Serbs and anti-communists. Tito, on the other hand, not only engaged the Germans effectively but also got the better in the civil war. Influenced largely by Fitzroy MacLEAN's reports (WC, V, 469) the British conclude that they and King Peter were backing the wrong horse. Under pressure from Stalin the Allies agreed at Teheran (28 Nov-1 Dec 43) to shift their support to Tito. King Peter reluctantly made this official after forming a new government on 17 May 44 in which TITO was war minister. By this time the British had withdrawn their last mission from Mihailovic, whom Tito drove from his headquarters at Ravna Gore four months later.

Mihailovic was captured by partisans on 13 Mar 46, convicted of collaborating with the Germans and Italians, and executed on 17 July 46.

MIKOLAJCZYK, Stanislaw. Polish statesman. 1901-66. Looming large in the problem of **Poland** as the "London Poles'" leading moderate he succeeded SIKORSKI as PM on 14 July 43. Later deputy PM of the Polish government reestablished in Warsaw in 1945, he was defeated in the elections of Jan 47 by Bolslaw BIERUT of the "Lublin Poles." Resigning rather than join the Soviet-sponsored government, Mikolajczyk fled nine months later and settled in the US.

MIKOYAN, Anastas Ivanovich. Soviet official. 1895-1978. He was an Armenian, born 25 Nov 95 in the village of Sanain. In 1915 he received a theology degree and joined the CP. Closely associated with Stalin against Trotsky, the dour and wily Armenian was people's commissar of external and internal trade from 1926, commissar of supplies in 1930, commissar of the fish industry 1934-38, and commissar of foreign trade 1938-46.

With Molotov he was out of favor during Stalin's last years and probably marked for liquidation. Saved by the emergence of his friend KHRUSHCHEV he briefly was the USSR's titular head—president of the Presidium of the Supreme Soviet—before retiring a little more than a year after Khrushchev's downfall in 1964. But Mikoyan remained a CC member 1923-76, was in the Politburo 1926-66, and held many other high posts. He died 21 Oct 78 in Moscow. His brother Artem I. Mikoyan and Mikhail I. Gurevich designed the MIG 1 aircraft in 1939-41.

MILCH, Erhard. German general. 1892-1972. The Luftwaffe's creator was born 30 Mar 92 in Wilhelmshaven. By 1914 he was an artillery lieutenant. After heavy action on both fronts he became an aerial observer in France and was selected on 1 Apr 18 for the GGS. Four months later Milch was promoted to captain. Although not a pilot he took command of Ftr Sqd 6 on 1 Oct 18 (weeks before the armistice).

Capt Milch resigned from the army in 1921 and four years later became director of the new national airline, Deutsche Lufthansa. He had a major role in secret efforts leading to the Luftwaffe's creation, and in 1933 became Goering's deputy as state secretary in the Reich air ministry. Goering had to order an inquiry into the persistent rumors that his deputy's father,

Anton Milch, was Jewish. This was disproved but investigators uncovered something else: the real father probably was a maternal great uncle, Carl Braeuer. (Irving, *HW*, xxx, and *Milch*, xvii, 4, photos facing p 236, and pages 308, 332-33.) Erhard Milch was appalled to learn that he was born of incest, worse in the Third Reich than being a Jew. The matter was resolved by his being certified as an honorary Aryan. Goering, his investigators, and Milch guarded their secret, and the legend was allowed to persist that the purely Aryan Milch in fact had a Jewish parent.

Although not a true military officer after 1921, Milch was given the rank of Generalmajor in 1934, Generalleutnant in 1935, Generaloberst in 1938, and field marshal on 19 July 40. His only command assignment was in Norway and Denmark as head of the 5th Air Fleet. But he had built the world's most powerful air force, shaping its doctrine, technical development, and industrial base, and being de-facto chief. Milch shares responsibility for fatal shortcomings apparent from 1940, particularly in the field of strategic air power and not being prepared for a long war. But even then, writes Irving, "his achievement was undeniable: faced with diminishing resources of a blockaded nation . . . and by annihilating air attacks, he more than trebled aircraft production between 1941 and 1944 . . ." (Irving, *Milch*, 341).

A true Nazi general who developed contempt for Goering but never lost faith in Hitler, the short, portly Milch was guided by personal friendships and animosities. "In later years," writes Irving, Milch "ruled the ministry by bluster and fear, by threats of courts martial and firing squad." (Irving, *Milch*, 341). His domination of the Luftwaffe ended on 20 June 44 when Goering made Milch resign as director of air armament and step down to be the Luftwaffe's IG. SPEER, who was minister of armaments and munitions from 7 Feb 43, diluting Milch's authority, now had charge of all military arms production. Milch stayed on begrudgingly as Speer's deputy, and the men remained close collaborators and friends. After Hitler's suicide, Milch withdrew to a castle on the Baltic Coast to awaited capture, which came on 4 May 45.

Brutally treated by British officers, Milch left for England with a cyanide capsule his mother had slipped him at their last meeting. (Irving, *Milch*, 299-300.) Harsh treatment at Nuremberg by American guards led Milch to testify on behalf of Goering, to the latter's amazement and deep gratitude. Belatedly charged himself with war crimes, mainly the recruiting of forced labor, Milch was condemned to life in prison but amnestied on 4 June 54. Vigorous almost to the end, he was an aviation consultant. Late in the 1960s Milch turned over his copious records to David Irving and collaborated closely during the last four years of his life on a monumental biography, *The Rise and Fall of the Luftwaffe: the Life of Field Marshal Erhard Milch* (Boston: Little, Brown, 1973). Meanwhile he had died, 25 Jan 72, at Wuppertal-Barmen.

MILLER, (Alton) Glenn. US band leader. 1904-44. An Iowan, he became a trombonist, arranger, and leader of one of the world's most popular dance bands. In late 1942 he gave up a highly remunerative contract with the Chesterfield program on CBS, broke up his band, and accepted a captaincy to become director of the USAAF Band. In late Dec 44 it was playing in recently liberated Paris and scheduled for the BBC's Christmas eve show. Miller, who was in England, disregarded bad weather warnings, and left for Paris late on 13 Dec 44 in a light, single-engine plane (UC-64A). Not until 11 days later was the public informed that Maj Miller's plane was missing. It probably went down in the Channel or the North Sea, but rumors have persisted for half a century in creating a mystery. A movie, *The Glenn Miller Story* (1953), and TV documentaries have played loosely with the facts. (Briggs, ed; Snyder, *Guide*.)

MITCHELL, Reginald Joseph. British aircraft designer. 1895-1937. Creator of the Spitfire, Mitchell was born in Talke, Staffordshire, son of a schoolteacher. In 1911 he became an apprentice in a locomotive plant and was trained as an engineer. But he had long been interested in flying, and in 1916 he joined the Supermarine Aviation works in Southampton as a designer. In three years Mitchell rose to be chief designer. His seaplanes won the Schneider Trophy and set speed records for a decade beginning in 1922. In 1931 his S-6B retained the trophy for Britain. When the air ministry announced requirements in 1934 for a new fighter, Sydney CAMM designed the Hawker Hurricane and Mitchell produced the Spitfire. After the first design for a low-winged, all-metal monoplane was a disappointment, the

second prototype was a winner. Flight trials began in Mar 36, and the first operational model was delivered in July 38. The British fighter was the first nasty surprise for the Luftwaffe, who never suspected that anything could beat the planes produced by Willi MESSER-SCHMITT, the Me 109 and Me 110. The ME 109 generally outclassed the Hurricane, so it was left for the Spitfires, and Hurricanes concentrated on German bombers. Some 19,000 Hurricanes were produced during the war to have a major role in whipping the Luftwaffe. Mitchell was dying of cancer when the RAF accepted his plane. (Briggs, ed.) A CBE in 1931, he did not live to be knighted. The designer's life and the story of his Spitfire (which Mitchell called a "bloody silly name") were told in the Leslie Howard movie *First of the Few* (1942).

MITCHELL, William "Billy" Lendrum. US general. 1879-1936. The controversial champion of US air power headed US military aviation in WWI as a brigadier general before becoming the US army's director of aviation. For publicly criticizing superiors who impeded development of military air power he was convicted by a court-martial in 1926 and demoted.

MITSCHER, Marc "Pete" Andrew. US admiral. 1887-1947. Mitscher is famous as commander of the fast carrier TF 38/58 in the Pacific.

He was born 26 Jan 87 in Hillsboro, Wisc. At the age of two he moved to Oklahoma when his father was appointed an agent with the Osage Indian tribe. He attended grade school and high school in Washington, DC. Unable to get a West Point appointment he entered Annapolis and was known as the "hell-raising Oklahoma Pete from the wild prairies" *(CB 44)*. Briefly suspended for hazing and an unremarkable student he graduated in 1910 (106/130). Six years later he became Naval Aviator No. 33. After serving on the navy's first carrier, *Langley,* and aboard the new CV *Saratoga,* the pioneering naval airman took command of the new CV *Hornet* in Oct 41. The following April he launched the DOOLITTLE raid on Japan. Roosevelt told a wondering world the planes had been based in "Shangri-La," the mythical mountain kingdom of the novel and movie *Lost Horizons.* The carrier captain himself could have been from there, having "a slight, wiry figure (he weighed only 135 pounds) and leathery, wizened face, usually seen under a long-visored lobsterman's cap. . . ." But like SPRUANCE he was "a simple, unassuming gentleman with a soft voice and quiet manners . . . averse to personal glorification and [he] would have avoided publicity if he could, but that was impossible. [He] 'made [newspaper] copy' in spite of himself." (Morison, VIII, 236.)

Promoted to rear admiral on 15 June 42 he briefly led carrier TF 17 while HALSEY was hospitalized, then headed the fleet air wing at Noumea from December until Apr 43, when he became naval air commander in the Solomons (Comairsols). He had control over US Navy, USMC, and Army Air Corps formations plus those of the Royal New Zealand AF. In Aug 43 the physically and mentally exhausted little admiral was ordered home to be commander fleet air West Coast but he returned to the Pacific five months later to head Carrier Div 3 in SPRUANCE's 5th Fleet. After making strikes in the central Pacific, Mitscher was promoted to vice admiral and put in command of Carrier TF 58, which supported landings at Hollandia and the Marianas before taking part in the battle of the Philippine Sea 19-20 June 44.

This was the "Great Marianas Turkey Shoot." Mitscher sent his planes in a vigorous, long-range pursuit of OZAWA's shattered carrier force. It was well after dark on an exceptionally black night when returning planes began circling TF 58 at 8:45 PM, and tired pilots were low on fuel. Despite the danger of lurking submarines Mitscher ordered his carriers to light up. The night recovery took two hours and, although only 20 US planes had been lost that day in action another 17 Hellcats, 35 Helldivers, and 28 Avengers were lost in deck crashes or in ditching. Of the 100 ditched pilots and 109 crewmen 101 were fished out that night. An additional 59 were saved the next day and later, leaving 16 pilots and 33 crewmen MIA. (Morison, VIII, 304).

Pete Mitscher supported the Palaus landings, then directed flights that showed Mindanao to be defenseless; this enabled the Leyte campaign to start ahead of schedule. Mitscher served as part of a force whose designation changed from the 5th Fleet when SPRUANCE was in command to be the 3d Fleet when HALSEY took it over. So the name of Mitscher's formation changed back and forth between TF 38 and TF 58.

Worn down by months of strike operations, Mitscher was relieved by McCAIN on 30 Oct 44; they swapped flags again on 30 Jan 44 for the Iwo Jima and Okinawa campaigns. Mitscher was relieved again on 28 May 45 by McCain. Soon thereafter, having taken a rest leave, the admiral became deputy CNO for air.

On 1 Mar 46 after declining appointment as CNO to take a seagoing billet, Mitscher assumed command of the newly created 8th Fleet in the Atlantic with the rank of full admiral. In September he became CinC Atlantic Fleet. While in this post he died 3 Feb 47 of a coronary thrombosis. (RCS.)

MODEL, Walther. German general. 1891-1945. A British student of some 800 of Hitler's generals finds that only Manstein, Kesselring, and "possibly Model" were in "the very front rank of commanders" (Brett-Smith, 7). He was fearless, even in talking sense to Hitler, tireless, and—of quintessential importance—eternally optimistic. Disliked by peers and superiors for his rough manner, he had another great leadership quality: from frequent presence at the front Model knew how much further to push his troops. From early 1944 he was "the fuehrer's fireman."

Model was born in Genthin, near Berlin, on 24 Jan 91. His father was a Royal Prussian director of music. (Mellenthin, *Generals,* 147.) Model became an infantry officer, seeing action around Verdun, was wounded several times, and won both classes of the Iron Cross. After commanding a regiment and serving in the **Truppenamt,** Lt Col Model headed the war ministry's technical warfare section from 1930. Although without special qualifications or aptitude in this field, he already was an early believer in motorization and in 1935 he took charge of an office responsible for creating new and improved weapons. Adding to the paradoxes of Model's career, he wrote an excellent study of Gneisenau (Goerlitz, *GGS,* 264, 443).

The vigorous Model, a straight-talker and relatively young, favorably impressed Hitler, Goebbels, and other high Nazis. This inevitably led to disapproval within the army's Old Guard, particularly after Model picked a Waffen-SS major to be his ADC (Mellenthin, *Generals,* 148). But the unorthodox, versatile officer, although pro-Nazi to the end, could not be called a "Nazi general."

His early WWII service was as a corps and army CofS, first in Poland and then in BUSCH's 16th Army in France. Generalleutnant Model took command of the 3d Pz Div on 13 Nov 40 (B&O, 74). In the 24th Corps, 2d Pz Gp, he won praise in Opn Barbarossa from Guderian (*Panzer Leader,* 336). On 1 Oct 41 Model replaced Reinhardt as head of the 41st Pz Corps in HOTH's 3d Pz Gp. He was engaged in the thrust from near Vitebsk to Kalinin and in the subsequent attempt to envelop Moscow from the NE. After Hoth's panzer army was driven back to around Vitebsk, Model left his corps on 14 Jan 42, succeeded by HARPE, and replaced STRAUSS as CG, 9th Army.

The 9th Army was in a very bad situation. Its headquarters were near Vyasma, and partisans were cutting rail lines to the rear. Forward elements were about 100 miles north, around Rzhev, in a long, narrow salient that was threatened on all sides. Briefed on the desperate situation the new commander was asked, "And what, sir, have you brought us . . . ?" With a show of surprise the monocled but unstuffy Model replied, "Myself." An eyewitness relates that "A burst of laughter relieved the tension." (Mellenthin, 149.) A few days later, 20 Jan 42, Model had a stormy session with Hitler. The general said the only way to save the 9th Army was to commit a panzer corps around Rzhev. Hitler replied that the panzer corps should instead be used on Model's NE flank around Gzhatsk, near Vyasma. "Who commands the Ninth Army, my Fuehrer, you or I?" said Model, adding—to the horror of those at the meeting—that as commander on the ground he could better formulate strategy than people in the rear studying maps. Model got his way, and events proved him right. (Mellenthin, 149-51.)

Almost immediately promoted, on 1 Feb 42, and nearly 10 years younger than most senior German army officers, Generaloberst Model held the Rzhev-Vyasma salient for a year. When finally authorized to withdraw in early 1943 he ordered systematic destruction of towns and their populations, for which the Russian later branded him a war criminal (Werth, *Russia,* 630-1).

From this long period of defensive warfare Model was ordered south for Opn Citadel, against the Kursk salient. The general was among the many who warned Hitler that the too-long-delayed offensive was doomed to failure. But the 9th Army attacked 5 July 43 from south of Orel and made headway until stopped on the 9th by a secondary line of defense. The Soviets then launched a long-planned counteroffensive on a large scale. Model was ordered to break contact (a very difficult operation) and move north of Orel to support Rudolf Schmidt 2d Pz Army, which had been penetrated. In the sort of "fire-fighting" at which he excelled, Model commanded Schmidt's army and his own during the period 13 July-5 Aug 43. But the Red tide could not be stemmed and Model was permitted to withdraw to the Desna River. For the rest of 1943 Model's 9th Army was driven back with AG Center. He ended up in the northern reaches of the Pripet Marshes along the historic Beresina River. (This is where Napoleon's retreating army of 37,600 troops escaped annihilation by 144,000 Russians on 29 Nov 1812.)

The "lion of the defense" was promoted 29 Jan 44 to head AG North, replacing the hard-pressed KUECHLER. Two months later Hitler finally sacked MANSTEIN and sent his "fireman" to succeed him. AG South was redesignated AG North Ukraine, and Model was promoted 1 Mar 44 to field marshal, one of the last Hitler created.

From 28 June 44 Model had the additional duty of commanding AG Center (vice BUSCH) as it was being annihilated in eastern Poland because Hitler refused to authorize strategic withdrawals. On 10 July Hitler disapproved of Model's proposal to establish a new defensive position behind the Dvina River. This led to virtual destruction of Model's old 9th Army and the 4th Army. But the Soviets paused to let logistics catch up, whereupon Model established a defense on the Vistula south of Warsaw.

Hailed by Hitler as Germany's savior in the east Model was given the Diamonds (17/27) on 17 Aug 44 and sent to save Germany in the west. Succeeding von KLUGE a few days later as OB West he promptly asked OKW for another 30 divisions and 200,000 individual replacements (Speidel, *Invasion,* 140). In charge only 18 days when Hitler recalled Rundstedt as OB West, and unequal to the task (Brett-Smith, 201), Model took over AG B in Holland and Belgium. He effectively regrouped substantial portions of his shattered organization and happened to have AG B Hq near Arnhem when the Allies undertook

Opn **Market-Garden,** 17-25 Sep 44. Model's personal leadership contributed significantly to the Allied failure.

Model was drawn increasingly into preparations for the Ardennes counteroffensive as Rundstedt (restored as OB West) decided to have as little as possible to do with it. (Liddell Hart, *Talk,* 272-73). Along with MANTEUFFEL Model did what he could to make the best of Hitler's foolish gamble.

The Rhineland campaign, which followed, then became one of Germany's greatest strategic defeats because Hitler refused to let Model withdraw behind the Rhine. AG B was encircled in the Ruhr pocket and annihilated. Model formally dissolved his command on 15 Apr 45 and broke out with a few others. Convinced the Americans would hand him over to the Russians as a war criminal, Model is believed to have shot himself on 21 Apr 45 in woods near Duisberg after an ADC refused to render this last service (Goerlitz, *GGS,* 494). The body was never found.

MOELDERS, Werner. German officer. 1913-41. Born 18 Mar 13 at Gelsenkirchen, "Vati" (Daddy) Moelders had 14 air victories in Spain and another 101 before being grounded in July 41 as a combat pilot. He was the first recipient of the Diamonds (1/27) on 14 July 41. The 28-year-old Col Moelders was then given two newly created posts: general of fighters (the title only, not the rank), and IG of fighter aircraft. En route to Ernst UDET's funeral he was killed on 22 Nov 41 when a plane in which he was a passenger crashed near Breslau. Moelders was succeeded by Adolf GALLAND.

MOLOTOV, Vyacheslav Mikhailovich. Soviet statesman. 1890-1986. Of bourgeois origins, he was born 9 Mar 90 in the village of Kukarka, now Sovetsk, in today's Kirov Oblast. He was the composer Alexander N. Scriabin's nephew and bore this surname as a child. He took part in the anti-tsarist revolution of 1905 when hardly dry behind the ears. The next year, while still a student, he joined the Bolshevik Party and began calling himself Molotov ("hammer"). At the St Petersburg Polytechnic School he became a natty dresser, sporting a pince-nez, bushy mustache, and developed a stuffed-shirt manner *(CB 40).* Throughout life he had a bad stammer.

Arrested in 1909 and exiled for two years, he edited *Pravda* (1912-17). By 1922 he was second secretary of the central committee and Stalin's right hand man. (Briggs, ed, "Molotov.") A Politburo member from 1925, he became premier in 1930. On 3 May 39 the faithful paladin, who had never left Russia, replaced LITVINOV as foreign minister, and the Old Bolshevik's first act was to throw a diplomatic bomb: the **Nazi-Soviet Pact,** 23 Aug 93. This was followed five days later by the secret protocol that partitioned Poland. On 6 May 41 STALIN made himself premier, Molotov stepping down to be deputy premier but remaining foreign minister. Molotov was a **GKO** member throughout the war, second in power only to Stalin. Although he played a vigorous role inside the USSR by rallying and sustaining the Soviet military effort, Molotov's primary concern remained in the field of foreign affairs. This included negotiating many nonaggression pacts and planning for the postwar period. Molotov is thought to have held talks in June 43 with Ribbentrop at Kirovograd to negotiate a separate peace, but they could reach no agreement on boundaries. That year Molotov was host at the Moscow Conference of foreign ministers. He attended all subsequent international war conferences, including the one at San Francisco to establish the UN *(see* GROMYKO). Molotov was largely responsible for the hard line leading to the Cold War.

He remained people's commissar for foreign affairs, then was Soviet foreign minister 1946-49. But he fell into "perilous disfavor" when Stalin "took it into his head that Molotov, perhaps his most loyal lieutenant, was in the employ of the American government" (Crankshaw, ed, *Khrushchev,* 553). Mrs Molotov was arrested in 1949 and not released until 1953 (HFS). Back as foreign minister, 1953-56, he opposed Khrushchev's de-Stalinization program, the reconciliation with Tito, and the policy of restraint in dealing with the Polish problem in 1956. The next year, after the 20th Party Congress, he was disgraced by Khrushchev, branded along with MALENKOV and KAGANOVICH as anti-party. Succeeded as foreign minister by Shepilov (who was followed by Gromyko), he was banished to far-away Ulan Bator, Mongolia, as ambassador. Molotov reappeared in 1960 as representative on the international atomic energy commission in Vienna.

The next year the 22d Party Congress charged him with complicity in Stalin's crimes, especially the **Great Purges** of the 1930s. Not seen in public again for almost a decade, he was readmitted to party membership and partially rehabilitated two years before dying in 1986 at the age of 86.

MOLTKE, Helmuth James von. German resistance figure. 1907-45. He was born 2 Mar 07 at Kreisau, Silesia, of a South African mother who had English blood. James was the great-great-nephew of Field Marshal Helmuth von Moltke the elder (1800-91), hence kin to the latter's nephew Generaloberst Johannes Ludwig von Moltke the younger (1848-1916).

The high-minded young count became an international lawyer, was called to the English bar, and had British and American friends in high places. In 1933 Moltke began forming the **Kreisau Circle.** From 1939 he was a legal adviser to the Abwehr, where he had a key role in the conspiracy directed by Hans OSTER. Initially he opposed staging a coup d'état, particularly assassinating Hitler; he was more interested in a new order for post-Nazi Germany. But for warning an associate of impending arrest, Moltke was jailed in Jan 44. During a year's incarceration he wrote his wife letters that were smuggled out by a prison chaplain. These were published in different versions as *A German in the Resistance. . .* (Oxford University Press, 1948). A later edition, edited and translated by Beate Ruhm von Oppen, is *Letters to Freya* (New York: Knopf, 1990).

Having written his wife on 20 Jan 45 that he would stand before FREISLER's people's court "as a Christian and nothing else," von Moltke was hanged three days later in Berlin's Ploetzensee prison.

MONNET, Jean. French economist and politician. 1888-1979. A businessman from a cognac family, he spent time stimulating US aircraft production to meet French contracts in 1938-39. He was chairman of the Allied economic coordinating committee in London when war broke out. Monnet offered his service to the British and was sent by Churchill to Washington with the British supply council. In 1943 he joined the Anglo American munitions assignment board in Algiers. Universally respected for having the "calm, cool, reasoning and self-disciplined mind which is supposed to be typically French . . . he was positively puritanical in his refusal to deviate from the straight line which led to his objectives" (Sherwood, 232). He worked to reconcile Free French factions, served as GIRAUD's economic adviser, and became commissioner of arms and supplies for the **FCNL.** In 1946 he produced the Monnet plan for economic recovery, becoming known as "Mr Europe."

MONTGOMERY, Alfred Eugene. US admiral. 1891-1961. The carrier admiral was born in Omaha, Neb, on 12 June 91. Graduating in the USNA Class of 1912 (29/156) he transferred to submarines in 1915 and became a pilot in 1922. After a succession of naval air duties, including command of CV *Ranger* and the Corpus Christi Naval Air Training Center, he was promoted to rear admiral on 29 May 42. In Aug 43 he took command of Carrier Div 17 in Carrier Gp 50.3 of Vice Adm POWNALL's TF 50. With this he struck Wake Island and Rabaul, supported the Tarawa and Marshall Island landings, and in early 1944 made the first strike on Truk. In Mar 44 he took command of Carrier Div 3 and TG 58.2 in MITSCHER's TF 58. Having distinguished himself in the Marianas campaign and the Battle of the Philippine Sea (19-20 June 44) he remained in the formation whose designation switched back and forth between TF 58 (under MITSCHER) and TF 38 (under HALSEY). He took part in the Leyte campaign and associated air actions. Ordered home in Jan 45, Rear Adm Montgomery headed Fleet Air West Coast for the remainder of the war. Subsequently he commanded the 5th Fleet 1946-49 as a vice admiral, then headed Naval Operating Base Bermuda until retirement on 30 June 51. He died 15 Dec 61 at Bremerton, Wash. (RCS.)

MONTGOMERY, Bernard Law. British general. 1887-1976. In North Africa he took command of the demoralized 8th Army, defeated ROMMEL, and drove him from El Alamein into Tunisia. After the campaign in Sicily and the first phases of the war in Italy, he took command of the 21st AG for the Normandy invasion and the final offensive into Germany.

The brilliant and eccentric general—whom the brilliant and eccentric Churchill would characterize as "indomitable in retreat; invincible in advance; insufferable in victory"—was an Ulsterman. Born 17 Nov 87 in London, fourth of nine children, he was the grandson of a dean of Canterbury (Frederick Farrar) and son of a bishop. Montgomery believed his military personality was formed early by a stern mother whose church duties left little time for the children. "If I could not be seen anywhere, she would say—'Go and find out what Bernard is doing and tell him to stop it.'" (*Memoirs*, 17.) But the boy worshipped his father, who was bishop of Tasmania for 12 years ending with the family's return to London in 1901. The son attended St Paul's School before entering Sandhurst; he graduated in 1908 with a class standing of 36th among the 170 who had entered 18 months earlier. Without independent means and not high enough at Sandhurst to qualify for the Indian Army, he joined the Royal Warwickshire Regt because it had a battalion in India. Here the new subaltern could exist on British army pay.

A maverick from the start, Montgomery formed a low opinion of prevalent military standards while serving his first three years on the NW Frontier and two in Bombay. He returned with the battalion shortly before the start of WWI and reached the front just after the BEF began its retreat from Mons (23 Aug 14). Seriously wounded after two months in action he was appointed to the DSO and hospitalized in England. He returned to the front early in 1916 as a brigade major. For the final six months of the war he was CofS, 47th (London) Div. Although he performed creditably, Montgomery was not marked as a "comer." But he did become an instructor at Camberley in 1926, six years after being a student there. In 1927 the 39-year-old bachelor married Betty Carver, widow of an officer killed at Gallipoli in 1915. The happy marriage ended after 10 years when Betty died of an unidentified insect's bite. There was one child, David, born in 1928.

The austere Montgomery was thereafter even more devoted to his profession. After being promoted to major general he went to Palestine in Oct 38 to command British forces quelling an Arab uprising. Returning to England, he took command of the 3d Div on 28 Aug 39, three days before Germany invaded Poland. Again rushed to France with the BEF, he had time to develop what he later referred to as a

formation that "did everything that was asked of it; it was like a ship . . . [that] answers to the slightest touch on the helm. . . . There were no weak links; all the doubtful commanders had been eliminated. . . ." (Montgomery, *Memoirs*, 57.)

The Germans struck on 10 May 40. The BEF maintained cohesion in retreat and Montgomery succeeded Alan BROOKE as head of the 2d Corps on 30 May, being promoted to lieutenant general (T), as is the British practice. The corps was on orders from London to be evacuated while the other was to be sacrificed as a covering force. But Montgomery convinced Lord GORT, whom he knew well, that if ALEXANDER were given charge of the 1st Corps he could save all British troops (*Memoirs*, 59-60). This came to pass.

Landing in England on 1 June 40, Lt Gen Montgomery returned to his 3d Div, which was being reequipped for a return to the Continent. But when the French surrendered on 17 June, the division was given a defensive mission on the south coast. Churchill and Montgomery met for the first time on 2 July 40. At dinner following an inspection tour the birdlike soldier, who had not impressed Churchill as being a man for the highest military command (WC, II, 263-64), gratuitously commented that he neither drank nor smoked and was 100 per cent fit. The PM "replied in a flash," the austere general remembered, "that he both drank and smoked and was 200 per cent fit" (*Memoirs*, 64). Montgomery remained in England for the next two years, rising in July 40 to command the 5th Corps, then in Apr 41 to take over the 12th Corps in Kent, and on 1 Dec 41 to command the South-Eastern Army.

The Western Desert

Alan BROOKE, CIGS, picked Montgomery to command the 8th Army under ALEXANDER as ROMMEL's offensive threatened Suez. But the assignment went to the general favored by Churchill, "Strafer" GOTT. The latter was killed while en route to his new post, and Brooke finally succeeded in having Montgomery named as Gott's replacement. (Bryant, *Tide*, 358-64.)

Alerted on 8 Aug 42 in England and reaching Cairo four days later, the new 8th Army commander took over on the 13th from Lt Gen W. H. Ramsden (acting head) and immediately began applying his meticulous methods under ALEXANDER's sympathetic supervision. More foxy not only in appearance but also in action than his famous opponent, the "Desert Fox," Montgomery quickly took the first round, at Alam Halfa, 31 Aug-6 Sep 42. Montgomery then won the decisive battle of El Alamein, 23 Oct-4-Nov 42. For this he was promoted to full general and knighted (KCB). (In 1945 he was advanced to GCB.)

As with the 3d Div in 1940, Montgomery now made the 8th Army in his own image. Part of his formula was to insist on having subordinates in whom he had complete confidence and who would be completely loyal. The "military messiah" (as Correlli Barnett calls him) undertook a ruthless purge. The veteran 30th Corps commander, Maj Gen W. H. Ramsden, asked for four days leave in Cairo after his unit performed well in the battle of Alam Halfa. "Montgomery was genial," writes Barnett. "Certainly, Ramsden," said he, "come back refreshed for the battle." But 36 hours later Montgomery sent for the general and brusquely told him he was being replaced by Oliver LEESE. (Barnett, 268.) The seasoned and capable A. H. Gatehouse (10th Armd Div) and LUMSDEN (10th Corps) were shipped back to England soon after the battle of El Alamein.

But the new broom also swept Rommel out of western Egypt, through Libya, to Tunisia. He conducted a sustained pursuit of 2,000 miles, proving himself to be a master of organization and training, of the set battle, of building and sustaining morale and physical fitness. He was sublimely heedless to well justified criticism of being too slow—too fussy about making careful tactical plans and about the 8th Army's "administrative tail." Perhaps Montgomery's strongest suit— much more appreciated by subordinates than by peers and superiors—was a flair for winning the confidence of his troops. "Most awkward to serve alongside, impossible to serve over, he was an excellent man to serve under," writes E. T. Williams in *DNB*.

Sicily and Italy

In Sicily he led the 8th Army up the eastern side of the island in a slow, grinding advance against the main enemy resistance (as he did later in Normandy) while PATTON (as in Normandy) gobbled up ground and headlines.

Largely because of this, and because of EISENHOWER's caution as supreme commander, Hans HUBE's elite German corps escaped annihilation and almost fatally slowed Montgomery's advance to support Mark CLARK's hard-pressed forces at Salerno. The British military hero became increasingly disliked by American generals, particularly Bradley. With two corps advancing in Italy to the Sangro River, in the right (northern) sector, Monty pressed on to KESSELRING's Winter Line.

Europe

On 31 Dec 43 he turned the 8th Army over to Oliver LEESE and returned to England as commander-designate of all ground forces in the cross-channel assault. Establishing headquarters in his old school, St Paul's, he replaced Bernard PAGET as head of the 21st AG. With Miles DEMPSEY's 1st British Army, Monty's formation for establishing the Normandy beachhead included Omar BRADLEY's 1st US Army. D day was 6 June 44. When Bradley's 12th AG was formed, on 1 Aug 44 (D+56), Montgomery's 21st AG retained the 2d British Army and acquired CRERAR's 1st Canadian Army.

Montgomery thought he was better qualified than Eisenhower to plan and direct the land battle in Europe. But the US provided most of the men, materiel, and logistical support, so Montgomery had a lost cause. Monty then contended that his 21st AG should make the main effort, a single thrust through the Low Countries into the North German Plain. For this he wanted logistical priority and two of the US armies of Bradley's 12th AG.

Again frustrated, Field Marshal Montgomery (from 1 Sep 44) got approval for a bold stroke in his zone that might have ended the war in 1944, but Opn **Market-Garden,** 17-25 Sep 44, was a costly failure. The field marshal admitted that his own mistakes exacerbated the exceptionally poor luck, but he contended that the operation failed primarily because it was not properly supported by higher authorities.

Then began Hitler's crap shoot in the Ardennes, a massive counteroffensive starting on 16 Dec 44 to split the Allied forces by a drive to Brussels and Antwerp. Bradley almost immediately lost land-line communications with his 1st and 9th US armies north of the "Bulge," having only Patton's 3d Army to the south available for counterattack. On 20 Dec 44 Eisenhower shifted the 21st AG boundary about 50 miles south, bisecting the Bulge, leaving Montgomery to direct defenses on the northern shoulder of the penetration. This gave the British field marshal operational control of two US armies, Simpson's 9th and Hodge's 1st. The 21st AG had a strong corps, Horrocks's 30th, ideally positioned to block the German drive to the Meuse at Dinant. By 26 Dec 44 the crisis had ended; the Germans had shot their bolt and were being driven slowly back.

The master of the set-piece battle had proved he could improvise brilliantly. But in a press conference on 7 Jan 45 Montgomery put the cat among the pigeons: he implied that he was the hero for heading off a disaster the Americans had created by failing to follow his strategy. If Montgomery could make the Western Desert too small for subordinates who did not hail him as the military messiah, Eisenhower did not consider Europe big enough for a disloyal subordinate. From London, Churchill and Brooke severely rebuked the troublemaker. Freddy DE GUINGAND, Monty's diplomatic CofS, quickly smoothed things out with his opposite number at SHAEF, Walter Bedell SMITH, and easily persuaded his now-contrite superior to write Eisenhower a profuse apology.

Having narrowly escaped being sacked, Montgomery continued his slow and methodical advance. Liberating the Netherlands and driving into Germany, he negotiated the German surrender in his sector on 4 May 45 and remained in Europe as CinC of the British Army of Occupation from 22 May 45.

Postwar

In the New Year's honors list of 1946 he was granted a peerage; he took the title Viscount Montgomery of Alamein, of Hindhead, in the county of Surrey *(DNB)*. In December 46 he was installed as a Knight of the Garter (KG). Succeeding BROOKE as CIGS on 26 June 46 he held that office until eased out in the fall of 1948—he had caused "two uncomfortable years for everybody" (ibid.). As a stopgap appointment he was named chairman of the Western Union's CinC committee (in the Cold War alliance of the UK, France, and the Benelux), with headquarters at Fontainebleau. He then was Eisenhower's deputy supreme commander when

SHAPE opened on 2 Apr 51. At SHAPE Hq, just outside Paris, Montgomery served as a sort of IG under three successive SACEURs until retiring 20 Sep 58 to live with his son David at Isington Mill, Alton, Hampshire. A prolific writer, he personally drafted *The Memoirs of Field-Marshal Montgomery* (1958); this ended an "uneasy friendship" with now-President Eisenhower *(DNB)*. His other books including *El Alamein to the River Sangro* (1948), *Normandy to the Baltic,* and *History of Warfare* (1968) were, for the most part, ghosted (ibid.).

Having "come to believe his own legend and to wrap himself in memoirs which excluded the inconvenient," he died 25 Mar 76 and was buried in a country churchyard at Binstead, a mile from Isington Mill. *(DNB.)*

MORAN, Charles McMoran Wilson, Baron. British physician. 1882-1977. On 24 May 40 the unconventional Sir Charles, president of the Royal College of Physicians and soon to be Lord Moran, had his first doctor-patient meeting with the self-indulgent PM Churchill. "I do not think the arrangement can last," the physician noted in his diary (Moran, 5). But the arrangement lasted a quarter of a century. And it is chronicled in what *DNB* editor E. T. Williams calls in his notice on Churchill a "distasteful book," *Churchill: Taken from the Diaries of Lord Moran. The Struggle for Survival, 1940-1965* (Boston: Houghton Mifflin, 1966). The less discriminating reader will find the book interesting for Lord Moran's political, military, psychological, and historical insights.

MORANE, Robert Charles. French aeronautical engineer. 1886-1968. Founder of the Morane-Saulnier Aircraft Co (1911) he furnished aircraft in both world wars and established the first French airline, forerunner of Air France.

MORELL, Theodore. German physician. 1887-1948. Of Huguenot origins, son of a schoolmaster, Morell was a ship's doctor before establishing a lucrative practice in Berlin. He catered to theatrical people as a skin and venereal disease specialist. In 1936 he cured Heinrich HOFFMANN of a serious infection, using the new drug sulfanilamide, and was introduced to Hitler, whom he cured of a serious gastric disorder. Morell was at Hitler's side for the next nine years as the fuehrer's physician. It was evident to Hitler's other doctors that Morell was a quack. Goering later dubbed him "Herr Reich Injection Master." But Morel got rich selling his patent medicines, often seeing that their use was made compulsory throughout Germany. The Wehrmacht used his "Russia" lice powder for government issue. As Hitler's twilight in the Berlin bunker approached he was being shot by Morell with more than 28 drugs, many of them untested amphetamines.

Abandoning his quarters in the Fuehrerbunker to the GOEBBELS family, the Reich injection master joined the flight to Obersalzberg. Those who took him into custody in 1945 saw "a gross but deflated old man, of cringing manners, inarticulate speech, and the hygienic habits of a pig. . . ." (Trevor-Roper, *Hitler*, 60.) The rotund physician could not heal himself; Dr Feelgood's health deteriorated rapidly after he was released from an American internment camp. Finally paralyzed, he died in misery at Tegernsee on 26 May 48.

MORGAN, Frederick Edgworth. British general. 1894-1967. "COSSAC" (below) was an artillery officer from 1913. Having served with the BEF in France in both wars he was promoted to major general in May 42 and given command the 1st Corps District in Yorkshire. Five months later he was transferred with his staff to make contingency plans for Eisenhower's use in North Africa. From 23 Apr 43 Lt Gen Morgan was CofS to the Supreme Allied Commander (Designate), or "COSSAC." The acronym was applied to the general as well as his Anglo-American staff that came to do the critical initial planning for the Normandy landings before EISENHOWER's staff took over. Morgan was a planner in SHAEF through V-E day, then Sir Frederick was UNRRA chief in Germany 1945-46. After retiring from the army he was controller of atomic energy from 1951, then controller of atomic weapons 1954-56. In *Overture to Overlord* (London: Hodder & Stoughton, 1950) the author tells of his experience as COSSAC. His memoirs are *Peace and War: A Soldier's Life* (London: Hodder and Stoughton, 1961).

MORGAN, William Duthie. British general. 1891-1977. He was CGS Home Forces, 1942-43, then GOC Southern Command. In Dec 44 Lt Gen Morgan became ALEXANDER's CofS, succeeding him as SACMED 1945-47.

MORGENTHAU, Henry, Jr. US secretary of the treasury. 1891-1967. Son of President Wilson's ambassador to Turkey, Henry Jr was born 11 May 91 in NYC. After spending time at Cornell without getting a degree he became a farmer on 1,400 prime acres located 15 miles from Roosevelt's Hyde Park. His public career began as a member of the US Food Administration in WWI. Having vigorously supported FDR's political career from the governorship of New York to the presidency, Morgenthau hoped to be secretary of agriculture. But he was made chairman of the Federal Farm Board, which eventually consolidated nine agencies into the Farm Credit Administration.

Morgenthau became treasury secretary on 1 Jan 34 and held the post 11 years. Lacking special qualifications for his task, the tall, taciturn, and hard-working Morgenthau was not generally considered to be a great secretary of the treasury but a competent one. He developed bond-sale programs to finance the war and tax plans to curb inflation. In July 44 he served effectively as chairman of the **Bretton Woods Conference.** As an old friend of the president he had an unwonted and unfortunate influence on foreign affairs. In 1941 he was convinced, as was Secretary of War STIMSON, that a hard line would force Japan to back down rather than risk war with the US (Buchanan, 34). He drew up the controversial Morgenthau plan, which called for reducing postwar Germany to a pastoral state. Although "the Morgenthau Plan had some impact on the early postwar military government of Germany" (ibid., 492) it died an unlamented early death.

Morgenthau resigned in July 45, three months after Truman succeeded FDR. He engaged in many philanthropies, worked with his biographer, John Morton Blum, on the multivolume work *From the Morgenthau Diaries,* and died 6 Feb 67 at in Poughkeepsie, NY, at the age of 75.

MORISON, Samuel Eliot. US historian. 1887-1974. Author of the 15-volume official history of the USN in WW II, the big, affable Bostonian was a famous Harvard professor, historian, and sailor. At his suggestion to Roosevelt, heartily approved by Navy Secretary Knox, Sam Morison was commissioned as a lieutenant commander, USNR, in May 42 to get first-hand experience in gathering material for his monumental naval history. Resigning his commission in 1946, but maintaining a sizeable staff in the Navy Dept and a small office at the Naval War College in Newport, RI, he published the final, 15th volume in 1962. Cited as Morison, the work is fully identified in the main bibliography. Having risen to captain in 1945, he retired from the USNR in 1951 as a rear admiral and died on 15 May 76 in Boston.

MORRISON, Herbert Stanley. British official. 1888-1965. His wartime offices included lord president of the council, home secretary and minister of home security, minister of supply (being MACMILLAN's chief), and member of the War Cabinet (WC, II & VI, passim).

MORSHEAD, Leslie. Australian general. 1889-1952. Originally a schoolmaster, he joined the army in 1914 and had an outstanding combat record at Gallipoli and in France. As a businessman he headed a reserve battalion. In 1939 he took command of the 18th Bde and from Feb 41 led the newly formed 9th Australian Div. He defended Tobruk against ROMMEL in the last eight months of 1941, winning the nickname "Ming the Merciless" from his admiring troops. Promoted to lieutenant general and knighted, Sir Leslie then headed Australian Imperial Forces in the Middle East. After being involved in the second battle of El Alamein he took the 9th Div to Australia in early 1943.

A year later he replaced Edmund HERRING in New Guinea as commander of the 1st Australian Corps, made up of his 9th Div and the 7th. In Apr 45 he led the corps from Australia to Morotai to make up a separate TF directly under MacArthur's Hq in Manila to liberate Borneo. Sir Leslie returned to civilian life after the war.

MOSKALENKO, Kirill Semenovich. Soviet military leader and official. 1902-85. Moskalenko was born in the village of Grishino, Donets region, on 11 May 02. A cadet in 1920 he became a battery commander that year and a CP member in 1926. After having normal military assignments Moskalenko headed an artillery brigade in 1938 and fought in the Soviet-Finnish War 1939-40. In the mass promotions of June 40 he was made a general major of artillery.

Gen Maj Moskalenko broke out of the Kiev encirclement on about 18 Sep 41 with some of his command group. Heading an operational group that took Yelets (Jelez) on 9 Dec 41 in the counteroffensive that saved Moscow he forced GUDERIAN to withdraw after making a lunge past Tula. Moskalenko then commanded the 38th Army from Mar 42 and in July 42 was made CG, 1st Tank Army. For the next month he was heavily engaged on the lower Don River.

His command group was moved from Kalach as cadre for Yeremenko's new Stalingrad Front Hq, after which Moskalenko led the 1st Guards Army from Aug 42. Early the next month he directed desperate counterattacks in the defense of Stalingrad. Another reorganization gave Moskalenko's staff to Vatutin as a cadre for the Southwestern Front Hq. Moskalenko himself took over the 40th Army in the Voronezh Front on Oct 42. Promotions came quickly, to general lieutenant in Jan 43 and colonel general the following September. The next month he assumed command of the reconstituted 38th Army in the Ukraine, remaining with it until the war ended.

As part of Khrushchev's "Ukrainian mafia" the general prospered professionally after the war and left valuable memoirs. He died on 17 June 85 in Moscow and, like Khrushchev, was buried in the **Novodevichy Monastery Cemetery.**

MOSLEY, Oswald Ernald "Tom." British Fascist leader. 1896-1980. Impeccably upper class but coming to oppose everything British except the monarchy, after becoming a Conservative MP for Harrow in 1918 at the age of 22, he was "an 'ex' almost everything—an ex-conservative, an ex–independent, an ex-Socialist, and an ex-leader of his own New Party" *(CB-40)*. It was said that "'on a fox hunt he would side with the fox'" (ibid.). The British tolerated his flamboyant leadership of the black-uniformed British Union of Fascists (or British Union) from its formation in 1932 after a visit to Italy. But on 23 May 40 they arrested him and his second wife, the Hon Mrs Diana Guinness, sister of Nancy, Jessica, and Unity Mitford. Detained until Nov 43, they were released because of Mosley's poor health.

After the war Sir Oswald made his home outside Paris at Orsay, returning on brief visits to Britain and standing unsuccessfully for Parliament in 1959 and 1966. To justify his earlier activities Mosley published *My Answer* (1946) and *My Life* (1968). Born 16 Nov 96 in Mayfair, London, eldest son of Oswald Mosley, fifth baronet, he died 3 Dec 80 at home in Orsay. *(DNB.)*

MOULIN, Jean. French resistance hero. 1899-1943. Born in Béziers (Hérault) and becoming a dedicated communist (Peter Wright, 240), Moulin was was a small, dark Provençal of outstanding intellect, energy, and charm. He rose rapidly in the civil service to be the Third Republic's youngest prefect. As refugees streamed south in June 40 he remained at his post in Chartres. For refusing to cooperate with the Germans on trumped-up charges that Senegalais troops were responsible for local atrocities, the prefect was jailed and tortured. He attempted suicide on 18 June by slashing his throat with broken glass. Taken unconscious to a hospital, he recovered to carry on in office until the Vichy government dismissed him in November.

Moulin was determined to join de Gaulle in London but while trying to organize an escape he toured the unoccupied zone and made contact with resistance leaders including Henri FRENAY. Reaching London through Lisbon in Sep 41, and impressing de Gaulle as being the man to form the resistance into a secret army, Moulin was trained for two months for this mission. With a new identity including a moustache "Max" landed by parachute near Arles on 1 Jan 42 with two companions. He convinced Frenay that his *Combat* organization needed the money, weapons, and radios that only de Gaulle could furnish. Giving Frenay 250,000 francs, half of what he had brought from London, Moulin then won over Jean Pierre Lévy and Raymond Aubrac of the *Francs-Tireurs Partisans* and Emmanuel d'Astier of *Libération*. Moulin organized the underground infrastructure of safe houses, letter drops, and radio nets. Resistance leaders continued to oppose unification, but de Gaulle decided to solve this by directing formation of a coordinating committee on which all groups would be represented without surrendering their separate identities. The stage was set by DEWAVRIN's mission to France, 23 Feb-16

Apr 43. Moulin then accomplished the gargantuan task of pulling together eight major resistance movements including the communists into the *Conseil national de la Résistance* (CNR). Moulin presided over the first plenary session on 27 May 43 at 48 Rue du Four in Paris. This was "His crowning achievement, and also his swansong" (Michel, 306).

A routine street search by police in Marseilles on 27 Apr 43 had netted one Jean "Lunel" Multon, deputy commander of the local cell. Turned by protracted torture, Lunel led the Gestapo on raids that arrested hundreds of his former associates in Marseilles. The traitor then was put to work for Klaus BARBIE in Lyons, where René "Didot" Hardy had been remarkably successful in sabotaging rail traffic. Lunel failed in several attempts to trap Didot in Lyons but intercepted an uncoded message setting up a meeting in Paris between Didot and one "Vidal." Barbie sent Lunel and another informer to help the Paris Gestapo set a trap for Vidal, who turned out to be the newly appointed commander of the secret army, Gen DELESTRAINT. Lunel then helped the Germans find and arrest two other important agents of the Paris resistance.

Hardy was ignorant of all this because the message had been left in a drop he no longer used. But the saboteur had other business in Paris and was headed there by train when arrested on 7 June. There is conflicting evidence as to what sort of deal Hardy made with Barbie in return for walking free and unharmed on 10 June. Hardy did not inform other resistance agents that he had been arrested, but Moulin knew that because of the arrests in Paris his own days were numbered.

For the vital task of replacing Delestraint and reorganizing the Secret Army before rival factions tore it apart, Max called for a meeting of top resistance leaders on 21 June. The place was Dr Frederic Dugoujon's villa and office in Caluire, a suburb of Lyons. Hardy, Henri Aubry (of Combat), and two others were waiting upstairs when Moulin arrived late, 2:45 PM, with Aubrac and two others. The doctor's receptionist assumed the newcomers were patients and showed them to the ground-floor waiting room. Moments later, Barbie burst into the upstairs room with a large group of armed men and, in excellent French, shouted "Hands up. German police." Quickly realizing somebody was missing he rushed downstairs, where Moulin and Aubrac pretended to be patients. After a quick, brutal interrogation, and still not identifying Moulin (Bower, *Barbie,* 71), Barbie herded his prisoners out of the house. But Hardy broke free and escaped, which has led many to assume that he was the traitor of Caluire, although this has never been proved.

Barbie subjected Aubry and two others to brutal interrogation over a 24-hour period before he learned from them which prisoner was Max. The Butcher of Lyons tortured Moulin for five days without learning anything from the man who knew everything. Barbie took his victim to Paris, where German doctors struggled to save his life and cover up the bungled interrogation. Still unconscious when put on a train for Frankfort, Moulin died en route, perhaps at Metz. By 9 July the body was returned to Paris and cremated at Père Lachaise. On 19 Dec 64 the ashes were placed in the Pantheon, France's "temple of glory" in Paris.

MOUNTBATTEN, Louis (Francis Albert Victor Nicholas). 1900-79. Lord Louis, the Earl Mountbatten of Burma, began his war service as commander of a destroyer flotilla. For two years he headed Combined Operations, and from Oct 43 was Supreme Allied Commander Southeast Asia. Only 45 years old when the war ended, he became the last Viceroy of India, First Sea Lord, and Chief of Defense Staff. He was killed by IRA terrorists.

The man later named Mountbatten was born at Frogmore House, near Windsor Castle, on 25 June 00. His father, then a captain in the Royal Navy, was Prince Louis of Battenberg, second cousin of King George V, and an Austrian by birth. Battenberg's mother was Princess Victoria, favorite granddaughter of Queen Victoria (by Princess Alice) and the eldest daughter of Louis IV, Grand Duke of Hesse. In declining the post of ambassador to Moscow in 1948, Mountbatten pointed out that the "Bolsheviks murdered my father's first cousin, two of my aunts on my mother's side, and five of my first cousins." As Mountbatten had to explain to the plebeian Ernest BEVIN, these were "The Tsar and Tsarina, their five children and the Grand Duchess Serge." (Hough, *Mountbatten,* 240.)

Becoming a strikingly handsome man, six feet four inches tall, "Dickie" entered the Royal Navy in 1913 as a cadet. His father now was

First Sea Lord, but because of Germanic birth was forced to resign early in the First World War. Battenburg was anglicized as Mountbatten, and the royal family changed its name from Saxe-Coburg and Gotha to the House of Windsor.

Prince Louis was a royal playboy and never one for intellectual pursuits including reading. With "his consuming vanity, his tactlessness, his pushiness, his shameless exploitation of the highest connections, his obsession with the royal blood, his bedazzlement with his own ideas," writes Alistair Cooke (below) Mountbatten was "a not a very engaging or even interesting man." Cooke notes that his official biographer (below) "felt compelled to stick on his desk a sign in block capitals: 'REMEMBER, IN SPITE OF EVERYTHING, HE WAS A GREAT MAN.'"

In 1922 he married the beautiful Edwina Cynthia Annette Ashley, granddaughter and heiress of the fabulously wealthy Jewish industrialist and banker Sir Ernest Cassel. It was a successful and enduring marriage but odd. "They were apparently only briefly passionate," writes Cooke. "Nevertheless, he was proud of her vivacity and beauty and hurt by her chronic infidelities, which were enough to divert his driving ambition into his career. . ." (op. cit., 106).

Brave and cheerfully confident, he was a popular and capable commander who undertook to master every task on shipboard, particularly communications. When the war started, Capt Mountbatten was on HMS *Kelly* with three other ships comprising the 5th Destroyer Flotilla. *Kelly* survived mine and torpedo damage in the North Sea before the Norwegian campaign started. When CARTON DE WIART was evacuated with his 5,000 troops from Namsos the night of 3-4 May 40, Mountbatten navigated treacherous waters to help escort the transports to safety. He saw even heavier action off Crete, where on 23 May 40 the flotilla was attacked repeatedly by Stukas. *Kelly* went down with 130 men, half the ship's complement. Mountbatten told the story to his long-time friend Noel COWARD, who made the fictionalized film *In Which We Serve* and played the lead.

Mountbatten was a junior captain of 41 years when Churchill selected him to succeed Sir Roger KEYES as head of what became Combined Operations. Taking over on 27 Oct 41, he launched 10 commando raids in six months. The first was a small operation by parachutists and seaborne troops on the night of 27-28 Feb 42 against a radar station at Bruneval, in northern France. A month later a raid blocked the dockyard at St Nazaire, the only repair facility for the pocket battleship *Tirpitz*. The disastrous **Dieppe raid,** 19 Aug 42, proved to have long-range benefits for the Normandy invasion.

Churchill meanwhile promoted Mountbatten to vice admiral, lieutenant general, and air marshal ahead of older and better qualified superiors. The upstart was put on the Chiefs of Staff Committee as Chief of Combined Operations. Other commando operations followed, and the British helped train US Rangers.

With another controversial appointment by the prime minister Mountbatten left England on 4 Oct 43 to establish the Southeast Asia Command (SEAC). In what was called a forgotten theater, morale and materiel shortages were so low that experts predicted offensive operations could not begin for two years (Tuchman, *Stilwell, 392*). But Lord Louis proved to be an effective leader, using personal charm, enthusiasm, diplomatic ability, and direct contact with London.

Burma's liberation began with in a bold campaign conceived and led by SLIM. In the fall of 1944 Mountbatten moved his headquarters from the stifling heat and political intrigue of Delhi, India, to Peredynia, Ceylon, above Kandy.

After directing the liberation of Burma, Mountbatten was unable to get landing craft needed for more ambitious operations in SEAC, but Singapore was occupied on 5 Sep 45. A week later Lord Louis met ITAGAKI, 7th Area Army commander, to sign the surrender instrument in Singapore. The ailing TERAUCHI personally surrendered later.

Mountbatten was selected in 1947 as the only man who could solve the problem of Indian independence. In a hurry to resume his naval career, Mountbatten cut the Gordian knot: he decided that the country should partitioned. Returning to England in June 48, and declining high civil positions then and later, he went to Malta as commander of the 1st Cruiser Squadron. In 1950 he became Fourth Sea Lord, and two years later was NATO Supreme Commander Allied Forces, Mediterranean. Churchill never forgave the last viceroy for what he had done in India, but there was a rapprochement in 1951. Again prime minister, Churchill gave Mountbatten the post once held by his father and one for which the son had long hungered, First Sea Lord (from 18 Apr 55). In 1960 Mountbatten became Chief of Defense Staff. Edwina died in her sleep, 20-21 Feb 60, while in Borneo on a whirlwind tour for her charities. In accordance with her special request, she was buried at sea four miles from Portsmouth.

Mountbatten retired in 1965 but remained active in many causes, primarily disarmament. Every August for several years he spent a month on a family estate in the Republic of Ireland, just 12 miles south of Ulster. On 27 Aug 79 he and several others were killed by a bomb planted in his fishing boat. There was nothing personal about the murder; IRA terrorists apparently wanted only to demonstrate that no target was immune. Lord Louis was 79.

An informal study by Richard Hough is *Mountbatten* (New York: Random House, 1981). The official biography, which Alistair Cooke calls "so thorough, so circumspect, so fair, so impeccably researched that there will be no need for any other" (*The New Yorker* Magazine, 9 Sep 85, 108) is Philip Ziegler, *Mountbatten* (New York: Knopf, 1985).

MUELLER, Heinrich "Gestapo." 1901-1945? He was born of poor Catholic parents on 28 Apr 01 in Munich. In WWI he won an Iron Cross 1st Class as a flight leader in Russia. Short, stocky, with massive hands, he was variously described as a crude peasant and "dapper"; and a captured British officer found him "a very decent little man."

Mueller began his career in the Bavarian police, specializing in surveillance of communists, of the emerging Nazi movement, and making a special study of Soviet police methods. Largely because of the latter expertise, HEYDRICH brought him from Munich to Berlin. The Bavarian policeman headed the Secret Political Police (Dept II) then, from Oct 39, Section IV, the Gestapo, of the **RSHA.** Subsection IV-A covered communism, sabotage, liberalism, and assassination; IV-B dealt with "sects" (Catholics, Protestants, Freemasons, and Jews). "Gestapo" Mueller was coldly efficient in running down and interrogating "enemies of the state," particularly Jews. Toward the end, however, he was suspected of being in touch with communists. After visiting the **Fuehrerbunker** to dispose of Hermann FEGELEIN, Mueller disappeared. His burial was recorded on

17 May 45, but the exhumed body was not positively identified (Wistrich).

MUELLER, Josef. German resistance figure. 1898-1979. "Ochsensepp" was born into a Bavarian peasant family in Steinwiesen, Upper Franconia. His nickname, best translated as "Oxen Joe," derives not from his ox-like physique, nerves, and subsequent resistance to Gestapo interrogation, but from having driven a pair of oxen to help pay his way through secondary schooling. (Deutsch, II, 113-114 & n.)

Dr Mueller was a 41-year-old Munich attorney and key figure in the Catholic resistance when recruited by Hans OSTER and commissioned to serve in the Abwehr office at Munich. Oberstleutnant Mueller was directed to use his Vatican connections for watching developments in Italy and to evaluate Allied attitudes toward making a peaceful settlement with Germany if an anti-Nazi conspiracy succeeded. On several visits to Rome during the fall of 1939 he got positive assurances from PIUS XII and through him from the British.

The **SD** long had Mueller under surveillance before finding cause to arrest him. It was not for several months after interrogating the wily Wilhelm SCHMIDHUBER, another Abwehr agent, that Heydrich moved on 5 Apr 43 to seize Mueller and other key conspirators. OSTER had time to get rid of many incriminating documents and an air raid destroyed many of Mueller's records.

Transferred from camp to camp, including Buchenwald and Dachau, Ochsensepp survived more than 200 interrogations without revealing anything. Chained hand and foot, put on a reduced prison diet, he was led to the gallows twice. As the end approached for the Third Reich and Hitler's orders for disposition of the **Prominente** became unclear, Mueller and a few others were loaded into a police van that joined a convoy of evacuees. But on about 3 Apr 45 he and two others were taken out and sent to Flossenburg, where on 9 Apr 45 Mueller "watched the tiny skin fragments of his friends [including CANARIS] floating in through the bars of his window from the crematorium . . ." (Deutsch, II, 114, 360). For unknown reasons Mueller then was sent back to the convoy—the **Niederdorf group** (Fey von

Hassell, 181, 185). Liberated with them on 4 May 45 the hardy survivor became minister of justice in Bavaria.

MUFTI OF JERUSALEM. *See* Amin el HUSSEINI.

MÜLLER. *See* MUELLER.

MURPHY, Audie. US military hero. 1924-71. With 28 medals Lt Murphy was the most highly decorated American of WWII. At the age of 18 he joined the army and took part in all the 3d Inf Div's campaigns from North Africa to Germany. During the Italian campaign he was one of only 235 original members of his company to survive. Having won all the army's other decorations for valor, and promoted to second lieutenant, he won the Medal of Honor on 26 Jan 45 for a highly publicized individual action in the Colmar Pocket. Ordering his men to take cover, this fugitive from the law of averages (to use the phrase of his buddy Bill MAULDIN, is credited with killing or wounding 50 Germans.

An attractive, articulate, boyish-looking Texan, Murphy played himself in the 1955 movie based on his autobiography, *To Hell and Back*, and was in about 40 other films.

MURPHY, Robert Daniel. US diplomat. 1894-1978. The tall, affable, cosmopolitan "diplomat among warriors" was the grandson of German and Irish immigrants and son of a railroad section hand (*CB 43*). Born 28 Oct 94 in Milwaukee, he entered the consular service in 1920 after putting himself through night law school and being admitted to the DC bar. From 1930 he was US consul in Paris, serving under three ambassadors. The last of these, BULLITT, made Murphy his deputy and counselor of embassy. When the French government fled south on 10 June 40, BULLITT and Murphy remained in Paris until 30 June. The ambassador then decided against presenting his credentials to the Pétain government and Murphy became chargé d'affaires at Vichy.

Suddenly summoned to Washington in September he was briefed by Roosevelt for a special mission: to explore the possibility of winning covert French support in North Africa for a US liberation. (Murphy, *Diplomat*, 70.) He got back to Vichy during the crisis leading to LAVAL's dismissal. Because of this Murphy did not have clearance for his visit until 18 Dec 40, before Adm LEAHY arrived as ambassador. (FDR was undertaking what came to be called his "Vichy gamble"—backing the Pétain government that Churchill spurned.)

But the career diplomat took only three weeks to accomplish what the State Department expected would require three months. Leaving Algiers on 5 Jan 41 for Lisbon, Murphy cabled a report from there 12 days later and included a draft of what became the Murphy-Weygand Agreement. This authorized the US to distribute food and clothing in North Africa and send 20 American observers to counterbalance 20 Germans of the armistice commission.

Murphy then spent almost two years directing what Macmillan accurately characterized as "a large-scale and ambitious Fifth Column operation" (Macmillan, *Blast*, 189; Murphy, 109 ff). Because Murphy was not permitted to tell his French collaborators when and where the landings would occur, the clandestine meeting near **Cherchell** on 22 Oct 42 may have done more harm than good (Murphy, 119). With no appreciation of the military problems involved but fully aware of how critical it was to have French cooperation, Murphy consequently recommended that the invasion be delayed several weeks. This brought much well-justified criticism of the frazzled fifth columnist (Clark, *Calculated Risk*, 91-92; Pogue, *Marshall*, II, 399).

It was Murphy who picked GIRAUD as the flagpole around which pro-Allied French commanders in North Africa were supposed to rally in welcoming the American liberators. Although highly recommended to Murphy by BETHOUART, MAST, and other high-ranking French generals whose judgment should have been reliable, Giraud proved to useless on African D-day (8 Nov 42).

With presidential authority since 17 October "to initiate any arrangement with Darlan which in my judgment might assist the military operation" (Murphy, 129), the diplomat was closely involved in the DARLAN "deal." When Harold MACMILLAN arrived as Murphy's British counterpart he thought Murphy should have been recalled. "Apart from being physically and mentally somewhat exhausted by two exceptionally heavy years, he was in a dangerously compromised position" after having had to work with "many unreliable and disreputable agents, as well as with keen but sometimes

over-enthusiastic patriots" (*Blast*, 189-90). But it was not until DE GAULLE established himself in July 43 that the American diplomat asked for reassignment.

Murphy became the president's personal representative on Italian affairs as the Allied invasion of Sicily was about to begin. Fourteen months later, on 4 Sep 44, Murphy reached Washington to be briefed for a new post as Eisenhower's adviser on German affairs. After Lucius CLAY succeeded McNARNEY as head of military government in Germany (OMGUS) on 15 Mar 47 Murphy was political adviser to both Clay (in Berlin) and Eisenhower (in Frankfort).

Following the Berlin airlift crisis of 1949 Murphy was ambassador to Belgium, and on 21 Apr 52 he became the first postwar US ambassador to Tokyo. Recalled suddenly to Washington in 1953, he headed the State Department's burgeoning office for UN affairs and soon had the additional duty of deputy under secretary for political affairs. This made Murphy the third highest ranking official in the State Department and holder of the highest post open to a nonpolitical appointee.

He retired in 1959 on reaching the mandatory retirement age of 65, declining to accept the ambassadorship to Germany because he did not believe the age limit should be waived. Living in NYC (where his daughter Rosemary was a prominent actress), Murphy became president of Corning Glass International. *His Diplomat Among Warriors* was published in 1964.

MURROW, Edward Roscoe. American radio broadcaster. 1908-65. Born in Greensboro, NC, he was reared in the State of Washington and graduated from Washington State Univ in 1930. He majored in political science, international relations, and speech, with drama as a major extracurricular activity. Murrow's first two years with the Columbia Broadcasting System were as director of talks and special events.

He went to London in May 37 as CBS's sole representative in Europe and with the assignment of organizing special events. Hitler provided more than anybody could have asked. Murrow revealed a flair not only for broadcasting but also for building a network of correspondents throughout the Continent. During the London blitz he became famous for nightly broadcasts that open calmly with, "This is London calling." Tall, lean, intense, exceptionally handsome, and with an ideal radio voice, Ed Murrow would have been perfectly cast for his own role in a movie. *(CB 42.)*

After the war he was a vice president of CBS and director of public affairs. He headed the US Information Agency 1961-64.

MUSELIER, Emile Henri. French admiral. 1882-1965. A vice admiral from 1939, in de Gaulle's London headquarters Muselier was appointed head of the Free French navy and merchant fleet on 27 Oct 40. His principal assistant in London was Capt Thierry d'ARGENLIEU.

Peter Wright, who joined MI5 in 1955 and rose to be assistant director, says this in his book *Spy Catcher* (1987): "De Gaulle faced persistent plots in London masterminded by his two Communist deputies, André Labarthe, a former *Chef du Cabinet* who was responsible for civilian affairs, and Admiral Mueselier [sic], who controlled military affairs. MI5 kept a close eye on these plots during the war at Churchill's instigation, and Churchill ordered the arrest of both Labarthe and Mueselier [sic] . . ." on 2 Jan 41. Wright errs however in saying this was during de Gaulle's absence for the Dakar fiasco, which took place more than three months earlier, and that the admiral was a communist—he was suspected of being a Vichy agent. But Wright goes on to say that "in 1964 we broke a [**Venona**] decrypt which showed conclusively that Labarthe had been working as a Soviet spy during this period" (Wright, 238-39).

As for Muselier, it was discovered that a DEWAVRIN protégé named Meffre ("Howard") had fed the British a forged document manufactured by one Colin with help from the Vichy consulate in London. The British apologized profusely to Muselier after holding him more than a week in prison. But de Gaulle blamed "British intelligence" and, far from being solicitous toward the victim took so little interest that Colin and Meffre were let off lightly by the British courts. (Werth, *de Gaulle*, 125.)

Muselier became a member of the French National Committee on 24 Sep 41. Exactly three months later he liberated the Vichy-controlled islands of St Pierre and Miquelon off Newfoundland, a unilateral action that infuriated Roosevelt. (The tiny islands loomed large in ASW.)

Muselier collaborated with the British in a futile effort to curb de Gaulle's consolidation of power but lost out in the struggle. Replaced by Adm Auboyneau in Mar 42 he wrote *De Gaulle contre le Gaullisme* (1946), which describes in great detail the French intrigues in London during the winter of 1940-41.

MUSSERT, Anton Adrian. Dutch puppet. 1894-1946. Great-grandson of a giant brawler and legendary wrestling champion but himself a midget of four feet 10 in elevator heels, Anton Mussert was born 5 May 94 in the village of Werkendan in southern Holland. After leaving the Delft Polytech Institute he had to settle for a civil service career with the Dept for Maintenance of Dykes, Roads, Bridges, and Canals. While rising slowly in the bureaucracy Mussert founded the odd-ball National Socialist Party of the Netherlands in 1931. Three years later (1934) the civil service ousted him for "pernicious political activity and treachery to the state."

Aping Hitler and Mussolini's parties, the Dutch Nazis adopted the black shirt, the fascist salute, and initially used a wolf's trap as its emblem! "Heil Hitler" was modified to "a sneeze-like 'Hou Zee,'" said to connote "Courage" or "Carry On." The slogan was "Mussert or Moscow." *(CB 42.)* In 1933 Mussert rallied only 600 to his first demonstration in Utrecht, the party's home base. Just a year later he had a turnout of 25,000 followers, and he polled nearly 300,000 votes in the 1935 general elections. But in the general elections of May 37, the last before the war, the no-nonsense PM, Dr Colijn, rallied to trounce the Dutch Nazi Party. Beaten at the polls, Mussert concentrated on organizing a fifth column. As a reward, in May 40 the conquering Germans suppressed all parties but his and installed Mussert as assistant to Reichkommissar of the Netherlands Artur SEYSSINQUART, who took over on 18 May 40 for the duration. The uncharismatic, teetotalling, non-smoking totalitarian midget visited Mussolini four times before finally being summoned by Hitler and chastised for not suppressing the stubborn Dutch resistance. Mussert reorganized his police to cooperate with the Gestapo in their roundups. Scores of Dutchmen were executed and thousands incarcerated as hostages. But on 11 Dec 41 the Dutch QUISLING was called back to Berlin and directed to get tougher. SS

Chief Himmler went to Holland the following May to show him how.

Queen WILHELMA proclaimed in late 1942 that a democratic Netherlands Commonwealth would be formed after the war, and Mussert made a bombastic radio address on 20 Dec 42 in anticipation of being anointed, shortly thereafter, as "leader of the Netherlands people." Hitler's pocket puppet was arrested 7 May 45 for collaboration; exactly a year later he was hanged at The Hague. *(CB 42.)*

MUSSOLINI, Benito Amilcare Andrea. Italian dictator. 1883-1945. Founder of Fascism, Il Duce (The Leader) ruled Italy from 1922 until overthrown on 25 July 43. After heading a puppet government on Lake Garda for a little more than a year he was murdered by communist partisans on 24 Apr 45.

The dictator was born on 29 July 83 in the village of Dovia (renamed Predappio), west of Ravenna in the lower Po Valley. Il Duce's mother was schoolteacher, and his father was a blacksmith who became the socialist mayor of Predappio. The boy was named for Benito Juarez, the Mexican who overthrew and executed Maximillian III. Rowdy from early childhood and reluctantly going into his mother's profession, Mussolini qualified at the age of 18 as a secondary schoolteacher but detested the work and brutalized his students *(CB 42)*. To avoid military service he spent about two years in Switzerland as a common laborer and beginning his career as an agitator and revolutionary. Returning to Italy in 1904 under a general amnesty he performed his obligatory military service with the 10th Bersaglieri Regt in Verona, before spending another three years as a teacher in Forì.

The first in a series of jail sentences for creating civil unrest came in July 08. He then edited a number of newspapers, ending up in Milan with the daily *Avanti,* and he gained authority in the Partito Socialista Italiana (PSI). He split with the party in 1914, along with the poet Gabriele D'Annunzio, and founded the newspaper *Popolo d'Italia*. In the fall of 1915 he was called for war service with the 11th Bersaglieri Regt. At this stage of his life the "indigent, bedraggled, and dirty" conscript, a stocky five feet seven inches tall, shed his vagabond image and shaped up to become a sergeant with an honorable if unheroic record.

(Kirkpatrick, *Mussolini,* 74.) The accidental explosion of a mortar round on 22 Feb 17 put him in hospitals for six months. After 27 operations and still on crutches, he was excused from further military service in Aug 17 and resumed editing *Popolo d'Italia.*

Meanwhile he had married Rachele Guidi on 16 Dec 15. Edda, future wife of CIANO, was already born (1910), as was Vittorio. Bruno, the first of five children born in wedlock, would become a military pilot and die in an air accident in Aug 41. Another son became a jazz pianist. The humble Rachele, whom Mussolini would call "the only woman whom I have ever really loved" (Kirkpatrick, 662), remained a devoted wife despite a succession of mistresses including Clara ("Claretta") Petacci from 1936.

In 1919 Mussolini began forming the ardently nationalistic Fasci di Combattimento, which became the Fascist Party. After the legendary March on Rome, 28 Oct 22, Mussolini was invited by King Victor Emmanuel III to form a new government. The murder on 10 June 24 of Giacomo Matteotti, Mussolini's most vociferous opponent, nearly nipped Fascism in the bud, but the new premier survived by showing personal outrage and pretending to direct a vigorous hunt for the assassins. But he paid a high price: "From that time onwards he was a prisoner of the 'hawks' in the sense that what started as a potentially supple Reformist Movement became a politically arthritic dictatorship" (L&W-B, Colin Coote, "Mussolini," 312).

Il Duce, however, raised national confidence from the depths. "He made the trains run on time," accomplished land reclamation on a grand scale, boosted wheat production, went far toward stabilizing the currency, and built the world's most modern navy and air force. Other programs, like trying to revive the glories of ancient Rome and raise the birth rate, became comic-opera.

Il Duce suspended parliamentary government in 1928 to become absolute dictator of a fascist corporate state. The bombastic tyrant genuinely respected the monarchy, which helped give him a broad popular base, and he achieved a long-needed modus vivendi with the Vatican by signing the Lateran Treaty in Feb 29.

Deteriorating relations with France pushed Italy into the German camp even before the Nazis took power in 1933. Mussolini's invasion of Ethiopia in 1935 became the most important single factor in destroying the League of Nations and collective security against aggression (Coffey, *Lion by the Tail,* xi). The Abyssinian adventure revealed how far Italy was short of world power status, but it showed Hitler how easily the western democracies could be manipulated and intimidated (ibid.). The war lost Italy its few remaining diplomatic ties with western Europe; Mussolini and Hitler inevitably became partners. Their first overt military collaboration was in the Spanish civil war, which Mussolini entered belatedly after Hitler rushed to FRANCO's side.

Although outraged by the Nazi takeover of Austria, the Anschluss of 12 Mar 38, Mussolini earned Hitler's undying gratitude by promptly condoning the act. Mussolini was invaluable to Hitler during the **Munich crisis** by setting up and conducting the conference of 29-30 Sep 38. The Pact of Steel, creating the Rome-Berlin Axis, was signed on 22 May 39. Mussolini did not expect to be ready for world war until 1943, but his negotiators shaped the agreement so it seemed to guarantee Italy safety from German aggression.

When Britain and France declared war against Germany on 3 Sep 39 Mussolini announced Italy's neutrality. But to participate in the spoils, he attacked the French on 17 June 40 after she had asked Germany for an armistice. GRAZIANI's four-day campaign was another fiasco. "It is the material that I lack," the Duce lamented. "A people who for 16 years have been an anvil cannot become a hammer within a few years." (*Ciano Diaries,* 17 June 40.) The pattern of Italian military defeat was continued by GRAZIANI in the western desert of North Africa and by the Duke of AOSTA in East Africa.

Not yet willing to be Hitler's jackal, Mussolini attacked Greece on 15 Oct 40 without alerting the Germans. But this was another Italian debacle. Having had to send ROMMEL to salvage the situation in the western desert, Hitler now dispatched German troops under LIST to conquer the Balkans.

After the German disaster at Stalingrad, where the the Italian 8th Army was among German satellite forces, Mussolini formed a new government on 5 Feb 43. Il Duce personally took over from CIANO as foreign minister. Two months later, after Axis troops were anni-

hilated in North Africa and the Germans were being driven back through the Ukraine, Mussolini visited Hitler at Salzburg and urged him to make a settlement with the USSR. Far from considering this, Hitler was making plans to occupy Italy, which was preparing to leave the Axis camp.

Before dawn on 25 July 43, two weeks after the Allies invaded Sicily, the grand council voted 19:7 to bring in the BADOGLIO government. Arrested as he was leaving the palace, Il Duce was bustled off in an ambulance to a succession of heavily guarded hiding places: the island of Ponza, the fortified port of La Maddalena on a tiny island three miles off Sardinia, and finally to the highest mountains of the Appenines, the Gran Sasso d'Italia. After his dramatic rescue by Otto SKORZENY on 12 Sep 43, Mussolini was flown immediately to see Hitler. The fuehrer, who maintained a high regard for his Axis partner, installed the sawdust Caesar under heavy SS protection as head of the "Salo Republic." Its seat was the village of Gargnano on the western shore of Lake Garda. As an early item of business Mussolini established a tribunal to avenge the coup d'état of 1943 (above). CIANO and DE BONO were among those ordered executed on 11 Jan 44.

The health of Il Duce, who once made a great show of virility, had deteriorated since 1940. In addition to ulcers, he is said to have long suffered from syphilis, which affected his brain, and also from paranoia and claustrophobia *(CB 42)*. His Salo Republic survived little more than a year. As Allied forces were about to start overrunning the Po Valley Mussolini moved his rump government to Milan on 18 Apr 45. After "seven phantom days" there (Kirkpatrick, 650 & n.) Mussolini fled northward in hopes of taking refuge in the Tyrol. Wearing a German greatcoat and helmet he was found hiding in a German army truck when partisans inspected the convoy at a check point in Dongo (on Lake Como). Following instructions from higher authority, the 52d Garibaldi Bde took elaborate precautions to protect their prize catch but communist leaders in Milan sent one "Colonel Valerio" (Walter Audisio) to take charge. When led to Mussolini's hiding place, Valerio pretended to be on a rescue mission. Il Duce and the heroic Clara (who had stayed with her master in violation of his instructions) were driven about a mile to the Villa Belmontone and machine gunned to death (Kirkpatrick, 671). The next morning, 25 April, their bodies and four others were hung by the feet at a gas station in Milan's Piazalle Loreto, where 15 Italian hostages had been killed some eight months earlier. That evening the cadavers were taken down on orders of Allied authorities, who had Mussolini buried secretly in a Milan cemetery. In 1946 the body was stolen by neo-fascists, hidden in a monastery at Pavia, found, and secretly reburied some 15 miles NW of Milan. In 1957 the body came to rest beside that of son Bruno in the home cemetery of San Cassiano in Predappio (originally Dovia). Mussolini had requested this in his last letter to Rachele, who also was buried there in due course. Clara Petacci lies in Rome.

Mussolini published many literary and political works. *My Autobiography* (1939), of dubious value, is supplemented by Max Ascoli, ed, *The Fall of Mussolini: His Own Story* (1948). Other standard works are V. E. de Fiori, *Mussolini,* (1928), Alexander Robertson, *Mussolini and the New Italy* (1928); C. H. Sherrill, *Bismarck and Mussolini* (1931); Gilbert Seldes, *Sawdust Caesar* (1935); Gaudens Megaro, *Mussolini in the Making* (1938); and Giorgio Pini, *Official Life of Benito Mussolini* (1939). An outstanding work, basis of the above sketch, is Ivone Kirkpatrick, *Mussolini: A Study in Power* (1964).

MUTAGUCHI, Renya. Japanese general. 1888-1966. As a regimental commander in China he lit the fuse for the Sino-Japanese war; in Burma he was primarily responsible for the disastrous "March on Delhi."

He was born 7 Oct 88 in Saga Prefecture, Kyushu, into the once-prominent Fukuchi family. This had fallen into decline, and after the early death his father and elder brother the boy was virtually an orphan until adopted as the son and heir of Moritsuni Mutaguchi. He graduated without distinction from the Military Academy in 1910 as an infantry officer but soon revealed a driving ambition. "Early on he seems to have made up his mind that the best chances for further promotion came through membership of the political cliques," writes Swinson (*Four Samurai,* 177). But he picked poorly. When a coup by the Cherry Society failed in 1930 he switched to the Imperial Way camp. Lt Col Mutaguchi (from 1930) became a section chief

of the army general staff in Tokyo in Jan 33 and was promoted in Mar 34 to colonel. After the insurrection of 26 Feb 36, in which Mutaguchi's role was uncertain, he was ordered out of Tokyo to command the Peiping garrison infantry unit (*Kogun,* 230). Still highly regarded by YAMASHITA and TOJO the colonel helped escalate the **Marco Polo Bridge** incident into open war with China (Swinson, 118). Having been promoted in Mar 38 Maj Gen Mutaguchi was assigned to Kwantung Army Hq, and four months later he became Yamashita's CofS in the 4th (Kwantung) Army. He was commandant of the military academy for two years starting in Apr 39. Two years later he took over the 18th Div in China.

As one of YAMASHITA's three divisional commanders in the Malayan campaign that took Singapore on 15 Feb 42 the brash, intensely ambitious Mutaguchi was a star. He went on to lead his 18th Div in Burma. WINGATE having showed that large scale operations in the jungle and mountains were possible, Mutaguchi conceived Opn U, the "March on Delhi." He believed reports that Indians would welcome a Japanese liberation. Under a major reorganization 15th Army Hq became the Burma Area Army Hq under Masakazu KAWABE in Mar 43. A new 15th Army Hq was activated under Lt Gen Mutaguchi on 18 March to comprise the 18th, 33d, and 56th Divs initially and soon was joined by the 31st. When his highly respected CofS, Maj Gen Obata, pointed out that not even one Japanese division, much less four, could survive in the remote and inaccessible Imphal plain, the Pattonesque Mutaguchi had Obata replaced by an officer of more positive logistical outlook.

As a preliminary to the March on Delhi, a strategic diversion (Opn **Ha-Go**) was launched on 4 Feb 44 in the **Arakan** coastal region against SLIM's 15th Corps. Thanks largely to the efforts of MESSERVY the British scored their first significant victory over the once-invincible Japanese.

But Opn U began nevertheless on 6 Mar 44 when three widely separated Japanese columns advanced from positions just across the Chindwin River. Attachments from Chandra BOSE's Indian division participated. Although expecting the offensive, the British were surprised by how fast it unfolded. In early April the Japanese cut off Imphal and Kohima, but the main effort of Lt Gen Kotoku Sato's 31st Div lost momentum and was unable to move another 30 miles NW of Kohima against Dimapur. Here SLIM was massing a corps for a counteroffensive to relieve Kohima and Imphal. By 3 June the Japanese position around Kohima was untenable; on 22 June the 88-day siege of Imphal was broken; then came the rains. Sato disregarded threats of a court-martial and began an unauthorized withdrawal. By mid-July, when Mutaguchi finally was ordered to retreat, his original force of 150,000 had lost 65,000 dead; 85 to 90 percent were sick or wounded. (Tuchmann, *Stilwell*, 454; see also Collier, *Far East*, 417.)

When the disaster ended, Mutaguchi sought to court martial his division commanders Sato and Lt Gen Motozo Yanagida, the latter for failure to pursue on the south flank with his 33d Div. But Sato and Yanagida were quietly retired, largely because Sato had prepared a good case against Mutaguchi and Kawabe. The latter was replaced by Heitaro KIMURA and Mutaguchi was relieved of command on 30 Aug 44 by Lt Gen Shihachi Katamura and he subsequently headed the junior course at the military academy.

Lt Gen Mutaguchi was arraigned for involvement in the Marco Polo Bridge incident but not charged with war crimes. The general was silent for almost two decades until A. J. Barker concluded in *The March on Delhi* (1963) that the campaign failed only because Sato had not moved against Dimapur. Mutaguchi wrote the foreword for Barker's book, then accepted the National Diet Library's request to write reminiscences for posthumous release. But the samurai could not wait. Attacking Kawabe and Sato, even leaving further denunciation in a pamphlet to be distributed at his funeral (Swinson, 252). He died 2 Aug 66 at the age of 76.

MUTO, Akira. Japanese general. 1883?-1948. A career army officer from Dec 13 he had long service in high staff positions including IG of military training on several occasions. In Prince KONOYE's last government he headed the military affairs bureau. But although prominent in the **Control Group** and in bringing on the Sino-Japanese war, Col Muto (from Aug 36) apparently disapproved of TOJO's policies as early as 1937. A major general from Mar 39 (*Kogun*, 230) and chief of the war ministry's military affairs bureau for almost four years from Sep 39 he was promoted again in Oct 41. After the Pearl Harbor attack two months later Lt Gen Muto visited influential friends including Foreign Minister Shigenori TOGO and former Prime Minister OKADA to urge TOJO's ouster (Toland, *Sun*, 258). But Muto hung on as Tojo's close adviser until exiled in June 43 (*Kogun*, 230) to command the 2d Imperial Gds Div in Sumatra. In Oct 44 (ibid.) he became YAMASHITA's CofS of the doomed 14th Area Army in the Philippines. Whatever the reasons for this surprising selection—the men were not old friends—Muto turned out to be Yamashita's most eloquent defender to the end. (Swinson, *Four Samurai*, 81.) Muto himself was hanged in Sugamo Prison on 23 Dec 48 with six other Class A war criminals.

N

NAGANO, Osami. Japanese admiral. 1880-1947. As chief of the naval general staff and deputy minister of the navy from Apr 41 to 21 Feb 44 Nagano was Japan's senior admiral.

Born in June 80 at Kochi City, Shikoku, of samurai ancestry, he had important connections with Japan's ruling elite *(CB 42)*. Nagano graduated from the naval academy in 1900 and rose steadily to the top of his profession, primarily in diplomatic assignments. He was naval attaché in Washington, he made good-will visits to the US in 1927 and 1933, he attended many international conferences, and he was known to western observers as bluff, genial, "picturesque and attractive" *(CB 42,* quoting John Gunther, *Inside Asia.* 60). Nagano was navy minister and commander of the combined fleet from Mar 36 to Jan 37 in the Koki HIROTA cabinet.

Like YAMAMOTO Nagano opposed the army's saber rattling and advised the emperor that Japan could not win a single great victory at sea (Toland, *Sun,* 86).

Recalled to the top echelon of government on 9 Apr 41 as Prince Fushimi's successor he was chief of the naval staff and deputy to Navy Minister Shigetaro SHIMADA. Nagano performed vigorously and well, giving Yamamoto pretty much free rein at sea but in Tokyo he continued to oppose the army's direction of grand strategy. When the Japanese high command was reorganized after military defeats continued, Tojo personally took over as army CofS from SUGIYAMA on 21 Feb 44 and ordered Shimada to dismiss Nagano. The navy minister apparently took over Nagano's post as an extra duty (Toland, *Sun,* 474) until Koshiro OIKAWA replaced Nagano officially on 2 Aug 44 (Morison, VI, 17n).

Nagano died 5 Jan 47 while awaiting trial for war crimes.

NAGUMO, Chuichi. Japanese admiral. 1887-1944. The aristocratic, diminutive, "extremely hot tempered" (Morison, IV, 125) Vice Adm Nagumo, despite lack of experience in naval aviation, commanded the principal body of Japanese aircraft carriers, the 1st Air Fleet. He led this in the Pearl Harbor striking force, through victories in the NEI, into the Indian Ocean, and at Midway, 3-6 June 42. Here a combination of bad luck and tactical errors cost him *Atagi, Kaga, Soryu,* and *Hiru*—four of Japan's six first-line carriers. Primarily responsible for the Japanese defeat in what proved to be the turning point of the naval war in the Pacific, Nagumo, understandably, lost his aggressiveness and effectiveness *(S&S).* He remained in action through the battle of Santa Cruz, 26 Oct 42, which, under KONDO's overall command, was a tactical victory but a strategic defeat that ended Nagumo's career as a carrier admiral.

Nagumo continued to serve devotedly, if not too brightly. After commanding a small force of patrol craft, barges, and ground troops in the defense of Saigon he and Gen Yoshitsugu SAITO committed suicide. A survivor who helped bury the admiral's body in an unmarked grave reported that Nagumo killed himself with a pistol shot on 6 July 44 (Morison, VIII, 337 & n.).

NAUJOCKS, Alfred Helmut. German adventurer. 1911-60. The son of a grocer, he was born 20 Sep 11 in Kiel. At the age of 15 the small, bright-eyed boy joined the Nazi Party and gained increasing repute as a street brawler, amateur boxer, "a fanatic and a specialist in violence" (Brissard, *SD,* 31). Having worked as a welder before studying engineering at Kiel Univ he moved to Berlin in the spring of 1932 and joined the small Nazi Security Police (SD) cell being organized there. Favorably impressing HEYDRICH he rose rapidly to the top echelon of SD and in due course had a prominent role in "dirty tricks" organized by SCHELLENBERG. In mid-Jan 35 he successfully executed a mission ordered by Hitler: tracking down and killing Rudolf Formis, operator of a secret radio station in Czechoslovakia that was broadcasting for Otto STRASSER's Black Front. In early Mar 39 Naujocks made sabotage attacks that looked like the work of Slovak nationalists (Hoehne, *Canaris,* 324). In one of several "provocations" staged to make it appear that the Germans were invading Poland in self defense, Naujocks planned and led the **Gleiwitz** incident of 31 Aug 39. For leading the SD team under Walter SCHELLENBERG in the **Venlo** incident on 9 Nov 39 Naujocks and Helmut Knochen were awarded the Iron Cross 1st Class.

Naujocks's official position from 1939 was head of the subsection within Amt VI SD Ausland under Heydrich that was charged with forging documents. These included false ID papers and other items used by secret agents. Naujocks's forgers figured prominently in the TUKHACHEVKY affair. But his most ingenious project was Opn **Bernhard**.

In 1941 Heydrich dismissed Naujocks for insubordination. Sent to the eastern front he served in the ranks of the Waffen-SS (Shirer, *Reich,* 519n.) and was wounded in 1943. The next year he turned up in Belgium as an "economic administrator" but soon was involved primarily in finding and assassinating Danish resistance members. Looking to save his skin the terrorist deserted to the Americans on 19 Oct 44 and was confined as a war criminal. He made a dramatic escape in 1946. Never brought to trial he settled in Hamburg as a businessman and is believed to have worked with SKORZENY in operating ODESSA. The self styled "man who started WWII" sold his story to the press. He died 4 Apr 60 in Hamburg. (Wistrich.)

NEAME, Philip. British general. 1888-1978. Short, wiry, a fine athlete, brainy, and brave (VC, DSO), he had combat service during the first world war as a brevet major in the Tank Corps. In 1939 Neame was deputy CofS of the BEF in France. Early the next year he took command of the 4th Indian Div in Egypt, brought them to a high degree of combat readiness, and in Aug 40 was promoted to lieutenant general and made GOC Palestine, Trans-Jordan, and Cyprus.

When WAVELL's forces were stripped down at the end of Feb 41 for operations in Greece Neame replaced "Jumbo" WILSON as commander of the widely dispersed British Desert Force in Cyrenaica. Smyth comments that Neame "probably knew a good deal more about the tactical handling of armoured formations than Wavell" but he was justifiably depressed by the condition of his troops and materiel. "Wavell seemed to resent Neame's frank summing up of the situation—and was beginning to realize that

his own appreciation was mistaken." (*Leadership,* 80, 82.) One significant thing Neame did, however, was to order in mid-March that Tobruk's defenses be restored and improved.

The British were facing Rommel's crack Afrika Korps, which was supported by the Luftwaffe's best tactical air formations. The Axis onslaught began 31 Mar 41, routing the British. Wavell arrived from Cairo and, having had little confidence in Neame from the start, ordered O'CONNOR up from Cairo to replace him. O'Connor arrived on 3 April but concluded that Neame (of whom he was a close friend and admirer) was handling the situation well. So Wavell confused the situation further by not relieving Neame but having O'Connor remain as an adviser! Both generals were captured on 6 Apr 42 when their driver got lost while en route from Derna to a new CP location at Timini.

After four unsuccessful attempts the two escaped from Castello De Vincigliata on 29 Mar 43. Neame spent the rest of the war as Lt Gov and CinC of Guernsey and its Dependencies. He was knighted (KBE) in 1946 and retired as a lieutenant general the next year. Curiously, he has no entry in *DNB*.

NEBE, Arthur. German police official. 1894-1945? Born 13 Nov 94, he became a policeman after serving in WWI. By 1924 he was a police commissioner, author of a standard text on criminology, and a recognized authority on criminal police work. In 1931 he entered the Nazi Party, the SS, and the **SD**. He went on to head the criminal police agency in the Prussian interior ministry, remaining when Goering took over that post in 1933 and reorganized the Third Reich's criminal police **(Kripo)**.

Nebe was at the height of his career in early 1938 as Kripo chief but already disillusioned about the Nazi regime when his subordinates chanced upon Berlin police records that incriminated senior officials. Nebe had a sincere desire to minimize damage to the high army command but he failed it this because Goering, Himmler, and Hitler gleefully took over and precipitated the BLOMBERG and FRITSCH affairs.

A close friend wrote that although Nebe always detested Himmler he regarded Hitler as "more dangerous but more unpredictably capable of good," as did Canaris. (Hoehne, 276, citing a 1949 story in *Der Spiegel.*) When Heydrich's **RSHA** was created by a decree of 27 Sep 39 Heinrich Mueller's Gestapo and Nebe's Kripo remained known by these acronyms but also as Amt IV and Amt V. (Brissaud, 303.)

Since 1938 Nebe had been keeping the Abwehr informed of what he learned from meetings with Himmler and Heydrich (Hoehne, 372). In the autumn of 1942 Nebe warned OSTER and his fellow conspirators that the Gestapo was preparing to arrest DOHNANYI and that he himself (Nebe) was under surveillance. The Gestapo knew Nebe was anti-Nazi but not until 22 Sep 44, after finding Abwehr records that incriminated CANARIS and so many others, did Nebe flee for his life. Heinrich "Gestapo" MUELLER took over Amt V as an extra duty.

Betrayed by a former mistress, Nebe is said officially to have been executed on 21 Mar 45 in Berlin (Wistrich). But there were reports of his being sighted in Turin in 1956 and four years later in Ireland with SKORZENY (Wistrich, II).

NEHRING, Walther K. German general. 1892-. Born 15 Aug 92 at Stretzin he joined Inf Regt 152 at Marienburg as an officer candidate in 1911 and was commissioned in 1914. On 8 June 15, two days after being promoted to Oberleutnant, he won the Iron Cross 1st Class.

Nehring was selected for general staff training in the postwar Reichswehr. Associated with GUDERIAN in building the panzer forces he was a colonel on Guderian's staff in Poland and in France. Promoted to Generalmajor on 1 Aug 40, he took command of the newly formed 18th Pz Div on 25 Oct 40 and was with Pz Gp Guderian in Russia. Nehring was awarded the RK on 24 July 41 for action around Borissow and on the Beresina River.

Leaving the division on 25 Jan 42 (B&O, 111) and promoted on 1 Feb 42, Generalleutnant Nehring took over the Afrika Korps (DAK) in late May 42. Rommel had driven the British 8th Army, then under RITCHIE, back to the Gazala line and Nehring promptly launched the envelopment on the south flank on 27-30 May that destroyed most of the British armor and left the 8th Army in a desperate situation.

Promoted to General of Panzer Troops on 1 July 42 (ibid.) Nehring made the main effort in the battle of Alam Halfa, 31 Aug-7 Sep 42.

Seriously wounded in an air attack on 31 Sep 42 the general was convalescing in Germany when Eisenhower invaded North Africa on 8 Nov 42. On that day KESSELRING, CinC South, ordered Nehring to Tunisia to form available troops into the 90th Corps and hold a beachhead while reinforcements arrived from Sicily. The panzer general arrived by air on the 16th and quickly organized a defense of his broad western front with available German and Italian units. On 19 Nov 42 he drove Georges BARRE's French forces from Medjez-el-Bab, a critical point some 30 miles west of Tunis by road and rail. But in a brief lapse of confidence Nehring abandoned Medjez-el-Bab and withdrew 15 miles to Tebourda as the 11th Br Inf Bde and **Blade Force** arrived at the head of K. A. Noel Anderson's 1st Br Army. The 11th Bde drove through Teborurda and on 30 Nov took Djedeida, within 12 miles of Tunis. Blade Force made further gains a few miles to the northwest. Nehring held a defensive position as the 10th Pz Div arrived from Sicily in the van of a German buildup; then he launched a counteroffensive that ended Eisenhower's "race for Tunis." But Kesselring and Alfred Berndt, Goebbels's agent in North Africa, recommended that Nehring, whom they considered too much of a pessimist, be replaced. OKW agreed and selected Hans Juergend von ARNIM, who arrived 5 Dec 42. Nehring left Tunisia three days later.

Returning to Russia and still highly regarded as a panzer leader, Nehring held a sequence high commands, first as CG, 24th Pz Corps, 10 Feb 43-27 June 44. Then he replaced Josef HARPE as acting commander of the 4th Pz Army until Hermann BALCK took over on 5 Aug 44 (B&O, 23). Meanwhile he was given the Golden Wound Badge in Sep 43 and awarded the Oakleaves (383/890) on 8 Feb 44.

After heading the 48th Pz Corps, 4-19 Aug 44 (B&O, 54), he returned to the 24th Pz Corps (B&O, 39). For defensive action in Poland Nehring was awarded the Swords (124/159) on 22 Jan 45 (Angola, I, 234). Group Nehring was driven back into Silesia (B&0, 38), where on 20 Mar 45 the general took over remnants of the 1st Pz Army from Gotthard HEINRICI. Nehring turned over command of the army to Wilhelm Hasse (B&O, 14-15) five days before was disbanded on 3 Apr 45 and surrendered to US forces on 9 May 45 (Angola, I, 235). After being released from POW camp he lived quietly in Duesseldorf.

NEHRU, Jawaharlal. Indian statesman. 1889-1964. Second only to GANDHI as a nationalist, Nehru was in jail from Oct 42 to June 45. After this he was prominent in MOUNTBATTEN's negotiations that lead to independence. Nehru also was involved romantically with Lady Mountbatten (Hough, *Mountbatten,* 224).

Pandit Nehru was Pakistan's prime minister and minister of foreign affairs from its formation in 1947. His autobiography is *Toward Freedom* (US edn. 1941).

NELSON, Donald Marr. US administrator. 1888-1959. Head of the War Production Board (WPB) until Sep 44, he then was with Patrick J. Hurley in China.

Nelson was born 17 Nov 88 in Hannibal, Mo. He majored in chemistry at the Univ of Missouri (1911) and joined Sears, Roebuck and Co (1912). A big, round-faced six-footer with a zest for hard work, he rose to be VP in charge of merchandising (1930-39). When the Office of Production Management (OPM) was created under William S. KNUDSEN on 7 Jan 41 Nelson took over its division of purchases. Because of troubles within the OPM the new Supply, Priorities, and Allocation Board was created in Sep 41 under Nelson.

FDR still was searching for somebody to head a single federal agency concerned with industrial mobilization. On 13 Jan 42 it was announced that the War Production Board (WPB) would be formed under Nelson to replace the OPM and the newer board. (*See* Sherwood, *R&H,* 474-77.) Nelson performed vigorously and effectively, if with bureaucratic turbulence. In early 1943 the feuding reached a peak within the WPB between Nelson and Charles E. Wilson (both disliked by the War and Navy Depts) and Ferdinand Eberstadt (whom the armed services favored). FDR finally addressed the crisis on returning from the Casablanca Conference; he decided to replace Nelson with Bernard M. Baruch (who had expected to get the job initially), but changed his mind (Sherwood, *R&H,* 699-700). Nelson then forced Eberstadt's resignation but soon fell out with Wilson. The squabbling featured press leaks and became so dangerous to the administration that FDR decided to remove Nelson from the battle of Washington by sending him to China with Patrick J. HURLEY. Soon after reaching Chungking on 7 Sep 44 with a meaningless assignment to "study the

Chinese economy" Nelson resigned from the WPA and was succeeded by Julius A. Krug as WPB chairman. Taken in like HURLEY by the China Lobby the big, burly businessman remained for the duration but he declined Chiang's request to direct China's postwar economic reconstruction (Tuchman, *Stilwell,* 496n.).

Nelson was president of the Society of Independent Motion Picture Producers (1945-47). With James F. BYRNES he wrote an official report titled "Industrial Mobilzation for War." Nelson also published *Arsenal of Democracy: The Story of American War Production* (1946).

NEURATH, Constantin von. German statesman. 1873-1956. The elderly, aristocratic, gentlemanly Baron von Neurath epitomized the "good Germans" who put career advancement ahead of moral aversion to Hitler's Third Reich. (Bracher, 320.) Consenting to be "conservative window dressing" for the Nazis (Bracher, 327), he ended up in Spandau as a major war criminal.

Freiherr von Neurath was born 2 Feb 73 in Klein Glattbach, Wuerttenberg. His mother was of the Swabian petty nobility and his father was a high court official in Wuerttenberg. The family was Protestant. Neurath entered the diplomatic service in 1901 and spent five years in London (1903-8). As a captain of grenadiers he was wounded in 1914, winning the Iron Cross 1st Class and being invalided back to the foreign service. After serving in Constantinople he was appointed ambassador to Copenhagen in 1919, to Rome in 1921, and to London in 1930. On 2 June 32 he became foreign minister under PAPEN, retaining the post under SCHLEICHER, and (supposedly at the request of HINDENBURG) under Chancellor Hitler. The old-school diplomat joined the Nazi Party in 1937. But the foreign office was gradually eclipsed by the RIBBENTROP Bureau—Neurath lacking the character and political acumen to oppose this effectively—and he was among the "uncooperative" officials whom Hitler suddenly sacked under the directive announced on 5 Feb 38. Neurath's offense was expressing alarm three months earlier when Hitler revealed his grandiose war plans in the conference recorded in the HOSSBACH memorandum.

Neurath held honorific posts before being named Protector of Bohemia and Moravia on 15 Mar 39, an appointment that was supposed to reassure western powers that the occupation of

Czechoslovakia would be benevolent (Wistrich). Although his Nazi subordinates took the initiative in oppressing the Czechs, Protector Neurath signed the new laws and decrees. But it soon became apparent that more drastic measures were needed because Czech resistance was gaining strength. The fuehrer summoned Neurath to Berlin for a dressing down on 23 Sep 41 and said that Reinhard HEYDRICH would be deputy-protector. Neurath refused to accept this arrangement but was allowed to take extended leave. HEYDRICH was mortally wounded on 27 May 42 and succeeded as acting protector by Karl Hermann Frank. On 25 Aug 43 Wilhelm Frick became protector, but real power was vested in his subordinate, Karl Hermann FRANK.

Neurath had a passive role in the anti-Hitler conspiracy. At Nuremberg he aroused compassion but was convicted on all four counts of **war crimes** and sentenced on 30 Nov 46 to 15 years in prison at Spandau. "The old gentleman," as other inmates called him, "amiable and calm," served eight years until increasingly bad health led to his release on 6 Nov 54. (Speer, *Spandau,* 166-257 passim.) He died 15 Aug 56 at Enzweihingen.

NIEMOELLER, Martin. German clergyman. 1892-1984. Known internationally for his courageous opposition to Nazism, he survived seven years in concentration camps to remain a world figure and leading pacifist in the Cold War. Niemoeller was born in Lippstadt, Westphalia, on 14 Jan 92. After a naval career, winning the *Pour le Mérite* as one of the most successful U-boat skippers in WWI, he was a farmer before undertaking to study theology. Ordination as a Lutheran minister came on 29 June 24. Three years later he was pastor of the Church of Jesus Christ at Dahlem, a Berlin suburb. His autobiography, *From U-Boat to Pulpit* (1933), expressed pleasure that the Nazi revolution had triumphed.

But the pastor took alarm when Nazi subordination of national institutions *(Gleichschaltung)* succeeded quickly with German churches almost everywhere. In opposition to the new German Christian Church or *Reichskirche* Niemoeller organized and led the Confessional Church *(Bekennende Kirche).* He and Dietrich BONHOEFFER immediatcly and publicly criticized the "Aryan paragraph" in a Nazi law of 6 Sep 33. Two weeks later Niemoeller called on clergymen to form the Emergency League, of which he became leader. On 27 Sep 33 the League published a major document opposing Nazi actions in the field of religion. After hundreds of Confessional Church leaders were arrested Pastor Niemoeller's turn came on 1 July 37. He was held for eight months in Berlin's Moabit prison before trial. The *Sondergericht* (Special Court for offenses against the State) found the pastor innocent of the main charge, "underhand attacks against the state." But the court convicted him of "abusing the pulpit," fined him 2,000 marks, and pronounced a jail sentence of seven months. Having already served the time he was set free but the Gestapo was waiting at the court room door.

Pastor Niemoeller spent the next seven years as a somewhat privileged prisoner, first at Sachsenhausen, then at Dachau. He declined freedom in return for silence. As one of the **Prominente** he was liberated at **Niederdorf** on 4 May 45.

The world-famous pastor was president of the Protestant church in Hesse and Nassau 1947-64. He lived in retirement at Darmstadt, remaining one of six presidents of the World Council on Churches.

NIMITZ, Chester William. US admiral. 1885-1966. As the senior US naval officer in the Pacific, CINCPAC/CINCPAO, with headquarters at Pearl Harbor, the quiet admiral from the Texas hill country had the biggest job in US naval history.

Nimitz was born 24 Feb 85 in Fredericksburg, Texas. His German ancestry has been traced to forebears who took part in the 13th century invasion of northern Livonia on the Baltic. Nimitzes were officers in the Swedish army after their homeland became part of Sweden. In 1648 a Maj Ernst von Nimitz settled near Hanover in NW Germany and continued the family military tradition, but later generations were wealthy merchants. The admiral's great-grandfather, Karl Heinrich Nimitz, squandered the family fortune and turned to the sea as supercargo on a merchant ship. Karl Heinrich Nimitz, Jr, went to sea at the age of 14 and in due course (1846) was a pioneering settler of Fredericksburg, Texas. In 1852 grandfather Charles Henry Nimitz (having anglicized his name) established a highly successful hotel in Fredericksburg. The steamboat gothic structure, fictional setting for an

O'Henry story, survives as seat of the Admiral Nimitz Center.

Despite his grandsire's tall tales of the sea, young Chester grew up knowing many army officers and set his sights on West Point. But no appointment was available so he ended up in Annapolis, graduating in 1905 (7/144).

Soon sent to the Philippines he took command of an old Spanish gunboat, *Panay,* whose name (not the same boat) would be famous in the **Panay incident** of 1936. Meanwhile another internal crisis was brought on in 1907 by Japanese war mongers, this stemming from American discrimination against emigrants to California after the Russo-Japanese War of 1904-5. The 20-year-old ensign was put in command of DD *Decatur* and given the mission of taking her into dry dock for overhaul. A biographer points out that SPRUANCE got his first destroyer at the age of 26, HALSEY at 30, and Ernest J. KING at 36 (Potter, *Nimitz,* 59), but the assignment came close to being a professional death sentence for Nimitz. In poorly charted Batangas Bay on the very black evening of 7 July 08 *Decatur* grounded on a mud bank. As required by regulations the ensign was court-martialed. But because of the circumstances and an excellent record he was let off with a reprimand. The memory caused Nimitz in later years to be lenient toward subordinates who made one mistake.

In 1909 Nimitz was assigned to the underwater service. This was much to his distaste, initially, but he became the navy's leading authority on submarines. In 1912 he commanded the Atlantic Submarine Flotilla, and the next year was sent to study diesel engines being built for the Germany navy. (The Texan was bilingual.) Commander Nimitz was largely responsible for having the dangerous and noxious gasoline engines of American "pig boats" replaced by the newly invented (1895) diesels. During WWI he was CofS in the Atlantic Submarine Force. Pioneering in a field spurned by navy careerists he set up at the Univ of Calif, Berkeley, what evolved into the naval **ROTC** program. While on this assignment, 1926-29, he was promoted to captain.

Nimitz subsequently commanded Sub Div 20, headed the San Diego destroyer base, was skipper of the cruiser *Augusta,* and was assistant chief of the bureau of navigation in Washington. (This actually dealt with personnel and its name later was changed accordingly.) Promoted to rear admiral in 1938 he commanded Cruiser Div 2, then BB Div 1, and the next year he took over as chief of the bureau of navigation. Although "air-minded" he never qualified as flyer and had no experience with carriers.

CINCPAC

On 16 Dec 41 he was notified by Secretary of Navy Knox that he was to take over immediately as CINC Pacific Fleet at Pearl Harbor. Delayed by bad weather, Vice Adm Nimitz arrived by Catalina flying boat on Christmas morning of 1941 to learn that Wake Island had just surrendered. A tall, silver-haired, physically fit officer about to have his 57th birthday, the newcomer took over officially as CINCPAC on 31 December and put on the four stars that went with the post. (He replaced Vice Adm William S. Pye, who had stood in for the ousted Husband E. KIMMEL.)

Most unusually for a new military broom, Nimitz did bring in or send for his own staff, nor did he purge the one inherited from Kimmell. (Compare Messiah "Monty" Montgomery's advent as GOC 8th Army.) But he gave his demoralized subordinates a new lease on life and set about rebuilding the Pacific Fleet.

CNO King had directed Nimitz to undertake carrier raids soon after assuming command, but no subordinate expressed enthusiasm for aggressive action until "Bull" HALSEY got back to Pearl Harbor. Nimitz would not forget this. With his task force, built around CV *Enterprise,* Halsey raided the Marshall Islands, and Frank J. Fletcher, with *Yorktown,* hit the nearby Gilberts. Although the strikes did little damage they were a valuable start.

If the Japanese had struck Pearl Harbor to buy a year's protection from the US Navy, Nimitz furnished a series of nasty surprises. The first was the DOOLITTLE Raid on Tokyo in Apr 42, from a deep-penetration task force built around CV *Hornet.*

In this same month Nimitz acquired an additional title that made him CINCPAC/CINCPAO. PAO is the acronym for Pacific Ocean Area, whose sub-areas were the North, Central, and South Pacific Ocean Areas. From headquarters in Pearl Harbor the three-star admiral visited forward positions, initially Guadalcanal and Midway.

With signal intelligence of the large-scale Japanese naval threat against Australia—the operation to take Port Moresby, New Guinea, by amphibious assault—Nimitz massed Allied naval forces that led to the Battle of the Coral Sea, 4-8 May 42. Although a tactical defeat, it was a significant strategic victory. The senior US naval officer on the scene, Frank Jack FLETCHER, drew criticism from officers including King for his performance. Nimitz's action was characteristic. After receiving Fletcher's oral report and then asking for a complete one in writing, Nimitz concluded that his subordinate had performed so well in a confusing situation that he should be promoted to vice admiral and awarded the **DSM**. (Potter, 68.)

Closely following this first major fleet action came the decisive US victory at Midway, 3-6 June 42.

After the US Navy's humiliating defeat in the night action off Savo Island, 9 Aug 42, Nimitz did not court-martial Adm Richmond K. TURNER or other commanders involved. When it became necessary to replace Robert L. GHORMLEY for shortcomings in the Guadalcanal campaign Nimitz was firm but considerate.

Strategic Offensive

For his drive across the central Pacific CINCPAC/CINCPAO secured his flank by clearing out Japanese bases in the Aleutians, first taking Attu in May 43. After landings in the Gilbert Islands, on Makin and Tarawa in Nov 43, suffering heavy losses, Nimitz overruled recommendations of his staff planners and major subordinate commanders on what to do next. SPRUANCE, TURNER, and Holland M. SMITH strongly favored a two-phase campaign that initially bypassed Kwajalein Atoll, heart of the enemy's Marshall Islands position (Morison, VII, 206). But Nimitz made the bold decision to bypass a ring of four strongly defended outer islands and go straight for Kwajalein. Finding this objective relatively undefended, the 4th Marine and 7th Army Divs took the atoll on 7 Feb 44, after a week's action, with only 372 killed, died of wounds, and MIA. Not a US ship was lost. (Morison, VII, 278.) The casualties were far fewer than in the Gilberts. Cincpac took Eniwetok a month later.

Now the army-navy disagreements over strategy came to a head. Throughout the war Nimitz met about every other month in California with Ernie King; he held high-level command conferences at Pearl Harbor; he visited the stay-at-home MacArthur on several occasions, notably in late Mar 44 with a small staff, in hopes of establishing better working relations.

But the impasse persisted. After his nomination for an unprecedented fourth term Roosevelt decided to resolve the conflict personally. At a meeting in Pearl Harbor, 26-28 July 44, MacArthur argued that reneging on his promise to return to the Philippines would shake conquered Asians' faith in America. Second, the general pointed out, his course of action would deprive the Japanese of what they had started the war for—the resources of Southeast Asia, principally the NEI. Nimitz and some of his staff were ultimately convinced, but Ernie King was unyielding. The CNO wanted Luzon bypassed so military assets could be massed to take Formosa (Taiwan) as a base for invading mainland China and joining forces with Chiang Kai-shek. But other JCS members won a compromise: Nimitz and MacArthur would converge on Mindanao; Washington would decide what happened next.

The Battle for Leyte Gulf, 23-26 Oct 44, came close to being an American disaster because HALSEY was faked out of position by a decoy force of carriers. Nimitz insisted vehemently that this should not diminish Halsey's reputation.

Appointment to the new five-star rank of Fleet Admiral was confirmed for Leahy, King, and Nimitz on 14 Dec 44. His war ended at the surrender ceremonies aboard *Missouri* on 2 Sep 45. Nimitz turned over the post of CINCPAC to SPRUANCE on 24 Nov 45 at Pearl Harbor and on 15 Dec 45 succeeded King as CinC US Fleet. Two years later he retired from military duty.

Postwar

In Mar 49 the admiral accepted a UN assignment as plebiscite administrator for Kashmir. But he never left the US, and after three months his large international staff was disbanded when India and Pakistan rejected UN truce proposals. (Potter, 437-50.) The admiral spent the next two years as a roving "good will ambassador" for the UN, making speeches throughout the US explaining UN issues and proposed solutions.

The admiral meanwhile was called to Washington (in 1949) for advice during "the revolt of the admirals." This resulted from the so-called unification of the armed services under the National Security Act. (Potter, 443 ff.) After Wisconsin's Sen Joseph McCarthy undertook his anticommunist witch hunt, President Truman established the Presidential Commission on Internal Security and Individual Rights on 23 Jan 51 with Nimitz as chairman. But the commission never functioned because a Senate committee headed by Pat McCarran of Nevada set up criteria for confirmation of the nine-member commission that were impossible to meet. In 1952 the admiral turned in his final resignation to the UN and sought the quiet life.

Turning down officers from universities, businesses, and industry he did become a regent at the Univ of California at Berkeley, and he took the responsibilities seriously. By the summer of 1963 the Nimitzes found their home in Berkeley too much of a burden and moved to navy quarters in the San Francisco area. After a severe fall later that year the admiral's health deteriorated. He died 20 Feb 66 and was buried under a regulation headstone at the Golden Gate National Cemetery.

The self-effacing admiral, who had refused to be "good copy" for war correspondents, would not write his memoirs nor authorize others to do it during his lifetime. But Nimitz carefully collected his papers and had them deposited in the Operational Archives of the Naval History Division in Washington. The Director of Naval History interested Alan Nevins in using these to write a biography, but ill health soon caused this eminent historian to abandon the task. It was taken over by E. B. Potter of the History Dept, USNA, whose definitive biography is *Nimitz* (Annapolis, Md: Naval Institute Press, 1976). Potter and the admiral had been coeditors of *Sea Power: A Naval History* (Englewood Cliffs, N J: Prentice-Hall, 1960). Of historical value also is the booklet *Nimitz: The Story of Pearl Harbor as Seen from the Japanese Perspective with the Relationship between Admiral Togo and Admiral Nimitz* (Fredericksburg, Texas: Admiral Nimitz Center, 1975.

NOBLE, Percy Lockhart Harnam. British admiral. 1880-1955. At the start of the war Sir Percy (KCB 1936) was CinC China. In Feb 41 he became CinC Western Approaches with a new headquarters at Liverpool to replace that of Adm Martin Eric Dunbar-Nasmith at Plymouth (WC, II, 601). During the next 18 months, before succeeded by Adm Sir Max Horton, Noble laid the foundations for successful ASW that eventually defeated the U-boat menace. He then headed the British Admiralty delegation in

Washington, DC, until replaced by James SOMERVILLE. (WC, V, 6; VI, 174.)

Born 16 Jan 80, Sir Percy retired in Jan 45 after being First and Principal Naval ADC to the king, 1943-45 and created GBE in 1944. He died in London on 25 July 55.

NOGUES, Charles Auguste Paul. French general. 1876-1971. At Rabat as high commissioner of Morocco when Patton's task force landed on 8 Nov 42, Nogues was considered by the Allies to be a Vichy villain in a class with BERGERET, BOISSON, and PEYROUTON.

The general was born in the village of Monléon-Magnoac, in the High Pyrenees Dept. After attending the Ecole Polytechnique (1897-99) and being commissioned in the artillery, Noguès was soon ordered to North Africa. His first duty was mapping the Oujda region of eastern Morocco. Then he served in Tunisia (1908-9) and in the Oran Division before joining the personal staff (*cabinet*) of the legendary Gen Louis Lyautey (1854-1934), resident general in Morocco. He later was in Lyautey's cabinet when the marshal was minister of war (1917). This experience under a master of colonial administration set Nouguès's course for life. After serving on the western front during WW I, finally CO of his artillery regiment and WIA, he held high staff positions in Paris before returning to Morocco. He fought in the final pacification of Morocco, held higher and higher posts in the **Maghreb** until 1936, when Leon BLUM named him IG of troops in North Africa and then resident general and CinC of troops in Morocco (16 Sep 36). Since 1925 the office had been held by a civilian. As a colonial administrator Noguès proved to be a worthy successor of the legendary Lyautey.

When France entered the war on 3 Sep 39, Noguès was CinC, North African Theater of Operations, with headquarters in Algiers, and during the **Phony War** Daladier briefly considered replacing GAMELIN with Noguès. Like Lyautey in 1914-18, his successor maintained order in the Maghreb despite detachment of many colonial army troops to the western front. After urging the fugitive government at Bordeaux not to sign an armistice, the proconsul declared he was willing to fight on in North Africa. This is according to Pierre Thibault, with benefit of historical perspective. (Larousse, "Noguès") But contemporary writers said the general opposed making North Africa a base for continued resistance. He is also accused of helping WEYGAND scotch REYNAUD's proposal in June 40 to save half a million young Frenchmen by calling up two mobilization classes and shipping them to North Africa for basic military training. (Pertinax, 289; Spears, II, 82). Noguès obeyed orders from Laval to arrest "resisters," including MANDEL, who reached Casablanca aboard the *Massilia* on 24 June 40.

After the armistice, Noguès reverted to his post in Morocco, WEYGAND taking overall military command in North Africa. In June 41, reaching the age for military retirement, the proconsul kept his civil authority in Morocco (as high commissioner) but turned over command of troops to JUIN.

Although anti-German, Noguès believed in following a strict neutrality, honoring terms of the armistice, and enforcing policies of Vichy. The high commissioner made it clear that he would oppose any Allied liberation, pointing out that it could trigger a native uprising. When BETHOUART tried to bring his chief over to the Allied side on the night of 7-8 Nov 42, Noguès had that general arrested for treason. In accordance with orders, many French troops and warships put up a stuff defense. Noguès received orders from Petain on 10 Nov 42 to take over the duties of DARLAN, who the marshal thought was an Allied prisoner in Algiers. Noguès agreed the next morning to a cease fire, but only after having the local German armistice commission attest that further resistance was senseless. Going to Algiers and finding that Darlan was at liberty, Noguès gave the admiral back his authority.

The general became a member of the Imperial Council that was constituted by Adm Darlan on 2 Dec 42. After the admiral's assassination on 24 Dec 42, Noguès presided over the session of the Imperial Council that, on the 27th, named Giraud civil and military chief in Africa.

As deputy high commissioner for French North Africa under GIRAUD, Noguès retained authority at Rabat because the Allies needed his support. Being responsible for order in Morocco, the proconsul was appalled when the free-wheeling FDR set up an audience with the sultan of Morocco on 22 Jan 43 (during the Casablanca Conference) and promised US support for Moroccan independence. (Larousse.)

In June 1943, when DE GAULLE gained control in North Africa and began settling political

scores with the "men of Vichy," Noguès was replaced by Ambassador Gabriel Puaux. On 20 June 43 Noguès took refuge in Lisbon. He was sentenced *in absentia* on 28 Nov 47 by the High Court of Justice to 20 years of hard labor and national indignity for obeying orders to resist the Allied landings. In June 54 the general presented himself to the High Court, which confirmed the sentence but immediately revoked it. Noguès returned to Portugal and maintained discreet contacts with Morocco. He died in Paris on 20 Apr 71 at the age of 95.

NOMURA, Kichisaburo. Japanese admiral. 1877-1964. As ambassador to Washington from 19 Feb 41, the one-eyed admiral was an innocent villain of the Japanese surprise attack on Pearl Harbor, 7 Dec 41.

He was born in Wakayama-ken in Dec 77, third son of Kisaboro Masuda. Orphaned young and left poor, he supported himself until adopted by Masatane Nomura and taking his name. Nomura graduated from the Naval Academy in 1898 with the Imperial Prize for scholarship. *(CB 41.)* After seeing action in the Russo-Japanese war 1904-5 he began a series of diplomatic missions. During WWI he was naval attaché in Washington and a student at Annapolis. Nomura rose steadily in his profession, commanding the 3d Fleet during the Shanghai incident of 1932. Several weeks after the military action ended, he lost his left eye when bombed by a Korean patriot. The tall, highly regarded, good-natured admiral retired from active naval duty but remained on the Supreme War Council. He was director of the Peers' School until serving as foreign minister 23 Sep 39 to 14 Jan 40 in the government of Gen Nobuyuki ABE.

Because he was known as a man of high character with many friends in America and was opposed to the militarists, Nomura was named ambassador to Washington. He arrived 14 Feb 41 and made a sincere if inept effort to reconcile national differences (Hull, *Memoirs,* 1097; Morison, III, 60, 65). In mid-Nov he was joined by special envoy Saburo KURUSU.

"Historians will linger for centuries over the character and detail of the Hull-Nomura negotiations," writes Bemis. "Already a massive literature has built up." (*Dipl Hist,* 869 and n.)

Yamamoto had insisted that the Americans have at least 30 minutes' warning of the Pearl

Harbor attack, and the emperor gave similar instructions. By 8 AM on Sunday 7 Dec 41 US authorities had deciphered the long message that Nomura was to hand Secretary of State Cordell HULL at 1 PM "The note did not declare war," writes Hull. "Neither did it break off diplomatic relations" (Hull, *Memoirs,* 1095); but it stated that further negotiations would be useless. Because of difficulties in his embassy code room Nomura did not have the complete note until 10:30 AM A final message instructed him to deliver this at 1 PM, preferably to Hull. The latter points out that "knowing the importance of a dead line set for a specific hour, Nomura should have come to see me precisely at one o'clock, even though he had in his hand only the first few lines of his note, leaving instructions with the Embassy to bring him the remainder as it became ready" (Hull, 1097). The meeting instead took place at 2:20 PM, more than an hour after the first wave of Japanese planes hit Pearl Harbor (ibid.).

"I have seen it stated that I 'cussed out' the Japanese envoys in rich Tennessee mountain language," writes Hull. As dictated from memory immediately after the meeting and released to the press, Hull concluded his very brief remarks with this observation: "I have never seen a document that was more crowded with infamous falsehoods and distortions—infamous falsehoods and distortions on a scale so huge that I never imagined until today that any Government on this planet was capable of uttering them." (Hull, 1096.) But this explanation leaves room for the legend that Hull muttered "scoundrels and piss-ants" as the visitors left.

The latter were interned until 1942 and repatriated. After the war Nomura published *My Mission to the United States.* He became president of the Japan Victor Co in 1952 and was in the House of Councilors.

NORRIE, Charles Willoughby Noke. British general. 1893-1977. A cavalryman who became a cool and able leader of mechanized forces (Barnett, *Generals,* 152), Norrie led his 1st Armd Div to the Western Desert in mid-Sep 41. CUNNINGHAM was grouping armored units into the new 30th Corps under Lt Gen V. Pope, but the latter was killed in an air accident shortly after assuming command. Taking over the "tank heavy" corps, Norrie moved promptly against Rommel's Afrika Korps with already available armored forces and was reinforced piecemeal by others as they reached the combat theater.

Norrie led the 30th Corps in AUCHINLECK's offensive, 18 Nov-31 Dec 41, then in the 8th Army's retreat before Rommel's second offensive, 21 Jan-7 July 42. In the confusion of RITCHIE's tenure as army commander, Norrie and his close friend GORT were unable to head off the mistakes that led to the catastrophic loss of British armor in battles on the Gazala line. At Tobruk, KLOPPER raised the white flag on 21 June 42 and Rommel pushed on. Norrie reached El Alamein on 26 June with his headquarters and organized the line on which the 8th Army held. But in the reorganization that occurred before 7 July 42 he was replaced by Maj Gen W. H. Ramsden, former head of the 50th Div. Returning to England, Norrie headed the Royal Armored Corps in 1943 *(S&S).*

NORSTAD, Lauris. US general. 1907-88. The tall, slender, Nordically handsome Norstad was one of the war's boy wonders. Born 24 Mar 07 at Red Wing, Minn, he graduated from West Point in 1903 (139/299), was commissioned in the cavalry, and transferred to the Air Corps. At the start of the war Norstad served in Army Air Force Hq until becoming A3, 12th AF, Mediterranean Theater. Promoted to brigadier general he became director of operations, Mediterranean Allied AF. In Aug 44 he went to Washington as deputy CofS, AAF, and CofS, 20th AF.

The 20th AF was the B-29 formation activated on 4 Apr 44 and commanded initially by K. B. WOLFE in India and China. Serving later under Curtis E. LEMAY Norstad helped pioneer a new era of air war. He was promoted to major general on 4 June 45 at the age of 38.

Norstad's postwar career advancement was even more meteoric. He headed the plans and operations div, WDGS, 16 Jun 46-30 Oct 47 *(AA,* 60); was acting vice CofS, USAF, in 1950; then was CinC USAF in Europe; CinC Allied Air Forces, Central Europe, 1951-53; a full general in 1952; air deputy at SHAPE in 1953; and Supreme Commander Allied Powers Europe (SACEUR), 1956-63. Norstad retired from seven years in the NATO post and joined the board of Owings-Corning Fiberglas Corp, of which he was CEO, 1967-72. The general died

12 Sep 88 at the Tucson Medical Center of severe arteriosclerosis.

NOVIKOV, Aleksandr Aleksandrovich. Soviet AF leader. 1900-76. Born 19 Nov 1900 he joined the Red Army in 1919, fought in the civil war, and in 1933 transferred from the infantry to the air force. After graduating from the Frunze MA he became CofS of the 450th Avn Bde under Iyeoronim P. Uborevich, who headed the Belorussian MD. When Uborevich was arrested and executed with TUKHASCHEVSKY in 1937 (Scarecrow) Novikov was removed from his post but not arrested (HFS).

The fortunate survivor was CofS of aviation in the Northwest Front during the war against Finland. Then he was aviation commander in the Leningrad MD, which became M. M. POPOV's Northern Front in June 41 after Barbarossa started. Novikov left Leningrad in 1942 to be people's commissar of defense for aviation. With the rank of general lieutenant he went as deputy commander of the Soviet AF to direct air operations of the new Volkhov Front, arriving in the same plane with VLASOV.

From Apr 42 to Mar 46 Novikov headed the Soviet AF, displaying remarkable ability as a Stavka representative coordinating aviation on many fronts during the war. He took part in Lend Lease talks and was an admirer of US aircraft received (HFS). Novikov was promoted to general colonel in early 43, after the Stalingrad victory, and he was the first marshal of aviation. On 21 Feb 44 he became the first of only two officers to be made chief marshal of aviation in WWII, the other being A. Ye. Golovanov. For directing air assaults on Berlin Novikov was twice a **HSU** (Apr and Sep 45).

Novikov was arrested on 24 Apr 46 at the instigation of Vasily STALIN as his father removed war heroes. The chief marshal of aviation's deputies, Marshals of Aviation Astakhov, Vorozheykin, and Falaleyev, were retired. Another deputy, Khudyakov, had been arrested in 1945 and was shot in 1950. (HFS.) After two weeks of constant interrogation the wartime chief of the purge-ridden Soviet AF was held in strict isolation for six years. He was released after Stalin's death Stalin in 1953 and rehabilitated. Novikov then held a succession of high posts: commander of long-range aviation, deputy CinC of the Soviet AF 1954-55, then commandant of the higher civil aviation school in Leningrad.

NYGAARDSVOLD, Johan. Norwegian statesman. 1879-1952. He worked in the US for six years as a young man before entering Norwegian politics in 1907 as a member of the Labor Party. In 1935 he formed a Labor cabinet. When the Germans occupied his country in June 40 Nygaardsvold escaped to London to head the government in exile until 25 June 45.

O

O'CONNOR, Richard Nugent. British general. 1889-1981. Educated at Wellington College and Sandhurst, the diminutive, bird-like O'Connor was commissioned in the Scottish Rifles (1909). A veteran of major actions in WWI, he won the MC and DSO with bar (1917 and 1918). After commanding the Peshawar Bde on India's NW frontier he was promoted to major general (1938) and posted to Palestine as military governor of Jerusalem and GOC 7th Div. In June 40 he took his division to Egypt and was given command of the small Western Desert Force in Egypt. Under his friend WAVELL, Lt Gen (T) O'Connor had the major role in planning and executing the highly successful counteroffensive of 9 Dec 40-7 Feb 41 against GRAZIANI. Facing heavy numerical odds, never having more than two divisions (30,000 troops) and a few hundred RAF pilots, he advanced 500 miles through unreconnoitered desert.

"The tactical decisions on which success or failure depended were his and the grim determination that inspired all our troops stemmed from his heart. It was his skill in calculating the risks, and his daring in accepting them, that turned what might have been merely a limited success into a victorious campaign with far-reaching effects on the future course of the war." (John HARDING, O'Connor's CofS, quoted by Smyth, *Leadership,* 63.) With fewer than 2,000 casualties he shattered 10 enemy divisions, took about 138,000 POWs including five generals, captured 400 tanks and 850 guns, and inflicted casualties that included 12,000 WIA and MIA. (Ibid.)

Wavell brought Philip NEAME in to head the forces left in Cyrenaica, which became the 8th Army, and O'Connor went to Cairo as GOC, British Troops in Egypt. After Rommel launched his first offensive on 24 Mar 41 and routed the British, Wavell concluded from a quick visit to 8th Army Hq that O'Connor should replace Neame. But when Sir Richard (KCB in 1941) arrived from Cairo on 3 Apr 42 he convinced Wavell that Neame should retain his post. Wavell then made the curious decision that O'Connor, who was Neame's friend and admirer, should remain as an adviser.

The two generals were captured three days later and sent to Italy as POWs. Neame masterminded an attempt in which he and O'Connor escaped 29 Mar 43 with Air Marshal Boyd. (CARTON DE WIART was recaptured.)

After commanding the 8th Corps from Normandy through breakout and exploitation to the north, O'Connor returned to India in 1945. First appointed to the Eastern Command, he then headed the North-West Army and was promoted to full general. Back in England he was on the Army Council as adjutant general 1946-47 and was elevated in the knighthood during his final year (**GCB**). Sir Richard retired in 1948. He was lord lieutenant, Ross and Cromarty, 1955-64, and lord high commissioner of the General Assembly, Church of Scotland (1964) and a Knight of the Thistle in 1971. (*Concise DNB.*)

O'DANIEL, John Wilson. US general. 1894-1975. Having risen from the ranks of the Delaware NG, the ebullient little (five feet six) "Iron Mike" got his nickname from a tough appearance and parade-ground voice. Col O'Daniel led the 168th RCT of the 34th Inf Div in the assault landing some 15 miles W of Algiers on 8 Nov 42. Promptly promoted to BG on 20 Nov 45 he then directed amphibious training for the 5th Army's landings in Sicily. Because TRUSCOTT was short of amphibious specialists, O'Daniel was assigned to the crack 3d "Rock of the Marne" Inf Div in Tunisia (*EP,* 1234).

After taking part in the Sicily and Anzio landings O'Daniel succeeded TRUSCOTT as division commander on 17 Feb 44, getting his second star on 30 May 44. The general innovated a catamaran "battle sled" of narrow, open-topped steel tubes in which a soldier, lying prone, was relatively safe from fire and anti-personnel mines as a medium tank towed a 12-man-team forward. An armored-personnel-

battlefield-expedient, the battle sled performed well enough to get a description and photograph in the US Army's official history. (Fisher, *Cassino to the Alps,* 130-2.)

In May 44 O'Daniel led his division in the Anzio breakout and on through Rome, which fell on 4 June. Then the 3d, 34th, and 36th Divs were pulled out to prepare for the invasion of southern France, and Iron Mike directed amphibious training and landing exercises near Naples, at Pozzuoli. Hitting the beaches around St Tropez on 15 Aug 44 he charged up the Rhone as the direct pressure force, taking the critical defile at Montélimar on the 28th. Although all of Friedrich WIESE's 19th Army might have been trapped if the hard-luck 36th "Texas" Div had seized a critical height in time, 57,000 Germans were captured. (*West Point Atlas*, Map 57.) The Marne division mopped up around Montélimar, while Truscott sent other forces north and east. After the link-up with Eisenhower's main body coming east from Normandy, O'Daniel advanced through the Vosges Mtns and reached Strassbourg on 26 Nov 44. His division then was sent south to help cut off the troublesome **Colmar Pocket,** 23 Jan18 Feb 45. In Wade HAISLIP's 15th Corps of PATCH's 7th Army, on the boundary with PATTON's 3d Army, he drove NE to hit the Siegfried Line south of Zweibruecken on 15 March. Breaking through, O'Daniel crossed the Rhine on 26 March and took part in the wheeling movement SE toward the Alps. In fierce house-to-house fighting he cleared Nuremberg, 17-20 April, took Augsburg and Munich, 27-30 April, and was around Salzburg and Berchtesgaden when the war ended. (*AA,* 521.)

Iron Mike commanded the Infantry School, 28 July 45-1 July 48, led the 1st Corps in the Korean War, being promoted to lieutenant general, and his final active duty was in South Vietnam as chief of the US military and advisory effort, 1954-55.

ODENDHAL, Jean Ernest. French admiral. 1884-1957. Born 14 Dec 84 in Brest (Finistère) Odendhal (or Odend'hal) was the son of a wholesale merchant. He took command of the naval war college in Mar 38 and was promoted to *vice-amiral* on 3 July 38. The admiral headed the French naval mission in London 1 Sep

39-1 June 40, being promoted during this tour of duty to *vice-amiral d'escadre* and awarded the British DSC.

Under a Vichy decree of 16 Nov 40 the admiral was president of the high commission on shipwrecks until his 56th birthday on 14 Dec 43. Thereafter on the retired list, Odendhal was named grand officer of the legion of honor in 1951. He died 19 Mar 57 at Bohars (Finistère). (Official records, French Navy.)

ODETTE. *See* Odette SANSOM.

O'DONNELL, Emmett, Jr. US general. 1906-71. "Rosy" O'Donnell, so known more for a cheery, Irish disposition than his pink complexion, was born 15 Sep 06 in Brooklyn. A West Point football star and later a coach there, he graduated in 1928 (228/261) and became an airman. In what allegedly was the first such flight in history, Maj O'Donnell led nine B-17s to Manila in Sep 41 as CO, 14th Bomb Sqdn, 19th Gp. When MacArthur's air force, under BRERETON, was caught on the ground by the initial Japanese attack on 8 Dec 41 (local date) O'Donnell managed to get airborne, to bomb two enemy warships, and to land despite flats in both wheels. When all his planes and fields were out of action, the ebullient Rosy O'Donnell formed what he called a "dismounted bombardment group" until he could fly to India with what was left of his squadron.

Having won three DFCs and the Air Medal (Cullum) he returned to the States in 1943, spent a year in Hq **AAF** and was promoted to BG. O'Donnell then he took command of the 73d Bomb Wing, 20th AF (B-29 Superfortresses) at Salina, Kan, and trained it for six months. Promoted on 22 Feb 44, Maj Gen O'Donnell flew his wing to Saipan later that year. On 24 Nov 44 he piloted the lead B-29 in a 3,200-mile round trip with 111 Superfortresses to bomb Tokyo for the first time since the DOOLITTLE raid of Apr 42. For this and later strategic bombing attacks on Japan he won the DSM, SS, and oak leaf clusters for his DFC and AM (Cullum).

On 1 Oct 48 the general became head of the Strategic Air Command's 15th AF with headquarters in Colorado Springs. He headed it until 1953 but during the Korean War was CG, FEAF Bomb Cmd (1950-51), winning the DSC. Promoted in 1953, the youthful Lt Gen O'Donnell spent six years as USAF director of personnel (DSC/P). He then he was CinC, Pacific Air Force, 1959-63, retiring as a full general to become national president of the USO and a board director with various companies. Hearty to the end (personal knowledge) he died suddenly on 26 Dec 71 at his home in McLean, Va.

O'HARE, Edward Henry. US ace. 1914-43. A naval pilot for whom the Chicago airport is named, "Butch" O'Hare graduated from the USNA in 1937 (252/323). In the first fight between carrier-type planes Lt O'Hare won the Medal of Honor and was promoted to lieutenant commander for downing five "Kates" on 20 Feb 42. The feat was performed about 400 mi ENE of Rabaul against land based planes and often in full view of cheering US crewmen of *Lexington* and its task force. One of O'Hare's victims tried to crash on the carrier. (Morison, III, 267.)

After winning a Navy Cross and additional fame as a "gallant and resourceful pilot, one of the best in the Navy" (Morison, VII, 143) he was killed on 26 Nov 43, the victim of a **snafu.** This occurred during what probably was the first radar-directed night action of a **CAP.** Before O'Hare and another Hellcat pilot could link up with the Grumman TBF Avenger that was supposed to control the action, the Avenger shot down "tail-end Charlie" of the incoming torpedo-bombers. Surprised, the Japanese broke formation and began firing on one another. In the ensuing melee O'Hare was shot down, "by whom nobody knows." (Morison, VII, 143).

OIKAWA, Koshiro. Japanese admiral and statesman. 1883-1958. A 1903 graduate of the naval academy and naval adjutant to Crown Prince Hirohito from 1915 to 1922, Oikawa was a vice admiral in 1938, when he commanded the Japanese Fleet in China. In 1939 he was a full admiral. Moving from his headquarters in Shanghai he took over from Zengo YOSHIDA as minister of the navy on 5 Sep 40. His selection was part of a program to put compliant admirals in top positions as the army-dominated government moved toward war. Although Oikawa openly accused Foreign Minister MATSUOKA of being "queer in the head" (Bergamini, 761 & n.) he forced the navy to accept the **Tripartite pact** (ibid., 794). Signed on 27 Sep 40 this led to the fall of the last KONOYE government on 16 Oct 41. Succeeded by the compliant Shigetaro SHIMADA, Oikawa was on the Supreme War Council until mid-Nov 43. He then headed the new Grand Escort Command Hq, controlling four escort carriers and the 901st Naval Air Group in a desperate but hopeless effort to reduce mounting Japanese merchant shipping losses to US submarines. (Toland, *Sun,* 478.)

On 21 Feb 44, as pessimism about the war's outcome mounted in Tokyo, Tojo ordered changes that included Osani NAGANO's dismissal of as chief of the naval staff.

Shimada apparently took the post as an extra duty (Toland, 474), but on 2 Aug 44 the emperor named Oikawa to the position (Morison, VI, 17n). Japanese naval defeats continuing and US forces beginning the conquest of Okinawa on 1 Apr 45, Oikawa was succeeded by Soemu TOYODA on 20 May 45 (Morison, VI, 17n.).

OKAWA, Shumei. Japanese militarist. 1886?-1957. The only Japanese war criminal released on grounds of insanity, he was charged with contriving the Mukden Incident (1931) and lesser plots. (*EB* obits.)

OKTYABRSKY, Filip Sergeyevich. Soviet naval officer. 1899-1969. Born 23 Oct 99 in the village of Lukshino, now in Kaliningrad Oblast, he entered the Red Navy in 1918 and joined the CP a year later. In Feb 38 he took command of the Amur Military Flotilla, and from Mar 39 headed the Black Sea Fleet. A rear admiral in June 40, Oktyabrsky was promoted to vice admiral in June 41.

He took part in what Soviet historians call the Western Ukraine Defense Operation, 22 June-6 July 41 (HFS), and as head of the entire Black Sea Fleet he directed Odessa's land defenses from 27 July 41. The admiral's evacuation of that city the night of 15-16 Oct 41 "was a major feat which shone out amidst the confusion and chaos which ruled elsewhere" (Erickson, *To Stalingrad,* 211). Two weeks later Oktyabrsky was in overall command of the Sevastopol defenses (against MANSTEIN) while I. Ye PETROV headed the Coastal Army. Evacuated by submarine at the last moment, 30 Jun 42, on orders from Moscow, Oktyabrsky continued to direct the Black Sea Fleet until May 43. Temporarily succeeded by Vice Adm Vladimirsky (Mitchell, *Soviet Sea Power*, 405) and stepping down to head the Amur Military Flotilla from June 43, he moved back to head the Black Sea Fleet in Mar 44. In that year he was promoted to full admiral.

Remaining Black Sea Fleet commander he was First Deputy CinC of the Navy until 1950. Oktyabrsky then took over the directorate in the Central Naval apparatus but was almost immediately retired. His offense was criticizing BERIA and BULGANIN over creation of a separate navy. In limbo for seven years he emerged in 1957 to head the Black Sea Higher Naval School and was made a HSU on 20 Feb 58. Two years later he joined the General Inspector's Group. The admiral died 8 July 69 in Sevastapol. (Scotts.)

OLDENDORF, Jesse Barrett. US admiral. 1887-1974. A burly Californian, born 16 Feb 87, "Oley" graduated from Annapolis in 1909 (141/174). In 1942-43 he was a rear admiral commanding the Aruba-Curaçao Area, with the main task of rescuing U-boat victims, then **NOB** Trinidad. During the period Apr-Dec 43 he commanded TF 24 convoy escorts based at Argentia in SE Newfoundland. In Jan 44 he assumed command of Cruiser Div 4 in HALSEY's 3d Fleet and for the next year led battleship-cruiser gunfire support groups. Oley took part in the Kwajalein Atoll landings that began 31 Jan 44, the Eniwetok landings that began 17 Feb 44 (see NIMITZ), then on 30 Apr 44 shelled Satawan (SE of Truk). His task group delivered preparatory fires before the Saipan landings, then supported the landings on Tinian, and Peleliu and Angaur, 13 Sep 44.

Leyte Gulf

Assigned to KINKAID's 7th Fleet for the Leyte campaign, Rear Adm Olendorf commanded all naval forces until Kinkaid arrived 20 Oct 44. (Morison, XII, 118.) There was little opposition to the landings on 17-20 Oct 44. But then came what a naval historial has called one of the greatest operations of all time (Morison,

XII, 159): fighting off the Japanese SHO-1 plan that is outlined under Takeo KURITA.

About noon on 24 Oct 44 Kinkaid alerted all ships in Leyte Gulf, including merchantmen, for a night engagement. He correctly estimated "that Nishimura's Southern Force would try to penetrate Leyte Gulf via Suriago Strait that night" (Morison, XII, 198). On short notice Olendorf moved out with his six old but modernized battleships, four heavy cruisers, four light cruisers, 28 destroyers, and 39 PT boats. They went forward to form what a landlubber would call an outpost line, its mission being to detect, delay, and deceive the attacker.

Nishimura's "C Force" approached with two battleships, a heavy cruiser, and four destroyers (Morison, XII, 431). The Battle of Suriago Strait opened just before midnight with sustained PT boat attacks until 2:15 AM Olendorf's force scored only one hit (on a destroyer) but sent invaluable contact reports. Flanking US destroyers began an hour of torpedo attacks at 2:45, knocking out one battleship and three destroyers, almost half the attacking force. But Nishimura steamed on and was engaged at 3:51 by the American cruisers. Three minutes later all six US battleships began shooting at targets revealed by radar.

Olley had realized the naval tactician's dream of "crossing the T." That is, he had maneuvered into line so all guns could fire broadside on a enemy that was in column, hence concentrated, able to use only forward guns, and having a dispersed target. Under a hail of heavy metal and his ships badly battered, Nishimura turned back at 4:10 AM. Ten minutes later he and most of the crew went down with the stricken flagship, BB *Yamashiro*. Only one other ship and crew of C Force survived, DD *Shigure,* whose steering engine was out of order.

But about 40 miles behind C Force came Vice Adm K. Shima's Second Striking Force. He had moved south from Japan with two heavy cruisers, one light cruiser, and four destroyers (RCS). Shima's light cruiser was hit by a PT boat on the way in (and later sunk by gunfire), but as late as 4:20 AM the Japanese admiral still thought he was coming to take charge of the battle. Five minutes later, not finding friend or foe, Shima ordered a withdrawal at high speed; in the pursuit phase he lost two destroyers. At 10:18 AM (25 Oct 44) the skipper of DD *Shigure* sent a message to Tokyo and KURITA: "All ships [of C Force] except *Shigure* went down under gunfire and torpedo attack." (Morison, 238.) This influenced KURITA's decision to withdraw (ibid.). The battles for Leyte Gulf were over. Olendorf and "Ziggy" SPRAGUE (opposing Kurita) were the heroes.

In Dec 44 Olendorf was promoted to vice admiral commanding BB Sqdn 1. On 3 Jan 45 his TG 77.2 left Leyte to support the landings in Lingayen Gulf. While at Ulithi to assist in planning the Okinawa campaign he and his CofS were badly injured on 11 Mar 45 when the boat taking them from shore to the flagship *Tennessee* hit a mooring buoy. Olendorf did not return to duty until 1 May 45. He subsequently commanded TF 95 off Okinawa with the primary mission of providing gunfire support until resistance ended on 22 June. TF 95 then provided radar picket stations whose primary mission was to ward off kamikaze attacks. Wounded in one of these in August he was invalided home and on recovery was commander of the 11th Naval District in San Diego. His last assignment was as Commander, Western Sea Frontier, from 1947 until retiring on 1 Sep 49 as a full admiral. He died 22 Apr 74 at the Portsmouth, Va, USNH.

ONISHI, Takijiro. Japanese admiral. 1891-1945. Born in Hyogo Prefecture (western Honshu), Onishi graduated from the NA in 1912 and was among the first Japanese military aviators. After serving in Britain and France as a resident officer (1918-20) he was promoted to lieutenant commander and he taught at the Kasumiga Ura Naval Air School (1925) before commanding the Sasebo Naval Air Unit. Joining the 3d Fleet Hq at Shanghai he helped plan the air assaults on the city in Feb-Mar 32 and was promoted to captain the next year. Onishi began advocating that carriers be the fleet's main striking force.

In Oct 41 Army CofS Sugiyama made a memorandum that, not public until 1967, sheds new light on Emperor Hirohito's personal involvement in the war. "In January 1941," the telegraphic-style document reads, "in answer to Commander of Grand Fleet Yamamoto, Emperor ordered Rear Admiral Onishi to research Hawaii attack." (Bergamini, 737 n.) Onishi turned the work over to Comdr Genda Minoru, who as head Japan's Self-Defense Air Force wrote after the war "that the attack would be extremely hazardous but would have a reasonable chance of success." (Quoted by Bergamini, 736.) A rear admiral from 1939 and 11th Air Fleet CofS from Jan 41, Onishi—a close friend of Prince Takamatsu's—is credited by most authorities with having had a prominent role with other members of the Emperor's Cabal in Genda's quick feasibility study during the first two weeks of Feb 41 (ibid.).

Having conceived of using kamikaze assaults against the converging US offensives of Nimitz and MacArthur toward the Philippines, Vice Adm Onishi (since 1943) was appointed 2 Oct 44 to command the 1st Air Fleet in Opn Sho Go. He flew into Nichols Field, near Manila, on 17 October as air strikes destroyed many Japanese planes and damaged their bases on Luzon. Reports two days later of mounting US activity in Leyte Gulf added urgency to the Japanese admiral's directive to launch his "divine thunder" (Millot, 37) in support of KURITA's main effort in the battle for Leyte Gulf, 23-26 Oct 44.

The admiral became vice chief of the naval staff in Tokyo on May 45 and was a die-hard advocate of fighting to the death. On hearing the emperor's surrender broadcast he committed suicide at home on 15 Aug 45.

OPPELN-BRONIKOWSKI, Hermann von. German general. 1899-. Born 2 Jan 99 in Berlin he followed his father into the army. In 1918 he was awarded the Iron Cross 1st Class. As an equestrian in the Berlin Olympics, 1936, the dashing cavalryman won a gold medal. In 1939 Maj Oppeln Bronikowski led a reconnaissance unit in Poland and took it west for the campaign against France. In Russia he commanded the 35th Pz Regt, then the 204th Pz Regt. On 1 Jan 43 Col Oppeln-Bronikowski was awarded the RK for actions near the Don River. After recovering from serious wounds, he commanded the 22d Pz Regt in France and on 28 July 44 was awarded the Oakleaves

(536/890) for action around Caen (Angolia, I, 256). He was given command of the hard-pressed 20th Pz Div in East Prussia on 7 Nov 44 and—despite his youth by German army standards—promoted on 30 Jan 45 to Generalmajor. Driven back to Berlin, and lacking tank replacements, his division was annihilated in May 45. Oppeln-Bronikowski meanwhile was among the last recipients of the Swords (142/159), awarded on 17 Apr 45 (Angolia, I, 257).

OPPENHEIMER, J(ulius) Robert. Nuclear physicist. 1904-67. Born in NYC, son of a highly successful Jewish businessman who had come from Germany at the age of 17, he was educated at Harvard (BA 1925), Cambridge, and Goettingen (PhD 1927). Frail, intense, and unwordly, the physicist taught at the Univ of California and the California Inst of Technology, 1929-47. Throughout the 1930s he built a reputation in theoretical physics, making important contributions to quantum theory. Oppenheimer's broad outside interests included foreign languages, art, literature, and politics. (Briggs, ed.)

After the **Manhattan Project** was created in late 1942 Oppenheimer helped out until COMPTON asked him to take charge of theoretical problems concerning the atomic bomb's design (Groueff, 41). When a leader was needed to coordinate work of the many scientists involved in the Manhattan Project Col (later major general) Leslie R. GROVES selected Oppenheimer. There was considerable objection from other scientists including Compton and Vannevar BUSH, who had doubts about the odd, young Oppenheimer's leadership qualities for the task. The FBI had a thick dossier to support the position that Oppenheimer should be denied a security clearance because of his earlier left-wing associations. (Groueff, 40 ff, 66, 251-60 passim), but Groves disregarded the evidence.

As director of the Los Alamos, NM, site, Manhattan Project Hq from 1943, Oppenheimer became "father of the atomic bomb." Its first test, 16 July 45 at Alamogordo, NM, was successful, and the first two bombs were promptly used on Hiroshima and Nagasaki, 6 and 9 Aug 95.

After the war Oppenheimer became director of the Inst of Advanced Study at Princeton. From 1947 to 1952 he also headed the general advisory committee of the Atomic Energy Commission (AEC). Because of his cold, abrasive manner toward those he did not respect, not to mention the normal professional jealousies, Oppenheimer had many enemies. The foremost was Edmund Teller, who gave the FBI a long secret, highly critical report that was the basis for official charges against Oppenheimer. He was accused (probably falsely) of having obstructed hydrogen bomb development and of consorting (probably innocently) with communists in the 1930s. (Oppenheimer's brother had been a card carrying communist.) It was concluded in late 1953 that the father of the atomic bomb was a security risk, although a loyal American. In June 54 he was stripped of all security clearances, a professional death sentence because almost all significant work in his field is classified. Putting up a brave front but in steadily deteriorating health the scientist retained his post at Princeton until shortly before dying of throat cancer on 18 Feb 67 at the age of 63.

ORLANDO, Vittorio Emanuele. Italian statesman. 1860-1952. When the Fascists gained power in his native Palermo in 1925, the senior statesman resigned from parliament and retired to private life. After Mussolini's fall in July 43 "southerners" Orlando and Benedetto CROCE were courted, along with other national figures, in efforts by various Italian statesmen to form viable new coalition governments. In 1944-46 Orlando was president of the chamber of deputies. He resigned in 1947 to protest signing of the Italian peace treaty, and as a senator opposed foreign policies that countered his strong sense of nationalism. Orlando had been prime minister, 1917-19. As leader of the Italian delegation to the peace conference of 1919 he had tried unsuccessfully to win territorial concessions in Dalmatia for Italy's entering the Allied camp. (*EB* obit.)

OSHIMA, Hiroshi. Japanese diplomat. 1886-1975. The eldest son of former war minister Ken-ichi Oshima (1858-1947), the soldier-diplomat was born in Tokyo. Closely associated with Germany throughout a military career starting in 1906 he was assistant MA in Berlin shortly after WWI. As a major general he was MA in Nazi Germany when Japan joined the Anti-Comintern Pact in 1937. Promoted meanwhile to lieutenant general, and made ambassador 1938 when Shigenori TOGO was transferred from Berlin to Moscow, Oshima was twice replaced temporarily in 1939 and 1940 as ambassador by Saburu KURUSU. After the latter signed the Tripartite Pact in Sep 40 Oshima was ambassador in Berlin for the rest of the war. He was convicted by US occupying powers of war crimes, sentenced to life imprisonment, but freed in 1955.

OSMENA, Sergio. Filipino statesman. 1878-1961. Born 9 Sep 78 in Cebu of humble parentage, a mestizo of Chinese and native blood, the tall, dignified, noncharismatic Osmeña became a lawyer. In 1906 he was elected governor of Cebu Prov and sent to Manila as a member of the house of representatives. After being speaker of the house, 1907-22, he became a senator and leading nationalist. On passage of the Independence Act of 15 Nov 35 he became Manuel L. QUEZON's VP and his principal political challenger. With five other high officials the two men were evacuated from Corregidor on 20 Feb 42 by the submarine *Swordfish*. Alternately a political ally and opponent of the more dynamic Quezon, and in Washington since May 42 with the government in exile, Osmeña became the second president of the Philippine Commonwealth after the long-ailing Quezon died on 1 Aug 44.

Although the new president of the Philippines was not highly regarded by MacArthur, who favored Manuel ROXAS, Osmeña accompanied MacArthur on his triumphal return to the Philippines, 20 Oct 44. Wading ashore on Leyte in the well-photographed group were the Philippine Army CofS Basilio Valdez, and Carlos ROMULO (MacArthur, *Reminiscences*, 216). Osmeña was there with great reluctance because he knew that as head of the civil government he had no real power; this was exercised by the imperious American general's civil affairs section. There also was disagreement over how to handle collaborators in LAUREL's puppet government: the Americans favored summary execution; Osmeña insisted on due process of law.

In presidential elections after the Philippines became independent on 4 July 46, Osmeña lost to Roxas.

OSTER, Hans. German resistance leader. 1888-1945. A Saxon born 9 Aug 88 in Dresden, Oster was the son of a Protestant clergyman. As a lieutenant during WWI he won several decorations for valor. Remaining in the army he began a long and close association with Canaris in 1931, when as a lieutenant colonel he was in Muenster as **Ib** on Col Franz Halder's 6th Div staff. The two men were kindred spirits politically, although incongruous in temperament. (Hoehne, Canaris, 259). Oster was brash, cynical, volatile, and a womanizer whom many peers and superiors (notably HOSSBACH) regarded as unfit for general staff duties (ibid). One of his personal traits, "irresponsible carelessness" (ibid.), led to an adulterous affair in 1932 for which he was brought before a court of honor and compelled to resign on 31 Dec 32. (This brings HEYDRICH to mind.) Four months later Oster got a post with Goering's "Research Department," a phone-tapping operation. Quickly tiring of this he entered the Abwehr as a civilian employee in counter-intelligence work and fell under the wing of GISEVIUS. When Canaris took over the Abwehr on 2 Jan 35 Maj Oster was classified as an *Ergaenzungoffizier,* and shortly after the **Munich crisis** of Sep 38 he was promoted to full colonel.

From 1938 Col Oster headed the Abwehr's Central Section (Abteilung Z), charged with organization and administration on behalf of the four other Abwehr sections. Promoted a year later, Generalmajor Oster was already an anti-Nazi conspirator and his office was ideally suited to support the anti-Hitler resistance, having the following staff sections: ZArch (records), ZK (central card index), ZKV (agents, central card index), ZReg (filing, administration of materials and equipment), ZB (foreign policy, under DOHNANYI), ZO (officers' personnel records), ZF (finance), and ZR (legal). (Hoehne, *Canaris,* endpaper chart.) Oster also was CofS to Canaris, who saw that the Abwehr was stocked with anti-Nazis and who was clever at maintaining a modus vivendi with HIMMLER and HEYDRICH.

But Canaris worried that his deputy "was so engrossed in his preparations for a *coup d'état* that he barely discerned the dangers that threatened his work," writes Hoehne. "Besides, he did not fear a surprise move by the Gestapo and could not conceive of one from any other quarter. The result was that, when the other side finally struck, he and his friends displayed an almost suicidal inability to cope." (Ibid, 515.)

Betrayal by Wilhelm SCHMIDHUBER led to DOHNANYI's arrest on 5 Apr 43 and the undoing of Oster and Dietrich BONHOEFFER. Oster misunderstood DOHNANYI's whispered message and was caught trying to pocket an incriminating document. But it was not for 10 days that outside pressure forced Canaris to dismiss his troublesome subordinate (15 Apr 43). The conspiracy crippled at a critical time, Oster was sent on leave and placed under house arrest in Leipzig. On 19 June 43 he was transferred to the "leadership reserve," and finally released from active duty effective 4 Mar 44. This authorized the Gestapo to put him under permanent surveillance. (Hoffmann, 294.)

"The blow suffered by the opposition [on 5 Apr 43] was so devastating and so dangerous that for the moment all thoughts of further action had to be abandoned," leadership of the conspirators passing to STAUFFENBERG. (Ibid.) After the latter's bomb attempt on 20 July 44 Oster and CANARIS were among the many arrested. KEITEL saved them and four other key Abwehr conspirators from the People's Court until after the Abwehr records of the conspiracy were found on 22 Sep 44. The documents included Oster's three-page study on how the coup d'état was to be conducted, but he and others were kept alive because the Gestapo hoped to get more information. On 6 Feb 45 the Gestapo began to move prize prisoners to concentration camps where they were in less danger of being killed by bombs or liberated by advancing enemy troops.

Discovery of the CANARIS diaries on or about 4 Apr 45 finally revealed the full scope of the conspiracy. After reading a few passages marked by KALTENBRUNNER, Hitler ordered immediate liquidation of the plotters. A summary trial of DOHNANYI was held at Oranienburg/ Sachenhausen on 7 April under

Standartenfuehrer Walter Huppenkothen and three associates (Hoehne, 592). That evening the same court, reinforced by SS Judge Otto Thornbeck, moved to Flossenbuerg. There at 4 PM on the 8th began the farcical trial of Oster, CANARIS, Dietrich BONHOEFFER, a Capt Gehre of the Abwehr, and ex-Army judge Karl Sack. Oster appeared first and, having abandoned hope, he not only vehemently admitted everything but also incriminated CANARIS. The latter appeared next and continued denying the charge of treason. But when Thornbeck called Oster back for a personal confrontation, CANARIS finally confessed. The others followed. That evening the court pronounced the death sentence on all men. Shortly after 6 o'clock the next morning, 9 Apr 45, Canaris was hanged, followed by Oster, Dietrich BONHOEFFER, and the two others. (Huppenkothen and Thornbeck were convicted in 1955 of abetting murder and sentenced to seven years of penal servitude.)

OUMANSKY, Constantine A. *See* UMANSKY.

OZAWA, Jisaburo. Japanese admiral. 1886-1966. One of the principal Japanese naval commanders throughout the war, Ozawa graduated from the NA in 1909. He was promoted to rear admiral in 1936 and the next year was appointed CofS, Combined Fleet. In 1940 he became a vice admiral and president of the NA. Two months before hostilities started in the Pacific he became responsible for naval operations in the South China Sea—the waters off the Malay Peninsula and the NEI. (Morison, III, 273.) Operating from Camranh Bay, Indochina, he put troops of the 16th Army ashore to take Sumatra and Java, from Jan to Mar 42.

Allied resistance including that of the **ABDACOM** crushed, Ozawa raised havoc with merchant shipping in the Bay of Bengal. With a TF built around CV *Ryujo* (5 CAs and many DDs) he hit Colombo, Ceylon, on 5 Apr 42 and Tricomalee on the 9th. (Morison, III, 384-85.)

Ozawa then commanded the main Japanese carrier force known as the Mobile Fleet, based initially at Lingga Roads, near Singapore. Soon after US amphibious forces hit Saipan on 15 June 44 the fleet was sent to destroy the dangerous new American offensive. But after events covered under KURITA the Mobile Fleet was decimated by Marc MITSCHER in the "Great Marianas Turkey Shoot."

The Japanese high command recalled Ozawa's crippled carrier fleet to the Sea of Japan in an effort to reconstitute it. But when the Japanese made their last major naval effort, which ended disastrously in the battle for Leyte Gulf, 23-26 Oct 44, Osawa's carriers were useful only as a decoy. (*See* KURITA.)

Reverting to his former position of Commander, 3d Fleet, Ozawa set up a forlorn hope to destroy US surface units supporting the troops on Okinawa. A task force was built around *Yamato,* which with *Musashi* (sunk under KURITA on 24 Oct 44) had been the pride of the Japanese navy. Having fuel only for a one-way trip and lacking adequate air cover, *Yamato* lasted one day after leaving the Sea of Japan, sunk on 7 Apr 45. (Morison, XIV, 199-208.) Ozawa, who had not accompanied TF Yamato, commanded the Combined Fleet from headquarters in Tokyo at war's end. He cooperated with MORISON on the naval historian's 15-vol history.

P

PACELLI, Eugenio. See PIUS XII.

PAGET, Bernard Charles Tolver. British general. 1887-1961. He was born 15 Sep 87 at Oxford, where his father was canon of Christ Church, becoming dean (1892) and bishop of Oxford (1901). Paget's maternal grandfather was dean of St. Paul's. (*DNB*.) Educated at Shrewsbury and Sandhurst, he was commissioned (1907) in the Oxfordshire and Buckinghamshire Lt Inf. After a winter in England with a battalion of this regiment he joined its 1st Bn in India and was on home leave when war broke out in 1914. Lt Paget was made adjutant of the regiment's new 5th (service) Bn and he accompanied it to France in May 15. Six months later he left the battalion to be brigade major of the 14th Lt Div and he promptly won the MC.

In Oct 17, having been promoted, Capt Paget left the trenches to be GSO 2 at 62d Div Hq and then moved up to BEF Hq. Already twice wounded he had his left arm permanently crippled in Mar 18, two months after winning appointment to the DSO. During the war he was mentioned four times in dispatches.

After distinguishing himself as commandant of the Quetta staff college in India and a general officer at the end of 1937, he was commandant at Camberley 1938-39 and was CIGS IRONSIDE's CofS briefly when that general took over the top British Army post from DILL. In Nov 39 Paget assumed command of the 18th Div, then stationed in East Anglia, getting the normal promotion to major general (T).

Summoned "literally on a moment's notice" in Apr 40 *(DNB)* Maj Gen Paget was sent to support Gen Otto RUGE's Norwegian forces. Hailed in these days of "too little too late," as "the hero of Trondheim" he extricated British and French troops from a hopeless situation. Returning to England he headed the new Southeastern Command, was promoted to lieutenant general in 1941, and was viewed as a candidate for CIGS. But Paget instead took command of the Home Forces in late Dec 41 when BROOKE left to be CIGS.

Sir Bernard (KCB in 1942) was promoted to general and for two years he performed brilliantly. Forming the 21st Army Group of 15 divisions for the Normandy invasion he prepared them for modern war in exercises that included the then controversial use of live ammunition and became hailed as Britain's troop trainer since the legendary Sir John Moore (1761-1809). But on 23 Dec 43 he was put aside as 21st AG commander by the more highly acclaimed Gen Sir Bernard MONTGOMERY.

Swallowing his disappointment, Sir Bernard became CinC, Middle East, in Jan 44. He showed diplomatic and military skill in frustrating French efforts to regain influence in Syria and Lebanon, and in dealing with the mutinous Greek army and naval forces of GEORGE II's troubled government in exile.

He retired at his own request in Oct 46. Honored by elevation in the knighthood to GCB, Paget was active for another decade until retiring to his home, The Old Orchard, Petersfield, Hampshire, where he died here suddenly on 16 Feb 61.

PALEWSKI, Gaston. French official. 1901-84. Born 20 Mar 01 in Paris into an expatriate family of Polish Jews, Palweski held degrees from the **Science-Po** and Oxford. As Paul Reynaud's chef de cabinet in 1934 he first met de Gaulle. Hélène de PORTES is commonly blamed for Palweski's sudden departure as Reynaud's devoted confidant on 19 Feb 39 (Pertinax, 107). But there is evidence that Reynaud sacrificed his paladin to placate Daladier, who was in power and who had an aversion to Palweski. Joining the French air force in 1940 Palweski was de Gaulle's political and military delegate in the Sudan and East Africa 1940-42 (de Gaulle, *Unity,* 170). Then he was responsible for restoring the administration of French territory as it was liberated.

Palweski was involved after the war in planning France's entry into the atomic club. With other Gaullist ministers he left the government on 6 Oct 55 but became ambassador to Rome

(1957-62) and was minister of scientific research, atomic affairs, and space (14 Apr 62-23 Feb 65). De Gaulle named Palweski president of the constitutional council in 1964, and for the next nine years he directed the drafting of a new French constitution. In 1969 he married Violette Talleyrand-Perigord, Duchess of Sagan and of Dino.

PAPAGOS, Alexander. Greek statesman. 1883-1955. Gen Papagos was minister of war by 1935 and army CofS the next year. As CinC of the Greek army he drove back the Italians who invaded on 28 Oct 40. But he could do little to stop the German assault that LIST launched on 6 Apr 41. The next month Papagos was arrested after an army coup preceded the Greek surrender. In 1943 he became a hostage in Germany, ending up in Dachau. Liberated by US troops in 1945, he became head of the Greek Rally Party. In 1949, after VAN FLEET was sent to head the US mission in the war against communism in Greece, US authorities prevailed on Papagos to head an army that badly needed purging. Promoted to field marshal, Papagos was premier when he died in 1955.

PAPANDREOU, Georgios Andreas. Greek statesman. 1888-1968. A great-grandson of Queen Victoria, Papandreou was born in Jan 88 at Patras. He became a lawyer and entered national politics in 1923. During most of the METAXAS dictatorship Papandreou was an exile on Greek islands, and after the German takeover he was jailed as a subversive.

British agents brought him to Cairo in an effort to establish some order in King George II's chaotic government-in-exile. Becoming premier on 26 Apr 44, Papandreou replaced the short-lived cabinets of Sophocles Venizelos and Emmanuel Tsouderos. Under British pressure the Caserta agreement of 26 Sep 44 pledged rival guerrilla chiefs Stephanos SARAPHIS and Napoleon ZERVAS to recognize Papandreou's political authority and the military authority of Lt Gen Sir Ronald Scobie's British forces. These landed in southern Greece on 4 Oct 44 and within two weeks Papandreou's Provisional Administration was in Athens. Two months later a Greek civil war was raging. On Christmas eve Churchill flew with Eden to Greece, where they were met by ALEXANDER, MACMILLAN,

and Ambassador Reginald W. Leeper. Churchill decided that Greek factions could be reconciled only by Archbishop Damaskinos, whom the king appointed regent on 30 Dec 44. (WC, VI, 322.) Papandreou was succeeded by Gen Plastiras as premier on 4 Jan 45 but remained prominent in Greek affairs.

PAPEN, Franz von. German statesman. 1879-1969. Papen was born 29 Oct 79 at Werl into a noble Prussian family of Catholic and monarchist convictions. Having grown into a wealthy dandy, army officer, and gentleman jockey, he was MA in Mexico City and Washington until expelled in 1916 by US authorities for inept espionage and sabotage efforts. Early in 1919 he left the army and entered politics to conspire with SCHLEICHER to destroy the Weimar Republic. Papen was chancellor briefly under HINDENBURG in 1932, then Hitler's vice chancellor from 30 Jan 33. Having hinted in a remarkable address on 17 June 34 that Germany needed more free speech, less Nazi terrorism, a multi-party system, and restoration of the monarchy, it is remarkable that Papen survived the **Blood Purge of 1934** a fortnight later. But for some reason Goering ordered him into virtual house arrest under SS guard for three days (Papen, 315). Refusing to accept Papen's resignation on 3 July 34 Hitler sent him to Vienna a month later when Chancellor DOLLFUSS was murdered.

As the minister to Austria, Papen proved to be useful until after the **Anschluss.** He was recalled on 4 Feb 39 and told on 7 April that he would be ambassador to Turkey. Papen accepted with great reluctance but performed competently. When Stalin learned in the summer of 1942 that the Pope and US government agents were approaching the ambassador about making a separate peace with the west and succeeding Hitler, an enraged Stalin ordered the ambassador's assassination. The attempt failed because the Bulgarian hit man lost his nerve and detonated his bomb prematurely, killing himself and only slightly wounding his victim. (Sudoplatov, 35, 115-16.) The Cicero affair involving Elyesa BAZNA took place on Papen's watch.

After Turkey abandoned her neutrality and severed diplomatic relations with Germany the ambassador left Ankara on 5 Aug 44. He had good reason to fear sharing the fate of "aristocrats" whom HITLER was having hunted down along with conspirators implicated in STAUF-FENBERG's 20 July 44 bomb plot. Being marked for liquidation by Stalin for reasons stated above did help either. But there was something else to worry Papen: he had drafted the political testament in which HINDENBURG recommended that Hitler revive the monarchy, and it was not until 1939 that the Gestapo had been made to stop trying to prove Papen had sent the original document to a Swiss bank vault (Papen, 440-41).

Hitler received Papen cordially, but the edgy ex-ambassador soon learned that the Gestapo was opening his mail and maintaining surveillance. As US forces approached his estate at Wallerfangen in the Siegfried Line he was ordered to move eastward with the retreating German forces. Papen was in Westphalia at the home of a married daughter at Stockhausen when US authorities took him into custody on 10 Apr 45. After four years under guard he was charged at Nuremberg only with conspiring to wage war. He was found to have supported the Nazis at critical times but, like NEURATH, had no trouble proving that he had always opposed the war (Davidson, *Trial,* 177). Acquittal on 1 Oct 46 having caused intense German resentment, a civil court on 1 Feb 47 pronounced him a "major offender" and sentenced him to eight years in a labor camp and forfeiture of property. After appeal and another trial he was freed in Jan 49 but fined 30,000 marks, stripped of his state pension, denied the right to hold office or work at anything but ordinary labor, and deprived of his driver's license! (Davidson, *Trial,* 176.)

His unrepentant, self-serving, but interesting autobiography is *Der Wahrheit eine Gasse* (Munich: Paul List, 1952), first translated into English translation as the *Franz von Papen Memoirs* (London: Andrew Deutsch, 1952). He died 2 May 69 in Obersasbach at the age of 89.

PARK, Keith Rodney. British general. 1892-1975. A senior RAF commander largely responsible for the "miracle of Dunkirk" and British victory in the Battle of Britain, Park was a New Zealander.

He was born 15 June 92 in Thames, NZ, youngest son of James Park, director of the Thames School of Mines and later Professor at the Univ of Otago. He received a solid mining education in New Zealand but went to sea as a purser. The outbreak of war in 1914 further arousing his sense of adventure, he volunteered as an artilleryman and won a regular commission in 1915 after fighting with the NZ Expeditionary Force at Gallipoli. In France he was "so severly wounded (for the second time) on the Somme that he was relegated to Woolwich as artillery officer instructor" (D. N. Davin in *DNB*). By 1917 he had recovered sufficiently to volunteer for the RFC, rising to command No. 48 Sqdn and win the MC and bar that year. In 1918 he joined the new RAF and was promoted to captain.

In Apr 40 the tall, lean, modest airman took command of No. 11 Fgtr Gp, the only one committed to cover the Dunkirk evacuation, 29 May-5 June 40. (Hugh DOWDING husbanded the other three for what he knew would follow.) With 16 of Ftr Cmd's 58 squadrons—about 200 Hurricanes and Spitfires—Park could keep only one squadron over the beachhead at a time. But by rotating them for the allowable 40 minutes of patrol time he maintained continuous air cover and (helped by bad weather) he gained local air superiority. The Luftwaffe was shocked to find itself outclassed by the Spitfire and its relatively green pilots.

Air Vice Marshal Park (promoted in July) had the major role in the Battle of Britain. Covering the main approaches SE London with No. 11 Group's main operations center at Uxbridge he had seven defensive sectors. Each had an operations room controlling three fighter squadrons of about 12 planes each. Getting radar reports of incoming German flights "Park, through his controller, would order the individual sectors to put up squadrons in accordance with his own swiftly conceived plan of battle, and the sector controllers would direct their individual squadrons from that moment" (Andrews, *The Air Marshalls* 108) Churchill frequently visited Uxbridge, a short drive from central London. After spending much of a particularly harrowing day there in mid-Aug 40, when at one point Park had committed his last squadron, Churchill coined the phrase "Never in the field of human conflict so much been owed by so many to so few." (*See* Ismay, 181-82.)

Although Dowding and Park are generally credited with winning the Battle of Britain, 8 Aug-31 Oct 40, PORTAL replaced both with their principal critics within a month after he became **CAS** on 25 Oct 40. DOWDING was succeeded by Sholto DOUGLAS, who promptly replaced Park with LEIGH-MALLORY. The RAF "intrigue," as the embittered Park called it, revolved around the **big wing controversy.**

Park was ordered to take a rest as head of a training group before being hustled out of Britain. But he still had full scope for his proven abilities: in the fall of 1941 he became **AOC** at Allied Hq in Egypt; and on 15 July 42 he was made AOC Malta. Here, after addressing the problem of defending the embattled island, covering supply convoys, and interdicting Axis shipping to North Africa, Park went on the strategic offensive. He furnished air support for British landing forces in Opn Torch (8 Nov 42), the drive to Tunisia, and the invasions of Sicily and Italy in 1943.

In Jan 44 he became Supreme Commander of Air in the Middle East. From Feb 45 he was MOUNTBATTEN's Air CinC in SEAC, directing air support for SLIM in Burma. Air Chief Marshal Sir Keith Park (KCB, 1945; GCB, 1946) retired in 1946 to his native New Zealand. He died in Auckland in 1975.

PASSY, Colonel. *See* Andrew DEWAVWARIN.

PATCH, Alexander McCarrell, Jr. US general. 1889-1945. "Sandy" Patch was born on 23 Nov 89 at Ft Huachuca, Ariz, son of a cavalry captain. Appointed from Pennsylvania he graduated from West Point in 1913 (75/93) and joined the 13th Inf Regt in Texas. He took part in the **Punitive Expedition** to Mexico and accompanied his regiment to France. Rising in little more than a year from captain to lieutenant colonel and taking part in all major US offensives, Patch was involved primarily in training, machine guns being his specialty. *(CB 43.)*

Patch performed normal peacetime duties, was a distinguished graduate of the C&GSS (1925), but had the remarkable experience of spending 12 years (in three tours of duty) as PMS&T at the Staunton MA in Va between 1921 and 1936. *(Cullum.)* He then was on the Infantry Board at Ft Benning, Ga, before being sent to the Alabama NG Hq at Montgomery, Ala.

Promoted to colonel, he headed the recruit camp at Ft Bragg, NC, before taking over the IRTC at Camp Croft, SC.

As the Japanese pushed into the South Pacific after attacking Pearl Harbor, the major Allied priority was to secure a LofC with Australia. Patch was rushed to New Caledonia, promoted to major general (10 Mar 42), and on Noumea he formed the Americal Div. Its 164th Regt reached Guadalcanal on 13 Oct 42 to reinforce VANDEGRIFT's Marines, who had been under heavy attack around Henderson Field since 7 Aug 42. Following with the rest of his division, Patch launched a counteroffensive. On 2 Jan 43 he took over the new 14th Corps Hq, Brig Gen Edmund Sebree assuming command of the Americal Div. *(AA, 572.)* Patch took overall responsibility for operations on Guadalcanal from VANDEGRIFT on 21 Jan, a fortnight before the last enemy resistance ended (9 Feb 43).

Two months later Maj Gen Patch assumed command of the 4th Corps Hq at Ft Lewis, Wash, concurrently heading the Desert Training Center, Nov 43-Jan 44 *(AA, 604)*. He then headed a staff split between and Algiers and Palermo that was planning the invasion of Southern France.

(Staff personnel were from PATTON's 7th Army Hq, and Mark CLARK had doubled as head of the 7th Army staff since 1 Jan 44. Clark was succeeded on 2 Mar 44 by Patch, who moved to Naples on 4 July 44.)

British strategists still favored invading the Balkans, but EISENHOWER insisted on the logistical need for Marseilles as a port. Not until after the capture of Rome on 4 June 44 and the Normandy landings two days later, did Patch finally know what combat forces he would have. He meanwhile got a third star as of 7 Aug 44.

Opn **Anvil,** later redesignated Dragoon, would begin with the 7th Army's having TRUSCOTT's 6th US Corps and the French 2d Corps, both in Adm Henry K. HEWITT's Western TF. Truscott would command these two corps in the assault landings on the French Riviera, 15 Aug 44, and in the exploitation phase up the Rhone Valley. Then DELATTRE DE TASSIGNY's French Army B, bringing ashore the 1st French Corps, would be under Patch's **operational control.** When DEVERS's 6th AG became operational on 15 Sep 44 at Lyons it comprised Patch's 7th

Army and what now was the 1st French Army under Delattre as its principal components. (*AA,* 490; W*est Point Atlas,* Map 57.)

Operating on the left of AG 6, next to Patton's 3d Army of Bradley's AG 12, Patch drove back elements of BLASKOWITZ's 19th Army through the Vosges. Then, in a masterfully coordinated effort with Patton, particularly in the matter of tactical air support, Patch executed Opn *Undertone*. This breached some of the strongest sections of the West Wall on the old border between Germany and Alsace Lorraine. By 21 Mar 45 Patch and Patton were **pinching off** the deep salient west of the Rhine defended by General of Infantry Hermann Foertsch's die-hard 1st Army. Still opposed by Foertsch, the 7th US and French 1st Armies wheeled southeast toward the phantom **National Redoubt.** Foertsch represented the AG G commander in the surrender to DEVERS on 5 Apr 44, ending the last armed resistance.

When Eisenhower ranked subordinates in value of services as of 1 Feb 45 he put Patch immediately ahead of army commanders HODGES and SIMPSON (*EP,* 2466). Returning to the US Lt Gen Patch commanded the 4th Army at Ft Sam Houston (San Antonio), Texas, from 23 July 45 until his death on 21 Nov 45 at the age of 55. (He was succeeded by WAINWRIGHT.) Posthumous promotion to full general came in 1954.

Five members of the Patch family were West Pointers, the last four of them infantrymen, and most died young. Capt Alexander M. Patch III (USMA 1942) was killed on 22 Oct 44 in Europe with the 79th Inf Div, winning the DSC, SS, BSM, and three Purple Hearts. A second grandson of Alexander senior was Richard King Patch (USMA 1945), who won a Purple Heart as a 75th Inf Div platoon leader in the during the Battle of the Bulge and was retired for physical disability as a captain in 1947. The third grandson, William Ashbrook Patch (USMA 1948), was WIA in Korea with the 24th Inf Div, winning the SS and retiring as a major general in 1978.

PATTERSON, Robert Porter. US official. 1891-1952. Judge Patterson was born on 12 Feb 91 at Glens Falls, NY, and reared there. He got his law degree from Harvard in 1915 and joined the New York City law firm of (Elihu)

Root, Clark, Buckner, and Howland to which STIMSON also belonged. He resigned in 1916, served with the 7th Inf Regt in the **Punitive Expedition.** Rising to major in the 306th Inf. Regt., ending up as a battalion commander in the **AEF,** he won the **DSC, SS,** and **PH.** In 1919 he joined the law firm of Murray, Aldrich, and Webb, practicing until 1930. During the Hoover administration he was judge of the US district court for southern NY, commuting from a farm at Garrison, NY (with a good view of West Point, across the Hudson River). Although a Republican, Patterson was appointed by FDR as judge of the US circuit court of appeals in March 1939. *(CB 41.)*

In July 40 he was a private at the Business and Professional Men's Training Camp at Plattsburg, NY, when called to Washington in July 1940 to be STIMSON's assistant secretary of war. Judge Patterson was undersecretary from 19 Dec 40, and TRUMAN's secretary of war after Stimson retired on 21 Sep 45. Leaving government service on 24 July 47 and resuming private law practice, Judge Patterson died in the crash of an airliner at Newark, NJ.

PATTLE, Marmaduke T. St John. Leading Allied ace. 1914-41. When shot down on 20 Apr 41, Sqd Ldr Pattle, a South African, was the leading Western fighter ace. His score never beaten, he had 41 air victories over the Western Desert and Greece. US Maj. Richard I. BONG was credited with 40 victories, followed by RAF Group Captains J. E. Johnson (38) and "Sailor" A. G. MALAN (35).

PATTON, George Smith, Jr. US general. 1885-1945. The highly controversial but authentic American hero was born on 11 Nov 85 at San Gabriel, Calif. His Jacobite ancestors had prospered as refugees in Virginia, and Patton's maternal grandfather, Benjamin Davis Wilson, founded the orange industry in California, planted the first vineyards, and gave his name to Mt Wilson.

Young George, who apparently suffered from a mild form of dyslexia, was tutored at home. On finally entering school at the age of 11 he "could neither read, write nor calculate, a handicap . . . which dogged him all the way to manhood." (Essame, 2-3). Patton grew into a handsome man of magnificent physique, some six feet two inches tall and burning for military glory. The *beau sabreur* image was marred only by a high-pitched voice.

Following his father and grandfather to VMI, George was there a year before entering West Point. He flunked out with Courtney H. HODGES but reentered to graduate in 1909 (46/103) with a commission in the cavalry. The next year he married Beatrice Ayer, whose family was even richer and more cultured than his own. She became a fiercely devoted wife, companion, and admirer of her husband's uninhibited antics (Pogue, *Marshall,* II, 405).

Patton was fifth out of 43 in the modern pentathlon at the 1912 Stockholm Olympics and he became the US Army's Master of the Sword. Nicknamed "Saber," he took courses at Saumur and with his wife, an avid sportswoman who had been schooled in France, traveled by car throughout regions he would see again in two wars. The couple later owned an oceangoing yacht, the future general becoming a skilled navigator. He also learned to fly.

As unofficial ADC to John J. Pershing on the **Punitive Expedition** of 1916, 2d Lt Patton led a raiding party in three automobiles that surprised the camp of Villista General Cardenas on 14 May 16. Personally killing the general and another man with his pistol, Patton returned to camp with the victims strapped like game trophies to the running boards.

Going with the AEF to France as Pershing's ADC again, Capt Patton was soon promoted. He declined command of an infantry battalion to head the AEF's newly created tank center. This was a risky decision professionally because tanks were an unproved weapon. In the US Army's first tank engagement Patton led the 304th Tank Bde. Later he was seriously wounded in the Meuse Argonne. The armistice was signed on Lt Col (T) Patton's 33d birthday, by which time he was wearing the DSC, DSM, SS, and PH.

Assigned to the tank center at Camp Meade, Md, Patton established a close friendship with EISENHOWER, his junior by five years. The two later served as majors on MacARTHUR's staff during the Bonus Army crisis of 1932.

World War II

In July 40 Col Patton formed a brigade of the 2d Armd Div at Ft Benning, Ga, after joining the new US Armored Force. Promoted on 1 Oct 40, Brig Gen Patton took over the division three

months later and on 4 Apr 41 got his second star. Despite notoriety in the **Louisiana maneuvers** for a foolhardy night movement of almost 400 miles at high speeds over country roads, Patton remained highly regarded by George C. Marshall (Pogue, II, 406). In Jan 42 he took command of the 1st Armd Corps Hq. Three months later this became the cadre for the Desert Training Center at Indio, Calif (*AA, 601*). Marshall then picked Patton to head the Western TF for the North African invasion, Opn **Torch.**

North Africa

Quickly liberating Morocco, 8-11 Nov 42, Patton remained as the senior American officer there. His 1st Armd Corps Hq, which had been part of TF A for Torch, was reactivated 1 Dec 42 and assigned to Mark CLARK's 5th Army Hq. The next month it was put under Patton to plan the landings in Sicily (*AA, 505*). Patton meanwhile replaced FREDENDALL, on 6 Mar 43, as head of the 2d Corps in Tunisia. Patton accomplished no tactical miracles, but with pearl-handled revolvers and an intimidating exhibition of personal leadership he imposed the strictest standards of military discipline on green US troops. He required officers and men to salute smartly, to button buttons, to shave daily out of one gallon of water rationed for all uses, and to wear neckties in action.

Sicily

Turning over command to Omar BRADLEY on 15 Apr 43 Patton returned to invasion planning. His 1st Armd Corps (reinforced) became the 7th Army on 10 July 43, being activated at sea while en route to Sicily. Lt Gen Patton, promoted 12 Mar 43, led the first American field army in action during WWII.

His force in Sicily, deployed on the left of Montgomery's 8th Army, consisted of Bradley's 2d Corps and TRUSCOTT's Provisional Corps. When Axis resistance was concentrated against the greater threat of Montgomery, Patton got permission to make a dash for Palermo, on the island's NW tip. This "demonstrated Patton's vigour and aggression," sniffs a British military historian, "but it threw into doubt his capacity for strategic thinking" (Mason, *Who Was Who,* 233). Whereas Montgomery had been assigned the main strategic effort, designed to trap the main enemy forces in the east and prevent their escape across the Strait of Messina to the Italian mainland, Patton's grandstanding spoiled the plan. "Old Blood and Guts" took Palermo and raced eastward across the north of Sicily to beat the British 8th Army to Messina. But most of KESSELRING's Italian and German troops escaped, thanks largely to Hans HUBE's efforts with his panzers. Patton consequently was passed over by BRADLEY, much his junior, to head US forces for the liberation of Europe.

The Slapping

Another reason for this was Patton's penchant for "adolescent caperings." He got bad publicity for ordering a peasant's donkey killed because its wagon blocked a bridge. Patton was the model for the villain in John Hershey's war novel *A Bell for Adano* (1944). On 10 Aug 43, a week before the campaign ended in Sicily, Patton was enraged to find "non-battle casualties" being admitted to the 93d Evac Hosp. "It's my nerves, sir," one soldier sobbed. "I can't stand the shelling any more." Patton lost control, called the patient a "yellow bastard," slapped him with his gloves or a hand, and screeched that there was no such thing as battle fatigue, only "goddamed cowards." (Bradley, I, 160.) War correspondents suppressed the story, which Eisenhower first learned of from routine medical reports and merely sent Patton "a sharp [but unofficial] letter of reprimand" and ordered him to go around making apologies to everybody including witnesses. (*Crusade*, 208-9.)

The War in Europe

Despite adverse publicity in Britain and the US over this evidence of emotional instability Patton was selected by Eisenhower to command the new 3d Army. This subordinated him to Bradley for the invasion of Europe. The headquarters staff began arriving in England on 12 Jan 44 from Ft Sam Houston, Tex, and Patton officially took command at midnight 25-26 Jan 44 (*AA,* 496). Meanwhile the famous American general was an ideal bogey in Allied deception plans. Leaving Sicily on 1 Jan 44 he visited the Middle East, where PAGET threatened the Balkans. Secret orders, leaked to German intelligence, then made Patton head of two phantom armies in England that tied down German strategic reserves in the Pas de Calais.

But Patton continued to caper. In a pep-talk to a US division he used outrageous, childish, and obscene language in a well-publicized perfor-

mance at which women were present. After promising to make no more public utterances, the general was prevailed on to say a few supposedly off-the-record words at the dedication of an Anglo-American service club. It was reported to Eisenhower that Patton said, in lauding this inter-allied effort, "Since it seems to be the destiny of America, Great Britain and Russia to rule the world, the better we know each other the better off we will be" (*EP,* 1837). Certain newspaper versions left out the Soviets, reporting that Patton said *Britain and America* should rule the world. "While his exact remarks . . . were incorrectly reported," Eisenhower cabled Marshall on 29 Apr 44, "I have grown so weary of the trouble he constantly causes you and the War Department to say nothing of myself, that I am seriously contemplating the most drastic action" (*EP,* 1837). The next day Eisenhower decided to send Patton home, but then—left by Marshall to make the final decision-changed his mind (*EP,* 1840-1). After the slapping incident, Patton had written his chief, "I am at a loss to find words to express my chagrin and grief at having given you, a man to whom I owe everything and for whom I would gladly lay down my life, cause to be displeased with me." (Quoted in *Crusade,* 210.) Eisenhower now told his groveling lieutenant, "You owe us some victories; pay off and the world will deem me a wise man" (ibid., 256).

Patton's 3d Army Hq was not operational until 1 Aug 44—D day plus 55—when Bradley's 12th AG Hq was formed. MIDDLETON's new 8th Corps (now part of the 3d Army) broke out of the beachhead at Avranches and sent its two armored divisions toward the ports of Brest, Lorient, and St Nazaire. Patton hurled his 12th, 15th, and 20th Corps through the Avranches gap to overrun Brittany quickly. As in Sicily, MONTGOMERY's British and Canadian troops drew the main German strength, so Patton made spectacular advances. But on 8 Aug, after taking Le Mans, he turned the 15th Corps north; five days later it drove to Argentan as UK forces approached from the north. The three remaining German armies of KLUGE's AG B might have been trapped, but Bradley could find no way to keep US and UK forces from clashing head on.

Ordered to halt his advance north, a disgusted Patton left Middleton's 8th Corps to clear the ports of Brittany and raced eastward across France with the rest of 3d Army. Breaking out of Seine River bridgeheads on 26 Aug 44 the 12th, 15th, and 20th Corps overran WWI battlefields. On 14 Sep 44 Patton's lead elements were just short of Metz on the north, Nancy in the center, and Epinal. On 30 Aug 44, after crossing the Meuse, Patton was halted four days by a gasoline shortage. (Logistical priority went to Montgomery.) Using captured gas and air supply the 3d Army met stiffening resistance as the Germans shifted reserves to contain his drive. A strong ring of forts around Metz, manned by first-rate troops, made Patton pay a heavy price. He finally called off Walton WALKER's bloody efforts of to take Ft Driant. Metz was encircled by 18 Nov 44, but was not surrendered until 13 December.

Battle of the Bulge

Because of superior staff work, for which he has not received sufficient credit, Patton not only saw the Ardennes crisis coming but also prepared to meet it. When Eisenhower had to give MONTGOMERY operational control of US field armies north of the Bulge, Bradley had only the 3d Army for a major counterattack from the south. It was perhaps Patton's finest hour, for which he put the wheels in motion even before leaving for an emergency conference with Eisenhower and Bradley at Verdun on 19 Dec 44. Despite bitter weather and icy roads, the 3d Army simultaneously planned and executed three of the most difficult operations in war: breaking off an offensive (in the Saar), wheeling across lines of communications of adjacent units, and attacking on another front. Alerted by radio intercepts, the Germans stiffened their defenses.

On 22 Dec 44, with the 8th, 3d, and 12th Corps from west to east, Patton began to push back BRANDENBERGER's 7th German Army on the southern shoulder of the penetration. Late on the 26th, the 4th Armd Div punched a narrow corridor into Bastogne after being in action since the 18th and having raced 150 miles in 19 hours. This forced MANTEUFFEL to withdraw his 5th Pz Army, and Brandenberger was driven back from the southern shoulder of the penetration in heavy fighting.

Final Operations

Shifting north for the Rhineland Campaign, Patton pushed slowly through the Siefried Line to overrun the Eifel and the Palatine. Collab-orating skilfully with PATCH's 7th Army (to the south), he then attacked a deep German salient west of the Rhine. His operation was climaxed by the 5th Inf Div's changing direction from south to east and making a surprise crossing of the Rhine at Oppenheim on 22 Mar 45. Having ordered up bridging equipment and a naval detachment with landing craft, Patton had four divisions across the Rhine by the evening of the 24th.

Then, in what Bradley called "as brash a venture as Patton dared during the entire war," he sent a task force to liberate a POW camp 50 miles inside the German lines. Reduced to a third of the orginally planned strength of 300 men, 19 tanks and assault guns, and 30 other vehicles, the column broke into Hammelburg on 28 Mar 45 after a two-day approach march. The liberated prisoners took to the hills, but exhausted survivors of the expedition surrendered the next morning because their retreat was blocked. Although Patton could hardly have known it, the POWs included his son-in-law Col John K. "Jake" Waters, USMA 1931, who had been captured at Kasserine Pass. Accused of sacrificing troops on a reckless venture to rescue his son-in-law, Patton said later that his only error during the war was not sending a larger force to Hammelburg. (Waters retired as a full general in 1966.)

Along with Bradley, Devers, and Hodges, Patton got his fourth star on 14 Apr 45. At various times his army had included six corps, the 3d, 5th, 8th, 12th, 15th, and 20th. Ordered to halt 35 miles short of Prague, when the Russians still were 100 miles from the Czech capital, Patton sent an expedition toward Vienna that saved the famous Lippenzaner horses from liberation by the Soviets.

Although unsuited professionally and temperamentally for the task, Patton was made military governor of Bavaria. Like other occupation authorities he violated directives barring Nazis from remaining in offices that only they—as former officials—were capable of performing to keep the shattered infrastructure and economy running. But the old horseman again fell victim to foot-in-mouth disease: "Well, I'll tell you," he said at a press conference on 22 Sep 45, "This Nazi thing. It's just like a Democratic-Republican election fight." Immediately replaced by TRUSCOTT, Patton took over 15th Army Hq from GEROW as president of the Theater

General Board, which was charged with making analytical studies of ETO operations. (*AA,* 503.)

On 9 Dec 45, a day before scheduled to go home for probable retirement, Patton was paralyzed from the neck down in an automobile accident. With Mrs Patton at his side, warning the doctors of his tendency toward embolism, the general who allegedly had had a premonition of death in battle died of an embolism on 21 Dec 45. He lies in the American military cemetery at Hamm, Luxembourg.

Evaluation

Much like the bombastic ZHUKOV, Patton was a thoughtful, sensitive, naturally mild man who deliberately cultivated the image of a swashbuckling military hero. Martin Blumenson, from whose writings the above characterization is drawn primarily, edited *The Patton Papers 1885-1940* (2 vols, New York: Houghton Mifflin, 1972). Patton's memoirs are *War as I Knew It* (New York: Houghton Mifflin, 1947). Biographies include those by Ladislas Farago, *Patton: Ordeal and Triumph* (New York: Obolensky, 1964), and Hubert Essame, *Patton: A Study in Command* (New York: Scribner's, 1974).

PAUL, Prince of Yugoslavia. 1893-1976. Tall, with a lofty forehead and aquiline nose, he looked like the effete prince he was. Paul's mother was a high-born Russian, and his cousin became king of Yugoslavia (below) in 1921. This was the year Prince Paul finally finished Oxford, having entered in 1910 but being pulled away by three Balkan wars and WWI. After building a white marble palace on the hills near Belgrade and stocking it with art masterpieces, Paul happily followed his scholarly and aesthetic pursuits until finding himself the principal regent (of three) after King Alexander was assassinated in 1934.

With realpolitik taking a particularly virulent form as Hitler gained strength, the Balkans boiled even more vigorously. Within Yugoslavia the Croats and Serbs sapped national stability. Prince Paul undertook to preserve neutrality. But on 25 Mar 41 he signed a pact with Nazi Germany that immediately precipitated a coup d'état. At dawn on 27 Mar 41 a group of Serb nationalist officers under Gen Dusan Simovic struck swiftly and installed PETER II as king.

Prince Paul, who had been en route by train to Zagreb, escaped through Greece to London. In 1943 he moved to South Africa.

PAUL I. King of Greece. 1901-64. Grandson of the founder of the royal house and third son of Constantine, Paul was appointed commander of the Greek Navy in 1935 when the monarchy was restored under his elder brother, George II. In Apr 41 Paul fled the invading Germans and went to Cairo with the government-in-exile. After the war he succeeded his brother, was crowned on 1 Apr 47, and reigned 17 years as Paul I. He was succeeded by his son Constantine. (*EB Yrbk.* obits.)

PAULUS, Friedrich. German general. 1890-1957. As commander of the German 6th Army he surrendered at Stalingrad on 31 Jan 43 and spent the rest of his life in the USSR and East Germany.

Paulus was a Hessian, born in Breitenau on 23 Sep 90. His father was an administrator in a reform school; his mother the daughter of its principal. From childhood he hoped for a career in the Imperial German Navy. Rejection because of lowly social background was a disappointment that, in the opinion of an aristocratic fellow officer who knew him well, "probably had some influence on the development of his nature, even if only subconsciously" (Mellenthin, *Generals,* 103). But Paulus was accepted as an officer in the German Army, where pedigree counted for much more than in the Navy. And he married a remarkable woman of the Romanian royal family, Elena Rosetti-Solescu. "That marriage, his own tall, elegant appearance, and his always immaculately correct uniform counted for a lot in his later life," comments Mellenthin (ibid.). Although writers persist in referring to him as von Paulus, he did not have that particle of nobility.

Before joining the 3d Baden Inf Regt as an ensign in 1910, Paulus studied law. During WWI he was appointed to the exclusive **GGGS** and in 1917 transferred to the Alpine Corps Hq. After the war he rose in the Reichswehr but had only a year of command experience, as a company commander of the 13th Inf Regt in Stuttgart while Rommel was there.

Paulus was a full colonel in early Oct 35 when he succeeded GUDERIAN as Gen Lutz's CofS in the new Armored Troops Command. This became the 16th Pz Corps on 4 Feb 38, with Guderian relieving Lutz and Paulus remaining briefly as CofS (Guderian, 49). Although the methodical, highly intelligent, and modest colonel was outstanding in this staff position, Guderian already had doubts about his decisiveness, toughness, and lack of command experience. Paulus also was particularly innocent politically (Goerlitz in *J&R*, 227-28; Guderian, 36, 49).

The quiet Generalmajor Paulus (as of 1939) became CofS to the dynamic REICHENAU, holding this post in the highly mobile 10th Army for the blitzkrieg in Poland and retaining it when Reichenau took over the infantry-heavy 6th Army in France the next year. On 3 Sep 40 Paulus succeeded HALDER as chief operations officer *(Oberquartiermeister I)* of OKH. This brought him into close contact with Hitler, who came to have a high regard for the consummate staff officer.

Because of this, and despite lack of command experience, in Jan 42 Paulus succeeded REICHENAU (now leading AG South) as head of the 6th Army. This exceptionally large army had the major role in opening phases of the German summer offensive of 1942. Largely because of Hitler's meddling, the 6th Army not only failed to take Stalingrad but also ended up trapped there. A tougher, more decisive, and more experienced general might have salvaged something of the campaign, but Hitler had picked the wrong man.

As disaster loomed at Stalingrad, anti-Hitler conspirators thought the time was ripe for senior generals to demand Hitler's resignation as supreme commander of the Wehrmacht. (Goerlitz, *GGS*, 428.) It was proposed that "collective action" begin by Paulus's breaking out of Stalingrad in disregard of orders to hold that critical pile of rubble. But the indecisive 6th Army commander refused to go along with the plan and professed undiluted faith in his fuehrer. As the situation became hopeless, Hitler made a last attempt at magic: because no German field marshal had ever failed to commit suicide rather than surrender, Hitler made Paulus a field marshal. But only few hours after being notified of the honor, Paulus surrendered along with his staff on 31 Jan 43. The 14th Pz Corps and 51st Army Corps already had raised the white flag,

and remaining pockets of resistance followed suit by 2 Feb 43.

The field marshal, "always correctly treated" (Mellenthin, 123), refused to cooperate with his captors until he learned what Hitler had done after the 20 July 44 assassination attempt to such old friends as FELLGIEBEL, HOEPPNER, and WITZLEBEN (ibid.). Paulus finally joined the League of German Officers in Russia, founded in the summer of 1943, and began making anti-Nazi propaganda broadcasts.

As a witness for Russian prosecutors at Nuremberg, and showing evidence of psychological pressure, he admitted personal guilt in helping plan a "criminal attack" on the USSR in 1941. But he did not incriminate JODL or KEITEL in any specific criminal act.

In Oct 47 Paulus and SEYDLITZ were said to be commanding several divisions composed mainly of Germans captured at Stalingrad. (Davidson, *Trial*, 361, 530, 542.) On release as a POW he lived in Dresden, dying there on 1 Feb 57 after a long illness.

PAVLOV, Dmitry Grigorevich. Soviet military leader. 1897-1941. He was born 4 Nov 97 in the village of Vonyukh, Kostroma region, an ethnic Russian and son of a peasant (HFS). In 1919 he joined the CP and the Red Army, remaining a private throughout WWI. Pavlov graduated in 1928 from the Frunze MA and three years later completed the Military-Technical-Academic courses. A specialist in armored warfare, Pavlov went to Spain as chief of the Soviet Volunteer Tank Force and in 1937 (when other "Spaniards" were falling victim to the Great Purges) he became an HSU! This is all the more ironic because in Spain, where the Germans were perfecting tactics and techniques of the blitzkrieg, Pavlov concluded that there was no future for large, independent armored formations!

With this wrong-headed outlook Pavlov became head of the Armed Tank Directorate in 1939, responsible on the eve of war for developing the Red Army's mechanized forces. Now with the rank of general colonel, he was a member of the Main Military Council from 24 July 40. Thanks largely to his bad advice and that of MEKHLIS to Stalin, defense minister VOROSHILOV, who also opposed mechanization, disbanded the mechanized corps in 1937. (Erickson, *To Stalingrad,* 15.) By May 40 it had been broken up into 35 brigades, with an additional 98 tank battalions assigned to rifle and cavalry divisions. (Seaton, *Stalin,* 91.)

Pavlov was promoted to general of the army (No. 4) on 22 Feb 41 and given command of the Western Special MD, which was redesignated the Western Front on 6 June 41. Covering 470 kilometers he faced BOCK's AG Center, which was supported by Kesselring's 2d Air Fleet. Against SHAPOSHNIKOV's advice (and astounding the Germans), Pavlov deployed three armies well forward with one in reserve. On STALIN's strict orders not to provoke the enemy, Soviet forces were in their peacetime deployment.

When Pavlov's intelligence officer reported before dawn on 22 June 41 that the invasion had begun, Timoshenko said on the phone that "Comrade Stalin has forbidden to open artillery fire against the Germans" and "there is to be no air reconnaissance more than thirty-five miles beyond the frontier." (Werth, *Russia at War,* 151.) Through gaps opened by two infantry armies GUDERIAN's and HOTH's panzer groups tore Pavlov's front apart.

Early on 29 June 41, YEREMENKO arrived unannounced at Pavlov's headquarters in Mogilev to say he was the new front commander. The newcomer brought Pavlov instructions to fly immediately to Moscow with his CofS, General Major V. Ye Klimovskikh, signals officer A. T. Grigoriev, and several others. Pavlov was arrested on 22 July, summarily tried, and shot. Also executed then or at some other date were Klimovskikh, Grigoriev, 4th Army commander A. A. Korobkov, plus commanders and commissars of the 60th and 30th Rifle Divs.

Until Stalin's death in 1953 Pavlov was held responsible for breaking up the mechanized corps in 1939 and for his front's collapse in 1941. During the Khrushchev era Stalin was blamed and Zhukov was faulted for not giving proper military advice. Zhukov blamed Voroshilov. (Seaton, *Stalin,* 105.)

PECHKOFF, Zinovi. French diplomat. 1884-1966. The natural and adopted son of Maksim Gorky, he joined the French foreign legion in 1914 and commanded it in 1937-40. Leaving Morocco for London Col Pechkoff

rallied to de Gaulle's Fighting French (as they were first known).

Col Pechkoff headed the Gaullist Mission to French West Africa in early 1943. Promoted to general he was the French delegate to China from Apr 43 to the end of the war. (Macmillan, *Diaries,* 27, 74.) Two years before his death in Paris at the age of 82 he returned on a special mission to tell Chiang Kai-Shek why France recognized the communist government.

PEIPER, Joachim. German officer. 1915-76. The man whose SS regiment committed the Malmedy massacre (below) was born 30 Jan 15 in Berlin of a military family. Well educated, fluent in English and French, tall, and easy going, Jochen (as he preferred to be called) joined Sepp DIETRICH's Liebstandarte-SS (LSSAH) in 1934. After attending OCS at Brunswick and being commissioned he had all subsequent service in the LSSAH except for TDY as one of HIMMLER's personal adjutants in 1938-39.

For reasons more bureaucratic than political he never joined the Nazi Party (Whiting, *Malmedy,* 17). Peiper led an SS company in Poland before moving up to head his battalion at the age of 25. Rising to regimental commander in Russia he won the RK on 9 Mar 43 for bravery around Kharkov, and the Oakleaves (377/890) on 27 Jan 44.

During the Ardennes counteroffensive of late 1944 Obersturmbannenfuehrer Peiper commanded a 5,000-man task force built around his 1st SS-Pz Regt. Spearheading Sepp Dietrich's 6th Pz Army he was near Malmedy on D+2 (17 Dec 44) when his troops captured Battery B, 285th FA Observation Bn. Facing the classic dilemma of what to do when impeded by POWs, some of Peiper's troops herded more than a hundred Americans into a snowy pasture and gunned them down. The task force hurried on, killing other POWs and some unarmed civilians, until the spearhead was cut off after crossing the Salm River and being encircled. Only 800 officers and men out of 5,000 escaped.

Investigation of the Malmedy massacre established that 71 Americans had been killed, not the 129 reported initially. The others survived by feigning death. An American military tribunal at Dachau condemned 43 SS officers including Peiper to death and 23 to life imprisonment. But US Senator Joe McCarthy initiated a new trial that revealed Piper had been tortured into confessing. The US Senate Armed Forces Committee took action that resulted in commutation of 31 death sentences in Mar 48, and the next month Gen Lucius D. Clay reduced the remaining death sentences to six from 12. But none of the accused was ever executed or served a full sentence. After 13 years in jail Peiper, DIETRICH, and other Malmedy defendants were released in the Stuttgart area on parole, then on probation. Still a hero to his SS veterans, Peiper died mysteriously in 1976. (Angolia, I, 229.)

PEIRSE, Richard Edmund Charles. British airman. 1892-1970. Peirse (rhymes with purrs) was born at Croydon, son of an admiral. After a short time at King's College, London, where he won a major motorcycle race (as PORTAL did at about this time) Peirse went to France in 1914 as a naval aviator. For daring attacks on U-boat pens at Ostende and Zeebrugge and surviving heavy AAA fire, in which he was wounded only once, he won the nickname "Lucky" along with a DSO. Luck and skill carried him through more action at Gallipoli and in Italy, and he was awarded the AFC.

Joining the new RAF, Peirse served on the air staff under Cyril L. N. Newall; in Apr 40 he became vice CAS and was knighted (KCB). In the sweeping reorganization after the Battle of Britain Sir Richard followed PORTAL as head of Bomber Command on 25 Oct 40. The organization continued to suffer such exorbitant losses while inflicting insignificant damages that Churchill, after having LINDEMANN and others get statistics, ordered a virtual ban on strategic missions. PORTAL's reputation on the line, he replaced Peirse with Arthur "Bomber" Harris on 22 Feb 42.

Sir Richard was sent to SE Asia, the "forgotten front," reaching Delhi in Mar 42 as AOC India. On 11 Dec 43, soon after MOUNTBATTEN's arrival to establish SEAC and infuse vigor into the Burma campaign, the US 10th AF and RAF Bengal Command were integrated into the Eastern Air Command, with Peirse as Allied Air CinC (*OCMH Chron,* 153). But Mountbatten lacked trust in Peirse and his opposite numbers, Gen George Gifford (Eastern Army) and Adm James SOMERVILLE (Eastern Fleet). The feeling was mutual (Hough, *Mountbatten,*

171). Problems were resolved during the first year, but the crisis came when MOUNTBATTEN moved his headquarters from Delhi to Kandy, Ceylon. Arguing that Kandy was dandy but too far from the action in Burma, Giffard and Peirse refused to go along. "Both were relieved of their command," writes Hough, "in October and November [1944]. It is no reflection on these commanders that the Burma campaign prospered after their departure." (Ibid., 196.)

Peirse returned to England and soon retired. Sir Richard's first marriage of 30 years having ended in divorce a year earlier, he married the divorced wife of AUCHINLECK in 1946. ACM Peirse died 5 Aug 70 at the age of 77 after a short illness.

PENIAKOFF, Vladimir "Popski." Leader of Popski's Private Army. 1897-1951. Born 30 Mar 97 in Belgium of cultured Russian parents and having Belgian citizenship. He was privately tutored until entering St John's College, Cambridge in 1914 as a self-styled "precious intellectual prig, with high scientific ambitions, and conscientious objections to war" (Peniakoff, vii). At the end of his fourth term he left Cambridge and enlisted as an artillery private in the French Army, which sent him to the western front with a minimum fuss about basic training. Spending the last year in hospitals and convalescent camps, he was invalided out of the French Army soon after the 11 Nov 18 armistice.

Peniakoff trained as an engineer but found little satisfaction in a succession of jobs. In 1924 he settled in Egypt and "devoted many years to the manufacture of sugar." (Ibid, viii.) "In the meantime I married and had two children, read, traveled, made a few friends, flew a plane, and motored in the desert in an indestructible Model A Ford, rudely nicknamed The Pisspot" (ibid.). Developing a love of the desert, usually alone, he became an expert at desert navigation with a sun compass and by the stars, "as a mariner does at sea" (ibid.). Belgium being neutral until 10 May 40, it was not until four months later, when GRAZIANI was massed on the Egyptian frontier, that the bulky, 43-year-old, ardent Anglophile found a sympathetic young medical officer who passed him as physically fit to fight. Commissioned a second lieutenant, and speaking Arabic, the Belgian's first service was as commander of one of four battalions of the

Libyan Arab Force of Senussi tribesmen who had escaped GRAZIANI's final "pacification" of their country in the late 1920s. The British 8th Army having suffered a series of disasters in the Western Desert and the Libyan Arab Force having been ineffectual, Middle East Hq approved formation of a company-size commando force of Senussi volunteers under Peniakoff. He wanted to join David STIRLING's Long Range Desert Group but was persuaded to operate independently. His "No. 1 Long Range Demolition Sqdn" became known as "Popski's Private Army" (PPA), even in official records. By the spring of 1942 he had packed his two daughters off to school in Durban, South Africa, and his wife, soon divorced on friendly terms, was in Cairo doing secret work for Middle East Hq.

The highly mobile PPA was mounted in Chevrolet 1 1/2 ton trucks until it got jeeps. The beloved Pisspot was soon scrapped as "beyond local repair" (ibid., 6-7). Popski's army was highly effective on rear-area reconnaissance and sabotage missions throughout the campaigns in North Africa before rejoining the 8th Army for the landing at Taranto, on the heel of Italy. The PPA continued its behind-the-lines operations, working frequently with the partisans. After more than six months of continuous action Popski lost his left hand and suffered other severe wounds on 9 Dec 44 around Rimini. In the final spring offensive of 1945 he conducted amphibious operations along the Adriatic coast to Chioggia, at the south end of the Lagoon of Venice, and bluffed a strong German force into surrendering without a fight. Landing craft took the PPA to Venice (an open city), where Popski celebrated by driving seven times around the Piazza San Marco, "the grandest salon in Europe" (Napoleon) and heretofore a stranger to the automobile. Moving north through the Julian Alps to Tarvisio, he made contact east of Klagenfurt with a Russian tank column.

By war's end Lt Col Peniakoff had been awarded the MC (1942), DSO (1945), and high orders of the Belgian croix de guerre (1940 and 1947). Making his home in London and becoming a FRGS, Popski published *Private Army* the year before his death on 15 May 51. The first American edition was published with excellent illustrations and maps as *Popski's Private Army* (New York: Bantam Books, 1980).

PERCIVAL, Arthur Ernest. British general. 1887-1966. Lt Gen Percival surrendered Singapore on 15 Feb 42, spent the rest of the war as a POW, but was liberated from a camp in Manchuria to be present with "Skinny" WAINWRIGHT at MACARTHUR's surrender ceremony on 2 Sep 45. Both generals then witnessed YAMASHITA's surrender in the Philippines.

The slender, toothy Brit began his career as a private and rose to command the BEF's 43d Div in France from early 1940. After the Dunkirk evacuation he headed the 44th Div on the English coast. Largely because of previous service in Malaya, 1936-38, Percival then took over the Malaya Command in the spring of 1941. Defenses of the great naval base at Singapore were oriented seaward, nothing covering the wide natural moat north of the 27-mile-long, 14-mile-wide island. Although the Malay peninsula (like the Ardennes) had long been considered to be a sufficient natural barrier, Percival asked in vain for six divisions with supporting troops and air forces. But he remained with two and a half ill-trained and badly led divisions.

Major Japanese fleet movements were reported on 6 Dec 41 but Percival was not authorized to react until YAMASHITA's crack troops began landing two days later in Siam. The Japanese brought about 200 tanks in what (like Korea in 1950) was not "tank country" and the defenders had none. On 10 December the invaders broke the first delaying position at Jitra, achieved air superiority, and sent Adm Tom PHILLIPS to the bottom with the only British capital ships in the theater, *Prince of Wales* and *Repulse*.

On 27 Jan 42 Percival ordered his surviving forces withdrawn to Singapore Island. Brigadier Ivan Simson, a highly capable engineer officer who had all necessary materials available, repeatedly urged his commanding general to authorize construction of defenses on the northern side of the island. At a late night meeting Percival finally told the frantic Simson: "I believe that defenses of the sort you want to throw up are bad for the morale of troops and civilians." (Barber, *Sinister Twilight,* 69.)

Percival had about 100,000 officers and men including Gordon BENNETT's 17,000 Australians and 33,000 British. "It is doubtful whether the Japanese have as many in the whole Malay peninsula," said Churchill in a cable on 10 Feb 42 to WAVELL on Java. There were about a million civilians in the city of Singapore, which was under constant air attack. The main Japanese assault on the island began the night of 8-9 Feb 42. It came, as expected, from the NW across Johore Strait. The 22d Australian Bde was driven back and although maintaining cohesion it abandoned the Tengah airfield without a fight. The another Aussie brigade unaccountably withdrew after brilliantly repulsing a second amphibious assault around the causeway from Johore Bahru. This left the road to Singapore city open. WAVELL paid a last visit at this critical juncture, on 10 Feb 42, and went over Percival's head to order a costly counterattack that dissipated reserves without accomplishing anything.

By Friday the 13th the Japanese had drawn the net around Singapore city, bringing field artillery to bear. A gaunt, red-eyed Percival surrendered unconditionally to Yamashita on Sunday, 15 Feb 42. In Britain's most humiliating defeat of the war, some 130,000 British, Australian, Indian, Malay, and local troops became POWs. About a million natives of Singapore, many of them Chinese, came under a harsh Japanese occupation. Thousands of men, women, and a handful of children suffered three and a half years of brutal internment. (*See* Barber, 290 ff.)

Percival published *The War in Malaya* (London: Eyre and Spottiswoode, 1949). He died in 1966, at 79, a broken man (Barber, 304).

PERESYPKIN, Ivan Terentyevich. Red Army signals chief. 1904-78. Born 18 May 04 in Protasovo, a village in the present Orel Oblast, he was in the Red Army 1919-20 and in 1923 fought in the civil war. He joined the CPSU in 1925. Peresypkin was chief of the Red Army's Main Signals Directorate 1941-46. He was the first Soviet Marshal of Signal Troops (1944) and postwar Chief of Signal Troops of the Soviet Army 1946-56. The authority on radio communications, author of several books in the field, he died 12 Oct 78 in Moscow. (Scotts.)

PETAIN, (Henri) Philippe (Benoni Omer). Marshal of France; head of Vichy government. 1856-1951. "They call me only in catastrophes," the already-elderly Pétain said 1917. Twenty three years later he was called for the last time.

Pétain was born 24 Apr 56 in NW France at Cauchy-à-la-Tour, near Arras, of solid peasant stock. He attended Jesuit and Dominican schools before graduating from St Cyr in 1878. For the next five years he served in the elite and newly formed Chasseurs Alpins ("Blue Devils"). With a hardy physique he would keep through a long life, the tall, blond, blue-eyed Pétain was a strikingly handsome figure. He was also was a man of few words.

After 36 years of outstanding service, primarily with troops, the 58-year-old Col Pétain had little prospect of further advancement when the Germans attacked in 1914. He had been in grade only since 1911 and was commanding the 33d Inf Regt at Arras. Lt Charles DE GAULLE, who as a student at St Cyr had heard the colonel condemn the prevalent French military doctrine of *l'offensive à l'outrance* (all-out attack at all times) was assigned at his own request to Pétain's 33d Regt in 1912.

The superannuated colonel had picked his retirement home when the guns of August 1914 changed his plans. In less than three months he rose to head the 33d Army Corps. A month after distinguishing himself near Arras in May 15 he was promoted to full general commanding the 2d Army. Two years later, 15 May 17, he succeeded Robert G. Nivelle as CinC on the Western Front. The 61-year-old general first had to quell the mutiny brought on by a reckless predecessor's mindless and murderous adherence to *l'offensive à l'outrance*. Showing good sense and compassion Pétain accomplished this before directing the successful defense of Verdun, where the Germans had hoped to bleed the Allied armies white. Two weeks after the armistice of 11 Nov 18, already a national hero, he was created a Marshal of France.

From early 1922 he was IG of the French army and CinC-designate in case of war. In this capacity he took the field to quell the Abd-el-Krim uprising in Morocco, 1925-26, associated in this Rif war with Francisco FRANCO. The marshal subsequently took Foch's seat in the French Academy (1929) and was VP of the Supreme War Council. After leaving active service in 1931 Pétain was recalled after the riots of 6 Feb 34 as minister of war (9 Feb-8 Nov 34). Declining the man-on-horseback role he refused to be a candidate for president and declined to join DALADIER's government.

The scholar Pierre Thibault points out that as holder of his country's highest military offices between the wars, Pétain was largely responsible for weaknesses revealed in 1940. Thibault blames Pétain for supporting the drastic reduction in mandatory military service, for instilling a defensive doctrine that included reliance on the Maginot Line, and for failure to appreciate the value of tanks and airplanes. (Larousse, "Pétain.")

The fateful rift between Pétain and his protégé de Gaulle (who had named his son Philippe for the marshal) dated from 1938. De Gaulle had written a popular history of the French army 10 years earlier that was to come out under Pétain's name. But the marshal decided against publication because the book too obviously was ghost-written. De Gaulle, hating to see his effort wasted, decided at the time of the Munich crisis of 1938 that the book might stimulate much-needed martial ardor so badly needed in a country weakened by political dissent and defeatism. So de Gaulle published *La France et son Armée* under his own name. What particularly outraged the venerable war hero was his subordinate's dedication: "To Marshal Pétain, who wished this book to be written; who, with his counsels, helped in the writing of the first five chapters, and, thanks to whom, the last two are the story of our victory." Unable to block publication or to have the dedication changed, Pétain forever bore de Gaulle a grudge. (Werth, *De Gaulle*, 86-87.)

Pétain's appointment as ambassador to Franco Spain on 24 Mar 39 was a transparent effort to remove him as a threat in Paris. But Paul REYNAUD recalled the 83-year-old national hero as minister without portfolio on 18 May 40. The common view is that the marshal was supposed to be a symbol, "a flag." De Gaulle later reported, however, that Reynaud admitted having very different political motives: because Pétain was suspected of being the screen for advocates of an armistice, "'It's better to have him inside than out.'" (de Gaulle, I, 53.)

French troops still were being slaughtered when the government fled to Bordeaux and the threat of civil war was real. On 11 June Reynaud told Churchill that Pétain advocated an armistice and on the 16th threatened to resign if his policy was not carried out. Reynaud stepped down, Pétain formed a cabinet and went on the radio shortly after noon on 17 June 40, when

DE GAULLE had fled to London. "With heavy heart, I tell you today that it is necessary to stop the fighting." French negotiators under HUNTZINGER left for Compiègne on the 20th; two days later the armistice was signed at Rethondes; it took effect on 25 June 40. France wanted an *armistice* rather than a *surrender* to preserve her surviving armed forces—the "Armistice Army"—and her powerful fleet. Only Frenchmen captured before the armistice were POWs. Vichy armed forces in metropolitan France and most of those in the colonies observed armistice terms, Axis commissioners being on hand at home and abroad to report compliance.

France was divided in two parts (*pace Caesar*). The Unoccupied Zone was demarked by a line from the Swiss frontier near Geneva, through Bourges, to a point on the Spanish border SE of Bayonne. Occupied territory in the south included Bordeaux, the Basque country, and the coast of the Bay of Biscay. The Vichy government was established on 2 July 40, and the *Etat Français* was established with Pétain as chief of state. The transfiguration was masterminded by Pierre LAVAL, an achievement that impressed Pétain with his clout.

"*Travail, Patrie, Famille*" ("Work, Country, Family") replaced "*Liberté, Egalité, Fraternité.*" Paxton faults Pétain for attempting "a substantial restructuring of domestic institutions"—his "National Revolution"—in a country notorious for political discord and now further torn apart by a humiliating defeat (Paxton, *Vichy*, 380-81). Vichy became increasingly repressive as its policies failed, DARNAND's *Milice* showing more ardor than the Germans in hunting Frenchmen.

Collaboration

As for "collaboration," a distinction must be made between what individuals did for personal reasons and what their leaders did for what they believed was in the national interest. There was little reason to believe in 1940 that Hitler would not win the war. Vichy persisted in seeking acceptance as a partner in Hitler's New Order for Europe, but Germany wanted only to control the territory and resources of a captive nation and deny French assets to enemies of the Third Reich.

"The two Montoire talks [22 and 24 Oct 40] were more remarkable for public effect than for anything said there," writes Paxton. Laval met with Hitler at the first session, Pétain coming for the second. It was agreed that France and Germany should work together, but neither Pétain nor Hitler got specific. (Paxton, 75.) The marshal went to Montoire primarily in hopes of getting French POWs released. The fuehrer, still furious over his recent meeting with FRANCO, was in no mood to comply.

LAVAL, the most persistent advocate of collaboration, was dismissed on 13 Dec 40 and succeeded by DARLAN. But after LAVAL returned to power in Apr 42 the old marshal was little but a figurehead.

As for Vichy's relations with the Allies, Britain did not recognize the Pétain government but America did. This led to the great difficulties with DE GAULLE, whom Pétain at Montoire had called a "blot on the honor of the French officer corps" (Paxton, 69). Roosevelt used Robert MURPHY and Adm LEAHY in what has been called "our Vichy gamble." The Allied landings in North Africa on 8 Nov 42 wrecked Pétain's hopes for a compromise peace with Hitler. When the Germans moved into Vichy France on 11 November the old marshal was concerned primarily with keeping his country from again becoming a battleground. He was thinking not only of the Allied liberation but also of the continuing threat of civil war after the Vichy government gave way to whatever Frenchmen attempted to put in its place.

Recession

On 20 Aug 44 the retreating Germans arrested Pétain, who called the papal nuncio and the Swiss minister to bear witness. (Larousse.) Dragged protesting from Vichy's Hôtel du Parc and virtually a prisoner, he was in Belfort, 21 Aug-8 Sep 44, then at Sigmaringen in the south of Germany. The marshal refused, despite German pressure, to continue the fiction of being head of state. Escorted by the Germans to Switzerland and getting authority to cross that country to the French border at Vallorbe, an honorable act said to have intensely disappointed de Gaulle, the old marshal was arrested by Gen KOENIG on 26 Apr 45.

Pétain was charged with "crimes against the internal security of the state" and "dealings with the enemy with a view to promoting their enterprises in conjunction with his own." (Roy, *Trial*, 14.) Pétain's defense attorneys argued that he

had done his best for France. The sentence on 15 Aug 45, by a vote of 14 to 13, was death with reprieve. De Gaulle promptly commuted this to life imprisonment.

Pétain was imprisoned 16 Aug 45 in the fort of Portalet. On 16 Nov 45 he was moved to the little Ile d'Yeu, an hour's ferry ride out in the Bay of Biscay. As the end approached, he was moved (29 June 51) from the Fort de la Pierre-Levée to the nearby Villa Luco. Here he died 23 July 51 at the age of 95. France buried her fallen hero in the island cemetery, not at Verdun, as he requested.

Much ink has been spilled over the elderly marshal's mental competence. "Contrary to a common postwar assumption," writes an American authority, "Pétain was not senile in 1940," and "Germans who met Pétain in 1943 still found him fresh and alert" (Paxton, 36, 382). At the beginning and end of his trial (having remained silent in between) the marshal of France stood erect and, without spectacles, read prepared statements in a clear, firm voice (Roy, 17). Not for another two years did an interrogator find Pétain to be genuinely senile (ibid., 388). Pierre Thibault concludes, on the other hand, that the elderly marshal had memory failures, periods of silence, and lapses of lucidity that were noticed, even by admirers, as early as 1941. *(Larousse.)*

PETER II. King of Yugoslavia. 1923-70. Born 6 Sep 23 into the Karageorgevich dynasty, Peter was the first son of Princess Marie of Romania. At the age of 11, just after entering school in England, he became King Peter II when his father, Alexander I, was assassinated by a Yugoslav fanatic in Marseilles on 9 Oct 34. Peter's cousin PAUL was regent until ousted by an anti-Nazi coup on 27 Mar 41. Hitler, who had counted on moving troops through Yugoslavia to support LIST's attack on Greece, ordered Yugoslavia crushed: the onslaught began on 6 Apr 41 with a terror bombing that devastated Belgrade and killed 17,000 people. Attacking the same day, German and Italian ground forces quickly overran Yugoslavia. Peter escaped through Greece to London with some ministers and set up a government in exile. Practically a British puppet, the young king had authority only to sign acts of his cabinet, which went through many changes to reconcile bitter animosities among Croat, Serb, and Slovak factions. Yugoslavia having been part of the Balkan entente with Greece and Turkey since 1934, the king signed an agreement on 12 Jan 42 with King GEORGE II of Greece for a Balkan Union. Peter hoped this would be expanded into a Central European Union to include the Czechs and Poles *(CB 43)*. The Soviets naturally opposed this, and Churchill—wedded to Alan BROOKE's Mediterranean strategy—spent much time on Balkan affairs. Roosevelt, on the other hand, remained ignorant in this field and the US had no consistent policy (Murphy, *Diplomat,* 220). On 17 May 44 the young king, after continually making cabinet reorganizations, dismissed Bodizar Puric, a Serb who had been named premier on 10 Aug 43 because he supported MIHAILOVIC. Dr Ivan Subasic formed a new administration that, in effect, endorsed TITO and ousted Mihailovic as war minister. The British being unable to have TITO accept the monarchy (WC, VI, 92-93), Peter II was deposed on 29 Nov 45 when the Yugoslav republic was proclaimed. Peter remained in exile with his queen, former Princess Alexandra of Greece, whom he had married in London despite British disapproval. Well provided for financially, and soon convinced that Tito was firmly entrenched, the ex-king reconciled himself to a carefree life of luxury in London and Paris. He had a large support from anti-Tito expatriates, particularly in the US, which he visited frequently. Peter II died 5 Nov 70 in Los Angeles aet 47. The American edition of his autobiography is *A King's Heritage* (1954).

PETLYAKOV, Vladimir Mikhaylovich. Soviet aircraft designer. 1891-1942. His two-engine Pe-2 was the Soviet answer to the Stuka (Ju 87) dive bomber and comparable to the US A-20 and British Mosquito (Kirk & Young, 39). An excellent 340mph light bomber, it took up about two-thirds of Soviet bomber production, 11,000 being turned out in WWII.

The designer was born 27 June 91 in Sambek, Rostov Oblast. In 1917-18 he worked in the laboratory of the "father of Russian aviation," Nikolay Ye. Zhukovisky (1847-1921), and from then until 1936 under TUPOLEV in the Central Aerodynamic Institute. Meanwhile he graduated in 1922, from the Moscow Higher Technical School/Bauman. In 1936 his four-engine long-range bomber TB-7 (renamed Pe-8) performed the remarkable feat of carrying five tons of bombs, but only 79 of this model were ever produced. During the Great Purges, which hit the aviation industry specially hard, Petlyakov was under special arrest in an NKVD "design bureau." After designing the Pe-2 he was released to work at the production plant in Fili. The facility was evacuated in the fall of 1941 to Kazan, where the designer died 12 Jan 42 in a plane crash.

PETROV, Ivan Yefimovich. Soviet military leader. 1896-1958. Ivan Yefimovich—Russia has many Petrovs—was born 30 Sep 96 in the village of Trubchevsk, Bryansk region. Lacking a peasant pedigree, the son of an artisan, he complicated his subsequent security clearances by studying at a theological seminary (Scarecrow), qualifying as a teacher, and graduating from a Tsarist military school in 1917. He saw action in Astrakhan before joining the Red Army and CP in 1918. During the civil war he commanded a brigade in Central Asia.

In 1937 he suffered the first of many almost-incredible professional setbacks when he was sacked for "lack of vigilance" (Scarecrow) as commandant of the Tashkent Infantry College. But Petrov had friends as well as enemies involved in his career, for in Mar 41 he formed a mechanized corps in the Central Asian MD and two months later he was a general major commanding the 2d Cav Div in the Ukraine. Opposing the onslaught of a German division and 18 Romanian divisions he commanded the Special Maritime Army 5 Aug-16 Oct 41 (Werth, *Russia,* 208). Official records show, however, that from Aug 41 he led the Black Sea Army's 25th Chapayev Inf Div.

After defending Odessa in 10 weeks of exceptionally heavy fighting directed by Adm OKTYABRSKY, Petrov was involved in the skillful withdrawal to the Crimea. As the admiral's deputy he then headed the special army command responsible for Sevastopol's land defenses.

For no stated reasons the Transcaucasus Front's military council (MC) removed Petrov on 24 Dec 41. Stalin rescinded the decision after the Sevastopol Defense Area's MC made an appeal (Kruzhin, 9). Moscow authorities ordered the admiral and the general to leave as MANSTEIN closed on Sevastopol. With other senior military and party leaders they escaped by submarine on 30 June 42. (Werth, *397*).

Petrov headed a new Black Sea army until Jul, when he took command of the 44th Army. This had been under Yakov T. CHEREVICHENKO, who took over the new Black Sea Group with the mission of defending Tuapse, a vital port. Against heavy attack through the western Caucasus Mountains by two corps (seven divisions) of Richard RUOFF's 17th Army, which put heavy pressure on the Black Sea Gp (Petrov's 44th, Ryzhov's 56th, and Kamkov's 18th Armies), Cherevichenko was hard pressed from 23 September. Although he had some success Cherevichenko was replaced on or about 14 Oct 42 by Petrov, who stopped the Germans a few miles outside Tuapse. This was due largely to heroic efforts by soldiers and civilians in building gun emplacements, digging anti-tank ditches, and felling trees to block roads (Werth, *568*). (See also Seaton, *R-G War,* 285, and the sketch on TYULENEV, who headed the Transcaucasus Front.)

Rewarded by promotion, Gen Lt Ivan Petrov was CofS, North Caucasus Front, from Mar 43. Two months later he succeeded MASLENNIKOV as front commander. A general colonel from 27 Aug 43, Petrov led the North Caucasus Front in the Novorossisk-Taman Offensive, 10 Sep-9 Oct 43, being promoted on the latter date to General of the Army (No. 15).

Petrov forced the German 17th Army to retreat across the Kerch Straits, and by the end of October had troops ashore on the eastern tip of the Crimea (Seaton, *R-G War,* 379-380). His North Caucasus (or Caucasus) Front now regrouped to form the Separate Black Sea Army, Petrov was directed to drive the 17th Army from the Crimea and liberate Sevastopol. Hitler had designated this a fortress—to be held at all cost. Petrov convinced the Stavka after a heated argument with Vice Adm Vladimirisky that he lacked means for more than expanding the Kerch bridgehead. Before he could get started, however, Petrov was suddenly relieved in early January and demoted one grade. This might have been the work of MEKHLIS (Scarecrow), but SHTEMENKO had genuine doubts about Petrov's competence and second thoughts about the Stavka's accepting his judgment over Adm Vladimirisky's (HFS).

In Mar 44 Gen Col Ivan Ye. Petrov (in his reduced rank) headed the 33d Army briefly until

stepping up in April to head the 2d Belorussian Front. But Stalin ordered him removed on 5 June 44. Again the circumstances were mysterious, but Petrov's nemesis Mekhlis had reappeared. The latter, as a member of the front's MC, had written to Stalin that the flabby Petrov was unqualified by ill health and professional incompetence to handle a major operation that was being planned (HFS). Only two months later, however, on 5 Aug 44, Petrov was given command of the 4th Ukrainian Front. He led this in the East Carpathian Offensive, 8 Sep-28 Oct 44, being restored to the rank of general of the army (No. 19) on 26 Oct 44 (Kruzhin, 9). After the Western Carpathian Offensive, 12 Jan-18 Feb 45, which took Cernauti, Petrov moved north into the sector where KONEV's 1st Ukrainians had been operating. But on 26 Mar 45 Petrov again was removed, "after an abortive offensive in the Carpathians" (Scarecrow). For this the 1st Pz Army under Erhard RAUS and then HEINRICI deserves much credit, but MEKHLIS, now on the military council of Petrov's front, seems again to have been the nemesis (Kruzhin, 9). The yo-yo Petrov succeeded SOKOLOVSKY as KONEV's CofS in from Apr 45 for the Berlin Offensive. Petrov retained the post when Konev's 1st Ukrainian Front moved south for the Prague Offensive, 6-11 May 45, becoming a Hero of the Soviet Union (1945).

Among those Stalin hustled to far-off places, Petrov headed the Turkestan MD from 15 July 45 to 1952. After Stalin's death in 1953 he held various honorific staff assignments in Moscow before dying there on 7 Apr 58. He is buried at the **Novodvichy Monastery**.

PEYROUTON, Marcel. French colonial administrator. 1887-1983. Born in Paris and becoming a lawyer with powerful personal and professional connections, Peyrouton made what the French call *la belle carrière*. This began in Tahiti, Madagascar, Togo, and Cameroun before he was André Maginot's assistant chef de cabinet in 1928. He was Tunisia's resident general 1933-36, held the same office in Morocco for a few months, showing good political instincts and an innate feeling for power. But for what Léon Blum's new popular front government perceived as unduly repressive action, to include setting up concentration camps on the edge of the Sahara for left-wing opponents of his reforms, the proconsul was exiled in Aug 36 to Buenos Aires as ambassador.

Reynaud restored Peyrouton to his post in Tunisia as honorary governor general in the Third Republic's dying days (9 June 40). But the veteran colonial officer quickly joined the Vichy administration as secretary general of administration and of police (18 July 40-16 Feb 41). He was responsible for many repressive laws. Purging the Corps of Prefects—to include Jean MOULIN—he had many of them put in house arrest. He supported passage of anti-Semitic statutes and had a major role surrendering anti-Nazi refugees to the Germans. Early victims were Fritz THYSSEN and his wife, followed a few weeks later (10 Feb 41) by socialists Rudolf Breitscheid and Rudolf Hilferding. (Larousse.) He got authority to appoint the mayors of communities having more than 2,000 people.

Highly regarded by Pétain (Pierre Thibault in Larousse, "Pétain"), he suggested to the old marshal on 4 Dec 40 that Flandin replace Laval, being supported by Darlan, Huntziger, and Baudouin. LAVAL was arrested on 13 Dec 40 and put in house arrest. Peyrouton claimed his motive was only to curtail collaboration with the Germans, which Laval was carrying too far, but his real reason probably was to protect his portfolio from Laval. (Larousse; Paxton, *Vichy*, passim.)

But Peyrouton had so alienated the Germans that Buenos Aires looked safer than Vichy. Turning over his duties to Darlan on 16 Feb 41, Peyrouton resumed his former ambassadorial post. He resigned on 28 Apr 42 after LAVAL returned to power and began settling old political scores. The following November, when the Allies landed in North Africa and made their deal with his friend DARLAN, Peyrouton volunteered his services. With an American passport (Larousse), the veteran colonial administrator reached Algiers in Jan 43. Darlan prevailed on Eisenhower to replace Yves Châtel with Peyrouton as governor general of Algeria. Announced on 19 Jan 43, the appointment caused an uproar on both sides of the Atlantic from the Free French and from Jewish organizations (*EP*, 910 & n4). The Allies were content to leave Peyrouton in the office he performed as a skilled colonial administrator. But the Free French had no such tolerance, and the ex-Vichyite resigned on 1 June 43 after de Gaulle reached Algiers.

He served in Syria as a captain of colonial infantry, but only briefly: the FCNL purge commission had the tainted official put in house arrest *(residence surveillée)* until 21 Dec 43 in southern Algeria, then in protective custody. The high court of justice order him deprived of liberty for five years and a day but acquitted him of "participating in an enterprise to demoralize the army and the nation." Peyrouton's memoirs are *Du Service public à la prison commune* (Paris, 1950).

PHILBY, Harold (Adrian Russell) "Kim." Soviet mole. 1912-88. History's most remarkable spy was the son of a famous explorer, orientalist, and civil servant, Harry St John Philby (1885-1960). Kim took his nickname early in life from the Kipling character.

Brilliant, arrogant, and licentious, Kim Philby joined the **Apostles** at Cambridge, the British CP, and was the first recruit of the **Cambridge Five.** Authorities disagree over whether this was in 1933 or 1934 and who deserves credit. Sudoplatov says it was Arnold Deutsch, not Aleksandr Orlov.

Philby's controller sent him to Vienna in early 1934 to learn German for the foreign service entrance examination and to start burrowing into the British establishment. In what was perhaps his only false step in a long career (Brown, *"C,"* 174) Philby married a militant Bolshevik, Frau Lizzy Friedman (Litzi Kohlmann). She was "almost certainly the person who recruited him to the Soviet cause" (Wright, *Spycatcher*, 324), although there is evidence he already had been hooked. But taking her to England on his passport was a taint of communism, that, added to his socialist associations at Cambridge, kept Philby from getting the necessary references for taking the examination.

Their ring in limbo for more than a year after their recruiter's departure, Philby and Burgess reestablished contact with Moscow through Lizzy Friedman (Wright, 228). Philby went to Spain in 1937 as a freelance war correspondent and Soviet agent. With his father's influence he then joined *The Times* (London) in May 37 as special correspondent with Franco's forces. Going on to France during the **Phony War** he returned to London in 1940 and entered MI6's

Sect V (Counterespionage) under Felix H. Cowgill. Philby soon drew the attention of Stewart Menzies, the SIS chief. Philby's keen nose for military intelligence led to a vital success in locating the **Bodden line**. Menzies ("C") consequently asked Philby on short notice to attend a Joint Intelligence Committee meeting that had "Bodden" on the agenda. "Who's that scruffy bugger?" whispered Chairman Cavendish-Bentinick to C as Philby sloped in wearing his father's WWI blouse, an orange shirt—as the chairman remembered—and old corduroy slacks. "Young Philby," Menzies hissed back. "St John Philby's son. He's with me. Good lad." The chairman, who knew of Kim Philby's bad company at Cambridge, commented, "Looks like a damned Bolshevik to me" but failed to follow up by asking for a security check. (Brown, 424.)

When MI6 prepared for the postwar era by recreating the anti-Soviet branch as Sect IX (Operations) in Sep 44 Philby was promoted over Cowgill to head it. Within a year the counterintelligence and anti-Soviet branches were united under Philby. The mole, a term created later by spy novelist John Le Carré, had arrived. His desk was just down the hall from C. In the last months of the war Philby intervened to block the defection of Konstantin Volkov, the KGB official in Istanbul who sent the British word that he would tell them all. Knowing he would be exposed, Philby delayed the procedures until the Soviets could liquidate Volkov.

The mole was appointed to the OBE for his war service and was one of the few that Menzies put in for honors. Made **CBE** on the New Year's Honors List of 1946. Philby is supposed to have invited a visiting American colleague, James Jesus Angleton, to the investure ceremony and Angleton claims to have remembered a curious remark that his host made as they left Buckingham Palace: "What this country needs is a good stiff dose of socialism." Angleton allegedly said later to Allen Dulles, "You know, he sounded like a Commie. I have a feeling in my bones about him." (Mosley, *Dulles*, 284.)

"It's a nice story," Philby told to a biographer, "but there's one rather big flaw in it": the mole had not attended the huge investure ceremony, opting to have the CBE sent to his residence. (Knightley, *Master Spy*, 140.) The purpose of the story, Philby explained, was that "Angleton

was suspicous of me early on and yet didn't do anything about it. Why? Because he wanted to use me for his own deception plans. It's an attempt to save face." (Ibid.)

Philby had been secretly helping an ally in WWII; it was a different ball game when the Cold War followed. He then served Moscow Center as intelligence officer in Istanbul before going to Washington as chief SIS LnO with the CIA and FBI.

When Vladimir Petrov defected on 3 Apr 54 he told a Royal Commission that BURGESS and MACLEAN, the first two moles, might have been alerted by a third man in the government. Foreign Minister Harold Macmillan told the House of Commons a few months later that he had "no reason to conclude that Mr. Philby has at any time betrayed the interests of this country, or to identify him with the so-called 'Third Man,' if indeed there was one." (Brown, 721.) Philby had gambled that if his treachery was known it could not be proved in court, and he had won.

Inevitably dismissed from MI6 he went to Beruit as a foreign correspondent for both *The Observer* and *The Economist* and renewed contact with Moscow Center. Proof of his treason finally came in late 1961 from a defector, Anatoli M. Golitsin. Philby disappeared on 23 Jan 63 and made his way to Moscow. Living here until his death in 1988 he published *My Silent War* (1968). A successor to Menzies, Sir Maurice Oldfield, would reveal only that the memoirs are accurate "as far as they go." (Brown, 743-44.) Perhaps the most authoritative work to date (1996) based on extensive correspondence and long interviews in Moscow, is that by Philip Kinghtly which is cited above and fully identified in the bibliography.

PHILIP, Prince of Hesse. German official. 1896-. He was a grandson of Queen Victoria and the elder twin son of Friedrich, Landgrave of Hesse, whose mother was the youngest daughter of Prussian Emperor Frederick III (1831-88). Philip married Mafalda (1902-44), daughter of Italy's King VICTOR EMMANUEL III. Having met Goering in WWI and renewed his acquaintance in 1927, Philip joined Hitler's entourage, was given the rank of SA Obergruppenfuehrer and made Gauleiter for Hesse-Nassau. The fuehrer treated the prince with deference and respect, using him for liaison with Rome, especially during the Anschluss. Philip also helped to get Italian art masterpieces for Hitler.

As for Princess Mafalda, in private the fuehrer called her a "tricky bitch" and had a low opinion of her intellect and feminine allure. Both Hitler and Goebbels suspected her of foul play in the sudden death of Bulgaria's King Boris III on 29 Aug 43, Mafalda having been at the court for several weeks visiting her sister, the queen. Philip was at Rastenburg 10 days later when the BBC announced the Italian surrender on 8 Sep 43. Long suspicious that Philip had been phoning coded messages through his wife, Hitler had the prince arrested that night. Goebbels noted two weeks later in his diary that Mafalda had been picked up, "acting exceptionally insolently and insultingly. . . ." She was mortally wounded on 24 Aug 44 during an air attack on Buchenwald that killed 80 guards and 400 prisoners. Her naked body was thrown on the stockpile for the camp crematorium. Philip was liberated on 4 May 45 with the **Niederdorf group.**

PHILLIPS, Tom Spencer Vaughan. British admiral. 1888-1941. Entering the Royal Navy in 1903 he served in the plans division as assistant director 1933-32 and as director 1935-38. A rear admiral in 1939, he was vice chief of the naval staff and deputy to Dudley POUND May 39-Oct 41. Tom Phillips was regarded as the Admiralty's brains during the first months of the war. But like POUND he was unpopular professionally for subservience to Churchill, for meddling in operational matters, and particularly for accusing seagoing officers of lacking aggressiveness.

Phillips, a hard-working officer given to fits of anger when his ideas were obstructed, bucked Churchill's decision in the autumn of 1940 (during the Battle of Flanders) to undertake retaliatory bombing of German cities. (Hitler responded with the Blitz of London.) The admiral was quite right in arguing the next year against diverting forces from North Africa for the ill-fated intervention in Greece, further alienating himself from the PM. (Roskill, *Churchill and the Admirals*, 198.)

In addition to lacking sea-going experience the desk admiral was "a prisoner of his fiercely expressed [prewar] convictions . . . that bombers were no match for battleships." (Sir William

Davis's letter of 1976 to RN historian Stephen Roskill, quoted in the latter's *Churchill and the Admirals*, 199.)

On Pound's instigation, apparently with Churchill's approval, and to the dismay of senior admirals (ibid.), the desk-bound Phillips was appointed in May 41 to command the embryo Eastern Fleet, whose creation he had urged. But he stayed in London as VCNS (*DNB*) until the following October. With the acting rank of vice admiral since 7 Feb 40, on Churchill's recommendation (*DNB*), he was promoted to acting admiral and sent to take up his duties at Singapore. It was one of Pound's and Churchill's major blunders.

The self-assured, jumped-up rear admiral whom his peers considered woefully unqualified for high command at sea and whom the outspoken James SOMERVILLE called "the Pocket Napoleon" (Phillips was a very short salt), reached Singapore shortly before the Japanese hit Malaya. His force was weak, unbalanced, and-despite the efforts of BROOKE-POPHAM—-it lacked the air support already shown in Norway and other earlier WWII operations to be essential. Pound and Churchill compounded their errors by reinforcing Phillips with the spanking new BB *Prince of Wales* and the modernized battle cruiser *Repulse*, the only capital ships the Allies now had in the western Pacific.

Just after visiting MacArthur in Manila, Phillips left Singapore the afternoon of 8 Dec 41 (local date) to attack Japanese landings some 500 miles north. With Force Z (the two big ships and four destroyers, Sir Tom hoped to make a surprise attack around Kota Bharu at dawn of the 10th. Fully realizing the need for fighter support, he left his CofS in Singapore to make arrangements. After passing east of the Anamba Islands Force Z was spotted at 1:40 PM by the most easterly of 12 Japanese submarines patrolling for just such a purpose (R&H, 163). Phillips did not know his position had been reported but he was not attacked that day by locally available Japanese air and subs because his location had been given inaccurately. Force Z continued on course but turned back at 8:15 PM after seeing three enemy aircraft and realizing that he had lost surprise.

Japanese torpedo planes from Saigon failed to find the British during the evening. Phillips altered course SW to investigate a report of enemy off Kuantan, 175 miles N of Singapore.

Shortly after midnight a Japanese sub sighted Force Z, launched an unsuccessful torpedo attack, and shadowed for five and a half hours. On 10 Dec at 10:20 AM, just after turning away from investigating what proved to be a false report, Phillips's force was found by air reconnaissance. For reasons still unknown, the admiral failed to report the contact or to ask for support from fighters that were on alert about an hour away at Sembawang.

Twenty seven high-level bombers made the first attack at about 11:30 AM but did no serious damage. The first torpedo bombers arrived 20 minutes later and got two hits on *Prince of Wales*. Perfectly coordinated and sustained bomb and torpedo attacks then sent *Repulse* down at 12:33 and *Prince of Wales* at 1:20 PM. The Japanese withdrew, and British destroyers rescued 2,081 of the 2,921 crewmen.

"Sir Tom went down with the *Prince of Wales;* and a whole naval era went with him," writes MacArthur. "Never again would capital ships venture into hostile waters without air power; Billy Mitchell [q. v.] had been right." (*Reminiscences,* 122.)

PICK, Lewis Andrew. US general. 1890-1956. A military engineer who graduated from **VPI** in 1914, Pick served with the AEF in France. In Dec 42 Brig Gen Pick began building the 478-mile Ledo Road ("Pick's Pike") with coolie labor, US heavy equipment, and having Chinese divisions to fight off the Japanese. From Ledo in NW India through N Burma the road crossed difficult jungle and mountain terrain in two years and 23 days to tie in with the old **Burma Road.** Pick led the first convoy into Kunming on 4 Feb 45 (*OCMH Chron,* 392). Pick's Pike and the Burma Road became the main land route for US supplies to the Chinese, and Chiang Kai-shek officially renamed it the Stilwell Road.

Promoted on 22 Mar 45 Maj Gen Pick succeeded Raymond A. WHEELER as Army Chief of Engineers on 1 Mar 49. He was promoted to lieutenant general in 1951 and headed the Corps of Engineers to Feb 53. Pick's postwar construction projects included the strategic air base at Thule, Greenland, and the Pick-Sloan system for flood control and irrigation in the Missouri River basin.

PILE, Frederick Alfred. British general. 1884-1976. Remembered for heading the Antiaircraft Command 1939-45, he was born 14 Sep 84 in Dublin, son of the lord mayor. Pile entered the Royal Artillery in 1904. By 1919 he was brevet lieutenant colonel in France, holder of the **MC** and **DSO.**

The gunner was an early advocate of mechanization, joining the Tank Corps in 1923 and later serving as assistant director of mechanization in the war office. In 1931 he inherited the title of baronet acquired by his father in 1900. As commander of the Canal Brigade 1932-36 Sir Frederick was responsible for the defense of Suez before heading the 1st AA Div of the Territorial Army.

In 1939 he took over the Antiaircraft Command as a lieutenant general (*CB 42*), remaining for the duration and being promoted to full general (*S&S*). His command included the guns, searchlights, and observer corps in the defense of London. The **Blitz of London** began 7 Sep 40 with a daylight raid by 372 bombers, causing Goering to exult, "London is in flames!" The initial assault lasted 23 consecutive days until the Germans switched their target to Coventry the night of 14-15 Nov 40 and then undertook the **"Baedeker raids."** The pounding of London resumed in December.

The spring of 1941 brought attacks on seaports in the south of England and on major cities like Liverpool, Manchester, and Birmingham. The Luftwaffe then shifted its main effort to the Russian front but assault on London peaked again in 1944-45 when **V Weapons** were operational.

A slim, amiable, urbane, quiet man, cool under pressure (*CB 42*), Pile worked closely and harmoniously with Churchill, Fighter Command, and the scientists who played a major role in coping with Luftwaffe technology. He pioneered the use of rocket batteries to increase firepower while greatly reducing costs (WC, II, 394).

PIUS XII (Eugenio Pacelli). Pope. 1876-1958. As spiritual leader of about 333 million Catholics in both warring camps Pope Pius XII had a major role in WWII but one that remains incompletely known.

Pacelli was a patrician with a two-century family tradition of church service. His grandfather founded the Vatican's semiofficial daily newspaper, *L'Osservatore Romana,* and his father was dean of lawyers of the Sacred

Tribunal of the Rota. Born 2 Mar 76 in Rome and intensely religious from childhood, Pacelli was a brilliant scholar and gifted linguist. In Rome's Capranica College he earned a doctorate in theology, philosophy, and law. Ordained 2 Apr 99, the tall, lean priest became a monsignor in 1911. He was nuncio to Bavaria from 1917 and titular head of the consular corps in Munich. In 1920 he went to Berlin as nuncio of all Germany. "Each of Pacelli's labors for the Holy See had enhanced his reputation as a veritable prince of diplomats—a model of what was discreet, trustworthy, and diplomatically surefooted" (Deutsch, II, 108). Returning to Italy in 1929 as an archbishop, he was made a cardinal. That year his brother Francisco helped draft the Lateran Treaty, which achieved a modus vivendi with Mussolini's Fascist government. The next year (1930) Pacelli became Vatican secretary of state, and when Hitler came to power in 1933 he negotiated a concordat for all Germany. But in 1937 Pacelli openly condemned the Nazi regime.

In one of the Vatican's fastest elections for centuries, three ballots, Pacelli was elected pope on 2 Mar 39 (his birthday). He was the first papal secretary in centuries to be pope, and the first Roman since 1730. *(CE.)* Succeeding Pius XI, whose policies he had helped shape, Pius XII made peace the theme of his reign.

The Vatican was committed by tradition, now buttressed by the Lateran Treaty, to be aloof from temporal disputes except when invited to be a peacemaker. But these were parlous times for a great church in the real world. There was brief speculation that the new pope would have to take refuge in America. Roosevelt and Pacelli had a special relationship since first meeting in 1936 *(CE)* and in 1940 FDR broke a 70-year US precedent by sending Myron Taylor as his representative to the Vatican. The new pope meanwhile snubbed the German emissary, RIBBENTROP. As for Bolshevik Russia and its avowed atheism Pius XII excluded the USSR from a proposed Vatican conference to preserve peace. At a meeting in May 35 Stalin asked Pierre LAVAL how many divisions the French had to contribute to their proposed collaboration. The visitor to Moscow is reported to have said, "Can't you do something to encourage religion and the Catholics in Russia? It would help me so much with the Pope." This is supposed to have elicited Stalin's famous quip, "Oho! The Pope! How many divisions has he got?" (WC, I, 135.)

On behalf of anti-Hitler conspirators in the fall of 1939, during the Twilight War, Josef MUELLER asked the Holy Father to intermediate between the conspirators and the British. Apparently after a day of deliberation the pope responded, "The German Opposition must be heard in Britain" and offered to be its voice. (Deutsch, 120-1.) "The risks to both the Pope personally and the Church were incalculable," writes Deutsch. This authority adds that the quickly made decision "to act as intermediary between a conspiratorial group in one belligerent state and the government of an enemy country can be reckoned among the most astounding events in the modern history of the papacy" (ibid.). The British did not realize they had a genuine chance to stop Hitler—perhaps the last—so the effort came to nothing. Dr Mueller nevertheless kept contact with the Vatican until the Hitler finally crushed the conspiracy after STAUFFENBERG's bomb attempt on 20 July 44.

Fear of atheistic communism did not permit the pope to call the German struggle with the USSR a crusade, as Hitler and Hitler's enemies alike urged. *(CB 41; CE.)* Charges of anti-Semitism against the pope—of failing to do more to save Jews—were loud during and after the war.

Pius XII issued many humanitarian appeals and concerned himself with the plight of prisoners and displaced persons. The Vatican sheltered political fugitives and aided the Allies covertly. As a sovereign neutral state, although of only 108 acres, the Papal See had ultra-modern communications. The Vatican exchanged diplomats with 37 countries and received reports from 60 papal legates and 1,300 bishops. *(CB 41.)* SS Gen Karl WOLFF got a special papal audience in May 44 when he was laying the groundwork for the secret surrender signed on 29 Apr 45.

The pope created no cardinals during the war but then showed his international outlook by bringing in so many non-Italians that they became the majority for the first time since the 15th century. Having officially remained politically neutral during the war, the Vatican then was increasingly anti-communist.

PLATT, William. British general. 1885-1975. Remembered for his successful campaigns in East Africa and Madagascar (1938-42) Sir William (KCB, 1941) was educated at

Marlborough and Sandhurst. In 1905 he was commissioned in the 4th Bn, Northumberland Fusiliers. Transferring to the 1st Bn and going to India he fought on the NW Frontier (DSO, 1908). Before returning to England in 1913 he visited the Far East and walked battlefields of the Russo-Japanese War. Platt served on the Western Front in 1914-18 and was severely wounded.

After attending Camberley and serving in India and Egypt (1920-26), he was assistant AG in the war office 1927-30. Platt then commanded at the battalion and brigade level. ADC to the king from 1937 until promoted in 1939 to major general he was posted to Khartoum as GOC, Sudan Defense Force, in Wavell's Middle East Command.

The Italians declared war on 11 June 40 and their troops from Abyssinia promptly overran British Somaliland but moved only a few miles across the Sudanese border to occupy Kassala and Gallabat. Emperor HAILE SELASSIE reached Khartoum from England on 3 July 40 to start rallying chieftains in western Abyssinia and to form an expeditionary force from Abyssinian refugees in the Middle East. Orde WINGATE arrived a few months later to advise the emperor and to organize raiders. The Italians evacuated Kassala and Gallabat on 17 Jan 41, two days before Platt began his conquest of Eritrea. The 4th and 5th Ind Divs plus Sudanese troops attacked into Eritrea from Kassala, while from Gallabat and vicinity the 9th Ind Bde enveloped SE to take Metemma (31 Jan 41) and start pressing north of Lake Tana toward the Italian stronghold at Gondar. Platt's main effort from Kassala, far to the north, resulted in heavy action in rugged mountains. The Indian divisions with an attached French foreign legion brigade took the fortress of Keren on 17 Mar 41 at a cost of 4,000 casualties while inflicting 3,000 on the Italians. Led by the foreign legion (de Gaulle, *Unity*, 170) Platt captured Massawa on 7 April, opening the Red Sea route for Allied ships. Detaching the 4th Ind Div for service in the western desert Platt moved south with his remaining force to collaborate with Alan CUNNINGHAM (coming from Kenya) in liberating Abyssinia. After a hard fight for Amba Alagi the 5th Ind Div captured the Duke of AOSTA, viceroy of Abyssinia. With the fall on 27 Nov 41 of Gondar, where Platt linked up with his 9th Ind Bde and the forces coming north from Kenya, East

African operations ended with an impressive British victory. Platt was knighted (KCB) in 1941.

Promoted to lieutenant general heading the new East African Command, Sir William was ordered on 1 July 42 to clear the remaining Vichy troops from Madagascar. On 10 September the 29th British Inf Bde captured the port of Majunga with little opposition. Joined by the 22d East African Bde and small columns of South African troops the 29th Bde captured critical points including the island's capital. The troublesome governor-general took to the bush with some of his staff but surrendered on 19 October after the British captured 750 POWs with no loss to themselves. (WC, IV, 237.) On 8 Jan 43 Platt formally turned over civil authority on Madagascar to LEGENTILHOMME. Promoted to full general in 1943 Platt was GOC East Africa for the rest of the war. He retired in 1946.

PLEVEN, René. French statesman. 1901-93. Born in Rennes on 15 Apr 01 and always a devoted Breton, Pleven joined the Action française as a law student and went on to get a degree in political science. When he failed to qualify as an inspector of finances Pleven reoriented himself toward an industrial career. Thanks to Jean MONNET he joined an English-based American firm—Automatic Telephone Co—and was director general for Europe 1929-39. Mobilized when France went to war, he became assistant chief of the French air mission to the US. When France fell in June 40 Pleven was back in London with MONNET as a member of the French economic mission (WC, II, 205). The two men worked on planning the Anglo-French political union, an idea overtaken by events.

Pleven rallied to de Gaulle in London and was directed to start making postwar plans for the colonies. On a mission to French Equatorial Africa with LECLERC and others, Pleven was instrumental in bringing over the governor of the Chad to de Gaulle (27 Aug 40). In Aug 41 Pleven went back to Washington, this time to improve relations with the Free French. On creation of the French national committee in London, 24 Sep 41, Pleven took charge of the vast field designated as Economics, Finance, and Colonies. He also coordinated the administration of civil departments. On reaching Algiers in late 1942, just after the Allied landings, he devoted all his efforts to the French colonies. As de Gaulle gathered the reins of power Pleven was commissioner for the colonies, 7 June 43-5 Sep 44. He stepped up to be minister for the colonies, 5 Sep-14 Nov 44, then was minister of finance.

Pleven went on to have a distinguished postwar career. Initially in finance and economics he was minister of defense in the governments of Georges Bidault, Pinay, Mayer, and Laniel (1949-54) Meanwhile, on the carrousel of French politics he went around twice as prime minister (*président du Conseil*) 13 July 50-28 Feb 51 and 11 Aug 51-7 Jan 52. He then held three ministerial portfolios: national defense (1952-1954), foreign affairs (two weeks in May 58), and justice (1969-1973).

Defeated in the 1973 elections after almost three decades as a deputy from his native Côtes du Nord Pleven retired from national politics. But he remained active as political director of a regional newspaper and president of the *Centre d'études et de liaison des interets bretons.* (Catherine Kawa sketch in Yvert.) He died 13 Jan 93 in Paris.

POPHAM, Brooke-. *See* BROOKE-POPHAM.

POPITZ, Johannes von. German resistance figure. 1884-1945. Born in Leipzig on 2 Dec 84, Professor Popitz was minister of finance for the state of Prussia, 1933-44. He was a monarchist and favored Crown Prince Frederick WILHELM (1882-1951) as Hitler's successor. From 1938 he was an active conspirator and on the secret cabinet list to be finance minister under GOERDLER. On 26 Aug 43 he had a meeting arranged by Carl Langbehn to sound out HIMMLER on an SS coup against Hitler. Thereafter under close surveillance and arrested on 21 July 44 after the bomb attempt, he was condemned to death by the People's Court. But HIMMLER ordered him kept alive, like Goerdler, for further interrogation and possible service in covert negotiations with the Allies. Popitz was hanged on 2 Feb 45 in Ploetzensee prison. (Wistrich).

POPLAVSKY, Stanislav Gilyarovich. Soviet military leader. 1902-73. Gen Maj Poplavsky, a Pole by birth, commanded a Red Army corps in Aug 44, then headed Polish field armies, the 2d and then the 1st. He was a general colonel at war's end. Poplavsky then commanded the

(Polish) Silesian MD until becoming head of Polish ground troops and chief inspector of the Polish armed forces for military training. In 1955 he was promoted to general of the army (HFS) in the Polish Army. The next year he returned to the USSR with Rokossovsky to be first deputy chief inspector of the USSR ministry of defence until Apr 58. At some point he was given the *Soviet* rank of general of the army. (Kruzhin, 8-9.)

POPOV, Dusko ("Tricyle"). Master spy. 1910-81. A Yugoslav from a prosperous upper-class family of Dubrovnik, Popov was schooled in France and England before finishing law studies in Belgrade and getting a doctorate at Freiburg Univ (1936-38). His close friend there was Johann "Johnny" Jebsen, a campus hero, anti-Nazi, and heir to the Jebsen & Jebsen shipping firm of Hamburg. Johnny joined the Abwehr as a lesser evil to carrying a rifle for the Third Reich and in the summer of 1940 asked Popov to become a secret agent. Popov got in contact with British intelligence in Belgrade, as did his brother Ivo. The Abwehr sent Dusko to Lisbon in Nov 40 as "Ivan" for training under SS Major Ludovico von Karsthoff, the station chief. Ivan reported to the local SIS bureau and flew to England on 21 Dec 40 at Abwehr expense. The SIS renamed him "Scout" and began his training as a double agent. The Germans were delighted to have a spy in England with the social background to get information that other agents would not find "in the street" (Popov, 31). SIS chief Stewart MENZIES called on the skilled services of a bright and alluring Austrian, Friedle Gaertner Sullivan (Popov, 73). A cabaret performer in London clubs who had Abwehr contacts, "Gelatine" was a double agent for MI5, one of C's regular weekend guests and his sister-in-law through her own sister, Lisel Gaertner, who had married Menzies's younger brother, Ian. (West, MI6, 208, and photo caption 3 following p 138.) Friedle walked Popov through British society, joining his network and moving quickly from "social mistress" to the other sort. Gelatine continued to send the Abwehr information in secret writing to the end of the war (Ibid., 208). When a "Dickie" Metcalfe ("Balloon") became the third man, so to speak, Popov was codenamed "Tricycle."

He established cover as an authentic import-export businessman, Yugoslavia still being neutral, and was run by the XX ("double-cross") committee. Popov memorized vast amounts of data to keep his complex cover-stories straight and he returned to Lisbon in January and Mar 41 for long debriefings by Karsthoff and for updated Abwehr instructions.

Popov and Johnny Jebsen met periodically in Lisbon and Madrid. The Yugoslav did not tell his anti-Nazi German friend he had become a double agent, but Johnny soon suspected it and approved. Their game changed when the Germans invaded Yugoslavia on 6 Apr 41.

SIS sent their double agent on a mission to the US in the fall of 1940. The unsuspecting Germans were delighted because they needed to rebuild their moribund spy net in America. With the FBI briefed and waiting, Tricycle flew out of Lisbon on 10 Aug 41 with $40,000 of German funds and a long list of questions the Abwehr wanted answered. Popov carried his secret material on a **microdot**, being the first agent to use this revolutionary method (Popov, 146).

But J. Edgar HOOVER decided that the "youngish traveler from the Balkans . . . the playboy son of a millionaire" was spying on the US (Popov, 200-1). The FBI covertly searched Popov's hotel room in NYC, finding the microdot message. Hoover proceeded to accumulate evidence that Popov was violating the Mann Act, which prohibits transporting women across state lines for immoral purposes! The subject of this interest was one of Popov's long-time playmates, French actress Simone Simon, who stayed with her mother in his NYC apartment building when not in Hollywood. The FBI seized Popov's radio and codes, barred him from access to their transmitting station, and began sending messages to the Abwehr.

Tricycle's Abwehr questionnaire asked for information about US defenses on Oahu that could have interested only the Japanese. Popov also knew that Canaris had sent Jebsen to Italy for a detailed report the Japanese wanted about the British attack on **Taranto.** But Hoover pigeonholed this information.

With no prospect of success in America, having exhausted his funds, and being out of contact with the Abwehr, Popov had the British recall him. Back to Lisbon in Oct 41, and still

in the Abwehr's good graces, Tricycle became involved in the highly successful deception plans for Allied landings in North Africa, Sicily, and Normandy. Popov reestablished contact with Johnny Jensen, who had been reassigned to Lisbon. In early 1943 Johnny became a British double agent, "Artist." He checked for MI6 to discredit reports that Germany was developing a 70-ton rocket capable of carrying a 10-ton atomic warhead. But he discovered in Sep 43 that the **V-1** was in mass production. (Popov, 260.) In mid-May 44 the SS kidnapped Jebsen in Lisbon and spirited him away to the Gestapo dungeon on the Prinz Albrechtstrasse. It turned out that he was suspected only of illegal financial dealings on behalf of influential Nazis, doing this for personal protection in the Nazi jungle. Jebsen withstood brutal interrogations and revealed nothing about his treasonous espionage games. Popov's final tour de force was finding and blackmailing one of his friend's "clients," a Dr Schmidtt, Walter Schellenberg's aide. Popov succeeded in having Johnny moved to **Oranienburg,** and the Tricycle ring went on strike until the Germans appeared willing to give their prisoner safe passage to Lisbon or Switzerland. Final negotiations were being made when Popov learned in late 1944 that Artist had been killed "while trying to escape."

The Tricycle ring deceived the Germans to the end. Having risen to lieutenant colonel in British intelligence, Popov tracked down the man most closely involved in his friend's arrest and death. This was a Kaltenbrunner hatchet man, Oberstrumbahnfuehrer Walter Salzer, a former employee of the Jebsen firm. Apparently Salzer had had Jebsen killed on Kaltenbruner's orders because "Herr Jebsen knew too much about some currency deals." (Popov, 316, 332.) Popov found Salzer and beat him unmercifully but was too revolted by the cowering, self-soiling victim to kill him.

Tricycle retired from the spy business, married, fathered three sons, and made his home in the south of France. His memoirs, with an introduction by Ewen Montagu, close associate in wartime London, are *Spy/Counterspy* (New York: Grosset & Dunlap, 1974). He died 21 Aug 81.

POPOV, Markian Mikhaylovich. Soviet military leader. 1902-69. Born 15 Nov 02 in the village of Ust-Medveditskaya, Volgograd

Region, son of a clerk, Markian Mikhaylovich served on the western front at the end of WWI. He joined the Red Army in 1920 and the CP in 1921. With old the rank of Kombrig he was CofS of the 1st Special Red Banner Army in Far East under Komkor G. M. Shtern (Marshal BLUYKHER's successor) for a year ending in July 39. M. M. Popov then commanded the 1st Red Banner Far Eastern Army.

Popov took command of the Leningrad MD on 14 Jan 41 and headed the Northern Front from its creation on 24 June 41. The next day Popov approved establishment of the main Leningrad defenses some 75 miles SW of the city along the Luga River, where fighting began on 12 July. VOROSHILOV arrived the same day to head the new NW Direction (or TVD). Popov's Northern Front meanwhile was redesignated the Leningrad Front on 23 Aug 41, the NW TVD was abolished on 24 Aug 41 for having been ineffective, and ZHUKOV was named to command the Leningrad Front. "The *Stavka* on 1 September severely reprimanded Popov and his officers for badly organized and insufficiently stubborn defense, and demanded 'more positive' measures," writes Erickson (*To Stalingrad,* 190). Voroshilov replaced Popov temporarily as front commander before Zhukov's arrival on 13 Sep 41 (Scotts; Seaton, *R-G War,* 150n). ZHUKOV's CofS was M. S. Khozin, who commanded the Leningrad MD in 1938.

Stalin learned about this time from the **Rote Kapelle** that Hitler had decided to encircle the city and starve it out. By 25 September, as defenses along the Luga line were being stabilized, LEEB was shifting strength south of the city. The crisis over for a while KHOZIN temporarily succeeded Popov as front commander in October.

Popov headed the 61st Army in the Bryansk Front 12 Nov 41-June 42 (succeeded by BELOV), the 40th Army to Oct 42, and was Yeremenko's deputy in the Stalingrad Front into Nov 42. He then took over the 5th Strike Army but was transferred almost immediately to head the 45th Tank Army. From Apr 43 he had the Reserve Front until it was reformed as the Steppe MD.

Promoted to general colonel he directed the Bryansk Front from June 43 until raised in rank to general of the army in command of the Baltic Front, which became the 2d Baltic Front in Oct

43. He was relieved and demoted in Apr 44. Gen Col Popov then was CofS of the Leningrad Front and of the 2d Baltic Front before returning to hold that post in the Leningrad Front. He headed the Lvov MD, 1945-46. In 1953, as chief of the Tavrida MD, he was restored to the rank of general of the army. (Kruzhin, 6.) In the Inspectorate from July 62 he died 22 Apr 69 in an accident and was buried at Moscow's **Novodvichy Monastery.**

POPOV, Vasily Stepanovich. Soviet military leader. 1893-1967. Born 27 Dec 93 in the village of Preobrazhenka, now in Volgograd Oblast, he served with the Don Cossacks in WWI. He joined the CP in 1919, was a Red Cavalry officer 1920-38 and a Frunze MA instructor in 1939. He commanded a rifle corps in the Finnish War and in June 41 was a general major heading the 28th Rifle Corps around Grodno.

In Sep 41 he became deputy commander of the 50th Army and with Ivan V. BOLDIN escaped the Vyasma encirclement early the next month. Retreating SE to Tula, which GUDERIAN bypassed on 17 Nov 41, Popov became Boldin's deputy for rear services when Boldin took command of the 50th Army on 22 Nov 41. On 3 December Popov began a penetration with a mobile force between Guderian's panzers and the German 43d Corps. After a week of house-to-house fighting, Popov took Kaluga and saved Tula (Erickson, *To Stalingrad,* 282; Zhukov, 350).

Popov commanded the 10th Army from Feb 42 and the following June was promoted to general lieutenant. Popov began forming the so-called 2d Tank Corps in the Stalingrad area in Sep 42. Having fewer than 50 tanks, most of them fit only for use in fixed positions, Popov formed a special command that held three critical strongpoints behind YEREMENKO's bridgehead as preparations were completed for the Stalingrad counteroffensive. (Erickson, 388, 432-33.)

In the last year of the war V. S. Popov headed the 70th Army. This was formed around Kovel on 17 Feb 44 in KUROCHKIN's 2d Belorussian Front. Popov's subsequent front commanders in the grinding battles through Belorussia into Pomerania were I. Ye. PETROV (from Apr 44) and ROKOSSOVKSY (from 5 June 44). In April and May 44

Popov was deputy commander of the 1st Belorussian Front.

A HSU in 1945 he headed a faculty at the Frunze MA. Popov spent a year with the General Staff before retiring in 1959. He died 2 July 67 in Moscow.

PORTAL, Charles Frederick Algernon "Peter." British air marshal. 1893-1971. Portal had primary responsibility for building and directing the RAF from Oct 40 to Jan 46. On both sides of the Atlantic he was called Britain's leading airman.

Described by a younger officer with some exaggeration as "fantastically ugly" (*CB 41*) Portal was tall (5 feet 11), "big boned but slight, with a beakish nose" and Huguenot heritage showing in his face and temperament. He was born 21 May 93 at Eddington House, near Hungerford, son of a countryman who had been a barrister *(DNB)*.

Childhood fascination with falconry led Peter (as he was always known to friends and relatives) to begin publishing articles about it at the age of 16. Entering Christ Church, Oxford, in Oct 12 he did well academically despite the hours he spent hawking, beagling, and motorcycling. In May 14 he won a famous motorcycle race against Cambridge, about the time Richard Peirse was winning a similar event. Passing his courses at Oxford he used his bike as a ticket to France in Aug 14 and was immediately promoted to corporal in the motorcycle section of the Royal Engineers. The not-quite-tireless messenger won attention by falling asleep on his wheels and crashing into the back of a staff car carrying Sir Douglas Haig *(DNB)*. But Portal was mentioned for valor in a BEF dispatch on 8 Oct 14 (for another deed), commissioned on 26 October, and about six weeks later given command of all riders in the 1st Corps Hq Signals Co.

He qualified as an aircraft observer in July 15 and graduated as a flying officer in Apr 16. For outstanding skill and gallantry during five months of the Somme offensive he was awarded the MC on 19 Jan 17, appointed to the DSO six months later and a year later awarded a bar. *(DNB.)* By war's end the 25-year-old Lt Col (T) Peter Portal had flown more than 900 operational sorties for tactical reconnaissance, artillery fire direction, and night bombing.

In 1927 he took over a bomber squadron (No. 7) and became known for developing techniques for improved accuracy. After air ministry staff assignments from 1930 he was sent to Aden in Feb 34 to command the British forces there. Portal demonstrated that air power alone could control hostile tribesmen, not by punitive action but by a sustained air blockade and threat of attack. For this almost bloodless achievement Portal was promoted to air commodore on 1 Jan 35. Late the following summer, when Aden was reinforced to face the challenge of Mussolini's Abyssinian adventure, Portal joined the Imperial Defense College staff. Here he sowed the seeds of inter-service cooperation and made friendships that would be valuable in the coming years.

Promoted to air vice-marshal in July 37 as the RAF expanded for war, Portal was director of organization in the air ministry for a hectic 18 months. Much of his work had to do with establishing more than 30 new air bases that would be vital in the Battle of Britain. On 1 Feb 39 Portal became air member for personnel with a seat on the Air Council. In the critical assignment of manning the expanding RAF he was promoted to air marshal on 3 Sep 39, when Britain declared war.

Portal headed the Bomber Command (BC) 4 Apr-4 Oct 40. Whereas Fighter Command performed brilliantly, RAF bombers bombed out—only the vernacular can express it. Planes could not find targets, much less hit them. Portal had barely assumed his duties when the problems first were apparent in Norway. BC's shortcomings were even more conspicuous when the Battle of Flanders began on 10 May 40. Only Portal's prompt demand for fighter cover saved the Blenheim medium bombers from complete annihilation *(DNB)*. But Portal shaped up his command so that it effectively hit Hitler's invasion ports and barge concentrations. The RAF's reprisal attack on Berlin caused little material damage but led the Germans to a critical error: shifting the Luftwaffe's main effort from Fighter Command's ground installations to London. This was decisive in the Battle of Britain.

Hailed by Churchill as "the accepted star of the Air Force" (WC, II, 20), Portal was knighted (KCB) in July 40 and on 25 Oct 40 he replaced Sir Cyril L. Newall as chief of the air staff (CAS). With the RAF's highest post came the rank of air chief marshal (T). Portal promptly changed the air strategy he previously had opposed, largely on humanitarian grounds: BC would start area bombing of German industry, abandoning attempts at precision bombing.

But Portal's first major problem was to resolve the **"big wing controversy."** Fighter Command chief Hugh DOWDING and PARK, who had led his most heavily committed fighter group, argued that the proposed change in strategy would slow response time, which would mean a greater loss of British property and civilian lives. With no radar in single-seated fighters of the time, RAF ground stations could pick up large enemy formations only at long range, then order a scramble and let pilots find targets. Dowding objected also that the big wing concept would cost the RAF more pilots over the Channel because they could not parachute to safety. Convincing arguments on the other side were made by opponents including Sholto DOUGLAS.

A month after assuming office, Portal replaced DOWDING with DOUGLAS, who promptly replaced PARK with LEIGH-MALLORY. Fighter Command began **big wing** operations, escorting bombers over France and making deep strikes. "At the time it was thought that the tactics had achieved extraordinary success" (Andrews, *The Air Marshals,* 135). But postwar statistical analysis showed that in destroying 114 Luftwaffe fighters over the Continent the RAF lost 426 pilots, more than in the entire Battle of Britain (ibid.). Portal meanwhile still had to address the disappointing performance of BC, which Richard PEIRSE now headed. The strain on Portal became alarming (WC, II, 700, 711). After a bitter year Portal brought in Sir Arthur HARRIS on 22 Feb 42 to replace Peirse.

Meanwhile the harried CAS blocked an attempt in the autumn of 1940 to transfer the RAF's Coastal Command to the Admiralty. Powerful proponents of this proposal were Albert V. Alexander, 1st lord of the Admiralty, and BEAVERBROOK, minister of aircraft production. But Portal won out by arguing that Coastal Command's weakness was due only to lack of resources, and with 1st Sea Lord Dudley Pound he worked out a solution: Coastal Command would be strengthened and formally placed under the Admiralty's **opera-**

tional control. A year later, in the autumn of 1941, Portal blocked Churchill's effort to recall TEDDER from the Middle East. Portal won another victory when Alan Brooke, CIGS, campaigned in 1942 for a very large and virtually separate air force dedicated to tactical air support. *(DNB.)*

During Portal's first two years in office, there was a question of whether he would measure up (Andrews, 155). In time for the invasion of Europe, however, Bomber Command's performance improved dramatically; with more powerful bombs and now achieving good precision, BC did more at night to support the **transportation plan** than US strategic bombers did by day. BC also became a reliable daylight force. (Andrews, Ibid., 262-63.)

Churchill was to say before the war ended, "Portal has everything." Tedder called his calm, unflappable chief "the real brains" of British strategic planning, superior to CIGS Alan BROOKE (Tedder, 532-33). Ian JACOBS wrote, "The Americans put their money on Portal. They would accept him as Commander-in-Chief over . . . all Allied air forces from Iceland to Bombay . . ." (Tunney).

Made a baron in 1945 the airman became the 1st Viscount Portal of Hungerford a year later. He died 22 Apr 71, at West Ashling House, after a brief struggle with cancer. Viscount Portal wrote no memoirs. (Denis Richards in *DNB.*)

PORTES, Hélène. French Egeria. c1910-40. With wealth and a title, the unlovely lady with the pretty name, Countess Hélène de Portes, was to Paul REYNAUD what the Marquise de Crussol was to DALADIER and what "Madame Soutien-Georges" was to her husband Georges Bonnet. Hélène de Porte's title came from marriage in about 1930 to Count Jean de Portes, whom she soon left in Marseilles with her father's prosperous shipping business on setting off to conquer Paris. Nobody has fathomed why the unkempt countess with the raucous voice had such a fatal allure to Reynaud. "Most probably it resided in his small stature," writes Horne. "As one Frenchman remarked, 'She made him feel tall and grand and powerful.' He needed and depended upon his Hélène, and . . . she in her turn, dedicated to seeing her hero reach the top of the political ladder, sustained him and goaded him in his strong ambitions." (Horne, *1940*, 178.)

Mme de Portes was christened "*la porte à côté*," the side door, but she became the front door to the premier's office. Hélène's mortal enemy was the Marquise de Crussol, a youthful-looking and rather handsome blonde whose Breton family had made a fortune in canning sardines. Punsters called her "*la sardine qui s'est crue sole,*"—the sardine pretending to be sole (the gourmet fish). Whereas the marquise worked quietly behind the scenes on Daladier's behalf, Reynaud's athletic mistress was brash, ruthless, vitriolic, and pushy. Reproached by his friend André Maurois for being hag ridden, Reynaud said, "Ah, you don't know what a man who has been hard at work all day will put up with to make sure of an evening's peace." (Horne, 179.) But she could not nag Reynaud into accepting that France should sue for an armistice. He resigned on 16 June 40 and fled from Bordeaux with Hélène by car. She died instantly on 28 June 40 when he ran off the road and hit a tree, or slammed on the brakes too suddenly; highly stacked suitcases hurled forward from the back seat, breaking the lady's neck. Not knowing this until he regained consciousness in a hospital, having been half scalped, Reynaud is alleged to have said "*Elle était la France.*" (Horne, 596; compare Pertinax, 311.) Mme Reynaud said a few days later to a friend, "And now, *chérie*, for my revenge." (Murphy, *Diplomat*, 61-62).

POUND, Alfred Dudley Pickman Rogers. British admiral. 1877-1943. Dudley Pound was born 29 Aug 77 on the Isle of Wight. His father was a barrister, and his mother was the former Elizabeth Pickman Rogers of Boston, Mass.

Pound entered the RN as a cadet in 1891 at the age of 14. In the Battle of Jutland in 1916, as flag captain in the battleship *Colossus,* he sank two cruisers, beat off two destroyers, and eluded a spread of five torpedoes. He then was posted to the Admiralty as head of a new section that evolved into the plans division, of which he became director in 1922. Pound was a vice admiral in 1930, and two years later was 2d Sea Lord and chief of naval personnel. In Jan 35 he was named to succeed Sir William Fisher as CinC Mediterranean. Because of the Abyssinian crisis the Admiralty

decided against the change but Pound volunteered to be Fisher's CofS. In 1936, when tension eased, Pound took the post for which he was so eminently qualified. For skilfully handling of a tricky political situation exacerbated by the **Spanish Civil War** Pound was knighted (**GCVO**) in 1937 and advanced later to **GCB** (1939).

Sir Dudley was appointed 1st First Sea Lord on 31 July 39 despite a brain tumor the fleet medical officer couldn't bring himself to tell the Admiralty about (Ludovic Kennedy, 107). The admiral also had a hip disease that kept him from sleeping well at night and, causing him to doze off during meetings. But Sir Dudley Lord was regarded with respect and affection by peers and superiors, particularly—for his compliancy—by Churchill. Some have credited Pound with winning the battle of the Atlantic, but the prime minister realized early in Mar 42 that the 1st Sea Lord was not up to remaining chairman of the Chiefs of Staff Committee. The admiral graciously yielded the post to Alan BROOKE. During the first Quebec conference, 14-24 Aug 43, Pound showed signs of serious health problems (Bryant, *Tide,* 571). Less than a month later Sir Dudley told Churchill (during the PM's visit to Washington) that he was no longer fit for duty. Vice Adm Edward N. Syfret took over until it was announced on 4 Oct 43 that Andrew "ABC" CUNNINGHAM would be 1st First Sea Lord. Pound died 21 Oct 43, Trafalgar Day, in a London hospital.

PRIEN, Guenther. U-boat skipper. 1908-41. His sinking of *Royal Oak* at Scapa Flow on 14 Oct 39 is one of the most remarkable exploits in naval history. The hero was born in Osterfeld on 16 Jan 08, became a sailor at the age of 15, and for two years was an officer on the Hamburg Amerika Line. In 1933 he went on duty as a naval officer. Although a similar attempt in WWI had cost the Germans two submarines, Lt Prien navigated U-47 through the one open channel into the Bay of Scapa Flow at nightfall on Friday, 13 Oct 39. Running on the surface to survey the harbor on what was picked as a dark night with a new moon, he found a northern light display almost too helpful. The raider discovered that the Home Fleet was at sea but he fired three torpedoes at the one big ship left. Only one exploded on the target; the others apparently being defective (*R&H,* 8). The skipper turned and fired from his stern tube, but there was another failure. Still on the surface, and undetected (the British thinking the explosion was internal), Pried cruised away and reloaded two tubes. A three-torpedo attack got three hits at 1:30 AM on 14 Oct 39; 45 minutes later U-47 was safely away, and *Royal Oak* was lost with 833 dead.

Prien went on to be credited with 28 merchant ships, 160,935 tons (Doenitz, 175). South of Iceland on the evening of 6 Mar 41 he led a wolfpack attack on an outbound convoy, OB 293, that cost the Germans two U-boats in sinking only two ships and damaging two others. Shadowing the well-escorted merchantmen he got too close and was surprised by a destroyer as a sheltering rain squall suddenly lifted. Depth charges damaged U-47's propeller shafts as she crash dived, and Comdr J. M. Rowland pursued on DD *Wolverine.* Rowland kept **ASDIC** contact and attacked again when his quarry surfaced after dark to run for safety. Prien dove again but renewed depth charge attacks finished him off. (Macintyre, 83.)

Prien's best-selling memoirs were translated into English after the war as *I Sank the Royal Oak.* "Prien was all that a man should be," wrote Doenitz, "a great personality, full of zest and energy and the joy of life. . ." (Doenitz, 175).

PU-YI, Henry. Puppet emperor of Manchuria. 1905-67. Last heir of the Manchu emperors, he was forced to abdicate in 1912 at the age of seven when the Chinese Republic was created. For the next 10 years he lived with an entourage in a corner of the old palace in Peking, growing into "a weak, vain, bespectacled pervert" (Bergamini, 440). The Japanese later moved him into their concession in Tiensin and in late 1932 made him regent in Manchuria. He was bestowed the title Emperor Kang Teh in 1934 but used the name Henry Pu-Yi in dealing with the west; in liberated China he was called the Emperor Hsuan-T'ung until the communist takeover, then Aisin Giro Pu Yi. Under that name he published *From Emperor to Citizen* (2 vols, Peking: Foreign Language Press, 1964, 1965). He died in Peking on 17 Oct 67 at the age of 61.

See Henry McAleavy, *A Dream of Tartary: The Origins and Misfortunes of Henry Pu Yi* (London: George Allen and Unwin, Ltd, 1963).

PULLER, Lewis Burwell "Chesty". US Marine officer. 1898-1971. When he reached Guadalcanal with his battalion of the 7th Marine Regt to join the 1st Marine Div in Sep 42 Lt Col Puller already wore two Navy Crosses for action in Nicaragua, 1931 and 1932. The night of 24-25 Oct 42 he won a third NC for holding a mile-long section of the line around Henderson Field. After army forces under PATCH relieved the Marines, Puller was XO, 7th Marines, for the Cape Gloucester operations that began on 26 Dec 43. When two battalion commanders were wounded, Lt Col Puller assumed overall command and attacked successfully. Awarded his fourth NC and promoted, Col Puller led the 1st Marine Regt ashore on Peleliu, 15 Sep 44. Despite 65 per cent casualties the regiment accomplished its mission.

Two months later the colonel returned to the States, where he commanded a training unit for the rest of the war. Puller won a fifth NC in Korea and retired in 1955.

PURKAYEV, Maksim Alekseyevich. Soviet military leader. 1894-1953. Purkayev was born 26 Aug 94 of peasant stock in the village of Nalitovo, which now bears his name in the Mordovian **ASSR.** He was drafted in 1915. The next year he graduated from the Saratov Ensigns' School and from 1918 was in the Red Army, joining the **CP** a year later. Originally an artilleryman, he served thereafter in the infantry. By 1936, after the normal staff, command, and service school assignments (graduating from the Frunze MA in 1936), he was commanding a division. In 1939 he was **MA** in Berlin briefly, leaving to be CofS, Western Special MD, which became M. P. Kovalev's Belorussian Front for the occupation of Poland in Sep 39. Purkayev retained the CofS post until Nov 39. In 1940-41 he was CofS in Kiev under ZHUKOV and his successor, KIRPONOS, who headed the Southwest Front for what the Soviets call the Western Ukraine Defensive Operations, 22 June-6 July 41. Purkayev escaped the Kiev encirclement and in November took command the 60th Army; this became the 3d Shock Army in December. In TIMOSHENKO's Northwest

Front he had a critical role in the Red Army's first successful strategic envelopment. This began against the Demyansk salient on 8 Feb 42, and the 3d Shock Army linked up near Saluchi with elements of V. I. Morozov's 11th Army to seal off about 90,000 Germans. Purkayev succeeded KONEV in Aug 42 as Kalinin Front commander and on 18 Nov 42 was promoted to general colonel (HFS).

After making the deep penetration to liberate Velikiye Luki, he took over the Far Eastern Front in Apr 43 and was promoted on 28 Oct 44 to general of the army (No. 28). His 2d Far Eastern Front, formed on 5 Aug 45, took Harbin and joined forces with the Pacific Fleet to overrun the southern half of Sakhalin Island and the Kuriles (Scarecrow). After the war he commanded the Far Eastern MD until Jan 47 (HFS). When the Soviet FE high command was reformed in May 47 Purkayev became its CofS and MALINOVSKY's first deputy CinC. From 1952 he headed the Directorate of Military Institutions of Higher Learning, the Training Establishments Board, then was minister of defense. General of the Army Purkayev died 1 Jan 53 in Moscow.

PYLE, Ernest Taylor. American war correspondent. 1900-45. "A frail little man, a gentle soul who hated war" (Morison, XIV, 241), he was born 3 Aug 00 on a farm near Dana, Indiana *(CB 41)*. After studying journalism for three and a half years at the Univ of Indiana he dropped out in 1923 to write for newspapers in his home state. In 1932 he became managing editor of the *Daily News* in Washington, DC. Three years later he left to become a roving reporter, avoiding big cities and writing about little things. In Nov 40 he flew via Lisbon to London and wrote a folksy, down-home column, "Ernie Pyle in London." This ran in 18 Scripps-Howard papers and 46 others *(CB 41)*.

When US troops entered combat in 1942 Ernie Pyle accompanied them from North Africa to Sicily, Italy, and France. In 1943 he was awarded the Pulitzer Prize for covering (like cartoonist Bill MAULDIN) the war as seen by the relatively few men who did the fighting. After the war in Europe ended he went reluctantly to the Pacific. He had filed only a few stories when he was killed 18 Apr 45 by a Japanese machine gunner on Ie Shima, an island near Okinawa.

Q

QUESADA, Elwood R(ichard) "Pete." US general. 1904-93. A bright, engaging, creative leader born 13 Apr 04 of Spanish-Irish descent, Pete Quesada (pronounced KAY sada) rose from the ranks to become an airman. He was promoted to brigadier general on 11 Dec 42 (AA, 925), given command of a wing, and a few weeks later he headed the 12th Ftr Cmd.

Brig Gen Quesada led the 12th over Tunisia, Sicily, Corsica, and Italy until becoming deputy commander of the Coastal Air Force (based in North Africa). Going to England in Oct 43 he took over the 9th Ftr Cmd and on 28 Apr 44 was promoted to major general. He supported the Normandy landings on 6 June 44 with his headquarters operating ashore on D+1.

The boyish-looking general was an innovator in a field shunned by many airmen outside the Luftwaffe. When he proposed suspending bombs from Spitfires the RAF protested that this was not only unseemly but impossible. Quesada replied that British planes in the 9th TAC were his, and they became fighter-bombers! He then fitted the big Thunderbirds with two racks, each carrying a 1,000-lb egg. The enterprising nonconformist next ordered a Sherman tank for experimental installation of the VHF radios that his air support parties had in jeeps. "For a while Quesada's tank failed to be delivered," writes Weigley, "because Ordnance could not believe that IX TAC was the right address for the recipient" (ETO, 165). The experiment worked, and ground-to-air control teams could operate near the head of armored columns and get air strikes faster.

Maj Gen Quesada became air force chief of intelligence in Apr 45. Two years later he retired with three stars.

.

QUEZON, Manuel. Philippines president. 1878-1944. Manuel Luis Quezon Antonio y Molina was born 19 Aug 78 in the isolated coastal village of Baler in eastern Luzon. Both parents were schoolteachers, and the mother had Spanish blood. (CB 41.)

Quezon was studying law when the Spanish-American War broke out in 1898. Enlisting as

Manuel Kison, he became known as a hot-tempered, tenacious soldier, rising to major and, after fighting the Spanish, he joined the insurrection that Douglas MACARTHUR's father eventually put down. After six months in jail he began training for the priesthood. The Catholic fathers in Manila decided he was better suited to managing a church farm outside the capital. Quezon soon returned to Manila where, working at a Catholic bank, he completed his law studies at the Univ of Santo Thomas. A fellow graduate in 1903 was Sergio OSMENA, who thereafter was alternately the dynamic Queson's political ally and opponent.

Quezon established a lucrative practice in Baler but soon entered politics. From provincial prosecuting attorney he moved on to be governor of Tayabas Prov. in 1906, resigning the next year to win election to the Philippine Assembly as a member of the Nacionalista Party. OSMENA became speaker of the house and Quezon was floor leader until beginning a long tour as resident commissioner in Washington 1909-16 and coming home a hero with the Jones Act. This gave Filipinos legislative power subject to veto by the American governor general. Quezon steadily increased his political base and was instrumental in winning additional US concessions on nationalist issues.

While the constitutional convention in Manila was at work in 1934 Quezon, who would be president of the Philippine Commonwealth from its founding the next year, undertook a mission to Washington that he considered to be of prime importance: establishment of an American military mission to direct the defense of the Philippines. Douglas MACARTHUR, then Army CofS, was of great help and encouragement. This led to America's most distinguished soldier becoming military adviser to the Philippines late in 1935. (James, MacArthur, I, 479 ff). Mrs Quezon would say later that her husband and the general came to be "like brothers" (James, II, 93).

Soon after the Japanese invaded in Dec 41 President Quezon took his family and government to Corregidor with MacArthur. He now was a very sick man, his tuberculosis exacerbated by dust from bombing and by dampness in the Malinta tunnel. When it became apparent that America could not save the Philippines the deeply depressed Quezon came up with a proposal: If the US offered to withdraw its troops and grant independence to the Philippines, Quezon would undertake to persuade the Japanese to do the same. The suggestion was forwarded to Washington on 8 Feb 42 with MacArthur's endorsement and the blessing of High Commissioner Francis B. Sayre. Washington was appalled, STIMSON calling the proposal "wholly unreal" (ibid, 93-96). But Quezon was invited to bring his family and government to Washington if possible. On 20 Feb 42 the president of the commonwealth (in pyjamas), and a party of 10 including OSMENA, left Corregidor aboard SS *Swordfish*. Via Panay and Australia they reached Washington in May 42. Having headed a government in exile, Quezon died 1 Aug 44 and was succeeded by OSMENA.

QUINAN, Edward Pellew. British general. 1884-1960. As British commander in Iran Lt Gen Quinan directed the brief campaign of 25-28 Aug 41 to secure the vital oil fields. (SLIM crushed the only serious resistance by Iranian troops.) Quinan became GOC 10th Army in Iran when AUCHINLECK assumed responsibility for Iran and Iraq on 5 Jan 42, Henry "Jumbo" WILSON having the corresponding post in Iraq as GOC 9th Army. (*OCMH Chron,* 12.) In 1943 Quinan went to India as Northwestern Army commander and retired that year.

QUISLING, Vidkun Abraham Lauritz. Norwegian quisling. 1887-1945. Born in Fyresdal, Norway, on 18 July 87, he was trained from childhood for a military career. After entering the army in 1905 as a field artillery officer he held many diplomatic assignments. These included serving as MA in Petrograd, 1918-19, in the Helsinki legation, on many League of Nations commissions and representing Norway on famine and refugee relief efforts in the Ukraine and the Balkans. Quisling married a native of Kharkov in 1923 and was fluent in Russian although ardently anti-communist. While on the legation staff in Moscow during 1927-29 he had charge of the British legation when the UK temporarily

broke diplomatic relations with the USSR and he was rewarded by appointment as honorary commander of the **OBE.**

Major Quisling was war minister 1931-32. But as a Farmer Party member out of step with a cabinet dominated by progressive laborites he resigned under pressure. Quisling formed the *Nasjonal Samling,* but the party never got a single member elected to the Storting (parliament). This threw the failed politician into the Nazi orbit.

Using businessman Wiljam Hagelin for liaison work Quisling visited Berlin in June and Dec 39. He got a favorable reception from Alfred ROSENBERG, who arranged for Quisling's followers to take a training course in August. On his second trip the Norwegian Nazi had a cold reception at the foreign office because of his known anti-Soviet sentiments. But he found an interested listener in RAEDER, who long had urged the invasion of Norway to secure naval bases. Meetings on 14 and 18 Dec 39 with Hitler prompted the fuehrer to order that planning for the invasion be undertaken, but without Quisling being made privy then or later. Hitler obviously realized that the burly Norwegian was a slim reed.

Even when FALKENHORST invaded Norway on 9 Apr 40 the Germans did not inform Quisling. Although he was a leader without followers the arrogant, dogmatic Quisling proclaimed himself head of government. King HAAKON refused to sanction the move. Hitler simply ignored it but did direct that the collaborator be given an "honorable position" and "held in reserve" (Petrow, 100). A puppet government was established 1 Feb 42 under Joseph TERBOVEN but Quisling never had enough popular support to help the Germans.

At the end of Jan 45, with the Soviets only 110 miles from Berlin, Minister President Quisling met with Hitler. A joint communique said that "Germany will restore the complete liberty and independence of Norway after victory," and Quisling apparently believed he would head the government. (Petrow, 350.) Refusing a last-minute chance to escape to Spain (Ziemke, *GNT,* 314) he was arrested 9 May 45 and confined. His trial began on 20 Aug 45; it was reported by the most foreign correspondents ever assembled in Norway. The charges ranged from theft, drunkenness, debauchery, and complicity in the murder of Jews to grand treason.

He made an impressive defense on minor charges but and pleaded lack of memory on the others. The trial was interrupted at midpoint for medical and psychiatric examination. Judged sane, he made an incoherent final argument that lasted eight hours and raised questions about the sanity ruling. Finding the accused guilty of all major charges including murder and treason, the court announced the death sentence on 10 Sep. Appeal was quickly rejected, as was a wifely petition of reprieve. Quisling was taken from his cell at 2 AM on 24 Oct 45 and executed half an hour later by a firing squad. (Petrow, 356.)

The fifth column, so effective in many other Nazi campaigns, was not a factor in Norway because of the German need for secrecy in the military planning (Ziemke, 112). "Quisling was from the first a source of political embarrassment and a military liability in that he contributed greatly to the failure of the intended 'peaceful' occupation" (ibid.). But dictionaries around the world had a new word: "quisling, n.: a traitor who collaborates with the invaders of his country esp. by serving in a puppet government" (Webster's Ninth New Collegiate).

R

RADFORD, Arthur William. US admiral. 1896-1973. A carrier division admiral during the war, "Raddy" rose to be JCS chairman. Born 27 Feb 96 in Chicago he attended high school in Grinnell, Iowa, was appointed to Annapolis from that state, and graduated in 1916 (59/177). During WWI he served in a battleship and was ADC to several admirals. In 1920 he qualified as a naval aviator, later having aviation assignments afloat and ashore. Before the outbreak of war in the Pacific he was CO NAS Seattle, 1937-40, XO of CV *Yorktown,* 1940-1, then he established and commanded NAS Trinidad in 1941. For two years beginning in Jan 42, when promoted, Capt Radford was director of aviation training (BuAer). He organized the vastly expanded program of training "and deserves great credit for keeping up high standards under pressure" (Morison, VII, 95-96n.). Requesting sea duty, in Apr 43 he was sent to the staff of Carrier Div 2. Three months later, promoted to flag rank, Rear Adm Radford took command of Carrier Div 11. He led this through the Gilbert Islands campaign, was CofS, Naval Air Pacific, Jan-May 44, and was assistant deputy CNO for air and alternate member of the special JCS Committee on Reorganization of National Defense.

Returning to the Pacific in Nov 44 to serve under MITSCHER as commander of Carrier Div 6 he took part in the Iwo Jima and Okinawa operations, then directing air strikes on Japan. Radford was deputy CNO for air from Dec 45 and worked on plans for the postwar navy. Promoted in May 46, a few months after his 50th birthday, Vice Adm Radford became head of the 2d Fleet in the Atlantic in Feb 47. The next year he was vice CNO, promoted to four-star rank. Radford figured prominently in the "revolt of the admirals" (*see* FORRESTAL).

On 7 Apr 49 Adm Radford became CinC Pacific Fleet, holding this post during the Korean War. He was JCS chairman 1953-57. Retiring 1 Aug 57 he died on 17 Aug 73 at Bethesda USNH, Md.

RAEDER, Erich. German admiral. 1876-1960. He was CinC of the German Navy from 1928 until succeeded by DOENITZ early in 1943. Erich Raeder was born 24 Apr 76 at Wandsbek in Schleswig-Holstein. His father was a language teacher who became headmaster of a **Realgymnasium** and his family of civil servants, farmers, pastors, educators, with a sprinkling of military officers, typified what Europeans call the haute bourgeoisie. With a good classical education Raeder became a sincerely religious, decent man. He entered the Imperial Navy in 1894 and quickly showed the diligence and ability that took him to the top. As CofS to Vice Adm Franz von Hipper from 1912 he saw action in WWI. He was promoted to admiral and head of the German Navy in 1928. Hitler confirmed him in this position after taking power in 1933.

Raeder found National Socialism repugnant but condoned it as a means of restoring Germany to great power status. He shared this outlook with army comrades, but unlike them was given a relatively free hand: Hitler hated salt water and admitted knowing nothing about this element. But Raeder had a powerful enemy in Reinhard HEYDRICH.

In 1935 Raeder refused promotion to grand admiral because this would make him senior to his army counterpart, FRITSCH, whom Hitler was not giving the rank of field marshal. But in 1936 Raeder took the title of admiral general that Hitler created for him. Not until 1939 did he accept the rank of grand admiral, last held in Germany by Alfred von Tirpitz (1849-1930). Raeder thought the rank would help him resist the pernicious influence of GOERING, who had been made a field marshal, and who used his dual capacity as head of the Luftwaffe and director of the German economy to hog industrial capacity the navy needed. Goering also blocked development of a separate naval air service, and the Luftwaffe's incompetence in the field of naval aviation kept Raeder from using surface and submarine forces with maximum effectiveness.

Raeder's guiding principle in rebuilding a navy to challenge the British was to concentrate initially on forces designed for raids and harassment. This led to construction of the superbattleships *Tirpitz* and *Bismarck,* "pocket battle-ships" like *Graf Spee,* cruisers like *Prinz Eugen,* and the submarine service. But Hitler's rush to war caught the German navy even less prepared than the army.

Raeder had long been convinced that he would need bases in Denmark and Norway for a war with the British. He also realized that they and the French would fight to deny Germany these bases. In Oct 39 Raeder sent Hitler his proposals for what evolved into the conquest of Norway. Philip VIAN's raid on the *Altmark* speeded up the timetable, leading to a rapid conquest in Apr 40 with the navy having a major role. Losses were so heavy that Raeder's force was crippled for months, but he got the bases he wanted, and the shipment of Swedish iron ore was guaranteed.

Always convinced that Britain was the main enemy, Raeder supported the planned German invasion of England. But the Luftwaffe first had to get air superiority. When Goering failed to win the Battle of Britain Raeder was one of the most vocal in convincing Hitler to call the off the cross-Channel attempt. He then argued against the invasion of Russia.

On several occasions the fuehrer backed down when Raeder threatened resignation—Hitler was prepared to take over the army personally but not the navy. But Hitler lost patience when Germany's splendid and costly new warships were sunk or bottled up in French and Norwegian waters. The fuehrer proposed scrapping inactive warships, whereas Raeder argued that they still tied up British naval strength.

Raeder's end came in late 1942 when *Luetzow* and *Admiral Hipper* failed to stop a large Arctic convoy and broke off action without authority. Hitler learned of the fiasco from foreign press reports and accused the navy of timidity. Raeder resigned on 30 Jan 43 and was succeeded by DOENITZ.

The elderly grand admiral was appointed Admiral Inspector of the Navy, which entitled him to a state funeral. But Hitler's final dig was not making the customary award of the Oakleaves to the departing chief. The Russians took Raeder and his wife prisoner at Potsdam. On charges of conspiring to wage aggressive war (specifically against Norway) and of war crimes (passing on the **Commando Order**) the Nuremberg tribunal sentenced the admiral to life imprisonment. The victors exonerated him of criminal charges in such areas as unrestricted submarine warfare (including the sinking of the *Athenia*) and of actually carrying out the Commando order. (Davidson, *Trial,* 380 ff.)

At Spandau the admiral became increasingly feeble in body, mind, and spirit. Thanks to extraordinary efforts by his lawyer, Walter Siemers, he was released in 1955. Raeder collaborated with a naval friend to produce a two-volume memoir, *Mein Leben* (1956-57). Due to the conditions under which written, the work is badly flawed (Deutsch, I, 95n). Raeder died 6 Nov 60 in Kiel at 84.

RAMCKE, Hermann Bernhard. German general. 1889-1968. General of Parachute Troops Ramcke commanded the 2d Para Div in the dogged defense of Fortress Brest, 7 Aug-19 Sep 44, for which Hitler awarded him both the Swords (99/159) and Diamonds (20/27) as of the latter date (Angolia, I, 93).

Ramcke was born on 24 Jan 89 and began his career as a cabin boy in the navy. Rising to **Feldwebel** as a member of the Marine Division in Flanders he won the highest Prussian decoration awarded to enlisted men for valor (the Militaerverdienstkreuz). Commissioned at this time, Leutnant Ramcke showed outstanding bravery through 1918 and joined a Freikorps in the Baltic states. He ultimately transferred to the army, was promoted to Oberleutnant, and subsequently joined the Luftwaffe. Lean and mean, Ramcke qualified at the age of 51 as a parachutist and was made a Generalmajor commanding the Parachute Assault Regt. He led this in the final phase of the airborne attack on Crete, being awarded the RK on 21 Aug 41. With German parachutists now relegated to ground operations, and his unit expanded to brigade size, he fought in North Africa. For a skilfully executed delaying action on Rommel's south flank in the battle of El Alamein he was awarded the Oakleaves (145/890) on 13 Nov 42. In the spring of 1943 he assumed command of the new 2d Para Div in Italy, later leading it on the eastern front until redeployed to France. On Hitler's orders he defended Fortress Brest, completely destroying its port facilities before surrendering to MIDDLETON on 18 Sep 44. "Pappy" Ramcke gave his captors constant concern, real and imagined, that he was about to escape (Angolia, I, 94). After being released Ramcke went into the concrete business. He died 5 July 68 at 79.

RAMSAY, Bertram Home. British admiral. 1883-1945. The third son of a 4th Hussars captain (later a brigadier general) he was born 20 Jan 83 at Hampton Court Palace, London. *(DNB.)* With his father on duty in India the boy joined *Britannia* in 1898 and from the age of 15 was largely in charge of his own affairs (ibid.). Never large physically, but a keen sportsman and athlete, he was independent and self-confident from an early age. Becoming a midshipman after a year of training on *Britannia,* he joined *Crescent,* flagship of the North American and West Indies station. It was a happy ship, he would remember. Promoted to sub-lieutenant in 1902 and getting a first taste of amphibious operations in Somaliland (1903-4) with a landing force, he was mentioned in dispatches and promoted to lieutenant.

For two years in WWI he held commands in the crack Dover patrol. The handsome, vigorous Ramsay rose rapidly. As a rear admiral, Home Fleet CofS, and King George V's naval ADC, he retired in Dec 38, at the age of 55, after 40 years in uniform. But less than a year later Vice Adm Ramsay was recalled to command the port of Dover. Britain had declared war (3 Sep 39), but the assignment appeared to be a sinecure for the superannuated "Bertie." Things livened up however for Opn Dynamo, the "miracle of Dunkirk," 29 May-5 June 40. Ramsay was knighted (KCB) and nicknamed "Dynamo."

With the acting rank of full admiral Sir Bertram was involved in directing the landings at Algiers and Oran (Opn Torch) on 8 Nov 42. After the victory in Tunisia he commanded the (British) Eastern Naval TF for the invasion of Sicily that began on 10 July 43. In what Morison has called the "greatest amphibious operation in recorded history, if measured by the strength of the initial assault," Ramsay controlled 795 vessels and 715 ship-borne landing craft. US Adm H. K. HEWITT had 580 ships and beaching craft in addition to 1,124 shipborne landing craft. (Buchanan, 167, citing Morison, IX, 28-29.)

Sir Bertram became British naval commander in the Mediterranean and was restored to the active list despite his age. On 29 Dec 43 he was named Allied Naval CinC for the Normandy invasion. He planned and directed the monumental undertaking, which involved some 1,800 vessels of the Eastern TF (British) and about 930 of the Western TF (under US Adm Alan G. KIRK). Five subordinate task forces in the initial assault on two American beaches and three British beaches were moved from five widely separated English ports. Followup waves came from other, more distant harbors, while all required naval and air escorts. This monumental planning effort led to Ramsay's promotion to full admiral.

After turning over to the US Navy the French ports from Le Havre, captured 12 Sep 44, and others to the south taken later, Ramsay kept responsibility for those to the north. He also directed the naval operations that cleared Walcheren Island and led to his crowning achievement, supporting CRERAR and SIMONDS in opening the port of Antwerp. (Morison, IX, 148n.)

Sir Bertram died shortly thereafter, on 2 Jan 45, with all aboard a plane allocated to his personal use. He was going from his headquarters outside Paris at St-Germain-en-Laye for a conference in Brussels with Montgomery when the plane crashed on takeoff from Toussus-le-Noble. He was buried at historic St-Germain-en-Laye. (G. E. Creasy in *DNB; CB 44.*)

RAUS, Erhard. German general. 1889-1956. "One of our best panzer generals" (Guderian, 421), although almost unknown to Hitler personally, the unsung hero (whose name some spell Rauss) was born 8 Jan 89 at Wolframitz, Austria. He served as an infantryman in WWI, remained in uniform, and by 1936 was a colonel. Two years later, after the Anschluss, Raus entered the Wehrmacht. In Poland the colonel led the 1st Lt Div's 4th **Schuetzenregiment.** The regiment was reformed under Generalmajor Werner Kempf as the 6th Pz Div for operations in the west (1940). Moving up to command the division's Schuetzenbrigade, serving in Opn **Barbarossa** with HOEPPNER's 4th Pz Gp of LEEB's AG North, Oberst Raus took part in the drive on Leningrad before moving south for the battles before Moscow. After helping close the Vyazma pocket on 26 Nov 41 Raus succeeded Franz Landgraf as acting division commander (mFb). Transferred to HOTH's 3d Pz Gp in

AG Center, the division was decimated, losing almost all its vehicles (*B&O,* 80). Remnants were shipped to France in May 42 for rest and reorganization (ibid.). At year's end the 6th Pz Div returned to the eastern front as the Red Army trap closed around Stalingrad.

Raus attacked NW toward Stalingrad on 12 Dec 42 as part of the 57th Pz Corps, Hoth's 4th Pz Army. Although outclassed by Russian T-34 tanks (Seaton, *R-G War,* 327), the 6th Pz Div drove to within 30 miles of the 6th Army perimeter and might have linked up if Paulus had tried to break out.

By now the Germans knew that a massive Soviet counteroffensive was coming. When Vatutin's northern wing broke through the 3d Romanian Army the still-powerful 6th Pz Div was detached from the 57th Corps to reinforce the Romanian delaying action on the Chir River (Seaton, 330).

Having led the division from 26 Nov 41 to 6 Feb 43, Raus continued a meteoric rise (by German standards). He was promoted 1 Jan 43 to Generalleutnant and on 1 May 43 to General of Panzer Troops commanding the 11th Corps (B&O, 81 & n.). For his part in MANSTEIN's epic defensive-offensive actions around Kharkov against Vatutin and Konev the hardfaced Raus was awarded the Oakleaves (280/890) on 22 Aug 43 (Angolia, II, 237).

The general stepped up to command the 47th Pz Corps 5-25 Nov 43, succeeding Joachim Lemelsen. Vatutin's 1st Ukrainian Front took Kiev on 18 November and Manstein counterattacked with the 4th Pz Army, of which Raus was part. The drive had considerable success until the weather broke on the 26th, overrunning part of I. D. CHERNYAKHOVSKY's 60th Army around Korosten and Malin. But the Germans could not retake Kiev and Raus has been criticized for being too cautious. (See Mellenthin, *Panzer Battles,* 249). But he simply did not have the resources: "The retaking of Kiev was in no way possible" (Seaton, 384n.). The general replaced Hermann HOTH on 26 Nov 43 as acting head of the 4th Pz Army; from 10 Mar 44 he was the permanent commander (*B&O,* 23). Raus then relieved Hans Hube as CG, 1st Pz Army, on 1 May 44 (*B&O,* 15). His promotion to Generaloberst was on 15 Aug 44 (Ibid.).

Transferred again and moved to meet the Soviet main effort now being made in the north, Raus replaced George Hans Reinhardt on 16 Aug 44 as head of the 3d Pz Army. After BAGRAMYAN broke through to the Baltic north of Memel in Oct 44 the veteran panzer army counterattacked successfully around Siauliai (Schualen) before taking up the desperate defense of East Prussia. Pushed back through Tilsit and Koenigsberg his 3d Pz Army Hq was withdrawn to organize the defense of Pomerania.

From 22 Feb 45 Generaloberst Raus's eight divisions, having a mere 70 tanks among them, held a 150-mile front on the Oder River around Kuestrin, some 40 miles east of Berlin. As Zhukov's eight armies, which had about 1,500 tanks, paused before resuming the offensive (Irving, *HW,* 775-76). Hitler summoned Raus for a "detailed exposition of the combat ability of your divisions" (quoted by Guderian, 420). Although attending officers in the Fuehrerbunker on the afternoon of 8 March thought Raus gave an excellent briefing, the fuehrer took an inordinate personal dislike to the general. "What a miserable speech," said Hitler after sending the general from the room and commenting inchoatcly that Raus whom the leader did not know as a fellow Austrian— "must be a Berliner or an East Prussian." Despite Guderian's outspoken defense of the general's competence (and ethnicty) Hitler ordered that Hasso von MANTEUFFEL (ironically an East Prussian born just outside Berlin!) replace Raus. The order was dated 10 Mar 45.

At least spared capture by the Russians, Raus surrendered to US forces. He died in 1956 at Bad Gastein.

REEVES, John Walter, Jr. US admiral. 1888-1967. "Jake" Reeves was born in Haddonfield, NJ, on 25 Apr 88 and he graduated from the USNA in 1911 (74/193). Reeves served in destroyers, taking part in the 1914 Vera Cruz expedition, then was in European waters. A naval aviator from 1936, he was XO of *Langley,* then CO, Fleet Air Base, Pearl Harbor. In Apr 40 he commissioned CV *Wasp* and was involved with her in resupplying Malta, Apr-May 42. The next month he was promoted to rear admiral commanding the Alaskan Sector, NW Sea Frontier, remaining until May 43 for operations to retake the Aleutians. He then headed Carrier Div 4, flag aboard CV *Enterprise,* for actions against Truk, Palau, Yap, Hollandia, and the Marianas. After taking part OZAWA's defeat in the 1st battle of the Philippine sea, Reeves became Commander, Western Carolines, in July 44. His mission was to develop Ulithi as the fleet's major support base in the Central Pacific. From Mar 45 he was based at Oakland, Calif, as head the Naval Air Transport Service.

He was chief of naval air training at Pensacola, Fla, from Mar 48 (promoted to vice admiral on 1 Apr 49) to retirement on 1 May 1950 with the rank of admiral. Reeves died 15 July 67 at the Pensacola USNH. (RCS.)

REICHENAU, Walter von. German general. 1884-1942. Because of his reputation as a revolutionary and a "Nazi-general," the German army's Old Guard kept Reichenau from the top posts for which Hitler recommended him on several occasions. But the maverick general proved to be an outstanding army commander in Poland, France (promoted to field marshal, and Russia before dying on 17 Jan 42 after a stroke.

A double-dyed aristocrat related by birth to Bohemian nobility and by marriage to titled Silesian families, Reichenau was born 8 Oct 84 at Karlsruhe. He entered the Imperial Army in 1903, was commissioned in the field artillery, and became a member of the elite **GGGS.** After serving in WWI Col Reichenau headed the Reichswehr chancellery under the Weimar Republic. As BLOMBERG's former CofS he was largely responsible for Hitler's picking that officer to be the first minister of defense when the Nazis came to power in 1933. Reichenau's reputation as a traitor to his class seems to have sprung from his conviction that Germany needed to break from the past. Although repelled by what he called "those swastikamen" around the fuehrer, Col Reichenau thought Hitler could accomplish this (as indeed he did!).

When Blomberg could not overcome army opposition to Reichenau's succeeding HAMMERSTEIN-EQUORD as head of the German army—the post going to FRITSCH—the war minister settled for Reichenau's being Chef der Ministeramt, thus Blomberg's closest associate, if not quite his deputy. Promoted for the new assignment, Generalmajor Reichenau had a leading role in Blomberg's efforts to align the German army with the Nazi Party and in establishing the army's supremacy over paramilitary forces like the Brownshirts (SA).

Succeeded by Keitel, Reichenau left Berlin on 1 Oct 35 to command the new 7th Corps Hq in Munich. Happy to be away from the political maelstrom he still hoped to be army CofS in Berlin if not the CinC (Goerlitz, *GGS*, 311). In the crisis of early 1938 that saw the ouster of BLOMBERG and FRITSCH, Hitler and Goering put pressure on the army by threatening to make Reichenau Blomberg's successor. By this maneuver the Nazi hierarchy succeeded in making the Old Guard settle for BRAUTCHITSCH, a weakling, as their puppet chief of the German Army. (Hitler himself took Blomberg's post.)

Excluded by fellow generals from a powerful political-military post in Berlin, where he might have been effective in curbing Hitler's excesses, the pariah proved to be an outstanding field commander. General of Artillery Reichenau led the highly mobile 10th Army in Poland. This, ironically, was in AG South, headed by RUNDSTEDT, the general who had led the Old Guard's opposition to his higher ambitions. Audacious personal leadership, in addition to professional prowess, was largely responsible for AG South's success. The athletic Reichenau appalled his peers by plunging into the Vistula to swim across at the head of his troops. This outdid the flamboyant ROMMEL in "leading from the front," and the less dainty PATTON, who merely urinated into the Rhine on reaching this famous barrier.

When Hitler announced his intention to violate Belgian and Dutch neutrality as part of his plan to conquer France, the "Nazi general" was one of the most vigorous opponents. Reichenau and his CofS, Paulus, first learned of this Nazi decision from Curt Liebmann on succeeding that general (whom Hitler sacked as a "defeatist") as 6th Army commander. "Thunderstruck," Reichenau commented that such an action would be "veritably criminal" and promised to use his personal influence to have Hitler reverse the decision. (Deutsch, II, 72-73.) Reichenau tried on at least two occasions, even speaking out about the brutalities in Poland. Not only failing, the general also alienated himself permanently with Hitler. (Ibid., 74-77, 236, 264.)

A colonel general on taking over the large 6th Army of 23 divisions, including two panzer divisions and heavy air support, Reichenau ironically had the role of advancing through Belgium. His mission was to draw the Allied strategic reserve out of position so RUNDSTEDT's main effort through the Ardennes would be more decisive. The 6th Army shattered defenses in the constrained Maastricht-Liége area, quickly overcoming the supposedly impregnable fortress of Eben Emael. When the 6th Army's panzers and air support were then diverted to reinforce RUNDSTEDT, Reichenau got OKW approval for a change of strategy: instead of continuing westward he was authorized to swing north of Lille toward Ypres, a maneuver that forced the Belgian army's precipitous surrender on 28 May 40.

For the final phase of the campaign on the west, the Battle of France, Reichenau took Pz Gp Kleist from Rundstedt for the decisive breakthrough from bridgeheads at Amiens and Peronne. But he made three errors that slowed his operations: he underestimated French resistance; he did not hold back his armor (as did LIST) until infantry cracked French defenses; and he did not mass his two panzer divisions for one decisive effort but "decided in favor of the pincer stroke from the two bridgeheads" (Liddell Hart, *Talk,* 140). Nevertheless promoted on 19 July 40 to field marshal, the dashing Reichenau, who numbered near-perfect command of English among his charms, was selected for a major role in the invasion of England (Opn *Sea Lion*).

But after Hitler abandoned the threat Reichenau's 6th Army was made the northernmost element of RUNDSTEDT's AG South for the invasion of Russia. With six infantry divisions in Opn **Barbarossa** he forced crossings of the Bug River just south of the Pripet Marshes. Kleist sent his powerful panzer group through these bridgeheads and moved swiftly toward Kiev. The 6th Army repelled powerful counterattacks that came out the Pripet Marshes on its northern flank and pressed on through Kiev to Belgorod. Hitler sacked RUNDSTEDT on 1 Dec 41 as Barbarossa came to grief around Rostov and Reichenau replaced him as head of AG South, with headquarters at Poltava. Reichenau prevailed on Hitler to let him continue a withdrawal to better defensive positions on the Mius River that Rundstedt had begun. But on 15 Jan 42 the new AG South commander suffered what Halder's diary entry called an "apoplectic fit." The general died two days later while being flown back to Germany, and his state funeral was on 24 Jan 42.

Liddell Hart characterizes Reichenau as "a strong personality and full of initiative, a man of action and instinct rather than of intellect . . .

ambitious, clever, highly educated, even a poet, [but] of a sturdy nature and a sportsman." (*Talk,* 86-87.) "The more that is learned about Reichenau," writes a leading American authority on the German resistance, "the greater force there is to the argument that he alone of the generals of the Nazi era demonstrated the combination of insight, courage, drive and sure brutality that could have stopped Hitler before disaster overtook the German nation and the world. But antagonism against him as 'the Nazi general' and his offenses against professional decorum closed the minds of many and prevented him from achieving a position from which he could have challenged the dictator." (Deutsch, I, 12.) This adds credence to rumors he had been murdered by the Nazis, although these have been discredited.

REINHARDT, Georg Hans. German general. 1887-1963. One of the Wehrmacht's outstanding panzer leaders, Reinhardt was born 1 Mar 87 at Bautzen. He became an army cadet in 1907 and the next year was a second lieutenant in the 107th Inf Regt. By 1937 he commanded the 1st Assault Bde, having become a Generalmajor, and he headed the 4th Pz Div from its formation on 10 Nov 38. He led the division in Poland, promoted to Generalleutnant on 1 Oct 39 and he was awarded the RK on the 27th of that month.

Slender, with an alert a bright face set off by pince-nez glasses, and wearing his cap with a jaunty tilt to the left, he looked more like a judge than the tough, capable field commander he proved to be.

Relinquishing command of his division on 4 Feb 40 (*B&O,* 76) Generalleutnant Reinhardt formed the small 41st Pz Corps (6th and 8th Pz Divs) on 15 Feb 40. In the drive through the heart of the Ardennes into Flanders he was between Hermann Hoth (on his right) and Guderian. Like these other panzer corps he was ordered to pause short of Dunkirk on 24 May but he attacked two days later across the Albert Canal south of Watten at two places.

Again promoted (1 Jun 40), General of Panzer Troops Reinhard led his 41st Pz Corps in the conquest of Yugoslavia (Opn Marita). OKH had not intended to use the corps in Marita but did so after Hitler ordered the 2d SS Mtz Div to advance from Timisoara, its assembly area in western Romania and, for "prestige reasons and propaganda purposes," to be the first into Belgrade. OKH insisted on having operational control over the force and made it a third prong in the drive on Belgrade. (DA Pamphlet 20-260, *Balkans,* 33.)

Reinhardt established his 41st Pz Corps Hq in East Prussia for Opn Barbarossa, the attack on Russia. His formation and Manstein's 56 Pz Corps formed HOEPNER's 4th Pz Gp of LEEB's AG North. On the left, with more than 60 per cent of Hoepner's armored strength, Reinhardt attacked on 22 June 41 from around Memel into Lithuania and advanced through marshy ground. In what probably was the high tide of the German offensive *(S&S)* he penetrated Leningrad's outer defenses on 12 Sep 41. On 5 Oct 41 Reinhardt assumed command of the 3d Pz Army (succeeding Hermann Hoth) in AG Center. In the next 10 days he made a deep penetration to Kalinin, 100 miles NNW of Moscow. Sideslipping south as Bock's AG Center massed its armor for an attempted envelopment of the Russian capital from the north he took Klin and pressed on to the Volga-Moscow canal. The Germans were then forced back by the Soviet winter counteroffensive that began on 6 Dec 41. Reinhardt was promoted 1 Jan 42 to Generaloberst and awarded the Oakleaves (73/890) on 17 Feb 42. The 3d Pz Army had a prominent part in the defensive fighting around Vitebsk, the counterattack through Vyasma, and subsequent action on the Moscow front.

Continuing to command the 3d Pz Army until 15 Aug 44, Reinhardt moved up to replace MODEL as head of AG Center, being succeeded Erhard RAUS *(B&O,* 21). The hard-pressed AG Center now was in the zone formerly held by AG North. There had been a quick succession of commanders—BOCK, KLUGE, BUSCH, and MODEL—as Hitler kept shuffling generals. The Russians had shifted their main strategic effort from the south to the center for their summer offensive of 1944. On a 400-mile front from around Riga to below Warsaw, AG Center was pushed back through Tilsit and Koenigsberg. He was awarded the Swords (68/159) on 26 May 44. But the situation got worse as the Soviets wheeled NW to overrun East Prussia. After continuing disputes with Hitler over making necessary withdrawals Reinhardt was relieved on 25 Jan 45 after receiving a serious head wound, being succeeded by RENDULIC.

He died on 22 Nov 63.

REITSCH, Hanna. German flyer. 1912-79. Born in Hirschberg, Silesia, now Jelenia Géra, Poland, daughter of an opththalmologist, she abandoned an early ambition to be a flying medical missionary and turned to professional flying. An attractive, fair-haired, blue-eyed little woman, almost insanely brave (Foley, *Skorzeny,* 103), and a rabid Nazi, Hanna was a leading stunt pilot when Ernst UDET selected her in 1937 to test military aircraft. The fearless Fraulein crashed while testing an early model jet airplane and emerged from months of hospitalization with such a fear of falling that she could not sit in a chair. But she gradually conquered the phobia and resumed her wild career. When she met Otto Skorzeny at Hitler's headquarters in the summer of 1944 they agreed to experiment with converting the V-1 buzz bomb for manned flight as a suicide weapon. When two pilots crashed on attempting to land, the authorities prohibited further attempts. But Hanna made Skorzeny lie to the base commander that the ban had been lifted, and she made a successful flight. "Those other two did not know how to bring down fast planes," she said simply. (Foley, 105.)

With Ritter von GREIM she made a dramatic visit to Hitler in his final days, landing 26 Apr 45 under fire on a shell-cratered Berlin avenue and flying back out a few days later. She was the first of 27 women to win the Iron Cross 2d Class, one of only two women awarded the Iron Cross 1st Class (Angolia, I, 32), and the only civilian so honored.

After 15 months at interrogation centers Fraulein Reitsch won many gliding championships, and in 1962 established a National School for Gliding in Ghana.

REMARQUE, Erich Maria. German writer. 1898-1970. Born 22 Jun 98 in Osnabrueck as Erich Kramer, he was the son of a bookbinder. Kramer entered the German army at the age of 17, served on the western front 1915-18, and was twice wounded. He became a sports reporter and wrote fiction in his spare time. The brutally realistic, semi-autobiographical first novel was *Im Westen nichts Neues* (1929); the ironic title was the stock phrase in war communiques, and the nom de plume Remarque comes from Kramer spelled backward. Translated as *All Quiet on the Western Front* (1929), the book was an international best-seller and a highly successful movie. A sequel, translated as *The Road Back* (1931), brought the author increasing criticism from the burgeoning Nazi Party, and *All Quiet* was among the books burned publicly in 1933. The Third Reich banned Remarque's works and revoked his citizenship. In 1939 the author moved to the US, where the film of his book was banned after America entered the war, being considered pro-German! (Hamilton, *Leaders,* 444, from an interview with Remarque.) The author became an American citizen in 1947, refused a German offer to restore his citizenship, and lived mainly in Switzerland. He continued to publish, but only *Arch of Triumph* (1946) came close to repeating his earlier literary success in deglamorizing war. Remarque died 25 Sep 70 in Ancona, Italy.

REMER, Otto Ernst. German officer. 1912-. The Nazi hero was born 18 Aug 12 in Neubrandenburg. As a major in the 1st Grenadier Regt, Grossdeutschland (GD) Div, Remer was awarded the RK on 18 May 43 for action around Byelgorod-Kharkov. His Oakleaves (325/890) were awarded 12 Nov 43 for action east of Krivoi-Rog while leading the redesignated 1st (SPW) Panzergrenadier Regt, GD. (Angolia, II, 274-75.)

Maj Remer commanded the Guard Bn "Grossdeutschland" outside Berlin at Doeberitz when orders came on 20 Jul 44 to execute Opn **Valkyrie.** Suspicious, the major reported to GOEBBELS for instructions and became a key figure in dooming the coup d'état. Hitler promptly promoted the tall, slender, strikingly handsome officer to Oberst, and in October his battalion was expanded into a regiment. Remer later headed the Fuehrer Escort Regt, which was redesignated a panzer brigade for action in the Eifel.

Promoted on 31 Jan 45, and wounded eight times during the war, Generalmajor Remer headed the postwar Sozialistische Reichspartei (SRP). Otto JOHN's security office gathered enough evidence to have the neo-Nazi party banned (John, 205) on 23 Oct 52. Remer meanwhile had been sentenced to three months in prison for slandering participants in the 20 July 44 plot as traitors. Sulzberger says that by 1953 the outlawed SRP had representatives in almost all government ministries, was organizing anti-Western activities, and was supporting former SS officers working behind the scenes in Egypt

with the junta headed by Col Gamal Abdel Nasser (*Candles,* 870).

RENDULIC, Lothar. German general. 1887-1971. One of the war's best but least known generals, Rendulic was born 23 Oct 87 at Wiener Neustadt into an old Austrian military family. Commissioned an infantryman in 1910 he saw heavy action with mountain troops on the Italian front in WWI. In 1920 he returned to the Univ of Vienna, got his PhD, and was promoted to major after attending the Austrian GS college. He was MA in London and Paris, expelled from the army for political activity in Paris.

When the Wehrmacht absorbed the Austrian army (after the **Anschluss**) Oberst Dr Rendulic saw his first action with the Wehrmacht in Poland. Three months later, 1 Dec 39, he was promoted to Generalmajor and given command of the 14th Inf Div. Rendulic led this across France in forced marches behind the panzers to the English Channel. In Kluge's 4th Army of AG Center he led the 52d Inf Div in the final surge south of Moscow, then commanded the 35th Corps in opposing the Soviet counteroffensive of 6 Dec 41-7 May 42. Promoted to Generalleutnant, he was awarded the RK on 6 Mar 42

After further action in Russia he was sent with his corps headquarters to the Balkans, where increasingly serious partisan warfare existed. For his role in bringing on the 9th Italian Army's surrender he was awarded the Oakleaves (271/890) on 15 Aug 43. At the same time General of Infantry Rendulic assumed command of the 2d Pz Army, which MODEL had led in Russia under Model. (Angolia, II, 231; *B&O,* 17.) Rendulic was promoted to Generaloberst on 1 Apr 44 for his successes against TITO in eastern Croatia.

In a major change of scene the Austrian went to Finland and replaced Eduard DIETL on 24 June 44 as head of the 20th Mountain Army. This was isolated and outnumbered two to one by the Finns, whom Stalin was pressuring to turn against the Germans. And the Soviets now were making their main strategic effort in the north and center. For his defense of **Kurland** Rendulic was awarded the Swords (122/159) on 18 Jan 45 (Angolia, I, 231). Eight days later he replaced SCHOERNER as AG North commander but had been at his new headquarters only 12 hours when ordered to take over from REINHARDT in AG Center. The "clever and subtle" Austrian "knew how to handle Hitler [who] had such faith in him that he now entrusted him with the desperate task of defending East Prussia" (Guderian, 401). In another mad reorganization the old AG North became AG Kurland; AG Center became the new AG North; and AG Vistula was created under HIMMLER.

Rendulic held Koenigsberg and Samland for some months as the battle for Pomerania was about to start (Seaton, 539). Then he replaced VIETINGHOFF on 11 Mar 45 in AG Kurland and beat off a major assault in his zone. But the situation in Austria had become desperate. "The Bolsheviks are outside Vienna!" BORMANN noted in his diary on 5 Apr 45 after AG South had retreated 50 miles. Hitler briefed Rendulic in the Berlin bunker on 6 April and sent him to take command of AG South from Otto Woehler.

Arriving a few days later Rendulic could do no more than concentrate forces east of the city while evacuating German wounded to the west. On 6 May 45 Generaloberst Rendulic ordered remnants of AG South to fight their way westward toward approaching US forces and avoid capture by the Russians. It was his last field order.

"As a soldier his nature showed a curious dualism," writes Goerlitz. "He took his National Socialism deadly seriously, and yet affected personally a most elegant style of life. He had a weakness for film shows at his headquarters which would be followed by genuinely entertaining conversation. On such occasions he seemed more like a representative of a dying order than a National Socialist." (Goerlitz, *GGS*, 444.)

Rendulic wrote a valuable military memoir, *Gekaepft Gesiegt Geschlagen* (Munich:"Welsermuehl" Wels, 1957). He died of natural causes in Jan 71 at Efferding, Austria.

REYNAUD, Paul. French statesman. 1878-1966. Grandson of a French soldier who served Maximillian in Mexico and remained to found a lucrative business in cotton textiles, Reynaud was born 15 Oct 78 in the French alpine village of Barcelonnette. His father had run the business in Mexico before moving the family to Paris and becoming prominent in politics. The diminutive Paul Reynaud attended Lycée Louis le Grand, studied law at the Sorbonne, became a highly successful lawyer, and married Jeanne Henri Robert, daughter of the legendary jurist.

Reynaud had qualities associated with a "runt complex": quick agility, cockiness, and intense ambition. He also had a mania for physical culture and sports like boxing, cycling, swimming, and walking. He was a Chinese art connoisseur, somewhat of a mandarin, and indeed Oriental in appearance. Enemies nicknamed him "Mickey Mouse" and "the cat."

Reynaud did not enter public life until he was 41 and he was always a maverick without a personal political base. Elected in 1914 as a deputy from his home district of Basses Alpes, he was defeated in 1924 but four years later was elected to represent the Bourse (financial) district of Paris. He held his seat until 1940, gaining a reputation for combativeness, brilliance in debate, and nonconformity while holding a variety of cabinet positions for the next few years. As the European dictators strengthened their hold and defeatism mounted in France, the devoutly patriotic Reynaud opposed appeasement, favored rearmament, and deplored Léon Blum's Front Populaire even more than the bankrupt politics of FLANDIN, LAVAL, BONNET, and DALADIER (a bitter enemy). Impressed by the ideas of de Gaulle, whom he first met in late 1934 after reading the colonel's book, and further influenced by PALEWSKI (Yvert, "Palewski"), Reynaud argued unsuccessfully on 15 Mar 35 in the chamber of deputies for an armored corps of seven divisions to be formed. (Larousse.) "As the small voice in the French wilderness, Reynaud represented the equivalent of Churchill (whom he hugely admired)," writes Horne; "but unfortunately he possessed neither the essential grandeur nor the support." (Horne, *1940*, 177.)

Reynaud became finance minister on 1 Nov 38 after the **Munich crisis** and the collapse of Blum's brief popular front government. He had considerable success, passing tough decrees to start cutting social reforms, to reduce domestic consumption, and to boost war production. The French reacted characteristically, calling a general strike on 30 Nov 38, but this was quickly broken *(CB 40)*. Further tightening screws, the finance minister lengthened the work week, raised taxes, and continued monetary reforms. On 25 Dec 39 he signed an agreement with the British for an economic and financial union, for pooling resources to fight a war, and for postwar collaboration.

Reynaud became premier after his arch-rival DALADIER was ousted on 20 Mar 40. Still with no party and few political allies he headed a "ministry of coalition, not a team" (Henri Michel quoted in Larousse). Reynaud visited London a week after taking office and signed a joint declaration (28 Mar 40) that neither nation would make a separate peace with Hitler. After the Germans invaded Norway (6 Apr 40) Reynaud promptly ordered French army and naval forces to support Lord CORK's expedition to Narvik.

Reynaud had been premier two months when Hitler attacked on 10 May 40. The French government survived by one vote and only with acceptance of Daladier as minister of national defense. Reynaud tried to replace the ineffectual GAMELIN as head of the French Army but was blocked by Daladier and President Lebrun. The premier however had Weygand brought secretly from the Levant to be on hand and he recalled PETAIN from Spain to join the cabinet. Reynaud wanted to make de Gaulle secretary of the War Cabinet, but the colonel refused to serve under Daladier. Hélène de PORTES prevailed in having Paul BAUDOUIN brought in as defense minister and she continued a bitter feud with Daladier's mistress, the Marquise de Crussol.

On 6 June 40 Reynaud finally succeeded in ousting Daladier and making de Gaulle minister of war. But he was frustrated in efforts to move the government and surviving French armed forces to North Africa, Weygand and NOGUES offering the strongest opposition. The Breton redoubt concept—holding a bridgehead in Brittany—was not accepted either. As the Germans wheeled south for phase two of their conquest, Reynaud and de Gaulle left Paris by car at midnight on 10-11 June 40. The rump government met twice at Cangé, Lebrun's chateau on the Loire near Tours. Here on 12 June Reynaud quashed Weygand's proposal to seek an armistice, but when the rump reached Bordeaux the capitulation clique rallied around PETAIN and forced Reynaud to resign on 16 June.

Later claiming to have declined on this day to be vice premier (Pertinax, 309), the ex-premier was interested in being ambassador to Washington. His personal tragedy then became comic-opera. Two trusted members of Reynaud's staff went through Madrid, believing they had diplomatic immunity. But Spanish police

inspected their luggage and found secret state papers, gold and currency worth millions of francs, and jewelry. (Mme de Portes had sent her children to America.) Reynaud apparently was not personally incriminated but his ambassadorial hopes were dashed. (Pertinax, 309; *CB 40*.) Reynaud nearly died on 28 June 40 in the car accident that killed Mme de PORTES.

Interned on 5 Sep 40 and arraigned for the abortive Riom trials, Reynaud was sentenced to life imprisonment. He was held in reasonable comfort until the Germans occupied the south of France and arrested him nine days later, on 20 Nov 42. After being imprisoned briefly at **Oranienburg** he was sent on 12 May 43 to the castle at Itter, in the Tyrol. With the Niederdorf group he was freed by American troops on 4 May 45.

The former premier was a witness at Pétain's trial. On 2 June 46 he was elected a deputy from the Nord Dept (adjoining Paris). In 1949, after his first wife had died, the 71-year-old Reynaud remarried and went on to sire three children. He supported de Gaulle in 1959, helping draft a new constitution, but later turned against the general.

Paul Reynaud died 21 Sep 66 in the Paris suburb of Neuilly.

REUTHER, Walter Philip. US labor leader. 1907-70. He was born 1 Sep 07 at Wheeling, W Va, son and grandson of labor organizers *(CB 41)*. Small, red-haired, and athletic, he completed three years at Wayne Univ while working as a night foreman in the tool and die room of the Ford Motor Co in Detroit. He and brother Victor then spent three years abroad, traveling primarily by bicycle, visiting automobile plants and labor groups from England to Russia and the Far East. In 1935 the brothers returned to Detroit on advice from friends that the opportunity had come to organize workers. By 1940 he was a top union leader, having organized the United Automobile Workers (UAW). Reuther held the UAW to their no-strike pledge during the war but supported their demands for a 30 percent pay increase. (*See* also John L. LEWIS and William S. KNUDSEN.) He headed the UAW of 1,600,000 members until his death in a plane crash.

REYNOLDS, Quentin. US writer. 1902-65. Initially a sportswriter for the New York *Evening*

World he was associated with *Collier's* magazine from 1933. Covering wartime England during the blitz he published the best-selling *The Wounded Don't Cry* and *London Diary* in 1941. That year he was Averell HARRIMAN's press secretary on a visit to Moscow. After US entry into the war he covered theaters of operations from the Mediterranean to the SW Pacific, writing hundreds of articles and the books including *Dress Rehearsal* (1943) and *Officially Dead* (1945). His autobiography is *By Quentin Reynolds* (1963).

RHEE, Syngman. Korean statesman. 1875-1965. The founder of independent (modern) Korea began his education under Japanese occupation forces before spending six years in American universities. His BA was from George Washington Univ, his MA from Harvard, and his PhD in 1910 was from Princeton. Having long worked for national independence Dr Rhee became president of Korea in 1945. A month after starting a fourth four-year term in Mar 60 he was ousted for election fraud. Rhee fled to Hawaii and died in exile.

RIBBENTROP, Ulrich Friedrich Willy Joachim von. German diplomat. 1893-1946. Hitler's much derided top diplomat was a Westphalian, born 30 Apr 93 in Wesel. He was the second son of Lt Richard Ribbentrop, a career artillery officer from an untitled west Prussian military family, and of Sophie Hertwig, who was from a wealthy family of Saxon landowners. Richard Ribbentrop moved with his family, which included a younger daughter, Ingebord, from Wesel to another pleasant garrison assignments in Kassel before being posted to Metz in 1901. Sophie died of TB in early 1902 after years as a beloved invalid, and Richard soon remarried. The new wife, Olga Margarete von Prittwitz und Gaffron, was charming and cheerful but the children—cherishing memories of their real mother—did not warm to her.

One of Joachim's schoolteachers in Metz, Frau Otto MEISSNER, characterized the handsome and charming boy as "the most stupid in his class, full of vanity and very pushy" (Weitz, 6). Aspiring to be a professional violinist and with a lust for foreign adventure, Joachim was allowed by his stern but reasonable father to end his schooling without sitting for the **Abitur.** A sympathetic "aunt," Gertrud von

Ribbentrop (1863-1943), used her small income to help send Joachim and his brother Lothar to a boarding school at Grenoble (1907). In the French Alps, and particularly during a winter sports vacation with their family at Arosa, in Switzerland, the boys acquired a taste for international life and foreign languages. Joachim's international outlook took another step in 1909 when an English friend of the family, a famous surgeon, invited the boys for an extended visit to his fashionable London home. Ribbentrop developed a genuine affection for British upper class life. But it was a romantic, superficial attraction to their style that failed to see their substance (Weitz, 9). After some experience as a clerk with a German importing firm in London, the 18-year-old Joachim and Lothar went to Canada, which had a large German presence. Taking readily to life in the new world, Joachim spent four years (1910-14) in a variety of jobs—bank clerk, timekeeper on a huge engineering project (reconstruction of the Quebec Bridge), clerk-timekeeper with the Canadian Pacific RR. The young Ribbentrop's idyll was interrupted by surgery in Montreal to remove a tubercular kidney, which is believed to have caused the drooping eyelid, "a sort of sad wink" that marked an otherwise handsome, fashionably bland face. (Weitz, 5.)

Ribbentrop returned to Germany for recuperation at the family home. Recrossing the Atlantic in 1913 he tarried briefly in NYC and Boston, where as a free lance newspaper reporter he got a taste of American journalism before joining his brother Lother in Ottawa to run a small wine import-export business. The suave German showed a flair for commerce.

On the outbreak of war in 1914 he escaped internment and made his way to Germany. Despite the missing kidney, Ribbentrop fought as a lieutenant with the 125th Hussar Regt until being WIA. Like his grandfather and father he won the Iron Cross 1st Class. Joachim later was on PAPEN's staff in America, going with him as temporary MA in Turkey. After being adjutant of the German delegation that signed the Versailles Treaty, Ribbentrop capitalized on postwar opportunities in his native Rhineland: currency speculation, corruption of customs officials (importing wine duty free), and he became a salesman for the French firm of Pommerey and Greno *(CB 41)*. While starting up a small wine business he met the rebellious, ambitions Annelies Henkell, whose family owned German's leading wine firm, Henkell-Trocken. They were married in 1920 despite her parents' strong disapproval. Never offered a position in the Henkell firm (Weitz, 27), he welcomed their offer of a partnership in the Berlin sales agency that represented Henkell (Weitz, 27).

Gaining entrée into high society, using his foppish charm along with genuine business sense, the "champaign salesman" prospered. He added "von" to his name in 1925 in a dubious deal with his "Aunt" Gertrud, who accepted a lifelong monthly support of 450 marks. The legal file on the arrangement was among the incriminating data acquired by Goering from the secret Prussian police files he got from Rudolf DIELS in 1933. (Aunt Gertrude lived until 1943, so the price was about 97,000 marks.)

The handsome, arrogant, empty-headed Ribbentrop had long considered entering public office, but it was not until 1 May 32 that he got on the Nazi bandwagon. Hitler had use for the recruit's social connections and his Berlin villa, which was ideal for clandestine meetings. Ribbentrop became Hitler's foreign affairs adviser and helped him form a cabinet in 1933.

The Ribbentrop Bureau was established the next year with a staff of 15. Initially a clipping service compiling digests of what foreign publications were saying about the Third Reich, the bureau grew to 300 enthusiastic and ambitious amateurs in what was a sort of independent foreign office. This was in line with Hitler's penchant for creating parallel and competing lines of bureaucracy, a technique of "divide and rule" that consolidated the dictator's power. Ribbentrop himself became a special ambassador, responsible to the fuehrer and bypassing NEURATH's foreign office.

With British, French, and American leadership paralyzed, Ribbentrop was a good salesman for Nazi Germany. He had considerable success at the London Naval Conference of 1935, where the British made concessions highly offensive to the French. Still highly regarded by Hitler and on friendly terms with Himmler, Ribbentrop was promoted on 13 Sep 36 to honorary SS Gruppenfuehrer after it was announced officially on 11 Aug 36 that he would be ambassador to London. Hitler was still eager to win the British over to a policy of nonintervention in Europe, particularly on the

anti-bolshevik front, and for this race Hitler prided himself on having picked the "best horse in the stable" (Weitz, 115).

Ribbentrop reached London with his wife and four children on 26 Oct 36 as ambassador extraordinary to the Court of St James, ambassador at large, and special adviser to the fuehrer. The envoy told Churchill in 1937 that he could have been foreign minister but had convinced Hitler it was more important that he "come over to London in order to make the full case for an Anglo-German entente or even alliance" (WC, I, 222). But the self-important, inexperienced, and not-too-bright envoy shocked even the Germans by his Gothic gestures on arrival. Annelies had the embassy rebuilt at an alleged cost of five million marks. An SS staff of guards and household personnel was installed. Ladies of the official circle were directed not to curtsey to British royalty. The embassy staff used the raised-arm salute. Official invitations went out in German, ignoring the custom of using the host-country language. (Responses came back in Turkish and Finnish!) In arrant disregard for diplomatic custom, an SS guard was posted at the embassy entry (Weitz, 117), and swastika flags were displayed on German buildings and official cars.

On presenting his credentials to King George VI on 5 Feb 37 the Nazi ambassador observed the custom of stopping three times to bow as he backed off. But each time he raised his right arm in a modified Hitler salute! It is not known whether he also intoned the customary "Heil Hitler!" The king is alleged to have smiled, but the British were outraged and the Germans were appalled. (Weitz, 122.)

His mission to the Court of St James becoming increasingly irrelevant, Ribbentrop spent the rest of 1937 shuttling between London and Berlin on what has come to be called "damage control." His principal achievement was negotiating the **Anti-Commintern Pact,** which required several visits to Rome.

From a very limited list of candidates to succeed the elderly and uncooperative Foreign Minister von Neurath—these being Rosenberg, Goebbels, Goering, and the professional diplomats Ambassadors von Hassell (in Rome) and von Dirksen (in Tokyo)—Hitler selected Ribbentrop. Taking over the foreign ministry on 4 Feb 38, Ribbentrop was closely involved with Hitler in the dramatic diplomatic maneuvers that followed. He exercised considerable initiative in working with QUISLING, but his most sensational achievement was the hastily contrived **Nazi-Soviet Pact** of 23 Aug 39. After this, however, "Nazi diplomacy as such scarcely existed" (Davidson, *Trial,* 147). Hitler personally directed what little there was; Ribbentrop was relegated to the background, but he did survive an attempted office coup in Apr 43 by a foreign office subordinate, Martin Luther (1895-1945). Not notably anti-Semitic in his early years, having many prominent Jewish friends, he later curried favor with Hitler by encouraging Germany's allies to support Nazi policies to exterminate European Jewery (Hamilton, *Leaders,* 234).

In the voluminous records of the Nuremberg trials there is not a favorable word about Ribbentrop, observes Davidson (*op. cit., 158, 166*). Found guilty on all four counts of war crimes, principally his involvement in the Nazi-Soviet pact of 1939 (above) and instigating anti-Jewish measures, Ribbentrop was sentenced to death on 1 Oct 46. He led the parade to the gallows at 1:11 AM on 16 Oct 46.

A self-serving memoir, written in prison and edited by his devoted widow, is *Zwischen London und Moskau* (Leoni am Starnberger See: Druffel, 1953). Of importance for biographical detail but of little historical value, it was translated as *The Ribbentrop Memoirs* (London: Weidenfeld & Nicolson, 1954).

RICHTHOFEN, Wolfram von. German general. 1895-1945. Himself a baron and cousin of "Red Baron" Manfred von Richthofen, he was born 10 Oct 95 in Gut Barzdorf, Silesia. After cadet school in Berlin he became an officer candidate with the 4th Hussar Regt in 1913, a Leutnant the next year, and saw action on both fronts. On 2 Mar 18 he qualified as a flyer and was assigned to the squadron whose first commander had been his famous cousin and whose last commander was GOERING.

Richthofen studied engineering (1919-22) before joining the Reichswehr. He took part in flying competitions and during 1929-33 was "on leave of absence" with the German mission in Italy. When GOERING brought the Luftwaffe out of the closet in 1933 Oberst Richthofen was one of Wilhelm Wimmer's two chief technical assistants to when UDET assumed the post. (Irving, *Milch,* 48.) In 1936 he went to Spain with the **Condor Legion,** first as a technical

adviser and then as leader of combat formations (Angola, II, 40). He became SPERRLE's CofS, was promoted in Sep 38 to Generalmajor, and later commanded the Legion until returning to Germany in May 39. (Wistrich.)

For the first years of the war he led the 8th Air Corps, which was equipped with Stukas. In Poland (where he also directed the virtual destruction of Warsaw) and in the blitzkrieg of the Low Countries and France, he delivered particularly effective tactical air support. On the western front his dive bombers were the aerial artillery for REICHENAU'S 6th Army in securing the critical crossing near Maastricht, Belgium, then in supporting KLEIST's thrust through Sedan. Early in the campaign he was awarded the RK (17 May 40) and then promoted to General of Fliers, skipping the rank of Generalleutnant (Angola, II, 40). In the Battle of Britain his 8th Air Corps had the mission of winning air superiority over the Channel, flying in daylight while other units attacked shipping and mined ports at night (Irving, *Milch,* 99). Like others of the Luftwaffe he was shocked to discover that Spitfires and Hurricanes outperformed Stukas.

Having failed against the RAF, the 8th AC was moved to the Balkans, where it had some difficulty in winning air superiority for the conquest of Greece, 6-21 Apr 41 (ibid., 121). But Richthofen was awarded the Oakleaves (26/890) on 17 July 41 after the battle for Crete. He then commanded the 2d AF in Italy before taking over Luftflotte 4, which supported MANSTEIN's AG South in Russia. Although he never believed the Luftwaffe could supply PAULUS's 6th Army once it was encircled in Stalingrad, Richthofen made a determined effort. He operated from a warm and well-equipped command train in the Black Sea town of Taganrog. For 72 days and nights, until German ground resistance ended on 2 Feb 43, the Luftwaffe delivered 8,350 tons of supplies. The price was 488 aircraft and about 1,000 crewmen lost. (Irving, *Milch,* 200.)

Despite this failure Richthofen became the Wehrmacht's youngest field marshal on 17 Feb 43 (Angola, II, 41), fourth of the Luftwaffe's five. Richthofen developed a brain tumor in Nov 44 and was retired from active duty. He died on 12 July 45 while in American custody. The tough, contentious airman's unpublished secret diary has been valuable to historians.

RICKENBACKER, Edward Vernon. US aviation figure. 1890-1973. "Captain Eddie" had 26 air victories in WWI, a score not surpassed by another American ace (Maj Richard I. BONG) until 1944. Born 8 Oct 90 in Columbus, Ohio, he was, in his own words, a "tough little kid with an uncontrollable temper" *(CB 40)*. The future ace left school at the age of 12 when his father died leaving a widow with two older and four younger children. After becoming a daredevil automobile racer, he won eight DSCs and the Medal of Honor as commander of the AEF's "Hat in the Ring" squadron. *(CB 40.)* In 1940 he left the presidency of Eastern Air Lines to advocate building up US military aviation. Remaining a civilian, he became a special observer for H. H. "Hap" Arnold and Secretary of War STIMSON. In Oct 42 he and others disappeared in the Pacific while returning from a trip to the USSR. After 21 days on a rubber raft they were spotted by a bomber from the newly established base on Funafuti Atoll in the Ellice group, 700 miles SE of Tarawa. A PT boat picked them up on 12 Nov 42. (Morison, VII, 78-79.)

RIDGWAY, Matthew Bunker. US general. 1895-1993. His father was a West Pointer appointed from New York to the class of 1883, "Matt" was born 3 Mar 95 in Virginia. The "army brat," appointed at large to West Point, graduated in Apr 17 (56/139) as an infantryman. Matt Ridgway became regarded almost unanimously by professional associates in America's small peacetime army, as "the man most likely to succeed" (personal information). As the US mobilized for war he was a full colonel. Serving on the WDGS in Washington he was engaged as late as Oct 41 with GEROW in making plans to meet a German invasion of Brazil from Dakar. (Pogue, *Marshall,* II, 54-55). Having impressed CofS George Marshall he succeeded Omar Bradley in June 42 as CG, 82d "All American" Abn Div.

Reaching Casablanca on 10 May 43 for the Sicilian campaign the division dropped around Gela. Although widely scattered in a poorly executed operation the parachutists reassembled in small groups to make a considerable contribution to the operation. The decimated division was withdrawn to Tunisia for reequipment, then returned to Sicily as reserves for the Salerno landings. The planned drop around Rome was called off by at the last minute by Maxwell TAYLOR. But the 82d was used on short notice to reinforce the hard-pressed Salerno beachhead. The 504th Para Regt dropped after dark on 13 Sep 43, the 505th the next night, and the 325th landed by boat. The division drove north from the beachhead to enter Naples on 1 Oct 43. Some units went on to fight in the Volturno valley and at Anzio .

Withdrawn from Italy the division went to Ireland in Nov 43 and then to England for invasion training. On D-day (6 June 44) the 82d and 101st Abn Divs landed by parachute and glider behind Utah beach. The badly scattered All Americans (who had much better luck than the 101st) reformed to take and hold vital points including Ste-Mère-Eglise. The 82d fought for 33 days in advancing from north of Carentan to St-Sauveur-le-Vicomte. The 82d was relieved on 8 July 44 and shipped back to England where Ridgway turned over command to GAVIN. Ridgway meanwhile had won two DSCs, the DSM, and the LM (Cullum).

In Sep 44 Ridgway took command of the 18th Abn Corps. He lead it through the Rhineland, Ardennes-Alsace, and Central Europe campaigns *(AA,* 508), winning another DSM, two Silver Stars, another LM, two BSMs (V), and a Purple Heart. On 4 Jun 45 he was promoted to lieutenant general.

Ridgway was CinC, Caribbean Cmd, 1948-49, before going to the Pentagon as deputy CofS to his classmate J. Lawton Collins. On the death of Walton H. Walker in Korea Ridgway took command of the 8th Army in the final days of 1950. Initially conducting an orderly withdrawal in the face of superior force, Ridgway began a counteroffensive on 25 Jan 51. Within two months the 8th Army had recrossed the 38th Parallel, virtually destroying the North Korean army's combat effectiveness in the process. With MacArthur's recall in Apr 51 Ridgway was promoted to full general and appointed CinC, Far East Command and SCAP. (James A. Van Fleet took over the 8th Army.)

Ridgway replaced Eisenhower on 30 May 52 as SACEUR and almost destroyed the international headquarters Eisenhower had created at SHAPE. "He surrounded himself with an all-American personal staff," writes Montgomery. "Morale began to decline. The crusading spirit disappeared." *(Memoirs,* 462.) Ridgway was replaced by Albert M. Gruenther on 11 July 53 and sent home to succeed Collins as US Army CofS. Now responsible for an army budget that President Eisenhower was determined to cut, Ridgway did not serve the normal four years. He retired in 1955 and promptly published *The Memoirs of Matthew B. Ridgway* (New York: Harper, 1956). Making his home in Pittsburgh, Pa, with his alluring young wife he was Chairman of the Board of Trustees, Mellon Institute Research, until 1960. Matt Ridgway died in Aug 93 at Pittsburgh.

RIEFENSTAHL, Leni. German movie maker. 1902-. The most innovative documentary film director of the early Nazi era—indeed in the history of the cinema—she was born 22 Aug 02 in Berlin. A robust beauty in the ideal Germanic mold, she was a dancer with the Russian Ballet and with Mary Wigman before catching the eye of theater director Max Reinhardt (1872-1943). She gave dance performances for Reinhardt before making a highly successful movie debut in *Der Heilige Berg,* "The Holy Mountain" (1925). While Marlene DIETRICH, an unfriendly contemporary rival, became famous for steamy and decidedly indoor performances, the wholesome Fraulein Riefenstahl was co-author, director, producer, and lead in a highly popular series of "mountain films." *Das Blau Licht,* "The Blue Light," won a gold medal in the 1932 Venice Biennale. Her last commercial film, a cliff hanger about Arctic sea rescue that featuring stunt flying by Ernst UDET, was *SOS Eisberg* (1933).

Hitler had long admired the actress for her screen roles, but she was oblivious to his existence until he took power in 1933. Invited to meet the fuehrer, the actress was so taken by his charisma that she agreed to make Nazi documentaries. The arrangement outraged Propaganda Minister Goebbels, who was not consulted, and he became a deadly enemy.

After false starts including "Victory of Faith" (about the 1933 Nuremberg rally), "Reichsparteitag" (about the 1935 party congress), Leni Riefenstahl gave new meaning to the word "spectacular" with "Triumph of the Will" (1935). This was built around the Nazi party rally staged by Albert SPEER at Nuremberg in 1934. Speer and Riefenstahl scripted events for the camera, and the film augmented Wagnerian opera effects with melodramatic and innovative photographic techniques. But the success of "Triumph" and subsequent documentaries was due to the producer's laborious, painstaking, and masterful editing from literally hundreds of miles of tape. Hitler gave the film its name, but the headstrong artist refused to make even minor changes.

"Triumph" was followed quickly by "Olympia," a four-hour, two-part epic about the 1936 Berlin Olympiad. It was not rivaled until Kon Ichikawa produced his film of the 1964 games *(S&S)*.

Although Goebbels's persistent hostility finally led to Leni Riefenstahl's losing Hitler's favor, she overcame great difficulties to make a remarkable "mountain movie" begun in Spain. She finished it as WWII ended but did not edit it for release. Blacklisted by the film industry she made a new career as a still photographer of primitive peoples in Africa. Her pictures were published in two remarkable books, *The Last of the Nuba* and *The People of Kau.* She published *Leni Riefenstahl: A Memoir* (New York: St Martin's, 1993). The same year she was featured in a three-hour, German-British biographical film, "The Wonderful, Horrible Life of Leni Riefenstahl." Still alluring and vigorous in her 90s, and still denying charges of political or romantic attachment to Hitler, the pioneering film maker was licensed as a scuba diver and turned to underwater cinematography.

RIGAULT, Jean. French politician. A monarchist and ex-**Cagoulard** whom Macmillan called "a mean, shifty, anti-British, shuffling creature" (Macmillan, 45), Rigault figured prominently in anti-Vichy activities that preceded Allied landings in North Africa on 8 Nov 32. Thanks to his friend Lemaigre-Dubreil (below), he had been director of the newspaper *Le Jour.* After the Vichy government suppressed the paper, Rigault reached Algiers in Dec 41. He and Lemaigre-Dubreil had been plotting to support an American liberation of North Africa and Rigault became one of Robert MURPHY's collaborators. Rigault helped to bring GIRAUD into the plot, attending the **Cherchell conference,** and was especially responsible for winning over BETHOUART. After the DARLAN deal Rigault had charge of "political and external affairs," meaning law and order. His police chief was Henri d'ASTIER, which may explain why GIRAUD had Darlan's assassin, Bonnier de la Chapelle, so summarily liquidated. Although a monarchist, Rigault helped convince the Comte de Paris, the durable French pretender, to get out of Algiers and focus on his lucrative agri-business in Morocco.

DE GAULLE's purge of the FCNL led Rigault to resign on 16 Mar 43 and withdraw from public life.

RITCHIE, Neil Methuen. British general. 1897-1983. He was educated at Lancing College and Sandhurst. Commissioned in the Black Watch (1914), Ritchie fought in France and Mesopotamia, was appointed to the DSO in 1917, and won the MC in 1918. Rising in four years from major to acting major general in 1940, Ritchie had been Alan Brooke's BGS with the BEF in France, 1939-40. He held the same post under Auchinleck in the Southern Command, went with the Auk to the Middle East Cmd as his deputy CofS. Maj Gen Ritchie "seemed surely destined for professional success because of his talents and not less because of his connections. He was rich . . . vigorous and thorough . . . very tall and very big. He was handsome and authoritative; good humoured in a slightly heavy manner. There was a bovine strength about him. Yet his brain was good." (Barnett, *Desert Generals,* 123.)

When Auchinleck had to relieved Alan CUNNINGHAM from command of the 8th Army on 25 Nov 41 he had a major problem in finding a successor. There was no time to get one from England. Because Opn **Crusader** was still in progress, it would have been disruptive to move up one of the army's two corps commanders, Willoughby Norrie and GOTT, and the Auk considered neither man particularly well qualified to replace Cunningham. Churchill and Alan Brooke urged Auchinleck to handle the field army himself, but the Auk thought his place as commander in the entire Middle East was in Cairo. This is why Ritchie was made "temporary" commander of the embattled 8th Army on 26 Nov 41.

Although self confident, impressing one observer as "fairly oozing energy and vigour" (quoted in Barnett, 124), he was much junior to his two major subordinates (Norrie and Gott) Ritchie's last command in combat had been as leader of a battalion in WWI. Auchinleck intended to compensate by spending much time at the front with Ritchie, to "hold his hand" iIbid.).

But the 8th Army proceeded to raise the siege of Tobruk and end Opn Crusader with a vigorous pursuit of shattered Axis forces through Cyrenaica to the El Agheila line. So Ritchie's appointment as army commander was made permanent.

Rommel came back with his second offensive on 21 Jan 42, much earlier than British intelligence thought possible. Shattered elements of the 8th Army were back on the Gazala line by 4 Feb 42, when another lull came. Despite warnings from subordinates and Auchinleck, Ritchie violated the fundamental rule of armor employment and parceled units out instead of massing them. When Rommel enveloped the British south flank around Bir Hacheim, the Afrika Korps being at the top of its game, Ritchie lost control of the battle, along with most of the 8th Army's armor. Auchinleck belatedly relieved Ritchie on 25 June 42, four days after KLOPPER surrendered Tobruk.

Given another chance at a lower level Ritchie led the 52d (Lowland) Div in the UK. For the Normandy operation he commanded the 12th Corps of Miles Dempsey's 2d Army in Montgomery's 21st AG. He was, of course, promoted to the commensurate rank of lieutenant general (T).

After the war, Sir Neil (KBE, 1945; KCB, 1947) headed the Scottish Cmd until promoted to full general and CinC, Far East Land Forces, with headquarters at Singapore, 1947-49. His final service was in Washington, DC, with the Joint Service Mission. In retirement he was chairman, Mercantile and General Reinsurance Co of Canada.

ROCKEFELLER, Nelson Aldrich. US official. 1908-79. Second son of John D. Rockefeller, Jr, he was born 8 July 08 at Bar Harbor, Maine, one of six children. Graduating from Dartmouth in 1930 he was involved with family enterprises to include being director of Rockefeller Center in NYC. He also was drawn to Latin America, an experience useful later when he was coordinator from Aug 40 of the Office of Inter-American Affairs (CIAA). In Dec 44 he became assistant secretary of state for Latin-American affairs. Nelson Rockefeller was Republican governor of New York from 1958 until resigning in Dec 73 to be Gerald Ford's vice president. Meanwhile he failed in 1964 and 1968 to win the Republican nomination for president. Not seeking further public office after his term expired in 1977 Rockefeller continued his involvement with art museums in NYC.

ROEHM, Ernst. German officer. 1887-1934. The odious chief of Nazi storm troops was born 28 Nov 87 in Munich, scion of an old Bavarian family of civil servants. Short, beefy, simple-minded and missing part of his nose from one of three WWI wounds, the swashbuckler also was homosexual. He joined the **DAP** in 1921, before Hitler, and formed its "gymnastics and sports" division. This became the **SA.**

Whereas Hitler approved giving the SA military trappings—knowing how Germans love and respect uniforms—the fuehrer never favored their becoming "even an auxiliary, let alone a rival, to the Army" (W-B, *Nemesis,* 204). But Major Roehm envisioned building more than a force of rowdies for political intimidation, and disagreements over this led to his removal in May 25. Hitler reorganized the SA under his own command and created the SS (ibid.). After five years in Bolivia with the unofficial military mission, Roehm was recalled to succeed Otto Wagener (1888-1971) on 5 Jan 31 (officially) as CofS of the SA. As *de facto* commander Roehm began a reorganization along military lines, now with Hitler's authority. The Brownshirts grew from 250,000 to 2.3 million by 1933, becoming a threat not only to the Reichswehr—whose strength was limited to 100,000 by the Versailles Treaty—but also to the Nazi Party, from which the SA had split. On the plausible but totally unfounded assumption that Roehm was planning a counter-revolution, and to placate the army (whose support he still needed), Hitler organized what became known as the **Blood Purge,** 29 June-1 July 34.

The fuehrer flew secretly to Munich, where at dawn on Saturday, 30 June, he linked up with SKORZENY's men and drove to the nearby resort of Bad Wiesse, where Roehm and his lieutenants were surprised in bed. The Brownshirt chief was herded into Munich's Stadelheim Prison to join those arrested earlier. After Dr Hans FRANK successfully raised legal objections to the wholesale execution of SA leaders, Roehm remained on the short list. At 6 PM on Sunday, 1 July 34, Theodor EICKE and Michael Lippert entered Roehm's prison room, and laid the Sunday edition of *Volkische*

Beobachter and a pistol on a table. The visitors left after telling the prisoner he would have 10 minutes alone. Under banner headlines the paper covered Saturday's events in Munich. When Eicke and Lippert heard no shot, they had a guard retrieve the pistol and entered the room shooting. Roehm was waiting with his chest bared. (Fest, *Hitler,* 486.)

ROESSLER, Rudolf "Lucy." Head of Red Army intelligence ring in Switzerland. 1897-1958. The long glossary entry on the **Lucy Ring** summarizes a complex story of its four networks, two dozen agents, and half a dozen other major actors involved.

One of history's most remarkable secret intelligence agents—careful writers will not call him a spy—Roessler was born 22 Nov 97 at Kaufbeuren, near Munich. From a family of highly respected, God-fearing Protestants, he was educated at Augsburg's **Realgymnasium,** where a schoolmate was Bertholt Brecht (1898-1956), the future playwright, poet, and theatrical reformer. (Read & Fisher, *Operation Lucy* [1980], 77; work cited hereafter as R&F.) Roessler's military service in 1914-18—from which he emerged as a corporal—gave him a valuable insight into how the German army worked (ibid, 78).

Roessler became a journalist in Bavaria and rose to edit an intellectual magazine, *Form und Sinn* (Form and Meaning), for three years before moving to Berlin in 1928. A small, intense, bespectacled man with thinning hair, he was a heavy smoker despite chronic asthma. His wife, Olga, also from Augsburg, was a pretty woman somewhat younger than her husband and content to be a simple hausfrau. They had no children.

Drawn to the theater, which was a powerful force in the waning years of the Weimar Republic, Roessler took over management of a theater association, the Buehnenvolskbund. He thrived in the intellectual world of the German capital, becoming a friend of author Thomas Mann and poet Stefan George. Admitted to the prestigious Herrenklub, Roessler enlarged his circle of influential social and political contacts, to include senior military officers. As a progressive conservative and patriot Roessler was ardently anti-Nazi but was considered by one literary colleague to be a dreamer devoted solely to the arts (ibid, 80).

When Hitler became chancellor in early 1933 Alfred ROSENBERG took over the highly profitable Buehnenvolskbund, at one blow depriving Roessler of both career and income. But the victim of Rosenberg's covetousness had been befriended by a Swiss student at the university of Berlin, an ardent young Marxist named Xaver Schnieper, son of a government minister in the canton of Lucerne. Schnieper persuaded the Roesslers to settle near Lucerne in the summer of 1934. Now 36 years old, Roessler established a book publishing house, Vita Nova (New Life). With German and Swiss financial backing he concentrated on producing antifascist works. In 1936 he began publishing a Catholic, liberal magazine, *Die Entscheidung* (The Decision), for a group of the same name that included Schnieper and Bernhard Mayr von Baldeg.

In May 39, on the eve of Hitler's war, Roessler's friends in Berlin sent him the parts of a late-model Wehrmacht radio-transmitter through customs in Basle. (Accoce & Quet, *A Man Called Lucy,* 43, cited hereafter as A&Q.) The moles—eight officers in OKW and two in OKL (ibid.)—also established secret channels, codes, and procedures for regular communication.

When the Swiss put frontier troops on a war footing, 29 Aug 39, Schnieper was called to active duty in Swiss military intelligence under Brigadier Roger MASSON. The brigadier condoned violation of Swiss neutrality on the condition that Roessler feed his material not only to the Swiss but also to Allied authorities.

German monitors quickly realized that Lucy was sending information to Moscow Center that could have come only from the top levels of the German high command. But it was not known until long after the war that MI6 was feeding **Ultra** intelligence to his net. In an operation set up under Walter Schellenberg to uncover the **Rote Kapelle** spy ring, the Germans finally homed in on radio transmitters in Geneva and Montreux that were sending reports to Moscow Center. Swiss police took Roessler and his principal associates into custody on 9 May 44 but held him for only four months. As covered in more detail under the **Lucy Ring,** the Swiss government held two well-publicized but somewhat inconclusive trials. Roessler was allowed to continue his life as a publisher in Switzerland.

In Mar 53, however, he was sentenced to a year in prison on charges of spying. All he had done, apparently, was write an analysis of military power in Europe for the Czech government,

using unclassified materials. But for some reason he sent the report from West Germany through Switzerland in a pot of honey, and Swiss police had been alerted. Schnieper was sentenced to nine months in jail as an accomplice.

The "greatest resistance worker" of WWII (*A&Q,* 127) took his secrets to the grave, as did Roger MASSON. Lucy is buried in the Swiss cemetery at Kriens beneath a simple plaque inscribed "Rudolf Roessler, 1897-1958."

ROKOSSOVSKY, Konstantin Konstantinovich. Soviet military leader. 1896-1968. From July 42 he was a front commander, ranking with Konev, Malinovsky, and Zhukov as one of "The Four Horsemen of the German Apocalypse" (*CB 44*).

Rokossovsky was born 21 Dec 96 in Velikiye Luki of a Russian mother and Polish father, a railroad machinist. Moving to Warsaw in 1900 with his family and orphaned at 14, he was apprenticed two years later to a stonemason. He grew into a huge man, six feet four inches tall, blue-eyed, handsome, ebullient, a "romantic figure" in the words used later by Western journalists (*CB 44*). In 1914 he volunteered for the Russian army, served as a dragoon, saw action on the western and northwestern fronts, and became a sergeant. He joined the Red Army in 1918 and the CP the next year. During the civil war he was in a Red Guard cavalry force, and in 1918-24 he led a cavalry unit in the Omsk region and on the Mongolian steppes (Scarecrow).

Deciding on an army career, Rokossovsky took the cavalry short courses in 1923, the Frunze MA higher short courses in 1929, and continued to command cavalry units. In 1929-30 he led the 5th Kuban Cav Bde in the Russian efforts to reestablish control of the Chinese Eastern RR. Zhukov and Rokossovsky, within less than three weeks of being the same age, served together at various times and remained close friends.

After taking command of the 5th Cav Corps in 1936, Rokossovsky was arrested in Aug 37 (during the **Great Purges**) on charges of being a counterrevolutionary. Beaten senseless and imprisoned under brutal conditions, he was released in Mar 40 on SHAPOSHNIKOV's request and restored to command of the 5th Cav Corps. A few months later, when mechanized corps again were formed, Rokossovsky was given the 9th Mecz Corps in Zhukov's Kiev MD. In June 41, when Zhukov was organizing reserves to stem the German drive on Moscow, Rokossovsky was rushed to the Smolensk region. The following August Gen Maj Rokossovsky formed the 16th Army and he was promoted a month later to general lieutenant. The young general, only 45, held the critical NW approaches to Moscow around Volokolamsk as Barbarossa fizzled in the early Russian winter. The 16th Army became known as a factory for producing **guards** units.

Badly wounded on 8 Mar 42 and hospitalized for three months (HFS) Rokossovsky returned to duty in mid-July and commanded the Bryansk Front until the Stalingrad defensive operations began. In September he took over the newly formed Don Front just north of Stalingrad, and in the Soviet counteroffensive (Opn Uranus) he constituted the northern wing. On completion of the encirclement he took over the grinding task of destroying die-hard elements of Paulus's 6th Army. On 15 Jan 43, a few weeks before the Don Front was dissolved, Rokossovsky was promoted to general colonel, and exactly a month later he assumed command of the Central Front. Promoted 28 Apr 43 to general of the army (No. 12), Rokossovsky led his front in Zhukov's great victory at Kursk-Orel in July 43, then drove almost 250 miles to cross the Dnieper and penetrate to the NE edge of the Pripet Marshes by late Nov 43. Meanwhile his force was redesignated the Belorussian Front on 20 Oct 43 and in Feb 44 it was subdivided, Rokossovsky then heading the 1st Belorussian Front. He was promoted to **MSU** (No. 16) on 24 June 44. (HFS.)

One of history's hardest military campaigns began on 24 June 44. In the first phase Marshal Rokossovsky quickly encircling five divisions of the German 9th Army around Bobruisk (27 June) then he was the southern wing of an operation that trapped large elements of the German 4th Army around Minsk (3 July 44). Leaving forces to reduce these pockets he swept west with parallel columns on a broad front to liberate the rest of Belorussia, taking Lublin on 23 July, Brest-Litovsk on 28 July, and reaching the Vistula River below Warsaw on 1 Aug 44.

What happened next is highly controversial. Rokossovsky has been accused of delaying his entry into Warsaw until the Germans crushed the uprising led by Bor-KOMOROWSKI. The rebuttal is that the pause was dictated by military (mainly logistical) realities and that the uprising was premature.

In the jockeying for the glory of taking Berlin STALIN gave ZHUKOV the nod. Zhukov took over the 1st Belorussian Front on 16 Nov 44 and Rokossovsky replaced Zakharov as the 2d Belorussian Front commander. M. S. Malinin, who had been Rokossovsky's CofS since Sep 42, now moved to serve Zhukov in that position for the rest of the war. Rokossovsky inherited Gen Col A. N. Bogolyubov, who had been Zakharov's CofS.

Whereas Zhukov got the glory of leading the main effort against Berlin, Rokossovsky encountered some of the war's most desperate resistance in taking East Prussia and Pomerania. He left the 2d Belorussian Front on 10 June 45, twice a HSU (1944 and 1945).

After the war Rokossovsky was CinC of Soviet Forces in Poland, 1945-49. On 2 Nov 49 he became a Marshal of Poland, CinC of the Polish army, MOD, and **PM.** He was forced to leave Poland for the USSR on 19 Oct 56 after the Gomulka crisis. He was chief inspector and deputy MOD, 1956-62, with a break to head the Transcaucasus MD, 1957-58. Then he was in the General Inspectorate Group of the Soviet MOD.

"The way in which dozens of [Soviet] memoirists recall with sympathy their service or their encounters with Rokossovskii has a warmth that seldom appears in descriptions of other military leaders" (Bialer, ed, *Stalin and His Generals,* 606n.).

He died 3 Aug 68 in Moscow and is buried in the Kremlin Wall.

ROMMEL, Erwin. German general. 1891-1944. "The Desert Fox" was born 15 Nov 91 at Heidenheim, NE of Ulm. His stoutly middle-class family had the admirable qualities of their native **Swabia.** Young Rommel was small for his age, quiet, docile, and at first a poor student. But he underwent a transformation in his teens:

Mentally, he began to give evidence of having inherited the mathematical talent of his father and grandfather [both school teachers]. Physically, he started to spend every spare moment in summer on his bicycle and in winter on skis. He passed his examinations with credit. He lost his dreamy abstracted air and reverted to the type of Wuerttemberg [*see* **Swabia**], "the home of common sense in Germany." He became hard-headed and practical—and very careful with his money, another Wuerttemberger characteristic. (Young, *Rommel,* 29.)

Rommel's earliest interests were in airplanes and gliders. He wanted to study engineering and find a career with the Zeppelin works at Friederichshaven. But his father disapproved, so in the summer of 1910 Rommel became an officer candidate in the 6th Wuerttemberg or 124th Inf Regt. As was customary he served first in the ranks, rising to sergeant. Attending the War Academy in Danzig from Mar 11 to Jan 12 and being commissioned, Leutnant Rommel rejoined his regiment. In Mar 14 he was assigned to a field artillery regiment at Ulm but returned to the infantry when war broke out. From his baptism of fire in France on 22 Aug 14 as a platoon leader the short, uncharismatic young officer was "the perfect fighting animal, cold, cunning, ruthless, untiring, quick of decision, incredibly brave" (Young, *Rommel,* 32). In Jan 15 he was awarded the Iron Cross 1st Class, having won the 2d Class four months earlier; in each action he received a leg wound that required hospitalization. On 10 Apr 15 Rommel joined a new Wuerttemberg mountain battalion that was a highly specialized formation of six rifle companies and machine gun platoons from which task forces could be tailored for specific missions. It was Rommel's introduction to "the nature of combat mobility." (Blumenson, "Rommel" in Barnett, ed, *Hitler's Generals,* 295.) He was a company commander in the campaign that quickly took Romania out of the war.

On leave in 1916 he married Lucie Maria Mollin. She was the handsome, high spirited daughter of a Prussian landowner, whom he had met five years earlier in Danzig, where she was a language student. Rommel's letters to "Dearest Lu" are the core of *The Rommel Papers* (below).

In May 17 Lt Rommel was back in France for three months before going to the Italian front. For a 50-hour action to capture Monte Matajur, SW of Caporetto, on 26 Oct 17, Rommel was promoted to captain and awarded the Pour le Mérite. Soon after this he and six men, roped together, swam the icy Piave river and captured the Italian garrison at Lognaroni. Capt Rommel returned from home leave spent the rest of the war as a staff officer, much to his disgust. (Young, 36-38.)

Despite this remarkable record Rommel never qualified for the General Staff, which his detractors—particularly in Germany—were (and are)

quick to point out. But he had a considerable reputation as a theoritician at the tactical level. This stemmed from the acclaim awarded his book *Infantrie greift an,* whose English language title is *Infantry Attacks* (1944). Based on his war experiences in Belgium, the Argonne, the Vosges, the Carpathians, and Italy, the book evolved from lectures at the Dresden infantry school, 1929-33. The Swiss Army adopted it as a manual and gave the author an inscribed watch. (Young, 30.) More important, Hitler admired the book. The men first met in 1935, when Maj Rommel's mountain battalion turned out as an honor guard. Rommel stoutly and successfully defied Himmler and Goebbels on the matter of posting a line of SS troops between his battalion and the fuehrer, this being a customary Nazi security precaution.

Promoted in Oct 35 Lt Col Rommel taught at the Potsdam War Academy. He subsequently headed the army security detachment with Hitler during the **Anschluss** in 1938 and the occupation of Czechoslovakia in 1939. The recently promoted Generalmajor Rommel was commander of troops with Hitler's mobile military head quarters in Poland in Sep 39. He found "the atmosphere of intrigue" intolerable (Goerlitz, *GGS,* 392) but profited from the association with Hitler to get command of the 7th Pz Div on 15 Feb 40.

"Over grade in age" (too young) by German army standards; lacking the requisite seniority, not to mention the crimson trouser stripes of the GGGS; Rommel had only three months to train what essentially was a new panzer division formed from STUMME's 2d Light Div.

France, 1940

For the assault in the west that began 10 May 40 Rommel's division and the 5th Pz Div (under Gen Lt Joachem LEMELSEN from 22 May 40) comprised Hermann Hoth's 15th Pz Corps of Kluge's 4th Army. The "perfect fighting animal" had quickly grasped the capability of armored forces. His first dramatic triumph was on the Meuse just north of Dinant, where he defied conventional military wisdom and made the assault crossing without waiting for large infantry formations to catch up. Rommel's troops became known as the "Ghost," or "Phantom" division, moving faster and farther than any other in modern military history, appearing out of nowhere, spreading confusion and the consequent terror. After racing across Flanders to the Channel, Rommel turned south and received the surrender of Cherbourg on 19 June 40. He then raced along the French coast to the Spanish border. These were "arguably the finest military exploits of his career," writes Douglas Home (Carver, ed, *The War Lords*. 277). But he had to wait six months for promotion to Generalleutnant on 1 Jan 41.

This was about the time Mussolini had to ask for help in North Africa, where WAVELL had routed GRAZIANI and was threatening Tripoli. Hitler immediately sent Luftwaffe units to bases in Italy and promised to have two German divisions in Libya by the end of May 41.

Understanding the value of military heroes, Hitler deliberately created two, being careful to pick men who lacked the political and intellectual qualities to be dangerous. Further, he saw that they performed in the wings. Eduard DIETL in Finland already was the "snow hero," so "Rommel in Africa was to be the sun-hero," writes Liddell Hart (*Talk*, 45). Rommel learned on 6 Feb 41 that he would command the new Afrika Korps and would have operational control over surviving Italian motorized forces in North Africa (*EP,* 99). The general reached Tripoli six days later for a personal reconnaissance and found that the situation was desperate. Graziani had been replaced by his chief of staff, Gen Gariboldi. Having come through Rome and the 10th Luftwaffe Corps Hq in Sicily, Rommel had the Italian Commando Supremo's approval for setting up a "forward strategy" to defend Libya.

I had already decided that in view of the tenseness of the situation and the sluggishness of the Italian command, to depart from my instructions . . . and to take the command at the front into my own hands as soon as possible, at the latest after the arrival of the first German troops. General von Rintelen, to whom I had given a hint of my intention in Rome, had advised me against it, for, as he put it, that was the way to lose both honor and reputation. (Liddell Hart, *Rommel Papers,* 101, hereafter cited as *RP*.)

General Rintelen, who was the OKW LnO, obviously was thinking about the problem of logistical support, the determining element of any military operation. But Rommel's attitude was that somebody with crimson stripes on his trousers could worry about that.

The Desert Fox

Rommel's first offensive, 24 Mar-30 May 41, was a masterpiece of desert warfare by a general with no experience in this field. With his heavier and faster panzer units, magnificently trained and equipped, plus powerful tactical air support, Rommel used audacity, vigorous personal leadership where the action was hottest, and superior tactical skill to shatter the thin shell of opposing British forces. (These had been thinned out to make up the BEF in Greece under Henry M. WILSON.) The man who was becoming famous as the "Desert Fox" pushed 1,500 miles to the Egyptian border. But, having overstretched his LofC, he had to pause, and the British had made a wise decision to hold Tobruk when Rommel bypassed it. In addition to being a much-needed port, Tobruk was a classic **"flanking position."**

WAVELL's counteroffensive of 15-17 July 41 to relieve Tobruk was repulsed by panzer forces that continued to outclass the British in materiel and tactics. AUCHINLECK replaced Wavell, was reinforced, and undertook an offensive, 18 Nov-31 Dec 41. This achieved surprise and forced Rommel to withdraw 1,500 miles to El Agheila. But the British Middle East Command again was weakened, this time because of the large-scale offensive of the Japanese in the Far East.

Rommel's second offensive, 21 Jan-7 July 42, again caught the overextended British 8th Army off guard and drove it back to the Gazala line, west of Tobruk. After a four-month pause to let his logistical support catch up, but with the Afrika Korps now in peak form, Rommel launched another offensive on 27 May 42. Using the same tactics that had been so successful, Rommel undertook to turn the south flank of the Gazala Line in a wide envelopment. Despite KOENIG's epic defense of Bir Hacheim with Free French forces, Rommel's panzers outclassed and virtually annihilated British armored formations and captured Tobruk from KLOPPER on 21 June 42. The Desert Fox was notified by radio of his promotion to field marshal, effective 22 June 42, Hitler personally presenting the baton three months later in Berlin. But Rommel's fortunes had reached high tide.

Enter Montgomery

Almost immediately after taking over the 8th Army in the El Alamein position, MONTGOMERY won his first round against Rommel at Alam Halfa, 31 Aug-7 Sep 42. Three weeks later, for the first time in his career except when wounded, Rommel had to report sick and be evacuated. Health had been a problem with Rommel from his first weeks of combat in 1914, when he had driven himself to exhaustion. Plagued from then with severe stomach trouble, he was bothered by rheumatism before going to North Africa. Subsequently he had frequent attacks of faintness. Doctors now reported he was "suffering from chronic stomach and intestinal catarrh, nasal diphtheria and considerable circulation trouble." (Liddell Hart, *RP*, 271n.)

Back to convalesce in Germany, the Sun Hero had his first doubts about Hitler's intentions to send substantial reinforcements to Africa. Then Rommel learned he was to take over an army group in the southern Ukraine, STUMME replacing him in the western desert. But Rommel had been in the hospital at Zemmering only three weeks when Hitler phoned at noon on 24 Oct 42 and said "Rommel, there is bad news from Africa. The situation looks very black. No one seems to know what has happened to Stumme. Do you feel well enough to go back and would you be willing to go?" (Young, 172.) Mongtomery had began the battle of El Alamein the preceding day.

Still very sick, the 50-year-old field marshal flew off at 7 o'clock the next morning, 25 Oct 42. Via Rome, where he checked on the always critical **POL,** and on through Crete, Rommel reached his headquarters by 8 PM. (Ibid.) (Around this time Geoffrey KEYES was killed in the commando raid against what was supposed to be Rommel's CP.)

Defeated decisively at El Alamein by 4 Nov 42, Rommel started the long retreat. Eisenhower began landing his forces a few days later in Morocco and Algeria, and the Germans quickly rushed reinforcements to hold a beachhead in Tunisia. Continuing his retreat, Rommel abandoned Tripoli on 23 Jan 43. Three days later Rommel was beginning to inspect the **Mareth Line** when he learned he was to be relieved. There were solid medical reasons, but the Italian and German high commands had long wanted the Desert Fox out. Hitler had distrusted his Sun Hero since Montgomery's victory at El Alamein, according to Hans SPEIDEL, "but he still wanted to make capital for himself with the German people out of the respectability of Rommel . . ." (*Invasion*, 158).

Free to pick his departure date and knowing that his opponent would be pokey, Rommel had the rear guard of his Panzer Army Africa into the line by 15 Feb 43.

Hans Juergend von ARNIM had headed the newly formed 5th Pz Army in Tunisia since 3 Dec 42 and had effectively blocked Eisenhower's "race for Tunis." But it was not for two months that Kesselring arranged a first meeting between Arnim and Rommel (9 Feb 43) to coordinate their operations. The first phase was a complete success—the battle of Kasserine Pass, 14-23 Feb 43. But this Allied disaster would have been much worse if Rommel had been permitted to exploit success by attacking Tebessa in strength and if it had not been for what he called "clumsy leadership by certain German commanders," notably ARNIM (*RP*, 400, 408). PATTON arrived to make up somewhat for the fiasco for which FREDENDALL was primarily responsible. A week after the 15th and 21st Pz Divs failed to penetrate British positions at Medenine on 5 Mar 43 Rommel left for Germany. Although now very sick and convinced that all hope of victory in Africa was gone, he wanted to fly back and evacuate his veterans or share their fate, but Hitler refused permission. (Young, 184.)

For all Rommel's brilliance in the desert campaigns he had justified the fears of superiors that he was not suited for a command above divisional level. (Some have said the same of Patton and Stilwell.) But Liddell Hart sums up the judgment of serious military historians by pointing out that Rommel was "apt to be riding around the battlefield," out of contact with his headquarters "when wanted by his staff for some important decision." (Liddell Hart, *Talk,* 47, 50.)

Intermission

After about six weeks of treatment at Zemmering Rommel spent some time at Hitler's headquarters. The Wehrmacht had reached high tide. PAULUS had surrendered his 6th Army at Stalingrad; ARNIM was about to surrender a comparable number of veteran German troops in Tunisia; the Allies were about to land in Sicily (10 July 43); and British intelligence had Hitler worried about an Allied invasion of the Balkans through Greece.

Rommel reached Salonika as CinC Southeast (*RP,* 430-31) on 23 July 43. Two days later MUSSOLINI was overthrown. The immediate danger, apart from what Italian troops in Albania would do, was that others would block the Brenner Pass. Rommel flew back to Hitler's Hq and soon was made commander of AG B Hq in Munich. When the threat to passages through the Alps did not materialize, he moved AG B Hq to Lake Garda and took command of all Axis forces in northern Italy (15 Aug 43). The pessimistic Rommel was scheduled to become supreme commander in all of Italy, but Hitler belatedly gave the nod to the eternally optimistic "Smiling Albert" KESSELRING.

Normandy

Leaving Italy on 21 Nov 43 Rommel went to France as IG of coastal defenses. He had the responsibility of examining all possible invasion areas from Denmark to the Alps. The so-called Atlantic Wall proved to be a propaganda myth. There were photogenic fortifications at places like Cape Griz Nez (opposite Dover). But the OKH, OKM, and OT had not been able to agree on a coordinated plan of defense. The Normandy coast of Calvados, where the Allies landed, "was practically unfortified when Marshal Rommel took over command." (Speidel, 43.) The organizational structure—order of battle— was a nightmare.

But Rommel made a prodigious effort. He ordered four belts of "foreshore obstacles," effective at all tide conditions, to be installed. To strengthen antiairborne obstacles he put "Rommel's asparagus," fields of stakes connected by barbed wire and many tipped with mines or artillery shells. He did not have time to add this final touch nor to complete the two outer belts of underwater obstacles. But AG B records show that more than 500,000 foreshore obstacles were emplaced by 13 May 44 and more than 4,000,000 land mines laid on the coast by the 20th. (*RP,* 457-60.)

Another major problem was Rundstedt's and Rommel's fundamental disagreement over strategy. The older marshal, who looked on Rommel as an upstart, envisioned the classic defense: a cordon on the shoreline with the strategic reserve well over 100 miles back, SE of Paris. Rommel's experience with Allied airpower in Africa and his study of the Salerno and Anzio landings convinced him that the Allies had to be stopped on the beaches. This required that immediately available reserves be well forward, otherwise Allied air supremacy would immobilize them. The other funda-

mental disagreement was over where the Allies would make their main landings. Rundstedt believed it would be at the Channel's narrowest area, the Pas de Calais; from Apr 44, according to SPEIDEL (whose evidence on this point has been questioned) Rommel rightly assumed it would be farther south, between the mouths of the Somme and the Seine, "with their harbors of Abbeville and Le Havre, the coast of Calvados [where it came] and the Cotentin peninsula with its port, Cherbourg" (Speidel, 23). Hitler's personal involvement caused a compromise, worse than a clean adoption of either concept.

Rommel became head of AG B on 1 Jan 44, subordinate to OB West (Rundstedt). This gave Rommel command of ground forces in the invasion area from just north of Antwerp to the Loire. (AG G under BLASKOWITZ covered the south of France.) The small operational staff of AG B occupied part of the historic Rochefoucauld chateau at La Roche Guyon, on the Seine some 40 miles below Paris.

When the landings came unexpectedly on 6 June 44 Rommel was in Germany trying to get two more panzer divisions and additional artillery. Hitler impeded defensive deployment by interfering with Rundstedt's actions, vetoing the proposals of commanders on the ground, imposing his own tactical concepts, and not letting divisions move without OKW authority. Despite Rommel's urging Hitler to visit the forward headquarters, the dictator continued to control from such a distance that even his sound decisions were overtaken by events. But Rundstedt and Rommel did have two meetings with Hitler soon after D day. The first was on 17 June at Margival, a specially prepared CP near Soissons. Rommel spoke out about Hitler's ignoring recommendations of subordinates without having adequate knowledge of realities. Rommel went so far at the second meeting, on the 29th at Berchtesgaden, as to ask Hitler how he imagined the war still could be won (Speidel, 480).

"The gulf between Field Marshal Rommel and Hitler had widened," SPEIDEL comments. "Hitler's mistrust, indeed his hatred, seemed to have grown." (Ibid., 98.) RUNDSTEDT was relieved of command two days after the 29 June conference but Rommel was not. On 15 July Rommel sent Hitler a three-page message saying that resistance could not last more than two or three more weeks in Normandy. "I must beg you to draw the conclusions without delay," the field marshal added in his own handwriting, then said to Speidel, "I have given him his last chance. If he does not take it, we will act." (Ibid., 117.) There is evidence that Rommel meant he would take the initiative in negotiating with the Allies. But fate intervened two days later.

On 17 July 44 the field marshal was critically wounded when three RAF fighters caught his staff car on the road. The driver was killed and Rommel was unconscious for a week, during which time the attempt was made on Hitler's life. Rommel was not won over by the conspirators until after D day, but even then he insisted that the fuehrer merely be arrested and tried, not assassinated. (Hoffmann, *Resistance,* 351-54, 375; Speidel, 68.) Suspicion about Rommel's involvement was raised, quite innocently, by the unfortunate Karl Heinrich von STULPNAGEL.

Death of Rommel

After hospitalization in France the partially recovered marshal was moved on 8 August, at his own request, to his home at Herrlingen, near Ulm. Rommel soon realized his life was in jeopardy and found a medical excuse to avoid orders to visit Berlin. But on 14 Oct 45 two generals came from Hitler with an ultimatum: suicide, with a state funeral and protection for his family and staff, or trial for high treason. After informing his wife, son, and ADC, that he would be dead in fifteen minutes, Rommel drove off a few hundred yards from the house with the visitors and took poison. Cause of death was given as a brain seizure. (Manfred Rommel in *RP,* "The Last Days," 495-506.) He was 52 years old. The funeral in Ulm was on 18 Oct 44 with Rundstedt reading an oration in Hitler's name.

Lucie Rommel, son Manfred, and Capt Hermann Aldinger, a long-time associate, saved most of Rommel's papers from the Gestapo. Taken by the Americans (and some of them, plus a large collection of photographs, being lost) these are the basis of the work edited by Liddell Hart, *The Rommel Papers* (New York: Harcourt, Brace 1953). Manfred Rommel and Fritz BAY-ERLEIN contributed important chapters. The first biography, perhaps still the best, is Desmond Young's *Rommel* (London: Collins, 1950). Also noteworthy are Ronald Lewin, *Rommel as Military Commander* (London: B. T.

Batsford, 1968), Charles Douglas-Home, *Rommel* (London: Weidenfeld and Nicholson; and New York: Saturday Review Press, 1973), and David Irving, *The Trail of the Fox: The Search for the True Field Marshal Rommel* (New York: Dutton, 1977). A perceptive essay by Martin Blumenson is in *Hitler's Generals,* edited by Correlli Barnett (New York: Grove Weidenfeld, 1989).

ROMULO, Carlos Peña. Philippine official. 1901-. He was born in Manila on 14 Jan 01, received his MA from Columbia Univ (NYC) in 1921, and became an English professor, newspaper publisher and editor in Manila. For articles based on a tour of the Far East to include unoccupied China and the **NEI** he won a 1941 Pulitzer Prize and became a marked man in Japan. As a reserve officer of the Philippine army Maj Romulo became MacArthur's press aide on 10 Dec 41. Later he broadcast "The Voice of Freedom" from Corregidor to troops on Bataan. The Japanese having put a price on his head, Romulo was among those chosen for evacuation to Australia, where he continued to be MacArthur's ADC and rose to the rank of brigadier general. With Pres OSMENA and Maj Gen Basilio J. Valdes he waded ashore with MacArthur on Leyte.

In 1944-46 Romulo was resident commissioner of the Philippines in the US, then he served with the UN. Among his publications is *I Saw the Fall of the Philippines* (1942).

ROOSEVELT, Anna Eleanor. US public figure. 1884-1962. Anna Eleanor Roosevelt (her maiden name) was born in NYC on 11 Oct 84. The painfully shy ugly duckling was a niece of Theodore "Teddy" Roosevelt's, at whose summer home she began spending vacations about the year Teddy became president (1901). Eleanor married her fifth cousin Franklin D. Roosevelt on 17 Mar 05. They had a daughter, Anna, the next year, followed by James (following), and a son who died 1909, then Elliot (following), and finally Franklin, Jr., and John. After her husband was stricken with polio in 1921 Eleanor defied a domineering mother-in-law to focus on keeping Roosevelt's political fortunes alive.

Eleanor Roosevelt was a large woman of tremendous vigor and personality who had a vital role in her husband's official life. From

1936 until shortly before her death she published a widely read syndicated column, "My Day," not missing a deadline in more than 25 years.

President Truman appointed Mrs Roosevelt to a high post in the UN. She finally withdrew from public life during the Eisenhower administration but accepted Pres John F. Kennedy's appointment to the UN as a delegate. She declined reappointment because of poor health after 1961, the year before she died.

ROOSEVELT, Elliott. US general. 1910-90. The "'stormy petrel of his family'" *(CB 46)* was born 23 Sep 10 in NYC. He was the third surviving child and second son, growing to a strapping six feet three inches. Non conformity began with not attending Harvard. After 18 months of marriage he was divorced from Elizabeth Donner of Philadelphia in July 33 and married Ruth Goodins of Texas. They established residence on a ranch near Fort Worth. Having become a pilot and aviation editor of Hearst newspapers, the president's son was accused publicly of lobbying for air lines and of contracting with German designer Anthony H. G. Fokker to sell US planes at high prices. In 1936 he turned to radio and was involved with a chain of 23 stations without investing money nor having any known office. In 1940 the venture went into receivership and Elliott began active service as an Air Corps Reserve officer with the rank of captain.

Highly regarded by H. H. "Hap" ARNOLD he took part during the summer of 1941 in aerial surveys of ferry routes over Greenland and the North Pole. He rose to the rank of colonel in Mar 43 while heading the NW Africa Photo Reconnaissance Wing. Continuing as an air reconnaissance specialist in Europe during 1944 he was with the US Strategic AF. On 3 Dec 44 he married Hollywood actress Faye Emerson after a divorce earlier that year by his second wife.

Public uproar over "bumping" three servicemen from an ATC plane to make room for his dog *(CB 46)* caused the Senate to delayed Col Roosevelt's promotion to brigadier general until 20 Jan 45. A scandal in June 45 involved a $200,000 debt to a prominent businessman that the late president's son had settled for $4,000.

Elliott accompanied his father to five international conferences, publishing a best-selling book in 1946 about his experiences, *As He Saw*

It. Churchill characterized the part about dinner table conversation at Casablanca as "rubbish" and writes disparagingly of Elliott's uninvited participation in a dinner party at Teheran of which Stalin was host. (WC, IV, 681; V, 373-74.) The petrel was active in the radio and airplane industries after leaving military service in Aug 45. He died 27 Oct 90 in Scottsdale, Ariz.

ROOSEVELT, Franklin D(elano). US president. 1882-1945. From 1933 until his death after winning an unprecedented fourth term FDR was President of the United States and Commander in Chief of US armed forces.

He was born 30 Jan 82 at Hyde Park, NY, an estate his father acquired on the Hudson River in 1867. Of "more or less patrician" stock *(CE)* and a distant cousin of Theodore "Teddy" Roosevelt (1858-1919) FDR was tutored at home before attending Groton. He graduated without distinction from Harvard in 1904. During these school years FDR came to admire President Teddy Roosevelt's championship of the "little man," his opposition to "malefactors of great wealth," and to what his illustrious forebear called the Square Deal.

In 1905 the Hudson River blue blood married a fifth cousin, Anna Eleanor ROOSEVELT; President Roosevelt gave his niece away. Franklin Roosevelt passed the bar examination in 1907, joined a prominent law firm, and entered politics. In 1910 he overcame entrenched Republican power in his district to win election as a Democratic state senator. For supporting Woodrow Wilson in 1912 as the Democratic Party's presidential nominee Roosevelt was appointed assistant secretary of the navy. During a long tenure, 1913-20, he advocated military preparedness and gained valuable experience in dealing with the Congress, industry, the military establishment, and labor. He also learned from Wilson's mistakes in disregarding popular opinion and the Congress when it came to enlightened foreign policy. (Sherwood, *Roosevelt and Hopkins,* 227.) Even this early the future president showed a penchant for expensive, grand-scale innovations in a trial-and-error, slap-dash manner.

Polio

Having run unsuccessfully for the US Senate in 1914 Roosevelt was a candidate in 1920 for vice president on the Democratic ticket with J. M. Cox. Harding and Coolidge won handily but Roosevelt became nationally known.

Then he was stricken with poliomyelitis on 10 Aug 21 while vacationing at the family summer home on Campobello Island, New Brunswick. Paralyzed from the waist down, he managed through a resolute effort during the next few years to recover partial use of his legs. Much of his therapy was at Warm Springs, Ga, where he established a polio foundation, spent most of his vacations thereafter, and retained a cottage that would become known as the Little White House. Eleanor meanwhile won over a domineering mother-in-law to help her husband remain active in politics. At the Democratic National Convention in 1928, the first year he was able to appear in public without crutches, Roosevelt delivered a strong statement of liberal principal in nominating Alfred E. Smith for president. *(CE.)* At the urging of Al Smith, ex-governor of New York, Roosevelt reluctantly ran for that office in 1928 and won narrowly. The new governor expanded Smith's liberal reforms, was reelected in 1930 with an overwhelming vote, and two years later was a successful presidential candidate.

The New Deal

The year 1933 was a time of world economic crisis on which Hitler capitalized to establish the Nazi regime in Germany. Mussolini was riding high in Italy. US Congressional leadership was bankrupt. Running on a "New Deal" platform and his record of reform and economic recovery in New York, Roosevelt carried all but six states in defeating Herbert Hoover. The jaunty, eternally optimistic Democratic candidate promised "direct, vigorous action," proclaiming that "the only thing we have to fear is fear itself."

Five days after his inauguration the new president declared a bank holiday on 9 Mar 33, stopping a dangerous run on banks. This was an important first step in restoring public confidence in government. Within the first 100 days the basic New Deal legislation was enacted by a compliant Congress that by year's end had authorized creation of a staggering list of "alphabetical agencies." These included the Federal Emergency Relief Administration, the Tennessee Valley Authority, the **CCC** ("tree army"), a number of farm programs under Henry WALLACE, the Home Owners' Loan Corporation, and a "Truth in Securities" Act that included creation of the Securities and Exchange Commission.

Most conspicuous to the public because of "We Do Our Part" stickers in store windows throughout the country was the National Industrial Recovery Act. This included guarantees to Labor on wages and hours. Back in March, meanwhile, morale was boosted by legalizing beer, a first step toward eliminating Prohibition. In Jan 34 the gold content of the dollar was stabilized. The next year saw passage of the Social Security Act and the Works' Progress Administration (WPA), which created public works to ease unemployment. Weak legs did not keep the otherwise physically powerful and tireless FDR from a man-killing schedule. He presided over White House meetings with innumerable special advisers, holding 337 conferences during the first term in office. (Hoover had held 66.) Making dramatic use of public radio, a relatively new medium, Roosevelt perfected a unique style of calm, confidence building oratory. While Hitler screamed and ranted, while Mussolini blustered and postured, FDR broadcast frequent "fireside chats" to court public support of his sweeping reforms. In frequent press conferences he wooed news reporters and editorial writers.

Part of the little group of intellectuals he had formed in New York went on to Washington. This provincial "brain trust" was reinforced by a horde of others, many derided as "crackpots." The president also had a stable of personal representatives who reported to him personally and preempted the role of the Cabinet and the Washington bureaucracy. By far the most prominent was Harry HOPKINS.

The Second Term

Roosevelt won reelected in 1936 by a greater landslide than in 1932. His challenger was Alfred M. Landon. But opposition rallied, and the pace of reform slowed. The Supreme Court found some basic New Deal acts unconstitutional. Roosevelt failed in a heavy-handed attempt to reorganize and "pack" the Supreme Court. He also was unsuccessful in an attempt to purge the Senate of some conservative Democrats. Adding to his troubles, an economic recession developed late in 1937; unemployment reached 10 million the next year, only three million fewer than when he took office.

Hitler and Roosevelt had great similarities in leadership style. Both disregarded conventional rules in seeking "action" and building morale. Both delayed vital decisions, priding themselves on intuition and pragmatism, thriving on improvisation and administrative disorder—an ancient technique of "divide and conquer" in dealing with subordinate officials. Both strove with great success to become remarkable orators, pioneering in the use of radio, and taking their message direct to the people. Historian A. J. P. Taylor makes the provocative observation that Hitler "stumbled on the economics of full employment, exactly as F. D. Roosevelt did . . ." (*Origins*, 70). The great difference was that whereas Hitler used conscription and rearmament to achieve quick economic and social triumphs Roosevelt used general welfare and America's tremendous economic resources to cure unemployment. Detractors argue that the US recovery was under way before the New Deal started, and that it continued not because of Roosevelt but in spite of him.

Roosevelt said in 1932 that the two most dangerous men in America were the Louisiana demagogue Huey P. "Share the Wealth" Long and General Douglas MacArthur! The reasoning was that "strong men" take over when the masses lose patience with the democratic process, which is what brought HITLER and MUSSOLINI to power.

Ironically these dictators deserve credit for ending the Depression in America. After the **Munich crisis** of 1938 a flood of orders came to US factories from Britain and France, virtually solving American's unemployment problem by 1939. Also a new breed of manufacturers like Henry J. KAISER got a head start in war production that soon needed was by their own country.

Foreign policy

Strong isolationism barred FDR's early efforts to join in European attempts at collective security. But one of Roosevelt's first diplomatic acts had been to recognize the USSR in late 1933. As for Latin America, his first inaugural address (4 Mar 33) launched the Good Neighbor policy. Implementing the pact that emerged from the Montevideo Conference, the president said on 28 Dec 33, "The definite policy of the United States from now on is one opposed to armed intervention." As Italy prepared to invade

Ethiopia in 1935, the president sought embargo power that would give him latitude to favor Haile SELASSI. Congress instead passed the Neutrality Act of 1935 which prohibited supplying arms to either side in a war. The revised act of 1937 retained this feature, but Roosevelt got a provision that belligerents could buy oil, scrap iron, rubber, cotton, and certain other items on a cash and carry basis. This favored the British, whose navy ruled the waves. But it also allowed Japan to buy war materials from the US right up until the Pearl Harbor attack.

When Japan moved into Manchuria in Oct 37 American public opinion was not ready for the president's proposal that aggressor nations be quarantined. But he did succeed in getting increased appropriations for America's absurdly weak armed forces.

American neutrality

Three days after Hitler's war broke out on 1 Sep 39 with the invasion of Poland FDR said in a fireside chat, "This nation will remain a neutral nation, but I cannot ask that every American remain neutral in thought as well." The reference was to Wilson's appeal in Aug 14 that Americans be "impartial in thought as well as in action." On 8 Sep 39 the president proclaimed a limited national emergency: this authorized expanding the US Army to a strength of 227,000 from 135,000. A fortnight later (the 21st) FDR urged Congress to repeal the neutrality act. Signed 4 Nov 39, this authorized cash-and-carry export of US arms and munitions.

Groundwork for "hemisphere solidarity" had been laid by the good neighbor policy (above); the Declaration of Panama (3 Oct 39) warned belligerents to refrain from actions in "sea safety zones" in the western hemisphere south of Canada (which had declared war on Germany). The president set the Manhattan Project in motion (11 Oct 39) for atomic bomb development, having been alerted by Albert EINSTEIN to its technical feasibility.

By the time Germany attacked in the west on 10 May 40, Roosevelt had gotten more than four and a quarter billion dollars for national defense and had established a production goal of 5,000 airplanes a year. Roosevelt was CHURCHILL's secret ally as Britain prepared to "go it alone." Shortly before the fall of France, Churchill proclaimed (4 June 40), "We shall defend our Island, whatever the cost may be . . . until, in

God's good time, the New World, with all its power and might, steps forth to the rescue and the liberation of the old." When Italy entered the war six days later Roosevelt said in a speech at Charlottesville, Va: "the hand that held the dagger has plunged it into the back of its neighbor." With neither popular support nor Congressional authority he added, "we will extend to the opponents of force the material resources of this nation. . . ." By the end of June 40 the president was sending obsolete arms and munitions to British ships waiting on American docks. "This, then, was Roosevelt's first tremendous wartime decision: to back the seemingly hopeless cause of Britain," writes Sherwood. "This decision was entirely his own. There was no time in his presidential career when he met with so much opposition in his own official family or when his position in the country was less secure." (Ibid., 150.)

Third term

Despite this Roosevelt ran for an unprecedented third term and won nomination on 18 July 40. Wendell WILLKIE eliminated isolationist candidates for the Republican nomination (DEWEY, TAFT, and VANDENBERG). Closing his campaign, Roosevelt told a Boston audience, "I shall say it again and again and again: Your boys are not going to be sent into any foreign wars." Sherwood points out that if Roosevelt had been honest with the public it probably would have been fatal politically. (Ibid., 151.)

Although Roosevelt had lost many powerful individual supporters, and a strong isolationist sentiment prevailed among the masses, the majority backed him. This was from a sense of responsibility to meet the war crisis or because they were getting rich. The president had called for a "great arsenal of democracy" in his fireside chat of 29 Dec 40. Three months earlier Churchill had concluded the "bases for destroyers" deal, getting 50 older but desperately needed US destroyers in return for 99-year leases on British air and naval bases in the Caribbean and Newfoundland. (WC, II, 398, 416.)

But Britain was running out of cash and Roosevelt himself hatched a solution to "get rid of the silly, foolish old dollar." He explained to the press that his concept could be compared with lending a $15 garden hose to a neighbor whose house was on fire: after saving his home the neighbor would return the hose undamaged or replace it. In the annual message to Congress on 6 Jan 41 FDR recommended the **Lend Lease** act (passed in March) that did so much to win the war with American supplies and foreign blood. The **Four Freedoms** for which the US would fight were enunciated in this same speech.

For all this international outlook Roosevelt remained an American politician's concerned with his personal fortunes. Subservient to public opinion he "had no strategy except a strategy of no strategy," writes Burns. "His main general policy was to wait on events—not any event, but one mighty event—to create the context for action." (Burns, 101.)

Whereas Churchill responded immediately and vigorously to support Stalin when the Germans invaded Russia on 22 June 41, "Roosevelt's first reactions to Russia's plight were sympathetic, expedient, and cautious. (Ibid., 103.) Stalin never forgot. The US Navy urged that this was the moment to start openly supplying escorts to Atlantic convoys. The Commander in Chief vacillated, finally ordering on 25 July 41 that only US ships would be escorted.

FDR meanwhile had authorized the repair of British ships and the training of RAF pilots in America, had transferred 10 Coast Guard cutters to the Royal Navy, had widened the American neutrality patrol zone to west Africa, and had placed Greenland under US guardianship. Greenland was of strategic importance for ferrying American aircraft to England and for US weather, radio, and radar stations. On 2 Apr 41 FDR authorized base construction to begin, making money available from his Emergency Fund. The first US troops left for the island on 17 June 41.

US forces started landing there on 5 Jul 41 to reinforce and eventually replace the British garrison established in May 40. All this followed delicate negotiations with Iceland and was a near act of war that FDR authorized with considerable trepidation.

The first of numerous conferences between Roosevelt and Churchill was on shipboard at Placentia Bay, Newfoundland, in mid-Aug 41. It established agreed aims in a jointly penned **Atlantic Charter.**

The War Years

In May 40 the US Fleet had transferred its base from the coast of California to Pearl Harbor on the order of the president with a view to checking Japanese expansion. Even reputable historians point out that FDR habitually used deception and deceit in attaining his aims, and he has been accused of sacrificing the Pacific Fleet at Oahu to get the "one mighty event" that rallied the public support for war he had been waiting for. The Pearl Harbor disaster was that event. "Yesterday, December 7, 1941—a date which will live in infamy—the United States of America was suddenly and delibeately attacked by naval and air forces of the Empire of Japan" he said in asking Congress to accept that because of this and concurrent attacks on Malaya, Hong Kong, Guam, the Philippine Islands, Wake Island, and Midway Island, "a state of war existed" between the US and Japan. (*See* Burns, II, 165-67.)

As a war leader Roosevelt meddled far less directly than CHURCHILL in military strategy. But as commander in chief (the title he favored) he established priorities not favored by the army and navy departments. Thriving on administrative chaos and disarray (Burns, 105) he disparaged Pentagon and State Department officials as "those people." One early presidential edict was to order "lots of planes" when the solution to American unpreparedness was not that simple. Another was to insisted that allies get materiel ahead of US forces.

In the field of foreign affairs, one of FDR's earliest initiatives was "our Vichy gamble" to recognize the Pétain government despite Britain's refusal to do so; this caused troublesome relations with de Gaulle that persisted long after the war. The president used Robert MURPHY to involve the US in French North Africa. Roosevelt was unsophisticated and indiscreetly outspoken in his anti-colonialism and his aversion to operations in the Balkans.

The Hudson Valley squire of Dutch ancestry had unreal and romantic ideas about China that caused problems throughout the war in dealing with Chiang Kai-shek. The president's conviction that he personally could charm "Uncle Joe" Stalin into accepting a reasonable postwar foreign policy also had unfortunate consequences.

The "unconditional surrender" policy, announced at the Casablanca Conference, was purely Roosevelt's. Master propagandist Goebbels seized on the unfortunate phrase to convince the Germans that they had no choice between victory or annihilation. Roosevelt was ignorant of European history and real-

politik. Overweening ego made him deaf to advice from Churchill and the few qualified American experts like KENNAN in his docile State Department. This had sad consequence for Poland in particular. Like most American leaders Roosevelt had a short-range view of politics and strategy, seeing only the need for the quickest and least costly victory. This played into Stalin's hands.

The Fourth Term

"That man in the White House" defied his worst enemies and the American founding fathers by running for a fourth term in Nov 44. He was a very sick man, but personal physician Vice Adm Ross T. McINTIRE pronounced his ailing patient fit. (On FDR's health problems *see* Parrish, *R&M*, 419-72.) Roosevelt dropped VP Henry WALLACE as his running mate, took Harry Truman, and won handily over Thomas E. DEWEY. Gen MacArthur was eliminated early from the race.

Military victory was in sight, thanks largely to FDR. He had mobilized US resources and had not wavered from the "Germany first" strategy. He alone was responsible for the vital concept of Lend Lease. Although duped by STALIN insofar as postwar Soviet intentions were concerned, he also helped get the maximum military assistance from the Soviets without their taking over the entire continent. And all this was done with remarkably little loss of American life. (Burns, 546.) Politically he had clearly defined and pursued high-minded goals including the Four Freedoms and the Atlantic Charter.

But the physically exhausted president faced mounting troubles over Poland, Greece, and China. During his final months Roosevelt suffered severe blows to his idealism. By persisting in supporting Chiang Kai-shek and finally recalling STILWELL the president set the stage for the communist takeover of China by the forces of MAO TSE-TUNG. At the Yalta Conference, 4-12 Feb 45, he danced to Stalin's tune, disregarding Churchill's warnings, and insisting that he could "handle Uncle Joe" by making concessions. Seeds of the Cold War were sown before the Yalta conference, but FDR has been held largely responsible for Stalin's postwar triumphs. The self-centered president also was seriously remiss in excluding Vice President Truman from foreign affairs.

FDR died suddenly on 12 Apr 45 at Warm Springs, Ga, after a stroke. Mourned throughout the free world he was buried in Hyde Park's rose garden beneath a simple stone giving only his name and the years he lived.

"There are no unbiased accounts of Roosevelt" *(CE).* More fully identified in the main bibliography are those by Sherwood, James MacGregor Burns, and Kenneth S. Davis.

ROOSEVELT, James. US officer. 1907-91. The president's eldest son and a USMC reserve officer, James was his father's personal secretary and ADC before the war. As XO of CARLSON's raider unit he won the Navy Cross. From Oct 42 he commanded the new 4th Raider Bn and took it to the Pacific but while training for the New Georgia operation he was hospitalized and evacuated. Returning to the Pacific in 1943 he was G2 on several high staffs. Col James Roosevelt ended active military duty in Oct 45 and retired from the USMC Reserve in 1959 with the rank of brigadier general. He was elected to Congress from California in 1954. Born 23 Dec 07, he died 13 Aug 91 at Newport Beach, Calif.

ROOSEVELT, Theodore, Jr. US general. 1887-1944. Eldest son of the 26th US president and a cousin of the 31st, FDR, he was born 13 Sep 87 and graduated from Harvard in 1908. In WWI Teddy Junior commanded the 26th Inf Regt of the 1st "Big Red One" Div and was wounded twice. He went on to be an explorer, author, and public figure. Small, wrinkled, hard-drinking, and raucous, he was elected in 1919 to the NY state assembly and he succeed Franklin D. Roosevelt as assistant secretary of the navy for the period 1921-24. Governor of Puerto Rico 1929-32 and governor general of the Philippines 1932-33, he became an editor at Doubleday, Doran & Co in 1935.

Col Roosevelt returned to active military duty in Apr 41 despite his advanced years, poor eyesight, fibrillating heart, and arthritis so bad he had to use a cane. Otherwise a fit fighting man, he took command of his AEF regiment. He was promoted to brigadier general on 17 Dec 41 and moved up to be assistant CG in the 1st Div. The next month he volunteered to parachute into the Philippines to bolster civilian morale as the former governor general. Army CofS George Marshall, a long-time friend who thought the idea had merit, informed MacArthur that Roosevelt was ready to drop in instantly. Word came back promptly: MacArthur wanted only "supplies and airplanes," not want any "outside agents." *(EP,* 91.)

Under "Terrible Terry" ALLEN the new "Big Red One" went to England and had its baptism of fire in North Africa on 8 Nov 42. The fragile but feisty ADC was in the thick of it. Eisenhower reported to Marshall on 3 Mar 43 that "Terry Allen seems to be doing a satisfactory job; so is Roosevelt" *(EP,* 1006). But Omar Bradley, and old friend of Allen's, already was convinced he would have to replace both generals for failure to comply properly with field orders and also for inability to maintain discipline when the division was out of the line. (Bradley, *Life,* 136.) The division rioted in Algiers before going to Sicily, where "Allen flubbed badly" in the initial assault on Troina on 1 Aug 43. A few days later Bradley relieved both generals. (Ibid., 195.) Clarence R. Huebner took over the US Army's premier division and shaped it up.

Roosevelt went to Corsica as the first US LnO with Juin's CEF and won high praise from the French commander *(EP,* 2024 & n.). Eisenhower and Marshall saw that their personal friends Allen and Roosevelt had another chance to show their undeniable fighting qualities. As ADC, 4th Inf Div, Roosevelt was the oldest American (at 56) and the only general to land with the first wave on Utah beach, 6 June 44. German resistance was insignificant but Roosevelt made such a contribution to success of the landing that Eisenhower decided to give him command of the 90th Inf Div. *(EP,* 2024.) The day before he was due to take over, Roosevelt had a fatal heart attack on 12 July 44. He was awarded the Medal of Honor posthumously.

ROSE, Maurice. US general. 1899-1945. A rabbi's son, Maurice Rose was promoted to brigadier general on 7 Apr 41 *(AA,* 926). He became CofS, 2d Armd Div, in 1942 and won his second star in Aug 44 for leading CCA in Opn Cobra as part of J. Lawton COLLINS's 7th Corps. *(AA* does not show that Rose was promoted beyond brigadier general, but all other sources give his rank as major general in Aug 44.)

Maj Gen Rose led the 3d Armd Div as part of the 7th Corps (Hodges's 1st Army) and he figured prominently in all of COLLINS's campaigns. In the Rhineland campaign he entered Cologne on 6 Mar 45, crossed the Rhine, and pushed toward Paderborn. To direct the final assault he was riding forward when trapped by four Tiger tanks that were manned by men of Paderborn's SS panzer training center. The Tigers appeared suddenly in the road behind Rose, and as they advanced in the failing light of 30 March he directed his jeep driver to race back past them. The jeep was sideswiped and pinned against a tree. "Rose, his aide, and his driver climbed out to surrender to a German soldier standing in the turret and wielding a burp gun. But as Rose reached either to unbuckle his pistol belt or to take his pistol from its holster, the German shot him down." (Ibid., 675.) He apparently lived through the night, some accounts giving 31 Mar 45 as the date of death. An investigation concluded that Rose, the highest ranking US Jew killed in WWII, was not the victim of an atrocity. (Ibid.)

ROSENBERG, Alfred. German official. 1893-1946. The Nazi party philosopher was born 12 Jan 12 in Reval, now Tallinn, Estonia. In an alien Baltic culture his family was German speaking and, like so many other **Auslanders** including Hitler was super-Germanic. But the Rosenberg genes were rumored to be Estonian and his farm-labor ancestors were said to have adopted the surname from a German landlord. Alfred Rosenberg's many Nazi enemies said in later years that he had French, Slavic, Estonian, or even Jewish blood. Some critics quipped that he must be the only Aryan Rosenberg in the world. (Davidson, *Trial*, 128.) But it is known that Rosenberg's immediate forebears in Riga were artisans and small business people.

The future ideologue of the Nazi party was better educated and more cultured than most of Hitler's entourage. Studying architecture at the Technical Institute in Riga he joined a pro-German student corps at a time when Estonia enjoyed a privileged position in Tsarist Russia. After the war broke out in 1914 the Germans threatened to take Riga, so the institute moved to Moscow. Rosenberg went along and married a schoolmate named Hilda he had known for years. But Hilda, from he would acquire a taste for literature, soon had to go the Crimea after developing tuberculosis. He spent much time

with her there before returning to Moscow in 1917 for his final examinations.

Rosenberg did not serve in the Tsarist Army or fight in the revolution, either in Moscow or after returning to Riga. Instead he made a few anti-Bolshevik speeches and wrote some propaganda to encourage the others to take arms in Estonia's fight for independence. Until 1918 his political outlook was so ambivalent he was free to concentrate on architecture and painting (ibid.).

Then joining the large White Russian colony in Paris, Rosenberg started feeding his long-standing racist prejudices on the works of Count Joseph Arthur de Gobineau and Houston Stewart Chamberlain. The Englishman's *Foundations of the Nineteenth Century* inspired the Balt to pursue his notions of Nordic racial superiority in London, but the British would not grant him the necessary travel permit. In Dec 18, therefore, he reached Munich, another center of White Russian émigrés. The Baltic Independence Commission was recruiting soldiers, but Rosenberg explained that he had a sick wife and pressing duties in Germany. (Hilda remained in Russia, later going to Paris, where she died after getting a divorce in 1923. Rosenberg remarried, had a daughter, and was a devoted family man. [Ibid., 128-29, 142-43].)

Rosenberg reached Munich in 1918 with a letter of introduction from a Baltic noblewoman to the poet and journalist Dietrich Eckart. Although somewhat repelled by the impoverished refugee, who has been described as having "the air of the supercilious intelligentsia," "dandified," and "perfumed" *(CB 41)*, Eckart was impressed by the drifter's potential as an anti-Semitic propagandist. Rosenberg quickly proved himself not only to Eckart but also to Hitler. As the Nazi Party's chief ideologist (Ibid., 125) the wild-eyed Balt was Faust to Hitler's Mephistopheles *(CB 41)*. When Julius STREICHER attempted to seize control of the movement in 1921 Rosenberg wrote the Nazi Party platform. On Eckart's death in 1923 Rosenberg became sole editor of the Party newspaper, *Voelkischer Beobachter*. He visited Hitler daily in the Landsberg fortress prison and probably had an influence on *Mein Kampf*'s muddled prose.

Rosenberg meanwhile published a number of books in which "Jewish depravity and the plan to conquer the world were exposed with the full apparatus of pseudoscholarship," as Davidson puts it. But "his grand synthesis" was *Der Mythus des Zwanzigsten Jahrhunderts* (Munich: Hoheneichen, 1930). In this he demanded "living space from the Soviet Union and a return in the Reich of the pagan myth of the blood." (Ibid., 133.)

In 1929 Rosenberg founded the Militant League for German Culture, which became the National Socialist Cultural Community. This spawned Robert LEY's "Strength Through Joy" movement. In 1930 the ideologue was elected to the Reichstag and during the next two years (before Hitler became chancellor) he was in the foreign office with missions to London and Rome. There was intense rivalry between Rosenberg and RIBBENTROP, who resembled each other physically and who both aspired to be foreign minister. They had equally little aptitude for foreign affairs, particularly in attempting to allay British misgivings about Nazism. Rosenberg's good will mission to England in May 33 reinforced British repugnance toward the Third Reich, particularly the anti-Semitism for which the emissary was a champion. (*CB 41*; Davidson, 132.)

In 1934 the paladin became the fuehrer's deputy in supervising ideological training and education of the NSDAP. About this time he also became the party's director of foreign policy, theoretically the supreme civil authority in occupied regions of the USSR. This authority became more real on 17 July 41 when Rosenberg was appointed minister for eastern territories. But he had little actual authority, primarily because of his own administrative ineptitude but also as a victim of Hitler's predilection to "divide and rule." Rosenberg's arch-enemy Erich KOCH became the real occupation chief in the Ukraine; GOERING directed economic affairs abroad and at home; HIMMLER held sway over an expanding SS empire; the Organization TODT handled infrastructure; and the army had its own civil affairs agencies.

In one of his many assignments on the eve of war Rosenberg founded the Central National Socialist University, which later would have many institutes for special research and teaching. Himmler set up a parallel organization. Both had the mission initially of plundering art, books, and archives, mainly from Jews and Free Masons. A "Rosenberg TF" (*Einsatzstab Reichsleiter Rosenberg*) collected not only "cultural goods" like art masterpieces but also clothing, medicines, furniture, rugs, and other household furnishings——anything that could be trucked off by the Wehrmacht, which had orders to support the effort logistically. Choice items, mainly books and archival material, went to the research institutes and private collections of Goering and others; mundane items of household goods were given to bombed-out Germans. Rosenberg claimed that the cultural plunder was not collected as private property but for German research and to keep it out of enemy hands.

Part of the Central Nazi Univ (above) was the Institute for the Investigation of the Jewish Question, established at Frankfort in 1939. Before Rosenberg began using this primarily to loot Jewish collections he said in a public speech that he did not advocate extermination but merely getting all Jews out of "the Greater German living space." It would be too dangerous to establish a separate Jewish state: the ideologue wanted all Jews isolated impotently on some island like **Madagascar.** Rosenberg did not favor full compliance with Hitler's **Commissar order** but proposed that lower ranking commissars should be spared for use as administrators in occupied areas.

When called by the Nuremberg tribunal Rosenberg was bewildered, broken, but unrepentant. He protested that Hitler had pursued the right course but that blood minded Nazis had misdirected the movement. Convicted on all four charges of war crimes, Alfred Rosenberg led the march to the gallows on 16 Oct 46.

ROSENTHAL, Joseph J. US photographer. 1911-. His photograph of the second flag raising on Mt Suribachi, Iwo Jima, at 10:37 AM on 23 Feb 45, may be the greatest of the war. Felix de Welden used the photograph as a model for his oversized bronze monument to the USMC near the main entrance to Arlington National Cemetery, Va.

ROTMISTROV, Pavel A. Soviet military leader. 1901-82. He entered the Red Army in 1919 and became a tank expert. A general major from June 40 he rose to be a general lieutenant commanding a tank corps at Stalingrad. Here in Dec 42 he stopped Erhard RAUS's attempt to reach Paulus's trapped 6th German

Army's. Rotmistrov then outfought Hermann HOTH's veteran 4th Pz Army before taking over the 5th Guards Tank Army in Feb 43 to begin a drive westward.

As part of Vatutin's Voronezh Front for the Battle of Kursk in July 43, he defeated HAUSSER's 2d SS Pz Corps around Prokhorovka in what has been called history's biggest tank battle. Rotmistrov went on to have a leading role in liberating the Ukraine, being promoted to general colonel in Oct 43 and becoming the first marshal of armored troops in Feb 44.

Immediately thereafter he was a star in Konev's capture of Uman on 10 Mar 44. Still under Konev he capped his combat career with a dash that encircled Berlin from the south. Deputy commander of the armored forces in 1944, as Khrushchev's protégé he became the first chief marshal of armored troops on 28 Apr 62 (HFS). Rotmistrov published military studies of exceptional value, the 2-vol *Istoriia Voennogo Ikusstva* (Moscow, 1963) and *Vremya i Tanki* (Moscow, 1972).

ROXAS y Acuña, Manuel. Philippines official. 1892-1948. Roxas (pronounced with a silent *x*) was born 1 Jan 92 at Capiz on Panay. Of native Filipino ancestry, he belonged to the largest ethnic group in the Islands, was taller than most of his countrymen, and had to learn Spanish. His mother tongue was Tagalog. Not a Catholic he became a 32d-degree Mason.

After graduating with honors in 1913 from the Univ of the Philippines College of Law in Manila he became governor of his native Capiz Province in 1919. On expiration of the two-year term he was elected to the house of representatives in Manila and became a protégé of QUEZON. In his first term he succeeded OSMENA as speaker of the house at the age of 31. Although a nationalist dedicated to independence he believed in American institutions. As a reserve officer Lt Col Roxas was MacArthur's ADC from 16 Dec 41. Ordered by Quezon to stay in the Philippines *(CB 46)* Roxas escaped from Corregidor to Mindanao, where he was virtually a POW for the duration. When the LAUREL cabinet surrendered in Apr 45 at Baguio it was announced that Brig Gen Roxas was "rescued," not "captured" (ibid.). Favored by MacArthur over OSMENA (see James, *MacArthur,* 700-1) Roxas won the postwar presidential election and was inaugurated

on 4 July 46. He died during his second, stormy year in office.

RUDEL, Hans Ulrich. German assault pilot. 1916-82. Born on 2 July 16 in Konradswaldau, son of a Protestant minister, the darkly handsome, good natured "tank buster" destroyed more than 519 Russian tanks, the Soviet BB *Marat* in Kronstadt harbor, a cruiser, a destroyer, and 70 landing craft. He flew 2,530 sorties, more than any other pilot, was wounded five times, and was downed 30 times by AAA.

On 1 Jan 45, at the age of 28, he became the only recipient of the Golden Oakleaves with Swords and Diamonds to the RK. On this date he was made a wing commander and promoted to full colonel. (Angolia, I, 48-50.)

Five weeks later (9 Feb 45) Rudel was only 50 miles from Berlin with one round of cannon ammunition left when he dove his Ju 87 on a Stalin tank. Having set the tank on fire he was jubilantly pulling up when his right leg was almost torn off by a 4cm AA shot. Another hit set his plane on fire. Almost blind and fainting from pain, he crash landed with instructions shouted by his radio operator over the intercom. Rudel was back six weeks later to fly combat missions with one leg missing and the other in a cast.

An unreconstructed nationalist and believing in the feudal values of chivalry and obedience he exiled himself to Argentina until 1953. He returned to join the neo-Nazi German Reich Party and was a successful businessman and USAF consultant. Rudel's rather wooden memoir of more than five years in action on the eastern front is *Stuka Pilot* (New York: Ballantine, 1958).

RUGE, Friedrich Oskar. German admiral. 1894-. Entering the navy in 1914 he served in the Baltic and led destroyer raids on the English coast. In 1920 he started specializing in mine warfare and began to establish a reputation as a military writer. Ruge participated in the Polish campaign of 1939; he was in charge of escorts, patrols, and subchasers from 1941; and he directed minesweeping off the Channel coast 1940-43. He was promoted to rear admiral in 1942 and to vice admiral in 1943.

After six months in Italy he became commander of Naval Forces West in Nov 43, working with ROMMEL in Normandy. From Aug 44 he was director of naval construction. After the war Ruge published *Entscheidung in Pazifik, Der Seekrieg 1939-1945,* and *Rommel und die Invasion* in addition to articles. Ruge was Inspector of the Bundesmarine from 1956 until retiring in Sep 61. He then lectured on military affairs at Tuebingen Univ and was president of the League of the Veterans of the Bundeswehr. (*J&R,* 317 ff, 472.)

RUGE, Otto. Norwegian general. 1882-1961. Col Ruge was IG of Infantry when promoted on 11 Apr 42, two days after the German assault, to command the Norwegian Army. Reaching GHQ at Rena, about 100 miles N of Oslo, on that day, Generalmajor Ruge found he had effective control over only the 2d Div. This unit was mobilizing under great difficulties—poor communications, conflicting orders from the capital (which the Germans controlled), and snow that formed deep drifts. (Ziemke, *GNT,* 69.)

Ruge's only possible course of action was to delay the German advance on the Trondheim area, where the hoped-for Allied expeditionary force would land. (Ibid.) Brigadier H. de R. Morgan's small, ill-equipped force, originally destined for Namsos, was diverted to Andalesnes. It landed unopposed on 18 April and pushed through snow drifts to Dombas, meeting Ruge, and being sent south in trucks to Lillehammer. Here the unseasoned British Territorials, without artillery and short on ammunition, took up positions just as the Norwegians began to collapse. In the first battlefield encounter between German and British troops Morgan's men—directed by Norwegian officers—held for 24 hours. Finally overwhelmed by German superiority in artillery, armor, and air support, Morgan and the Norwegians withdrew from one delaying position to another. Most were scattered into small groups and captured, but some escaped into Sweden.

"Norwegian civilians turned against the retreating soldiers with a vengeance," writes Petrow. "One British soldier complained that Norwegian resentment was 'as strong against the British for letting the country be ravished by the Germans as against the Germans for doing it.'" (*The Bitter Years,* 86). PAGET reached Andalesnes on 24 April, followed the same day by French reinforcements, and took command of the hard-pressed British and French expedition. But Paget began reembarking on 30 April from

Andalesnes and nearby Molde, on orders from London, a day behind King HAAKON and his party. Ruge left aboard a British destroyer on 1 May, joined the king to continue resistance around Narvik, and declined to leave his troops. A member of Ruge's staff signed the surrender on 10 June 45. (Petrow, 97.) The Norwegian general was a POW for the duration, ending up in a German camp.

RUNDSTEDT, Karl Rudolf Gerd von. German general. 1875-1953. One of the Wehrmacht's highest ranking, most durable, and most highly respected commanders, he was born 12 Dec 75 in Aschersleben, near Magdeburg (Saxony). Rundstedt's father was of the military aristocracy; his mother of the well-to-do bourgeoisie. A captain in 1914 Rundstedt fought in Alsace before becoming a staff officer. For the rest of the war he was a chief of staff at the division and corps level, serving principally on the eastern front and attaining the rank of major. Remaining in uniform, promoted to lieutenant colonel in 1920, the relatively elderly general was commanding the 3d Inf Div and the Berlin MD (Wehrkreis III) in 1932. He tried to resign when Chancellor von PAPEN declared martial law that year and ordered troops to eject ministers of the Social Democratic Prussian state government from their offices. But Rundstedt then performed the unpleasant task. "It is said that he was so gracious and sympathetic in arresting his unresisting friends that they harbored no resentment and were glad the job had been done by him rather than anyone else!" (*CB 41*). True or not, the story illustrates the finesse for which Rundstedt continued to be known.

When BLOMBERG nominated the pro-Nazi REICHENAU to succeed HAMMERSTEIN-EQUORD as head of the German Army, Rundstedt and LEEB were the two senior troop leaders who blocked the move. But Rundstedt was among the Old Guard generals who failed to muster opposition to the growing Nazi threat to the army. According to one German historian he endorsed Hitler's personally assuming overall command of the Wehrmacht when Blomberg was ousted (Andreas Hillgruber in Carver, ed, *The War Lords,* 188). Promoted on 1 Mar 38 Col Gen Rundstedt retired at his own request on 31 Oct 38 after the **Munich crisis.**

The 64-year-old general was recalled less than a year later when mobilization was ordered. With Erich von Manstein as his deputy, Rundstedt led AG South into Poland. After a near-perfect campaign he headed army occupation forces, 1-20 Oct 39. Succeeded by the unfortunate BLASKOWITZ and taking over AG A for the campaign in the west, Rundstedt was quick to see the merits of the MANSTEIN plan and urge its adoption by OKW (Manstein, 124).

AG A had the major role in the Battle of Flanders. With seven panzer divisions, three motorized divisions, and 35 infantry divisions, Rundstedt penetrated the "impassable" Ardennes and drove to the English Channel. Not yet a true believer in panzers, he convinced Hitler that the tanks should be halted until infantry divisions caught up for a conventional assault on the Dunkirk beachhead. This enabled the Allies to execute the almost-miraculous **Dunkirk evacuation** (26 May-4 June 40). The general later blamed Hitler for a controversial decision that was primarily his own. (*See* Shirer, *Reich,* 731-38.)

When the Germans undertook the exploitation to the south, the Battle of France, Rundstedt turned the Maginot Line from the west, sent troops to the Swiss border, then moved through Lyons to trap the French Army of the Alps.

Rundstedt was promoted to field marshal on 19 July 40 and his AG A was given a major role in the threatened invasion of England. The field marshal assumed correctly that this probably was only a bluff, and when Sea Lion was called off he took command of occupation forces with the additional mission of preparing coastal defenses in Holland, Belgium, and France.

On 14 Mar 41 he turned over AG A to his friend WITZLEBEN and two weeks later was heading AG South for Opn Barbarossa. Knowing the eastern front from his experiences in WWI Rundstedt tried to convince Hitler that Russia could not be conquered in a quick campaign. Failing this, the field marshal succeeded in having the main strategic effort made initially against Leningrad, where the Finns were expected to be of assistance. Rundstedt argued, wisely, that the main objective should then be Moscow. This broad strategic concept was adopted to the extent of making AG South's role in the Ukraine secondary. But Rundstedt remained pessimistic. On 4 May 41 he said to

LEEB, "So see you again in Siberia" (Blumentritt in *F&R,* 45).

Rundstedt attacked 22 June 41 with six field armies—52 infantry divisions and five panzer divisions. His northern boundary bisected the Pripet Marshes, and his main effort into the Ukraine was made from this flank. Jumping off from southern Poland he moved SE with Reichenau's 6th Army (6 divisions), Kleist's 1st Pz Gp (5 panzer divisions and 9 others), and Stuelpnagel's 17th Army (13 divisions). To the far south, advancing from Romania, were Schobert's 11th German Army (7 divisions) and Antonescu's Romanian Army (14 divisions). Three more divisions were in reserve.

Rundstedt made slow progress for the first few weeks as LEEB's AG North and BOCK's AG made spectacular gains toward Leningrad and Moscow. It was not until early August, some six weeks into Barbarossa, that AG South scored its first major success: it destroyed large Soviet forces near Uman and pushed into the Dnieper bend. HITLER meanwhile made what perhaps was his major error of the war, stopping the advance of BOCK's AG Center on Moscow in the center and diverting much of its strength north toward Leningrad and south into the Ukraine. Rundstedt sent Kleist's 1st Pz Gp north to cooperate with Guderian's 2d Pz Gp and the 2d Army in the encirclement of Kiev. Here the great battle of annihilation ended on 26 Sep 41, when the last of some 665,000 Russian prisoners were taken. With organized resistance now virtually crushed, Rundstedt directed most of his forces east toward Kharkov and Rostov while wheeling the 11th Army south to overrun the Crimea. Here MANSTEIN would achieve another great victory.

The doyen of the officers' corps had retained reasonably good relations with Hitler, but now the first of three breaks occurred. A man "with whom patience had never been a strong point" (Manstein, 69), and who had always been pessimistic about Barbarossa, Rundstedt strongly opposed continuing the offensive as winter approached. He also was overextended physically after months of pushing himself too hard. Early in November, his headquarters at Poltava, the elderly warrior collapsed of a heart attack. Refusing to be evacuated he pushed on through determined resistance and his panzers took Rostov, "Gateway to the Caucasus," on 21 Nov 41. By the 29th TIMOSHENKO had driven the

Germans out and the fuehrer, on a rare visit to the front, blamed Rundstedt. The tired field marshal snapped back that the fault lay with OKW for persisting in a bad strategy against his advice. "Hitler looked for a moment as though he were about to hurl himself on Rundstedt and tear his Knight's Cross from his uniform," writes Goerlitz, and "Brauchitsch promptly had a heart attack" (*GGS*, 402-3). Hitler characteristically took no immediate action but as AG South pulled back to a defensive position on the Mius River he sent orders on 30 Nov 41 to stop and fight in place. "It is madness to attempt to hold," Rundstedt wired back. "In the first place the troops cannot do it and in the second place if they do not retreat they will be destroyed. I repeat [sic] that this order be rescinded or that you find someone else." Rundstedt thought this threat would make Hitler change his mind. (Hillgruber, previously cited, 194.) But Hitler promptly wired back, "I am acceding to your request. Please give up your command." (Postwar interrogation report quoted in Shirer, *Reich*, 861.) REICHENAU took command of AG South the next day, 1 Dec 42, promptly phoned Hitler, and was authorized to continue the retrograde! "So we are exactly where we were yesterday," wrote HALDER in his diary. "But time and strength have been sacrificed and Rundstedt lost." (Ibid., 861 n.) The fallen field marshal left Poltava on 3 Dec 41, allegedly at his own request and on grounds of ill health. REICHENAU died six weeks later, and Rundstedt represented Hitler at the funeral!

France

The Pearl Harbor attack, 7 Dec 41, brought America into the war finally. Because the threat of an Allied landing on the Continent now was real, Rundstedt could find patriotic reasons for accepting Hitler's invitation in Mar 42 to resume active duty. The blunt but loyal field marshal, whom Hitler always trusted and who became more easy going in later years (Irving, *HW*, xxxi), spent most of his time thereafter as OB West. His headquarters were in the Paris suburb of historic Saint-Germain-en-Laye.

His mission was to defend 1,700 miles of Atlantic coast and 300 miles along the Mediterranean. The Atlantic Wall of permanent fortifications with huge naval guns turned out to be largely propaganda. Priorities for manpower and materiel went to the eastern front. Accepting that he could not keep the Allies from getting ashore,

Rundstedt adopted the time-tested strategy of establishing coastal strong points—a defensive cordon to determine where the Allies were making their main effort—and a large strategic reserve of highly mobile panzer forces.

When ROMMEL reached France in late 1943 he had a fundamentally different strategic approach. This and the subsequent conduct of operations are covered under ROMMEL. But Rundstedt had serious political problems in addition to his military responsibilities. The first problem arose when the Allies landed in North Africa on 8 Nov 42 and he was ordered to occupy Vichy France three days later. He had several "soldier to soldier" meetings with Pétain and won the Frenchman's confidence. In the delicate business of delineating German and Italian occupation zones in SE France, Rundstedt overcame national animosities to reach a satisfactory agreement. But when the Italians defected to the Allies on 8 Sep 43 OB West was faced with disarming the Italian 4th Army in its zone between the Rhone and the Alps and sending in German troops. Largely because of the respect in which he was held by the Italian high command, and because of intelligent orders, Rundstedt solved this problem amicably. (Hillgruber, cited herein, 195-6.)

"Von Rundstedt was surprised by the strength of the Allied landing in Normandy on 6 June 44 and especially by the massive use of air power" (ibid., 197). He and ROMMEL had two unsatisfactory conferences with Hitler, the last at Margival on 29 June 44. When Keitel phoned on 1 July he learned that four crack German divisions had failed that day to wipe out the British salient near Caen despite bad weather that had grounded Allied aircraft. "What shall we do?" Keitel wailed. "Make peace, you fools," Rundstedt snapped back, "what else can you do?" Hitler immediately ordered KLUGE to take over as OB West. Still in the fuehrer's good graces Rundstedt left St Germain the evening of 3 July for rest and medical treatment at Bad Toelz.

A month later he complied with Hitler's order to preside over a court of honor with Guderian and Keitel to deal with officers accused of being involved in the assassination attempt of 20 July 44. The court of honor acted primarily from conviction that all officers were bound by their personal oath of loyalty to Hitler as legal head of state. Using flimsy evidence that the accused did not have an opportunity to refute, the court of honor dismissed many innocent officers from the Wehrmacht, which removed them from military jurisdiction so FREISLER's People's Court could try them. (Bracher, 459.) Shortly after SPEIDEL's arrest on 7 Sep 44, writes Manfred Rommel, Speidel's "name was mentioned, together with my father's, before the Army Court of Honour. But the 'Rommel Case' was not discussed officially. (Liddell Hart, *RP*, 501.) Almost certainly without knowing the circumstance of his death (Mellenthin, *Panzer Battles,* 312) Rundstedt represented Hitler and gave the eulogy at Rommel's state funeral on 18 Oct 44.

Rundstedt quite realistically "looked upon any plan for a *coup d'état* in wartime as unrealistic," which is why he and so many others—who also appreciated Hitler's great popular support— never joined any conspiratorial effort (Goerlitz, *GGS,* 413).

Meanwhile, only two months after being replaced as OB West by KLUGE, Rundstedt was summoned to Rastenburg on 4 Sep 44 and reinstated. Australian journalist-historian Chester Wilmot comments that Rundstedt was senile by this time, had "lost his grip," and for the second time "virtually 'sold out' to Hitler." German historian-journalist Goerlitz probably is closer to the mark in saying Rundstedt "was not unmoved by Hitler's appeal to his patriotism." (Wilmot, 189; Goerlitz, *GGS,* 413.)

The Ardennes and the Rhineland

With Germany collapsing on all fronts at the end of 1944 only Hitler and a few die-hard associates saw reason to soldier on. The fuehrer decided to gamble all on a counteroffensive through the Ardennes to take Brussels, the great port of Antwerp, and split Eisenhower's forces. "When I received this plan early in November I was staggered," the field marshal told Liddell Hart in a postwar interview (*Talk,* 275). After trying to have the operation reduced in scope, "as always, he ultimately gave in," writes Goerlitz, and "confined himself to private sarcasm and lent his name . . . to a scheme which went wholly beyond Germany's strength" (ibid., 484). Rundstedt received a 250,000-mark birthday gift from the fuehrer on 12 Dec 44, an embarrassment he dealt with by immediately putting the money into a special bank account he never touched. The Knight's Cross was normally awarded only for personal valor, but Hitler's hand had to be behind Rundstedt's receiving the RK on 30 Sep 39 for service in Poland and OB West, the Oakleaves on 1 July 44 and the Swords (133/159) on 18 Feb 45. (Angolia, I, 244.)

His third and final dismissal came on 10 Mar 45, when KESSELRING became OB West with headquarters at Bayreuth. Rundstedt was taken prisoner in Bad Toelz by the US 36th Inf Div on 1 May 45. Long ailing, he suffered a heart attack during interrogation at Wiesbaden. With other senior German officers he went to the UK and was confined in hospitals and POW camps until July 48. He cooperated fully with historians including Liddell Hart, who would write, "the more I saw of Rundstedt the better impression he made" (*Talk,* 71; see also HORROCKS, 185).

Released from POW status he was confined in Germany awaiting trial. But no real charges could be made, so he was freed in May 49. In ill health and obscurity he lived with his wife first in two small rooms near Celles, then in a three-room apartment in Hanover. Field Marshal von Rundstedt was the "target of serious criticism from the most varied quarters" in Germany after the war (Hillgruber, ibid., 188). He wrote no memoirs but, the year before his death, contributed a short foreword to a laudatory biography by his long-time CofS, Guenther BLUMENTRITT, *Von Rundstedt: The Soldier and the Man* (London: 1952). No German edition was published. Rundstedt died 24 Feb 53 in Hanover, a year after his wife. He was buried at the city's Stocken cemetery with only a few relatives and friends present.

RUOFF, Richard. German general. General of Infantry Ruoff commanded the 5th Corps of Kluge's 4th Army in France and the same corps in Russia as part of Erich Hoeppner's 4th Pz Gp in AG North. Moving to the Moscow front he succeeded Hoeppner on 8 Jan 42 as CG of what was now the 4th Pz Army, being was promoted to Generaloberst on 1 April (*B&O,* 24). Exactly two months later he changed places with Hermann Hoth, taking over the 17th Army on the extreme right flank of Bock's AG South. Initially opposite Ilyum on the upper Donetz, his army was shifted 350 miles south for an attack on Rostov and an exploitation through the western Caucasus to the Black Sea. Group Ruoff was made up of his own 17th Army of five infantry divisions and Dumitrescu's 3d Romanian Army of one infantry and three cavalry divisions (Seaton, *R-G War,* 280). Taking

Rostov on 28 July 42 he then drove 175 miles south in two widely separated columns with the mission of taking the Taman Peninsula and the Black Sea ports of Novorossisk (with its great naval base) and Tuapse (75 mi SE). Ruoff captured Novorossisk on 6 September from Yakov CHEREVICHENKO's Black Sea Gp (redesignated the Maritime Gp on that day). Within a month of fierce fighting in the west Caucasus Mts Cherevichenko stabilized the situation briefly, but Ruoff resumed his offensive to take Novorossisk and get within a few miles of Tuapse. I. Ye. PETROV replaced Cherevichenko on about 17 Oct 42 and both sided paused.

For the next year Ruoff was heavily engaged in the west Caucasus and was driven back by Petrov's front to a beachhead in the Kuban. On 4 Sep 42 Hitler, who had come forward to visit Manstein's AG South Hq at Zaporozhe, authorized the hard-pressed 17th Army's withdrawal across the Strait of Kerch to the Crimea. After being summoned to a conference with Hitler at Manstein's headquarters on 8 Sep 43 (*Lost Victories,* 462) Ruoff turned over command of his army to Erwin Jaenecke. (Seaton must be wrong in saying this happened earlier, in July 43 [*R-G War,* 379].) Ruoff subsequently had no major role in the war.

RUPERTUS, William Henry. US general. 1889-1945. As ADC, 1st Marine Div, Brig Gen Rupertus led the force that secured Tulagi on 7-8 Aug 42 and then went to Guadalcanal. In July 43, when VANDEGRIFT left, Rupertus took command of the division and was promoted on 26 Dec 43. Maj Gen Rupertus headed the division for the Cape Gloucester landings on 15 Sep 44 and two months later at Peleliu. Becoming Commandant of the Marine Corps Schools at Quantico, Va, on 25 Mar 45, he died later that year of a heart attack.

RUTHERFORD, Ernest, 1st Baron. British physicist. 1871-1937. Known as the father of nuclear physics, he was the son of a New Zealand farmer. He went from Canterbury College, Christchurch, NZ, to Cambridge on a scholarship and worked with J. J. Thomson (1856-1940), discoverer of the electron in 1897. The New Zealander began his independent work at McGill Univ in Canada (1895-98) and then held the chair of physics at the Univ of Manchester (1907-19) and was awarded the

Nobel Prize in chemistry in 1908 for discovering that radioactive elements transform into other elements. In 1911 he and associates discovered that the atom was constructed around a small central mass with much of the atom being empty space. In WWI he worked with Arthur H. COMPTON on aircraft development and for ways to detect submarines.

Rutherford returned to his chair at Manchester after the war but left in 1919 to succeed Thomson as Cavendish professor of physics and director of Cambridge's Cavendish Laboratory. In 1920 he announced his discovery that matter could be artificially transmuted. Lord Rutherford (1931) was still active as director of one of the world's greatest centers of nuclear physics study when he died unexpectedly in 1937 after surgery for a strangulated hernia. Among his disciples was (Sir) John D. COCKCROFT. (Briggs, ed.)

RYAZANOV, Vasiliy Georgiyevich. Soviet air force officer. 1901-51. Born 25 Jan 01 in the village that is now Balakhna, Gorky Oblast, Ryazanov was the son of a peasant. In 1920 he joined the Red Army and Communist Party, graduated in 1926 from military pilots' school and in 1935 from the AF Academy. Starting as a colonel in Sep 42 and a general lieutenant of aviation by 1943 Ryazanov, headed the 1st Gds Assault Avn Corps on various fronts in succession (SW, Southern, Kalinin, NW, Voronezh, Steppe, and finally the 2d and 1st Ukrainian Fronts). He was twice a HSU (1944 and 1945). After the war he had various air force commands and Ukrainian political posts before dying on 8 July 51.

RYCHAGOV, Pavel Vasilyevich. Soviet air force leader. 1911-41. Rychagov was born in Moscow Prov, son of a peasant. A fighter pilot in the early 1930s, he served in Spain (20 victories; HSU in 1936), and became a leading advocate of tactical air support. Immediately after returning from Spain he volunteered for service in China and became military attaché there, leading fighter forces against the Japanese at **Lake Khasan** and directing a bomber attack on the Japanese air base on Taiwan (Scarecrow). Succeeded by his assistant MA, ZHIGAREV, in May 38 he returned to Moscow (HFS) before being air force commander of the 1st Separate Red Army in the Far East (ibid.).

During the Winter War in Finland 1939-40 he commanded the air force of one of MERETS-KOV's field armies.

Not yet 30 years old, not only a brilliant pilot but also a talented commander, he was one of 13 promoted in 1940 to general lieutenant of aviation and in August of that year he was appointed chief of the Soviet AF. All countries had fundamental disagreements over air force doctrine but the Soviet AF was particularly severely plagued. Gen Lt (Avn) Rychagov undertook to form 106 new units but had raised only 19 by the end of May 41. As for new airfields, few of the authorized 190 or so were finished by that date. (HFS.) Stalin had asked during a meeting of the Main Military Council in Apr 41 why the aircraft accident rate was so high. Rychagov said it was because of bad planes: "They make us fly in coffins." Stalin abruptly closed the meeting and walked out. Replaced by Pavel F. ZHIGAREV, his first deputy since Dec 40, Rychagov was arrested a week later. Within two months (by early June) the NKVD confined two other former Air Force chiefs, A. D. Loktionov, Ya. V. Smushkevich. Severely beaten by Beria's men in hopes of getting confessions, Rychagov was among 25 senior officers shot 28 Oct 41 without trial. His wife, Maria Nesterenki, commander of an aviation regiment, also was executed. Rychagov was rehabilitated in 1954. (Scotts.)

RYDER, Charles Wolcott. US general. 1892-1960. "Doc" Ryder was born 16 Jan 92 in Kansas and graduated from West Point in 1915 (39/164). In France with the 16th Inf Div he won two DSC's, the SS, and the PH. The tall, slender, distinguished-looking Brig Gen Ryder was commandant of cadets at the USMA 1937-41. Leaving to be CofS, 6th Corps, he took over the 34th Inf Div in May 42 and was promoted to major general on 21 June 42.

The 34th was the first US division sent to the ETO, where it trained in Ireland and on the Scottish coast. British involvement in the North Africa landings (**Torch**) minimized to get better French cooperation, Ryder planned and led the Eastern TF landings at Algiers on 8 Nov 42. British Gen Kenneth A. Noel ANDERSON arrived the next day to relieve Ryder, who returned to lead his 34th Div for operations in Tunisia and Italy. After the 34th distinguished itself by penetrating the Gustav Line at Cassino in early Feb 44 the division landed at Anzio on 24 March to reinforce the beachhead. Overcoming stiff resistance to start breaking out on 23 May 44 the division fought its way along the coast to take Leghorn on 19 July 44. Physically and mentally exhausted, Ryder was then relieved without prejudice (Fisher, 281), replaced by Maj Gen Charles L. Bolté, and kicked upstairs (personal information) to head the 9th Corps in the US from 2 Sep 44. Maj Gen Ryder took his headquarters to Japan on 25 Sep 45 for occupation duty, remaining until 20 Dec 48. Ryder then served in Washington until retiring 28 Feb 50, still a major general. He died 17 Aug 60 at Vineyard Haven, Mass.

RYTI, Risto Heikki. Finnish statesman. 1889-1956. Ryti (pronounced ruh-tie) practiced law before entering politics to become the world's youngest finance minister in 1921. He formed a coalition government on 1 Dec 39, the day after the Soviets attacked Finland. As president from 19 Dec 40 (after the death of Kyosti Kallio) he cooperated with the Soviets but when Hitler attacked Russia in June 41 he nominally joined the Axis. Finland reoccupied territory taken by Russia but refused to join in the German offensive against Leningrad. It has been contended, however, that the Finns would have done so if LEEB's AG North had not stopped its attack south of the city (Werth, *Russia,* 361). But when the Soviets attacked Finland again in June 44 Ryti promised Hitler he would not make a separate peace. The pro-German president resigned suddenly on 1 Aug 44, being replaced by MANNERHEIM and arrested on 6 Nov 45. Charged as a collaborator and war criminal Ryti was sentenced to 10 years in prison but freed in 1949 for ill health.

S

SABU (Dastagir). Indian-born actor. 1925-63. Son of an Indian mahout, he played the title role in *Elephant Boy* (1937), a movie based on Kipling's *Jungle Book*. As a ward of the British government he attended an English public school, made several more movies, and settled in Hollywood in 1941. A tail gunner in WWII he completed 42 missions. Sabu made his last film in 1956.

SACHS, Alexander. Russian-born economist. 1893-1973. Picked by SLIZARD and other scientists to warn FDR that construction of an atom bomb was possible, he read EINSTEIN's letter to FDR on 11 Oct 39. *(S&S.)*

SAFFORD, Laurence Frye. US naval officer. 1894-1973. As an intelligence expert, particularly in codebreaking, "Sapho" Safford was frustrated by superiors in issuing warnings that Japan clearly was preparing to launch a surprise attack in 1941. The problem stemmed from the US Navy's intramural bureaucratic battles with regard to military intelligence, particularly dissemination.

Safford graduated from Annapolis in 1916 (16/177), served initially with submarines, and in Jan 24 took charge of the new Research Desk in the Code and Signals Section of Naval Communications in Washington. A brilliant, eccentric, unstarched officer "whose uniform was always rumpled and looked as though he had slept in it" (Edwin Layton, 32), Sapho created the Radio Intelligence Organization (RIO) and began to study electrical cipher machines. In addition to improving signal security, he analyzed intercepted Japanese radio traffic, collaborating with Col William FRIEDMAN.

For his early efforts Safford had the 1918 Japanese Navy Secret Operations Book and subsequent editions. Intercepts of messages from Japanese Navy war games revealed that the Japanese knew of US war plans and were planning countermeasures. (RCS.) In 1941, however, territorial battles within US Navy Hq kept him from properly disseminating intelligence. T. S. WILKINSON, Director of Naval *Intelligence*

from 15 Oct 41, and Safford, under the Director of Naval Communications, were restricted to *collecting* enemy information. But *evaluation* and *dissemination* were the responsibility of the Deputy CNO for war plans, Rear Adm Richard Kelly "Terrible" TURNER, who refused to release any messages that did not reflect his personal evaluations of the Japanese threat. To circumvent this Safford arranged to have the rumpled Lt Comdr Joseph J. Rochefort, a brilliant cryptanalyst and expert linguist, transferred to head the intercept station at Pearl Harbor. Here Rochefort worked directly with the intelligence section of the Pacific Fleet. From Sep 41 intercept stations in the Pacific were tracking Japanese naval and merchant ships. Two months later all merchantmen were in home ports, and in October an intercept revealed that the Japanese consul in Honolulu had been given a grid targeting system for reporting US ship movements in Pearl Harbor. Turner did not allow Safford to pass these and other indications of impending war to Pacific Fleet Hq, the reasons being that they contradicted conclusions that the Japanese intended to make their first strike in SE Asia. On 3 Dec 41 Safford learned that the Japanese embassy in London and the consulate in Honolulu had instructions to destroy all classified records. But he was authorized to send this information only to Adm Thomas C. HART, CinC Asiatic Fleet, for "action," with Adm Husband E. KIMMEL, CinC Pacific, only an "information addressee." On 4 December Guam received Safford's message to destroy codes and code machines, but Pearl Harbor was not informed. Early on the Sunday morning of 7 Dec 41, American cryptologists in Washington delivered decoded transcripts of the message to NOMURA instructing him to inform Cordell HULL that US peace proposals were rejected. Defense of Hawaii was an Army responsibility, but CNO Harold R. STARK offered to send a flash warning to Pearl Harbor by USN communications. Army CofS MARSHALL responded that he could have a message to Pearl Harbor delivered just as fast, but it arrived after the attack started.

Safford was promoted to captain in Feb 42 and made assistant director of Communications for Cryptographic Research. For seven years he continued to develop improved crypto systems, moving into teletype, facsimile, and ultimately TV, eventually inventing 20 coding systems and devices. The captain testified at Pearl Harbor hearings that CINCPAC had been only partly informed of all Washington knew before 7 Dec 41.

In Jan 49 Safford became special assistant to the director of the Armed Forces Security Agency. Placed on the retired list on 30 June 51 as a captain, he remained on active duty as special assistant to the Security Branch of Naval Communications until 2 Mar 53. Safford died 15 May 73 in Bethesda, Md.

His limited-distribution report, *The Undeclared War, History of RIO,* covers the work of his Radio Intelligence Organization (above) from 1920 to 4 Dec 41. Dated 15 Nov 43 it was subsequently declassified. (RCS.)

SAINT EXUPERY, Antoine (Jean Baptiste) de. French airman and author. 1900-45. The internationally famous airman and author was born in Lyons on 29 June 00. His father's ancestral home is St Exupéry-les-Rochers (Corrèze), in south central France; his mother's forebears were the Boyer de Fonscolombe family, to whom Fragonard and other 18th century painters dedicated works *(CB 40).* "Saint Ex," as friends called him, began his schooling at Le Mans, where Dominican fathers found him noisy and difficult. But he went on to have an admirable record in literature and philosophy under the Maristes at the Swiss college of Fribourg. *(CB 40*; official French AF records, cited hereafter as OR.)

During long vacations in the region west of Lyons, where one of France's first airfields was located, Saint Exupéry watched trial flights, talked to pilots, and learned something about engines. After brief naval-school training, and failing to pass examinations for acceptance as a student pilot, Saint Exupéry completed his mandatory military service and on 10 Oct 22 was commissioned as a second lieutenant of the army reserve. Becoming a pilot at his own expense, he joined a fighter group and was discharged as a first lieutenant of reserves.

Turning naturally to civil aviation, Saint Exupéry had a long, adventurous career, and

proved to have a remarkable literary ability. His first book, *Night Flight,* won the Prix Femina in 1931. *Southern Mail* (1933) was followed by *Wind, Sand and Stars* (1939), which was awarded the French Academy's Grand Prix. In 1938 the now-famous airman and author was in the crew of a flying boat that crossed the Atlantic in an experiment for Air France. The tall, massive aristocrat was working on a novel in America when war broke out on 1 Sep 39. He returned to France on the last boat, was commissioned as a captain, and was ordered to Toulouse as an instructor.

The not-so-young celebrity's initial requests for combat duty were disapproved because he had suffered injuries in numerous air accidents (OR), but on 3 Dec 39 he finally managed assignment to a photo reconnaissance group. Promoted to major and flying the Bloch 174, he had seven combat missions during the period 29 Mar-9 June 40, all but one being high-altitude photographic flights. In the most dramatic one he took off from Orly (Paris) with fighter support on 23 May (D+13 of the invasion) and followed a route over German-occupied Cambrai to Arras, where BEF commander Lord Gort had counterattacked two days earlier in hopes of slowing the advance of Pz Gp HOTH (which included Rommel). Over Arras Saint Ex braved intense ground fire to continue his mission until the plane was almost torn apart.

His 1st Sqdn, 2/33 Recon Gp, reached Algiers on 20 June 40, three days after Pétain asked for an armistice, and Saint Exupéry left the unit about a month later. In August he went to the US for three surgical operations he needed. Saint Ex was as driven to write as to fly and he stayed in America to publish *War Pilots* (which included an account of his mission to Arras), *The Little Prince,* and *Letter to a Hostage.*

After the Allies landed in North Africa (8 Nov 42) the internationally known author-airman undertook to resume his military career. In Algiers he became prominent in GIRAUD's resistance to Gaullism, which he consistently condemned as "a fascism without a doctrine" (quoted in Smith, *OSS,* 180). US imposed age restrictions delayed the famous airman's initial efforts but he finally got around them to fly long-range photographic missions over France before rejoining his old squadron. Equipped with the P-38 Lightning, flying high altitude sweeps over the south of France, he had eight more missions. The last was from Corsica over Savoy on 31 July 44, where Saint Exupéry disappeared, ironically in the region where his love of flight had begun. Inevitably, rumors of political assassination were bruited (ibid).

SAIONJI, Kimmochi. Japanese elder statesman. 1849-1940. Coming from the old Fujiwara aristocracy from which all court nobles were drawn, the Marquis Saionji was active in the Meiji restoration. He then had a long exposure in Europe to western liberal ideas. After being premier in 1906-08, and 1911-12, he retired from party politics a few years later. In 1919 he headed the Japanese delegation to the Paris Peace Conference. Elevated from marquis to prince in 1922, "the last genro" (elder statesman) had great influence on the formation of governments as ultranationalists vied for control. With generally liberal and moderate views he tried to curb the trend toward packing cabinets with generals and admirals, his final and perhaps greatest achievement being to push his protégé Prince KONOYE into the premiership in 1937. This proved to be of no avail, but as HIROHITO's principal political tutor from about 1915 the remarkable old courtier left a stamp that lingered after his death on 24 Nov 40. A biography by Bunki Omura is *The Last Genro* (1937).

SAITO, Yoshitsugu. Japanese general. 1890-1944. A "stodgy, colorless cavalryman" (Toland, *Rising Sun,* 487), Lt Gen Saito headed a horse procurement unit before going to Saipan in Apr 44. His Northern Marianas District Group, the Saipan and Tinian Island Area (*Kogun,* 106), comprised Saito's 43d Div and a Col Oka's 47th Independent Mixed Bde (Morrison, VIII, 167). Imperial Hq saw no need for a first-rate general on Saipan, a rocky little island of the Marianas, and little had been done to fortify or garrison it. But the American wanted Saipan's airfields for B-29s. Although Saito had full responsibility for the island's defense (Morison, VIII, 167) he was junior to Vice Admirals Chuichi NAGUMO and Takeo Takagi, who both had headquarters on Saipan but few surviving forces.

The Marines hit the beaches on 15 June 44, overcoming ground defenses within a few days but still having to deal with pockets of die-hard resistance. Too old and sick to lead the esti-

mated 3,000 officers and men who died the night of 6-7 July 44 in the war's biggest banzai attack, Saito committed suicide on the 6th at about 10 AM. Authorities disagree on how Saito and NAGUMO died and whether they were together, but each apparently performed the first step of *seppuku* before an aide dispatched them with a pistol. Saito's cremated remains, identified by a POW, were buried with military honors by US Marines under Holland M. SMITH. Takeo Takagi (herein) also died in the campaign. Although some Japanese survived for years in caves, most of the 30,000 other troops and about 22,000 of approximately 32,000 civilians (including native Chamorros) died. On 11 and 12 July 44, in one of the war's most ghastly spectacles in which entire families were involved, hundreds jumped or were pushed from cliffs on the northern end of the island. (Morison, VIII, 338.)

SAKAI, Saburo. Japanese ace. 1916-. Credited with downing 64 Allied planes, most of them as a Zero pilot, he began his combat career over China. After service in the Philippines and Java he was based at Rabaul. The ace was on the long return flight from Guadalcanal in Aug 42 when he realized too late that a plane suddenly appearing behind him was American. Although badly hit and almost blind he landed safely. The left eye was lost, and the other was saved only by an excruciating operation and long convalescence. Sakai trained other pilots until permitted in mid-44 to fly combat missions again. Despite loss of depth perception he scored several more victories and was promoted to ensign in late 1944.

Japan's greatest living fighter pilot was almost unknown after the war, but with Martin Caidin and Fred Saito he published a lively war memoir, *Samurai!* (New York: Dutton, 1957)

SAKONJU, Naomasa. Japanese admiral. 1890-1948. He graduated from the naval academy in 1912 and from the start of the war in 1941 was a rear admiral serving as naval attaché in Thailand. Two months after leaving that post in July 43 he headed Transport Div 16. After the Allied landing on Biak, 27 May 44, Sakonju was involved in extensive countermeasures. The first was Opn Kon, for which he had the mission of moving the 2d Amphib Bde, some 2,500 strong, from Mindanao to Biak for a counterattack. The effort was suspended because surprise was lost in the first phase, and a followup effort failed. (Morison, VIII, 118-30.) Sakonju then headed Transport Unit 1 for Matome UGAKI's Opn A-Go. But this was aborted because Ugaki had to rush north to rendezvous with OZAWA in the Philippine Sea. Other efforts to reinforce Biak were defeated.

During the Leyte campaign, after the Japanese decided to make a major effort to reinforce and hold the island, Sakonju headed the SW Area Guard Force (or Transport Unit) of SHIMA's 2d Striking Force. Sakonju was detached on 23 Oct 44 to land 2,000 troops from Mindanao on the far side of Leyte at Ormoc early on 26 Oct 44. His flagship CA *Aoba* had been disabled by a torpedo hit from a submarine outside Manila Bay on the 23d, and the transport unit lost CL *Kinu* and DD *Uranami* around noon on the 26th in the Visyan Sea, but Sakonju accomplished his mission. (Morison, XII, 196n, 239.) The admiral subsequently had considerable success in landing reinforcements on Leyte. In Dec 44 he was promoted to vice admiral and made CofS, China Area Fleet. Four years later he was he was executed for war crimes.

SALAZAR, Antonio de Oliveira. Portuguese head of state. 1899-1970. The son of a small landowner, Salazar was born in Vimieiro, Beira Alta Province. He was educated at a seminary and took minor orders before entering the Univ of Coimbra in 1910 and becoming a leading economist. Army putschists in 1926 recruited him as finance minister to restore the country's finances but, finding hopeless confusion in the government, he resigned in five days. In 1928 he returned as finance minister and he became premier in 1932. (Briggs, ed, *20 Cent Bio.*)

After completely reorganizing the government, the "little gray man"—a recluse, ascetic, and devout Jesuit—became a virtual dictator. In the age of European dictators, Dr Salazar headed the mildest and least oppressive. *(CB 41.)* Throughout WWII he maintained a strict neutrality. But the Portuguese were pro-British, the two countries having close economic ties and an alliance dating from 1386, and Dr Salazar was somewhat more neutral toward the Allies. In Aug 41 he began negotiating an agreement for American protection from a German attack. After arduous negotiations in which George

KENNAN had a major role, the strong man granted the US base rights in the Azores on 8 Oct 43. A stroke ended Salazar's long rule in 1968.

SANSOM, Odette Marie Celine. British secret agent. 1912-. The daughter of Gaston Brailly, Odette was born in Amiens and reared in Normandy. She married Roy Sansom, an English friend of the family. Odette was living in Somerset with three young daughters in the spring of 1942 when she responded to a call for snapshots of the French coast. This led **SOE** to recruit her for setting up a ring at Auxerre. After three unsuccessful attempts at overnight air delivery SOE landed her in the south of France from a small boat in Nov 42.

Peter "Raoul" CHURCHILL prevailed on her to abandon her mission in Auxerre and join his "Spindle" ring. As covered under Peter Churchill in more detail, Abwehr Sgt BLEICHER arrested the two agents during the night of 15-16 Apr 43. Unbroken by torture she spent a year at Fresnes prison in Paris before being sent to Ravensbruck in May 44 for execution. But she was spared because the camp commandant believed the cover story that she was married to Peter Churchill and that he was kin to Winston Churchill, hence of possible value as a hostage.

After the war Odette was awarded the **George Cross** and lionized by the press. She married Peter in 1947 but divorced him in 1955.

SASAKI, Minoru. Japanese general. 1893-. A cavalryman, born 1 Jan 93 and a major general in 1939, he became CG, 4th Cav Bde, then CofS, 6th Army. (*Kogun,* 234.) After heading the army's mechanized dept from Aug 42, he commanded the Nanto (Southeast) Detachment at Munda, New Georgia. "Completely baffled" when Americans landed on 30 June 43 a few miles south on Rendova Island (Morison, VI, 150) Sasaki frustrated Maj Gen John H. Hester's initial efforts to take Munda Field on 7 July with the 43d Div. The Japanese reinforced Munda's garrison during the night of 12-13 July 43 with 16 barges of troops from Vila and had another 1,200 more en route by destroyer. Maj Gen Oscar W. Griswold, CG, 14th Corps, took command of the New Georgia Occupation Force the night of 15-16 July, Hester remaining as CG, 43d Div. Sasaki gave up the base on 4 Aug 43 after a valiant but futile defense by some 10,000 men. (*Kogun,* 66; Morison, VI, 180. The latter work indexes the general as *Noboru* Sasaki.)

Sasaki was reassigned to 8th Area Army Hq a month or so after losing Munda and was promoted in Oct 44 to lieutenant general (*Kogun,* 234).

SAUCKEL, Ernst Friedrich Christoph. German official. 1894-1946. "The greatest slaver of all time" (Davidson, *Trial,* 506), "Fritz" Sauckel directed mobilization of German and foreign workers to include POWs.

He was born 27 Oct 94 in Hassfurt am Main, only child of a postal clerk. Thanks to his mother's earnings as a seamstress he attended a **Gymnasium** until the age of 15. He then was a merchant seaman on German, Norwegian, and Swedish ships. A POW in France for almost five years, Fritz acquired a thirst for politics from his fellow captives and endured primitive living conditions that led him later to question complaints of foreign workers held in Germany.

In 1927 Sauckel became Gauleiter of Thuringia and member of the Landtag. On Hitler's gaining power in 1933 he was appointed Reishsstathalter of Thuringia and elected to the Reichstag. On BORMANN's recommendation he was Plenipotentiary for Labor Allocation from 21 Mar 42. (Albert SPEER had nominated Karl Hanke.) The almost bald, baby-faced Sauckel, who quipped that if you met the devil tomorrow he would look like a charming fellow, carried out his duties "with tireless efficiency as well as with a gross, brutal goodwill (Davidson, *Trial,* 504).

Sauckel initially had more than five million foreign workers, including POWs, in Germany; from seven to 10 million were added during the war. Sauckel once boasted that not more than 200,000 came voluntarily. The slaver never considered that he was violating international law.

The careers of Speer and Sauckel were closely linked. Having worked for Speer in Weimar and Berlin, Sauckel remained his subordinate in the Third Reich. With the titular rank of general in the SS and SA, Sauckel made all Gauleiters nominal members of his staff. He carried out his promise to work with "fanatical devotion" and employed anybody he could use as slave dealers and handlers. But Sauckel also intrigued constantly against his chief, Speer, who came to need more and more labor, and Hitler said later

in the war: "I made a great mistake when I appointed Sauckel" (Speer, *Memoirs,* 333).

Sauckel was convicted by the Nuremberg tribunal of crimes against humanity and war crimes. He was hanged on 11 Oct 46.

SAUCKEN, Dietrich von. German general. 1892-. Born in the village of Fischhausen, East Prussia, on 16 May 92, he was WIA seven times in WWI and awarded three decorations for valor. Oberst Saucken led a regiment in Poland, Holland, and France. Still a colonel, he was acting commander of the 4th Pz Div, 27 Dec 41-2 Jan 42, in AG Center Center and AG South. Promoted 1 Jan 42 to Generalmajor, on 1 Apr 43 to Generalleutnant, he continued to head the division during the periods 31 May 43-Jan 44, and from March to 30 Apr 44. (*B&O,* 76.) The slightly built, fine-featured, youthful Saucken was promoted to General of Panzer Troops on 1 Aug 44. Leaving the 4th Pz Div as it was driven toward Latvia, he ultimately command a corps, then the 2d Army, as the war moved into East Prussia. Around Danzig he was CinC of the special Army Command (AOK), and on 9 May 45 was the 27th and last recipient of the Diamonds (No. 27), awarded by Doenitz as chief of state (Angolia, I, 105). Surrendering to the Russians he was held for ten and a half years, until 1955. The general then lived in Bavaria.

SAUNDERS, La Verne George. USAF general. 1903-88. "Blondie" Saunders was born 21 Mar 03 in Stratford, South Dakota, but appointed to West Point from Pennsylvania. The nickname was reverse English, "Blondie" being a black Irishman. (Pete Martin sketch in *These Are the Generals,* 246 ff.) The easy going, soft-spoken, squarely built farm boy was a star football player and later an innovative and successful assistant coach at West Point. Graduating in 1928 (214/261) he promptly took flight training with the famous Kelly Field, Tex, class that included Curtis LE MAY. His 11th Bomb Gp of 16 B-17s was the first USAAF formation involved in the Guadalcanal Campaign (*C&C,* IV, 27).

He was promoted to brigadier general on 25 Dec 42, one of the US Army's youngest. Shortly before this he had crash landed a crippled B-17 off the Shetland Islands. With part of his forehead hanging over an eye, and a badly wounded hand, Saunders paddled two miles to shore on a rubber raft with the few survivors. Found by natives, they were rescued 24 hours later. (Pete Martin, above.)

Brig Gen Saunders commanded the 58th Bomb Wing of B-29 Superfortresses and the 20th Bomber Command in the CBI, 1943-44, serving under his Kelly Field classmate, Curt Le May. He was retired for physical disability in 1947 as a brigadier general and died on 16 Nov 88 in Aberdeen, SD (Cullum).

SCHACHT, Hjalmar. German economic minister. 1877-1970. Born of Danish ancestry in Tingleff, Schleschwig-Holstein, on 22 Jan 77, Hjalmar Schacht was reared in the US, where his father became an American citizen. The future financial wizard completed his studies in Germany. As a banker he became Reich currency commissioner in 1923 and earned a reputation world wide for saving the German economy from run-away inflation. Among the financiers who backed Hitler, he became Nazi minister of economics in 1934 but, despite accomplishing wonders, was soon an obstacle to Hitler's ambitions. In 1936 Schacht was subordinated to GOERING in economic affairs. Finding the situation intolerable he resigned in Nov 37 as minister of economics and plenipotentiary for the war economy but remained president of the Reichsbank. To keep the growing rift with the Nazis from alarming them unduly he accepted the title minister without portfolio.

About six feet three inches tall, Schacht was a man of Old World culture and charm whose four-inch-high celluloid collar was a trademark. In 1938 he was separated from a rabidly Nazi wife who reported his candid private comments on the Hitler regime. Three years later the 58-year-old financier married an attractive young woman, 30 years his junior, and sired two daughters. (SKORZENY married one of Schacht's nieces in 1954.) Although not wholeheartedly committed to the anti-Nazi resistance, Schacht was arrested on 21 July 44 and held in concentration camps. He was rescued on 4 May 45 with the **Niederdorf** group. Jailed for trial at Nuremberg as a war criminal he was found not guilty. But a de-Nazification court sentenced him to eight years at hard labor as a "major offender." After appeal he was released on 2 Sep 48 but not finally cleared until two years later. Then 73 years old he launched a successful new career as an adviser to Third World countries (Wistrich) and made another personal fortune as a banker. Having published works on his accomplishments in the Weimar Republic he dealt with his Third Reich experiences in *Abrechnung mit Hitler* (1949) and *76 Jahre meines Lebens* (1961).

Schacht died in his sleep on 8 Aug 70 in Kroev.

SCHELLENBERG, Walter. German official. 1910-52. An arch-villain of the Nazi regime, only 35 years old when his career ended, SS Gruppenfuehrer Schellenberg directed German foreign intelligence and counter-intelligence during most of the war. He was born 16 Jan 10 at Saarbruecken, seventh child of a piano manufacturer. After France occupied the Saar in 1918 the Schellenberg family moved into nearby Luxembourg and had fallen on hard times when Walter entered the Univ of Bonn in 1929. Small (five feet nine), stocky, but well-put-together, he studied medicine for two years before deciding that law promised quicker and more regular pay because it would lead to a government job. (Kahn, *Hitler's Spies,* 255.) He got a doctorate in law. On 1 May 33, a month after being accepted in the SS, he became Nazi Party member No. 3,504,508. The delay in joining would be a political problem in years to come. (Ibid.)

The young lawyer came to Himmler's attention in 1934 by giving of a lecture on German law that was particularly hard on the Catholic church. Schellenberg entered the SD on 2 July 34, just after the **Blood Purge** (Brissaud, *SD,* 73), and Himmler brought him to Berlin the next year. Long apprenticeship in the SS included visiting Italy to organize security for a visit by Mussolini to Berlin. But he used the opportunity to gather information on Italian foreign policy. (Ibid., 256.) Beginning to show his special aptitudes, the young lawyer created special units of both party and government personnel for HEYDRICH's use in the occupation of Czechoslovakia. This innovative principle led to organization of HEYDRICH's RSHA, in which Schellenberg took charge of Amt IV E. Under the Gestapo (Amt IV) Group E handled counterintelligence. Schellenberg's first coup, in which he participated with NAUJOCKS, became the **Venlo incident.** His next exploit is covered in a full chapter of the adventurer's memoirs titled "A Plot to Kidnap the Duke of

Windsor" (*The Labyrinth*, 107 ff). Conceived probably by Ribbentrop to repeat the trick at Venlo, this failed for reasons that have never been explained. (*See* WINDSOR.)

Other counter-intelligent exploits of Amt IV E were establishment of the "Kitty Salon," an elegant VIP brothel full of electronic listening devices. Pioneering the use of **radiogoniometry** in secret intelligence work Schellenberg took the lead, starting in late 1941, in virtually destroying the large-scale Soviet spy ring **Rote Kapelle** and went on to decapitate Rudolf ROESSLER's "Lucy" ring in Switzerland. Professional jealousy in the foreign office kept him from involvement in Elyesa BAZNA's Opn "Cicero."

Meanwhile the 31-year-old SS Sturmbannfuehrer rose to be Himmler's right hand man and heir apparent. The men were almost twins professionally, and Schellenberg says in his memoirs that he would have succeeded HEYDRICH as head of the RSHA but for his youth. (KALTENBRUNNER got the plum.) Boyish and charming but his pasty face scarred from student duels, Schellenberg was a good horseman (riding almost daily for several years); he was a crack pistol shot and shared a passion for swordsmanship with his boss Heydrich—they fenced almost daily. But the young lawyer, known for exceptionally precise enunciation, was considered effete by street-brawler types of the Nazi peerage, and his anti-Semitism was almost pro forma.

Having a flair for bureaucratic infighting and being increasingly close to Heydrich and Himmler the lawyer finally achieved his ambition of ousting Heinz Jost and replacing him as acting chief of the **RSHA** VI. The appointment was announced 21 June 41, the eve of Opn **Barbarossa**. This made him responsible for secret service matters outside of Germany, to include his former counterespionage activities. But despite close personal contact with the crafty Abwehr chief CANARIS—for years they rode horseback almost daily—Schellenberg was slow to learn about the resistance movement that Hans OSTER headed within the Abwehr.

By early 1945 Schellenberg's Amt VI had 12 groups and 48 desks. *See* Kahn, *Hitler's Spies*, 260-71, for a good summary of the bureau's operations and accomplishments.

As it was obvious that Hitler's Germany was headed for oblivion, Gruppenfuehrer Schellenberg took the initiative in putting out peace feelers through Count BERNADOTTE. (KALTEN-

BRUNNER made a parallel effort.) On 6 May 45 he reached Stockholm to begin what proved to be unsuccessful negotiations. Making his last phone call to Flensburg (Doenitz's Hq.) three days later, and put under house arrest in the village of Trosa, he wrote (at Bernadotte's suggestion) the "Trosa memorandum" about these negotiations.

Schellenberg surrendered in June 45 when faced with extradition from Sweden. He was not charged as a major war criminal but was a prosecution witness. In testimony on 4 Jan 46 he tried to incriminate the army in crimes committed by the SS (Davidson, 558). After a 15-month session on the "Wilhelmstrasse Case" against WEISAECKER *et al*, Schellenberg was sentenced by a US tribunal on 14 Apr 49 to six years in prison, time running from his arrest in June 45. In early June 51 he was granted clemency after undergoing a serious operation for liver disease. He took refuge incognito in Switzerland but was soon discovered and asked to leave. Settling with his wife at Pallenza on Lake Maggiore, Italy, seriously ill and financially strapped, the Nazi resented not being considered sufficiently important to be watched by the police. And he was miffed that the Americans picked GEHLEN rather than him to organize an intelligence service against the Russians. In continual pain, showing mental unbalance, and drafting his memoirs with assistance from a German journalist, he put off a liver operation too long and died in Turin's Clinica Fornaca on 31 Mar 52. His unmarked grave, Fossa No. 1763, is in the 3d Ampliamento, Campo Est. A white marble slab, inscribed "Walter Schellenberg, 1910-1952," disappeared after being placed by Italian friends. (Brissaud, *SD*, 17, 23n4.)

The posthumous *Memorien* (Cologne: Verlag fuer Politik und Wirtshaft, 1956) has been translated and edited by Louis Hagen as *The Schellenberg Memoirs* (London: André Deutsch, 1956) and *The Labyrinth: Memoirs of Walter Schellenberg* (New York: Harper, 1956). Allan Bullock's introduction to the latter work has valuable biographical data and the complex tale of how the fascinating but historically untrustworthy book was written and published.

SCHIRACH, Baldur von. Nazi official. 1907-74. The Reich youth leader who became Gauleiter of Vienna, was born in Berlin on 9

Mar 07. Both his paternal grandmother and mother were American. "He was the kind of young man the Germans call *schwaermerish*," Davidson points out, "a lad with sentimental longing for adventure linked to high pursuits and a love of poetry, tales of derring-do, and literary discussions that do not place too great a strain on one's intellectual capacities." (*Trial*, 285.) Involved with the Young Germans' League from the age of 10, picking up the prevalent anti-Semitism, and becoming a rabid Nazi, Schirach was the ideal leader for what involved into the Hitler Youth (*Hitlerjugend*). Upper-class, chubby, and somewhat effeminate but the hero of his movement, Schirach was viewed dimly by Nazi associates, especially Martin BORMANN. But Hitler championed the youth leader. In early 1940 Schirach enlisted in the German Army, rose to lieutenant, and won the Iron Cross 2d Class in France.

He became governor and Gauleiter of Vienna in Aug 40, turning over active leadership of the Hitler Youth to his former assistant, Arthur Axmann, but remaining inspector of the Hitler Youth and Reich leader of youth education.

With his wife, daughter of Heinrich HOFF-MANN, and four children, Schirach moved into the governor's palace in Vienna and took on "so many jobs, he could be accused of participating in almost all the inequities that took place" (Davidson, 303). These included "resettlement" of Jews from Vienna to Poland and use of slave labor. But by 1943 Schirach had lost all influence with Hitler, thanks largely to Martin BORMANN's enmity of and the Gauleiter's objections to the more inhumane actions. Schirach surrendered in June 45 after working in disguise as interpreter for the Americans. At Nuremberg he conceded guilt in the "resettlement" program but maintained he knew nothing about the death camps. Belatedly seeing the evil of Nazism, and influenced largely by Albert Speer he denounced Hitler before the tribunal. On 1 Oct 46 the Gauleiter was convicted of crimes against humanity. In 1966, a year after completing a full 20-year sentence in Spandau, he published a sincere apologia, *Ich Glaubte an Hitler* (I Believed in Hitler). Schirach died in his sleep at a small hotel in Kroev on 8 Aug 74, at the age of 67. (Wistrich.)

SCHLABRENDORFF, Fabian von. German resistance figure. 1907-80. A lean, aesthetic-looking young nobleman and lawyer, he had important connections in Germany and abroad. His great grandfather, Baron von Stockman, was Queen Victoria's private physician and confidential adviser; his wife was the daughter of pre-war State Secretary Herbert von Bismarck and once Schlabrendorff's chief in the Prussian ministry of the interior. Schlabrendorff was an early and active member of the anti-Nazi resistance and did his most important work as an ADC to TRESCKOW. The men were not related (W-B, *Nemesis*, 514n), on a point on which some authorities err. He and TRESCKOW planted the bomb that failed to go off in Hitler's plane on 14 Mar 43. After being closely involved in other assassination plans and in organizing the conspiracy, Schlabrendorff was implicated in the STAUFFENBERG *Attentat*. He suffered unbelievable tortures without breaking, outwitting interrogators and not being revealed as a major resistance figure. He was waiting in the courtroom to face the People's Court when a major air raid struck Berlin on 3 Feb 45. An American bomb hit the building, killing Judge Ronald FREISLER and destroying the records of most surviving conspirators. His trial, postponed five times until 16 Mar 45, resulted in acquittal on grounds that the one charge against him (a very minor one) had come from being tortured. But Schlabrendorff was held in various prisons including Dachau until liberated by American troops on 4 May 45 with the **Niederdorf group.** He became a prime source of information about the resistance, his story first appearing as *They Almost Killed Hitler* (New York: Macmillan, 1947) and *Revolt Against Hitler* (London, 1948). These works became *Offiziere gegen Hitler* (rev ed, Zurich, 1951).

SCHLEICHER, Kurt von. German general. 1882-1934. He was born 7 Apr 82 in Brandenburg of venerable ancestry. In 1900 he became a subaltern in Paul von Hindenburg's old regiment, the 3d Foot Guards, and began a friendship with son Oscar von Hindenburg.

"If Hans von Seeckt was the sorcerer of the Reichswehr," writes Wheeler-Bennett, "it was reserved for Kurt von Schleicher to play the unsavory and tragic role of the Sorcerer's Apprentice. He was, indeed, the evil genius of the later Weimar Period, symbolizing in himself all the worst traits of the General in politics." (W-B, *Nemesis*, 182.)

Schleicher rose to be MOD, then was chancellor for 18 months. Succeeded on 30 Jan 33 by

Hitler, the political general resumed the post of war minister with the Nazi's promise he would soon have a more important assignment But Generalleutnant Schleicher and his young wife were murdered in their home by an SS detachment at about 11:30 AM on Saturday 30 June 34, the start of the **Blood Purge.**

SCHMELING, Max (Siegfried). German boxer. 1905-. The most successful boxer in German history and a parachutist during the war, Schmeling was born near Berlin, in Klein Luckow, on 28 Sep 05. He was world heavyweight champion, 1930-32, and in 1936 defeated Joe Louis in a stunning upset (Studies of Louis's fights had revealed a fatal flaw.) No Nazi, liberal-minded, and having a Jewish manager, Schmeling—despite himself—became a symbol of German racial superiority. But the American "Brown Bomber" destroyed this myth in two minutes and four seconds of the 1938 rematch.

Still a national hero, Schmeling served in the Wehrmacht as a parachutist, jumping into Crete with the assault wave. After the war, although over 40, he attempted a comeback and won a few fights, but retired from boxing after being beaten in 1948 by another old-timer. From 1957 he owned the franchise on a Coca Cola plant in Hamburg-Wandesbeck. Schmeling's autobiography was published in 1967 as *Ich boxte mich durchs Leben* (I Boxed all my Life).

SCHMIDHUBER, Wilhelm. Anti-Hitler conspirator. A Munich businessman who was also the honorary Portuguese consul in that provincial capital, Dr Schmidhuber was a reserve officer attached to the Abwehr. Described as "a flabby, greedy man" (Brown, *Bodyguard,* 302) he gained DOHNANYI's confidence and learned something about the anti-Hitler conspiracy, particularly the activities of Josef MUELLER. He also was involved in **"Opn 7."** When German guards at Cehba on the Czech frontier found dollars in the baggage of a Jewish family in Apr 42 the Jews said Dr Schmidhuber had furnished the funds. (Ibid.) The Gestapo arrested the doctor for this and other illegal currency transactions, and Schmidhuber sent Canaris a message that he would tell what he knew about the conspiracy if not given protection as an Abwehr agent. CANARIS indignantly refused because he did not believe Schmidhuber knew enough to be a

threat. It was a fatal mistake. From bits and pieces the Gestapo got on a trail that led to destruction of Hans OSTER's cell in the Abwehr. (Hoffmann, *Resistance,* 293.)

Dr Schmidhuber survived to pick up his business in Munich, steadfastly denying any connection with the anti-Hitler conspiracy. But contrary evidence is convincing. (Deutsch, II, 116n.)

SCHMIDT, Paul. Hitler's interpreter. 1899-1970. Born 23 June 99 in Berlin, Paul Schmidt was the foreign office's chief interpreter 1935-45. Like many others in his remarkable trade he could memorize vast chunks of material—in his case up to 10 minutes at a time—and recite it back, translated. The simultaneous interpreter wrote minutes of what he heard and saw, to include his impressions of personalities involved. Highlights are in his book *The Secret History of German Diplomacy, 1935-1945* (New York: Macmillan, 1951). In 1952 the diplomat and professional interpreter became director of the Munich Language and Interpreter Institute. He died 21 Apr 70 in Munich. (Snyder, *Ency of 3d Reich; S&S.*)

SCHMUNDT, Rudolf. German general. 1896-1944. Oberstleutnant Schmundt replaced HOSSBACH on 1 Apr 38 as Hitler's Wehrmacht adjutant. He was an avowed Nazi, known to other officers as "John the Disciple," and in the words of Desmond Young was "very good-looking, very intelligent, very ambitious and very 'smooth,'" (quoted in Brett-Smith, 193). Still a colonel in 1940, Oberst Schmundt kept the war diary at Hitler's Hq and was one of the few within the inner circle who had Hitler's respect on army matters. Basically decent but weak-willed and ingenuous, he was a close friend of Rommel and von TRESCKOW (whose activities Schmundt did not suspect). After HALDER's dismissal in late Sep 42 there was what Goerlitz calls a "reintroduction of the old almighty Adjutant-General's department of the General Staff," of which Schmundt was, in effect, the chief (*GGS,* 420). As head of the army personnel office (*Heerespersonalamt*) and promoted, General of Infantry Schmundt directed officer assignments and promotions. Schmundt underwent a progressive disintegration of personality and became a pitiable figure whose only refuge was the bottle. (Deutsch, I, 126,

274-75 & n.) Blinded and horribly burned in the 20 July 44 bomb attempt against Hitler, Schmundt died on 1 Oct 44.

SCHOERNER, Ferdinand. German general. 1892-1973. A robust, plebeian, brutal Bavarian, the Third Reich's next-to-last field marshal, Schoerner was named in Hitler's final testament to succeed the fuehrer as head of the Wehrmacht.

Schoerner was born in Munich on 12 May 92, son of a police officer. He served there with the Royal Bavarian Prince's Own Infantry before attending the Universities of Munich, Lausanne, and Grenoble. This schooling for a teaching career and subsequent foreign duty made Schoerner an outstanding linguist. On the outbreak of war in Aug 14 he went back to his regiment and was commissioned two months later. Like ROMMEL, Leutnant Schoerner quickly excelled in mountain warfare on several fronts, both of them winning the Pour le Mérite in the Battle of Caporetto. Returning to the western front and fighting around Verdun and Rheims he suffered a severe head wound. After the armistice of 1918 Lt Schoerner fought with Freikorps Epp in the Ruhr and Upper Silesia before joining the Weimar Army. In 1922 he was selected for the **GGS.**

He disliked staff work. After serving since 1934 in Berlin, Oberstleutnant Schoerner took command of the 98th Mtn Regt on 1 Mar 37 and was promoted Oberst four days before leading his regiment into southern Poland on 1 Sep 39. He was 47 years old. The 98th and 99th Mtn Regts had a critical role in the hard fighting to capture and hold Lvov (or Lemberg), 12-21 Sep 39.

He led the 6th Mtn Div in the west (1940), being promoted to Generalmajor on 1 Aug 40. Still heading 6th Mtn Div for the campaign in Greece (6-16 Apr 41) he penetrated the Metaxas Line, pursued to Salonika, pushed through Olympus Pass to drive the New Zealanders from Thermopylae, and was awarded the RK on 20 Apr 41. Working with the 2d Pz Div he helped take Larissa and pursue vigorously to Athens. One of Schoerner's regiments was detached for the assault on Crete.

Transferred to the Arctic with his 6th Mtn Div, he held the Litsa front in the extreme north despite winter conditions (1941-42) in which all the division's Greek mules were lost. Promoted

on 15 Jan 42, Generalleutnant Schoerner assumed command of Mountain Corps Norway that day (Ziemke, *GNT,* 329). He was well on the way to becoming the most unpopular general in the German Army. "During the first winter in Lapland, he demonstrated his disdain for adversity by admonishing his troops to live by the slogan 'The Arctic Does Not Exist' (*Arktis ist nicht*)." (Ibid., 221-22.)

A major Soviet counteroffensive to wipe out the threat from DIETL's Army of Lapland to their supply route from the west to Murmansk began in late Apr 42. Against overwhelming strength, personally leading counterattacks, Schoerner held his front. He was promoted to General of Mountain Troops on 1 June 42, and in a reorganization was made CG, 19th Mtn Corps until 23 Oct 43. (Ziemke, 329.)

"From now on Hitler sent in Schoerner whenever the German line began tottering," writes F. W. von MELLENTHIN (*Generals,* 178). Leaving Lapland on 23 Oct 43 for the Ukraine he was appointed CinC, Nikopol Army Detachment. Hitler was determined to hold the historic industrial center of Nikopol on the Dnieper not only because of its manganese deposits but also because it had an important air base within range of the Ploesti oil fields. Schoerner was awarded the Oakleaves (398/890) on 17 Feb 44 for his performance but withdrew when about to be overwhelmed. In Hungary he ordered Draconian measures, including execution, of all AWOLs found in rear areas. (Brett-Smith, *Hitler's Elite,* 204.) Held in such high regard by Hitler that he could defy the "never retreat" order when he thought the situation demanded, Schoerner was appointed in early-Mar 44 to head the National Socialist Command Staff of OKH. He was supposed to infuse the army with his own Nazi zeal, but the assignment did not suit the old warrior. He clashed with Martin BORMANN, whose military ignorance was notorious but who also resented having anybody around Hitler who was not a Party crony.

Schoerner got away from his desk with a promotion to Generaloberst on 31 Mar 44 and appointment to succeed MODEL as head of AG South. In a situation calling for strategic ability, the general was out of his depth. Leaving major decisions to others, he roared about the battlefield exhorting the troops. But the Bavarian mountaineer served his command well by again defying Hitler's orders, evacuating Odessa and saving the new 6th Army from the fate of its predecessor at Stalingrad under PAULUS. "Hitler simply had to put up with it," comments F. W. von Mellenthin (ibid., 181).

On 21 July 44 Schoerner rushed to another fire, taking command of AG North. This was a vestige of its former self, pushed back into Estonia and north Latvia, and there had been a quick succession of generals who failed to work miracles expected by Hitler. In reverse chronological order these were Johannes Friessner, Georg Lindemann, and MODEL, who had been preceded by KUECHLER (with a long tenure) and LEEB. The Soviets were making a major effort against AG North after virtually annihilating AG Center. Schoerner withdrew from Estonia when faced with certain annihilation by the fronts of GOVOROV and MASLENNIKOV. When BAGRAMYAN and YEREMENKO threatened his new position, Schoerner abandoned more of the Baltic States to defend Riga. From here he was driven into Courland (Kurland) by 10 Oct 44, 33 divisions cut off as BAGRAMYAN reached the sea north of Memel. The Germans continued to hold Memel, and the situation in the Baltic States was temporarily stabilized.

On 1 Jan 45 Schoerner was awarded the Diamonds (23/27) and on 17 January he left AG North to relieve Harpe as CG, AG Center. German armies on this front had faced a battle of annihilation from the Soviet summer offensive of 1944 through the winter offensive of 1945. Faced with overwhelming odds Schoerner notified Hitler, well in advance this time, that he could not hold all positions. Instead, he intended to trade space for time and let German refugees escape across the Oder. During these desperate months, however, "the People's General," aka "the Bloodhound," set up drum-head courts that for the smallest transgressions ordered the execution of privates and colonels alike (Wistrich). An appreciative fuehrer made the bloody Bavarian a field marshal on 5 Apr 45, the next to last awarded a baton. (The last, three weeks later, was GREIM.) Hitler's political testament of 29 Apr 45 named the field marshal his successor as Wehrmacht commander in chief.

Schoerner was a prisoner of the Soviets for nine years. On his release, 28 Jan 55, he was surprised to learn on returning to Munich that he was charged with murdering subordinates during the war's last months. The principal accuser was the field marshal's former CofS Generalleutnant Oldwig von Natzmer. Belgian authorities also wanted the ruthless Bavarian for war crimes he allegedly committed in 1940. And Schoerner had enemies among those opposing West German rearmament and conscription (Mellenthin, 186).

A civil court acquitted the field marshal of most charges but sentenced him to four and a half years in prison for manslaughter and froze his pension. Veterans of the 6th Mtn Div raised funds that about recompensed their rough general: he had ruled through fear but had cared for his men (ibid.). Schoerner died 6 July 73 in Munich at the age of 81.

SCHULDT, Heinrich (also Hinrich). German general. 1901-44. Born in Blankensee on 14 June 01 Schuldt served in the Reichsmarine, 1922-28, and was commissioned. He joined the SS in 1933, rose to command a company in the SS Liebstandarte Adolf Hitler, and moved up to head the 4th SS Totenkopf Regt. In action behind enemy lines in AG Center the regiment was reduced to a strength of 180 effectives but still accomplished its mission. This won Schuldt the RK, awarded 5 Apr 42. (Angolia, I, 162.)

After moving up to lead a brigade on the eastern front he was promoted to SS Oberfuehrer and given command of the crack 2d Latvian SS Volunteer Bde. He was mortally wounded on 15 Mar 44 in a defensive action. On 24 Mar 44 he was posthumously awarded the Swords (56/159) and given the rank of Generalmajor der Waffen-SS. (Ibid.)

SCHULENBURG, Friedrich von der. German general. 1865-1939. A famous forebear, General Count von der Schulenburg, was the senior minister in Berlin when Napoleon humiliated the Prussian army at Jena in 1806 (Goerlitz, *GGS,* 28). The subject of this sketch was the Crown Prince's CofS on the western front in France when Germany signed the armistice of 1918. As the Prussian defeat in 1806 was rightly attributed to incompetence on the home front, many Germans in 1918 attributed their defeat to a **"stab in the back."** Seeing Hitler as the country's savior the highly decorated old Count Friedrich and his sons joined the Nazi Party, the father in 1931. As valuable window dressing he was given high honorary ranks in the SA and SS. But when Hitler offered him the war minister post vacated by BLOMBERG the elderly count declined on grounds of failing health. He died about 18 months later. (Deutsch, I, 46, 115-16 & n.)

SCHULENBURG, Friedrich Werner von der. German diplomat. 1876-1944. Count von der Schulenburg was ambassador to Moscow from 1935. As one of the last in the old school of German diplomats in the east he sincerely believed that Russo-German collaboration was possible. Shocked by Hitler's decision to invade the USSR, and recalled in June 41, he offered his services to the German resistance after the Stalingrad disaster of early 1943. KLUGE had agreed to smuggle the elderly count through the lines as a negotiator but reneged on learning that renunciation of Hitler was part of any deal the former ambassador said he would try to make with Stalin (Gisevius, 506). The Germans considered parachuting the count behind the lines, but there is no evidence he was willing (W-B, *Nemesis*, 616-17). Found to be listed by the conspirators as alternate foreign minister to HASSEL Count von der Schulenburg was executed on 10 Nov 44.

SCHULENBURG, Fritz Dietloff von der. German resistance figure. c1895-1944. Youngest son of Count Friedrich von der Schulenburg (1865-1939), Fritz Dietloff was attracted intellectually to communism while a student at Goettingen but became a National Socialist. (Gisevius, 487.) Two years as a police official under Erich KOCH in East Prussia dispelled his illusions. Deciding to be "Hitler's Fouché," as he told August Winnig (Deutsch, I, 46), referring to the police minister who turned against Napoleon, Count Fritz joined the anti-Nazi resistance. In July 37 he became deputy police president under Count Wolf Heinrich von Helldorf in Berlin and soon was the principal figure in the "Counts' Group" of about 10 regulars (ibid.). After the FRITSCH affair of 1938 he was linked with the Abwehr group headed by Hans OSTER (Deutsch, I, 47 & n.). As Deputy Oberpraesident of Silesia from 1939 he belonged to the **Kreisau Circle.** Toward the end he had a major influence on STAUFFENBERG (Gisevius, 487). On the conspirators' cabinet list

as state secretary the count was quickly arrested after the 20 July 44 bomb attempt against HITLER. He was hanged on 10 Aug 44.

A biography by Albert Krebs is *Fritz-Dietlof Graf von der Schulenburg: Zwischen Staatsraison und Hochverrat* (Hamburg, 1964).

SCHULZ, Adelbert (also Adalbert). German general. 1903-44. Born 20 Dec 03 in Berlin and reared there, he was a policeman briefly before being commissioned in the Wehrmacht in 1934. Schulz took part in the occupation of Austria and the Sudetenland and was in the 25th Pz Regt when it was added to the 2d Light Div on 18 Oct 38 to become the 7th Pz Div. Generalmajor Erwin Rommel succeeded Generalleutnant Georg Stumme as division commander on 15 Feb 40, and Capt Schulz was CO, 1st Co, 25th Pz Regt, when awarded the RK on 29 Sep 40 for action in France. Going on to lead his company in Russia he was awarded the Oakleaves (47/890) on 31 Dec 41. As regimental commander of the 25th, Oberstleutnant "Panzer Schulz" was presented with the Swords (33/ 159) on 6 Aug 43 for action around Kharkov with the 4th Pz Army. Promoted in November, Oberst Schulz promptly won the Diamonds (9/27), presented on 14 Dec 43. (Rommel was the only other army officer wearing the Diamonds at that date.)

He succeeded Manteuffel on 21 Jan 44 as CG, 7th Pz Div (*B&O*, 83). A week later Panzer Schulz was in a command car, leading an attack at Schepetowka, west of Kiev, when hit in the head by a shell fragment (28 Jan 44). The general died before he could be evacuated. (Angola, 1, 75.)

SCHULZ, Friedrich. German general. 1897-1976. Born 15 Oct 97, he volunteered as an officer candidate in Sep 14 and joined the 54th Inf Regt. By 1939 Schulz was a staff officer in OKH. He distinguished himself as CofS, 43d Corps, in Russia. Oberst Schulz was awarded the RK on 29 Mar 42, promoted to Generalmajor, and assigned as CofS in Manstein's 11th Army in the Crimea. "Apart from being a man of great personal courage, he had . . . a special awareness of the privations and needs of the fighting troops, as well as a most equable nature" (Manstein, *Lost Victories,* 236). Going on to be Manstein's CofS in AG Don through the winter of 1942-43 he took command of the 28th Jaeger Div. He rose to the rank of General-leutnant and was acting commander of the 3d Pz Corps 27 Nov 43-9 Jan 44 (*B&O, 32*). Schulz then led the 59th Army Corps of the 1st Pz Army (Seaton, *R-G War,* 422), being award-ed the Oakleaves (428/890) on 20 Mar 44 (An-golia, I, 247). General of Infantry Schulz next headed the 17th Army of HARPE's AG A, pulling it back in relatively good order and abandoning Cracow on 19 Jan 45. The next day SCHOERNER succeeded Harpe. AG A (the 17th Army and the 1st and 44th Pz Armies of HEINRICI and Fritz Hubert Graeser) fell back on a 300-mile front to SW Silesia. Schulz was awarded the Swords (135/159) on 26 Feb 45 for his role in SCHOERNER's disorderly retreat before KONEV's 1st Ukrainian Front. (Seaton, ibid., 537, 559.) Schulz died 30 Nov 76 in Freudenstadt (Angolia, I, 247).

SCHUMAN, Robert. French politician. 1886-1963. He was born in Luxembourg of a long-established family in German Lorraine. He earned a law degree from the university of Strasbourg (1910), practiced at Metz, and was a deputy from Thionville (Moselle) 1919-40. As an authority on handling displaced persons in long-disputed Alsace-Lorraine he was named undersecretary for refugee affairs on 21 Mar 40. He retained this post when Pétain succeeded Reynaud on 16 June 40. Although Schuman voted the next month to give the marshal full powers he declined to join the Vichy govern-ment and returned to Metz, where the Germans arrested him on 14 Sep 40 for protesting their expulsions. He was incarcerated for seven months at Neustadt, then put in house arrest. Escaping in Aug 42 and making his way first to Lyons, he conducted clandestine operations from many monasteries, notably the famous Abbey of Ligugé, just south of Poitiers.

Schuman returned to Metz shortly before the city was liberated on 20 Nov 44. Reelected a deputy from the Moselle Department, he was minister of finance in two cabinets, 24 June 46-19 Nov 49, before heading his own gov-ernment. Schuman is best known for his efforts to form a European common market for coal and steel.

SCHUMANN, Maurice. French politician. 1911-. Born in Paris of Belgian-Alsacian ancestry he became a journalist with the Havas agency. After serving in London 1932-35 and Paris, he became the agency's assistant chief of *grand reportage* in 1939. A Catholic since 1937, he also was political editor of *l'Aube,* a Christian-Democrat newspaper. He warned Frenchmen of the fascist threat in two books, *le Germanism en marche* (1938) and *Mussolini* (1939).

Schumann became a LnO to the BEF in Sep 39, was captured on the Somme, but escaped to become de Gaulle's spokesman in London on the BBC. He went to Algiers with de Gaulle on 30 May 43. As a member of LECLERC's armored division he saw the liberation of Ale-nçon, Paris, and Strasbourg. Famous in France for his wartime broadcasts, and highly regard-ed by de Gaulle, Schumann became a success-ful postwar politician.

SCHUSCHNIGG, Kurt von. Austrian states-man. 1897-1977. Schuschnigg was born 24 Dec 97 at Riva on Lake Garda. His father was an Austrian army officer who became a general. The son was schooled by Jesuits, fought on the Italian front in the first world war, and got a law degree. As a member of the Christian Social Party he rose rapidly in the new Austrian state to be minister of justice in 1932. Austrian Nazis decided when Hitler came to power in 1933 that their time had arrived also, and Civil war erupt-ed in Feb 34. Nazi thugs fatally wounded Chancellor DOLLFUSS on 25 July 34, and Schuschnigg became chancellor 10 days later after a coup d'état failed.

When MUSSOLINI took a strong position against German intervention Hitler repudiated the Austrian Nazis and relative quiet prevailed for a time. In 1936 Schuschnigg reintroduced compulsory military service, defying the 1919 treaty that had established Austria, but eliminat-ed the one remaining military militia, the *Heimwehr.* Schuschnigg was skilful in playing rival factions against each other, at home and abroad, but he gradually lost support as the eco-nomic situation worsened. His policy of making concessions to the Nazis was crippled when the Rome-Berlin Axis was formed.

Schuschnigg was forced to resign on 11 Mar 38 after the **Anschluss.** Held until 28 May 38 in a tiny room of the Hotel Metropole, Gestapo Hq in Vienna, he spent almost seven years in German concentration camps until liberated with the **Niederdorf** group on 4 May 45. Two years later he emigrated to the US and became a professor of government at the Univ of St Louis, Mo. Having lived two decades in America, naturalized in 1956, he returned to Austria in 1967 to spend his final years. Schuschnigg published *The Brutal Takeover: The Austrian ex-Chancellor's Account of the Anschluss of Austria by Hitler* (New York: Atheneum, 1971).

SCHWARZKOPF, H(erbert) Norman. US general. 1895-1958. Born in New Jersey on 28 Aug 92 and graduated from West Point on 20 Apr 17 (88/139) he was commissioned in the cavalry (Cullum). Having been wounded in France, Schwarzkopf resigned as a captain in 1920 and was superintendent, NJ State Police, 1921-36. He had charge of investigating the LINDBERGH baby kidnapping in 1932. Schwarzkopf returned to active military duty in 1939 and was G2, 44th Div (NJ-NY NG) until 1940. Then Schwarzkopf served in the Near East as a police officer and in 1942 he was chief of the military mission to Iran. A brigadier general of the reserve on 2 July 47 (*AA*, 930) Schwarzkopf retired as a major general, AUS, in 1957. He died 25 Nov 58 in West Orange, NJ.

His son, General H. Norman Schwarzkopf, USMA 1956 (43/480), commanded US forces in the Persian Gulf war, 1991.

SCHWEPPENBURG. See GEYR VON SCHWEPPENBURG.

SCOBIE, Ronald MacKenzie. British general. 1893-1969. Assuming command of a division in Oct 41 he landed at Tobruk that month to relieve the besieged Australian garrison. In AUCHINLECK's counteroffensive, when CUNNINGHAM drove ROMMEL back Cyrenaica, Scobie made limited objective attacks from Tobruk. He then was commander of beleaguered Malta in 1942 before becoming CofS, Middle East Command, in 1943.

The next year he led British occupation troops to Greece. His mission was to reinstall King PETER II, whose faction-plagued government in exile in Cairo finally had a cabinet headed by PAPANDREOU. After landing on 4 Oct 44, Scobie directed the heavy fighting necessary to put down SARPAPHIS's communist insurrection. He remained in Greece until 1946 to cope successfully with communist efforts to take over the country.

SCOONES, Geoffrey Allen Percival. British general. 1893-1975. From 1939 he was on the staff of CinC India, becoming director of operations and intelligence. On 29 July 42 he took command of the 4th British Corps with headquarters at Imphal in **Assam**. There was little fighting until MUTAGUCHI's "march on Delhi" jumped off on 8 Mar 44. Lt Gen Scoones undertook a classic defense-offense strategy, withdrawing initially to strong positions from which to counterattack. The first phase was accomplished by 5 April and the hard-fought counteroffensive reopened the Imphal-Kohima road by 23 June 44. Mutaguchi's exhausted army dropped back in defeat.

Scoones was promoted to head Central Command, making way for the more aggressive MESSERVEY to take over the 4th Corps, and in 1946 was promoted to full general.

SEAGRAVE, Gordon Stifler. US missionary surgeon. 1897-1965. Born in Burma, son, grandson, and great-grandson of missionaries, he returned to the US at the age of 12. In 1922, soon after receiving his MD from Johns Hopkins Univ, he returned to Burma (*CB 43*). With limited medical experience, skimpy resources, and having to training his own nurses from the Shan and Kachin tribes, he had practiced for almost 20 years when the Japanese invasion came. The surgeon was commissioned a major in the US Medical Corps and attached to STILWELL's Chinese forces (Allen, *Burma*, 72). Retreating to India with Stilwell he returned to Burma in 1944 and continued setting up and directing field hospitals. Many of his units supported Merrill's Marauders.

In 1950 the Burmese government convicted Seagrave of aiding rebel tribesmen and sentenced him to 10 years in prison but he served only 10 months until cleared of treason and freed. The legendary doctor was a muscular man who described himself as "short and ugly"; his devoted Burmese nurses called him "Daddy" (*CB 43*).

Dr Seagrave's books, published to raise funds for his work, included *Burma Surgeon* (1943) and *My Hospital in the Hills* (1955). Active to the end, he died in 1965 at Namhkan, Burma.

SEECKT, Hans von. German general. 1886-1936. Although long off the stage when Hitler's war began, Hans von Seeckt, called "the Sphinx" for his enigmatic silence, figures prominently in the literature of WWII. He worked out an ingenious scheme for evading Versailles Treaty restrictions to rebuild the Great German General Staff and the German Army. "Under the leadership of von Seeckt," writes Wheeler Bennett, "the Bendlerstrasse turned its back on sterile political ambitions, upon facile patriotic indignation and barren military adventures. The brains of the Army were concentrated upon the all-important task of its own internal reconstruction." (W-B, *Nemesis,* 96.)

Von Seeckt was born 22 Apr 86 into a military family in Silesia. A Generalmajor from 1915, CofS, 12th Austro–Hungarian Army, he became CofS, Turkish Army, in 1917. He was neutral during the Kapp putsch of 1920, emerging to succeed HINDENBURG as chief of the outlawed General Staff on 7 July 19. In his first message to the army von Seeckt said, "The form changes, but the spirit remains as of old. It is the spirit of silence, selfless devotion to duty in the service of the Army. General Staff officers remain anonymous." (Ibid., 97.) As Chief of the Army Command, or Reichswehr, the trim, monocled Prussian covertly used the newly formed **Truppenamt** to reconstitute the outlawed general staff (ibid.). The Versailles treaty limited the German army to a strength of 100,000, but the Sphinx rotated new levies of high-quality reserve officers and enlisted men through the Reichswehr to form an ever-growing cadre for mobilization. Seeckt also used the Reichswehr to oppose communist uprisings, and he ordered the Bavarian army to put down Hitler's **Munich Beer Hall Putsch** in 1923. Initially opposing Nazism the general reached an accommodation when HITLER became accepted as the one hope for restoring German national power. The Sphinx signed the agreement under which German pilots and tank crews were trained in Russia.

An ardent monarchist, Generaloberst von Seeckt was dismissed on 8 Oct 26 after offering a military post to a son of ex-Crown Prince Wilhelm. But his task was done. In 1930 he was elected to the Reichstag and was soon in open alliance with the Nazis. He was chief of the German mission to train the Nationalist Chinese Army for 10 months beginning in May 34. The field-gray eminence died 29 Dec 36 in Berlin.

SENGER UND ETTERLIN, Fridolin Rudolf von. German general. 1891-1963. One the war's finest commanders at the division and corps levels, a Prussian distinguished for uncommon qualities of culture and high moral principle, Frido von Senger was born 4 Sep 91 in Waldshut. After attending Eton he served as a volunteer in the Freiburger (76th) FA before being a Rhodes scholar 1912-14. The tall, graceful, but exceptionally homely German aristocrat comments in his memoirs that he was tremendously influenced by his experience at Oxford (Senger, 5, 42).

Rejoining his regiment when war broke out in Aug 14 he was promptly commissioned as a second lieutenant of reserves. In 1917 he was given a regular commission with seniority retroactive to from 19 Feb 13. At war's end he married Hilde Margarethe von Kracht, later identified in his memoirs only as "P," and drifted unenthusiastically into a military career. Aloof from postwar civil turmoil he joined the Reichswehr's horse cavalry and became a world-class equestrian. After two years at the cavalry school in Hanover (1919-21) and four hectic years with the cavalry inspectorate in Berlin, Oberstleutnant Senger took over the 3d Cav Regt at Goettingen in the autumn of 1938 and was promoted the following March to colonel.

"I never completed a course at any military school," he writes, and "On passing the required examination, I was considered too old to take up the career of a General Staff officer." Instead of deploring this he rejoiced: "How glad I was to escape the misery of repeated changes of domicile, and to be able to remain with my horses!" (Senger, 43).

After leading his horse-cavalry regiment in Poland, Senger took command of a motorized brigade that supported Rommel's drive through France to Cherbourg. For the next two years he was chief German LnO with the Franco-Italian armistice commission, being promoted 1 Sep 41 to Generalmajor.

From this cushy assignment he went to the eastern front. Commanding the crack 17th Pz Div, which was down to 30 tanks and lacked adequate motor transport for its infantry elements, he moved south for a leading role in Hermann Hoth's 4th Pz Army's failed attempt to link up with Paulus's 6th Army in Stalingrad. Still in the 4th Pz Army he took part in MANSTEIN's defensive-offensive operations in the

SW Ukraine. Senger was promoted to General-leutnant on 1 May 43, and six weeks later he was chief LnO with the Italian army in Sicily.

Senger was highly successful in coordinating the operations of Italian forces with those of Hans HUBE. The high-level LnO served next on the army commission for administration of Corsica and Sardinia and performed skilfully in extricating German troops. These four months were not made easier by his distaste for National Socialism being exceeded only by his disdain for Fascism.

Again returning with a vengeance to the war Senger succeeded Hans "the Man" Hube on 23 Oct 43 as the 14th Pz Corps commander in Italy. For the next six months he faced heavy odds in checking repeated attacks on the 5th US Army front. A general of panzer troops from 1 Jan 44 he was particularly successful in the battles for Cassino. "His objectiveness makes his evidence about the unjustified destruction of the Abbey of Monte Cassino by bombing all the more impressive and convincing," comments Liddell Hart in his foreword to Senger's memoirs (page 7). The general figured prominently in KESSELRING's remarkable defensive operations, serving in Joachim LEMELSEN's 14th Army from 5 June 44. "His narrative of the closing stages of the war in Italy is . . . fascinating, and a real contribution to history" (ibid.). After being involved in Karl WOLFE's politically dangerous peace negotiations Senger was a POW from 22 May 45 to 18 May 46. Freed in Holland after leaving a camp in England he reached Goettingen by train from Hanover in the middle of the night and walked the rest of the way home. "I wondered how I would summon P. without arousing all the others," he writes. "Very quietly I stepped into the garden behind the house and gave the low whistle that was our special signal. P. appeared on the veranda."

His memoirs, which Fred Majdalany called "important as well as fascinating," were published as *Krieg in Europa* (Cologne and Berlin: Keipenheuer & Wisch, 1960). The US edition is *Neither Fear nor Hope* (New York: Dutton, 1964).

SEYDLITZ-KURZBACH, Walter Kurt von. 1888-1976. After surrendering at Stalingrad he headed an anti-Nazi propaganda organization in the USSR.

Walter von Seydlitz-Kurzbach was born on 22 Aug 88 at Eppendorf-Hamburg. After about 16 months as an artillery officer candidate he was commissioned on 27 Jan 10. Oberst Seydlitz commanded the 102d Arty Regt in Poland (Sep 39). He led the 12th Inf Div in France and was awarded the RK on 15 Aug 40. With AG North in Opn **Barbarossa** he was promoted to Generalmajor on 1 Dec 41 (still commanding the 12th Inf Div). For action with the 16th Army on the S flank of AG North he was given the Oakleaves (54/890) on 31 Dec 41.

Seydlitz then had the major role in a desperate action to relieve the German 2d Corps in the Demyansk pocket. (The action was against the NW Front of P. A. Kurochkin, whose deputy was the redoubtable VATUTIN.) At dawn on 27 Mar 42 Seydlitz hit between the 1st and 11th Shock Armies with overpowering artillery and air support. In 30 days of heavy work he penetrated one defensive line after another to reach the Lovat River and link up with the 2d Corps. (Erickson, *To Stalingrad,* 332.) In June 42 Seydlitz was promoted to General of Artillery and given command of the 51st Corps. When this was trapped with the 6th Army in Stalingrad Seydlitz tried unsuccessfully in November to convince PAULUS to attempt a break-out. Then, after Paulus made an unauthorized withdrawal to strengthen his position, Hitler removed the 51st Corps from his operational control.

Seydlitz surrendered before Paulus did on 31 Jan 43, for which Hitler sentenced him to death *in absentia.*

The Russians prevailed on Seydlitz to head the anti-Nazi League of German Officers. Taking over in the summer or fall of 1943 he performed the same propaganda functions as did the Free Germany National Committee, formed a year earlier. PAULUS joined after the 20 July 44 attempt on Hitler's life. Ironically, Paulus's change of heart convinced the Russians that they no longer needed Seydlitz (Wistrich), but in Oct 47 the two turncoats were said to be commanding several divisions composed mainly of Germans captured at Stalingrad. (Davidson, *Trial,* 361, 530, 542.)

With most other captured senior generals Seydlitz was released by the Soviets in 1955, but the Germans held him another nine months until the *in absentia* death sentence was finally annulled in July 1956. (Wistrich.) He died 28 Apr 76 in Bremen.

SEYSS-INQUART, Artur von. Nazi official. 1892-1946. An ethnic German, Seyss was born 22 July 92 at the village of Stannern, near Iglau, Austria, where his father was a secondary school teacher. The family moved to Vienna when Artur was 15. He studied law before seeing action in Russia and on the Italian front in WWI. Seyss (pronounced sice) was wounded seriously and decorated for valor while serving in the Tyrolean Imperial Chasseurs (*Kaiserjaeger*). In 1917 Seyss got a law decree while on furlough, and after the war his practice prospered mildly. (Davidson, *Trial,* 447.) Devotedly Catholic and anti-Semitic the attorney believed the only hope for Austria was **Anschluss,** and he joined the German Brotherhood, one of many secret nationalist organizations dedicated to achieving this goal. Intelligent, pleasant, and ambitious, Seyss became state counselor in May 37. When Hitler coerced SCHUSCHNIGG into aligning his government more closely with the Third Reich, the Austrian chancellor selected Seyss as a man he could work with. Becoming minister of the interior on 16 Feb 38 Seyss succeeded SCHUSCHNIGG on 2 Mar 38 and was chancellor until the Germans took over four days later. Davidson comments that Seyss had not wanted to be a Trojan horse, and after being forced into that role treated Schuschnigg well, taking him home in his own car. (Ibid, 452, 454.).

Rewarded with the rank of SS Generalleutnant (15 Mar 38) he served until 30 Apr 39 as Reich governor (Statthalter) of the new German province called Ostmark. He then was minister without portfolio in Hitler's cabinet *(S&S).* Seyss set up the **Generalgouvernment** in Poland, being in the country briefly from 12 Oct 39 and serving as Hans FRANK's deputy. So far Scyss had done nothing to warrant later charges of war crimes (Davidson, 457).

Seyss became Reich Commissioner (Reichkommissar) of the Netherlands on 18 May 40 and remained for the duration. Directly subordinate to Hitler, he was the supreme civil power of the German government in Holland and had complete legislative authority. In his political testament Hitler named his fellow Austrian foreign minister, but DOENITZ picked Count Schwerin von Krosigk.

An honest, basically decent bureaucrat who claimed to have done his best for the Dutch (ibid.), Seyss was convicted at Nuremberg of war crimes and crimes against humanity. He was charged with presiding over the shipment of art treasures and industrial and economic resources to Germany along with levies of forced labor. Of 140,000 Dutch Jews, only 8,000 survived in hiding and only 5,450 came home from camps in Poland and Czechoslovakia. (Davidson, 466 and n). The proconsul was hanged on 16 Oct 46 in Nuremberg prison.

SHAPOSHNIKOV, Boris Mikhaylovich. Soviet military leader. 1882-1945. The highly regarded but physically ailing Shaposhnikov was CGS from May 37 to 14 Aug 40, and again from 29 July 41 to 26 June 42.

He was born 2 Oct 82 at Zlatoust, a city in the southern Urals. His father was a distillery manager and his mother a schoolmistress (Scarecrow). In 1901 he joined the Tsarist army, becoming an officer two years after graduating from the Moscow Military College. Shaposhnikov subsequently rose to command infantry and Cossack units in Turkestan, attaining the rank of colonel. Demobilized in 1918, he joined the Red Army and during the civil war was chief of operations for the field staff.

Non-peasant origin, good education, a cultured manner, and Tsarist army background made Shaposhnikov politically suspect. Not until 1930 was he granted Party membership, although this still was 10 years ahead of most other former officers of the Russian rmy (HFS). Meanwhile the general, although not among the early marshals of the Soviet Union, was the Red army's CGS from 1928. But in 1931 he was replaced by a younger rival, Tukhachevsky, who is said to have conspired to have his superior ousted (Sudoplatov, 90). Demoted to head the Frunze MA, Shaposhnikov sat on the special court in 1937 that condemned TUKHACHEVSKY on trumped-up charges of treason. His former rival executed in May 37, Shaposhnikov immediately succeed the doomed Marshal A. I. Yegorov as CGS and deputy commissar of defense. Sharing Tukhachevsky's progressive doctrinal views, the more experienced Shaposhnikov also had the executive ability to modernize and revitalize the Red Army. As author of the three-volume *Mozg armii* (*The Brain of the Army*), published 1926-29, he was known internationally. But political insecurity made the CGS unduly submissive to Stalin and senior political generals like MEKHLIS and VORO-

SHILOV. The CGS could not keep D. G. PAVLOV from disbanding the Red rmy's large armored formations in Nov 39. The Finland fiasco a few months later resulted from Stalin's allowing MERETSKOV to ignore Shaposhnikov's advice, but "his was evidently the brain behind the revised Soviet operational plans" with which TIMOSHENKO finally won the Winter War of 1939-40 (Erickson, *To Stalingrad,* 17).

A marshal of the Soviet Union on 7 May 40, the CGS was succeeded by MERETSKOV on 14 Aug 40 because of ill health but he remained deputy commissar of defense. In the crisis following the German invasion that began on 22 June 41, Shaposhnikov's strategic plans for defense were rejected for those of MEKHLIS, which is one reason why the scapegoat D. G. PAVLOV did not have a fighting chance. Shaposhnikov served very briefly in the field as TIMOSHENKO's CofS 21-29 July 41. But he was called back suddenly as CGS when ZHUKOV left that post for the front. Shaposhnikov served 11 months this time before bad health again intervened. Replaced on 26 June 42 by his protégé VASILEVSKY the old Tsarist remained on the Stavka and as deputy commissar of defense (May 42-June 43). His principal duty now was revising military manuals (Scarecrow). He headed the General Staff Academy from June 43 and served as a Stavka member until 17 Feb 45. Long in failing health, he died 26 Mar 45 of tuberculosis in Moscow at the age of 62. Boris Mikhaylovich Shaposhnikov's ashes are in the Kremlin Wall.

SHCHADENKO, Yefim Afanasyevich. Soviet leader. 1885-1951. In a class with the villainous KULIK and MEKHLIS (Khrushchev, 163), Shchadenko was born in Kamensk, Rostov Province, the son of a worker. His CP membership dates from 1905 (Scarecrow). Before Oct 17 he was a tailor's assistant, then he became active in the revolution, helping establish the Soviet regime in the Don area. In 1918 he joined the Red Army, commanded a cavalry detachment, and in 1920 fought against Generals Denikin and Wrangel. He was assistant commandant (political) at the Frunze MA before joining the military council of the Kiev MD, 1937-38. For the next two years he was chief of the main personnel board of the defense ministry, then chief of the main musters board and

deputy MOD. In Kiev and Moscow he was active in finding victims for the **Great Purges.** "In the autumn of 1941 Mekhlis and Shchadenko still worked hand in glove," writes Seaton, citing GORBATOV, "and . . . could effect the arrest and imprisonment of senior army commanders" (*Stalin,* 127). In 1943, with the rank of general colonel, he was on the Southern Front's military council until forced by bad health to become inactive. He died 6 Sep 51.

SHCHERBAKOV, Aleksandr Sergeyevich. Soviet official. 1901-45. "One of the most contemptible characters around Stalin during the war . . . a poisonous snake," writes Khrushchev, to which the editor adds, "Fat, spectacularly gross, treacherous, and drunken, he was very close to Stalin, and during the war many in Russia believed that he was a probable successor to Stalin" (*Khrushchev,* 171 and n.).

Shcherbakov was born 10 Oct 01 in Ruza, near Moscow, of working class parents. Having been a printer's apprentice in Rybinsk (later renamed for him), he joined the Red Guards in 1917 at the age of 16. Active throughout Russia in party work, Shcherbakov also edited a newspaper and became secretary of the USSR Writers' Union in 1934. Two years later he replaced Khrushchev as 1st Secretary of the Moscow Party Organization, serving to 1945. From 1941 he was a candidate member of the Politburo and a party secretary.

In June 42 he succeeded MEKHLIS as head of the Red Army Political Directorate and Deputy Commissar of Defense, and he also headed the Soviet Information Bureau. In Dec 42 he was promoted to general lieutenant, and the next year to general colonel. After a long illness he died 10 May 45 of a heart attack. His ashes are in the Kremlin Wall.

SHERMAN, Frederick Carl. US admiral. 1888-1957. "Ted" Sherman was born in Port Huron, Mich, on 27 May 88. He won honors at Annapolis in boxing, lacrosse, and sailing, graduating in 1910 (24/131). Aboard battleships until 1914, he then was ordered to take submarine training. After serving in H-1 and commanding H-2 he fitted out and commanded 0-7 on Atlantic patrols during WWI. Subsequent duties included command of Sub Div 9 and two destroyer divisions. Despite his age, 48, he qualified as a naval aviator in 1936.

In June 40 Sherman took command of CV *Lexington* and with HALSEY in CV *Enterprise* was near Midway when Pearl Harbor was attacked on 7 Dec 41. He took part in HALSEY's subsequent operations, commanding the *Lexington-Yorktown* group in Mar 42 off New Guinea, and was promoted on 3 Apr 42 to rear admiral. In the Battle of the Coral Sea, planes from *Lexington* sank the Japanese carrier *Shoho* on 7 May 42. But *Lexington* was crippled the next day by planes from Taekeo Takagi's carriers. After several hours of unsuccessful damage control Sherman gave orders to abandon ship and was the last to leave.

Rear Adm Sherman served briefly on Ernest J. King's staff before returning to the south Pacific in November to command Carrier TF 16 (RCS). In HALSEY's 3d Fleet of SOPAC (supporting MacArthur) he led successful carrier strikes in the South Pacific. Sherman took over Carrier Div 2 with flag aboard CV *Enterprise* for the Solomons campaign. In July 43 he moved aboard CV *Saratoga* to head Carrier Div 2 for strikes against Rabaul and for landings on Bougainville and the Gilberts in November. From then until Feb 44 his raids on bases in the south and central Pacific sank 46 ships and destroyed nearly 350 planes. (RCS.)

Redeployed for a rest, he was Commander, Fleet Air, West, from March to Aug 44. He returned to action for the Leyte campaign. As Commander TG 38.3/58.3 he was stationed east of Luzon as the northernmost element of HALSEY's 3d Fleet. His task group bore the brunt of land based air attacks from Clark Field and Manila on 24 Oct 44: CL *Princeton* sank after taking a bomb that exploded below decks; CL *Birmingham* was badly damaged; and five destroyers were hit. But on the same day Sherman's planes attacked KURITA's Force A in San Bernadino Strait, helping sink the super-battleship *Musashi*. Some three weeks later, 11 November, Sherman's group destroyed an effort by Adm Naomasa SAKONJU to convoy 15,000 troops to reinforce Sosaku SUZUKI on Leyte.

Sherman then took part in the audacious fast carrier raids in the South China Sea and into Japanese home waters. After supporting the landings on Iwo Jima and Okinawa, and making further raids to Japan, Sherman was promoted in July 45 to vice admiral and given command of the 1st Carrier TF, Pacific Fleet, for the rest of the war.

Ted Sherman headed the 5th Fleet from January until 3 Sep 46, retiring from active duty on 1 Mar 47 as a four-star admiral. He died 27 July 57 at the San Diego USNH of a heart attack.

SHERMAN, Forrest Percival. US admiral. 1896-1951. A leading naval strategist during and after the war, Forrest Sherman was born 30 Oct 96 in Merrimack, NH, but reared in Melrose, Mass. He spent a year at MIT awaiting appointment to Annapolis (from Maine), then graduated high (2/199) in the early section of the Class of 1918. Sherman went to the Mediterranean for escort and patrol duty, served briefly on a destroyer in the Atlantic, and after the war was on a battleship and on two destroyers. He was an aide to Commander, Control Force, before taking flight training in 1922. After a year in a fighter squadron and two as an instructor at Pensacola, he attended the Naval War College, 1926-27. Sherman then was aviation officer for Adm Claude C. Bloch during the latter's service as Commander, Battle Force, and then as Commander, US Fleet, 1937-40. Early in 1940, Comdr Sherman was assigned to the Navy War Plans Division when Harold R. STARK was CNO.

In addition to a brilliant mind Sherman had skill as a mediator while serving on the Canadian-US Joint Board. He accompanied the CNO to the Churchill-Roosevelt meeting at Argentia in Aug 41. Six months later he was transferred to the Joint War Plans Committee. Promoted in May 42, Capt Sherman took command of the 14,700-ton CVL *Wasp* when she was moved from the Atlantic for landings on Guadalcanal that began 7 Aug 42. Hit by three torpedoes on 15 Sep 42, the carrier was turned into an inferno and had to be abandoned. Capt Sherman spent two hours in the water with survivors, suffering internal injuries from US depth charges directed against Japanese submarines. On recovery he became CofS to John Towers, the new Commander, Naval Air, Pacific. Sherman so impressed NIMITZ as a mediator in a difficult command relationship with Towers that Sherman became Nimitz's CofS at CINCPAC Hq in Nov 43. He was promoted at this time to rear admiral. The following March Sherman was made chief of war plans, Nimitz's alter ego and often CINCPAC's representative at conferences in Washington.

In Dec 45 Nimitz made Sherman his deputy CNO for operations. Promoted at this time, Vice Adm Sherman was responsible for strategic intelligence, fleet operations, and training. He worked with presidential adviser Clark Clifford and Lauris NORSTAD on negotiations for what became the National Security ("Unification") Act of 1947. In Jan 48 Sherman became Commander Naval Forces in the Mediterranean, and later was commander of the 6th Fleet. The "revolt of the admirals" cut short Louis Denfeld's tour as CNO after only two years, and Sherman succeeded him on 2 Nov 49. Promoted at this time to full admiral, he was the youngest ever to have the post and the first airman to hold it in peacetime. As CNO he was among the first to support Truman's recall of MACARTHUR in early 1951.

He died 22 July 51 in Naples after a series of heart attacks while on a trip to negotiate for bases in Spain.

SHIGEMITSU, Mamoru. Japanese statesman. 1887-1957. A career foreign service officer considered a moderate, he served briefly after the first world war as consul at Portland, Maine, and for many years in China. The diplomat lost his left leg in 1932, and NOMURA lost an eye, when a Korean terrorist tossed a bomb into a group of Japanese celebrating their victory in Shanghai. Shigemitsu was ambassador to Moscow in 1938 and negotiated a settlement that preceded the final Russo-Japanese clash at **Khalkhin Gol.**

From late 1938 he was ambassador to London. After Japan joined the Axis the ambassador tried to give assurances that this did not mean war with Britain. Recalled in June 41 he spent two weeks in Washington conferring with NOMURA and US officials.

It was hoped in the west that Shigemitsu would succeed MATSUOKA as foreign minister. But he was sent two days after the Pearl Harbor attack (7 Dec 41) as ambassador to the Chinese puppet regime at Nanking. He took the lead in convincing TOJO that success of the Co-prosperity Sphere depended on ceasing to treat China as a colony (Toland, *Sun,* 449.) In Apr 43 Shigemitsu was made foreign minister (changing posts with Masayuki Tani) and he had considerable success in extending his "good neighbor" policy throughout the rest of Asia. (Ibid.) Although supposedly hoping to negotiate a peace, in Dec 43, the second

anniversary of the Tripartite Pact, he made a speech calling for Japan and Germany to fight on. Shigemitsu was replaced by Shigenori TOGO when the Kantaro SUZUKI cabinet was formed on 5 Apr 45, but on 17 Aug 45 he came back as foreign minister in the "surrender government" of HIGASHIKUNI.

In great pain from a new artificial leg Shigemitsu hobbled up the gangway of *Missouri* and then up a ladder for the surrender ceremony on 2 Sep 45. With 24 others he was convicted of war crimes but was the only one found not guilty of the conspiracy charge. He and KOISO also were the only ones convicted of negligence in not preventing atrocities. Sentenced to seven years' imprisonment Shigemitsu later was foreign minister several more times. On the last occasion he served to within a few weeks of his death on 25 Jan 57.

SHIMADA, Shigetaro. Japanese admiral. 1883-1976. Navy minister in the TOJO government formed on 18 Oct 41, he was picked by the elder statesmen (*genro*) for his reputed sympathy for the army's political outlook (Morison, VI, 20). The admiral was so faithful as to be called "Tojo's briefcase carrier" (*kaban-mochi*). When TOJO relieved SUGIYAMA as army CofS on 21 Feb 44 and personally took over the ousted general's duties Tojo ordered Shimada to follow suit and personally succeed NAGANO. "Kill Tojo and Shimada!" signs appeared in some navy offices after the Japanese lost Saipan in early July 44 (Toland, *Sun,* 507). With great reluctance Tojo ordered Shimada to resign, which he did on 18 July 44. The next day Tojo had to resign, and YONAI succeeded Shimada.

Given life imprisonment for war crimes, the admiral was free by 1956 and lived another 20 years.

SHORT, Walter Campbell. US general. 1880-1949. Remembered as the army commander responsible for the defense of Pearl Harbor, Walter Short was born 30 Mar 80 in Fillmore, Ill. A physician's son, he graduated from the Univ of Illinois in 1901 and accepted a commission as an infantry officer the next year. He went to France during the first world war but served exclusively in noncombat assignments, mainly as a training officer. As assistant commandant at the Infantry School, Ft Benning, Ga, he was promoted to brigadier general in 1936. A month after the war started in Europe he took command of the 1st Inf Div, and in the expansion of 1940 he was promoted to major general commanding the 1st Corps. Four months later, on 8 Feb 41, he took command of the Hawaiian Dept, being promoted on that date to lieutenant general. A week earlier Husband E. KIMMEL had become CINCPAC with headquarters at Pearl Harbor.

The surprise attack hit Oahu on 7 Dec 41, and both senior commanders were recalled 10 days later, Short replaced by Delos C. Emmons and Kimmel by Chester NIMITZ.

Short reverted to his permanent rank of major general on 18 Dec 41 and retired at the end of Feb 42. Having served 40 years, the 61-year-old general became traffic manager of the Ford Motor Co. in Dallas, Tex., the following September (*CB 46*).

The Roberts Commission, first of eight Pearl Harbor investigations, found Kimmel and Short guilty primarily of not coordinating with each other to defend the Hawaiian Islands. An army investigation found Short himself derelict in directing proper staff work. There was public clamor to court-martial both commanders but they waived the two-year statute of limitations.

The general made no public statement until the last Pearl Harbor investigation began on 15 Nov 45, arguing then that he had not been given adequate warning from Washington and had lacked the resources to defend Oahu. The conclusion after eight months of inquiry was that officials both in Washington and Hawaii were derelict. The smallish, dapper general, never given the court-martial he now requested and maintaining his conscience was clear, died in Dallas, Tex, on 3 Sep 49 at the age of 69.

SHTEMENKO, Sergei Matveevich. Red Army operations officer. 1907-76. Born 20 Feb 07 in Volgograd Oblast and becoming a brilliant staff officer, Shtemenko took part in the invasions of Poland and Finland, 1939-40, while a student at the Academy of the General Staff (GS). He then rose in the GS Office of Operations from lieutenant colonel serving as senior assistant to a section chief in 1940 to be deputy chief in Aug 41. Still a lieutenant colonel when the Germans invaded on 22 June 41, he then was made chief of a section. In Apr 43 he became first deputy chief under ANTONOV, succeeding Antonov on 25 May 43 and holding the critical post until Apr 46. Confident and brash (HFS), the youthful

Shtemenko not only survived close contact with Stalin, whom he genuinely admired, but also prospered professionally, being a general colonel before the war ended.

On 12 Nov 48 he was made a general of the army (No. 30) and CGS. In Dec 52, only two months after being elected a candidate member of the CC CPSU and while Stalin was still alive, he suffered the first in an unexplained series of career reverses. Demoted and replaced by SOKOLOVSKY, he went to Germany as CofS of the occupation forces. In 1953, during the post-Stalin power struggle that made BULGANIN head of the Soviet armed forces, Shtemenko was recalled from Germany, demoted, and not seen for three years. (Kruzhin, 10.) In 1956, when ZHUKOV was MOD, Shtemenko became head of the GS Main Intelligence Directorate. The next year he was promoted back to general colonel. His professional fortunes seeming to wax and wane with those of ZHUKOV, in 1957 Shtemenko again was demoted and given minor posts (first deputy CG, Volga MD, then of the Transcaucasus MD). (Ibid.) In Feb 68 he was once again promoted to general of the army; six months later he was CofS, Warsaw Pact Armed Forces, and masterminded the invasion of Czechoslovakia. (HFS.) He died 23 Apr 76 in Moscow (HFS), two months after his 69th birthday.

Excerpts from Shtemenko's interesting articles on operations of the Soviet general staff are in Bialer's *Stalin and His Generals* (1969). His memoirs are *General'nyi Shtab v Godoy Voiny* (2 vols, Moscow, 1968, 1973).

SIKORSKI, Wladislaw. Polish statesman. 1881-1943. First head of the "London Poles," he was born 20 May 81 in Tuszow, near Sandomierz, central Poland *(CB 40)*. Sikorski was conscripted into the Austro-Hungarian Army in 1905, was placed on the reserve list a year later as a lieutenant, and resumed his education in the Polytechnic Institute of Lvov. During and after the first world war he served under Marshal Josef Pilduski, winning praise from Marshal Foche for outstanding generalship in the Franco-Polish campaign of 1920 that routed the Bolsheviks outside Warsaw. (WEYGAND headed the French mission.) Sikorski was CGS in 1922 when asked to form a government after the assassination of Pres Narutowicz. For the next six years he held various cabinet posts until dismissed in 1928 by Pilduski. He meanwhile had retired from the army in 1926.

When Poland fell in 1939 Sikorski was named to head a cabinet in exile. This was located at Angers until the fall of France, then in London. The highly regarded general worked effectively to form new combat units from tens of thousands of Polish military refugees. In the diplomatic field he effected a rapprochement with the Czechs and had considerable success with the Soviets. But after Wladislaw ANDERS's release from POW status to form a Polish army in Russia, Soviet-Polish relations were severely set back by revelations of the **Katyn Forest massacre.** The general was again making progress toward accommodation with the Russians when killed on 4 July 43 in a plane crash near Gibraltar. Foul play was suspected but never proved. MIKOLAJCZYK took over as head of the London Poles.

SIKORSKY, Igor Ivan(ovich). US aircraft designer. 1889-1972. Born in Kiev on 25 May 89 he fled the Russian revolution, leaving behind $500,000 in government bonds and real estate (*CB 40*). Via Paris and London he reached America in Mar 19, virtually penniless and speaking no English. Already well established as an aircraft designer and producer he formed (in 1923) what became the United Aircraft Corporation's Vought-Sikorsky Aircraft Division after the 1929 stock market crash. He had been naturalized in 1922. Sikorsky specialized in large flying boats and pioneered development of heavy-lift helicopters.

SIMONDS, Guy Grenville. Canadian general. 1903-74. A career officer, Maj Simonds went overseas in Dec 39 with McNAUGHTON'S staff of the 1st Cdn Div. He served on Montgomery's staff in North Africa before becoming the Canadian army's youngest general officer and taking command of the 2d Cdn Div. After H. L. N. Salmon's death on 29 Apr 43 in an aircraft accident Simonds succeeded him as head of the 1st Cdn Div, the only Canadian division in the Sicily campaign (Nicholson, *Italy,* 30). The young and inexperienced Simonds pushed north rapidly on the 8th Army's left flank against elements of the elite Hermann Goering Div before wheeling NE against an Italian division to skirt Mt Etna. Put in reserve as the campaign drew to

an end, Simonds and his troops had won Montgomery's admiration (*Memoirs,* 166). Monty would later call Simonds "the best product on the Allied side" (*S&S*).

After crossing to Italy he was invalided out with jaundice, soon after 22 Sep 43, and not back with his division until 15 Oct 43. Two weeks later he left again, this time to await arrival of his new command, the 5th Cdn Armd Div. After leading both infantry and armor in action he returned to England with a brilliant reputation and took command of the 2d Cdn Corps on 30 Jan 44. As part the British 2d Army, 4-31 July, he was heavily engaged south of Caen with vicious counterattacks by EBERBACH's strong panzer forces. Always an effective innovator, Simonds pioneered the Allied use of armored personnel carriers known as "Kangaroos" (Stacey, II, 210n.) CRERAR's 1st Cdn Army Hq was operational on 23 Jul 44 and about a week later it was assigned Simonds's corps and the 1st British Corps.

After failing to trap the Germans by closing the gap at Falaise, CRERAR's army broke out of the Normandy bridgehead and moved north along the Channel coast to overrun V-1 launching sites and take badly needed ports. Montgomery then gave Crerar the mission of clearing the Scheldt estuary and opening access to the much-needed port of Antwerp. Simonds argued for a combined operation against the western tip of Walchern Island. He proposed that dykes be bombed to flood the large portion of the island below sea level and that Germans still above water be pounded day and night by bombers. To further demoralize the enemy, all flights of heavy bombers headed to and from targets in Germany should be routed over Walchern! When patrols reported that the enemy was sufficiently demoralized, parachute and amphibious assaults would be launched after a final bombing and artillery shelling had driven the enemy into their holes. (Stacey, II, 369-71.) Crerar initially disapproved the unconventional strategy but then decided it was worth a try. But Crerar needed hospitalization for jaundice so he turned over command of the army to Simonds temporarily. Simonds was refused the use of airborne troops and not allocated the great bombing effort he wanted. This probably delayed the opening of the port of Antwerp and certainly ran up the price in Allied casualties (Stacey, II, 425). But the operation was a success. Crerar sent

Simonds the message: "My sincere congratulations . . . the battle reputation of the First Cdn Army has never stood higher" (Ibid.).

After his final campaigns under CRERAR Lt Gen Simonds headed Cdn Forces in the Netherlands and was Canada's CGS, 1951-55.

SIMPSON, William Hood. US general. 1888-1980. "If Simpson ever made a mistake as an army commander, it never came to my attention," wrote Eisenhower (*Crusade,* 416).

He was born in Texas on 19 May 88 near Weatherford, west of Fort Worth, son of a Confederate veteran. Almost last in the USMA Class of 1909 (101/103), he served with Pershing's **Punitive Expedition** in Mexico before going to France. Under Maj Gen George Bell, Jr, CG, 33d Inf Div, he rose from aide de camp to CofS. He was awarded the DSM and SS.

Simpson was on the WDGS 1928-32 and in June 40 took command of the 9th Inf Regt, 2d Inf Div. Ten months later he was given command of the army's infantry replacement training center, then he commanded several infantry divisions before becoming CG, 12th Corps, and being promoted to lieutenant general on 13 Oct 43. Simpson then took over the 4th Army Hq when it was separated from the Western Defense Command. The staff moved from San Jose, Calif, to the Presidio, then in Jan 44 to Ft Sam Houston, Texas.

After Simpson's staff provided cadre for the 8th Army Hq he took an advance party to the UK in Apr 44. But to avoid confusion with the British 8th Army of western desert fame the new US field army was redesignated the 9th on 22 May 44 (*AA,* 500). Simpson established his headquarters at Bristol on 29 June, D+23. The 9th US Army became operational on 5 Sep 44 in Omar Bradley's 12th US AG. With five infantry divisions of Troy Middleton's 8th Corps and supporting troops Simpson had "Fortress Brest" as his first major objective. Hermann RAMCKE surrendered to MIDDLETON on 18 Sep 44. The 9th Army also contained German pockets at Lorient and St Nazaire and covered the 12th AG's southern flank along the Loire as far east at Orleans. Rear area operations completed, Simpson moved his headquarters in early October to a position opposite the Siegfried Line between US 1st and 3d Armies. Less than a month later it moved to the north

flank of American forces. Because of these deployments, Simpson for a while had units dispersed in five countries, France, Holland, Belgium, Luxembourg, and Germany. From the Ardennes crisis in Dec 44, through the Rhine crossing and envelopment of the Ruhr Simpson was in Montgomery's 21st (British) AG. He then reverted to Bradley's 12th (US) AG.

The tall, completely bald "Big Simp" was nominated for a fourth star as the war ended but a serious stomach disorder forced him to retire on 30 Nov 46 as a lieutenant general. He was promoted to general on the retired list in 1954 and died 15 Aug 80 in San Antonio.

SKORZENY, Otto. German officer. 1908-67. A burly six-feet-four-inches tall, always physically fit, marked by a conspicuous dueling scar from the left cheekbone to the tip of his massive jaw, the "commando extraordinary" was born 12 June 08 in Vienna. He was an ethnic German whose family—and name—came from the East Pomeranian village of Scorzencin. As an engineering student in Vienna he fought 15 of the ritual sabre duels popular among certain Teutonic types. In the 10th of these encounters Skorzeny's left cheek was laid open, sewn up on the spot without anesthetic, and the meeting went on for the prescribed time.

Believing that union with Germany was his country's only way out of its desperate economic predicament Skorzeny joined the Austrian Nazi Party in 1930. He was useful to the Nazis during the **Anschluss** (1938), showing a cool head in crises and becoming KALTENBRUNNER's protégé.

The 31-year-old Skorzeny was busy as part owner of a Vienna construction firm when faced with conscription. To avoid the monotony of army life he tried to join the Luftwaffe for pilot training but was rejected for age. After five months' training with a Luftwaffe communications depot in Vienna he volunteered for the elite SS-Leibstandarte Adolf Hitler (**LAH** or LSSAH). Becoming an artillery officer-cadet on 21 Feb 40, the day his daughter was born, he left to join the regiment's reserve battalion in the Berlin area. The fighting had ended when his unit moved through France into the Netherlands and prepared for the invasion of England that never came.

Sent to Yugoslavia for the Balkan campaign newly commissioned Leutnant Skorzeny was leading his platoon on a patrol when approached by a much larger but unsuspecting enemy force. Ordering his men to hold their fire, the hulking lieutenant jumped up, commanded his surprised opponents to surrender, and took 63 prisoners including three officers. The action brought promotion to Oberleutnant for "bravery in the face of the foe" (not for good thinking) but it showed Skorzeny that cool nerves and discipline can achieve more than hot lead.

The Viennese giant served in Russia until invalided home at the end of 1942 with a severe head wound, gall stones, and an Iron Cross. Classified "fit for home service only" he rode a desk in a repair depot until the spring of 1943. Hitler had become more inclined toward drastic measures after Rommel's defeat at El Alamein, the Stalingrad disaster, and Roosevelt's unconditional surrender announcement at Casablanca. On 20 Apr 43 Skorzeny was promoted to captain and named "Chief of Germany's Special Troops, Existing or to be Created in the Future" (Foley, 33). He set up shop near Berlin in a hunting lodge at Friedenthal (Valley of Peace!), inheriting three "spy schools." With an Austrian comrade, Karl Radl, as his deputy he began assembling "special forces" and studying records of British commando raids. He was particularly interested in Robert E. LAYCOCK's attempt to eliminate Rommel and he grasped the importance of hitting at the "brains" of the enemy (Tunney). Initial missions in the Middle East and Russia failed largely because higher headquarters imposed political and military obstructions (Wistrich).

Mussolini

But Hitler picked Capt Skorzeny on 26 July 43 to find and rescue Mussolini. With STUDENT's support the feat was undertaken on 12 Sep 43. Crash landing in a glider within a few feet of a small hotel on a 6,000-foot-high plateau in the Gran Sasso massif, Skorzeny and nine others neutralized the Carabiniere guard without firing a shot and quickly persuaded the rest of the 250-man garrison to surrender. Cramming the Duce between his knees in a Storch piloted by Student's personal pilot he made a miraculous escape from the plateau and flew to Rome. In Vienna, en route to Hitler's Hq, Skorzeny was awarded a Knight's Cross and notified of his promotion to major.

In a flush of enthusiasm Hitler directed Skorzeny to form a battalion of special forces for every front and authorized him to take 4,000 officers and men from the **Brandenburg Div.**

Pétain-Tito

Hitler also asked for two more political hits: kidnap Pétain and get Tito dead or alive. (There were reports that the Vichy head of state might defect, or that the Free French might take drastic action to neutralize his continued support of the Nazis. Tito had become too much a thorn in Hitler's side.) Skorzeny spent a month slinking around Vichy incognito before being ordered home and sent to get Tito. Flying to Belgrade, and unable to learn from German intelligence where the partisan leader was, Skorzeny spent a month driving through the country with two NCOs to find out. Locating Tito's secret headquarters in the Drvar Valley of western Bosnia, the commando chief prepared to infiltrate Tito's well guarded and virtually inaccessible cave with men disguised as partisans. When he undertook the necessary coordination with German forces in the region he found that their general would not abandon his own plans for a hamhanded conventional military operation with bombers and airborne troops. Tito escaped this blow.

Skorzeny had a role in restoring order in Berlin after STAUFFENBERG's failed attempt to kill Hitler on 20 July 44, reaching the Bendlerstrasse with Kaltenbrunner at 1 AM on 21 July to halt the summary executions (W-B, *Nemesis,* 662).

Adm Horthy

The next adventure was in Budapest when Hitler learned that the Hungarian regent, Adm HORTHY, and his son Nicholas, were about to conclude a separate peace with the Soviets. This exposed a million German troops in the Carpathians to annihilation. In a dramatic shootout Skorzeny broke into a house where Nicholas was meeting with Soviet emissaries on Sunday 15 Oct 44 to initial the surrender pact. The young Horthy was waving his arms in vigorous protest when the huge Austrian had him rolled into a handy rug, trussed with a curtain rope, heaved into a truck, and taken to an awaiting plane for same-day air delivery to Germany. (Foley, *Skorzeny,* 94.)

Adm Horthy went on the radio at 2 PM to issue an outraged protest and announce that he had concluded an armistice with the Soviets. But his war office did not follow through with the prescribed orders for their armies to observe the regent's directive, so Skorzeny moved swiftly in the confused situation to stop Hungarian field forces from defecting. Rejecting BACH-ZELEWSKI's offer to use the monstrous 25-inch mortar he had brought from Warsaw, Skorzeny bluffed his way past Hungarian guard detachments into Adm Horthy's castle. The regent had fled the castle to seek protection from a German general who was related to the ex-Kaiser, but—his son a hostage—Horthy promptly announced his abdication. A few days later Skorzeny escorted the durable strong man to Germany.

His reputation enhanced, "the most dangerous man in Europe" was promoted to lieutenant colonel and awarded the **German Cross in Gold.** Although he remained active most of Skorzeny's subsequent missions were aborted—overtaken by events. After the Market-Garden failure Montgomery was using the two great Rhine River bridges at Nijmegen to build up a dangerous bridgehead, and powerful German attacks by ground and air forces had failed to take out the structures. But 15 of Skorzeny's frogmen did. Planting half-ton U-boat torpedoes under water on the massive pylons they blew a 70-yard gap in the railroad bridge and so badly damaged the highway bridge that it had to be replaced by a **Bailey.**

Opn Griffin

Hitler gave Lt Col Skorzeny a critical role in the Ardennes counteroffensive of Dec 44 (Opn **Griffin**). The fuehrer wanted his miracle man to raise an armored brigade of English-speaking personnel dressed in American uniforms and using enemy US materiel including 20 Sherman tanks! The bogus tank brigade was supposed to follow smaller units through the 6th SS Pz Army after it made a penetration and then to take the Meuse River bridges intact. Other commandos had the mission of creating chaos. But American uniforms and vehicles were not delivered in anything like the numbers promised. There were only two Sherman tanks, 10 "American armored cars," and 15 jeeps; a few German Fords were painted olive drab and some Czech and French cars were used.

German tanks and wheeled vehicles were painted in US colors with the conspicuous white stars. (Foley, 115.) With nothing like the necessary time for preparation there were other snafus. When the breakthrough still had not been made after 48 hours Skorzeny had his brigade throw off their disguises and advance like a standard formation. Finding a soft spot at Malmedy on 21 Dec he launched a two-pronged attack. But without artillery and having only 10 tanks left he was driven back by American reserves. By the end of the day Skorzeny had a head wound that almost cost him his right eye. A week later he was authorized to break contact and withdraw.

As for the "American" detachments, only 28 men ever got through the lines (Foley, 126), not the planned-for 50 jeep loads. Most of the bogus-GIs betrayed themselves by failing password and quiz tests and politely requesting "petrol" from roadside gas stations. But a few English-speaking commandos in Allied uniforms spread confusion among easily-confused US forces in rear areas.

Opn Griffin failed to capture the Meuse bridges, but its very name (from the mythical bird of prey) lent credence to the hoax that Skorzeny's mission was to assassinate Eisenhower, Montgomery, Omar Bradley, and possibly others. "Spies work in Allied uniforms," Eisenhower reported to George Marshall on 1 Jan 45, "and it appears certain that there was a definite assassination plot" (*EP,* 2391). Not until interviewing Skorzeny as a POW after his surrender did the Americans realize they had been had: Gen Walter Bedell SMITH so informed disgusted Allied war correspondents.

Field Commander

At the end of Jan 45 the commando chief was ordered to set up a bridgehead on the lower Oder River around Schwedt, some 80 kilometers NE of Berlin. This was in Himmler's AG Vistula, whose headquarters did not know how close the Russians were. On his first and only conventional military mission, Skorzeny ended up with a division-size command, a mixed bag of some 15,000 troops, and his outposts were holding off the Russians when he was recalled at the end of Feb 45. Although the BBC announced otherwise, Skorzeny was not promoted to Generalmajor, but he was awarded the Oakleaves to his RK. Ordered to organize an Alpine redoubt with headquarters in Hitler's Bergestgaden enclave, he and Karl Radl found that none of the necessary preparations had been made. The war had been over for 10 days when Col Skorzeny, Karl Radl, and two other officers, all in uniform and armed, descended from their mountain hideout and surrendered on 13 May 45.

Trying to Surrender

It wasn't easy. The American sergeant they first approached had never heard of the most dangerous man in Europe and was too busy to mess with prisoners. But the GI arranged for a jeep ride to Salzburg, where the bewildered commandos had to wait outside a hotel until their victors finished the lunch hour. A US major then sent the Germans off to pick up orders, which had to be signed in another town. Finally the conquering heroes woke up from their siesta, asked the Germans to wait in a room, and then broke through doors and windows, armed to the teeth, to "capture" their still-armed supplicants. (Foley, 152-53.)

Skorzeny was a prosecution witness at Nuremberg (Davidson, *Trial,* 159), after which he and fellow SS officers were arraigned before a US military court at Dachau in 1947. The prosecution dropped charges of murdering the American soldiers whose uniforms were later used in the Ardennes, and the commando chief was acquitted of wrongdoing in the latter act. Testifying on Skorzeny's behalf, YEO THOMAS pointed out that he himself had dressed French resistance agents in German uniforms. After a long trial that was skilfully handled by Lt Col Robert D. Durst, Skorzeny was cleared of all charges but not set free. It appeared that Denmark and Czechoslovakia wanted him extradited. This turned out not to be true but still he was held. At the request of the US Army Historical Section he and Radl prepared an account of the Mussolini rescue. Held in the interrogation cell at Oberusel, he had English lessons from Mildred "Axis Sally" GILLARS and while on parole he visited Hanna REITSCH in Oberusel. When his de-Nazification process continued to be delayed, Skorzeny wrote to Yeo Thomas for advice. "Escape!" replied the White Rabbit. Smuggled from a camp at Darmstadt in the trunk of a car on 27 July 48 he received hints that German authorities were glad to be rid of him. There were no charges, but the public thought he should be punished for *something.*

Postwar

After recuperating for several months in the mountains near Bergtesgaden, joined by his wife and eight-year-old daughter, he emerged from hiding to drive around Germany and France freely but as inconspicuously as possible. The Russians made two attempts to kidnap him (Foley, 4). Skorzeny finally accepted domicile in Spain on a **Nansen** passport and established a successful engineering firm in Madrid. Here, in 1954, he married a niece of Hjalmar SCHACHT's, Ilse Francisca Judhge. The Allied Control Office in Madrid, which investigated ex-enemy aliens, approved requests for travel documents, and the German court of Hessen finally cleared him of Nazi crimes. After publishing *Skorzeny's Special Missions* (New York: McGraw-Hill, 1957) the adventurer emerged periodically from the shadows. In 1959 he bought a summer estate in Kildare, Ireland, where he spent several months a year, and he also had a house in Mallorca. In the mid-1960s he was reported to be in Africa working with pro-Belgian mercenaries in Katanga and French ultra-rightists fleeing Algeria. It has been written that with the alias Robert Steinbacher, and with left-over Nazi funds, he founded Die Spinne (The Spider) and helped some 600 former SS men escape from Germany.

He died 5 July 75 at the age of 67 in a Madrid hospital of a lung ailment. This sketch draws on the obituary by Joseph Novitski, *Washington Post,* 8 July 75, page C 4. Biographies are C. Whiting, *Otto Skorzeny* (1971) and Charles Foley, *Commando Extraordinary* (The Noontide Press edition, (1988).

SLESSOR, John Cotesworth. British airman. 1897-1979. Born at Ranikhet, India, 3 June 97, the future air marshal was the son of a major of the Sherwood Foresters. Like so many other great military men, he was less interested in hard work at school than in making friends and enjoying life. (Max Hastings in *DNB*.) Childhood polio left him lame in both legs and, in the words of an army medical board in 1914, "totally unfit for any form of military service" (ibid.). With family influence he was commissioned in the RFC on his 18th birthday. Four months later he was in hot but futile pursuit of a zeppelin night raider over central London (ibid.).

The ardent young airman flew strafing and bombing missions in the Sinai and the Sudan with No. 17 Sqdn until invalided home in the spring of 1916 with a thigh wound and the MC. As a flight commander in No 5 Sqdn he flew in France for a year ending in June 18. Assigned to the new RAF as a flight lieutenant he became sufficiently disenchanted to leave the service, but two months of civilian life drove him back to the RAF in early 1920.

Between the wars he became a disciple of TRENCHARD and, like PORTAL, was "marked as an officer of exceptional ability, charm, and force of personality" (ibid.). His book *Air Power and Armies* (1936) propounded what became the British air doctrine of making war against enemy morale, which was known to be more vulnerable on the home front (ibid.). After being director of plans at the Air Ministry from 1937 he went with the British team to Washington at the end of 1940 for three months of staff talks to coordinate Allied war plans should the US enter the war.

At the end of these "ABC" discussions in Mar 41 he took over No. 5 Group of Bomber Command and was promoted to air vice marshal. It was a time when only RAF bombers could take the war to Germany, and Bomber Command's performance was poor. After a frustrating year Slessor became assistant chief of the air staff (policy) as PORTAL tried desperately to buck up Bomber Command. Slessor also worked with USAAF officers in planning a combined air offensive. In the Anglo-American disagreement over strategic air war the British insisted on night bombing as the only viable option, and the Americans insisted they could made a go of daylight bombing. Slessor saw military and political reasons to support the USAAF position. But Portal had convinced Churchill to urge that US production concentrate on **Lancasters** and that the USAAF abandon plans for daylight bombing. Slessor convinced Portal and Air Minister Sir Archibald Sinclair that their position might lead the US to shift all their strategic bombers to the Pacific (Allen Andrews, 218). At the Casablanca conference, in Jan 43 Slessor was largely responsible for the compromise outlined under SPAATZ. The decision also was made at Casablanca to direct more RAF resources against U-boats.

On returning to England from the conference Slessor headed Coastal [Air] Command. It was a particularly critical time; the British were los-

ing the Battle of the Atlantic and PORTAL was fighting to keep the Admiralty from taking over Coastal Command. In what has been called "the role for which he is best remembered" *(DNB)* he did much to start winning the Battle of the Atlantic. A splendid administrator and coordinator of air and naval forces of the UK, US, and Canada, he showed outstanding personal leadership in getting the best out of officers and men. Slessor was promoted in 1943 to air marshal and knighted that year (KCB).

After a year in Northwood as chief of Coastal Cmd Sir John somewhat reluctantly succeeded TEDDER as head of RAF formations in the Mediterranean and Middle East. Slessor also was Ira EAKER's deputy commander of MAAF, which supported the Italian campaign, the Yugoslav partisans, and made a vain attempt to supply the Warsaw insurgents under Tadeusz Bor-KOMOROWSKI.

Having remained in the Mediterranean until Mar 45 Slessor spent the next three years as air member for personnel. He was promoted to air chief marshal in 1946 and elevated in the knighthood to GCB in 1948. He headed the Imperial Defence College until Jan 50, then succeeded Tedder as CAS with rank as marshal of the RAF. He retired in 1953 to Somerset and remained active in many fields. As a theoritician of air power he published *Strategy for the West* (1954), and *The Great Deterrent* (1957), meaning air power. His lively autobiography is *The Central Blue* (1956).

Sir John Slessor died 12 July 79 in a hospital at Wroughton in Wiltshire. (Max Hastings in *DNB*.)

SLIM, William Joseph. British general. 1891-1970. A "ranker" whose promotion to field marshal did not keep the tough, lantern-jawed, unsmiling but very witty general from looking like a sardonic old sergeant, Bill Slim found full scope for his genius as 14th Army commander in Burma.

He was born in Bristol on 6 Aug 91. Too poor for a regular army career (the pay barely covering a dress uniform) he volunteered as a private in 1914. But he was promptly commissioned (22 Aug 14) in the Royal Warwickshire Regt. Posted to Mesopotamia, he went to fight in Gallipoli at Cape Helles and Angat, being WIA and invalided out of the army. He managed by undisclosed means to get back in *(CB 45)* to serve in Flanders before returning to Mesopotamia and winning the Military Cross in the campaign to capture Baghdad. Again WIA, again declared medically "unfit for duty," Slim again got around the medics.

From 1919 he was with the Indian Army, commissioned the next year as a regular in the 6th Gurkha Rifles. After graduating at the top of his Quetta Staff College class in 1926 he taught at Camberley 1934-37. Two years later he was commandant of the Senior Officers' School at Belgaum, India *(CB 45)* and by 1939 he was a brigadier. Sent to the Sudan and getting to know Orde WINGATE well, Slim took command of the 10th Ind Bde. At the start of William PLATT's offensive he was wounded in an air raid near Gallabat in Jan 41 and missed most of the campaign in Abyssinia and Eritrea. But in two months he recovered sufficiently for duty with WAVELL's staff of the Middle East Command. Slim assumed command of the 10th Ind Div when its last brigade reached Basra on 7 May 41. With the customary temporary promotion Maj Gen Slim moved swiftly through Iraq, northern Syria, and Iran, being appointed to the DSO.

After commanding the 10th Ind Div less than a year Slim went on short notice to India, where Wavell now coped with a massive Japanese advance in SE Asia. Again promoted, Lt Gen Slim took command of all British, Burmese, and Indian Army troops in Burma on 19 Mar 42. His 1st Burma Corps Hq was initially at Mamyo, NE of Mandalay. This freed ALEXANDER to coordinate with the Chinese armies that soon came under STILWELL. By now the Japanese invasion was well under way and Alexander issued orders on 1 May 42 for a "sauve qui peut." Slim and Stilwell retreated to India, the tatterdemalion "Burcorps" reaching Imphal on 20 May 42. Slim's surviving troops, 28 guns, 50 trucks, and 30 jeeps became part of Geoffrey Scoones's 4th Corps in Assam and Slim assumed command of the 15th Corps Hq in Calcutta.

With priorities going to other war fronts, it was more than a year before the Allies could mount an effort to retake Burma. But while Stilwell worked to rebuild two Chinese divisions that had reached India, Slim did the same with Imperial forces. In mid-Mar 43 he was sent to report on what might be done to restore British military fortunes in Arakan. Three months later he undertook a limited offensive to recapture Akyab (Slim, 123), but it was another fiasco.

After MOUNTBATTEN arrived in late 1943 to head SEAC Bill Slim was named to head a new army, the 14th, made up of his 15th Corps (still in Arakan) and Scoones's 14th Corps (in Assam). The second Arakan campaign started off badly because the Japanese had planned a powerful "spoiling attack" that hit soon after the 15th Corps jumped off. Thanks largely to MESSERVY the British had their first victory over the junglewise Japanese.

MUTAGUCHI's large-scale and ambitious "march on Delhi," Opn U-Go, began on 7 Mar 44. Slim conducted a valiant and successful defense of the bases he needed in Assam, principally Kohima and Imphal. He was reinforced by Montagu Stopford's 33d Ind Corps and had good tactical air support. Slim also used a new logistical system of air supply developed to support the long-range penetration groups of WINGATE and MERRILL. A hard-fought, wide-ranging campaign stopped the Japanese and started driving them back. On 11 July KAWABE ordered a general withdrawal, and Japanese survivors of the disaster were back across the Chindwin by 1 Aug 44. A few days later Stilwell's Chinese took **Myitkyina** with material assistance from Merrill's Marauders.

Now the stage was set for Sir William (knighted in late 1944) to launch Opn Capital from Assam into central Burma. The campaign featured large-scale deception tactics—dummy headquarters, bogus radio traffic, and fake guns and vehicles—to create the impression that the principal objective was the obvious one, Mandalay.

On 3 Dec 44 Lt Gen Montagu Stopford's 33d Corps moved SE on a broad front across the Chindwin River toward Mandalay. Five days later the 4th Corps, now under MESSERVY, kicked off from far on the right (west) flank. Messervy moved through virtually impassable terrain but met surprisingly light resistance. So Slim executed "Capital extended": instead of having Messervy turn east and attack Mandalay from the flank, he sent him farther south in a **turning movement.** This captured the large, virtually undefended supply base some 60 miles south of Mandalay at Meiktila in an action from 27 Feb to 3 Mar 45. Kimura needed time to realize he was not dealing with a mere raid but he then diverted elements of four divisions south from Mandalay to meet the unexpected threat to his LofC. The British had to use air resupply for three weeks, but the 17th Ind Div held Meiktila. Stopford's 33d Corps, its task facilitated, took Mandalay (9-20 Mar 45) and moved down the Irrawaddy, switching flanks with Messervy.

The British strategy split central Burma down the middle as Messervy continued due south to enter Rangoon without opposition on 3 May.

In a turbulent general reorganization for mopping up, and before the planned amphibious operations in Malaya, Sir William left his 14th Army on 7 May 45. Succeeded by Stopford he took home leave before replacing LEESE as commander of Allied Ground Forces SE Asia (ALFSEA). Promoted to full general in August, Slim returned to England at the end of 1945 to head the Imperial Defense College. In 1948 he succeeded MONTGOMERY as CIGS and was made a field marshal. Slim next served as Gov Gen of Australia 1953-60 and was raised to the peerage in 1960 as the 1st Viscount Slim. He died in London on 14 Dec 70 at the age of 79.

"Bill Slim is considered by many people to have been the finest commander Britain produced in the last war. He combined the best qualities of Monty and Alex" (Smyth, 221). Slim also published one of the war's finest memoirs, *Unofficial History* (London: Cassell, 1959); the shortened US edition is *Defeat Into Victory* (New York: McKay, 1961).

SMIGLY-RYDZ, Edward. Polish statesman. 1886-1943? In 1935 the marshal succeeded Pilduski as the virtual dictator of Poland. As CinC in 1939 he has been blamed for deploying his armed forces poorly to meet the German invasion and for relying on horse cavalry to fight panzers. He escaped to Romania, returned to join the resistance, and is believed to have been killed in 1943 by the Germans. Smigly is an acquired name meaning "Lightning."

SMITH, Allan Edward. US admiral. 1892-1987. "Hoke" Smith was born 19 Jan 92 at Detroit, Mich. Attending the Univ of Michigan before entering the Naval Academy he graduated in 1915 (130/179). At Annapolis he played baseball and was captain of the basketball team. Most of his early service was on battleships. In Feb 25 he became XO of the gunboat *Villalobos*

in the Yangtze River Patrol in China. At Changsha he won the Silver Life Saving Medal for rescuing an enlisted man from drowning. Stateside service thereafter included two tours in the navy's Judge Advocate General department, during which time Smith got a law degree from George Washington Univ and was admitted to practice before the US Supreme Court.

In June 40, after completing the senior course at the Naval War College and serving a year on the faculty, he fitted out and commanded Mine Division 5 (converted destroyers). In June 40 he took over Destroyer Div 3. A captain from Mar 41, Smith became operations officer of Battle Force Pacific Fleet (later TF 1), then he was CofS from May 42. In Sep 42 he went to Washington for a year of staff duty before commanding BB *South Dakota*. Operating with fast carriers he saw action in the Marshall Islands, supported the Makin operation in Nov 43, then returned to the Marshalls in Jan 44. He provided shore bombardment for the landings on Kwajalein and in the Marianas.

Promoted to rear admiral in Mar 44 he assumed command of Cruiser Div 1 for three bombardments of the Kuriles. In July 44 he took over the 17th Naval District (Alaska and the Aleutians) and the next month he commanded Cruiser Div 5 in the 3d Fleet. After taking part in Bull HALSEY's operations to include Leyte, Iwo Jima, and Okinawa he became head of Service Sqdn 10 on 29 July 45 . The squadron operated huge supply and repair bases in forward areas and, with more than 1,000 ships, prepared to provide logistical support for the invasion of Japan.

Hoke Smith was SPRUANCE's CofS at the Naval War College from Jan 46 and the school's acting president in the first half of 1948. He then commanded Atlantic Fleet Battleships Cruisers with flag aboard BB *Missouri*. After commanding Cruiser Force, Atlantic Fleet, until Sep 50 Hoke Smith took over TF 95 during the Korean War. Eventually he commanded ships of 10 nations and was nicknamed "The Duke of Wonsan." Returning to the US in July 51 and being Commandant 13th Naval District in Seattle, he retired on 1 Feb 54 as a vice admiral. Smith died on 2 July 87.

SMITH, Holland McTyeire. USMC general. 1882-1967. "Howlin' Mad" Smith was born 20 Apr 82 in Seale, Ala, son of a lawyer in Montgomery. Attending the Alabama Polytechnic Institute, a military school at Auburn, he discovered Napoleon and decided to become a career officer (Smith, *Coral and Brass,* 29). A champion sprinter but less of a scholar he spent two years at the Univ of Alabama and in 1903 was awarded a law degree and admitted to the bar. When Smith considered an army career but found he would have to wait a year for a commission a helpful congressman suggested joining the Marines. "What are the Marines?" Smith asked in all candor. (Ibid., 32.) He found out. Commissioned on 29 Mar 05, he came to rank second only to VANDEGRIFT in the USMC.

Some time before 1916 he acquired the nickname "Howlin' Mad." In France with the AEF Smith commanded the 8th Co, 5th Marine Regt and won the Croix de Guerre with Palm. Between the wars he and BARBEY pioneered amphibious warfare. In Mar 37 Col Smith became director of operations and training at Marine Hq in Washington, which gave him primary responsibility for building a Marine Corps amphibious force. In Sep 39 he took command of the 1st Marine Bde and, promoted to major general, went to Cuba for amphibious training. In Feb 41 the brigade, more than doubled in size, was redesignated the 1st Marine Div and sent back three months later to the US. In June 41 Smith assumed command of what became the Amphibious Force, Atlantic Fleet.

A short, heavy-set man with a moustache and round, thin-rimmed glasses, a hard face, and ever-present cigar, Howlin' Mad looked more like an elderly business tycoon than a fighting general. He was 60 years old and serving at Quantico, Va, in 1942 when a medical board found him physically unfit because of severe diabetes. This turned out to be a lab technician's mistake, but when the general reached the West Coast in Sep 42 to head the amphibious training center a routine physical checkup found the same medical problem. The events, he would write, "set me to wondering, too, about a conspiracy that could deprive a man of an opportunity to fight for his country by killing him with a medical certificate." (Ibid., 102.)

Continuing to form Marine divisions at Camps Elliott and Pendleton on the coast, and with an artillery unit inland at Nilan, near El Centro, he also trained army forces for landings in the Aleutians. Inspection trips took him to the Pacific and Smith became increasingly de-

pressed about not getting in the fight. Nimitz finally relented, and Holland Smith reached Honolulu on 5 Sep 43 as CG, Fleet Marine Force, Pacific. His chain of command was: 1) NIMITZ at the top as CINCPAC/CINCPAO through; 2) SPRUANCE, who headed the Central Pacific Force, and; 3) Kelly TURNER, who headed the 5th Amphibious Force to; 4) Smith, "VAC," or V [5th] Amphib Corps. (Ibid., 109, 113.) VAC's opposite number in the South Pacific was Roy S. GEIGER, whose 1st Marine Amphibious Corps was redesignated the 3d Amphibious Corps in Apr 44.

For the assault on Makin, 20-23 Nov 43, Holland Smith had operational command over Col Gardiner Conroy's 165th Regt of Ralph Smith's 27th US Army Div. Lt Col James ROOSEVELT, USMC, who had been XO in CARSON's Raiders on the famous raid to Makin, went along with Col Conroy as an observer. When Holland Smith visited the island on D+2 he found that the corpse of Col Conroy, killed by a sniper on D day, had lain for two days "in full sight of hundreds of men" (ibid., 126). Shocked by this and displeased by other evidence of poor training and discipline the Marine general on his return to Pearl Harbor told Nimitz "that had Ralph Smith been a Marine I would have relieved him on the spot." (Ibid.)

The landings on "bloody Tarawa" also began on 20 Nov 43. In the first large-scale assault on a strongly held beach the amphibious doctrine developed largely by Holland Smith proved to be sound, although there were many weaknesses in its implementation, mainly in the area of communications. (Buchanan, 286.) To the public and many military critics the casualties were exorbitant (almost 1,000 Marines killed and more than 2,000 wounded), but this was under 20 per cent (ibid.). Commenting quite incorrectly that the island had no strategic importance and should have been bypassed, Smith writes "Tarawa was a mistake" (Smith, 134). Morison disagrees strongly, as did Spruance and Turner. (Morison, VII, 183n.) For one thing, quickly constructed air bases in the atoll halved the distance bombers had to fly, reducing their vulnerability and increasing their payload. (Buchanan, 286.) But the experience at least convinced the JCS that NIMITZ was right in bypassing two islands in the Marshalls, Maloelap and Wotje, and concentrating forces on the largest, Kwajalein. This was secured on

1 Feb 44, and Eniwetok was taken 16 days later, Ralph Smith's division again performing poorly in Smith's opinion.

To now only one Marine, Vandegrift, who became USMC commandant, had three-star rank; on 15 Mar 44 Holland Smith became the second. Lt Gen Smith then led his corps on Saipan, D day being 18 June 44. With great reluctance he took Ralph Smith's division along, this being the only army division available in Hawaii. (Smith, ibid., 168.)

Despite constant prodding Ralph Smith could not keep pace. After consulting Turner and with written authority from Spruance, the Marine general relieved the army general of command on 24 June 44 for lack of aggressiveness. Maj Gen Sanderford JARMAN took over the division temporarily.

"Relieving Ralph Smith was one of the most disagreeable tasks I have ever been forced to perform," writes Holland Smith, who says he personally liked the man and considered him "professionally knowledgeable." (Smith, ibid., 173.) But the New York National Guard division was suffering from what Holland Smith called "militia-itis"—officers and men retaining hometown personal and political affiliations, which meant that proper military standards were not enforced. (Ibid., 168-69.) Holland Smith went on to take Tinian, three miles off Saipan, in a shore to-shore operation. Japanese resistance on the two islands ended 1 Aug 44.

Howlin' Mad Smith then headed the new Fleet Marine Force, Pacific, which combined his 5th corps (VAC), now under Maj Gen Harry Schmidt, with Geiger's 3d Amphibious Corps (mentioned earlier). The 3d Corps, with the 77th US Army Div, took Guam in July and Aug 44.

Geiger captured Iwo Jima, 19 Feb-25 Mar 45, almost 6,000 Marines and nearly 23,000 Japanese being killed and more than 17,000 Marines wounded. Geiger's corps was in BUCKNER's 10th US Army for the Okinawa campaign, 1 Apr-21 June 45. This was the last Pacific island taken and the most costly.

Smith returned the next month to Camp Pendleton, Calif, and directed training until retiring in May 46 after 41 years of military service. He died on 12 Jan 67.

SMITH, Julian Constable. USMC general. 1885-1975. A brigadier general when the war

started, he had been involved with Holland M. SMITH in developing amphibious doctrine. In the spring of 1943 he took command of the 2d Marine Div. Being promoted, Maj Gen Smith led TF 53 in the bloody battle for Tarawa Atoll beginning on 20 Nov 43, his division reinforced by the 2d Bn, 8th Marines. Julian Smith was relieved on 4 Dec 43 by Capt Jackson R. Tate, USN, who became Commander, Advanced Base, Tarawa. (See Holland M. SMITH for Tarawa's importance.) Doubling as CG, Expeditionary Troops, 3d Fleet, he took the southern Palaus and on 23 Sep 44 occupied Ulithi, which became the hub of US naval operations in the western Pacific. (S&S.) Smith returned to the States three months later and retired in Feb 46.

SMITH, Ralph Corbett. US general. 1893-. In Nov 42 he took command of the 27th "New York" Div, a National Guard unit that had been in Hawaii for six months (AA, 530). Smith led elements of his division in Adm R. K. Turner's amphibious assault on Makin Atoll in the Gilbert Islands that began 21 Nov 43. Taking command ashore on 22 Nov, beating off a final counterattack that night, Smith secured the atoll in the next two days. He detached a battalion of the 106th Regt to support the attack on Eniwetok Island, 19-26 Feb 44. Already in bad odor with USMC Gen Holland M. "Howling Mad" SMITH, Ralph Smith began landing his division on Saipan under cover of darkness on 16 June 44 (D+1) to support the 2d and 4th Marine Regts. The New Yorkers helped establish the beachhead and take Aslito airfield on the 18th. A banzai attack overran part of the division during a pitched battle on 7 July, after Ralph Smith's troops mopped up pockets of resistance in difficult terrain. (AA, 530.)

The "Marine Smith" sacked the "Army Smith" on 24 June 44 for lack of aggressiveness in the final offensive, replacing him temporarily with Maj Gen Sanderford JARMAN. Howling Mad Smith's action led to an "interservice wrangle" (Buchanan, 522) that lasted long after the war. Recalled to Hawaii, Ralph Smith took command of the 98th Div on 15 July 44. The division, whose peacetime headquarters was in upper New York State, had been in Hawaii since the preceding April, its presence supposedly a secret. The division never saw action but provided replacements, and Smith left it before the unit went to Japan on occupation duty. The general retired 31 Oct 46, having been awarded two Silver Stars, two Legions of Merit, and the Purple Heart.

SMITH, Walter Bedell. American general. 1895-1961. Known from his middle name as "Beetle" Smith and famous as Eisenhower's brilliant but dyspeptic CofS, he was born on 5 Oct 95 at Indianapolis, Ind. A German grandfather was a veteran of the Franco-Prussian War of 1870. Smith enlisted in the Indiana NG at the age of 16 and was given an RA commission in 1918. He was WIA and decorated while serving with the 4th Inf Div of the AEF for four months.

Completing the advanced course of the Infantry School in 1932, he remained at Ft Benning, Ga, for a year to teach. After graduating from the **AWC** in 1937 he returned to Benning as secretary of the school under Marshall. He then went to Washington (above), serving with the rank of brigadier general during the period 31 Aug 41-3 Feb 42 (*AA*, 54).

Ike's 'small, pouchy' chief of staff 'with a red face and stern eyes in a dynamo'" (Cole, *Ardennes*, 413) "had a sense of humor and could be conspicuously successful as a diplomat, but the hard fight upward and an intestinal disorder that bit like an ulcer had left an angry streak in him that made him ugly and even brutal when crossed. . . . Weigley, *ETO*, 503). Smith was the lean and hungry type Marshall needed for a ruthlessly efficient office, and he leaned on him heavily as Secretary General Staff and Secretary of the Combined Chiefs of Staff in 1941-42. In an Army where he depended on officers like Eisenhower and Bradley to do their jobs quietly, to conciliated, to persuade, he required others like Smith who could hack a path through red tape and perform hatchet jobs when time and tradition and the dead hand of the past threatened to block progress. Smith was [later] the perfect complement to Eisenhower." (Pogue, *Marshall*, II, 408.)

Marshall finally released Beetle Smith in mid-Sep 42 to be Eisenhower's CofS in London. Smith held the post for the duration, being promoted to lieutenant general on 14 Feb 44.

Smith yearned for the postwar job in Germany that went to Lucius D. CLAY but instead was ambassador to Moscow, 1946-49. He was CG, 1st Army Hq, Governor's Island, NYC, 29 Mar 49-30 Sep 50, then CIA director until retiring from active duty on 31 Jan 53, a full general from 1 July 51. Gen Smith was undersecretary of state until resigning in 1954 and becoming vice chairman of the American Machine and Foundry Co.

Beetle Smith published *My Three Years in Moscow* (1950) and *Eisenhower's Six Great Decisions: Europe, 1944-45* (New York: Longmans, Green and Co., 1956). He died 9 Aug 61. in Washington, DC.

SMUTS, Jan Christiaan. South African statesman. 1870-1950. Long a venerable world figure, Jan Smuts was born 24 May 70 of Afrikaner parents on a farm near Riebeck West, Cape Colony. He was a brilliant student who won the highest honors in law at Cambridge. Renouncing British citizenship, and entering law practice in Cape Town, Smuts became chief of Boer commandos in 1900 and led them against the British until May 04. By then he concluded that South Africa's future lay in reconciliation of Boer and British interests. Smuts was a leading politician in efforts under Louis Botha to create the Union of South Africa. Stern and authoritarian, he used military force against a miner's strike and a Boer uprising in 1914. *(CE.)* As a general in SW and E Africa he claimed to have overcome German military resistance by Nov 16, but it continued another two years until the armistice. Meanwhile going to London and sitting on the Imperial War Cabinet, Smuts was so highly regarded that the high command considered making him commander in Palestine or even in France. An apochryphical story circulated that Botha cabled: "Don't do it Jannie. You and I know you are no general." Remaining in London 1917-18 and reluctantly signing what he thought was the unduly punitive Versailles Treaty, Smuts drafted a memorandum that in substance became the covenant of the League of Nations.

Smuts was prime minister of South Africa after Botha's death in 1919. The Nationalists attained power in 1924 with J. B. M. Hertzog as PM, but Smuts took the post again in Sep 39 as an advocate of war with Germany. He doubled as CinC of South African forces and Churchill consulted him on strategy. A field marshal from 1941, the slim, soldierly Smuts spent most of WWII in London and was largely responsible for South Africa's furnishing some of the Commonwealth's finest combat forces. (KLOPPER surrendered 10,500 crack South African troops at Tobruk on 18 June 42, almost a third of those fielded to that date.)

Smuts attended the San Francisco Conference in 1945 and was active in drafting the UN charter. "It is after the war that worries me," he had confided to TEDDER, "it will take years and years of patience, courage, and faith" (Tedder, 688). But Smut's international outlook lost favor as internal problems intensified, and D. F. Malan ousted him as premier of the Nationalist Party. Smuts died shortly thereafter, 11 Sep 50, at his home near Pretoria.

Smuts was author of a philosophy expounded in his *Holism and Evolution* (1926 and 1936). He published *Africa and Some World Problems* (1930). His collective speeches were published as *Plans for a Better World* (1940). Biographies are by Sarah Millin (1936), F. S. Crawford (1943), and Rene Kraus (1944).

SOBENNIKOV, Petr Petrovich. Soviet military leader. 1894-1960. Although he joined the Red Army in 1918 Sobennikov was not a CP member until 1940. From Mar 41 Gen Maj Sobennikov commanded the 8th Army under F. I. KUSNETSOV in the Baltic MD. In a reorganization begun when the Germans attacked on 22 June 41 five fronts were created: the Northwest, Western, Southwest, Northern, and Southern Fronts. According to some records Sobennikov immediately took over the Northwest Front (22 June) but the effective date was 4 July 41. The next month he was succeeded by Gen Col P. A. Kurochkin and stepped down to command the 43d Army (which Kurochkin had headed originally). Sobennikov left the army in Oct 41 and did not figure again in the war. After heading the **Vystrel** courses, 1955-59, he died the next year. (Scotts.)

SODENSTERN, Georg von. German general 1889-. Short, plump, bespectacled, pedantic-looking, and prosaic, he was one of Germany's most highly regarded operational planners. In 1932 he was in the **Truppenamt** with Jodl, Keitel, Krebs, Model, and Speidel. Halder hoped to push him into the top operational post in Berlin that went to JODL on 23 Aug 39. (Goerlitz, *GGS,* 264, 351.)

As WITZLEBEN's CofS on the eve of war Sodenstern was a charter member of the anti-Hitler conspiracy. In Mar 40 he succeeded MANSTEIN as Rundstedt's CofS and remained in that post through the campaigns in France and the USSR. He remained CofS of AG South after RUNDSTEDT's departure, serving under Reichenau and Weichs (1942-43). Rejoining Rundstedt in OB West for the intensified planning to meet the Allied landings, Generalleutnant von Sodenstern was promoted to general of infantry and given command of the 19th Army Hq in Avignon. He controlled troops BLASKOWITZ's AG of G on the Riviera but before TRUSCOTT began landing on 15 Aug 44 he was replaced by WIESE. He disappeared from the history books but survived the war (Irving, *HW,* 457n.)

SOKOLOVSKY, Vasily Danilovich. Soviet military leader. 1897-1968. The future MSU and Konev's long-time CofS was born 21 July 97 into a peasant family in the village of Kozliki, near Grodna, then in Poland. He entered the Red Army in 1918 but did not join the CP until 1931 (HFS). During the civil war he fought on the eastern, southern, and Caucasus fronts, rising to be CofS, 32d Rifle Div. After graduating from the Red Army Military Academy of the General Staff in 1921 he saw more combat in Central Asia. In 1930-35 he commanded a rifle division then was CofS, Ural MD.

Having been CofS, Moscow MD, since May 38 Sokolovsky was promoted to general lieutenant in June 40 along with Chuykov, Golikov, Konev, Malandin, Vatutin, and Yeremenko. When his old friend ZHUKOV succeeded MERETSKOV as CGS on 14 Jan 41 Sokolovsky became deputy CGS. But he soon left to be TIMOSHENKO's CofS in the Western "Direction" (see **Glavkom**). He retained the post under ZHUKOV, doubling as CofS Western TKV and of the Western Front July-Sep 41. Gen Lt Sokolovsky remained in this front as CofS to Zhukov and Konev during various reorganizations.

After being in the Battle of Moscow and the massive Soviet counteroffensive Sokolovsky was promoted to colonel general in June 42. Moving up from CofS he succeeded KONEV as Western Front commander in Feb 43 and was promoted to general of the army

(No. 7) on 27 Aug 43, after a month-long struggle to take Elnya, gateway to Smolensk. (Seaton, *R-G War,* 388.)

As the long-lived Western Front was about to be deactivated, Sokolovsky turned over command to CHERNYAKHOVSKY in Apr 44 and resumed the post as CofS to Zhukov, who was about to replace VATUTIN as CG 1st Ukrainian Front. For the rest of the war Sokolovsky spent long periods in the field between tours of duty in Moscow. He was Konev's CofS during the Lvov-Sandomir offensive in July-Aug 44; for two months in the East Carpathian operations; in the Vistula-Oder offensive, 12 Jan-3 Feb 45; and in the Berlin offensive. During the last month of the war he was Zhukov's deputy in the 1st Belorussian Front. (HFS.)

In 1945 he became a HSU and the next year was promoted to MSU (No. 18). After having been Zhukov's deputy CinC of occupation forces in Germany, he succeeded Zhukov in Mar 46 and was in Berlin three years before becoming 1st Deputy Minister of War. Retaining that post in Moscow he was CGS from June 52 to Apr 60, succeeding SHTEMENKO. Finally he was General Inspector and head of a group of leading military commanders working on nuclear war doctrine. Their conclusions were published as *Military Strategy* (1962, 1963, and 1968), Sokolovsky being editor and contributor. (HFS.) He died 10 May 68 in Moscow and is buried in the Kremlin Wall.

SOMERVELL, Brehon Burke. US supply chief. 1892-1955. Lt Gen Somervell headed the Army Service Forces from 1942 and was promoted to full general on 6 Mar 45.

The logistics genius was born 9 May 92 in Little Rock, Ark, only son of a doctor; his mother had been a school teacher. When the boy was 15 years old he moved to Washington, where his parents founded Belcourt Seminary, a successful finishing school on S Street for young ladies. *(CB 42.)*

Bill Somervell (as he was called) graduated from West Point in 1914 (6/107). He was known as somewhat of a dandy in his cadet years, and later as "a quick-tempered, impulsive officer" (C. J. V. Murphy, below, 171). Commissioned as an engineer, he was on graduation leave in Paris when war broke out. He reported to the embassy, was made assistant MA, and was given the task

of distributing more than $1,000,000 in gold to US citizens being repatriated. After following in the wake of Pershing's **Punitive Expedition** to build roads he went to France with the AEF's first engineering detachment. He directed rear-area construction and was on leave at the front, as a captain, when given the opportunity to replace a captured officer as G3 of the 89th Inf Div. Somervell saw action in the Meuse Argonne offensive and was a temporary lieutenant colonel when the war ended. After being a supply officer at 3d Army Hq in Germany he went home with a DSC and DSM and reverted to the rank of captain.

The "brilliant engineer," an Old Army jibe that was no joke in his case, had come into a comfortable legacy when given a choice assignment. In 1925 he accompanied Walter D. Hines on a survey of navigation on the Rhine and Danube Rivers for the League of Nations. Then he went to Turkey with Hines in 1933 for an economic study requested by Kemal Ataturk. In 1936-40 he was WPA administrator in NYC, which Harry L. HOPKINS called the most difficult WPA job in the nation. "The curious rules of WPA condemned him to operate in a kind of economic never-never land in which the worthless and the worth-while were administratively indistinguishable," wrote Charles J. V. Murphy; "in which archery contests, block dances, poison ivy and ragweed projects were appraised on the same basis as the $40,000,000 LaGuardia *[sic]* airport," whose construction he directed. (*These Are the Generals,* 176-77.) His seven predecessors had lasted a matter of months; Col Somervell held the job nearly four years. Promoted to brigadier general, he headed the Quartermaster Construction Div from 11 Dec 40, then was G4 WDGS, 25 Nov 41-9 Mar 42 (*AA,* 62). The SOS (later the Army Service Forces) was established on the latter date under Maj Gen Somervell (*OCMH Chron,* 28). Soon promoted to lieutenant general, Somervell commanded the Army Service Forces for the rest of the war. Representing the army's interests, he waged a private war with Donald M. NELSON's WPB over war production control.

He was promoted on 6 Mar 45 to full general and on 30 Apr 46 he retired a director in many corporations. Thereafter Somervell died 13 Feb 55 at Ocala, Fla. (Cullum.)

SOMERVILLE, James Fownes. British admiral. 1882-1949. He was born 17 July 82 at Weybridge, Surrey. Descended from the Hood family of naval heroes he joined *Britannia* as a cadet in 1897, was a lieutenant in 1904, and became one of the navy's leading radio specialists. In this capacity he was appointed to the DSO in 1916 for service in the Dardanelles. A rear admiral from 1933, he commanded the Mediterranean destroyer flotillas 1936-38. During the Spanish Civil War, when the Republicans threatened to bombard Palma, Majorca, in 1936, Somerville evoked naval seniority and took operational control of the German pocket battleship *Deutschland* and the Italian destroyer *Malocello* to form an "international squadron" that promptly removed the threat.

In Apr 38 he was invalided home from his post as CinC East Indies and retired for an illness diagnosed as pulmonary TB. Somerville recovered completely but navy doctors would not reinstate him.

Knighted (KCB) in 1939, Sir James was declared fit for light duty when Britain went to war. He made lively BBC broadcasts before undertaking important work in developing naval radar. In May 40 he volunteered to serve under Adm Sir Bertram H. RAMSAY in what became the "miracle of Dunkirk." There being no further question about his fitness for full duty Somerville was named commander of the newly formed Force H. Based at Gibraltar, this was built around the carrier *Ark Royal* and the battle cruiser *Hood*. After the French signed the armistice on 22 June 40 Churchill gave Somerville the nasty task of dealing with the French navy's main striking force at **Mers-el-Kebir.**

Continuing to operate from Gibraltar, Vice Adm Somerville made a devastating gunfire attack on Genoa (9 Feb 41), delivered a carrier air attack on Leghorn, escorted convoys through the Mediterranean, and had the decisive role in crippling *Bismarck* on 26 May 41 (see LUETJENS). Knighted for the second time (KBE 1941), Sir James received a signal from "ABC" Cunningham, "Congratulations, but isn't twice a knight at your age rather overdoing it?" (L. Kennedy, below, 155).

Somerville took over the Eastern Fleet from Sir Geoffrey Layton in Mar 42, after Adm Tom PHILLIPS lost *Prince of Wales* and *Repulse* off Malaya, and was made an admiral (retired list) on 6 Apr 42. NAGUMO had been conducting carrier raids into the Indian Ocean since Japan went to war and Somerville had to make a strategic withdrawal from his base on Ceylon to Kilindini, Kenya. But the British admiral operated from a secret base at Addu Atoll in the Maldive Islands and had headquarters at Bombay. Reinforced as the tide of war turned, Sir James attacked Diego Suarez, Madagascar, and pushed back eastward until relinquishing command in Aug 44. That month he was reinstated on the active list and honored by advancement to GCB (*DNB*).

In Oct 44 he succeeded Adm Sir Percy Noble as head of the British Naval Delegation in Washington (where he had taken part in talks in May 43). Promotion to admiral of the fleet came when the next vacancy occurred in May 45. On retiring for the last time in 1946 Sir James was advanced in the knighthood to GBE.

Somerville was "one of the Navy's characters," writes Ludovic Kennedy (following), "a big congenial man full of humour and vitality. . . . He maintained, says his biographer [below] 'a schoolboyish approach to all things, a youthful zest and sense of fun combined with an uninhibited simplicity of expression . . . an unconscious urge to be the centre of the stage and act the unorthodox admiral . . . [which] brought him enemies as well as friends'" (Ludovic Kennedy, *Pursuit,* 155-56). He was a trim, square-jawed man, and a physical fitness addict.

In retirement at Dinder House, Wells, in Somerset, the property inherited in 1942 from his father, the admiral was active as lord lieutenant. He died 19 Mar 49 at Dinder House. A biography by Donald Macintyre is *Fighting Admiral: The Life and Battles of Admiral of the Fleet Sir James Somerville* (London: Evans Bros., 1961).

SOONG, T. V. (Sung Tsu-wen). Chinese official. 1894-1971. Born in Shanghai on 4 Dec (?) 94, he was the third child and only son in what became China's most powerful family. T. V.'s father, Charles Jones Soong, had gone to Boston with an uncle and studied to be a Methodist missionary. The senior Soong returned to Shanghai, made a fortune in enterprises including Bible publishing, and sent his six children to schools in America.

Three Soong daughters attended Wesleyan and married men who became prominent. Ailing (b. 1888) married H. H. KUNG. Ching-ling (b. 1890) married Dr SUN YAT-SEN. Mei-Ling (b. 1896) married Chiang Kai-shek on 1 Dec 27, given away by her brother T. V. in a well-publicized Methodist ceremony. (*See* Emily Hahn, *The Soong Sisters*. Garden City, NY: Garden City Publishing Co, 1945. This is a reprint of the 1941 Doubleday, Doran & Co ed.)

The stocky, moon-faced T. V. Soong studied economics at Harvard, graduated in 1915, and then spent two years at Columbia Univ. After working for an international banking firm he returned to China where Dr Sun recruited him to manage the Salt Administration in Kwangtung and Kwangsi Prov. But Soong soon took over the new Central Bank of Canton, being chairman 1935-43. (*China Yrbk 1970-71*, 640.)

Soong's relationships with his siblings were strained—with Mme Chiang because he was a political threat to her husband; with Mme Sun because he wasn't pro-communist. As finance minister after Dr Sun's death on 12 Mar 25, Soong raised funds from Shanghai bankers to help Chiang consolidate nationalist power, and he brought about vital tax reforms. But in 1933 Soong resigned all posts after disagreing with his brother-in-law over high military expenditures and the issue of new bonds.

When the Sino-Japanese war broke out in 1937 Soong worked with Chou En-lai to forge a Nationalist-Communist alliance against the Japanese. Again finance minister, then foreign minister from 21 Dec 41, he spent much time in Washington and had easy access to the White House. John Gunther characterized Soong in 1939 as "diffident and direct by turn; not afraid to be rude, and intolerant of bores; enormously competent" (*Inside Asia*, 201-2). Although a generally honest intermediary, Soong could be devious. Once he confused both sides by altering a particularly blunt message from the White House to Chiang (Tuchman, *Stilwell,* passim.).

T. V. Soong suddenly fell from grace in China at the end of 1943 and was eclipsed by H. H. Kung. Analyzing how this came about, John S. Service points out first that "Chiang and Soong have always had difficulty in getting along with each other: Chiang is dictatorial, Soong out-spoken and strongwilled" (Esherick, ed., *Service,* 78). But problems seemed to have come to a head because both Gen and Mme Chiang thought Soong was too independent in foreign affairs, a field they preferred to dominate. Soong also enraged Chiang and alarmed H. H. and Mme Kung by implying that he—Soong—should take over as economic tsar to straighted out China's critical economic problems. When the final break with Chiang came in early 1944 Soong remained foreign minister but his powers were sharply curtailed. Kung soon took control of the Bank of China and the national economy (ibid., 80-83), but Soong retained control of the Bank of Canton a few months more.

Soong was president of the Executive Yuan, 1945-47, and governor of Kwantung Prov 1947-49. He moved to NYC shortly before the Nationalists fled the mainland in 1949, and the next year declined Chiang's invitation to join the expatriate government on Taiwan.

The 76-year-old T. V. Soong died suddenly on 25 Apr 71 in San Francisco after food lodged in his windpipe during a private dinner party.

SORGE, Richard. Soviet spy. 1895-1944. One of the most successful spies in history, Sorge operated for five years in Tokyo without being detected and another three years before his ring was broken up on 18 Oct 41. During this time he sent Moscow accurate and timely detail of almost all intended major Japanese and German military and diplomatic decisions. The Soviets had such confidence in Sorge's reports that they shifted desperately needed reserves from Siberia to defend Moscow and to launch their large-scale counteroffensive in the winter of 1941-42.

Grandson of a man who had been secretary to Karl Marx, Sorge was born at Baku, in the Caucasus. His father was a German engineer working there for a German oil firm. Sorge's mother was Russian, a quiet, decent woman who lived with her children in Berlin after being widowed when the future spy was only a few years old. (Willoughby, below, 133.) In 1914-18 Sorge served on both fronts as an enlisted man and was twice wounded. During long convalescences he read avidly and became a Marxist. He joined the Hamburg branch of the new German communist party late in 1919, got a doctorate in political science, then was a teacher, coal miner, and journalist. In 1924 he began his career as a professional communist, making such a reputation in Germany that he was sent to Moscow. Here he joined the CPSU and spent three years as a Comintern agent. Sorge then went abroad as a secret agent, posing as a correspondent for an obscure German magazine. Three years later, for some reason having become interested in China and Japan, he transferred to the Red Army's 4th Bureau (Intelligence) and was sent with two others to China. They had instructions to avoid local communist groups, these having recently been bloodied by CHIANG KAI-SHEK. Instead they were to set up a spy ring to target the Japanese. Dr Sorge reached Shangahi in Jan 30, and six months later he took charge of the operation there. Posing as a Nazi journalist he recruited more than a dozen dedicated communists. Two who proved to be key men were journalist Ozaki Hozumi (1901-44) and radio master technician Max Klausen. The recently arrived Agnes Smedley (1894-1950) was with the group briefly in Shanghai. Sorge established cells throughout China and into Manchuria.

In 1933 Sorge was ordered to Tokyo. Through Hozumi, who had become unofficial adviser to the cabinets of Prince KONOYE, he learned governmental secrets; carousing with German embassy officials he picked up diplomatic secrets. His closest and most valuable German source was Eugen Ott, the military attaché who became ambassador. Another was Joseph Meisinger, who reached Tokyo in the fall of 1940 as police attaché, meaning Gestapo chief. SCHELLENBERG, whose judgment on such a matter can be trusted, called Meisinger "one of the most evil creatures among Heydrich's bunch of thugs."

Sorge himself looked and acted more like a Nazi storm trooper than one of history's greatest secret agents. He was a large man with a full head of thick brown hair, cruel eyes, sensuous lips, and was a notoriously heavy drinker and womanizer. He was in Tokyo five years before his ring was even known to exist, and it was another three years before secret police **radi-ogoniometry** located his transmitter. The confession of the communist Ito Ritzu more or less accidentally gave the Japanese the scent that had so long eluded them. Sorge and his principal assistants were arrested on 18 Oct 41, shortly after he reported that the Japanese were planning the Pearl Harbor attack. His earlier achievements were signaling that Japan

was aligning itself with Germany (signing the **Anti-Comintern Pact** and joining the Tokyo-Berlin-Rome Axis [27 Sep 40]), and Sorge sent an unheeded warning to Moscow Center that Hitler planned to invade the USSR. But the spy's greatest contribution to the Soviet war effort, mentioned earlier, was information that the **Strike South Faction** had prevailed.

After a long, careful investigation, the Japanese sentenced Sorge and Ozaki to death in Sep 43. Allowed to appeal, they were not executed until 7 Nov 44! Of the other 15 in the Sorge ring, two were given no sentence, two got life sentences, and the others received up to 15 years. Eight of the latter, including radio operator Klausen, survived to be released by Allied authorities in Oct 45. The others meanwhile had died or had been freed.

See Maj Gen Charles A. WILLOUGHBY, *Shanghai Conspiracy: The Sorge Spy Ring; Moscow, Shanghai, Tokyo, San Francisco, New York* (New York: Dutton, 1952). The author, MacArthur's intelligence chief and closely involved with the denouement in 1945, provides much documentary evidence.

SPAATZ, Carl Andrew. USAAF general. 1891-1974. To sum up his career, "Tooey" Spaatz commanded the 8th AF in the UK, directed US air operations in North Africa, then was TEDDER's deputy in the Mediterranean Allied AF, and he commanded US strategic air forces in Europe for the invasion of Europe. After V-E day he directed the final air assault on Japan. Gen Spaatz was subsequently the first CofS of the independent US Air Force.

Carl Spatz (sic) was born 28 June 91 at Boyertown, Pa, of German ancestry. In 1937 he changed his name to Spaatz, pronounced "spots," to make it look less Germanic—more Holland Dutch than Pennsylvania Dutch. The red haired, freckled-faced "Tooey" acquired the nickname at West Point because he had a facial resemblance to a colorful upperclassman. This cadet, Francis J. Toohey, was the "goat" (last man) in the class of 1913 (93/93)! (Cullum). Spaatz graduated from West Point in 1914 (57/107).

Quickly bored with infantry life in Hawaii, Spaatz got himself sent to the Aviation School at San Diego, Calif. In 1916 he became one of the US Army's first 26 aviators (*CB 42*). Based initially at Columbus, NM, and San Antonio,

Tex, he served in Pershing's **Punitive Expedition** (Cullum). With the AEF in France he headed the aviation training center at Issoudon (*CB
42*). Putting theory into practice during a 19-day
period of temporary duty he shot down three
German planes and was awarded the DSC.

After the normal peacetime assignments
Maj Spaatz was awarded the DFC in early
1929 for setting an endurance record of slightly more that 150 hours aloft. His copilot was
Capt Ira EAKER.

Col Spaatz went to England in 1940 as an
observer during the Battle of Britain. After the
Luftwaffe's first terror raid on London, 7 Sep
40, he jubilantly wired H. H. "Hap" ARNOLD,
"The British are winning. They've forced the
Germans to bomb at night." (Andrews, *The Air
Marshals*, 175.) Spaatz returned to the US that
month to head the Air Materiel Command. In
July 41 he became Arnold's CofS and deputy
commander of the US Army Air Force. In the
shake-up after the Pearl Harbor attack, 7 Dec 41,
Spaatz took over the AF Combat Command,
succeeding Lt Gen Delos C. Emmonds, who
replaced Walter SHORT in Hawaii.

Spaatz's 8th AF was activated on 28 Jan 42
(*AA*, 219) to supply strategic bombers for duty
with the RAF. Brig Gen Spaatz himself reached
London on 18 June 42 (*OCMH Chron,* 42) and
was promoted shortly thereafter to major gener-
al. After the North African landings, 8 Nov 42,
Maj Gen Spaatz established the Northwest
Africa Air Force Hq in Algiers on 1 Dec 42
(ibid., 72), replaced in the UK by Ira Eaker.
Spaatz took control of Western Desert AF on 21
Feb 43 (ibid., 94).

With Hap Arnold and Ira Eaker, Spaatz had
led the fight against the British over daylight
versus nighttime bombing. Churchill remained
adamantly opposed to the former. But Eaker,
with support from SLESSOR, persuaded the PM
at Casablanca in Jan 43 "to make an astonishing
surrender," which delighted Hap Arnold (Allen
Andrews, 221). It was then agreed that the
Americans would continue daylight bombing
while the RAF continued to work at night. The
resulting around-the-clock strategic air assault
became more effective as both the RAF and US
perfected their methods. (*See also* PORTAL.)

When TEDDER's Mediterranean Allied Air
Forces (MAAF) was activated on 20 Dec 43
Spaatz was its CofS and deputy commander.
Comprising RAF, USAAF, French, and Italian

units the MAAF conducted all Allied air operations from the Middle East through Malta
to Gibraltar.

For Opn **Overlord** Spaatz received orders on
22 Dec 43 to take command of US Strategic Air
Forces in Europe (USSAFE). TEDDER became
Eisenhower's deputy, being replaced in the
MAAF by Ira Eaker, who reached the MTO in
mid-Jan 44 after being authorized to stay in the
UK long enough to brief Spaatz and DOOLIT-
TLE. (*OCMH Chron,* 156.)

Promoted on 11 Mar 45 to four-star rank,
Tooey Spaatz established the US Army Strategic
Air Forces on Guam (18 July 45) and directed
the final air assault on Japan. In 1946 he succeeded Hap ARNOLD as commander of the
Army Air Force and then was the first CofS of
the independent US Air Force, 1947-48. Retiring
after reaching the top of his profession, the pioneer airman died on 14 Jul 74 in Washington at
the age of 83.

SPEARS, Edward Louis. British officer and
author. 1886-1974. Called "a poet laureate of the
wars" (S. L. A. Marshall), he was born in Paris
on 7 Aug 86, son of a noted lexicographer,
Alexander Spiers. (Tired of having the name
mispronounced he changed the spelling to
Spears in 1918.) Contrary to what Churchill
says, Spears was not "Half French by birth"
(WC, II, 109): both parents were British. But
Spears was educated privately on the Continent
and spoke impeccable French.

As a subaltern in the 11th Hussars, he was
working in Paris with the French War Office on
a bilingual cipher book when war broke out in
Aug 14 and he was made LnO between the
French 5th Army Hq and BEF Hq. The masterful
account of this experience was published as
Liaison 1914 (1930). Rising to brigadier by
1917, when named head of the British military
mission in Paris, he wore the MC, the Croix de
Guerre with three palms, the Legion of Honor
(Commander), and four wound stripes.

Spears, CBE (1919) and CB (1921), sat in
Parliament as a National Liberal (1922-24), then
as a Conservative (1931-45). He pursued extensive business interests and published *Prelude to
Victory* (1939). Before becoming premier, Churchill visited France with Spears. In 1940, Spears
was promoted to major general and sent to Paris
as British LnO to the French PM and MOD
(WC, II, 748). Ideally suited for the assignment,

"Spears could say things to the high French personnel with an ease and force which I have never seen equalled," wrote Churchill (WC, II, 109). His highly personal account of the experience is *Assignment to Catastrophe* (2 vols, 1954 and 1955).

Spears fled from Bordeaux to London with DE GAULLE and was primarily responsible for convincing Churchill that his passenger was the man most likely to rally French colonial forces to the Allied cause. Churchill sent Spears with a military mission to the Middle East in early 1941 as his personal representative to the Free French in Africa. The emissary found that de Gaulle balked at honoring CATROUX's agreements with the British representative, Sir Miles Lampson, about postwar arrangements with Syria and the Lebanon. The latter were unhappy as French mandates and de Gaulle was not ready to promise them independence after the war. London pressed Spears to sort out the differences between de Gaulle and Churchill.

As the first British minister to the Syrian and Lebanese republics, 1942-44, Spears was pro-Arab and anti-French *(DNB)*. His forceful handling of the situation led to harsh criticism not only from de Gaulle but also from Eisenhower's headquarters in Algiers, where MACMILLAN represented British interests. In assuming his ministerial duties in 1942, Spears also sat on the Middle East War Council, and he was knighted (KBE). His experience in the Middle East is recorded in *Fulfilment of a Mission* (1977).

After the war Sir Edward resumed civilian pursuits and in 1953 he was created first baronet. He published *Two Men Who Saved France: Pétain and de Gaulle* (1966) and *The Picnic Basket* (1967), the latter about his youth. Having been chairman of the Ashanti Goldfields between the wars, he became president of the company in 1971.

In 1918 he had married the well-known American novelist Mary Borden (of the Borden's Milk family), who equipped and ran field hospitals and ambulance units during both wars. Starting in France in 1940, she then supported the Free French throughout the campaign in North Africa, in the Levant, and again in France. Her memoir of the experience is *Journey Down a Blind Alley*. This first wife died in 1968, and the next year Sir Edward married the daughter and granddaughter of the famous generals and military writers Sir Frederick B. Maurice (1771-1851) and Sir John F Maurice

(1841-1912). Spears died 27 Jan 74 at a nursing home in Windsor. (Charles Mott-Radclyffe in *DNB.*)

SPEER, Albert. German official. 1905-81. Hitler's court architect from 1933, Speer (pronounced shpare) succeeded TODT in early 1942 and from late the next year headed German war production.

Albert Speer was born in Mannheim on 19 Mar 05, the son and grandson of architects. The family had substantial means and social status. With a good secondary education, excelling in mathematics, he began studying architecture in 1924 at the Munich Institute of Technology, and in 1925 Speer entered the Institute of Technology in Berlin-Charlottenburg. He got his architect's license in 1927 and a few months later became an assistant at the institute. Speer thought he was well on the way to fulfilling a fortune teller's prophesy: "You will win early fame and retire early," she had told him in 1918, (Speer, *Memoirs,* 12). Now gainfully employed, Speer married a girl he had loved for six years. The honeymoon was spent boating and tenting on the solitary and forested chain lakes in Mecklenburg, writes Speer. "We launched our boats in Spandau. . . ." (Ibid.)

Profoundly impressed by Hitler's eloquence but never an active nor enthusiastic Nazi (Speer, *Memoirs,* 17), Speer met Hitler accidentally in July 33 and learned that the fuehrer particularly admired some private work Speer had done for several Nazi bosses. Hitler instantly liked the tall (six feet four) young patrician, who, "wild to accomplish things," thought he had found his Mephistopheles, who "seemed no less engaging than Goethe's" (Ibid., 31).

The architectural critic Ada Louise Huxtable wrote in 1970 (reviewing Speer's memoirs): "To call Speer a gifted architect who fell under Hitler's spell is poppycock. He was not gifted. As an architect, he was mediocre at best. The poverty of his architectural vision was matched only by Hitler's . . . [but] his taste was better than Hitler's, and he knew it. . . . The Speer style was a self-cancelling blend of ostentatious display and total sterility of the neoclassical wedding-cake school. It suited Hitler well." (*NYT* Book Review Sect, 1 Nov 79, p. 25.)

Hitler was delighted with his new Reichstag building, which the young architect designed in the heroic style and constructed in record time. The court architect designed settings for spectacular Nazi ceremonies, reaching a tour de force at a Nuremberg rally with 130 anti-aircraft searchlights, most of the Luftwaffe's reserve stock. (Leni RIEFENSTAL immortalized the spectacle.) By 1939 his designs for a new Berlin were about finished, and Hitler intended for Speer to push ahead despite the war to have construction completed by 1950. The vulgarly ostentatious plan, most of it depicted in scale models Hitler loved to prowl around, featured a Great Hall with a dome 726 feet high and 825 feet in diameter (about the length of super-battleship *Bismarck*). A stadium at Nuremberg for 400,000 spectators was another project for which plans were completed and a test section built. This "architectural megalomania," as Speer candidly calls it, was his bond with Hitler to the bitter end. As this approached, Hitler said "Speer is still the best of them all." On trial not long thereafter at Nuremberg, Speer said, "If Hitler had had any friends, I would certainly have been one of his close friends" (*Memoirs, 462n, 515*).

Speer's organization grew to 65,000 German workers as it was inexorably diverted to war construction. He put up buildings for the Wehrmacht before taking on the tasks of repairing bomb damage and building air raid shelters. He was involved in putting up some of the elaborate headquarters facilities used by Hitler throughout Europe. But it was not until the end of 1941 that the fuehrer gave into Speer's long-standing suggestion that his organization concentrate on repairing the railroad system wrecked by the Soviets in their withdrawal. Then Fritz TODT gave Speer responsibility for the entire Ukraine. (*Memoirs, 185*.) Both men were visiting Hitler at Rastenburg (Speer for the first time) and were scheduled to fly out together at 8 AM on 9 Feb 42. Speer changed his plans five hours before the departure because Hitler had kept him up all night. TODT was killed after the plane mysteriously exploded, and Speer was appalled at immediately being named his successor. (Hitler brusquely rejected a bid by Goering.)

Quite apart from the staggering task of grasping the organizational reins dropped by Dr Todt, Speer had many administrative obstacles. Hitler (like FDR) had an almost pathological aversion to orderly administration, deliberately creating "roles and missions" conflicts over which only he could mediate. Speer prided himself on being an apolitical technocrat interested only in problem solving. The war effort was hampered by

Hitler's steadfast refusal to impose austerity measures within Germany. Romantic notions of German womanhood deprived the country of the female labor recruited within other nations. (German homes had tens of thousands of domestic servants, most of them "slave labor.") Critically needed workers were producing consumer goods. Martin BORMANN represented the powerful Gauleiters under whose jurisdiction non-essential factories and services functioned. HIMMLER had a highly profitable system of factories within the concentration camps, further exacerbating the labor shortage.

When bombing reduced aircraft production by two thirds in early 1943, MILCH, who had great admiration for Speer, agreed to merge the Air and Armaments ministries. This was accomplished by creating a Fighter Aircraft ("Jaeger") Staff. Hitler approved despite objections from Goering, who now was almost entirely removed from the economic scene. Milch and Speer sat on the Jaeger staff from Mar 44 and also on the Central Planning Board. Thus Speer was in a position to devote his talents to the naval and Luftwaffe armaments fields (if these services invited him to do so).

By the autumn of 1943, little more than six months after taking on his new duties, Speer had had remarkable success despite the mounting intensity of Allied bombing. But he could sense he was losing Hitler's support, and some of his key deputies, notably SAUCKEL, connived with his enemies, like Bormann. A bad situation was exacerbated by a medical problem. Persistent knee pain forced Speer to enter a hospital near Berlin on 18 Jan 44. "Sickness on the part of a minister of the Third Reich involved some special difficulties," he comments wryly (*Memoirs, 327*). Speer soon had good reasons to suspect that his doctor had instructions to keep the patient from returning to duty quickly, if ever! (Ibid., 332.) He escaped from the notorious Karl Gebhardt to another clinic only when heavy air raids convinced this care giver that Speer was the target. With a phone and secretaries Speer continued to work as best he could. But enemies within the Nazi bureaucracy capitalized on his indisposition.

Only four days after Speer's return to Berlin on 8 May 44, 1,000 bombers of the US 8th AF hit fuel plants in central and eastern Germany. Primary targets until then had been single elements of German production like ball-bearings and airframes. Now concentrating on fuel production the Allies finally found the Achilles heel. In retrospect, Speer concluded he had lost the technological war (Ibid., 346).

But in 1944 he produced seven times as many weapons as had others in 1942, six times as much ammunition, and five and a half times as many armored vehicles, using only 30 per cent more workers. (Davidson, *Trial,* 484.)

Speer's remarkable success [writes Davidson] came from his gift of improvisation and his clear sense of how to organize. He used beltlines and manufactured standardized parts in scattered factories so that if one factory was destroyed, the finished tanks, or whatever, could still be produced. He gave bonuses, threatened punishments, and got rid of as many administrative bureaucrats as he could. The last accomplishment was close to his heart; he was grateful for the fire that destroyed thousands of documents in his ministry, and he used the occasion to drop a long list of officials from their jobs. (Ibid., 491.)

Hitler's continual shifting of manufacturing priorities was perhaps a more serious problem for Speer than round-the-clock bombing. Collaboration between the minister of production and DOENITZ resulted in a remarkable program of U-boat construction. Formerly it had taken almost a year to build a boat in drydock. Separate sections of the new and improved ones were fabricated inland, sent to shipyards, and assembled in two months. In the first quarter of 1945, production reached 42 U-boats a month. About a third were destroyed by bombing at shipyards, but the loss would have been higher if the work there on a boat had not taken only two months. (*Memoirs,* 272 ff, 544n; Doenitz, 354 ff.)

Speer's remarkable accomplishments continued to be hampered by competition with HIMMLER, who with Hitler's blessing was building his own SS industrial empire. The Reichsfuehrer-SS was rich in slave labor but lacked the technical expertise at Speer's disposal. An uneasy partnership evolved. Use of slave labor and closing his eyes to SS barbarities in the concentration camps were the crimes of which Speer was convicted at Nuremberg. Although he could not refute the principal charges, Speer could point out that in the interest of efficiency, if not morality, he had saved lives. Speer pre-

scribed shorter hours and better working conditions because this increased output. He curbed Himmler's plans for setting up more concentration camp factories, because these were inefficient. Speer fought to leave production facilities in occupied countries. These policies saved thousands from the SS. But Speer acted only because efficiency and humanity happened to be parallel in his technocracy, whereas in Himmler's SS underworld they crossed.

By the narrowest of margins Speer missed being innocently implicated in the 20 July 44 coup. The conspirators' organizational chart had a box labeled "Armaments: Speer," a post that also would have made him head of the Home Army. What saved him was the pencil annotation, "If possible" and a question mark. (Speer, *Memoirs,* 392.)

The Minister of Armaments undertook to kill Hitler in mid-Feb 45. His decision was prompted by a friend's pointing out a passage in *Mein Kampf* that said a nation must be saved by any expedient from destruction. Berliners were discussing this, but the friend added that in another part of the 1935 edition was the statement that if a state was being led to doom, "the rebellion of every single member . . . is not only a right, but a duty." (Speer, *Memoirs,* 429.) In what he admits was a plan "with a touch of the ridiculous" (ibid.), he confided in only one man, Dieter Stahl, head of munitions production. Having designed the Fuehrerbunker, Speer had access to its ventilating system. But before Stahl could get him the right kind of gas, Hitler ordered a 10-foot chimney built on the ground-level intake Speer intended to use. Remembering from his WWI experience that gas is heavier than air, Hitler had anticipated the danger. Only slowly recovering from fear that his plot had been detected, Speer then devoted himself to frustrating Hitler's "scorched earth" directives. Using deception when his arguments with the fuehrer failed, Speer was highly successful in saving infrastructure he knew Germany would need for postwar recovery.

Until almost the very end Speer visited Hitler in the bunker. Sometimes the two spent hours discussing architectural plans for the Thousand Year Reich. The final parting at 4 AM on 24 Apr 45 (T-R, 141) was perfunctory: "So, you're leaving? Good. Auf Wiedersehen." (Speer, *Memoirs,* 485.) Hitler named Deputy Minister of Armaments Karl Sauer to succeed Speer in the DOENITZ government, where Speer spent the last days of the war doing what he could to frustrate the scorched earth edicts.

At Nuremberg he was found guilty of counts three and four: war crimes and crimes against humanity. Speer had knowingly used slave labor; he had been present when Hitler directed SAUCKEL to bring in foreign labor by force and when a quota of at least four million was set. Speer was a good witness. Accepting that German leaders had a common responsibility for Hitler's evil regime, he made a fool of the Soviet prosecutor: when Gen Raginsky attempted to show that single-minded dedication to war tasks was reprehensible the Nazi arms minister replied (nothing to lose), "I believe that was the custom in your State, too."

Waiving the right to appeal, accepting his sentence of 20 years in prison, Speer wrote a few weeks later in his diary, "there are things for which one is guilty . . . simply because the scale of the crimes is so overwhelming . . . (Speer, *Memoirs,* 523).

Serving the full maximum sentence, he was released from Spandau Prison (Berlin) a few seconds ahead of SCHIRACH, on the stroke of midnight on 30 Sep-1 Oct 66. During 20 years in Spandau he smuggled out more than 25,000 pages of notes. These were written secretly in a minuscule scrawl on bits of whatever he could get, including toilet paper. Until the notes could be smuggled out by sympathetic guards they were concealed in a shoe lining and in leg bandages worn to relieve phlebitis. He spent the first 21 months on the first draft of his memoirs. From then to the last day he wrote notes for a prison diary. For almost three years after release he conducted research for the final draft of the memoirs. His efforts and those of good editors make the work one of the most solid and interesting in the field, although what some find disarming in the certified war criminal's writing is a "tone of artful honesty" to many others.

Published originally in as *Erinerungen* (Frankfurt/Main-Berlin: Ullstein, Propylaen, 1969), the memoir was translated as *Inside the Third Reich* (New York: Macmillan, 1970). This was followed by *Spandauer Tagebuecher* (same place and publisher, 1975), translated as *Spandau: The Secret Diaries* (same place and publisher, 1976).

SPEIDEL, Hans. German general. 1897-1984. Known primarily as ROMMEL's CofS in France in 1944 he was the first German general of WWII appointed to a top NATO command. Speidel was a **Swabian,** born in Metzingen, Wuerttemberg, on 28 Oct 97, and related to Ludwig BECK. He became a career officer in 1914 and served in the postwar **Truppenamt.** In 1925 he received a PhD, summa cum laude, from the Univ of Tuebingen, where his father was a professor. After being assistant MA in Paris, Speidel was chief of section "West" in the Foreign Armies Div of the GS. As CofS in KUECHLER's 18th Army, Lt Col Dr Hans Speidel received two French officers who came under a flag of truce early on 14 June 40 to surrender Paris (Horne, *1940,* 563). As a corps CofS briefly thereafter he issued instructions to German troops for taking the surrender of the 2d French AG in Lorraine on 23 June 40 (Mellenthin, *Panzer Battles,* 22). Speidel remained in Paris as Otto von STUELPNAGEL's CofS until going to the eastern front in Mar 42 for two years. He started in KLUGE's AG Center, seeing action around Vyasma, then moved to BOCK's AG South and saw action around Kharkov. During the Stalingrad campaign he was in WEICHS's AG B, serving in the NW sector.

In delaying actions through the Ukraine "the highly capable General Speidel" was CofS of Woehler's 8th Army of Manstein's AG South (ibid., 240.) When ROMMEL took over AG B in France he asked for his fellow Wuerttemberger as CofS and Generalleutnant Speidel reported to La Roche Guyon on 14 Apr 44. The officers had never served together, writes Col Truman Smith, who had known Speidel in 1935-39 while serving as US Army MA in Berlin. "Yet each rapidly acquired respect for the other's character and ability." (Smith's introduction to Speidel, *Invasion,* xi). After ROMMEL was critically wounded on 17 July 44 Speidel retained his post under KLUGE and MODEL. The CofS played a major role in sabotaging Hitler's orders to CHOLTITZ for the demolition program in Paris (ibid., 143-44).

On 5 Sep 44, when AG B was being driven back to the Siegfried Line, Speidel was suddenly replaced by Hans Krebs, summoned to Berlin, and arrested two days later. The Gestapo had a confession from Lt Col Caesar von Hofacker of Gen Karl Heinrich von Stuelpnagel's staff that on a visit to La Roche Guyon on 9 July 44 he had discussed the STAUFFENBERG assassination plot with Speidel. The latter skilfully denied this. When Hofacker was called in, showing signs of physical abuse, he shielded Speidel during a long joint interrogation and withdrew his previous testimony. (Irving, *Fox,* 435.) The court of honor headed by RUNDST-EDT did not dismiss Speidel from the army, which would have thrown him at the mercy of the Peoples' Court, even though Keitel told the court that Hitler believed Speer was guilty of treason. The owlish, professorial Speidel outwitted inquisitors (including Ernst KALTEN-BRUNNER) through two major interrogations and many lesser ones by remaining calm, almost indifferent in professing that neither he nor Rommel could possibly have been involved in the conspiracy. (*See* Young, *Rommel,* 247-49.) Speidel was held prisoner for seven months without betraying anybody or being brought to trial. Hitler and the Gestapo were convinced that evidence of his treason would eventually be found. Finally moved from the Albrechtstrasse cells to Urna, near Lake Constance on the Swiss border, he masterminded an escape with more than 20 others, whom a Catholic priest hid until Allied troops arrived. (Ibid.)

After the war Speidel was a professor of modern history at Tuebingen, a consultant to the European Defense Community, and an adviser with HEUSINGER to the FRG. He negotiated with the French in 1951 on German rearmament. When NATO was formed, Speidel commanded Allied Land Forces in Europe, Apr 57-Sep 63. He retired 21 Mar 64 to resume academic work at Tuebingen and to write. (Wistrich.)

The translation of his *Invasion 1944, Ein Beitrag zu Rommels und des Reiches Schicksal* (Tuebingen and Stuttgart: Rainer Wunderlich Verlag Hermann Leins, 1949), was translated as *Invasion 1944: Rommel and the Normandy Campaign* (Chicago: Henry Regnery, 1950). The slim volume of 176 pages (unfortunately not indexed) is almost universally praised for severe objectivity and historical value. But David Irving warns that the author had self-serving motives for building the "myth" that Rommel (hence Speidel as well) was a major figure in the anti-Hitler conspiracy. "He admitted quite frankly to another German general in an American prison camp in 1946: 'I intend making

Rommel into the hero of the entire German people.'" (Irving, *Fox,* 450-51.)

SPERRLE, Hugo. German general. 1885-1953. One of the most senior Luftwaffe commanders, a field marshal from 1940, he was born 7 Feb 85 at Ludwigsburg, son of a brewer. He grew into an ox-like, brutal-looking man who would rival Goering in corpulence and sybaritic living. Speerle began his career as an infantry officer, became a pilot in WWI, headed the air detachment of a Freikorps in 1919, and reverted to the infantry when the German military air force was banned under terms of the Versailles treaty. He joined the Luftwaffe in 1935 as a Generalmajor, going to Spain late the next year to head the **Condor Legion.** Turning the legion over to RICHTHOFEN and promoted to General of Flyers, he soon headed Air Fleet (Luftflotte) 3 with headquarters in Munich.

When Hitler began using military intimidation as an instrument of foreign policy he joked that Speerle and REICHENAU were valuable as his "two most brutal-looking generals."

Speerle did not participate directly in the Polish campaign but his Luftflotte 3 and Kesselring's Luftflotte 1 were fully engaged in the 1940 assault on the west. Speerle remained in France as the sole air commander in the west after 21 May 41. When the Allies landed in Normandy three years later his Western Air Command had only 198 bombers and 125 fighters with which to oppose 3,467 bombers and 5,409 fighters (Bekker, 355).

Almost 18 months earlier Goebbels wrote that Hitler was so irritated by reports of Speerle's high life in Paris, at the Palais du Luxembourg, that "The Fuehrer wants to recall him." The ax fell on 18 Aug 44, when Otto Dessloch replaced the porky Speerle. He was tried at Nuremberg for war crimes but acquitted of all charges. The Luftwaffe field marshal died in Munich on 4 Apr 53.

SPRAGUE, Clifton Albert Frederick. US admiral. 1896-1955. "Ziggy" was born in Boston on 8 Jan 96 and educated at the Roxbury Latin School. A good student and athlete, he was in the three-year class of 1918 at Annapolis, graduating on 28 June 17 (43/199). Three years later he became a naval aviator. As commander of seaplane tender *Tangier* at Pearl Harbor on

7 Dec 41, Capt Sprague was credited with firing the first shots at the Japanese.

The chubby, thorough, and conscientious Sprague next served as CofS Gulf Sea Frontier, where the U-boat menace was critical. He then headed the Seattle Naval Air Station before commissioning the second CV *Wasp*. This was completed in Nov 43 and Capt Sprague commanded her in the fast carrier TF that raided Marcus and Wake Islands. He then was involved in SPRUANCE's assault in the Marianas. With MITSCHER's TF 58 he took part in OZAWA's defeat in the first Battle of the Philippine Sea in mid-15 June 44 and was promoted to flag rank.

As commander of Escort Carrier Div 25 he supported the virtually unopposed conquest of Ulithi that began on 15 Sep 44. Rear Adm Sprague was the principal hero in the Battle for Leyte Gulf on 25 Oct 44: against seemingly impossible odds he launched an air strike that befuddled KURITA into making an improper deployment of a force that could have annihilated the six escort carriers of "Taffy 3" in minutes. But Sprague sent in destroyers for desperate torpedo attacks and in the "ultimate of desperate circumstances" forced KURITA to abandon his mission of destroying the vulnerable amphibious forces in Leyte Gulf (Morison, XII, x). The cost to Taffy 3 was three out of six CVEs and three destroyers. "Among the pilots who flew from the carriers that he commanded," writes Morison, "he was noted for his constant thought for their safety. Modest and retiring by nature, he used to give his senior, Rear Admiral Thomas Sprague, all the credit for stopping Kurita off Samar; but 'Tommy' Sprague, with equal generosity, ascribes the victory to his junior." (Morison, XII, x; the naval historian dedicates Volume XII of his official history to Clifton Sprague.)

The bulldog admiral moved up in Feb 45 to command Carrier Div 2 for the rest of the war.

Ziggy Sprague commanded the Navy Air Group for the nuclear bomb tests at Bikini in 1946, then headed Carrier Div 6 (1948-49), the 17th Naval District, and the Alaskan Sea Frontier (1949-51). He retired 1 Nov 51 as a vice admiral and died 1 Apr 55 at the San Diego USNH, Calif. (RCS.)

SPRAGUE, Thomas Lamison. US admiral. 1894-1972. "Tommy" Sprague, carrier admiral in the Pacific, was born in Lima, Ohio, on 2 Oct

94 and attended the state university before entering the US Naval Academy. He graduated in 1917 (19/199) with the first section of the Class of 1918.

In 1921 he qualified as a naval aviator. For a year from June 40 he was XO in CVL *Ranger* and was promoted. Capt Sprague then fitted out and commanded seaplane tender *Pocomoke*, operating out of Argentia, Newfoundland, on ASW patrols. On 3 Mar 42 he commissioned CVE *Charger,* commanding her until the following December. After being CofS to ComFlt Air at Quonset Point, RI, then to ComNavAirLant at Norfolk, Va, on 16 Aug 43 he commissioned CV *Intrepid* and led her through the Marshalls Islands campaign under Rear Adm Alfred E. Montgomery.

Tommy Sprague was with the three carrier groups under MITSCHER hitting shipping around Truk when half a dozen radar-equipped "Kates" counterattacked after dark on 17 Feb 44. At about 11 PM *Intrepid* took a torpedo hit that killed 11 men, wounded 17, flooded several compartments, and jammed the rudder. Sprague steered by engines to withdraw with an escort to Eniwetok. (Morison, VII, 321.) *Intrepid* suffered so many mishaps during several months of repairs that she was nicknamed "The Evil I" (ibid.), but Sprague got his battered ship back to San Francisco, a 6,000 mile trip.

Promoted to rear admiral, he served as ComFltAir Alameda, Calif, May-July 44, then led Escort Carrier Div 22 in the Pacific. With this he supported the Marianas landings in August, then those at Morotai in New Guinea (16 Sep 44) and Leyte (20 Oct 44).

In the Battle for Leyte Gulf Tommy Sprague commanded **Taffy** 1 (Carrier Divs 22 and 28) as well as Rear Adm Felix B. Stump's Taffy 2 and "Ziggy" SPRAGUE's Taffy 3. (The two Spragues were not kin, and the USN presumably does not form forces from an alphabetical roster.) Heavily attacked by land based planes from Luzon that supported KURITA's column, whose mission was to destroy the US amphibious fleet in Leyte Gulf, he put up a fight that figured prominently in the Japanese admiral's decision to withdraw.

Tommy Sprague moved up in early in 1945 to head Carrier Div 3 off Okinawa. In July and August he led TG 38.1 of the Fast Carrier TF for the final raids on Japan. At year's end he became deputy chief, Bureau of Naval Personnel, then headed that office 1947-49 and was promoted in Aug 49 to vice admiral. The following October he became ComNavAirPac. Retiring 1 Apr 52 as a full admiral. Recalled to active duty in 1956 he was involved in air and naval base negotiations with the Philippine government. He died 17 Sep 72 in a convalescent hospital at Chula Vista, Calif, of cardiorespiratory failure. (RCS.)

SPRUANCE, Raymond Ames. US admiral. 1886-1969. Considered by many to be the most outstanding US naval commander of the war, the handsome, highly intellectual, taciturn Spruance was tactical commander in the decisive victory at Midway. He continued to head the 5th Fleet in the Pacific until after the Japanese surrender.

Spruance was born 3 July 86 in Baltimore. After schooling in New Jersey and Indiana he was appointed from the latter state to Annapolis, graduating with the 1906 early section of the class of 1907 (24/209). His "passed midshipman" period served on the world cruise of the Great White Fleet, he was commissioned 13 Sep 08 as an ensign.

A career specialty in electrical engineering began with a year's study in Schenectady with the General Electric Co. Between the wars he commanded destroyers and took the senior Naval War College course 1926-27 to start a long and affectionate association that ended in 1946 with achievement of his long-standing desire to head the NWC (RCS).

After commanding BB *Mississippi* from 1938, in early 1940 Spruance became Commandant 10th Naval District with headquarters at San Juan, PR. A captain since 1932, he was promoted to rear admiral on 14 Dec 40. In July 41 the Caribbean Sea Frontier was added to his district. About three months before the 7 Dec 42 attack on Pearl Harbor, Spruance went to the Pacific as head of Cruiser Div 5. After the war started, Spruance was HALSEY's second-in-command in TF 16, built around *Enterprise* and *Hornet*. The task force took part in the early raids that NIMITZ ordered on Japanese bases in the Central Pacific.

When a skin problem hospitalized HALSEY he got Nimitz's approval for Spruance to take over as TF 16 commander. Although not an aviator and having been in relatively subordinate command positions (Buell, *Spruance,* 435), the quiet, highly-regarded admiral was thoroughly

familiar with the complex planning and hence able to work with Halsey's staff. TF 16 refueled on 31 May 42 and took position 326 miles NW of Midway to cut off the Japanese who were thought, on the basis of signal intelligence, to be headed in great force toward that strategic American base. "Black Jack" Fletcher caught up on 2 June with his TF 17, built around the hastily repaired *Yorktown,* and took overall command. The Battle of Midway, 4-5 June 42, was well under way when *Yorktown* was crippled and Fletcher waived seniority to give Spruance tactical command. *Yorktown* eventually was lost, but four enemy carriers were sunk in a crushing American victory. Spruance thus had the major role in what proved to be the turning point in the naval war against Japan.

When Halsey returned to duty Spruance became Nimitz's CofS on 18 June 42, was promoted to vice admiral on 19 June 43, becoming Nimitz' deputy. Having had a key role in planning the major naval effort in the Pacific, "the quiet admiral" left his staff post in Pearl Harbor to execute it. From 5 Aug 43 he was Commander, Central Pacific Force, his force redesignated the 5th Fleet a month later. Alternating between directing offensive operations and planning them, Spruance had overall command in the assault on the Gilberts (20 Nov 43) and on the Marshalls (31 Jan 44). On 21 Feb 44 he was promoted to full admiral.

Spruance headed the amphibious force that assaulted the Marianas (15 June 44), where three divisions made the main landing. Four groups of MITSCHER's TF 58 and a group of six modern battleships had a two-fold mission: to cover the landing and to draw the Japanese Combined Fleet into a decisive engagement. OZAWA had little choice but to accept the challenge, loss of Saipan being a threat to the home islands, so the Japanese admiral churned on for what resulted in the First Battle of the Philippine Sea 19-20 June 44. Spruance scored a decisive victory and followed up with a vigorous pursuit that turned into the "Great Marianas Turkey Shoot." This started with a bold and successful strike at long range as darkness approached. Mitscher urged his chief also to pursue with his fifth group of surface ships, but Spruance had submarine reports that another enemy fleet was prepared to attack the landing force if he left it unprotected. This fear proved to be groundless, but Spruance acted on information at hand and later was faulted for losing a great opportunity to reap the rewards of pursuit. The inevitable comparison is made between this probably correct decision and HALSEY's probably wrong one later in the Second Battle of the Philippine Sea (Leyte Gulf). Years later one admiral gave a thoughtful final comment: "Halsey should have been in the Marianas and Spruance at Leyte" (RCS).

To plan the Iwo Jima and Okinawa assaults Spruance returned to Pearl Harbor in Aug 44. He then commanded these operations, which began on 19 Feb and 1 Apr 45. The next month Spruance was relieved at sea by HALSEY and began planning the invasion of Japan that never came. After attending surrender ceremonies aboard *Missouri,* 2 Sep 45, he succeeded NIMITZ as CinC Pacific Fleet on 24 Nov 45. Spruance lost out narrowly to HALSEY when a choice had to be made between the two for the new five-star rank of fleet admiral. (*See* Buell, 435-36.) But the Congress recognized the quiet admiral's remarkable career by approving that he, unlike others, get retired pay for life at the full rate of a four-star admiral (ibid.).

On 1 Mar 46 Spruance became president of the NWC, a billet he had long wanted (RCS). He held the assignment until 30 June 48, retiring the next day. He was ambassador to the Philippines 7 Feb 52-1 Apr 55. Now 69 years old and living quietly in Pebble Beach, Calif, he refused to be involved in the "revolt of the admirals" over integration of the armed forces. Although willing to talk with friends and family about his career, Spruance refused to write his memoirs or let others do so. (Buell, 424.)

The death in 1969 of his son Edward, a captain in the navy, marked the start of a final decline in the admiral's health. He rarely spoke after this but when an old lady complained of having had three strokes he quipped "Three strokes and you're out" (Buell, 428). Spruance died quietly at home on 23 Dec 69. As arranged with Nimitz, Turner, and Charles LOCKWOOD he was buried under a regulation headstone in the Golden Gate National Cemetery, just south of San Francisco at San Bruno. *See* Thomas B. Buell, *The Quiet Warrior: A Biography of Admiral Raymond A. Spruance* (Boston and Toronto, Little, Brown, 1974).

STALIN, Joseph. Dictator of USSR. 1879-1953. A Georgian whose real name was Iosif

Vissarionovich Dzhugashvili, "Koba" to his closest friends, he was born 21 Dec 79 at Gori, near Tiflis. His father, variously described as "a worker in a shoe factory" *(CB 42)* and "a drunken cobbler" (Crankshaw, 220), is said to have treated his son cruelly. But a pious mother got the boy headed toward priesthood. Stalin ("made of steel," the alias he eventually settled on) did well enough in the Gori Theological School to enter the Tiflis Orthodox Seminary in 1893. Five years later he joined the covert **RSDRP** and in 1899 was expelled from school for "unreliability" (Scarecrow). Stalin's mother would lament that but for this "he might now be a bishop" instead of being in the Kremlin *(CB 42).* Becoming a professional revolutionary, he was arrested by tsarist police in 1902, exiled to Siberia, but he escaped to resume subversive activities in Tiflis in 1904. After Lenin split the RSDRP Stalin joined the Bolsheviks, who were less popular locally than the Mensheviks, hence less numerous, so Stalin was able to form "his own small but compact power base." (Crankshaw, "Stalin," in Carver [ed.] *The History Makers,* 221.) He is said to have been an ordinary police informer from 1906, the year he staged a hijacking that netted the party a large sum from the money convoy of a Tiflis bank. (LITVINOV was given the task of laundering the loot in Paris.)

By 1907 the short (five feet four), squat, slender young Stalin was the Bolshevik boss in Baku, being twice more arrested and deported (1908 & 1910). A fellow prisoner commented on his outstanding memory and "aptitude for striking secretly by the hands of others while remaining in the background." (Quoted by Seaton, *Stalin,* 16.) The upper ranks of the revolution considered him still a nonentity, "a colorless drone" (Kennan, *Russia and the West,* 234) or a "gray blur" in the oft-cited quip of N. N. Sukhanov (who would die for it).

But Lenin liked what most others in the party disliked about the rough and ready Georgian (Crankshaw, 221). In St Petersburg when the Bolsheviks broke with the Mensheviks in 1912 and established the **RSDRP (b)** Stalin was elected to its Central Committee. He became the first editor of *Pravda* on 5 May 12. Arrested the next year and sentenced to exile in Siberia for life he was amnestied after the Feb 17 revolution. Meanwhile Stalin had been found unfit for military service, presumably because of obstetrical palsy in his left arm. He returned from the Turukhanha area on 12 Mar 17 and a few days later resumed editorship (with Lenin) of *Pravda* (Medvedev, 7). In Oct 17 he was on Trotsky's Military Revolutionary Committee (Scarecrow) but had no active role in the insurrection (Crankshaw). However, from that event to 1922 he was People's Commissar of Nationalities, and from 1919 was also People's Commissar of Peasants' Inspection.

During the civil war he organized the defenses of **Tsaritsyn** and **Petrograd**. Associates in these celebrated victories would form Stalin's inner circle of cronies, most notably BUDEN-NY, KULIK, TIMOSHENKO, and VORO-SHILOV. In Apr 22, at Lenin's suggestion, Stalin was elected secretary general of the Central Committee. In late 1923 he launched the campaign against Trotsky, political heir apparent to Lenin, who died 21 Jan 24. The "Lenin Testament" recommended that Stalin be replaced as secretary general, his former protégé having proved to be "too crude" for the high post and too obviously intent on monopolizing power. But the 13th Party Conference of 1924 could not muster the votes to oust Stalin, who succeeded Lenin in the triumvirate with Kamenev and Zinoviev. From 1927 Stalin was sole leader of the party (having ousted Trotsky, Kamenev and Zinoviev).

Although he had no official position in the government he dominated it as head of the Politburo. His first five years were a brutal battle for survival. Stalin continued and extended Lenin's New Economic Policy (NEP) with a view to reconciling the peasantry with the Soviet regime (*CE,* "Stalin").

Collectivization

The NEP having brought considerable agricultural prosperity, Stalin changed course in 1928 and ordered the campaign of forced collectivization (said to have been his own brainchild). "There was the liquidation of the kulaks [wealthy peasants] as a class, which ravaged a considerable portion of the middle peasants as well," writes Medvedev. "Entire villages and Cossack *stanisty* were transported to the north." (*Let History Judge,* 69.) Volkogonov (identified below) estimates that 8,500,000 to 9,000,000 peasants suffered in this drive during the period 1928-33. Many were shot for resisting reset-

tlement, many died en route to Siberia, and hundreds of thousands starved to death. They were stripped even of seed for the next crop. In 1928 Stalin also launched the first Five Year Plan, giving priority to military production, but without sufficient capital, industrialization had a stumbling start. Agricultural production dropped, but Stalin exported great quantities of grain (ibid.) and a man-made famine of staggering proportions occurred.

A personal crisis for Stalin had come in 1908 when his beloved first wife Ekaterina Svanidze died of typhus. She was a Georgian, "and with her died my last warm feelings for all human beings," he said. (Conquest, *Terror,* 67). In 1919 he married Nadzezhda ("Nadya") Alliluyeva, sister of Paul Alliluyev, an Old Bolshevik associate of Stalin's who then was Commissar of the Armored Forces. The young wife and her peasant mother nagged Stalin about "butchering the people" to carry out collectivization. Nadya committed suicide on 9 Nov 32, leaving a letter that was political as well as personal. Stalin seems to have been genuinely saddened by the suicide but to him the letter meant primarily that he should be more suspicious about having enemies everywhere. (Conquest, 67-68.)

Stalin's first major cleansing of the party and the government apparatus to remove his enemies was in 1929-32, By 1933, when Hitler and Roosevelt came to power at the height of the Great Depression, Stalin had domestic matters sufficiently under control to worry more about foreign affairs. Contrary to what might be assumed, "Stalin did not want other states to be communist. He was concerned only that they should be weak, or that they should at least expend their strength not against him but against each other" (Kennan, 239). "Good relations with the United States and concerns for American reactions to Soviet moves constituted a cornerstone of Stalin's foreign policy" (Ulam, 290-1). LITVINOV succeeded in getting American diplomatic recognition of the USSR in 1933.

It was not until 1934 that Stalin awoke to the threat of Nazi Germany to eastern Europe in general and to the Ukraine in particular. Collective security becoming attractive, he joined the League of Nations (18 Sep 34), signed a treaty with France (2 May 35), and reoriented the **Comintern.** German reoccupation of the Rhineland (7 Mar 36) showed

Stalin he had to fight Hitler or reach an accommodation. Hitler had used the menace of bolshevism to great effect in seizing power, and anti-fascism was a fundamental communist ideal. Stalin therefore needed to play for time, and at this he was very good.

To get his own house in better order Stalin made YAGODA head of the secret police (GPU), thus gaining personal control of this instrument of terror, and—inspired by the Nazi **Blood Purge** of 1934—Stalin began the **Great Purges.** When the Spanish civil war broke out and FRANCO got military support from Hitler and Mussolini, fear of fascism prompted Stalin to send tanks, planes, and advisers to oppose FRANCO and his German and Italian allies. Republican ideals of the Spanish civil war being dangerous, Stalin had almost all "Spaniards" liquidated on their return to Mother Russia.

The **Anschluss** (Mar 38) and **Munich crisis** (Sep 39) convinced Stalin that collective security was no security. On 10 Mar 39 Stalin threw his archenemy Hitler a broad hint by saying in a speech that Russia had no intention of pulling anybody else's chestnuts from the fire. Now courted by the British and French as well as the Germans over the fate of Poland, Stalin sought the highest bidder. Deciding this was Hitler, Stalin replaced Foreign Secretary Litvinov with Molotov on 3 May 39.

One of Stalin's basic principles was to avoid involvement with countries not on his borders, but these extended from Europe to the Far East. The Chinese communists were of no interest to Stalin but he saw in the Kuomintang a potentially valuable anti-imperialist force if it could develop a powerful army. Stalin had CHIANG KAI-SHEK and other Nationalists brought to the USSR for military schooling and then sent Soviet military advisers to China. As for Japan, Stalin concluded that in this case his best foreign policy was collective security with America.

Border fighting with the Japanese in the Far East led Stalin to fear a two-front war. This drove him to sign the Nazi-Soviet Pact on 23 Aug 39, which ironically was the very day that ZHUKOV ended the Japanese threat in Mongolia by his stunning victory at **Khalkhin Gol.** This strengthened Japan's Strike-South faction, which meant the Soviets ultimately could move large forces from the Far East to oppose the Germans: Siberian troops, dressed for the occasion, appeared with the bitter Russian winter of 1941-42 to made Hitler look more and more like Napoleon.

If the world was stunned by Stalin's nonaggression pact with Hitler (herein), Stalin was appalled by how fast Hitler overran Poland. Under a secret protocol the Red Army occupied its half—78,000 square miles; 13,000,000 people.

Stalin's behavior was particularly enigmatic in the following months. He enraged Hitler by taking over the Baltic countries and attacking Finland on 30 Nov 40. Hitler was even more alarmed when Stalin moved into Bessarabia and Bukovina on 28 June 40. None of this was in the secret protocol. Stalin made an uncharacteristic error in Nov 40 by assuming that Hitler was playing from weakness by inviting him to join the Three Power Pact (Japan, Italy, and Germany); the Soviet leader demanded more concessions in the Balkans and eastern Europe. Hitler decided to "crush the Soviet Union in a quick campaign," as he said in the directive for planning Opn **Barbarossa.**

Stalin meanwhile scored a diplomatic coup by signing a treaty with Japan on 13 Apr 41. Until then the dictator had held no official governmental post (above) but on 6 May 41 he created a sensation by taking over from MOLOTOV as Chairman of the Council of Peoples' Commissars. This made him the actual head of government, a move presumably to impress the world, Hitler in particular, with how serious he was personally about meeting challenges against Russia. Molotov stepped down to be deputy **premier** but remained foreign minister. (Ulam, 279, 309, 310.) Stalin meanwhile infuriated the fuehrer further by accusing in him in *Pravda* of spreading the war by attacking Yugoslavia, which capitulated on 17 Apr 41 as the Germans overran Greece.

But Stalin started behaving even more strangely in private. "He'd obviously lost all confidence in the ability of our army to put up a fight," writes Khrushchev from observing him in the Kremlin on visits from Kiev in mid-June 41. "It was if he'd thrown up his hands in despair and given up after Hitler crushed the French army and occupied Paris." (Khrushchev, 166.) There are many other similar reports, but recent scholarship indicates Khrushchev errs in saying that Stalin was virtually in shock for

11 days (ibid., 169); it was more like three days (below). The following seems to be an accurate scenario based on new evidence Dmitri Volkogonov gives in *Triumph and Tragedy* (New York: Grove Weidenfeld, 1991) and supplementary material from Harriet F. Scott.

Barbarossa

Stalin called a Politburo meeting on 22 June 41 after Zhukov (CGS) informed him that an invasion had started. On Stalin's order Molotov phoned the German ambassador, who said Germany had declared war. Although communications with the front had been knocked out and the extent of the disaster not known for four or five days, Stalin at first believed that the invaders could be stopped and thrown back. Being a politician concerned with survival in power he had Molotov give the people the bad news. (HFS.)

On that long first day Stalin raged around the Kremlin making harsh demands and threatening military and political subordinates. Without waiting for formalities he set up the supreme command (the **Stavka**). Late in the day he sent people to find out what was going on: SHAPOSHNIKOV and KULIK to D. G. PAVLOV's central sector; ZHUKOV to Kiev.

On D+1, 23 June, after German troops had advanced up to 60 kilometers and had overrun the Red Army's designated forward concentration areas, Stalin tried unsuccessfully to phone Pavlov. The latter's front had collapsed, no gasoline or vehicles being available for reserves. Stalin still believed the situation could be stabilized in a few weeks.

But on finally having reports of the debacle and as the first great encirclement formed around Minsk, on the "dry" route to Moscow that Napoleon had used in 1812, paralyzing shock hit Stalin. He was in this state during the period 28-30 June 41, making senseless demands in the Kremlin and phone calls to the field, sometimes being incommunicado for hours in his large office suite or dacha.

While Stalin was in this state of mental paralysis Molotov concluded that the GKO should be established. With MALENKOV, VOROSHILOV, BERIA, N. A. Voznesensky, and MIKOYAN he went to see Stalin in his dacha. "Why are you here?" the dictator asked, suspecting that it was to arrest him (HFS). Told that they wanted him to take charge as head of

the new agency, the GKO, and put the country on a war footing, Stalin agreed somewhat listlessly. But he then began to recover. Twice on 29 June he appeared at the Commissariat of Defense, his eyes bloodshot from lack of sleep. The GKO was formed the next day and Stalin's first act was to order the arrest of D. G. PAVLOV and his staff.

The people were waiting to hear from their supreme leader, whom they still trusted. Although never an orator, Stalin made an effective radio address on 3 July that rallied the country for the "great patriot war."

The short-lived **Glavkom** system was set up under three of Stalin's cronies, TIMOSHENKO, BUDENNY, and VOROSHILOV. The position of commander in chief had not existed since the revolution but Stalin was persuaded to take that post and chairmanship of the Stavka. This arrangement was effective on 10 July 41, giving Stalin all political, economic, military, and diplomatic power for the duration. (HFS.) Stalin was commissar of defense also, but while things went badly his signature did not appear on any documents or orders. (Khrushchev, 169-70.) Not until the Stalingrad victory in early 1943 did he admit to being supreme commander in chief (Seaton, *Stalin,* 106-7) and start using the title of marshal which he had gotten in 1941 (**MSU.** No 9). Not until 26 June 45, well after V-E day, did Stalin become Generalissimus [*sic*] of the Soviet Union (HFS).

While using the GKO-Stavka apparatus to direct military operations and insisting that senior staff officers spend most of their time at the front, Stalin seldom left the Kremlin. He visited a war zone only on 3 and 5 Aug 43. This apparently was a "photo opportunity" to make propaganda films. The supreme commander went to the Western and Kalinin Fronts, where Sokolovsky and Voronov met him well to the rear. (Seaton, 190, citing SHTEMENKO, I, 178-79.)

In dealing with the western allies who had saved his bacon in the first few months but on whom he depended throughout the war, Stalin made exorbitant demands, especially for **Lend Lease.** Like Chiang Kai-shek he kept postwar goals in mind while demanding more. Stalin effectively used his phenomenal memory and mastery of technical detail (Ulam, 292) and nobody was his peer at correlating military and civilian requirements. Thinking of everything, he devised crafty and elaborate ways of deceiving his people about the foreign origin of **Lend Lease** materiel.

Stalin became increasingly strident on the second front issue. He even accusing the west of wanting Russia to be bled white. He had considerable justification for this accusation, as he did for the claim that the Soviets made the greatest sacrifices and scored the greatest triumphs in crushing the Third Reich. While the western allies, particularly the Americans, planned military operations with little regard for postwar politics, Stalin made no such mistake. (*See* LITVINOV.) At Teheran, Yalta, and Potsdam (excusing himself from other conferences on grounds that he had a war to fight), "Uncle Joe" was the acknowledged master.

It has been said that Bulganin was working with him as early as 1944 on how to keep war heroes from taking political advantage of their prestige (Erickson, 257). Stalin started removing famous wartime commanders after V-E day. Foremost among thousands of victims were Zhukov, Novikov, Tolbukhin, Rokossovsky, Meretskov, Voronov, Vatutin, Chernyakhovsky, Bagramyan, Konev, Malinovsky, and Kuznetzov. (Medvedev, 469; Wolfe, 66n64.).

About Stalin's own performance as a war leader, Seaton concludes that "if he is to bear the blame for the defeats of the first two years of the war, he must be allowed the credit for the amazing successes of 1944" (*Stalin,* 271). In the Cold War Stalin demonstrated that if "War is merely the continuation of policy by other means" the converse of Clausewitz's dictum is valid.

Although he aged rapidly after 1945, almost immediately showing signs of senility (Djilas, 151-52), Stalin was fully in control almost to the end. This came on 5 Mar 53, at Kuntsevo, near Moscow, less than a month after he had a stroke. The Man of Steel was 10 weeks past his 74th birthday.

As part of the de-Stalinization program launched under KHRUSHCHEV and in accordance with a decision of the 22d Party Congress his embalmed body was removed from the elaborate Red Square Lenin-Stalin mausoleum on 31 Oct 61 and reinterred near (not in) the Kremlin Wall.

"Whatever standards we use to take his measure, in any event—let us hope for all time to come—to him will fall the glory of being the greatest murderer in history. For in him was joined the criminal senselessness of a Caligula with the refinement of a Borgia and the brutality of Tsar Ivan the Terrible." (Djilas, *Conversations With Stalin,* 187.)

What has been called "the First Glasnost Biography," Dmitri Volkogonov's *Stalin: Triumph and Tragedy* (Moscow, 1988; New York and London, 1991) has important revelations from previously inaccessible personal and official archives.

STALIN, Vasily Iosifovich. Soviet air force officer. 1921-62. Joseph Stalin's son by second wife Nadezhda (Nadya) Sergeyevna Alliluyeva (d. 1932), he was a "clever but headstrong" boy (Khrushchev, 291) who turned into a thoroughgoing rotter. He married TIMOSHENKO's daughter in 1940 (or about then, according to HFS). Although ill suited for military service, already "a coarse, semiliterate alcoholic" (Medvedev, 469n), he was given a special sufferance for admission to flying school and, despite a poor record, he got his wings in 1941. The spoiled son was air force chief of inspection until his father had him dismissed in the spring of 1943 for "moral degeneracy." Sent to the front after 10 days in custody he rose from commanding an air regiment to heading a corps. Vasily was a general lieutenant by the time he reached his 29th birthday in 1950.

Joseph Stalin ordered his son relieved in May 52 for insubordination and misconduct after Vasily proved to be incapable even of keeping up with his course at the General Staff Academy. After his father's death in 1953 the prodigal son, still in the Soviet AF, raised such a ruckus with accusations of foul play that Defense Minister Bulganin ordered him to leave Moscow for duty elsewhere. Refusing, Vasily Stalin was discharged from the service and shortly thereafter (28 Apr 53) arrested and sentenced to eight years imprisonment for intrigue and abuse of position. Khrushchev had him released in Jan 60 but because of continued alcohol related misconduct he was reincarcerated two months later to complete his sentence. In the spring of 1962 he was freed because of bad health and banished from Moscow. Debilitated from alcoholism, he died

19 Mar 61 in Kazan and was buried there in the Dzhugashvili family grave.

STALIN (Dzhugashvili), Yakov Iosifovich. 1908-43. "Chapev" was Joseph Stalin's eldest (legitimate) son. Volkogonov says he was two months old when his mother, Yekaterina, died of typhus. (Volkogonov, 4. Others say she died in 1917.)

The shy, unprepossessing boy, known as Yakov Iosifovich Dzhugashvili, did not join the household until 1926, the year Svetlana was born and Vasily was four years old. Although well cared for my his young stepmother (ibid, 149), Yakov was never on good terms with his hard, work-addicted father (Ibid.; Conquest, 68; Khrushchev, 291).

Honest and decent, but emotionally crippled and not a good student, Yakov attended the Moscow Railway Engineering Institute before working in a power station and being accepted at the Red Army Artillery Academy. He was given command of a battery in the 14th Howitzer Regt as a first lieutenant or captain (authorities differ). At some time in his early years Yakov became so depressed by his father's coldness that the tried to shoot himself. "Ha! You missed," was Stalin's only sympathy as the boy began a long convalescence from an arm wound. (Volkogonov, 149.)

In action from the start of war on 22 June 41 he surrendered with thousands of others near Vitebsk on 16 July 41. Variously identified as Capt or 1st Lt Stalin, he was photographed with German officers as a defiant POW and is said to have warned interrogators that Moscow would be defended to the end and that a very capable group of new Soviet military commanders was emerging. (Erickson, *To Stalingrad*, 221-22.) The Germans gave wide circulation to a broadside with an alleged photo of Yakov talking with two of his captors (Volkogonov, II, 430).

Joseph Stalin had Yakov's wife, Julia, imprisoned under Order No. 274 of 1941 that all POWs were to be considered traitors and their families punished (see Kinship edicts) and refused even to consider Count BERNADOTTE's offer to try his son's release. (Svetlana Alliluyeva Stalin, *Twenty Letters to a Friend*, 172 & 196; Volkogonov, II, 430). The father later refused a German offer to exchange Yakov for PAULUS (Medvedcv, 468n).

Delores Ibarruri published memoirs in 1985 that said a special force perished in 1942 while attempting to free Yakov from Sachsenhausen, something previously unreported and neither "corroborated or disproved" (Volkogonov, II, 150-1). His strength failing as the Germans moved him through Hammelburg, Luebeck, and Sachsenhausen, losing interest in his worth as a Prominente, Chapev ended his ordeal on 14 Apr 43. Either by refusing to enter his POW barracks or by hurling himself on the wire, he was killed by a guard.

STANGL, Franz Paul. Nazi war criminal. 1908-71. Born in Altmuenster, Austria, on 26 Mar 08, he joined Austrian police in 1931. Late in 1940 he became superintendent of the Euthanasia Institute at Schloss Hartheim, then from Mar 42 he served in Poland under Odilo GLOBOCNIK. SS Capt Stangl was commandant of the extermination camps at Sobibor (until Sep 42) and Treblinka.

He was a quiet, polite, friendly man who was not motivated by sadism nor even by anti-Semitism, writes Wistrich; he became known as the "best camp commander in Poland" because he had a talent for efficient mass murder. After the camp uprising on 2 Aug 43 he was involved in antipartisan operations in Yugoslavia and in a large-scale construction project that used half a million Italian laborers.

Stangl was interned after the war for his antipartisan activities, his earlier war crimes not being known in 1945. Handed over to Austrian authorities, he walked out of Linz prison late in 1947 and escaped via Rome to Syria. After working there for three years and being joined by his family, he moved with them to Brazil in 1951. Not until 10 years later did the Austrians officially put his name on the list of wanted war criminals, although they had known for some years about his role in murdering almost a million people. (Wistrich.) Arrested in Brazil on 28 Feb 67 and extradited, he was sentenced on 22 Oct 70 to life imprisonment. Stangl died at Dueseldorf on 28 June 71 of a heart attack.

STARK, Harold Raynsford. US admiral. 1880-1972. Stark was born in Wilkes-Barre, Pa, on 12 Nov 80 and graduated from the USNA in 1903 (30/50). As a plebe he acquired the nickname Betty from having to recite what the Revolutionary War hero John Stark allegedly said to inspire his militia before the Battle of Bennington, Vt, in 1777. (The version on the battlefield monument at Bennington is "There are the redcoats and they are ours or this night Molly Stark sleeps a widow." Mrs Stark's name was Elizabeth, but Molly (as in Molly Pitcher) was a common sobriquet. What plebe Stark popped off was something more like "We win today or Betty Stark's a widow tomorrow" [RCS].)

Stark began sea duty aboard Adm David G. Farragut's Civil War flagship *Hartford,* the last full-rigged ship on active service. By 1914 he was skipper of DD *Patterson.* For a particularly smart bit of shiphandling into a tricky Maine harbor with Assistant Secretary of the Navy Franklin D. Roosevelt aboard he acquired a permanent friend in the future president. (RCS.)

When the US entered WWI Stark took a squadron of five old coal-burning destroyers from Manila through monsoons in the Indian Ocean to reach Gibraltar in fighting trim. He was awarded the DSM and assigned to Adm William S. Sims's staff in London. The experience in coordinating US-British naval operations in European waters would later prove valuable.

Exactly a month before the Germans attacked Poland on 1 Sep 39 Stark succeeded LEAHY as CNO. He overcame strong isolationist sentiment in Congress to get authorization to start constructing additional ships and bases for WWII, thus deserving much credit for the critical first efforts to build the US navy that fought the war. When FDR directed creation of the Atlantic Neutrality Patrol the new CNO decided that the fastest way to provide ships was to refurbish old destroyers that had been laid up for years. Congress specified when granting the funds that no ship could be transferred or otherwise disposed of unless the CNO certified that it was not needed for national defense. This presented a problem when Roosevelt and Churchill negotiated the "bases for destroyers" deal in 1940. Stark compromised only because the US national defense benefitted from the exchange.

Adm J. O. Richardson was finishing maneuvers off Hawaii with the US Pacific Fleet when FDR ordered him to remain at Pearl Harbor rather than return to the West Coast. Both Richardson and Stark protested, the latter pointing out several objections: Pearl Harbor lacked adequate repair and overhaul facilities, spare parts, ammunition stocks, fuel, or rations. Further, families would be abandoned on the West Coast. The president insisted that the US fleet's presence in Hawaii would deter Japan from moving south while the British and Dutch were tied up in Europe. Richardson was relieved of command, but Stark stuck it out.

As for approved national strategy, the CNO was left with the Orange Plan of the 1920s. This called for an offensive against Japan in the central Pacific while Britain secured the Atlantic. "Orange" was quickly overtaken by events. With German U-boats and commerce raiders winning the Battle of the Atlantic, Stark reversed priorities: the US Navy would have to fight a holding action in the Pacific while doing everything possible with limited resources to help keep Britain in the war. US-UK senior staff talks in Washington in early 1941 ended with approval of the "Germany first" strategy. The US Navy's primary mission thus became defense of the Western Hemisphere and support of Atlantic convoys.

As for the Pacific, Stark recognized that the little Asiatic Fleet, based in the Philippines under Adm. Thomas C. HART, was vulnerable. But he quite correctly refused to send it reinforcements. Instead, he kept the Pacific Fleet of Adm Husband E. KIMMEL concentrated at Pearl Harbor and worked on building up its base facilities. From decoded intercepts of Japanese radio traffic made possible by Capt. L. F. SAFFORD and others involved in the "Magic" program, it was apparent to Stark that a military crisis was approaching in the Pacific. He passed frequent warnings to all principal commanders. But toward the end of 1941 the CNO shared the view that the first enemy attack would come not at Pearl Harbor but in the Far East. When the critical intercept of the long message to NOMURA was decoded early on 7 Dec 41, indicating that something momentous was scheduled for 7:30 AM Pearl Harbor time, Stark offered to send a flash message by USN communications. But army CofS MARSHALL, assured him that the army would get it there just as fast. The warning arrived after the attack started.

The US Congress and public clamored for scapegoats. Although Ernest J. KING probably was right in saying privately at the time and later that the army (having responsibility for the defense of Pearl Harbor) was more guilty than the navy, the CNO was relieved but his army counterpart, George Marshall, was not. Stark turned over his functions to KING on 7 Mar 42 after a meeting with the president.

The admiral became FDR's personal representative in London on 30 Apr 42. From 1 Oct 43 he also commanded the 12th Fleet with responsibility for USN forces in British waters and off the coasts of Europe. He was charged with training and providing maintenance for US naval forces in his area and readying them for the Normandy invasion. Stark also was de facto ambassador to de Gaulle's Free French government and he dealt with other governments in exile. His most important function, well performed, was liaison with the British Admiralty and Churchill himself.

Having passed retirement age a year earlier, and the war in Europe won, Stark was succeeded by Kent HEWITT on 15 Apr 45. He testified at one of the many Pearl Harbor investigations, and the view persisted that he was partly responsible for the disaster of 7 Dec 41. (*Washington Post* obit.) Although still highly respected within the navy and considered by many to be a scapegoat, Stark was barred by FORRESTAL from any further position of responsibility in the navy (ibid.). Retired on 1 Apr 46, and living to the age of 91, the admiral died 20 Aug 72 at his home in Washington after a heart attack.

STAUFFENBERG, Nicholas (Claus) Philip Schenk von. German officer. 1907-44. The only anti-Nazi conspirator who came close to eliminating Hitler (on 20 July 44), Count von Stauffenberg was born 15 Nov 07 in Greifstein Castle, Upper Franconia. He was a Swabian from a highly cultured Catholic family that had produced many military aristocrats. On his mother's side Claus was a great-grandson of Gen August von Gneisenau and was related to Yorck von Wartenburg, both of whom were German heroes in the wars against Napoleon. His father had been privy chamberlain to the last king of Wuertenburg. The boy grew into a tall, slender, strikingly handsome man with a brilliant mind and a passion for liberal arts as well as for horses and sports.

At 19 he became an officer cadet in the celebrated Bamberger Ritter (17th Bamberg Cav

Regt). Two years after attending the War Academy in Berlin he was selected for the General Staff (1938), and in 1939-40 was on the staff of HOEPNER's 6th Pz Div in Poland and France, Stauffenberg joined the OKH Organization Dept in June 40. He became a specialist in forming volunteer units from POWs, especially anti-Bolsheviks. During the first 18 months of Barbarossa he spent much time in the USSR, becoming more and more appalled by Nazi barbarities. Falling in with two leading anti-Hitler conspirators, TRESCKOW and his aide SCHLA-BRENDORFF, Maj von Stauffenberg (promoted in 1942) used his staff visits to sound out senior commanders about opposing Hitler. Getting nowhere, in Feb 43 he requested and was granted a combat assignment.

Maj von Stauffenberg was operations officer of the 10th Pz Div, which had been driven back into Tunisia. On 7 Apr 43, during the last days of the German victory around Kasserine Pass, he was critically wounded when his staff car ran into a mine field and was attacked by aircraft. The major lost his left eye, two fingers of the left hand, his right forearm, and had injuries to an ear and knee.

Oberstleutnant Stauffenberg decided during convalescence that he had a sacred mission to have Hitler killed. His first assignment on returning to duty on 1 Nov 43 was as CofS to the General Army Office (*Allgemeine Heersamt*). The Gestapo had arrested DOHNANYI on 5 Apr 43 and Canaris was pressured into dismissing Hans OSTER 10 days later. Stauffenberg assumed leadership of the conspiracy when it seemed to be fatally crippled. His first task was to replace Oster as "business manager," but the young count was soon recognized as

the first natural leader to emerge from within the ranks of the plotters, a leader who could command at once the devotion of both soldiers and civilians to an extent to which neither Beck nor Goerdeler, with all the respect they very properly enjoyed, could ever have attained. Not for nothing was he nicknamed the '*Bambererger Reiter*' from his remarkable resemblance to the famous thirteenth-century statue in the Cathedral of his native city. (W-B, *Nemesis,* 600-1, where photographs make the author's point.)

Conspirators in OKW connived for Oberst Stauffenberg (as of 1 June 44) to become Gen Friedrich FROMM's CofS in the Replacement Army, which had the primary mission in Opn **Valkyrie.** The war reached a new crisis five days later when the Allies landed in Normandy.

Stauffenberg believed it was necessary to kill Goering and Himmler along with Hitler and he had had to abort at least six attempts from 26 Dec 43 because all three men were not present. (W-B, ibid., 633-34.) The final attempt was on Tuesday 20 July 44 when (beside the point but with a certain irony) there was a full solar eclipse (Otto John, 146). Himmler and Goering would not be not present during the attempt, but Stauffenberg decided he had to proceed. The chosen weapon was a captured British time bomb developed by the SOE; it was small enough to fit into a briefcase but had tremendous power and—most important—a silent timing mechanism.

Hitler's conference normally would have been held in an underground bunker where concussion would have optimum effective. But the bunker was closed for repairs and the meeting took place in a large wooden hut that had three windows opposite the long side of the table at which Hitler would stand over maps. There were places around the table for 23 others including two stenographers. (W-B, ibid, 638 [diagram].) Entering the room with Keitel at about 12:40 PM, when HEUSINGER had begun his briefing, Stauffenberg was presented to Hitler (apparently for the first time) and told he would be next. The colonel, who had set the fuse for a 10-minute delay, moved to a corner of the table near Col Heinz Brandt and said he would leave his briefcase on the floor there while making a phone call. Finding the briefcase in his way, Brandt pushed it farther under the table and against a heavy upright support on the side away from Hitler. Keitel was asking nervously for Stauffenberg, whose turn was about due, when a tremendous explosion occurred. The time was between 12:42 and 12:50. Three detonations sent up thick smoke flecked with yellow flame. An officer, unhurt after being blown through one of the shattered windows, ran toward the guard-house shouting "*Attentat! Attentat!*" (W-B, ibid., 641).

The official stenographer was killed immediately, Brandt, SCHMUNDT, and KORTEN were

fatally injured, and almost all others were injured. The fuehrer, who had been standing with his body leaning over the table, lost his trousers at the belt line. His hair was set on fire, his right arm was partially and temporarily paralyzed, and both ear drums were damaged. (Ibid.) The victims thought first that the bomb had been dropped by a plane, then that it had been tossed through a window or planted in the floor. (Ibid.) It was some time before the truth was known.

Having seen all this from a safe distance and assuming there were no survivors, and not knowing that FELLGIEBEL would fail in his vital communications role, Stauffenberg and his orderly officer bluffed their way through the three security posts to a waiting plane. Three hours later they landed at Rangsdorf, a 45-minute drive from central Berlin. At 3:45 PM the colonel phoned his staff office and was appalled to learn that "Valkyrie" had not been broadcast! Gen Friedrich Olbricht, Fromm's deputy, explained that the conspirators had received word from Rastenburg of the explosion but that a bad telephone connection left them without confirmation that Hitler was dead.

Reaching the dithering generals at the Bendlerstrasse around 4:30 PM the colonel took charge. "He went from telephone to telephone in his effort to try and carry the deputy commanders in the provinces along with him," writes Goerlitz, "adjuring one, encouraging another, issuing peremptory orders to a third, always displaying what seemed to be a sixth sense in the choice of the manner and tone most suited to the person concerned" (*GGS,* 470).

The coup still might have succeeded if others had acted in Berlin. But Generals BECK and WITZLEBEN, who were to take over as head of state and OKW commander, had been slow in reporting for duty and had then failed to act. The plan was that FROMM, as Replacement Army commander, would order troops to comply with Opn **Valkyrie** or that the general be arrested and succeeded by Olbricht. Because of their oath of allegiance to Hitler most German officers would not join the conspiracy until assured they had been released by the fuehrer's demise, by death or otherwise. Olbricht went to Fromm's office and told him that orders for **Valkyrie** must go out because Hitler was dead. Not knowing that communications to Rastenburg had been restored after being blocked as part of the plot,

Olbricht volunteered to let Fromm reassure himself by phoning OKW. KEITEL answered immediately. "Everything is as usual here," said the latter. "Where, but the way, is your Chief of Staff, Colonel Count Stauffenberg?"

The conspirators then arrested Fromm, but he violated parole and phoned for help. Then came an official radio announcement, after 6:30 PM, that the fuehrer would address the nation that evening. Certain junior officers in the Bendlerstrasse got weapons, started policing the corridors, and rounded up putschists including Beck, Hoepner, Stauffenberg, and Olbricht. Fromm then appeared brandishing a pistol and, believing that his own safety lay in silencing his collaborators, ordered their liquidation forthwith. BECK opted for suicide. HOEPNER was allowed to live and take his chances in court. Others including Stauffenberg, who needed assistance after having been wounded in the back about two hours earlier, were herded into a courtyard. In the glare of truck headlights, they were executed by one volley of machine pistol fire from troops under Maj Otto REMER. Having remained silent during his brief captivity, Stauffenberg died shouting "Long live Free Germany," or something similar. The Bendlerstrasse headquarters building was subsequently was renamed for him.

STEINER, Felix. German general. 1896-1966. He was born 23 May 96 in Ebenrode and was an officer in WWI. In 1935 Steiner was among the few who left the Reichswehr for what became the Waffen-SS, making him a rare SS officer professionally qualified for high command. After fighting in Poland and France SS-Gruppenfuehrer Steiner commanded the SS Division "Wiking" in the east and was awarded the Oakleaves (159/890) on 23 Dec 42. Early in 1944, having been promoted, Obergruppenfuehrer Steiner took command of the 3d SS Pz Corps facing FEDYUINSKY's 2d Shock Army in the Oranienbaum bridgehead near Leningrad (Seaton, R-G War, 409). Again promoted, General of the Waffen-SS Steiner was awarded the Swords (86/159) on 10 Aug 44 after a defensive action that reduced his army corps to 200 men (Angolia, I, 194-95). Early in 1945 Steiner assumed command of the 11th Army for the defense of Pomerania, now opposing ROKOSSOVSKY (Seaton, 540). In the final defense of

Berlin, Hitler ordered Steiner on 21 April to pick elements of several shattered divisions and attack SE to seal the gap through which Zhukov's right wing was pouring. Hitler hoped Steiner would link up with a force under WENCK that was driving NE toward Potsdam. But with no more than 15,000 men and lacking heavy weapons, Steiner could accomplish little. Withdrawing to avoid capture by the Russians, he surrendered to the British on 3 May 45 at Lueneburg. The remarkable field commander wrote of his Waffen-SS campaigns in the book *Armee der Geaechteten* (Army of Outlaws). He died 17 May 66 in Munich. (Ibid.)

STEPHENSON, William Samuel. British SIS LnO in US. 1896-1989. A very wealthy, Canadian-born industrialist, WWI ace, amateur world boxing champion and electronics expert, the diminutive "Little Bill" Stephenson was sent to NYC in 1940 to replace Sir James Paget as head of the SIS station. For cover he was formally appointed Passport Control Office rand was assigned LnOs from MI5 and SOE. As "director of British security coordination" Sir William coached "Wild Bill" DONOVAN, the new OSS chief, on British SIS tactics and techniques.

The "man called Intrepid" also was the channel for intelligence and other matters between Roosevelt and Churchill for the duration. (*S&S*; Nigel West, *MI6*, 123.)

Soon after leaving his NYC office, in Sep 45 he found that the Canadian government intended to surrender the defector Igor Gouzenko, a young cipher clerk who had worked in Moscow and Ottawa, to avoid a diplomatic incident with the Soviets. Sir William's timely intervention enabled western counterintelligence to the arrest and convict the atomic spy Dr Alan Nunn May and 18 others in 1946. The defector later provided leads to the Cambridge Five. (See West, MI6, 130 ff.)

Stephenson and DONOVAN founded the World Commerce Corp after the war (Smith, OSS, 192). He died 3 Jan 89 (NYT obit, 3 Feb [sic] 89.)

STETTINIUS, Edward Reilly, Jr. US official. 1900-49. "Little Stet," whose illustrious father had been a J. P. Morgan partner, was born in Chicago on 22 Oct 00. He grew into a strikingly handsome man with white hair and heavy black eyebrows offsetting a ruddy complexion. Before leaving the Univ of Virginia in 1924 without graduating he was offered a job in Detroit with the General Motors Corp. In 1930 he became assistant to the president, and the next year he went to Washington as a liaison man. He joined the US Steel Corp in 1934 and in May 40 he resigned as chairman of the board to head the new National Defense Advisory Commission. "Before arriving in Washington at the age of thirty-eight, wrote Dean Acheson, "he had gone far with comparatively modest equipment (*Present,* 99); diplomatic historian Herbert Feis called Stettinius a man of "mediocre mind and shallow."

After serving under William S. KNUDSEN in the Office of Production Management, established within the Office for Emergency Management in Jan 41, he was appointed Lend Lease administrator late that year. Of this experience he published *Lend Lease: Weapon for Victory* (New York: Macmillan, 1944). Stettinius became undersecretary of state in Oct 43 and the next year had direct responsibility for the Dumbarton Oaks Conference. Little Stet succeeded Cordell HULL as secretary of state on 1 Dec 44, going with FDR to Yalta and being a delegate to the UN conference at San Francisco. Stettinius resigned his cabinet post in June 45 and served the next year as US representative to the UN. *See also* Campbell, Thomas M. and George C. Herring, eds, *The Diaries of Edward R. Stettinius, Jr., 1943-1946* (1975).

STILWELL, Joseph Warren. US general. 1883-1946. "Vinegar Joe" commanded US forces in the China-Burma-India Theater (CBI), was Chief of the Joint Staff under CHIANG KAI-SHEK, and was the agent for receipt and distribution of Lend Lease in CBI. He held these titles from Feb 42 until recalled in Oct 44. Stilwell then was CG 10th Army on Okinawa after BUCKNER's death on 18 June 45.

The controversial general was born 19 Mar 83 in Florida while his talented but flighty father was there briefly in the lumber business. Joe was reared at the family home in Yonkers, NY, in a region where the Stilwells had been since 1738. Two forebears had been senior officers during the American Revolution. Young Joe acquired his father's facility with words, developed a strong aversion to religion, and had a life-long taste for athletics and physical fitness.

In high school he got glowing reports for mental, moral, and physical qualities. Too young on graduation in 1889 for college, he was kept in high school for postgraduate work. The 16-year-old Stilwell relieved the inevitable boredom by organizing a band of troublemakers, the Big Four, whose pranks led to their expulsion. Family tradition has it that Dr Stilwell then told his son of "a nice place up the Hudson where you can play tennis" (Tuchman, *Stilwell,* 12).

Stilwell did well at West Point. He was a good athlete (cross-country, track, crew, basketball, and football); he excelled in French, showing the language aptitude that would loom large later; he achieved the rank of cadet lieutenant; and in 1904 he graduated 32th in a class of 124.

Commissioned an infantryman Lt Stilwell served 14 months in the Philippines before returning to West Point. He taught English, French, Spanish, and history (during the fourth year) and coached basketball, baseball, track, and football. On summer leaves in 1907-09 he visited Latin America, ostensibly to sharpen his Spanish but really for adventure. On foot, mule, and horseback he explored the back country of Guatemala and Mexico.

After further troop duty in the Philippines and a 17-day visit to China in 1911 (a few weeks after Sun Yat-sen toppled the Manchu dynasty) he had a second tour at West Point, teaching English, history, and Spanish (1913-17). Stilwell won the DSM in France as an intelligence officer, serving initially at GHQ before being G2, 4th Corps and helping plan the Saint-Mihiel offensive. Maj Stilwell developed great affection for the French and a loathing for the British.

Stilwell's three tours of duty in China between 1920 and 1939 let him see major changes take place in the ancient country. As a language officer in 1920-23 he witnessed the rise of the warlords; he was with the 15th Inf, 1926-29, as Chiang Kai-shek consolidated power; and as MA, 1935-39, he had a ringside seat for the Japanese invasion. When US involvement in war appeared to be inevitable, Col Stilwell faced mandatory retirement for age when 10 of his West Point classmates already were generals.

But when George C. Marshall became CofS he put Stilwell's name second on the list of nominees for a star. Marshall's high regard for the nonconformist and imaginative infantryman had been established years earlier but was heightened by watching him perform as head of the tactical section of the infantry school at Ft Benning, Ga. Stilwell got his second star after commanding the 7th Inf Div (1 July 40 to 26 July 41) and the 3d Corps (to 21 Dec 41).

CBI

Stilwell was earmarked for operations in North Africa when Hugh A. DRUM took himself out of the running to head a mission to China and Stilwell got the job. He reached India on 25 Feb 42, the day his promotion to lieutenant general was confirmed. Singapore had fallen and the Japanese were invading Burma. After conferring in New Delhi with the British and meeting briefly in Lashio with Chiang (who was visiting Chinese troops in Burma), Stilwell proceeded to Chungking. Here he integrated officers and men of a previously established mission under MAGRUDER to create "American Army Forces, China, Burma and India" (USAFCBI). Its headquarters opened at Chungking on 4 Mar 42, two days before Stilwell had his first conference with the Chiangs to explain his instructions.

An immediate problem, however, was that Chiang was timid about risking his 5th and 6th Armies that were supposed to be helping the British defend Burma. Stilwell left for Burma on 11 Mar 42 with Chiang's promise that he would command Chinese forces there. He set up headquarters just NE of Mandalay at Maymyo. The Old China Hand was establishing relations with Chinese generals when Harold ALEXANDER arrived as Allied commander in Burma (succeeding WAVELL). The situation was beyond salvaging, and on 2 May 42 Alexander ordered a general retreat to India. Stilwell sent part of his staff by air to New Delhi but refused to leave himself in the plane sent by H. H. ARNOLD. Abandoning his Chinese troops, Stilwell reasoned, would have a bad psychological effect.

With a small staff he retreated 60 miles north from Maymyo to Wuntho as most of Chiang's divisions fled NE into China. Stilwell then headed west toward India, having ordered his advance party to start setting up training camps. Finally having to abandon most vehi-

cles after crossing the Chindwin River, he personally led the "walkout." The entire group of 114 reached India after making marches of about 15 miles a day over jungle trails and mountains to link up with the road to Imphal, India. (Tuchman, 298, 417 [map].) Stilwell reached Delhi on 24 May and concluded a press conference with: "I claim we got a hell of a beating. We got run out of Burma and it is humiliating as hell. I think we ought to find out what caused it, go back and retake it."

Washington told Stilwell that no US troops were available for his CBI. (MERRILL had taken part in the walkout but his Marauders would not be formed until later.)

The Chiangs received Stilwell cordially in Chungking, even promising to recommend his promotion to full general so he would be effective in getting logistical support for China. But the honeymoon ended quickly and violently when BRERETON's heavy bombers and air transports were ordered from India to Egypt, where Rommel was threatening Suez after taking Tobruk on 21 June 42; B-24s en route to India also were diverted to the British. An outraged CHIANG fired off his "Three Demands." Stilwell's effectiveness under his original instructions had ended, and a new game began.

Now Stilwell undertook to organize the CBI *theater of operations,* these words having been specifically excluded in setting up the USAFCBI (herein). Mindful of his earlier mandate (*see* the first paragraph of this sketch), which gave him the primary duty of functioning as CofS to Chiang as *US representative in China for matters including Lend Lease,* Stilwell established an office in Chungking with only tacit approval from Washington.

During the next six months Vinegar Joe was preoccupied with organizing the far-flung CBI theater. In New Delhi, India, he created the "Branch Office, Hq American Army Forces, CBI." This headquarters issued orders in the name of the "Theater Commander." An "area command" was set up at Kunming "to make the city's shift from a Burma Road terminal to an air ferry discharge and a major base for Chennault as smooth as possible" (R&S, *CBI,* 193). The Services of Supply (SOS) headquarters was at Karachi until 27 May 42, then in New Delhi, where 10th AF Hq also was located. Ramgarh became the training center for Chinese troops in India. Chiang gave Stilwell command of the Chinese Army in India, remnants of the 22d and 38th Divs.

Nepotism was one of Vinegar Joe's faults: son Joe ("Cider Joe") was G2 of the Northern Combat Area Command (NCAC); sons-in-law Col Ernest Esterbrook and Maj Ellis Cox were LnOs with Chinese divisions (Tuchman, 421).

Chiang soon was working to have Stilwell and other troublesome Old China Hands replaced. Presidential assistant Lauchlin CURRIE recommended on 24 Aug 42 that Vinegar Joe, his CofS Haydon L. BOATNER, Ambassador Clarence E. Gauss, and T. V. SOONG be reassigned. Roosevelt did not act on this advice nor on Soong's proposal on 15 Sep 43 for a reorganization of the Chinese Theater that excluded Stilwell. This effort failing, Soong sought other ways. Vice President Henry A. WALLACE weighed in with a recommendation to Roosevelt on 28 June 44 that Stilwell be replaced or else given a deputy who had authority as a presidential assistant. Next came Patrick Jay HURLEY, sent after the president promised to relieve Chiang of his cross. But George Marshall continued to believe that only Stilwell could get Chiang's field forces to fight the Japanese. It consequently was agreed that Vinegar Joe would retain command of Chinese troops in Burma and China's Yunnan Province but would no longer be responsible for Lend Lease. But Chiang and the China Lobby persisted, the Generalissimo asking FDR on 11 Oct 44 to recall Stilwell immediately. Vinegar Joe got his marching orders a week later. Chiang was told no American officer would succeed Stilwell as commander of Chinese forces but that WEDEMEYER was available as Chiang's CofS. This too came to pass.

Recalled

Stilwell left Chungking on 21 Oct 44. He stopped at various CBI installations to say good-bye and reached New Delhi on the 24th. And "two days later, after 32 months of unslackened pursuit of the least attainable American goal of the war, he wrote the last diary entry of his mission: 'Shoved off—last day in CBI'" (Tuchman, 504).

He had been promoted to full general a few weeks earlier, 1 Aug 44, and had the consolation in being junior only to Marshall, Eisenhower, MacArthur, and H. H. Arnold (*AA*, 910). The war hero's return during the last week of the presidential election created political turmoil and the administration took extraordinary precautions to keep him isolated from the press.

Stilwell requested a "bust" to major general so he could take over a division. Detractors quipped that this was his proper command level. But Vinegar Joe did not abandon hope of returning to China, considering himself the obvious candidate to replace MacArthur if this also troublesome theater commander were recalled (Tuchman, 517). On 23 Jan 45 Stilwell became head of Army Ground Forces, whose mission was training and equipping combat units. Three months later the army-navy conflict in the Pacific had been resolved by making Nimitz and MacArthur coequal theater commanders. Stilwell used the pretext of an inspection trip to find an assignment in the Pacific and, having declined MacArthur's offer to be his CofS, was in Honolulu en route home when he got a message from MacArthur: "Command Tenth Army," it read. "Return to Guam at once." BUCKNER had been killed on Okinawa.

Only mopping-up operations remained when Stilwell took over from the interim commander, "Sandy" JARMAN, on 23 June 45. Vinegar Joe succeeded Nimitz on 31 July as military governor of the Ryukyus. "I am eminently suited to something else," he would write (Tuchman, 523). After three and a half months on the job, on 18 October he returned to Washington for a brief tour as president of the War Equipment Board. The general was delighted to be assigned in Jan 46 to the Presidio of San Francisco, a few hours from his home in Carmel, as head of the Western Defense Command.

After a month observing the two atomic bomb tests at Bikini in the Marshall Islands he returned looking ill and complaining of fatigue. Medical tests showed liver trouble, and surgery on 3 Oct 46 revealed stomach cancer and metastasis to the liver. Doctors were mystified that he had no pain. Stilwell died in his sleep shortly after noon on 12 Oct 46. The funeral was private, and his ashes were scattered over the Pacific.

The Stilwell Papers (New York: Sloane, 1948), a book edited by Theodore White from wartime letters and diaries, created a sensation. The original documents, plus other papers of a private nature, supplemented by extensive interviews of CBI personnel, were used by Charles F. Romanus and Riley Sunderland for the volume of the US Army's official history, *Stilwell's Mission to China* (Washington: OCMH, 1953). The rest of the family archives were made available to Barbara W. Tuchman (an Old China Hand) for writing *Stilwell and the American Experience in China, 1911-45* (New York: Macmillan, 1971).

STIMSON, Henry Lewis. US statesman. 1867-1950. Secretary of war, 1940-45, he was born 21 Sep 67 in NYC. After attending Phillips Andover Academy he graduated from Yale in 1888 and Harvard Law School in 1890. Becoming a lawyer and an understudy of the great Elihu Root he served in the later's firm. (Its name went through various changes to become Winthrop and Stimson by 1901.) Five years out of law school he was appointed by President Theodore Roosevelt to be US District Attorney for the Southern District of NY. As a Republican gubernatorial candidate whose opponents called Stimson the "human icicle" he was defeated in 1910 but made secretary of war, 1911-13, under President Taft.

Having served in the NY National Guard 1898-1907 he went to France as a lieutenant colonel of the 305th FA Regt. Although approaching the age of 50 he was promoted to command the 31st FA. Col Stimson was President Calvin Coolidge's representative in arbitrating a dispute over the presidency of Nicaragua in 1927, Governor General of the Philippines, 1927-29, then Hoover's Secretary of State, 1929-33. He stopped the State Department's code-breaking program on grounds that "Gentlemen do not read each other's mail." More realistically, however, after the gentlemen of Japan pursued conquest in Manchuria he established the "Stimson Doctrine" that the US would not recognize territories or diplomatic agreements acquired by aggression.

Returning to private life after Franklin D. Roosevelt's election in 1933 Stimson supported the president's often-unpopular foreign policies. In June 40, as Hitler overran France, Col Stimson made a radio speech urging military preparedness and support of France and Britain. FDR yielded to the urgings of Felix Frankfurter and others to draft Stimson, a prominent Republican, into the Democratic administration as secretary of war (Burns, *Roosevelt*, 38).

Just short of his 73d birthday but "still keen and resilient," in the words of Burns, Stimson was "an indomitable, world-minded, richly experienced war administrator" (ibid.). He was also a rallying point for other Republicans who had long felt excluded from government (ibid.). But Stimson was read out of his party.

The elderly squire marshalled America's overwhelming industrial and economic resources, backed effectively at first by army CofS Marshall. But from Feb 42, soon after the US went to war, Roosevelt made Marshall start bypassing the secretary on matters of "strategy, tactics, and operations" (Pogue, *Marshall*, III, 69). This was prescribed soon after FDR had talked blithely with the visiting Churchill about the possibility of giving American reinforcements to the British if, because of the Pearl Harbor disaster, they might not get through to MacArthur in the Philippines (Burns, 182). Stimson protested through Hopkins, who relayed back to him a denial from Roosevelt and Churchill that they had actually agreed on any such thing. British minutes of the meeting showed otherwise, and Stimson threatened to resign if the president persisted in this sort of thing. (Ibid.)

Stimson was a solid rock in the meerschaum of Roosevelt's storm flecked administration. With good sense and sound international insights he cooled Democratic liberals on such matters as repudiating the DARLAN deal (Burns, 296-97) and on the MORGENTHAU Plan. He also worked to discourage needless destruction of German economic resources that he foresaw would be needed for postwar recovery (Buchanan, 453, 490). In his diary the secretary railed at Mrs Roosevelt's "intrusive and impulsive" influence in many areas, especially in agitating for racial integration of the army despite the president's letting the navy continue absolute exclusion of Negroes (Burns, 266). The secretary of war was closely involved with scientific development programs, particularly the **Manhattan Project,** which the army ran.

In office from 10 July 40, Stimson retired on 21 Sep 45 (*AA,* 49) his 78th birthday. Undersecretary Robert J. PATTERSON took over. With McGeorge Bundy he published *On Active Service in Peace and War* (New York: Harper 1948). His historically important diary and papers are in the Yale Univ Library.

STIRLING, David Archibald. British officer. 1915-. "The Phantom Major," as the Germans dubbed him, was a Scots Guards officer who went to the Middle East with Robert E. LAYCOCK's commando unit. In July 41 he was authorized to organize a special force to raid deep behind enemy lines. As covered in more detail in the glossary entry **Special Air Service** (SAS) he took that cover name. After the initial operation by parachute failed Stirling began having the Long Range Desert Group deliver his raiders by air. The Phantom Major was promoted after expanding SAS from 66 officers and men to regimental size. Lt Col Stirling's 1st SAS Regt continued to score commando triumphs, operating at one time from the Kufra oasis some 500 miles S of Tobruk.

The six-foot-six-inch phantom was captured 10 Jan 43 when a specially trained German unit surprised his column in Tunisia. Stirling escaped, made his way to a group of Arabs, but they sold him to the Germans for ll pounds of tea. (Liddell Hart, *RP,* 393.) Stirling spent the rest of the war at **Colditz** after four failed escapes from the camp in Italy at Gavi.

The SAS remained in existence throughout the war, unlike other special forces created by CARLSON, LAYCOCK, MERRILL, and WINGATE, and it was expanded to three regiments. With a modified role it remains one of the British Army's elite units.

STOPFORD, Montagu George North. British general. 1892-1971. He commanded the 33d Indian Corps in the defense of Assam in early 1944 and then led it in the liberation of Burma.

At the start of the war he was chief instructor at **Camberley,** leaving to command the 17th Inf Bde in France. After covering the BEF's retreat to Dunkirk he headed the London Division 1941-42 until becoming commandant at Camberley. In Nov 43 he took over the 33d Indian Corps Hq, which was rushed to defend Assam when MUTAGUCHI began the "march on

Delhi" in early 1944. Advancing on a broad front, Japanese columns cut the Kohima-Imphal road and threatened to move farther into India. A small garrison of 1,500 British and Indian troops held Kohima against great odds, and Lt Gen Geoffrey Scoones's 4th Corps was invested at Imphal.

Stopford moved with remarkable speed across India and by Apr 44 his corps had driven the enemy from around Kohima. He then covered 52 miles in seven days through monsoon weather to link up on 22 June 44 with elements of the 4th Corps coming north from Imphal. (Allen, *Burma,* 294.) This made Masakazu KAWABE decide on 3 July to order a general withdrawal. With this hard-fought victory in what has been called the world's worst terrain and climate for military operations, SLIM formulated a bold strategy to reconquer Burma in collaboration with US-sponsored Chinese troops under Dan SULTAN (who had replaced STILWELL). As covered in more detail under SLIM, the 4th Corps under MESSERVY moved south from Assam on the 14th Army's right (west) flank while—on a much broader front initially—Stopford's 33d Indian Corps advanced east and then turned south. On 20 Mar 45 Stopford took Mandalay after Messervy had seized and held Meiktila far to the south. Stopford pushed southward, down the Irrawaddy, to link up with the 15th British Corps. (This unit, from Assam, had taken Rangoon on 2 May 45 by amphibious assault.) Stopford succeeded SLIM as 14th Army commander on 7 May 45 and later replaced him as CinC Allied Land Forces in South East Asia, 1946-47.

STRACHWITZ, Hyazinth von Gross-Zauche und Camminetz, Graf. German general. 1893-1968. Count (Graf) Strachwitz was born 30 July 93 at Grossstein into an family that traced its lineage back seven centuries (Angolia, I, 77). He began military service as a cadet at Lichterfelde, was commissioned in the "Garde du Corps" Regt at Potsdam, and showed outstanding courage on the western front. Between the wars the affable-looking aristocrat kept up his reserve status, rising to Oberleutnant. As a company-grade officer he fought in Poland and France before spending the rest of the war on the eastern front. As a major commanding the

1st Bn, 2d Pz Regt, 2d Pz Div, he was awarded the RK on 25 Aug 41. Still with the battalion Oberstleutnant Strachwitz was awarded the Oakleaves (144/890) on 13 Nov 42, promoted to full colonel, and given command of the Grossdeutschland Pz Regt. Strachwitz was awarded the Swords (27/159) on 28 Mar 43. Leading a panzer battle group in AG North he was awarded the Diamonds (11/27) on 15 Apr 44 and promoted to Generalmajor. (Angolia, I, 77-78.) According Angolia's sources he took command of the Pz Lehr Div at this time, but other authorities show him holding this position from 8 June 44 to early the following December (B&O, 130; see also Fritz BAYERLEIN).

Surrendering to US forces, Strachwitz was held until 1946. He died 25 Apr 68 (Angolia, I, 135).

STRASSER, Gregor. German politician. 1892-1934. At one time Hitler's most dangerous rival, Gregor Strasser was born 31 May 92 at Geisenfeld, Lower Bavaria. In WWI he was a volunteer in the 1st Bavarian FA Regt, winning both classes of the Iron Cross. Settling in Franconia after becoming a chemist and pharmacy owner he served in the Epp Freikorps, was commander of a storm battalion with HIMMLER as his adjutant, an early Nazi Party member, and a close collaborator of Hitler's. During the Munich putsch in 1923 Strasser led an SA detachment and was imprisoned briefly. Going to north Germany he established a large following as leader of the region's social-revolutionary wing of the Nazi Party. Gregor and younger brother Otto became publishers of the *Berliner Arbeiterzeitung,* the *NS-Briefe* (which GOEBBELS edited), and Gregor's independent *Kampfverlag.* Gregor Strasser grudgingly accepted Hitler's leadership after Hitler left jail and unexpectedly established supremacy within the Nazi Party. But the two had irreconcilable differences. Strasser was champion of the progressive wing, he advocated strict socialism, and he opposed Hitler's program of winning support from industrialists and the Junkers.

The showdown came in Dec 32 when HINDENBURG called SCHLEICHER to form a government and invited Strasser to be vice chancellor. Hitler and Goering vigorously challenged this maneuver to divide the Nazis, and in the ensuing crisis Strasser resigned all party positions on 8 Dec 32 and abandoned politics to be administrator of a large chemical firm.

Now a marked man, Gregor was arrested around noon on 30 June 34, in the **Blood Purge,** and taken to Gestapo Hq. Without any inkling of the charges he was shot from behind after being told he was being moved to an individual cell. "Let the swine bleed to death," Heydrich is reported to have said (Gisevius, 158). The death was reported as suicide.

STRASSER, Otto. Nazi deviationist. 1897-1974. Born in Windsheim on 10 Sep 97, Gregor's younger brother (herein), Otto was educated as a lawyer but became a skilled journalist with a highly intellectual view of socialism. The Strasser brothers rallied early to National Socialism, had a major role in Hitler's early rise to power, but split with him over the issues of capitalism and socialism. The crisis followed a seven-hour conference the night of 21-22 May 30 during which "Otto Strasser's reasoned attack on the inconsistencies of his position hit Hitler hard" (Fest, *Hitler,* 293). Otto advocated revolution and headed critics of Hitler's "legal" course of action (Heiden, *Hitler,* 348-49). The fuehrer denounced Otto Strasser in an open letter as a "parlor Bolshevik" whose adherents were "political boy scouts" (ibid.). Otto responded with the pamphlet "Cushioned Ministerial Seats or Revolution" and on 4 July 30 his papers announced "The socialists are leaving the NSDAP." Hitler made the voluntary purge official by telling Goebbels, Gauleiter of Berlin, to expel Strasser and his followers from the party. Goebbels, as editor of *Angriff,* was particularly happy to comply because Otto's daily *Berliner Arbeiterzeitung* (which Gregor had founded in 1924) soon reverted to weekly publication whereas *Angriff* subsequently became a daily. (Heiden, 350.)

Otto went to Prague and formed the "Black Front"—the Union of Revolutionary National Socialists. With Walter Stennes, and Maj Buchrucker, former leader of the "Black Reichswehr" (W-B, *Nemesis,* 92 and n, 227n), Otto Strasser headed émigré activities against Hitler, producing a fortnightly newspaper, *Die Deutsche Revolution,* and a long series of books attacking Hitler and his leadership. Although claiming 10,000 followers (not including Gregor) the **Black Front** was never a serious threat to Hitler. The Strasser brothers where high on the hit list for the **Blood Purge** of 30 June 34; Otto had a narrow escape but Gregor STRASSER did not.

Five years later the Nazi press charged Otto, who was safe in Switzerland, with being associated with the alleged attempt to assassinate Hitler in the Munich beer cellar explosion on 8 Nov 39 that precipitated the **Venlo incident.** The Nazi deviationist subsequently lived in Montreal, where Walter C. Langer interviewed him while writing *The Mind of Adolf Hitler* (1972). Recovering German citizenship after the war, Otto Strasser failed to win support for his brand of Nazism but continued to publish virulent anti-Semitic works. He died 27 Aug 74 in Munich. (Wistrich.)

STRATEMEYER, George Edward. USAF general. 1890-1969. An outstanding air strategist in the Far East during WWII and in the Korean War, Stratemeyer was born 24 Nov 90 in Ohio. He graduated from West Point in 1915 (145/ 164), "the class the stars fell on," and was CofS, Army Air Forces, 1942-43.

Named to coordinate air forces in the India-Burma sector Maj Gen Stratemeyer reached India on 7 Aug 43 (*OCMH Chron,* 116, 125) but MOUNTBATTEN, disregarding Stilwell's objections, integrated his air forces under ACM PEIRCE. (The British had about two thirds of the squadrons in the SE Asia Command, but the US soon had the preponderance of transport planes.) In Peirce's Eastern Air Command Stratemeyer had Air Marshal John Baldwin's 3d TAC AF. This comprised three elements: the US Northern Air Sector, which supported Stilwell and protected the air route over the **Hump** to China, plus two RAF groups, the 221st, cooperating with the British 4th Corps on the main front and the 224th Gp supporting the 15th British Corps in Arakan. (Slim, 182, 183.)

Stratemeyer warned on 16 Nov 43 that he would not be able to deliver the required tonnage over the Hump for the controversial CHENNAULT plan in 1944, and the priority of Chennault's 14th AF in China had to be lowered. (*OCMH Chron,* 147.) New organizational prob-

lems arose as Curtis E. LEMAY prepared to move his B-29s of the 20th Bomb Command (BC) from the US to India execute the Chennault plan. A directive on 30 Jan 44 put the new bomber force under Stilwell with Stratemeyer exercising operational control (ibid., 166). The arrangement was changed two weeks later: Stratemeyer was made responsible only for the 20th BC's administration in India but he was authorized to recommend its operational use in the SEAC-China area. (Ibid., 173.)

SLIM and Stratemeyer issued a joint directive on 4 Feb 44 to Chindit commander Orde WINGATE and Philip C. COCHRANE, US commander of No 1 Air Commando, for long-range penetration operations in Burma. (Slim, 224.) Stratemeyer inactivated his 3d TAF on 21 Nov 44. This freed the RAF groups (above) to fly close support for the British corps they had been supporting in Burma and Arakan (Ibid., 333).

When CHENNAULT resigned in a huff on 6 July 45 as head of the 14th AF, Lt Gen Stratemeyer (as of 28 May 45) was named over Chennault's head to be air chief in China. (Tuchman, 520, 523.) After the war he briefly headed the Far East AF under MacArthur (*AA,* 26) before becoming CG, Air Defense Command, 1946-49 (Cullum). He was CG, FEAF, again until retiring in 1951 for physical disability. Lt Gen Stratemeyer died 9 Aug 69 in Winter Park, Fla, at the age of 78.

STRAUSS, Adolf. German general. A quiet, prudent and experienced commander whom Hitler considered politically reliable, Strauss was a Generalmajor in 1935. He took command of the 22d Inf Div at Bremen, was promoted to general of infantry, then he headed Wehrkreis II and the 2d Corps Hq at Stettin. His CofS until Hitler found out about it and ordered a change was the fuehrer's former army adjutant Friedrich HOSSBACH.

After leading the corps in France as part of Kluge's 4th Army the general was promoted to head the 9th Army. He was scheduled to land in England between the Isle of Wight and Brighton, but when Sea Lion was called off he moved his headquarters east for Opn **Barbarossa.** For initial operations in Russia the powerful 9th Army of some 12 infantry divisions was on the north flank of BOCK's AG Center.

In the final drive on Moscow Strauss attacked in the north on 19 Nov 41 with operational control over HOTH's powerful 3d Pz Gp. By 1 Dec 41 BOCK's last, desperate effort had failed and the Soviets launched their large-scale winter counteroffensive, driving the 9th Army from Kalinin (15 Dec 41) and Staritsa, then threatening Gen Albrecht von Schubert's the 23d Corps Hq in Rzhev. KONEV was encircling Schubert's exhausted and frost-bitten forces when Hitler put out the order, "9th Army will not retreat another step." Generaloberst Strauss was relieved of command on 12 Jan 42, ostensibly at his own request and for ill health. (Brett-Smith, 100.) Replaced by Model and not further employed, the capable, experienced Strauss was one of seven senior commanders to go.

STREICHER, Julius. German official. 1885-1946. Perhaps the most ignominious figure of the Third Reich, Streicher was born 12 Feb 85 in the upper Bavarian village of Fleinhausen. He became an elementary school teacher, like his father. In the first world war Streicher was a lieutenant in the Bavarian army, winning both classes of the Iron Cross.

In 1919 he co-founded an anti-Semitic party (Wistrich) and presented it the next year to Hitler as a gift (Davidson, *Trial,* 43). He joined the Nazi Party in 1921 and four years later was appointed Gauleiter for Franconia with headquarters in Nuremberg. Here he founded and edited (1923-45) a rabid weekly newspaper, *Der Stuermer.* which became "the world's best-known anti-semitic publication with its crude cartoons, repellent photographs of Jews, its stories of ritual murder, pornography and its coarse prose style." (Wistrich.) The paper and tireless speaking tours gave Streicher a large political following. He went too far with his favorite weapon of slander by printing that Goering had fathered his daughter Edda by artificial insemination (Davidson, 4). Goering ordered an investigation of Streicher's personal life and business dealings that led to his being deprived in 1940 of all party offices including Gauleiter (Ibid.). Meanwhile, in 1928 he had been dismissed from his teaching post for unbecoming conduct and scurrilous attacks on the Weimar Republic.

But Streicher continued to edit *Der Stuermer* and remained on good terms with Nazi hier-

archs including Hitler. The coarse, foul-mouthed Jew-baiter, among the few whom the fuehrer addressed with the familiar *Du,* was devoted to the fuehrer from start to finish. He is said to have coined the name Hitlerjungend. Indicted at Nuremberg for conspiring to commit aggressive warfare and for crimes against humanity he "made a poor appearance on the witness stand with his shaven bullethead and incoherent fulminations against his enemies who were all around him. He seemed both insane and criminal" (Davidson, 51.) Streicher's IQ, as tested at Nuremberg, was 102, lowest of the 22 defendants.

Calling his trial and conviction "a triumph for world Jewery," he went to the scaffold on 16 Oct 46 his last words were "Heil Hitler."

STRONG, Kenneth William Dobson. British officer. 1900-82. Graduating from Sandhurst in 1920 and commissioned in the Royal Scots Fusiliers he was assistant MA in Berlin before the war. In 1939-41 Lt Col Strong was chief of the War Office's German section (GSO 1, MI14). He then commanded 4/5 Royal Scots Fusiliers until appointed **BGS** (Intelligence) in Eisenhower's AFHQ in Algiers at the end of 1942. Promoted in 1943 Maj Gen Strong remained with Eisenhower as chief of intelligence when SHAEF was established in 1944. After the epic intelligence failure at SHAEF before the Battle of Bulge the general, long suspect for pro-American bias, was a target of British critics.

Maj Gen Strong was the postwar director general of political intelligence in the Foreign Office. On retirement from the army in 1947 he continued to hold high governmental posts and was knighted in 1952. Sir Kenneth published *Intelligence at the Top: The Recollections of an Intelligence Officer (1968)* and *Men of Intelligence: A Study of the Roles and Decisions of Chiefs of Intelligence from World War I to the Present Day* (1971).

STRUBLE, Arthur Dewey. US admiral. 1894-1963. "Rip" Struble was born 28 June 94 in Portland, Ore. He graduated in 1915 from the USNA (12/179) and specialized in battleship gunnery, damage control, and taught engineering at Annapolis. Struble was XO of BB *Ari-*

zona for a year starting in May 40. Promoted to captain he commanded CL *Trenton,* which operated out of Panama. In June 42 he returned to Washington as head of the Central Division in OpNav. Promoted 1 Nov 43, Rear Adm Struble went to London as Alan G. KIRK's CofS and was involved in the early planning and training for the Normandy invasion.

He reached the Pacific in Aug 44 to command Amphib Gp 9 of the 7th Amphib Force and directed some of the initial landings in the Philippines—the one between Panaon and Leyte (20 Oct 44), three landings of the 6th Ranger Bn on outer islands in Leyte Gulf (17-18 October), and the 77th Inf Div assault at Ormoc (7 December). The admiral then commanded the Visayan Attack Force for MacArthur's expedition to take Mindoro, 15 Dec 44-3 Jan 45. (Morison, XIII, 18-19; *West Point Atlas,* 145, 148, 153.)

The main convoy to Mindoro was about to round the southern cape of Negros into the Sulu Sea, shortly before 3 PM on 13 Dec 44, when a loaded-to-kill kamikaze Val sneaked in low from astern CL *Nashville* and crashed abaft Struble's cabin. Both Japanese bombs exploded along with the plane, killing or mortally wounding at least 190 officers and men. Adm Struble, his staff of about 50, and war correspondents transferred to DD *Dashiell.* (RCS; Morison, XIII, 23-24.)

Subsequently taking part in the landings at Subic Bay, Zambales, Lingayen, Corregidor, Negros, Panay, Macajabon, and Mindanao, Rip Struble supported operations through the southern Philippines until Aug 45. He then directed all minesweeping and clearance operations in the Western Pacific until June 46, when he became Commander, Amphibious Force, Pacific Fleet. Promoted in Apr 48 Vice Adm Struble was deputy CNO for operations and naval deputy in the JCS until May 50.

He then commanded the 7th Fleet and planned MACARTHUR's three major amphibious operations of the Korean War: the "impossible" one at Inchon in Sep 50, the landing a month later at Wonsan, and the withdrawal of Marine and Army troops from Hungnam and Wonsan completed on 24 Dec 50.

Leaving the Korean theater in Mar 51 Struble headed the 1st Fleet in the eastern Pacific for a year, then served with the JCS and was US Naval Representative on the Military Staff Committee of the UN 1952-53. For the next two years he was the committee chairman. Retiring 1 July 56 with the rank of admiral he died 1 May 83 at Chevy Chase, Md.

STUDENT, Kurt. German general. 1890-1978. The commander of the world's first airborne division was born 12 May 90 in Birkhonz and was commissioned in 1912. The next year Leutnant Student (pronounced schtu DENT) became a flyer. After action on both fronts, piloting reconnaissance and bomber aircraft, he rose to the rank of captain. Transferring back to the infantry, he flew his first glider in 1921 and became an avid enthusiast of the sport (Mrazek, 30). Every year between 1924-28 he was an observer of Soviet air maneuvers and had a high regard for the Red Army (ibid.). He joined the new Luftwaffe in 1934 after being an air adviser and having an important role in creating the new German air force.

Student became chief of the parachute and glider arm and in 1938, as a Generalmajor, secretly forming the first parachute battalion. His 7th Air (Para) Div was not used in Poland because Hitler did not want to compromise the existence of his secret weapon. But elements of the division were used with great effect in Norway, Belgium, and the Netherlands.

Their most spectacular success was at Eben Emael. Hitler conceived of the idea that the "impregnable" fort might be taken by landing heavy shaped charges in gliders on its top, which was a large grassy field. On 27 Oct 39 the fuehrer summoned Student hastily for an opinion on whether this operation was feasible; the general returned a day later to say it was, and Hitler gave him the go-ahead. The fuehrer also ordered Student to capture the Albert Canal bridges at Canne, Vroenhoven, and Veltwezelt by glider assault before they could be blown; this would enable ground troops to take part in the final assault on the fort. (Mrazek, 34.)

In a coup de main that stunned the world and whose details long were secret, Student used 500 glider troops to take Eben Emael on 10 May 40 while 4,000 parachutists dropped around the Hague and Rotterdam. Dutch counterattacks at the Hague frustrated the mission temporarily, but Generalleutnant Student, commanding the 7th Flieger Div, personally directed establishment of an airhead at Rotterdam and was awarded the RK on 12 May 40 (Angolia, II, 256). But a stray "friendly" bullet hit the airborne pioneer in the head, wounding him so badly he did not return to duty until Jan 41.

Proposed airborne assaults on Northern Ireland or the Cornwall-Devon peninsula were ruled out as unfeasible, and an effort against Gibraltar was abandoned because FRANCO would not permit passage of eight divisions across Spain for the ground link-up.

As CG 11th Fliegerkorps Student was involved in planning the assault on Crete (Opn **Merkur**) 20 May-1 June 41 and had operational control of the airborne troops involved but Hitler (who was skeptical of the operation) did not authorize him to participate personally. Because of excessive losses, 4,000 of the nearly 6,500 German KIA were airborne troops, Hitler concluded that no more large-scale airborne operations should be undertaken. German airborne troops (in the Luftwaffe) were used in the ground role, where they proved to be redoubtable, particularly in Italy under Richard "Arno" HEIDRICH. Some were held in strategic reserve.

Student himself continued to direct airborne training and planning. In Rome he made plans to capture Malta but the operation was called off for reasons covered under KESSELRING. General der Flieger Student was awarded the Oakleaves (305/890) on 27 Sep 43 for "defensive actions" (Angolia, II, 256). The date of award is suspect because Student supported SKORZENY's rescue of Mussolini from the Gran Sasso in Italy on 12 Sep 43.

When the British took Antwerp, 4 Sep 44, Student was directed to form and command the 1st Parachute Army. With this scratch force of Luftwaffe and naval personnel, many of them semi-invalids, Student spent the rest of the war opposing Montgomery's advance through Holland to the Rhine. One reason for the failure of Opn Market-Garden was that the German airborne pioneer happened to be very near the drop zones and to have the additional good luck of being presented with a complete set of orders for the operation. (They were recovered from a downed American glider.)

In Nov 44 Student took command of AG H, formed in Holland of the 1st Para Army and the 25th Army. On 28 Jan 45 BLASKOWITZ succeeded Student, who was sent to organize a new parachute division in Germany. But he returned in mid-Apr 45, as a desperate situation deteriorated, to head the 1st Para Army around Bremen. Less than two weeks later, on 28 Apr 45, he was named to succeed HEINRICI as commander of AG Vistula. "Hitler regarded him as one of his most energetic generals," writes Albert SPEER, "and felt he could depend on him all the more in this situation because he thought the man was rather stupid" (Speer, *Memoirs,* 476). Actually, Generaloberst Student was an officer of exceptional ability with a fresh, thoughtful approach to problems and a talent for picking his major subordinate commanders well. (Brett-Smith, 146.) But Student had an unusually slow manner of speech that made him seem foolish to Hitler iIbid., 145).

The war ended before he could comply with this last order and Student surrendered to the British. Interviewed in 1970 at his home in Bad Salzuflen, he impressed an American military historian as being an intense man but neither a Prussian martinet nor a Nazi diehard, (Mrazek, 29).

STUELPNAGEL, Karl Heinrich von. German general. 1886-1944. He was one of four Prussian generals—cousins—who were prominent just before or during WWII. Generals Edwin and Joachim von Stuelpnagel were retired from the army by 1932 but Edwin was head of a group devoted to physically hardening German youth (the *Reichsjuratorium fuer Jugendgertuechtigung*) and Joachim was business manager of the *Berliner Boersenzeitung.* (Goerlitz, *GGS,* 264.)

Karl Heinrich, the subject of this sketch and a cousin of Otto's (following), was a major heading the army's operations section in 1918 (ibid., 216). He returned to the post on the eve of WWII, was close to Beck and Halder (ibid., 328), he and he and his cousin Joachim von Stuelpnagel were among the few generals whom anti-Hitler conspirators could count on (Deutsch, I, 47). Heinrich also was involved in futile efforts during the FRITSCH crisis in early 1938 to defend the army from Hitler's take-over. Leaving Berlin in June 40 after the French collapse he spent the next six months on the Armistice Commission.

Stuelpnagel then commanded the 17th Army in Russia until 5 Oct 41, when he reported sick, apparently after incurring the displeasure of Brauchitsch, who gave the army to HOTH. (Seaton, *R-G War,* 192n.)

On 3 Mar 42 he replaced his cousin Otto von STUELPNAGEL as military commander of France and Governor of Paris, carrying on a brutal enforcement of Nazi policies. But he remained an active conspirator, being the more useful as a friend of ROMMEL's since their days at the Dresden infantry school. Believing STAUFFENBERG's Attentat on 20 July 44 had succeeded, Stuelpnagel ordered the arrest of more than 1,000 Gestapo and SS men in France. Then he learned that Hitler was alive! En route to face conspiracy charges he left his car near Verdun and bungled a suicide attempt that left him blind from a bullet in the forehead. He was recovering consciousness after an operation when for some reason he called out "Rommel!"

The blind general was condemned to death by Judge FREISLER, led by the hand to the gallows in the Ploetzensee prison courtyard on 30 Aug 44, and his body hung from a butcher's hook. (Wistrich.) [350]

STUELPNAGEL, Otto von. German general. 1878-1948. Administrator of France and the Channel Islands and Military Governor of Paris, 1 Nov 40-6 Feb 42, Otto von Stuelpnagel, one of four well-known Prussians with that surname (see preceding entry) was born 16 June 78 in Berlin. At 20 he was commissioned in the 2d Prussian Infantry Life Guards. For alleged crimes of murder and theft against French civilians during WWI he was extradited for trial in France but acquitted.

In postwar Germany Otto was among those who worked covertly to destroy the Weimar Republic and he became a rabid Nazi. In the late 1920s he headed the Reichswehr's motor transport staff, was promoted to Generalmajor on 1 Feb 29, and he soon joined what became the Luftwaffe. Although he rose to General of Flyers and was highly regarded he returned to the army in 1939 as deputy commander of Wehrkreis XVII. The tour turned out to be brief: Stuelpnagel was retired as a General of Infantry when Hitler purged the army of "uncooperative" officers. Restored

to that rank when recalled in 1940, but too old for a more active command, in Oct 40 he was given the occupation posts in France mentioned earlier.

The elderly Prussian general was basically fair-minded but he imposed severe measures against French who challenged occupation laws. Finally disgusted with his own reign of terror, but later claiming he delayed resignation only to "prevent worse things happening," he was succeeded on 3 Mar 42 by his cousin Karl Heinrich (herein). The French charged Otto with war crimes, again. After a failed suicide attempt in Dec 46 the general hanged himself in Paris' Cherche Midi prison on 6 Feb 48.

STUMME, Georg. German general. 1886-1942. The short, good-humored Stumme suffered from chronic high blood pressure that gave his face a permanent flush. The troops called him "Fireball," and the monocled little general, although old for front line duty even by Wehrmacht standards, had a flair for seizing tactical opportunities. Generalleutnant Stumme took over the 2d Light Div on 1 Oct 38 and led it into Poland a year later. On 18 Oct 39 he began converting the unit into the 7th Pz Div, which ROMMEL took over on 15 Feb 40. Stumme moved up to head the recently formed 40th Army Corps at Lubeck. He led this in the west, winning promotion to General of Cavalry on 1 June 40.

The 40th Corps went to Romania in Feb 41 and then to Bulgaria for the Balkan campaign. Stumme made the main effort as the right wing of LIST's 12th Army. His two divisions, the 9th Pz and 73d Inf, drove west separately into Yugoslavia and wheeled south to join at Monastir on 9 Apr 41 (D+3). Forcing the Monastir gap Stumme took part in the conquest of Greece that ended 27 Apr 41, and he was promoted a week later to General of Panzer Troops. He joined Adolf Strauss's 9th Army of Bock's AG Center in Aug 41 for the operation to take Velikie Lukie. His 40th Corps was motorized on 25 Aug 41 and redesignated the 40th Pz Corps on 6 Sep (*B&O,* 44). On 18 Oct 41 his tanks entered Mozhaisk, the last major town west of Moscow and a mere 65 miles away. But he soon faced the massive Soviet counteroffensive and was on the defensive during the long Russian winter.

In June 42 Stumme was transferred to the Kharkov sector of BOCK's AG South for the large-scale offensive toward Stalingrad and the Caucasus.

He immediately became the scapegoat for a subordinate's serious security violation on 19 June 42: the Soviets captured a set of operational plans carried in a light plane by a senior staff officer of the 23d Pz Div. Hitler held Stumme and his CofS, BOINEBURG-LENGSFELD, responsible and ordered them court-martialled. But the fuehrer decided not to alter the compromised plan (Seaton, *R-G War,* 262), which is why it was a month before Stumme officially turned over command to GEYR VON SCHWEPPENBURG (*B&O,* 45). Stumme was "busted" back to General of Cavalry and sentenced to five years of fortress arrest. But the army group commander, Bock, succeeded in having the jail sentence commuted.

When ROMMEL prepared to come home on sick leave he recommended that Guderian be sent to take over temporarily as commander of Panzer Army Africa. But Stumme was selected, although Rommel did not think the general was fit physically for the task. (Liddell Hart, *RP,* 292, 305.) Stumme reached North Africa on 19 Sep 42, and when Rommel left three days later both generals were optimistic about blocking the expected British offensive (WARLIMONT, in *J&R,* 200-1).

The Battle of El Alamein began on the evening of 23 Oct 42 with a 20-minute artillery preparation. Other than prohibiting use of limited German artillery ammunition to hit forward assembly areas (where troops are particularly vulnerable) Stumme faithfully followed the plan left by Rommel. Early the next morning he was in his command car near Hill 21 when seriously wounded by British infantry covering the Alarm Track. His driver raced for the rear and did not realize until reaching safety that the general had fallen out, apparently after having a heart attack. Stumme was reported MIA until his body was found and identified about 24 hours later.

STUMP, Felix Budwell. US admiral. 1894-1972. The carrier admiral was born in Parkersburg, W. Va, on 15 Dec 94 and graduated from Annapolis in Mar 17 (59/182). He served first in a gunboat and then in a cruiser on escort duty in the Atlantic, 1917-18. Qualifying as a naval aviator in 1920 he went on to get an MS degree from MIT in aeronautical engineering.

After heading the maintenance division of BuAer 1937-40, then being XO of CV *Enterprise,* Stump assumed command of *Langley* in Sep 41. She was the US Navy's first carrier, on which Stump had commanded experimental Torpedo Sqdn 2, and she had been converted into a seaplane tender. From Manila Stump took her to Australia after war broke out, and from Jan 42 he had charge of **ABDACOM**'s combined operations center. Two months later, when ABDACOM was dissolved, he became air officer, Western Sea Frontier. Capt Stump commissioned the new CV *Lexington* in Feb 43, fighting her during the period Sep-Dec 43 through operations at Tarawa, Wake, the Gilberts, and Kwajalein. Torpedo damage in the latter action required repairs on the West Coast, after which Stump commanded her in operations against Mille and Palau (Mar-Apr 44). Promoted to rear admiral he headed Escort Carrier Div 24 in the Marianas landings (June-Aug 44) and the Leyte campaign in October.

In the decisive battle for Leyte Gulf against KURITA he had six escort carriers of **Taffy 2.** With **Taffy 1** and **3,** commanded by the two SPRAGUEs, he had the critical role in forcing a vastly superior Japanese force to turn back. (Morison, XII, 286.) His division subsequently supported the landings at Mindoro, Lingayen Gulf, and Okinawa (Mar-May 45).

In June 45 Stump became chief of Naval Air Technical Training, which finally settled at Memphis, Tenn. In Dec 48 he was promoted to vice admiral heading Naval Air, Atlantic Fleet, and remained in the Atlantic to command the 2d Fleet, 1951-53. Promoted to admiral on 10 July 53 he took over the unified command in the Pacific as CINCPAC. Stump was involved in the final action of the Korean War and the beginning of the end for the French in Indo-China. In Mar 55 he became military adviser to SEATO (SE Asia Treaty Orgn). President Eisenhower asked the admiral to stay beyond normal retirement in 1956, and in Feb-Aug 58 he reverted to the post of CINCPAC when US efforts escalated in SE Asia. The admiral retired from active duty on 1 Aug 58 and died 13 June 72 at McLean, Va.

SUGIYAMA, Gen. Japanese general. 1880-1945. Having vigorously advocated war as "the only possible answer" to Japan's problems, and speaking for the most ardent militarists in opposing compromise to this position, the fiery Sugiyama was army CofS during most of the war.

In events leading to war Sugiyama was army vice CofS and a senior member of Tojo's **control faction** during the **26 Feb 36 insurrection.** Unpunished and unrepentant, the **Imperial Way** general was war minister in several cabinets. He was first appointed on 2 Feb 37 to the one headed briefly by Gen Senjuro Hayashi and retained the portfolio when Prince Konoye formed his first of three cabinets on 31 May 37. The **Marco Polo Bridge Incident** occurred almost immediately, and the war minister said, "Crush the Chinese in three months and they will sue for peace." Succeeded as war minister on 30 Aug 39 by Gen Shukoru Hata, Sugiyama became army CofS.

Still a leading hawk he urged a dubious Tojo to set a target date in 1941 for a surprise attack in the Pacific, meanwhile drawing out diplomatic negotiations. The former war minister assured a very skeptical emperor, whom he had assured that China would be defeated quickly, that the Japanese army and navy could conquer Malaya and the Philippines in five months. (Toland, 97.) Having been wrong twice, Sugiyama ardently opposed evacuating Guadalcanal and Buna when they became untenable, never ceasing to believe that the true samurai spirit could overcome all obstacles. Field Marshal Sugiyama (from 1943) warned Tojo that he was making Hitler's mistake in trying to combine political and military direction of the war. Tojo realized it was impossible to devise a proper strategic defense with such a man as army CofS, and on 21 Feb 44 he took over the latter's office as an additional duty.

After Tojo's resignation on 18 July 44 Sugiyama was war minister, again, in the Koiso-Yonai government. When Kantaro SUZUKI's "surrender cabinet" replaced this on 5 Apr 45 Sugiyama was succeeded as war minister by Gen Korechika Anami and put in command of the Mainland Defense Force. The field marshal committed suicide in his office on 12 Sep 45, shooting himself in the heart; his wife took cyanide and fell on a dagger. *Notes of Field Marshal Sugiyama,* compiled by the Japanese Army GS, was published by Hara Shobo (Tokyo, 1967).

SULLIVAN BROTHERS. US sailors lost in 1942. All five assigned to the new CL *Juneau,* they died with most of the crew off **Savo Island** when the crippled ship was torpedoed the night of 12-13 Nov 42. The brothers were born in Waterloo, Iowa, between 1914 and 1920. The two elder, George and Francis, had served in the USN, 1937-41. With Joseph, Madison, and Albert, they enlisted on 3 Feb 42 after a friend died at Pearl Harbor, 7 Dec 41, aboard BB *Arizona.* DD-537, *Sullivan Brothers,* was christened by their mother and joined the fleet on 30 Sep 43. After long service she became a memorial ship at Buffalo, NY.

SULLIVAN, William Aloysius. US naval salvage expert. 1894-1985. He directed the clearing of captured ports including Casablanca, Tunis, Bizerte, Palermo, Naples, Cherbourg, Le Havre, and Manila.

Born 27 Aug 94 in Lawrence, Mass, Sullivan attended MIT a year before entering the USNR on 1 Dec 17 and he remained in the service. From 10 Apr 41 he was Head of Salvage Section in the Bureau of Ships. He was salvaging the 83,423-ton troopship *Lafayette,* ex-*Normandie,* which had burned and capsized on 9 Feb 42, when ordered to Casablanca on 23 Nov 42 with his crews of divers and other specialists. His last job, starting in Feb 45 in Manila, was the most difficult because the Japanese were better than Europeans at marine demolition (Morison, XIII, 206). Sullivan retired 1 May 48 as a rear admiral. In the 1950s he headed the Sullivan Engineering Co in Tokyo. (RCS.) He died 6 Sep 85, La Jolla, Calif.

SULTAN, Daniel Isom. US general. 1885-1947. Born in Mississippi, Dan Sultan was commissioned in the Corps of Engineers on graduation from West Point in 1907 (9/111). He was on the staff and faculty 1912-16 then in Manila constructing fortifications on Corregidor 1916-18. Sultan served on the WDGS, 1918-19 (DSM), the Nicaragua Canal Survey 1929-31 (DSM) then was Engineer Commissioner in the District of Columbia 1934-38.

Despite lack of command experience he was a contender for the post of army CofS that went to George C. Marshall. Sultan headed the 38th Inf Div in the US for a year beginning in Apr 1941, then (according to Cullum but not AA) the 7th Corps. As the army's senior major general he was sent in 1943 to be Stilwell's deputy in Delhi. "Dan Sultan is the best thing that ever happened to the theater," Stilwell said of the officer who relieved him of many logistical and command burdens. (Tuchman, *Stilwell,* 423.)

Promoted 2 Sep 44, Lt Gen Sultan replaced Stilwell on 27 Oct 44 as head of what until three days earlier was the NCAC (Burma); Sultan's new title was CG, US Forces, India-Burma Theater (*AA,* 612). WEDEMEYER replaced Stilwell vis a vis CHIANG KAI-SHEK. Turning over his duties to Raymond A. "Spec" WHEELER on 23 June 45 (*AA,* 613), Sultan was the IG, US Army, from 14 July 45 until his death in Washington on 14 Jan 47 (*AA,* 752) at the age of 61.

SUMMERSBY, Kay. Eisenhower's driver. 1908-75. Born McCarthy-Morrogh in County Cork, Ireland, she was in the British Transport Service and was Eisenhower's driver from July 42 until Oct 44. Then commissioned in the WAC she became DDE's private secretary and member of his inner circle for the rest of the war. It was widely believed she was a mole, planted to keep the British informed of American planning, and it was rumored that her boss had an unrequited romantic attachment. In 1946 she resigned the WAC commission and in 1950 became a US citizen. She was married to Reginald H. Morgan 1952-58. Under the name of Kay Summersby she published *Eisenhower Was my Boss* following up years later with *Past Forgetting: My love Affair with Dwight D. Eisenhower* (1975).

SUN LI-JEN. Chinese army officer. 1900-88. A native of Anhwei Prov, Sun Li-jen (pronounced sun-lee-ren) was a VMI graduate with a BS from Purdue Univ. In 1941 his 38th Chinese Div was in Burma under William SLIM, who writes of their first meeting: "He was a slight but well-proportioned man . . . alert, energetic, and direct. Later I found him a good tactician, cool in action, very aggressively minded, and in my dealings

with him, completely straightforward." (Slim, 47). But STILWELL and H. L. BOATNER, Old China Hands, saw that Sun remained an Oriental, particularly in his barbaric treatment of subordinates and in intriguing with Chaing Kai-shek for removal of Americans he disliked. (*See* Tuchman, *Stilwell,* 329, 393, 394.) From 1943 Lt Gen Sun headed the New 1st Chinese Army of the **NCAC.** He had a prominent role in retaking Ledo and in liberating central Burma in 1944-45. According to the Purdue Alumni Office, whose last card entry is in 1988, Sun Li-jen died that year in Taiwan. VMI has no record.

SUN YAT-SEN. Chinese nationalist leader. 1866-1925. Son of a peasant, Sun Yat-sen (Sun Zhong Shan) was born in Kwantung province. He was reared in Hawaii, where he received a Christian education and learned western ways. After studying medicine in Canton and Hong Kong, graduating in 1892, Dr Sun was exiled in 1895 for involvement in an unsuccessful anti-Manchu uprising in Canton that year.

In 16 years abroad, mostly in Japan, he gathered support at home and abroad for his Alliance Society (1905). CHIANG KAI-SHEK was among Dr Sun's many overseas Chinese student adherents in Japan. Returning to China during the 1911 revolution that overthrew the Manchu dynasty he was elected president of the provisional government.

Conservative opposition caused Dr Sun to resign the post in 1912 after Gen Yuan ousted the Kuomintang. Sun Yat-sen led an unsuccessful counterrevolution the next year and was expatriate until regaining power in 1923 with substantial Russian help. Mikhail Borodin provided guidance for establishing a new Chinese government along communist lines with power in the hands of a small elite.

The "father of modern China" died 12 Mar 25 of cancer. CHIANG KAI-SHEK, who commanded a Nationalist army that consolidated Kuomintang power, eventually won out over WANG CHING-WEI in the struggle to succeed Dr Sun.

His widow was Ching-ling Soong (b. 1890), one of T. V. SOONG's and Mme CHIANG KAI-SHEK's remarkable sisters. A critic of the

Kuomintang and its anti-communist policies Mme Sun lived quietly in Chungking during WWII as the largely honorary vice chairman of the People's Republic of China. She was extremely popular with visitors.

SUTHERLAND, Richard Kerens. US general. 1893-1966. Born 27 Nov 93, MacArthur's controversial CofS (1939-45) has been described by one of many hostile eyewitnesses as "a natural climber trying to advance his own interests at the expense of the other fellow . . . one person out here . . . that I will never trust until the day he dies . . . bright and efficient and meaner than hell . . ." (Luvaas, ed, EICHELBERGER, *Dear Miss Em,* 99n, 186, 195). The judgment is mitigated only slightly by MacArthur's biographer: "A superb golf player and a dashing gentleman in the presence of ladies, Sutherland was such a loner that few other than [his deputy, Brig Gen Richard] Marshall knew much about his personal life. . . . The immediate headquarters staff accepted his faults and considered him an efficient chief of staff 'who got the job done no matter what it took,' but some who tangled with him would have agreed with the later evaluation by an Australian: 'Sutherland was the wrong kind of chief of staff for MacArthur, whose foibles he would not offset but nourish.'" (James, *MacArthur,* II, 78.) One of the few commanders to stand up to Sutherland (and win) was the airman George C. KENNEY.

On recommending him for promotion to lieutenant general (as of 20 Feb 44), MacArthur called his CofS an officer who has "demonstrated outstanding strategical and tactical judgment, command and executive ability, and great personal courage and leadership in actual combat. While not so designated officially, he has actually performed all the functions of deputy commander." (Ibid.) The hatchet man was one of his aloof chief's few confidants (James, 77). He retired 30 Nov 46 as a lieutenant general, wearing the DSC (OLC), DSM (OLC), Silver Star (awarded by MacArthur in 1942), LM, and CR (*Army Register,* 1957).

SUZUKI, Kantaro. Japanese official. 1867-1948. Suzuki was born 24 Dec 67 near Tokyo. His 40 years of military service ended in 1927 with retirement as vice minister of the navy and appointment to the Supreme War Council. In 1929 he succeeded the famous Admiral Heiachiro Togo (1847-34) as Grand Chamberlain and member of the Privy Council. With the emperor's confidence and affection Suzuki was the channel through which the admirals and generals had access to the throne. Suzuki was shot through the heart during the **26 Feb 36** insurrection. Narrowly surviving the assassination attempt he withdrew from public life but remained an adviser to the emperor. In Aug 44 he became president of the privy council and was later a member of the Jushin (council of senior statesmen).

The elderly baron reluctantly accepted the emperor's call to head the "surrender government," being an almost unanimous choice. Assuming office on 5 Apr 45 he undertook the delicate task of negotiating the best possible terms without precipitating a civil war. By July he had approached the Soviet Union in a vain attempt to get their mediation for terms short of unconditional surrender. On 10 Aug 45, two days after the Russians declared war and invaded Manchuria, Suzuki offered to surrender if the emperor retained the throne. The atomic bombs meanwhile had been dropped on Hiroshima and Nagasaki, 6 and 9 August, but Suzuki still could not prevail on his government to authorize surrender. HIROHITO finally made the decision when the PM called on him to do so. On 14 August Suzuki announced acceptance of Allied terms, with V-J day set for the 15th. Suzuki resigned on that day and was succeeded by Prince HIGASHIKUNI.

Suzuki was a tall, heavy, but well-built man, a devout Taoist, and free of personal ambition. He did not marry until 1915, and when he became PM in 1945 his only son, Hajime, left the Agriculture Ministry to serve as bodyguard. "Don't accompany me to death," said the father. "I have come a long way but you still have far to go."

They lived through the surrender trauma of 1945 because the expected assassins made the mistake of going to Suzuki's home only after first raiding his office. The family escaped by car after having to have it pushed to start the engine. The admiral's two houses were destroyed. When foreign correspondents finally succeeded in arranging an interview about two weeks later the former PM was still in hiding. He died three years later of natural causes.

The baron's younger brother, Takao Suzuki, was a highly respected general who retired to be chief priest of the Yasukuni Jinja, or Special Government Shrine. Takao's son, Suguru Suzuki, was the navy's youngest lieutenant commander when given the mission of scouting Pearl Harbor's defenses before the surprise attack on 7 Dec 41.

SUZUKI, Sosaku. Japanese general. c1895-1945. Known primarily for his defense of Leyte, Sosaku Suzuki was commissioned in Dec 12 as an infantryman and from 1920 was a member of the general staff. (*Kogun*, 236.) He was promoted to major general in July 38 and the next year became deputy CofS, China Expeditionary Army (ibid.). A lieutenant general in Mar 41 he was YAMASHITA's CofS in the 25th Army for the Malayan campaign. He then had administrative posts in Tokyo, primarily involved with transportation, before taking command of the new 35th Army Hq at Cebu City in Aug 44.

His mission was to defend the central and south Philippines. Since April the 16th Div had been preparing defenses on Leyte, but the high command had not decided on the tactics (whether to defend the beaches or move farther inland to avoid naval preparatory fires) or the strategy (whether to fight the main battle for the Philippines on Leyte). Suzuki compromised with a sort of outpost line of strongpoints overlooking the beaches. (Morison, XII, 136; *West Point Atlas,* Map 145.) YAMASHITA reached Manila on 5 Oct 44 to head the 14th Area Army Hq. Only two weeks later, on the 18th, Krueger's 6th Army began putting four divisions ashore from Leyte Gulf, achieving complete surprise. Suzuki sent three divisions through the Camotes Sea (the west coast) through Ormoc to reinforce the 16th Div, which withdrew to the center of Leyte. Suzuki has been charged with sending a constant flow of optimistic reports that led Yamashita to decide to send him reinforcements to hold Leyte at all cost. The best

evidence is that IGHQ (Tokyo) dictated this course of action.

Yamashita correctly concluded after the Battle for Leyte Gulf (25-26 Oct 44) that Suzuki's position was untenable. But on orders from IGHQ the 21,000 Japanese originally on Leyte were augmented by 13,000 on 2 November and by the same number during the next two weeks.

The Japanese were driven back into pockets that had no hope of surviving. On 22 Dec 44 Yamashita relieved Suzuki of holding the island at all cost and directed him to continue resistance in positions of his own chosing and for only as long as possible. By Christmas day, when the island's last port, Palompon, was lost, Yamashita signaled that he was writing off the 34th Army. Suzuki fought on until the original 47,000 on Leyte were reduced to about 12,000, some 750 being evacuated to Cebu.

The die-hard Suzuki, whom associates called him a sensitive man "of great heart," "straight as bamboo" (Toland, *Sun,* 533), went to sea on 18 Mar 45 in a small boat with part of his staff. After reaching Cebu City (about 70 miles due west) and finding that US forces were taking the island, Suzuki headed south with his little band in five dugouts toward Mindanao, where a pocket of Japanese held out. Only one boat made it. Suzuki was killed on 17 Apr 45, a week under way, when American planes spotted him off Negros. (Toland, *Sun,* 703.) He was promoted posthumously to full general (*Kosun,* 236).

SUZUKI, Teiichi. Japanese general. 1888-. An economics expert and specialist on China he retired from the Army in Apr 41 as a lieutenant general to head the Cabinet Planning Board. For the preceding seven years he had been employed in "planning and executing the economic exploitation of China" (Bergamini, 1100). After having a major role in mobilizing and administering the war economy he lost his post when TOJO resigned on 18 July 44. Sentenced to life imprisonment as a war criminal, he was released in 1956.

SZILARD, Leo. Nuclear physicist. 1898-1964. With Enrico FERMI he produced the first atomic chain reaction on 2 Dec 42. The

Hungarian-born scientist had been an associate of Einstein's after receiving his PhD from the Univ of Berlin in 1922 and working in the capital for 10 years. Szilard left Nazi Germany for London in 1933 and began his work in nuclear physics. In 1938 he became a guest researcher at Columbia Univ in NYC. When war broke out the next year the physicist recognized the possible military applications of his work and was appointed to the US Advisory Committee on Uranium. With Eugene Wigner and other scientists he wrote a letter to President Roosevelt warning that production of an atomic bomb was possible. Alexander SACHS read the letter to FDR on 11 Oct 39, and the next year Szliard and FERMI were put in charge of developing the bomb. The project started at Columbia and moved to the Univ of Chicago. Szilard became a US citizen in 1943. Soon horrified by what he had done to introduce atomic weapons, and devoting the rest of his life to having them banned, he stayed in the Univ of Chicago's metallurgical lab but gave up nuclear physics in 1946. On the faculty as professor of biophysics until Apr 64 he died only a month later (30 May 64) at La Jolla, Calif, after beginning work there at the Salk Institute for Biological Studies.

T

TAFT, Robert Alphonso. American statesman. 1889-1953. Elder son of President William Howard Taft (1857-1930), who blighted the career of Douglas MACARTHUR's father, Robert himself was an unsuccessful Republican candidate for president in 1936, 1940, 1948, and 1952.

Taft was born 8 Sep 89 in Cincinnati and was first in his classes at Yale and at the Harvard Law School (1913). Elected to the US Senate in 1938 and twice thereafter, he became spokesman of the Republican conservative wing, opposing Roosevelt's New Deal (particularly its fiscal policies) and close involvement in European affairs. Senator Taft was intelligent and ambitious but shy, an inept political organizer and a poor speaker. "Robert Taft retained throughout his life the provincial attitude toward Europe of the good burghers of Ohio River cities like Cincinnati, where he resided" (Blum, *V Was for Victory,* 271). But he later backed US participation in the UNO. The senator's career was cut short by cancer on 31 July 53.

TAKAGI, Takeo. Japanese admiral. 1892-1944. The able but cautious Rear Adm Takagi led a powerful support force off the Philippines before defeating DOORMAN in Feb 42 in the Java Sea. Three months later Vice Adm Takagi scored a slim tactical victory in the Coral Sea. He ended up commanding the 6th (Submarine) Fleet, based on Truk. In the spring of 1944 he moved his few surviving forces to Saipan, where Yoshitsugu SAITO was the army commander and Vice Adm Chuichi NAGUMO also had headquarters. It is presumed that Takagi was killed or that he committed suicide like SAITO and Nagumo, but this is not known. (Morison, VIII, 337n25 & 417.)

TAKAHASHI, Ibo. Japanese admiral. 1888-1947. As a senior vice admiral commanding the 3d Fleet, based at Formosa, he supporting the invasion of the Philippines and the NEI but subsequently had no significant role in the war.

TANAKA, Giichi. Japanese official. 1863-1929. His name is associated with the so-called "Tanaka Memorial," published 1929, and that allegedly was a Japanese blueprint for imperialism. But the document is believed to have merely been a report Prime Minister Tanaka made to the throne for the Far Eastern Conference of 1927 that foreign ministry officials and army commanders from Korea and Manchuria attended to formulate policy. Tanaka is thought to have urged merely that the new Emperor HIROHITO concentrate on economic rather than military expansion. No copy of the original document was ever found. By the time of the Tokyo war crimes trials the "Tanaka Memorial," long cherished by Allied propagandists, was generally acknowledged to be a Chinese forgery.

TANAKA, Raizo. Japanese admiral. 1892-1969. The intense, fine-featured, and foxy Rear Adm Raizo Tanaka trained DD Sqdn 2 and led it with great success as commander of the Davao and Jolo Attack Gp in the Philippines. He was based on Davao for early operations in the NEI and then at Ambon. In June 42 he lead the Transport Gp of Nobutake KONDO's Midway Occupation Force from Guam but saw no significant action. During the Guadalcanal campaign, still under KONDO, he became known as "Tanaka the Tenacious" for heroic efforts of the "Tokyo Express." After thoroughly outclassing numerically superior opponents off **Savo Island** in the night battle of Tassafaronga, 30 Nov-1 Dec 42, the admiral was relieved for well-warranted criticism of superiors, whom he advised to abandon Guadalcanal. (*See* Morison, VI, 22). He had no further command at sea.

TANAKA, Shinichi. Japanese general. 1893-. Born in Hokkaido, and graduating from the MA in 1913 as an infantryman (*Kogun,* 236) Col Tanaka was a section chief in the army's Military Affairs Bureau from Mar 37. From Feb 39 he was CofS, Mongolia Garrison Army. He returned to Tokyo and in due course was CofS of the Inspectorate Div, Lines of Communication. Promoted in Oct 41 Lt Gen Tanaka became chief of the military operations section at **IGHQ** with duties that included inspections in French Indo-China, Thailand, and the Philippines. (Ibid.) Although "a plump, comfortable-looking officer in a toupee" (Tuchman, *Stilwell,* 416) Tanaka was impulsive and hot headed: urging a greater effort in early Dec 42 to reinforce Guadalcanal he assaulted Kenryo SATO and in a drunken rage called Premier Tojo a damn fool *(bakayaro).* For this he was removed from his high staff position in Tokyo (Toland, *Sun,* 423-24) and posted to Count TERAUCHI's Southern Army Hq in Saigon.

In Mar 43 Lt Gen Tanaka succeeded Renya MUTAGUCHI in Burma as commander of the renowned 18th Div. In adversity he proved to be "a soldier of outstanding capacity who maneuvered his resources superbly and knew how to make the best of what he had" (ibid.). Driven back by STILWELL's forces in Yunnan and Burma in 1944, his disease-ridden troops were encircled in Kamaing and reduced to about half strength before breaking out. Tanaka had been virtually abandoned by HONDA, who was using all reserves in a futile effort to recapture Myitkyina, and this led to rapid deterioration of relations between the generals. Tanaka was CofS of the Burma Area Army after Heitaro KIMURA replaced Masakazu KAWABE as CG in Aug 44. The CofS was somewhat ineffectual because of his preoccupation with administrative details but he held his post until wounded in May 45 and hospitalized for the duration. After the war he was active in the National Defense Society.

TASSIGNY. *See* LATTRE DE TASSIGNY.

TAYLOR, Maxwell Davenport. US general. 1901-87. A pioneer in airborne warfare, he commanded the 82d Abn division artillery in the Sicilian campaign and later was CG, 101st Abn Div. The suave, intellectual, handsome Max Taylor, who had an exceptional aptitude for learning languages, used to say that he did not like to jump from airplanes but liked associating with men who did.

Taylor was born 26 Aug 01 in Keytesville, Mo, son of an attorney. He graduated from West Point in June 22 (4/102) and was first captain.

As assistant SGS in Washington he was promoted to lieutenant colonel 17 days after the 7 Dec 41 attack on Pearl Harbor. In July 42 he became CofS, 82d Abn Div, getting his first star on 4 Dec 42 and becoming division artillery commander.

After jumping into Sicily he volunteered for the a secret mission to Rome. On 3 Sep 43 the BADOGLIO government had signed an armistice with the Allies and Eisenhower was to announce this just before Mark CLARK began an amphibious assault at Salerno on 9 September. Taylor was to determine whether an air drop on Rome was feasible, which depended on whether the city and its air fields were still in Italian hands. The general and an intelligence officer landed by patrol boat near Rome and proceeded by Red Cross ambulance to meet Italian officials in the city. The emissary found that KESSELRING had reacted with unexpected rapidity to secure Rome, overcoming Italian garrisons. Badoglio informed Eisenhower of this development and even warned that the armistice announcement should be postponed. On Taylor's recommendation the airborne operation was called off, but Eisenhower made the surrender announcement as planned.

When BADOGLIO and the king fled Rome, Taylor became senior US representative on the commission that, among other things, convinced the new Italian government to declare war on Germany.

The general took command of the 101st Abn "Screaming Eagles" Div in the UK and got his second star on 31 Mar 44 at the age of 42. On D-day, 6 June 44, he jumped with the first wave into Normandy behind Utah beach. Having won the Silver Star for the Rome mission he was awarded the DSC and the British DSO. After 33 days in action the Screaming Eagles shipped back to Britain, where they were assigned to BRERETON's 1st Allied Abn Army on 10 Aug 44.

The 101st landed in Holland on 17 Sep 44 for Opn **Market-Garden.** Taylor's troops immediately took Vechel, held the Zon bridge, and that day and the next they seized St Oedenrode and Eindhoven. Opheusden changed hands several times before the Germans were driven out on 9 Oct 44, and the division secured the Eindhoven bridgehead. Having patrol actions until 28 Nov 44 the Screaming Eagles then went to France. Taylor was severely wounded during the 73-day campaign and was out of action for two weeks. In addition to the automatic PH he was awarded a second SS.

Taylor was in Washington on TDY when the Ardennes counteroffensive started on 16 Dec 44. "Tony" McAULIFFE consequently became the hero of Bastogne but Taylor flew back on Christmas Eve and rejoined his troops after the 4th Armd Div made the link-up late the next day. Fighting until 17 Jan 45 to reduce the **Bulge,** the division patrolled in Alsace along the Moder, sending a three-company assault across the river on the 31st. Withdrawn to Mourmelon, France, on 26 Feb 45 for a month of rehabilitation, the division moved into the Ruhr pocket to mop up and handle military government duties. Then resuming the pursuit across Germany, Taylor reached Bergtesgaden before V-E day.

He became superintendent at West Point on 4 Sep 45, at 44 the youngest since MacArthur (who had been Taylor's "supe"). Taylor headed the Berlin Command 1949-51 and in the latter year was promoted to lieutenant general. Then he was DCS for operations until 1953, when he got his fourth star and took command of the 8th Army in Korea. He was CG, Army Forces Far East, 1954-56; CinC, Far East Command, 1955; then Army CofS, 1955-59. Retiring from military service to be chairman of the board of the Mexican Light & Power Co Ltd 1959-60 the general became president of the Lincoln Center for the Performing Arts in NYC as this monumental project was being completed. Returning to active duty as military adviser to the president 1961-62 he was JCS chairman 1962-64 and ambassador to South Vietnam in 1965. Then he was special consultant to the president, 1965-69, head of the Institute for Defense Analysis, and president of the Foreign Intelligence Advisory Board, 1965-70.

Max Taylor died 19 Apr 87 at Walter Reed Army Hospital at the age of 85.

TAYLOR, Myron Charles. US envoy to the Vatican. 1874-1959. Born in Lyons, NY, on 18 Jan 74, Myron Taylor was an Episcopalian of early Quaker stock. (*CB 40.*) Until 1927 he was an attorney and textile executive, thereafter with the US Steel Corp, rising to be CEO. Hitler had overrun Poland and was poised to attack France and the Benelux when FDR appointed Taylor his personal representative to the Vatican on 23 Dec 39. Critics objected that this violated the doctrine of separation of Church and State, but the president persisted in what he hoped would support Pope PIUS XII's peace efforts. The first American minister to the Papal States since Rufus King departed in 1868, Taylor sailed on 17 Feb 40 with ambassadorial rank. Except for a break in 1942-44, when denied reentry to Italy after a trip to the US, Taylor held his post until 1950, having been reappointed by Truman.

TEDDER, Arthur William. British airman. 1890-1967. Born 11 July 90 at Glenguin in the County of Stirling, where his father lived while exercising his civil service appointments, Tedder was educated at Whitgift and Magdalene College, Cambridge. He won academic honors, ending with the postgraduate Prince Consort Prize for history in 1913. After playing professional rugby briefly, he served a few months in Fiji as a colonial servant. Unfit for army service because of a minor knee injury, although in 1914 he had taken a reserve commission in the Dorsetshire Regt in 1914, he was accepted two years later by the RFC. Flying bombing and photo missions in 1916 he so impressed TRENCHARD that he was given command of No. 70 Ftr Sqdn in early 1917. After a year in action, he served in the UK with a training unit until sent to Egypt in 1918. With two years of war service, mentioned three times in dispatches, he was commissioned in the new RAF (1919). Thereafter he had a major role in developing the service he had joined.

In 1929 he became a member of the RAF Staff College at Cranston, leaving with the rank of group captain. He headed the Air Armament School (1934-36) and for the next two years was director of training in the Air Ministry. He was AOC in Singapore (1936-38), being promoted to air vice marshal (1937).

Tedder took the new post of director general of R&D in the Air Ministry in 1938, continuing this work when the Ministry of Aircraft Production was created. He clashed inevitably with the supercharged Lord BEAVERBROOK when the latter became the minister in 1940, and "the Beaver" passed on to Churchill the sense that Tedder an obstructionist.

Tedder went to Cairo in late 1940 as deputy air commander (AOCinC) Middle East, replacing Sir Arthur Longmore in June 41, when Longmore was recalled after the British debacle in Greece and Crete. As Middle East Air Force (MEAF) commander Tedder adopted a new air doctrine that was the key to his immediate success in the desert and later in the Mediterranean and northern Europe. Having concluded that the RAF had to integrate air strategy more closely with ground operations, as the Luftwaffe did, he reasoned further that ground commanders must dictate target selection.

Tedder was knighted (KCB) on the 1942 New Year's honors list and promoted during the year.

Air Chief Marshal Tedder continued to support the offensive that drove ROMMEL's Panzer Army Afrika toward the armies of Eisenhower that were approaching Tunis.

Under a command reorganization in Apr 43 for final destruction of Axis forces in North Africa Tedder moved up to be Eisenhower's deputy with the title Air Commander in Chief, Mediterranean. This was the beginning of an enduring and harmonious relationship between the two leaders. Tedder's major subordinate commands were the MEAF, now under William Sholto Douglas (who had been Tedder's deputy for three months), Carl "Tooey" Spaatz's US NW Africa AF (NAAF), and RAF, Malta.

After the conquest of Tunisia, Sicily, and the invasion of mainland Italy, Tedder was appointed on 28 Dec 43 as Eisenhower's deputy supreme Allied commander and the senior Allied airman. When he reached London in Jan 44 Tedder began a delicate command relationship. His immediate superior was Portal; his immediate subordinates was Leigh-Mallory who as head of the Allied Expeditionary AF was responsible for air support of the invasion. Under Leigh-Mallory were the two Allied strategic air force chiefs, "Bomber" Harris and Spaatz. These two disagreed with Leigh-Mallory over priorities and operational concepts about what air support would do the landing forces most good, and they refused to coordinate US and British strategic air efforts. Spaatz refused to take orders from Leigh-Mallory.

All this Tedder gloomily reported to Portal in February. The obvious solution [writes Andrews] was to place Tedder, as Eisenhower's deputy, in command superiority to Harris and Spaatz. Eisenhower and the American Chiefs of Staff, and also Churchill, favoured this. The British Chiefs of Staff resisted. Only on 14 April, seven weeks before the invasion, was the technical superstructure creating a supreme air command recognized officially. From this moment the overall direction of the air war, which had hitherto been exercised by Portal on behalf of the Combined Chiefs of Staff, was in the hands of Tedder. It continued thus until, on Portal's representation in September, command of the strategic bombers was taken from Tedder and remitted now to Portal and Arnold jointly, although exer-

cised through their deputies [Air Marshal Sir Norman] Bottomley and Spaatz. (Andrews, *The Air Marshals,* 261-62.)

Based on his successful experience in North Africa and Italy, where he had perfected close tactical air support, Tedder also believed in making a massive effort to isolate the battlefield by going after the enemy's entire communications system. Hence he was a proponent of the **Transportation Plan.** HARRIS objected that Bomber Command (BC) still lacked the requisite accuracy, but Tedder ordered specimen night attacks on six French targets, and these revealed that BC had made giant steps since its disappointing earlier performance. SPAATZ remained wedded to targeting the Luftwaffe's fighter command and German industry. Churchill was the most formidable opponent of the Transportation Plan because of the civilian casualties and the damage to historic structures. But "Tedder's communications plan was somewhat grudgingly accepted" (Ibid., 263).

Subsequently he successfully directed the air war in Europe. During the controversies among senior British and American leaders, ground and air commanders, he won almost universal admiration for sustaining tactical and strategic air support. But Montgomery continually criticized Tedder for being too pro-American. Largely because of American pressure, notably from Spaatz, it was announced on 15 Oct 44 that Tedder would personally take over the tactical air force leadership from the abrasive LEIGH-MALLORY. Shortly thereafter it was decided that high-level coordination of air efforts were needed with the Russians as the Allies closed in on Germany. Tedder went Moscow in Jan 45 for talks with Stalin and others, and on returning to SHAEF around 29 Jan 45 he learned of a move to have him replaced by Alexander.

This came about because Churchill had decided that Alexander deserved a larger role now that Italy was a minor theater of war, and Eisenhower admitted asking for this general. Alan Brooke wrote in his diary that the change "might assist in keeping Ike on the rails in the future" and Montgomery agreed (Tedder, 661). It also was proposed that Tedder become Portal's deputy. But on second thought the proponents of the change, including Eisenhower and Montgomery, decided to leave the command arrangement unchanged. Aside from the bad public relations aspects of relieving Tedder, Eisenhower had begun to worry about Alexander's interfering with his direct relations with army group commanders; Tedder had had responsibility only for the air war and rear area administration. (Tedder, 662-64.)

On 8 May 45 he led the Allied delegation that signed the surrender instrument in the ruins of Berlin.

After retiring from the RAF in 1950 Lord Tedder, 1st Baron of Glenquin, spent a year as chairman of the British Joint Services Commission in Washington before becoming chancellor of Cambridge Univ in 1951. He died 3 June 67 in Surrey at the age of 76. His lively, scholarly, candid, and objective war memoirs are *With Prejudice* (Boston: Little, Brown, 1966).

TERAUCHI, Hisaichi. Japanese general. 1879-1946. Field Marshal Count Terauchi commanded the Southern Army throughout the war.

Closely related to Emperor Hirohito, the general was born in Yamaguchi Prefecture, son of Viscount General Misatake Terauchi (1852-1919), who was governor general of Korea in 1910 and prime minister of Japan, 9 Oct 17-29 Sep 18. The son graduated in 1900 from the military academy and received further military training in Germany and Austria (1909) before teaching at the military academy. Terauchi rose to command the 5th Div and to be CofS of the Korea Army, then he headed the Formosa Army. Promoted to full general in Oct 35 the suave, elegant, and aristocratic old count was made a military councillor the next year for the first of several times. As a member of the Control Faction that came out on top in the **2 Oct 36** crisis he was the army's choice as war minister in the Koki HIROTA cabinet (9 Mar 36-23 Jan 37). HIROHITO had assigned Hirota the task of restoring civil order, and Terauchi was cooperative initially. But after settling scores with opposing military cliques and getting the Control Faction firmly established—further cemented political bonds with Tojo and Sugiyama—Terauchi took the lead in ousting Hirota.

Count Terauchi was IG of military training and a military councillor (again) until Aug 37, when he became CG North China Area Army.

From Dec 38 he again was a military councillor. (*Kogun*, 237.)

Terauchi assumed command of the Southern Army on 6 Nov 41 and met four days later with Adm Yamamoto in Tokyo to conclude a "central agreement" on how they would direct their "stupendous scheme of conquest" (Morison, III, 71). Starting with four field armies and having his headquarters in Saigon (which the Japanese had taken over from the French in July 41) Terauchi had the task of conquering the Southern Resources Area. He moved his headquarters to Singapore after Yamashita took the place on 15 Feb 42, and Terauchi's command continued to be known as the Southern Army even after it included several area armies.

Field Marshal Count Terauchi (promoted in June 43) moved to Manila in May 44 after the IGHQ in Tokyo decided belatedly to make the Philippines a "principal area of decisive battle." The elderly nobleman was an effective administrator and logistician but an inept strategist. His many mistakes in crippling the campaign of a brilliant subordinate are covered in some detail under YAMASHITA. Terauchi left his final instructions for defense of the Philippines and moved his headquarters back to Saigon on 17 Nov 44. He had been one of three nominated to replace Tojo, but the latter committed one of his last big blunders in recommending that the count be left in the field.

The far-flung Southern Army now faced disaster on all fronts. The Burma Area Army, created in Mar 43 as part of Terauchi's command, had suffered a crushing defeat and its chief, Kawabe, had been sacked along with the controversial Mutaguchi. The Allied counteroffensive under MOUNTBATTEN, with William SLIM making the main effort, was driving into Burma and preparing to continue the offensive into Malaya and the NEI. Bad news from Burma (the fall of Mandalay) and of defeats in the Philippines caused the old field marshal to suffer a stroke on 10 Apr 45. He recovered partially and remained in Saigon because his staff concealed the truth about his health, but in early August the emperor ordered him home. On 10 August, about a week before he planned to leave, Terauchi learned from a US commercial radio bulletin that the emperor was negotiating a surrender. When HIROHITO's broadcast on 15 Aug 45 made this official Terauchi prevailed on his subordinate commanders to lay down their arms.

Not fully in command of his faculties and unable to travel (which Mountbatten's doctor confirmed in Saigon) the field marshal sent deputies to negotiate surrender of his far-flung armies. Because Mountbatten could not be dealing with the senior enemy commander he named "Boy" Browning to sign the surrender in Rangoon on 28 August and in Singapore on 12 Sep 45.

Terauchi sent for his two ceremonial swords, one dating from 1292, which he surrendered to Mountbatten in Saigon on 30 Nov 45. The British commander, who like Terauchi was kin to his country's royal family, was solicitous of a prisoner who obviously had little longer to live and who normally would have committed suicide. The privileged captive was living in a bungalow near Johore Bahru, Malaya, attended by a small entourage and having periods of lucidity, when he died 12 June 45. (Allen, *Burma,* 543-52.) Only this saved him from prosecution as a major war criminal.

TERBOVEN, Joseph. Nazi proconsul in Norway. 1898-1945. Of Roman Catholic parentage, he was born 23 May 98 in Essen. Despite his youth Terboven served as a lieutenant in WWI (Wistrich) and was educated at Freiburg. He was involved in Hitler's **Munich Beer Hall Putsch,** 8-9 Nov 23, joined the NSDAP in Essen, and from 1930 was a Nazi deputy to the Reichstag. On Hitler's taking power in 1933 Terboven was made a Prussian State Counselor and Gauleiter of Essen. He rose to be Oberpraesident of the Rhine Province on 5 Feb 35. In Sep 39 he became Reich Defense Commissioner for Wehrkreis VI, his office in Muenster (Wistrich).

Terboven then took the position with which his name is primarily associated, Reichskommissar for the Occupied Norwegian Territories from 24 Apr 40. A brutal proconsul, dominating the ineffectual QUISLING, he attempted to infringe on military authority. In June 43 FALKENHORST put him off with the promise that if the Allies ever invaded Norway the Reichskommissar would retain civil authority everywhere except in the immediate combat zones. By Mar 45 Terboven concluded that an Allied invasion would overrun most of Norway,

leaving him as the principal German authority in the country. "This thought he communicated to [Generaladmiral Hermann] Boehme, who agreed and suggested that when the time came, he take over the post of chief of the military government under the Armed Forces Commander," the latter being the admiral. "Terboven countered with a suggestion that he be made Boehme's deputy in all except tactical matters." (Ziemke, 313.) The OKW was greatly alarmed by this proposal, approved in principle by Hitler but fought off by KEITEL and JODL, because it would make all Gauleiters political commissars as in the Red Army (ibid.). On 8 May 45, the day the German surrender was announced, Terboven committed suicide in his bunker.

THEOBALD, Robert Alfred. US admiral. 1884-1957. "Fuzzy" Theobald, who had a minor role in WWII operations but is well known as an author, was born 25 Jan 94 in San Francisco. He spent a year at the Univ of California before entering Annapolis and graduating early, on 12 Sep 06, in the first section of 86 midshipmen in what officially is the Class of 1907. He ranked ninth among 209 graduates and 57 nongraduates of this class.

Theobald commanded a destroyer landing force at Santo Domingo in 1916 before becoming gunnery officer of BB *New York,* flagship of the squadron serving with the British Grand Fleet. Theobald was XO, Naval Post Graduate school at Annapolis, 1919-21, and head of the school 1924-27 after serving with the Destroyer Command, Asiatic Fleet. XO BB *West Virginia* 1927-1929, he attended the Naval War College 1929-30 before becoming secretary of war plans in the Navy Department and member of the Joint Army-Navy Planning Commission 1930-32. Theobald was CofS Destroyers, Pacific Fleet, until 1934; he held high planning positions at the Naval War College 1935-37; and he commanded BB *Nevada* 1937-39. Capt Theobald was CofS to Adm Claude Block, CinC, US Fleet, then commanded Cruiser Div 3 before being ordered to the Navy General Board in Feb 40. On 1 Sep 40 he was promoted to rear admiral commanding DD Flotilla 1, Pacific Fleet. After Pearl Harbor the admiral was Commander, Destroyers, Pacific Fleet before NIMITZ personally selected him to head the North Pacific Fleet. Theobald reached

Kodiak on 27 May 41 to command a main body of five cruisers and four destroyers. As a newcomer to what was primarily an army theater of operations the admiral was properly tactful (Morison, IV, 166). But the cautious Theobald was soon at loggerheads over strategy with the dynamic Gen BUCKNER and his air corps officers, a conflict that paralyzed operations in the Aleutians (Garfield, 184). After months of asking to be relieved, Theobald was replaced on 4 Jan 43 by the aggressive KINKAID and put on the shelf as commander of the 1st Naval District and Navy Yard in Boston. Retiring 1 Feb 45 as a rear admiral and living in Boston, Theobald published *The Final Secret of Pearl Harbor: The Washington Contribution to the Japanese Attack* (New York: Devin-Adair, 1954). He also wrote the introduction and voluminous in-text notes for the US edition of Capt Andrieu d'Albas's highly regarded *Death of a Navy: Japanese Naval Action in World War II* (New York: Devin-Adair, 1957). The admiral died 13 May 57 in Boston.

THOMA, Wilhelm Ritter von. German general. 1891-1948. "The most famous of the original German tank leaders next to Guderian," Thoma was a "tough but likeable type [who] would have been perfectly happy as a knight errant, challenging all comers at any cross-road. . . ." (Liddell Hart, *Talk*, 90. The author devotes nine pages to his postwar interview with Thoma.)

A veteran of the first world war, "famous for his icy calm and exceptional bravery" (Guderian, 180), Thoma took command of the first German tank battalion in 1934 and then spent three years as head of all German ground troops supporting Franco. Soon after leaving Spain in June 39 and writing his final report Thoma briefly commanded a tank regiment before taking over the tank brigade of the 2d Pz Div in Aug 39. As part of List's 14th Army of AG South for the attack on Poland (1 Sep 39) his tank brigade was supposed to make a frontal attack on Jablunka Pass, some 60 mi SW of Cracow. But at Thoma's suggestion the division's motorized brigade undertook this conventional mission while Thoma made a remarkable 50-mile **turning movement** through heavy woods and mountainous terrain—not losing a tank—to achieved complete surprise.

Thoma became Director of Mobile Forces after the Polish campaign and in Oct 40 he was sent to recommend whether German reinforcements should be sent to support GRAZIANI's lumbering offensive in North Africa. The panzer pioneer submitted a negative report, primarily because of the logistics problems. But Rommel, whom he briefed, already was planning the operations that would make him famous as the Desert Fox.

Generalmajor Thoma replaced Hans-Juergen von Arnim in Opn **Barbarossa** as acting commander of the 17th Pz Div on 17 July 41. In Guderian's 2d Pz Group he saw action in the Smolensk and Kiev encirclements, he and Model being slightly wounded on 2 Sep 41 (Guderian, 209). Exactly a month after leaving the 17th Panzers he commanded the 20th Pz Div in the Moscow region until 30 June 42. Promoted to head an army corps, Generalleutnant Thoma was then ordered to assume command of the **Afrika Korps.** He reached North Africa on 20 Sep 42.

(Thoma told Liddell Hart he was sent *to relieve Rommel* and arrived about 20 Sep 42. STUMME arrived *a fortnight later* "to take charge of the African theater as a whole," Thoma recollected, relegating Thoma to "command of our troops at the front, facing the El Alamein position." [Ibid., 163.] As outlined in the sketch of STUMME that general seems actually to have reached North Africa on 19 Sep 42, three days before Rommel left on sick leave. See also **Afrika Korps** for what's wrong with Thoma's recollection as quoted above from Liddell Hart's work.)

Montgomery began the battle of El Alamein with tremendous preparatory fires on the evening of 23 October and STUMME was reported MIA the next morning. Thoma was acting commander of Panzer Army Africa until ROMMEL returned from Germany on the 25th. Promoted to General of Panzer Troops as of 1 November (B&O, 30n) and having resumed command of the Afrika Korps, Thoma was so disgusted by Hitler's refusal to authorize any withdrawal that he seemed to have become suicidal. On 4 November, as the British ground through Rommel's lines, Thoma raced from one critical point to another in a tank that took several hits before finally being set on fire. The general was thrown clear, and Fritz Bayerlein saw him standing in an intense cross-fire, "rigid and motionless as a pillar of salt, with his canvas bag still in his hand" (Flower, ed, *Courage*, 472).

Taken prisoner by forward elements of the 10th Hussars the latter-day knight errant was Montgomery's dinner guest that night before going into captivity. Other than Rudolf HESS he was Britain's most distinguished POW until joined by von ARNIM. Thoma died 30 Apr 48 in Starenberg, Germany, a few months after being released.

THOREZ, Maurice. French Communist Leader. 1900-64. The "French Stalin" was born 28 Apr 00 at Noyelles-Godault (Pas de Calais). Son and grandson of coal miners, he went to work at the age of 12 in the screening process or as an errand boy (Larousse) at the coal mines of Dourges (some 25 km NE of Arras) and soon was a militant unionist. Thorez joined the French Socialist Party in 1919 and a year later he helped create the French Communist Party (SFIC). He was the party's secretary general 1930-46 and a deputy from the working-class Paris suburb of Ivry-sur-Seine 1932-39.

Thorez changed course politically at least three times on the eve of war. In 1934 he dropped an anti-socialist stand to form an alliance with the SIFO that later made Léon BLUM's **popular front** government possible (in 1936). He dropped an anti-military position when the Franco-Soviet pact was signed in 1935. Finally, after being anti-Nazi he applauded the Nazi-Soviet Pact of 23 Aug 39.

Thorez then called for his followers to answer the call to arms and he set the example. But he deserted the army after Daladier outlawed the Communist Party on 26 Sep 39 (because the Soviets invaded Poland). In separate actions Thorez was sentenced to 11 years in prison and stripped of French citizenship. After making his way to Moscow by a route and on dates unknown (Larousse), Thorez faithfully relayed Stalin's orders to France for the next five years. He returned to France on 27 Nov 44 under a special amnesty, his plane passed one taking de Gaulle to Moscow. "Please wait a little before you shoot him," Stalin is alleged to have joked with de Gaulle. "You may find him useful."

Threat of a communist putsch was very real in postwar France but Thorez immediately (30 Nov 44) issued instructions for communists to focus on helping win the war and on rebuilding industry. To the surprise of friend and foe Thorez then came out in favor of disarming and disbanding irregular groups. The communist leader evi-

dently "was paying de Gaulle a quid pro quo for his return to France and for the [recently-signed] Franco-Soviet pact. Moreover, he [Thorez] was probably not displeased to take the Party he had abandoned for five years back into his own hands by disarming his comrades who had remained and fought in France." (Robert Aron, *Liberation,* 415-16.)

Thorez became a deputy from the Seine-et-Marne department on 21 Oct 45 and held the office thereafter. He was elected minister of state on 21 Nov 45, doubling as vice president of the Council from 24 June 46, and again holding the dual position during the period 24 June-12 Dec 46. In the Nov 46 election he came within a few votes of becoming premier, one fifth of all French voters by that time being communists. Thanks to Thorez France had become perhaps the only western European country that communists could have taken over by legitimate, parliamentary action. But he was ousted as secretary general in 1947 for refusing to support Paul Ramadier.

The communist chief was a stocky man, five feet ten and looking like a prizefighter. But he became "a man of considerable culture" and "one of the few Marxists who laugh" (*CB 46,* quoting *Newsweek* and *Time).* In ill health during his final years, Thorez died 11 July 64 while a passenger on a Soviet liner in Istambul harbor.

THUEMMEL, Paul. Secret agent. 1902-45. Best known as "Franta" and variously identified as "a Saxon aristocrat" and "a former baker" (Paine, *Abwehr,* 109; Ivanov, *Target Heydrich,* 87), Thuemmel was a German who acquired the credentials of a nickel-plated Nazi. He wore the party's gold badge and moved in the highest social and official circles. An old friend of Himmler's and later in the confidence of Canaris, he was completely unsuspected for many years of being a traitor.

Paul Thuemmel began intelligence work for the Germans in 1928 and gave the Nazis his services as Hitler rose to power. But as "Voral," code number A54, he collaborated with Czech intelligence in the early days of the republic (Ivanov, 88). Thuemmel became an Abwehr agent in 1933. The next year Canaris sent him to the Dresden office, where he continued to give the Czechs high-level Nazi secrets to include a warning that Hitler would take Czechoslovakia on 15 Mar 39. About this time Canaris sent Thuemmel to Prague as chief of Military Intelligence for the Balkans (Paine, 109). Through contacts in foreign capitals Franta relayed reports to President Benes in England, but the London Czechs lost radio contact with Prague in the summer of 1940. France had collapsed, and the British were straining to find out about Hitler's threatened cross-channel assault, Opn **Sea Lion.** So the SOE and London Czechs arranged for underground leaders in Prague to make contact with Thuemmel. Secret instructions described him as a man of about 40, of medium height, "strong features, and rather staring eyes" (Ivanov, 89). Capt Vaclac Moravek ("Ota") succeeded in meeting "Voral-Franta" and quickly overcoming his distrust. The two worked closely thereafter, Ota being one of the "Three Kings" comprising the British-sponsored Central Committee for Internal Resistance (UVOD) and the only one to know Franta's identity. The men kept in contact through intermediaries and met when necessary. London again began getting the spy's reports. One of particular value was that **Sea Lion** was "postponed" and another, toward the end of Oct 40, that **Barbarossa** was being planned. Franta also warned the Czech underground through UVOD of people and addresses under surveillance, of proposed arrests, and of informants (Ivanov, 91).

But the Germans found the underground's last radio transmitter on the night of 4-5 Oct 41, again breaking the Prague-London link. Eager to restore this, the SOE dropped three parachutists, the Silver A team, into the Bohemian hills on 29 December. Silver A was headed by Lt Alfred Bartos, who had orders to find Moravek and make contact with Thuemmel. Dropped separately from the same aircraft were the Anthropoids, who were joined by Sgt Josef Valcik of the A team for the assassination of HEYDRICH.

It, however, was not until 14 Mar 42 that Bartos could radio London that he had found Moravek, and by this time the Gestapo was closing in: Thuemmel had been arrested on 13 Oct 41 but freed on 25 November when the Gestapo could find no conclusive charges; Heydrich— who arrested several highly placed Germans on suspicion of being Franta—had Thuemmel brought in again on 27 Feb 42 for questioning. The Abwehr officer denied being Franta and protested that he was just doing his job in penetrating OVOD; that was why he had contact with Moravek and the other miscreants Heydrich was hunting. A bamboozled court-martial referred the case to Himmler, who conferred with Canaris (!) and ordered the prisoner released. (Paine, 110.) Thuemmel pretended he would help set a trap for Moravek (Ivanov, 93). The latter now was working to get Franta safely out of Prague and was to meet an agent in a park near Thuemmel's apartment the evening of 21 Mar 42. But the Germans knew this, having thoroughly penetrated the underground, and they arrested Thuemmel for the third time on 20 Mar 42. Probably not knowing this, hence not getting his usual warning from Franta, Moravec walked into a Gestapo trap. Versions vary on what happened, but Moravec apparently committed suicide after being mortally wounded in a fierce shootout. The OVOD also was dead.

Thuemmel was convicted of high treason and spent three years in a cell in the fortress of Terezin. He was shot to death in the last days of the war.

THYSSEN, Fritz. German industrialist. 1873-1951. Son of the man who is generally credited with founding the German iron and steel industry, Fritz Thyssen was a Rhinelander born in Muelheim on 9 Nov 93. As an ardent nationalist he was convicted by French occupation forces in 1923 of organizing passive resistance. That year, through Gen Erich Ludendorff, he gave Hitler's fledgling party 100,000 gold marks. (Wistrich.) The cultured, devoutly Catholic Thyssen found Nazism abhorrent but, like many other Good Germans, saw Hitler's movement as Germany's one hope for revival.

Having succeeded his father in 1926 as head of an industrial empire based in the Ruhr, Thyssen joined the National Socialist Party in 1931. Two years later, as the Nazis took power, GOERING finally arranged a meeting between the steel baron and Hitler that brought Ruhr industrialists into the Nazi camp. When Hitler became head of state Goering appointed Thyssen Prussian State Councilor for life. The industrialist was fully awakened to the evils of Nazism when Hitler invaded Poland on 1 Sep 39 and said publicly "Whoever is not with me is a traitor and shall be treated as such." Thyssen drove to Switzerland the next day and made his way to France. His citizenship revoked, property confiscated, and later branded a communist, he quickly wrote *I Paid Hitler* (New York & Toronto: Farrar & Rhinehart, 1941). Thyssen was trying to make his way to South America when the Vichy police arrested him on Christmas day 1940 and delivered him the next day to German police agents. Thyssen and his wife were held in Germany throughout the war and liberated with the **Niederdorf group** on 4 May 45.

A German court found the tycoon guilty of being a "minor Nazi" and ordered him to give 15 per cent of his available property to the fund for victims of Nazi persecution. Thyssen died in Buenos Aires on 8 Feb 51 at the age of 77. His wife Amalie and daughter, Countess Anita Zichy-Thyssen, continued to live in Argentina with what was left of the family fortune.

TIMOSHENKO, Semen (Semyon) Konstantinovich. Soviet military commander. 1895-1970. A Ukrainian, born near Odessa in the village of Furmanka, Bessarabia, on 18 Feb 95, the son of a peasant, he was drafted in 1915. As a machine gunner he fought the Germans and became an NCO. In 1917 he was jailed for striking an officer, but the revolution freed him the same year from completing the prison sentence. Timoshenko became a hero of the civil war, fighting at Tsaritsyn (Stalingrad), dashing to the gates of Warsaw in 1920, and being wounded five times in the Crimea. In these early years he formed an enduring friendship with Stalin. *(CB 41.)*

Virtually illiterate, the veteran of many battlefields started a long period of schooling after the civil war. At the Frunze MA he was distinguished only for the comment "Well, this is not like going into battle" (*NYT* obit, 2 Apr 70). But he graduated in 1922 and in 1933 was deputy commander of the Belorussian MD. He then headed, in turn, the Northern Caucasus, Kharkov, and Kiev MD. Meanwhile, when the first Supreme Soviet was created in 1937, Timoshenko was made a member and remained one for life.

In the Soviet occupation of Poland in 1939 he led the Ukrainian Front, moving on Lvov and later into the Lublin area (Kennedy, *Poland,* 125). He concluded the Winter War against Finland on 13 Mar 40 after succeeding MER-ETSKOV (7 Jan 40) and apparently using the strategy conceived by SHAPOSHNIKOV. The powerfully built, poker-faced Slav, who had not

a hair on his rather flat head, was now a national hero and was known internationally. He was 45 years old when made a marshal (MSU No. 7) and a Hero of the Soviet Union on 7 May 40. The next day he became commissar of defense (vice VOROSHILOV) and about this time his daughter married Vasily STALIN, the dictator's shiftless son. Timoshenko was ill-suited for high command, having "much of the cavalry non-commissioned officer about him" and like Yeremenko and Zhukov "being particularly blunt and outspoken, offensively so to his subordinates, according to his colleagues" (Seaton, *Stalin,* 131). But the civil war hero appreciated the fundamentals of discipline, morale, and realistic training, and he undertook to reform the Red Army along lines he had found successful in the Winter War. He also followed Stalin's general directions for discarding military traditions unsuited to modern war. (Bialer, 574n97.)

But Defense Minister Timoshenko must share the blame with Stalin for the debacle that began on 22 June 41. He belatedly accepted the warning of **GRU** chief F. I. GOLIKOV that a German attack might be imminent, but when D. G. PAVLOV's intelligence officer reported that the invasion actually had begun, Timoshenko's response was, "Comrade Stalin has forbidden to open artillery fire against the Germans" and "there is to be no air reconnaissance more than thirty-five miles beyond the frontier." (Werth, *Russia at War,* 151.) The commissar of defense finally galvanized into action and took charge in Moscow until STALIN emerged from his stupor on 2 July. Two days later Marshal Timoshenko left for the battlefield.

As **Glavkom** of the critical "Western Direction" in the central zone and also as commander of the Western Front (HFS) he flew to Gnezdoyo, near Smolensk. His deputy was YEREMENKO. Stalin meanwhile pulled himself together and took over from Timoshenko as head of the new **Stavka** on 10 July and as commissar of defense. The marshal stepped down to be Stalin's deputy commissar of defense.

With fresh troops and remnants of Pavlov's forces along a frontage of almost 200 miles Timoshenko had some success in delaying the Germans. But by 3 July 41, when all fighting stopped in the Bialystok pocket, the Western Front ceased to exist. Five days later the Germans had 290,000 Russian POWs, 2,500 tanks, and 1,500 guns. What saved Moscow was Hitler's order on 19 July that weakened BOCK's AG Center by diverting GUDERIAN's panzers south toward Kiev and HOTH's panzers north toward Leningrad. On 12 Sep 42 Timoshenko was ordered south as Glavkom in the Ukraine, and he reached Poltava the next day, when ZHUKOV landed at Leningrad (Seaton, *Stalin,* 113). Because Stalin refused to authorize withdrawals until it was too late, Guderian closed the northern side of a trap that netted 665,000 prisoners in the Kiev encirclement. On orders from Moscow, Timoshenko was flown out along with Budenny and Khrushchev.

Thereafter he commanded the Southwest *Theater* while remaining head of the Southwest *Front,* succeeding KIRPONOS. The Russian rout continued, panzers entering Rostov, "Gateway to the Caucasus," on 19 Nov 41. With reinforcements from the hard-pressed defenses of Moscow the marshal retook Rostov 10 days after it had fallen; it was the first successful Soviet counteroffensive of the war.

During the period Jan-Mar 42 Timoshenko was back on the Finnish front, where his operations were a complete failure. Timoshenko had peaked out. Back in the Ukraine for the mismanaged Kharkov counteroffensive in May 42 his forces were so decimated that the theater headquarters was disbanded and Timoshenko was demoted to command only the Southwest Front (Seaton, *R-G War,* 273). He left this to head the new Stalingrad Front briefly, 12-22 July 42, being succeeded by V. N. GORDOV. In August Timoshenko was quietly removed from the Stalingrad Front to succeed P. A. Kurochkin as head the Northwest Front, Oct 42-Mar 43 (ibid.). Then relieved by Konev the civil war hero and old crony of Stalin's was through in the field. He held training commands thereafter and was Stavka's representative in several large operations—in the Ukraine, around Leningrad and Riga, and finally around Vienna (ibid., 555).

Timoshenko has been described as "suspicious and testy, still living the glories of the Civil War, jealous and contemptuous of the younger officers and staffs." (Seaton, *Stalin,* 203, citing SHTEMENKO, I, 271-77.)

After the war he headed the South Ural MD 1946-49 and Belorussian MD for a while in 1946, then again in 1949-60. Twice a **HSU**

(1940 and 1965) the old warhorse died of cancer on 31 Mar 70 in Moscow and was buried in the Kremlin Wall.

TINKER, Clarence Leonard. USAF general. 1887-1942. An Osage Indian born 21 Nov 87 near Edgin, Kans, Tinker graduated from Wentworth MA in Lexington, Mo. He entered the Philippine Constabulary in 1908 as a second lieutenant and was given an RA commission four years later. Maj Tinker earned his wings in 1920. With an outstanding record in leading pursuit and bomber units *(CB 42),* known for personal courage and executive ability, he was promoted to BG on 1 Oct 40. From 18 Dec 41 (*AA,* 595) he headed the Hawaiian AF, which was redesignated the 7th AF on 5 Feb 42 and placed under Maj Gen Tinker's command on 29 March (Craven and Cate, I, 454). His mission, in addition to assisting in the defense of the Hawaiian group, was to train combat crews, and do modification and maintenance for combat units in the south and SW Pacific (ibid.). The general was reported MIA on 7 June 42 while leading the 7th AF in the Battle of Midway. Tinker AFB is (1995) a major USAF maintenance installation in Oklahoma.

TIPPELSKIRCH, Kurt von. German general. Generalmajor von Tippelskirch was director of army intelligence (Ob IV) in the first years of the war, heading both its branches, Foreign Armies East and West. Succeeded by Generalmajor G. Matzky in the summer of 1941 he commanded the 30th Inf Div; his hardest action was in the Valdai Hills, S of Leningrad. Tippelskirch was promoted to head the 12th Corps from 1943 and was CG 4th Army from May to July 44. Badly injured in a plane crash and invalided back to Germany, he returned briefly to OKH as Ob IV (Goerlitz, *GGS,* 448).

Again promoted, General of Infantry Tippelskirch was CG 14th Army in Italy. Located along the west coast north of Leghorn the general, on his own initiative, launched Opn Winter Thunderstorm (Wintergewitter) on 26 Dec 44 to demoralize the African-American 92d "Buffalo Division." Elements of this green outfit were deployed in the Serchio Valley, a quiet sector. Although little more than a reconnaissance in force, Opn Wintergewitter caused a stampede that left a 500-yard gap.

The "German success seemed to threaten a breakthrough on the 92d Division's Serchio valley front" (Fisher, 409). US reserves stabilized the line by 28 Dec 44, and the crack 442d Japanese-American regiment sent patrols well north of the original **MLR** before meeting any resistance. The US 5th Army G2 thought Winter Thunderstorm was in some way associated with the Ardennes counteroffensive, but this was far from true; in fact Hitler ordered the acting theater commander, VIETINGHOF, "not to undertake such operations in the future without prior approval from supreme headquarters" (Fisher, 410). But Tippelskirch's initiative halted all Allied offensive operations in Italy until the spring (ibid.).

His winter sports vacation ending on 17 Feb 45, when LEMELSEN took over as CG 14th Army, Tippelskirch was rushed to face the final Soviet offensive in northern Germany. In April he resumed command of the 4th Army briefly before taking charge of a scratch force designated the 21st Army. About this time, 29 Apr 45, KEITEL named Tippelskirch to succeed HEINRICI as commander of AG Vistula until STUDENT arrived (Seaton, R-G War, 580-81). The official US Army history says that "Lt Gen [sic] von Tippelskirch" surrendered the 21st German Army to the 82d Abn Div on 2 May 45 (OCMH Chron, 528). An acute observer and analyst of military operations, Tippelskirch told LIDDELL HART that Hitler was completely right in his 1941 "veto on any withdrawal, but his great mistake was to repeat it in 1942 and later, when conditions were different" (Talk, 217-18). The general had much of interest to say on how easily he and other German field commanders found it to deal with Red Army offensives when free to establish flexible defenses. He published a valuable military history of WWII, Die Geschichte des zweiten Weltkreiges (Bonn, 1951 and 1954).

TISO, Joseph. Slovak puppet. 1887-1947. The right wing Catholic priest was born 13 Oct 87 into a prosperous peasant family at Velka-Bytec in Slovakia, then part of Austro-Hungary. When Msgr Andrew Hlinka, founder of the Slovak Popular Party and the notorious Hlinka guards, died in August 1938, the eve of the Munich crisis, the short, square, gormandizing Msgr Tiso

succeeded him as head of the Slovak People's Party. Capitalizing on Czechoslovakia's misfortunes—Hitler's occupation of the **Sudetenland**—Tiso claimed autonomy for Slovakia; on 6 Oct 38 he became PM of the new government in Bratislava.

The nationalist priest did not favor Nazism, particularly its solution of "the Jewish question," nor did he support the Hlinka guards. But he hoped that by cooperating with Hitler he could establish an independent federal state. While Czech President HACHA took military measures to block the defection of Slovakia and Ruthenia, the Nazis continued to conduct covert operations in Czechoslovakia, and the Hungarians prepared to retake their lost lands in Slovakia.

Hitler summoned Tiso to Berlin for a brief meeting on the evening of 13 Mar 39 and said that if Slovakia really wanted freedom he was ready to guarantee it independence. Tiso quickly promised to cooperate. (W-B, Munich, 342.) After a similar meeting two days later with HACHA, Hitler occupied Czechoslovakia.

The Germans granted Slovakia autonomy with Tiso remaining PM, and bestowed independence on 15 Mar 39. The next day, as planned by Tiso and Hitler, the state became a German protectorate. In Oct 39 Tiso was made president of a clerico-fascist regime that cooperated with the Germans, an arrangement benefiting the Germans militarily and the Slovaks economically.

US authorities arrested Tiso on 8 June 45. He was convicted of war crimes on 15 Apr 46 and was hanged three days later.

TITO. Yugoslav resistance leader. 1892-1981. Josip Brozovitch (or Broz), who used many aliases before settling on Tito in 1934, was born in May 92 in Croatia. In 1914 he was conscripted into the Austro-Hungarian army after an impoverished childhood and a hard life as an apprentice mechanic. Having spent the last years of the war as a POW in Russia he returned to what had become Yugoslavia. The royalist government outlawed the communists in 1920 after they had been successful in a national election, and many workers and trade unionists including Tito became revolutionaries. In 1928 he was arrested and given a five-year prison sentence, which saved him from the Yugoslav government's savage measures against communists in 1929-32. On release Tito worked in Moscow for the **Comintern** 1934-35, then, according to Louis Adamic, he operated in France 1936-38 to send thousands of Balkan anti-Fascists to take part in the Spanish Civil War (*CB 43*). Having thus survived the extermination of many leading Yugoslav communists during the **Great Purges** he rose after many adventures to be general secretary of the Yugoslav CP. Virtually unknown to the outside world, even rumored to be a woman, Tito was well prepared for guerrilla warfare long before the Germans subjugated Yugoslavia in June 41. He changed his title to CinC of the Slovenian Front, soon known as partisans, and operated underground in Belgrade for months while planning military and political action in the countryside. Initially he dealt with non-communist conspirators, but his support was primarily from Croatians.

The partisans scored their first military successes in Montenegro in July 41 after many German divisions had left to fight in Russia, and Tito moved his headquarters from Belgrade into the mountains. But the resistance forces became engaged in a bitter civil war, as in Greece. Most of MIHAILOVIC's Chetniks were Serbs, who had a long ethnic animosity toward Croatians and who also had traditional monarchist values. The rivals reached an understanding on 27 Oct 41 (Djilas, *Wartime,* 88) but their forces had a bloody clash two weeks later in Serbia.

Churchill, who had a great interest in the Balkans whereas FDR did not, came to realize that the royalist Mihailovic was the wrong resistance leader to back in Yugoslavia. The PM was under Soviet pressure to support the communist faction, and Fitzroy MACLEAN reported that Tito was much more effecting against the Germans. The decision was made at the Teheran Conference (28 Nov-1 Dec 43) to shift Allied support to Tito. King PETER II reluctantly went along with changing horses in mid-war, forming a new government on 17 May 44 under Ivan Subasic (1892-1955) that was acceptable to Tito, who was made war minister. The British meanwhile had withdrawn their last mission from MIHAILOVIC.

The Germans reinforced combat troops in the Balkans as partisan activity became more serious, and in Feb 44 Hitler sent SKORZENY to kill or capture Tito. The partisan chief narrowly escaped from his secret headquarters in

the Drvar Valley of western Bosnia and had to keep running until withdrawing in June 44 to Vis Island in the Adriatic. As TOKBUKHIN's 3d Ukrainian Front approached four months later Tito cooperated in liberating Belgrade on 20 Oct 44.

He became premier in Mar 45, at which time his British mission left. Eight months later the constituent assembly declared Yugoslavia a republic under Marshal Tito. Rejecting British and Soviet efforts to divide Yugoslavia into spheres of influence he moved inexorably from Soviet dominance until finally making a clean break in June 48. Tito died 4 May 81, three days before his 90th birthday.

TIULENEV, I. V. *See* TYULENEV.

TIZARD, Henry Thomas. British scientist. 1885-1959. Tizard was born 23 Aug 85 at Gillingham, Kent, and educated at Westminster School and Magdalen College, Oxford. Here he won honors in mathematics (1905) and chemistry (1908), his tutor being Nevil Sidgwick. After starting research under Sidgwick at Oxford he spent a semester in Berlin, where he and LINDEMANN began a long association. Tizard joined the Royal Garrison Artillery in 1914 and established effective new methods for training recruits. In June 15 he became an experimental equipment officer in the RFC and in 1917 he began testing new aircraft. Working under Bertram Hopkinson, director of aeronautical R&D, Tizard was again associated with Lindemann. Both men overcame vision problems to become pilots so they could perform flight tests. When Bertram Hopkinson was promoted to be RAF controller of experiments and research in late 1917 Tizard was promoted to lieutenant colonel and made his deputy. Tizard moved into the top spot after Hopkinson died in 1918.

The next year Tizard returned to Oxford and did pioneering work on aviation fuel that led to new understandings of internal combustion engines. (Harold Hartley in *DNB.*) Between the wars Tizard was more and more involved in using science to solve practical problems, particularly in national defense. He was on the Aeronautical Research Committee from 1919.

When air exercises in 1934 focused attention on Britain's vulnerability to air attack, various people concluded independently that Britain's best scientists should adddress the problem. In a letter to *The Times* in Aug 34 Lindemann proposed setting up a sub-committee of the Committee of Imperial Defense (CID) but when he sent Whitehall his suggestion a short time later he was outraged to learn that the air ministry had already formed such a committee. Its chairman was Tizard! Lindemann assumed this was a plot to circumvent his own proposal.

At its first meeting, 28 Jan 35, the "Tizard committee" heard the report of WATSON-WATT that led to the development of radar. Churchill and Lindemann succeeded in having a CID committee created to address *political* and *financial* problems of air defense (ibid.) and this new body held its first meeting in Apr 35. Tizard was a member, and his group became a sub-committee responsible for research. Then Churchill joined the CID committee in June 35 and had Lindemann made a member of the Tizard sub-committee!

The prime minister's protégé was so abrasive, however, that the Tizard committee operated only a year before a wave of resignations broke it up in June 36. Four months later it was reconstituted without Lindemann. *(DNB.)*

Sir Henry (KCB in 1937) was primarily responsible for continuing the successful development of radar. Early in 1938 he enlisted the support of COCKCROFT, which proved to be invaluable, and Lindemann also had R. V. JONES brought into the air ministry to deal with scientific intelligence. When Churchill became PM in May 40 and retained Lindemann as his scientific adviser Tizard's position was increasingly difficult.

The climax came on 21 June 40 when R. V. Jones briefed Churchill and senior RAF officials on the chilling evidence that the Germans were using a revolutionary new navigational device, the **Lorenz beam**, code named *Knickebein.* Tizard "rejected the theoretical posibility of the *Knickebein* beam," writes Ronald Lewin, but Lindemann recognized the threat. "Tizard had committed professional suicide," Lewin continues. "Realizing this he went straight from the meeting to his club . . . and wrote out his resignation as Scientific Advisor to the Air Staff." (Lewin, *Ultra*, 79-80n.) Beaten out by his rival, Tizard resigned all air ministry commitments except chairmanship of the Aeronautical Research Committee. Later he was a semi-official adviser to successive ministers of aircraft pro-

duction, sitting on the Aircraft Supply Committee from the autumn of 1940 and representing the air minister on the Air Council from June 41. He also took the initiative in bringing about maximum scientific and technical interchange between Britain and the US. With COCK-CROFT as his deputy he led a scientific mission to the US in the fall of 1940. But Tizard now had so little influence in Whitehall that in 1942 he accepted the presidency of Magdalen College, Oxford. He returned to Whitehall in Jan 47 to chair the defense research policy committee and the advisory council on scientific policy. Raised to GCB in 1949 he retired in 1952 to his home at Fareham, Hampshire. He thereafter devoted most of his energies to education and became honorary doctor of 10 universities. Sir Henry Tizard died at home on 9 Oct 59 of a cerebral hemorrhage. (Harold Hartley in *DNB*.)

TODT, Fritz. German engineer. 1891-1942. The highly-regarded head of the Third Reich's construction empire was born 4 Sep 91 at Pforzheim, Baden, into an upper class family. He won the Iron Cross during WWI and was wounded while flying as an observer. After getting a doctorate in engineering he joined the Munich firm of Sager and Woerner, which specialized in building roads and tunnels, and he rose to be manager.

In 1930 Dr Todt published a paper titled "Proposals and Financial Plans for the Employment of One Million Men." Soon after Hitler came to power in 1933 Todt was made head of the new state-owned Reichsauto-bahnen corporation and he was directed to build a national highway system that military planners had laid out. The Autobahn undertaking was well under way before the world realized that this "unemployment project" was creating a system of high-speed roads suited primarily for military use and only secondarily for the civilian economy. But to get maximum propaganda value from a highway plan decades ahead of its time the Nazis gave aesthetics priority over cost effectiveness.

Dr Todt had helped found the National-sozialisticher Bund Deutscher Technik. Over the years he not only centralized efforts of major technical facilities under his Head Office for Technology but also drew engineers and managers of the German construction industry into a single, gigantic effort. This is one reason why he responded so effectively to Hitler's demand in 1938 that the West Wall be built on a crash basis to protect Germany's western frontier while the Wehrmacht conducted offensive operations on the eastern front.

Martin Bormann and Hermann Goering became Todt's major competitors and enemies within the Nazi hierarchy. Although a loyal party member of the early years, Todt "maintained his personal independence in his relations with Hitler," who "paid him and his accomplishments a respect bordering on reverence" (Speer, *Memoirs,* 193). The quiet, withdrawn technocrat eventually held three top positions: Minister of Armaments and Munitions; head of the OT, which was in charge of highways, navigable waterways, and power plants; and from late 1941 he had responsibility for restoring the road and rail system in occupied Russia. He also directed construction of major works on the Atlantic Wall.

The mammoth OT had bureaucratic faults, many elements being administratively top-heavy. But it had innovative features like separate units of physically handicapped personnel assigned special missions within their capabilities and with special medical staffs.

The plane he normally used was in maintenance and temporarily replaced by a He 111 when Todt flew to Rastenburg for a meeting with Hitler. A few minutes after leaving for Munich at 8 AM on 9 Feb 42 the plane exploded, killing all aboard. Sabotage naturally was suspected but no evidence ever found. Todt was succeeded by SPEER, who had been scheduled for the flight but canceled out! (*See* Speer, *Memoirs,* 191-93.)

TOGO, Shigenori. Japanese diplomat. 1882-1950. Togo was born on Kuyshu into the illustrious Satsuma clan. His name properly pronounced approximately like Tohngo (Toland, *Sun,* 120n), Shigenori Togo was not related to the famous Adm Heihachiro Togo (1847-1934).

Entering the foreign service, Togo became a moderate and was highly regarded professionally although considered rude by many associates for his candor. He married a German in 1920 at the start of a tour as second secretary in the Berlin embassy, where he rose to be counselor in 1929 and ambassador in 1937-38. Togo then was ambassador to Moscow and he returned to

Tokyo with a knowledge of western ways and as a firm advocate of friendship with the Soviets.

Although suffering since 1940 from pernicious anemia Togo was foreign minister in the Tojo government from 16 Oct 41 until resigning in protest on 1 Sep 42. At this time he was elevated to the House of Peers. As a moderate familiar with the west he was brought back as foreign minister after 5 Apr 45 in Kantaro SUZUKI's "surrender cabinet." On 26 July 45 he persuaded it not to reject the **Potsdam Declaration** outright. Togo was one of three members of the Supreme Council who, two weeks later (9 Aug 45), favored capitulation but he refused to join the HIGASHIKUNI government. Sentenced to 20 years for war crimes, he died in prison on 23 July 50. Meanwhile he wrote memoirs of Japan's diplomacy in WWII, *Jidai-no Ichimen (One Aspect of the Age).* Son-in-law Fumihiko Togo translated the book as *The Cause of Japan* (1956).

TOJO, Hideki. Japanese prime minister. 1884-1948. Third son of an army lieutenant, he was born 30 Dec 84 in Tokyo. Schoolmates called him "Fighting Tojo," and in later years he was nicknamed "Razor Brain." Hard-working, hard-headed, hard-nosed, peering through thick glasses, the scrawny but wiry Tojo (five feet four) was an uncomplicated man dedicated to his profession and highly respected professionally. He was considered incorruptible, selecting subordinates on the basis of merit alone, and he had a burning desire to establish Japan's supremacy by force of arms.

Tojo's military career included service in Switzerland from 1919 and in Germany from 1921 (*Kogun,* 237). A major general in 1933, he became the Kwantung Army's chief of military police in Sep 35 and was promoted 14 months later to lieutenant general. He was CofS, Kwantung Army, from Mar 37 until returning to Tokyo in May 38 to be vice minister of war for six months in the first KONOYE cabinet. Tojo left this post to be IG of army aviation in Dec 38. (*Kogun,* 237.)

A bold strategic thinker who advocated a pre-emptive strike on China, he had alarmed planners by urging in 1938 that Japan fight Russia and China concurrently. He was pro-German and anti-Russian.

He served in three KONOYE cabinets, vice premier and finally rising to minister of war from 18 July 41. When the new, moderate Fn Min Shigenori TOGO demanded Japanese troop withdrawals from China and Korea Tojo objected so vehemently as war minister that he petrified the Konoye cabinet. "The way of diplomacy isn't always a matter of concession; sometimes it is oppression," he shouted; withdrawal from overseas would be "a stain on the history of the Japanese Empire!" (Toland, *Sun,* 112-13).

The general was prime minister after Konoye resigned on 16 Oct 41, remaining war minister and the army's leading spokesman. He was a full general by Sep 42. (*Kogun,* 237.) The militarists had finally triumphed but there was no dramatic change in Japanese foreign policy. Tojo had a legalistic mind and—having supported Japan's joining the Axis—he took **Tripartite Pact** obligations seriously. He backed the foreign office's efforts to seek a diplomatic solution to problems with the US and other Western powers. But, US diplomacy not being noted for a conciliatory attitude toward Japan, Tojo quickly concluded that his country had a choice between economic strangulation or war. In addition to being premier and war minister, Tojo became home minister in 1941 and briefly succeeded TOGO as foreign minister 1-17 Sep 42.

Tojo assumed more authority as it became increasingly apparent that Japan was losing the war. On 21 Feb 44 he took over as CGS from SUGIYAMA and, at the same time, had the subservient minister of the navy, SHIMADA, sack NAGUMO and assume command of the Imperial Navy. But about a week after the US capture of Saipan put the home islands within American bomber range Tojo resigned on 18 July 45 after failing in an effort to effect a reorganization that would leave him in power.

To sum up, Tojo had unquestioned control over Japan's civil and military establishments during the long period from 18 Oct 41 to 18 July 44 (Reischauer, *Japan,* 197). But as head of a totalitarian state that soon was in the sort of difficulties inviting a dictatorship on the western pattern, and although he had no lack of qualifications for the role, Tojo "neither received nor asked for dictatorial powers." He was a "Right Wing Conservative rather than a revolutionary." (Collier, *Far East,* 79.)

Tojo continued to have great influence among hard-liners, and he called (in vain) for an army-dominated cabinet when Gen Kuniaki KOISO resigned as PM on 4 Apr 45 after more military

disasters. Adm Kantaro SUZUKI's surrender cabinet consequently was formed. Only three days after establishing himself in Tokyo on 8 Sep 45, MacArthur ordered the arrest of the first alleged war criminals. Journalists and what looked like a lynch mob almost immediately besieged Tojo's modest Tokyo home in Setagaya. "Tell this yellow bastard we've waited long enough," a heroic American MP officer shouted. "Bring him out." Tojo attempted suicide by shooting himself in the chest with a pistol. He was nursed back to health for a tedious and controversial trial, sentenced to death on 12 Nov 48 and hanged on 23 Dec 48.

TOKYO ROSE. Radio propaganda announcer. 1916-. The person most commonly known by this name was born 4 July 16 in Los Angeles, Calif, as Iva Ikuko Toguri. She was an American citizen of Japanese descent and a UCLA graduate. Trapped while visiting a sick aunt in Tokyo she married a Portuguese named d'Aquino.

Later claiming to have been coerced, she began making daily 15-minute broadcasts in English for the Japanese Broadcasting Corp. She was paid $40 a month. One of several called "Tokyo Rose" by American listeners she broadcast as "Anna," taking the name from "announcer." After Tojo's ouster on 18 July 44 and Japan's defeat seeming certain, she called herself "Orphan Annie"—a homeless stray. Like "Axis Sally" (Mildred E. GILLARS) and numerous others in Europe, Tokyo Rose was essentially a disk jockey who played popular, nostalgic American music that hooked millions of homesick listeners. "Commercial messages" to undermine American morale had little effect. Mrs d'Aquino was held for two years without trial. Charged with eight counts of treason she was convicted on 6 Oct 49, fined $10,000, and sentenced to 10 years in prison. After serving six years she was released in 1956 for good behavior. In 1975, being an Oriental gift shop clerk, Mrs d'Aquino completed payment of the fine. President Gerald Ford granted her petition for pardon, without comment, on his last day in office, 19 Jan 77. She presumably was alive in 1933, when M.H. Mahoney published *Women in Espionage.* (CRS.)

TOLBUKHIN, Fyodor Ivanovich. Red Army officer. 1894-1949. Born 16 June 94 in the village of Androniki, Yaroslavl Prov, the future marshal was the son of a peasant artisan. In 1911 he became a bookkeeper and in 1915 he entered the army to rise from dispatch rider to battalion commander. He joined the Red Army in 1918, serving as a district (Volost) military commander until 1919, then as a staff officer through 1920 *(Scarecrow)*. He took command of the 72d Inf Div in 1937, was accepted the next year in the CP (belatedly because of his insufficiently earthy pedigree?) then was CofS, Transcaucasus MD, and was promoted to general major in June 41. Two months later, as the Wehrmacht drove into south Russia, Tolbukhin was D. T. KOZLOV's CofS in the Transcaucasus, Caucasus, Fronts. (Ibid.)

Tolbukhin was among the many dismissed in the search for scapegoats after KOZLOV's abortive offensive in Mar 42. He had run afoul of MEKHLIS but SHAPOSHNIKOV was not entirely satisfied with Tolbukhin's explanation of the fiasco. (Erickson, *To Stalingrad,* 456.)

The general was recalled in July 42 to command the 57th Army at Stalingrad. He was promoted to general lieutenant and picked to make the main effort in the great counteroffensive that started on 20 Nov 42. Erickson points out that Tolbukhin had two outstanding qualities: "great professional skill and a deal of experience." He also was a trainer: in a two-night series of war games involving the forthcoming operation, Tolbukhin schooled his major subordinate commanders and told them to do the same down to the battalion commander level. Although ill with diabetes, on 20 Nov 42 Tolbukhin insisted on supervising the attack (Erickson, ibid., 456, 466) and he personally took Paulus's surrender on 1 Feb 43.

That month Tolbukhin took command of the 68th Army in Timoshenko's Northwestern Front. He was involved in the unsuccessful efforts to eliminate the salient around Demyansk, which the Germans evacuated by 18 March. In this month Gen Lt Tolbukhin took command of the Southern Front astride the lower Don. He was promoted to general colonel on 28 Apr 43 and less than five months later (22 Sep 43) to general of the army (No. 13). The next month his formation was redesignated the 4th Ukrainian Front for the drive to the Black Sea. After liberating strategic Perekop he cooperated with YEREMENKO in the hard fight to reconquer the Crimea, which Hitler had ordered held at all

cost. The Soviet Black Sea Fleet's timidity allowed the Germans to evacuate most of their Sevastopol garrison but the port city was captured on 9 May 44 at a cost of almost 100,000 German casualties. The rest of the Germans and Romanians surrendered four days later.

Still on the south flank Tolbukhin succeeded Malinovsky in May 44 as commander of the 3d Ukrainian Front for the rest of the war. An MSU (No. 17) on 12 Sep 44 at the age of 50, he signed the armistice with Bulgaria in Moscow on 28 Oct 44. The town of Dobric in Bulgaria was renamed for him. Cooperating with MALINOVSKY in overrunning Bulgaria, Romania, Hungary, and Austria, and pushing into Yugoslavia, Tolbukhin took part in the capture of **Budapest** and Vienna (13 Apr 45). After the war he headed the Southern Group of Forces in Bulgaria and Romania until it was dissolved in 1947 after the peace treaty was signed. His last assignment was as head of the Transcaucasus MD. He died 17 Oct 49, his ashes were buried in Red Square, and a monument to him was erected in Moscow. In 1965 he was posthumously made a Hero of the Soviet Union.

TOYODA, Soemu. Japanese admiral. 1885-1957. One of many Toyodas prominent in the Japanese Navy at the same time, he graduated from the naval academy in 1905. Three months before the Pearl Harbor attack on 7 Dec 41, he was promoted to full admiral and given command of the Kure Naval Station. In Nov 42 he became a member of the Supreme War Council, and in May 43 he took command of the Yokosuka Naval Base.

His appointment as CinC Combined Fleet was announced on 5 May 44, when Mineichi KOGA had been missing for more than a month. Toyoda carried on with efforts to bring on a decisive surface engagement but revamped Koga's "Plan Z" to produce "A-Go," issued 3 May 44. This led to OZAWA's decisive defeat by MITSCHER in the Battle of the Philippine Sea, 19-20 June 44. From headquarters in Tokyo, Toyoda directed the Battle of Leyte Gulf, 23-26 Oct 44. This last major effort of the Japanese Navy to win a major action ended in disaster. (*See* OLDENDORF and KURITA.) On 20 May 45 Toyoda succeeded Koshiro OIKAWA as Navy CofS. Although noted for pungent anti-army remarks during the war

(Toland, *Sun,* 446), the admiral joined Generals ANAMI and UMEZU as a principal opponent of HIROHITO's surrender efforts. After the war he cooperated with Samuel E. MORISON in giving details of Japanese action in the Battle of the Philippine Sea.

TOYODA, Teijiro. Japanese admiral and statesman. 1885-. Generally confused with his naval academy classmate Soemu TOYODA, he retired in 1941 as a full admiral and held various ministerial posts thereafter. In the second KONOYE cabinet he was minister of commerce and industry, 4 Apr-16 July 41. In the third KONOYE cabinet he was foreign minister, 18 July-16 Oct 41, succeeding Yosuke MATSUOKO. In the Kantaro SUZUKI cabinet, 5 Apr 17 Aug 45, he doubled as minister of munitions and of transportation and communications. In 1941, meanwhile, he became president of the Nittetsu-Nihon Iron Manufacturing Company's Mining Co, then was chairman of Tekko Toseikai (Iron & Steel Control Co).

TRENCHARD, Hugh Montague. "Father of the RAF." 1873-1956. A member of the House of Lords since 1936, the 1st Viscount Trenchard of Wolfeton retained great influence during WWII as creator of the RAF and as a venerable authority on air power.

Lord Trenchard was born 3 Feb 73 and entered the army in 1893. After fighting on the Indian frontier and in various African colonies (dangerously wounded with the Canadian Scouts during the Boer War), he was about to retire in 1912 at the age of 39 after being a brevet major for 10 years. But he paid for flying lessons and joined the RFC, leading the 1st Wing in France in 1914 and taking command of the RFC the next year as a brevet colonel. In 1916 he was promoted to major general, meanwhile having developed the infant air force. In Apr 18 he resigned as Chief of the Air Staff in London after disagreeing over policy with Lord Rothmere. Churchill reinstated him the next year as CAS and at this time Trenchard became Britain's first air marshal. Before retiring in 1930 Sir Hugh (KCB in 1918) developed the RAF as a separate service, an independent air force, a concept the US would not follow until after WWII, in 1947. Trenchard was Metropolitan Police Commissioner, 1931-35, and

chairman of the United Africa Company of the Unilever group, 1936-53. He died 10 Feb 56, a week after his 83d birthday.

TRESCKOW, Henning von. German general. 1901-44. Perhaps the most dedicated and persevering anti-Hitler conspirator, Tresckow was born in Magdeburg on 19 Jan 01. Despite a Prussian upbringing as a Pomeranian gentleman farmer he had an aversion to militarism and became a successful stockbroker after serving as an officer in WWI.

But he joined the Reichswehr in 1924 and by 1939, as lieutenant colonel, he had a burning conviction that Hitler had to be eliminated as a threat to Germany and to the world. Tresckow first tried to find like-minded senior generals but had no success with Rundstedt, Manstein, nor with his uncle Fedor von Bock. Generalmajor von Tresckow served on Bock's staff in AG Center Hq and assembled a group of anti-Hitler conspirators that "in 1942-43 was the heart and soul of Opposition planning . . . on the eastern front" (Deutsch, I, 372n40). His ADC was Fabian von SCHLABRENDORFF (to whom, contrary to common belief, he was not kin). Planted as aides in Bock's office were two other staunch anti-Nazis, Counts Hans von Hardenberg and Heinrich von Lehndorff. Giving up on enlisting Bock but having been assured that his uncle would take no initiative in suppressing a putsch, the aides resolved to cope without him.

Their earliest plan was to arrest Hitler during one of his infrequent visits but the wary fuehrer and elaborate SS security made this impossible. So the conspirators concentrated on assassination. An attempt failed narrowly on 14 Mar 43. Tresckow and Schlabrendorff put a British bomb in a package allegedly containing two bottles of brandy that one of Hitler's escort officers was carrying back on the plane from a visit to Kluge's AG Center Hq in Smolensk. The "gift" for an officer at Rastenburg was supposed to destroy Hitler's plane shortly before it reached Minsk, a 30-minute flight. But Hitler landed safely at Rastenburg! Schlabrendorff contrived a visit there the next day, switched packages, and found that the bomb's detonator had malfunctioned. At least four other plots failed because officers with bombs in overcoats could not get close enough to Hitler at the right moment. After OSTER was eliminated from the conspiracy, Tresckow and Schlabrendorff identified STAUFFENBERG as the man for a final effort. This failed on 20 July 44. The next morning Tresckow said good-bye to Schlabrendorff, drove to the front, moved past forward outposts, faked a gunfight with two pistols, and blew off his head with a hand grenade. His wife Erika had assisted Margarete von Oven in secretly typing orders and letters for the conspirators. These were hidden in OLBRICHT's office safe, and details are known because SCHLABRENDORFF lived to write about the conspiracy.

TRIBUTS, Vladimir Filippovich. Soviet naval commander. 1900-77. A vice admiral from June 41 and an admiral in 1943, he commanded the Baltic Fleet throughout the war. His main base was Leningrad, where he was born on 28 July 00. Tributs joined the Red Navy in 1918 and took part in the civil war. A CP member from 1928, he was made a vice admiral in June 41 and a full admiral in 1943. Meanwhile, he had been CofS, Baltic Fleet, from Feb 38 and its commander from April 1939. Like other Soviet admirals with the exception of Black Sea commander OKTIABRSKY, Tributs made no significant splash in 1941-45.

After the war he was deputy CinC, Troops for the Far East for Naval Forces, and held various other high posts before retiring in 1961. Author of several books in the Baltic Fleet during the Great Patriotic War, he died in Moscow on 30 Aug 77.

TROTSKY, Lev Davidovich. Russian revolutionary. 1879-1940. Son of a Jewish colonist named Bronshteyn in the south Ukrainian village of Yanovka in Kherson Prov, the famous revolutionary was born 7 Nov 79. He was 19 years old when first arrested and sent to Siberia. But Trotsky escaped abroad in 1902, sided with the Mensheviks, and in 1905 became chairman of the Petersburg soviet. Again arrested and exiled to Siberia, he escaped while en route. In 1908 he founded *Pravda,* but this was discontinued in 1912 when an opposition paper of the same name appeared with Stalin as editor. From 1914 Trotsky was an exile in Switzerland, France, Spain, and the US. After the Feb 17 revolution he went to St Petersburg and sided with the Mezhrayonetsky faction of the **RSDRP,** which was midway between the Bolsheviks and

Mensheviks. In Feb 18 he became people's commissar of military affairs and he later was chairman of the Revolutionary military council.

Trotsky was instrumental in organizing the Red Army and in restoring the Navy, having a major—if controversial—role in bringing about the Bolshevik victory in the civil war. His authority was challenged by STALIN, to whom Trotsky lost out in the power struggle to succeed the ailing Lenin, who died on 21 Jan 24. He was ousted in 1925-29 from all official posts and eventually deported to Turkey.

Deprived of citizenship in 1932 he lived abroad and continued trying to organize a counterrevolution. During the Great Purges Trotsky was condemned to death in absentia and a special NKVD group was formed to carry out the sentence. It did not succeed until 20 Aug 40, when an agent penetrated the elaborate security of a house near Mexico City and delivered the fatal blow with a mountaineer's ax. (Medvedev, 35 ff, 178-79.)

TRUMAN, Harry S. American statesman. 1884-1972. Less than a month before the German surrender he became the 33d president of the US after Roosevelt's death on 12 Apr 45.

Truman was born 8 May 84 at Lamar, Mo, and reared on a farm near Independence. Unable to afford college and denied admission to West Point because of bad eyesight he became the only 20th century US president who was not a college graduate. He took over the family farm in 1906, a year after joining the Missouri National Guard. Truman's first leadership experience, which would mark his emergence from 33 years as a virtual nonentity, was as commander of Co D, 129th FA, in France. In 1919 he married a childhood sweetheart, Elizabeth (Bess) Wallace, and set up a haberdashery business which failed in 1921. T. J. Prendergast, who was influential in the Kansas City Democratic machine, appointed Truman overseer of highways for Jackson Co, Mo. Still supported by Prendergast he was county judge for Jackson Co, 1922-24, attending night law school in Kansas City and becoming involved in local politics. Elected to the US Senate in 1934 he quickly made his presence known, particularly as an enterprising and able member of investigative committees. When Prendergast finally got comeuppance as a corrupt political boss and was jailed in 1938 for tax evasion,

Truman suffered from guilt by association. Roosevelt briefly withdrew his support for Truman's reelection to the Senate, but the feisty little man from Independence had established himself not only as an honest politician but also as a fighter. He weathered what might have ended his career and went on to greater things as war approached. Starting his second term in 1941 he introduced a resolution to create the Special Committee to Investigate the National Defense Program, a "watchdog" body of which he was chairman. The Truman Committee became one of the most important in Congress (Buchanan, 315) in due course exposing profiteers, dishonest contractors and labor leaders, reducing waste, and winning praise for integrity and efficiency.

At the 1944 Democratic convention Truman was nominated as vice president after Roosevelt heeded advice to discard Henry A. WALLACE as a running mate. "One of President Roosevelt's most serious acts of omission," however, "was his failure to keep his Vice President informed of significant international developments." (Buchanan, 499.) The new president knew nothing about the atomic bomb project until briefed by STIMSON shortly after taking office on 12 Apr 45. Nor did he have the background to influence Eisenhower's critical political-military decision not to make Berlin the primary objective as US and Soviet troops closed for the kill.

On 8 May 45, after less than a month in office, Truman announced the surrender of Germany. With virtually no experience in foreign affairs and with a new secretary of state, James F. BYRNES, who had little more, the president attended the last international meeting of the war. But he delayed start of the Potsdam Conference until 17 July 45 so he could arrive with the knowledge that the first test of the atomic bomb (the preceding day) had succeeded. Taking the leadership reins firmly, at Potsdam he overrode the JCS recommendation to stop Lend Lease to the British occupation troops in Europe. But he accepted the JCS recommendation to encourage the Soviets to enter the war against Japan.

After issuing a surrender ultimatum to the Japanese, the **Potsdam Declaration,** and having it promptly rejected, Truman authorized use of the atomic bomb on Hiroshima and Nagasaki, 6 and 9 Aug 45. The president then led the nation in the Cold War, which resulted primarily from Roosevelt's failure to cope properly with Stalin's postwar plans. Truman inherited also the problems in China that stemmed from Roosevelt's illusions about Chiang Kai-shek as a national leader. Despite last-minute efforts of George C. Marshall, whom the president selected for the mission, China was lost to the communists under Mao Tse-tung. After the UNO was created with headquarters in NYC and funded primarily by the US it proved incapable of coping with the world's postwar economic and political crises. So Truman threw himself into directing US foreign affairs and proved to be a quick learner. When Churchill abruptly abandoned efforts to save Greece from a communist takeover, another problem Roosevelt had neglected, the Truman Doctrine was announced in Feb 47. This committed the US to taking over from the British on a large scale to oppose Soviet expansion into the Balkans. A few months later the (George C.) Marshall Plan was undertaken to restore the European economy.

"Give 'em hell Harry" very narrowly won reelection in 1948 after a whistle-stop campaign against Thomas E. DEWEY. The race was so close that the Chicago *Daily Tribune* came out with the banner headline DEWEY DEFEATS TRUMAN.

NATO was established in 1949 for military defense of Europe. When North Korean attacked South Korea in June 50 there was every reason to believe that this was a Soviet diversion for a moving into western Europe, starting WWIII. Truman proclaimed a national emergency in Dec 50 and ordered a shift to wartime production. The same month he approved Eisenhower's appointment to head the military arm of NATO as **SACEUR.**

Facing up to the problem of MacArthur's exceeding his authority as military commander in the Far East Truman peremptorily recalled the national hero in Apr 51, taking much popular criticism for doing the right thing. "If you can't stand the heat, get out of the kitchen," was one of the president's homely aphorisms. Another was expressed in a sign on his desk in the White House: "The buck stops here." The president of the world's greatest power said he would be happy with the epitaph he had seen in a western frontier cemetery: "Here lies N. N.— he tried his damnedest."

In Mar 52 Truman announced he would not run for a third term. Succeeded by Eisenhower and slowly coming to be respected as one of America's great presidents, he retired to private life and published his memoirs in 1955-56. He lived to the age of 88, dying on 26 Dec 72. A highly regarded biography is Jonathan Daniels, *The Man From Independence* (Philadelphia, 1950).

TRUSCOTT, Lucian King, Jr. US general. 1895-1965. After heading a task force in Patton's invasion of Morocco and then being Eisenhower's field deputy in Tunisia, he commanded the 3d Inf Div, the 6th Corps, and finally the 5th Army, seeing action in Italy, southern France and Germany.

Truscott (pronounced as one syllable) was a recently promoted cavalry colonel when he favorably impressed Eisenhower early in the war while the men served together briefly at Ft Lewis, Washington *(S&S)*. A few months later Brig Gen Truscott went to the UK for duty with the Combined Operations staff and formed the first US Ranger unit. A hard, charismatic leader, he was a strict disciplinarian with a passion for hard training. Like Patton he affected unorthodox dress: enameled helmet, white silk scarf, weathered leather jacket, cavalry breeches and boots.

Truscott was the principal US observer with the **Dieppe Raid** on 19 Aug 42. Promoted later that year Maj Gen Truscott led the Northern Attack Group TF in the assault on Morocco, 8 Nov 42. His troops were the 60th Inf Regt of the 9th Inf Div and the 66th Armd Regt of the 2d Armd Div. Landing near Mehdia they were unable to overcome French colonial troops defending Port Lyautey and the nearby airfield *(OCMH Chron,* 65) but had a major role in convincing NOGUES to order a cease fire in Morocco.

During the Tunisian campaign Truscott was Eisenhower's field deputy. He then returned to the States and in Mar 43 succeeded LUCAS as head of the 3d ("Rock of the Marne") Inf Div *(AA,* 521). For the landings in Sicily on 10 July 43 his division was reinforced by CCA of the 2d Armd Div and the 3d Ranger Bn to form the westernmost element of Patton's 7th Army. During the Italian campaign that followed, Truscott led the 3d Div at Salerno, across the Volturno, and on to Cassino. After withdrawing

his division off the line for rest and more amphibious training he sent it ashore at Anzio on 22 Jan 44 in the 6th Corps of John P. Lucas. As dissatisfaction with Lucas mounted, Truscott turned his division over to "Iron Mike" O'DANIEL and on 17 February moved up to be deputy corps commander. Six days later he replaced Lucas as head of the 6th Corps. *(OCMH Chron,* 173, 175.) He led the corps from Anzio to enter Rome on 4 June 44.

Now foremost expert in amphibious operations, Truscott directed planning and training of the 6th Corps for the invasion of southern France as the assault force of PATCH's 7th Army. Landing on 15 Aug 44 with three divisions abreast between Nice and Toulon, he moved north into the Vosges Mountains. After crossing the Moselle and closing toward the Rhine River and being promoted on 2 Sep 44, Lt Gen Truscott turned over command of his corps to Edward H. Brooks on 25 Oct 44 *(OCMH Chron,* 311).

Truscott replaced Mark Clark as 5th Army commander on 16 Dec 44 in a major reorganization of Allied forces in Italy. Eight months earlier Eisenhower had considered Truscott as a replacement for Patton as 3d Army commander before the invasion of France, expressing regret that Truscott was no longer free *(EP,* 1840-41). But Truscott did succeed Patton as 3d Army commander and military governor of Bavaria when PATTON committed his final outrage after V-E day. *(See* PATTON for details of both episodes.)

In addition to being an outstanding combat commander, Truscott was author of outstanding war memoirs, *Command Missions* (1954).

TSUJI, Masanobu. Japanese army officer. 1903-68. The legendary and savage Col Tsuji, the "God of Operations," figured prominently as an staff officer in almost every major Japanese military operation. He was born in Ishikawa Prefecture in 1903 *(Kogun,* 238). In 1930, a year before graduating from the War College, he was recruited into the **Emperor's Cabal.** As a military academy instructor in 1934 Tsuji headed the group that exposed the cadet plot for a coup d'état. Posted to the Kwantung Army Maj Tsuji saw action in the border warfare that ended with Zhukov's triumph in 1939 at **Khalkhin Gol** (or Nomonhan), going immediately thereafter to join the 11th Army staff at Hankow.

Tsuji had proved to be a brilliant, fearless staff officer but he became increasingly notorious for fanatic idealism and savage conduct. He inspired devotion among younger officers but acute distaste from many superiors. But Tsuji is said to have had "mysterious sources of power and probably direct access to Tojo" (Swinson, *Four Samurai*, 65) and the fire-eater "was thought to have the ear of the Imperial family" (Allen, *Burma*, 382).

Perhaps because Tojo finally wanted to get him out of Tokyo, Lt Col Tsuji was assigned in Nov 40 as Yamashita's operations chief on Formosa while planning was under way for the brilliant campaign down the "impassable" Malay peninsula to take Singapore. Tsuji's unorthodox but highly effective intelligence and training efforts earned him the sobriquet "God of Operations" and promotion to colonel. Remaining in Singapore he allegedly was primarily responsible for having some 5,000 Chinese murdered on charges of having supported British colonialism (Toland, *Sun,* 295).

When Masaharu HOMMA reported on 10 Feb 42 that his 14th Army needed rest and reorganization before taking Bataan, an outraged Imperial Hq assigned Tsuji to Homma's operations staff (Swinson, 65). The colonel had a role in the conquest of Bataan that far exceeded his rank and position. Violating a cardinal rule of staff work, he issued orders to field commanders. Countermanding Homma's instructions that POWs be treated humanely Tsuji ordered field commanders to give no quarter and the savage colonel is said to have been primarily responsible for the **Bataan death march.**

Acting as if he feared war might go out of style the colonel got himself ordered to Guadalcanal in Oct 42. Tsuji had a significant role in planning the ill-advised counteroffensive that involved sending the 2d Div to Guadalcanal. But he accepted responsibility for the defeat that followed. "I underestimated the enemy's fighting power and insisted on my own operations plan, which was erroneous," he admitted to CofS SUGIYAMA. Saying he deserved "ten thousand deaths" the God of Operations asked to stay on the island, but on 3 Nov 42 he was recalled to Tokyo for staff duty.

Hot-headed, insolent with superiors, and justly critical of how the war was being conducted, Tsuji was sent back to China in Aug 43 and then ordered to Burma in the spring of 1944 as G2 of the new 33d Army. Under Masaki HONDA, who took command on 30 Apr 44, the Burma Area Army was soon in deep trouble as the Allied counteroffensive got going. From Myitkyina the 33d Army was driven through Mandalay to Meiktila and Pyawbwe in desperately contested actions. MESSERVY's corps closed on the latter place in mid-Apr 44 to put Honda's Hq heavy fire from medium tanks, small arms, and artillery. Signs of panic were developing when Col Tsuji stripped naked beside a well and was sluicing himself when a fellow staff officer ran up in full combat fig. "I'm having a cold shower," said the God of Operations. "Won't you join me?" The comedy nipped a panic in the bud. (Allen, *Burma*, 465.) But a less amusing event had happened earlier: "Colonel Tsuji's biographer," writes Allen, "cannot rid his subject of the accusation that he cooked and ate the liver of the pilot of a downed P40, and even persuaded the unwilling Army commander, Lieutenant-General Honda to nibble a piece." (Ibid., 609; see also 382.)

As the campaign ended, Tsuji was ordered to join TERAUCHI's Southern Army Hq in Saigon. From there he escaped to gain protection as an adviser to the Chinese Nationalists in their war against the communists. He returned to Japan in 1949, wrote several books (below), entered politics, and in 1961 he disappeared in North Vietnam. Seven years later he was declared officially dead.

Among his books in English translation are *Underground Escape* and *Singapore— The Japanese Version* (London: Constable, 1962). His memoir of service in Burma, published in 1962, is *Jugo tai-ichi (Fifteen to One,* A biography by Kyuei Sugimori is *Sanbo:* [staff officer] *Tsuji Masanobu* (Kawade Shobo Shinsha, 1982).

TUKHACHEVSKY, Mikhail Nikolaevich. Soviet marshal. 1893-1937. Although Tukhachevsky died in 1937, the most famous military victim of the **Great Purges**, his name looms large in the history of WWII. Born 3 Feb 93 on the Aleksandrovskoye Estate, he was the son of a Russian nobleman and a peasant woman. As a guards officer Tukhachevsky won six decorations before being captured in 1915. Fellow POWs at Fort 9 at Ingolstadt were Maj Georges CATROUX and Capt Charles DE GAULLE; the Russian escaped in

1917 after three attempts. Despite his youth Tukhachevsky had a brilliant record in the civil war as a commander of large forces. Long-lived hostility existed between him and Stalin over blame for mistakes in this war, particularly because Stalin and Voroshilov blocked transfer of cavalry reinforcements to support Tukhachevsky's advance on Warsaw from the Vistula River line. (WEYGAND's French mission advised the Poles.) Tukhachevsky rose quickly to be **CGS**, 13 Nov 25-5 May 28. In 1935, when only 42, he was among the first five **Marshals of the Soviet Union** (No. 5). The next year he visited England and France before heading the Red Army Military Training Board. In this and other assignments he had some success in improving Soviet military doctrine and modernizing the armed forces. In a minor act that in retrospect might be seen as portentous he approached Stalin at least once about offering J. Walter CHRISTIE a substantial stipend for aid in developing Red Army tanks. "The Russians displayed great admiration for Christie [and commented] 'it is unfortunate that he was born in the imperialist camp and hence not given the chance to exploit his ideas to the full.'" But Tukhachevsky was rebuffed for "succumbing to western bourgeois teachings and ideas." (Quoted by Milsom in his *Russian Tanks,* 41.) In his extensive travels in western Europe the youthful marshal "had behaved with that particular indiscretion which seems, unless vigorously and continuously suppressed, to be a national characteristic. He had acted at the same time the part of diplomat, roving military attaché, and socialite." (Clark, *Barbarossa,* Quill Ed [1985], 33).

Having gone so far as to make contact in Paris, openly, with one General Miller, head of the tsarist officers in exile (ibid.) he was viewed as a threat to Stalin and his cronies. So it came to pass that on 26 May 37, only five weeks after taking command of the Volga MD, Tukhachevsky was arrested with seven other senior officers including I. E. Yakir and I. P. Uborevich. "From files that are now [1994] being published we know that the criminal charges against Tukhachevsky and other high-ranking military leaders were consciously fabricated" (Sudoplatov, 87). But there is convincing evidence that almost all conventional views of the Tukhachevsky affair are wrong, especially BENES's role in sending Stalin evidence (fabricated by HEYDRICH). "The documents have

never been found in the KGB or Stalin archives. The criminal case against Tukhachevsky is based entirely on his confession, and there is no reference to any incriminating evidence received from German intelligence," says the Soviet secret service official who was in a position to know (Sudoplatov, 91.) A special session of the USSR supreme court pronounced the death sentence, and Tukhachevsky was executed the night of 11-12 June 37. His mother, a sister, and two brothers were executed later; three sisters and the marshal's daughter were arrested but survived imprisonment. The fate of his wife after being arrested is unknown. (Conquest, *Terror,* 219-26, passim; Scarecrow.)

TUPOLEV, Andrey Nikolayevich. Soviet bomber designer. 1888-1972. During and after the war Tupolov designed some of the world's best aircraft, doing much of his early work as a prisoner in a NKVD design bureau.

Born 10 Nov 88 in northern Pustomazovo within the present Kalinin Oblast, he was never a party member. The designer graduated from the Moscow Higher Technical School in 1918. With a professor from the school, Nikolay Yegorovich Zhukovsky (1847-1921), he organized the Central Aerodynamic Institute and was its director 1918-35.

Tupolev's TB-3 (ANT-6) was operational in 1930 as a heavy bomber, but its production ended in 1936. A four-engine, long-range (1,250 mile) plane with a maximum speed of 155 mph and only a two-ton payload, it was used until 1944 as a transport, then phased out. In 1936 his SB-2 (ANT-40) twin engine bomber became operational. All metal, with a 250 mph top speed, it was tested successfully in Spain and was popular there. Tupolev's work was part of the Soviet emphasis on bombers, which by the end of 1936 comprised 60 per cent of the Red AF inventory. Along with almost all other Soviet aircraft designers, numbering in the hundreds, he was arrested in 1938. The false charges against Tupolev and most of the others were passing technical secrets abroad. According to one authority (Erickson, *To Stalingrad,* 34) he was superseded by PETLYAKOV, but the latter also was jailed. Specially confined in three main groups, Tupolev's, Petlyakov's, and Myasishchev's, the men worked and slept in NKVD prison-bureaus called *shargas.* (In his book *First*

Circle Solzhenitsyn tells of similar "closed" bureaus in the postwar period.)

Incarcerated until late 1941, Tupolev developed the Tu-2, a ground-support dive bomber. It had limited service from 1943, 2,500 being produced, but was outperformed by Petlyakov's Pe-2, of which 11,500 were produced. After the war Tupolev designed many passenger planes and bombers, the Tu-104, 114, 124, 134, 154, the supersonic Tu-144. At one time the planes he designed held 78 world records. (HFS.)

He died 23 Dec 72 in Moscow at the age of 84.

TURNER, Richmond Kelly. US admiral. 1885-1961. "Terrible Turner" to the US Navy, he was "the alligator" to the Japanese because of his amphibious operations (RCS). He was a brilliant innovator in this little-known field and was a tough taskmaster from Guadalcanal, the first offensive, to Okinawa, the last.

Turner was born 22 May 85 at Portland, Oregon. Near the top of the USNA Class of 1908 (5/201) he became a gunnery specialist. At the advanced age of 42 Commander Turner got his wings in 1927 and had important aviation assignments afloat and ashore. Promoted to captain in 1935 he attended the Naval War College and remained as head of the Strategy Section. He returned to sea as skipper of CA *Astoria,* then in Oct 40 became director of war plans for CNO STARK. The tall, slender, sourlooking and abrasive captain was known for his hot Irish temper and heavy drinking off duty. (Buell, *Spruance,* 255, 424-25.) He functioned in Washington before the war under an antiquated staff system that made him responsible not only for operational planning but also for the end product of military intelligence. Chief of Naval Intelligence Theodore S. WILKINSON collected *information* about the enemy, but Turner was charged with *evaluation* and *dissemination.* (Morison, III, 134.) Disregarding recommendations of other staff officers Turner flatly refused to send clear warnings to KIMMEL as it became more and more apparent that war in the Pacific was imminent. Like almost all others in authority, Turner believed the Japanese would begin hostilities in the western Pacific, not at Pearl Harbor. But when disaster struck there Turner still refused to admit personal blame and was an anti-Kimmel witness at later investigations. After the US declared war Turner took on additional duties as assistant CofS to Ernest J. KING with responsibility for planning amphibious operations in the Pacific.

The 57-year-old admiral left Washington in July 42 to command Amphibious Forces, South Pacific. Aboard the transport *McCawley* and subordinate to Ghormley he directed amphibious support for the Guadalcanal campaign, 7 Aug 42-9 Feb 43. He was severely criticized for the defeat of Victor A. CRUTCHLEY, RN, his second in command, in the first Battle of Savo Island, the night of 8-9 Aug 42, but an investigation concluded that no one officer could be held responsible for all the mistakes involved. Turner was awarded the Navy Cross and the debacle did not impede his subsequent advancement. (Paolo E. Coletta in Stephen Howarth, ed, "Turner," 367, 373.)

He then headed TF 61 for the Russell Islands assault that month, moving on to New Georgia and Rendova. There on 30 June 43 a torpedo stopped *McCawley* dead in the water but her gunners got 17 of the 25 "Bettys" that tried, unsuccessfully, for the kill (Morison, VI, 151).

On 24 Aug 43 Turner was designated Commander, 5th Amphibious Forces, Pacific, with the 3d and 5th Amphibious Forces as major components. He formed a new staff and got permission to have an administrative command ashore so he could be at sea. (Coletta, ibid., 370.) With no amphibious force flagship yet available he flew his flag aboard BB *Pennsylvania* for the conquest of the Gilbert Islands late in 1943. He disagreed with NIMITZ's strategy for the Marshalls campaign, saying the proposed assault on Kwajalein was "reckless and dangerous." When Nimitz gave him five minutes to decide whether he wanted to keep his command Turner "Smiled and said, 'Sure I want to do it.'" (Coletta, ibid., 372, citing Dyer, *Turner,* II, 738-42.) For his performance Kelly Turner was nominated on 10 Feb 44 for promotion to vice admiral, which the Senate confirmed the next month.

As head of 5th PhibFor he directed all subsequent major amphibious operations in the central Pacific. From the new command ship *Rocky Mount* he directed TF 51 in the Marianas, beginning 15 June 44 with the assault on Saipan, on Iwo Jima in Feb 45, and on Okinawa, beginning 1 Apr 45. Two months later, having ceased to command 5th PhibFor, he was promoted to full admiral and on Guam began planning for the invasion of Japan.

When this was called off Turner was on the General Board briefly until Dec 45, when appointed USN Representative on the UN Military Staff Committee. After serving in NYC and London he retired 30 June 47 to the comfortable home he had long had at Carmel, Calif. An avid reader, incessant talker (*CB 44*), and now a complete alcoholic, Terrible Turner died on 12 Feb 61 at nearby Monterey. Like NIMITZ, Charles LOCKWOOD, and SPRUANCE (the latter a close neighbor and good friend), he was buried beneath a regulation headstone at the Golden Gate National Cemetery just south of San Francisco at San Bruno.

See George F. Dyer, *The Amphibians Came to Conquer: The Story of Admiral Richard K. Turner,* 2 vols (Washington, DC, 1971).

TWINING, Nathan Farragut. US general. 1897-1982. Wartime commander of the 13th, 15th, and 20th AF, he rose to be USAF CofS and JCS Chairman.

"Nate" Twining was born 11 Oct 97 in Wisconsin, appointed to West Point from the Oregon NG and was in the wartime class that finally graduated on 11 June 19 (138/284). After the Pearl Harbor attack he was assigned in the South Pacific, initially as CofS to Millard F. Harmon, who commanded USAAF in the region. On 13 Jan 43, as a brigadier general, he took command of the new 13th AF with headquarters at Espiritu Santo, New Hebrides. Promoted to major general, he headed the Solomons Air Command (COMAIRSOLS) from 25 July 43, replacing MITSCHER. On 20 Nov 43 he was succeeded by Maj Gen Ralph J. Mitchell, USMC (*OCMH Chron*, 148).

Maj Gen Twining then headed the 15th AF, 3 Jan 44-26 May 45 (*AA*, 598). Activated under DOOLITTLE on 1 Nov 43 for shuttle bombing in coordination with the 8th AF, based in the UK, it waged a five-month offensive against the Ploesti oil refineries in Romania. Operations were directed mainly by Twining. Promoted to lieutenant general on 5 June 45, he succeeded Curtis LEMAY as CG 20 AF, 1 Aug-15 Oct 45 (*AA*, 598).

Twining headed the Alaskan Dept, Nov 1947-50, before going to Washington as vice CofS, USAF, with promotion to full general. Moving up in 1953 to be CofS, he completed active duty as Chairman of the JCS, 1957-60. The general died in San Antonio, Texas, on 29 Mar 82.

TYULENEV, Ivan Vladimirovich. Soviet military commander. 1892-1978. Born 28 Jan 92 into a worker's family he entered the army in 1913 and rose to be a junior officer. In 1918 he entered the Red Army and the party after serving a year in the Red Guard. As a cavalry division leader during the civil war Tyulenev served in Budenny's 1st Cavalry Army, helping to suppress the Kronstadt rebellion in 1921 (HFS) and from 1923 he commanded cavalry units from brigade to corps level. In 1936 he was appointed deputy inspector of Red Cavalry

From Feb 38 he headed the Transcaucasus MD, being promoted to general of the army (No. 3) on 4 June 40 (Khruzin). Meanwhile he headed the 12th Army of the occupation forces in Poland before taking command of the Moscow MD in Aug 40 at the age of 51. At 3 AM on Sunday 22 June 41, hours after being ordered by Stalin to put Moscow's AA defenses on 75 percent of combat readiness, the general was summoned to the Kremlin and told to leave immediately and set up the new Southern Front. Based on the Odessa MD, the sector was relatively quiet as Rundstedt's AG South made its main effort farther north and annihilated KIRPONOS's Southwest Front. But by 1 Sep 41 Antonescu's Romanian Army and German 11th Army had cut off Odessa and the Crimea.

Tyulenev received a leg wound in late September and was evacuated to a Moscow hospital. After fuming in rear-area assignments, on 19 Jan 42 he became deputy to Budenny, **Glavkom** in the SW Direction (or TVD). Two months later he returned to head the Transcaucasus MD, from which troops had gone to Iran on 25 Aug 41 to link up with the British division of William SLIM. In May 42 Tyulenev's sector was redesignated the Transcaucasus Front.

His mission originally was to guard the borders of neutral Turkey and secure Lend Lease supply lines in NW Iran. But Tyulenev soon had more pressing business to the rear, and by Sep 42 he had absorbed the troops of what had been Malinovsky's Southern Front and Budenny's North Caucasus Front (Seaton, *R-G War*, 159). Meanwhile the German AG A under LIST and then KLEIST, overran vital oil fields in the Caucasus, reached the Caucasus mountains, and threatened the Red Navy's Black Sea bases. But without a sea lane for supplies, the Germans lost momentum, and by late August the Transcaucasus Front was pulling itself together.

Rallying reserves from somewhat unwilling mountain tribes (who had little love for Mother Russia), and receiving reinforcements across the Caspian Sea from central Russia, Tyulenev went on the offensive. But he quickly was plagued by political and military interference. BERIA, present as GKO representative, berated field commanders, generals, proposing to arrest Malinovsky, and telling Tyulenev he would "break his back" (Seaton, *Stalin,* 162). Moscow also bombarded the general with criticism of alleged shortcomings and gave detailed instructions on how to operate.

Late in 1942 Tyulenev got orders for several grandiose campaigns to trap Kleist's AG A in the Caucasus. But the terrain became virtually untrafficable because of flooded lowlands and snow in the mountains through which I. Ye PETROV's Black Sea Group was supposed to strike north from around Tuapse. Tyulenev and Petrov had begun planning a more limited offensive toward Maikop, but the GKO-Stavka in Moscow flatly disapproved. Then Kleist's AG A began withdrawing from the Caucasus toward the German bridgehead at Rostov. On 24 Jan 43 MASLENNIKOV's Northern Troop Group (HFS) was made independent of Tyulenev as the new North Caucasus Front. This absorbed Petrov's Black Sea Group on 16 Mar 43, and Tyulenev returned to his mission on the frontier. He remained head of the Transcaucasus Front until July 45, by which time the Red Army was making its final drive into Germany.

Tyulenev commanded the Kharkov MD until July 46. His final duty until being retired in May 58 was on the staff of the defense ministry. He died in Moscow on 15 Aug 78, the year he was made a HSU, and he was buried in Moscow's **Novodvichy Monastery Cemetery.** Two excerpts of his brief and somewhat lyrical memoirs, *Cherez tri voiny* (1960), are in Bialer's *Stalin and His Generals.*

U

UDET, Ernst. German airman. 1896-1941. Born 26 Apr 96 in Frankfort/Main, he was a leading ace by 1918 (26 kills) and an outstanding stunt pilot after the war. He was featured with Leni RIEFSTAHL in her film *SOS Eisberg.* Udet also was good at designing fighter planes. Bohemian and convivial, a wily cartoonist, and close friend of MILCH's, he was on bad terms with Goering. Their animosity stemmed from Udet's ejecting the Reichsmarschall from the Richthofen Veterans' Association for false claims of air victories as the famous squadron's commander (Irving, *Milch,* 49). Udet joined the Luftwaffe in June 35 as a colonel and a year later was appointed head of its technical department. He rose to the high rank of colonel general and Director of Air Armament but Udet lacked the requisite temperament, character, and professional ability. The morning of 17 Nov 41, under the influence of narcotics and cognac, he shot himself after making a distraught phone call to an estranged mistress (Irving, *Milch,* 138-39). Goering dictated a press notice that Udet had accidentally shot himself while testing a new weapon and would have a state funeral.

UMANSKY, Konstantin Aleksandrovich. Soviet diplomat. 1902-45. His name often spelled Oumansky, to the befuddlement of researchers (personal knowledge), he was Soviet ambassador to the US 10 May 39-8 Dec 41. He was succeeded (the day after the Pearl Harbor attack) by LITVINOV, his former patron.

Born in the south Ukraine's Nikolaev region on 14 May 02 he was the youngest ambassador in Washington for a major power, not 37 years old on taking office. (GROMYKO later beat this record by becoming ambassador in 1943 at the age of 34.) Umansky worked for **TASS** from 1918 and graduated from the Univ of Moscow in 1921. He started acquiring linguistic skill while spending part of his military service as a diplomatic courier, then he worked as TASS foreign editor from 1922 and later was its correspondent in Rome and Paris. In 1930 he became chief of the Press Division of the Commissariat of Foreign Affairs and was unpopular among American correspondents in Moscow for heavy-handed censoring of their stories. Nor did the short, chubby, dapper, but stuffy Umansky endear himself to Americans after he became counselor to the Soviet embassy in Washington from 1936 and chargé d'affaires from June 38.

Umansky became ambassador on 10 May 39, the day his former patron LITVINOV first was ousted and three months before the **Nazi-Soviet Pact** was signed. These were chilly times for a Russian diplomat in the US, but the climate in Washington warmed after Germany attacked the USSR on 22 June 41. The ambassador was involved in setting up Lend-Lease, accompanying GOLIKOV as interpreter as he met in late July 41 with US officials in Washington, and he was appointed to serve with Harry HOPKINS and Arthur Purvis on an inter-governmental committee on aid to Russia. (Stettinius, *Lend Lease,* 123-24.) In his last telegram from Washington, which was dated 9 Sep 41, Umansky said inter alia that he planned to fly to London three or four days later. (Scotts, citing Soviet records.) This is significant because it is difficult to establish the final date he served in Washington. He was in Moscow for the talks on 29 September that led to signing of the **Lend Lease** agreement (the Moscow Protocol) on 1 Oct 41. (Stettinius, Ibid., caption of photo facing page 128.)

GROMYKO was acting ambassador in Washington until LITVINOV presented his credentials on 8 Dec 41, the day after Japan attacked Pearl Harbor.

In 1943 Umansky was appointed ambassador to Mexico City, where he was killed 25 Jan 45 in an plane crash.

UMBERTO. Italian Crown Prince. 1904-83. The Prince of Naples (and of Piedmont), VICTOR EMMANUEL III's only son, was born 15 Sep 04. He was genetically enhanced by his mother, Princess Elena, the large, manly daughter of King Nicholas of Montenegro. The crown prince grew into a tall (six feet two), handsome, athletic playboy who lacked intellect and personality. He attended the Royal MA at Turin and rose rapidly to become IG of Infantry. When Italy entered the war on 10 June 40 Umberto commanded the Northern Army on the French frontier, and in Oct 42 he was promoted by the Duce to Marshal of Italy. After Mussolini's ouster on 25 July 43 the monarchy retained a brief lease on life. As Lieutenant General of the Realm the crown prince became regent after the Allies took Rome on 5 June 44. Two years later he succeeded to the throne for a 35-day reign as King Umberto II. A national plebiscite abolished the monarchy by a close vote and Umberto went into exile in Portugal, where he died 18 Mar 83.

UMEZU, Yoshijiro. Japanese general. 1882-1949. Umezu was born in Jan 82 in Oita Prefecture on the southern island of Kyushu. Commissioned an infantryman in 1904, he graduated from the war college in Nov 11 and was promoted the next year to captain (*Kogun,* 239). After various European assignments and with solid staff, command, and service school experience he was promoted to major general in Aug 30. He took command of the China Garrison Army in Mar 34, was promoted five months later to lieutenant general after concluding the **Ho-Umezu Agreement** on or about 10 June 35.

Lt Gen Umezu moved into politics after the **26 Feb 36** insurrection, becoming vice minister of war in the HIROTA cabinet and in two succeeding governments. When the last KONOYE cabinets fell on 5 Jan 39 he was appointed commander of the Kwantung Army and Ambassador Plenipotentiary to Manchukuo and was promoted to full general in Aug 39.

Umezu became the Japanese Army's CofS on 10 July 44 when Tojo vacated the post along with that of prime minister. He had been a candidate for the latter position, along with HATA, KOISO, and TERAUCHI, but Privy Seal KIDO considered him unsuited (Toland, *Sun,* 528). In the SUZUKI cabinet Umezu opposed surrender but begrudgingly came around to backing HIROHITO's decision to accept Allied terms and was in the delegation that signed the surrender instrument aboard *Missouri.* Serving a life sentence for war crimes he died of cancer on 8 Jan 49.

URQUHART, Robert Elliott. British general. 1901-88. Born 28 Nov 01, educated at Saint Paul's school in London, he was commissioned in the Highland Light Infantry (24 Dec 20). He was a huge, amiable Scot, over six feet tall, robust and athletic *(CB 44).* As an acting lieutenant colonel in Dec 40, assigned to headquarters of the crack 51st Highland Div, Urquhart saw action in the western desert from the summer of 1942 to the final Allied victory in Tunisia (13 May 43). The next month he was appointed to the DSO and promoted in July to brigadier commanding the 231st Malta Bde.

The brigade was made up of West Country troops who were hardened by service on Malta but without field experience. Redesignated the 231st Inf Bde and operating independently most of the time, the Malta Brigade performed well in Sicily and Italy. It won high praise for its part in the desperate fight for Regalbuto, 30 July-2 Aug 43 (Nicholson, 148-49) and for amphibious operations near Pizzo in the Gulf of Sant' Eufemia on 8 Sep 43 (ibid., 220). Urquhart was seriously wounded in this action, and Montgomery awarded him a bar to his DSO on 23 Sep 43.

Although he lacked airborne experience the big Scot was given command of the 1st Br Abn Div in England and promoted to major general. The "Red Devils," who had jumped in North Africa and Italy but not in Normandy, were given the most difficult mission in Opn **Market-Garden**—to take and hold the Lower Rhine bridges at Arnhem. (Strategic details are sketched under **Market-Garden.**)

With the 1st Air Landing [glider] Bde plus the 1st and 4th Parachute Bdes Urquhart himself landed by glider on Sunday 14 Sep 44 with about 8,000 troops. These had intermediate objectives some six to eight miles west of their final objective, the bridge in Arnhem. Unknown to British intelligence, despite warning from the Dutch underground, Bittrich's 2d SS Pz Corps was just north of Arnhem. Model had recently established his CP in Oosterbeek, a western suburb of Arnhem. Student also was on the scene, and the Germans soon had the complete plans of Market-Garden (taken from a downed American glider).

The Red Devils secured the north end of the 2,000-foot-long bridge but could not get across before SS Pz Grenadiers secured the other end. Urquhart meanwhile was cut off from his head-quarters for a critical 39 hours—in hiding behind enemy lines. The 9th and 10th SS Pz Divs moved in through Arnhem from the north to put the British under siege, the 10th Panzers taking the Arnhem bridge on 20 September and pushing south to block the linkup effort. The 9th Panzers and other units encircled survivors of the British airborne division in a bridgehead west of Oosterbeck. On the south (left) bank of the Rhine, opposite Oosterbeck, Maj Gen Stanislaw Sosabowski's 1st Polish Bde of about 2,000—delayed more than two days by bad weather—by this time had a perimeter around Driel. But they could not cross the 1,200-foot-wide river. The 2d Household Cav made a circuitous envelopment to link up with the Poles on 22 September. It was D+8!

Some 2,200 survivors of Urquhart's 8,000 officers and men were evacuated secretly from the right bank during the night of 25-26 September in assault boats manned by Canadian and British combat engineers. The Red Devils and Sosabowski's Polish Bde withdrew some 10 miles south to the Nijmegen bridgehead. Urquhart's division of about 10,000 (including the 2,000 Poles) lost about 1,200 KIA and 6,642 MIA. The Germans had 3,000 casualties including 1,100 KIA. (Ryan, *A Bridge Too Far,* 591).

For his heroic failure Maj Gen Urquhart was made a **CB** on 29 Sep 44.

Reverting in 1945 to his permanent rank of colonel he served in the War Office as director, Territorial Army (TA) and Army Cadet Force until 1946. Urquhart was promoted back to major general and was GOC, 16th Abn Div, TA, 1947-48. He retired without further promotion to be a company director in Glasgow and he published *Arnhem* (New York: Norton, 1958).

USHIJIMA, Mitsura. Japanese general. 1887-1945. Commandant of the Japanese MA from 1942, Lt Gen Ushijima was given command of the 32d Army on Okinawa in Aug 44 and of the entire land garrison when the landings started on 1 Apr 45. He then had 77,000 ground troops and about 20,000 Okinawan militia and labor troops. (Morison, XIV, 102.) The Japanese surprised the attackers by not putting their main defenses on the coast, where they would be subjected to overpowering US naval gunpower and air attack. Instead of this Ushijima concentrated on the southern end of the 60-mile long island, organizing three concentric lines around the natural fortress of Shuri Castle, which was on a volcanic mountain. In the Oriental tradition he also set up reverse-slope defenses behind the standard forward-slope positions, connecting them with tunnels. The rocky terrain was honeycombed with well-defended caves. US troops consequently suffered heavy losses.

The battle began on 1 Apr 45, and three days later the Marines cut the island in half and wheeled south toward Ushijima's main positions. A month later the Japanese general ordered massive counterattacks that had some success, but by 19 June he accepted that the campaign was lost. After ordering the garrison to die fighting he and his CofS took their lives at 3 AM on 22 June 45 by seppuku.

V

VAN FLEET, James Alward. US general. 1892-1992. Van Fleet was born 19 Mar 93 in New Jersey and appointed to West Point from Florida. Joining the West Point "class the stars fell on" he graduating in 1915 (92/164) and soon won the SS and PH in France.

The big, impressive Col Van Fleet commanded the 8th Inf Regt, 4th Div, with distinction from 1941 (Cullum) but remained in grade long after his classmates Eisenhower, Bradley, and many others became generals. When Army CofS George Marshall visited the Normandy beaches he was told by Eisenhower that one regimental commander deserved an on-the-spot promotion. Learning that the officer's name was Van Fleet, Marshall responded with some heat that he been scratching that officer from promotion lists for years because he had been known in the Old Army as a drunkard. It turned out that the chief of staff had confused Van Fleet, almost a complete teetotaller, with an officer named Van Vliet! (This oft-told tale, repeated by C. L. Sulzberger [*Candles,* 468], is well confirmed. Cullum lists a Maj Gen Robert C. Van Vliet and his son as ex-cadets [non graduates] in the classes of 1897 and 1915 the latter being Van Fleet's class!).

Marshall did penance for his homophonic error by promoting the burly, vigorous, clean-living regimental commander immediately. Brig Gen Van Fleet was assistant commander of the 2d Div (under Maj Gen W. M. Richardson). Having been awarded the DSC, SS, BSM, CR, CIB, and PH as a colonel in Normandy, as assistant division commander he won the SS, LM, two BSMs and another Purple Heart (Cullum). Taking over the 90th Inf Div on 15 Oct 44 (from Maj Gen R. S. McLain) he was promoted to major general on 15 Nov 44 (two DSCs, the DSM, and the LM). On 17 Mar 45 Van Fleet succeeded Maj Gen John Millikin as CG 3d Corps (DSM). *AA* does not confirm the Cullum entry (like all of them submitted by the graduate) that in 1944 he returned to command his old division, the 4th, before becoming CG, 90th Div.

Promoted on 19 Feb 48, Lt Gen Van Fleet headed the mission to support the Greek government in its civil war against communist rebels (1948-50). He then commanded the 2d Army in the US before taking over the 8th Army in Korea from Ridgway on 14 Apr 51 (*AA* rev ed, 641). Promoted to general on 1 Aug 51 (ibid.) he retired on 31 Mar 53. Having undertaken various socio-political initiatives in Korea (to the displeasure of US authorities in Tokyo and Washington [private information]) the highly decorated general was chairman of the American-Korean Foundation from 1953. He then was president of Van Fleet Ranch & Citrus Growers in Florida, dying 23 Sep 92 in Polk City, Fla.

VANDEGRIFT, Alexander Archer. USMC general. 1887-1973. "Sunny Jim" was a modest, quiet Marine with many distinctions: the first to lead a US Marine division in combat since WWI, the 18th Commandant of the USMC, and the first Marine to hold four-star rank.

He was born in Charlottesville, Va, on 13 Mar 87. Inspired by a Confederate grandfather who had been a captain in Pickett's charge at Gettysburg he applied for an appointment to West Point. But his congressman had no vacancy, so Vandegrift spent two years at VMI before being commissioned in 1909 as a second lieutenant, USMC. Vandegrift took part in the expedition to Nicaragua (1912), to Vera Cruz (1914), and as a first lieutenant in 1915 fought in Haiti against the Cocos. He then was with the Haitian gendarmarie 1916-18 and 1919-23. Four years later he served in China as S3 to the legendary Gen Smedley D. "Old Gimlet Eye" Butler.

After duty in the USMC Budget Bureau, and two years at Quantico as personnel officer (G1) Fleet Marine Force he returned to China in Aug 35 as XO of the Marine detachment in the Peiking embassy. Promoted in Apr 36 Col Vandegrift went to Washington as military secretary to USMC Commandant Holcomb, them as a brigadier general he was assistant commandant. Just before the Pearl Harbor attack he became assistant CG 1st Marine Div, and in Mar 42 took command of the division as a major general.

Maj Gen Vandegrift directed landings of the 1st Marine Div on Guadalcanal and in the desperate defense of Hickham Field. He triumphed over tremendous difficulties in this hastily planned operation, the first US offensive campaign of the war, which CNO Ernest J. KING insisted on undertaking despite MacArthur's objections. There was no time for the normal rehearsals of what is the most intricate of military operations, an amphibious assault; military intelligence was woefully lacking; the full division was not available initially nor was logistical support fully organized; Marine and naval personnel were green and their commanders were more so, notably Adm GHORMLEY. But "with a few good men" and outstanding personal leadership, Vandegrift held Henderson Field until US Army reinforcements arrived (below). The Marine general won the Navy Cross early in the campaign and was later awarded the Medal of Honor. After turning over command on the island 21 Jan 43 to Alexander M. PATCH, Jr, forward elements of the Americal Div having gone into action on 13 Oct 42, Sunny Jim took command of the 1st Marine Amphibious Corps in July 43. He was planning the assault on Bougainville when replaced by Maj Gen Charles D. Barrett. But the latter was killed in an accident so Vandegrift returned to direct the Bougainville landings on 1 Nov 43. GEIGER took over when the beachhead was secured, and Vandegrift was appointed USMC commandant-designate in Washington. Lt Gen Vandegrift became commandant in 1 Jan 44, and on 4 Apr 45 got his fourth star, the first Marine to hold this rank on active duty. He died 8 May 73 after 18 months as a patient at the Bethesda NH, Md.

VANDENBERG, Arthur Hendrick. US Senator. 1884-1951. A US congressman from Michigan since 1928, he was born 22 Mar 84 in Grand Rapids. His mother and father were of colonial New York Dutch origin. Young Arthur went to work at the age of nine after his father, a harness manufacturer, was ruined financially in the panic of 1893. "Son, always be a good Republican," allegedly was the death bed advice of the father who blamed the Democrats for his fall. Arthur worked as a clerk in a cracker factory after completing high school and rose to be managing editor of the Grand Rapids *Herald*. After 20 years with that paper, and becoming established as an author of works including several studies of Alexander Hamilton (*CE*) he was appointed to fill a Senate vacancy in 1928. Elected "with the largest plurality ever given any Michigan candidate" (quoted in *CB 40*), Vandenberg became a power in the Republican Party and a principal presidential possibility from 1940. He was long an ardent isolationist but after the Japanese attack on Pearl Harbor he began advocating US leadership in world affairs. Critics would accuse the senator of having a shifty political outlook, one editorial writer saying he had stood "squarely on both sides of every issue of the past 10 years" (ibid.) But by 1945 the Midwestern senator had a strong international outlook. FDR made him a US delegate to the UN conference in San Francisco and Vandenberg became a leading Senate advocate of the UN charter. He also gave strong support to the Marshall Plan. The senator was the uncle of Hoyt S. VANDENBERG.

VANDENBERG, Hoyt Sandford. USAF general. 1899-1954. Exceptionally young for such high command and strikingly handsome—actress Marilyn Monroe (1926-62) named him one of the three men she would like to be marooned with on a desert island—Lt Gen Vandenberg commanded the 9th AF 2 Aug 44-23 May 45 (succeeding BRERETON), was a full general in 1947 at the age of 49, and he headed the USAF 1948-53.

A nephew of Arthur H. VANDENBERG, the airman was born 24 Jan 99 in Wisconsin and appointed to West Point from Michigan. He graduated in 1923 (239/262) and joined the Army Air Corps. A meteoric professional rise began in June 39 with assignment to H. H. "Hap" ARNOLD's staff in Washington. Promoted to BG three years later he was ordered to the UK as an air planner for the impending invasion of North Africa, Opn **Torch.** Subsequently flying some 20 missions while performing staff duties, he was DOOLITTLE's CofS in the 12th AF 1942-43. In 1944 he was given a second star, and took over from BRERETON on 2 Aug 44 as CG 9th AF in Europe (*AA, 596*). He returned to Washington as chief of army intelligence 26 Jan-9 June 46 (*AA, 58*) and a year later he became director of central intelligence (DCI) as head of the Central Intelligence Group (CIG). This was a new post created by President Truman, who had abolished "Wild Bill" DONOVAN's OSS and who took a dim view of peacetime espionage. But as the Cold War heated up and the president was deluged with information from overseas, on 22 Jan 46 he created the National Intelligence Authority (NIA) and the post of director of central intelligence (DCI). The first DCI was Rear Adm Sidney W. Souers, chief planner of the reorganization, who agreed to stay on for only six months. Souers directed the work of a small staff, the central intelligence group (CIG), whose task was to screen the voluminous data from collection agencies and present it in a daily intelligence summary. Vandenberg succeeded Souers on 10 June 46. Promptly nicknamed "Sparkplug" and "visibly anxious to use the [CIG] post . . . as a stepping-stone to his air force career" (Christopher Andrew, 167), Vandenberg had been in office less than a month when he proposed legislation to establish an independent central intelligence agency. Free from the control that had been exercised over the CIG by the armed forces and the State Dept, this evolved into the CIA.

Returning to the air force in May 47 and promoted that year to full general, the second youngest since U. S. Grant (1864), Vandenberg was vice chief of the USAF before succeeding SPAATZ as head of the USAF in 1948. He retired from that post on 30 June 53 for physical disability and died of cancer on 2 Apr 54 in Walter Reed Army Hospital. Christopher Andrew's work of 1995 is the source of intelligence history given above. A scholarly biography, from which Andrew took the Marilyn Monroe nomination (above), is Philip S. Mellinger, *Hoyt S. Vandenberg* (Bloomington and Indianapolis: Indiana University Press, 1989).

VASILEVSKY, Aleksandr Mikhailovich. Red Army CofS and field commander. 1895-1977. The son of a priest, Vasilevsky attended theological seminary before becoming a tsarist army officer. He was a captain on entering the Red Army in 1919. During the civil war Capt Vasilevsky was a deputy commander of the 429th Rifle Regt. From 1931 to the end of 1934 he was chief of the Red Army's department of combat training after commanding the 144th Rifle Regt. In 1935 he went to the Volga MD as

head of the combat training department. He attended the newly established GS Academy 1936-37 and until June 39 was chief of the operations training section.

Impure pedigree (herein) kept Vasilevsky out of the CP until 1938. Thus certified he was first deputy chief of operations from 1939 to May 40, moving up as a SHAPOSHNIKOV favorite to headed the operations directorate during VATUTIN's prolonged absences after 23 June 41 (D+1 of **Barbarossa**). On this date he "narrowly escaped being sent [instead of VATUTIN] to Leningrad to help out Voroshilov" but soon "began, on Stalin's instructions, to spend most of his time in visits or attachments to the fronts" (Seaton, *Stalin,* 128). Only Zhukov was Stavka representative in the field more than Vasilevsky, who like Zhukov often coordinated actions of more than one front (HFS).

In June 42 Vasilevsky succeeded SHAPOSHNIKOV as CGS. "Vasilevsky, like Shaposhnikov, was a man of education, culture and tact, and of charm and modesty," writes Seaton, and "he was also circumspect in his relationship with Stalin and the party . . ." (Seaton, *Stalin,* 131).

Vasilevsky was promoted to MSU (No. 10) in Feb 43 at the age of 48. From 23 June to 7 Aug 44 he coordinated operations of the 1st Baltic and 3d Belorussian Fronts while Zhukov directed the 1st and 2d Belorussian Fronts to their left (south). Stalin wanted his CGS then to supervise operations in East Prussia so they could be ended quickly to free forces for Zhukov's assault on Berlin and so Vasilevsky could go to the Far East with two or three of the better armies for operations against the Japanese. But when CHERNIAKHOVSKY was killed Vasilevsky succeeded him on 21 Feb 45 as CG 3d Belorussian Front. After the final offensive in the west, and having spent 22 of his 34 months as CGS away from Moscow on various fronts (Bialer, ed., 683), Vasilevsky turned over his duties as CGS to ANTONOV in Feb 45 and directed the campaign that crushed the Japanese, 9-20 Aug 45.

Vasilevsky replaced Antonov as CGS in Nov 48 and four months later he succeeded Bulganin as defense minister (Seaton, *Stalin,* 266). From Stalin's death in 1953 until his retirement in Dec 57 he was first deputy minister of defense. (Bialer, ed, 639). His memoirs are *Delo Vsei Zhizni* (Moscow, 1974).

VANSITTART, Robert Gilbert. British diplomat. 1881-1957. Born 25 June 81 at Wilton House, Farnham, into a distinguished family, he spent an unusually long seven years at Eton. He excelled in ball games but also had a rare distinction of winning both the Prince Consort prizes in French and German in the same year. Entering the diplomatic service he was posted to Paris in 1903, transferred to Teheran in 1907, and to Cairo in 1909. Two years later he began his service in the Foreign Office (FO). Long an outspoken opponent of "communism, Deutschism and homosexuality" he became permanent under secretary (head of the FO) on 13 Nov 29 and was knighted (KCB) that year.

Sir Robert promptly created what became called "Vansittart's Private Detective Agency," a loose association of businessmen and travellers (mainly in Germany) set up by Claude DANSEY. After eight arduous years during a critical period of history in which he was ardently anti-German, hence increasingly out of step with the government, and tarnished by association with the HOARE-Laval pact, Sir Robert was replaced by CADOGAN on 1 Jan 38 and "kicked upstairs." (Churchill, I, 241.) Keeping his room in the FO he became "chief diplomatic adviser to His Majesty's Government," an ad-hoc post lacking real authority (ibid.). Vansittart soldiered on, declining the embassy in Paris (ibid), until retiring in 1941 and being created Baron Vansittart. In the House of Lords and publicly he continued a vigorous anti-Nazi campaign. "'Van' to his many friends, 'Bob Vansittart' to the fringe, and just Vansittart to the rest" (*DNB*) he died 14 Feb 57 at his home at Denham.

DNB calls his posthumous autobiography, *The Mist Procession* (1958), "one of the outstanding contemporary accounts of the time."

VATUTIN, Nikolay Fedorovich. Soviet military leader. 1901-44. He ranked with Rokossovsky and Konev as a field commander, but like VASILEVSKY is all the more remarkable for having first distinguished himself as a senior staff officer in Moscow. An ethnic Russian and son of a peasant, he was born 16 Dec 01 in the village of Chepukhino, Belgorod region (HFS). The stocky Slav joined the Red Army in Apr 20 and the CP in 1921. He graduated from the Poltava Infantry School in 1922, from the Frunze MA in 1929 and from the first class of the GS Academy in 1937 (HFS), becoming CofS Kiev MD. In Poland Sep-Nov 39 he was TIMOSHENKO's CofS in the Ukrainian Front (HFS). Then he headed the GS Operations Directorate in Moscow; as of June 40 he was first deputy CGS with the rank of general lieutenant (Scarecrow).

A few hours before the German assault of 22 June 41 Vatutin was with CGS Zhukov and MOD Timoshenko in the first frantic meetings called by Stalin (Seaton, *R-G War,* 21). When Zhukov left the next evening for Kiev to assess the situation on Budenny's front Vatutin was acting CGS 23-26 June 41. About a week later he became P. P. Sobennikov's CofS in the Northwest Front (Erickson, *To Stalingrad,* 147). Although officially in this post until May 42 (HFS) he went to Leningrad in Sep 41 as Stavka representative and was VOROSHILOV's CofS briefly. When Konev's Kalinin Front was formed on 17 Oct 41 to defend Moscow's critical northern flank Vatutin was Konev's CofS and commander of an operational group of four infantry and cavalry divisions plus a tank brigade.

After distinguishing himself in the winter counteroffensive, Vatutin returned to the Northwest Front as Kurochkin's CofS. He took part in the drive toward Vitebsk on 9 Jan 42 that failed to reduce the Demyansk salient (Seaton, *R-G War,* 235 and n).

In early May 42, Vatutin returned to his former post in Moscow, which had been held temporarily by his close associate Gen Maj Vasilevsky . But on 14 July 42 Vatutin left Moscow permanently and replaced GOLIKOV until October in the recently established and collapsing Voronezh Front. Despite a stubborn defense, he lost Voronezh on 6 July 42. In the reorganization for the Soviet counteroffensive at Stalingrad, and promoted on 12 July 42, Gen Col Vatutin took command of the new Southwest Front on 22 Oct 42 (HFS). On 19 Nov 42 he attacked on the north wing of the double envelopment, routing Italian and Romanian defenders and advancing 75 miles in three days. On 29 Mar 43, as others concentrated on final destruction of Paulus's 6th Army in Stalingrad Vatutin took command of all forces on the outer encirclement ring. Advancing into the Donets Basin on a 150-mile front he was crossing the river around Voroshilovgrad by 1 February in heavy fighting against counterattacks by the 4th Pz Army of Manstein's AG Don.

A general of the army (No. 9) in February Vatutin took part in the grinding offensive through the Ukraine. Around 17 Mar 43 he again succeeded the unfortunate GOLIKOV as CG, Voronezh Front, heading it, with Khrushchev as commissar, until it became the 1st Ukrainian Front on 20 Oct 43 in a final redesignation. His major actions were at Kharkov, Orel, Kursk, and Kiev.

Vatutin was ambushed on 29 Feb 44 by BANDERA guerrillas some 75 miles north of Kiev in the Korosten area. Wounded in the hip, he died 15 Apr 44 at Kiev and is buried there. ZHUKOV meanwhile personally assumed command of the front.

A "brilliant military leader" although "highly emotional" and poor at delegating responsibility, Vatutin owed much to "exceptional industry and breadth of strategic thinking" but also to assiduous logistical planning. (Zhukov, *Memoirs,* 209, 232, 508, 512).

VERCORS (Jean Bruller). French artist and writer. 1902-. Taking his pseudonym from the **Vercors** region of France, Jean Bruller was well known as a graphic artist when he founded the clandestine *Editions de Minuit* (the Midnight Press) in occupied Paris. His idea was to give French writers a third option to collaboration or silence. "This is a great honor," the essayist Jean Guéhenno wrote in his diary when asked to contribute. "By attaching so much importance to our thoughts, a tyrannous power forces us to recognize just how singular and outrageous they are. We had not dared to believe we were so interesting." Some 40 titles, more than 25 volumes, were edited, printed, and distributed under the Gestapo's nose. Bruller primed the pump with *Le Silence de la mer* (1942), a major novel about the power of silence as a form of protest—the silence of deep waters beneath raging waves. It was not for almost three decades that Bruller, using the name Vercors, published his war memoirs as *The Battle of Silence* (New York: Holt, Rinehart and Winston, 1968, first American edition).

VERSHININ, Konstantin Andreyevich. Soviet air marshal. 1900-73. A colonel in June 41 he rose to marshal of aviation in 1944, having commanded the 4th Air Army throughout much of the war. Vershinin was born 21 May 00 in the village of Borkino, now in Kirov Oblast. A tall man of good military bearing, he was CinC Air Forces and deputy MOD 1946-49 and again in 1957-69. He died 30 Dec 73 in Moscow. (HFS.)

VIAN, Philip Louis. British admiral. 1894-1968. The tall, graggy, publicity-shy "Vian of the Cossack" had a combination of personal daring and professional ability that made him one of the war's most outstanding naval commanders.

Of Huguenot ancestry he was born 15 June 94 in London, the son of Alsager Vian and the former Ada Frances Renault. After attending Hillside School he graduated from the RN colleges of Osborne and Dartmouth, becoming a midshipman in 1912. During and after WWI he served on destroyers, specializing in gunnery. Getting his fourth stripe in 1934 Capt Vian took command of DD *Cossack* after Britain declared war on 3 Sep 39 and was transferred to convoy escort duty. In Feb 40 he was in European waters when the search began for the German supply ship *Altmark,* which was sneaking back from Capt Hans LANGSDORFF's defeat in *Admiral Graf Spee* off the Rio Plate, Uruguay. Released British captives had reported that hundreds of merchant seamen were aboard *Altmark.*

The latter's skipper, Capt H. Dau, hid for nearly two months before heading home. With good luck and bad weather he eluded detection until spotted on 14 Feb 40 by British aircraft. Dau took refuge in Jossing Fjord, within Norwegian territorial waters, while *Cossack* closed in with another destroyer and a cruiser. Vian was ordered to enter the fjord and establish that *Altmark* was violating Norwegian neutrality by entering her waters with POWs. Two Norwegian gunboats met *Cossack* and told her skipper that *Altmark* was unarmed, had been examined, and that she had permission to proceed through Norwegian territorial waters.

Vian withdrew for instructions, which Churchill sent him personally: unless the Norwegians convoyed *Altmark* to Bergen with a joint Anglo-Norwegian guard on board "you should board *Altmark,* liberate the ship, and take possession . . ." (WC, I, 562).

That night Vian entered the narrow fjord without a pilot and using searchlights. Boarding one of the Norwegian gunboats he was told that *Altmark* had been searched twice and that no

POWs were found. Capt Dau meanwhile got under way, tried to ram *Cossack,* and went aground. Vian tied up along side and sent Lt Comdr Bradwell Turner (his first lieutenant) and Petty Officer Norman Atkins over at the head of a boarding party. After a fight in which four Germans were killed, five wounded, and several captured, Turner bellowed down a broken-open hold: "Any British down there?" As Stephen Howarth reconstructs the oft-told but much-distorted story, "A clamor of voices came back: 'Yes—we're all British!' 'Come on up then,' Turner called, and someone on deck [nobody knows who] shouted: 'The navy's here!" (Editor Stephen Howarth's sketch of Vian in *Men of War,* 495.) The boarders found two AA guns and four machine guns, and 299 British seamen were found hidden throughout the ship (WC, I, 563). Vian was awarded the first of his three DSOs but not, as myth has it, the VC.

The "Altmark Affair" caused Hitler to speed up his long-contemplated invasion of Norway (*see* FALKENHORST) during which Capt Vian commanded the 4th DD flotilla. He escorted troop transports in the withdrawal from Namsos, having his flagship *Afridi* sunk on 3 May 40 but not allowing any British transport to be hit. Back aboard *Cossack* he won a bar to his DSO for Opn **DM,** which destroyed a German convoy off Norway in Oct 40, and a second bar for his audacious torpedo attacks the night of 26-27 May 41 on *Bismarck.* (See under LUETGENS.)

In the Mediterranean

Just 47 years old when promoted to rear admiral (July 41) and ordered to Alexandria, Rear Adm Vian led task forces of cruisers and destroyers in the Mediterranean, engaged primarily in convoy protection. Vian was so aggressive in the 1st Battle of Sirte against IACHINO on 17 Dec 41 that the Italian admiral withdrew because he falsely assumed a British battleship must be within supporting distance. Having survived this indecisive action, Vian lost his flagship CL *Naiad* on 11 Mar 42 to U-565. The 2d Battle of Sirte, 22 Mar 42, was a four-and-a-half hour action between Vian's four light cruisers and 11 destroyers and Iachino's force of one light and two heavy cruisers, 10 destroyers, and BB *Littorio.* The Nelsonesque Vian took advantage of poor visibility, rough water, and bad Italian gunnery to frustrate Iachino's efforts against a four-ship convoy en route from

Alexandria to Malta. The Luftwaffe destroyed most of the convoy a day later as it unloaded a mere 5,000 tons at Malta (*R&H,* 202), but this resupply enabled the island to hold out until the next convoy got through three months later. Vian was knighted (KBE) for the action.

Sir Philip landed SIMMONDS's 1st Cdn Div in Sicily on 10 July 43 (*R&H,* 338) and headed the Support Carrier Force (TF 88) off Salerno, 9-16 Sep 43.

Final Actions

Ordered to the UK for the cross channel attack, he headed the Eastern Naval TF that put Miles DEMPSEY's 2d British Army ashore in Normandy on 6 June 44. The next day (the king's official birthday) he was given a higher order of knighthood, **KCB.**

Moving to the Far East as the naval war in Europe wound down, from Nov 44 Sir Philip commanded a carrier task force of the Eastern Fleet based in Trincomalee, Ceylon. He joined the British Pacific Fleet in Australia for the Okinawa campaign and remained in the Far East until 1948. After this he was 5th Sea Lord in charge of naval aviation before commanding the Home Fleet, 1950-52. On retirement he was promoted to admiral of the fleet and made GCB. His terse, self-effacing memoirs are *Action This Day* (1960).

In his perceptive sketch Stephen Howarth (already cited) points out that the book's tone of modesty and "'generosity toward those who served under him'" as another authority put it, "were two aspects of Vian's make-up," but one grateful beneficiary, Rear Adm Royer Dick, said "He wasn't like that at all." His writing, in this book and in reports, was clear, economical, and precise. But the man himself was "stupendously rude," and in his later years was "vain and snobbish, socially awkward and rude." (Howarth, ibid., 492-93.) This detracts nothing from his reputation as "a superb sea-warrior" (ibid.) and will surprise nobody who has a knowledge of exceptional military leaders. He died 27 May 68.

VICTOR EMMANUEL III. King of Italy. 1869-1947. Born 11 Nov 69 in the Palace of Capodimonte in Naples, the Prince of Naples was the only son of King Umberto I and of Margherita of Savoy. He suffered physically and mentally from 10 centuries of royal inbreeding, growing to slightly over five feet tall and having weak legs disproportionately short for the torso. King Umberto prescribed a Spartan regimen for his son, whose first tutor was a stern English woman who stressed moral values along with the three Rs. (*CB 43*.) Despite his limited intellect the Prince of Naples developed a near-perfect command of French and English, an encyclopedic memory, and a certain native shrewdness (ibid.).

In the royal tradition he was educated as an army officer and was a lieutenant general at the age of 25. In 1896 he married the gigantic, athletic Princess Elena of Montenegro, who bore UMBERTO. Ascending to the throne in 1900 he remained popular through the first world war and spent most of his time in the field. He is said to have had two long conversations with Corporal Benito Mussolini in hospitals and to have been favorably impressed.

In the political foment following the war the king concluded that the Fascist movement was Italy's best hope. Thus began the generally cordial political collaboration between the puny king and the macho Mussolini. Victor Emmanuel remained a useful figurehead when Il Duce was ousted on 25 July 43.

The night of 8-9 Sep 43, after the Italian surrender was announced, BADOGILO and the royal family were besieged in the ministry of war building. They escaped early the next morning from Pescara in two corvettes and reached Brindisi early on the 10th to set up a government in Allied-held territory. But the king had become increasingly ineffective with old age and his people were increasingly disaffected. He relinquished power to UMBERTO after the Allies took Rome on 5 June 44 and abdicated in 1946 when a plebiscite narrowly voted to end the monarchy. Going into exile in Alexandria, Egypt, with Queen Elena, he died there on 28 Dec 47.

VIETINGHOFF-SCHEEL, Heinrich Gottfried von. 1887-1952. A self-confident old Prussian infantryman of the Guards, although not a heroic figure—bearing a strong resemblance to Hitler—Generalleutnant Baron von Vietinghoff **(genannt)** Scheel became the first commander of the 5th Pz Div on 24 Nov 38. After serving in Poland with BUSCH's 8th Corps of LEEB's 14th Army (*B&O*, 78) he left the division on 17 Oct 39.

Promoted on 1 June 40 to Gen of Pz Troops von Vietinghoff led the 46th Pz Corps from 1 Nov 40 and was assigned to Weichs's 2d Army for the conquest of Yugoslavia. From a base in western Hungary he sent one column SW to Zagreb and another SE and S to Sarajevo. Then joining GUDERIAN's 2d Pz Gp of BOCK's AG Center in Russia, he fought under GUDERIAN and his successor, Rudolf Schmidt, in the 2d Pz Army, until leaving the 46th Pz Corps on 10 June 42 (*B&O*, 48).

Vietinghoff was commanding an army in occupied France when ordered to Italy on 9 Aug 43 to head the all-German 10th Army created on the 22d to oppose Allied forces that had overrun Sicily and were preparing to invade southern Italy. His army was made up of reinforcements being rushed to KESSELRING in central Italy while ROMMEL formed a new army group to defend the Po Valley. With limited resources and a new command group, Generaloberst Vietinghoff (as of 1 Sep 43) showed remarkable initiative in opposing Mark Clark's anticipated landings at Salerno on 9 Sep 43 and Montgomery's advance to link up from the south. Thanks largely to outstanding work by his veteran CofS Generalmajor Fritz Wentzel (Senger, 181) Vietinghoff conducted a masterful delaying action from the Volturno River to the Gustav Line, which KESSELRING was organizing across Italy. Here the 10th German army held fast through the Winter Line campaign of 15 Nov 43-15 Jan 44.

After MACKENSEN's 14th Army of Kesselring's AG C was formed to deal with the Anzio landings (22 Jan 44) the 10th Army operated on the eastern (Adriatic) flank against the British 8th Army. Vietinghoff was on leave to receive his Knight's Cross from Hitler on 11 May 44 when the final assault began around Cassino (Fisher, 42 & n). He returned promptly to be involved in the action and subsequent withdrawals through Rome, across the Arno, and into the north Apennines.

Vietinghoff was acting commander of AG C from 23 Oct 44, when KESSELRING was severely injured, until the field marshal's return on 15 Jan 45. From then until 11 Mar 45 Vietinghoff temporarily commanded AG Kurland (formerly AG North), replacing RENDULIC, then he succeeded KESSELRING on 23 Mar 45 as supreme German commander in Italy. The Allied 15th AG was poised to break out of their positions in the northern Apennines for a final offensive into the Po Valley that began in early April. Supporting Karl WOLFF's surrender arrangements, Vietinghoff signed the document that ended hostilities at 2 PM on 2 May. After having a fortuitous role in saving the **Niederdorf group** he went into captivity with von SENGER and LEMELSEN. Released in 1946 he died in 1952 at Pfronten (*B&O,* 79).

VINSON, Frederick Moore. American jurist. 1890-1953. Born in Louisa, Kentucky, on 22 Jan 90 he was in the US House of Representatives 1923-29 and 1931-38. With an aptitude for mathematics and statistics Vinson was noted as a fiscal expert. He resigned from Congress to be a federal judge in Washington until in May 43, then succeeding James F. BYRNES as director of the Office of Economic Stabilization. In July 45 he became Truman's secretary of the treasury and the next year he succeeded Harlan F. Stone as Chief Justice of the US Supreme court, dying in office and being followed by Earl Warren.

VISHINSKY. See VYSHINSKI

VLASOV, Andrey Andreyevich. Soviet turncoat. 1901-46. One of Stalin's favorite generals until he was captured in June 42, he subsequently headed the anti-Soviet Russian Liberation Army. Vlasov was born 16 Dec 01 in the village of Chepukhino, Nizhni-Novgorod province, now Kursk Oblast. A local German merchant provided money for his education, but in 1917 the seminarian left his studies to join the Red Army. Fired with Bolshevik ardor, the very tall (six feet seven), bespectacled Vlasov soon decided he preferred the smell of gunpowder to incense. He rose during the civil war to command what was called a division (considerably smaller than a standard **division.**) In 1938-39 he was a military adviser in China, returning to lead the 99th Inf Div into Bessarabia as a general major. In 1940 his unit was officially acclaimed as one of the Red Army's best trained (Scarecrow).

From the start of Barbarossa on 22 June 41 Vlasov led the 4th Mech Corps in delaying actions around Przemysl and Lvov before taking over the 37th Army and the Kiev Fortified Area. He led some of his troops out of the encirclement before Kiev fell on 19 Sep 41 and went to Moscow two weeks later to command the specially reinforced 20th Army with the rank of general lieutenant. In the Soviet counteroffensive he attacked 5 Dec 41 to take part in the recapture of Klin and to become officially hailed as one of the eight outstanding heroes in the Battle of Moscow.

As the situation worsened around Leningrad, Vlasov arrived on 9 Mar 42 to be MERETSKOV's deputy in the new Volkhov Front (Salisbury, *900 Days,* 528n). Effective 16 April (ibid.) he took over the 2d **Guards Army** after N. K. Krykov fell ill and the elite force was about to be trapped deep inside German positions. His last supply route was cut on the 19th. In marshes and woods made untrafficable by spring thaws his 130,000 men held under heavy air and ground attack while MERETSKOV conducted heroic relief efforts.

On 24 June Vlasov ordered his men to form small groups and fend for themselves, and he was run to ground on 13 July 42. As a protégé of MALENKOV, who was a mortal foe of ZHDANOV's, Vlasov figured in Kremlin politics (Salisbury, 533). The party line was that "the cowardly and supine Vlasov . . . fearing to answer for his defeat, defected" (*Istoriya,* II, 555). Like all Soviet lies this had some truth, but the Germans were more precise in seeing Vlasov as an exceptionally able Russian who had lost faith in Stalinism.

After making himself useful in anti-Soviet propaganda the defector worked to establish his National Russian Government in alliance with but not subservient to the Nazis. The latter's hierarchy had mixed views on how to deal this proposal, and on several occasions Vlasov threatened to give up and be a mere POW. But finally, on 14 Nov 44, the Russian general was allowed to issue a Nazi-approved manifesto from Prague reflecting the aims of his Committee of Liberation of the Peoples of Russia. Addressing all those who were under Soviet oppression he slipped in the phrase "there can be no greater crime than the forced enslavement of another nation." Hence the book title *Against Stalin and Hitler* adopted by Strik-Strikfeldt, the German Balt who commanded the special camp set up for the Vlasov movement.

The long, lanky Vlasov organized a Russian army of two divisions, one of which helped the Czech resistance liberate Prague on 5 May 45 as

Soviet and US troops approached (Bethell, 71). It was their one bright moment. In accordance with the Yalta repatriation agreement US authorities turned Vlasovite POWs over to the Soviets. On 12 May 45, near Hanover, an American escort surrendered Vlasov, who by then was a broken man seeking solace in the bottle. The Soviets announced on 2 Aug 46 that Vlasov and some associates had been executed. *See* Salisbury, 528-33, and the work by Strik-Strikfeldt (listed in the bibliography).

von BRAUN. See BRAUN, Werner.

VOROBYEV, Mikhail Petrovich. Soviet military engineer. 1896-1957. The Red Army's senior military engineer was born 29 Dec 96 in Khasavyurt, now Dagestan ASSR, son of a telegrapher. After attending a mining institute, Vorobyev was drafted in 1916. He entered the Red Army as an officer in 1918 and the CP a year later—curious in view of his non-peasant origin. Having graduated in Apr 29 from the Military Engineering Academy he stayed for graduate work. His dissertation, published as *Obstacles: Construction, Application, Overcoming* (Leningrad: Dzherzhinsky Military-Engineering Academy, 1932), became the Bible of Soviet engineering troops. (HFS.)

After being commandant of the Leningrad Military-Engineering School in 1936 he was appointed IG of Engineer Troops of the Soviet Army in July 40. In June 41 he was a General Major of Engineer Troops, with rank backdated to 4 July 40. Shortly after the Germans invaded he was made Chief of the Engineering Directorate and later was Chief of Engineer Troops in the Western Front. Vorobyev directed construction of Moscow's defenses in 1941. From Apr 42 to 1952 he was chief of Engineer Troops. Duties included organizing mining operations and pontoon bridge construction. Promoted to General Lieutenant of Engineer Troops on 29 Mar 43, to General Colonel on 16 Sep 43, and Marshal of Engineer Troops on 21 Feb 44, the first to hold this rank and the only one until 1961 (HFS).

It seems that for 10 years, 1942-52, he was Chief of Engineer Troops. Then he was Chief of Engineer Troops in the Kiev MD until appointed deputy chief of Construction Troops, 1954-56. In 1956-57 he was assistant to the commander of the Baltic MD for Construction Troops. He died on 12 Jun 57 at the age of 60.

VORONOV, Nikolai Nikolaevich. Red Army artillery chief. 1899-1968. Son of a clerk, he joined the Red Army in 1918 and the CP a year later (despite his non-peasant provenance). He commanded a battery during the civil war and was a POW in Poland 1920-21. Returning to command an artillery battalion in 1924, leaving to attend the Frunze MA 1927-30, then heading an artillery regiment until 1932 he was posted to Rome as a military attaché. He returned from Italy to be a chief of divisional artillery (1933), commandant and commissar of the Artillery Officers School (1934-36) and military adviser in Spain until 1937. Voronov returned to Moscow to be chief of the Soviet army's artillery (*Nachal'nik artillerii*). His responsibilities included national air defense, and the fortunate "Spaniard" also was first deputy to the nefarious KULIK. The latter took over as *Nachal'nik artillerii* in June 40 and operated the office with Voronov as the senior of his three deputies (Erickson, *To Stalingrad,* 17). Voronov had the consolation of being promoted to general colonel when his authority was reduced, and when KULIK was demoted in July 41 he stepped back up to be chief of artillery and also was appointed deputy commissar of defense.

A favorite of Stalin's (HFS) the tall, imposing Voronov created the "artillery offensive" and the uniquely Soviet concept of using artillery. The Red Army employed artillery not merely an arm for *supporting* infantry and armor (the doctrine of most other armies) but for taking and hold ground. The Germans could testify to the success of this revolutionary doctrine, as could Americans who later faced Soviet-inspired Chinese communist artillery in Korea. (US artillerists, who won equal respect on the battlefield, rejected the Soviet concept and continued to favor a more flexible employment.)

Voronov's Main Artillery Administration was charged with developing and providing all types of weapons for all arms of the Red Army. Voronov therefore was blamed along with Kulik, probably unfairly, for shortcomings in this area. He was among those available to the

GKO-Stavka throughout the war for planning and supervising the execution all major military operations. In 1943 his title became *Commander* of Artillery. That year he became the first of three promoted during the war to Marshal of Artillery. (The others, in 1944, were N. D. YAKOVLEV and M. N. CHISTYA-KOV.) Voronov was raised to Chief Marshal of Artillery on 12 Feb 44. (HFS.)

He remained head of all Red Army artillery until 1950, was president of the Academy of Artillery Sciences to 1953, and Commandant of the Artillery Academy until retirement in 1958.

VOROSHILOV, Kliment Yefremovich. Soviet military commander. 1881-1969. The vainglorious and generally incompetent Voroshilov remained prominent throughout the war simply because he never lost favor with Stalin. He was born 4 Feb 81 in the Ukrainian village of Verkhneye, near Dnepropetrovsk. The son of a railroad worker he had two years of schooling before becoming a metal worker at the age of 14 and a revolutionary shortly thereafter. In 1903 he joined the Russian Social Democratic Party. After a prison term and exile in 1907-14 he was active in Lugansk (later Voroshilovgrad) and at Petrograd.

He was a crony of Stalin's from early in the revolution, an original member of the Bolshevik faction, and a creator of the secret police and of the Red Cavalry. During the civil war he commanded large formations including the 5th Ukrainian Army. Voroshilov defied the Central Committee's military directives and was insubordinate to Trotsky, things that endeared him to Stalin but contributed to disaster in the Soviet-Polish war of 1920 (Erickson, *To Stalingrad,* 5).

But Stalin valued political reliability above ability and retained his crony as his leading military expert. Commissar of Defense Voroshilov (1925-40) opposed mechanization and in 1937 disbanded the mechanized corps. (Erickson, ibid., 15.) He was in the first batch of marshals (MSUs) created in late 1935. Goading Stalin on with vile and reckless accusations (HFS) during the **Great Purges.** Only he and BUDENNY survived the fate of the other first five marshals, Blyukher, Tukhachevsky, and A. I. Yegorov.

In early Aug 39 Voroshilov led the fruitless secret talks in Moscow with the British and French on opposing Hitler, and three weeks later Stalin signed the infamous **Nazi-Soviet Pact.** Senior officers had severely criticized Voroshilov's leadership as early as 1928 (Erickson, op. cit., 15), but he was not replaced as commissar of defense (by Timoshenko) until 8 May 40, after the fiasco in Finland.

As the top leadership in Moscow was frantically reorganized after the Germans launched Barbarossa on 22 June 41 the incompetent Voroshilov was selected as one of three **Glavkom**s. He reached Leningrad on 12 July but the Glavkom position was eliminated at the end of August. Voroshilov lasted a week as POPOV's successor in the Northwest Front (5-12 Sep 41) before ZHUKOV arrived (Erickson, Ibid., 189).

The day before his recall to Moscow, and having every reason to believe he would be shot (like D. G. PAVLOV), he is said to have gone to the front in hopes of being killed. But the old Stalin crony spent the rest of the war in honorific posts, organizing reserves in the Urals, heading Asian armies against the Japanese at the end of the war, and then serving in Hungary as chief of the Control Commission until 1947. After the war he fell from grace, virtually ostracized by Stalin and even suspected of being "an English spy and God knows what else" (Khrushchev, 281). On Stalin's death in 1953 he became titular head of the USSR as chairman of the Supreme Soviet Presidium, succeeded in 1960 by Brezhnev.

Eighteen months after retiring for ill health, Voroshilov suddenly was denounced in 1961 at the 22d Party Congress for anti-party activities in the 1950s. But in 1962 he was reelected to the Presidium after confessing his trespasses. Marshal Voroshilov returned to the limelight when KHRUSHCHEV fell in 1964. He died 2 Dec 69 in Moscow and is buried in the Kremlin Wall.

VOROZHEYKIN, Grigory Alekseyevich. Soviet airman. 1895-1974. Born in the village of Berezniki in the present Kalinin Oblast on 16 Mar 95 he joined the Red Army in 1918, fought in the civil war, but was not a CP member until 1927. By Jan 41 he had risen to be commander of aviation in the Volga MD. Five months later, when the war started, he commanded aviation in the 21st Army until August and then held the same post in the Central Front before going to Moscow as AF CofS until Mar 42. After heading an assault aviation group until May he spent the rest of the war as first deputy commander of the Soviet Army AF. Marshal of Aviation Vorozheykin (in 1944) headed the Military Air Academy faculty 1953-59, dying 30 Jan 74 in Moscow. (HFS.) [150]

VYSHINSKY, Andrei Yanuaryevich. Soviet statesman. 1883-1954. A leading Soviet jurist who became notorious internationally as a prosecutor during the **Great Purges**, he represented the USSR during the war as Molotov's deputy minister of foreign affairs.

Vyshinsky was born in Odessa, son of a Polish chemist, and he began his communist career in 1902 as a Menshevist. Arrested and jailed several times for activities in the Caucasus he and his wife were wounded in 1907 by political terrorists. Vyshinsky graduated in law from the Univ of Kiev in 1913, remained to prepare for a professorship, but was expelled for political activities. He then held teaching and literary positions. When the Bolshevists took power in Nov 17 he defected to the Menshevists (his original political persuasion), joined the Red Army in 1919 and the CP a year later. He lectured at Moscow U for the next two years and held several governmental posts thereafter while advancing his career as a criminal lawyer and prosecutor.

He reached a peak (or a valley) as state prosecutor during the Great Purges and "obediently carried out Stalin's will, trampling all principles of justice and morality" (Scarecrow). The reward was election to the Central Committee in 1939 and appointment on 7 Sep 40 as Molotov's deputy commissar of foreign affairs. Vyshinsky never reached the higher policy-making heights nor became a member of the Politburo but he laid the groundwork for Soviet postwar domination by organizing satellite governments, notably in Latvia (1940) and Romania (1945).

In 1943 he began representing the USSR in the Allied Mediterranean Commission. "I watched with fascination his manipulations which laid the foundation for Soviet policy in Western Europe," wrote Robert MURPHY (*Diplomat,* 211). Often vituperative and even abusive in formal debate, he was highly effective in private conference and in what Murphy termed "undercover maneuvers" (Ibid.).

Vyshinsky attended most of the inter-Allied and UN meetings starting with the Potsdam conference in 1945. On 4 Mar 49 he succeeded MOLOTOV as foreign minister. When Molotov resumed this post on 6 Mar 53 after Stalin's death Vyshinsky reverted to his former status and became permanent representative of the USSR at the UN. His brief career was characterized by frequent use of the veto, adding *nyet* (the Russian *no*) to the vernacular. Death silenced the 71-year-old Vyshinsky on 22 Nov 54 in New York.

W

WAGNER, Gustav. German death camp leader. 1911-80. Born and reared in Vienna, he joined the illegal Austrian Nazi party in 1931. Three years later, wanted by the police for such subversive acts as putting up Nazi posters and painting swastikas on walls, he fled to Germany and found a home in an SA guard detachment before transferring to the SS. In 1940 he went back to Austria as a guard at Schloss Hartheim, near Linz, where mental patients were killed in accordance with directives from the Foundation for Institutional Care in Berlin.

Sgt Wagner was ordered to Poland in Mar 42 as second in command at Sobibor and he doubled as Franz STANGL's deputy at Treblinka. Himmler presented him with a decoration in Sep 43 for his murderous efficiency, and he was promoted to Oberscharfuehrer (master sergeant).

On furlough when the uprising occurred at Sobibor on 14 Oct 43 the sergeant was reassigned to NE Italy, soon followed by his chief, Odilo GLOBOCNIK and his SS detachment, who were based at Trieste. Allied liberators took Wagner prisoner but he was released from an American POW cage under a false identity. The fugitive did construction work in Graz before linking up with Fritz STANGL in 1947 and escaping through Rome and Syria to Brazil. Gaining permanent residence on 12 Apr 50 he lived incognito, freely, in a Bavarian style house near Sao Paulo for three decades until unmasked by two journalists on 20 Apr 78 at a celebration of Hitler's 89th birthday. He was arrested 30 May 78, but Israel, Austria, and Poland all failed in their extradition efforts.

The unrepentant Oberscharfuehrer Wagner said in a secretly taped BBC documentary—first aired 18 June 79—"I had no feelings. It just became another job." He committed suicide on 15 Oct 80 in Sao Paulo. (Wistrich).

WAGNER, Robert. Nazi official. 1895-1946. The gauleiter was born 13 Oct 95 in Lindach. An infantryman in WWI, he was a Reichswehr officer until jailed in 1924 for participating Hitler's Munich Beer Hall Putsch (8-9 Nov 23). Wagner became Gauleiter in Baden in Mar 25.

After the fall of France in 1940 he was Gauleiter of Alsace-Baden, and in October of that year, as the chief of civil administration, he organized the sudden deportation of more than 6,500 Jews from to the unoccupied zone of France. Condemned by a French military court he was executed 14 Aug 46 in Strasbourg. (Wistrich.)

WAGNER, Winifred. Expatriate Englishwoman. 1894?-1980. She was born Winifred Williams in Hastings, Eng, in 1894 or 1897 (the latter date given by Wistrich). Orphaned before the age of two, she was adopted eight years later by Karl Klindworth, a German musician. In 1915 young Winifred married the middle-aged Siegfried Wagner (1869-1930), son of Richard Wagner (1813-83). Frau Wagner met Hitler in 1923 and became an ardent supporter. Their friendship deepened after she was widowed in 1930, and by 1933 it was rumored they might get married. The union, if Hitler had been the marrying kind, would have been plausible from many points of view including Hitler's adoration of Richard Wagner's ardently Teutonic music and equally ethnocentric political philosophy. Retaining a special place in Hitler's affections, Winifred ran the Bayreuth Festival from her husband's death in 1930 until 1945, when she was forced to turn her duties over to sons Wieland and Wolfgang. (Wistrich.) She continued to live at Bayreuth, still admiring Hitler, and saying in 1973: "To have met him is an experience I would not have missed" (Hamilton, *Leaders*, 206).

WAINWRIGHT, Jonathan Mayhew. US general. 1883-1953. Succeeding MacArthur as commander in the Philippines and promoted 19 Mar 42, Lt Gen "Skinny" Wainwright surrendered his forces on 6 May 42 and spent the rest of the war as a POW.

Wainwright was born 2 Aug 83 in Walla Walla, Wash. His father, USMA 1875 (24/43), died as a cavalry major in 1902 during the Philippine insurrection.

A grandfather was Commandant Jonathan Mayhew Wainwright, USNA Class of 1867 (38/87), which graduated in 1863; he was fatally wounded in action against pirates off the coast of Mexico in 1870. (By 1991 there were 10 other Wainwrights in the USNA *Register* including another Jonathan Mayhew Wainwright, appointed from Maine, in the class of 1959.)

Skinny Wainwright graduated from West Point in 1906 (25/78) as a cavalryman. With the 1st Cav Regt he took part in the Moro Expedition of 1909 in the Philippines and after returning to the States with his regiment was on the Cavalry Rifle Team that competed in the National Matches. In 1918 he was CofS the 82d Inf Div before holding this position in the 3d US Army, rising to lieutenant colonel.

In 1936 he took over the 3d Cav Regt at Ft Myer, Va. Promoted two years later to brigadier general and given a brigade in San Antonio, Texas, he got his second star in Sep 40 and was ordered to the Philippines. After the Japanese landings on 8 Dec 41 (local date) he commanded the North Luzon Force in its withdrawal to Bataan and was awarded the **DSC** (7 Feb 42).

MacArthur left Corregidor on 11 Mar 42 for Australia but it was not until the 19th that Wainwright was promoted to lieutenant general and officially made CG US Army in the Far East. (*AA, 612, 915.*) This was "deconstituted" and superseded by US Forces in the Philippines (USFIP) on 21 Mar 42, when Wainwright established his headquarters in Malinta Tunnel on Corregidor. He left Maj Gen Edward P. King with orders to hold Bataan at all cost, and Wainwright was optimistic about this being possible. But when King began surrendering on 9 Apr 45, without authority, Wainwright proclaimed "Corregidor can and will be held." Less than a month later the Japanese made their first landings on the Rock, and next day, 6 May 45, the American general raised the white flag. He took a launch to meet HOMMA on Bataan and was told three days later, "your high command ceases and you are now a prisoner of war" (*AA, 612*). Wainwright was awarded the Medal of Honor.

He and PERCIVAL were liberated in time to attend the Japanese surrender ceremonies aboard BB *Missouri* (2 Sep 45). Wainwright also attended those in the Philippines at Baguio.

Promoted on 5 Sep 45 to full general he succeeded Patch the following June as CG 4th Army Hq in San Antonio (*AA, 497*). Retiring from active duty on 31 Aug 47 (*AA, 910*) and living in San Antonio he died there on 2 Sep 53.

WAKE-WALKER, William Frederick. British admiral. 1888-1945. Born 24 Mar 88 at Watford, younger son of a solicitor, he left school to become a naval cadet in Jan 03. After the normal service aboard *Britannia* and at sea, he passed first class in all exams at Greenwich and won a prize. He rose rapidly in the Royal Navy and was appointed to the OBE in 1919 for war service. (*DNB.*) He had begun as a torpedo specialist and became an expert in marine mines.

After commanding *Revenge* in the Home Fleet for a year, Wake-Walker was promoted to flag rank on 10 Jan 39, given a senior officer's war course, and he led the 12th Cruiser Sqdn in the Northern Patrol when war broke out. (*DNB.*) At the end of Oct 39 he was assigned to the Admiralty as rear admiral in charge of mine laying. A month later, when German magnetic mines were identified, he became responsible for coordinating countermeasures. The British had developed such a weapon but pigeonholed the plans (personal information) because countermeasures— degaussing—were easy but very expensive. Wake-Walker consequently had conspicuous success in dealing quickly with what could have been a much more serious threat.

On 29 May 40, three days after the Dunkirk evacuation began, Wake-Walker went to the Dover station as "commander of sea-going ships and vessels off the Belgian coast" (quoted in *DNB*). After six days and nights under almost constant attack off the beaches, responsible primarily for the "little ships," the superannuated admiral had a major role in bringing off the "miracle of Dunkirk." For this he was appointed CB.

After commanding the newly formed mine laying squadron from June 40, then Force K (Malta) with flag aboard CV *Formidable,* Wake-Walker took command of the 1st Cruiser Sqdn in Jan 41 . Patrolling the **Denmark Strait** on 23 May 41 he picked up and shadowed the powerful raiders *Bismarck* and *Prinz Eugen* as they steamed south to begin operations against Atlantic convoys. Wake-Walker defied great odds to trail *Bismarck* until the RN closed for the kill. (This is outlined in considerable detail under Guenther LUETJENS, the unfortunate victim.)

Appointed CBE for this action the elderly salt hauled down his flag in Feb 42. Two months later he was promoted to vice admiral and appointed 3d Sea Lord and controller of the RN. His main responsibility was to develop landing craft. Knighted (KCB) in 1943 Sir William was promoted on V-E day (8 May 45) to vice admiral. Broken in health, he died suddenly in London on 24 Sep 45 a few hours after formally accepting the appointment as CinC Mediterranean. (*DNB.*)

WALDHEIM, Kurt. Austrian diplomat and UN secretary general. 1918-. Son of a civil servant, he was a law student when drafted into the German army in 1939. Waldheim was a Wehrmacht interpreter and intelligence officer in Greece and Yugoslavia until discharged in 1943 for wounds. He got his law degree in 1944, entered the diplomatic service a year later, and was UN secretary general 1972-82.

After being research professor of diplomacy at Georgetown Univ in Washington he became president of Austria in 1986. Political enemies contested the election with charges that the internationally known Waldheim had been associated with Nazi atrocities. After first denying all accusations, Waldheim admitted that he had not properly revealed his war record but stoutly denied charges of any war crimes. A court cleared Waldheim of charges relating to his war record but the onus of deception remained on his election.

WALKER, Walton Harris. US general. 1889-1950. Born in Texas, he graduated from West Point in 1912 (73/95). After serving on the Vera Cruz expedition in Mexico (1914) he commanded a machine gun battalion in France, winning two Silver Stars. In 1941 he transferred to the newly established Armored Force and became known for hard and effective tank training (Cole, *Lorraine,* 17). Maj Gen Walker commanded the 3d Armd Div Jan-Aug 42, took over the 4th Armd Corps, and remained when this became the 20th Corps in Oct 43. Walker concurrently headed the Desert Training Center, Nov 42-Mar 43. (*AA,* 506, 509, 575, 604.)

Sent to Normandy with his 20th Corps Hq to be part of Patton's 3d Army, Walker took over the 19th Corps for about two weeks in late June 44 when Charles H. Corlett was sick (Weigley, *ETO,* 130). The 20th Corps became operational in early August, and Walker won the DSC shortly thereafter for his part in the Seine crossings (Cole, 17). Like his idol Patton, the short, chubby, hard-faced Walker was a "blood and guts" commander who appeared unconcerned about taking heavy casualties. Facing determined resistance around historic Metz he sent troops against Ft Driant (or Kronprinz) on 27 Sep 44 without proper military intelligence or air support. He persisted more than two weeks until Patton ordered a halt to the ill advised effort. (Cole, 260 ff.) In another "smash and grab" operation he captured and held the critical Saar River bridge at Saarlautern, giving Patton flank protection on the Moselle for the drive on Frankfort. (Weigley, *ETO,* 398-90.)

Promoted 15 Apr 45, Lt Gen Walker left his corps a few weeks later to command 5th Army Hq in Chicago (*AA,* 497). He remained until sent to Japan as CG 8th Army, succeeding Eichelberger on 3 Sep 48 (*AA,* 500). When **unified commands** were established in Dec 46 Walker headed the US Army element (*AA,* 26). On the outbreak of war in Korea in 1950 he took his 8th Army (which included his old 20th Corps Hq) into combat. S. L. A. Marshall, a close student of the Korean War, called Walker's defense of the Naktong Line "a military classic" (*S&S,* "Walker").

The Pattonesque Walker had his idol's weakness of wanting to be driven at dangerously high speeds (private information). He was killed 23 Dec 50 when his jeep driver lost control on an icy road in Korea. Walker's posthumous promotion to full general was dated 20 Dec 50 (*AA* 2d ed, 330).

WALLACE, Henry Agard. US Vice President. 1888-1965. Born 7 Oct 88 on a farm in Adair Co, Iowa, Wallace graduated from Iowa State College in 1910. He was the third-generation editor of his family's magazine *Wallace's Farmer,* he helped develop several important strains of hybrid corn, and he was a respected agricultural economist. Entering politics in 1932 and helping swing Iowa into the Democratic party, the tall, rustic Wallace became a prominent New Dealer. He was Secretary of Agriculture, 1933-1940, a position his father had held under Warren Harding.

Although considered by many to be an impractical idealist and a political liability, Wallace was Roosevelt's second vice president (1941-45). Duties included being Chairman of the Board of Economic Warfare and of the Supply Priorities and Allocations Board. The latter merged with the new War Production Board in 1942, and Wallace clashed with Jesse Jones, head of Reconstruction Finance Corporation. The VP lost the subsequent political battle and his Board of Economic Warfare was abolished.

Active in foreign affairs, Wallace left Washington on 20 May 44 for a tour of the Far East and the USSR. Reaching Chungking in June, when problems of US cooperation with Chiang Kai-shek were reaching another crisis, the VP was impressed by the CHENNAULT Plan and recommended Stilwell's recall. But his solution was not accepted (Buchanan, 478).

Wallace returned to Washington 10 July 44, only days ahead of Roosevelt's run for a fourth term. The president was personally fond of his VP and did not take a strong position on retaining him on the ticket. But although Wallace led TRUMAN on first ballot he subsequently lost the nomination. In 1945 Truman made Wallace Secretary of Commerce, ousting Wallace's old adversary Jesse Jones. But Wallace was forced to resign in 1946 over opposition to Truman's handling of the Cold War. Wallace was editor of the *New Republic* (1946-48), then he helped launch the new Progressive Party. This drew most of its support from the extreme left, but Wallace did not win a single electoral vote in running against Truman as the party's presidential candidate. He retired to resume his agricultural research.

WALLENBERG, Raoul. 1912-47. Swedish diplomat. Scion of a wealthy Swedish banking family and known to the Budapest business community since 1938, Wallenberg was sent back to the Hungarian capital in 1944 to save Jews from deportation to Auschwitz. The American Jewish Joint Distribution Committee funded the mission, and the Swede was chosen by Iver Iksenby, US representative on the War Refugee Board, and Dr Marcus Ehrenpreis, both located in Stockholm. (Sudoplatov, 268 & n.)

Wallenberg saved thousands of Jews by issuing Swedish passports and having frequent negotiations with German security officials before he had to go underground in Sep 44.

Wallenberg also had frequent dealings with a Soviet agent named Kutusov who reported that the Swede was collaborating with German intelligence. "Thus Wallenberg had left himself open to forced recruitment as our agent: join us or be exposed as a German agent," writes Sudoplatov (ibid).

Not knowing whether he was a guest or a prisoner (ibid), the Swede was taken to Soviet authorities outside Budapest on 12 Jan 45 and three days later was seen leaving Budapest in a car with several others. Wallenberg traveled to Moscow in a luxury railroad car and given the VIP treatment initially.

From the beginning of 1944 the Wallenbergs had had clandestine contacts the Soviet government on making peace with Finland, where the family had important capital investments. "Stalin and Molotov wanted to blackmail the Wallenberg family . . . to use its connections for favorable dealings with the West," writes Sudoplatov. "By early July 1947 Wallenberg's case was stalled," the ex-NKVD officer continues. "Wallenberg had refused to cooperate and he was eliminated, at the same time that the leadership continued to tell the Swedes that they knew nothing of his fate." (Sudoplatov, 265-76.) Soviet documents show that Wallenberg died 17 July 47, probably by lethal injection, in a super-secret cell of the Lubyanka (ibid).

WALLIS, Barnes Neville. British aeronautical engineer. 1887-1979. The inventor of super bombs, which Sir Henry TIZARD called the "finest individual technical achievement of the war" (*DNB*), Wallis was born 26 Sep 87 at Ripley, Derbyshire. He was the second son of a general practitioner who moved to London, where the doctor became so handicapped by poliomyelitis that Mrs Wallis had to struggle and make great sacrifices for a family that included three sons and a daughter. The devoted mother, with whom Wallis remained very close, made her son as a devout Anglo-Catholic for life, inspired him to do well in school, and sacrificed to support him there.

Wallis entered Christ's Hospital school in London at the age of 12 by way of a competitive examination. He excelled particularly in English, mathematics, and science, despite frequent illness and attacks of migraine that would become more debilitating through the years.

Because of his family's straitened conditon he left school at the age of 17 to start making a living as an engineering apprentice. He showed a genius for design in the new field of aviation and was soon doing pioneering work in the geodetic system of aircraft construction. In the 1920s he worked with H. B. Pratt, J. E. Temple, and (Sir) C. Dennistoun Burney on designing commercial dirigibles, culminating with the highly successful R-100. But the strain of four years' work led to a nervous breakdown in 1928. After recovering on Lake Geneva with his wife, Wallis began a long career with Vickers Aviation at Weybridge. There he worked with the chief designer, R. K. Pierson, to develop long-range aircraft. Wallis applied his knowledge of duraluminum construction and basketweave geodetic structure first to developing a biplane fusilage and then a monoplane wing. This provided the great stiffness needed for large fixed-wing monoplanes. The first Pierson-Willis triumph was the single-engine, two-man Wellesley; this was followed by the twin-engine, midwing Wellington bomber. Nearly 12,000 (through Wellington X) were built by 1945. But Wallis continued to use fabric covering, not realizing the structural advantages of metal covering used by Roy Chadwick of Avco, Manchester, for his four-engine Lancaster, which became operational in Mar 42. The most successful of Britain's heavy bombers, the Lancaster far outclassed the Wellington.

Wallis, meanwhile, had become convinced that strategic bombers should concentrate on knocking out German sources of industrial power. To this end he turned his own priorities to inventing a special bomb to breach the great Moehne dam that supplied the Ruhr. He came up with the revolutionary concept of a spherical skip-bomb, secrets of which were not revealed until the 1960s. Wing Comdr Guy GIBSON's "dam busters" in Lancasters flew the dicey mission with complete success on the night of 16-17 May 43.

Wallis went on to produce much bigger deep penetration bombs—"Grand Slam" and "Tall Boy"—for use from high altitude, often with dramatic success as Bomber Command improved its aim, on the launching sites of V-weapons and submarine pens. After the war Wallis went on to ingenious engineering accomplishments in fields as diverse as submarine and bridge design that, while apparently feasible technically, were abandoned for lack of backing. Not formally retiring from Vickers until 1971, at the age of 84, he had been made an almoner at his old school, Christ's Church, in 1945. He established a foundation for educating the children of RAF personnel at Christ's Church, and as school treasurer he raised almost a million pounds. His many honors included election as FRS in 1946, knighthood in 1968, and honorary doctorates from six major British universities. Sir Barnes died 30 Oct 79 in Leatherhead Hospital. (*DNB*.)

WANG CHING-WEI. Chinese turncoat. 1884-1944. The puppet was born in Canton, the son of a scholar. He became one of Dr Sun's principal assistants and a favorite, serving until Sun died in 1925. In the long struggle for succession, Wang lost out to Chiang Kai-shek's right-wing faction but remained high in the government. He was vice president of the Kuomintang when war with Japan began in 1937, and he went to Chungking with Chiang's government. Branded a traitor for insisting that collaboration with Japan was in China's best interest, Wang fled from Chungking, reached Hanoi in 1938, and eventually made his way to the occupied area of China. The only Chinese leader of any stature they had won over, Wang, was installed by the Japanese in Nanking on 30 Mar 40. Hundreds of thousands of Chinese eventually followed him into the enemy camp (White, *Thunder,* 143) but, largely because the Japanese continued to brutalize the countryside, the puppet government in Nanking never gained popular support.

Hirohito broke precedent to give Wang a private audience on 22 Sep 43 to discuss ways of reaching a compromise with Chiang. But the turncoat still could not persuade Chiang to seek peace. (Bergamini, 992.) Already sick when he met with Hirohito, Wang died 14 months later of cancer.

WARBURTON-LEE, Bernard Armitage Warburton (sic). British naval officer. Died 1940. Generalmajor Eduard DIETL, CG 3d Mtn Div, reported at 8:10, 10 Apr 40, that he had taken Narvik, "grand prize of the Norwegian campaign" (Ziemke, *GNT,* 46, 87). Ten German destroyers, three carrying Dietl's main force, were under Commodore Paul Friedrich Bonte.

It was not until late on the preceding day that First Lord of the Admiralty CHURCHILL had authorized subordinates to use their initiative. Capt Warburton-Lee commanding the 2d DD Flotilla (*Hardy, Hunter, Havock, Hotspur,* reinforced by *Hostile*) and located at the entrance to West Fjord, signalled "Going into action" (WC, I, 597).

In the mist and snowstorms of April 10, the five British destroyers steamed [some 30 miles] up the fiord, and at dawn stood off Narvik. Inside the harbour were five enemy destroyers. In the first attack the *Hardy* torpedoed the ship bearing the pennant of the German Commodore, who was killed; another destroyer was sunk by two torpedoes, and the remaining three were so smothered by gun-fire that they could offer no effective resistance. (Ibid., 597-98.)

The mined harbor held 23 merchantmen including five under the British flag. Destroying six German ships in a first attack, and calling up *Hotspur* and *Hostile* from reserve to sink two more with torpedoes, Warburton-Lee was withdrawing after little more than an hour of unopposed action when his luck turned. Two enemy destroyers emerged behind him from Herjangs Fjord but did not close. The British captain was engaging them at 7,000 yards when three other destroyers, which he had passed at anchor in Ballangen Fiord, attacked from the rear. The heavier German guns soon knocked *Hardy* out of action, mortally wounding Warburton-Lee and killing or wounding all his officers but one. Lt Stanning took the wheel and fought until forced to beach. Meanwhile *Hunter* was sunk; *Hotspur* and *Hostile* were damaged; but the Germans were in no condition to pursue. On the way out *Havock* met and destroyed the 8,460-ton transport *Raunfels*, which was carrying most of Dietl's resupply of ammunition. (R&H, *Chron,* 24.) Survivors of *Hardy* reached shore with their commander's body and held out until rescued by a destroyer. German air superiority from land-based planes kept the British from occupying Narvik immediately, the effort having to wait some six weeks for Lord CORK's expedition. Warburton-Lee was awarded the VC posthumously.

WARD, Orlando. US general. 1891-1942. He was born in Missouri on 4 Nov 91 and appointed to West Point from Colorado. Ward graduated in 1914 (86/107) as a cavalryman and served

in Mexico with Pershing's punitive expedition (1916-17). With the 3d Inf Div in France he won a Silver Star (Cullum). Transferring to the artillery, he was on the staff and faculty of the Field Artillery School.

Brig Gen Ward was secretary of the WDGS 3 July 39-30 Aug 41 (*AA,* 54). Promoted 10 Mar 42 and given command of the 1st Armd Div he led it in Algeria and Tunisia. But Ward's relationships with FREDENDALL got increasingly worse. Physically and mentally exhausted after the Kasserine Pass fiasco, 19-20 Feb 43 (*EP,* 969), but still highly regarded by Eisenhower (Ibid.), and awarded the DSC, SS, and PH, he turned over command two months later to Ernie HARMON (*AA,* 573).

Returning to the States he headed the Tank Destroyer Center before being Field Artillery School commandant, 12 Jan-30 Oct 44. (Cullum; *AA,* 366).

Shortly before leaving this position he was given command of the 20th Armd Div in the US and he landed it at Le Havre on 16 Feb 45 (*AA,* 584). Finally attached to Lt Gen Wade H. Haislip's 15th Corps of the 7th Armys at Wurzburg, Germany, on 23 Apr 45, Ward led his division across the Danube on the 28th against sporadic resistance and into Munich on 30 Apr 45. The division was moving toward Salzburg on V-E day.

Maj Gen Ward commanded the 5th Corps from June to 7 Sep 46, the Replacement and School Command for a few weeks, the 6th Inf Div in Korea from Oct 46 to 1 Jan 49. On 1 Apr 49 he replaced Maj Gen Harry J. Maloney as Chief of the Historical Division and took over production of the highly regarded, multi-volume official history, *The United States Army in World War II.* Ward retired in 1953 as a major general and died 5 Feb 72 in Denver, Colo. (*AA,* 506, 524, 604, 736; Cullum.)

WARLIMONT, Walter. German general. 1894-1976. As Jodl's deputy for five years in the OKW operations staff and author of *Inside Hitler's Headquarters, 1939-45,* Warlimont has been called "by far the most vivid personality" in the military triumvirate closest to Hitler. "With the ease and grace of manner of a Rhinelander, he complemented the drab mediocrity of Keitel and the academic reserve of Jodl, [but] his social facility masked an acute and vibrant mind well attuned to the main chance." (W-B, *Nemesis,* 430.)

A dark-haired man of medium height, he was a Catholic, born 3 Oct 94 in Osnabrueck, the son of a publisher of Walloon ancestry. (The family maintained ties in Belgium.) Becoming an artillery cadet and going on to the Danzig MA, he was commissioned in June 14. Warlimont saw action on the western and Italian fronts as a firing battery officer, an adjutant at the battalion, regimental, and brigade level, and as a battery commander. (Warlimont, 582.)

At war's end he joined the Maercker Freikorps as a lieutenant. In 1922 he entered the Reichswehr and was promptly selected for general staff training. Given three months of "language leave" in England in 1926, appointed later that year to the GGGS as a captain, Warlimont was ordered to Berlin as second assistant to the CGS. Soon posted to the defense ministry's economics section, he also served in the foreign armies intelligence section. In May 29 he began a year with the US Army studying industrial mobilization and married an American. Maj Warlimont went to Spain in Sep 36 as military plenipotentiary to Franco. Having been promoted, Lt Col Warlimont returned to Germany in 1937 for troop duty, rising from command of a battalion to be acting head of the 26th Arty Regt at Duesseldorf and being promoted to colonel.

Now 43 years old and highly regarded by Keitel (Hitler's CofS in OKW) Oberst Warlimont was ordered to Berlin in Sep 38 as head the Home (or National) Defense branch. Two months later he succeeded JODL as acting head of the operations office (**Wehrmachtamt**) at a critical period of reorganization. Warlimont drafted the plan creating a single staff to serve one supreme military commander; this became Hitler's **Wehrmacht Leader Staff,** headed by JODL. Somewhat resentful about not getting the top position, Warlimont became Jodl's deputy chief of the operations staff. Serving from Sep 39 to Sep 44 he attended Hitler's major command conferences and drafted most of the principal operational plans and directives. He was promoted to Generalmajor on 1 Aug 40; to Generalleutnant on 1 Apr 42; and to General of Artillery exactly two years later.

Warlimont worked loyally with Jodl but he never was a toady of Hitler's nor was he an anti-Nazi conspirator. (*See* Deutsch, II, 77-79 and notes.) But field commanders held the aloof, scrupulously correct Warlimont in low esteem for his lack of combat experience and apparent disdain for their problems.

The staff planner seemed to have escaped Stauffenberg's 20 July 44 bomb attempt with only minor injuries but within weeks he was found to be suffering from a serious concussion that became disabling. In Sep 44 he was replaced by a Gen Winter, "transferred to the OKH Command Pool" (Warlimont, 583), and not recalled after recovering.

Warlimont was a key witness at Nuremberg before himself being on the dock in the "OKW trial." On 28 Oct 40 he was sentenced to life imprisonment for war crimes and crimes against humanity, charges that Walter Goerlitz finds "hardly comprehensible" (op cit, 168). The sentence was commuted in 1951 to 18 years, and six years later the general was released from Landsberg Prison. He died 9 Oct 76 at Kreuth in Upper Bavaria at the age of 82.

Warlimont's Nuremberg testimony is of great historical value, as is his book *Inside Hitler's Headquarters, 1939-45* (London, Weidenfeld & Nicolson, 1964). Also important is his "Interpretation and Commentary on the Jodl Diaries, 1937-54," which the US National Archives has on microfilm.

WARREN, Earl. US politician and jurist. 1891-1974. The large, affable, controversial Warren was born 19 Mar 91 in Los Angeles, son of a master builder of railroad cars. As California's attorney general 1938-43 he had a leading role in putting Japanese-Americans in concentration camps. He was elected governor in 1942 and 1946, and was viewed as a dark horse Republican presidential possibility in 1944 but refused to be drafted. Four years later he was nominated for VP on the ticket with Thomas E. DEWEY.

Warren was chief justice of the most activist and liberal US Supreme Court in American history, holding office 1953-69. In 1964 he headed the still-disputed inquiry into Pres John F. Kennedy's assassination. Warren died 9 July 74 in Washington, DC.

WATSON, Edwin Martin. Presidential assistant. 1883-1945. "Pa" Watson was born in Alabama, appointed to West Point from Virginia, and graduated in 1908 (99/108). He was an additional ADC to Pres Woodrow Wilson, 1915-17 (*S&S*). As a field artilleryman with the 2d Inf Div in France (having transferred from the infantry) he won two Silver Stars. After being MA in Belgium 1927-31 Watson was Roosevelt's ADC, 1933-39, then his secretary. Known as "Pa" for a benign appearance and manner, he was a major general from 1 Oct 40 and on the retired list from 1944. Watson died at sea on 20 Feb 45 while returning with the president from Yalta.

WATSON-WATT, Robert Alexander. British scientist. 1892-1973. The radio pioneer was a Scot in the family of James Watt (1736-1819), who invented the steam engine. Watson-Watt graduated in 1912 from University College, Dundee, with a BS in engineering. Interested in radio waves, he became the meteorologist at the Royal Aircraft Factory, Farnborough, and worked on locating thunder storms. In the 1930s he came into contact with TIZARD and worked out the theoretical basis for **radar**. In early 1935 Watson-Watt and his assistant, A. F. Wilkins, sent the Tizard committee a proposal titled "The Detection of Aircraft by Radio Methods" that resulted in his directing development of airborne radar sets and radar stations. By the summer of 1940 these formed a system that had a major role in winning the Battle of Britain.

The Scots scientist was director of communications development in the Air Ministry (1938) and Scientific Adviser on Telecommunications in the Ministry of Aircraft Production (1940). His major accomplishments included work on operational research and the Instantaneous Visual Radio Detection Finder (HF/DF, or "Huff-Duff"). CB and FRS in 1941, knighted in 1942, Sir Robert was awarded £52,000 after the war for his work on radar. He set up a consulting firm and remained active. Published works were *Three Steps to Victory* (1957) and *Man's Means to his Ends* (1961). The scientist died 5 Dec 73 at Inverness. (R. V. JONES in *DNB*.)

WAVELL, Archibald Percival. British general. 1883-1950. The son and grandson of generals, Wavell was born at Colchester on 5 May 83, educated at Winchester, and in 1901 he graduated at the top of his class at Sandhurst. Three days after turning 18 he was commissioned in the Black Watch. (Bernard Fergusson in Carver, ed., *The War Lords,* "Wavell.")

By 1908 the young officer had won five decorations in the Boer War and had two citations for service on India's NW frontier. A brilliant scholar, he was first in the entry examination to **Camberley** and one of only two graded "A" on graduation (ibid.). After two years as a language student in Russia he joined the BEF in Nov 14 as brigade major in the 3d Div. Seven months later, at Ypres, he lost his left eye and won the **MC**. After eight months with the Russian army in the Caucasus (to June 17) he was LnO from the CIGS to Sir Edmund Allenby in Palestine. Later he was brigadier general staff of the 20th Corps in Palestine, then he held this post under Allenby when the latter became High Commissioner and CinC in Egypt.

The tough, stocky Lt Gen Wavell (as of 1938) was known for his brilliant mind and contempt for convention. The ideal infantryman, he once said, was a cross between a poacher, a gunman, and a cat-burglar (Bernard Fergusson in *DNB*). Wavell was an odd bird himself, in many respects, one conspicuous trait being his long silences and general inarticulateness.

In July 39 Wavell was given the mission of creating the Middle East Command. With headquarters in Cairo and few troops, none trained or equipped for modern war, he was charged with protecting a vast area that included the vital Suez canal and oil reserves of the Middle East. After war was declared on 3 Sep 39, and particularly after Italy entered the war on 10 June 40, Wavell showed remarkable generalship on separate fronts from East Africa to the Egyptian frontier (western desert) to the Levant and Iraq. Although reinforced by crack troops of the Indian Army and the Dominion, Wavell was outnumbered everywhere. Worse, he had to put up with CHURCHILL's meddling. Their first clash was over British Somaliland, when the PM disapproved Wavell's sound decision to save the valuable garrison by evacuating the protectorate. GODWIN-AUSTEN did this successful, "and relations between . . . Churchill and Wavell were never very happy thereafter," comments Fergusson with monumental understatement *(DNB)*.

In an "elaborate bluff" (ibid.) Wavell detached the crack 4th Indian Div from William PLATT's Sudan Defense Force and used it in stopping GRAZIANI's advance, 13-16 Sep 40. The Western Desert Force under Richard O'CONNER then launched a counteroffensive on 9 Dec 40 that had sensational success. With only 36,000 troops the British virtually annihilated 14 Italian divisions and by 7 Feb 41 cleared all of Cyrenaica. But Churchill then made the unfortunate decision to defend Greece. "A word from him [Wavell] would have erased the enterprise at any of several stages," David Mason points out, "but he never gave it." (*Who's Who*, "Wavell.") Bernard Fergusson, on the other hand, says this:

> In two respects he had been misled: the Greeks had accepted . . . that they would withdraw from their exposed positions to a line on Aliakmon River more in keeping with the weakness of the joint armies; Wavell's intelligence had assured him that the German ground forces in North Africa, whose arrival was known to be imminent, would not be able to take the field until mid-April at the earliest. But the Greeks did not shorten their line; and the Germans appeared in strength on the frontiers of Cyrenaica before the end of March. By that time a high proportion of Wavell's army, and much of the best of it, was irrevocably committed in Greece; and by the middle of April, both Greece and Cyrenaica had been lost, Tobruk was invested, and vast quantities of fighting troops, military technicians, tanks, and material were in enemy hands. *(DNB.)*

Wavell had directed on 2 Dec 40 that the Duke of AOSTA's Italian forces be driven from East Africa and on the 10th he ordered the 4th Indian Div back to the Sudan. From here William PLATT attacked north to join Alan CUNNINGHAM for the conquest of Eritrea and Ethiopia, completed by 27 Nov 41.

ROMMEL meanwhile launched his first offensive, 24 Mar-30 May 41. Wavell's excellent decision to hold the vital port of Tobruk (as recommended by John HARDING) created a **flanking position** that forced Rommel to halt some 50 miles inside Egypt on the Gazala Line. Wavell then launched Opns Brevity and Battleaxe to relieve Tobruk, but by 17 June 41 these had ended in disaster. Churchill by now had a strong aversion to Wavell, although the general's peers, subordinates, and most superiors including the CIGS, Alan Brooke, still held him in high esteem. But the ever-meddling prime minister took military matters in his own hands, and in early June he decided that Wavell would switch posts with Auchinleck, who was CinC in India. The post at this time was a sinecure; Wavell commented that he was expected merely to "hold the baby" while the war was won in Europe.

But on 7 Dec 41, only five months after Wavell's arrival at Delhi, the Japanese attacked in the Pacific and SE Asia. On 28 Dec 41 Wavell was appointed commander in Burma, and a week later he was handed the ABDA Command as Supreme Allied Commander Southwest Pacific but with precious little to command. Japanese forces, superior in numbers, materiel, and leadership, advanced rapidly, and Wavell faced a hopeless situation. But one of his decisive acts was a disaster: wanting time for US air reinforcements to join the ABDA Command Wavell ordered the convoy carrying the well-equipped 18th Div to Singapore rather than to Burma. Consequently the division was lost when PERCIVAL surrendered Singapore on 15 Feb 42. Hostilities in the NEI ended 8 Mar 42, and two months later the Japanese had conquered Burma. (ALEXANDER arrived with time only to extricate what was left of Allied forces in Burma and lead them back to India.)

Wavell was promoted to field marshal in Jan 43 and the following July was raised to the peerage as Viscount Wavell, 1st Earl of Cyrenaica and of Winchester. As the new peer began the daunting task of liberating Burma, one of his first steps was to send for WINGATE. He also tried to reoccupy the coastal region of Arakan, but the operation—directed by SLIM—was a big failure.

Beginning a new phase of his career, Wavell became viceroy of India on 19 June 43, succeeding Linlithgow (Victor Alexander John HOPE). Auchinleck returned as CinC India, and Mountbatten arrived a few months later to direct military operations in the new SE Asia Command (SEAC). Viceroy Wavell then devoted himself to resolving Hindu-Moslem differences as an essential first step toward the long-promised grant of independence to India. Lacking guidance from London the viceroy freed Congress leaders who had been in jail since their rebellion in 1942. The India problem was exacerbated when ATTLEE succeeded Churchill as PM in July 45 and the labor government failed to enunciate a clear policy until Feb 47. At this time Wavell's replacement by MOUNTBATTEN was "simultaneously announced with some abruptness" *(DNB)*. Wavell was made an earl with the additional title "Viscount Keren, of Eritrea and Winchester." (Keren or Cheren is the mountain stronghold in Eritrea captured on 28 Mar 41 by William PLATT's forces.)

Wavell returned to London. Still vigorous, he was active in literary societies and in 1946 he became colonel of the Black Watch. In this capacity he visited its allied regiments in Canada and South Africa. He had been chancellor of Aberdeen Univ since 1945 and had honorary degrees from that school and others including Cambridge, Oxford, and McGill. He became lord lieutenant of the County of London in 1949.

The field marshal died 24 May 50 in London, not long after first showing signs of illness. The host of famous men at his funeral did not include Churchill. Wavell was buried at his old school, Winchester.

Although notoriously inarticulate and uncommunicative in conversation and conference, Wavell produced highly praised books: *The Palestine Campaigns* (1928), *Allenby* (1940), *Generals and Generalship* (1941), *Allenby in Egypt* (1943), an anthology of poetry *Other Men's Flowers* (1944), *Speaking Generally* (1946), and *The Good Soldier* (1947).

WAVERLY, 1st Viscount. *See* John ANDERSON.

WEDEMEYER, Albert Coady. US general. 1897-89. His paternal grandparents settled in Atlanta, Ga, after emigrating from near Hanover, Germany, in 1830. Wedemeyer was born 9 July 96 in Omaha, Neb, and reared there. He graduated from West Point in 1919 (270/285), served in Tiensin, China, with the 15th Inf 1930-32, graduated from the C&GSS, and attended the German War College (*Kriegsakademie*), 1936-38. Tall, suave, able, and ambitious, Maj Wedemeyer was assigned to the War Plans Div, WDGS, in 1941. He worked closely with his father-in-law, Lt Gen Stanley D. Embick, head of the Defense Commission, on preparing what was distributed from his office as the Victory Plan. This revealed the approved US military strategy for the coming war, and only four copies existed.

One fell into the hands of Robert R. McCORMICK's *Chicago Tribune,* whose issue of 5 Dec 41 published the most important parts (Wedemeyer, 15 ff). The newly promoted lieutenant colonel of German ancestry, a recent graduate of the *Kriegsakademie,* was suspected of lax security or outright treason. Extensive FBI investigation never discovering how the plan was leaked, and Wedemeyer survived professionally. In Oct 43, a month after being promot-

ed, Maj Gen Wedemeyer was "eased out to Asia" (Wedemeyer, 249) as Mountbatten's deputy CofS for planning. The new SEAC commander refers to his American subordinate as "a tricky customer but very loyal to me" (Hough, *Mountbatten,* 171).

Wedemeyer succeeded Chennault on 31 Oct 44 as head of US Forces, China Theate, (ia, 613). Chiang Kai-shek had finally gotten rid of the Old China Hands who knew how to cope with his corrupt and ineffective Kuomintang (Burns, *Roosevelt,* 589). Stilwell's recall left his former CBI split into Wedemeyer's China Theater and Daniel I. SULTAN's India-Burma Theater. Wedemeyer was promoted to lieutenant general on 1 Jan 45 and he stayed in China until 1 May 46. He then headed 2d Army Hq (Ft George G. Meade, in Md) 1946-47; the Plans and Operations Div (the Pentagon) 31 Oct 47-15 Nov 48 (*AA,* 60); and 6th Army Hq (at the Presidio of San Francisco) in 1949 (Cullum) before retiring 31 July 51 as a lieutenant general. Promoted 4 Aug 54 to full general, he published *Wedemeyer Reports!* (New York: Holt, 1958) and died 17 Dec 89 at Ft Belvoir, Va.

WEICHS ZUR GLON, Maximilian Maria Joseph von. German general. 1881-1954. Von Weichs was born 12 Nov 81 at Dessau into a devout Catholic family. In 1900 he became an officer cadet in the 2d Bavarian Hv Cav Regt and six years later was its adjutant. A captain by 1914 he fought as a cavalryman and later was a staff officer. Rittmeister Freiherr von Weichs joined the Reichswehr in 1919 and by 1928 was a lieutenant colonel commanding the 18th Cav Regt. Promoted in 1933 Generalmajor von Weichs was associated with Guderian in developing mobile forces and in December of that year he became CG 3d Cav Div at Weimar. The following June he headed a training division set up to give panzer instruction to existing units (Guderian, 35). Continuing to win promotion, Generalleutnant von Weichs headed the 1st Pz Div 1 Oct 35-30 Sep 37 (*B&O,* 68), becoming a General of Cavalry in 1936 (Brett-Smith, 170). He then commanded the 13th Army Corps Hq at Nuremberg with duties that included staging the highly publicized annual Nazi Party rallies.

The tall, lean, rather bald cavalryman, whose horn-rimmed spectacles made him look more like a priest or college professor than one of Germany's best generals, was among the 16 "uncooperative" senior officers Hitler had retired in early 1938 after the FRITSCH affair. Soon recalled, he led a corps into Poland under BLASKOWITZ on 1 Sep 39. A year later he commanded the 2d Army of three corps that RUNDSTEDT used in the Battle of Flanders for flank security and for exploitation in the Battle of France. Promoted 19 July 40 Generaloberst Weichs commanded the ground forces that quickly conquered Yugoslavia. In July 41, after the start of Barbarossa, his 2d Army Hq took over eight divisions in BOCK's AG Center. The new army's first operation was against Brest Litovsk (taken 24 June 41, or D+2) after which it helped mop up pockets bypassed by the panzers. When Hitler diverted the main effort south, Weichs scored a major victory in August 41 near Gomel, taking some 80,000 prisoners. The next month he was on Guderian's west flank for the Kiev encirclement.

The general was on sick leave for two months before resuming command of the 2d Army in mid-Jan 42. Still under Bock, but now in AG South, he had a wide front on the northern flank between Orel and Kursk. By summer he headed "Group von Weichs," comprising his own army, Hoth's 4th Pz Army, and the 2d Hungarian Army. He attacked toward Voronezh on 28 June 42 to start the large-scale offensive toward Stalingrad and the Caucasus.

On 15 July 42 Weichs succeeded BOCK. His AG B had four armies, from north to south the 2d German, 2d Hungarian, 6th German, and 4th Panzer. As the latter two armies closed on Stalingrad, AG B was reinforced by the 8th Italian, and 3d and 4th Romanian Armies. When AG Don was formed on 20 Nov 42 MANSTEIN took over Weichs's 3d and 4th Romanian Armies, the 4th Pz Army, and PAULUS's 6th Army (now trapped in Stalingrad). Some German authorities have argued that Weichs should have protested Hitler's decision that Paulus not attempt a breakout (Brett-Smith, 171).

In the first phase of the Soviet counteroffensive around Stalingrad, 19 Nov 42-1 Jan 43, VATUTIN's SW Front shattered the 8th Italian Army. Then Vatutin was joined by GOLIKOV's Vorozhezh Front (to the north) for the exploitation which drove AG B back on a 200-mile front. AG B was disbanded, its troops assigned to Manstein's new AG South, but Weichs was promoted to field marshal as of 1 Feb 43 and sent to the Balkans. As commander of AG F (some 600,000 guerrilla-beset German, Bulgarian, and other satellite troops) he was known variously as CinC Southeast and CinC Balkans. With headquarters first in Belgrade, and from 5 Oct 44 at Vukovar (83 mi NW), the field marshal was charged with defending Bulgaria, Yugoslavia, Albania, and Greece. Hitler prohibited withdrawal of overextended German forces, and as TOLBUKHIN pushed through Hungary into Austria, AG F was virtually annihilated.

Guderian nominated his old friend to head the "Pomeranian Army" being organized for the last-ditch defense of northern Germany (Guderian, 403). Hitler said the field marshal was too old and tired, but his real objection was that an ardent National Socialist was needed. So Himmler took the command on 24 Jan 45. But Weichs was awarded the Oakleaves and on 22 Mar 45 he joined seven other field marshals in retirement.

Arrested by US authorities but never charged with war crimes, a POW until 1948, he died 27 Sep 54 at Schloss Roeseberg, near Bonn.

WEISS, Pierre (Theodore). French general. 1889-1970. Weiss was born 17 Oct 89 at Nancy. He had university degrees in literature and law, and in 1914-18 was cited for valor, first as a light cavalryman and subsequently as a pilot. Weiss became a pioneering airman who won world records for long-distance flights, one in 1930 from France to India, and another the next year from France to Ethiopia. He conducted aerial surveys of the Sahara and is credited with inventing the technique of aerial refueling. Weiss also was acclaimed as an author of articles and books, many based on his experience as a military aviator.

He was promoted to général de brigade on 2 July 38 and to général de division on 1 Mar 40. Having specialized in military education and training, the general was responsible for military schools in Algiers before taking command of air forces in Tunisia. Weiss being known to advocate Allied intervention in North Africa, the Vichy government ordered him retired on 15 Dec 40. The Free French recalled him to active duty on 22 Oct 43 as military governor of Algiers.

Because of his having a law degree Weiss was public prosecutor when Vichy's former minister of interior, Pierre Picheu, was convicted and executed (de Gaulle, *Unity,* 200-3). In 1944, after the Allied victory in North Africa, Weiss commanded French air forces in Tunisia.

WEISS, Wilhelm. German journalist. 1892-1950. Germany's leading journalist in WWII was a Bavarian born 31 Mar 92 in Stadsteinach. He was a captain in WWI and lost his left leg as a flyer. After editing *Heimatland* and *Voelkische Kurier* he joined the *Voelkische Beobachter* on 1 Jan 27 as Alfred ROSENBERG's assistant and was the actual editor-in-chief for several years before having the title in 1938. Goebbels meanwhile had made Weiss head of the Reich Association of the German Press (*Reichsverband der Deutschen Presse*) in 1934. A quiet, compliant man of only average intelligence (Wistrich), Weiss became increasingly dissatisfied with restrictions imposed by Hitler and Reich Press Chief Otto DIETRICH. Although he did not rigorously enforce the Editor's Law "he never repudiated or distanced himself in any way from the Nazi system" (Wistrich). On 15 July 49 a de-Nazification court sentenced the journalist to three years of incarceration (which he had already served) and to other penalties. Weiss died 24 Feb 50 while his appeal was pending. (Wistrich.)

WEIZSAECKER, Ernst von. German diplomat. 1882-1951. Freiherr von Weizsaecker was born 12 May 82 in Stuttgart. He entered the navy in 1900, saw some action in the first world war but then served on the staff of the naval delegation to the Imperial GHQ. Starting a diplomatic career in the Weimar Republic (1920) he was minister to Norway 1931-33 and to Switzerland 1933-36 before heading the foreign ministry's political department under NEURATH. In Apr 38, when Hitler reshuffled his senior foreign service officers, he replaced Neurath with RIBBENTROP, Von HASSEL with Hans Georg von Mackensen as ambassador to Rome, and Weizsaecker became what a German scholar calls "the new State Secretary of the old school." He confidently expected to channel Hitler's foreign policy into conventional lines, but was quickly excluded from even minor matters. (Bracher, 327-28.) In 1943 he was made ambassador to the Holy See.

Weizsaecker was arrested in June 47, tried in the "Ministries Case" at Nuremberg, sentenced to seven years in prison, but released under amnesty in 1950 and he promptly published his memoirs, *Erinnerungen* (Munich, 1950). The work's many discrepancies of fact are revealed in Lewis Namier's *In the Nazi Era* (London, 1952); the self-serving memoirs are useful only if compared with published official documents (W-B, *Nemesis,* 416n). The diplomat died 4 Aug 51 at Lindau am Bodensee.

WELLES, Sumner. US diplomat. 1892-1961. Born 14 Oct 92 in NYC, he was educated at Groton, graduated from Harvard in 1914, and was on close personal terms with FDR and his family. The tall, austere, homosexual Welles joined the foreign service. Rising to be ambassador to Havana in 1933, he was strongly criticized by Cubans for exerting US pressure but he persisted until a new government was established to exclude Leftists. Welles then figured prominently in the Pan-American Conference of 1936, originating the slogan "good neighbor policy," and the next year he became under secretary of state. Welles controlled all appointments and transfers within the State Department and Foreign Service and he was closely involved in Far Eastern and European affairs.

In the spring of 1940, during the Phony War, FDR sent him to see European heads of state about preserving peace, an experience he related in *The Time for Decision* (New York: Harper 1944). Welles also had an important role in the Rio Conference of Jan 42.

Bringing a long-standing feud between presidential favorites Welles and BULLITT to a head, the latter advised Roosevelt on 23 Apr 41 that keeping the homosexual Welles in public office "was a menace to the country since he was subject to blackmail by foreign powers . . . and a terrible public scandal might arise at any time . . ." (Orville Bullitt, ed, *For the President,* 513). The president replied that he had seen official reports of Welles's criminal sexual offenses but "found it convenient" to do nothing (ibid.) and thought the news media would not make the charges public. A year later, however, FDR turned against BULLITT after becoming convinced that the latter was spreading gossip and leaking official reports. Welles held office for almost another 18 months until the long-time favorite became so blatantly disloyal to both FDR and Cordell HULL that the president finally dismissed him (Hull, 1230). Replaced by Edward R. STETTINIUS, Jr, Welles retired on 30 Sep 43.

WESSEL, Horst. Nazi martyr. 1907-30. Son of a Protestant military chaplain, Horst Wessel was born in Bielfeld, Westphalia, on 9 Sep 07. He quit law school and joined the Nazi Party in 1926. A combination of idealist and criminal, the weak-chinned, pointy-nosed Wessel quickly became an effective Brownshirt leader. There is only circumstantial evidence that he was a pimp, as commonly alleged. But he was living in a Berlin slum with an ex-prostitute, Erna Jaenecke, when her vengeful former protector, one Ali Hoehler, finally tracked them down with the help of their landlady, a Frau Salm. With a communist gang Hoehler burst in on the couple and had a scuffle that left Wessel with a fatal pistol wound in the face. Horst Wessle lingered 40 days until dying on 23 Feb 30.

One of GOEBBELS's first propaganda triumphs was to make Wessel into a martyr, a Nazi idealist murdered by communists. A dirge whose lyrics the renegade had patched together from several sources and called "Raise High the Flag" became the "Horst Wessel Song." Whatever its cultural poverty the song served the Nazis well.

After Hitler came to power in 1933, Rudolf DIELS took Ali Hoehler from jail and murdered him in the Mecklenburg wood (Friedrich, *Deluge*, 317). Erna Jaenecke and Frau Salm had already disappeared.

WESTPHAL, Siegfried. German general. 1902-. The son of a major, Westphal was born in Leipzig. As Rommel's highly regarded operations officer (Ia) Lt Col Westphal loomed large in the North African campaign. In the spring of 1943 he became one of the army's youngest generals when made Kesselring's CofS for the Sicilian and Italian campaigns. In early Sep 44 he succeeded BLUMENTRITT as RUNDSTEDT's CofS in OB West, rising to General of Cavalry. Cool, quick to make decisions, and intolerant of mediocrity, he was known by some as the "Paperwork Pedant," but he earned the highest praise from Rommel, Kesselring, and Rundstedt. Westphal's valuable *Heer in Fesseln* (Army in Fetters) (Bonn, 1950) was translated as *The German Army in the West* (London: Cassell, 1952).

WEYGAND, Maxime. French general. 1867-1965. Successor to Gamelin on 19 May 40 as supreme Allied commander in Flanders and later a candidate to rally French forces in North Africa to the Allies (the post that went to GIRAUD), Weygand was known to his detractors as "the little bastard." This was literally if not figuratively correct: a very small man physically he also was illegitimate. Born 21 Jan 67 in Brussels, Weygand is widely believed to have been the woods colt of King Leopold II of the Belgians (he of the infamy in the Congo) and a German from the Saar. Paternity also has been ascribed to Austrian Emperor Maximillian of Mexico (1864-67) by a Mexican mistress. Yet another of many suppositions is that the general was the son of a Belgian industrialist by a Polish woman.

Weygand was reared on the Belgian estate of the childless Empress Charlotte and educated at the prestigious Lycée Louis le Grand in Paris before attending St Cyr, 1886-88. He acquired French citizenship to improve his career prospects. The small, jaunty cavalryman had his only taste of combat as a lieutenant colonel of the 5th Hussars in the battle of Morhange, 18-23 Aug 14. Five days later (Larousse) Marshal Ferdinand Foch selected the colonel, more or less at random (Horne, *1940*, 480), to be his CofS. Promotion to brigadier general came in 1916, and to lieutenant general by 1918. When Poland's Marshal Jozef Pilduski desperately appealed for French support in July 20 he asked for Foch but got Weygand. With a mission of 600 French officers Weygand defeated poorly handled Bolshevik forces at the gates of Warsaw on 16-24 Aug 20.

Leaving Foch's side in 1923 to be high commissioner in Syria, Weygand was the French army's CGS in 1930. Replaced by GAMELIN he then headed the French Army 1931-35 as vice president of the Higher Council of War and CinC designate in case of war. Alert to the dangers of Hitlerism, the general denounced French defeatism, opposed the vociferous advocates of curtailing military service, and was a leading critic of Léon BLUM's popular front government. Initially he opposed signing a military accord with the Soviets but reversed his position in 1934 after receiving a laudatory report on the Red Army by Col de LATTRE DE TASSIGNY. As a belated nod to the future of mechanized warfare he ordered the formation of an armored division.

Weygand was retired on 21 Jan 35, having reaching the mandatory age limit of 68, and he was named administrator of the Suez Canal company. Although prominent in right-wing, royalist, and clerical activities, Weygand refused ministerial posts that could have led to his becoming head of state (Larousse). Instead, he pursued an already-distinguished literary career for which the French Academy had elected him to take Marshal Joffre's chair in 1931.

World War II

Gamelin recalled him in Aug 39 to head the Eastern Mediterranean Theater of Operations. Taking his post in Beirut on 31 Aug 39, hours before Hitler invaded Poland, Weygand made grandiose plans for an Allied second front in the Balkans that featured bridgeheads at Salonika and Constantsa. He also conceived, at Daladier's behest, a far-out plan to cripple the German war effort by bombing the Soviet oil centers of Baku and Batum! (Larousse.)

Looking like a well preserved old gentleman jockey the vigorous 73-year-old Weygand returned to France on 17 May 40. REYNAUD had summoned him secretly to be on hand to succeed GAMELIN as Allied commander in chief. During the change of command ceremony on 19 May the new generalissimo implied he would perform another Miracle of the Marne: "I have the secrets of Marshal Foch!" he boasted.

Exhausted Allied troops, many of them disorganized and demoralized in their ninth day of the blitzkrieg, were retreating on a broad front. Relentless air attack had destroyed almost all communications, so Weygand had only a hazy picture of the extremely fluid strategic situation. It was known that the German spearhead was nearing the English Channel in a "panzer corridor" that split the Allies in Flanders from French forces to the south. Cut off in the north were the hard-pressed Belgian Army under King Leopold III and two remaining elements of Gaston Billotte's 1st French AG (comprising Lord Gort's BEF and Georges Blanchard's 1st French Army).

The newly anointed generalissimo promptly went to visit senior commanders in the northern pocket, reaching historic Ypres, Belgium, at 3 PM on 21 May. No others having arrived, Weygand talked first to Leopold in a series of conferences over the next four hours in the town hall. (Three Belgian ministers were on hand, having learned only by chance of the meeting, but the king refused to let them join the discussion.)

The Weygand Plan

Weygand said he wanted Belgian forces withdrawn from the Escaut (Scheldt) to defend along the Iser River. This would abandon more Belgian territory but shorten and secure the strategic left flank so the BEF could counterattack. The King of the Belgians, understandably unenthusiastic and giving his putative nephew the impression he considered the situation hopeless, promised to think it over.

Billotte finally arrived and was briefed on what was shaping up as the "Weygand plan." In broadest terms, the first phase called for Billotte to counterattack south from around Cambrai with the BEF and several of Blanchard's divisions to link up around Bapaume with another thrust coming north from the Somme. "If Blanchard and Gort had been at the Ypres meeting," writes an authority, it seems improbable that Weygand could have returned to Paris harbouring any serious belief that the northern armies could ever attack concertedly on anything like the scale that he would be promising in front of Reynaud and Churchill twenty-four hours later." (Horne, *1940*, 512.)

Weygand steadfastly believed that Gort had avoided the meeting at Ypres because the British commander had decided unilaterally to save the BEF. Billotte waited in Ypres to brief Gort, who arrived about an hour after Weygand's departure, then left to see Blanchard, who unaccountably had not been summoned to Ypres. BILLOTTE had a fatal car accident while en route to tell Blanchard about his role in the Weygand plan.

On 26 May 40 the Allied generalissimo ordered all cut-off forces in the north to retreat toward the port of Dunkirk, having directed Adm ABRIAL three days earlier to organize a bridgehead that was to be held at all cost. The British decided on that same day to undertake the **Dunkirk evacuation,** but Weygand only belatedly informed his admiral.

Weygand regrouped south of the Somme and the Aisne, as planned, a not insignificant accomplishment. French defenses held fast on 5 and 6 June before the Wehrmacht broke through and began a massive exploitation to the south. Weygand now began to show less concern about his hopeless task than about preserving French honor (hence his own).

Armistice

On 13 June he recommended seeking an armistice, and two days later he categorically opposed the alternative of capitulation. France's greatest danger after a humiliating military defeat was civil war, Weygand and many including Pétain believed quite correctly, and it was essential to preserve at least a token military force for maintaining order. Other considerations were that *capitulation* would have made all surviving forces POWs, and Reynaud could move the government, many troops, the fleet, and much of the air force to continue the war from North Africa and France's many other overseas bases.

PETAIN replaced REYNAUD in Bordeaux on 17 June 44 as head of government, and the armistice was signed five days later. Briefly Vichy minister of defense, 16 June-6 Sep 40, Weygand organized the armistice army but clashed with the pro-German LAVAL and was named on 6 Sep 40 to replace ABRIAL in Algiers. Taking his post in October after recovering from an air accident, he held a specially created position: delegate general and commander in chief of land and air forces in the African colonies. The proconsul interpreted the armistice terms narrowly in reorganizing and rearming the formidable 120,000-man Army of Africa. The Weygand-Murphy agreement of 26 Feb 41 authorized aid shipments to the people of North Africa, an arrangement that slipped in 20 US observers to counterbalance 20 Germans of the armistice commission.

American and British journalists, whose speculations perhaps were inspired by Gaullists to have the general sacked (Murphy, 78), fueled suspicions that Weygand was plotting an uprising. The Germans pressured Vichy into recalling the general on 18 Nov 41. He was succeeded by Adm Raymond Fénard, whose authority was reduced to that of delegate general with Weygand's former military authority. Taking over his predecessor's quarters, the admiral became DARLAN's secret link with Robert MURPHY.

Weygand was retired and forbidden to revisit North Africa (Larousse). He resided in his villa near Antibes, where US agents sounded him out in Jan 42 about joining the Allied cause and where GIRAUD did likewise the next summer. Weygand declined on ethical grounds (Larousse). When the Allies landed in North Africa (8 Nov 42) Pétain called Weygand to Vichy for advice. The general recommended resuming the war with Germany. Three days later he joined AUPHAN in urging Pétain to protest Germany's taking over the unoccupied zone. SS troops arrested the general on 12 Nov 42 at St Pourcian-sur-Sioule (28 km NNW of Vichy) as he headed for cover in Guéret. As for GIRAUD, from 5 Dec 43 he was interned first at a castle in Mecklenburg then at Itter, in the Tyrol. He was liberated on 5 May 45, arrested five days later, but hospitalized in the Val de Grâce. As a witness at PETAIN's trial he accused Reynaud of showing weakness (*défaillance*) in 1940. Himself charged before the High Court of Justice with "acting against internal state security" (as part of the Vichy government). But for steadfastly refusing to collaborate militarily he was granted leniency and released on 9 May 46. All charges were dropped two years later and all his rights and privileges restored.

Although many of his books including *Histoire de l'Armée Française* (1938) are highly regarded, Weygand's three volumes of autobiography—the best known of them translated as *Recalled to Service* (1947)—have little historical value. Weygand died in Paris in 1965 at the age of 98.

WHEELER, Raymond Albert "Spec." US general. 1885-1974. Born in Illinois on 31 Jul 85, he graduated near the top of his West Point class in 1911 (5/82). "Spec" Wheeler, his nickname being cadet slang for "brilliant," saw action with the AEF as a combat engineer in France and rose to be a colonel in the 4th Inf Div (SS, DSM). Between the wars he directed large-scale construction projects, highways and railroads. Col Wheeler headed the Persian Gulf Mission when it was set up in 1941 to supply the USSR after the Germans cut off normal routes from the west. After America entered the war BG Wheeler was ordered on 27 Feb 42 to command the **SOS** in CBI but he remained chief of the Iranian mission until 3 Apr 42 (*OCMH Chron,* 26, 31). From headquarters at Delhi, India, Wheeler expedited materiel to Stilwell in Burma, and in Nov 42 he surveyed the Chinese supply situation in preparation for an offensive the following spring (ibid., 64). From the end of 1942 he directed constructing of the **Ledo road** and of airfields in **Assam.** Maj Gen Wheeler headed US Army Forces, CBI, 24 Apr-8 June 43 when STILWELL was absent (*AA,* 613). Wheeler was MOUNTBATTEN's Allied Principal Administrative Officer from 15 Nov 43 in SEAC Hq (Hough, 171), being promoted to lieutenant general on 21 Feb 44 (*AA*, 911). Wheeler replaced STILWELL on 12 Nov 44 as Mountbatten's deputy (*OCHM Chron*, 306, 324). Lt Gen Wheeler succeeded SULTAN as CG USF India-Burma Theater 23 June-29 Sep 45 (*AA*, 612).

After the war he was Chief of Engineers 1 Oct 45-28 Feb 49 (*AA*, 98). Retiring 28 Feb 49 Lt Gen Wheeler was Engineering Advisor to the International Bank for Reconstruction and Development from that year to 1964. After the Suez crisis of 1956 he astonished the engineering world by reopening the Suez Canal in record time. Spec Wheeler died 8 Feb 74 at Walter Reed AMC.

WHEELER-BENNETT, John Wheeler. British historian. 1902-75. An outstanding authority on Germany, Wheeler-Bennett was born 13 Oct 02 at Kenston, in Kent. His father, Wheeler Wheeler-Bennett was a wealthy merchant in London; his mother, Christina Hill McNutt, was Canadian. (A. J. Nicholls in *DNB*.) It has been rumored even in scholarly circles that Wheeler-Bennett was Kaiser Wilhelm's illegitimate son (personal information). "He had a remarkable facial resemblance to the Kaiser and would often joke about it," writes Nicholls.

In Apr 16, while attending school in Westgate, he was shell shocked in an air raid and developed a severe stammer. This was not cured for 15 years, one of his doctors being the one who treated George VI. (Ibid.) But poor health, a problem through life, kept him from going on from Malvern College to Oxford. Wheeler-Bennett became the unpaid personal assistant to Gen Neill Malcolm, who had headed the military mission in Berlin immediately after the armistice of 1918 and who encouraged the young man to study foreign affairs, particularly the situation in Germany. After a stint in the publicity department of the League of Nations Union (1923-24) he established an information service on international affairs and published or edited several periodicals in this field. On Malcolm's advice he went to live in Germany in 1929 to study the increasingly political situation.

This led to Wheeler-Bennett's becoming an outstanding authority on Germany with much of his information and insights coming from inside sources. Heinrich BRUENING was a particu-

larly close associate and friend. The Englishman had been called from Berlin to meet Malcolm in Switzerland when the ROEHM purge started on 30 June 34. Learning that his rooms in the Kaiserhof had been ransacked, and assuming he was on the Nazi hit list, Wheeler-Bennett did not return to Germany. But on several occasions he was an unofficial link between high German officials (excepting Nazis) and the British foreign office. Physically unfit for military service, Wheeler-Bennett was in Washington from 1939 as a personal assistant to the British ambassador (Philip Henry KERR, then Lord HALIFAX from 24 Jan 41).

The emissary traveled widely in America to present the British viewpoint, he helped establish the British Information Services in New York, and he was with the Political Warfare Mission in Washington. In May 44 Wheeler-Bennett joined the Political Intelligence Department in London, rising to be assistant director-general. Having been away from German since 1934 he returned after the war as an adviser to British prosecutors at Nuremberg and as editor of captured German foreign office archives.

In 1945 he married Ruth Harrison, a Virginian, and established a home at Garsington Manor, near Oxford. He taught there at New College but also at the Universities of Virginia, New York, and Arizona. Of his many historical works written after leaving Germany in 1934 the greatest (oft cited cited in this biographical dictionary) is *The Nemesis of Power: The German Army in Politics, 1918-1945* (1953). Also pertaining to Hitler's War is *Munich: Prologue to Tragedy* (1948). He wrote the official biography of King George VI (1958). Autobiographical books are *Knaves, Fools and Heroes* (1974), *Special Relationships* (1975), and *Friends, Enemies, and Sovereigns* (1976).

Knighted in 1959 (KCVO) and elevated in that order in 1974 (GCVO) Sir John died 9 Dec 75 in a London hospital.

WHITE RABBIT. *See* YEO-THOMAS

WHITEHEAD, Ennis C. US general. 1895-1964. In the summer of 1942 Col Whitehead became deputy commander of KENNEY's 5th AF in MacArthur's SWPA. He was a major general from Mar 43 and Kenney's successor as 5th AF commander, 15 June 44-29 Dec 45, getting his third star on 5 June 45. (*AA*, 594, 991.) After the war Lt Gen Whitehead headed the Far East AF with headquarters in Tokyo.

WIART, Carton de. See CARTON DE WIART.

WIESENTHAL, Simon. Nazi hunter. 1908-. Born in Buczacz, Poland, trained as an architect, he spent three years in German concentration camps. (Briggs, ed.) Wiesenthal helped US authorities gather evidence for the Nuremberg trials. He established the Documentation Center on the Fate of the Jews and their Persecutors in Linz, Austria, in 1947. Devoting his life to hounding Nazi war criminals he also used his records to help holocaust survivors and worked with Israeli agents when the center closed in 1954. He opened the Jewish Documentation Center in Vienna in 1961 and published books including *I Hunted Eichmann* (1961), *The Murderers among Us* (1967), and *Every Day Remembrance Day* (1986).

WILHELM. German royal family. Kaiser Wilhelm II (1859-1941) fled to Holland on 10 Nov 18, ending the Hohenzollern dynasty in Germany. Two sons and a grandson figured in Hitler's Third Reich.

Crown Prince Frederick Wilhelm von Hohenzollern, "Little Willie," 1882-1951, the kaiser's eldest son, entered cadet school in 1900 and commanded the 5th Army in 1914. The next year he was titular head of the army group that failed in the campaign of attrition around Verdun. Little Willie followed his father into exile in the Netherlands after the armistice of 11 Nov 18 and on 1 Dec 18 renounced his succession rights. In Nov 23 Chancellor Gustav Stresemann invited the crown prince back to Germany with the condition that he stay out of politics. But in 1932 the crown prince urged Berliners to vote for Hitler, and the next year he joined the Nazi motorized corps (NSKK). Although he twice announced unconditional fealty to the fuehrer and wore the Nazi badge ostentatiously Hitler wanted no part of the Hohenzollern dynasty and Little Willie lacked the qualities to have any active role in the Third Reich. He died in Hechingen on 20 July 51, the seventh anniversary of STAUFFENBERG's failed bomb attempt on Hitler's life.

Little Willie's eldest son, Prince Louis Ferdinand Wilhelm (1906-40), who had spent five years in a Ford factory, died of battle wounds in France on 26 May 40 (Shirer, *Reich,* 907n).

August Wilhelm (1887-1947), known as "Auwi," was the kaiser's fourth of six sons. He rose to the rank of colonel in WWI, then was a bank clerk and automobile company employee, and in 1930 he joined the Nazi Party. Although ardently pro-Hitler, Gruppenfuehrer August Wilhelm was arrested during the **Blood Purge** of 30 June 34. Goering asked his old friend Auwi what he and SA Group Leader Karl Ernst had discussed in a recent phone conversation, which the SD had recorded. When the puzzled prince replied that Ernst was merely saying Aufwiedersehen before taking a trip abroad, Goering said he was glad Auwi had decided to spend a few days in Switzerland, and added, as the prince looked bewildered, "Have I not told you that you have the dumbest face in the world?" (Frischauer, 106, citing Heiden's original 1936 edition of *Der Fuehrer* [1944.]

Anti-Nazi conspirators ruled out Auwi as a candidate for restoration to the throne, picking instead Wilhelm II's youngest surviving son, Prince Oskar of Prussia (Shirer, *Ibid.,* 907n). A German de-Nazification court sentenced Prince Auwi in May 48 to two and a half years in prison. Having already served this time in pre-trial confinement he was released, dying a few months later, on 25 Mar 49 in Stuttgart.

WILHELMINA, Queen of the Netherlands. 1880-1962. She took the throne in 1898 and became highly popular. When her country was overrun quickly in May 40 she fled to London with her government. Returning home after the war she formally abdicated on the 50th anniversary of her reign, in 1948, in favor of daughter Juliana.

WILKES, John. US admiral. 1895-1957. Born in Charlotte, NC, on 26 May 95, he was the great-grandson of the Antarctic explorer and Civil War hero Commodore Charles Wilkes (1798-1877). After serving aboard a surface ship in WWI John Wilkes commanded submarines 1919-33 and was navigating officer of *Indianapolis* 1935-37. When Adm Thomas C. HART took over the Asiatic Fleet in Oct 39 Capt Wilkes moved his Sub Div 14 to Manila from San Diego and Pearl Harbor. He organized the first seven new P-class boats and six ancient S-boats as Sub Sqdn 5. "This . . . was—potentially—the most lethal arm of the insignificant Asiatic Fleet at this time" (Blair, *Silent Victory,* 77).

But the potential far exceeded the reality, due primarily to defective torpedoes. (Guenther PRIEN and other U-boat skippers also had this problem.) After the initial Japanese landings Capt Wilkes operated from Manila. He was designated Comsubs Asiatic Fleet on 8 Dec 41 when Hart took most of his Asiatic Fleet southward, leaving Wilkes with 29 boats and the inshore patrol (Morison, III, 193). This was soon withdrawn also, Wilkes reaching Surabaya in SS *Swordfish* on 7 Jan 42 to establish a new base and undertake the unconventional mission of resupplying Corregidor and evacuating personnel. After runs by *Seawolf, Seadragon,* and *Sargo* it was the turn of *Swordfish.* She lay on the bottom off Corregidor all day (20 Feb 42) and surfaced at sunset to pick up 10 people in Pres QUEZON's party (including VP OSMENA). Landing them on Panay the sub went back for another group including US High Commissioner Francis B. Sayre and members of his family and staff. On 3 Feb 42 SS *Trout* delivered ammunition to Corregidor and returned with gold the Japanese could have used in neutral countries. (Blair, ibid., 172-75; Morison, III, 203.)

Wilkes moved his base to Freemantle on 1 March and was designated Comsubs SW. Replaced 26 May 42 by Charles A. LOCKWOOD, Jr, and awarded the DSM, he left the Pacific to be skipper of the new CL *Birmingham.* After supporting the landing in Sicily (10 July 43) he left the next month to begin training a 4,000-unit landing craft force for D day in Normandy. From 26 June 44 (D+20) he was Comdr US Ports and Bases, France, being promoted to rear admiral.

He had the administrative command of Amphibious Forces Pacific Fleet from May 45 to Dec 45. When the planned invasion of Japan was called off he again crossed the world to be Comsubs Atlantic Fleet and became Commander Naval Forces Germany in 1948. He retired from this post on 30 June 51 as a vice admiral and died 20 July 57 at the Bethesda USNH in Maryland.

WILKINSON, Theodore Stark. US admiral. 1888-1946. "Ping" Wilkinson was born at Annapolis on 22 Dec 88. He graduated first in his 174-man USNA Class of 1909 and won the Medal of Honor at Vera Cruz in 1914 for leading a landing party. During WWI he served in the Bureau of Ordnance and thereafter had normal staff and command duties leading to flag rank.

He became Director of Naval Intelligence (DNI) on 15 Oct 41. It was a bad time to be thrown into that job, but Rear Adm Wilkinson's career survived the Pearl Harbor disaster that occurred just three weeks later. His office was responsible only for gathering information, which it had done well. Evaluation (which turns *information* into *intelligence*) and dissemination were the responsibility of Adm R. K. TURNE. (Morison, III, 134.)

Wilkinson was DNI until Jan 43, when he became HALSEY's deputy in the South Pacific Area, and on 15 July 43 he took over the 3d Amphibious Force from R. K. TURNER. Proving to be a brilliant planner and commander "Ping" Wilkinson showed rarer qualities: consideration toward subordinates, amiability with peers, and a talent for being cooperative with superiors, notably MacArthur. (Morison, VI, 14-15.) He planned and executed the leapfrog operations that took Cape Torokina, Green Islands, North Georgia, Vella Lavella, Treasury Island, and Bougainville. Rear Adm Wilkinson then planned the Palau Island landings and was promoted before starting to execute them on 15 Sep 44.

Vice Adm Wilkinson led 3d Amphibfor on to Leyte and Lingayen Gulf, leaving Kinkaid's 7th Fleet on 18 Jan 45 to start planning the Kyushu landings (which were called off).

Shortly after being assigned to the JCS Strategy Committee the admiral was drowned on 21 Feb 46 when his car was driven off the ferry at Norfolk, Va.

WILLKIE, Wendell Lewis. US industrialist. 1892-1944. The large, exuberant, unassuming Willkie, born 18 Feb 92 at Elwood, Ind, and a highly successful corporation lawyer, was a major figure in WWII without ever holding public office or controlling a political machine. Opposing the New Deal but supporting FDR's foreign policy the dark horse challenger and overnight political phenomenon got 22 million popular votes to FDR's 27 million but lost 82 to 449 in the electoral college.

The midwesterner then undertook far-ranging trips abroad as one of FDR's personal representatives. Sent to China as the Japanese were overrunning Burma he impressed Mme Chiang Kaishek as being "very charming" but "an adolescent" (Burns, *Roosevelt*, 377). Old China Hand Barbara Tuchman comments that Willkie's "impressions were notable for his capacity to accept what he was told or shown [by the Chinese] at face value. He was to pass them on to the American public in ten newspaper installments and a book . . ." (Tuchman, *Stilwell*, 333). His *One World* (1943) was probably the most influential book published during the war; it was followed by *An American Program* (1944). His untimely death came on 8 Oct 44.

WILSON, Henry Maitland. British general. 1881-1964. The elephantine, good-natured "Jumbo" Wilson held high commands in the Middle East and Mediterranean throughout the war. "His military reputation was one of the few which escaped Churchill's criticism," writes Tunney.

Wilson was born 5 Sep 81 into a Suffolk family of impressive military ancestry including Lords Ragland and Cardigan of the Crimean War. Wilson got the nickname Jumbo at Eton. He was a veteran of the Boer War and WWI and was the first to command a completely mechanized British formation. From 1939 Lt Gen Wilson headed the British Army of the Nile with headquarters in Cairo. In 1940 he planned the strategy that kept GRAZIANI's huge army off balance, sending R. N. O'CONNOR in early June to command the Western Desert Force. Wilson then collaborated with WAVELL in the counteroffensive of 9 Dec 40-7 Feb 41 and he became military governor of Cyrenaica.

When the British sent an expeditionary force of their best troops, fully equipped at the expense of other units in the Middle East (WC, III, 220), Jumbo Wilson assumed command on Mar 41 of Greek and British Imperial units on the Aliakhmon line in Greece. It was a forlorn hope, but Wilson conducted a masterful delaying action.

Later in 1941 he headed British forces in Palestine, Transjordan, and Syria. After suppressing the revolt in Iraq, Wilson led a campaign to bring Syria into the Allied camp. Jumping off from northern Palestine and Trans-Jordan the night of 7-8 June 42 and moving north against the Vichy French forces of Fernand Dentz, he commanded the 7th Australian Div, 4th Indian Bde, and LEGENTILHOMME's recently formed 1st Free French Div. Over-coming superior combat power, Wilson linked up with British units from Iraq, and on 11 July he concluded an armistice that gave the Allies control of Syria and Lebanon.

Wilson then was CinC Persia-Iraq Command and GOC 9th Army. When Churchill undertook in Aug 42 to replace AUCHINLECK as CG 8th Army he thought Wilson and GOTT were the best candidates to succeed the "the Auk." But CIGS Alan BROOKE had been led to believe that Jumbo was too old and tired, so the job went to MONTGOMERY. "Luckily I discovered my mistake in time," wrote Brooke, "and made full use of him during the remainder of the war." (Bryant, *Tide*, 358.)

Succeeding ALEXANDER in Feb 43 as CinC Middle East, Wilson was responsible inter-alia of for sending missions to MIHAILOVIC and TITO in Yugoslavia. On 8 Jan 44 Wilson replaced EISENHOWER as commander of Allied forces in the Mediterranean with the title Supreme Allied Commander, Mediterranean Theater (SACMED). Promoted at this time to field marshal, Wilson had administrative responsibility for broad questions of policy and strategy, and for maintaining good relations between US and British forces. ALEXANDER directed the war in Italy, but SACMED planned the landings in Southern France.

On 16 Dec 44 he turned over command to Alexander and succeeded the late Sir John DILL as Head of the British Joint Staff Mission in the US, remaining in Washington until 23 Apr 47.

The field marshal was elevated to the peerage in 1946 as the 1st Baron Wilson of Libya and Stowlandtoft. He became Constable of the Tower of London 1955-60 and made his last public appearance on St Andrew's Day 1964. Suddenly taken ill at his retirement home in the Chilterns (Aylesbury), he died 31 Dec 64. *(DNB.)*

WINANT, John Gilbert. US ambassador. 1889-1947. Born 23 Feb 89 in NYC of wealthy parents he was educated at St Paul's School in Concord, NH, and Princeton. Graduating in 1912 the tall, dark, slender, quiet, and Lincoln-esque Winant *(CB 41)* was a teacher and assistant rector at St Paul's before serving as a military aviator in France. Turning to politics and first elected governor of NH in 1925, the year he was awarded an MA in government studies from Princeton, he was state governor again in 1931-34. As a Liberal Republican he was director of the International Labor Organization in Geneva, 1939-41, and on 6 Feb 41 he was named to succeed Joseph P. KENNEDY as ambassador to London. In late 1943 he was appointed US representative on the European Advisory Commission, and George F. KENNAN became his adviser. "A man of quiet personal charm" (*S&S*), popular and highly effective throughout the war and well into Truman's administration, he committed suicide in 1947.

WINDSOR, Edward, Duke of. Ex-King Edward VIII. 1894-1972. Edward Albert Christian George Andrew Patrick, later Duke of Windsor, was born 23 June 94 at White Lodge, Richmond Park (a royal residence 10 miles WSW of London). Though Edward was the name he signed officially, he was David to family and close friends. (Bryan and Murphy, cited hereafter B&M, *The Windsor Story*, 57.) Edward attended the RN Colleges at Cranston and Dartmouth (1907-11). His father becoming King George V in 1910, Edward was created Prince of Wales that year on his 16th birthday. The heir apparent left Oxford in 1914 at the end of his second year and was commissioned in the Grenadier Guards. Although not a "parapet popper" who went over the top as a troop leader, the prince avoided rear-area assignments and spent most of the Great War at the front. "No one begrudged him his Military Cross, his Croix de Guerre, and his other decorations and citations. . . ." (Ibid.)

Edward was known internationally between the wars for extensive "Empire tours," accompanied much of the time by his second cousin and close friend Louis MOUNTBATTEN. Handsome and personable although a not-so-bright playboy, he developed an aversion to restrictions of his royal legacy, becoming pro-American and pro-German (B&M, 107, 171-72). He and his like-minded friend Sir Oswald MOSLEY (1896-1980) were "outraged by the 'old men' in power" and believed "'something must be done' to cure their country's ills but did not themselves accomplish very much" (David Cannadine, *The New Yorker*, 5 Aug 91, page 9)

The Prince of Wales met Wallis Warfield Simpson in 1930. She was an American of impecunious but genteel origins (distantly related to the royal family), born 19 June 96 in Baltimore. A *belle laide*, vampish, quick-witted, and hotheaded, Wallis had married Lt Earl Winfield Spencer, USN, in 1916 and quickly found herself the victim of a drunkard and wife abuser. After a long separation, and several indiscreet liaisons, Wallis got a divorce in 1927 and the next year was happily married to an American-born London businessman, Ernest Aldrich Simpson.

Six years after meeting "Wallie" the Prince of Wales succeeded George V as Edward VIII (20 Jan 36). Madly in love for the first and only time, and not keen about being king, his new role, Edward undertook to have Mrs Simpson accepted as his morganatic queen. The royal family had long disapproved of the liaison but now the public, with whom Edward had been very popular (*DNB*) was outraged. Despite CHURCHILL's heroic efforts the abdication crisis ended with Edward's giving up the throne on 11 Dec 36. Succeeded by his brother GEORGE VI, whose first act was to confer the title of Duke of Windsor on Edward, he married Wallis Simpson in Paris on 3 June 37. This was less than a week after her second divorce was final, and she became Duchess of Windsor. But Wallis was prohibited from sharing her husband's royal rank. She was addressed as "Your Grace," not Your Royal Highness (like her husband), and was not entitled to a curtsey (as he was to a bow). The duchess legally changed her name to Wallis Warfield, so she is properly indexed as "Windsor, Wallis Warfield" (*CE*).

Although the duke considered Paris a "ghastly place" (B&M, 488), not speaking French well, not enjoying night clubs, and having few British friends to talk with, the French exempted him from taxes (ibid.). Among several properties the Windsors had a *hôtel particulier* at 24 Blvd Suchet in Paris and the Château de la Croë at Cap d'Antibes on the Riviera. On the pretext of studying "labor conditions" in a country where labor unions had been smashed, the duke made a two-week visit to Germany in Oct 37 with Wallis as guests of the Nazi government. Although escorted by the uncouth Dr Robert LEY rather than by one of the industrialists they would have preferred, the Windsors were given red carpet treatment. Interpreter Paul SCHMIDT wrote in his diary that he saw "nothing whatever to indicate whether the

Duke really sympathized with the ideology and practices of the Third Reich, as Hitler seemed to assume he did" (B&M, 391).

When Britain went to war on 3 Sep 39, Windsor volunteered his services again. He finally was made a major general and LnO with the "Number 1 Military Mission from the War Office" to GAMELIN's GHQ at Vincennes. His duties during the **Phony War** were negligible, and after the Germans invaded France the duke concentrated on getting himself and the duchess off the Continent. Making his way to Lisbon, and again applying for an assignment, Windsor was disappointed to learn he was to be Governor General of the Bahamas.

The Germans contrived an elaborate scheme to capitalize on the duke's displeasure. There were rumors that he was about to break politically with his government. Inspired probably by Schellenberg's triumph in the **Venlo Incident** and the trick proposed perhaps by Ribbentrop (Kahn, *Hitler's Spies,* 259), the Germans planned to lure the duke and duchess close enough to the frontier for a team under Schellenberg (with help from Spanish troops) to whisk the couple into Spain. The intrigue failed for reasons that have not been fully documented, but when the pertinent German secret records were published, the duke issued a statement on 1 Aug 57 denying he had considered defecting.

The Windsors sailed from Lisbon on 1 Aug 40 for the Bahamas. The bored exiles, who traveled frequently to the US, were criticized for tactlessness and dereliction of duty. Not waiting for his term to expire, the duke requested that his resignation be effective on 15 Mar 45. After waiting in the US for transportation the couple returned to France in Sep 45. Windsor still hoped for a government post but Attlee turned him down in 1948 as Churchill did in 1951. Never regretting his decision to marry Wallis, who remained the devoted if somewhat domineering consort, and living mainly in Paris, the duke died there, at home, on 28 May 72 of cancer of the throat. Given a state funeral attended by the distraught duchess, who had visited England several times but still was not accepted by the royal family, he was buried in the lawn at **Frogmore.** The duchess died at home in Paris in 1986 and was buried beside her husband

The duke published *A King's Story* (New York: Putnam, 1947). The definitive biography,

by a writer who never met the Windsors, is Frances Donaldson's *Edward VIII* (London: Weidenfield and Nicholson, 1974). A work by two outstanding writers who did know the couple well is J. Bryan III and Charles J. V. Murphy, *The Windsor Story* (New York: Morrow, 1979). Wallis's memoirs are *The Heart Has Its Reasons* (New York: McKay, 1956).

WINGATE, Orde Charles. British general. 1903-44. An eccentric, controversial, but exceptionally able soldier, he is best known for organizing and leading long-range penetration columns in Burma he called the **Chindits**.

Wingate was born 26 Feb 03 at Naini Tal, India, eldest son of an Indian Army officer who established a mission to tribes on the NW Frontier and Baltistan. Wingate's paternal grandfather was a missionary to the Jews of Hungary, and other highly uncommon forebears were a distinguished Persian scholar and the philanthropist Granville Sharp. *(DNB.)* Orde Wingate got his puritanism and profound knowledge of the Bible from his parents, who were Plymouth Brethren.

After being a day boy at Charterhouse he graduated from Woolwich in 1923 and was commissioned in the Royal Artillery. He was athletic, interested in observing wildlife, and he became an outstanding horseman. Significantly, he was not keen on team sports. Wingate studied Arabic at the School of Oriental Studies in London before deciding in 1927 to continue his studies in the Sudan. He got there at his own expense—the first stage by bicycle to Brindisi—and served five years in the Sudan Defense Force 1928-33. On completing this service he spent five weeks exploring on foot in the Libyan desert.

Wingate was in England with artillery units until getting a transfer in late 1936 to the intelligence staff in Palestine. The Arabs were rebelling against Jewish immigration and Wingate soon became intensely involved in the Zionist cause. He organized, trained, and led irregular forces in raids against Arab terrorist bases, being wounded in July 38 and winning appointment to the **DSO**. For several months Wingate served under WAVELL, who in July 39 began creating the Middle East Command.

Wingate was in England as brigade major of an AAA unit when the war started on 1 Sep 39. He was about to attend a course at **Camberley** when Wavell sent for him in the autumn of 1940. Italy had entered the war and Wingate was given the mission of supporting William PLATT's Sudan Defense Force. From the base at Khartoum Wingate organized "Gideon Force" for raids against Italian outposts near the Abyssinian border. His Gideon Force augmented by Sudanese, Ethiopians under a small cadre of British officers and NCOs, Wingate and Emperor HAILE SELASSIE crossed the frontier in Jan 41 when PLATT undertook his counteroffensive against the Duke of AOSTA, and with fewer than 2,000 remaining troops Wingate and the emperor entered Addis Ababa on 4 May 41.

Seriously ill after this arduous campaign, Wingate spent several months in a Cairo hospital and became so depressed that he attempted suicide. Long neurotic, he apparently became a cyclothyme—"a manic-depressive passing from moods of profound despair in which he believed that God (who had chosen him for some great work) had abandoned him, to a zestful euphoria in which everything pointed to fulfilment." (Allen, *Burma,* 121.)

Wavell had returned to India as CinC and he again sent for Wingate, who arrived in May 42 as the Japanese completed their conquest of Burma. But Wingate had time for a quick reconnaissance of what has been called the world's worse terrain in which to fight a war, and he got some insight into Japanese military mentality. Wingate quickly conceived of forming long-range penetration groups that would be supported by air for long periods. Wavell concurred, promoted Wingate to brigadier, and the **Chindits** were on.

Starting with an unlikely and unenthusiastic force of city-bred men, the 13th King's Liverpool Regt, the new brigadier formed the 77th Indian Bde. Wingate disliked the Indian Army in general and the **Gurkhas** in particular, a feeling that was mutual (Allen, 122). But Gurkhas eventually formed five of the eight Chindit columns, the others being British. The 142d Commando Co, specializing in sabotage and demolition, comprised survivors of "Mad Mike" CALVERT's Bush Warfare School. After rugged training and careful logistical planning for complex operations that depended on the then-novel use of air supply, and whose artillery would be tactical aircraft, Wingate led 3,000 Chindits into north Burma in Feb 43. They returned two months later to India after

proving that long-range penetration operations were feasible and effective but extremely difficult and costly. Only about 600 of the 2,000 who came back were ever again fit for duty. But Wingate was awarded a bar to his DSO.

Churchill, after a brief meeting with Wingate in London, took the raider (and his wife!) on a few hours' notice to the Quebec conference in Aug 43 (WC, V, 67-68). The decision was made at the conference to expand the Chindits to division strength and to create an American counterpart, which became Frank W. MERRILL's "Marauders." Wingate was promoted to major general about this time and made commander of the Special Force. It comprised of the Indian (Gurkha) 77th and 111th Bdes and the 14th, 16th, and 23d independent brigades, the latter formed from the Br 70th Div. Col Philip G. COCHRAN's US 5318 Air Unit was charged with transporting, supplying, and evacuating Wingate's forces (*OCMH Chron,* 170).

On 5 Feb 44 the Special Force (or 3d Indian Div [*OCMH Chron,* 178]) began moving SE from Ledo into Burma with the mission of facilitating the advance of Stilwell's Chinese Expeditionary Force (CEF) SW from Yunnan, China.

Wingate had operated successfully for only a few weeks before MUTAGUCHI's "March on Delhi" dictated a change in Allied strategy. Drawn into conventional battles for which they were not suited, the Chindits suffered prohibitive losses, one brigade being reduced to only 118 of 2,200 officers and men fit for duty. This reinforced the conventional military wisdom that "special forces" achieve little while sacrificing many highly trained men and requiring much military effort (Hatch, *Montgomery,* 304-5).

The controversy was raging when Wingate died in a plane crash on the evening of 24 Mar 44. "Stories were told afterwards that Wingate was advised against flying because of storms," writes a biographer, "and that with characteristic impetuosity, he overruled his American pilot, Lieutenant Hodges. All this is imagined. . . . There were isolated storms, but in the main the weather was fine." (Sykes, 534, quoted by Allen, *Burma,* 347.) What happened? Probably the B-25 Mitchell was thrown out of control after suddenly hitting one of the "isolated storms," which were hard to avoid at night (Slim, 268-69). The wreck was found on a hillside, its nose pointed back toward Imphal; there were no survivors. (Allen, 344-48.) "With him a bright flame was extinguished," wrote Churchill (WC, V, 566), and the Chindits were never the same under LENTAIGNE.

Wingate was buried in Arlington National Cemetery, Va. *(DNB)*. Wavell wrote the two-page *DNB* sketch of Wingate, and a full biography by C. Sykes is *Orde Wingate* (London: Collins, 1959).

WINKELMAN, Henri. Dutch general. 1876-1952. The very elderly and badly behind-the-times general was recalled from retirement and made CinC of Dutch forces in early 1940. His conventional defenses along river lines lasted less than five days against the German blitzkrieg. At last light on 14 May 40 he ordered his troops to end their resistance, and the next day he signed the official surrender documents at 11 AM.

WIRTH, Christian. German SS officer. 1885-1944. "The savage Christian" was born 24 Nov 85 in Oberbalzheim, Wuerttemberg. As an NCO in WWI he won the **Militaer-Verdienst-kreuz.** Wirth practiced law in Stuttgart, where by 1939 he was high in the **KRIPO.** The ex-attorney became such an expert in euthanasia programs that he was made a roving inspector throughout the Third Reich and in 1942 the tall, broad-shouldered, uncouth sadist was sent to direct four death camps including Maidenek and Treblinka. Eventually coming under Odilo GLOBOCNIK he lived alone in Lublin and worked from daily reports. Late in 1943, after a special investigation revealed corruption and crimes in the concentration camp system, Wirth was ordered to destroy his installations. Promoted to SS-Sturmbannfuehrer and sent to Trieste, he was killed on 26 May 44 by Yugoslav partisans or by a Jewish vengeance squad. (Wistrich.)

WISLICENY, Dieter. German SS official. 1911-48. Born 13 Jan 11 in Regularken, and a failed theology student, the Sturmbannfuehrer was active as Adolf EICHMANN's deputy in bargaining for Jewish lives in Greece, Hungary, and Slovakia, and in arranging mass deportations. The Czechs hanged the SS major on 27 Feb 48 in Bratislava for complicity in mass murder. (Wistrich.)

WITZLEBEN, Erwin von. German general. 1881-1944. The future field marshal, who in the opinion of a leading American authority "stands in a special place of honor among the generals who at one time or another formed part of the military Opposition" (Deutsch, I, 44), was born 4 Dec 81 in Breslau. He began his military career in 1901 and served on the western front in WWI. At the start of the Nazi era he was a senior general of the Old Guard who controlled all troops in the Berlin area as Wehrkreis III commander.

Witzleben apparently began considering an anti-Hitler putsch no later than the summer of 1937, long before the FRITSCH affair caused other senior officers to begin conspiring (Deutsch, I, 44). But serious illness incapacitated the general on critical occasions, in early 1938 and in early 1942, when he was ready to lead his troops in a coup. (Goerlitz, *GGS*, 313, 413.)

Witzleben was one of the "uncooperative" officers whom Hitler ordered into early retirement after the BLOMBERG and FRITSCH affairs of early 1938, but like most of the others he was quickly recalled. For the campaign against France he commanded 1st Army on the north of Leeb's AG C, being deployed in a defensive role in the Lower Palatinate (between the Moselle and the Rhine). In Phase 2, the Battle of France, 5-25 June, his army attacked near Saarbrucken to penetrate the Maginot Line in an action of little more than psychological significance—most defenders having been pulled back. He then fanned out to overrun most of Alsace-Lorraine.

Witzleben got his baton in Hitler's wholesale creation of field marshals on 19 July 40 and remained in France as OB West. The anti-Hitler conspiracy reached a new peak in the winter crisis of 1941-42 brought on by the failure of Opn **Barbarossa** in Russia. Witzleben was planning to march on Berlin when—with characteristic indecision—he decided to postpone action; long overdue for hemorrhoid surgery he decided he should be in perfect physical shape before moving. But Hitler did not dally: he put Witzleben back on the retired list, replacing him as OB West by Rundstedt.

The field marshal spent the next two years at his country estate some 50 miles SE of Berlin. Opn **Valkyrie** called for him to succeed Hitler as Wehrmacht commander if a coup succeeded,

and he authenticated the orders STAUFFEN-
BERG drafted for issue on the fateful day.
Witzleben received word in the early afternoon
of 20 July 44 that Stauffenberg's bomb had
killed Hitler. Heading for Berlin to lead the revolution the field marshal tarried for several
hours at **Zossen** and did not reach the Bendlerstrasse until shortly before 8 PM. In full uniform, baton and all, he spent 45 minutes with
BECK and Stauffenberg before concluding that
the coup had failed. Apparently thinking that
lack of active participation would save his own
skin the elderly field marshal drove back to
Zossen and then home.

Arrested the next day and subjected to degrad-
ing treatment during interrogation he was hailed
before the People's Court in Berlin on 7-8
August with seven others including Erich
HOEPNER. Deprived of his suspenders and
false teeth he was verbally assaulted by Roland
FREISLER in a barbarous show trial. A few
hours after being convicted of high treason on
8 Aug 44 he was among the eight major conspirators stripped half naked and hung (not
hanged) by piano wire from meat hooks while
movie cameras recorded the scene for Hitler.

WOLFE, Kenneth B. US general. 1896-1971.
"K. B." Wolfe supervised development of the B-
29 Superfortress, brainchild of H. H. ARNOLD.
A brigadier general from the spring of 1943, he
led the 20th Bombr Wing of B-29s from its base
near the Boeing factory in Wichita, Kan, to
India. K. B. directed the first, largely experimental raids that started in June 44 from India.
After moving his wing to bases established in
China under the CHENNAULT Plan he returned
to the States and continued B-29 development
and production. As a major general from 8 Nov
44 Wolfe went to Okinawa in Aug 45 as 5th AF
CofS to Ennis WHITEHEAD. Acting CG from
Oct Wolfe headed the 5th AF 29 Dec 45-4 Jan
48 (*AA,* 594). See also Curtis E. LEMAY.

WOLFF, Karl Friedrich Otto. German general. 1900-75. "Little Karl" is remembered
mainly for negotiating the early surrender in
Italy. He was born 13 May 00 in Darmstadt,
son of a wealthy district court magistrate
(Wistrich). As a very young Guards lieutenant
he won both classes of the Iron Cross during
WWI. After the armistice Wolff was in the
Hessian Freikorps until May 20 then was a

commercial clerk in various firms for five years
before owning an advertising enterprise in
Munich. (Wistrich.) The affable, prim Little
Karl joined the Nazi Party in 1931 and completed SS officer training the next year with an
impressive record. In July 33 he became
Himmler's adjutant and two years later he was
made the Reichsfuehrer's personal CofS. Wolff
was elected to the Reichstag from Hesse in
1936 and received the Golden Party Badge on
30 Jan 39 when he became Himmler's LnO at
Hitler's Hq (OKW). After HEYDRICH left
Berlin for Prague on 23 Sep 41 Wolff was virtually HIMMLER's deputy, promoted in 1942
to Obergruppenfuehrer and Generaloberst of
the Waffen-SS.

Losing favor with his morally fussy chief by
becoming involved in a divorce, Wolff was
sent to Italy in Sep 43 as Higher SS and Police
Leader. The fallen paladin displeased Berlin
further by having an audience with the Pope
in May 44 and promising to do all he could to
shorten the war. By early 1945 the SS general was convinced that the war was lost, and he
apparently knew that HIMMLER was among
those extending peace feelers. Wolff made his
own move in early Mar 45. Through Swiss
and Italian intermediaries, notably the industrialist Luigi Parilli, Wolff began lengthy
negotiations with Allen DULLES in Berne.
US Gen Lyman LEMNITZER and British Gen
Terence Airey entered Switzerland covertly to
negotiate for Gen Alexander's AFHQ in Italy.
Despite Russians objections—perhaps because of their plans for Tito to seize Trieste
and other Italian territory—the separate surrender was signed 29 April and became effective on 2 May 45. Gen von VIETINGHOFF,
Wehrmacht supreme commander in Italy, supported Wolff's surrender arrangements, and
Little Karl placated his superiors in Berlin by
arguing that as German military governor of
north Italy and plenipotentiary to MUSSO-
LINI's Salo government he had acted only to
head off a takeover by the powerful communist Garibaldi partisan brigades.

Worn out by his dangerous work and finding it had not won the Germans in Italy some
special status with the Western allies Wolff
was hospitalized during the winter of 1945-46
for paranoia (S&A, 201n52). The British did
not bring the SS Obergruppenfuehrer before
the tribunal in Venice that convicted Kessel-

ring of war crimes in Italy, and Wolff was not a defendant or witness at Nuremberg (ibid.). In 1946 a German court sentenced him to four years of hard labor, but the senior surviving SS officer (after KALTENBRUNNER) spent only a week in prison and in Aug 49 was finally cleared of war crimes in Italy in a little-publicized British trial.

Wolff prospered in Cologne as an advertising executive and published his memoirs in 1961, the year after EICHMANN was brought to justice. Eichmann's trial cast a new light on "'the SS General with the clean waistcoat'" (quoted by Wistrich) and on 18 Jan 62 Wolff was arrested again. The SS general was charged with committing genocide and other crimes before going to Italy. He was sentenced on 30 Sep 64 to 15 years of penal servitude and loss of civil rights for 10 years. Freed in 1971 Karl Wolff lived comfortably in Munich until his death in 1975.

WOOD, Edward Frederick Lindley. British statesman. 1881-1959. *See* HALIFAX, 1st Earl of.

WOOD, (Howard) Kingsley. British official. 1881-1943. He was born 19 Aug 81 at West Sculcoates, Hull, son of a Wesleyan clergyman who for nine years was minister of Wesley's chapel in London. Kingsley Wood was educated at the nearby Central Foundation Boys' School. In 1903 took honors in his law finals after reading under a solicitor and he practiced in the City until elected in 1911 as Municipal Reform member on the London City Council. Knighted in Jan 18 Sir Kingsley was elected to Parliament the following December and he represented West Woolwich until his death almost 25 years later.

A short man (five feet five), plump, brisk, precise, puritanical and genial (Helen M. Palmer in *DNB*) Sir Kingsley held many high offices before Stanley Baldwin appointed him in May 38 to head the air ministry. "To this eleventh-hour task Wood brought all his customary assiduity" *(DNB),* taking over a ministry that needed overhauling, lacking experience in this field, and with war clearly on the horizon Sir Kingsley established the Empire Air Training Plan and at least doubled the RAF's fighting strength. (Ibid.) But the effort exhaust-

ed him, so in Apr 40 the little trouble shooter changed places with Sir Samuel HOARE to become lord privy seal. A month later. when his close friend Churchill became PM, Sir Kingsley was named chancellor of the exchequer and member of the War Cabinet.

He faced staggering problems as air raids wreaked havoc: Britain had to pay for American arms as dollar reserves declined; wartime inflation reared its head; and a compulsory insurance scheme was needed. Sir Kingsley quickly established a council of advisers that included economist J. M. Keynes, who was given a room in the Treasury. Wood was preparing to present his "pay as you earn" scheme for further improving the war economy when he died suddenly on 21 Sep 43 (WC, V, 162) and was succeeded by John ANDERSON.

WRIGHT, Carleton Herbert. US admiral. 1892-1973. "Boscoe" Wright was born 2 June 92 in New Hampton, Iowa. Graduating from the USNA in 1912 (16/156) he became an ordnance specialist and had more than half of his 23 years of peacetime service ashore. At the start of the war in Europe he was in the Atlantic as skipper of CA *Augusta,* which took Roosevelt and Churchill to their meeting at Argentia Bay, Newfoundland, in Aug 41.

Promoted on 15 May 42 Rear Adm Wright was given command of the cruiser unit of "Bull" Halsey's carrier group in the Solomons. Still lacking combat experience, he then moved up on short notice to replace KINKAID as head of a hastily assembled and green formation of five cruisers and six destroyers. (Morison, V, 293.) Off **Savo Island** in the night battle of Tassafaronga, 30 Nov-1 Dec 42, Wright's TF 67 surprised a weaker force of eight destroyers under the redoubtable Raizo TANAKA that was running the **Tokyo Express** to Guadalcanal. One enemy destroyer was sunk and others damaged, preventing the landing of reinforcements and supplies. But Japanese torpedos sank CA *Northampton* and crippled three destroyers. NIMITZ decided to replace Wright, Halsey drafting "Pug" AINSWORTH, who happened to be visiting the South Pacific Area. Wright manfully accepted blame for his shortcomings; he was awarded the Navy Cross and sent to Washington for a brief stint of staff duty.

Given another chance at sea Wright proved himself as commander of Cruiser Div 4 in the Aleutians, at Makin, and in the Marshall Islands in late 1943. But the following January he was back on shore, spending the rest of the war as head the 12th Naval District in San Francisco. His mission was to insure a steady flow of personnel and equipment overseas.

In Mar 46 he became IG, Pacific Fleet and Pacific Ocean Area, then he was deputy high commissioner, Pacific Islands Trust Territory, and deputy commander, Marianas 1947-48. Retiring 1 Oct 48 as a vice admiral he died 27 June 70 at Claremont, Calif. (RCS.)

WRIGHT, Jerauld. US naval officer. 1898-. "Jerry" Wright was born in Massachusetts on 4 June 98. He was the son of Lt Gen William Mason Wright, ex-USMA 1886, who commanded the 35th Inf Div, AEF, and later the Philippine Dept (Cullum). Appointed from NJ Jerry graduated from Annapolis in 1917 (93/199). Early in the war he was a captain commanding CL *Santa Fe* in the Pacific. Recalled to Washington he was ordered to London where he and Rear Adm B. H. Bieri were the most important US naval officers on the combined staff planning the invasion of North Africa (Morison, II, 182).

When GIRAUD agreed to meet Eisenhower at Gibraltar the French general stipulated that the submarine picking him up in the south of France be American. None being available, the Royal Navy specialist in secret submarine operations, Lt N. L. A. JEWELL, was sent with HMS *Seraph*, and Capt Wright went along as *Seraph's* figurehead skipper. (Morison, II, 186 & n.)

Capt Wright then was involved in planning the Sicily and Salerno landings before returning to the Pacific. He commanded cruisers until promoted in Nov 44. Rear Adm Wright commanded a diversionary force in the Okinawa campaign that drew heavier air attack than the main landing on 1 Apr 45 (Morison, 108, 111, 154).

A vice admiral after the war he was CINC US Naval Forces Eastern Atlantic and the Mediterranean and he held high NATO posts until retiring 31 Jan 60 as a full admiral.

Y

YAKOVLEV, Alexandr Sergeyevich. Soviet aircraft designer. 1906-89. Born 1 Apr 06, son of a clerk, Yakovlev joined the Red Army in 1924, became a technician in the Red AF, but was not a CP member until 1938. Meanwhile he designed his first plane (Air-1) in 1927 before studying in the Zhukovsky Military Air Engineering Acaemy 1927-31. He visited France, England, Germany, and Italy, and he designed fighters that proved to be among the best in the war. His YAK-1, first flown in Mar 39, went into production the next year and entered service in 1941. Two thirds of wartime Soviet fighter production, or 36,000 planes, were the YAK-1 and its modification, the YAK-3 (Bialer, ed, 570n58). Usually paired with Sergei ILYUSHIN's Il-2, they became mainstays of the Soviet fighter forces. The YAK-9U (operational late in 1944) was "one of the first Soviet plancs to compare favorably with contemporary Western aircraft" *(S&S)*.

Yakovlev tells in his memoirs how Stalin relegated him to the post of deputy in charge of R&D when A. I. Shakhurin succeeded M. M. Kaganovich as People's Commissar of the Aviation Industry on 9 Jan 40. After Stalin brushed aside Yakovlev's protests that at the age of 34 he was too young to be chief of R&D, that he was a designer, not an administrator nor a politician, he complained of being coerced, "Stalin burst out laughing," writes the hand-cuff volunteer, "But we are not afraid of coercion. . . . After all, coercion is the midwife of revolution." (Quoted in Bialer, 100.) The dictator's coercion led to Yakovlev's designing 75 aircraft that went into production, 66,000 of all types being manufactured.

With the military rank of general colonel-engineer from 1946 the reluctant chief of Red AF R&D held his post until 1948. He later designed one of the first Soviet jet aircraft and the YAK-24 heavy helicopter. Passenger planes were the YAK-40 and 42. Yakovlev aircraft have won 50 world records. Seven excerpts from his memoirs, *Tsel' zhizni* (Moscow, 1966), and a biographical sketch are in Bialer's *Stalin and His Generals.* The autobiography was published in English as *The Aim of a Lifetime* (Moscow: Progress Publishers, 1972). *See* also TUPOLEV.

YAKOVLEV, Nikolay Dmitriyevich. Soviet military officer. 1898-1972. As Chief of the Main Artillery Directorate and member of the Military Artillery Council of the Red Army 1941-46 he directed arms development and production. Yakovlev was born in Straya Russa, now Novgorod Oblast, on 31 Dec 98. He fought in WWI, joined the Red Army in 1918, served through the civil war, but was not a CP member until 1923. After routine artillery assignments he was chief of artillery in the Belorussian, North Caucasus, and Kiev Military Districts 1937-41 before being in the invasion of Poland and the war with Finland. He then took up the assignment mentioned earlier and in 1944 was promoted to Marshal of Artillery (No. 2). In 1946-48 he was 1st Deputy Commander of Artillery of the Armed Forces, USSR, in addition to the other duties. In Nov 48 Yakovlev became deputy Minister of the Armed Forces for artillery and missiles.

Yakovlev was arrested on 31 Dec 51 as BERIA and L. Z. MEKHLIS began a new purge of the military high command that started with ZHUKOV. He and others withstood months of endless interrogation without incriminating themselves or any others. But even after Stalin's death on 5 Mar 53 he remained in prison until Beria's arrest on 26 June 53.

Yakovlev immediately was appointed 1st deputy CinC of National Air Defense. He was retired to the General Inspector's Group in 1960 and died in Moscow on 9 May 72. (Scotts.)

YAMAGUCHI, Tamon. Japanese admiral. 1892-1942. A student at Princeton and military attaché in Washington before the war and a rear admiral from 1938, Yamaguchi was one of the Japanese Navy's most highly regarded officers and was considered as a possible successor to Yamamoto (Morison, IV, 137). In 1940 he took command of the 2d Carrier Div and with CVs *Hiryu* and *Soryu* he took part in the Pearl Harbor attack on 7 Dec 41, remaining under Chuichi NAGUMA for the raid into the Indian Ocean and subsequent operations. His flagship *Hiryu* was fatally hit in the battle of Midway. "As commanding officer of this carrier division I am fully and solely responsible for the loss of *Hiryu* and *Soryu*," he said solemnly in an address to 800 survivors at 2:30 AM on 5 June 42. "I shall remain on board to the end. I command all of you to leave the ship and continue your loyal service to His Majesty, the Emperor." (Morison, IV, 396.) Despite pleas from his staff the admiral took a length of cloth to lash himself to the bridge and went down with *Hiryu* when she and *Akagi* were sent to the bottom by Japanese torpedoes later that morning. Yamaguchi was made a vice admiral posthumously.

YAMAMOTO, Isokoru. Japanese admiral. 1884-1943. CinC of the Japanese Combined Fleet 1939 until his death on 18 Apr 43 Yamamoto was born on 4 Apr 84. He was the seventh child of Sadakichi Takano, a cultured but impoverished schoolmaster of the samurai class. The father soon became headmaster of the primary school in nearby Nagaoka on the bleak and isolated west coast of Japan's main island. Proud of his hard childhood Isokoru referred to himself later in life as "a country boy" who became "just a common sailor."

But he was most uncommon. Standing second out of 300 applicants when entering the Naval Academy at the age of 16 he graduated four years later as seventh in his class. As an ensign he quickly had his baptism of fire. He was aboard the cruiser that covered the flagship of Adm Heihachiro Togo (1846-1934) in one of history's most decisive naval battles, the destruction of the Russian Battle Fleet off Tshushima in 1905. In the final action he was wounded in the right leg and left hand, losing two fingers. (Potter, *Yamamoto*, 3-13.)

Soon after his parents died the 30-year-old lieutenant commander was adopted by the prominent Yamamoto family, whose name he assumed. (Isokoru comes from "fifty-six," the father's age when the boy was born. Yamamoto is a Japanese name meaning "base of the mountain.") Promoted about this time to commander and assigned to Imperial Naval Hq in Tokyo he finally married. The couple had no sooner set up housekeeping than Yamamoto was sent (alone) to Harvard. For the next two years, 1916-18, he studied economics, concentrating in the field of petroleum. But he also learned what he could about military aviation, which was winning its wings over France. Comdr Yamamoto was a hardworking student, so good that several American oil companies offered to hire him. But

the earnest Oriental, a slight figure of medium height who "radiated intelligence and energy" (d'Albas, 9), delighted American hosts with parlor tricks such as standing on his head and doing traditional Japanese dances with dinner plates. Athletic from childhood, he took to baseball, and—already proficient in the Japanese versions of checkers (*go*) and chess (*shogi*)—he became formidable at bridge and poker.

Capt Yamamoto (from 1923) was director of the new air training base at Kasumigaura for 18 months before being naval attaché in Washington 1925-27. He took command of the 1st Air Fleet in 1930, and the next year was promoted to rear admiral in charge of the navy's technical service. He had visited American aircraft factories, had become a pilot at Kasumigaura, and he had recognized that airplanes would relegate battleships to a secondary role. The Japanese were moving into Manchuria and Yamamoto capitalized on the national emergency to stimulate the Japanese aircraft industry into developing modern designs.

Having been a delegate to the London Naval Conference of 1929-30, Rear Adm Yamamoto headed the Japanese delegation to the London conference of 1934. En route he put off ill-informed gentlemen of the press by pretending not to know English, but on reaching Southhampton he told reporters in fluent English, "Japan can no longer submit to the ratio system." He was referring to the 5:5:3 formula for US, UK, and Japanese battleships. It was rumored in Japan that militarists intended to assassinate the entire delegation if they returned in defeat, but Yamamoto was welcomed home as a hero after these restrictions were removed. Becoming vice minister of the navy under Mitusmasa YONAI, the air-minded admiral opposed the program launched immediately under terms of the new treaty to build the gigantic *Yamato* and *Musashi*. "These battleships will be as useful to Japan in modern warfare as a *samurai* sword," he said privately (Potter, *Yamamoto*, 30). Aircraft carriers *Akagi* and *Kaga* already were in service, but they would be joined by the faster and more modern *Shokaku* and *Zuikaku*. Although unable to overcome traditional reliance on surface units, duction of long-range flying boats and the Zero fighter.

Anathema to ultra-nationalists who were rushing Japan into a war, the admiral opposed Japan's joining the **Tripartite Pact** in 1939. When asked by Premier KONOYE at this time what the Japanese navy was capable of doing in a world war, Yamamoto allegedly said he would "run wild" for six months to a year but that he had "utterly no confidence" in what would follow. (Morison, III, 46 & n; Potter, 43.) His widely quoted boast of dictating peace in the White House was a US propaganda version of a very different statement. *The peace the Japanese Army wanted* could be dictated only in the White House, he said; *the Navy could not win it for them.* (Morison, VI, 128n, citing James A. Field, Jr, USNI *Proceedings*, Oct 49). Navy Minister Yonai worried about the personal safety of his deputy, even though the latter was fatalistic. After ordering that Yamamoto accept a personal police guard, Yonai finally sent him to sea.

Thus the country boy from Nagaoka reached the top of his profession in mid-Aug 39: promoted to full admiral he became CinC Combined Fleet. Yamamoto devoted himself to improving not only naval technology but also the leadership of senior officers. From 1930 he had insisted on tough, realistic training in foul weather and at night. "I regard death in training the same as a hero's death in action," he said in 1930 (Potter, 23), accepting that peacetime training fatalities would save lives in battle. American moms and recruiting officers were not yet ready to accept this obvious fact.

On the other hand Yamamoto may be faulted for the fact that no Japanese ship had radar when the war started; all US Navy ships did. Not until early 1943 did all Japanese warships receive their first, primitive, radars. (d'Albas, 9n.)

Pearl Harbor

The surprise attack on Pearl Harbor, 7 Dec 41, was Yamamoto's idea. Approved only after much opposition, it was inspired by the carrier-based British raid against the Italian fleet at **Taranto,** 11 Nov 40. (This glossary entry has considerable detail including how the US failed to get the word of Japanese interest in the Taranto raid.)

The Pearl Harbor attack was one of the most stunning achievements in the history of war. Execution required near perfection. Achieving strategic and tactical surprise, 353 Japanese planes from six carriers almost completely wrecked the US Pacific Fleet. By a great stroke of luck, however, the all-important US carriers happened to be safely at sea.

Yamamoto now could "run wild" for a few months but he remained subordinate to authorities in Tokyo, where the army controlled overall direction of the war. The admiral, however, was able to formulate naval strategy.

Powerful Japanese fleets supported the Malayan campaign, the conquest of the NEI, and the drive into the Solomons and New Guinea. Raids ranged into British colonies as far west as Ceylon. In pushing to isolate Australia the Japanese had heavy carrier losses in the Battle of the Coral Sea, which forced them to turn back from an attempt to take Port Moresby by amphibious assault.

Central Pacific

In mid-Apr 42 Yamamoto's staff visited Tokyo to start working out Plan AF for the seizure of Midway, which they wanted as an advance base. More important, however, was that by drawing the US Navy into a major engagement Yamamoto could mass eight Japanese carriers against the two he believed the US had left in the Pacific: with these eliminated the Japanese fleet could threaten the American west coast and possibly win the war. US planes had struck Marcus Island, only 1,000 miles from the Imperial Palace, on 3 Mar 42. Six weeks later the **DOOLITTLE** raid threw Japan into consternation, and Plan AF suddenly gained overwhelming support.

The decisive US victory at Midway, 3-6 June 42, turned the tide in the Pacific. It was made possible largely because of **Magic** radio intercepts, which enabled the Americans to mass their limited resources at the right place. Bad Japanese naval intelligence and errors by Adm NAGUMO, who commanded the carrier force, played a major role.

Only six months after his triumph at Pearl Harbor, Yamamoto had suffered the first major Japanese naval defeat since the 16th century. Biographer Potter devotes a chapter to the admiral's failures: having conceived a good strategy, he failed to follow the Napoleonic dictum of mustering all available force for the main effort; he did not position himself to control the action; lacking "the Nelson touch" he failed to brief major subordinate commanders fully on the plan; he was careless about deploying reconnaissance and screening forces; but perhaps his greatest fault was overconfidence, like Robert E. Lee at Gettysburg 99 years earlier.

Morison is less damning. "The Japanese fleet was intact, except for the carriers; and the Northern Area Force had occupied Kiska and Attu" in the Aleutians. (Morison, IV, 159.) But the great carriers *Akagi, Kaga, Hiryu,* and *Soryu* were lost; these constituted 43 per cent of the Japanese carrier tonnage in operation. More important was loss of veteran pilots and maintenance crews. The Americans lost only one of their three carriers, *Yorktown,* which had been repaired after the Battle of the Coral Sea; *Enterprise* and *Hornet* remained in action.

South Pacific

The Midway defeat made the Guadalcanal campaign more critical to Yamamoto. Neither side wanted another major engagement, but with his headquarters now on Truk the Japanese admiral used various unorthodox tactics to support the 15,000 Japanese troops blockaded on Guadalcanal. He was quite successful with what Americans came to call the Tokyo Night Express but that the Japanese called the "Rat Express" or "Ant Freight" (Toland, 386-87); Yamamoto was prepared to lose half of the small, fast destroyers engaged, but these ended up suffering no damage. A major Japanese effort to make a substantial landing of troops and heavy equipment was defeated by the Americans in the Battle of Cape Esperance, 11-12 Oct 42. But Yamamoto stepped up his efforts, sending more troop transports and using big battleships in a diversionary effort, shelling Henderson Field. The Battle of the Santa Cruz Islands, 26-27 Oct 42, was the decisive action in which outnumbered US forces kept the reinforcements from landing. CV *Hornet* was lost but three of Nagumo's five carriers had to withdraw for repairs. Japanese carriers did not reappear for two years, and then merely as OZAWA's decoy force in the Battle for Leyte Gulf, 23-26 Oct 44.

The Naval Battle of Guadalcanal, 12-14 Nov 42, meanwhile ended Japanese efforts to recapture the island, but Yamamoto now started his "submerged freight service." Whereas all destroyers survived the "Rat Express," 20 of 38 submarines subsequently were lost. But the Japanese evacuated 13,000 troops from Guadalcanal in a remarkable operation the Americans never detected.

The admiral was preparing for a final, massive effort to retake Henderson Field on 1 Feb 43 but Gen Hitoshi IMAMURA arrived as over-all commander before this could start. With Hirohito's broad hint that he should make a maximum effort to hold Lae now that Buna was lost, Yamamoto ordered another major operation to get reinforcements through. This met a bloody repulse in the Battle of the Bismarck Sea, 2-4 Mar 43. More losses were incurred without having any good results when Yamamoto sent out large air strikes that cost him many more veteran naval pilots.

"I do not know what to do next," Yamamoto wrote to an old friend (Potter, 300). To bolster morale he decided to visit forward bases on 18 Apr 43. (This was the first anniversary of the DOOLITTLE raid.) A Japanese message in ordinary naval code was sent five days ahead of time with the precise trip itinerary and details of security arrangements. Imamura, who had narrowly escaped ambush over Bougainville, warned Yamamoto of the danger he was incurring, and one of the admiral's closest friends flew in to Rabaul and pleaded that the trip be canceled. "When I saw that foolish message," he said, "I told my staff, 'This is madness.' It is an open invitation to the enemy." (Bergamini, 976.)

Operation Vengeance

US monitors in Hawaii and the Aleutians intercepted the message on 13 April and relayed it to naval intelligence in Pearl Harbor and Washington. Nimitz asked only a few questions before deciding to eliminate Japan's best admiral and the man responsible for Pearl Harbor (Morison, VI, 128). He ordered Halsey to see whether the operation was feasible. Squadron leaders on Guadalcanal said it was. Notifying Washington of his decision, Nimitz told his subordinates to proceed. Capt ZACHARIAS of ONI, who had direct access to Roosevelt, "had his staff collect an in-basketful of precedents for international assassination . . ." (Bergamini, 977). Navy Secretary Knox, who also had the message intercept, gave his blessing only after consulting the navy advocate general on the legality of the action, asking churchman about its morality (ibid.), and checking with H. H. "Hap" Arnold and Charles Lindbergh on its feasibility (Potter, 302-3).

P-38 Lightnings from Henderson Field on Guadalcanal were equipped on short notice with auxiliary gas tanks provided by George Kenney. Losing one of 18 planes on take-off (Bergamini, 978) Maj John W. Mitchell led his flight at an altitude of 30 feet—wave-top level—on a deviating, 410-mile course of exactly two hours and fifteen minutes. Right on schedule, at 9:30 AM on 18 Apr 43, the expected two camouflaged Mitsubishi Betty bombers were spotted at 2,000 feet as they approached Kahili field on Bougainville. Capt Thomas G. Lamphier fought off three Zekes before attacking the plane he correctly guessed had Yamamoto aboard. Two bursts sent the burning plane into the jungle. Moments later Lt Rex T. Barber sent the other Betty into the water. Having tangled with six escorting Zekes, downing three while losing one plane, Mitchell led the flight home safely. All US planes had bullet holes and two had lost an engine. (Potter, 303-8.)

Yamamoto's corpse was found in dense jungle near the shattered and burned bomber; another 10 bodies were in the plane. Three badly injured survivors from the other plane included the admiral's long-time CofS Matomi Ugaki, his paymaster, and his communications officer. For security reasons, the operation was not reported by US authorities. Mitchell and his pilots were decorated, sent home, and told to keep Opn **Vengeance** a secret. Many facts were not reported until after the war, and some details remain unclear.

Mineichi KOGA replaced Yamamoto, but the Japanese waited a month, until 21 May 43, to report that their greatest hero, "while directing general strategy in the front line in April of this year engaged in combat with the enemy and met a met a gallant death in a war plane." He was given a state funeral, only the 12th since 1900, and Yamamoto was promoted posthumously to fleet admiral. Hitler made him the only foreign recipient of the **Swords** (Angolia, I, 276).

YAMASHITA, Tomoyuki (Hobun). Japanese general. 1888-1946. Many authorities call Yamashita (pronounced ya' mash' ta) the greatest Japanese general of the war. But the Tiger of Malaya, who captured Singapore on 15 Feb 42, was in such disfavor with superiors in Tokyo for his involvement in the **26 Feb 36** coup that he was relegated to virtual exile in Manchuria until it was too late for him to have any major role in the war. Sent in early 1944 to take command in the Philippines, but his hands tied by superiors including the incompetent Count TERAUCHI, he fought to the end. His subsequent trial on orders from MacArthur, and his execution as a war criminal, were viewed by friend and foe as a miscarriage of justice.

Yamashita was born 8 Nov 88 in the village of Osugi Mara, Kochi Prov, Shikoku. (*Kogun,* 240; other sources have 1885 as the year of birth.) He is indebted to his mother not only for a giant physique (six feet one) but also for the means to have a better schooling than his father could have afforded as a village doctor. Yamashita undertook a military career after showing little academic aptitude or temperament for medicine. But as a military cadet he graduated fifth in his class at the Hiroshima MA and was commissioned in 1906 as a second lieutenant of infantry. (*Kogun,* 240; other sources say he graduated from the military academy in 1908.) Yamashita quickly became highly regarded as a bright, witty, hard-working officer who avoided military cliques (Swinson, *Four Samurai,* 81). Sixth in his War College class of 1916 he began a happy if childless marriage that year to a general's daughter, Hisako Nagayama.

A member of the general staff from early 1918 and given choice assignments, Yamashita was sent to Europe as a military student and assistant military attaché in Switzerland and Germany (1919-1922). After serving in the War Ministry, teaching at the war college, and being promoted to lieutenant colonel, he was MA in Vienna and Budapest (concurrently) from Feb 27. Again promoted, Col Yamashita was CO, 3d Inf Regt, for eight months before heading the Army Affairs Section of the Military Affairs Bureau from Apr 31.

For reasons never fully understood he became involved in the factionalism that marked Japan's march to war. As a disciple, almost a son, of Sadao ARAKI, who headed the **Imperial Way** clique, he had a prominent if ambiguous role in the **26 Feb 36** insurrection. As this fizzled out he distanced himself from the conspirators to mediate among senior officers of the Imperial Way and of TOJO's **Control Faction** and appeared to be profoundly depressed about incurring imperial displeasure (Swinton, 90). But while advising several others to take the traditional Japanese course of suicide Col Yamashita himself acted more like a round-eyed Occidental than a samurai. As a relatively junior officer whose role apparently was minimal he got off lightly. According to some authorities he was taken off the promotion list for a year when shipped off to Korea as commander of the 40th Inf Bde. But this is contradicted by evidence that he was promoted to major general a month after the coup (*Kogun,* 240).

In Aug 37, a month after the Sino-Japanese war started, Yamashita took over the China Garrison Mixed Bd, and he was promoted three months later to lieutenant general. In July 38 he began a 14-month tour as CofS, Northern China Area Army. Gen Yamashita took command of the 4th Div in Sep 39 when border fighting ended in Manchuria and Hitler attacked Poland. When Lt Gen Yamashita returned for duty in Tokyo the newly appointed Minister of War Tojo got rid of him by sending him at the end of 1940 to Europe for six months with a military inspection team to German and Italian forces. Yamashita's report stressed the need for air power, mechanization of the army with emphasis on medium tanks, and creation of parachute units. He also advised strongly against initiating war against Britain, the US, or the USSR until the Japanese armed forces were modernized. (*Kogun,* 26-27.) Tojo disregarded this last recommendation and many of the others. Still in bad odor with the emperor and much of the top brass in Tokyo, Yamashita was sent in July 41 to head the Kwantung Defense Army.

Singapore

Lt Gen Yamashita had been in grade four years and had no prospects for higher command when he took over the 25th Army, which was being formed and given special jungle training for the Malayan campaign. The bold strategy for taking of Singapore had been approved at an Imperial Conference on 6 Sep 41 and Yamashita was subordinated to TERAUCHI, an old political enemy whose Southern Army Hq was in Saigon. One of the new army commander's few contributions to the planning was to reduce the strength of his force to three divisions (the 5th, 18th, and Imperial Gds) from the five offered. (Yamashita wanted to ease the burden of logistical support.) Yamashita began the Malayan campaign with attacks at 4:30 AM on 8 Dec 41 (local date) on airfields in northern Malaya and Singapore. Landing hundreds of miles north of Singapore and sending his specially trained force though jungles the British had long considered to be passable only to

explorers, the "Tiger of Malaya" took Johore on 31 Jan 42, landed his troops on Singapore Island on 8 February, and accepted PERCIVAL's surrender of the city and 100,000 troops on 15 Feb 42.

But Lt Gen Yamashita received no kudos and no promotion. Neither Hirohito nor Tojo wanted a military hero at home, and insiders realized that Yamashita's role in the coup of 26 Oct 36 had not been forgiven. Yamashita's fears of being assassinated on orders from Tojo during the final stages of his campaign cannot be dismissed as paranoia (Swinson, 106). Ostensibly on grounds of preserving secrecy, he was told not to visit Tokyo en route take over his 1st Area Army Hq at Mutankiang in E Manchuria. The Tiger of Malaya left Singapore on 17 July 42 and bore his exile without complaint, partially consoled by promotion to general in Feb 43.

The Philippines

The Japanese had lost Guadalcanal and their fortunes were ebbing when Yamashita learned on 25 Sep 44, two months after Tojo's resignation, that he would command ground forces in the Philippines. The IGHQ had decided in Mar 44 to make their last stand strategically in the islands, which had been merely a rear operational base. "Why bother about defense plans?" Yamashita's high-living predecessor, Lt Gen Shigenori Kuroda, had said. "The Philippines are obviously indefensible."

Yamashita himself had no illusions. "It's my turn to die," he said to his CofS. Rushed through briefings in Tokyo but his departure for Manila delayed by weather until 5 Oct 44, the general insisted on being presented to the emperor. Terauchi had moved his Southern Army Hq to Manila, six months too late for making adequate plans. Japan's greatest soldier acted vigorously despite serious obstruction by Terauchi, one of Japan's most incompetent generals. Terauchi made Yamashita send reinforcements to Leyte, where Sosaku SUZUKI, Yamashita's friend and former CofS in Malaya, was conducting losing campaign.

When Yamashita learned on 13 Dec 44 that MacArthur's forces were making a major landing on Mindoro, barely 150 miles south of Manila, he finally was able to stop dissipating his resources and concentrate on the defense of Luzon. Terauchi had left for Saigon on

17 Nov 44 but he retained operational control in the Philippines. Yamashita resisted orders from Tokyo and Saigon to undertake a counter-offensive against Mindoro, and a few days before Christmas he finally got authority to direct operations without interference from higher headquarters.

By this time Suzuki's army on Leyte was written off. Yamashita had more than 250,000 troops, but many divisions were hastily formed of noncombatant units, shipwreck survivors, and other scrapings of the manpower barrel. The Americans had complete air and naval superiority. Only two days before US forces started landing on Luzon (9 Jan 45) Yamashita was given operational control over shore-based naval units and command of the 4th Air Army, although the latter soon left. About a week earlier, service troops of the 3d Maritime Transport Command had come under orders of Yamashita's 14th Area Army. Whether this included 17,000 elite troops of the 31st Naval Defense Force in and around Manila is uncertain, but the point would become vital (below).

Yamashita issued orders, which the navy strongly opposed, that Manila not be defended. He also directed that 4,000 POWs throughout Luzon be freed when the Americans landed. (Swinton, 206-7.) On 26 Dec 44 he established headquarters 20 miles north of the capital at Ipo and ordered that some 152,000 troops constitute the Shobu Group with headquarters at Baguio. Two smaller formations were on southern Luzon, around Clark Field, and on Bataan. But Yamashita lost contact with these troops during the campaign. As his situation deteriorated under guerrilla and air attack, and with little left of his communications system, Yamashita started moving his headquarters on 17 Apr 45 from Baguio to Bamgbang, 50 miles farther inland.

Exactly two months later he moved 16 miles north to Kiangan, now on foot. When Yamashita realized by late July that food stocks would be exhausted in six weeks he made his final plans: able-bodied men would break out to form small groups for protracted guerrilla warfare; others would launch suicidal banzai charges; he and his devoted CofS, Airka Muto, would commit seppuku. But the news came by commercial radio on 14 Aug 45, about two weeks before this plan was to be carried out, that Japan was suing for peace. Eyewitnesses reported that Yamashita seemed to age 10 years over night, and the staff

was so concerned about his committing suicide that a young officer was ordered to keep watch. "Don't worry, I won't go to heaven alone," the general is alleged to have said on noticing this. "That'll do no good. My duty is to get the soldiers back home. So relax and go to bed." (Swinton, 218.)

War Trial

Two week later Yamashita decided to surrender himself as proposed by a message dropped from an American plane. After an emotional farewell on 2 Sep 45 he walked with an ADC down a mountain path into captivity. Formally charged on 8 Oct 45 with violating the "laws of war," he was subjected to a trial of nearly six weeks beginning on the 29th. The findings and sentence were delayed almost two days for announcement on the fourth anniversary of Pearl Harbor (7 Dec 45).

The Japanese had committed acts of incredible barbarism while Yamashita commanded in the Philippines, but the main issue was whether he had any personal control over the troops involved, particularly the 31st Naval Defense Force stationed in and around Manila (herein). It also was pointed out that MacArthur's military commission lacked authority, civil courts in the Philippines having reopened. Sufficient doubt was raised on legal and moral grounds to get a stay of execution for almost two months. The Philippino Supreme Court declined to act on the appeal. The US Supreme Court ruled 6:2 that it could not interfere with MacArthur's handling of the case. Pres Truman announced on 8 Feb 46 he would not grant clemency, and Yamashita was hanged on 23 Feb 46.

YEFREMOV, Mikhail Grigoryevich. Soviet military leader. 1897-1942. He was born in the village of Tarusa, near Kaluga, on 3 Nov 97. Yefremov's grandfather was hanged in 1905 for rebelling in the Imperial Navy and his father was killed by kulaks. After being a worker in Moscow and a junior officer he entered the Red Guards in Oct 17, the Red Army in 1918, and the CP in 1919. During the civil war he rose from division to corps commander. In 1927 he was an adviser in China. After taking the military short courses a year later and attending the Military-Political Academy Yefremov graduated from the Frunze MA in 1933. Four years later he took over the Volga

MD from TUKHACHEVSKY, then headed the Transbaykal MD until arrested in early 1938 and imprisoned. In a letter to VOROSHILOV he summarized his honorable service and said "I beg you to stop my suffering and torment." (Scotts, citing Volkogonov, book 1, part 2, 163.) The plea went unanswered formally but the prisoner was released.

He commanded the Orel MD in 1940, was promoted to general lieutenant, and then he headed the Transcaucasian MD. In June 41 he was appointed first deputy IG of Infantry.

Gen Lt Yefremov's first combat service in Hitler's War was closely linked with that of F. I. KUZNETSOV, who commanded the 21st Army and, concurrently from 21 July 41, the short-lived Central Front. In mid-July Yefremov led the 21st Army in a desperate attack toward Bobruisk. He succeeded Kuznetsov in the Central Front 25 Aug 41. The front was deactivated a few day later and Yefremov formed the 33d Army at Naro-Fominsk from units of Zhukov's Reserve Front. Early on 1 Dec 41 he bore the brunt of a final, desperate lunge by Kluge's 4th Army along the Minsk-Moscow Hwy. His defenses around Naro-Fominsk shattered, threatening to split his army from the 5th Army and wreak havoc in Zhukov rear areas, Yefremov promptly took command of a composite group formed on Zhukov's orders. Counterattacking on 2 December in the Yushkovo-Burtsevo with "a rifle brigade, a couple of [T34] tank battalions, ski troops and a *Katyusha* unit (Erickson, *To Stalingrad,* 266) he drove Kluge's troops back. This was part of the Russian winter counteroffensive, but by mid Apr 42 Yefremov's army was encircled around Dorogobuzh, near Smolensk. Trying to link up with the 43d Army, only a mile or so away, the general was mortally wounded on 19 Apr 42 in the village of Zhari. Exhorting his men to fight on he shot himself in the temple. A monument to Yefremov was erected in Vyazma (Scarecrow). [465]

YEGOROV, Aleksandr Ilich. Soviet military leader. 1883-1939. The son of a stevedore, he was born 25 Oct 83 in the village of Buzuluk in what became the Orenburg region. Aleksandr Ilich attended the Kazan Junker Infantry School in 1905, served as a colonel in WWI, and in 1918 joined the Red Army and CP. He became CGS in 1931 and was one of the first

five marshals (of the Soviet Union) created in 1935. Arrested in May 37 soon after becoming first deputy Commissar of Defense and succeeded by SHAPOSHNIKOV, he was shot on 22 Feb 39.

YEN, W. W. (Yen Hui-Ching). Chinese diplomat. 1877-1950. Born in Shanghai he received his BA from the Univ of Virginia in 1900 and a doctorate in literature from the National Peking Univ in 1906. He entered the diplomatic service and became minister to the US, Germany, Sweden, and Denmark. After holding high national offices to include that of premier he was ambassador to the USSR. As China's chief delegate to the League of Nations in 1933 he brought charges of aggression that caused the Japanese to leave the League. In 1949 he headed an unofficial delegation in a failed effort to form a coalition government with the communists. [100]

YEO-THOMAS, Forest Frederic. British secret agent. 1902-64. The "White Rabbit" of the French resistance was born in London on 17 June 02. His family, which was of Welsh origin, had been in Dieppe for several generations. By adding two years to his age the stocky, athletic boy joined Pershing's AEF and served in 1918 as a dispatch rider. Still eager for action "Tommy" fought in Poland against the Red Army and was captured. He escaped execution by strangling a guard. Back in France he had a variety of jobs from 1921 until becoming secretary to the high-fashion house of Molyneux in 1932. Having been found too callow to fight in the first world war he was ruled too long in the tooth for the second go-round. But the RAF finally accepted the rare Welshman. He rose from sergeant in 1939 to be an intelligence officer posted to a Polish air squadron in 1941. The next year he wrangled assignment to the Special Operations Executive and became responsible for planning in the French section. The duty included working with DEWAVRIN in organizing the French resistance.

On the first of three SOE missions he (now codenamed "White Rabbit"—becoming "Shelley" to the Germans—and Dewavrin ("Colonel Passy") jumped into Normandy on 26 Feb 43. As planned, they made contact with Pierre "Professor" Brossolette, an outstanding secret service agent, and undertook to win over the many contending resistance groups to a "Secret Army" that recognized de Gaulle as the Free French leader. Dewavrin and Yeo-Thomas returned to London in April with Brossolette after having remarkable success. Jean MOULIN formed his National Resistance Council (CNR) a month later with representatives of all eight major resistance groups including communists.

But the Abwehr promptly arrested several CNR members including Moulin on 21 June 43. The Welsh Rabbit and Brossolette returned to France in Sep 43 to repair the damage. Shelley was on the Lyons-Paris train when he had the harrowing experience of finding that his amicable and unsuspecting companion was Klaus BARBIE!

Scheduled to meet a **Lysander** for his return to England (leaving Brossolette to handle operations in France) Yeo-Thomas was hidden in a hearse to pass German check points. After arranging through Churchill to get the secret army better logistical support, the White Rabbit returned to France in Feb 44 to take over from Brossolette, who had been arrested.

Yeo-Thomas was betrayed just before he sprang an elaborate effort to rescue Brossolette from prison in Rennes. With German-speaking partisans in enemy uniform, fake release papers, a captured car, and a vehicle done up to look like a prison van, the White Rabbit intended for the van to block the gate so the prison guards could be killed, if necessary.

But Shelley violated a cardinal rule of spies by waiting a few minutes outside the Passy Metro station when his contact was late (Farago, *Foxes,* 189). Despite prolonged torture and brutal imprisonment conditions he revealed nothing significant. From Paris' Fresnes prison he was moved through Compiàgne to Buchenwald. On the eve of his scheduled execution in Sep 44 he and two others escaped by assuming the identity of Frenchmen who were dying of typhus. The Rabbit was a hospital orderly at Rehmsdorf until the camp was evacuated on the approach of Allied troops in Apr 45. He organized an escape from the prison train when it stopped for typhus victims. Sick and starving, he was recaptured by German troops. Posing as a POW, he went to Stalag Grunhainigen, where he organized another escape but collapsed after getting away. The 10 other escapees risked their

own safety to get Yeo-Thomas into the hands of advancing US troops.

At the Buchenwald war crimes trial he gave evidence that helped send 22 guards and doctors to the gallows (Foley, *Skorzeny,* 173). The White Rabbit testified as a witness for Skorzeny that Allied resistance forces had done things for which the German commando chief was on trial. This put the military tribunal in the position of condoning a double standard for victors and vanquished, which contributed materially to Skorzeny's acquittal. After Skorzeny's de-Nazification process was inordinately delayed, the German took the advice of Yeo-Thomas: "Escape!"

In many ways the consummate secret agent, Yeo-Thomas was awarded the **George Cross,** the MC with bar, two French decorations, and the Polish Cross of Merit. He returned to Molyneux in 1946 but in such damaged health that he had to resign two years later. But he recovered sufficiently to be Paris representative of the Federation of British Industries in 1950. Yeo-Thomas died 26 Feb 64 in Paris. *See DNB;* M. R. D. Foot, *SOE in France* (1968) and Bruce Marshall, *The White Rabbit* (1953).

YEREMENKO, Andrey I. Soviet military officer. 1892-1970. A senior commander of large formations including the Stalingrad Front, Yeremenko was a burly, baby-faced, ready-fisted Ukrainian whose origins as a cavalry NCO remained apparent.

The son of a peasant, he was born 14 Oct 92 near the present Voroshilovgrad. In the Russian army from 1913 he saw action on the southwest and Romanian fronts before being demobilized in 1917 and going home to organize a partisan detachment and join the Red Army and CP in 1918. After June 19 he headed reconnaissance units then was CofS of a cavalry brigade. For the rest of the civil war he was assistant to a regimental commander in the 14th Cav Div of the 1st Cav Army, fighting in the Caucasus and in the southwest. From Dec 29 he commanded a cavalry regiment, moving up to head a cavalry division in 1937 and two years later to lead the 6th Cossack Cavalry Corps into Poland. The next year (1940) he took his corps into Lithuania and became garrison chief in Vilnius.

After 20 years as a horse cavalryman he took command of a mechanized corps in June 40, promoted at this time to general lieutenant along with Chuykov, Golikov, Konev, Malandin, Sokolovsky, and Vatutin.

Barbarossa

Yeremenko was attending high-level war games in Moscow in mid-Dec 39 when ordered to command the 1st Red Banner Far Eastern Army. But on 19 June 41 Timoshenko ordered him back to Moscow, where he arrived on the 28th after a five-day train ride to take a plane from Novosibirsk. Yeremenko reached D. G. PAVLOV's Western Front Hq on the 29th with orders to take command of the shattered front with MALANDIN as CofS. Soviet encyclopedias do not show that Yeremenko ever commanded the Western Front (Scotts) but some sources confirm his claim to heading it 29 June-2 July 41.

TIMOSHENKO arrived on 4 July with the dual role of **Glavkom** and Western Front commander. Yeremenko and Budenny, whose entire Reserve Front was taken over by the Western Front, became Timoshenko's deputies. The front had collapsed when PAVLOV was recalled on 29 June and by 3 July 41 it ceased to exist when all fighting stopped in the Bialystok pocket. Five days later the Germans had 290,000 Russian POWs, 2,500 tanks, and 1,500 guns (Erickson, *To Stalingrad*, 106).

On 16 Aug 41 (Scotts) the Bryansk Front was created under Gen Lt Yeremenko, "the sort of fellow we want in a tight corner" Stalin said to Vasilevsky after first meeting Yeremenko (Seaton, *Stalin*, 111). "I will smash this scoundrel Guderian without any doubt," Yeremenko assured Stalin on 25 Aug 41 despite Shaposhnikov's and Zhukov's expressed doubts about the new front's combat effectiveness. Yeremenko launched an offensive in the Smolensk-Vyasma-Yelna against an AG Center weakened by GUDERIAN's temporary absence, shortage of reserves, and partisan activity. This caused BOCK some concern before he drove it back in greater disorder than Stalin realized. Yeremenko organized strong defensive positions during the lull that followed. But the "scoundrel Guderian" returned from the Ukraine and launched a surprise attack on 30 September that shattered the Bryansk Front. Yeremenko was severely wounded south of Orel on 13 Oct 41 by bomb splinters and was hospitalized for almost

two months. Although displeased with Yeremenko's failure to measure up, Stalin impulsively promoted him to general colonel and named the stout fellow commander of the 4th Shock Army in the NW Front. After leading a successful attack the general was again severely wounded, on 13 Feb 42.

Command Confusion at Stalingrad

Yeremenko was still lame when ordered from a Moscow hospital on 2 Aug 42 to a GKO meeting in the Kremlin. The situation around Stalingrad was desperate as the Germans closed in, and Stalin could not agree with the Stavka on how to reorganize the command structure. Timoshenko had commanded the Stalingrad Front since 12 July 42, but GORDOV had replaced him 10 ten days later. Yeremenko was ordered to take over "a front in the Stalingrad area." But at a meeting the next day he objected to Stalin's dividing responsibility for Stalingrad's defense between two fronts whose boundary was the Tsaritsa river gorge. Stalin abruptly refused to change his obviously unsound arrangement and Yeremenko left for Stalingrad the next day (4 Aug 42) without a staff. He headed the short-lived Southeast Front (7 Aug-28 Sep 42), which had operational control over troops in the Stalingrad area, with Khrushchev as commissar. These two were promptly in cahoots, initially sharing a crowded command post in the Tsaritsa River gorge with V. N. Gordov's Stalingrad Front. To patch up the unity of command problem Gordov was subordinated to Yeremenko on 13 Aug 42. Gordov remained head of the Stalingrad Front, however, while the actual (if unofficial) command of his SW Front passed to Yeremenko's deputy front commander, F. I. Golikov. The front commanders hence doubled as Yeremenko's deputies in his new capacity, but the ex-sergeant still did not like the new arrangement. "Instead of directing the battle through Gordov and Golikov," writes Seaton, "he began to act as the field commander for both forces, passing orders direct to armies and holding consultations with the military councils and army commanders of both fronts" (*Stalin*, 152). The former cavalry noncom was notorious for punching subordinates, acceptable behavior in the Red Army and jovially encouraged by Stalin, but he may have gone too far even by Russian standards of behavior in also slugging a military council member (*Khrushchev,* 170). HOTH's 4th Pz Army and PAULUS's 6th Army attacked on 23 Aug 42 for what they thought would begin the final assault. ZHUKOV arrived on the 29th to take overall charge of the epic battle. Another reorganization on 9 Sep 42 renamed the Stalingrad Front the Don Front (under ROKOSSOVSKY) and Yeremenko's SE Front was renamed the Stalingrad Front on 28 Sep 42 (Scotts). But Stalin apparently was about to sack Yeremenko for failure to stop the relentless German drive into the rubble of Stalingrad when Khrushchev intervened to save the unpopular general. (*Khrushchev,* 195-96). When a new reorganization was made in Dec 42 for the great Soviet counteroffensive Yeremenko was passed over, ROKOSSOVSKY getting the honor of making the main effort with his Don Front. The heartbroken and furious Yeremenko, who wept bitterly over the decision (*Khrushchev,* 198), had to transfer his 57th, 62d, and 64th Armies to Rokossovsky and take over the Southern Front on 1 Jan 43. With this until the next month (Scotts) he pushed MANSTEIN out of the Caucasus.

Destruction of AG Center

In Apr 43 Yeremenko was transferred to the Kalinin Front and was promoted on 27 Aug 43 to general of the army (No 16). Next he commanded the 1st Baltic Front, in October and November 43, for the advance on Smolensk.

He then led the special Independent (Black Sea) Army in the eastern Crimea in a well-conceived amphibious operation that started on 17 Apr 44 from bridgeheads established during the winter, and he moved west along the southern coast and pursued the Germans into Sevastopol. (Werth, *Russia,* 831.) This cleared the way for TOLBUKHIN to liberate the Crimea.

Heading the 2d Baltic Front from Apr 44 he took part in the offensive starting on 23 June, drove deep into Latvia, and took Dvinsk. He then waged a hard-fought campaign against SCHOERNER's AG North, taking Riga (13 Oct 44) in cooperation with Bagramyan's 1st Baltic Front on his left.

Yeremenko moved back south to head the 4th Ukrainian Front in 1945 from March to July, pushing north of the Carpathian Mountains into Czechoslovakia.

Postwar

After the war until 1958 he commanded the Carpathian, W Siberian, and N Caucasus MDs. Yeremenko then joined MALINOVSKY and ROTMISTROV in the group of General Inspectors who were Khrushchev's apostles in the war of words following the Great Patriotic War. Erickson comments that Yeremenko's *Stalingrad* (Moscow, 1961) "is not wholly reliable and is somewhat one-sided, with almost no attempt at corroboration or identification of documentary items quoted." He died 19 Nov 70 in Moscow and was buried in the Kremlin Wall.

YONAI, Mitsumasa. Japanese admiral. 1880-1948. A career officer, the conservative, antimilitarist Yonai was navy minister from 2 Feb 37 until succeeded by Zengo YOSHIDA when Nobuyuki ABE's cabinet was formed on 30 Aug 39. Adm Yonai then was premier 16 Jan-22 July 40. Resuming his former post as navy minister, he served until TOJO became PM on 18 Oct 41. Succeeded by SHIMADA he had had a major role in building one of the world's most modern and powerful fleets. In retirement he was among those (notably Sokichi Takagi) who secretly began advocating a negotiated peace when the war turned against Japan, but he then declined to resume his post from Shimada when Tojo proposed this in a desperate effort to remain premier. The elderly Yonai insisted, quite accurately, that as "an admiral, not a politician" he was unqualified to lead the government out of her plight. When Tojo was ousted in July 44 the admiral declined the office of premier but agreed to return as navy minister in Kantaro SUZUKI's new cabinet and to double as the nominal co-premier but actually as vice-premier. In a much quoted statement he said that Japan's situation was hopeless after MacArthur took Leyte in late 1944 (Morison, XII, 338). The Suzuki ministry fell on 5 Apr 45, just after US forces landed on Okinawa. Yonai remained in the Supreme Council for the Direction of the War and had a leading part in convincing other members to accept that surrender was inevitable. During his last few years the admiral was involved in the development of Hokkaido.

YORCK VON WARTENBURG, Peter. German resistance figure. 1903-44. Born 17 Nov 03 in Klein Oels, Silesia, Graf von Wartenburg was the great-great-grandson of the Prussian general of the same family name who figured prominently in defeating Napoleon. After studying law and politics at Bonn and Breslau, he entered the civil service and became a senior government counselor. In 1939 he served in Poland as a lieutenant. He was a founder with Helmut von MOLTKE of the **Kreisau Circle** and a cousin of STAUFFENBERG's. The three were anti-Hitler conspirators primarily out of Christian convictions (Wistrich). Attached from 1942 to the War Economy Office, Yorck was among the first arrested after the 20 July 44 bomb attempt on Hitler's life. The young count said in his last letter to his wife, "I believe I have gone some way to atone for the guilt which is our heritage." Brought with the first batch of accused before the People's Court of Roland FREISLER on 8 Aug 44 he was hanged the same day.

YOSHIDA, Zengo. Japanese admiral. 1885-. Fourth son of Mine Yohachi, he was born in Saga Prefecture. Changing his name when adopted by Yujiro Yoshida, he rose after graduation from the Naval Academy in 1904 to be captain of the battleships *Kongo* and *Matsu*. He took command of the Combined Fleet in Dec 37, succeeded YAMAMOTO as vice-minister of the navy in July 39, and replaced YONAI as minister of the navy in Nobuyuki ABE's cabinet, which was formed 30 Aug 39 (the eve of Germany's invasion of Poland). "He is a good Navy Minister," Yamamoto said at the time, "We can sleep easily while he is charge" (Potter, *Yamamoto,* 41). But Yoshida did not live up to expectations in opposing the militarists dominated by the army. Broken in health he resigned 5 Sep 40 to protest Japan's signing of the **Tripartite Pact.** Succeeded by a weaker man, Koshiro OIKAWA, he was promoted to full admiral and made CinC Japanese Fleets in China. In 1944 he became CinC, Yokosuka Naval Station, and during the last months of the war he was on the Supreme War Council.

YOSHIKAWA, Takeo. Japanese official. 1912-. Under an alias, Tadashi Morimura, he reached Honolulu on 27 Mar 41 as an assistant to vice consul Otajiro Okuda, who was under Consul General Nagao Kita. The former ensign had four years of intelligence training as an undercover agent for American operations. After furnishing valuable information for the surprise attack on Pearl Harbor he was arrested on 7 Dec 41 along with Kita and others of the consulate. He was repatriated in the general exchange of diplomats.

YOUNG, Desmond. British officer. 1892?-1966. A British army officer and WWI veteran, he was captured near the 10th Indian Bde Hq on the Gazala line around Bir Harmat in June 42. He escaped, joined Auchinleck's staff, and rose to the rank of brigadier. His *Rommel* (London: Collins, 1950) has been called Rommel's first and perhaps best biography. It became a film, "The Desert Fox," with James Mason playing the lead. Young's autobiography is *Try Anything Twice.*

Z

ZACHARIAS, Ellis Mark. US naval officer. 1890-1961. "Zach" was born 1 Jan 90 in Florida. He graduated from Annapolis in 1912 (79/156), "one of the few Jewish naval academy graduates of his generation" (Layton, 59). After going to Japan in 1920 for language and area study he specialized in naval intelligence. But his sea duty included command of CA *Salt Lake City* in the North Pacific Nov 40-May 42 and of BB *New Mexico* in the Gilberts, Marshalls, and Marianas Sep 43-July 44. (RCS.)

Capt Zacharias meanwhile had headed the Office of Naval Intelligence (ONI) Far East desk and had been intelligence officer of the 11th ND in San Diego before returning to Washington. He became deputy director of the ONI in 1942. With ready access to Roosevelt the captain had a major role in making the controversial decision to assassinate YAMAMOTO.

Marshall and the JCS had advised the White House to accept plans for the war against Japan to last as long as 1949. "The results of this policy were the costly invasions of Iwo Jima and Okinawa," writes a former ONI staffer identified below. "A large-scale invasion of Kuyshu, one of the main islands of Japan, was scheduled to take place in the fall of 1945 with a force of millions and casualties estimated at one million men." (Farago, *War of Wits*, 26.)

In Feb 45 an office was created under Zacharias to correlate information about Japan's war effort from many intelligence agencies including code breakers and the OSS. In a one-page memo the captain concluded that the Japanese, isolated in the four home islands, were losing their will to resist, and he concluded his summary of 12 points with: "It is known that foreign broadcasts are monitored in Japan and transcripts have a comparatively wide distribution." The captain proposed the following policy goal: "To make unnecessary an opposed landing in the Japanese main islands, by weakening the will of the High Command, by effecting cessation of hostilities, and by bringing about unconditional surrender with the least possible loss of life to us consistent with early termination of the war." (Ibid., 29.)

The Zacharias recommendations went to the president with a supporting operations plan. Roosevelt read and penciled comments on the paper but died before directing any action. Pres Truman studied the Zacharias plan on 8 May 45 (V-E day), and it became the basis for subsequent US policy. (Ibid.)

From Apr 45 the captain directed the navy's psychological warfare against enemy morale, personally broadcasting in Japanese and hinting that the Japanese might hope for terms less drastic than unconditional surrender. As head of Op-16-W he had an enterprising subordinate, Ladislas Farago, who, on his own initiative, wrote anonymously to the editor of the *Washington Post* to suggest that the US might offer the Japanese more lenient terms than unconditional surrender. The letter, published on 18 July 45, was taken by some US reporters as an official trial balloon floated by Zacharias. The captain not only approved of Farago's act but also repeated the advice in a subsequent broadcast (Toland, *Sun,* 770n). Zacharias assured the Japanese on 28 July 45, before the A-bombs were dropped, that surrender need not mean an end to the emperor's authority nor Japanese national sovereignty (Bergamini, 81 & n). This message was relayed by US ships steaming perilously close to the coast (ibid.) and the Japanese picked it up on home radios. The maverick captain thus had a significant role in facilitating HIROHITO's efforts to bring about a surrender.

Zacharias retired 1 Nov 46 as a rear admiral and promptly published *Secret Missions: The Story of an Intelligence Officer* (New York: Putnam's, 1946). The author had trouble getting official clearance because he dealt with his long fight to establish an effective naval intelligence service, he cited some of its early wartime weaknesses, and he put much of the blame for the Pearl Harbor disaster on local commanders (RCS). Zacharias and Farago collaborated on *Behind Closed Doors* (New York: Putnam's, 1950), a survey of cold war intelligence operations since 1946. The admiral died 27 Jun 61 in West Springfield, NH.

ZAKHAROV, Georgy Fedorovich. Soviet military commander. 1897-1957. Born 5 May 97 to peasants in a village of Saratov Prov he graduated from the Chistopol Ensigns' School in 1916 and became a junior officer. In 1919 he joined the Red Army and CP, rising to command a company during the civil war.

Zakharov graduated from the Frunze MA in 1933 and from the GS Academy six years later. Characterized by SHTEMENKO as "hot-tempered" and "self-righteous" he was prone to lecture subordinates on tactics, which he had taught at the Military Engineering Academy (Scotts). In 1939-41 he was CofS, Ural MD, leaving on the outbreak of war with Germany to be CofS, 22d Army, Western Front. As a general major he was CofS, Bryansk Front, Aug-Oct 41, then he replaced YEREMENKO as front commander until November. The next month Zakharov became Zhukov's deputy in the Western Front and in May-Aug 42 he was Budenny's deputy in the North Caucasus. Zakharov then was YEREMENKO's deputy in the Southeast and Stalingrad Fronts Aug-Dec 42, following him to the Southern Front.

In Feb 43 he took command of the 51st Army. From the following July he headed the 2d Guards Army in what then was TOLBUKHIN's Southern Front, leading it in the reconquest of the Don Basin. In Tolbukhin's 4th Ukrainian Front he entered the Perekop Peninsula in Oct 43 and established a bridgehead from which he attacked on 8 Apr 44 in the final campaign to liberate the Crimea.

After the recapture of Sevastopol (9 May 44) he commanded the 2d Belorussian Front, Jun-Nov 44, succeeding Ivan Ye. PETROV, and being promoted 28 July 44 to general of the army (No. 21). Georgy Fedorovich led his front through the liberation of Belorussia until the reorganization of mid-Nov 44. This stemmed from Stalin's decision to take over Zhukov's coordinating role in the campaign and the advance on Berlin: Zhukov took over the 1st Belorussian Front from Rokossovsky, who replaced Zakharov as CG, 2d Belorussian Front, and Zakharov stepped down to head the 4th Guards Army from Nov 44 until Mar 45. Serving in the 4th Ukrainian Front (in which YEREMENKO succeeded the unfortunate Ivan Ye. PETROV as front commander in Mar 45). The 4th Guards Army drove into northern Romania, across the Danube, and took part in

the storming of **Budapest.** After the war Zakharov commanded the South Ural MD before heading the Eastern Siberian MD. From 1950 he directed the **Vystrel** Higher Officers' Courses, and from Sep 54 he was deputy head of the Main Military Training Board for Ground Forces (Scarecrow). G. F. Zakharov died 26 Jan 57 in Moscow.

ZAKHAROV, Matvey Vasilevich. Soviet military commander. 1899-1972. Born 17 Aug 99 in the village of Voylovo, Kalinin region, son of a peasant, he was a fitter at a plant in Petrograd before volunteering for the Red Guard in Apr 17 and the Red Army in 1918. Meanwhile he took part in the Bolshevik uprising in Oct 17 and the storming of the Winter Palace. During the civil war he commanded artillery units. He had the normal military school assignments, the **Frunze** in 1928, the Operations Faculty in 1933, the General Staff MA in 1937, thereafter having most of his service as CofS in higher headquarters.

At the start of war in June 41 he was a general major in the Rear Services Directorate, then he was given the new post of CinC Air Forces. His responsibilities were administrative, much like those of the Main Artillery Administration (*see* MEKHLIS). During the war he was CofS on various fronts, mainly under Konev (Kalinin, Steppe, 2d Ukrainian), then in Romania and the Far East under Malinovsky (2d Ukrainian and Transbaykal Fronts). Some writers (and indexers) notwithstanding, it was not M. V. Zakharov but Georgy F. Zakharov (herein) who was Yeremenko's CofS and deputy at Stalingrad.

In Feb 45, having become general of the army (No. 26) the preceding May and **HSU** for service against the Japanese *(S&S)*, Matvey Vasilevich became deputy CG, Far Eastern MD. After holding other high staff positions he commanded Soviet troops in Germany 1957-60. The only officer promoted to the rank between 1955 and 1961 he became a marshal of the Soviet Union (No. 26) in 1959 and got a second HSU gold star in 1971.

ZANGEN, Gustav Adolph von. German general. After the Allied landing at Anzio on 22 Jan 44 and MACKENSEN's assuming command of the 14th Army the latter general's former responsibilities passed to General of Infantry von Zangen. Soon promoted, he commanded a rear-area **Armeegruppe** that was designated Armee Abteilung von Zangen. This was built around the 77th Corps Hq and had three missions: sending combat replacements south, countering partisans, and building defenses along the Adriatic coast.

Generaloberst Zangen then succeeded Salmuth in Holland as CG, 14th Army, on 23 Aug 44 (Stacey, II, 296). After skilfully evacuating most of his army across the Scheldt he was sent to defend the Coblenz area before the Ardennes counteroffensive started on 16 Dec 44. Facing Hodges on the West Wall he was unable to convince MODEL (CG, AG B) that the Americans would make a direct attack in the Remagen sector, and loss of the Rhine River bridge there on 7 Mar 45 changed the entire balance of the Allied offensive into Germany. The 14th Army's 22d Corps defended the south flank of MODEL's AG B along the Rhine until eventually overrun.

Resistance in the Ruhr pocket ended 18 Apr 45 and Zangen became a POW. After the war he provided valuable reports, narratives, and interviews (Toland, *The Last 100 Days,* passim).

ZANGEN, Wilhelm. German industrialist. 1891-1971. He was born in Duisburg on 30 Sep 91. A member of the Nazi Party from 1927 and of the SS, Wilhelm Zangen was an excellent businessman and technician who became the Third Reich's War Economy Leader. He also was chairman of the board of the Mannesmann tube rolling mills in Duesseldorf from Dec 34 to 1957. Zangen died 25 Nov 71 in Duesseldorf. (Wistrich.)

ZEITZLER, Kurt. German general. 1895-1963. Zeitzler was Army CofS after HALDER's exit on 24 Sep 42; he was succeeded by Guderian on 20 July 44

Coming to be nicknamed "Thunderball" *(Kugelblitz),* the burly, dynamic general was born in Cossmar-Luckau on 9 June 95, son of a Protestant pastor. Having commanded an infantry regiment in the Great War he remained in uniform and was one of Hitler's early supporters in the officer corps. With a pleasant round face and toothbrush mustache he even looked somewhat like the fuehrer. In 1934 he joined the first panzer forces. Four years later, having risen to lieutenant colonel, Zeitzler served under WARLIMONT in JODL's new

Wehrmachtfuerungstab. During the Munich Crisis of 1938 he dealt with Hitler's military aide Maj Rudolph SCHMUNDT and the men developed a close friendship that helps explain much of Zeitzler's rapid professional advancement. (Seaton, *R-G War,* 304).

Zeitzler commanded a regiment briefly before being appointed CofS to KLEIST, whose 22d Corps in LIST's 14th Army of became operational in Poland on D+4. Zeitzler then was CofS of Kleist's Pz Gp in the drive through France beginning in May 40. After making a secret reconnaissance in the mountains of SW Bulgaria as LIST prepared to invade Greece, Col Zeitzler was Kleist's CofS in Greece and south Russia.

The colonel was a master of the staff work for fast-moving operations involving large formations and that called for improvisation and good logistical planning. Kleist lavished praise in postwar talks with Liddell Hart on his CofS' performance from France through Greece to the Ukraine *(Talk,* 57-58). Hitler, tiring of military professionals who insisted on doing everything "by the book" and impressed by what he had heard about the colonel, sent for him in early 1942 for an interview. Shortly thereafter, in April, Zeitzler was assigned to OB West, in France, as Rundstedt's CofS. Promoted at this time, Generalmajor Zeitzler was primarily responsible for making the **Dieppe Raid** of 19 Aug 42 an Allied disaster.

Hitler appointed Zeitzler Army CofS a month later, after relieving HALDER on 24 Sep 42. Immediately promoted to Generalleutnant, less than six months after having been a colonel, Zeitzler was soon a Generaloberst. But he held a position that now bore no resemblance to what it had been. Keitel, Jodl, and senior field commanders considered him totally unqualified but consoled themselves with the hope that Thunderball's good personal rapport with the fuehrer would compensate for lack of professional credentials. The newcomer made a valiant effort that included sweeping changes in command and staff procedures. "Zeitzler has introduced a new method of work at GHQ," Goebbels wrote approvingly in his diary on 20 Dec 42, "clearing the desk . . . [so] the Fuehrer is relieved of a lot of detail, and everything doesn't depend upon his decision" (Lochmer, 253). But it was quickly apparent that the new CofS was inadequate for what was an impossible task and Hitler realized he had not found his "General of the Revolution" (Goerlitz, *GGS*, 420, 424). Zeitzler showed courage in shouting back at Hitler on occasion and he argued unsuccessfully against decisions that caused the Stalingrad disaster. But Guderian concludes that Zeitzler and the fuehrer shared responsibility for the epochal failure at Kursk, Opn **Citadel,** the last German hope to turn the tide in Russia. The CofS protested Hitler's "no withdrawal" edicts that led to isolation of AG North in the summer of 1944 and the virtual annihilation of AG Center. Zeitzler tendered his resignation at least four times, first after the Stalingrad disaster, but the fuehrer replied "A general is not entitled to abandon his post." (*See* Zeitzler's chapter on Stalingrad in *F&R*.)

But the general did precisely that on 30 June 44, simply walking away on grounds of ill health. Adolf HEUSINGER took over temporarily. Colonel General Zeitzler was formally retired as of 20 July when Guderian became CofS. Hitler took the extraordinary step in Jan 45 of dismissing the German Army's next to last CofS from the army and forbidding him to wear his uniform. Zeitzler died 25 Sep 63 at Hohenassachau in Upper Bavaria. (Wistrich.)

ZEMKE, Hubert A. US ace. 1914-94. Leader of the 56th "Wolfpack" Ftr Gp of P-47 Thunderbolts in Europe, Col Zemke had 47 aces in his 8th AF unit. He himself was credited with 17 3/4 planes. ("Assists" caused fractions in the US scoring system.) His P-51 broke up in a storm on 31 Oct 44 and he spent the rest of the war as a POW. Zemke died 30 Aug 94.

ZERVAS, Napoleon. Greek partisan. 1891-1957. A regular army officer involved with the Greek Republican Guard, he was dismissed in 1926 and was exiled to France in 1933. In 1938 he returned, and in 1942 he joined the Greek National Democratic Army (EDES). Col Zervas cooperated closely with British sabotage teams that operated against German and Italian occupation forces but devoted most his guerrilla efforts against Gen Stephanos Seraphis's communist-dominated National Popular Liberation Army (ELAS).

Zervas lost the first phases of the civil war but gained the upper hand politically after British troops returned to Greece. In early 1947 he became Minister of Public Safety as the long civil war intensified.

ZHADOV, Aleksei Semenovich. Soviet military leader. 1901-77. He was born 30 Mar 01 in the village of Nikolskoye in what is now the Sverdlovsk Region, Orel Oblast. A general major commanding the 4th Abn Corps in D. G. Pavlov's Western Front he used two brigades on 28 June 41 in a failed attack on the rear of German spearheads approaching the Berezina River, where the shattered 4th Army was attempting to form a defense.

General Major Zhadov succeeded Malinovsky on 16 Oct 42 as CG 66th Army in Rokossovsky's Don Front and had a defensive role in the Don-Volga isthmus as the Stalingrad counteroffensive was organized. He was promoted to general lieutenant in Jan 43 and the following April his unit was redesignated the 5th Guards Army, which fought most of the rest of the war under KONEV. In early July 43 Zhadov's army and ROTMISTROV's 5th Guards Tank Army were detached from the Steppe Front to VATUTIN's Voronezh Front for a decisive role in the Battle of Kursk. Back in the Steppe Front he helped liberate Belgorod on 5 Aug 43, then was heavily engaged against MANSTEIN's AG South. He remained in Konev's front when it was redesignated the 2d Ukrainian Front on 20 Oct 43. Having been promoted again in Sep 44 Gen Col Zhadov attacked on 14 Feb 45 to encircle Breslau, and on 25 Apr 45, in KONEV's final offensive that split Germany, Zhadov's forces met 1st US Army patrols near Torgau.

He was promoted to general of the army (No. 37) in 1955 while serving as first deputy CinC of Ground Forces.

ZHAVORONKOV, Semyon Fyodorovich. Soviet Naval AF commander. 1899-1967. Born 23 Apr 99 in a village of Ivanovo Oblast of peasant paternity he became a textile worker in 1910. Still so employed he participated in the Oct 17 revolution in Vichug. The next year he graduated from the Moscow Party School, helped crush the anti-Soviet revolt in Yaroslavl, and started his rise from Red Army private to battalion commander. In 1934 he qualified as a military pilot. The **Great Purges** hit the navy particularly hard, and as a survivor Zhavoronkov took command of the Soviet Naval AF in 1939 and retained the post throughout WWII. In 1944 he became a marshal of aviation, one of only eight created during the war and the only naval officer (Scotts).

ZHDANOV, Andrey Aleksandrovich. Soviet official. 1896-1948. He was born 26 Feb 96 at Mariupol, a town 100 miles NW of Moscow that now bears his name. Zhdanov's father was a public school inspector, and the son had a good secondary education before becoming a revolutionary in 1912. Most of his work was in the Urals and Tver, where he spread Bolshevist propaganda among the troops and edited a newspaper, *Tverskaya Pravda.* From 1934 Zhdanov was secretary of the Central Committee, and Stalin picked him to take over the party leadership in Leningrad after Sergei Kirov's assassination on 1 Dec 34. Ambitious and unpopular but capable, Zhdanov acquired such power that no business could be conducted in the area without his approval. As a new member of the Politburo in 1939 he made a report to the 18th Party Congress that led Stalin to halt the Great Purges (Clarkson, *History of Russia,* 620). As a member of Stalin's inner circle but had an unfortunate influence in swinging foreign policy away from the west and into the Nazi orbit.

On 19 June 40 Zhdanov reached Tallinn, Estonia, to install a Soviet regime and in the first days of August the USSR annexed the three Baltic States of which he had become overlord. Zhdanov advocated the attack on Finland and became a member of the military council of MERETSKOV's Volkhov Front, and his popularity with Stalin fell temporarily when the first phase of the Winter War failed.

It was on the advice of Zhdanov and KULIK that Stalin made the disastrous error of cutting production of small-caliber tank guns on the eve of Barbarossa (Scotts, citing Volkogonov) but Zhdanov proved his mettle as a military council member during the 29-month siege of Leningrad (Salisbury, *Leningrad,* 181, 320n) and he was given the military rank of colonel general in 1944.

From that year he worked for the Central Committee, **CPSU (B),** on cultural and ideological measures, particularly music and literature (Scarecrow). A prolific author of pamphlets, speeches, and published reports, he imposed his tastes in launching an artistic and literary purge in Aug 46, and effects of the *Zhdanovshchina* were felt for more than a decade. Zhdanov headed the Soviet-British Control Commission for Finland from 1944 to 1947, then organized the **Cominform.** He died

on 31 Aug 48 from chronic heart and lung disease and is buried at the foot of the Kremlin wall. His son Yuri was married briefly to Stalin's daughter Svetlana.

ZHIGAREV, Pavel Fyodorovich. Soviet air forces leader. 1900-63. Born of peasants in Tver Province on 19 Nov 00, the name rendered also st Zhigaryov (Scarecrow), he was a cavalryman (1922) before completing flight training (1927). In Nov 37 he went to China for a year as assistant military attaché in charge of Soviet volunteer pilots, and in May 38 he succeeded RYCHAGOV as MA. (HFS.) The following September Zhigarev became chief of the combat training directorate of the Soviet AF (1938), then he was chief of aviation in the 2d Detached Red Army in the Far East. In 1940 he was one of 13 promoted to general lieutenant of aviation, and in December of that year he became RYCHAGOV's first deputy chief of the Main Directorate of the AF.

Succeeding his unfortunate superior in Apr 41 (HFS), Zhigarev was given the title Commander of Air Forces in June 41. But he was replaced by NOVIKOV in Feb 42 and relegated to command the aviation of the Far Eastern Front. In Aug 45, when Russia went to war against Japan, he led the 10th Air Army of MERETSKOV's 2d Far Eastern Front.

Zhigarev was CinC, Soviet AF, Sep 49-Jan 57. He also was deputy defense minister from Apr 53, when he was promoted to marshal of aviation (No. 10). On 11 Mar 55 he became a chief marshal of aviation (No. 3). Chief of the civil air fleet from Jan 57, he was commandant of the Air Defense Academy from 1959 until his death in 1963.

ZHUKOV, Georgi Konstantinovich. Soviet field marshal. 1896-1974. Perhaps the greatest general of the war, he was born 1 Dec 96 (HFS) in the village of Strelkovka, near Kaluga, about 60 miles E of Moscow.

Zhukov was a peasant reared in crushing poverty but three years in the parish school gave him a life-long appetite for self education. At the age of 10 he started a long, arduous apprenticeship in Moscow as a furrier, qualifying as a craftsman. But the future looked bleak until he was drafted on 7 Aug 15 and selected for the cavalry. Good luck continuing (Napoleon always wanted to know in evaluating an officer whether he was lucky) the ex-furrier became a junior officer in the elite 10th Cav Div, winning two St George crosses, being WIA, and surviving typhus. He joined the Red Army in 1918 and was in the 1st Cav Army during the civil war.

Having grown into a thickset, extraordinarily powerful and exceptionally vigorous man a bit under middle height, Zhukov was rather handsome despite a heavy jaw. He was always a poor mixer socially *(CB 42)* but could be a good companion (below). Joining the CP in 1919, taking part in the defense of Tsaritsyn (which became Stalingrad) and again wounded, with Zhukov, Budenny, Timoshenko, and Voroshilov he was a charter member of Stalin's inner circle.

In 1923 Zhukov commanded a cavalry regiment as the Red Army began modernization. "He seemingly devoured every book, paper and study he could lay his hands on during these hectic days" (Erickson in Carver, ed, *The War Lords,* "Zhukov," 246). "He knew the military classics from Caesar to Clausewitz" (Salisbury's introduction to Zhukov's memoirs, cited below, 14). Formal military schooling included the Cavalry Short Courses in 1925, Higher Short Courses in 1930, and the Leadership Refresher Courses at the Frunze MA, 1929-30 (HFS). He was involved in writing the new field manuals.

Zhukov's field service from 1922 was in the Belorussian MD (HFS) while mechanized forces were being developed. He had no prewar service in Germany, Spain, or China, contrary to what has been written (Erickson, *The Soviet High Command,* hereafter cited as *SHC,* 430; HFS).

Politically suspect for close association with A. I. Yegorov and I. P. Uborevich, both of whom were liquidated (Scarecrow), Zhukov had the unnerving experience of getting no answer to a telegram he sent to Stalin for support (Scotts). But he ended up being charged only with "political shortsightedness" (ibid.) and was not arrested, thus narrowly escaping the **Great Purges.**

After commanding one cavalry corps after another he became deputy CG, Belorussian MD, toward the end of 1938 and took command of the elite 4th Cav Div. (According to some sources he had first headed this in Mar 33.)

Khalkhin Gol

Zhukov first made his mark in Outer Mongolia, where an undeclared border war with the Japanese had been going on. Ordered to the Far East on 1 June 39 after Marshal BLYUKHER was liquidated, Zhukov methodically built an overwhelming combat superiority including a 4:1 advantage in tanks, routing the Japanese at **Khalkhin Gol** (Nomonhan) in Aug 39. Made a Hero of the Soviet Union, he MERETSKOV and TYULENEV were the first three given the new rank of **General of the Army** on 7 May 40.

Battle of Moscow

Later in 1940 Zhukov commanded the Kiev MD and in June he directed the invasion of Bessarabia in Romania. In war games at the end of a big military conference at the Kremlin in late Dec 40 Zhukov directed "enemy forces" and D. G. PAVLOV commanded "friendly forces." After Zhukov's paper panzers ripped through Pavlov's defenses and CGS MERETSKOV was caught unprepared to critique the exercise, Zhukov was suddenly named to replace him. The change was dated 14 Jan 41, Zhukov needing time to wrap up his affairs in Kiev (HFS).

The evening of 22 June 41, the day the Germans invaded, Zhukov flew to Kiev on Stalin's orders for a four-day visit to assess the situation on Budenny's front. On 29 June Zhukov recommended allowing the armies defending Kiev to fall back, and that a counterattack be launched against the Yelnya salient. (Here GUDERIAN's panzers were only 150 miles from Moscow.) When Stalin roared that abandoning Kiev was unthinkable and the idea of retaking Yelnya was "nonsense" Zhukov asked to be relieved. "Don't be so hot-headed," Stalin said calmly. "We'll talk it over and then call you." Some 40 minutes later, Stalin told Zhukov he would be replaced as CGS by the ailing SHAPOSHNIKOV and given the Reserve Front to "take that job" at Yelnya. (Zhukov, *Memoirs,* 288-89). The enemy was driven from Yelnya by 6 Sep 41.

The immediate threat to Moscow was eased even more by HITLER's weakening Bock's AG Center by diverting its panzers toward Kiev and Leningrad. Although generally in charge of defending Moscow, Zhukov headed the Reserve Front from 30 July. TIMOSHENKO commanded the Western theater of operations or TVD, 10 July-10 Sep 41, and also the Western Front (Scotts).

When the situation in Leningrad became critical Zhukov was called to the Kremlin on 9 Sep 41 and ordered to replace VOROSHILOV. The general flew reached Leningrad by air the next day, but within less than a month threat to Moscow was even more critical and on 6 October Stalin recalled his chief fire fighter to Moscow. Only after reaching Western Front Hq on the 11th did Zhukov learn that he was to replace its commander, Konev, who took over the new Kalinin Front. Thus Zhukov became the principal hero in the Battle of Moscow, stopping the Germans after their leading troops could see the Kremlin spires. He then mounted the large-scale winter counteroffensive of 6 Dec 41-7 May 42. Although this bogged down because the Red Army was not yet ready for such a massive effort (particularly in the matter of logistics), it not only saved Moscow but also gave the Germans their first strategic defeat.

Stalin's Military Deputy

On 26 Aug 42 Zhukov became deputy supreme commander in chief of the Red Army (**RKKA**) and Navy. The next day he was made the leading representative of the **Stavka**, thus second only to Stalin in military authority. After assessing the situation at Stalingrad he recommended making the counteroffensive that came to be called Opn Uranus, 19 Nov 42-2 Feb 43. This was the turning point of the war (along with the earlier British victory at **Alamein**). But after he had directed *planning* of Uranus, Zhukov was ordered to turn its *execution* over to Vasilevsky and undertake another mission. On 17 Nov 42 he left the Stalingrad area to coordinate attacks of the Kalinin and West Fronts to pin down enemy strategic reserves during "Uranus" (Seaton, *R-G War,* 309). In early Jan 43 he was sent with Voroshilov to Leningrad, where they organized a double envelopment by the Leningrad and Volkhov Fronts, the latter under MERETSKOV. After only seven days of fighting the two fronts linked up on 18 Jan 43 to break the blockade. (Zhukov, *Memoirs,* 425-26.)

The next month Zhukov became a Marshal of the Soviet Union (No 11), junior in the military hicrarchy only to Stalin and the CGS, Vasilevsky. (KULIK had been demoted, TIMO-

SHENKO shelved, and SHAPOSHNIKOV moved to a less arduous post.) Showing he had administrative as well as command ability, Zhukov proceeded to bring the Soviet armed forces to peak strength.

Kursk

He had a dominant part in planning and directing the execution of the great Battle of Kursk in July 43. "Kursk destroyed any hope of Germany achieving a stalemate in the east; it banished for ever any hope of victory: the strategic initiative had passed irreversibly to the Red Army. . ." (Erickson, Carver, ed, *War Lords,* "Zhukov," 254). The marshal continued to have overall direction of the large-scale operations that liberated Kiev on 21 Nov 43 and he went on to clear the Ukraine. Zhukov took command of the 1st Ukrainian Front after VATUTIN was mortally wounded on 29 Feb 44. Vatutin had set the stage for annihilating what was left of Manstein's defenses on the Dnieper, but Erickson points out three flaws in Zhukov's handling of the 1st Ukrainian Front in his three months as its commander: in late March he failed to reinforce his outer front and the inner front; reconnaissance was defective; and many command posts were isolated from subordinate units. (Ibid.) One-armed Hans "The Man" HUBE consequently fought his 1st Pz Army free from encirclement in the Korzun salient (about 75 miles SSE of Kiev), although Hube lost almost all his heavy equipment. But his offensive and that of Konev's 2d Ukrainian Front effectively shattered the German AG South and their big unearned bonus was Hitler's finally deciding to remove MANSTEIN.

Destruction of AG Center

Now the Soviets undertook to destroy an even more formidable German force, AG Center. The relentless Russian war of attrition continued to be aided immeasurably by Hitler's insistence that all his commanders hold all ground at all times at all costs. Opn **Bagration** began the night of 23-24 June 44 on a frontage of 620 miles against well organized defenses. In accordance with Soviet doctrine they had overwhelming combat superiority, 3:1 in the number of divisions, 4:1 in armor, and almost 5:1 in aircraft. (Erickson, ibid.) Under Zhukov's overall charge as Stavka representative in the field Rokossovsky's 1st Belorussian Front took Bobruisk in only five days, penetrating 70 miles on a frontage of 120 miles and encircling two panzer corps.

British and US forces had finally opened the second front in Normandy on 6 June 44 but now Stalin wanted to finish off the Germans alone. The Soviet high command had sharp disagreements about how to do this and which commander would have the honor of taking Berlin. The nod went to Zhukov but Stalin decided in the fall of 1944 to direct the campaign. Zhukov therefore ended his former duties as coordinator and in Nov 44 he took over the 1st Belorussian Front from Rokossovsky, who replaced Zakharov as CG, 2d Belorussian Front. But disagreements over grand strategy continued. Zhukov wanting more time for logistical support to catch up, and he worried that the northern flank of his drive on Berlin could be threatened from East Prussia and Pomerania. CHUYKOV later accused Zhukov of being so preoccupied by this possibility that he missed the opportunity to rush into Berlin in 1944 and end the war.

Konev, who had the assigned mission of driving south of Berlin to the Elbe, proposed that he also attack Berlin from the south. The general staff agreed, Stalin dismissed all these recommendations and directed also that the Stavka (which he headed) would henceforth control all fronts.

Berlin

Having been given the honor of taking Berlin, Zhukov attacked on 16 Apr 45 but was quickly stopped. "In a transport of fury and disappointment at the delay, Zhukov, flaying all about him, decided to commit his armour at once and literally hurled Katukov and his 1st Guards Tank Army into the attack. By sheer weight of metal Zhukov broke through, using armour and infantry in concentric attacks to force his men forward and into Berlin." (Erickson, ibid., 257.) Konev meanwhile had been authorized to turn his armor north toward Berlin, and the capital surrendered on 2 May 45. He remained there almost a year as head of Soviet occupation forces.

The Man

Zhukov was a rude, brutal, and capricious commander. P. I. BATOV records one episode,

Zhukov's surprise inspection of his 65th Army sector in June 44. "The corps commander is to be removed," ordered Zhukov. "The commander of the 44th [Guards Div] is to be sent to the penal company." (Bialer, 417 ff.) (The sentences were reduced to a severe reprimand for the corps commander and reassignment of the other.)

But SHTEMENKO recalls Zhukov's softly playing his accordion on nights before battle when the marshal could not sleep (HFS). "He was a literate, even a cultured man," writes Salisbury. "But he deliberately presented himself as rude, profane, abusive, domineering." (Salisbury introduction to Zhukov memoirs, 14.)

Postwar

Wearing three Gold Star Medals as a Hero of the Soviet Union (1939, 1944, 1945) and second only to Stalin in national popularity Zhukov was among the many to suffer the tyrant's vengeance. (Others are listed under STALIN.) Beria's poisonous accusations led to the marshal's recall from Berlin in Apr 46 as head of Soviet occupation forces. He was made CinC of all Soviet Ground Forces, a position of even greater prestige, but within three months he was virtually exiled as head of the Odessa MD. This saved Zhukov from Beria and the **Lubyanka** (HFS) but he was expelled from the Central Committee (CC) that year, and in Feb 48 he went into deeper oblivion as head of the Urals MD.

The marshal's first resurrection came the day after Stalin's death on 5 Mar 53, Zhukov being made first deputy defense minister. He stood in the honor guard at Stalin's bier. On 30 June 53 he furnished the troops that enabled political leaders to arrest all top NKVD officials, Zhukov holding the pistol on Beria and later prodding the Politburo into bringing Beria and his aides to trial and execution. Zhukov became defense minister in Feb 55 when his friend Khrushchev took power. (They had known each other since before the war.)

In 1956 the marshal put military pressure on Poland and sent troops to brutally crush the uprising in Hungary, getting his fourth Gold Star Medal as a HSU. In June 57 he provided air force planes to fly CC members to Moscow and vote down a Politburo majority that was prepared to oust Khrushchev. As MOD the marshal undertook to correct the damage Stalin had done to the armed forces in the postwar years.

But Zhukov was suddenly replaced by his deputy MALINOVSKY on 26 Oct 57, stripped of all political posts except party membership and was retired. Why? Probably because Khrushchev knew that his defense minister, like KONEV later, would oppose his plans to shift priority from conventional to nuclear forces. But it may also have been that Khrushchev, like Stalin, had come to realize that the leading war hero was a political threat.

Living from 1957 in a pleasant dacha outside Moscow the non-hero wrote heavily censored articles about his battles. These were published in 1965-68 and translated as *Marshal Zhukov's Greatest Battles,* with a valuable introduction, commentary, and editorial notes by Harrison E. Salisbury. In 1965, meanwhile, Leonid Brezhnev brought the war hero out of the shadows, doing this apparently to curry favor with the Red Army. Millions of copies of his long-suppressed memoirs subsequently were sold, a new edition being published under Mikhael Gorbachev's *glasnost.* Zhukov died 18 June 74 and was buried with all honors in the Kremlin Wall.

ZIEGLER, Heinz. German officer. 1894-1964. Generalleutnant Ziegler was Hans Juergend von ARNIM's CofS in the 39th Pz Corps in Russia and went with him to Tunisia. After blocking Eisenhower's "race for Tunis" Arnim put Ziegler in charge of the counteroffensive that began on 15 Feb 43 and routed Fredendall's green US troops around Kasserine Pass. Ziegler commanded the Afrika Korps in Tunisia shortly before it surrendered on 9 May 43 *(RP,* 418) but he was evacuated. General of Artillery Ziegler succeeded LEMELSEN as 14th Army commander in the last days of the war in Italy.

ZOG (Ahmed Bey Zogu). King of Albania. 1895-1961. Born 8 Oct 95 near Burgayeti, son of the most powerful Moslem clan chieftain in northern Albania, "Ahmed of the family of Zog" (that word meaning *bird*) was educated in Istanbul. He came home in 1912, the year Turkey ("the sick man of Europe") granted Albania autonomy after a general uprising. With a cousin he led their Mati tribe in driving back Serbian invaders. *(CB 44.)* After years of fighting invaders and establishing his tribal hegemony Ahmed Zogu was made interior minister and commander in chief of Albanian armed forces. He became premier on 3 Dec 22 as a representative of the Yugoslav Party, was forced to flee on 10 June 24 to Belgrade from an Italian-supported revolution, but launched a successful counter-revolution in Yugoslavia and was again elected premier on 6 Jan 25. A fortnight later the Albanian Republic was proclaimed with Zog as president with almost dictatorial powers. Having ordered a $5,000 wardrobe from Paris—rose-colored breeches and lots of gold braid *(CB 44)*—and proclaiming himself Zog I on 1 Sep 28, the King of the Albanians began cautiously making reforms.

His notoriously backward country is strategically sited to block access to Italian and Yugoslav ports in the Adriatic. King Zog used this geographical advantage to play off Italy and Yugoslavia against each other in return for the financial and political support he needed. But the country of Machiavelli won out. Zog concluded the Treaties of Tirana in 1926 and 1927 with Italy, which promised respect for Albania's territorial status quo, but Italy used its financial leverage to gain more and more concessions. Mussolini, like his Axis partner Hitler, wanted Lebensraum, and in 1934 he gained the right to colonize certain areas. Albanian discontent with King Zog's reforms led to Moslem insurrections in 1937.

Taking advantage of the distraction caused by the Munich Crisis and Hitler's unopposed move into Czechoslovakia, Mussolini attacked Albania on 7 Apr 39 and established control with little opposition over a country the Italians had virtually owned for decades. King Zog's young, half-American queen (the former Hungarian Countess Geraldine Apponyi) fled in an ambulance to Greece with the four-day-old Crown Prince Skander and two of Zog's sisters. The king followed a day later with 115 courtiers and 10 heavy cases of valuables. Having squirreled a vast fortune abroad, and now appropriating much of the Albanian treasury, he went on through Turkey to a chateau near Versailles. In 1940 the refugee king was admitted to England as a private citizen. His country meanwhile was joined with Italy in a personal union under King Victor Emmanuel III, and a puppet government was installed.

The Germans restored Albanian independence after the Badoglio government surrendered Italy to the Allies on 3 Sep 43 and established a government. Communist partisan leader Enver Hoxha, in alliance with Tito, controlled most of the country by Nov 44, and he took over to rule Albania ruthlessly until his death in 1985.

Ex-King Zog meanwhile had lived in France since the liberation, dying in Paris.

ZORN, Hans. German general. 1891-1943. A Bavarian born 27 Oct 91 in Munich, he had an outstanding combat record in WWI and joined the Reichswehr. Generalmajor Zorn commanded the 20th Inf Div (Mtz) in Russia and was awarded the RK on 27 July 41. He headed the 40th Pz Corps for a month beginning 15 Aug 42 with the rank of Generalleutnant, then was promoted on 1 June 42. General of Infantry Zorn led the 46th Pz Corps 1 Oct-21 Nov 42 and again from 21 June 43. KIA near Krassnaja-Roschtocha on 2 Aug 43 he was posthumously awarded the Oakleaves. (Angolia, II, 245-46; *B&O*, 48.)

ZUCKERMAN, Solly. British scientist and civil servant. 1904-94. The 1st Baron Zuckerman (1971), who loomed large as a scientific adviser on strategic bombing decisions, was born in South Africa. There he received a university degree in anatomy (1923) before moving to England in 1926 and getting a medical degree. As a biologist and research anatomist to the London Zoological Society (1928-32) he made pioneering studies of primates in captivity and published these as *The Social Life of Monkeys and Apes* (1932). Dr Zuckerman was research associate at Yale University (1932-34),

then demonstrator and lecturer at Oxford's Dept of Human Anatomy (1934-45).

His first task as a scientific adviser in WWII was to study the effects of bombing on people. Zuckerman concluded that casualties were due primarily to indirect effects of blast, which led him to the controversial conviction that the enemy could be *bombed* into submission. Largely on his recommendations the Italian island of Pantelleria was "captured" by bombing alone. His concepts of a "communications offensive" gaining acceptance, the Italian rail net then became a major target.

In planning for the assault on northern Europe Zuckerman urged that massive strikes on German population centers and industry should continue, with minimum diversion to support the cross-channel attack (Tedder, 510). It having been demonstrated that railroad nets could be destroyed by scientific selection of targets and by the timing of attacks, "Zuck" was largely responsible for the **Transportation Plan.** Captured railway records in Italy and northern Europe showed that the communications offensive was tremendously effective militarily (Portal, 609-10).

After the war Zuckerman was professor of anatomy at Birmingham Univ until 1968. Concurrently he did much to influence development and technology in Britain, serving on many commissions and being chief scientific adviser to the Ministry of Defense 1960-66 and to the government 1964-71. A fellow of the Royal Society in 1943, knighted in 1956, he was honored with an Order of Merit (OM) in 1968 and a life peerage in 1971. His publications include *A New System of Anatomy* (1961), *Scientists and War* (1966), and *Nuclear Reality and Illusion* (1982).

GLOSSARY

Glossary of abbreviations, definitions, events, issues, terms, and other items indicated by **boldface** in the body of this work. **Boldface** also indicates a cross reference to a separate glossary entry.

A

A day/A hour. Scheduled start of an amphibious assault. See also D day.

A1, A2, etc. US air staff officers corresponding to **G1, G2,** etc. and **S1, S2,** etc.

AA/AAA. Antiaircraft/Anti-aircraft artillery. See also **Ack-Ack.**

AAC & ACC (Italy) **The Allied Advisory Council** in Italy was set up after the **Allied Control Commission (Italy).**

AAF. 1. (US) Army Air Forces. 2. Allied Air Force(s).

A bomb. Atomic bomb.

ABC. American-British [staff] Conversations in Washington, Jan-Mar 41.

ABDACOM. American-British-Dutch-Australian Command, 31 Dec 41-25 Feb 42. WAVELL established its headquarters at Batavia, Java, on 15 Jan 42, dissolving it shortly before hostilities ended 8 Mar 42 in the NEI.

Abitur. German high school exam taken to move from the **Realgymnasium** into the university. It corresponds to the French baccalauréat ("bachot") or the British A-level examination.

ABMC. American Battle Monuments Commission.

Abn. Airborne.

Abteilung (Abt). A German staff branch or section, also a detachment or other separate body of troops.

Abwehr *(Amt Auslands Abwehr).* OKW military intelligence organization headed by CANARIS until 12 Feb 44, when Hitler ordered it placed in Himmler's SS. To the distress of Britain's MI6 (under Stewart MENZIES), this consolidated overlapping and competing **police and secret services of Nazi Germany.**

ACC. 1. Allied Control Commission (Italy); 2. Allied Control Council (Germany).

Ace. Unofficial designation for an aircraft pilot or submarine skipper with at least five victories, except in Germany. *See* **Experte.**

Acft. Aircraft.

Ack-Ack. Antiaircraft fire or guns. "Ack-Ack" is the WWI **phonetic alphabet** rendering of "AA."

ACMF. Allied Central Mediterranean Force.

ACTC (US). Air Corps Tactical School.

ADC. 1. Aide de camp; 2. Assistant Div Cmdr (US).

Adjutant. A minor administrative officer in the US armed forces but more important elsewhere. A French *adjoint* is a deputy or second-in-command; a German *Adjutante* is an important staff officer, high-level liaison officer, or *chef de cabinet.*

Admiral of the Fleet and General of the Army (US). The new five-star rank was bestowed in Dec 44 to the following (dates of rank are in parentheses): 1. Adm LEAHY (15 Dec, retroactive to 15 Nov); 2. Gen George C. Marshall (16 Dec); 3. Adm Ernest J. KING (17 Dec); 4. MACARTHUR (18 Dec); 5. EISENHOWER (20 Dec); and 6. H. H. ARNOLD (21 Dec 44).

Admiral of the Fleet of the Soviet Union. A postwar rank corresponding to Marshal of the Soviet Union and to Admiral of the Fleet in other countries. It was not awarded until Mar 55, when given to I. S. Isakov (1894-1967) and N. G. Kuznetsov (1902-74).

aka. Primarily police jargon for *alias,* standing for "also known as," it is a jocular space-saver in this work.

AEF. American Expeditionary Forces in France 1917-18 under Gen John J. Pershing (1860-1948).

AF. Air Force(s)

AFC (UK). Air Flying Cross (**RFC** and **RAF**).

AFHQ (Allied Force Hq). 1. Eisenhower's Allied Forces Hq (SHAEF); 2. Redesignation of **SACMED** Hq when ALEXANDER took it over on 16 Dec 44.

Afrika Korps (DAK). The famous formation was created by a Fuehrer Order of 11 Nov 40 after GRAZIANI's defeat in Cyrenaica. ROMMEL reached Tripoli on 6 Feb 41 to head "German Troops in Africa," redesignated the German Afrika Korps on 23 Feb 41. (Hitler picked the name.) In his first offensive, 24 Mar-30 May 41, Rommel led the DAK from El Agheila to the Egyptian frontier (bypassing Tobruk). But after personally commanding the Afrika Korps only six months, Rommel moved up on 15 Aug 41 to head Panzer Group Africa, and on 30 Jan 42 his force of German and Italian mechanized divisions was designated Panzer Army Africa. This also was known during the period 1 Nov 42–22 Feb 43 as the German-Italian Panzer Army (*B&O*, 29n).

Although the term "Rommel's Afrika Korps" is improperly used for operations after 15 Aug 41, the DAK continued to be Rommel's Sunday punch. For most of its existence the DAK comprised only two panzer divisions plus independent units. The latter were the 15th Pz Div and 5th Lt Div, which became the 21st Pz Div. The 90th and 164th Lt Inf Divs and RAMCKE's Parachute Bde were attached briefly in the summer of 1942. But none of these independent units was organic to the DAK. (*See* Davies, *Handbk*, 166-68.)

DAK commanders after Rommel were Ferdinand Schaal, but he was too ill to take over, and his successor, Philip Mueller-Gebhard, was invalided home in mid-Sep 41. So for two months the Afrika Korps was essentially leaderless. CRUEWELL arrived in Oct 41 and was captured on 29 May 42. His successor, NEHRING, was WIA on 31 Sep 42 and replaced temporarily by DAK CofS BAYERLEIN. Von THOMA took over shortly before the battle of El Alamein started on 24 Oct 42, but he was captured on 4 Nov 42. Bayerlein resumed command (*RP*, 325) until Gustav Fehn arrived on 23 Nov 42. As the end approached in Tunisia, the world-famous formation (comprising the 90th Light Div, 164th Light Africa Div, and 15th Pz Div) was under Fritz BAYERLEIN as Messe's CofS in the 1st Italian Army. Official records show Johann Cramer as the last commander, 4-13 Mar 43, although it was headed by Gen Lt Ziegler on 7 Mar 43, according to Rommel (*RP*, 418).

AG. **Army group.** See also (Soviet) **Front.**

AGF. US Army Ground Forces. Created 9 Mar 42 to replace GHQ as the agency responsible for combat training in the US, AGF was headed by McNAIR until 25 July 44, then by Ben LEAR.

AGH. US Army General Hospital, as in Walter Reed AGH.

agrégé. A person certified by a French university as qualified for the rank of assistant professor in a specified academic field.

AIF. Australian Imperial Force(s). Separate from the militia and formed for overseas service, "From the beginning [of the war in 1939] the A.I.F. became virtually a separate army with its own seniority lists and system of promotion (Keogh, 65)." The term AIF is used for all Australian Imperial Forces but also for specific formations, as in reference to the "6 Division, Second Australian Imperial Force."

El Alamein, Egypt. A coastal village 65 miles west of Alexandria and 40 miles north of the Quattara Depression. British defenses between these flanks stopped ROMMEL's second offensive, 21 Jan-1 July 42, and were the scene of his defeat by MONTGOMERY, 23 Oct-4 Nov 42. The Battle of El Alamein and PAULUS's defeat at Stalingrad, 14 Sep 42-2 Feb 43, were the turning point of WWII.

Alamo Force (TF Alamo). With the same headquarters as KRUEGER's 6th Army, Alamo Force was created to give MacArthur **operational control** over US forces that should have been under Australian general BLAMEY, who was nominal commander of all Allied land forces in the SWPA. MacArthur's subterfuge added to US-Australian animosity (Collier, *FE*, 346). Alamo Force mopped up in New Guinea, seized the islands of Kiriwina and Woodlark (July 43), captured the W end of New Britain Is and Saidor (15 Dec 43-10 Feb 44), then took the Admiralties, Hollandia-Aitape, and Biak. Its troops reverted to KRUEGER's control for the Leyte campaign.

Aldershot. A major training center 32 mi SW of London.

ALFSEA. Allied Land Forces Southeast Asia.

Allgemeine SS. Literally the "general SS," it was the prewar SS, composed of part-time volunteers.

Allied Advisory Council (Italy). Set up after the **Allied Control Commission** (Italy), it had representatives of all Allied nations once at war with Italy and was directed to "deal with day to day questions other than military preparations and . . . make recommendations to coordinate Allied policy with regard to Italy." (*EP*, 1511n.)

Allied Control Council (Germany). In accordance with an agreement at **Yalta**, a quadripartite body was established in Berlin to administer occupied Germany. It was composed initially of Eisenhower, de Lattre, Montgomery, and Zhukov. A comparable body in Austria, on which Mark CLARK originally sat, was the Inter-Allied Council.

Allied Control Commission (Italy). Established by Eisenhower after signing the 8 Sep 43 armistice with BADOGLIO, and set up with US and UK personnel to see that the Badoglio government complied with surrender terms. (*EP*, 1510n.) See also Advisory Council (Italy).

Allied Military Government of Occupied Territories (AMGOT). British and American teams were formed to follow combat forces and take over the military government of liberated areas. US civil affairs sections were under the **G5**, whose directives came from the civil affairs division of the **WDGS**, established in Washington on 1 Mar 43. The British had a comparable staff section, and the Combined Civil Affairs Committee of the CCS coordinated US-UK efforts.

AM. Air Medal. A minor US decoration, originally for meritorious achievement while participating on a flight in any capacity, it soon was awarded merely for being on five combat missions. Most of the 1,166,471 Air Medals distributed during the war (*AA*, 675) went to USAAF personnel, but officers and men of other services were eligible. *See* **Bronze Star Medal.**

American Volunteer Group (AVG). "Flying Tigers" formed by CHENNAULT in China. In flagrant violation of the Neutrality Act, and with help from T. V. SOONG and Thomas G. CORCORAN, Chennault created the highly publicized force. Recruits were American civilian pilots and military flyers who resigned to seek adventure. With fewer than 20 obsolescent planes initially, three squadrons were operational in time to attack Japanese bombers over Burma on 24 Dec 41. The Flying Tigers eventually included about 90 pilots, of which 20 were lost; 200 planes scored 300 kills. The AVG was disbanded in July 42, when the China Air Task Force was

formed. This was succeeded by Chennault's 14th AF, activated at Kunming on 10 Mar 43 and inactivated 6 Jan 46 in the US. Many Flying Tigers stayed in the successive formations. (*AA*, 597-98.)

"Amerika." Hitler's special train (Fuehrer-sonderzug).

AMET. Africa-Middle East Theater (of operations).

AMGOT. Allied Military Government of Occupied Territories.

Amphib. Amphibious.

Amphibfor (US Navy). Amphibious force.

Amt (Ger). Bureau or office.

Anschluss, 12 Mar 38. Meaning "fusion," the word was applied to the Nazi takeover of Austria. Although inevitable on economic and ethnic grounds, the actual event was improvised suddenly by Hitler to capitalize on a mistake made by SCHUSCHNIGG.

Anti-Comintern Pact. The brainchild of Ribbentrop, whose ally was geopolitician Karl Haushofer, the pact was signed in Berlin between Germany and the Japanese government of Koki HIROTA on 25 Nov 36. Ostensibly a reaction to the popular front policy adopted in July-Aug 35 at the seventh and last congress of the Communist International, the pact named communism the chief threat to world peace. But Japan gained more freedom to expand in China, Germany recognizing Japan's regime in Manchuria, and the pact had secret provisions for assistance if either country fought the USSR. Hungary and Spain joined in 1939. The Anti-Comintern Pact was extended in Nov 41 for another five years but it meanwhile was the basis for the **Tripartite Pact,** signed 27 Sep 40. See also **Axis** and **Comintern.**

Anvil-Dragoon. The Allied invasion of southern France in Aug 44 had the code name Anvil until this was changed because of a security violation to the word Dragoon.

ANZAC. Australian-New Zealand Army Corps.

Anzac Force. Formed on the break-up of TF 14, because CV *Saratoga* was crippled on 11 Jan 42 by a torpedo, the Australia-NZ (Anzac) Force covered the approaches from the major Japanese base at Rabaul to NZ and Australia. Made up initially of the Australian CA *Australia,* CA *Canberra,* CL *Hobart,* two destroyers and a few corvettes, all under British Rear Adm J. G. CRACE, Anzac Force was soon beefed up by US ships, BB *Chicago* and two destroyers. From early Feb 42 US Vice Adm H. F. Leary commanded Anzac Force under the operational control of Adm E. J. KING, US CNO. The force was dissolved on 22 Apr 42 after the Battle of the Coral Sea (Morison, IV, 25n).

AOC (Br). Air Officer Commanding.

Apostles, The. One of the secret societies at Cambridge, it had a long history of opposition to the Church of England and the ruling class. **The Cambridge Five,** two of whom allegedly were "lovers" (Burgess and Blunt), were recruited from the society.

Arakan. Region of SW Burma on the Bay of Bengal that includes Akyab Is.

Arcadia conference, 24 Dec 41-14 Jan 42. A meeting in Washington of Churchill, Roosevelt, and their service chiefs to coordinate strategy.

ARCOS raid, 1927. The Soviet Trade Delegation had the offices of its All Russia Cooperative Society (ARCOS) Ltd at 49 Moorgate in London. On orders from MI5 the offices were raided by police in 1927 to reveal extensive espionage activity (Peter Wright, 33).

Ardeatine Caves Massacre, Rome, 24 Mar 44. The day after a bomb killed 33 Waffen-SS officers in Rome, the Germans executed 335 hostages in caves of the Via Ardeatina.

Ardennes campaign (Battle of the Bulge), 16-25 Dec 44. Hitler's brainchild, opposed by advisers, it was a massive counteroffensive through the Ardennes to take Antwerp and drive a wedge between American and British forces. Although lacking the necessary resources, principally air support, the operation achieved surprise and had considerable success initially. EISENHOWER gave MONTGOMERY **operational control** of BRADLEY's US forces north of the penetration because Bradley had lost contact with them. While Montgomery directed counterattacks on the north shoulder, the critical road junction at Bastogne was held by McAULIFFE, and PATTON mounted a counteroffensive from the south.

Argentia Bay Conference, Newfoundland, 9-12 Aug 41. Churchill and Roosevelt met for the first time, agreed on the "Germany First" strategy, and signed the **Atlantic Charter.**

Arlington National Cemetery, Va. Just across the Potomac from Washington, on the grounds of the Custis mansion that was R. E. Lee's home (by marriage), this national cemetery was established during the American Civil War.

Armee (Ger). A field army. (The German Army was *das Heer,* as in **OKH.**)

Armistice, Franco-German, 22 June 40. Signed for the PETAIN government by HUNTZINGER at Compigne on 22 June 40, it set up a commission to oversee French compliance on the continent and in the colonies. By negotiating an armistice rather than a surrender the French gained advantages to include saving her navy and surviving field forces (which remained under the French government at Vichy).

Army, field. A field army headquarters plans and directs operations of assigned divisions, normally (except in the Red Army) through two or more intermediary **corps** headquarters.

Army Air Forces (USAAF). Created on 9 Mar 42 under H. H. "Hap" ARNOLD as one of three major subordinate commands of the US Army (others being the **AGF** and **SOS**) it gave virtual autonomy to what had been the US Army Air Corps.

Army Group (AG). Two or more field armies. See also, Soviet **Front.**

Arty. Artillery.

ASDIC. The acronym comes from the Allied Submarine Detection Investigation Committee, under whose auspices it was developed in 1918. Working under water somewhat like **radar,** it lulled British naval planners into believing the U-boat would not be a serious menace in the future. Despite severe shortcomings initially, ASDIC became an effective element of **ASW.**

Assam. Province of NE India on the border with Burma.

Assault army (Sov). One reinforced for a specific campaign. Unlike a **shock army** or one composed of **guards units,** an assault army was not a permanent formation.

Assistant/deputy CofS (US). All four general staff officers heading the personnel, intelligence, operations, and logistics divisions of a US Army headquarters—the G1, G2, G3, and G4—are assistant chiefs of staff. But there is normally only one deputy CofS, and only in higher headquarters. Other countries follow much the same practice.

ASSR. Autonomous Soviet Socialist Republic.

ASW. Anti-submarine warfare.

AT. 1. Anti-tank (gun). 2. USN oceangoing tug.

ATC (US). Air Transport Command.

Atlantic Charter. In a joint declaration signed 12 Aug 41 off Newfoundland, Churchill and Roosevelt agreed to war goals. Highlights were that neither sought "aggrandizement territorial or other" and that all peoples— including the vanquished—were entitled to self determination and a fair share of the world's economic resources.

At large. USNA or USMA cadet not appointed from a state. The usual significance is that he was the son of an army or navy officer.

Attentat (Ger)/attentat (Fr). An assault or attempt at a crime like assassination. The failed STAUFFENBERG attentat on Hitler occurred 20 July 44.

AUS. Army of the US (as contrasted with the **RA).**

Auschwitz (Oswiecim). About 33 mi W of Cracow, Poland, the former military base was first used by the Germans in May 40 as a **concentration camp** for Poles. The facility had 28 brick barracks that in 1943 held 10,000 men, women, and children. Auschwitz I became the **Stammlager** (base camp) for 39 subcamps whose construction began in Mar 40.

Auschwitz II at Birkenau, 1.5 mi from Oswiecim, was the death camp. Thirty times the size of the Stammlager, it had about 300 wooden barracks with rows of wooden bunk beds for some 100,000 men, women, and children who were held in 1943.

Auschwitz III at Monowitz, 5 mi from Oswiecim, was a slave labor camp for a huge I. G. Farben rubber plant. Like "lucky ones" at other labor camps, inmates of Auschwitz III were men under the age of 40 and boys of 18 or 19.

Almost all others were taken direct from the railroad station to gas chambers at Birkenau, a few specimens being reserved by MENGLE for his experiments. Life expectancy in labor camps was about six months, except for inmates on special duty as guards, orderlies, clerks, etc. Used-up prisoners ("Gypsies") went to gas chambers and four crematoriums at Birkenau. An estimated two million were gassed and cremated there between 1942 (after the **Wannsee**

Conference) and the fall of 1944. The SS then demolished and abandoned most facilities to destroy evidence of the "holocaust" before the Red Army arrived on 27 Jan 44. Commandant Rudolf Franz Hoess (1900-47) testified at Nuremberg that about 140,000 inmates passed through his hands. In 1993 a multi-million-dollar project was begun to preserve what remains at Auschwitz-Birkenau, to include buildings, fences, watch towers, gas chambers, ovens, collected personal effects, and nearly two tons of human hair.

As for the latter, prisoners were shorn on arrival, if selected for labor, or after being gassed. Hair was cured, baled, and sold at 20 pfennig per kilogram to felt and textile manufacturers.

Red Army troops liberated the camps on 27 Jan 45.

Auslandsdeutscher. German living abroad.

Auslandsorganisation (AO). Known variously as the Foreign Countries Organization, the Foreign Organization, or Overseas Branch, headed by Ernst Wilhelm BOHLE, it oversaw affairs of overseas Germans. The AO overlapped functions of the Third Reich's diplomatic service (Bracher, 322-23).

Avalanche. Code name for Allied amphibious assault on Salerno, Italy, 9 Sep 43.

AVG. American Volunteer Group in China (above).

AWC. US Army War College at Ft McNair, Washington, DC.

Axis. The "Berlin-Rome Axis," a statement of common interests signed on 21 Oct 36, became a formal military alliance, the "Pact of Steel," on 22 May 39. The **Tripartite Pact** of 27 Sep 40 created the Tokyo-Berlin-Rome Axis. Hungary, Romania and Slavokia joined on 20, 23 and 24 Nov 40. Bulgaria and Yugoslavia signed up on 1 and 25 Mar 41. Croatia joined on 15 June 41, having declared independence on 10 Apr 41. Finland was a German ally after Hitler invaded Russia on 22 June 41 but never formally joined the Axis. See also **Anti-Comintern Pact.**

B

B-17 Flying Fortress (US). Designed for self-defense in daylight operations, it was the only prewar long-range aircraft (tested in 1935) that flew as a first-line plane in 1941-45. With modifications, "Forts" were the backbone of the US strategic air war.

B-24 Liberator (US). A long-range heavy bomber, it had greater range and payload than the B-17.

B-29 Superfortress (US). Brainchild of H. H. "Hap" Arnold, it was the biggest and most advanced bomber of WWII. Under Curtis LeMAY the B-29 had a major role in the defeat of Japan.

"Baedeker raids." So called by the British, alluding to Karl Baedeker's travel guides, they were in retaliation for incendiary raids on historic Luebeck. The Luftwaffe's targets, many bombed several times during a period of about two months beginning 24 Apr 42, were Exeter, Bath, Canterbury, and Norwich. Coventry had been blasted earlier. The RAF responded by devastating 600 acres of Cologne in the first 1,000-bomber raid of the war, 30-31 May 42.

Bagration, Opn. Soviet campaign in Belorussia that destroyed AG Center, 22 June-29 Aug 44.

Bailey bridge. Designed early in the war by Sir Donald C. Bailey, and promptly adopted by the US Army (and others), this was a steel bridge that came in panels and could be erected in many variations for quickly bridging a gap of almost any width.

Baltic States. Estonia, Latvia, and Lithuania.

Bar. 1. British equivalent of the US oakleaf cluster to indicate a subsequent award of the same decoration. (The second award is perversely called a "first bar," and so on.) 2. British campaign medals of WWII are issued with appropriately inscribed bars—"Battle of Britain" on the 1939-45 Star, for example.

Barbarossa. German code name for their invasion of the USSR that started on 22 June 41.

Bataan death march. After some 78,000 US and Filipino survivors of the Luzon Force were surrendered by Maj Gen Edward P. King, Jr, on 9 Apr 42, most were marched 65 miles from Mariveles to San Fernando. Clubbed, beaten, bayonetted, denied food, water, and mercy, the surviving POWs ended up at Camp O'Donnell, near Tarlac, to begin 40 months of captivity.

Battle of Britain, 8 Aug-31 Oct 40. After their lightning victories on the continent, the Germans concentrated on taking Britain out of the war. A prerequisite was to defeat Hugh DOWDING's RAF Fighter Command. It was nip and tuck until Goering (directing the war from his estate, Karinhall, outside Berlin) made the critical error of shifting the Luftwaffe's main effort from destruction of Fighter Command to undertake the London **Blitz.**

Battle of the Bulge. Popular name for the **Ardennes campaign,** which drove a deep penetration (bulge) into the American line.

Battles of Flanders, 10 May-2 June 40, and of France, 5-22 June 40. Terms commonly used for the first and second phases of the German conquest.

Bazooka. A recoilless rocket launcher first used with revolutionary effect by US troops in North Africa. The name comes from a musical instrument that physically resembles the weapon. Normally fired from the shoulder by one man and an assistant, or from a mount in a light vehicle, it had a 2.36-in, 3.5-pound projectile with a **shaped charge.** Effective range was 400 yards. Other countries quickly fielded comparable weapons, the **Panzerfaust** and Panzerschrecht, and the British PIAT.

BB. Battleship. A USN designation, it is used in this work (and others) for battle ships of other countries.

BBC. British Broadcasting Corporation. Its overseas service had a major role in the war, giving concise and accurate news to friend and foe, to captive people, and passing coded messages to the resistance.

BC. 1. Battle cruiser (RN); 2. RAF Bomber Command; 3. various USAAF bomber commands worldwide.

BCT. Battalion combat team. See also **RCT.**

Beer Hall Putsch, 8-9 Nov 23. See **Munich Beer Hall Putsch.**

BEF. British Expeditionary Force to France in 1914-18 and 1939-40.

Befehlshaber (Ger). Commander of a formation.

Belsen. See **Bergen-Belsen.**

Bendlerstrasse. Berlin street address of the German Ministry of Defense. The building was renamed for Count von STAUFFENBERG.

BENELUX. Belgium, the Netherlands, and Luxembourg.

Benning. One of the US Army's centers of education and training, The Infantry School at Ft Benning, Ga, figures prominently in WWII literature because so many officers associated there with George MARSHALL went on to high command. Benning was the Infantry **OCS**; it provided basic and advanced courses for all **company grade** infantry officers; and it was the center for airborne training.

Berchtesgaden. Village in SE Bavaria about 10 mi S of Salzburg overlooked by Hitler's **Berghof.**

Bergen-Belsen. Established in 1941 on Lueneburg Heath in NW Germany to handle sick POWs, this became one of the more infamous **concentration camps.** The SS took over the camp in 1943 for Jews and invalids. As the Red Army approached other camps in 1944, Bergen-Belsen's population mushroomed from 8,000 to 60,000. Survivors were dying of typhus at the rate of 500 a day when the British liberated the camp on 15 Apr 45.

Berghof. Hitler's mansion on the Obersalzberg overlooking **Berchtesgaden.** It was heavily bombed in Mar 45 and occupied by US troops on 7 May 45.

Bernhard, Opn. The plan to undermine the British economy with forged bank notes was credited to NAUJOCKS but masterminded by SS Col Fritz Schwend. The sophisticated counterfeiting operation, set up in a concentration camp, was technically a success, the paper money passing examination even by some Bank of England experts. Opn Bernhard failed in its economic mission but the bogus bank notes were useful in paying secret agents including the spy BAZNA ("Cicero") and, allegedly, in financing the ODESSA network. Schwend escaped to a life of luxury in Peru.

BG (US). **Brigadier general.**

BGS (UK). Brigadier General Staff. A **brigadier** serving as CofS.

Big Three. These were Churchill until succeeded by Attlee on 28 July 45, Roosevelt succeeded by Truman on 12 Apr 45), and Stalin.

Big wing controversy. Bitter disagreement developed within the RAF during the Battle of Britain over the refusal of Hugh "Stuffy" DOWDING, chief of Fighter Command, to adopt the "big wing" strategy. This was advocated principally by Douglas BADER, Sholto DOUGLAS, and LEIGH MALLORY. Dowding refused to alter his successful strategy of scrambling fighter squadrons to attack as fast as possible. The main criticism of the big wing strategy was that it took more time to "mass" a "big wing" than critics thought was warranted by results. Douglas argued that it was better to destroy 50 enemy bombers after they hit than to down 10 of them on their way to the targets.

Bismarck. A German battleship, the world's newest and most powerful, it was sunk by the British on 27 May 41 after a dramatic chase across the Atlantic that is covered under LUETJENS.

Bismarck Sea. Name given during the war to the waters between New Britain, Papua, the Trobriand Islands, and the Northern Solomons. (Morison, III, 387n.)

Black and Tans troubles in Ireland, 1919-21. Irish republican demands for a free Ireland led to violence against the Royal Irish Constabulary (RIC). The British beefed up the constabulary with British ex-soldiers, who wore a temporary uniform that led to the nickname Black and Tans.

Black Dragon Society. In 1901 a member of the Genyosha, a secret society dating from 1881, founded the Kokuryaki. "This name has been dramatically translated in the West as the 'Black Dragon Society,'" writes an authority, "but it was actually based on the Chinese name for the Amur River, and was meant to suggest that Japan's natural strategic frontiers were on this northern boundary of Manchuria" (Reischauer, *Japan,* 182). The Japanese government had virtually destroyed the so-called Black Dragon Society by 1940, but its name and that of the Genyosha remained a convenient scapegoat for any sinister act of ultranationalism. One victim was HIROTA.

Black propaganda. Deceptive information to attack enemy morale.

Black Reichswehr. Officially the Work Command, and so nicknamed because of its black uniforms, it was a sort of Free Corps **(Freikorps)** created by von SEECKT to defend East Prussia and Silesia after Poland won its war against the Red Army in 1920-21. Formed mostly from ex-Freikorps members, and eventually numbering about 20,000, the Work Command operated under instructions from von Seeckt. The force was commanded by a civilian, von Schwarzkopfen (a former colonel of the GGS). He was under the supervision of Oberstleutnant Fedor von BOCK (CofS, Wehrkreis III), who got his orders from a Truppenamt section that included Majors von SCHLEICHER and HAMMERSTEIN-EQUORD. (Dupuy, *GGS,* 211.)

Blackshirts. Fascist and Nazi **(SD)** storm troopers.

Blade Force. A mobile task force of armor, infantry, artillery, and engineers formed in Algiers, it reached the Tunisian front on 18 Nov 42. After pushing from Bejda in the direction of Bizerte, Blade Force had to withdraw as the "race for Tunis" failed.

Bletchley Park. A country estate near London to which the GC&CS moved from **Broadway** in early 1941, Bletchley accommodated a great variety of codebreakers. Decoded radio messages were evaluated to become intelligence classified "**Ultra** Secret." The population at Bletchley grew from 1,800 in the spring of 1941 to 9,000 (Brown, *"C,"* 396-97). Under the control of MENZIES, the station was directed until Feb 42 by Alastair Denniston, then by his former deputy, Cmdr Edward Travis.

Blitzkrieg ("lightning war"). Featuring close cooperation between panzers and the Luftwaffe, the word first gained currency in Poland (Sep 39).

Blitz of London. It began on 7 Sep 40 with a daylight raid of 372 bombers, and after a two-day break continued for 23 consecutive days. The pounding of London resumed in Dec 40 and lasted until the following spring. But the London blitz gave DOWDING's Fighter Command the respite it needed to win the **Battle of Britain.**

Blood Purge of 29 June—1 July 34 in Germany and Austria. Commonly called "the night of the long knives," officially Opn Hummingbird (*Kolibri* in German), the purge was ordered primarily to destroy the SA (Brownshirts) leadership. With the support of SKORZENY, HITLER personally directed actions in and around Munich to "terminate" ROEHM and his principal lieutenants. Goering, Himmler, and Heydrich controlled Opn Hummingbird from Berlin. Killings there and throughout Germany and Austria began on Friday, 29 June 34,

the majority taking place the next day, but continuing through Monday. The estimated 478 victims (Deutsch, I, 17) included Gen and Frau von SCHLEICHER, Gregor STRASSER, and two of von Papen's advisers. Hitler won praise from the generals, including Hindenberg, for keeping his promise that the Brownshirts would not be a threat to the national army.

"Blue Max." the German Imperial Army's **Pour le Mérite**.

Bodden line. A chain of 16 infra red and sonic ship reporting stations being constructed by the Abwehr, with Spanish naval assistance, to report on traffic through the Straits of Gibraltar. Radio intercepts in June 42 contained the code word "Bodden," which Kim Philby's research revealed had something to do with the sea bottom. This led to discovery of the Abwehr's project and a diplomatic protest to Franco, who ordered the Bodden line dismantled before it was a threat to Opn Torch.

Bodyguard. A highly successful group of six deception plans, 36 subordinate plans, and "scores of associated stratagems" to cover the Normandy landings on 6 June 44. The major deception operations were Fortitude North (against Norway), Fortitude South (the Low Countries), Ironside (Bay of Biscayne), Royal Flush (NE Spain around Barcelona), Vendetta (south of France), Zeppelin (western Greece), and Russian operations north and south (Black Sea). See Anthony Cave Brown, *Bodyguard of Lies* (1975).

Boffin. British term of unknown origin for a scientist working for the government on wartime problems.

Bolero. Code name for the buildup of US forces in the UK.

Bolsheviks. A communist faction ("the majority") created by Lenin in 1902 that finally won out over the Mensheviks ("the minority") in 1912 and split from the Russian Social Democratic Workers's Party (RSDRP) as the RSDRP(b). The latter became the CP(B), all-Union Communist Party (Bolsheviks), in 1925-52, being redesignated the CPSU in 1952. Meanwhile "Bolshevik," which Russians generally do not capitalize (Scotts), became the common name, particularly among foreign enemies, for all Soviet communists.

Boomerang, Opn. Elaborate (and successful) deception programs supporting Opn **Bodyguard** to cover the Normandy landings of 6 June 44.

Br. British.

Brandenburg training center. Abwehr personnel were trained here before Canaris ordered creation of "Construction and Training Company Brandenburg" in Oct 39. Many recruits were Balts and **Volksdeutchen,** and native Germans also were selected for fluency in foreign languages. Under Genmaj Erwin von Lahousen's Abwehr Div II (sabotage and special duties), they were parceled out to the operational control of army corps commanders, receiving orders through the corps intelligence section. (Paine, *Abwehr,* 156.) As the force grew into Theodor EICKE's Brandenburg Div it suffered the common fate of special forces: employment in costly conventional operations. So SKORZENY was authorized to take some 4,000 officers and men from the Brandenburg Div for his "special troops." The SS commando unit for special tasks was called **"Oranienburg."**

Bretton Woods Conference, NH, 1-22 July 44. In one of the longer-lasting efforts toward establishing the UN it was agreed at this meeting to establish the International Monetary Fund and the International Bank for Reconstruction and Development.

Brevet (Bvt). A temporary promotion given usually for exemplary service, it originally was a way to honor officers for gallantry. (Modern awards and decorations—medals—are a relatively recent military innovation.) The British continued to use the brevet system in WWI, but in America it was so abused as to be meaningless even before the excesses of the Civil War era.

Bridgend POW Camp No 11, South Wales (UK). Several hundred senior German POWs of all armed services and the SS were held here for interrogation and classification. The German camp leader was Georg von Seidel, ex-QMG of the Luftwaffe. Historians including Basil LIDDELL HART interviewed the inmates and had them record their experiences. To his later distress, Otto JOHN helped classify prisoners as anti-Nazi, indifferent, incurable.

Brigade. To "brigade" is to combine several battalions or regiments, often temporarily, into a brigade under one commander, a brigadier in the UK but normally a colonel in the armed forces of other countries.

Brigadefuehrer. The Waffen-SS rank equivalent to army Generalmajor.

Brigadier. British Army rank immediately above full colonel and below major general, so called because the officer normally commands a **brigade.** The British abolished the grade of brigadier *general* in 1918, hence a brigadier is not a **general officer** and a US brigadier general is not a "brigadier." British officers in moments of camaraderie may address American colonels as "brigadier." The Bri-tish Army rank of colonel is primarily an administrative rank (for doctors and officers in management positions). See also **BGS.**

Brigadier general (US). With one star for rank insignia the US brigadier general has few foreign counterparts other than the French général de brigade, who wears *two* stars.

Broadway (London). British military intelligence was located from 1924 in a large building at No. 54 Broadway, behind 21 Queen Anne's Gate, the Passport Control Office. "Broadway" housed SIS, including the GC&CS until this moved in the spring of 1941 to Bletchley. Stewart Menzies, SIS chief from 1939, had his offices at Broadway and his official residence (connected by a secret passage) at 21 Queen Anne's Gate.

Bronze Star Medal (US). A minor decoration in two grades, one for valor and the other for merit in ground action against an enemy of the US. It was authorized for front line or rear area actions that did not qualify for a higher award. Instituted on 4 Feb 44 but awarded retroactively to 7 Dec 41, the BSM was created to be bestowed as liberally to ground forces as the AM was to flying personnel. But only 395,379 BSMs actually were awarded up to 30 June 47, whereas 1,166,471 Air Medals were awarded during the same period. (*AA,* 674-75.) After V-E day the BSM was awarded automatically to all holders of the combat infantryman badge (CIB) or medical badge.

Brownshirts (SA). Nazi storm troopers. *See also* Blackshirts.

Brty. A battery, or company-size unit of artillery, normally 4 to 6 guns.

BuAer, BuPers, etc (USN). Bureau of Aeronautics, of Naval Personnel, etc (most designations being self evident).

Buccaneer. Proposed amphibious operation against the Andaman Islands cancelled at the Cairo Conference because MOUNTBATTEN's SEAC was not given the necessary priority in landing craft.

Buchenwald. Located on a wooded hill four miles from Weimar, it was one of the first **concentration camps** and perhaps the most notorious after Ilse KOCH's husband became commandant in 1939.

Budapest. A twin city astride the Danube, the capital of Hungary. Located on flat ground, Pest fell quickly to the Red Army on 18 Jan 45. Buda, the older city and a natural fortress on high ground and topped by the gigantic governmental palace, was held by the Germans until 13 Feb 45. This significantly slowed the Soviet advance on Vienna.

Buergerbraeukeller *(Bürgerbräukeller)*, Munich. A Nazi landmark, this was an early meeting place for Hitler's supporters, site of the Nazi CP for the **Munich Beer Hall Putsch** of 8-9 Nov 23, and of the Hitler-assassination attempt of 8 Nov 39 that led to the **Venlo incident** of 9 Nov 39.

Bulge, The. The deep German salient created in the **Ardennes campaign,** 16-25 Dec 44.

Bundesrepublik Deutschland (Federal Republic of [West] Germany). Established 21 Sep 49 with Dr Conrad Adenauer as chancellor until 1963, it became a sovereign independent country on 5 May 55. Bundestag, Bundesrat, and Bundeswehr were new names for the German diet, upper chamber, and armed forces.

Burma Road. The NE section of this vital motor route ran 717 miles from Kunming, China, to the head of the easterly branch of the British-owned Burma RR at Lashio, Burma. The airline distance was 320 mi. *(Webster's Geogr Dict,* 174.) Before the Japanese captured Canton on 21 Oct 37 the Chinese began improving the old spice and caravan trail into a one-lane, light-surface road. Opened in Dec 38 (ibid.), it became China's only supply line from the west, having a riverboat and rail link from Rangoon to Mandalay (for a total distance of about 2,100 miles). Graft and various inefficiencies had reduced traffic to only 4,000 tons a month by mid-41, but Daniel ARNSTEIN quadrupled the flow by year's end. After the Japanese took Lashio on 29 Apr 42, allied supplies had to be flown from India to China across **The Hump.** For about a year starting in Sept 1943 Col Leo Dawson directed reconstruction of the Burma Road, 25 miles of which the Chinese had demolished in the Salween River canyon. When the Allies recaptured Mongyu on 27 Jan 45, completion of the Ledo Rd, renamed at that time for Stilwell, allowed the link-up of the **Ledo Road** from India.

Buzz-bomb. British nickname for the V-1.

Bvt. **Brevet.**

Byrnes Note. US Secy of State James C. BYRNES drafted this with two masterfully ambiguous paragraphs to get around the Australian view that HIROHITO should perhaps be charged as a war criminal. Broadcast on commercial radio to Japan from Washington on 11 Aug 45, the note included provisions that "From the moment of surrender the authority of the Emperor and the Japanese Government to rule the state shall be subject to the Supreme Commander of the Allied Powers" and that the "ultimate form of Government of Japan shall . . . be established by the freely expressed will of the Japanese people." The note accelerated the Japanese surrender.

C

c. Circa (about), as in c 1900.

C&GSC. Postwar designation of the C&GSS.

C&GSS (US). The Command and General Staff School at Ft Leavenworth, Kans, evolved from officers' schools that had been there since 1881. In 1928 the course was changed back to two years from one year, and the name was changed from General Service Schools to the C&GSS. In 1935 it reverted to a one-year course attended by 250 selected officers *(AA,* 355), mostly captains and majors. Between the two world wars about 4,000 RA and 500 NG and Reserve officers graduated (ibid). From Dec 40 Leavenworth gave accelerated courses to thousands of officers. After the war the C&GSS became the Command and General Staff College.

CA/CL. USN designations for heavy and light cruisers.

CAC (US). Coast Artillery Corps.

Cactus. US code name for the Guadalcanal-Tulagi area.

Cagoulard. The name comes from *cagoule,* a hood worn by monks and penitents. Like the Ku Klux Klan, the Cagoule went through many evolutions (Pertinax, 335). By the 1930s it was an extreme-right, secret terrorist group of Frenchmen who opposed Léon Blum's **popular front.**

Cairo, Egypt. Headquarters of the British Middle East Command, home for Greek and Yugoslav governments in exile, Cairo was the site for various high-level meetings including the two-part Cairo Conference. For the first of these, "Sextant," 22-27 Nov 43, Churchill and Roosevelt were joined by Gen and Mme Chiang Kai-Shek to discuss the future role of China. Churchill and FDR then had the **Teheran Conference** with Stalin. The second phase at Cairo, "Eureka," 28 Nov-1 Dec 43, firmed up plans for the invasions of Normandy and southern France, which ended hopes for MOUNTBATTEN's Op **Buccaneer.** China was certified as a world power in the Cairo Declaration of 1 Dec 43.

Camberley. British army staff college corresponding to the US **C&GSS.**

Cambridge Five. Starting around 1933 Kim PHILBY, Guy Burgess, Donald Maclean, Anthony Blunt, and John Cairncross were recruited by the Soviets. The five operated as moles in high places during and long after the war (below).

As members of the **Apostles** and the Communist Party of Great Britain (CPGB) the Five were recruited by a remarkable succession of **"illegals."** Authorities disagree widely as to the identity of these talent scouts and recruiters. The first seems to have been the former Hungarian priest and tutor of international affairs, Theodore Maly. "Theo" was followed in 1936-37 by the equally effective "Otto," who probably was a Czech, but MI5 never learned his identity (Peter Wright, 227).

Sudoplatov, writing in 1994, discredits the long-accepted view that Alexandr Orlov (formerly Nikolski) recruited Philby, Burgess, and Maclean in that order. But recently available KGB files show that Andrew Deutsch operated in England ahead of Orlov, who was in London from the summer of 1934 until the fall of 1935, and that Deutsch enlisted Philby.

Orlov, London resident in the summer of 1934 but having to leave in the fall of 1935, defected in July 38. He lay low for 15 years (for his own safety) but never exposed the Cambridge group. (Sudoplatov, 34n, 44-46.)

For more than a year after Otto's departure "the ring remained in limbo, out of touch [with Moscow] and apparently abandoned" (Peter Wright, 228). Then Litzi PHILBY provided a new link through her close friend and fellow Comintern agent Edith Tudor Hart, whose connection with Moscow was through Bob Stewart of the CPGB. This link disappeared when several high officials of the CPGB were convicted of espionage directed against the Woolwich Arsenal Munitions Factory. "Had we run the case on longer, we might well have captured the most damaging spies in British history before they began" (ibid).

The Russians reestablished contact with the Cambridge Five at the end of 1940 and redirected their efforts to military intelligence. The new controller was Anatoli "Henry" Gromov or Gorski, who worked under diplomatic cover. Gromov left for Washington in 1944 to run Donald Maclean and was replaced in London by Boris Krotov, an officer of the **NKGB.** Krotov controlled the Cambridge Five throughout the war and after.

The first moles to be exposed were Burgess and Maclean. Philby was "the third man" who alerted them in time to defect in 1951. Philby was strongly suspected at this time but not unmasked until 1963. Late that year an American, Michael Whitney Straight, told the FBI that Blunt had recruited him as a Soviet agent at Cambridge in the 1930s (Wright, 213). Confronted with this evidence by MI5 Blunt confessed in Apr 64 and was given immunity in return for a full confession. Tall, wispy, and homosexual, Blunt had been a high official in MI5. He had remained briefly after the Burgess-Maclean affair of 1951 and the departure of Cairncross from Britain (following). Philby needed Blunt, who was a useful informant in MI5 on how the hunt for moles was progressing. But Blunt was anxious to pursue his career as an art expert, and, by a queer irony, he was appointed Keeper of the Queen's pictures.

He was the queen's third cousin once removed. His treason was revealed to MI5 in late 1963 but in return for full cooperation he was given full immunity and his secret was not revealed by the government. Having been knighted, Sir Anthony remained at Buckingham Palace until publicly exposed in 1979 and stripped of his knighthood.

The fifth man, John Cairncross, was promptly identified by Blunt as the missing spy. He had served in the Treasury in 1940, moved on to the **GC&CS**, and joined MI6 in 1944. The Scot had given the Russians unedited **Ultra** messages while MI6 was feeding edited versions of the same material to Moscow Center through the **Lucy ring.** As noted in that entry, the Soviets could tell by comparing messages from Cairncross and Lucy that MI6 had penetrated their Swiss network. Cairncross had been a suspect since 1951, Treasury information in his handwriting had been found in the hastily abandoned flat of Burgess, but the fifth man denied being a Soviet spy and said he did not know that his friend Burgess was. Peter Wright found Cairncross to be entirely unlike the other moles, "a clever, rather frail-looking Scotsman with a shock of red hair and broad accent" who wanted to make a clean breast of it and come home from France. (Wright, 222). He confessed in 1964. Three years later he visited England when promised repatriation if he could help MI5 get an admission from the man he claimed to have recruited him. But the elderly James Klugman, previously known only as an overt CPGB activist, refused to be wheedled or coerced into confessing he had been a covert Soviet agent. Cairncross returned to exile (ibid).

The defectors died in Moscow, Burgess in 1963, Maclean in 1983, and Philby in 1988. Blunt died in 1983. Cairncross was living in Paris and writing his memoirs (Sudoplatov, 34-35n), when he returned to Britain in Mar 95. In failing health at the age of 79 he lived only six months.

CAP. Combat air patrol (to cover a naval force).

Captain. In most countries the army rank of captain is immediately above first lieutenant and below major; it equates to lieutenant of the navy. A naval captain, who wears four stripes on his blouse and a silver eagle on the shirt collar, is equivalent in rank to full colonel in most armies, air forces, and marine corps. Naval captains and lieutenants should be introduced as "of the Navy" if out of uniform.

Carriers, US. See **CV, CVE,** and **CVL.**

CAS (Br). Chief of [the] Air Staff, the RAF's senior officer. His principal staff officers have titles like "Assistant CAS (policy)."

Casablanca Conference, 14-23 Jan 43. As allied victory in North Africa seemed assured, Churchill, Roosevelt, and the CCS met near Casablanca in the Anfa Hotel and surrounding villas. US planners reluctantly agreed to postpone the cross-channel attack on Europe until 1 May 44, allowing for the invasions of Sicily and Italy, operations expected to take Italy out of the Axis. It was decided at Casablanca also that ALEXANDER would become Eisenhower's deputy in Algiers (leaving his Cairo headquarters). In a feeble attempt to reconcile the **French factions** of DE GAULLE and GIRAUD, Roosevelt persuaded the two antagonists to shake hands for a historic photograph. FDR announced his **unconditional surrender** declaration at the final press conference.

Casualty. The imprecise term includes **DOW, KIA, MIA,** and **WIA.**

CB (Br). **Companion** of the Bath.

CB ("Sea Bee"). A US naval construction battalion or its personnel.

CC. 1. Combat command within a US armored division, whose **SOP** called for formation of all divisional units into CCA, CCB, and CC Reserve. 2. **Central Committee of the CPSU.**

CCC. The US Civilian Conservation Corps was created in early 1933 by Roosevelt to get depressed youth off the streets for work including large-scale reforestation. The US Army was given the task of handling what became known as the "tree army."

CCS. Combined (US—UK) Chiefs of Staff.

Cdn. Canadian.

CEF. Chinese Expeditionary Force of about 12 weak divisions under Marshal WEI Li-huang in Burma, 1945.

Center, The (in Moscow). Vernacular designation for the Soviet central intelligence service.

Central Committee (CC) of the **CPSU.** Comprising party members from the government, armed forces, and the arts and sciences, the CC legalized work of the exclusive **Politburo** (Scotts).

Central Intelligence Agency (CIA). A postwar evolution of the **OSS** through the short-lived **CIG,** the controversial secret empire was created under the new National Security Council by the National Security Act of 26 July 47. The CIA was headed first by Rear Adm Roscoe H. Hillenkoetter, who was followed in Oct 50 by Gen Walter "Beetle" Smith. Allen DULLES, Smith's deputy, moved up to be the agency's first civilian director, 1953-61.

Central State Security Directorate (USSR). Name sometimes used for the **Main State Security Directorate.**

CEO. Chief Executive Officer (of a commercial enterprise), who normally works through a chief operating officer.

CFLN or CNL. The Free French Comité Français de la Libération Nationale created 3 June 43 in Algiers with DE GAULLE and GIRAUD as co-presidents. See also **French factions.**

CIA. US Central Intelligence Agency (above).

CG. Commanding general (US). The British equivalent is GOC (Army), AOC (RAF), and NOC (RN).

CGS. Chief of the General Staff. *See also* CIGS.

Chad (officially Tchad). Now the northern division of what was French Equitorial Africa, Chad is bounded on the north by Libya's Fezzan and Cyrenaica districts. In late 1942 LECLERC led the "Chad column" on a remarkable march north to join Montgomery's 8th Br Army.

Changkufeng Hill, Manchuria. *See* Khalkhin Gol.

Chantiers de la jeunesse. Meaning "youth work camps" (roughly) these were first created in France during the summer of 1940 as an emergency measure to move young unemployed men of draft age from the cities to camps where they could be physically and morally uplifted by work in the forests. By Jan 41 the Vichy government had turned the program into a form of national service. (Paxton, *Vichy,* 164.) An armed detachment of the organization was used by pro-US conspirators to secure Algiers in Opn Torch (8 Nov 42).

Cheka, 1917-22. The Extraordinary Commission Against Counterrevolution, Sabotage, and Speculation (Cheka) was a secret police force established immediately after the 1917 Revolution. See also **Police and secret services of the USSR.**

Cherchell conference, 22 Oct 42. As part of final preparations for the 8 Nov 42 landings in North Africa, GIRAUD's representatives in Algiers asked for a secret meeting with senior officers of Eisenhower's staff (Smith, *OSS,* 58-59). Robert MURPHY picked a spot about 75 miles west of Algiers near Cherchell, where a fellow conspirator, Henri Tessier, had an isolated villa near the beach. Mark CLARK, Lyman LEMNITZER, and Capt Jerauld Wright (USN) went from Gibraltar to the rendezvous in Lt N. L. A. Jewell's *Seraph,* a British sub. Under cover of darkness the Americans landed in rubber boats and were met by Murphy and Vice Consul Ridgeway Knight (ibid). Gen Charles E. MAST and his staff officers were waiting at Tessier's house. The French provided valuable information about troop dispositions, installations, and reiterated willingness to collaborate (*EP,* 639). But Clark was not authorized to tell the French what they needed to know about when and where the landings would be. Mast believed he had several weeks to make final arrangements, whereas he actually had 17 days. The troublesome command problem was only obfuscated at Cherchell, where all Clark could promise was that Giraud would have the overall command "as soon as possible." (Murphy, 119.) DARLAN had only recently sent hints he might shift allegiance to the Allies, and his offer had to be considered.

Tessier's Arab servants suspected smugglers were responsible for the suspicious activity on the beach, and the authorities offered generous rewards to informers. Tipped off by the servants, French police burst in on the meeting. Murphy and company put on a show of revelry while the Americans hid in a wine cellar until they could head for the beach. Because of heavy surf the rubber boats capsized before the party got back to the submarine, Clark losing his coat, shirt, trousers, and 750,000 francs in gold coins he had brought to give the Algiers cabal. This and other comic aspects of the adventure have diverted attention from the fact that the Cherchell conference did not prepare the French to render maximum assistance to Operation Torch.

Chetniks. From *ceta,* a company of guerrillas who fought the Turks in the Balkan wars and WWI, Chetniks was the name TITO's supporters gave to MIHAILOVIC's. (Djilas, *Wartime,* passim.)

Chef de cabinet. The French word "cabinet" means office, bureau, or study, hence the term—common throughout Europe, not just in France—is self-explanatory. It might best be translated as chief private secretary (Pertinax, 190). The British are comfortable with "private secretary." American journalists settle for the vague term "aide," and the White House has adopted the military term "chief of staff."

China Lobby. Chinese and American supporters and agents of CHIANG KAI-SHEK fueled FDR's illusions that Chiang could make China a world power; Old China hands knew better.

Chindit(s). A corruption of *Chinthe,* the mythical dragon that guarded Burmese temples, the name was picked by WINGATE for his long-range penetration forces in Burma.

CIA (US). Central Intelligence Agency. A postwar outgrowth of "Will Bill" DONOVAN's **OSS.**

CIB. **Combat Infantryman Badge.**

"Cicero." *See* Elysea BAZNA.

CIG (US). Central Intelligence Group. Set up after the abolishment of "Wild Bill" DONOVAN'S **OSS,** its second chief, Lt Gen Hoyt S. VANDENBERG, began the transition of the CIG into the **CIA.**

CIGS (UK). Chief of the Imperial General Staff. Alan BROOKE officially took over the post from DILL on 25 Dec 41.

CinC. Commander in Chief.

CINCAF. Commander in Chief, Allied Forces.

CINCLANT. Commander in Chief, Atlantic Fleet (US).

CINCMED. Commander in Chief, Mediterranean.

CINCPAC/CINCPAO. NIMITZ's titles as CinC, Pacific, and CinC, **Pacific Ocean Areas.**

CINCSWPA. CinC, **Southwest Pacific Area** (MacArthur).

CL/CA. USN designation for light and heavy cruisers.

CMG (Br). **Companion** of St Michael and St George.

CNL. The Free French Committee of National Liberation, also called the **FCNL.** See also **French factions.**

CNO (US). Chief of Naval Operations.

CNS (UK). Chief of Naval Staff.

Co. Company, military or commercial. (In medieval times a company of military mercenaries was a commercial company whose investors shared the loot and other profits.)

Cobra, Opn. Code name for US 1st Army breakout from the Normandy beachhead west of St Lô in July 44.

Colditz. A large, high-walled, supposedly escape-proof castle in SE Germany where some 600 Allied prisoners of all ranks and nationalities eventually were housed. Most were there because of persistent escape attempts elsewhere, but others were **Prominente.**

CofS. Chief of Staff.

Colmar pocket, 20 Jan-9 Feb 45. Hitler ordered bypassed remnants of Friedrich Wiese's 19th German Army to hold the bridgehead around Colmar on the Upper Rhine after de Lattre's 1st French Army cleared Belfort Gap and pushed through Mulhouse to the Swiss border in late 1944. De Lattre had recently had LECLERC's 2d Div transferred to his army, but a disagreement over the strategy for eliminating the Colmar pocket led to Leclerc's rejoining Patch's 7th Army in mid-Dec 44 (*EP,* 2362n). When Eisenhower suggested to DEVERS, CG 6th AG, that Patch send one of his corps south to attack Colmar from the north while de Lattre attacked from the south, Devers said this was unnecessary because the 19th German Army had "ceased to exist as a tactical force." This proved to be very wrong, and a heavy reinforcement of the 1st French Army by three US divisions (Frank Milburn's 21st Corps of the 7th Army) was needed to eliminate the Colmar Pocket by 9 Feb 45. (*West Point Atlas,* Map 64a.) Devers's bad judgment "exerted a profound and adverse effect on our operations" said Eisenhower in his official report (Wilmot, 570).

Com-. USN abbreviation for "Commander," as in ComCruDiv (Commander, Cruiser Div), ComNavAirLant (Commander, Naval Air,

Atlantic Fleet), and ComFltAir Quonset (Commander, Fleet Air, Quonset, RI).

Combat Infantryman Badge (CIB). Authorized 27 Oct 43 to give more recognition to the Queen of Battles (which had trouble getting recruits) it was awarded only to infantry officers and men in combat at the *regimental or lower* level. No other criteria were established officially except that the badge was awarded at the discretion of regimental commanders, many of whom authorized automatic issuance. The CIB features a miniature Revolutionary War rifle in sterling silver on a 3-in-long rectangular infantry-blue enamel field that has a silver frame encircled by a silver wreath. The CIB is worn on the left breast above all ribbons.

Combined Chiefs of Staff (CCS). A US-UK command committee set up in Washington after the Arcadia Conference ended on 14 Jan 42, it comprised the three US service chiefs (Marshall, King, and Arnold) and representatives of their British counterparts.

Combined operations. Amphibious operations involving forces from more than one armed service (Army, Navy, Marines, AF, and sometimes the Coast Guard or others). See Roger KEYES and MOUNTBATTEN.

Comdr. Commander.

ComFltAir (USN). Commander Fleet Air.

Companion (of various British orders). One of several grades, third, in the case of the **OBE,** and one rank below knight. See also **knighthood.**

Company grade officer. A captain or lieutenant, the category below "field grade."

Commando. The name used in the Boer Wars for a unit of partisans was picked by the British in WWII for **special forces** conducting guerrilla operations. "Commando" came to mean individuals as well as formations.

Cominch. Commander in Chief US Fleet.

Cominform. Organized in 1947 by ZHDANOV, it succeeded the Comintern (below).

Comintern. Communist International, established by Lenin in 1919 under Grigori Ye. Zinoviev (1883-1936) as chairman of the External Committee guided the communist movement outside the USSR with the objective of causing world revolution. The Comintern attracted dedicated and courageous Trotskyist communists who operated in foreign countries as **"illegals,"** the most effective Soviet recruiters and controllers of secret agents. The 7th and last conference of the Comintern in July-Aug 35 adopted a **popular front** policy, reflecting STALIN's decision to side with democratic states against fascism. This prompted formation of the **Anti-Comintern Pact.** The Comintern was abolished on 22 May 43 but reorganized in 1947 as the Cominform.

Commando order. Prompted by the **Dieppe raid** (19 Aug 42) and having found Allied orders authorizing commandos to kill prisoners who were a hindrance to carrying out a mission, Hitler issued the Commando Order on 18 Oct 42. It directed that "all enemies [captured] on so-called Commando missions" be turned over immediately to the SD and "slaughtered to the last man."

Commissar (USSR). People's Commissars or "Narkoms" (from *Narodnyy Komissar*) hold posts at the ministerial level. In the spring of 1918 the Soviets adopted the system of military-political commissars (used in French Revolutionary armies of 1792-93) to control former Tsarist military personnel. As party representative the commissar (*voenkom*) countersigned all orders issued by commanders. Voenkoms were abolished in Aug 40 after becoming a serious problem for field commanders, but they returned to duty after the Germans invaded the USSR in June 41.

After 9 Oct 42, the strategic situation having stabilized, military-political commissars were restricted to indoctrination, troop welfare, assisting in military administration, and sitting on **military councils.** Although no longer having veto power, the commissar could make or break military careers by using his special communications channels. Most commissars were so experienced militarily that they could take over from commanders who became casualties, and many (like KONEV) left the corps of commissars to be **line officers.** Military commissars wore regular uniforms but had a stitched-on red star with hammer and sickle as a sleeve emblem. After Oct 42 they had military-political rank from Junior Politruk to Army Komissar 1st Rank.

Commissar order *(Kommissarbefehl).* Three months before the start of **Barbarossa** Hitler directed that normal rules of war should not be observed in Russia. On seeing the first draft of what became the "commissar order" almost all officers protested that it was criminal. WARLIMONT produced a watered-down version that Hitler approved on 6 June 41. It called for immediate liquidation of **commissars** captured while fighting in battle areas. Those taken in rear areas because of doubtful behavior were to be turned over to the SD. (Davidson, *Trial*, 335-36.) Others would be spared. Because the order still was criminal, it was not issued in writing but passed on orally.

Companion of the Bath (CB) and other orders. "Companion" is the honor conferred before a **knighthood,** hence the bearer is not addressed as "Sir" Whomever.

COMSOPAC. USN Commander, South Pacific.

Com Z (US). The Communications Zone, formerly the SOS, in the **ETO,** headed by J. C. H. LEE.

Concentration camps of the Third Reich. The first were established in Prussia by GOERING and in Bavaria by HIMMLER. Need for the camps arose when prisons were overcrowded with communists and socialists charged with responsibility for the **Reichstag fire** of 27 Feb 33. (Bracher, 358.) After opening Estewengen and **Dachau** in 1933, Himmler took charge of all camps and the next year started building more. Among the earliest, located conveniently near SS Hq in Berlin, were Sachsenhausen and Oranienburg. The latter was a "detention center" before becoming headquarters in 1938 for Theodor EICKE (who then was Inspector of Concentration Camps). Other early camps were Quednau (near Koenigsberg); Hammerstein (Pomerania); Lichtenburg (near Merseburg); Werden (Essen); Brauweiler (near Cologne); the SS Columbia House special prison in Berlin; Boergermoor and Papenberg (both in the Ems region); Duerrgoy and Kemna (both near Breslau); and Sonnenburg (at Warthe, near Frankfurt/Oder).

Others were **Buchenwald** (1937); the granite quarries of **Flossenburg** and **Maut-hausen,** both in the Upper Palatinate (1938); **Ravensbrueck** (for women) and **There-sienstadt** (both opened in 1939). New camps set up in 1940 or soon thereafter were Neuengamme, near Hamburg; **Bergen-Belsen;**

Gross-Rosen, in Lower Silesia; Stutthof, near Danzig; and Natzweiler or Natzwiller, in the Vosges about 25 mi WSW of Strasbourg.

In Poland, **Auschwitz** opened in May 40. After the Wannsee Conference, 20 Jan 42, many new facilities were built in Poland, where Odilo GLOBOCNIK took charge of Belzec, Kulm (Chelmno), **Maidenek** (Lublin), Sobibor, and **Treblinka.**

Full information of HIMMLER's mass murder program was restricted to himself and perhaps only 70 who ran the camps (Irving, *HW*, 393). But reports of widespread corruption within the system led KALTENBRUNNER to have an independent lawyer make an investigation in 1943. Starting at Buchenwald, Dr Konrad Morgen built cases against 200 camp officials including Ilse KOCH and her husband Karl, the commandant. When Morgen discovered that systematic mass murder was taking place in the camps, Christian WIRTH told him that this was on Hitler's orders. Believing Wirth, and realizing the danger of blowing the whistle, the investigator continued to prosecute individual camp officials in hopes that this would, indirectly, expose the greater crimes. But Morgen submitted his more alarming findings to Kaltenbrunner, who claimed at Nuremberg in 1946 that both he and Hitler were shocked by the report. On 17 Oct 44 the fuehrer demanded an accounting from Himmler and Oswald Pohl (1892-1951), who directed "economic" aspects the concentration camp system—getting maximum return on the slave labor and collecting booty from victims. David Irving cautions that "we have only Kaltenbrunner's account of all this" and no corroborative documentary evidence has been uncovered (*HW,* 718). But in Oct 44 Himmler ordered the death camps closed and evidence of the killing destroyed (ibid). See also **Final solution.**

Condor Legion. Composed of Wehrmacht volunteers, the Condor Legion was assembled at Seville, Spain, by 6 Nov 36 to support FRANCO's Nationalist. The larger Luftwaffe component, under Hugo SPERRLE with Wolfram von RICHTHOFEN as CofS, ultimately had about 5,000 personnel with 200 aircraft (Irving, *Milch*, 50) organized as follows: a battle group of four bomber squadrons of 12 Ju 52s; a fighter group of the same composition flying He 51s and Me 109s; a squadron of reconnaissance, seaplane, and experimental aircraft; and AA units. The aircraft operated mainly without radios.

A German army unit of about 2,500 officers and men under Generalmajor Walter WAR-LIMONT picked up the two armored units of four panzer companies of four tanks each that had been in Spain for three months under von THOMA, who had been training Franco's troops and acting as a general military adviser.

The legion later had an attached "North Sea Group" of gunnery, mine, and signal specialists operating from BBs Deutschland and *Graf Speer.* (Thomas, *The Spanish Civil War,* 316-17.)

Conferences, Allied. Chronologically, the major Allied conferences were at **Argentia Bay, Washington** (3), **Casablanca, Quebec** (2), **Cairo, Teheran, Yalta,** and **Potsdam.**

Control Group. One of the **Japanese political factions.**

Corps, army. A *headquarters* subordinate to the field army. Normally headed by a lieutenant general, it plans operations, directs training, and is assigned two or more divisions plus supporting troops to execute the plans. Composition of a corps varies as operations proceed. The Red Army used the corps echelon primarily for mechanized formations. So many Soviet senior commanders had been lost by Dec 41 that only six of the original 62 corps headquarters remained, divisions being directly subordinated to army commanders. But Red Army cavalry corps began to be formed at this time. Soviet AF corps formations were eliminated from strategic (long-range) aviation but retained for air defense. Early in 1942, however, guards rifle corps started being formed, followed in March by tank corps, and from September by new mechanized corps. (Scotts; Seaton, *R-G War,* 112n.)

COSSAC. CofS to the Supreme Allied Commander (Designate), a post held by Frederick MORGAN to start planning the Normandy invasion.

CP. 1. Command post; 2. Communist Party.

CP(B). All-Union Communist Party (Bolsheviks), 1925-52. It evolved from the RSDRP, and in 1952 was redesignated the **CPSU.** See also **Bolsheviks.**

CR. US Commendation Ribbon. Established in 1945, it was awarded retroactively on the rec-

ommendation of a major general or above to personnel who had served well during WWII.

Cranston. RAF staff college.

Cranwell. RAF cadet college.

Cross of Lorraine. An ancient symbol with modern associations: in 1918, the return of Lorraine to France from Germany; in 1941, the sign adopted by de Gaulle's Fighting French (later Free French).

Crusader. Code name for AUCHINLECK's counteroffensive, 18 Nov-31 Dec 41, that relieved Tobruk and drove ROMMEL back to El Agheila.

Crystal Night (Kristallnacht), 9-10 Nov 38. The night of pogroms throughout Germany and Austria was triggered by the fatal shooting of a minor German diplomat, Ernst vom Rath, on 7 Nov 38 by a 17-year-old Polish-German Jew, Herschel Grynszpan, in the German embassy in Paris. Vom Rath died on the afternoon of 9 Nov, when the 15th annual celebration of the **Munich Beer Hall** putsch was being held in Munich. Nazi leaders, particularly Goebbels, had wanted a provocation to launch drastic anti-Jewish policies (Schwab, 191); this was it. But Grynszpan's act let the Nazis make it appear that the widespread anti-Jewish rioting was spontaneous and not organized.

At least 267 synagogues and almost all Jewish cemeteries were desecrated; 7,500 stores and at least 177 homes were looted and destroyed. Property damage totaled about a billion **marks.** At least 91 people were murdered, 36 were seriously injured, and numerous suicides included entire families. About 30,000 men and boys were incarcerated briefly in concentration camps, where hundreds died. Total deaths attributed to Crystal Night, directly or indirectly, are estimated at 2,000 to 2,500. (Schwab, 26-27.) Walter FUNK is credited with coining the lighthearted name Crystal Night as an allusion to the shattered plate glass shop windows.

Cub. The L-4 Piper Cub, produced by the (W. T.) Piper Acft Co of Lock Haven, Pa, was used by the US Army primarily for directing field artillery fire. But with **VSTOL** characteristics, it performed innumerable chores as a "flying jeep." Some 7,000 L-4s were used during the war by the USAAF and Signal Corps (*CB 46.*)

CV. US aircraft carrier, large. The pre-Pearl Harbor US carriers were *Lexington* and *Saratoga* (both 33,000 tons, 34 knots, 86 planes), *Ranger* (14,500 tons, 30 knots, 72 planes); *Yorktown* (19,800, 34, 85), *Wasp* (14,700, 30, 84), and *Hornet* (20,000, 34, 81). Built and commissioned during the war were 16 CVs of the *Essex* class (27,100 tons, 33 knots, 103 planes). Essexes that replaced lost carriers were *Hornet, Lexington, Wasp,* and *Yorktown. See* Morison, XV, 29 ff, for all USN ships and aircraft.

CVE. Escort carrier ("baby flattop").

CVL. Light aircraft carrier.

CVO (Br). Commander of the Royal Victorian Order.

CZ. Canal Zone (Panama and Suez).

D

D day. Military planners use "D day" for the date any operation is scheduled to begin, "H hour" being the starting time. "A day" and "A hour" are used also in connection with amphibious assaults, as on Leyte, PI.

Dachau. From 20 Mar 33 an old powder factory in this small town, 10 mi NNW of Munich, was the site of one of the first **concentration camps.** In June 33 Theodor EICKE became commandant and made the camp a model and training center for camps established later. Mass executions were not conducted at Dachau, but murderous medical experiments were. Liberated by US troops on 29 Apr 45, when it held 32,000 prisoners, Dachau has been preserved as a monument.

DAK. Deutsches **Afrika Korps.**

DAP (Deutsche Arbeiter Partei). German Workers' Party taken over by HITLER in the early 1920s and built into the Nationalist Socialist (Nazi) German Workers' Party (NSDAP).

Dartmouth. Royal Naval College, a two-year program from which students go on as cadets to become midshipmen.

DCG. Deputy commanding general.

DCGS. Deputy chief of the general staff.

DD. 1. Destroyer. 2. Duplex drive amphibious vehicle propelled in the water by its wheels, tracks, or a propellor.

DE. Destroyer escort.

Death march. See **Bataan death march.**

Death's Head (Totenkopf) SS. The Death's Head Hussars were an elite unit of the Imperial German Army. Their old commander, Field Marshal August von Mackensen, still appeared in full military fig during the first days of Hitler's chancellorship and was among the few officers of the Old Guard to speak out against Nazi excesses. The name of the Death's Head Hussars and their skull-and-crossbones insignia were purloined by Theodor EICKE for the branch of the SS he formed in 1934 to guard **concentration camps.** Eicke's 3d SS Totenkopf Div was formed in 1939 with a cadre from the **Totenkopfstandarten,** and in Apr 41 it was made part of the Waffen-SS.

Decorations, medals, and awards. See individual entry.

Denmark Strait. A 130-mile-wide passage between Iceland and Greenland, it is narrowed by pack ice. Frequent fog and rough weather made the strategically located strait a favored haunt of German surface raiders.

Dept. Department.

Deputy People's Commissar (Zam Narkom). The term suggests a relatively exclusive position, but a deputy commissar was one of many who headed subordinate offices in the numerous people's commissariats like those of defense or state security. There also were subordinates with the title first deputy. (HFS.)

Diamonds. An order of the German **Knight's Cross (RK).**

Dieppe raid, 19 Aug 42. Although useful in testing amphibious techniques and German coastal defenses in France, the operation was a costly disaster in which 5,000 of the 6,000 ground troops were Canadian, 4,000 of them actually engaged. Total Cdn casualties in nine hours were 3,367. No fewer than 1,946 of these were captured, more Cdn POWs than during 20 months in Italy and more than during 11 months of fighting from D day in Normandy to V-E day. Cdn dead exceeded 900, about 70 of whom died in captivity, chiefly from wounds. (Stacey, I, 387.) Of the other 1,000 ground troops engaged, 275 were lost, including 45 killed. (Ibid.) See also MCNAUGHTON.

Direction. A Soviet theater of military action, or TVD, commanded by a Glavkom (Scotts).

Division. Army divisions (a concept adopted by Napoleon) are the smallest military formations organized for sustained, independent field operations. Most are composed of infantry, but many are motorized, armored, airborne, or made up of mountain troops. A WWII US Army division numbered about 15,000 officers and men in three regiments, with an artillery unit of about **brigade** size, plus **organic** engineer, signal, medical, and other units. German and Red Army divisions were of about the same size and composition initially, but they frequently fought on with only a few thousand survivors. Soviet cavalry and infantry divisions were often reduced to a combat strength as low as 3,000 and 8,000 (Seaton, *R-G War*, 94n). "Division" is used also to designate other military formations of varying composition, particularly in the navy.

Djebel. Arabic word for a rocky prominence, used in accounts of operations in Tunisia. "Gibraltar" derives from Jebel al Tari, "Mount of Tari" the 8th century Moorish conqueror.

DM. Light minelayer.

DM or RM. Deutschmark or Reichsmark (in 1944 the equivalent of US $0.25).

DMS. High speed minesweeper.

Doolittle Raid on Tokyo, 18 Apr 42. Lt Col James H. Doolittle's squadron of 16 Army B-25 Mitchell Bombers was carried on the deck of Capt Marc Mitscher's CV *Hornet* of Vice Adm William F. Halsey's TF 16 (which included CV *Enterprise*). Each with four 500-lb bombs and 1,141 gallons of gasolene the planes began launching in choppy seas at 8:24 AM on 18 Apr 42 (Tokyo time, E Longitude date) when 668 miles from the heart of Tokyo. This was 150 miles short of the planned launching position because picket boats, outside the expected stations, had detected TF 16 at about dawn. By 12:35 the 13 bombers assigned targets in Tokyo began attacking military targets, meeting little resistance. Three other planes, carrying only incendiaries, had targets in Nagoya, Osaka, and Kobe. They also achieved surprise, although the plane assigned to Osaka probably hit Nagoya instead.

The raid did no serious material damage—although more than hoped for—and no plane was lost over Japan—but the moral effect on the Japanese and on the US home front was immense. One serendipitous result, however, was that the Japanese decided to push their defensive perimeter to Midway, an effort that led to the battle that turned the war against them.

Preparations to recover the B-25s at fields in China were not ready, and weather over the mainland was bad. One plane, having developed fuel trouble, landed in the "friendly" airfield at Vladivostok, was impounded, and the crew interned. (They escaped to Persia 13 months later.) The 15 others made for China, where four made crash landings and the crews of 11 B-25 jumped when their fuel ran low. Doolittle was one of 71 of the 80 pilots and crewmen who survived the raid. The Japanese captured the pilot and two crewmen of one plane that ditched near Ningpo and all five from another bomber that bailed out near Nanchang. The Japanese executed 2d Lts Dean E. Hallmark and William G. Farrow, and Sgt Harold A. Spatz; a fourth died in prison. Lt Ted W. Lawson, one of the plane commanders, published *Thirty Seconds over Tokyo* (1943) with the help of Bob Considine. (Source: Morison, III, 389-98.)

DOR. Date of rank (often retroactive).

DOW. Died of wounds. *See* **casualty.**

Dragoon. Code name for the 1944 invasion of southern France after the original one, Anvil, was compromised.

DSC (US). Distinguished Service Cross, second highest US decoration for valor (after the Medal of Honor), 4,434 being awarded during the war.

DSM (US). Distinguished Service Medal, a decoration for "exceptionally meritorious service . . . in a duty of great responsibility," hence awarded almost exclusively and almost automatically to generals and admirals who performed competently. The distinguished service is not required to be performed in wartime nor against an armed enemy. In WWII 1,439 DSMs were awarded. (*AA*, 673.)

DSO (UK). Distinguished Service Order. A high British award to military officers for valor or merit. One is "appointed to" the DSO, but reputable sources (including the *DNB*) allow DSOs to be "awarded" or "won." The medal is worn on a blue and red ribbon, a bar indicating subsequent awards. (FREYBERG had four.)

DUC. US Distinguished Unit Citation.

Dueppel. German name for **"window,"** coming from the German town where it was first identified.

DUKW ("duck"). Amphibious truck (US).

Dumbarton Oaks Conference, Washington, 21 Aug-7 Oct 44. As a preliminary to the San Francisco Conference of 1945 that created the UNO, this meeting had US, USSR, and UK representatives who were joined in the last week by Chinese. The conference proposals were published 9 Oct 44.

Dunkirk Evacuation, 26 May-4 June 40. The British decided on 20 May 40, after the Allies lost the Battle of Flanders, to evacuate their troops to England through Dunkirk, the last available French port north of GUDERIAN's "panzer corridor." Adm Bertram RAMSAY organized Opn Dynamo, which began 26 May. Adm WAKE-WALKER was sent to Dover on the 29th to command the host of big and little craft involved. Weygand meanwhile had ordered ABRIAL to form and hold a beachhead. Learning of the British evacuation only when it started (26 May), Abrial began organizing his own evacuation, and the first French convoy left on the 29th. The last officers and men left the beaches and jetties of Dunkirk on 4 June 40. They carried only individual weapons and personal equipment, but "the miracle of Dunkirk," in which DOWDING's RAF Fighter Command had a significant role, saved some 215,000 British and 123,000 French troops.

Dunkirk stop order. As Rundstedt's AG A prepared to wheel north and wipe out the Dunkirk beachhead after reaching the English Channel in late May 40, OKW ordered Rundstedt to halt and leave the work to the Luftwaffe and Bock's AG B. The latter was marching through Belgium with the 6th and 18th Armies. In one of his few acts of initiative, Brauschitsch (OKH) had directed on 24 May 40 that KLUGE's 4th Army, which had operational command over the panzer divisions, be moved from AG A to AG B. Bock would then annihilate the beachhead. But Halder exercised his right as OKW CofS to disapprove, and Hitler agreed.

Dyle plan. The unfortunate Allied strategy of opposing a German invasion in the west by wheeling French and BEF forces into Belgium to defend the Dyle-Escaut River line. Allied planners assumed the Germans would make their main strategic effort through the Low Countries, as in 1914. This in fact was their original intention, but the Wehrmacht finally adopted the so-called MANSTEIN plan, which featured a main effort through the Ardennes. Allied execution of the Dyle plan on 10 May 40 put the French right where the Germans wanted them.

DZ. Drop zone for airborne troops and supplies, to include covert operations. An LZ (landing zone) is used for gliders or supply planes.

E

E-boat (Ger). A small, fast torpedo boat.

E-officer (Ger). See *Ergaenzungoffizier.*

EAC. **European Advisory Committee.**

Eagle Squadrons. Three Spitfire units of US pilots flying in the RAF, the first formed in the fall of 1940, served over Europe and in the Mediterranean until transferred to the US 8th AF on 29 Sep 42.

Eben Emael. A supposedly impregnable Belgian fortress on the Albert Canal that fell quickly on 10 May 40, with gliders of STUDENT's force playing the critical role.

Einsatzgruppe(n) ("action group[s]"). SS/SD task forces set up to exterminate Jews, communists, partisans, and others proscribed by Nazi racial and political policies. (Stein, *Waffen SS,* 300.) Einsatzkommandos were special killer units within Einsatzgruppen.

Eleven Reliables. Selected as majors in 1921, at a meeting organized by HIGASHIKUNI to work covertly on a variety of revolutionary programs under HIROHITO (who had just become regent), they were the cadre of the **Emperor's Cabal.** Most famous of the Reliables were Kenji DOIHARA, Itagaki SEISHIRO, and TOJO. Others were Komoto Daisaku, Rensuke ISOGAI, Yoshio Kudo, Masakasu Matsumura, and Yamaoka Shigeatsu. (Bergamini, 326 & n.)

EM (US). Enlisted men ("other ranks" in the UK).

Emperor's Cabal. Formed around the Eleven Reliables (herein), it was one of the **Japanese political factions.**

Enigma. A cipher machine used by the Germans (and later the Japanese) for high-level radio transmissions. The British codebreaking center was at **Bletchley.**

Ergaenzungofficier (E-officer). One (like Hans OSTER) who had been dismissed from the German officer corps by a court of honor but recalled and made eligible for reinstatement.

Erinerungen (Ger). Memoirs.

Ersatz (Ger). Literally a substitute, as in "ersatz coffee," the word was used also for a reserve or replacement military formation of field army or smaller size.

ETO and ETOUSA. US European Theater of Operations and European Theater of Operations, US Army.

European Advisory Commission. With ambassador to London John G. WINANT as US delegate and George F. KENNAN as his political adviser, this body was concerned almost exclusively with postwar arrangements in Germany.

ex-cadet (USMA). One admitted to West Point but not graduated.

Experte(n). The Luftwaffe's informal designation of a pilot who distinguished himself over a long period. The Germans disdained the designation of ace for a pilot with five or more kills, its top scorer, HARTMANN, eventually having 352 victories. German pilots with up to 20 kills might still not be rated as an Experte. (Sims, *The Greatest Aces,* 21.)

F

FA. Field artillery.

Fahnenjunker. Officer candidate (cadet); ensign.

Fall (Ger). Literally "case," Fall became synonymous with "operation," as in Fall Gelb (yellow), the German attack in the west in May 40; Fall Rote (red), the exploitation into the south of France in June 40; Fall Gruen (green), Czechoslovakia; and Fall Weiss (white), Poland.

Fallschirm (Ger). Parachute.

FCNL. English language acronym for French Council of National Liberation. *See* **CFLN,**.

FEAF. Far Eastern AF.

FEC. French Expeditionary Corps (formed by JUIN).

Feldwebel. German senior sergeant in a line (combat) unit.

Festung Europa ("European Fortress"). German term applied to countries conquered by 1940. *See also* **National Redoubt.**

Fezzan. A vast region of oases in SW Libya that the Italians had made part of Tripoli in 1912. CATROUX led Free French forces from Lake Chad to drive out some Italian garrisons in 1940-41, after which LECLERC conquered the Fezzan and linked up with the 8th British Army.

FF. **Free French.**

FFI. French Forces of the Interior (under the **FCNL**).

Field army. A combat formation of two or more army **corps,** normally under a full (four-star) general.

Field grade officers. Majors, lieutenant colonels, and colonels, who are above "company grade" and below **general officers.**

Field marshals of the 3d Reich. The Kaiser named only 5 in 1914-18; Hitler created 25 (19 in the Army and 6 in the Luftwaffe). The first of the fuehrer's creation was Blomberg (1 Jan 33), who was followed by Goering (4 Feb 38).

Interrupting his Reichstag speech on 19 July 40, Hitler named 9 field marshals in the army and 3 in the Luftwaffe. The later were Milch, Kesselring, and Sperrle. In the army were Brauchitsch, Keitel (but not Halder), Rundstedt, Bock, Leeb, List, Kluge, Witzleben, and Reichenau. Goering was given the new rank of Reichsmarshall, senior to all others.

Then came Rommel on 21 June 42 after capturing Tobruk; Kuechler on 30 June 42; Manstein on 2 July 42 after taking Sevastopol; and Paulus on 31 Jan 43 at Stalingrad (in the vain hope he would not be the first German field marshal ever to surrender).

Although Hitler said he would make no more field marshals, it apparently was with retroactive DOR to 1 Feb 43 that the following were appointed: Busch, Kleist, and (No. 21) Weichs. These were followed by Model, 1 Mar 44, Richthofen (Luftwaffe), 17 Feb 45, Schoerner, 5 Apr 45, and Greim (Luftwaffe), 26 Apr 45.

Fifth column. Toward the end of the Spanish Civil War, as four Nationalist columns closed on Madrid, Gen Emilio Mola Vidal told foreign correspondents that Madrid would fall to a "fifth column" working secretly within the city. But a historian of that war says "Lord St Oswald (at the time a reporter on the Republican side) has a claim to have coined the phrase some weeks before." (Thomas, 317n.) "Fifth columns" of subversives, their psychological effect often magnified by enemy-inspired rumors (black propaganda), loomed large in Hitler's early conquests.

Final Solution (Endloesung). The Jewish population in Europe decreased in 1939-45 to 3.1 million from 9.2 million, and some 6 million died of abuse or were killed.

Although Hitler called in his Reichstag speech of 30 Jan 39 for "extermination of the Jewish race in Europe," and various agencies of the Third Reich pursued this goal from the start of the war on 1 Sep 39, it was not until 31 July 41 that Goering ordered HIMMLER to find a "total solution to the Jewish question in the German sphere of influence in Europe."

The **Wannsee conference** of 20 Jan 42 set the many interested governmental agencies to making a coordinated effort under the direction of Adolf EICHMANN. The **Madagascar plan** for forced resettlement of millions of Jews was never adopted, but 30,000 to 50,000 prosperous Jews were forced to emigrate after being "processed" through various camps including Auschwitz and Thersienstadt.

Commenting on Adolf EICHMANN's oft-cited report to Himmler in Aug 44 that approximately six million Jews had died, four million from natural causes (!) in the camps and the rest shot by mobile units (Snyder, *Hitler's Elite,* 227), one authority notes that these rough estimates presumably excluded hundreds of thousands of non-Jews including Gypsies (Bracher, 430 and n59).

First Sea Lord (UK). The senior RN post, it was held initially during the war by POUND and finally by Andrew ("ABC") CUNNINGHAM. Lesser posts include that of Fifth Sea Lord.

Flag officer. An admiral, so called because entitled to display a flag indicating rank.

Flak. German abbreviation for Fliegerabwehrkanonen (or Flugabwehrkanonen), anti-aircraft guns. Allied pilots used the term for enemy AA *fire.*

Flanking position. More or less self-descriptive term for a defensive position established or retained (like Tobruk in the spring of 1941) that stops or slows an attacker (Rommel, in this case) because he cannot pass it without exposing his flank.

Flossenburg. A concentration camp in lower Bavaria near Weiden where Dietrich BONHOEFFER, CANARIS, OSTER, and others were hanged on 9 Apr 45. Remaining personnel were moved three days later to **Dachau** as US troops approached.

Flying Tigers. *See* American Volunteer Group.

Fortitude. Among the major deception plans of **Bodyguard** were Fortitude North (against Norway) and Fortitude South (landings in the Low Countries).

FMF. Fleet Marine Force, or USMC personnel shipboard.

FO. British foreign office.

Four Freedoms. Enunciated by ROOSEVELT in his annual message to Congress on 6 Jan 41 as what he thought America should fight for, they were freedom of speech, of religion, from fear, and from want.

Fr. Father (of the church).

Free French. Supporters of DE GAULLE against the Vichy government of PETAIN. See also **FCNL.**

Fregattenkapitaen. German naval officer immediately junior to Kapitaen and above Korvettenkapitaen. It corresponds to commander in most other navies, including the USN.

Freiherr. Hereditary German military title of nobility usually rendered in English (somewhat imprecisely) as Baron. See also **Ritter** (Count).

Freikorps. Illegal but officially sanctioned "free" (or volunteer) corps formed with a cadre of former army officers and EM to replace the Germany Army defeated in 1918. Operating from the Baltic to central Europe, Freikorps opposed left-wing anarchists and revolutionaries including Germans, Poles, and Russians. Freikorps veterans made up the bulk of the 20,000-man Work Command or Black Reichswehr.

Freiwillige (Ger.). Volunteers.

French factions. These divided basically into those supporting PETAIN or DE GAULLE. The latter's Free French movement evolved from the *Conseil de Défense de l'Empire* established by DE GAULLE at Brazzaville on 27 Oct 40. Its successor, the French National Committee, was created 24 Sep 41. Then came DARLAN's **Imperial Council** (21 Nov 42). After DE GAULLE reached Algiers the French Council of National Liberation (FCNL or CFLN) was established 3 June 43. De Gaulle forced the resignation of co-president Giraud on 9 Nov 43, and then enraged Roosevelt by having BOISSON, FLANDIN, and PEY-ROUTON arrested; NOGUES escaped. On 26 May 44 the FCNL ("Algiers Committee"), now dominated by de Gaulle, acclaimed itself the Provisional Government of the French Republic.

FRG. Postwar Federal Republic of Germany **(Bundesrepublik).**

FRGS. Fellow of the Royal Geographical Society (London).

FRS. Fellow of the Royal Society (London).

Frogmore. British royal lodge half a mile from Windsor Castle.

Front, Soviet. Not synonymous with but roughly equivalent to an army group, Soviet fronts had more or less **organic** air and tank armies in addition to field armies.

Frunze MA (Soviet). The GS Academy of the RKKA until 1921, located in Moscow and named for CGS Mikhail V. Frunze (1885-1925), it became the most prestigious of 17 Soviet military schools at its official level. (Scott and Scott, *Armed Forces of the USSR,* 356.) Higher academic courses were added in the early 1930s, but in 1936 these were moved to the Academy of the GS. Thereafter the Frunze was a three-year course preparing junior officers for staff and command duties at the regimental and divisional level. During the **Moscow panic** the Frunze moved to Tashkent, remaining Oct 41-May 43. The Frunze, like its closest US equivalent the **C&GSS,** had accelerated courses during the war.

Ft. Fort.

Fuehrer (Ger). Generally, any leader or officer; specifically, Hitler.

Fuehrerbefehl/Fuehrererlass. The first is an order ("befehl") from Hitler; the second a decree or edict ("erlass") from him.

Fuehrerbunker. Designed by Albert SPEER and constructed 50 feet under ruins of the new Chancellery, the bunker had 18 very small rooms and a narrow central passage. From 19 Jan 45 Hitler operated the OKW from various Berlin locations, but he spent his last days in the Fuehrerbunker. Other nearby shelters beneath their bombed offices accommodated BORMANN, GOEBBELS,

Brigadefuehrer Mohnke (commandant of the Chancellery), and their staffs.

Fuehrersonderzug. Hitler's special train "Amerika."

G

G1, G2, etc. In the US Army, **General Staff** officers are: G1 (Personnel and Administration), G2 (Intelligence); G3 (Operations and Training), G4 (Supply, or Logistics), and a WWII newcomer, G5 (Civil Affairs). Each is officially designated Assistant CofS. **Special Staff** officers (at regimental and battalion levels and functioning under the **XO**) are designated S1, S2, etc. Corresponding USAAF staff officers were the A1, A2, etc. Other countries have comparable designations but use different numbers.

Garbo. A Spanish-born double agent whom the British ran in what "Connoisseurs of double cross have always regarded . . . as the most highly developed example of their art." (John C. Masterman, quoted in Brown, *Bodyguard,* 481.) Garbo convinced the Abwehr that he had 14 agents and 11 well-placed contacts, whereas actually he worked alone in Lisbon. A one-man **orchestra,** he fabricated 400 secret letters and 2,000 radio messages that successfully deceived the Germans between the end of 1942 (Torch) and D-Day (6 June 44), using almost $200,000 in Abwehr funds. See J. C. Masterman, *The Double-Cross System* (1972).

Gau/Gauleiter. A Gau was a territorial region of pre-Nazi Germany, Austria, and Russia. The Nazi Party established political control within Greater Germany by reviving the Gau concept, but they created the Party office of Gauleiter (Gau leader). Eventually there were 42 Gaue plus Ernst BOHLE's **Auslands-organisation.** Berlin and Vienna were Gaue within the Mark Brandenburg and Lower Danube Gaue. Appointed by Hitler for political reliability, not aptitude, Gauleiters originally reported only to the fuehrer but during the war they took orders from Martin BOR-MANN. Many doubled as provincial president (Reichsstatthalter).

GBE (Br). Knight or Dame, Grand Cross, Order of the British Empire.

GC&CS (Br). Government Code and Cipher School. From 1924 it was housed with SIS at

54 Broadway in London until moving to Bletchley Park and becoming operational there in the spring of 1941. Its director, under the control of MI6 Chief Menzies, was Cmdr Alastair G. Denniston until Feb 42, then (after a palace revolt over administration) by Cmdr Edward Travis. At this time the school was renamed the Government Communications Hq with Menzies as director general. (Brown, *"C,"* 396-402.)

GCB (Br). Knight Grand Cross of the Bath, the order above KCB. Six top US military leaders were awarded the honorary GCB, the next Americans being Presidents Ronald Reagan and George Bush (30 Nov 93). Americans do not kneel at the investure, are not tapped on the shoulder, and are not entitled to be called Sir.

GCIE (Br). Knight Grand Commander of the Indian Empire.

GCMG (Br). Knight Grand Cross of St Michael and St George.

GCSI (Br). Knight Grand Commander of the Star of India.

Gebirgstruppen (Ger). Mountain troops.

Geheime (Ger). Secret, as in **Geheime Staats**-**po**lizei (Gestapo) or SS (Secret State Police).

Gen. General.

Genannt (Ger). Called, surnamed, known as. E.g., VIETINGHOFF (genannt) Scheel.

General. The title is ancient, but the rank or grade of general officer is relatively modern. This glossary has separate entries for most general officer ranks mentioned in the biographical sketches, but the following recap by major country should be useful.

American general officers.

The hierarchy in ascending order, is Brig Gen (1 star), Maj Gen (2 stars), Lt Gen (3), General (4), and General of the Army (5 stars in a circle). Promotions after 7 Dec 41 were about 1,400 US officers to brigadier general, about 500 to major general, and 57 to lieutenant general. Twelve men were promoted during the war to full general: Joseph Stilwell had the rank as of 1 Aug 44; the others, promoted at one day intervals in the period 5-13 Mar 45, were Walter Krueger, Brehon B. Somervell, Joseph T. McNarney, Jacob L. Devers, George C. Kenney, Mark W. Clark, Carl Spaatz, Omar N. Bradley, and Thomas T. Handy. Promoted a month later

were George S. Patton (14 Apr 45) and Courtney Hodges (15 Apr 45). Malin Craig, a four-star general as Army CofS, was recalled in his old rank for the period 26 Sep 41-25 July 45. Jonathan M. Wainwright was promoted 5 Sep 45 to full general, three days after attending surrender ceremonies aboard *Missouri*.

US Generals of the Army with DOR from 16 to 21 Dec 44 were, in order of seniority, George C. Marshall, MacArthur, Eisenhower, and H. H. ARNOLD. (Of course, all had already been promoted to full general.)

British general officers.

The hierarchy is about the same as in most other countries including the USA. A notable exception is the grade of **brigadier** (who normally commands a brigade or a regiment). The British rank of brigadier general was abolished after 1918, so their lowest ranking general officer is a major general (who normally leads a division). The succession then is lieutenant general and general, as in the US Army. The highest British Army rank is field marshal, equating to US General of the Army. The British have the practice of almost automatically giving an officer temporary rank, pay, and perquisites of a higher assignment. Hence a brigadier moved up to head a division would immediately be a temporary major general; if reassigned for purely administrative reasons (without prejudice) he would, if possible, be posted to a vacancy calling for most recent temporary rank; otherwise the British officer would revert to his former rank. (This is a splendid old system the more recent US Army has refused to adopt.)

French generals.

The lowest is a général de brigade, who, unlike the American brigadier general, wears *two* small stars. The reason is that a single one of these small stars would be almost indistinguishable where insignia of rank are worn, on the sleeve and cap of the French army uniform. This is apparent in wartime photos of Général de Brigade Charles de Gaulle, a "two-star general" literally but, by American standards, a "one-star" general. The French add a star for each higher rank: général de division (three stars in a triangle), général de corps d'armée (four stars in lozenge), général (a fifth star above the lozenge).

German generals.

From Oberst (colonel), a German officer was promoted to Generalmajor, then Generalleutnant. Next, corresponding to US lieutenant general, came the following ranks, awarded within all arms of the Wehrmacht: General der Infanterie, Artillerie, Gebirgstruppen (mountain troops), Kavallerie, Nachrichtentruppen (signal troops), Panzertruppen, Pioniere (combat engineers), Luftwaffe, Flieger (fighter aircraft), Fallchirmtruppen (parachute troops), Flakartillerie, and Luftnachrichtentruppen (air force signal troops).

The next highest German ranks (which have separate glossary entries) were Generaloberst (colonel general) and Generalfeldmarschall. See also the entry Field Marshals of the Third Reich. Goering alone held the top rank of Reichsmarschall. There were about 800 German generals in Hitler's War.

Japanese general officers.

Saburo Hayashi and Alvin D. Coox give the following tabulation in *Kogun,* 220:

	Regulars	Res & recalled	Total
General and field marshal	19	2	21
Lieutenant general	384	100	560
Major general	623	473	1,432

Brigadier general No strictly comparable Japanese rank.

Soviet general officers.

There is no rank of general in the USSR, which is why the identification "Soviet military leader" must be used instead of "Soviet general" (Scotts). The Red Army had no rank corresponding to the US brigadier general; the first general officer rank was general major, followed by general lieutenant. The rank corresponding to US full general was *introduced* on 7 May 40, but it was not until 4 June 40 that the first three recipients, Meretskov, Tyulenov, and Zhukov were listed in *Pravda,* with 4 June 40 as their date of rank. However, the awarding ceremony was almost a month later. The promotion list being alphabetical in cryllic, Zhukov was at the top; this has led to the false

assumption that he had seniority over the other two (Scotts).

Peter Kruzhin, cited as RL 89/75, lists 29 Red Army officers promoted to General of the Army (G/A) through 1945, and a total of 59 through 1955. He gives some exact dates of rank, and I have added others. Kruzhin's research shows that after the first three promotions (above), the next two, on 22 Feb 41, were to the unfortunate D. G. PAVLOV and APANASENKO. Nobody was promoted to G/A in 1942, but there were 10 in 1943, 8 in 1944, and 6 in 1945. The last of these was to BULGANIN (No. 59), after which the next promotion went in 1948 to SHTEMENKO, whose post war nemesis, ironically, was Bulganin.

Corresponding to Soviet General of the Army is Marshal of Aviation, of Armored Forces, of Artillery, of Signals, etc. The next higher Soviet ranks are Chief Marshal of Aviation, Armored Forces, and Artillery, after which is **Marshal of the Soviet Union.**

General Colonel (USSR). A Soviet military rank above Gen Lt and below Gen of the Army. In Germany, however, the relative rank is reversed, **Generaloberst** (colonel general) being higher than Gen of Inf, etc.

Generalfeldmarschall (Ger). The rank is equivalent to field marshal in the many countries that have such a rank and to US General of the Army (5 stars). The corresponding Waffen-SS rank is Reichsfuehrer-SS. *See also* **Field Marshals of the Third Reich.**

Generalgouvernement (in Poland). Most of Poland's 150,500 sq mi were incorporated by Germany and the USSR, but 39,000 sq mi were left as "occupied Poland" or "the general government." Civil authority was under Karl Hermann FRANK as governor general, depriving Gen BLASKOWITZ of the normal military-government authority and creating a situation previously unknown in history. To exacerbate the Hitlerian abnormality, Himmler's SS had authority over **concentration camps** to include their extermination programs (added later).

General Inspectors' Group (Sov). Commonly known as the Inspectorate, it has been called the "military rest home for marshals" of the Soviet Union (Erickson, *To Stalingrad,* 296).

Generalkommando (Ger). Armeekorps Hq. See also **corps,** previously.

Generalleutnant (Ger) and Gen Lt (Sov). The ranks equate to major general in the US and UK, not to lieutenant general.

Generalmajor (Ger) and Gen Maj (Sov). The lowest German and Soviet **general officer** rank, equivalent to US brigadier general.

Generaloberst (Ger). Translated colonel general, the rank is normally equated with full general in the UK-US hierarchy.

General of Infantry, etc. (Ger). A rank above Generalleutnant and below Generaloberst, equivalent to US and British lieutenant general (although some authorities incorrectly equate the rank with US-UK lieutenant general).

General of the Army (US). A five-star rank equivalent to field marshal. Generals of the Army, with DOR from 16 to 21 Dec 44, were (in order of seniority) George Marshall, MacArthur, Eisenhower, and H. H. "Hap" Arnold.

General Staff (GS). The staff of a general officer commanding a division or larger formation. Such a general staff is controlled by a chief of staff. Subordinate staff officers are *assistant* (not *deputy*) chiefs of staff (e.g., "Assistant CofS G1" in the US). See also **G1, G2,** etc. and **German general staff.**

Genyosha. Predecessor of the **Black Dragon Society.**

George Cross (UK). A very high decoration for valor at great personal risk, primarily for civilians but awarded also to military personnel whose act did warrant a military medal, the George Cross was instituted in Sep 40 and awarded to only about 105 men and women until 1947. It is a Greek (square) cross in gold with a central medallion inscribed "For Gallantry," and suspended from a short, square, purple ribbon. (*Medals,* 130.) See also the following entry.

George Medal (UK). Instituted with the **George Cross,** and also primarily for civilians, the George Medal was awarded to men and women for acts of great bravery falling short of criteria for the George Cross. Of approximately 1,900 George Medals issued from Sep 40 (when created) until 1993, some 1,030 went to civilians, 455 to the army, 200 to the RAF, 150 to the RN, and 45 to the Merchant Navy. (*Medals,* 130.)

German Cross in Gold. About 3,000 awarded in 1939-45, for gallantry, it ranked above the Iron Cross 1st Class and just below the Knight's Cross. (Manfred Rommel note in *RP,* 39.)

German General Staff (GGS) or Greater German General Staff (GGGS). Dating from 1808, it evolved into "a *corps d'élite* within the [German] military caste" (W-B, *Nemesis,* 6). Outstanding officers were selected early in their careers and given a succession of staff and command assignments. They were distinguished by broad crimson stripes on their trousers, and unlike staff officers in many other armies were respected for their superior staff and command training. Article 160 of the Treaty of Versailles dictated that "The Greater German General Staff and all similar organizations [sic] shall be dissolved and may not be reconstituted in any form." Such was the reputation of the GGGS among the victors. Von SEECKT evaded the edict by establishing the **Truppenamt,** and the crimson stripes reappeared after Hitler renounced restrictions of the Versailles treaty.

Germanen ("Germanics"). Non-Germans of Nordic blood.

Geschwader. A Luftwaffe air wing. Until 1943 a Geschwader of fighters comprised three Gruppen (24 to 36 planes); from 1943 it had four Gruppen (32-48 aircraft). (Sims, Aces, 130.

Gestapo (**Ge**heime **Sta**atzpolizei). Literally the secret state police, "Gestapo" is commonly misused for all German police and secret service organizations, notably the **Abwehr.** The Gestapo was a creature of the Nazis that evolved from an office set up by Rudolf DIELS in Apr 33, and its name was coined at this time. Police records inherited from the State of Prussia, which Goering headed, were used promptly against BLOMBERG and FRITSCH. The Gestapo became more and more independent of the Prussian administration but remained under Goering's sole jurisdiction. When Himmler moved to take over the Gestapo his first step was to have Diels replaced by one of his own people. Heydrich fabricated false charges against Diels that finally forced Goering to oust his protégé. But the Gestapo was headed for less than a month by a Nazi party hack, Paul Hinkler, and DIELS won reinstatement by using the threat of blackmail on Goering. When Hitler finally made the State of Prussia part of the Third Reich (10 Apr 34) Diels had to turn over the Gestapo to Heinrich MUELLER. (Arthur NEBE's Kripo also became part of Himmler's SS.) In the Oct 39 reorganization the Gestapo became Amt IV of the RSHA, Heinrich Mueller remaining chief. Gestapo Hq and the Gestapo prison were at 8 Prinz Albrechtstrasse in Berlin.

GGGS/GGS. Great German General Staff/German General Staff.

GH. General hospital.

GHQ. General Hq. The US GHQ of WWII was superseded by AGF but "GHQ" was later used for other headquarters.

GI (US). Derived from "government issue," and originally the self-depreciating term for American draftees who prided themselves on being "civilians in uniform," it became popular first as journalistic shorthand (beloved by headline writers). Webster notes that GI did not enter the language in this sense until 1943. GI acquired the additional meanings of "strictly military" and to clean (floors or equipment) in preparation for inspection.

GKO (USSR). The State Committee of Defense (Gosudarstvennyy Komitet Oborony) had responsibility for all aspects of the war, political, economic, and military. Operational from 30 June 41, it had a basic membership of eight, Stalin being chairman and Molotov his deputy. Early members were Malenkov, Voroshilov, and Beria. Added in 1942-45 were Voznesensky and Mikoyan; Kaganovich, a non-person after the war, is believed to have been a member in 1942-45. Bulganin joined in Nov 44.

Glavkom (Glavnokomanduyushchy). This title for supreme commander in a theater of operations (TVD) was abolished in the 1920s but revived briefly in the first days of the war when an intermediate command link was needed between Moscow and the "fronts." VOROSHILOV headed the Northwestern TVD, BUDENNY theidSouthwestern TVD, and TIMOSHENKO the Western TVD. VOROSHILOV's position was eliminated on 27 Aug 41. Timoshenko's Western TKV was abolished 10 Sep 41, but revived 1 Feb 42 with Zhukov being rushed from Leningrad to be CinC. The Western TKV was abolished 5 May 42, when the **Stavka** took direct control of the fronts. Timoshenko meanwhile replaced Budenny as Glavkom SW, which existed 10 July-26 Sep 41 and 16 Oct 41-21 June 42 (HFS). TIMOSHENKO also commanded the SW *Front* Sep-Dec 41, and Apr-July 42. Meanwhile, BUDENNY headed a new North Caucasus TKV, 21 Apr-19 May 42. The first four Glavkoms, all headed by Stalin cronies, failed to provide the badly needed intermediary link between Moscow and the "fronts." At the end of the war, however, VASILEVKY was Glavkom of Soviet Troops in the Far East, 1 Aug-20 Dec 45, for the brief campaign against the Japanese.

Gleiwitz incident, 31 Aug 39. This was conceived by HEYDRICH and led by NAUJOCKS as a provocation for the invasion of Poland that was to begin a few hours later. SS commandos in Polish uniforms took over the radio transmitter on the border town of Gleiwitz in Upper Silesia. Still posing as Poles, they made a bogus broadcast calling for war. Using the corpse of a condemned German criminal, they left behind "evidence" that the raiders had been Polish.

GMT. Greenwich Mean Time (Zulu hour in messages).

GOC (Br). General Officer Commanding (= US CG).

"Good Germans." English term used commonly for those Germans they did not believe deserved the same disapprobation as the Huns of WWI or the Nazis of WWII.

GP. General purpose (bombs).

GOSPLAN. Soviet State Planning Committee.

Goumiers. Fierce Berber tribesmen from the Atlas Mountains, Goumiers first served as French colonial light infantry in 1908. Formed soon thereafter as the Tirailleurs Marocains, they helped pacify hostile tribes in the high Atlas of Morocco and fought with distinction in France during both world wars. Demobilized after the Franco-German armistice of 1940, they emerged from the mountains in Nov 42 to rejoin the French African Army. Goumiers served in Goums of 175 to 200 men under a cadre of 10 to 12 highly-selected French officers and NCOs. The officers were from the top of their St Cyr class—a notable one being JUIN—and had authority that included the power of summary execution for offenses like rape. Four to five Goums make a Tabor. Goumiers fought under JUIN in Tunisia and Italy, and under de LATTRE in France and Germany.

GPU/NKVD, 1922-23. Gosudarstvennoye Politischeskoye Upravleniye (State Political Administration)/Narodny Kommissariat Vnutrennikn Del (People's Commissariat of Internal Affairs). As pointed out under **Police and secret services of the USSR,** the GPU/ NKVD followed the **Cheka** and preceded the **OGPU.**

Graf (Ger). Count, as in Graf Zeppelin.

Great Purges in the USSR, 1936-38. They were touched off by the assassination on 1 Dec 34 of Sergey M. Kirov, one of Stalin's most trusted colleagues in Leningrad. Sudoplatov finds "no evidence that Stalin ordered the murder of Kirov to eliminate him as a rival center of power" but used his assassination "to fabricate a grand conspiracy against Kirov and himself; he exploited the situation to eliminate all those suspected as rivals or disloyal opponents . . ." (Sudoplatov, 55). " What is clear, however," writes Volkogonov, admitting that considerable mystery remains, is that the murder was not ordered by Trotsky, Zinoviev, or Kaminsky, "which was soon put out as the official version. Knowing what we know about Stalin [as late as 1988], is certain that he had a hand in it. The removal of two or three layers of indirect witnesses bears his hallmark." (Volkogonov II, 208.) After the liquidation on Stalin's orders of "socially-alien elements" the purges started with political and military officials but extended to the general public. The first show trial in Aug 36, the "Trial of the 16," allegedly proved that TROTSKY was masterminding a counter-revolution. All defendants, including Kamenev and Zinoviev, were shot immediately. The elaborately staged "Trial of the 17" in Jan 37 sought to establish that the conspirators intended to use German and Japanese armed forces against the USSR (Clarkson, *Russia,* 616). N. I. Yezhov, STALIN's new **NKVD** chief, won the death penalty for 13, who were shot. But Karl Radek, Grigori Sokolnikov, and two others got only 10-year prison sentences (ibid).

In early June 37 it was announced that TUKHACHEVSKY and seven others of the Red Army high command had been executed for "espionage and treason" in the service of unnamed foreign powers. At least half of 75,000 officers in the Soviet Army, Navy, and AF—the entire top echelon—were then shot or imprisoned. Their trials were secret, pre-sumably because military men "were of tougher fibre than civilian Old Bolsheviks" (Clarkson, 617).

About three million were executed or died as prisoners, and about eight million went to the camps. (Many were freed after the Germans launched Barbarossa.) Few foreigners, including Hitler, believed the USSR could fight a war within the next decade, a conviction reinforced by the Red Army debacle in Finland in Dec 39.

"Green Devils." The sobriquet won by Richard HEIDRICH's 1st Para Div for their dogged defense of Cassino.

Group (Ger). 1. In the German army a *Gruppe* (group) was larger than a corps but smaller than a field army. 2. In the Luftwaffe a fighter Gruppe was a formation of 8-12 planes, three to four Gruppen making a **Geschwader.** 3. An RAF or USAAF air group was made up of three to four squadrons, the numbers depending on the type of aircraft.

GRU. Soviet Main Intelligence Directorate of the Ministry of Defense—the intelligence element of the general staff.

Gruppenfuehrer. Waffen-SS rank equivalent to **Generalleutnant.**

GSO (UK). General Staff Officer.

Guards units, Sov. For outstanding performance four Red Army divisions were redesignated guards units on 18 Sep 41. The honor subsequently was extended to units up to field army. For example, Gen Col Mikhail S. SHUMILOV's 64th Army was the 7th Gds Army after he took the surrender of PAULUS at Stalingrad. Eventually there were 11 guards armies and 6 guards tank armies, all numbered in sequence. Guards units got better rations, and on 21 May 42 "guards" was added to military rank, as in "Guards Junior Sergeant." (Scotts.)

GULAG. (Glavnoye Upraveleniye Lagerov or Main Camp Administration). Stalin ordered the GULAG created in the early 1930s under what became the **NKVD.** Like German **concentration camps** Soviet *raiony* (camps) were needed for the swelling numbers of political prisoners. But because of the USSR's great demand for labor, particularly in remote regions, the GULAG soon directed much of the country's logging, mining, and construction of roads and canals. (Medvedev, 394.)

Gurkhas. Nepalese soldiers of Britain's Indian Army, Gurkhas were organized into units up to division size. They served with great distinction in the Near East, East Africa, the Western Desert, Sicily, Italy, and Burma. A few battalions survived dismemberment of Britain's Indian Army as palace guards and shock troops. News of their dispatch to the Falklands allegedly hastened the Argentine capitulation in 1982.

H

Hauptmann. German army captain except in the cavalry, where the rank is **Rittmeister.**

Hauptsturmfuehrer. Waffen-SS rank equivalent to Hauptmann.

He. HEINKEL aircraft of the Lufthansa and Lufftwaffe.

HE. High explosive (artillery shells and aerial bombs).

Heavy weapon. An imprecise term generally meaning a weapon not designed to be carried, like a rifle, as an individual load. The **Vercors** maquis called in vain for heavy weapons in June 44.

Hedgehog. An isolated position with all-around defense.

Heer (Ger). Army, as in OKH and Heeresgruppe (Army Group).

Hero of the Soviet Union (HSU). The highest Soviet award for valor or service, individual or collective, the title is bestowed with the Gold Star Medal, a simple five-pointed star suspended from a short red ribbon. The medal is worn on the left breast above all other decorations. A separate medal is worn for each award, ZHUKOV sporting four. The HSU *title* was introduced 16 Apr 34 and first bestowed on seven airmen who rescued crew and passengers from the icebreaker *Cheluskin* in Feb 34. The *medal* was authorized 16 Apr 39. Starting 29 July 36 the HSU was awarded with the Order of Lenin (created 1930). About 36,000 Gold Stars were presented in 1941-45. (*Medals.*)

HIAG der Waffen SS. A veterans' organization, the *Hilfsorganisation auf Gegenseitikeit* publishes a magazine, *Der Freiwillige,* has a library, holds annual conventions, "and lobbies incessantly for legitimacy for its members." (Stein, *Waffen SS,* 252-53.)

Hitlerjugend. Hitler Youth. It was organized in June 33 and headed until Aug 40 by Baldur von SCHIRACH, who remained inspector of the Hitler Youth and Reich leader of youth education when his assistant, Arthur AXMANN, took over as active head of the organization. In 1936 the Hitler Youth became the only youth organization permitted in Germany, and from 1939 it conscripted children for service. Segregated by age, the Hitlerjugend were given intensive training and indoctrination as future leaders. The last photo of Hitler was taken as he inspected a group of about 1,000 boys under Axmann in Berlin whose principal mission was to hold the Wannsee bridges until WENCK's relief column arrived.

Hlinka People's Party and Hlinka Guards. Monseigneur Andrew Hlinka, founder of the Slovak Popular Party, died in Aug 38 and was succeeded by Josef TISO. But his name continued to be that of the political party and its notorious Hlinka Guard.

HMAS, MHCS, HMNZS, HNMS. His (Her) Majesty's Australian Ship, Canadian Ship, New Zealand Ship, Her Netherlands Majesty's Ship.

Hoare-Laval proposal. Worked out by the British foreign secretary and his French counterpart as a basis for further negotiations, this was a step toward appeasing Mussolini by recognizing some of his claims in Ethiopia while leaving HAILE SELASSIE limited sovereignty. The alternative being world war, Hoare recommended that the Cabinet endorse the plan and forward it to the League of Nations. Leaked to the French press and picked up by Fleet Street, the proposal brought violent protest from Britain's conservative party. Sir Samuel HOARE manfully refused to withdraw his approval of the plan and had no choice but to resign.

Home Force(s). The British territorial command charged with home (UK) defense and with organizing and training units for service overseas. Wartime commanders were IRONSIDE, BROOKE, and PAGET.

Hossbach Memorandum. On his own initiative the redoubtable Col Friedrich HOSSBACH wrote up minutes of the 5 Nov 34 conference in which Hitler first revealed his foreign policy objectives. Astonished listeners, in addition to Hossbach, were BLOMBERG, NEURATH, FRITSCH, RAEDER, and GOERING. The gist was that **Lebensraum** would be acquired in Austria and Czechoslovakia before the Wehrmacht overran Poland and the

Ukraine. The Hossbach Memorandum was a key document for the prosecution at Nuremberg, having been generally unknown until the German archives were captured. A. J. P. Taylor has questioned the authenticity of the Hossbach Memo on grounds that Hitler hardly would have shown his hand this early to known political enemies. (See Taylor, *Origins,* identified in the bibliography.)

Ho-Umezu Agreement (or Pact), 10 June 35. In a flagging effort to create an appearance of Sino-Japanese cooperation "Hirohito's inner circle of Big Brothers" (Bergamini, 600) took advantage of the crisis brought on by their Tiensin garrison. Arrogant Japanese NCOs had been swaggering through Tiensin and Peking looking for a pretext to provoke an incident, and the Japanese were not yet quite ready for this. Lt Gen UMEZU and Gen Ho Ying-Chin (for Chiang Kai-shek) "signed a document known to this day only as the Ho-Umezu Pact. . . . China promised to prevent her citizens from 'scowling' at Japanese soldiers and to cede all but civil police powers in the bulk of north China to representatives approved by Tokyo." With open conflict as the alternative, CHIANG (who hoped to retire) accepted what might be perceived as face-saving terms. (Ibid.)

Hq. Headquarters.

HS. High School (US) or, quite different, a German *Hochschule,* which is an academy, college, or university (often in a special field such as music, technology, or agriculture). A German *Hochschueler* is a univeristy student.

HSU. **Hero of the Soviet Union.**

Hump, The. A series of 17,000-foot mountain ranges, with visibility frequently zero, it was crossed by US cargo planes with supplies from India to China after the **Burma Road** was cut and before the **Ledo Road** was built. From a slow start in Apr 42, 650,000 tons were delivered by V-J day.

Husky. Code name for Allied invasion of Sicily in July 43.

Hv. Heavy.

I

Ia, b, c, etc. German **general staff** positions corresponding (with different numbers) to US Army G1, G2, G3, etc. Equating roughly with the US G3, the German Army Ia is the senior operations officer (or chief of operations) and ex-officio deputy CofS. The Ib (G4) is responsible for logistics (supply), and the Ic (G2) handles intelligence.

IBT. India-Burma Theater (of operations).

IG. Inspector General.

IGHQ. Imperial General Headquarters (Tokyo).

IGS. Imperial General Staff (Tokyo).

"Illegals." Soviet secret agents, mostly **Comintern,** who operated outside the USSR under false identity and without diplomatic immunity. "Legals" function covertly from embassies, consulates, trade delegations, etc. Although holding Soviet citizenship, "illegals" often were not ethnic Russian but Trotskyist communists who all knew each other and who built "the finest spy rings history has ever known" (Peter Wright, 227). There are two types of illegal: those who live undercover for five to 15 years building a network and awaiting an assignment from **Moscow Center;** and those sent to penetrate hostile intelligence services. (Sudoplatov, 12n.)

Stalin recalled most illegals in 1938 for liquidation, believing that as Trotskyites and foreigners they were a threat to him (Peter Wright, 227). Control of illegals passed to the **GRU** when the USSR went to war.

"Great illegals" included Theodore Maly, "Otto," and Arnold Deutsch, all involved with the **Cambridge Five.** Others were Richard SORGE in China and Japan; Alexander Rado, with the Lucy ring in Switzerland; Leopold Trepper, creator of the **Rote Kapelle;** Ruth "Sonia" Kuzchinski, who trained Allan FOOTE in Switzerland, married Len Brewer, and then ran the atomic spy ring from Oxford, 1941-44; and Mr and Mrs Henri Pieck, who worked as Dutch illegals in prewar Britain; Walter Krivitsky; and Ludwik (aka Ignace Reiss) and Elizabeth Poretsky. The latter published her autobiography, *Les Nôtres;* which had at least one valuable fact censored before appearing in English as *Our Own People.* (Peter Wright, 226.) Krivitsky was murdered after refusing recall orders and defecting. Mrs Pieck lived as a widow in Amsterdam, and Sorge's widow, Christiane, lived in a seminary near NYC.

Another famous illegal was known in the west as Aleksandr Orlov. After a remarkable career that included early work with the

Cambridge Five he defected in 1938 but did not expose the ring. After 15 years underground in the US he published *The Secret History of Stalin's Crimes* (New York: Random House, 1953) and *A Handbook of Intelligence and Guerrilla Warfare* (Ann Arbor, Mich, 1962).

Imperial Council (Fr). Set up by DARLAN in Algiers by a proclamation of 21 Nov 42 to comprise "senior Vichy officials and officers present and willing to participate in the war against Germany" (Paxton, *Vichy,* 282). Headed by Adm Darlan until his assassination on 24 Dec 42, then by GIRAUD, the council included the African proconsuls: NOGUES (Morocco); Yves CHATEL (Algeria); and BOISSON (West Africa). In addition were GIRAUD, JUIN; and BERGERET. (Pertinax, 552.)

Imperial Defense College (Br). Established in 1920, it was a staff and command school for officers of all armed services who had completed their own service schools (like **Camberley**).

Imperial Way Group. One of the **Japanese political factions.**

IMT. International Military Tribunal at Nuremberg.

Inf. Infantry.

Inspectorate (Soviet). *See* **General Inspectors's Group.**

Integration (US). The National Security Act of 1947 "integrated" the US Army, Navy, Marine Corps, and AF. Passage of the act followed bitter partisan warfare waged by high ranking veterans of WWII, particularly "the revolt of the admirals." Ironically, its main effect was "disintegration," H. H. "Hap" ARNOLD achieving the long-sought goal of an independent USAF and the USMC getting more autonomy. To create unified civilian control, however, the post of Secretary of Defense was created. The first, tragic incumbent was FORRESTAL. Details of the integration act are in the *Army Almanac,* 37 ff.

Intelligence. Military intelligence is derived from *evaluating* data (information) about the enemy collected from all sources to include the observation of front line troops to surveillance of telephone and radio communications. (See **Magic, Radiogoniometry,** and **Ultra.**) A distinction therefore must be made between raw *information* and the resulting *intelligence;* the words are not synonymous.

Interallié. Created by Roman "Valentin" GARBY-CZERNIAWSKI as the first Allied intelligence net in occupied France, Interallié became the largest and most important. Its first radio message to London went out from near the Trocadero on 1 Jan 41. The cipher clerk and broadcaster was Mathilde CARRE, who introduced transmissions with "The Cat reports. . . ."

The net had 120 agents and four transmitters when disaster struck in Nov 41. Maj Czerniawski was visiting London when the Germans arrested and "turned" his agent in Cherbourg, Raoul Kiffer. Kiffer betrayed 21 helpers and revealed Valentin's hideouts. Sgt BLEICHER ("Col Henri") caught Czerniawski asleep in his apartment at St-Germain-en-Laye (near Paris) the morning of 17 Nov 41. Bleicher found incriminating documents, and bagged the Cat later that day in the net's headquarters in the Rue Léandre. The Cat and Kiffer led Bleicher to almost 100 Interallié agents, most of them within three days. As covered in more detail under Mathilde CARRE, Abwehr operators took over the Interallié radio network without arousing suspicions in London.

International Military Tribunal (IMT). At Nuremberg it tried the 22 senior Nazis accused of **war crimes.**

"Ironbottom Sound." The SE end of **"The Slot,"** so nicknamed because of many sinkings in the Battles of **Savo Island.**

IRTC. Infantry Replacement Training Camp or Center (US).

Izvestia. The word meaning *news, Izvestia* was the official USSR newspaper.

J

Jaeger (Ger). Literally "hunter," the word is used for light infantry (rifle) troops, for fighter pilots, and for fighter aircraft.

Jagdgeschwader (JG). Luftwaffe fighter wing.

Japanese political factions. When HIROHITO became regent in 1921 after a visit to Europe, HIGASHIKUNI (based in Paris) took the first steps in forming the **Emperor's Cabal.** The **Eleven Reliables** were picked for the cadre. Others joined from the University Lodging House, the (Teiichi) SUZU-

KI Study Group, and the Cherry Society. Around 1930 the Cabal split. The majority, dissatisfied with HIROHITO's national strategy, formed the **Imperial Way Group** and backed the **Strike North Faction.** But after the **26 Oct 36** insurrection was put down, HIROHITO intervened personally. Under the interim premiership of Korechika ANAMI, Sadao ARAKI and other leaders of the Imperial Way were retired from the army. Survivors of the purge were ISHIWARA, YAMAMOTO, and YAMASHITA. The Imperial Way clique and Strike North Faction were further discredited by the Japanese defeat at **Khalkhin Gol** in 1939. Some had been genuinely anti-bolshevik, but most (including DOIHARA) were motivated by conviction that Manchuria had all Japan needed in the way of natural resources and space for colonization. Many were accused of being "pacifists in war paint" who thought Japan should avoid war with the west (Bergamini, 1099).

The smaller element of the Cabal, which remained loyal to the emperor and (like him) backed the Strike South Faction, formed the Control Group. "The name . . . was meant to appeal to those who feared possible lack of self-control in Hirohito's policies for Japan" (Bergamini, 1086). Members were Teiichi SUZUKI, DOIHARA, ITAGAKI, and Kuniaki KOISO (ibid.). The Control Group won out, leading Japan into war with the west.

JCS. Joint Chiefs of Staff (US). It comprised service chiefs Marshall, King, and Hap Arnold, presided over by LEAHY as chairman.

Jervis Bay incident, 5 Nov 40. Under Capt Edward S. Fogarty Fegen (1895-1940) this lightly armed merchant cruiser was the sole escort of a 37-ship convoy eastbound from Halifax (HX.84). E of Newfoundland, at dusk, she sighted *Admiral Scheer* (Capt Theodor KRANCKE). Ordering the convoy to make smoke and scatter into the twilight, Fegen sacrificed his ship and crew in an uneven, 22-minute battle that enabled all but five of HX.84 to escape. Fegen was awarded a posthumous VC, and a passing Swedish ship rescued the few surviving British crewmen.

Jinking. Evasive maneuvers by aircraft.

JG. 1. Jagdgeschwader (Luftwaffe fighter wing). 2. Junior grade (as in Lt., jg, USN).

JMAG. Joint Military Assistance Group (postwar).

JPS. Joint Staff Planners (US).

K

Kaliningrad. Formerly **Koenigsberg,** E. Prussia.

Kamikaze ("divine wind"). Japanese suicide attack. Vice Adm. Onishi of 1st Air Fleet trained the original class of the Kamikaze Corps, which made its first organized attack off Samar on 25 Oct 44 against escort carriers *Santee* and *Suwannee* (Morison, XII, 166). Japan expended 2,550 kamikaze planes; 5,350 were left and 5,000 new pilots were being trained when the war ended (Morison, XIV, 352). Although they inflicted considerable damage, the kamikazes were introduced too late and not used in sufficient mass to have a significant role in the war.

Kampfgruppe (Ger). Battle group.

Kampfzeit (Ger). Time of Nazi struggle to take over Germany (1919-33).

Kapellmeister (Ger). Meaning orchestra leader, the term was used for the head of a spy network.

Kapitaen (Ger). 1. Captain of the Navy. 2. A Luftwaffe title (not a rank), as in **Staffel** Kapitaen MARSEILLE. See also **Kommodore,** etc.

Kapitaenleutnant. German naval officer equating to lieutenant commander, USN.

Kapitaen sur See. German naval rank equivalent to German army Oberst (colonel) and USN captain.

Kapo. German convict in charge of concentration camp inmates.

Kapp Putsch, Berlin, 13-17 Mar 20. A monarchial, antirepublican coup in Berlin, led by Wolfgang Kapp and Gen von Luettwitz, forced the **Weimar government** to flee to Stuttgart. Prompt army intervention and a general strike of the trade unions soon restored order.

Katyn Forest massacre. Goebbels noted in his diary on 9 Apr 43 that the Germans had found Polish mass graves near Smolensk (Lochner, *Goebbels Diaries,* 318). The Germans claimed that the victims had been taken prisoner during and after the campaign of 1939 in Poland, moved to POW camps in the USSR, and massacred in the spring of 1940. Cadavers at Katyn (there were many others elsewhere) included some 4,000 military officers, intellectuals, high-ranking clergymen, and others of the Polish elite. Goebbels invited outsiders to examine the evidence, but Stalin said it was a propaganda trick and blocked efforts of the Western Allies, including the London Poles, to accept safe passage to confirm the German charges. C. L. BISSELL admitted to Congress in 1950 that he had taken part in an officially sanctioned US cover-up to keep from alienating Stalin, whose promised military support in final actions against Japan in Manchuria was deemed essential. It was reasonably well established by this time that massacre of Poles, here and elsewhere, was as charged by Goebbels. Publication of Pavel Sudoplatov's memoirs in 1994 (see Bibliography) leaves no doubt. In Appendix Five the former KGB general gives a top secret letter of 5 Mar 40 from Beria to Stalin recommending the massacre of 25,700 Polish prisoners taken during and after the Russian occupation of eastern Poland in 1939. (The English translation is from *RFE/RL Research Report,* vol 2, no 4, 22 Jan 94, p 22, which the author used with permission. RFE/RL is Radio Free Europe/Radio Liberty.) See also ANDERS.

Katyusha rockets. Katyusha. A class of solid-fuel, recoilless, rocket launchers commonly fired from racks of 32-48 tubes, Katyushas—which Germans called the "Stalin (pipe) organ"—were an area-saturation weapon. The fused projectiles varied from 75mm to 16-in, they ranged up to 6,500 yds, and they were fired from artillery batteries, tanks, other vehicles, or from boats. In addition to their devastating power of physical destruction on troop formations, tanks, and artillery, Katyushas had demoralizing pyrotechnic and acoustic effects. German troops, many of them routed in their first encounter with the weapon at Smolensk in Mar 41, called them Stalin (pipe) organs.

KBE. Knight Commander of the Order of the British Empire.

KCB. Knight Commander of the Bath (UK).

KCIE. Knight Commander of the Indian Empire (UK)

KCMG. Knight Commander of St George and St Michael (UK).

KCSI. Knight Commander of the Star of India (UK).

KCVO. Knight Commander of the Royal Victorian Order (UK).

KG. Knight of the Order of the Garter (UK).

KGB. The Soviet Committee of State Security, Chief Investigative and Intelligence Agency, KGB was created after the war under Beria. (It had existed earlier as the NKGB, then the MGB.)

Khalkhin Gol (Nomonhan), 20-30 Aug 39. After the Battle of Lake **Khasan,** ZHUKOV was ordered to end the Japanese threat in the Far East. He took over a force designated Soviet-Mongolian Troops and began a campaign that ended with a decisive Red Army victory in the battle of Khalkhin Gol. Zhukov's success resulted from masterful use of airpower, armor, and surprise. Ending the undeclared border war in Mongolia, Zhukov's victory (hushed up by the Japanese) virtually eliminated Soviet concern about fighting a two-front war. Ironically, the **Nazi-Soviet Pact** was signed on the very day (23 Aug 39) the Soviet victory was sealed.

Khasan, Lake, Battle of, 31 July-11 Aug 38. One of several Russo-Japanese actions along the Khalka River, which is the boundary between NW Manchuria and Outer Mongolia. The Japanese made significant gains in the undeclared frontier war, leading to the arrest (and subsequent execution) of Marshal BLYUKHER, CinC in the Far East. He was succeeded temporarily by G. M. Shtern, who headed the FE Front until ZHUKOV arrived to take over the disorganized Russian forces and defeat the Japanese at **Khalkhin Gol.**

KIA. Killed in action.

Kinship or "kith and kin" edicts. Under a policy dating from the Russian revolution, the Soviets punished family members of "traitors" including Yakob STALIN and Marshal TUKHAVSHEKY. The Germans also had long had a "prisoners of kin" policy, which they called **Sippenhaft.**

Knickebein. Luftwaffe code word for the **Lorenz beam.**

Knight Commander of the Bath (KCB). A British order of **knighthood.**

Knighthood (Br). There is a complex hierarchy of British knighthoods including Knight of the Order of the Garter (KG), of St Patrick (KP), of the Thistle (KT); Knight Commander of the Bath (KCB), of St George and St Michael (KCMG), of the Order of the British Empire (KBE), of the Indian Empire (KCIE), and of the Star of India (KCSI). The knight grand cross of various orders exists above these simple knighthoods, the GCB being Knight Grand Cross of the Bath, GCIE being Knight Grand Commander of the Indian Empire, GCMG being Knight Grand Cross of St. Michael and St. George, and GCSI being Knight Grand Commander of the Star of India. (*Who Was Who* [in the UK], *1941-1950*, xiii-xiv.)

Knighthood entitles a man and his wife to be addressed as, for example, Sir Winston and Lady Clementine Churchill. Women knighted in their own name, like prima ballerina Margot Fonteyn, are addressed as Dame Margot.

Six top US military leaders of WWII were awarded the honorary GCB, the next Americans being Presidents Ronald Reagan and George Bush (30 Nov 93). Lower honors have been awarded to foreigners. Americans do not kneel at the investure, are not tapped on the shoulder, and are not entitled to be called Sir or Dame.

Knight's Cross or Ritterkreuz (RK). Created by Hitler as the highest decoration *for valor,* although the RK was awarded later in the war for "command achievements" (Manfred Rommel, *RP,* 39n). The Knight's Cross was bestowed on slightly more than 7,000 of more than 15,000,000 who fought in 1939-45. With permission and source citations I have made extensive use of Lt Col John R. Angolia's works (see bibliography) for the following summary and also for biographical data on many German officers in this dictionary.

When Hitler reinstituted the Iron Cross on 1 Sept 39 it was prescribed that "The cross for a higher class must be preceded by that of a lower class" (Angolia, I, 25). The progression was: Iron Cross 2d Class, Iron Cross 1st Class, **German Cross in Gold,** then Knight's Cross (RK) of the Iron Cross.

The RK with Oakleaves was created 3 Jun 40, and 890 were awarded during the war, eight to foreigners. The RK with Oakleaves and Swords was created in 1941; awards numbering 159, one posthumously to YAMAMOTO, the only foreigner. Of the RK with Oakleaves, Swords, and Diamonds, also created in 1941, only 27 were awarded. The Golden Oakleaves with Swords and Diamonds, instituted 29 Dec 44 by Hitler,

was intended to honor Germany's 12 bravest men, but the sole recipient was Hans RUDEL (1 Jan 45). Goering alone got the Grand Cross of the Iron Cross, presented 19 July 40 along with the unique rank of Reichsmarschall.

Both classes of the Iron Cross went to enlisted men (EM) but very few received the Iron Cross 1st Class (Manfred Rommel, RP, 39n). The highest German decoration for EM was the Militaerverdienstkreuz. The Iron Cross 2d Class was presented to 27 women, the first being Hanna REITSCH; she was one of only two women recipients of the Iron Cross 1st Class (Angolia, I, 32) and the only civilian. The other was Red Cross Sister Ilse Schulz (in North Africa).

Koenigsberg Fortress. Surrendered on 9 Apr 45 by Otto LASCH after a long siege, the historic port city and region of East Prussia was assigned to the USSR at the Yalta conference of 1945 and renamed Kaliningrad in 1946.

Kommodore, Kapitaen, Kommandeur. German *naval ranks* and *Luftwaffe titles* for commodore, captain, and commander.

Korvettenkapitaen. German naval rank equivalent to German Army major and USN commander, junior grade.

KP. 1. Knight of the Order of St. Patrick (UK); 2. Kitchen police (US).

Kreisau Circle. Formed in 1933 by Count Helmuth James von MOLTKE as a social group that met at his Kreisau estate, it became "perhaps the most widely publicized and certainly the most 'glamorized' facet of the whole anti-Hitler resistance movement" (W-B, *Nemesis,* 544). A founding member was Count YORCK VON WARTENBURG. The circle eventually had a formidable membership: Horst von Einsiedel, Carl Dietrich von Trotha, Aldolf Reichwein, Hans Peters, Hans Lukaschk, Carlo Mierendorff, Theodor Stelzer, Adam von Trott zu Solz, Hans-Bernd von Haeften, Harald Poelchau, and Jesuit Fathers Augustin Roesch, Aldred Delp, and Lothar Koenig. Others were Theo Haubach, Eugen Gerstenmaier, Paulus von Husen, Julius LEBER, Hans Schoenfeld, and many others on a less intimate and permanent basis. The Kreisau Circle had cross-connections to many socialists and trade unionists. (Hoffmann, 33.)

Kriegsgefangenenwesen. The Nazi POW administration headed by Gottlob BERGER at the end of the war.

Kriegsmarine. German Navy, headed by the OKM.

Kripo (Kriminalpolizei). The criminal police department of Goering's Prussian ministry of the interior, it was on a level of the organizational chart with DIELS's Gestapo. In Apr 34 the Kripo and **Gestapo** became subordinate agencies of Heydrich's Political Security Police (Sipo). When HEYDRICH's **RSHA** was created in Oct 39, the Gestapo and Kripo became Amt IV and V, still under Sipo. (Brissaud, Tables A-C, pp 300-3.) Arthur NEBE headed Kripo until forced to go underground in early 1945. Kripo was taken over by Heinrich ("Gestapo") MUELLER as an extra duty.

Kristallnacht, 9-10 Nov 38. See **Crystal Night.**

KT (Br). Knight of the Order of the Thistle.

Kuibyshev. The river port on the Volga, called Samara until 1935, became temporary capital of the USSR on 16 Oct 41, when the **Moscow Panic** started. Some 550 mi SE of Moscow, near the Trans-Siberian RR, "Europe's backdoor to Asia" was the site of many postwar trials and executions.

Kuomintang-Communist agreement, 3 July 37. A truce for Chinese collaboration against the Japanese.

Kwangtung Army (Kanto-gun). The Japanese army in Manchuria.

L

L-4 Piper Cub (US lt acft). See **Cub.**

LAH or LSSAH. Sepp DIETRICH's "SS-Leibstandarte Adolf Hitler" (elite bodyguard)

Lake Khasan. See Khasan, Lake.

Lancaster. The RAF's most successful heavy bomber, operational from Mar 42, it was a 4-engine, twin-tail plane with considerable onboard firepower for defense. The Lancaster could fly 1,600 miles at 210 mph with 14,000 pounds of munitions. *(S&S)*

Landesgruppe. Nazi party organization in a country outside Germany.

Landing craft (LC). These included the LCA (assault), LCI (infantry), LCI(L) (infantry, large), LCP (L) (personnel, large); LCT (tank); and LCVP (landing craft, vehicle and personnel). Landing ships included the **LSD** and **LST.**

Landwehr. German military reserve corps of men between the ages of 35 and 45.

Leavenworth, Ft. Site of the **C&GSS.**

Lebensraum. Literally "living space" in the geopolitics of HAUSFHOFER, it became the Nazi code word for expansion into central and eastern Europe.

Ledo Road. US Army engineers took over from the British in late Dec 42 to build the road from Ledo, in **Assam,** India, into Burma through **Myitkynia** to connect with the **Burma Rd.** Under R. A. WHEELER's overall responsibility Lewis A. PICK completed the 478-mile road on 7 Jan 45.

Légion des volontaires Français contre le bolchevism (LVF), or 638th Inf Regt. Pierre LAVAL was seriously wounded while reviewing the first contingent leaving Versailles for Russia on 27 Aug 41. The LVF was transformed on 18 July 42 from a private, volunteer force into "la Légion tricolore."

Legion of Honor. Created by Napoleon, the decoration is awarded in various degrees from Chevalier to Grand Cross to French and foreign civilians and to military personnel for service to France. The *Cross* of the Legion of Honor is for the highest military valor.

Leningrad. Founded in 1703 as St Petersburg, it was the capital of Russia 1712-1917 until Moscow became the capital. The great port city meanwhile was renamed Petrograd in 1914, Leningrad in 1924, and on 6 Sep 91 the name St Petersburg was restored.

Leutnant. German military rank corresponding to US Second **Lieutenant.** (Oberleutnant = 1st Lt.)

Leyte Gulf, Battle for, 23-26 Oct 44. In a daring gamble to break up the massive US amphibious assault on Leyte Island in the east Philippines the Japanese launched Opn Sho I. Adm Takeo KURITA, leading the main effort, met heroic resistance in the Battle off Samar and abandoned his mission.

LH. French **Legion of Honor.**

Lidice (lid' uh see), Czech, 9-10 June 42. As the Germans undertook a program of reprisal for the assassination of HEYDRICH (who died 4 June), Frank visited Berlin and was instructed by Hitler to destroy the village of Lidice, shooting its male inhabitants and deporting its women and children. Why? The Germans knew that one native of Lidice was serving with the Czech army in Britain, but other reports of subverve activity in the village (an arms cache and secret radio transmitter) later proved to be unfounded. Only after the reprisal did the Germans learn that some of the British-trained assassination agents had been given addresses in Lidice for contacts. (Mastny, 215-16).

The operation began at 10 PM on 9 June, when German troops, police, and members of the Czech gendarmerie encircled the village. The inhabitants were registered, and movable property including livestock was evacuated. At dawn a special squad of the Regular Police herded the male population into a farmhouse yard and shot 173 men and boys. The German later executed 26 inhabitants of Lidice who had not made muster on 9 June, including nine night-shift workers and a miner who had been in the hospital with a broken leg (ibid.). Army engineers razed the village on 10 June (ibid.), a film crew recording the event (S&S).

The 198 women were sent Ravensbrueck, where about 50 died (ibid.). Of 98 children, 81 were deemed racially unsuitable and later killed, probably in the gas chambers at Chelmno, Poland. The other children were adopted by German families. The villages of Bernartice and Lezaky suffered much the same fate, but Lidice became the universal symbol of Nazi barbarity. Never rebuilt, its name was taken by a Czech-American community in Illinois on 12 July 42 (*Webster's Geog Dict*) and a town in Mexico *(S&S)*. Exactly two years after the mass murder at Lidice a somewhat similar atrocity took place at **Oradour sur Glane** in France.

Lieutenant. The most junior commissioned officer in the US Army, Air Force, and Marines is a 2d Lt (gold bar), who aspires to the rank of 1st Lt (silver bar). US Navy ranks are Lieutenant (junior grade), corresponding to the army's 1st Lt, and Lieutenant, corresponding to army captain.

Lieutenant general. The rank above **major general.** A licutenant general in most armies equates in rank to US major general.

Limpet (mine). An explosive designed to cling to the hull of a ship, usually with magnets.

Line, the. Regular army forces as opposed to **territorial** and reserve forces (*UOD*). Also,

the combat element of a force (front line). A US Army line officer belongs to a combat arm (as opposed to a technical or administrative *service*). A US Navy line officer (wearing a star above his sleeve or shoulder board insignia of rank) is one eligible for command at sea (as opposed to an officer of the staff, who wears an oak leaf).

LM. US Legion of Merit. A decoration for meritorious service; 20,273 were awarded in 1939-47, almost exclusively to colonels and generals.

LnO. Liaison officer.

LofC. Line of communications. It includes all land, sea, and air routes for supplies, reinforcements, and other support.

LORAN (*Long range radio navigation*). First used in the USN from 1944, Alfred L. LOOMIS being a principal developer, Loran works somewhat like *radar.* Short-pulse radio signals from two points (for triangulation) are picked up by a receiver that measures the difference in arrival time. Prepared tables make it possible to determine location of the receiver quickly. In addition to being an aid to navigation, loran was a breakthrough in ASW. Improved versions (Loran-C) have been invaluable in mapping.

Lorenz beam. Codenamed **Knickebein,** it was a navigational system used by the Luftwaffe at night or in bad weather to find bombing targets. One station sent a pair of closely parallel radio beams within which a pilot stayed until hitting another beam from a station on a flank. Failure to recognize the threat discredited TIZARD in Churchill's eyes, to LINDEMANN's advantage.

Louisiana maneuvers of 1941. The first and only maneuver involving two American field armies (*AA,* 495), it was a maker and breaker of reputations. On the winning side was Walter KRUEGER's Blue Force, with EISENHOWER as CofS and BRADLEY figuring prominently. Ben LEAR headed the Red Force, with which PATTON made himself conspicuous.

LSD. Landing Ship, Dock.

LSSAH (or LAH). Leibstandarte SS Adolf Hitler, formed by Sepp DIETRICH.

LST. Landing Ship, Tank. For debarking troops and supplies over the beach, the LST was a large, ocean-going vessel with a flat bottom enabling it to get close to a beach. Two large doors and a ramp made landing possible from the bow.

Lt. 1. Lieutenant; 2. Light, as in Lt Inf (meaning lightly equipped) or Lt Arty.

Lubyanka. The Moscow building at 2 Lubyanka St housed offices and prisons of Soviet security services from 1917. The Kommandatura of the NKVD, where executions were carried out, were in the internal jail. The "second block" of the jail was a hotel-like facility for special prisoners. See **Police and secret services of the USSR.**

Lucy ring, Switzerland. So named for Rudolf "Lucy" ROESSLER (because he operated from Lucerne), the ring was set up by the Soviets but (it was learned long after the war) controlled by the British. Brigadier Roger MASSON, head of Swiss military intelligence, protected the Lucy ring in return for being furnished material that was in the interest of his country and the Allies. Masson established liaison between the Bureau Ha, a formerly private intelligence agency under Hans Haussmann, and the Lucy ring.

The so-called Lucy ring evolved from four Soviet-run networks controlled by resident director Sandor Alex "Dora" Rado from Sep 38. He was a respected Hungarian geographer whom Red Army intelligence (**GRU**) sent to Geneva in the summer of 1936. Rado's cover was a map publishing business, Geopress. Quiescent until war broke out, Rado and his wife Hélène ("Lène") then became active and expanded his net. Ruth "Sonia" Kuczynski (following) arranged for a code book and instructions on secret radio procedures to be brought from Brussels by Victor "Kent" Sukulov, who then was deputy chief of what became known as the **Rote Kapelle.** Dora recruited Edmond "Edward" Hamel, owner of a local radio shop, to build a set and operate it with his wife Olga, who proved to be highly capable. As the workload increased, Rado (who had radio experience in the merchant marines) recruited Margrit "Rosie" Bolli as a courier and additional radio operator.

Alexander Allan "Jim" FOOTE had been ordered to Geneva by British intelligence in Sep 36 for insertion as a double agent. His contact was the alluring Sonia, a German Jewess born Ruth Kuczynski, who at the time was acting resident director and operator of a ring based near Montreux. She directed Foote's training, sent him to Munich, and from 23 Aug 39 he was her radio operator. On taking over the net from Sonia he moved to Lausanne on 15 Dec 40 and thereafter was the principal radio link between the Lucy net and Moscow Center. But Foote also had a vital administrative role. Through Max "the Cobbler" Havijanic in Basle he supplied passports ("shoes" in the language of espionage). The Cobbler worked through the elderly Anna Mueller, who served as a letter drop and call address for agents who needed directions. She handled the transfer of operating funds from Soviet agents in France and Germany, and Anna maintained contact with a network in Germany. Her agent in Munich was Foote's fiancée, Agnes "Mikki" Zimmermann.

Rachel "Sissy" Duebendorfer operated her net from the International Labor Office (ILO) in Geneva with Paul Boettcher (her common-law husband), Christian "Taylor" Schneider, and Walter "Brant" Fluckiger. Strapped for funds, Sissy was readily recruited by Claude DANSEY, thus becoming another link with MI6 for Ultra material. But, much more important, Sissy brought Lucy into the net. This came about when she sent Schneider (above) to answer Roessler's advertisement for part-time editorial help in his publishing business. Sissy passed material to Rado for transmission to Moscow Center. Because the Russians would accept nothing without knowing the source, Rado called it "Lucy."

Otto "Pakbo" Puenter, a highly respected journalist, operated a net from Berne under the cover of his press service, the International Socialist Agency (INSA). Puenter's net had highly placed sources in Italy, Austria, and Germany. On a visit to Spain during the civil war Puenter met the Russian intelligence officer with the Republicans, "Carlo," and agreed to share his INSA material with the Loyalists. This meant it would go to Moscow Center, and the link was maintained when Carlo went to Paris and became known as "Kolia." In turning over his duties as Swiss resident director to Rado in Sep 38, Kolia introduced Rado to Pakbo and the two collaborated thereafter.

Lucy's incredibly accurate, timely, and detailed reports were dismissed initially by the Russians and the Western Allies as disinformation planted by the Germans. It was too good to be true, and Lucy refused to reveal his sources so "customers" could evaluate them. But Roessler's credibility was accepted by Moscow Center after Rado authorized the transmission of his warnings about the impending German assault in Russia, Opn **Barbarossa.**

It was not known until long after the war that Lucy's most important information was from **Ultra.** The myth that it came from Roessler's 10 highly placed moles in OKW was a perfect cover story. But Roessler's genius was as an evaluator or analyst of military information based largely on his mastery of German order of battle material. For this he needed his own inside sources.

Lucy's only big failure was in the spring of 1943, when he had little Ultra traffic and had to rely almost entirely on his own sources. This was because Hitler had joined Manstein in the south of Russia, where the master of mobile warfare was about to conduct a large-scale counteroffensive. With no need for Manstein to clear his decisions with OKW in Rastenburg, Bletchley had little radio traffic, hence little Ultra intelligence. Reports to Moscow Center from Switzerland still bore Lucy's imprimatur, but most of the intelligence during this period was from Pakbo's net, not Ultra. When VATUTIN reported that his SW front was about to be overwhelmed in Kharkov, front line intelligence at variance with Moscow Center's, Stalin told Vatutin the Germans were at the end of their tether and that he should hold Kharkov at all cost. This led to a Soviet disaster in the third battle of Kharkov, which ended 16 Mar 43 with a loss of no fewer than 52 Red Army divisions.

Lucy's credibility was quickly redeemed by the great Soviet victory around Kursk, 5-16 July 43, Opn Citadel. Thanks largely to Ultra information fed through Lucy, Stalin was reading Hitler's hand before and during what has been acknowledged by most historians as the turning point of the war. It also was the end of Ultra material being fed to Moscow Center on a regular basis; Britain no longer needed to do so.

Walter SCHELLENGERG slowly closed in on Lucy after **radiogoniometry** eventually found he was operating from Switzerland. When German codebreakers isolated the word "Everhard" in the welter of incomprehensible code groups, a bibliophile recognized the name of a hero in Jack London's novels. This led to cracking the Lucy ring's code, but Foote was so clever in changing codes and wavelengths that the Germans never learned the full content of his transmissions.

MASSON stayed a step ahead of the Germans in his dangerous game. But the Italian surrender on 3 Sep 43 put the Swiss in new peril from German troops on their southern border. In one of their secret meetings Schellenberg convinced Masson that Hitler still might be provoked into violating Swiss neutrality and a task force was making preparations. A special formation under Lt Maurice Treyer of the Swiss army radio-intelligence service, operating separately from Masson's agency, was ordered to use **goniometry** equipment to listen around Geneva for Wehrmacht radio transmissions that might reveal hostile German intentions. Within 10 days Treyer's men picked up two suspicious transmitters. Correctly suspecting Soviet spy activity, the lieutenant informed the local police rather than military intelligence. (But for this, Masson might have protected the Lucy ring a little longer.) A fortnight after this initial success (in which he had heard Olga Hammel and Margrit "Rosie" Bolli) the lieutenant located a third transmitter in Lausanne and reported this also to the local police. The Hammels, Margrit "Rosie" Bolli, and her lover, Hans "Romeo" Peters, were arrested in police raids on 14 Oct 43. Rado panicked, warned Foote (now the only radio contact with Moscow Center), went into hiding, but kept contact with Foote. The latter suspected his days were numbered but continued communicating with Moscow until arrested on 20 Nov 43. The rest of his story and that of Rado are told in the sketch of FOOTE.

Rachel "Sissy" Duebendorfer and Paul Boetcher were arrested on 19 Apr 44, and the police found material that led to the arrest of Roessler and Schneider on 9 May 44. Unable to build a case that would not reveal too many embarrassing state secrets, the Swiss released Roessler four months later, in Sep 44 (the same day as Foote).

Roessler and Schneider were brought to trial on 22 Oct 45 in Berne and charged with helping the intelligence service of a foreign power, Germany! (Read & Fisher, *Lucy,* 211-

12.) Lucy had sent three messages about the new Oerlikon cannon, which was manufactured in Switzerland and shipped to Germany. But the judge set Lucy free under a Swiss law that no punishment need be imposed if an accused had acted in the best interest of the state. Schneider was sentenced to 30 days in prison. The other accused in this trial, Rachel "Sissy" Duebendorfer and Paul Boettcher, had fled in 1945. The Swiss court sentenced them in absentia to two years in prison. (See Read & Fisher, *Lucy,* 211, and Accoce & Quet, *Lucy,* 234. The latter say the couple spent 12 years in Siberian work camps before settling in Leipzig. Op cit, 13, 243.)

The Gestapo lured Anna Mueller into Germany in Aug 43 with a bogus message about a sick relative and arrested her. She held up under brutal interrogation and harsh imprisonment in irons, revealing nothing, and lived to come home after a long hospitalization. Agnes "Mikki" Zimmermann, Foote's fiancée, was taken by the Gestapo and she went mad under torture.

Otto "Pakbo" Puenter was never arrested, probably because trial would reveal that he had acted in the best interests of Switzerland and in close collaboration with the Swiss federal police. (Read & Fisher, *Lucy,* 231.) He continued his journalistic career in Berne.

Rado and his wife went into hiding on 14 Oct 43. After 11 arduous months they were smuggled into France the night of 16-17 Sep 44 in a milk train. Both were sick, Lène from chronic bronchitis and her husband from severe rheumatism. They reached Paris on 24 Sep, soon after FOOTE, where the rest of Rado's story is outlined.

The Swiss opened their second trial of Lucy ring on 30 Oct 47 in Lausanne. The accused this time were the Hamels and Margrit "Rosie" Bolli in court and the Rados and Foote absent. Roessler was a witness. Like him, the accused were charged not with what they actually did but with giving the Germans technical details of the Oerlikon. Of the absentees, Foote was given 30 months in prison, a 8,000 franc fine, and confiscation of his bank account and the 3,255 francs that had been found on him when arrested. Rado was fined 10,000 francs, sentenced to three years in prison, and barred from Switzerland for 15 years. His wife, who was living in France, was sen-

tenced to a year in prison and 10 years's expulsion. (Reade & Fisher, *Lucy,* 217.)

Of the three small fry actually in the court room the Hamels and Margrit "Rosie" Bolli were given less than a year in prison and modest fines. They then led normal lives in Switzerland. The Hamels were divorced in the 1970s, but he continued to operate his radio shop in Geneva.

Luftflotte. Air Fleet.

Luftwaffe. The Aero Club of Berlin, which GOERING established in Feb 33, was unveiled in Mar 35 as the new German Air Force. Goering remained head of the Luftwaffe, but MILCH was its real creator.

LVF. See Légion des volontaires Français.

Lysander ("Lizzie"). This chubby **VSTOL,** a high-winged, single-engined, two-seater monoplane with a glassed-in cabin and fixed landing gear was produced by Westland for the RAF in a number of specialized models. With a 890 hp radial Bristol Mercury engine it could reach almost 220 mph, and with external tanks could fly 450 miles. Two .303-cal machine guns fired forward and one from the rear cockpit. *(S&S.)* Painted black, the Lysander was a workhorse of Sqdn Ldr John Nesbitt-Dufort's "Moon Sqd." This overnight shuttle service for the SOE lost only 13 Lysanders in four years during which some 800 secret agents were taken in and out of France on 180 missions. (Miller, *The Resistance,* 44.) Lysanders were used also for air-sea rescue, liaison, air reconnaissance, artillery spotting, strafing, and precision bombing.

LZ. Landing zone for gliders or supply planes. A DZ (drop zone) is for parachutists and supplies.

M

MA. 1. Military attaché; 2. Military Academy.

MAAF. Mediterranean Allied Air Force.

Madagascar plan. Drafted in 1940 by Franz Rademacher, a foreign office subordinate heading the Jewish desk in Martin LUTHER's "Germany" dept (Abteilung Deutschland), the plan called for France to cede Madagascar to Germany for use as a huge ghetto where four million Jews could be isolated, paying their own way, after more than 25,000 Frenchmen were evacuated. Adolf Eichmann was put in charge of carrying out the plan, which was seriously considered after the Wannsee conference (20 Jan 42) but never adopted.

Mad Mullah. Muhammad Abdill Hassan was given this name by the British, although he was certainly not insane nor, strictly speaking, a mullah. The Sheikh, who graduated to the honorific title Sayyid (Lord or Master), led insurgencies in British Somaliland for 21 years until his death on 23 Nov 20. Among those who fought the Mad Mullah are CARTON DE WIART, "Freddie" DE GUINGAND, and Claude DANSEY.

MAF. (US) Marine Amphibious Force.

Magic. Originally a code name for translations of intercepted Japanese diplomatic messages, "Magic" became the term for US programs to break *all* Japanese codes.

Maginot Line. A 200-mile band of French fortifications along the border with Germany, it extended north from near Belfort to Thionville. The Belgians reneged on extending the line along their border with Germany, leaving the supposedly impregnable line with an exposed left flank, which the Germans "turned" in May-June 40. Named after André Maginot, French minister of defense, 1929-32, the line became a monument to the folly of relying on fixed defensive systems, particularly in modern war.

Maghreb. Africa north of the Sahara with the exclusion of Egypt. *Maghreb* is Arabic for "west." The maghreb includes Libya, but the term is applied mainly to the former Barbary States of predominantly Berber people in NW Africa. See Andrew Boyd and Patrick van Rensburg, *An Atlas of African Affairs* (New York: Praeger, 1962), 48-49.

Maidenek. A concentration camp just outside Lublin, Poland, it was one of four under Christian WIRTH. An estimated 1.5 million were murdered at Maidenek in two years. Found by the Red Army on 23 July 44, it was the first Nazi death camp revealed to the world.

Main effort. Military attacks, tactical and strategic, have resources allocated to one main effort; one or more secondary efforts normally are made, and often with feints, diversions, or demonstrations (to fake out enemy reserves).

Main line of resistance (MLR). Defensive positions behind outposts and delaying positions.

The MLR is held "at all cost" (i.e., to death) unless permission is given to withdraw.

Main (or Chief) State Security Directorate (USSR). A department of the NKVD, it was headed by BERIA from Dec 38.

Major General. Because few countries have the rank of brigadier general a major general is the lowest-ranking general officer in most countries other than France and the US. Hence a major general in the British, German, or Soviet army does not rank with a US major general but with a US brigadier general. The major general originally was a *sergeant-major* general, which is why a modern major general is junior to a lieutenant general.

Malmédy massacre, Belgium, 17 Dec 45. As Joachim PEIPER's SS task force spearheaded the 6th Pz Army (of "Sepp" DIETRICH) in the Ardennes offensive it was slowed on the second day by the capture of Battery B, 285th FA Observation Bn, near Malmédy. Some of Peiper's troops herded POWs into a snowy pasture and gunned them down. It turned out that 71 Americans were killed, not the 129 reported initially; the others lived by feigning death. Peiper, DIETRICH, and other Malmédy defendants were released on parole after 13 years in jail, then put on probation. Further details are in the sketch of Joachim PEIPER.

Manchukuo. Japanese name for their pseudo-independent state set up in Feb 32. Manchukuo came to include the three provinces of Manchuria and the province of Jchol.

Manchurian Incident, 1931. See Mukden incident.

Manhattan project. Created to develop and produce the first US atomic bombs, it was under the administrative control of Col (later Maj Gen) Leslie R. GROVES. As CG of the specially created Manhattan (NY) district of the US Army Corps of Engineers, he had administrative control over scientific work, engineering, and construction of what became known as the Manhattan project. Major installations were at Oak Ridge, Tenn; Los Alamos, NM; and Hanford, Wash. Without Congressional authorization and in the strictest secrecy the Manhattan project eventually employed 125,000 people and cost more than $2 billion.

Maquis. The word comes from the Italian *macchia* ("spot") and has long been used for regions of Corsica covered by scrub growth or brush and often infested with bandits. French guerrillas of 1940-45 called themselves *maquisards* and their movement the *maquis*.

Mareth Line. Built by the French to defend their protectorate of Tunisia from the Italians in Libya, it was demilitarized after the June 40 armistice but still formidable when Rommel occupied it for a last stand in his retreat from Montgomery. Gen Giovanni MESSE commanded Axis forces in the line when the British broke through on 27 Mar 43.

Marco Polo Bridge Incident, Peking, 1937. An exchange of shots between sentinels on 7 July 37, apparently accidental, was used by local Japanese commanders to bring on the Sino-Japanese war.

Marita. Code name for German invasion of Greece.

Mark (Ger). The Deutschmark (DM), later the Reichmark (RM), had an official exchange value of 25 US cents until 1969.

Market-Garden, 17-25 Sep 44. Code name for MONTGOMERY's attempt to cross the Lower Rhine at Arnhem and **turn** the West Wall. "Market" was the airborne assault; "Garden" the ground link-up. In Market, BRERETON's 1st Abn Army was to take five critical bridges in a 65-mile-long corridor through which the ground link-up would come. As part of "Boy" BROWNING's 1st Abn Corps, Roy URQUHART's Br 1st Abn Div was to land around Arnhem, the critical objective and farthest bridge; James GAVIN's 82d US Abn Div would drop around Nijmegen (some 10 miles south of the Rhine); and Max TAYLOR's 101st US Abn Div would take the closest objectives, bridges just north of Eindhoven (one at St Oedenrode and two at Veghel). The ground linkup would be spearheaded by Maj Gen Allan's Br Guards Armd Div of HORROCK's Br 30th Corps, which was supposed to reach Arnhem by D+2.

Unknown to British intelligence (despite warning from the Dutch underground), the crack 2d SS Pz Corps of "Willi" BITTRICH was just north of Arnhem, and MODEL had recently established his CP in a western suburb of Arnhem, (Oosterbeek). STUDENT, father of German airborne forces, also happened to be on the scene, and from a downed American glider the Germans got the complete plans for Market-Garden! To compound all this bad luck, five days of bad weather slowed reinforcement and resupply of the airheads.

The landings began Sunday 17 Sep 44. At Arnhem the Red Devils secured the north end of the 2,000-foot-long Rhine River bridge but a small force on the other side kept them from crossing to complete their mission. Bittrich's SS panzer divisions moved in from the north to put the British under siege and then drove a wedge between those at the bridge and the rest of their division. The Germans secured the bridge on 21 Sep and captured its defenders.

Forward elements of the linkup force made contact the next day, D+5, three days behind schedule. As covered in more detail under URQUHART, the few Allied survivors at a bridgehead west of Arnhem retreated through the corridor.

As for operations around Nijmegen, Browning (who landed here to set up his corps headquarters) had told Gavin that the 82d Abn must secure high ground southeast of the city before taking the 1,960-foot-long highway bridge. But "Jumping Jim" decided before leaving England that a battalion might take the great bridge on D day by rushing it before the Germans were ready. He gave instructions for the battalion to move out promptly after landing, and to approach Nijmegen from the east to avoid the built-up area. His orders were misunderstood as to time and route: the battalion was slow leaving the drop zone; it approached the town from the south; and it did not arrive until after dark. The Germans consequently had time to secure the only bridge available to the linkup force. Not until D+5 (22 Sep) did forward elements of the Guards Armd Div reach Arnhem, a day too late to save the Red Devils at the bridge.

At Eindhoven, Max Taylor's 101st Abn took its objectives, opening the route for the Guards Armd Div., which reached Eindhoven on D+1 and Nijmegen on D+2. Like the 82d at Nijmegen, the "Screaming Eagles" held their airhead against determined German counterattacks.

Allied airborne and ground forces in Market-Garden lost more than 17,000 officers and men killed, wounded, and missing in the nine-day operation.

Marshals of the Soviet Union. The first five, created in 1935, were BLUYKHER (shot), BUDENNY, VOROSHILOV, A. I. Yegorov (shot), and TUKHACHEVSKY (shot). Appointed in 1940 were KULIK (subsequently demoted), TIMOSHENKO, and SHAPSONIKOV. In 1941 STALIN became MSU No. 9. Next came VASILEVSKY and ZHUKOV, both in Feb 43. There were six in 1944 who in alphabetical order were: GOVOROV, KONEV, MALNOVSKY, MERETSKOV, ROKOSSOVSKY, and TOLBUKHIN. BERIA was the last wartime MSU. Then came SOKOLOVSKY (1946), BULGANIN (1947), BAGRAMYAN (1947). Five were created during the KHRUSHCHEV regime: S. S. Biryuzov, CHUYKOV, YEREMENKO, A. A. Grechko, and K. S. Mosalenko. The next, ending the names of those who had held high positions during the war, were G. F. Zakharov (1959) and F. I. Golikov (1961).

Maru. Japanese for "ship."

Massilia affair, 20-26 June 40. With cabinet approval to establish a new government in North Africa after PETAIN's armistice in metropolitan France, some 30 French legislators took the chartered liner *Massilia* from Port-Vendres (on the Mediterranean near the Spanish border) to Casablanca. Here the "resisters," including DALADIER and MANDEL, were put in protective custody by NOGUES on orders from LAVAL (Pertinax, 459). Duff COOPER and Lord GORT made a vain attempt, on instructions from the British cabinet, to make contact in Morocco with the *Massilia* group as their confreres in Vichy voted the Third Republic out of existence.

MATAF. Mediterranean Allied Tactical AF.

MBE (UK). *Member* of the **OBE,** a knighthood. An MBE is distinct from an *officer* of the OBE, who is not a member of the **knighthood.**

MC. 1. Military Cross, a high British decoration for valor. The ribbon is a broad black stripe on a white field. 2. Military Council of a Soviet military **front.**

MD. Military district, Soviet or German, as in Kiev MD or Berlin MD.

ME. 1. **Middle East.** 2. **Main effort.**

Me 109. A single-seat, single-engine German fighter with squarish wing tips, it was designed by Willi MESSERSCHMITT to specifications first established in 1934 (as were those for the Hurricane and Spitfire). The Messerschmitt fighter went through several modifications until the Me 109G supplanted all others by the end of 1942 (S&S). More Me 109s were produced in 1940-45 (30,124) than any other warplane, and with the earlier output of more than 2,300 from 1937 it may lead all other combat planes in total production (*S&S*).

Me 262. The world's first operational jet airplane, it had a top speed of 540 mph. Armament was twenty-four 50mm rocket missiles and four 50mm cannon. Production was 1,294, perhaps a quarter of which survived testing and had the fuel to fight (Bekker, 356). The Me 262 needed a hot pilot for what was essentially an experimental plane of advanced design, but Adolf GALLAND's JV-44 threw a scare into the Allies and proved that he had been right in arguing for better use of fighters in the defense.

Mecz. Mechanized (completely equipped with motor transport and sometimes with armored vehicles also).

Medals of Honor (US). *See* **MH.**

Mediterranean strategy. Strongly advocated by Churchill and CIGS Alan BROOKE, it was opposed on military grounds by US military planners and on political grounds by Stalin (who wanted no British presence in central Europe).

Mensheviks (plural Menshivists or Menshiviki). A communist faction (from a word meaning "less"), they formed the minority and less revolutionary group, in opposition to the extremist **Bolsheviks** ("larger") wing. The latter won out, the formal break coming in 1912 when the **RSDRP(b)** was created with STALIN on its **Central Committee.**

Mers-el-Kebir, 3 July 40. Adm Marcel Gensoul's French fleet, in harbor here just W of Oran, Algeria, suffered heavy losses when attacked by James SOMERVILLE after refusing the alternatives dictated by Churchill for all French naval commanders in waters controlled by the Royal Navy: join the British, or turn their ships over to the British, or sail to the West Indies and out of German reach. Gensoul refused all these alternatives, thus being the only French admiral to honor the Franco-German armistice agreement. Somerville did his duty, opening fire at about 6 PM on 3 July 40. In addition to destroying the ships, the British killed about 1,300 Frenchmen and wounded about 350. The affair virtually destroyed what little willingness the French Navy had left to join the British against the Germans.

mFb, mdFb, mstFb. German Army command designations meaning, roughly, "charged with command." When the regular commander was absent, a replacement was assigned with one of these designations. Both of the first two abbreviations are for "mit der Fuehrung beauftrangt"; mstFb is for "mit der stellvertretenden Fuehrung beauftrangt." (B&O, 143.)

MG. 1. Military Government; 2. Machine gun.

MH. Medal of Honor, the highest US decoration for valor, 289 being awarded in WW II (AA, 672). Although bestowed "in the name of Congress" it is the Medal of Honor, not the Congressional Medal of Honor.

MI (Br). Military intelligence.

MI5 (Br). Security Service handling counterintelligence within the UK.

MI6 (Br). Secret Intelligence Service (SIS) responsible for overseas operations. MI6 was established in 1909 under Mansfield Smith Cumming, RN, who was followed by Hugh "Quex" Sinclair and Steward MENZIES. Carrying on the practice begun by Cumming, MI6 chiefs were always known within "The Firm" by the designation "C." The Firm was responsible for espionage overseas, whereas secret operations within British territory were handled by MI5. MI6 sections after 1939 were: I Political; II Military; III Naval; IV Air; V Counterespionage; VI Industrial; VII Financial; VIII Communications; IX Ciphers (from Sep 44, it was the anti-Soviet section); X Press. In had "stations" at Vienna, Tallinn, Riga, Brussels, Sofia, Prague, Copenhagen, Helsinki, Paris, Berlin, Athens, in Japan, Rotterdam, Oslo, Warsaw, Lisbon, Bucharest, Madrid, Stockholm, Berne, Vladivostok, Beirut, New York, and Buenos Aires. (Brown, "C," 129-30.) See also SIS.

MI9. Escape and Evasion Service branch of SIS.

MIA. Missing in action, some of whom are later reclassified POW, DOW, KIA, and WIA.

Microdot (mikropunkt). A German development first used by Dusko "Tricycle" POPOV on his trip to America in Aug 41. With a microphotographic process it put a page of text or a drawing on a piece of film the size of the dot over a typewritten or printed letter *i*.

Middle East. Despite Churchill's objection that Egypt, Palestine, and Syria were the *Near* East, the Middle East being Iran and Iraq, all these countries were in the British "Middle East Command" until early Aug 42. At this time, when Alexander succeeded Auchinleck as CinC Middle East, his command covered only Egypt, Palestine, and Syria. Iran and Iraq were detached as a separate theater of operations of that name. (WC, IV, 460 ff.)

Militaerverdienstkreuz. The highest German decoration for valor awarded through 1918 to enlisted men.

Military Council (Sov). It comprised the **front** commander, his CofS, and the political member (commissar).

MI(R). Research branch of SIS

MIT. Massachusetts Institute of Technology, Cambridge, Mass.

MLR. **Main line of resistance.**

MOD. Minister or Ministry of Defense, an abbreviation used in this book as a spacesaver. In the postwar USSR the position corresponded roughly to the US Secretary of Defense and Chairman of the JCS combined (Scotts).

Molotov cocktail. Normally a glass bottle filled with gasoline and having an improvised wick, it was lit and thrown at the air-intake or open hatch of a vehicle, usually incinerating the crew. The simple and effective weapon was used in Spain (1936-39) but Finnish soldiers of the Winter War (1939-40) named it the Molotov cocktail.

Moscow Center. Headquarters of the USSR security service or central intelligence service.

Moscow Panic, 16 Oct 41. With the Germans less than 100 miles away, the Soviets ordered evacuation of many governmental departments and of the diplomatic corps from Moscow to **Kuibyshev.** The **Frunze MA** moved to Tashkent. Stalin, the **GKO,** and **Stavka** stayed in Moscow, where a state of siege was declared on 19 Oct 41 because of general panic and widespread looting.

Mosquito (RAF). A two-engine plane built of wood, it was conceived as a bomber so fast (over 400 mph) it did not need guns. The Mosquito was designed by the DE HAVILLAND Acft Co as a private venture and accepted by the RAF only after seeing the designer's son Geoffery (Jr) fly phenomenal tests in Nov 40. Perhaps the most versatile military aircraft ever built, in addition to being one of the fastest of its day, the Mosquito was good day or night as a precision bomber, fighter, or reconnaissance plane. About 7,000 were produced during the war.

MP (Br.). Member of Parliament.

mph. Miles per hour.

Msgr . Monseigneur/Monsignor.

Mtzd. **Motorized.**

MRP (Fr). Mouvement Populaire Républicain. Postwar political party of great clout that evolved out of one established during the war by BIDAULT and fellow Catholics.

MSU. **Marshal of the Soviet Union.**

Mtn. Mountain, as in 10th US Mtn Div.

MTO. Mediterranean Theater of Operations.

MTOUSA. Mediterranean Theater of Operations, US Army. It replaced NATOUSA on 1 Nov 44 (AA, 606) with McNARNEY as head until succeeded in Dec 45 by J. C. H. LEE (AA, 609).

Mukden Incident, 18 Sep 31. A few feet of the South Manchurian RR were blown mysteriously while the Japanese were conducting night maneuvers around Mukden. Allegedly conceived by DOIHARA without official blessing, and blamed on the Chinese, the incident was the work of ultra-nationalists in the Kwantung Army as an excuse for imposing Japanese control over Manchuria. It was the proximate cause of WWII.

Mulberry. Code name for artificial ports originally dreamed of by Churchill in 1915. Mulberry B in the British zone off Arromanches handled 680,000 tons of equipment, 40,000 vehicles, and 220,000 men between mid-July and 31 Oct 44. Mulberry A off Omaha Beach (16-19 June 44) was broken up by high seas and portions were sent to Mulberry B. The mulberry off Cherbourg was finished on 27 June 44 but also broke up in heavy weather.

Munich Beer Hall Putsch, 8-9 Nov 23. With headquarters in the Buergerbraeukeller, HITLER directed a coup that failed in a whimper but gave him national prominence for the first time. The beer hall was used for annual commemorations. A bomb explosion on 8 Nov 39, 20 minutes after Hitler's exit, wrecked the hall and led to the **Venlo incident.**

Munich crisis, 1938. Threatening war over the **Sudetenland,** Hitler met with Chamberlain, Daladier, and Mussolini in Munich on 29-30 Sep 38. The Munich Agreement (or Pact), signed about 2 AM on 30 Sep 38, allowed Hitler to occupy the Sudetenland unopposed.

MVD. Soviet Ministry of Defense.

Myitkyina, Burma. Pronounced myi chee nah, located on the left bank of the upper Irrawaddy near the China border, it is the most important town in N Burma. The river port and land communications center was captured by the Japanese in Apr 42 and was Stilwell's main intermediate objective in 1944. Frank D. MERRILL's Marauders led the way. But Stilwell's G2 (his son) badly underestimated Japanese strength in the town (as was not revealed until after the event) and regular forces were needed before the Allies took Myitkyina on 3 Aug 44.

N

NAAF. NW African AF.

NAAFI (Br). Navy Army Air Force Institute, which is comparable to the US post exchange service.

Nanking, Rape of. Starting 13 Dec 37 two Japanese divisions of about 35,000 officers and men under Gen Iwane MATSUI got out of control after entering Nanking (Nanjing), capital of Nationalist China. The invaders had finished a hard-fought 170-mile advance in four months from Shanghai. In a two-month orgy the Japanese executed as many as 200,000 Chinese, raping at least 5,000 women, girls, and children before killing them (Bergamini, 4). The Japanese systematically destroyed about a third of the city. Because of many foreign eyewitnesses the massacre was well publicized abroad, and in 1948 Matsui was hanged as a war criminal.

Nansen passport. Issued to stateless people, it is named for the Norwegian arctic explorer, scientist, statesman, and humanitarian Fridtjof Nansen (1861-1930)

Narkom. From Narodnyy Komissar, Narkom is the common Russian name for People's Commissars and Commissariats (HFS).

NAS (US). Naval Air Station.

National Guard (US). A non-regular (or civilian) component of the US armed forces that evolved from the militia, the national guard receives state and federal support. A state's national guard is commanded by the governor until called out—federalized—by the president of the United States. (*AA*, 308-23.)

National redoubt myth. To slow the US advance, GOEBBELS created the fiction that 100 German divisions were preparing to make a last stand in the Alps. Eisenhower and Bradley were taken in by the story, rushing forces toward the chimera. As Weigley points out in a 17-page chapter on "The National Redoubt," this last propaganda triumph of Goebbels had the ironic effect (for the Germans) of leaving Berlin to the Russians. (Weigley, *ETO*, 700.)

NATO. 1. North African Theater of Operations (wartime). 2. North Atlantic Treaty Organization (postwar).

NATOUSA. North African Theater of Operations, US Army. Commanded by DEVERS until he was succeeded by McNARNEY, 22 Oct-1 Nov 44 (*AA*, 606), NATOUSA was then deactivated and MTOUSA was created. McNarney remained CG until succeeded in Dec 45 by J. C. H. LEE (*AA*, 609).

Navy Cross (US). The second highest USN decoration for valor, ranking just under the Medal of Honor.

"Navy junior." US Navy counterpart of "Army Brat." See also "At large."

Naval War College (US). Located at Newport, RI, the venerable and prestigious NWC provides academic and professional courses for naval officers marked for high staff and command positions.

Naxos. U-boat-mounted **radar** search receiver.

Nazi. A member of the Nazi Party, strictly speaking, but carelessly used to mean any German of the Third Reich.

Nazi-Soviet Pact (Soviet-German Nonaggression Pact or Molotov-Ribbentrop Pact), 23 Aug 39. Negotiated in less than 24 hours by MOLOTOV and RIBBENTROP, both of whom signed it in Moscow on 23 Aug 39, it cleared the way for Hitler to invade Poland on 1 Sep 39, the start of world war. The pact of 23 Aug was followed five days later by a secret protocol that gave the Soviets eastern Poland and Bessarabia plus a sphere of influence extending into Finland and the Baltic States. Stalin promised Hitler strategic materials and foodstuffs in exchange for industrial equipment and machinery (*S&S*). Other agreements and secret protocols followed. The world was shocked primarily because anti-Bolshevism had been a major element of

HITLER's foreign policy. And Stalin lost much of his support from communists outside the USSR

NC. US **Navy Cross** (above).

NCAC. US Northern Combat Area Command (Burma). Established at Ledo, India, on 1 Feb 44, the NCAC was under STILWELL until 27 Oct 44, then headed by Daniel I. SULTAN.

ND Cemetery, Moscow. See **Novodevichy Monastery.**

NEI. Netherlands East Indies.

Neptune. Code name for naval portion of Opn **Overlord.**

NG (US). **National Guard.**

NH. Naval hospital.

Niederdorf group. As the Allies overran Germany the **Prominente** were moved south from concentration camps with the thought that some might be used for barter as hostages. But the Nazis did not want them to be liberated by Allied troops. Traveling by truck and bus with an SS escort, and accompanied by what apparently was a mobile gas chamber, the groups converged at Dachau and then crossed the Brenner Pass into Italy. Because of Hitler's ambiguous orders, Otto BERGER did not know whether he was supposed to kill all hostages before they could be liberated, or shoot only certain ones. Capt Sigismund Payne Best, a tall, impressive, German-speaking British intelligence officer who had used his five years as a POW after the **Venlo incident** to acquire a profound knowledge of the SS, convinced the guards that he was an important Allied personage with authority to hold them accountable (Anthony Cave Brown, introduction to Fey von Hassell, *Hostage*, xii). At dawn on 27 Apr 45 the convoy approached the small Tyrolean village of Niederdorf (Villabassa). Vehicles were parked under guard so escort officers could seek instructions. Col von Bogislav Bonin, one of the prisoners, pulled his rank on the guards and walked with a companion to the village. There he saw von VIETINGHOFF, an old army friend who now was the German commander in Italy, and whispered that help was needed urgently. About an hour later a Wehrmacht detachment arrived to surprise and disarm the SS escort officers. According to one member of the group (who kept notes) Himmler sent an order that all the prisoners be executed on 29 April to keep them from being liberated. (Fey von HASSELL, op cit, 205.) Other accounts imply that only Léon BLUM, Gen von FALKENHAUSEN, Hjalmar SCHACHT, and Fabian von SCHLABRENDORFF were in danger of being shot (Shirer, *Reich,* 1074). Wehrmacht troops protected the hostages until they were freed by American troops on 4 May and sent to Capri for processing.

Kurt von SCHUSCHNIGG, wrote that the Niederdorf group had 136 prisoners from 17 nationalities (*Takeover,* 16). Fey von Hassel remembers that there were "120 of us" at Niederdorf (op cit, 205). Germans included Pastor NIEMOELLER, Joseph "Ochsensepp" MUELLER, HALDER, Fritz THYSSEN, and Prince PHILIP of Hesse. Hostages under the **kinship edicts** included nine STAUFFENBERGs, seven GOERDELERs, and two HAMMERSTEIN-EQUORDs.

"Night and Fog" (*Nacht und Nebel*) policy. Knowing that the greatest fear is of the unknown, Hitler conceived of and named Nacht und Nebel as a weapon of psychological terror. This directed that members of the resistance, mainly in France, would simply disappear after being arrested. Family and friends would not know whether they were dead or alive. The policy was announced in Sep 41, and on 7 Dec 41 the OKW decree was signed by Keitel. Files of such prisoners were annotated "NN."

"Night of the Long Knives." A name commonly considered synonymous with the **Blood Purge of 1934.**

NKGB (Narodny Kommissariat Gosudarstvennoye Bezopasnosti or People's Commissariat for State Security). The NKGB, under BERIA, was the Soviet security service Feb-July 41, and 1943-46. See **Police and secret services of the USSR.**

NOC (Br). Naval officer commanding.

Nomonhan incidents. Japanese name for actions leading to what is generally called the battle of Khalkhin Gol (1939).

Novodevichy Monastery Cemetery, Moscow. Repository for Soviet officials denied the honor of burial in the Kremlin Wall or in Red Square. KHRUSHCHEV lies in a far corner. (Scotts.)

NS. New Style or Gregorian, calendar. The Russian calendar was 13 days behind the west until Jan 18, when the Old Stye was brought into line with the New Style. Hence the "February Revolution" of 1917 took place in March (NS), and since 1918 the 24 Oct 17 outbreak of the "October Revolution"—the storming of the Winter Palace—has been commemorated on 7 November (NS). See **OS.**

NSA (US). Postwar National Security Agency, which evolved from the US Armed Forces Security Agency. Among its triumphs was the **Venona** codebreaking operation.

NSC. National Security Council (US). Established 26 July 47 as the highest statutory body involved exclusively with national defense, it includes the president, secretary of state, secretary of defense, and "service secretaries" (Army, Navy, and AF).

NSDAP. The Nazi party, Nationalsozialistische Deutsche Arbeitpartei or National Socialist German Workers' Party.

Nuremberg and Tokyo Trials. See **War Crimes Trials.**

Nuremberg decrees. At the 1935 annual Nuremberg rally of the Nazi Party, Goebbels announced anti-Jewish laws later passed by the Reichstag. The laws debased Jews to noncitizens, excluding them from all professions and from marriage or sexual relations with non-Jews.

NWC. US **Naval War College.**

O

Oakleaf cluster (OLC). A small bronze device added to the ribbon of a US award in lieu of a subsequent medal. The British award a bar, whereas the Soviets gave another medal for recipients to wear.

Oakleaves. An order of the **Knight's Cross** (RK).

OB. 1. Order of battle. A listing of military formations and their commanders, sometimes with locations. The term is used also for the aggregate of formations itself.

2. Oberbefehl (supreme command), Oberbefehlshaber (CinC), and Oberkommando. The names, as in OB West, are used for the individual commanding a large territorial region as well as for his headquarters and its field units.

OBE (UK). Order of the British Empire. In precise usage one is only "appointed to" the OBE. But impeccable authorities—

notably the *DNB*—occasionally refer to a person as having *won* or been *awarded* the OBE. Although among the highest of honors, the OBE is known lightheartedly as "other bugger's effort" (which might characterize almost all decorations). See also **MBE.**

Ober (Ger). Used in many prefixes, the word means "over" (see following entries) or "upper" (as in Oberammergau and Obersalzberg).

Oberbefehlshaber (Ob). CinC of a large military formation, as in Oberbefehlshaber des Heeres (ObdH), CinC of the Army.

Oberfuehrer. Waffen-SS rank with no German Army equivalent, senior to **Oberst** and junior to **Generalmajor.**

Obergruppenfuehrer. Waffen-SS rank equivalent to German Army Gen of Inf, etc., and to US-UK Lt Gen.

Oberkommando. The command (or commander) of a field army or higher echelon, as in OB West, **OKH, OKM, OKL,** and **OKW.**

Oberquartiermeister (Ob). The title is used by German general staff officers responsible for various functions. Roman numerals are used for those at OKH, and Arabic for unit staffs in the field.

As Oberquartiermeister IV, for example, Generalmajor Tippelskirch headed two intelligence branches of OKH, Foreign Armies East and West. The Ob 4 on a field army or lower field staff would the formation's intelligence chief. Other designations: 1 (operations); 2 (organization); 4 (training); 7 (military science)

Oberstleutnant. Equivalent to US-UK Lt Col.

Oberstgruppenfuehrer. Waffen-SS grade equivalent to Generaloberst (Col Gen).

Obersturmfuehrer. Waffen-SS rank equivalent to German army Oberleutnant (US-UK 1st Lt).

Oblast. Before the Russian revolution of 1917 the Oblast was the basic territorial administrative unit that previously had been called a region. The Okrug is a subdivision of an Oblast or of an autonomous republic (**ASSR**).

OCMH. The Office, Chief of Military History. It published the multi-volume *U. S. Army in World War II,* the official history written by outstanding historians.

OCS (US). Officer Candidate School, a 90-day course for commissioning wartime officers ("ninety day wonders"), succeeding the OTC (Officer Training Corps) of earlier wars.

Octagon. Second **Quebec Conference.**

ODESSA (*Organization der SS Angehoerigen*). A secret organization set up to help SS members (Angehoerigen) and other Nazis escape to Latin America and subsist there.

It allegedly was created by SKORZENY and NAUJOCKS. SS Col Fritz Schwend, mastermind of Opn **Bernhard,** is said to have supported ODESSA after escaping to Peru.

Office for Emergency Management (OEM), US. Rather than give wartime duties to existing agencies, Roosevelt created many "offices" under the authority of the Reorganization Act of 1939. The Office for Emergency Management (1940), within the president's Executive Office, coordinated and directed the following:

Office of Civilian Defense (May 41), directed first by Fiorello H. LA GARDIA, with Eleanor ROOSEVELT as assistant director. The OCD's mission was to cooperate with state and local governments for protection of civilians "in emergency situations." When La Guardia resigned 10 Feb 42 (followed by Mrs Roosevelt) and was succeeded by James M. Landis, **OCD** had about 3.5 million volunteers and 7,000 defense committees. The numbers grew in two years to 11 million volunteers and 11,400 local councils. (*S&S.*)

Office of Economic Stabilization. Established in Oct 42 to stabilize wages and the cost of living. BYRNES was OES director until succeeded by Judge Fred Vinson.

Office of Price Administration (OPA). Originally the Office of Price Administration and Civilian Supply in the **OEM** (previously), it became the OPA in Aug 41. At this time its civilian supply duties (which had been handled by the labor leader Sidney Hillman, who had founded the CIO in the 1930s) were transferred to the **War Production Board.** On 16 Jan 42 the OPA became a separate agency with responsibility for coordinating price and control and rationing. Successive directors were Leon Henderson, Prentiss M. Brown, and Chester Bowles. (*S&S.*)

Office of Production Management (OPM). The agency, whose director was William S. KNUDSEN and whose associate was Sidney Hillman, had broad powers over supply of materials for national defense and war production. OPM had jurisdiction over national defence purchases; small business activities;

and research and statistics. OPM's functions were transferred to Donald M. NELSON's **War Production Board** by an executive order dated 16 Jan 42. (*S&S.*)

Office of the Coordinator of International Affairs. Nelson A. ROCKEFELLER was the first head.

Office of War Information (OWI). Created 13 June 43. Headed by Elmer Davis, whose celebrated deputies were Robert E. Sherwood, Leo Rosten, and Milton S. EISENHOWER.

OGPU/GPU (USSR). See **GPU/OGPU** and **Police and secret services of the USSR.**

OKH–OKL–OKM–OKW (Ger). The acronyms are for **Oberkommando** des Heeres (Army), der Luftwaffe, der Marine (Navy), and der Wehrmacht (the entire armed forces). OKH, OKL, and OKM were subordinate to OKW.

Okrug (USSR). A subdivision of an Oblast or of an autonomous republic (or ASSR).

OKL. **Obercommando** der **Luftwaffe.**

OLC (US). **Oakleaf cluster.**

Old China Hand. The self-designation of a westerner who has lived long enough in the Orient to reach the third stage in appreciating Chinese inscrutability. The first stage is: "It's impossible"; the second stage is, "Now I understand them"; and the third is, "The western mind will never understand the Oriental mind but this is how to deal with it." Chiang Kai-shek and the China Lobby finally succeeded in having Roosevelt recall Old China Hands like "Vinegar Joe" Stilwell and send over men like Patrick HURLEY and WEDEMEYER.

OM (Br). Order of Merit.

OMGUS. Office of Military Government for Germany, headed by McNARNEY until 15 Mar 47, then by Lucius CLAY.

Omaha Beach. The D day landing area in Normandy of the US 5th Corps on 6 June 44.

OP. Observation post.

Operation. Word used in the code name for a campaign, for example Opn Torch.

Operational control. This gives a commander authority to assign combat missions to another formation, but not to exercise *administrative* authority over the unit. For example, he could not relieve or reassign its personnel.

Operation(s). "A military action, mission, or maneuver including its planning and execution" (*Webster's Ninth New Collegiate Dictionary,* "operation," 6 a). To the Germans and Soviets, however, "operations" (or "the operative art") has the additional meaning of something midway between **tactics and strategy.**

Operations research (OR). Pioneered by the British and yielding excellent results, particularly in **ASW** and air strategy, OR used scientists (**"boffins"**) to help solve military, economic, and other wartime problems. P. M. S. BLACKETT is credited with discovering OR.

Opn. A military **operation.**

OpNav. USN Bureau of Naval Operations (Washington).

"Oranienburg" (Ger). An all-purpose SS commando unit of **RHSA** Amt VI.

Operation 7. A plan conceived by Abwehr Chief Canaris and executed by DOHNANYI to disguise a group of Jews as Abwehr agents and exfiltrate them to Switzerland. The Gestapo's interrogation of Dr Wilhelm SCHMIDHUBER in the spring of 1942 uncovered the operation, with fatal results for Dohnanyi and the German resistance.

Oradour-sur-Glanc. This village in SW France (HauteVienne) was destroyed on 10 June 44 by troops of the SS 2d Pz Div after a sniper killed an SS officer, or, according to some accounts, the maquis abducted an officer. Unlike the premeditated atrocity at **Lidice,** the Oradour massacre apparently was spontaneous. Waffen SS troops butchered 642 men, women, and children, then destroyed the village. The unreconstructed site has been preserved as a memorial.

Orchestra, chapel, or choir (*Kapelle* in German). Espionage vernacular for "spy net," as in Rote Kapelle (Red Orchestra).

Orders of British nobility. See **Knighthood.**

Ordre de la Résistance de l'Armée (ORA). A covert organization of French regular army officers on "armistice leave." Engaged secretly in military intelligence and counterintelligence, the ORA was supposed to reactivate the French army for a national uprising or to support any Allied landing in France. ORA Hq was in Paris, secreted in the Bureau of Foods. It had subordinate staffs at regional and department levels, and LnOs with each branch of the army and each regiment.

Organic unit. A permanent part of a military formation, as opposed to one attached temporarily or assigned.

Organisation Todt (OT). A semi-military agency created and headed by Fritz TODT. The OT had charge of the entire German construction industry at home and in occupied territories. Albert SPEER succeeded Todt when the latter was killed 8 Apr 42.

Orpo (Uniformed Municipal Police). In Frick's ministry of the interior from Mar 33 to Apr 34, under Kurt Daluege. Orpo and **Schupo** were then in Himmler's SS on an organizational level with Heydrich's **Sipo** and **SD.**

OS. Old Style (or Julian) calendar. Dates in Russia lagged those in the west by 12 days in the 1800s and by 13 days from 1900. The Soviets adopted the **NS** or Gregorian calendar in Feb 18, but readers should assume that dates of birth and less blessed events in Russia are given in NS unless OS is specified.

Osborne. The two-year Royal Naval College that boys attend before having 2 years of additional schooling at **Dartmouth** and becoming naval cadets.

OSS. US Office of Strategic Service under "Wild Bill" DONOVAN. It became the postwar CIA.

Ostland. Baltic countries and White Russia.

OT. **Organization Todt.**

OTC. 1. (US) Officer Training Corps, succeeded by OCS. 2. (UK) Officer in Tactical Command.

"Other ranks" (UK). Enlisted personnel.

Overlord, Opn. Code name for the Allied cross-channel attack that hit the Normandy beaches on 6 June 44. The naval part was Opn Neptune.

OWI. US Office of War Information.

P

P (*Porpoise*) class and S (*Salmon*) class of US subs were authorized under the 1933 building program that authorized construction of 3 more carriers, 7 battleships, 11 cruisers, 108 destroyers, and 26 submarines. The latter, commissioned 1935-39, were similar to but larger than the *Cachalot-Cuttlefish* design and powered by the new lightweight high-performance diesel engines developed by private industry. (See Blair, *Silent Victory*, 64-77, passim.)

Pacific Ocean Areas (US). Under NIMITZ, it included all of the Pacific except MacArthur's SW Pacific Area. The POA was divided into the North, Central, and South Pacific Areas.

Panay incident, 12 Dec 37. At the end of Gen Iwane MATSUI's brutal campaign to take **Nanking** the US gunboat *Panay* and three Socony-Vacuum tankers were attacked repeatedly by Japanese naval planes while at anchor on the Yangtze about 60 miles north of Nanking. *Panay* sank with three killed and 14 critically wounded; two tankers were set on fire, the other grounded on a mud flat, and an undetermined number of Chinese workers were killed and wounded.

Panzer. The word comes from Panzerkampfwagen (armored battle vehicle) and was applied also to armored formations.

Panzer Army Africa. Evolving from **Pz Gp Africa,** which was operational from 30 Jan 42, the army was also known briefly as the German-Italian Pz Army, 1 Nov 42-22 Feb 43 (*B&O,* 29n). Its assigned commander was ROMMEL until 23 Feb 43, although during the "Desert Fox's" frequent sick leaves Pz Army Africa was commanded temporarily by CRUEWELL (9-19 Mar 42), STUMME (22 Sep-24 Oct 42), and von THOMA (24-25 Oct 42). Rommel's AG Africa Hq was created 23 Feb 43, shortly before he left Tunisia; it comprised Pz Army Africa and the new 1st Italian Army, which Generale d'Armata MESSE headed 23 Feb-13 May 43 (when it surrendered).

Panzerfaust. Common name for the German *Faustpatrone,* modeled on the **bazooka.**

Panzer Grenadiers. German motorized infantry formations were upgraded to semi-armored status and redesignated Panzer Grenadiers. Formed to accompany **panzers,** they became elite troops and often were used independently.

Panzer Group Africa. Moving up from his **Afrika Korps,** ROMMEL commanded Panzer Group Africa, 15 Aug 41—29 Jan 42, then **Panzer Army Africa.** These formations included Italian and German units.

Panzer Groups and Panzer Armies 1, 2, 3, and 4. Under KLEIST, GUDERIAN, HOTH, and HOEPNER for the initial phase of Barbarossa, Pz Gps 1 and 2 were known from 6 Oct 41 as panzer armies, and Pz Gps 3 and 4 were so designated on 1 Jan 42 (Seaton, *R-G,* 236n36).

Panzerschiffen. To circumvent the Versailles Treaty, Germany built three "pocket battleships": *Admiral Graf Spee* (see Hans LANGSDORFF), *Admiral Scheer* (see Theodor KRANCKE), and *Deutschland*. At a little over 10,000 tons, but with six 11-in turret guns in addition to 8-in and 6-in guns, they were no match for conventional battleships. But their speed of more than 26 knots and radar made pocket battleships effective commerce raiders.

Panzertruppe. German tank corps.

PC. Privy Councillor.

Pearl Harbor investigations. Buchanan lists eight, noting that "No clear-cut findings have emerged" (I, 77n). The first was the (Justice Owen J.) Roberts Commission, 18 Dec 41-23 Jan 42. The last was the Joint Congressional Committee on the Investigation of the Pearl Harbor Attack; this started on 15 Nov 45 and submitted its 39-vol report on 20 July 46. The Roberts Commission Report included its own hearings and supporting documents plus records of the other investigating agencies. The majority report "tended to absolve the Washington administration of responsibility and to place the blame on those in command in Washington," notes Buchanan. The minority report blamed officials in both Washington and Hawaii (ibid.).

Peenemuende. In 1936 the German army and the Luftwaffe jointly purchased part of Usedom, a secluded island just off the Baltic Sea coast. Here they conducted R&D for **V weapons.** Allied intelligence discovered only slowly that something important was happening at Peenemuende. The island was hit by a massive air attack during the night of 17-18 Aug 43, but most of the damage was to non-essential facilities and Dornberger had the bomb rubble left undisturbed so the British believed they had destroyed the base. Consequently, enemy bombers did not come back for nine months, and with new manufacturing facilities in the Harz mountains the rocket program forged ahead with a setback of only six months.

Peking incident. See **Marco Polo Bridge Incident.**

People's Court. See Roland FREISLER.

Petersburg, See Petrograd and Leningrad.

Petrograd. From 1914 to 1924 this was the name of the WWII **Leningrad.**

PH. US **Purple Heart.**

Phonetic alphabets. For clarity in message transmission, words like Alpha, Bravo, and Charlie are used for letters. These words were adopted in designations like **Ack-Ack,** "Alpha Force," and "Zulu [Z] time" (for Greenwich Mean Time).

Phony War. American name for the 8-month stalemate in the west after the Franco-British declaration of war on 3 Sep 39 and the German assault on 10 May 40. Chamberlain called it the Twilight War, the British press favored *Sitzkrieg,* and the French spoke of *la drôle de guerre.* The period before the German assault was marked by patrolling, minor raids, and an exchange of propaganda.

PI. Philippine Islands.

"Pinch out." A term for what happens to an advancing formation when its prescribed boundaries converge to a point. The "pinched out" unit normally reverts to the reserve.

Plunder. Code name for the principal assault crossing of the Rhine by the 21st AG of MONTGOMERY.

Pluto. Pipeline Under the Ocean supplying **POL** to the Normandy beachhead.

PM. Prime Minister. (The British PM is addressed as "Prime Minister," not "Mr Prime Minister".)

PMG (US). Provost Marshal General.

PMST or PMS&T. Professor of Military Science and Tactics, the officer heading **ROTC** programs in US schools.

POA (US). Pacific Ocean Area (under NIMITZ).

"Pocket battleship." See Panzerschiffen.

Pointblank. Code name for Allied strategic bombing of German industry from June 43 to the spring of 44, targeting plants used for production of fighters and **POL.**

POL. Petroleum, oil, and lubricants, a logistical term.

Poland. The Germans overran western Poland on 1-28 Sep 39 and annexed large portions of the country. The rest of German-occupied Poland became the **General Government** under Karl Hermann FRANK. Disagreement over the status of postwar Poland between the western and eastern Allies, primarily Churchill and Stalin, became known as the Polish problem. (About all Roosevelt understood about this was that he had a large Polish-American constituency.) The "London Poles," the government-in-exile, under SIKORSKY until 4 July 43 and then under MIKOLA-JCZYK, eventually lost out to the Soviet-sponsored "Lublin Poles." MIKOLAJCZY-CK briefly headed a postwar government until forced to flee in 1948, and Poland soon was a Soviet satellite.

Police and secret services of Nazi Germany. At OKW Wilhelm CANARIS's **Abwehr** was the principal intelligence agency until Himmler's SS absorbed it under an order dated 12 Feb 44. Meanwhile, the five SS agencies, most of which were switched around on the organization charts in Apr 34 and Oct 39, were these: **Kripo** (criminal police), **Gestapo** (state secret police), **Schupo** (civil security police), **Orpo** (uniformed municipal police), and the **SD** (party security police). When the all-powerful **RSHA** was created under Reinhard Heydrich on 27 Sep 39 it absorbed the **Gestapo** and **Kripo** under a new office, the Sipo (Political Security Office).

For the changing status and relationship of these principal agencies see the charts in Brissaud, *SD,* 291-303. More detailed charts are in Hoehne, *Canaris,* 138-39, and 158.

Police and secret services of the USSR. These evolved from the Tsarist Okhrana, whose headquarters from 1917 were at 2 Lubyanka St (or Dom Dva, House Number 2), which contains the infamous prison. The first Soviet agency succeeding the Okhrana was the **Cheka,** 1919-22. Next were the **GPU/NKVD,** 1922-23, and the OGPU (Unified State Political Administration). The OGPU was replaced in July 34 by the NKVD (Narodny Kommissariat Vnutrennikh Del) or People's Commissariat of Internal (or Domestic) Affairs, an interior agency of which was the GUGB (Glavnoye Upravleniye Gosudarst-vennoye Bezopasnosti, or Main Administration of State Security). The NKVD was headed briefly by Genrikh Yagoda (1891-1938), whom STALIN removed to install N. I. Yezhov as the **Great Purges** got under way in 1936. BERIA took over the NKVD in Dec 38. The NKGB (Narodny Kommissariat Gosudarstvennoye Bezopastinosti), or People's Commissariat of State Security (or Public Safety) existed briefly as part of the NKVD from 3 Feb to 20 July 41, then the NKGB reappeared in July 43 as a separate agency on a level with the NKVD. Both the NKGB and NKVD directed espionage and counterespionage, STALIN having a devotion to duality.

The NKGB was the Soviet Security Service from 1943 until 1946. At the end of the war the NKGB was elevated to the status of a ministry as the MGB (Ministersvo Gosudarstvennoye Bezopastinosti), or Ministry of State Security. Following Stalin's death in Mar 53, Lavrenti Beria made his agency a larger ministry, the MVD or Ministry of Internal Affairs (Ministersvo Vnutrennikh Del), which he headed until his arrest in June 53. The MVD existed until 1954. Then the KGB or Committee for State Security (Komitet Gosudarstvennoye Bezopasnosti) was established, downgrading the security apparatus from an independent ministry to a committee of the Council of Ministers. With creation of the KGB the NKGB disappeared for good. (Scotts; Sudoplatov, xxiii, 398n.) KGB Border Guards and NKVD Internal Troops were part of the Soviet Armed Forces until 1989 (Scotts). Further changes came in Aug 91 (after the coup against the government of Mikhail Gorbachev) and in Dec 93, when Russian president Boris Yeltsin abolished the Ministry of Security (Ministersvo Bezopasnosti) and replaced it with the FSK, Federal Counterintelligence Service (Federal Sluzhba Kontrazvedki).

Politburo. Political Bureau, **CPSU (b).** Limited to 15 full members and nine candidate members, all coming from the large **Central Committee,** the Politburo controlled the USSR by deciding the most important political, economic, and internal Party questions (Scotts).

Popular front. A political alliance of convenience, usually of leftists, against a common opponent. Communists were fond of forming popular fronts as a step toward taking power. See **Comintern.**

Post/posting. British parlance for the American terms "assign" and "assignment" ("he was posted to India").

Potsdam conference and declaration (17 July-2 Aug 45). Primarily to make plans for postwar Germany and for final operations against Japan, the **Big Three** met at Potsdam (near Berlin) after V-E day. Their surrender ultimatum to Japan, the Potsdam declaration of 26 July 45, was ignored until atomic bombs destroyed Hiroshima and Nagasaki on 6 and 9 Aug 45. HIROHITO then prevailed in having his government accept the ultimatum and he announced the Japanese surrender on 14 Aug 45.

Pour le Mérite ("Blue Max"). Frederick the Great created the decoration in 1740 and gave it this French name because he disliked his mother tongue. The medal was a large, enamelled Maltese cross displayed at the throat on a blue ribbon, hence its sobriquet. The Blue Max was Germany's highest award for valor until Hitler introduced the **Knight's Cross,** but it continued to be worn by many recipients including GOERING and ROMMELL.

POW. Prisoner of war.

Pravda. Official Bolshevik Party newspaper. STALIN became its first editor on 5 May 12 and a year later he was exiled to Siberia. *Pravda,* **Izvetzia** and *Red Star,* the Red Army newspaper, were the USSR's official news organs.

Premier. The word is used commonly for "prime minister." In the USSR the Chairman of the Council of Peoples' Commissars, called Premier or Prime Minister by many western writers, was the actual head of state. STALIN took the post from MOLOTOV on 6 May 41. Titular head of the USSR was the President of the Presidium, a post held from 1938 to 1946 by M. I. KALININ.

PRO (Br). Public Records Office.

Profumo affair. A British security scandal that broke in Mar 63, when Minister of War John Profumo resigned after first denying to the House of Commons that he was sharing the services of a call girl with a Soviet naval attaché. She was Christine Keeler, whom Profumo had met at the swimming pool of Cliveden, the stately home made famous by Nancy ASTOR. The scandal brought down the government of Harold MACMILLAN, who also had told the House that Kim PHILBY was not the "third man" of the **Cambridge five.** One of many security British scandals of the time, it was refreshing in that it involved good clean heterosexuality.

Prominente. These were eminent political prisoners in Germany whom the Nazis gave special treatment in waning months of the war

because of their potential barter value. Hitler's term of contempt for them was the Purple International. Although the Germans finally ordered their execution, most Prominente were liberated along with **Sippenhaft** prisoners. The war memoirs of Fey von HASSELL (see bibliography) have the names of most Prominente and the photo of a "guest list" signed by about 50 Prominente and Sippenhaeftlinge at Niederdorf.

Prussia. A large German state of which GOERING became minister of the interior and head of the Prussian Police and Gestapo when Hitler was appointed German chancellor on 30 Jan 33. The Nazis were quick to incorporate the Prussian government into the Third Reich.

PTT (Fr). Postes, Telephone, Télégraph.

Punitive Expedition (to Mexico), 15 Mar 16-7 Feb 17. With crippling political restraints like not being allowed to use the railroads Gen John J. Pershing led American forces into Mexico against the bandit Pancho Villa. Many WWII officers, notably PATTON, got their baptism of fire in the wild goose chase.

Purple Heart (US). From 1932 until Sep 42 it was awarded for merit as well as war wounds. Thereafter it went only to those classified KIA, WIA, or DOW.

Purple International (Gesellschaftsklasse). Hitler's term of contempt for the **Prominente.**

PX (US). Post Exchange, an army and AF store for military personnel and authorized camp followers. The NAAFI is the British counterpart.

Pz. Panzer.

Q

Quebec Conferences. "Quadrant," 14-24 Aug 43, was attended by FDR, Churchill, the CCS, and (for the first time) a Chinese representative. The US successfully opposed UK efforts to project their **Mediterranean Strategy** into the Balkans. FDR prevailed in getting agreement that an American would command Overlord, and it was reaffirmed that the operation would start by 1 May 44. The SEAC was created under MOUNTBATTEN. Formation of MERRILL's Marauders was authorized. Civil authority of the **FCNL** was recognized in French territories overseas. Foreboding news came during the conference that Stalin was recalling pro-Western Amb LITVINOV from Washington.

The second Quebec Conference ("Octagon"), 12-16 Sep 44, was held to coordinate US-UK strategy as Allied victory appeared imminent. The principal agenda item was postwar treatment of Germany, to include establishing four Allied occupation zones. The MORGENTHAU plan was tentatively approved. Churchill pressed for redeployment of the Royal Navy to reinforce the US Navy in the Pacific; Adm E. J. KING successfully opposed the offer, although the RN carried out some separate operations.

R

RA. Regular army (US).

RAAF. Royal Australian Air Force [singular].

R&D. Research and development.

Radar. "Radio detection and ranging" determined characteristics like distance and movement of an object by reflecting ultra-high-frequency radio waves from it. R. A. WATSON-WATT's work led to the first successful test on 26 Feb 35, and operational radar stations were constructed on England's east coast in time to be decisive in the **Battle of Britain.**

Radiogoniometry. A technique for locating radiotelegraph transmitters. A simple radio receiver ("gonio") with the usual aerial replaced by a pivoting frame gets the strongest signal when the frame points straight at a radio that is transmitting. With two or more gonios a transmitter can be located by triangulation. The Germans used radiogoniometry to break spy rings including the Berlin branch of **Rote Kapelle,** Rudolf "Lucy" ROESSLER's ring in Switzerland, and SORGE's ring in Japan. The system loomed large also in HEYDRICH's war on the Czech underground.

RAF (Br). Royal Air Force, successor to the Royal Flying Corps (RFC). The RAF's major components in WWII were Fighter, Bomber, and Coastal Commands.

Rainbow 5. US Army-Navy plan for a two-front war, defeating "Germany first" while conducting a holding action in the Pacific.

Ranks of US Army officers and insignia of rank. From top to bottom, these are General of the Army (5 silver stars in a circle), General (4

silver stars in a row), Lt Gen (3), Maj Gen (2), Brig Gen (1), Col (silver eagle), Lt Col (silver leaf), Major (gold leaf), Capt (2 silver bars—"railroad tracks"), 1st Lt (1 silver bar), 2d Lt (1 gold bar). See separate entries on these ranks.

Ranks of US Naval officers and collar insignia of rank. From top to bottom, Adm of the Fleet (5 stars), Adm (4), Vice Adm (3), Rear Adm "upper half"—(2 stars); Rear Adm "lower half"—(1 star); Capt (eagle), Commander (silver leaf), Lt Cmdr (gold leaf), Lt (2 silver bars), Lt Junior Grade (one silver bar); Ensign (gold bar). See separate entries on these ranks.

Ratissage ("rat-hunt"). A French counterespionage term adopted by the British for the Abwehr-Gestapo-SS manhunt that followed an SOE coup de main. (Brown, *"C",* 411.)

Rastenburg. East Prussian town (now Polish) near which Hitler's principal headquarters, "Wolf's Lair" (Wolfsschanze), was located in mosquito-infested but cool woods. The fuehrer spent most of the war there, primarily for personal security but also to get away from the business of civil government and to be nearer the eastern front (Keegan, *Mask,* 275). An inner compound of wooden huts accommodated the OKW operations staff and had offices for the Reich press chief, foreign office representative, the armaments minister when visiting, LnOs from the navy and Luftwaffe, and Hitler's personal staff. Wolfsschanze had a superb communications center and an air strip for the many official visitors. OKH was 8 miles away at Mauerwald, connected by a small-gauge RR.

RCAF. Royal Canadian Air Force.

RCT (US). Regimental Combat Team. A reinforced US regiment.

Realgymnasium. German secondary school corresponding (except in its higher academic standards) to the US high school. The college entrance exam was the **Abitur.**

Red Army. The "Workers' and Peasants' Red Army" (RKKA) included the Navy and Air Force. In 1946 it was renamed the Soviet Army. (Scotts.)

Red **Orchestra.** See Rote Kapelle.

Regulars. Professionals of a regular army, air force, or navy.

Reich. German for "country."

Reich Security Main Office. **RHSA.**

Reichsfuehrer-SS. Reich leader of the SS (HIMMLER).

Reichsfuehrung-SS. High command of the SS.

Reichskanzlei. Chancery of the Reich Chancellor, directed by Hans Heinrich LAMMERS.

Reichsmarschall. The highest German military rank, held only by GOERING.

Reichssicherheitshauptnamt. *See* **RSHA.**

Reichstag. German Parliament.

Reichstag fire, 27 Feb 33. The Nazis capitalized on the mysterious event—if they did not rig it—to outlaw the German Communist Party and win the elections of 5 Mar 33 that brought HITLER to power. The fire apparently was started by a half-witted Dutch youth, Marinus van der Lubbe (1909-34), acting alone. In the trial presided over by GOERING, Bulgarian communist Georgi DIMITROV was acquitted after turning the tables on Goering. But there is evidence that this confrontation also was faked and that Dimitrov had immunity.

Reichswehr. Defensive Land Forces of the **Weimar Republic** (1919-33) succeeded by the Wehrmacht. (The Reichswehr had no air force.)

Reiter SS. (Horse) Mounted SS, the first unit of which was commanded by Hermann FEGELEIN. See also Ritter.

Reserve (res). 1. The armed forces of most countries comprise a small "regular establishment" of career personnel and many part-time officers and men of the mobilization "reserve." The **US National Guard** is another "civilian component," and it is roughly comparable to British "territorial" formations. 2. In military operations a reserve is a force not committed initially but positioned to be used in emergencies or to exploit success.

Rezident. An **NKVD** station chief (Sudoplatov, 14).

RFC. Royal Flying Corps. On 1 Apr 18 the WWI RFC became the **RAF.** It was headed by TRENCHARD as chief of air staff (CAS).

Rhineland crisis, 1936. Renouncing the Locarno Pact of 1925, HITLER ordered troops into the demilitarized Rhineland on 7 Mar 36. World opinion generally condoned the act, rationalizing that only Hitler could save Germany from chaos and that a strong Germany was needed to protect western civilization from the Soviets. France and Britain, unwilling to risk war for which they were unprepared, took no action. It was later known that German commanders had orders to withdraw if they met any opposition at all. The operation was the first in a series of bloodless conquests that led the German high command (and others) to think that Hitler's intuition was infallible.

Riom Trial. On 19 Feb 42 the Vichy government put former leaders of the defunct Third Republic on trial publicly. Pétain hoped to make them scapegoats for France's humiliating collapse in 1940. The accused included three former premiers, Léon BLUM, Eduard DALADIER, Paul REYNAUD, former air ministers Pierre COT and Guy LA CHAMBRE, and former CinC GAMELIN. Cot did not recognize Vichy's authority and, unlike La Chambre, did not return from America to face trial. Georges MANDEL was not brought before the Riom tribunal but was dealt with separately. Embarrassed by the brilliant defense put up by BLUM and others, Pétain suspended proceedings in April. Particularly because so many official French archives were destroyed, records of the Riom trial have great historical value. For a summary see Pertinax, Appendix 4, pages 594-98.

Ritter (Ger). Literally "rider," this ancient military title usually is translated as "Count" (Eng) and "Chevalier" (Fr). See also **Freiherr, Graf,** and **Reiter SS.**

Rittmeister. German cavalry captain (Hauptmann).

RK (Ritterkreuz). **Knight's Cross** of the Iron Cross.

RKKA. Workers' and Peasants' **Red Army.**

RM or DM (Ger). Reichsmark or Deutschmark. At the official rate of exchange, which remained reasonably stable throughout 1939-45, the mark was worth US $0.25.

RMC. Royal Military College. The British RMC is at **Sandhurst,** the Canadian RMC at Kingston, Ontario.

RN (UK). Royal Navy.

RNAS. Royal Navy Air Service, formed July 14.

RNC. Royal Naval Colleges (two years) at Osborne and Dartmouth.

RNR (UK). Royal Navy Reserve.

ROTC (US). Reserve Officer Training Corps. To provide officers for the newly created Officers Reserve Corps, ROTCs were established in the fall of 1916 at 37 colleges (most of them land-grant) and at nine military and other schools. Approximately 100,000 ROTC graduates served in WWII. (*AA,* 327.)

Rote Kapelle (Red **Orchestra,** Chapel, or Choir). German code name for the largest Soviet spy ring in Europe. Leopold Trepper set up the first cell in Brussels for GRU (military intelligence) by the fall of 1938 (Trepper, 97). The next summer he was joined by "Kent," Anatoli Markovich Gurevich (aka Victor Sukulov), a secret service officer on a Uruguayan passport issued to Vincent Sierra. OKW was informed in late Sep 41, three months after the start of Barbarossa, that 250 "little evening concerts" had been transmitted to Moscow from heretofore unsuspected secret radio stations.

(Trepper claims that from May 40 to Nov 42 his various groups sent more than 1,500 radio transmissions to Moscow Center, and that it was not until June 41 that the Germans decoded the first of no more than 250 they ever broke. Trepper, 425.)

Sonderkommando Rote Kapelle was formed under the direction of HEYDRICH's **RSHA** to coordinate efforts of SCHELLENBERG's SD, Heinrich MUELLER's Gestapo, Adm CANARIS's Abwehr, and Gen Fritz Thiele's Funkabwehr (signal intelligence). Administrative director of the Sonderkommando was Friedrich Panzinger (Trepper, 435). The collaboration of feuding intelligence forces came after a meeting in Hitler's presence to address the problem. With good luck and **radiogoniometry** the Germans eventually ran key secret agents to ground in Berlin, then in Brussels, and finally in Paris. Although the Rote Kapelle was never completely broken up, its effectiveness was greatly impaired. The damage spread into Switzerland after Kent revealed all he knew about the **Lucy spy ring** and became virtually a mole in the Rado network.

Long after the war Trepper published *The Great Game: Memoirs of the Spy Hitler Couldn't Silence* (New York: McGraw Hill, 1977).

Rotte. A Luftwaffe formation of 2 fighters, 2 Rotten making a Schwarm. A Staffel had 3 or fewer 4-fighter units, but usually comprised 8 to 12 aircraft. A Gruppe had 3 Staffeln; and 3 Gruppen (4 as from 1943) constituted a Geschwader. (Sims, *Aces,* 130.)

RR. Railroad.

RSDRP/RSDRP(b). The Russian Social Democratic Workers' Party was created in 1898. When the Bolsheviks broke with the Mensheviks in 1912 they established the RSDRP(b), electing STALIN to its **central committee.**

RSHA. The SS Reichssicherheitshauptnamt (RSHA) or SS Hauptamt, in English the Reich Security Main Office (RSMO), was an all-powerful bureau of Himmler's SS Hq set up under HEYDRICH by a decree of 27 Sep 39. Left over from SD in the new RSHA were Amt I (Personnel) and Amt II (Administration). New divisions were Amt III (Interior), Amt IV (Gestapo), Amt V (Kripo), and Amt VI (Foreign Intelligence).

Although the RSHA proved to be overly beaucratized, excessively compartmentalized, and its efficiency further hampered by security restrictions, it served Heydrich well in his climb for supreme power in the SS. When Heydrich was mortally wounded on 27 May 42 Himmler personally headed the RSHA until Kaltenbrunner took it over in Jan 43.

RSMO. English acronym for the SS **RSHA.**

Russian. In 1941 the USSR had more than 170 races speaking 140 languages and numbering about 190 million people. Only 20 racial minorities had more than half a million people, and 14 minorities made up 94 percent of the population. The Great Russians totalled more than 90 million; their standards and language (known universally as "Russian") had long been imposed throughout the USSR. Ukrainians and White Russians, with distinct languages and cultures, numbered about 40 million and slightly fewer than 10 million, respectively. (Seaton, *R-G,* 95-96.)

S

SA (Sturmabteilung). Originally a "gymnastics and sports division" of the **NSDAP** created in 1921, by the end of 1929 it numbered 100,000 (Bracher, 167). The SA grew to around a million, "Brownshirts" threatening to dominate not only the **Reichswehr** but also the Nazi revolution. After its creator ROEHM was liquidated in the **Blood Purge** of 1934, the SA no longer was a significant military force, being eclipsed by the **SS.**

SAC. Supreme Allied Commander.

Sachsenhausen. A principal **concentration camp.**

SACEUR. Postwar acronym for Supreme Allied Commander Europe, whose headquarters at **SHAPE,** were originally near Paris. Eisenhower was the first SACEUR, with MONTGOMERY as his deputy. The second incumbent was RIDGWAY, who was quickly succeeded by A. M. Gruenther.

SACMED. Supreme Allied Commander in the Mediterranean. The *title* was retained by Harold ALEXANDER after succeeding "Jumbo" WILSON on 16 Dec 44, but designation of the *headquarters* was changed from SACMED to AFHQ.

St. Petersburg. Original name of **Leningrad.**

Sandhurst. The RMC in Sandhurst Parish, Berkshire, is imprecisely called "the British West Point." The USMA (like the USNA) has a 4-year course, almost exclusively academic, from which cadets are commissioned in all combat arms and most of the technical services of the US Army. But the RMC is a two-year course leading to a commission in the infantry or cavalry. (**Woolwich** commissions artillery and engineer officers.)

San Francisco Conference, 25 Apr-26 June 45. After much haggling at **Yalta** about organizing the UNO, and with much preliminary work done at the **Dumbarton Oaks Conference,** representatives of the Big Four and 40 other states met at San Francisco to create the United Nations Organization (UNO). GROMYKO (Molotov's successor) temporarily halted proceedings on 27 May 45 by insisting that the Security Council, where the USSR had the veto, could decide whether a dispute could even be discussed (Buchanan, 502). But the UN Charter was signed on 26 June 45.

SAS. Special Air Service. When David STIRLING wanted a name for his new commando force he took that of the imaginary Special Air Service. This was a dummy formation on the British order of battle set up (with elaborate deception measures) to make the Germans believe there was a British airborne brigade in the Middle East (when there was none). Stirling did not depend on air transport, nor were enemy airfields his primary targets, except initially. But the War Office, deceived along with the rest of the world, eventually put Stirling's SAS under control of the Airborne Forces. (Foley, *Skorzeny,* 204n.)

Savo Island, Battle(s) of. Up to six Battles of Savo [Island] were fought near the SE end of "the **Slot,**" route of the Tokyo Express between Savo, Guadalcanal, and Florida Islands. First and most famous was the night action of 8-9 Aug 42 between Gunichi MIKAWA and Richmond Kelly TURNER. "Second Savo," or the battle of Cape Esperance, 11-12 Oct 42, was between Arimoto GOTO and Norman SCOTT. The next was off Santa Cruz, 26-27 Oct 42, Nobutake KONDO and Chuichi NAGUMO opposing Thomas KINKAID, George MURRAY, and Willis LEE. Subsequent night engagements, also called the Battle of the Solomons or the naval battle of Guadalcanal, were on 12-13 Nov 42 (Hiroko ABE v. Daniel J. CALLAGHAN and Norman SCOTT), and on 14-15 Nov 42 (involving Raizo TANAKA, Nobutake KONDO, and Willis LEE). Variously called the battle of Tassafaronga or Lunga Point, also the fourth, fifth, or sixth Savo, was the night action of 30 Nov-1 Dec 42. Because of heavy losses the area was called "Ironbottom Sound."

SBD. The Douglas Dauntless, "probably the greatest dive bomber of the war" (Kirk & Young, 48), was the standard USN and USMC dive bomber. Although slow, lightly armed, and short ranged, it led all other aircraft in Japanese tonnage sunk. With a rear-facing gunner, it also had the lowest ration of losses in the USN (ibid.).

S Class US submarines (S boats). *See* **P (Porpoise class).**

SCAP. Supreme Commander, Allied Powers, title of MACARTHUR and his successor, RIDGWAY, as head of occupation forces in Japan.

Schuetzenbrigade/Schuetzenregiment. Motorized light infantry unit of a panzer division.

Schupo (Civil Security Police) or Schutz-polizei. From Mar 33 to Apr 34 the Schupo and **Orpo** were in Frick's Ministry of the Interior. Then they were put in Himmler's SS on an organizational level with Heydrich's **Sipo** and **SD.**

Sciences Po (politiques). Popular designation for the prestigious *Ecole Normal Superieure de la rue d' Ulm* in Paris. The school is known also as "rue d'Ulm."

Scorched earth policy. Destruction of crops, stock, buildings and other infrastructure to deny their use to an enemy.

SD (Sicherheitsdienst or Security Service). It began functioning on 10 Aug 31 in the Munich Brown House under Reinhard HEY-DRICH as an intelligence office of the Nazi Party. The office, still under Heydrich, became the SD on 19 July 32. During the period Mar 33—Oct 39 HEYDRICH's SD had two offices: Amt I (Counterespionage Abroad), under Herbert Melhorn, and Amt II (Intelligence at Home), under Franz Six. With creation of the **RSHA** under Heydrich on 27 Sep 39 the SD was the Nazi Party's sole intelligence agency. The SD from Oct 39 had Amt III (Interior) under Otto Ohlendorf and Amt VI (Exterior), which was first under Heinz Jost, then Schellenberg. See also RSHA.

Sea Lion, Operation. The German plan for a cross-channel invasion of England, called off after the **Battle of Britain.** There is good reason to believe that Sea Lion was never more than a bluff.

SEAC. **Southeast Asia Command.**

SEC (US). Securities and Exchange Commission

Second front controversy. The Soviets clamored from early in the war for their western allies to open a second front to ease German pressure on Russia. After America entered the war (7 Dec 41) US military planners advocated a direct attack from England across the Channel at the earliest opportunity. But the **Mediterranean strategy** was pursued initially. Having continued to demand that the US and UK open a real second front, Stalin contended after the Normandy landings began on 6 June 44 that his armed forces already had assured the ultimate defeat of Germany. See also Sledgehammer.

Second/seconding (Br). Removing an officer temporarily from his primary assignment for other duty, as on a staff or in another organization. Temporary duty (TDY) in US military parlance.

"Senegalese." The term includes not only the redoubtable French colonial troops from Senegal but also those from other black African ex-colonies. Unlike the mountain-hardy **Goumiers,** the Senegalese do not perform well in winter weather.

Seppuku. A samurai's ritual suicide by disembowelment, commonly called hara (or hari) kiri ("belly cutting").

SGS (US). Secretary (of the) General Staff. With a small super-staff, or secretariat, the SGS is an officer interposed between the chief of staff of a senior headquarters and heads of staff sections (G1, G2, etc.). Those selected for SGS assignments, particularly in Washington, are officers (like EICHEL-BERGER) marked for accelerated promotion in wartime.

SHAEF. Supreme Headquarters, Allied Expeditionary Force, headed by Eisenhower. Also called **AFHQ.**

SHAPE. Supreme Headquarters Allied Powers [in] Europe, headquarters of **SACEUR.**

Shaped (or hollow) charge. The effect of explosives is greatly enhanced by creating a cone-shaped cavity that focuses the blast in what is known as the "Monroe effect."

Shingle. Code name for Allied operation at Anzio, Italy, beginning 22 Jan 44 under LUCAS.

Shock army, Soviet (Udarnaya armiya). A rifle army with greatly increased **organic** artillery. There eventually were five permanently constituted shock armies, numbered sequentially. See also **assault army** and **guards units.**

Sicherheitsdienst (SD). SS security and intelligence service.

Sicherheitspolizei (Sipo). SS security police.

Sippenhaft (kinship edict) or Sippenhaftung (kin arrest). Revived by the Nazis with particular enthusiasm after Claus von STAUFFEN-BERG's 20 July 44 bomb plot failed, this was an ancient German law for taking action against family members of those charged with political crimes against the state. (Fey von Hassell, x.) Minor children were renamed and raised as Fuehrertreu, good little

Nazis. In Buchenwald at one time and marked for death were 10 members of the STAUFFENBERG family and eight of the GOERDLER family. Probably for their value as hostages, surviving Sippenhaeftlinge (prisoners of kin) were evacuated with the **Prominente** in the **Niederdorf group.**

Sir. An honorary form of address, as in Sir Winston, that comes with British **knighthood.**

SIS (Br). Although often used as a synonym just for MI6, the British Secret Intelligence Service also included MI5 and the GC&GS (eventually at Bletchley). As the chief of MI6 Stewart MENZIES also headed the SIS.

Skip-bombing. Conceived of by KENNEY and his ADC, Maj William Benn, while en route to the SWPA in the fall of 1942, the innovative technique was quickly perfected by Kenney's airmen. With one or more conventional time-delay bombs the pilots would approach a ship broadside at 200 mph and 200 feet above the waves to release at a range of 300 yards. Ideally the bomb or bombs would skip across the water into the ship's side, arm, sink to the optimum depth, and blow a hole in the ship's side or bottom. The technique came to be used in the Pacific by planes as large as the B-17 and B-24. British dam busters under Guy GIBSON used skip bombing in mid-1943 wtih devastating effect on German industry in the Ruhr. *(S&S.)*

Sledgehammer. Code name for a contingency plan to make a limited objective cross-channel attack in 1942. It was to exploit a crack in German morale or to be a desperation move to aid the Russians.

Slot, The. Narrow body of water in the Solomon Islands between Rabaul and Guadalcanal ending off **Savo Island.** It was the route of the **Tokyo Express** and became known also as Ironbottom Sound because of heavy losses in naval engagements called collectively the battles of **Savo Island.** (Morison, V, 81.)

Snafu (US). GI epithet for "situation normal, all fouled up."

SOE (UK). Special Operations Executive. British organization created 22 July 40 with headquarters in London to direct resistance operations in all countries occupied by the Germans and Japanese.

Sonderkommando (special command), as in Sonderkommando **Rote Kapelle.** "Special commands" were used in civil government areas, where some were extermination squads comparable to an **Einsatzkommando.** (Stein, *Waffen SS,* 303.)

SOP. Standing (sic) Operating Procedure. Instructions to be followed automatically under specific circumstances.

SOS (US). Services of Supply.

Southeast Asia Command (SEAC). Under MOUNTBATTEN, it was established at the Quebec ("Quadrant") Conference that ended 24 Aug 43. China was excluded, Stilwell remaining responsible in this area to Chiang but doubling as deputy to Mountbatten in SEAC.

Southwest Pacific Area (SWPA). Under MacArthur, SWPA comprised Australia; the Solomons (after 2 July 42); New Guinea and archipelagos to the NE including New Britain, New Ireland, and the Admiralties; the Philippines; and all of the **NEI** except Sumatra.

Soviet-German Nonaggression Pact. See Nazi-**Soviet Pact** of 23 Aug 39.

"Spaniard." Name given to Soviets who served in the **Spanish Civil War** against Franco. The Red Army contingent soon began to "show its teeth" to attached NKVD members (Clark, *Barbarossa,* 34) and picked up dangerous republican notions. Most "Spaniards" consequently were early victims of the **Great Purges.**

Spanish Civil War, 18 July 36-31 Mar 39. After **popular front** election victories in France and Spain, a rebellion broke out in the Army of Africa. FRANCO led it in the capture of Medilla, in Morocco, on 18 July 36. In planes furnished by Hitler he moved the army to Spain, where on 1 Oct 36 the insurgents appointed him Chief of the Spanish State. Franco's Nationalists defeated the Republicans, or Loyalists, in a bloody three-year war. Italy and Germany were Franco's principal supporters; the USSR backed the Republicans. Britain and France arranged an international agreement against intervention. Perceived as a struggle between Fascists and non-Fascists, the war attracted many foreign volunteers.

Special forces. Units trained for irregular warfare behind enemy lines, or "special operations."

Special staff (US). See **G1,** etc.

Spitfire. RAF fighter plane. After the Air Ministry announced requirements in 1934 for a new fighter, Sydney CAMM designed the Hawker Hurricane and R. J. MITCHELL produced the Spitfire. Mitchell's first operational model was delivered in July 38. The Spitfire I came as a nasty surprise to the Luftwaffe, who thought nothing could beat the Me 109 and Me 110, and in the Battle of Britain gave Germany the first hint it would again be defeated. The RAF fighter was only a bit faster (except at high altitude) than the Me 109 but had a big edge in maneuverability, visibility from the cockpit, and concentrated fire power. The German fighter was better at climbing and diving, and its guns had a longer effective range. The RAF flew 21 variations of the famous fighter during the war, some 19,000 being produced.

Sqdn. Squadron.

Squadron (Sqdn). Cavalry and air force terms for what might roughly be called a "company-size" formation. A fighter or fighter-bomber squadron had 25 planes, about 40 officers, and from about 250 to 175 **EM**. A US medium bomb sqdn. had 16 planes, 67 officers, and 310 EM, whereas a US heavy (4-engine) bomb squadron had 12 B-17 or B-24 planes, 67 officers, and 360 men. (*AAF Guide,* 21.)

SS. 1. US Silver Star decoration, awarded for valor to 73,651 officers and EM during the war. 2. **Schutzstaffel** (Protection Squad). Originally the Nazi Party's elite bodyguard, established in 1932, the black-uniformed SS grew into a huge political and industrial empire under HIMMLER. Its armed element was the **Waffen-SS.**

"Stab in the back" theory. After the armistice of 1918 many Germans asserted they had not been defeated in batttle but betrayed by cowardly and profiteering civilians. One result, other than giving demagogues a platform plank, was to convince the Western Allies that the next time they would leave the Germans no doubt. Hence **the unconditional surrender** policy.

Staffel (Ger). A Luftwaffe **squadron.**

Stahlhelm (Steel Helmet). A nationalist organization of German military veterans formed 23 Dec 18, it became a powerful, right-wing political force. There being room for only one political party in Hitler's Third Reich, the

Stahlhelm was incorporated in the SA by a decree of 1 Dec 33. But there was trouble between Storm Troopers and Stahlhelm veterans, so on 17 Feb 34 the Stahlhelm was renamed the National Socialist League of Ex-Servicemen. The Stahlhelm was revived as a veterans' organization in 1951.

Stalingrad. A desperate Soviet defense in which the principal commander was CHUYKOV preceded the counteroffensive of 19 Nov 42-2 Feb 43 that destroyed PAULUS's 6th Army and marked the turning point of the Russo-German war. The city was Tsaritsyn until 1925, and it was renamed Volgograd as part of de-Stalinization.

Standartenfuehrer. Waffen-SS rank equivalent to German Army Oberst.

Stavka (Stavka Verkhovnogo Glavno Komandovaniy). Headquarters of the Supreme High Command, the Stavka (which had existed in Tsarist days) was revived on 23 June 41 and reorganized on 10 July 41. The new Stavka originally comprised Budenny, Molotov, Timoshenko, Voroshilov, Shaposhnikov, Zhukov, and N. G. Kuznetsov. Under the **GKO,** the Stavka had a permanent staff and communications center and was responsible for operations of land, air, and sea forces. (HFS.)

"Storch" (stork). A **VSTOL** plane whose design concept was MILCH's, it was produced by Fieseler over the objections of many including UDET and RICHTHOFEN. The Storch proved to be invaluable for battlefield command and control tasks, for courier and liaison work, and on special missions like SKORZENY's rescue of MUSSOLINI. See VSTOL for comparable British and US light aircraft.

Storm trooper. A **Blackshirt** or **Brownshirt.**

Strategy and tactics. See under **operation(s).**

Strike North and Strike South Factions. Further identified under **Japanese political factions,** these were supporters of a main strategic effort north against the USSR or south against the British, French, and Dutch colonies in SE Asia.

Stuka (Ju 87). The name "Stuka," from Sturzkampffugzeug, the Luftwaffe term for all dive bombers *(S&S),* was monopolized by the Ju 87. In the blitzkrieg victories of 1939-40 the Stuka was one of the Wehrmacht's most feared weapons. With pinpoint accuracy as a dive bomber, and valuable as aerial artillery in close support of armor, the ugly, hawk-like bird of prey terrified ground troops with its screaming 1,100 hp engine (later boosted to 1,400 hp) and siren device. Its shortcomings in speed, maneuverability, and defensive armor became painfully apparent in the Battle of Britain, when the RAF's fighters, particularly Spitfires, found the Stuka easy prey. But the Ju 87 continued to be effective, especially against green American troops in Tunisia. Production of the Ju 87 in various models was 5,709 planes from 1937 to 1944 (*S&S*). The Ju 87D, operational from 1940, was supplanted by the two-engine, streamlined Ju 88 bomber and night fighter.

Sturmbannenfuehrer. Waffen-SS rank equivalent to German army major.

Sudetenland. The mountains of NW Czechoslovakia, long home for about three million ethnic Germans, included the country's elaborate frontier defenses. The **Munich crisis** led to the agreement of 30 Sep 38 that left Hitler free to occupy the Sudetenland.

Surrender of Germany and Japan. The DOENITZ government of Germany, represented by JODL, surrendered to Eisenhower on 7 May 45 in Reims, France, at 2:41 AM. Shortly after midnight of 8-9 May 45, on Stalin's insistence, another instrument was signed in Berlin by representatives of all four nations of the Allied high command (French, UK, US, and USSR). Meanwhile, V-E day was proclaimed on 8 May 45. V-J day was proclaimed on 16 Aug 45, two days after HIROHITO surrendered the Japanese *armed forces* unconditionally. The Soviets, who had not entered the war against Japan until eight days earlier, only reluctantly assented to MacArthur's representing all the Allies (as **SCAP**) in signing the formal instrument of surrender aboard *Missouri* on 2 Sep 45. On orders from MacArthur, MOUNTBATTEN waited until after this to reoccupy Singapore and the mainland of Malaya. Japanese surrenders in **SEAC** consequently did not take place until 12 Sep 45. US Adm Daniel E. BARBEY directed the surrender of Japanese forces in Korea on 9 Sep 45 (Western Hemisphere date), about a month later, after large bands of well-armed Japanese held out until they could surrender to Americans. (Barbey, 342-44.) Hostilities were declared

terminated by US presidential proclamation on 31 Dec 46 [sic] (*OCMH Chron,* 551).

Swabia (*Schwaben*). A SW Bavarian district nearly coextensive with Wuerttemberg, a duchy in medieval Germany, inhabited originally the Suevi (hence the name) and the Alamanni. The modern capital is Augsburg; other principal cities being Ulm, and Konstanz. (*Webster's Geog Dict.*) Swabians/ Wuerttembergers like ROMMEL and SPEIDEL were known to other Germans for decency, thrift, common sense, and about all other qualities of Good Germans.

Swords. An order of the **Knight's Cross** (Ger).

Swordfish. A carrier-based torpedo bomber dating from 1936, the fabric-covered, 138mph "String Bag" performed valiantly throughout the war, notably in the raid on **Taranto** and in bringing *Bismarck* to bay.

SWPA. Southwest Pacific Area (under MacArthur).

T

(T). Following a rank, as in "Captain (T)," this indicates temporary, "wartime," or "emergency" rank. Temporary rank bringing all the authority and perquisites of permanent rank, the significance was primarily legal and administrative. In most countries an officer reverted to his permanent rank when the war emergency ended.

T-34. The Soviets' standard medium (26-ton) tank from 1940, the T-34 was perhaps the best tank of the war. It had a simple diesel engine (500 hp), good armor, excellent firepower, and superb mobility in snow and mud.

Tabor. A formation of **Goumiers,** about 200 of whom make a Goum; four to five Goums make a Tabor.

Tactics and strategy. "Tactics is the art of using troops to win battles," wrote Clausewitz; "strategy is the art of using battles to win wars." Sir Archibald WAVELL has defined tactics about the same way but says "strategy is the art of bringing forces to the battlefield in a favorable position." See also **Operation(s).**

TAF. Tactical Air Force.

Taffy (USN). The radio voice call of US naval task groups usually made up of six escort carriers and eight destroyers or destroyer escorts. (Morison, XII, 125.) The most famous was Clifton A. F. "Ziggy" SPRAGUE's Taffy 3 off Samar Island in the Battle for Leyte Gulf.

Tanaka Memorial. *See* TANAKA, Giichi.

Tank destroyer (TD). A controversial US Army vehicle developed on the later-discredited theory that the best way to fight enemy tanks was with lightly armored, hence faster and more maneuverable units.

Taranto, Italy, 11 Nov 40. The raid by British naval aircraft on the Italian port and naval base showed that a surprise attack by carrier-based planes could sink battleships in the shallow water of a harbor. The British had found that torpedoes could be rigged to work in less than 42 feet of water, and that Italian torpedo nets did not extend beyond maximum draft of the battleships (to the harbor bottom). Attacking "on the deck" in clear moonlight, 21 **Swordfish** were launched in two waves from CV *Illustrious,* which was 170 miles off shore. Only 12 planes carried torpedoes, the rest having flares or bombs. The new battleship *Littorio* and two older ones, *Cavour* and *Caio Duilio,* were crippled. "ABC" CUNNINGHAM had two planes lost and two damaged.

Taranto harbor having about the same depth as Pearl Harbor, Yamamoto asked the Germans for details of the attack. (Sudden appearance of Japanese marine biologists in large numbers at Taranto might have aroused suspicion.) When Foreign Minister Matsuoka visited Berlin in Mar 41 with a contingent to iron out military aspects of the Tripartite Pact, he relayed Yamamoto's request for a more adequate report. Canaris gave the job to Johann Jebsen, double agent Dusko "Tricycle" POPOV's friend. (Popov, 142-43.) When POPOV went to Washington a few months later he had a long list of questions from the Abwehr about installations in Hawaii! POPOV devotes a chapter of his memoirs (p. 192 ff) to the charge that J. Edgar HOOVER pigeonholed the information, and the accusation is supported by Sir John Masterman's memoirs, *The Double-Cross System* (1972).

Task force (TF). A military formation, army or navy, under one commander and tailored for a specific operation.

TASS. Telegraphic Agency of the USSR, or state news agency.

Tchad. Variant spelling of Chad, a region of north central Africa where LECLERC's "Chad column" was formed.

TD. **Tank destroyer.**

TDY. Temporary duty.

Teheran Conference, Iran, 28 Nov-1 Dec 43. While Churchill and Roosevelt met at **Cairo** Stalin agreed on short notice to meet them for a conference at Teheran. It was the first time the Big Three got together. Roosevelt had long believed he could charm "Uncle Joe" into closer collaboration, and—to the annoyance of Churchill—accepted accommodations in the Russian embassy. The Big Three hit the high point of their relations, agreeing generally on grand strategy and on some postwar matters. Stalin accepted that the Western Allies would not open the long-awaited **second front** in France until May 44. The British failed again in efforts to project their **Mediterranean strategy** into central Europe. The Western Allies agreed tentatively to Stalin's territorial claims in East Prussia and eastern Poland, compensating Poland with German territory. Stalin volunteered to attack Japan after Germany was defeated. Final agreement on the last two matters was achieved at **Yalta.**

Temporary (wartime emergency) rank. Wartime promotions in most armed services are temporary, at least initially. The British have a splendid system of almost automatically giving an officer temporary rank commensurate with his assignment, making it therefore possible to reassign the officer to a lower position. US policy, on the other hand, was to withhold temporary promotion (in the **AUS**) until it appeared the officer would remain in the higher position; this made it virtually impossible to reassign him to a lower position. Temporary rank in the UK and US services entitled officers to the pay and authority of "regular" or "permanent" rank but not to seniority on the "regular" list. Unless otherwise stated, readers should assume that wartime ranks mentioned in this book are temporary. This is sometimes designated with a parenthetical T as in Lt Gen (T).

Territorial/Territorials. Member/members of territorial military formations, as opposed to "regular" units of the national armed services. The territorial establishment in the UK and some of its Commonwealth countries is comparable to the US National Guard.

TF. Task Force.

TG. Task group.

Thersienstadt. A concentration camp established in 1939 in N Bohemia, it was designated at the **Wannsee Conference** of early 1942 as site of an "old people's ghetto" for Jews over 65 years old. (Bracher, 427). This was part of EICHMANN's program to give the **Final Solution** a better face. But of 141,000 German, Czech, Austrian, and Dutch Jews who went to Thersienstadt and signed over their assets to the **RSHA,** 23,000 survived and 33,000 died (ibid., 428).

Tirailleurs. European light infantry originally, they are known in modern times as French colonial troops of North Africa.

T/O&E. Table of Organization and Equipment. This US term, with equivalent designations in other countries, prescribes the official authorization of personnel and materiel for each military formation.

Tokyo Express. Almost nightly Japanese naval operations down the **Slot** organized by YAMAMOTO to reinforce the Guadalcanal garrison. Americans dubbed them the Tokyo Night Express but to the Japanese they were the "Rat Express" or "Ant Freight" (Toland, 386-87). Several engagements to block them are known collectively as the battles of **Savo Island.** (Morison, V, 81.)

Tokyo Raid, *See* Doolittle Raid.

Tokyo war crimes trials. See War crimes trials, following.

Torch, Operation. Allied landings in Morocco and Algeria, 8 Nov 42.

Totenkopf (Death's Head) formations. The Death's Head Hussars were a famous unit of the Imperial German Army whose name and skull-and-crossbones insignia were taken by Theodor EICKE in 1934 for his concentration camp guards. These were organized during the war into Totenkopfwachsturmbanne (Death's Head Guard *Battalions*), which were under the camp commanders. In addition, some 35,000 officers and men of 14 reinforced SS Totenkopfstandarten (Death's Head *Regiments*) performed military police duties in the west and conducted executions and deportations in the east. But by the time Barbarossa started, other SS or police units

had taken over these duties and Totenkopfstandarten were disbanded; their personnel joined units of the Waffen-SS. Transfers between the Totenkopfwachsturmbanne (guard battalions) and Waffen-SS field units took place throughout the war, and many guards previously unfit for field service were assigned to field units of the Waffen-SS as the Third Reich collapsed. (Stein, *Waffen-SS,* 258-63, 303.)

Meanwhile, Eicke's 3d SS Totenkopf Div was formed in Oct 39 with a cadre of some 6,500 of the most experienced troops of three Death's Head regiments. The division's record is sketched under EICKE.

Toulon. Here LABORDE scuttled the French fleet on 26 Nov 42.

Transportation Plan (Overlord). Over powerful objections on moral and political grounds, and largely on the basis of studies by ZUCKERMAN, the large-scale strategic bombing of French rail centers, open tracks, and bridges began in May 44. With great destruction of life, property, and historic sites, rail traffic was cut almost in half by 9 June 44.

Treblinka. A **concentration camp** where most Warsaw Jews were taken, it was just outside Lublin, near **Maidenek.** At Treblinka and Sobibor, Franz STANGL directed the killing of 700,000 people, whom his guards stripped of vast wealth in money and jewelry.

Trident. Code name for US-UK conference in Washington, 12-25 May 43.

Tripartite Pact (Germany, Italy, Japan), 27 Sep 40. Transforming the **Anti-Comintern Pact** into a formal alliance, on the initiative of Mussolini, who anticipated war with the western powers, the signatories agreed on mutual aid if attacked by a power not involved in Europe or China, meaning the US. Recognizing the **Soviet-Nazi-Pact,** Japan thus joined the Axis (after some last-minute hesitation) and alleviated Stalin's fear of a two-front war. Saburu KURUSU negotiated the agreement in Berlin, significantly widening the split among Japanese political factions and causing the KONOYE government to fall.

Troop Carrier Command. Special organization of aircraft used to transport airborne troops and supplies.

Truppenamt. The Reichswehr ministry, which was set up under terms of the Versailles Treaty to replace the old Prussian War Ministry, had two major agencies. These were the Heeresamt (Army Office) and Truppenamt (Troop Office). With a deliberately misleading name, the Truppenamt of about 60 officers, initially under Hans von SEECKT, 1919-20, undertook covertly to replace the outlawed Great German General Staff. BLOMBERG was Truppenamt chief, 1926-29, followed by HAMMERSTEIN-EQUORD, by Wilhelm Adam in 1930, and by Ludwig BECK on 1 Oct 33. Two years later the Truppenamt became the new German General Staff of the OKH.

Tsaritsyn. Renamed Stalingrad in 1925 to honor the man who directed its defense in the Civil War.

"Turn." As used in tactics and strategy, to "turn" an enemy defensive position is to make a wide movement around a flank to threaten a critical point in the rear. A turning movement is so called from its *effect* on the enemy, not the nature of the maneuver; it is not an envelopment or flanking attack. "Turn" also has the secret intelligence sense of changing allegiance.

TVD. Soviet theater of military action or "strategic direction" (napravleniye). See also **Glavkom.**

26 Oct 36 insurrection in Japan. Some 1,400 officers of Sadao ARAKI's **Imperial Way** faction surrounded the Imperial Palace on 26 Oct 36 and demanded elimination of hostile government officials. HIROHITO violated imperial tradition by intervening to assure that the coup was crushed. Col Yamashita, whose role was ambiguous, distanced himself from the conspirators, falling back behind a shield of neutrality and becoming an intermediary between senior officers of the Imperial Way and the Control Faction, which Tojo headed. Two coup leaders took their own lives, and the insurrection collapsed. More than a dozen officers and several civilians were shot for treason on 12 July 36. Several officers were retired, including Araki and War Minister Kawashima, an Imperial Way adherent.

Twilight War. (*See* Phony War).

U

U-boat. German submarine (*Unterseeboot*).

UDT. Underwater Demolition Team.

Ukraine. A major portion of the (former) USSR. See also Russian.

Ultra. "Ultra Secret" originally was the *security classification* for **intelligence** from German radio messages encoded with their **Enigma** machine and decoded at **Bletchley.** "Ultra," like "**Magic,**" came to mean the intelligence itself.

UN/UNO. The term United Nations was adopted 1 Jan 42, after Churchill and FDR held their first Washington conference, "Arcadia," 22 Dec 41 *(S&S)*. The United Nations Organization was set up by the **San Francisco Conference** that convened on 25 Apr 45.

Unconditional surrender policy. Roosevelt proposed that the Allies offer Axis powers nothing less than unconditional surrender, publicly announcing it at Casablanca on 24 Jan 43, to the dismay of Churchill and others, and it became official Allied policy. Roosevelt chose to pretend he had been suddenly inspired at Casablanca by U. S. "Old Unconditional Surrender" Grant's rhetoric at Ft Donelson, Tenn, in 1863, when Simon Bolivar BUCKNER asked for surrender terms. But FDR actually had conceived his unconditional surrender idea before coming to Casablanca. (*See* Parrish, *R&M,* 336-41.)

It has been generally accepted that the unconditional surrender policy prolonged the war appreciably by convincing German diehards that they must fight to the last cartridge. But it has been argued that this is merely one of the myths concocted by senior German generals on trial at Nuremberg. (*See* Otto JOHN, 189.)

Undertone. Code name for US 6th AG offensive to penetrate West Wall and establish a Rhine bridgehead near Worms in Mar-Apr 45.

USNH. US Naval Hospital.

UNRRA. **UN** Relief and Rehabilitation Administration.

Untermensch(en). Literally "subhuman," and long used for *gangster* or *thug,* the Nazis adopted the term to mean like Jews, Gypsies, and Slavs.

Untersturmfuehrer. Waffen-SS rank equivalent to German army Leutnant (US-UK 2d Lt).

UPI (US). United Press International.

USAAF. US Army Air Forces (plural).

USAFBI. US Army Forces, British Isles.

USAFFE. US Army Forces, Far East.

USAFIA. US Army Forces in Australia.

USAFIME. US Army Forces in the Middle East.

USAFMTO. US Army Forces, Mediterranean Theater of Opns.

USAFMEAF. US Army Forces Middle East Air Forces.

USFIP. US Forces in the Philippines.

USMA. US Military Academy at West Point, NY.

USMC. US Marine Corps. See also FMF.

USMEAF. US Mediterranean Air Force .

USN. US Navy.

USNA. US Naval Academy, Annapolis, Md.

USNH. US Army Navy Hospital.

USSR. Union of Soviet Socialist Republics (Soyuz Sovyetskikh Sotsialisticheskikh Respublik). It was formed originally in 1922, picked up additional republics, and was dissolved on 5 Sep 91.

Utah Beach. US 7th Corps landing area in Normandy on 6 June 44.

V

V weapons. So named by German propagandists, the V was for Vergeltungswaffe, meaning a reprisal or vengeance weapon.

V-1 (FZG-76) "buzz bomb" or "doodlebug" was an inexpensive, unmanned monoplane with a pulse-jet gasoline engine in a "stove pipe" protruding a few feet over the tail. Launched from a concrete ramp about 150 feet long, it had pre-set guidance and delivered a one-ton warhead of high explosive on an area target. Flying bombs began attacking London on 13 June 44 from sites along the Channel coast that all were overrun by the first week of Sept 44. V-1 then were delivered against targets on the Continent, principally Antwerp, by a squadron of modified He 111 bombers. The V-1 flew at a maximum altitude of 4,000 ft. Noisy and easily visible, it was a very effective terror weapon because there was no predicting, after its put-put engine went silent and the bomb plunged, where it would hit. With 80 percent of the missiles expected to hit within an 8-mile circle at the maximum range of about 130 miles, a little more than 4,600 exploded in England. But these did great damage to property, not to mention British sang froid. In collaboration with SKORZENY, Hannah REITSCH proved that a pilot could fly and land a modified V-1 so it could be developed into a suicide bomb launched from airplanes or submarines. Hitler was enthusiastic, but the program, conceived late in the war, did not go forward.

V-2 (A-4) rocket. Developed by von BRAUN (under DORNBERGER) the weapon was tested successfully on 3 Oct 42 but was not operational until 6 Sep 44, when two exploded after being launched on Paris. The V-2 assault on London began two days later. The 46-ft., 13-ton liquid-fuel rocket hit Mach 1 in less than 30 seconds. It had a range of more than 200 miles and a one-ton, high-explosive warhead. Unlike the V-1, the V-2 could be fired from almost any small clearing. Being supersonic, it was almost impossible to intercept. About 1,359 were fired against England, killing about 2,500 people and injuring about 6,000. London, the primary target, took 517 hits that killed more than 2,700 civilians (Johnson, *V-1/V-2*, 195).

V-3. A huge cannon, it never progressed beyond **R&D.**

V-E day, 8 May 45. Victory in Europe Day proclaimed.

V-J day, 14 Aug 45. The Japanese surrendered on this date, signing the surrender instrument on 2 Sep 45.

V-Mann (Vertrauensmann). Literally a "trusted person" he was a reliable source used by German intelligence agencies.

Valkyrie (*Walküre*). Opns Valkyrie and Rheingold were conceived in 1941 to raise emergency replacements for combat units on the eastern front. The plans, conceived by Friedrich FROMM, who commanded the Home or Replacement Army inside Germany, called for mobilizing limited duty men including convalescents. But as the concept evolved to include handling a POW or slave-labor uprising within Germany, units throughout Germany were given specific missions to perform on receipt of the codeword "Valkyrie."

After STAUFFENBERG took over direction of the anti-Hitler conspiracy from Hans OSTER a decision was made to use the Replacement Army for the coup, if necessary without Fromm's cooperation (Hoffmann,

298). Stauffenberg then established a network of reliable contacts within the **Wehrkreise** to act on receipt of the code word "Valkyrie," which they would take to mean that HITLER was dead. (*See* Hoffmann, 301 ff.)

Venlo incident, 9 Nov 39. In a gangster-like raid across the international border near Venlo in SE Holland an SD team kidnapped two British agents, their driver, and a Dutch liaison officer. An alleged assassination attempt against Hitler had taken place in Munich the preceding night. It probably was concocted by Goebbels to boost Hitler's popular support, and for maximum propaganda value the Germans wanted to blame foreign enemies. Hence the kidnapping. The Venlo incident, one of the SD's most masterly "dirty tricks," destroyed SIS operations in the Low Countries and Germany at a critical time; it fatally compromised Dutch neutrality; and it humiliated the British. Official records are not scheduled for release until 2015 at the earliest.

The business started after Claude "Col Z" DANSEY made contact in Paris through Dr Klaus Spieker (or Spiecker). Col Z was trying to strengthen his network inside Germany and the distinguished émigré had ideal qualifications as a recruiter and contact man. (Read & Fisher, *Col Z*, 202-3.) This was true, but the guileless Spieker, no judge of tricky types, enlisted the help of Dr Franz Fischer, a convicted embezzler, and Johannes "Hans" Travaglio, who was "so unlikely a spy that he could only exist in real life" (ibid). What Spieker did not suspect was that Fischer and Travaglio had the mission of infiltrating refugee circles in France and Holland. When Dansey went on with other work, never meeting either man, whom he probably would have seen through, the naive Dr Spiecker convinced Col Z that they could be used as British agents. Accordingly, Dansey directed his experienced Z man in Holland, Capt Sigismund Payne Best, to check into Fischer as a possible recruit. Payne Best (his proper surname) found that Fischer was a man to avoid but was told by Stewart Menzies, acting chief of MI6, not only to meet him but also to join forces with Maj Richard H. Stevens, the SIS chief at The Hague. The tall, monocled Payne Best

found Stevens to be "a pleasant little man" but an ignoramus in the field of espionage (ibid, 208). After the two British agents first met on 4 Sep 39 Fischer introduced them to Travaglio. As "Maj Solms" the former Luftwaffe officer and retired opera singer claimed to be on the staff of an OKL general. Despite growing apprehension, Payne Best received orders from both Stewart "C" Menzies and Dansey to continue the march.

The two British agents coordinated with the chief of Dutch intelligence, Maj Gen J. W. van Oorshot, who put Lt Dirk Klop ("Lt Coppens") on their team to assure safe passage for the Germans. Oorshot rationalized that was not a violation of Dutch neutrality because peace negotiations were involved. (Read & Fisher, *"Col Z,"* 213.)

On orders from SD chief Reinhard HEYDRICH on 15 Oct to take charge of the case, Walter SCHELLENBERG set up a CP in Duesseldorf. Five days later he sent "Lt Grosch" (Hauptsturmfuehrer Christiansen) and another officer to make the initial contact. Klop and Fischer went by taxi to meet the emissaries at the small frontier town of Zutphen while Payne Best and Stevens waited at a nearby cafe. The discussions took place in Arnhem and went well until cut short by police, who had been alerted by two soldiers who got suspicious after overhearing the group speaking German at the cafe. (Ibid., 215-16.)

The Germans had penetrated SIS operations in Holland, and their objective initially was limited to burrowing in further. But Schellenberg now saw the possibility of being invited to continue the negotiations in London and learn even more. British objectives had been to find what they could about the anti-Nazi resistance, but Prime Minister Chamberlain got a better idea: to have Payne Best find out whether the Germans were planning a main strategic effort through the Low Countries, as in 1914. Menzies, anxious to improve his chances at getting the vacant post of MI6 chief, ignored Payne Best's growing qualms and instructed him to continue the meetings. So did Col Z. (Ibid, 210, 212.)

Schellenberg recruited a distinguished-looking friend, Prof Max de Crinis, to attend the next meeting as "Col Martini" and pretend to represent the conspiring generals.

The colonel's aides would be "Capt Schaemmel" (Schellenberg) and Lt Grosch (named perviously). Klop and Payne Best's driver, a thoroughly trusted Dutchman named Jan Lemmens, picked up the Germans on the frontier at Dinxperlo on Monday 30 Oct. The meeting at Dansey's office of his Continental Trade Service Co in The Hague began at 3:30 PM. As senior officer Col Martini maintained a dignified silence while the charismatic Capt Schaemmel proceeded briskly to make an excellent impression as spokesman for a putative cabal of anti-Nazi generals who planned to arrest Hitler and set up a new government. The Generals were prepared to negotiate an armistice; they offered significant concessions in return for a peace treaty that would return German's pre-1918 colonies; and they wanted to know what terms the British and French would offer. It was all quite credible. Payne Best drafted a protocol for submission to London and gave the Germans a radio for maintaining contact.

There was a week's delay while the British and French coordinated their response, and, as evidence of sincere British interest at the highest level, Menzies told Stevens that "the matter must be prosecuted with energy" (ibid, 218). After meetings on 7 and 8 Nov at the Cafe Backus in Blerik, only 200 yards from a customs post on the frontier, Schellenberg promised to bring his general the next day.

But on the evening of the 8th a powerful bomb virtually destroyed the Buergerbraukeller in Munich only moments after Hitler had left the hall. It making sense to blame foreign agents, Himmler ordered Schellenberg to kidnap Payne Best and Stevens when they came for the next meeting. Soon after noon on 9 Nov Payne Best reached the Cafe Backus at the wheel of his 1937 Lincoln Zephyr with Lt Klop beside him. The Dutch chauffeur and Stevens were in the rear seat. Backing into the parking lot, Payne Best saw Schaemmel, who waved from the cafe verandah. Seconds later a large open car wheeled out from behind the customs house, drove through the barrier (Schellenberg, 78), and screeched into the parking lot. Lt Klop dismounted and in a dramatic pistol duel put two shots into the touring car before being dropped. The others, too confused to resist,

were handcuffed and thrown into the SS car, which backed across the border. "Lt Coppens," bleeding profusely from wounds in the head and right shoulder, was evacuated in the Lincoln Zephyr. Lt Klop died in a Duesseldorf hospital within a couple of hours but was identified by his papers as a Dutch officer. Jan Lemmens eventually was repatriated and became a prominent member of the Dutch resistance.

The Nazi press had a field day. "England threw the bomb so that it could find an escape from the embarrassment caused by its reverses," said the official *Voelkischer Beobachter* on 23 Nov 39. The front page of this issue had a mug shot of Otto STRASSER with those of the British captives as the ringleader and his underlings. Praise was lavished on Maj Schellenberg for the coup.

The British agents cooperated fully with interrogators and spent the rest of the war as POWs. Payne Best learned that the 8 Nov 39 bomb attempt had been ordered by Goebbels to revive Hitler's badly sagging popular support. Two SS agents had found a skilled woodworker, George Esler, in Dachau and offered him freedom in return for helping frustrate an alleged plot to assassinate Hitler. Esler was to hide a time-bomb in a pillar of the Buergerbraeukeller that would kill the would-be assassins after Hitler was spirited out ahead of schedule. The night after the attentat the same men took Esler to within 400 yards of the Swiss-German border post at Bregens and released him with a large amount of currency and a postcard. Esler was told that German frontier guards would wave him through on seeing the card. But the guards arrested the carpenter as a currency smuggler. Gestapo agents found the postcard, which had been embellished with an X on the pillar in which the bomb had exploded. Esler insisted he had acted alone, correctly reasoning that this was his only chance. The Nazis, hoping to have a postwar show trial, saved Esler, Payne Best, and Stevens as friendly witnesses. But an SD order of 9 Apr 45 directed the Dachau commandant to liquidate Esler during the next air raid. It was to be "pretended that 'Eller' suffered fatal injuries."

Payne Best was evacuated with the **Niederdorf group** and had a prominent role in protecting it from last-minute execution.

Met by British authorities when the group landed at Naples, but never charged with giving the Germans details of the SIS organization in London and The Netherlands, he was given indefinite leave. He published *The Venlo Incident* (London: Hutchinson, 1951), an informative but less-than-candid book about his war experiences.

See Read & Fisher, *"C,"* 201-29, and Schellenberg, *The Labyrinth,* 63-92.

Venona operation (Br). The British code name for a postwar codebreaking operation (originally Bride, then Drug), Venona resulted from the triumph of Meredith Gardner. He was in the agency that became the **NSA.** Called "the greatest counterintelligence secret in the Western world" and "by far the most reliable intelligence of all on past penetration of Western security" (Peter Wright, 179, 238), it enabled the West to read portions of previously undecipherable Soviet messages of the war years. Venona led to exposure of such Soviet agents as the **Cambridge Five,** prewar French Air Minister Pierre COT, the Free French government in London, and atomic spies including Klaus Fuchs. See Peter Wright, *Spycatcher* (New York: Viking, 1987).

Vercors Plateau. In the French alps southwest of Grenoble in the Drôme and Isère Depts, the Vercors features a large central plateau about 30 by 12 miles in size. Surrounded by mountains and with one of Europe's largest forests, it had been a base for about 3,500 partisans of the Vercors maquis since the fall of 1943. After the Allies landed in Normandy on 6 June 44 the Germans decided to wipe out this partisan stronghold. Their first attack, on 13 June 44, was repulsed. A few weeks later the OSS dropped a 15-man team to urge the maquisards to behave like proper guerrillas and avoid pitched battles. On 25 June the OSS began daylight supply drops throughout France; one-fifth reached the Vercors but only rifles were delivered, none of the heavy weapons needed for conventional defense. On Bastille Day, 14 July, the cocky maquisards proclaimed the Free Republic of the Vercors, and some 80 US bombers dropped hundreds of rifles and machine guns but still no mortars or other heavy weapons. The Luftwaffe strafed the drop zone as a prelude to massive attacks by converging infantry columns supported by artillery and tactical air. On 21 July more than 200 SS troops landed in 20 gliders on an airstrip the maquisards had hacked for the expected Allied reinforcement. This surprise "vertical envelopment" was coordinated with two ground attacks and continued air and artillery support. The guerrilla defenses collapsed on 23 July. SS troops had been massacring civilians, maquisards, and noncombatants alike, but now there was a large-scale slaughter. Having killed 750 guerrillas, the Germans murdered 700 civilians in reprisal. Vassieux en Vercors was dive bombed and then burned by ground forces with villagers inside.

Verfuegungstruppen. Prewar predecessor of the Waffen-SS.

Veritable. Code name the Canadian attack between Maas and Rhine Rivers (21st AG zone) in Jan-Feb 45.

Verlag. German publishing house.

VF. USN designation for fighter aircraft force aboard a carrier.

VGK. Soviet Supreme High Command.

VIP. Very Important Person (granted special attention).

VMI. The Virginia Military Institute, Lexington, Va.

Volksdeutsche. Ethnic Germans outside the Third Reich.

Volksgrenadier. Honorary designation given to German infantry divisions for an outstanding record.

Volst. Former small rural district of Russia.

Volvograd. **Stalingrad.**

von. This particle of Teutonic military aristocracy was permitted in post-monarchist Germany after the first world war but not in Republican Austria (Deutsch, I, 375n). Writers commonly err in grafting the von particle onto the names of Gen of Inf Guenther Blumentritt, Field Marshal Ernst Busch, Generaloberst Franz Halder, and (particularly) Field Marshal Friedrich PAULUS.

VP. Vice president.

VPI. The Virginia Polytechnic Inst and State Univ, Blacksburg, Va, a rival of VMI and Texas A&M as a cradle of military officers.

VSTOL. "Very short takeoff or landing" aircraft.

Vystrel Higher Officers' Courses (USSR). The one-year courses are for **field grade officers.** *Vystrel* means "the shot," and instruction is concentrated on field work with various weapons.

W

Waffe (Ger). A weapon or branch of the military service as in Luftwaffe and Waffen-SS.

Waffen-SS. The "armed SS" evolved from the Verfuengstruppe, scattered battalions of which were organized from 1 Oct 36 by Paul HAUSSER. (*See* Stein, *Waffen SS*, 9 ff.) The Waffen-SS had no more than four regiments until after the campaign in Poland, where they showed some shortcomings as combat troops. Formation of divisions then began, there finally being 38 of these—600,000 officers and men (ibid, 286). With high entrance requirements, outstanding training on a par with that given British commandos and US Rangers, plus intense political indoctrination, they fought with fierce effectiveness and sustained a higher casualty rate than other Wehrmacht units. As fanatical Nazis, many members indulged in atrocities, a matter explored in detail by Stein (op cit).

Wake Island defense, 8-23 Dec 41 (local dates). A strategically located little volcanic atoll of three islands in the mid-Pacific, it came under the jurisdiction of the US Navy at the end of 1939. Comdr Winfield Scott Cunningham arrived 28 Nov 41 to establish a naval air station, but he left defensive preparations and tactical command to Maj James DEVEREUX, USMC. (Morison, III, 228.) The garrison included 500 Marines, 70 other military men, 70 Pan American Airways personnel, and 1,150 civilians who were building an airfield. Twelve obsolete Grumman Wildcats (F4F-3s) were flown in from CV *Enterprise* on 4 Dec 41. The island had no radar.

The first Japanese planes hit Wake at noon on Monday 8 Dec 41 (local date), five hours after the island received a radio message that Pearl Harbor was under attack. Following two days of bombing and strafing, a Japanese force under Rear Adm Kajioka arrived for an amphibious assault. With remarkable accuracy, and without adequate fire-control equipment, the three two-gun batteries of 5-inch guns sank two destroyers, from which at least 500 Japanese were lost. The two surviving Wildcats downed two of 18 bombers, a third

bomber was shot down from the ground, and four more flew away smoking. With only one American killed, it was a great day for the US Marine Corps, writes Morison. But he notes that "The message SEND US MORE JAPS, attributed to Devereux that day, was never sent by him or anybody else." (Ibid, 234n17.)

Kajioka returned with a much stronger force of ships, air support, and assault troops on 23 Dec, and at 2:50 AM Cunningham (not Devereux) sent the message "ENEMY APPARENTLY LANDING." At 5 AM he signaled, "THE ENEMY IS ON THE ISLAND. THE ISSUE IS IN DOUBT." Cunningham's final dispatch, at about 6:30 AM, reported that the island was ringed by enemy ships. Shortly after 7 AM Devereux informed his superior that organized resistance could not last much longer. When Cunningham realized that the planned relief expedition had been delayed, he decided at about 7:30 to surrender and notified Devereux. The Marine commander did what he could to inform his subordinates and, "with a sergeant carrying a rag lashed to a swab handle, walked forth to meet the nearest Japanese officer." (Ibid., 252-53.)

Having lost about 820 killed and 330 wounded, the Japanese captured 1,616 Americans, of whom 470 were military men. Bodies of 49 Marines, 3 sailors, and about 70 civilians were left on the island. (Ibid.)

A relief force, Adm Frank FLETCHER's TF 14 built around CV *Saragota*, was ordered to stop for refueling destroyers, which were running low (ibid., 243n29). When only 425 mi NE of Wake at 8 AM on 23 Dec (east longitude dates), he turned north and headed back to Pearl Harbor (ibid, 239 [chart]). Adm W. S. Pye, temporary successor to KIMMEL, had cancelled the relief effort.

Walküre. See **Valkyrie.**

Wannsee Conference, 20 Jan 42. To address the **Final Solution,** Adolf EICHMANN was directed to set up this meeting in the picturesque Wannsee suburb of Berlin. Chairman Heydrich and some 14 senior officials undertook to organize "parallel lines of action" among agencies that already had been involved in the deportation, resettlement, genocide, or other means of purging the Third Reich of "undesirables." One immediate consequence of the conference was establishment of mass murder machinery in **concentration camps.**

War crimes trials. The main counts were: 1) Conspiracy to commit crimes alleged in other counts; 2) Crimes against peace (e. g., involvement in planning and waging aggressive war); 3) War crimes (to include violating the codes and covenants of war); and 4) Crimes against humanity (like genocide, use of forced labor).

The International Military Tribunal (IMT) at Nuremberg, 20 Nov 45—31 Aug 46, charged only two dozen senior Nazis of the 35,000 on which the UN War Crimes Commission had dossiers in 1945. Between 1947 and 1953 various Allied military tribunals tried about 10,500 people, pronounced slightly more than 5,000 sentences, and executed a few more than 800 prisoners.

The International Military Tribunal of the Far East (IMT-FE) was set up by MacArthur in Tokyo, and 25 former government officials were tried for crimes against peace. The first seven principals, including TOJO, were condemned to death on 12 Nov 48 and hanged on 23 Dec 48; 18 others were sentenced to long terms in prison, but many were freed for ill health. Various other tribunals, sitting outside Tokyo, brought some 5,000 findings of guilty and executed more than 900 victims including YAMASHITA.

War Manpower Commission. US agency created 16 Jan 41 to replace the OPM.

War Plans Division, WDGS. Created in 1921 to prepare staff officers for war service, it made strategic plans for the use of field forces; on mobilization its officers were supposed to take the field as the GHQ staff (*AA*, 252). Although never performing as foreseen, the War Plans Div. became a nursery of high generals including EISENHOWER.

War Production Board (WPB). Created 16 Jan 42, this US agency was charged with planning and supervising production and distribution of raw materials and manufactured goods. The WPB replaced the Office of Production Management and the Supply Priorities and Allocations Board (OPM). As part of the reorganization labor leader Sidney

Hillman (1887-1946), who had been associate director of the OPM, became director of the WPB's labor division. WPB Chairman Donald M. NELSON was replaced in Sep 44 by Julius A. Krug, who continued the agency's politically troubled but relatively successful efforts. *(S&S.)*

Warsaw uprisings. The Warsaw Ghetto Uprising, 18 Jan-16 May 43 resulted in the death or capture of more than 56,000 Jews and destruction of a ghetto that had shrunk to about 900 by 300 meters in size (*S&S*). SS Brigadefuehrer Jurgen Stroop (1901-51) wrote a detailed report called "The Warsaw Ghetto Is No More." The heroic, suicidal resistance to further deportation—some 300,000 Jews had been "resettled" to Treblinka in the summer of 1942—inspired uprisings at Vilna, Cracow, Lodz, and other Polish cities. (Ibid.)

The second warsaw uprising, 1 Aug-2 Oct 44, began with Bor-KOMOROWSKI's Home Guard taking control of Warsaw in just three days. But a merciless action to restore order and destroy the Polish capital was directed by BACH-ZELEWSKI.

Washington conferences. Roosevelt and Churchill met three times in Washington during the war. "Arcadia," 22 Dec 41, reaffirmed the "Germany first" strategy and issued the United Nations Declaration (adopted 1 Jan 42). The second conference, 25-27 June 42 (no code name), dealt with strategy for 1942-43. At "Trident," 11-17 May 43, US-UK agreement was reached on opening the second front in Europe by 1 May 44, a massive air offensive on Continental targets including **Ploesti,** and the US offensive in the central Pacific.

WD. War Department (US).

WDGS. (US) War Department General Staff. Created by Secy. of War Elihu Root in 1903 and reorganized in 1921, it was modeled loosely on the Great German General Staff. But to avoid the onus of the Prussian prototype, US officers were not assigned permanently to the general staff. "General Staff with Troops" was the designation for those on the general staffs in field units of divisional and higher echelon. **The War Plans Division** existed in the WDGS from a reorganization of 1921. (*AA*, 35, 252.)

Wehrkreis (defense sector). A German military district or home base area for a number of army divisions, corresponding to a stateside US Army "corps area." Numerical designations and headquarters cities were: I, Koenigsberg; II, Stettin; III, Berlin; IV, Dresden; V, Stuttgart; VI, Munster; VII, Munich; VIII, Breslau; IX, Kassel; X, Hamburg; XI, Hanover; XII, Wiesbaden; and XIII, Nuremberg. In 1940, after Greater Germany included Austria, Czechoslovakia, the Danzig Corridor, and most of Poland, the following Wehrkreis were added: XVII, Vienna; XVIII, Salzburg; XX, Danzig; and XXI, Poznan. Wehrkreis I was extended from E Prussia into N Poland. (Davies, *German Army Hdbk*, 19-21.)

Wehrmacht. The German armed forces, 1935-45, succeeding the Weimar Republic's **Reichswehr** and preceding the postwar **Bundeswehr**, it included the army, Navy, and Air Force (Luftwaffe). The Ministeramt became the Wehrmachtamt, which was "virtually, though not in name, a commander in chief's office . . . made up of Staff officers from all three fighting services" (Goerlitz, *GGS*, 280). The first Wehrmacht commander, BLOMBERG, was succeeded by HITLER.

Wehrmachtamt. An office that evolved from the Ministeramt when the **Wehrmacht** was created in 1935.

Wehrmachtfuehrungsstab (Armed Forces Operations Staff). A super-staff section also known as the Fuehrer's Leader Staff, it was headed by JODL with WARLIMONT as a deputy.

Wehrmacht Leader Staff. See previous entry.

Weimar Republic. Interwar German government, 1919-33.

Wellington College. A privately operated school near London named for the famous duke, it had the principal objective of preparing boys, mainly sons of army and navy officers, for a career in the regular army.

WIA. Wounded in action.

Wilhelmstrasse. Berlin foreign office address.

Winchester. British public school attended by many future generals and admirals.

"Window." **Radar**-jamming metal foil developed by the Western Allies and first identified by the Germans at **Dueppel.**

Wing. Normally, two or more air groups (of two to four squadrons, each with a headquarters) constitute a wing. Two or more of the latter make a "command."

Whitehall. A London street between Trafalgar Square and the Houses of Parliament along which the principal British governmental offices are located. (*Webster's Geog Dict.*)

Woburn Abbey. Headquarters of British **black propaganda** broadcasts.

Wolfsschanze (Wolf's lair). Hitler's Hq at **Rastenburg.** Wolfsschanze II was near Soissons, France.

Woolwich. The Royal Military Academy from which cadets are commissioned in the Royal Artillery and Engineers. (*See also* **RMC.**)

WPB (US). **War Production Board.**

WPD (US). War Plans Division.

WRGH. Walter Reed (US Army) General Hospital, Washington, D. C.

WSA (US). War Shipping Administration

WW I. World War I, 1914-18.

WW II. World War II, 1939-45.

X

XO. Executive officer. At the regimental and lower echelons of the US Army, the XO is second in command (a deputy at higher echelons). In the US Navy and USMC the XO is second in command of a ship or ground formation.

Y

Yalta (or Crimea) conference, 7-12 Feb 45. After several delays, the Big Three met at the Black Sea resort about 30 mi SE of Sevastopol. With diplomatic and military staffs, they addressed final plans for defeating the Axis powers and shaping the postwar world. Code names were "Argonaut" for the earlier US-UK staff talks at Malta ("Cricket") as well as those at Yalta ("Magneto").

Disclosure of all Yalta agreements did not become public until 25 Mar 47, and much of the secrecy was for valid military reasons. But ROOSEVELT's critics accused him of being duped by Stalin at Yalta as CHAMBERLAIN was by Hitler at Munich. Secret accords gave the USSR Japanese territory (northern Sakhalin and the Kurile Islands), plus concessions at the expense of China.

Yalta agreements also recognized Soviet claims to the Koenigsberg district of E Prussia and to a 200-mile-wide slice of eastern Poland, moving the boundary to about the Curzon Line of 1919. In compensation, the western frontier of Poland was extended (pending the final peace settlement) to the Oder-Niesse line in E Germany. Particularly shamefully, the US and UK agreed to forcible repatriation of Soviet refugees including Cossacks and troops raised by VLASOV. Germany was divided into four occupation zones, British, French, Soviet, and US, which would be under an **Allied Control Council.** Germany would pay reparations in kind, would be destroyed as a military power, and it was reasserted that **war crimes** trials would be held.

Conferees haggled long over organization of the UN, but they scheduled a conference at San Francisco for 25 Apr 45 to make final arrangements. The **Polish problem** was addressed but not resolved.

Yuan. China's premier is president of the Executive Yuan, which supervises the ministries and two dozen agencies. Four subordinate Yuans, or government councils, are named Control, Examination, Judicial, and Legislative.

Z

Z agent or Z man/woman (Br). One working for the following service.

Z Organization (Br). A semi-private, semi-official, British intelligence service set up in Europe by Claude "Col Z" DANSEY in 1936. It evolved from an independent intelligence service Dansey began forming from Rome in 1930 because VANSITTART was dissatisfied with the existing SIS, particularly in political and economic matters. Within five years "Vansittart's Private Detective Agency" had a network of businessmen, politicians, public figures and other informants, many of them Germans. In Berlin the major player was Group Capt Malcolm Grahame Christie, the air attaché. In 1936 DANSEY and MI6 chief Sinclair began building Orgn Z, using Dansey's existing apparatus. But Orgn Z also was set up to parallel MI6 and replace it if necessary. Dansey established his main office in London, using his position on the board of Alexander Korda's British Lion Films for cover. Z agents and informants became members of Korda's empire, ostensibly running its local offices throughout Europe and using the company's communications. Z moved his headquarters to Zurich after war broke out on 1 Sep 39. When the appointment of Stewart MENZIES as MI6 chief was confirmed on 28 Nov 39, Dansey returned to London as his assistant chief. Col Z now controlled all British military intelligence except Ultra. The main body of the Z Orgn became the Swiss section of SIS and ran most of the agents inEurope. But Col Z kept control of a few Z agents whom nobody else in SIS knew about. (*See* Read & Fisher, *Col Z*, 166-91 and 230.)

Zossen. German Army Hq (OKH) about 35 km S of central Berlin. OKH Hq secretly moved to this village shortly before Hitler invaded Poland (1 Sep 39) and remained throughout the war.

BIBLIOGRAPHY
And List of Authorities Cited

CAPITAL LETTERS indicate authors and others who have a biographical sketch in the main body of this book, except in the case of major figures whom the reader should assume has an entry. Most English-language works of importance are published in London as well as New York, but only one edition will be cited below.

A

AA. *The Army Almanac* (below).

AAF Chron. *The Army Air Forces in World War II: Combat Chronology, 1941—1945.*

AAF Guide. *The Official World War II Guide to the Army Air Forces* (reprint of 1944 ed.). New York: Bonanza Books, 1988.

A&Q. Accoce and Quet (next entry).

Accoce, Pierre and Pierre Quet. *A Man Called Lucy.* New York: Coward-McCann, 1967.

Addington, Larry H. *The Blitzkrieg Era and the German General Staff, 1865-1941.* New Brunswick, N.J.: Rutgers, 1971. An excellent work whose focus is on the campaigns of 1939-41 as seen by HALDER.

Alanbrooke. See Bryant, Arthur.

Alexander of Tunis. *The Alexander Memoirs 1940-1945.* John North, ed. London: Cassell, 1962.

Allen, Louis. *Burma: The Longest War: 1941-45.* New York: St Martin's, 1984.

Ambrose, Stephen E. *The Supreme Commander: The War Years of General Dwight D. Eisenhower.* New York: Doubleday, 1970.

The American Heritage Pictorial History of World War II. Narrated by C. L. Sulzberger. New York: American Heritage, 1966.

Andrew, Christopher. *For the President's Eyes Only: Secret Intelligence and the American Presidency from Washington to Bush.* New York, HarperCollins, 1995. By a Cambridge history professor and a leading scholar of intelligence history, this has been called "the most important book ever written about American intelligence" (David Kahn).

Andrews, Allen. *The Air Marshals: The Air War in Western Europe.* New York: Morrow, 1970. This outstanding work features "Hap" Arnold, "Stuffy" Dowding, "Bomber" Harris, Portal, Tedder, and Goering.

Angolia, John R. *On the Field of Honor: A History of the Knight's Cross Bearers.* 2 vols. San Jose, Calif.: R. James Bender Publishing, vol. 1, 1979; vol. 2, 1980. The works include a history of the Iron Cross and the RK, photographs of recipients, and valuable biographical data to include dates of awards and brief citations.

Arendt, Hannah. *Eichmann in Jerusalem: A Report on the Banality of Evil.* New York: Viking, 1963.

The Army Air Forces in World War II: Combat Chronology, 1941—1945. Compiled by Kit C. Carter and Robert Mueller. Washington: Government Printing Office, 1973.

The Army Almanac. A Book of Facts Concerning the Army of the United States. Washington: Government Printing Office, 1950. This scarce book, current as of Oct 48, and invaluable for histories of US Army organizations including the USAAF, and wartime careers (including promotion dates) of officers. A new, commercial edition is Gordon Young Russell, ed., Harrisburg, Pa: Stackpole, 1959, cited as *AA rev.*

Army Register, US. See *US Army Register.*

ARNOLD, Henry H. *Global Mission.* New York: Harper & Bros., 1949. My page citations are to the British edition, Hutchinson & Co. Publishers LTD, 1951.

Aron, Robert. *France Reborn: The History of the Liberation, June 1944-May 1945.* New York: Scribner's, 1964. An authoritative work.

——. *The Vichy Regime 1940-44*. New York: Beacon, 1958.

Ashman, Charles, and Robert J. Wagman. *The Nazi Hunters: The Shattering True Story of the Continuing Search for Nazi War Criminals*. New York: Pharos Books, 1988.

Assembly. Association of Graduates (AOG), USMA. West Point, NY. A periodical useful for its obituaries. The AOG also publishes the annual *Register of Graduates* (below).

Atlas of the Second World War. Peter Young (ed). New York: G. P. Putnam's Sons., 1974 (first American edition).

ATTLEE, Clement R. *As It Happened*. London: Heinemann, 1954.

Avon, Earl of. See Anthony Eden.

B

Barber, Noel. *Sinister Twilight: The Fall and Rise Again of Singapore*. London: Collins, 1968.

BARBEY, Daniel E. *MacArthur's Amphibious Navy: Seventh Amphibious Force Operations, 1943-45*. Annapolis, Md: US Naval Institute, 1969.

Barnett, Correlli. *The Desert Generals*. New and enlarged ed. Bloomington, Ind: Indiana University Press, 1982.

——. (ed), *Hitler's Generals*. New York: Grove Weidenfeld, 1989. A companion volume to Keegan (ed), *Churchill's Generals* (below), it is in the same format and of the same high quality.

Baudot, Marcel, et al. eds. *Historical Encyclopedia of World War II*. Outstanding work of reference for its long, signed articles including "Atomic bomb" (8 pp) and "Yugoslavia" (3 pp).

B&O. Short title for Bender & Odegard, below.

Behr, Edward. *Hirohito: Behind the Myth*. New York: Vintage Books, 1990. Originally published: New York, Villard Books, 1989.

Bekker, Cajus. *Hitler's Naval War*. Garden City, NY: Doubleday, 1974.

——. *The Luftwaffe War Diaries*. Tr and ed Frank Ziegler. Garden City, NY: Doubleday, 1968.

Bender, Roger James, and Warren W. Odegard. *Uniforms, Organizations and History of the Panzertruppe*. San Jose, California: R. James Bender Publishing, 1980. The work is of particular value for dates during which panzer units from army to division level were commanded by a succession of officers. Notes give promotion dates and some other biographical data.

Bergamini, David. *Japan's Imperial Conspiracy: How Emperor Hirohito Led Japan into War Against the West*. New York: Morrow, 1971. A controversial work that is particularly useful for authoritative insights into Japanese leadership.

Best, S. P. See Payne Best, Sigismund.

Bethell, Nicholas. *The Last Secret: The Delivery to Stalin of Over Two Million Russians by Britain and the United States*. New York: Basic Books, 1974.

Bialer, Seweryn (ed). *Stalin and His Generals: Soviet Military Memoirs of World War II*. New York: Pegasus, 1969. An well edited anthology by a leading authority.

Bidwell, Shelford. *The Chindit War: Stilwell, Wingate and the Campaign in Burma 1944*. New York: Macmillan 1980.

Bird, Michael. *The Secret Battalion*. Holt, Rinehart and Winston, 1964.

Blair, Clay, Jr. *Silent Victory: The US Submarine War Against Japan*. Philadelphia and New York: J. B. Lippincott Company, 1975.

BLEICHER, Hugo. Ian Colvin, ed. London, William Kimber, 1954.

Blum, John Morton. *V Was for Victory: Politics and American Culture During World War II*. New York and London: Harcourt Brace Jovanovich, 1976.

——. *From the Morgenthau Diaries*. I. *Years of Crisis, 1928-1938* (1965); II. *Years of Urgency, 1938-1941* (1965); III. *Years of War, 1941-1945*. (1967). Boston: Houghton Mifflin, 1965 & 1967.

BONHOEFFER, Dietrich. *No Rusty Swords*. London: Collins, 1965.

Bower, Tom. *Klaus Barbie: Butcher of Lyons*. London: Michael Joseph, 1984.

Bradley, Omar N. *A Soldier's Story* (New York, Holt, 1951).

——. *A General's Life* (New York: Simon and Schuster, 1983).

Bracher, Karl Dietrich. T*he German Dictatorship: The Origins, Structure, and Effects of National Socialism.* New York: Praeger, 1970.

Brett-Smith, Richard. *Hitler's Generals*. San Rafael, Cal: Presidio, 1976. Has good sketches of 82 leaders; 36 portraits.

Briggs, Asa., Consulting ed., *A Dictionary of 20th Century World Biography.* Oxford-New York: Oxford University Press, 1992.

Brissaud, André. *The Nazi Secret Service.* Paris: Plon, 1972; London: The Bodley Head, 1974; New York: W. W. Norton & Company, Inc., 1974.

Brown, Anthony Cave. *Bodyguard of Lies.* New York, Evanston, San Francisco, London: Harper, 1975. An exhaustive study by a British journalist of "the clandestine war of intricate deceptions that hid the secrets of D-Day from Hitler. . . ."

——. *"C" : The Secret Life of Sir Stewart Menzies, Spymaster to Winston Churchill.* New York: Collier Books, Macmillan, 1989.

Bryant, Arthur. *The Turn of the Tide* (1939-1943) and *The Triumph of the West* (1944-1945), both subtitled *A History of the War Years Based on the Diaries of Field-Marshal Lord Alanbrooke, Chief of the Imperial General Staff.* Garden City, NY: Doubleday, 1957 and 1959.

Buchanan, A. Russell. *The United States and World War II.* 2 vols. New York: Harper, 1964. A well-documented work covering all aspects of American participation, military, diplomatic, and the home front.

Bullitt, Orville H., ed. *For the President, Personal and Secret, Correspondence Between Franklin D. Roosevelt and William C. Bullitt.* Boston: Houghton Mifflin, 1972.

Bullock, Alan. *Hitler: A Study in Tyranny.* Rev ed. New York: Harper, 1962. Outstanding in an overcrowded field, this revision of a work first published in 1952 includes a definitive bibliography of first-hand sources.

Burns, James MacGregor. *Roosevelt: The Soldier of Freedom.* New York: Harcourt Brace Jovanovich, Inc., 1970.

BUTCHER, Harry C. *My Three Years with Eisenhower.* New York: Simon & Schuster, 1946.

Butow, Robert C. *Japan's Decision to Surrender.* California: Stanford University Press, 1954.

Byas, Hugh. *Government by Assassination.* New York: Knopf, 1942.

C

C&C. Short title for Craven and Cate (below).

Caidin, Martin. *The Tigers Are Burning.* New York: Hawthorne, 1974. (About the battle of Kursk.)

Calvocoressi, Peter, Guy Wint, and John Pritchard. *Total War: The Causes and Courses of the Second World War.* 2d ed, rev, New York: Pantheon; London: Viking, 1989. This revision of a highly regarded book first published in 1972, when **Ultra** remained classified, updates the scholarship and expands treatment of the Tokyo war crimes trials..

Cambridge Biographical Dictionary. Magnus Magnusson, general editor; Rosemary Goring, assistant. New York: Cambridge Univ Press, 1990. Like so many other excellent works published too late to help me much, this mighty tome nevererthless was valuable in providing dates of those who died in the 20 years I soldiered on.

Campbell, Thomas M. and George C. Herring, eds. *The Diaries of Edward R. Stettinius, Jr., 1943-1946.* New York: New Viewpoints, 1975.

Canadian Army Official History. See Stacey, C. P., and Nicholson, G. W. L.

Carell, Paul. *The Foxes of the Desert.* New York: Dutton, 1960; reprint edition, New York: Bantam Books, 1972.

——. *Hitler Moves East, 1941-1943.* Boston: Little, Brown, 1965.

Carver, Michael (ed). *The War Lords: Military Commanders of the Twentieth Century.* Boston: Little, Brown, 1976. The work includes 31 chapters on prominent military leaders. Because most of the essays are by well-known authorities I include their names in the source citations.

CB 1940-46. *Current Biography Yearbook* (below).

CE. Columbia Encyclopedia (below).

China Handbook 1937-1945 New Edition with 1946 Supplement. New York: Macmillan, 1947.

China Yearbook 1970-71. Taipei, Taiwan, China: China Publishing Co, nd.

CHURCHILL, Winston S. *The Second World War.* 6 vols. Boston: Houghton Mifflin, 1948-53. Volume numbers and publication dates: I. *The Gathering Storm* (1948); II. *Their Finest Hour* (1949); III. *The Grand Alliance* (1950); IV. *The Hinge of Fate* (1950); V. *Closing the Ring* (1951); and VI. *Triumph and Tragedy* (1953).

CIANO, Galeazzo. Hugh Gibson, ed. *The Ciano Diaries, 1939-43.* Garden City, NY: Doubleday, 1946. My page citations are from this early edition. Another was published under the same title in New York by H. Fertig in 1973.

Clark, Alan. *Barbarossa: The Russian-German Conflict, 1941-45.* New York: Morrow, 1965. My page citations of this classic are to the paperback edition, The New American Library, Inc. (Signet Books), 1965.

CLARK, Mark W. *Calculated Risk.* New York: Harper, 1950.

———. *From the Danube to the Yalu.* New York: Harper, 1954

Clarkson, Jesse D. *A History of Russia.* New York: Random House, 1969 (2d ed).

Clayton, Anthony. *Three Marshals of France: Leadership after Trauma.* London: Brassey's, 1992. Good coverage of JUIN, DE LATTRE, and LECLERC.

Clifford, Clark. With Richard Holbrooke. *Counsel to the President, A Memoir.* New York: Random House, 1991.

Collier, Basil. *The Second World War: A Military History from Munich to Hiroshima—in One Volume.* New York: Morrow, 1967.

———. *The War in the Far East 1942-1945: A Military History.* New York: Morrow, 1969.

Collier's Encyclopedia. This standard reference work was a useful source, particularly in providing the names of about 300 candidates for inclusion in this biographical dictionary.

Collins, Larry, and Dominique Lapierre. *Is Paris Burning ?* New York: Simon and Schuster; Pocket Cardinal, 1965. I have used the latter for page citations.

The Columbia Encyclopedia in One Volume, 2d ed. New York: Columbia University, 1950. According to many authorities this is the best of its kind.

The Concise Dictionary of National Biography From Earliest Times to 1985. London: Oxford University, 1992. In three volumes, A-F, G-M, N-Z, this new edition contains summaries of major entries in the main *DNB* (below) from the earliest times, plus those who died up to 1985.

Connell, J. *Auchinleck: A Critical Biography.* London: Cassell, 1959.

———. *Wavell.* 2 vols., M. Roberts, ed. London: Cassell, 1969.

Conquest, Robert. *The Great Terror: Stalin's Purge of the Thirties.* London and New York: Macmillan, 1968.

Craig, Gordon A. *Germany 1866-1945.* New York and Oxford: Oxford University, 1978.

———. *The Politics of the Prussian Army, 1640-1945.* New York and Oxford: Oxford University 1956.

Crankshaw, Edward. Soviet authority, editor of *Khrushchev Remembers* (See under Khrushchev, below).

Craven, Wesley, and James Lea Cate, eds. *The Army Air Forces in World War II.* 7 vols. Chicago: University of Chicago, 1948.

Cullum. Short-title for West Point's *Register of Graduates* (below). See also *Assembly.*

CUNNINGHAM, Andrew B. *A Sailor's Odyssey: The Autobiography of Admiral of the Fleet, Viscount Cunningham of Hyndhope* (New York and Boston: Dutton, 1951).

Current Biography Yearbooks. New York: The H. W. Wilson Company, 1940-1945.

D

DAB. The Dictionary of American Biography (following).

Dallek, Robert. *Franklin D. Roosevelt and American Foreign Policy, 1932-1945.* New York: Oxford University, 1979.

Davidson, Eugene. *The Trial of the Germans: An Account of the Twenty-two Defendants before the International Military Tribunal at Nuremberg.* New York: Macmillan, 1966.

Davies, W. J. K. *German Army Handbook.* New York: Arco, 2d US ed, 1977.

Dawidowicz, Lucy S. *The War Against the Jews 1933-1945.* New York: Holt, Rinehart and Winston, 1975.

Davis, Kenneth S. *Experience of War: The United States in World War II.* Garden City, NY: Doubleday, 1965.

———. *FDR: The Beckoning of Destiny, 1882-1928* (New York: Putnam's, 1973)

Deane, John R. *The Strange Alliance: The Story of Our Efforts at Wartime Cooperation with Russia.* New York: Viking, 1947.

DE GAULLE, Charles André Joseph Marie. *War Memoirs: The Call to Honour, 1940-1942.* Vol I. New York: Viking, 1955.

———. *War Memoirs: Unity, 1942-1944.* Vol II. New York: Simon and Schuster, 1959.

———. *War Memoirs: Salvation, 1944-45.* Vol III. New York: Simon and Schuster, 1960.

———. *The Complete War Memoirs of Charles de Gaulle.* New York: Simon and Schuster, 1972.

DE GUINGAND, Francis *Operation Victory.* London: Hodder and Stoughton, 1947.

———. *Generals at War.* London: Hodder and Stoughton, 1964.

De la Bere, Ivan. *The Queen's Orders of Chivalry.* London: Spring Books, rev ed 1964. An authoritative work by a former Secretary of the Central Chancery of Knighthood, 1945-1960.

Deutsch, Harold C. *Hitler and His Generals: The Hidden Crisis, January-June 1938.* Minneapolis: University of Minnesota, 1974. ST: Deutsch, I.

———. *The Conspiracy Against Hitler in the Twilight War.* Minneapolis: University of Minnesota, 1968. ST: Deutsch, II.

DEWAVRIN, André Pierre. See Passy, Colonel.

Dictionary of American Biography, The. New York: Scribner's, 1981. This 17-vol set includes Supplements 1-7 and includes prominent Americans who died up to 31 Dec 65. Supplement 8 (1966-70) is available separately.

London: Oxford University, various years. Works cited by the short title DNB are the separate volumes that cover approximately a decade each. The reader can tell from the death date in my biographical sketches which volume of DNB to consult. For example, the citation "(DNB)" for a statement in the entry on Winston Churchill, who died in 1965, refers the reader to a volume whose full title is *The Dictionary of National Biography, 1961-1970;* it was published in 1981, reprinted with corrections in 1987, and has been periodically reprinted. See also The *Concise DNB,* above (under C).

Dictionary of National Biography, The.

Dictionnaire de la 2e Guerre Mondiale. 2 vols Paris: Larousse, 1979 & 1980. A monumental work in the publisher's best tradition.

Djilas, Milovan. *Conversations With Stalin.* New York: Harcourt, Brace & World, Inc., 1962.

DNB. Short title for *The Dictionary of National Biography.*

Doenitz, Karl. *Memoirs.* London: Weidenfeld & Nicolson, 1959.

Dornberger, Walter. *V-2.* London: Hurst & Blacket, 1954.

Dulles, Allen. *The Craft of Intelligence.* New York: Harper, 1963.

———. *Germany's Underground.* London and New York: Macmillan, 1947.

———. *The Secret Surrender.* New York: Harper, 1966.

Dupuy, R. Ernest and Trevor N. Dupuy (son). *Encyclopedia of Military History.* Fairfax, Va: Historic Evaluation and Research Organization (HERO), 1984.

Dupuy, Trevor N., Curt Johnson, and David L. Bongard, eds. *The Harper Encyclopedia of Military Biography.* Edison, NJ: Castle Books, 1992. Published by arrangement with HarperCollins. Although the 3,000 sketches go back into antiquity this work includes many WWII military figures, some of them not well known to the general public.

Dupuy, T. N. *A Genius for War: The German Army and the General Staff, 1807-1945.* Englewood Cliffs, N. J.: Prentice Hall, 1977.

E

Earle, Edward Mead, ed, in collaboration with Gordon A. Craig and Felix Gilbert. *Makers of Modern Strategy*. Princeton: Princeton Univ, 1943.

EB Yrbk obits. *Encyclopaedia Britannica Yearbook* obituaries. Because these appear in the yearbook following the subject's death, publication dates are not given as part of citations.

EDEN, Anthony (Earl of Avon). *The Memoirs of Anthony Eden* (3 vols). American editions, published by Houghton Mifflin, Boston, are *Full Circle* (1960), *Facing the Dictators* (1962); and *The Reckoning* (1965).

EICHELBERGER, Robert L. *Our Jungle Road to Tokyo*. New York: Viking, 1950. See also work edited by Jay Luvaas.

EISENHOWER, Dwight David. *Crusade in Europe*. New York: Doubleday, 1948. My page citations are from the Permabooks Special Edition, New York: Garden City Books, 1952.

———. *At Ease, Stories I Tell to Friends*. Garden City, NY: Doubleday, 1967. Not a joke book, as the unfortunate title implies, *At Ease* is a collection of interesting autobiographical anecdotes that have historical merit.

Eisenhower Papers. See *Papers of. . . .*

Engle, Eloise and Lauri Paananen. *The Winter War: The Russo-Finnish Conflict, 1939-40*. New York: Scribner's, 1973.

EP. Eisenhower Papers, listed below under *Papers of. . . .*

Erickson, John. *The Soviet High Command: A Military-Political History, 1918-41*. New York: St Martin's Press, 1962.

———. *The Road to Stalingrad: Stalin's War with Germany,* Vol. I. New York, Evanston, San Francisco, London: Harper, 1975. Good biographical details.

———. *The Road to Berlin. Continuing the History of Stalin's War with Germany*. Boulder, Colo, Westview Press, 1983.

———. *Biographical Dictionary of the USSR*. (I have not found publication data.)

Essame, Hubert. *The Battle for Germany*. New York: Scribner's, 1969.

———. *Patton: A Study in Command*. New York: Scribner's, 1974.

Esposito, Vincent J., Chief editor. *The West Point Atlas of American Wars*. Vol. II, 1900-1953. New York: Praeger, 1959. The invaluable work includes 169 large, uncluttered "situation maps" on WWII campaigns with text on facing pages. The atlas was designed to accompany Stamps and Esposito, eds, *A Military History of World War II* (cited below).

F

Facts on File. New York: Facts on File, Inc. Citations are to monthly issues.

F&R. Short title for work edited by Seymour Freiden and William Richardson, *The Fatal Decisions*.

Farago, Ladislas with Ellis M. ZACHARIAS. *Behind Closed Doors*. New York: Putnam's, 1950. A survey of cold war intelligence operations since 1946.

Farago, Ladislas. *The Game of the Foxes: The Untold Story of German Espionage in the United States and Great Britain during World War II*. New York: McKay, 1971.

———. *Patton—Ordeal and Triumph*. New York: Ivan Obolensky, 1964.

_____. *War of Wits: The Anatomy of Espionage and Intelligence*. New York: Funk & Wagnalls, 1954.

Feis, Herbert. *The China Tangle*. Princeton, N. J.: Princeton University, 1953.

———. *Churchill, Roosevelt and Stalin*. Princeton, N. J.: Princeton University 1957.

———. *The Road to Pearl Harbor*. Princeton, N. J.: Princeton University, 1950.

Fergussen, Bernard. *Beyond the Chindwin*. London: Colins, 1945. Major Fergusson (1943), later Lord Ballantrae, led a column of Chindits in Burma under both WINGATE and LENTAGNE.

———. *The Watery Maze: The Story of Combined Operations*. London: Collins, 1961.

Fest, Joachim C. *Hitler*. New York: Harcourt Brace Jovanovich, 1974.

Fisher, Jr, Ernest F. *Cassino to the Alps*. Washington: Center of Military History, United States Army, 1977.

Fleming, Peter. *Operation Sea Lion: The Projected invasion of England in 1940—An account of the German preparations and the British countermeasures*. New York: Simon and Schuster, 1957.

Flower, Desmond, and James Reeves, eds. *The War, 1939-1945*. London: Cassell, 1960. The US edition is *The Taste of Courage: The War, 1939—1945*. New York: Harper, 1960. A valuable anthology with excerpts from memoirs, highlighting the entire war. Good bibliography and index. Desmond Flower was head of Cassel & Company, Ltd.

Foley, Charles. *Commando Extraordinary: A Biography of Otto Skorzeny* with an introduction by Sir Robert LAYCOCK. Costa Mesa, Calif: The Noontide Press, 1988.

Foot, M. R. D. *Resistance*. McGraw-Hill, 1977.

——. *Six Faces of Courage*. Eyre Methuen, 1978.

——. *SOE in France*. Her Majesty's Stationery Office, 1966.

FOOTE, Alexander Allen. *Handbook for Spies*. New York: Doubleday, 1949.

Fourcade, Marie-Madeleine. *Noah's Ark*. New York: Dutton, 1974. The alluring Mme Fourcade directed the Alliance intelligence net of almost 3,000 secret agents in France who had the code-names of animals.

FRANK, Anne. *Anne Frank: The Diary of a Young Girl*. New York: Random House, 1952.

Freiden, Seymour, and William Richardson (eds). *The Fatal Decisions*. New York, Sloane, 1956. New York: Berkley Books (paperback), 1958. Chapters by high ranking Germans are "The Battle of Britain" (Werner KREIPE), "Moscow" (Guenther BLUMENTRITT), "El Alamein" (Fritz BAYERLEIN), "Stalingrad" (Kurt ZEITZLER), "France" (Generalleutnant Bodo Zimmerman, operations officer of OB West, then of AG D), and "The Ardennes" (Hasso von MANTEUFFEL). My page references are from the paperback edition.

FRENAY, Henri. *The Night Will End*. New York: McGraw-Hill, 1976.

Frischauer, Willi. *Himmler*. Boston: Beacon Press, 1953.

——. *The Rise and Fall of Hermann Goering*. Boston: The Riverside Press Cambridge, Houghton Mifflin Company, 1951.

FULLER, J. F. C. *The Second World War*. New York: Meredith Press, 1968.

G

Gaddis, John Lewis. *The United States and the Origins of the Cold War, 1941-1947*. New York and London: Columbia University, 1972.

Gaevernitz, Gero von S., ed. *They Almost Killed Hitler*. New York: Macmillan, 1947. SCHLABRENDORFF's account of his role in the anti-Hitler conspiracy as told to Gaevernitz. The slim volume of 150 pages is a valuable primary source.

Gallo, Max. *The Night of the Long Knives*. New York: Harper, 1972. (Eng trans from the French.)

Garraty, John A. and Jerome L. Sternstein, eds. *Encyclopedia of American Biography*. New York: Harper & Row, 1974.

GAULLE, Charles de. See DE GAULLE.

GAVIN, James. *Airborne Warfare*. Washington, DC: Infantry Journal Press, 1947.

——. *War and Peace in the Space Age*. New York: Harper, 1959.

GEHLEN, Reinhard. *The Service: The Memoirs of General Reinhard Gehlen*. New York: World, 1972.

Geroi Sovetskogo Soyuza (Heroes of the Soviet Union) Moscow: Voyenizdat, 1987. 2 vols. Ed. I. N. Shkadov.

Gilbert, Felix, ed. *Hitler Directs His War*. (New York: Oxford University, 1950.

Gilbert, G. M. *Nuremberg Diary*. New York: Farrar, Straus, 1947. This is a US psychiatrist's account of his experiences with major war criminals on trial at Nuremberg.

GISEVIUS, Hans Bernd. *To the Bitter End*. Boston: Houghton Mifflin Company, 1947.

Goerlitz, Walter. *History of the German General Staff: 1657-1945*. New York: Prager, 1954. Half of the book is on WW II. A comparable work, also a classic, is cited by the short title Craig, *Politics*.

Gordon, Harold J. Jr. *Hitler and the Beer Hall Putsch*. Princeton: Princeton University, 1972.

Graham, Dominick, and Shelford Bidwell. *Tug of War, The Battle for Italy: 1943-4*. New York: St Martin's, 1986.

Groueff, Stephane. Manhattan Project: *The Untold Story of the Making of the Atomic Bomb*. Boston: Little, Brown, 1967.

Guingand, de. See De Guingand.

GUDERIAN, Heinz. *Panzer Leader*. New York: Dutton, 1954.

Guillaume, Augustin. *Soviet Arms and Soviet Power: The Secrets of Russia's Might*. Washington, DC: Infantry Journal Press, 1949.

Gunther, John. *Inside Asia*. New York: Harper, 1939.

——. *Inside Europe*. New York: Harper, 1936-1940.

H

H&C. Short title for work by Terry Hughes and John Costello.

HBC. "The History Book Club *Review*." A monthly publication with authoritative reviews of current selections.

Hayashi, Saburo, and Alvin D. Coox. *Kogun: The Japanese Army in the Pacific War*. Quantico, Va: Marine Corps Association, 1959. First published as *Taiheiyo senso rikusen gaishi*. Tokyo: 1951. A valuable reference.

H&Z. See work on GEHLEN by Heinz Hoehne & Hermann Zolling.

HALDER, Franz. *Diary, 1939-42*. Arnold Lissance, ed and trans. Nuremberg: (US) Office of Military Government for Germany, 1947. A typescript produced for the trial prosecutors at Nuremberg from seven volumes of Halder's handwritten MS— much of it in Gabelsberger shorthand—the work was mimeographed, in German and English. This text had wide circulation among historians until publication of the following work in 1963.

——. *Halder: Kriegstagbuch*. Hans Adolf Jacobson, ed. 3 vols. Stuttgart: W. Kohlhammer, 1963.

——. *The Halder War Diary, 1939-1942*. Charles Burdick and Hans Adolf Jacobsen, eds. Novato, Calif: Presidio, 1988. A one-volume abridgement of the 1963 German edition.

——. *Hitler as War Lord*. London: Putnam's, 1950.

HALIFAX, Lord. *Fullness of Days*. New York: Dodd, Mead, 1957.

Hamilton, Charles. *Leaders and Personalities of the Third Reich, Their Biographies, Portraits, and Autographs*. San Jose, Calif.: R. James Bender, 1984.

HANFSTAENGL, Ernst "Putzi". *Unheard Witness*. Philadelphia and New York: Lippincot, 1957.

HARRIS, Arthur. *Bomber Offensive*. New York & London: Collins, 1947.

Harrison, Gordon A. *Cross-Channel Attack*. Washington: Office of the Chief of Military History, Department of the Army, 1951.

Hassell, Fey von. *Hostage of the Third Reich: The Story of My Imprisonment and Rescue from the SS*. New York: Scribner's, 1989. The author is the daughter of Ulrich von HASSELL, below.

HASSELL, Ulrich von. *The von Hassell Diaries, 1938-1944: The Story of the Fight against Hitler inside Germany*. Garden City, NY:, Doubleday 1947. The unabridged German edition was published in 1946, and other versions have been printed.

HCD. Harold C. Deutsch (following).

HFC. Harriet Fast Scott (*see* Scotts, following).

Higham, Robin. *Air Power: A Concise History*. New York: St Martin's, 1972.

Historical Encyclopedia of World War II, The. Marcel Baudot, Henri Bernard, Hendrik Brugmans, Michael R. D. Foot, Hans-Adolf Jacobsen, eds. New York and Oxford: Facts on File, 1980 and 1989 (paperback). This is the English-lanugage edition of *Encyclopédie de la Guerre 1939-*

1945 (Paris and Tournai: Casterman, 1977). WWII specialists will appreciate the impressive list of editors. The 1989 paperback edition has additional material by Alvin D. Coox (an authority on Japanese involvement) and Thomas R. H. Havens. Although very skimpy on biographies, the work deals in sometimes highly technical detail on special topics. Under "Atomic bomb," for example, Henri Bernard devoted seven and a half pages to the subject, including schematic figures and complex equations dealing with the physics involved.

HITLER, Adolf. *Mein Kampf,* New York: Reynal & Hitchcock, 1939.

Hoehne, Heinz, & Hermann Zolling. *The General was a Spy. The Truth About General Gehlen and His Spy Ring.* Introduction by Hugh Trevor-Roper. New York: Coward, McCann & Geohegan, Inc, 1972. .

Hoffmann, Peter. *The History of the German Resistance 1933-1945.* Cambridge, Mass: MIT, 1977. A painstaking study of the conspiracies "within the officer corps and conservative groups like the **Kreisau circle,**" having little to say "on the personalities involved, their motives, their thoughts. . . ." (Walter Laqueur, *NYT* Book Review, 3 Apr 77, 47.) Typically, the American publishers inflated the more-precise German title, "Resistance, Coup d'état, Assassination," to promise more than the author intended. "[A] handbook rather than a history, including valuable maps and diagrams, and 200 pages of footnotes," the work "does not mention the anti-Nazi activities of Socialists, Communists and the churches." (Ibid.) This should not detract from what otherwise has been hailed as a classic. Since 1970 the author has held the Chair of German History at McGill Univ, Montreal.

Horne, Alistair. *To Lose a Battle: France 1940.* Boston: Little, Brown, 1969.

Howarth, Stephen, ed. *Great Naval Captains of World War II.* New York: St. Martin's Press, 1993. The anthology has military biographies of 31 men, Japanese, German, British, and American, by good naval historians.

Hoyle, Martha Byrd. *A World in Flames: The History of World War II.* New York: Atheneum, 1970. An outstanding one-volume narrative concentrating on military operations.

Hoyt, Edwin P. *The Battle of Leyte Gulf: The Death Knell of the Japanese Fleet.* New York: Weybright and Talley, 1972.

Blue Skies and Blood: The Battle of the Coral Sea. New York: Eriksson, 1975. .

———. *How They Won the War in the Pacific: Nimitz and His Admirals.* New York: Weybright and Talley, 1970.

Hughes, Terry, and John Costello. *The Battle of the Atlantic.* New York: Dial, 1977.

Humble, Richard. *Hitler's Generals.* New York: Doubleday, 1974.

Hutton, J. Bernard. *Hess: The Man and His Mission.* New York: Macmillan, 1970.

I

Institute for the Study of the USSR (Munich, Germany). See *Who Was Who in the USSR* (Scarecrow Press).

Trial of the Major War Criminals before the International Military Tribunal, Nuremberg, 14 November 1945-10 October 1946. 42 vols. Nuremberg, 1947-49. The official English-language text of the proceedings and of the documents produced. (The latter are of great historical value.)

Trials of War Criminals before the Nuremberg Military Tribunals under Control Council Law No. 10, October 1946-April 1949. 15 vols. Washington: US Government Printing Office, 1952.

Irving, David. *The Trail of the Fox: The Search for the True Field Marshal Rommel.* New York: Dutton (Thomas Congdon Books), 1977.

———. *Hitler's War.* New York: Viking, 1977.

———. *The Rise and Fall of the Luftwaffe: the Life of Field Marshal Erhard Milch.* Boston: Little, Brown, 1973.

Istoriya Velikoy Otechectvennaya Voyny Sovetskogo Soyuza 1941-1945 (History of the Great Patriotic War of the Soviet Union 1941-1945). 6 vols. P. N. Pospelov, ed, Moscow: Voyenizdat, 1961-1965.

J

J&R. Short title for work by H. A. Jacobsen and J. Rohwer (below).

Jackson, W. G. F. *The Battle for North Africa 1940-43*. New York: Mason/Charter, 1975.

Jacobsen, H. A. and J. Rohwer (eds). *Decisive Battles of World War II: The German View*. New York: Putnam's, 1965. This is the translation by Edward Fitzgerald of *Entscheidungsschlachten des Zweiten Weltkrieges* (Frankfurt am Main: Bernard & Graefe, 1960). An exceptionally solid work including eight pages of sketch maps, it has an introduction by Cyril Falls, a preface by Hans SPEIDEL, and chapters by well-known writers (many of them eyewitnesses) like Walter WAR-LIMONT, Walter Goerlitz (see his works, previously cited), and Hasso von MANTEUFFEL. As the title indicates, the work covers Dunkirk, The Battle of Britain, Crete, The Battle for Moscow 1941, the Mediterranean in 1942, Stalingrad, the U-boat war, Normandy, "The Collapse of Army Group Center in 1944," and the Ardennes. Eleven "chronicles" give the background of the war and provide transition between chapters. I cite the work as "J&R" followed by the individual contributor, e. g.: J&R, Rudolf Hofmann.

Japanese Biographical Encyclopedia and Who's Who 1964-65. A monumental work of 2,377 pages.

JOHN, Otto. *Twice Through the Lines*. New York: Harper, 1972. Introduction by H. R. Trevor-Roper. The work was published in Germany as *Zweimal kam ich heim* (Econ Verlag Gmbh., 1969).

K

Kahn, David. *The Code Breakers*. New York: Macmillan, 1967.

——. *Hitler's Spies: German Military Intelligence in World War II*. New York: Macmillan, 1978.

Keegan, John (ed). *Churchill's Generals*. New York, Grove Weidenfeld, 1991. Up to the standards of its distinguished editor, the work has chapters on top British commanders, concentrating on analysis but including a valuable chronology of each man's life.

——. *The Mask of Command*. New York: Viking, 1987. The highly regarded work includes a valuable chapter on Hitler as a soldier.

——. (ed). *The Rand McNally Encyclopedia of World War II* (cartography by Richard Natkiel). Chicago, New York, San Francisco: Rand McNally (A Bison Book), 1977.

——. (ed). *Who Was Who in World War II*. New York: 1978.

KENNAN, George F. *American Diplomacy: 1900-1950* (Boston: Little, Brown).

——. *Russia and the West Under Lenin and Stalin*. Boston: Little, Brown, 1960. My page references are from the paperback Mentor Books edition.

——. *Memoirs: 1925-1950*. Boston: Little, Brown, 1967.

——. *Memoirs; 1950-1963*. Boston: Little, Brown, 1971.

Kennedy, Ludovic. *Pursuit: The Chase and Sinking of the Bismarck*. London: Collins, 1974.

Kennedy, Robert M. *The German Campaign in Poland*. Department of the Army Pamphlet 20-255. Washington, D C: Government Printing Office, 1956.

Keogh, E. G. *The South West Pacific 1941-45*. Melbourne: Grayflower Productions, 1965. An Australian military history of the AIF by the editor of the Australian Army Journal (1948-1964).

Kessel, Sim. *Hanged at Auschwitz*. New York: Stein and Day, 1972. A small volume by a survivor of 23 months in German concentration camps.

KESSELRING, Albert. *Soldat bis zum letzen tag*. Bonn: Athenaeum Verlag, 1953. The British edition preserves the title unaltered, *A Soldier to the Last Day* (UK). The American edition is *Kesselring: A Soldier's Record* (Novato, Calif: Presidio Press, 1989).

Khrushchev, Nikita. Crankshaw, Edward, ed. *Khrushchev Remembers*. (Boston: Little, Brown, 1970). See KHRUSHCHEV sketch for questions of authenticity.

——. *The Last Testament*. Boston: Little, Brown, 1974.

——. *The Glasnost Tapes*. Boston: Little, Brown, 1990.

Knightley, Phillip. *The Master Spy: The Story of Kim Philby*. New York: Knopf, 1989. By a leading author of works on espionage including *Philby the Spy Who Betrayed a Generation* (London,

Deutsch, 1968) this exceptionally clear biography is based on extensive correspondence with Philby and long interviews with the expatriate in Moscow.

Kozlov, M. M., ed., *Velikaya Otechectvennaya Voyna 1941-1945. Entlsiklopediya (The Great Patriotic War 1941-1945. Encyclopedia)* Moscow: Soviet Encyclopedia, 1985.

Kruzhin, Peter. "Soviet Generals of the Army," Radio Liberty Research (RL 89/75), 28 Feb 75. Cited as RL 89/75. This is a monograph recapitulating the history of the rank, listing the officers who received it, and giving some data on their "fate or present position."

L

L&W-B. Short title for Longford, Lord, and John Wheeler-Bennett (eds), *The History Makers.*

Langer, William L. (comp & ed). *An Encyclopedia of World History.* Rev ed. Cambridge, Mass.: Houghton Mifflin, The Riverside Press, 1952.

——. *Our Vichy Gamble.* New York: Knopf, 1947.

——. *The Undeclared War 1940-1941.* New York: Harper, 1953.

——. *The Mind of Adolf Hitler.* New York: Basic Books, 1972.

Layton, Edwin. *And I Was There.* New York: Morrow, 1985.

Larousse. Short title for *Dictionnaire de la 2e Guerre Mondiale.* 2 vols Paris: Editions Larousse, 1979 & 1980. A monumental work that is hard to find.

LEAHY, William D. *I Was There.* New York: Whittlesey House, 1950.

LEMAY, Curtis E., with MacKinley Kantor. *Mission with LeMay* (Garden City, NY: Doubleday, 1965).

Leuchtenburg, William E. *New Deal and Global War. The Life History of the United States.* Vol. II: 1933-1945.

Lewin, Ronald, ed. *The British Army in World War II: The War on Land.* New York: Morrow, 1970.

LIDDELL HART, B. H. *The German Generals Talk.* New York: Morrow, 1948. Based on his interrogations of captured German generals in 1945. Published in England as *The Other Side of the Hill* (1948).

——. *History of the Second World War.* New York: Putnam's, 1971.

——. (ed.) *The Red Army.* New York: Harcourt, Brace, 1956.

——. ed (with the assistance of Lucie-Maria Rommel, Manfred Rommel, and Fritz BAYERLEIN). *The Rommel Papers.* New York: Harcourt, Brace, 1953.

Life, editors of. *World War II.* Time-Life Books. Individual volumes are cited by author's name and volume title.

Lingeman, Richard R. *Don't You Know There's A War On? The American Home Front, 1941-1945.* New York: Putnam's, 1970.

Lochner, Louis P., ed & transl. *The Goebbels Diaries, 1942-1943.* Garden City, NY: Doubleday, 1948.

Loewenheim, Francis L., Harold D. Langley, and Manfred Jonas, eds. *Roosevelt and Churchill: Their Secret Wartime Correspondence.* New York: Saturday Review Press/E. P. Dutton, 1975.

Longford, Lord, and John WHEELER-BENNETT (eds). *The History Makers: Leaders and Statesmen of the 20th Century.* New York: St Martin's, 1973.

Lucas, James. *Panzer Army Africa.* London: Macdonald and Jane's Publishers, 1977.

Luvaas, Jay, ed. *Dear Miss Em: General Eichelberger's War in the Pacific, 1942-1945.* Westport, Conn: Greenwood, 1972.

M

MacDonald, Charles B. *Command Decision.* Kent Greenfield, ed. London: Methuen, 1960.

——. *The Mighty Endeavor.* New York: Oxford University, 1969.

——. *US Army in World War II: The Siegfried Line Campaign.* Washington, D. C.: Office Chief of Military History, Department of the Army, 1963.

Macintyre, Donald. *The Naval War Against Hitler.* New York: Scribner's, 1961.

Macksey, Kenneth. *Guderian: Creator of the Blitzkrieg.* New York: Stein and Day, 1975.

———. *The Partisans of Europe in the Second World War.* New York: Stein and Day, 1975.

MACMILLAN, Harold. *Winds of Change, 1914-1939.* New York: Harper, 1966.

———. *The Blast of War, 1939-1945.* New York: Harper, 1967.

———. *War Diaries: Politics and War in the Mediterranean, January 1943-May 1945.* New York: St Martin's, 1984.

Makers of Modern Strategy. See Edward Mead Earle et al.

Mann, Golo. *The History of Germany Since 1789.* New York: Praeger, 1968.

MANSTEIN, Erich von. *Lost Victories.* Chicago: Henry Regnery, 1958. Anthony G. Powell, ed and tr; foreword by LIDDELL HART.

Marshall, Bruce. *The White Rabbit.* Boston: Houghton Mifflin, 1953. About YEO-THOMAS.

Mason, David. *Who's Who in World War II.* Boston, Toronto: Little, Brown, 1978.

Mastny, Vojtech. *The Czechs Under Nazi Rule: The Failure of National Resistance, 1939-1942.* New York and London: Columbia Univ, 1971.

Mayo, Linda. *Bloody Buna.* Garden City, N Y: Doubleday, 1974.

Medals: A Wordsworth Colour Guide. Ware, Hertsfordshire, Eng: Wordsworth Editions, Ltd, 1993. A small-format work (approx 3 X 4-in) of excellent color photographs and authoritative text on about 200 of the world's best known medals, ribbons, and attached clasps, bars, and oak leaves.

Medvedev, Roy. *Let History Judge: The Origins and Consequences of Stalinism.* New York: Knopf, 1972.

MELLENTHIN, F. W. von. *German Generals of World War II: As I Saw Them.* Norman, University of Oklahoma, 1977.

———. *Panzer Battles.* Norman, University of Oklahoma, 1956.

Merriam, Robert E. *The Battle of the Bulge.* New York: Ballentine Books, 1957. This is the abridged (paperback) ed, of *Dark December* (New York, Ziff-Davis, 1947).

Michel, Henri. *The Shadow War: European Resistance 19391945.* New York, Harper, 1972.

Miller, Russell, and the Editors of Time-Life Books. *The Resistance.* Alexandria, Va; Time-Life Books, 1979.

Mitchell, Donald W. *A History of Russian and Soviet Sea Power,* New York; Macmillan, 1974.

MONTGOMERY, Bernard Law. *El Alamein to the River Sangro; Normandy to the Baltic.* London: Barrie & Jenkins in association with The Arcadia Press, 1973. (*Normandy to the Baltic* was privately published by Printing & Stationery Service, British Army of the Rhine, 1946, then by Hutchinson & Co., 1947. *El Alamein to the River Sangro* was published by Hutchinson in 1948.)

———. *The Memoirs of Field Marshal The Viscount Montgomery of Alamein, K. G.* London: Collins, 1958.

Morehead, Alan. *Montgomery.* London; Hamish Hamilton, 1946.

MORGAN, Frederick. *Overture to Overlord.* London: Hodder & Stoughton, 1950. The author tells of his work as **COSSAC.**

———. *Peace and War: A Soldier's Life.* London: Hodder and Stoughton, 1961.

MORISON, Samuel Eliot. H*istory of the United States Naval Operations in World War II.* 15 vols. Boston: Little, Brown, 1962.

Morton, Louis B. *US Army in World War II: The War in the Pacific, The Fall of the Philippines.* Washington, DC: Center of Military History, United States Army, 1953 (reprinted 1989). Professor Morton was my friend and mentor until his premature death during the early stages of this book's development.

Mosley, Leonard. *Hirohito, Emperor of Japan.* Englewood Cliffs, NJ: Prentice Hall, 1966.

Mrazek, James E. T*he Fall of Eben Emael, Prelude to Dunkirk.* Washington and New York: Robert B. Luce, Inc., 1970.

MURPHY, Robert. *Diplomat Among Warriors.* New York: Doubleday, 1964.

N

Nicholson, G. W. L. *The Canadians in Italy, 1943-1945.* Ottawa: Roger Duhamel, FRSC, Queen's Printer and Controller of Stationery, 1966. By the Deputy Director, Historical Section, General

Staff, this is Vol. II in the Official History of the Canadian Army in the Second World War. Cited as Nicholson, *Italy.*

O

OCMH Chron. Short title for *Chronology 1941-1945.* Washington, DC, Office Chief of Military History, 1960. Compiled by Mary H. Williams and indexed by N. J. Anthony.

O'Donnell, James P. *The Bunker.* New York: Houghton Mifflin, 1978. Has valuable material supplementing Trevor-Roper's, *The Last Days of Hitler* (1947).

OUD. *The Oxford Universal Dictionary,* below.

The Oxford Universal Dictionary on Historical Principles. 3d ed revised with addenda, C. T. Onions, ed. Oxford: The Clarendon Press, 1955

P

Paine, Lauran. *The Abwehr, German Intelligence in World War Two.* London: Robert Hale, 1984. By the author of several works in the field of intelligence, this small book has fresh insights.

The Papers of Dwight David Eisenhower: The War Years. Alfred D. Chandler, Jr, ed; Stephen E. Ambrose, associate editor. 5 vols. Baltimore, Md: Johns Hopkins, 1970.

Parrish, Thomas. *Roosevelt and Marshall: Partners in Politics and War; the Personal Story.* New York: Morrow (Quill), 1989. Masterful, lively, and insightful.

——, ed; S. L. A. Marshall, chief consultant ed. *The Simon and Schuster Encyclopedia of World War II.* New York: Simon and Schuster, 1978. With specialists contributing many of the more-than-4,000 entries, many of them biographical, this is the best US reference book in its field.

——. *The Ultra Americans: The US Role in Breaking the Nazi Codes.* New York: Stein and Day, 1986. Published in paperback as *The American Codebreakers: The US Role in Ultra.* Chelsea, Mich: Scarborough House, 1991.

Passy, Col (André Pierre DEWAVRIN). *Souvenirs.* 3 vols. Monaco: Solar, 1947 and 1949; Paris: Plon, 1951.

PATTON, George S. Jr. *War as I Knew It.* Boston: Houghton Mifflin, 1947.

Payne Best, Sigismund. *The Venlo Incident.* London: Hutchinson, 1950.

Pospelov, P. N., ed. See *Istoriya Velikoy. . . .*

Pogue, Marshall. *George C. Marshall: Education of a General, 1880-1939.* New York: Viking, 1963. Cited as Pogue, *Marshall,* I.

——. *George C. Marshall: Ordeal and Hope, 1939-1942.* New York: Viking 1966. Cited as Pogue, *Marshall,* II.

——. *George C. Marshall: Organizer of Victory, 1943-1945.* New York: Viking, 1973. Pogue, *Marshall,* III.

——. *George C. Marshall: Statesman 1945-1959.* New York: Viking, 1987. Pogue, *Marshall,* IV.

——. *The Supreme Command.* Washington, DC: Office of the Chief of Military History, Department of the Army, 1954.

POPOV, Dusko ("Tricycle"). *Spy/Counterspy.* New York: Grosset & Dunlap, 1974.

Porten, Edward P. Von der. *The German Navy in World War II.* New York: Galahad Books, 1969.

Price, Frank James. *Troy H. Middleton: A Biography.* Baton Rouge: Louisiana State, 1974.

Price, G. Ward. *Giraud and the African Scene.* New York: Macmillan, 1944.

Paxton, Robert O. *Vichy France: Old Guard and New Order, 1940—1944.* New York: Knopf, 1972.

Pertinax (André GERAUD). *The Gravediggers of France: Gamelin, Daladier, Reynaud, Pétain, and Laval; Military Defeat-Armistice-Counterrevolution.* Garden City, New York: 1944.

Pugh, Marshall. *Frogman: Commander Crabb's Story.* New York: Scribner's, 1956.

R

Radio Liberty Research. Peter Kruzhin, "Soviet Generals of the Army," dated 28 Feb 75. Cited as RL 89/75.

The Rand McNally Encyclopedia of World War II. John Keegan, general ed. Chicago, New York, San Francisco: Rand McNally & Co. (A Bison Book), 1977.

Read, Anthony and David Fisher. *Operation Lucy: Most Secret Spy Ring of the Second World War.* New York: Coward, McCann & Geohegan, 1981.

———. *Colonel Z: The Secret Life of a Master of Spies* [Claude M. DANSEY]. New York: Viking, 1985.

Register of Graduates and Former Cadets of the United States Military Academy, Cullum Memorial Editions. West Point, NY: Association of Graduates, 1980 and 1990. A "Cullum Memorial Edition" is published every decade to include all classes; intermediate annual volumes omit the classes of 1802 to about 1909.

R&H, *Chron.* Short title for the following work.

RCS. Roy C. Smith, Capt USNR (Ret), consultant on US naval entries.

Rohwer, J. and G. Hummelchen, *Chronology of the War at Sea.* 2 vols. London: Greenhill Books, 1992: Arco, A comprehensive, well edited reference that identifies all naval craft, commanders, and actions cited.

Romanus, Charles F., and Riley Sunderland, *Stilwell's Mission to China.* Washington: Office of the Chief of Military History, 1953.

RL 89/75. Monograph by Peter Kruzhin (above).

Romilly, Giles and Michael Alexander. *Hostages of Colditz.* New York: Praeger, 1973. First published as *The Privileged Nightmare* (London, 1954), this is by two **Prominente** who shared a cell in **Colditz** for two years.

Roy, Jules. *The Trial of Marshal Pétain.* New York: Harper, 1968. Journalistic but first rate.

Roskill, Stephen. Capt Roskill, RN 1917-18, a naval historian of extraordinary gifts and literary style, wrote *The War at Sea 1939-1945* (London: HMSO, 1954-61). Roskill is the author or editor of many other works including *Churchill and the Admirals,* (New York: Morrow, 1978.).

Rudel, Hans Ulrich. *Stuka Pilot.* New York: Ballantine, 1958.

Ryan, Cornelius. *A Bridge Too Far* [Opn **Market-Garden**]. New York: Simon and Schuster, 1974.

———. *The Last Battle.* New York: Simon and Schuster, 1966.

———. *The Longest Day.* New York: Simon and Schuster, 1959.

S

S&A, *Sunrise.* Short title for work by Bradley F. Smith and Elena Agarossi (following).

S&E, *WWII.* Short title for work edited by T. Dodson Stamps and Vincent J. Esposito (following).

S&G. Short title for work edited by Fabian von Schlabrendorff (following).

S&S. Short title for *The Simon and Schuster Encyclopedia of World War II* (following).

Salisbury, Harrison E. *Marshal Zhukov's Greatest Battles.* New York: Harper & Row, 1969.

———. *The 900 Days: The Siege of Leningrad.* New York: Harper & Row, 1969.

Scarecrow. Short title for *Who Was Who in the USSR* (following).

SCHUSCHNIGG, Kurt. *The Brutal Takeover: The Austrian ex-Chancellor's Account of the Anschluss of Austria by Hitler.* New York: Atheneum, 1971.

Seaton, Albert. *The Russo-German War 1941-45.* New York and Washington: Praeger, 1971.

———. *Stalin as Military Commander.* New York: Praeger, 1976.

SCHELLENBERG, Walter. *The Labyrinth: Memoirs of Walter Schellenberg* (New York: Harper, 1956).

Scott, Harriet Fast. Promotion Lists, "Soviet Armed Forces"

Scott, Harriet Fast and William F. Scott. *The Soviet Art of War.* Boulder, Colorado: Westview Press, 1982.

——. *Soviet Control Structure*. New York: Crane, Russak and Company, Inc., 1983.

——. *The Armed Forces of the USSR*. Boulder, Colorado: Westview Press, 1979. My citations are this first edition, which has been revised several times.

——. *Soviet Military Doctrine: Continuity, Formulation, and Dissemination*. Boulder, Colorado: Westview Press, 1988.

Scotts. This citation is used for William F. Scott and Harriet Fast Scott who edited my Soviet sketches and glossary entries pertaining to the former USSR. Their principle sources are identified below by shortened titles only but with full publication data elsewhere.

    1). Kozlov, ed., *Entlsiklopediya* (1985).

    2). *Sovektskaya Entlsiklopediya* (1976-1980).

    3). *Geroi Sovetskogo Soyuza* (1987).

    4). *Istoriya . . . 1941-1945* (1961-1965).

    5). Volkogonov, D. A. Stalin 2 vols (1989).

    6). Periodicals: a. *Voyenno-Istoricheskiy Zhurnal;* b. *Sovetskiy Voin* (Soviet Soldier); c. *Pravda;* d. *Krasnaya Zvezda* (Red Star).

Sherwood, Robert E. *Roosevelt and Hopkins: An Intimate History*. New York: Harper, 1948.

Shirer, William L. *Berlin Diary: The Journal of a Foreign Correspondent, 1934-1941*. New York: Knopf, 1941.

——. *The Rise and Fall of the Third Reich: A History of Nazi Germany*. New York: Simon and Schuster, 1960.

——. *The Collapse of the Fourth Republic*. New York: Simon and Schuster, 1969.

Shiroyama, Saburo. *War Criminal: The Life and Death of Hirota Koki*. Tokyo/New York (distr by Harper & Row, 1977).

Shkadov, I. N. (ed). *Geroi Sovetskogo Soyuza* (Heroes of the Soviet Union). 2 vols. Moscow: Voyenizdat, 1987.

The Simon and Schuster Encyclopedia of World War II. See Thomas Parrish, ed.

Sims, Edward H. *Fighter Tactics and Strategy 1914-1970*. New York: Harper, 1972.

——. *The Greatest Aces*. New York: Harper & Row, 1967.

Sixsmith, K. G. *Eisenhower as Military Commander*. New York: Stein and Day, 1973.

SLESSOR, John C. *Air Power and Armies*. See biog. sk.

——. *Strategy for the West* (1954).

——. *The Great Deterrent* (1957)

——. *The Central Blue* (1956). His lively autobiography.

SLIM, William. *Defeat into Victory*. New York: McKay, 1961. (A shortened edition of one published in London, 1956.)

Smith, Bradley F., and Elena Agarossi. *Operation Sunrise: The Secret Surrender*. New York: Basic Books, 1979. The work rebuts much of Allen DULLES's account in *Secret Surrender* (New York, 1966).

Stein, George H. *The Waffen SS: Hitler's Elite Guard at War, 1939-1945*. Ithaca, N.Y.: Cornell, 1966.

Smith, Denis Mack. *Mussolini's Roman Empire*. New York: Viking, 1976.

Smith, E D. *The Battles for Cassino*. New York: Scribner's, 1975.

R. Harris Smith. *OSS: The Secret History of America's First Central Intelligence Agency*. Berkeley and Los Angeles, Calif: University of California, 1972.

Smyth, John. *Leadership in War, 1939-1945*. New York: St Martin's, 1947. Brigadier Sir John Smyth, VC, writes from sound professional insight and considerable personal knowledge of prominent British commanders of 1939-45.

Snell, John L. *The Outbreak of the Second World War: Design or Blunder?* Boston: Heath, 1965.

Snyder, Louis L. *Encyclopedia of the Third Reich*. First paperback edition, New York: Paragon, 1989. Reprinted from 1976 edition published by McGraw-Hill. Dr Snyder, a history professor at The City College and The City University of New York, and a master of secondary sources, has published many useful works (following).

——. *Hitler's Elite: Biographical Sketches of Nazis who Shaped the Third Reich*. New York: Hippocrene, 1989. Includes Goering, Himmler, Streicher, Roehm, Hess, Goebbels, Bormann, Rosenberg, Ribbentrop, Schirach, Heydrich, Kaltenbrunner, Eichmann, Rudolf Hoess, Josef Kramer, Ilse Koch, Mengele, Morell, and Skorzeny.

——. *Snyder's Historical Guide to World War II*. Westport, Conn: Greenwood, 1982.

——. *The War: A Concise History, 1939-1945*. New York: Messner, 1960.

SPEARS, Edward L. *Assignment to Catastrophe*. Vol 1: *Prelude to Dunkirk; July 1939-May 1940*. Vol 2: *The Fall of France; June 1940*. New York: Wynn, 1954 & 1955. Cited as *Spears* I & *Spears* II.

SPEER, Albert. *Inside the Third Reich*. New York: Macmillan 1970.

——. *Spandau: The Secret Diaries*. New York: Macmillan, 1976.

SPEIDEL, Hans. *Invasion 1944: Rommel and the Normandy Campaign*. Chicago: Henry Regnery, 1950.

Stacey, C. P. *Six Years of War: The Army in Canada, Britain and the Pacific*. Ottawa: Roger Duhamel, FRSC, Queen's Printer and Controller of Stationery, 1966. By the Director, Historical Section, General Staff, this is Vol I in the Official History of the Canadian Army in the Second World War. Cite as *Stacey*, I.

——. *The Victory Campaign: The Operations in North-East Europe, 1944-1945*. Ottawa: Roger Duhamel, FRSC, Queen's Printer and Controller of Stationery, 1966. Vol. III in the Official History, cited as Stacey, II. See also Nicholson, G. W. L.

Stamps, T. Dodson, and Vincent J. Esposito, eds. *A Military History of World War II* (2 vols) with Atlas. West Point, NY: The United States Military Academy, 1956.

Stein, George H. *The Waffen SS, 1939-1945. Hitler's Elite Guard at War*. Ithaca, NY: Cornell University Press, 1966.

STENNINIUS, Edward R., Jr. *Lend-Lease: Weapons for Victory*. New York: Macmillan, 1944.

STIMSON, Henry L. and McGeorge Bundy. *On Active Service in War and Peace*. New York and Toronto, 1948.

Strawson, John. *The Battle for North Africa*. New York: Scribner's, 1969.

——. *Hitler's Battles for Europe*. New York: Scribner, 1971.

Strik-Strikfeldt, Wilfried. *Against Stalin and Hitler: Memoir of the Russian Liberation Movement, 1941-1945*. New York: John Day, 1970. Translated from the German. The author commanded the German camp that was the center the VLASOV movement.

Strong, Kenneth. *Men of Intellignce: A Study of the Roles and Decisions of Chiefs of Intelligence from World War I to the Present Day*. New York: A Giniger Book in association with St Martin's, 1971.

Sudoplatov, Pavel, and Anatoli (son), with Jerrold L. and Leona P. Schechter. *Special Tasks: The Memoirs of an Unwanted Witness—A Soviet Spymaster*. Boston: Little, Brown, 1994. The author is a former NKVD-KGB general lieutenant who served until KHRUSCHEV purged the KGB in 1953. Jailed until 1968, he was under a gag order until 1992. In his most sensational chapter, "Atomic Spies," the author claims his agents convinced Robert OPPENHEIMER, Enrico FERMI, Leo SZILARD, Bruno Pontecorvo, Alan Nunn May, Klaus FUCHS and other scientists in the US and UK to "share atomic secrets with us." Sudoplatov writes that Niels BOHR knowingly gave vital technical assistance to a Soviet scientist involved in the USSR's nuclear bomb program. Scholars have called the book a disgrace, and nuclear physicists including Nobel laureate Hans Bethe, Edward Teller, and the American Physical Society of 43,000 physicists have denounced it. On a lower level and better documented, Sudoplatov sheds new light on the murder of TROTSKY (on Stalin's orders) and the liquidation of Raoul WALLENBERG. Sudoplotov says the ROSENBERGs were spies, although of marginal importance, and that Alger HISS gave information to a Soviet spy cell in Washington *before the war* but later refused to collaborate. The spymaster identifies the enigmatic Rudolf Abel as William FISHER. It is too early for a considered judgment on Sudoplatov's overall credibility, although many of his charges—particularly in "Atomic Spies"—are demonstrably false. But the memoirs can no more be rejected in toto than accepted.

Sulzberger, C. L. *A Long Row of Candles: Memoirs and Diaries [1934-1954]*. Toronto, Ontario: Collier-Macmillan Canada, 1969.

Swinson, Arthur . *Four Samurai: A Quartet of Japanese Army Commanders in the Second World War*. London: Hutchinson, 1968. The book deals with HOMMA, MUSAGUCHI, TSUJI, and YAMASHITA.

T

Taylor, A. J. P. *The Origins of the Second World War*. New York: Athenaeum, 1962. A highly revisionist work by a famous Oxford don arguing that Western powers forced Hitler to blunder willy-nilly into war. "Whatever our feelings about Mr. Taylor's disturbing thesis," writes WHEELER-BENNETT, "we cannot but be grateful to him for having challenged and provoked us to re-examine the evidence. . ." (W-B, *Munich,* reissued edition, x).

——. *The Second World War: An Illustrated History*. New York: Putnam's, 1975. (1st American ed.) The excellent text is enhanced by remarkable illustrations.

These Are the Generals. Introduction by Walter Millis. New York: Knopf, 1943. The book comprises 17 feature articles (profiles) from the *Saturday Evening Post, Collier's,* and *Life* magazines. Authors are David G. Wittels (BUCKNER, EICHELBERGER, DEVERS, McNARNEY), General Johnson Hagood (MARSHALL), Clare Boothe Luce (MacARTHUR), Demaree Bess (EISENHOWER), Carey Ford and Alastair MacBain (H. H. ARNOLD), Carl W. McCardle (Mark CLARK), John T. Whitaker (McNAIR and W. R. WEAVER), Ted Shane (PATTON), Charles J. V. Murphy (SOMERVELL), Leigh White (VANDEGRIFT), William Clemens (CHENNAULT), Mark Murphy (FREDENDALL), and Pete Martin (L. G. "Blondie" SAUNDERS).

Thomas, Hugh. *The Spanish Civil War*. New York: Harper, 1961. Long hailed as the best popular history in its field.

THYSSEN, Fritz. *I Paid Hitler*. New York: Farrar & Rinehart, 1941.

Toland, John. *The Last 100 Days*. New York: Random House, 1966.

——. *The Rising Sun: The Decline and Fall of the Japanese Empire, 1936-1945*. New York: Random House, 1970.

Toliver, Raymond F., and Trevor J. Constable. *Fighter General: The Life of Adolf Galland*. Introduction by Gen James H. DOOLITTLE. Zephyr Cove, Nev: AmPress, 1990.

Trepper, Leopold. *The Great Game: Memoirs of the Spy Hitler Couldn't Silence*. New York: McGraw-Hill, 1977. Trepper set up and directed the **Rote Kapelle**.

Trevor-Roper, H. R. *The Last Days of Hitler*. New York: Macmillan, 1947. An old study that many historians consider to be still unexcelled. See more recent work by James P. O'Donnell, *The Bunker.*

Tuchman, Barbara. *Stilwell and the American Experience in China*. New York: Macmillan, 1970, 1971. This popular work by an **Old China Hand** complements the official history by Charles F. Romanus and Riley Sunderland.

Tunney, Christopher. ***Biographical Dictionary of World War II***. New York: St Martin's, 1972. This small but comprehensive work was among the first in its field.

Turner, Henry Ashby, Jr (ed). *Hitler: Memoirs of a Confidant*. New Haven, Conn., and London: Yale University Press, 1985. First published in German, 1978, these memoirs of the virtually unknown Otto Wagener (1888-1971) give an invaluable insight into the personality and thinking of Hitler and his entourage during the period 1929-33. Cited as Wagener.

U

[USMA] Register of Graduates and Former Cadets. West Point, New York: 1990. The *Register* is published annually with earlier classes omitted; a comprehensive edition (from 1802) is issued at the start of each decade. (A "former cadet" is a "non-graduate.") See also *Assembly,* above.

[*USNA*] *Register of Alumni.* Annapolis, Md.: The United States Naval Academy Alumni Association, Inc, annual. Biographical data are so drastically abbreviated as to have little historical value, unlike the notices in the USMA Register (above).

Ulam, Adam B. *Expansion and Coexistence: The History of Soviet Foreign Policy, 1917-67.* New York and Washington: Praeger, 1968.

U.S. Army Register, Vol 1, United States Army Active and Retired Lists, 1 January 1957. Washington: Government Printing Office, 1957..

V

Verrier, Anthony. *Assassination in Algiers.* New York and London: Norton, 1990.

Volkogonov, Dmitri. *Stalin: Triumph and Tragedy.* Ed and trans: Harold Shukman. London and New York: Grove Weidenfeld, 1991. The original title is: *Triymf i Tragediya: I.V. Stalin: politicheskii portret I. V. Stalina.* (2 vols, 1989.) The author, a Georgian born in 1879, joined the Red Army in 1945, rose to the rank of general lieutenant, and became deputy chief of the main political section. Apparently having full access to all Stalin's personal and official archives the author produced "the first Glasnost biography" of Stalin. The Scotts (identified above in a separate entry) used the Russian editioin; I used the one-volume English language edition of 1991, cited as Volkogonov II.

W

Wagener memoirs. See work edited by Henry Ashby Turner Jr.

W-B, *Nemesis.* Short title for Wheeler-Bennett work cited below.

W&M. Short title for work by Windrow, Martin and John Mason (below).

WARLIMONT, Walter. *Inside Hitler's Headquarters* 1939-1945. London: Weidenfeld & Nicolson, 1964.

Warner, Geoffrey. *Pierre Laval and the Eclipse of France.* London: 1968). A highly regarded work.

Webster's Geographical Dictionary: A Dictionary of Names and Places, With Geographical and Historical Information and Pronunciations, Illustrated with Many Maps in the Text and with Twenty-four Maps in Full Color. Springfield, Mass: G. & C. Merriam Co, 1959.

WEIGLEY, Russell F. *History of the United States Army.* New York: Macmillan, 1967. This classic work includes useful WWII material.

——. *Eisenhower's Lieutenants: The Campaign of France and Germany, 1944-1945.* Bloomingdale: Indiana University, 1981.

Werth, Alexander. *De Gaulle: A Political Biography,* New York: Simon and Schuster, 1965, 1966.

——. *Russia at War, 1941-1945.* New York: Dutton, 1964. The author of this valuable work is a Russian-born journalist who emigrated to England after the Revolution of 1917. He has published many important books about the USSR and France including the biography cited above.

West Point Atlas. Short title for work whose chief editor was Vincent J. Esposito (listed above).

WHEELER-BENNETT. John W. *The Nemesis of Power: The German Army in Politics 1918-1945.* London: Macmillan, 1954.

——. *Munich: Prologue to Tragedy.* New York: Duell, Sloan and Pearce, reissued 1962.

White, Theodore H., and Annalee Jacoby. *Thunder out of China.* New York: William Sloane, 1946.

Who Was Who, Vol IV, 1941-1950. London: Adam & Charles Black, 1951.

Who Was Who. Vol V, 1951-1960. London: Adam & Charles Black; New York, Macmillan, 1961.

Who Was Who in the USSR. Institute for the Study of the USSR (Munich, Germany). Metuchen, NJ: Scarecrow Press, 1971.

WIESENTHAL, Simon. *The Murderers Among Us.* New York: McGraw-Hill, 1967. These are the Nazi-hunter's memoirs.

Williams, Mary H., comp. *US Army in World War II: Special Studies; Chronology 1941-1945.* Washington, DC: Office Chief of Military History, Department of the Army, 1960.

Wilmot, Chester. *The Struggle for Europe*. New York: Harper, 1952. The Australian author, a BBC correspondent in WWII, has a British slant that provides a useful balance to works by American writers.

Windrow, Martin and Francis K. Mason. *A Concise Dictionary of Military Biography: Two Hundred of the Most Significant Names in Land Warfare, 10th-20th Century*. Reading, Eng: Osprey, 1975.

Winterbotham, F. W. *The Ultra Secret*. New York: Harper, 1974.

_____. *The Ultra Spy: An Autobiography*. London: Papermac (Macmillan paperback), 1991. Cited as Winterbotham, *Autobiography* (see below).

_____. *The Nazi Connection*. New York: Harper, 1978. The author has added now-declassified secrets that, as head of the MI6 air section in WWII, he was not able to disclose in *The Ultra Secret*. His *Autobiography,* in turn (above), reworks and adds personal data to the earlier books.

Wistrich, Robert (S.). *Who's Who in Nazi Germany*. New York: Bonanza, 1984. This invaluable reference book has nearly 350 careful and analytical sketches of significant persons of the Third Reich to include many little-known artists and authors. As editor of the Wiener Library *Bulletin* in London for five years until 1980 the author had access to rare source material to include personnel files, documentary evidence, press clippings, and published works. Wistrich updated his book in 1995, providing new material and missing death dates. Cited as Wistrich II, the revised edition was published simultaneously in London, the US, and Canada, by Routledge (11 New Fetter Ln, London EC4P 4EE, and 29 West 55th St, NYC, 10001.

World War II. Time-Life Books. Alexandria, Va, 1976 onward. I cite the many individual voumes by author's name and title (e. g., Miller, *Resistance*).

Wright, Peter. *Spycatcher: The Candid Autobiography of a Senior Intelligence Officer.* New York: Viking, 1987. By the former assistant director of MI5, and long barred from publication, *Spycatcher* has new material on the **Cambridge Five** and the **Venona** decrypts.

Y

Young, Peter, ed. See *Atlas of the Second World War.*
——. *World War 1939-45: A Short History.* New York: Crowell, 1966.
——. *Rommel.* London: Collins, 1950.
Yvert, B. *Dictionnaire des Ministres.* Paris: Perrin, 1990.

Z

ZACHARIAS, Ellis M. *The Broken Seal: The Story of Operation Magic and the Pearl Harbor Disaster.* New York: Random House, 1967.

ZHUKOV, G. K. *The Memoirs of Marshal Zhukov.* New York: Delacourt Press, 1971. The original Russian edition of 1969 appeared in English translation in the UK in 1971 (Jonathan Cape).

——. *Marshal Zhukov's Greatest Battles.* New York and Evanston: Harper & Row, 1969. The work has a valuable introduction, commentary, and notes by editor Harrison E. Salisbury.

Ziemke, Earl F. *The German Northern Theater of Operations 1940-1945.* Department of the Army Pamphlet No 20-271 Washington: US Government Printing Office, 1960.